The Oxford History of the United States

David M. Kennedy, *General Editor*

ROBERT MIDDLEKAUFF
THE GLORIOUS CAUSE
The American Revolution, 1763–1789

GORDON S. WOOD
EMPIRE OF LIBERTY
A History of the Early Republic, 1789–1815

DANIEL WALKER HOWE
WHAT HATH GOD WROUGHT
The Transformation of America, 1815–1848

JAMES M. MCPHERSON
BATTLE CRY OF FREEDOM
The Civil War Era

DAVID M. KENNEDY
FREEDOM FROM FEAR
The American People in Depression and War, 1929–1945

JAMES T. PATTERSON
GRAND EXPECTATIONS
The United States, 1945–1974

JAMES T. PATTERSON
RESTLESS GIANT
The United States from Watergate to Bush v. Gore

GEORGE C. HERRING
FROM COLONY TO SUPERPOWER
U.S. Foreign Relations since 1776

FROM COLONY TO SUPERPOWER

U.S. Foreign Relations
since 1776

GEORGE C. HERRING

OXFORD
UNIVERSITY PRESS
New York   Oxford

OXFORD
UNIVERSITY PRESS

Oxford University Press, Inc., publishes works that further
Oxford University's objective of excellence
in research, scholarship, and education.

Oxford   New York
Auckland   Cape Town   Dar es Salaam   Hong Kong   Karachi
Kuala Lumpur   Madrid   Melbourne   Mexico City   Nairobi
New Delhi   Shanghai   Taipei   Toronto

With offices in
Argentina   Austria   Brazil   Chile   Czech Republic   France   Greece
Guatemala   Hungary   Italy   Japan   Poland   Portugal   Singapore
South Korea   Switzerland   Thailand   Turkey   Ukraine   Vietnam

Copyright © 2008 by Oxford University Press, Inc.

Published by Oxford University Press, Inc.
198 Madison Avenue, New York, NY 10016

www.oup.com

First issued as an Oxford University Press paperback, 2011

Library of Congress Cataloging-in-Publication Data
Herring, George C., 1936–.
From colony to superpower : U.S. foreign relations since 1776
/ George C. Herring.
p. cm. — (The Oxford history of the United States)
Includes bibliographical references and index.
ISBN 978-0-19-507822-0; 978-0-19-976553-9 (pbk.)
1. United States–Foreign relations.   I. Title.
E183.7.H44 2008   327.73–dc22   2008007996

5   7   9   8   6   4

Printed in Canada
on acid-free paper

For Dottie

Acknowledgments

One of the great pleasures of completing a project like this is to be able to thank publicly the many institutions and people who helped along the way. The John Simon Guggenheim Foundation provided the financial support that, combined with a University of Kentucky sabbatical, enabled me to get started. The Rockefeller Foundation funded a month's stay in the incomparably beautiful and uniquely stimulating environment of Bellagio, Italy, a sojourn that allowed me to shape the final chapter and gain interesting feedback from people in numerous fields of intellectual inquiry. Deans Rick Edwards and Steve Hoch of UK's College of Arts and Sciences provided encouragement and funds for research, as did chairs Jeremy Popkin and David Hamilton of the History Department, my professional home for thirty-six years. Bob Flynn, Keely Jones Green, Shelby Lynn Marshall, and Stephanie May assisted with the research.

Many colleagues and friends gave generously of their time and expertise. John Behlolavek, Jerald Combs, William Freehling, Daniel Walker Howe, Howard Jones, Lawrence Kaplan, Warren Kimball, Thomas Knock, Jeffrey Matthews, Robert McMahon, Melvin Small, Mark Stoler, and Randall Woods read individual chapters covering periods of their specialties and offered invaluable suggestions. Andy Fry shared with me his vast knowledge of nineteenth- and early twentieth-century U.S. foreign policy by reading and commenting on the first half of the manuscript. Steve Wrinn, director of the University Press of Kentucky, cast his sharp editorial eye on numerous chapters. Former Transylvania University English professor Charlie Holmes read the entire manuscript, and the comments provided by this non-specialist keenly interested in international relations were very useful. Robert Divine, Walter LaFeber, Fredrik Logevall, and Jeremi Suri evaluated the manuscript for Oxford University Press and sent me detailed commentary and invaluable criticism and suggestions.

The Boone Seminar furnished weekly diversion in the form of highly competitive tennis and spirited trash talk as well as stimulating conversation about world affairs. After more than ten years on this project, I appreciate more than ever the outstanding work being done by my colleagues in the history of U.S. foreign relations. Their productivity made my task daunting. The quality of their work also made it exciting. It was great fun to continue to learn new things after more than forty years in the field.

Vicki Vaughn of the Patterson School of Diplomacy and International Commerce, where I spent my last semester, arranged for copying, packing up, and mailing out an early draft to various readers. Patiently and with all good humor, Peter Harris bailed his Luddite father-in-law out of computer foul-ups.

I have had the good fortune with this project to work with the best editors an author could hope for. I was enormously flattered when the late Sheldon Meyer, the dean of history editors, invited me to write this volume. I would like to think that he would be pleased with the result. The late C. Vann Woodward read one chapter and offered warm encouragement. Peter Ginna at Oxford helped plan the book. Series editor David M. Kennedy read chapters promptly and thoroughly. His excitement about the project gave me a huge boost. He offered countless suggestions on style and substance, especially in framing the arguments. Susan Ferber has been a wonderful editor, keenly interested in the project, attentive, helpful in every possible way, a superb critic. India Cooper is simply the best of copy editors—and a delight to work with. Caitlin Craven secured the photographs and permissions. Joellyn Ausanka skillfully managed the production process.

Finally, above all, and for so many reasons, I thank Dottie Leathers, my co-worker of nearly forty years, my wife of thirteen. This book is dedicated to her with all my love.

George C. Herring
Lexington, Kentucky

Contents

Maps

Editor's Introduction

From Colony to Superpower is the sole topical volume in *The Oxford History of the United States*, whose eleven other titles all address discrete chronological periods between the European discovery of the Americas and the dawn of the twenty-first century. George C. Herring has thus taken on a formidable challenge: crafting a coherent historical narrative around the theme of foreign relations through more than two hundred years of American nationhood, while neither ignoring nor repeating material covered elsewhere in the series.

He has succeeded more than admirably. To be sure, readers of other *Oxford History* volumes will find familiar items here, from the War of 1812 to the high-stakes diplomacy of the Civil War era, the geo-political strategies of World War II, and the disillusioning debacle of Vietnam. But Herring, a renowned scholar of the Vietnam imbroglio, brings strikingly fresh perspective to his accounts of each of those episodes, and many others. He also artfully weaves them into what is undoubtedly the single most comprehensive interpretation of the entirety of America's foreign relations yet written.

From Colony to Superpower is not a mere textbook, faithfully recounting all salient episodes in the history of American diplomacy—though its coverage is so thorough that it will surely become an authoritative reference work. Herring's accomplishment is greater than that. He has written not simply a history of American diplomacy, but a history of diplomacy's role in shaping America's unique history and its singular identity, as well as its effects on the wider world. He also has much to say about the stubbornly distinctive character of American statecraft, from the time of the Founders to the present.

His opening pages remind us of the often-neglected truth that foreign policy was the indispensable midwife to the birth of the American republic. Thomas Paine's celebrated pamphlet of 1776, *Common Sense*, simultaneously made the case for government based on the sovereignty of the people and for independence as a means to secure foreign support for the Revolutionary cause. It is not too much to say that Paine thereby drafted the foundational document of American foreign policy, one that blended high philosophical principle with clear-eyed consideration of the national interest—and infused American foreign policy from the outset with a powerful ideological flavor.

With a masterful recounting of Paine's story, Herring launches his grand narrative. It is a rich tale of the continuing interplay between soaring ideals and gritty reality, aspiration and compromise, accident and purpose, and the will of the United States and the often contrary will of countless other international actors. And it is a tale of the halting, even muddled, progression of the United States from a struggling state trying to establish its authority over the still-raw North American Atlantic seaboard to a sophisticated "hyperpower" whose influence reached into every corner of the planet, for better or for worse.

The infant nation's first diplomatic task was to protect its experiment in representative government from foreign interference. As George Washington's fabled Farewell Address made clear, it was essential to that task that the nation be ever vigilant against "the insidious wiles of foreign influence," that it avoid the entanglements of foreign alliances or even partiality to any other power, and that it recognize the limits to its own capacity and adapt its foreign policy to its abilities as well as to its ideals and its interests. Yet, Herring writes, Washington also dreamed of a time when the United States would "possess the strength of a Giant and there will be none who can make us afraid." He and others in the founding generation envisioned an America that would usher in a *novus ordo seclorum* (new order of the ages) in the international as well as in the domestic sphere. But they knew that theirs was not the generation that could hope to achieve such an extravagant goal.

The next immediate task of American diplomacy was to advance the project of continental expansion. As Herring brilliantly shows, North America in the nineteenth century was not a vacant wilderness awaiting pioneers to tame it. It was, rather, an arena of international intrigue and a cockpit of sometimes explosive rivalries. At various times British, Spanish, French, Russian, and Mexican contenders clashed with the Americans for dominance over the continent—as did the several Indian tribes that warily watched white encroachment on their ancestral lands. Indeed, it is among the many strengths of Herring's account that he insists on understanding Indian policy as foreign policy, with immense consequences for both national security and national expansion. He also explodes the common assumption that Americans were uniquely peace-loving. As he pointedly observes in his Introduction, "each generation has had its war."

By the nineteenth century's close, the United States had consolidated its grasp on its continental domain and began to look outward with ever-swelling ambitions. The Spanish-American War of 1898 and President Theodore Roosevelt's dispatch of the "Great White Fleet" on a world-girdling show of strength in 1907 heralded the arrival of a potential new great power on the international stage, even as the world was rapidly growing more interconnected and more volatile. But many Americans carried into the modern era the habits of inwardness and the tendency to take national security as a free gift of Nature that had prevailed in the Republic's first century. Some wanted to maintain that posture indefinitely. Others, including Roosevelt, yearned to see the nation seated among the circle of great powers that presumed to arbitrate the world's destinies. Still others, conspicuously including Woodrow Wilson, hearkened back to the transformative dreams of the Founders. As Wilson put it in 1914: "What are we going to do with the influence and power of this great nation? Are we going to play the old role of using that power for our aggrandizement and material benefit only?" As Herring shows, those simple questions have overhung the foreign policy of the United States ever since, as successive generations of Americans have continued to question whether and how, and to what ends, American power should be exercised in the international arena.

Wilson's questions came into especially sharp focus in 1945, when World War II's conclusion deposited the United States, in Winston Churchill's memorable phrase, "at the summit of the world." America now came into the fullness of its powers, not merely as one among many international players, but as an increasingly influential hegemon that led the way to the most sweeping transformations in international institutions, norms, and behaviors since the Treaty of Westphalia in 1648. How history managed to cast the United States in that role, and how well or badly it played its part, are lucidly analyzed in the pages that follow.

Herring also treats the reader to a parade of colorful personalities who have shaped America's diplomacy: a trio of Adamses, including John, the dour second president who contrived to avoid taking an overmatched United States into war with France; his shrewdly prudential son, John Quincy, the author of the Monroe Doctrine and the cool realist who declared the United States "does not go abroad in search of monsters to destroy"; and the silky diplomat Charles Francis Adams, Lincoln's cunning and diligent minister to the Court of St. James during the Civil War. We also get a pair of Roosevelts (Theodore and Franklin), a brace of Bushes (father and son), and numerous generals and admirals, as well as various missionaries, journalists, theorists, traders, settlers, and adventurers who put their mark on the nation's relationships with others.

The highest aim of the *Oxford History of the United States* is to bring the very best historical scholarship to the widest possible readership, in books that are at once original, analytical, and narratively compelling. *From Colony to Superpower* satisfies all those criteria handsomely. It is an exceptionally welcome addition to the series.

David M. Kennedy

From Colony to Superpower

Introduction

In his last years in office, an embattled President George Washington yearned for a time when his nation would "possess the strength of a Giant and there will be none who can make us afraid."[1] More than two hundred years later, at the dawn of the twenty-first century, the United States had achieved a position of world power Washington could not have dreamed of. Pundits hailed a "unipolar moment."[2] Comparisons were drawn with ancient Rome, the only historical example that seemed adequately to describe America's global preeminence.

This volume recounts the rise of the United States from a loose grouping of small, disparate colonies huddled along the Atlantic coast of North America and surrounded by often hostile Indians and the possessions of unfriendly European powers to a commanding position in world politics and economics. It focuses on U.S. foreign policy and seeks to place it in the context of an ever changing international system. It also examines the deeply shaping role played by foreign relations in the evolution of America's domestic institutions and values.

Foreign policy has been central to the national experience from the outset. External assistance was essential to the birth of an independent United States; concerns about international commerce and foreign threats decisively influenced the form of government created in the Constitutional Convention of 1787. Foreign policy molded the political culture of the new nation. It was instrumental in securing the young republic's political experiment and the outcome of the Civil War. During the nation's second full century and beyond, it has become even more critical to the prosperity and security of the United States. The enduring idea of an isolationist America is a myth often conveniently used to safeguard the nation's self-image of its innocence. In fact, from 1776 on, the United States has been an active and influential player in world affairs. Foreign policy has had a huge impact on American life.

Americans think of themselves as peace-loving, but few nations have had as much experience at war as the United States. Indeed, beginning

1. Quoted in Burton Ira Kaufman, *Washington's Farewell Address: The View from the Twentieth Century* (Chicago, 1969), 170.
2. The phrase was coined by *Washington Post* columnist Charles Krauthammer.

with the American Revolution, each generation has had its war. Armed conflict has helped to forge the bonds of nationhood, nurtured national pride, and fostered myths about the nation's singular virtue and indomitableness. From the American Revolution to the present, wars have also set the mileposts on the nation's road to world power.[3] America's nineteenth-century conflicts provided the means to conquer a continent and acquire overseas territory. Europe's extended and bloody twentieth-century civil war laid low the traditional great powers, shifting the center of gravity of world politics and economics across the Atlantic to the United States. The collapse of the Soviet Union at the end of a half century of Cold War left the United States the lone superpower in a unipolar world.

Throughout its history, the United States has taken a distinctive approach toward foreign policy. A set of assumed ideas and shared values have determined the way Americans viewed themselves and others and how they dealt with other peoples and responded to and sought to shape events abroad.

From the birth of the nation—even when there was little cause to do so—Americans have shared a faith in their nation's destiny.[4] The Revolutionary generation did not hesitate to use the word *empire*, although for them the word meant something different from what it meant to Europeans. Jefferson envisioned an "empire of liberty," a necklace of independent republics spread across North America. For the generation of the 1840s, America's Manifest Destiny was to spread across the continent and even beyond. When the United States thrashed Spain in 1898, it signaled to Americans—and others—the mature nation's emergence as a major power. "The greatest destiny the world ever knew is ours," ambassador John Hay crowed from London.[5] Amidst the carnage of World War I, Woodrow Wilson proclaimed for the United States what he believed to be its rightful role as world leader. Although his ideas were rejected by Americans in his own lifetime, they lived on to inspire U.S. leaders into the twenty-first century. Such was the nation's power and influence after World War II that the twentieth century came to be called the American Century. In the 1990s, Secretary of State Madeleine Albright would refer to the United States as the "indispensable nation."

Americans have held decidedly mixed views about the international order and their place in it. On the one hand, they have been allured by the riches of the world. Their lust for trade with other countries led them to

3. Geoffrey Perrett, *A Country Made by War* (New York, 1989), 558–59, 562.
4. Michael H. Hunt, *Ideology and U.S. Foreign Policy* (New Haven, Conn., 1987), 19–45.
5. David Healy, *U.S. Expansionism: The Imperialist Urge in the 1890s* (Madison, Wisc., 1970), 39.

rebel against Britain's mercantilist restrictions in 1775. Early Americans viewed international commerce as essential to their economic well-being and their political freedom alike. Adopting ideas from European Enlightenment thinkers, some even saw free trade as a means to transform the very nature of international life.[6] As the nation shifted from a commercial to an industrial economy, foreign markets and investment outlets continued to be seen as crucial to the nation's prosperity and stability. To be sure, Americans have often heatedly debated the importance of domestic versus overseas markets and the priorities to be assigned to the protection of domestic industries or the stimulation of foreign trade, making tariff policy at times a highly contentious issue. Yet from the Revolution to the present, the pursuit of economic self-interest has ensured a high level of global involvement.

On the other hand, Americans have often seen themselves as a people apart. The Revolutionary generation rebelled not only against Britain but also against Old World ways. European history formed a "summary of the evils which America has escaped," a Kentucky lawyer rejoiced in the early nineteenth century.[7] Americans associated conventional dealings among nations with royalty and found them repugnant. They rejected realpolitik and decried traditional diplomacy, in Thomas Jefferson's words, as "the pest of the peace of the world."[8] They saw themselves as heralds of a *novus ordo seclorum*, a new world order, in which enlightened diplomacy based on free trade would create a beneficent system that would serve the broader interests of mankind rather than the selfish needs of monarchs and their courts. In the early national period, Americans flaunted their distinctiveness by rejecting the trappings of European diplomacy, even the customary formal dress, and by refusing to appoint ambassadors, a rank associated with European royalty. As the United States emerged to world-power status, it made its peace with conventional diplomatic practices. But Americans continued to see themselves as different from their European forebears and as harbingers of a new world order. For Wilson, the Great War more than ever exposed the insanity of European power politics, prompting him to set forth a vision for reforming world politics and economics according to *American* principles. Open diplomacy, disarmament, freedom of the seas, free trade, and self-determination for nationalities, in his view, would promote peace and prosperity for all peoples.

6. Felix Gilbert, *The Beginnings of American Foreign Policy: To the Farewell Address* (New York, 1965), 44–75.
7. Quoted in Peter S. Onuf and Nicholas Onuf, *Federal Union, Modern World: The Law of Nations in an Age of Revolution* (Madison, Wisc., 1993), 139.
8. Quoted in Gilbert, *American Foreign Policy*, 72.

From Massachusetts Bay Colony founder John Winthrop's invocation of a "city upon a hill," through Jefferson and Wilson, to George W. Bush's born-again zeal, Americans have continued to see themselves as a chosen people with a providential mission, "God's American Israel," the Puritans called it.[9] They have taken pride in their presumably unique innocence and virtue, "the most moral and generous people on earth," in Ronald Reagan's words.[10] They have felt a special obligation to extend the blessings of freedom to others. Beginning with John Quincy Adams's and Henry Clay's eloquent debate over U.S. support for the Greek rebellion against Turkey in 1821, they have often disputed whether that mission could best be fulfilled by what Adams called the "benignant sympathy of our example"—by creating a society at home worthy of emulation—or by active intervention.[11] Depending on the state of the nation, its position in the world, and the proclivities of its leaders, they have varied in their zeal to spread the blessings of liberty, but they have retained a sense of special virtue and unique destiny.

The ideal of a providential mission has spurred a drive to do good in the world, manifested in the work of merchants, missionaries, and educators, often the advance guard of the nation's foreign policy. It also undergirded the Wilsonian dream of the United States as world leader and a world reformed according to its principles. In the twenty-first century, the extension of freedom has even been declared a basis for U.S. security. "The survival of liberty in our land increasingly depends on the success of liberty in other lands," George W. Bush proclaimed in 2005. "The best hope for freedom in our world is the expansion of freedom in all the world."[12]

This sense of a special destiny has at times also spawned arrogance. Disdain for native peoples and Mexicans fueled America's rush across the continent, pushing the Indians steadily westward to the verge of extinction and wresting from Mexico one-third of its territory. Similar sentiments led to the imposition of colonial rule on Filipinos and Puerto Ricans and to the establishment of protectorates throughout much of the Caribbean. From an ill-fated incursion into Canada in 1775 to the 2003 invasion of Iraq, America's sense of its grand historical mission has even justified spreading the blessings of liberty by force. Certain of their righ-

9. Richard Van Alstyne, *Empire and Independence: The International History of the American Revolution* (New York, 1965), 4.
10. Ronald Reagan, *An American Life* (New York, 1990), 296.
11. Adams's July 4, 1821, speech may be found at www.fff.org/freedom/1001e.asp.
12. Second inaugural address, January 20, 2005, www.whitehouse.gov/inaugural.

teousness, Americans have confidently expected to be welcomed as liberators. The ironic result, in many cases, has been to invigorate nationalist opposition.

Attitudes about race have reinforced this sense of cultural superiority. The United States came into existence as a slaveholding nation, and slavery exerted a potent impact on its foreign policy until its abolition after the Civil War. Slavery was supported by pseudo-scientific nineteenth-century ideas about a hierarchy of race that assigned the top rank to white Anglo-Saxons and lower positions to other races based on darkness of skin color.[13] Americans' views on race along with their sense of cultural superiority made it easy to justify expansion and empire. In their dealings with "barbarous" Mediterranean and Malay "pirates," "bigoted" and "indolent" people of Spanish descent, and "inscrutable" Vietnamese, Chinese, and Japanese, nineteenth-century Americans often adopted a high-handed approach based on a sense of racial superiority. Scientific racism was discredited in the twentieth century, but more subtle forms have exerted persisting influence over U.S. interactions with other peoples and nations.

The ideological fervor and messianic streak that have stamped U.S. foreign policy have been balanced by offsetting tendencies. Pragmatism is basic to the American character, and in diplomacy U.S. officials have often manifested a willingness to compromise to achieve vital goals. Indeed, diplomats and policymakers such as Benjamin Franklin, Abraham Lincoln, and Franklin D. Roosevelt went further by developing a uniquely American brand of practical idealism, conforming to the nation's professed principles while vigorously pursuing important interests. When they have clung to ideological positions and refused to compromise, as with Jefferson and James Madison in responding to British trade restrictions between 1805 and 1812 and Wilson with the League of Nations in 1919–20, they have met defeat.

United States policymakers have also been swayed by what Jefferson in the Declaration of Independence called a "decent respect for the opinions of mankind." Their determination to live up to their ideals and concern for their standing before at least some other nations have at times put checks on the nation's more aggressive tendencies. Wars and military occupations have produced revelations of atrocities and torture, provoking political backlashes that forced changes in policy. As Richard Nixon and Henry Kissinger's amoral "realism" demonstrated, policies can not survive

13. Hunt, *Ideology*, 46–91.

indefinitely without some foundation in the nation's most cherished principles. "The American conscience is a reality," columnist Walter Lippmann wrote at the height of the Cold War. "It will make hesitant and ineffectual, even if it does not prevent, an un-American policy."[14]

Unilateralism, often mistakenly called isolationism, has also formed a powerful and enduring strain in U.S. foreign policy. From the outset, Americans chose *not* to isolate themselves from the world, preferring to reap the wealth offered by commerce with other countries. The term *isolationism* did not come into common usage until World War I. But a unilateralist approach seemed natural and essential to people who saw themselves as morally superior and understandably feared entanglement in Europe's wars and contamination from its cancerous politics. The turbulent experience of the infant republic in fending off foreign threats underscored the urgency of abstaining from Europe's alliances and wars. Unilateralism also derived from geography. The United States was "blessed among nations," French ambassador Jules Jusserand observed in the early 1900s: "On the north she had a weak neighbor; on the south, another weak neighbor; on the east, fish, and on the west, fish."[15] Indeed, through much of the nineteenth century and beyond, geography conferred upon the United States an advantage few nations have enjoyed—the absence of major foreign threat—permitting it to avoid binding foreign commitments and to expand and prosper with minimal distraction from abroad. This free security has made the nation highly sensitive to threats, so that when they occur Americans have sometimes exaggerated them.

As early as the turn of the twentieth century, some Americans began to argue that a world reduced in size and made more dangerous by advances in military technology rendered traditional policies outdated. But it would take the Second World War and especially the Japanese attack on Pearl Harbor on December 7, 1941, to shatter the notion that the United States was safe from foreign threat. During the Cold War era, an embattled nation turned unilateralist ideas on their head. The historical experience of free security helped to generate an exaggerated sense that the United States might be threatened by events anywhere. During the heyday of the Cold War, John F. Kennedy could even declare tiny Guyana in northern South America vital to U.S. security. The United States took on

14. Quoted in William M. LeoGrande, *Our Own Backyard: The United States in Central America, 1959–1980* (Chapel Hill, N.C., 1998), 551.
15. Quoted in Steven Walt, *Taming American Power: The Global Response to American Primacy* (New York, 2005), 39.

commitments to scores of nations, established military bases throughout the world, and provided billions of dollars in economic and military assistance to allies. Such was the power of the unilateralist tradition, however, that even after a half century of global commitments, it resurfaced in the radically altered international environment of the post–Cold War era.

Unilateralism served the United States well during its first century and a half, but it also bred a certain smug parochialism and a suspicion of international institutions, as well as indifference and even hostility toward other cultures and peoples. In part as a result of their historical separation from the mainstream of world affairs, historian Fredrik Logevall has observed, Americans were spared the necessity of negotiating and making concessions to survive and prosper. They have never been "wholly comfortable in the messy world of European style politics and diplomacy, with its emphasis on pragmatic give and take leading to imperfect solutions."[16]

America's democratic political system has also given a distinctive cast to its foreign policy. Political parties originated from the bitter internal struggle over ratification of the Jay Treaty with Britain in 1794. Since that time, foreign policy has often been the object of fierce partisan dispute. Party differences have sparked vigorous debates over the nation's role in the world. At times, partisan politics have obstructed effective diplomacy. On other occasions, opposition parties have put needed constraints on policymakers and helped rein in ill-advised policies.

As in most other countries, U.S. foreign policy has normally remained the province of elites, but leaders must pay heed to the democratic process. On occasion, an aroused public has pushed the government to act. Interest groups focusing on issues like armament or disarmament, human rights, and trade issues have relentlessly promoted their agendas. Huge influxes of immigrants have flooded the United States at various times in its history and produced ethnic constituencies that, from the Irish in the late nineteenth century to the modern-day Cuban and Israeli lobbies, have sought to sway the government to adopt policies favoring their countries of origin, sometimes producing initiatives that run counter to broader U.S. interests. More often, public indifference or apathy has created impediments for policymakers, bringing about in the twentieth century sustained and increasingly sophisticated efforts to inform, "educate," and manipulate public opinion. At times, policymakers have resorted to

16. Fredrik Logevall, *Choosing War: The Lost Chance for Peace in Vietnam* (Berkeley, Calif., 1999), 384. See also Logevall, "A Critique of Containment," *Diplomatic History* 28 (September 2004), 488.

distortions and lies to sell their programs. They have exaggerated foreign threats to gain public and congressional support. Having done so, they sometimes boxed themselves in, forcing a vigorous response to perceived dangers to avoid the risk of domestic political backlash.

By dividing foreign policy powers between the executive and legislative branches of government, the U.S. Constitution added another level of confusion and conflict. The executive branch is obviously better suited to conduct foreign policy than a larger, inherently divided legislature whose members often represent local interests. George Washington set early precedents establishing presidential predominance. In the twentieth and early twenty-first centuries, the growing importance of foreign policy and the existence of major foreign threats have vastly expanded executive power, producing what has been called the imperial presidency. Congress from time to time has asserted itself and sought to regain some measure of control over foreign policy. Sometimes, as in the 1930s and 1970s, it has exerted decisive influence on crucial policy issues. For the most part and especially in the realm of war powers, the president has reigned supreme. Sometimes, chief executives have found it expedient to seek congressional endorsement of their decisions for war if not an outright declaration. Other times and especially in periods of danger, Congress has witlessly rallied behind the president, neglecting to ask crucial questions about policy decisions that turned out to be badly flawed.

America's peculiar approach to foreign policy has long bemused and befuddled foreign observers. Referring specifically to the United States, that often astute nineteenth-century French observer Alexis de Tocqueville warned that democracies "obey the impulse of passion rather than the suggestions of prudence." They "abandon a mature design for the gratification of a momentary caprice."[17] In the early years, European diplomats tried to exploit the chaos that was American politics by bribing members of Congress and even interfering in the electoral process. More recently, other nations have hired lobbyists and even public relations experts to promote their interests and images in the United States.

Despite claims to moral superiority and disdain for Old World diplomacy, the United States throughout its history has behaved more like a traditional great power than Americans have realized or might care to admit. United States policymakers have often been shrewd analysts of world politics. They have energetically pursued and zealously protected inter-

---

17. Melvin Small, *Democracy and Diplomacy: The Impact of Domestic Politics on Foreign Policy* (Baltimore, Md., 1996), xi.

ests deemed vital. In terms of commerce and territory, they have been aggressively and relentlessly expansionist. They exploited rivalries among the Europeans to secure their independence, favorable boundaries, and vast territorial acquisitions. From Louisiana to the Floridas, Texas, California, and eventually Hawaii, they fashioned the process of infiltration and subversion into a finely tuned instrument of expansion, using the presence of restless Americans in nominally foreign lands to establish claims and take over additional territory. When the hunger for land was sated, they extended American economic and political influence across the world. During the Cold War, when the nation's survival seemed threatened, they scrapped old notions of fair play, intervening in the affairs of other nations, overthrowing governments, even plotting the assassination of foreign leaders. From the founders of the eighteenth century to the Cold Warriors two hundred years later, they played the great game of world politics with some measure of skill.

Popular notions to the contrary, the United States has been spectacularly successful in its foreign policy. To be sure, like all countries, it has made huge mistakes and suffered major failures, sometimes with tragic consequences for Americans—and other peoples as well. At the same time, it has sustained an overall record of achievement with little precedent in history. In the space of a little more than two hundred years, it conquered a continent, came to dominate the Caribbean and Pacific Ocean areas, helped win two world wars, prevailed in a half-century Cold War, and extended its economic influence, military might, popular culture, and "soft power" through much of the world. By the beginning of the twenty-first century, it had attained that "strength of a Giant" that Washington longed for.

Ironically, as the nation grew more powerful, the limits to its power became more palpable, a harsh reality for which Americans were not prepared by history. The nation's unprecedented success spawned what a British commentator called the "illusion of American omnipotence," the notion that the United States could do anything it set its mind to, or, as one wag put it, the difficult we do tomorrow, the impossible may take a while.[18] Success came to be taken for granted. Failure caused great frustration. When it occurred, many Americans preferred to pin it on villains at home rather than admit there were things their nation could not do. Despite its vast wealth and awesome military power, the United States had to settle for a stalemate in the Korean War. It could not work its will

18. D. W. Brogan, *The American Character* (New York, 1956), 207–8.

in Vietnam or Iraq, nations whose complex societies and idiosyncratic histories defied its efforts to reshape them.

The emergence of a new twenty-first-century threat in the form of international terrorism and the devastating September 11, 2001, attacks on New York's World Trade Center and the Pentagon underscored another hard reality: that power does not guarantee security. On the contrary, the greater a nation's global influence, the greater its capacity to provoke envy and anger; the more overseas interests it has, the more targets it presents to foes, and the more it has to lose. Weaker nations can deal with a hegemonic nation by combining with each other or simply by obstructing its moves.[19] Even America's unparalleled power could not fully assure the freedom from fear that George Washington longed for.

19. Steven Walt, "Taming American Power," *Foreign Affairs* (September/October 2005), 105–20, and *Taming American Power*, 109–79

1

"To Begin the World Over Again"

Foreign Policy and the Birth of
the Republic, 1776–1788

"We have every opportunity and every encouragement before us, to form the noblest, and purest constitution on the face of the earth," revolutionary pamphleteer Tom Paine wrote in late 1775. Paine's words came at a time when the American colonists in their struggle with Great Britain suffered military defeat and economic distress. They were bitterly divided between those who sought independence and those who preferred accommodation. Only thirty-seven years old when he arrived in the United States in 1774, Paine had been a corset maker and minor British government functionary. His best-selling pamphlet *Common Sense* made an impassioned appeal for independence. It was "absurd," he insisted, for a "continent to be perpetually governed by an island." A declaration of independence would gain for America assistance from England's enemies, France and Spain. It would secure for an independent America peace and prosperity. The colonists had been dragged into Europe's wars by their connection with England. Without such ties, there would be no cause for European hostility. Freed of British restrictions, commerce would "secure us the peace and friendship of all Europe because it is in the interest of all Europe to have America as a free port."[1]

Paine's call for independence makes clear the centrality of foreign policy to the birth of the American republic. His arguments hinged on estimates of the importance of the colonies in the international system of the late eighteenth century. They suggest the significant role foreign policy would assume in the achievement of independence and the adoption of a new constitution. They set forth basic principles that would shape U.S. foreign policy for years to come. They hint at the essential characteristics of what would become a distinctively American approach to foreign policy. The Revolutionary generation held to an expansive

---

1. Thomas P. Slaughter, ed., *Common Sense and Related Writings* (Boston, 2001), 89, 90, 93.

vision, a certainty of their future greatness and destiny. They believed themselves a chosen people and brought to their interactions with others a certain self-righteousness and disdain for established practice. They saw themselves as harbingers of a new world order, creating forms of governance and commerce that would appeal to peoples everywhere and change the course of world history. "We have it in our power to begin the world over again," Paine wrote. Idealistic in their vision, in their actions Americans demonstrated a pragmatism born perhaps of necessity that helped ensure the success of their revolution and the promulgation of the Constitution.[2]

I

From their foundation, the American colonies were an integral part of the British Empire and hence of an Atlantic trading community. According to the dictates of mercantilism, then the dominant school of economic thought, the colonies supplied the mother country with timber, tobacco, and other agricultural products and purchased its manufactured goods. But the Americans also broke from prescribed trade patterns. New England and New York developed an extensive illicit commerce with French Canada, even while Britain was at war with France. They also opened a lucrative commerce with Dutch and French colonies in the West Indies, selling food and other necessities and buying sugar more cheaply than it could be acquired from the British West Indies. Americans benefited in many ways from Britain's mercantilist Navigation Acts, but they staunchly resisted efforts to curb their trade with the colonies of other European nations. They became champions of free trade well before the Revolution.[3]

The American colonies were also part of a Eurocentric "international" community. Formed at the Peace of Westphalia in 1648, this new system sought to end years of bloody religious strife by enlarging the stature and role of the nation-state. Based in part on concepts developed by Hugo Grotius, the Dutch political theorist and father of international law, Westphalia established principles such as the sovereign equality of states, the territorial integrity of the state, non-interference by one state in the

---

2. Ibid., 113; Felix Gilbert, *The Beginnings of American Foreign Policy: To the Farewell Address* (New York, 1965), 37–43. See also David W. Fitzsimons, "Thomas Paine's New World Order: Idealistic Internationalism in the Ideology of Early American Foreign Policy," *Diplomatic History* 19 (Fall 1995), 574–78.
3. Max Savelle, *The Origins of American Diplomacy: The International History of Anglo-America* (New York, 1967), 540–44.

domestic affairs of others, peaceful resolution of disputes, and the obligation to abide by international agreements. After Westphalia, diplomacy and war came under the purview of civil rather than religious authority. A corps of professional diplomats emerged to handle interstate relations. A code was produced to guide their conduct. François de Callières's classic manual of the eighteenth-century diplomatic art affirmed that negotiations should be conducted in good faith, honorably, and without deceit—"a lie always leaves a drop of poison behind." On the other hand, spies were essential for information gathering, and bribes—although that word was not used—were encouraged. Negotiation required keen powers of observation, concentration on the task at hand, sound judgment, and presence of mind, de Callières explained. But a "gift presented in the right spirit, at the right moment, by the right person, may act with tenfold power upon him who receives it." It was also important to cultivate the ladies of the court, for "the greatest events have sometimes followed the toss of a fan or the nod of a head."[4]

Far from eliminating war, the new system simply changed the reasons for fighting and the means of combat. Issues of war and peace were decided on the basis of national interest as defined by the monarch and his court. Nation-states acted on the basis of realpolitik rather than religious considerations, changing sides in alliances when it suited their foreign policy goals.[5] Rulers deliberately restricted the means and ends of combat. They had seen the costs and dangers of unleashing the passions of their people. They had made substantial investments in their armies, needed them for domestic order, and were loath to risk them in battle. Once involved in war, they sought to avoid major battles, employed professional armies in cautious strategies of attrition, used tactics emphasizing maneuver and fortification, and held to unwritten rules protecting civilian lives and property. The aim was to sustain the balance of power rather than destroy the enemy. War was to be conducted with minimal intrusion into the lives of the people. Indeed, that master practitioner of limited war, Prussia's Frederick the Great, once observed that war was not a success if most people knew it was going on.

In the international system of the eighteenth century, Spain, the Netherlands, and Sweden, the great powers of an earlier era, were in decline, while France, Great Britain, Austria, Prussia, and Russia were ascending. Separated by a narrow channel of water, Britain and France

4. Ronald Hoffman and Peter J. Albert, eds., *Peace and the Peacemakers: The Treaty of 1783* (Charlottesville, Va., 1986), ix–xii.
5. Paul Kennedy, *The Rise and Fall of the Great Powers* (New York, 1987), 73.

were especially keen rivals and fought five major wars between 1689 and 1776. The American colonies became entangled in most of them.

The Seven Years' War, or French and Indian War, as Americans have known it, has been aptly called the "War That Made America."[6] That conflict originated in the colonies with fighting between Americans and French in the region between the Allegheny Mountains and the Mississippi River. It spread to Europe, where coalitions gathered around traditional rivals Britain and France, and to colonial possessions in the Caribbean and West Indies, the Mediterranean, the Southwest Pacific, and South Asia. Winston Churchill without too much exaggeration called it the "first world war." After early setbacks in Europe and America, Britain won a decisive victory and emerged the world's greatest power, wresting from France Canada and territory in India and from Spain the territories of East and West Florida, a global empire surpassing that of Rome.[7]

As is often the case in war, victory came at high cost. Americans had played a major part in Britain's success and envisioned themselves as equal partners in the empire. Relieved of the French and Spanish menace, they depended less on Britain's protection and sought to enjoy the fruits of their military success. The war exhausted Britain financially. Efforts to recoup its costs and to pay the expenses of a vastly expanded empire—by closing off the trans-Appalachian region to settlement, enforcing long-standing trade restrictions, and taxing the Americans for their own defense—sparked revolutionary sentiment among the colonists and their first efforts to band together in common cause. The disparate colonies attempted to apply economic pressures in the form of nonimportation agreements. Twelve colonies sent delegates to a first Continental Congress in Philadelphia in the fall of 1774 to discuss ways to deal with British "oppression." A second Continental Congress assembled in May 1775 as shots were being fired outside Boston.

American foreign relations began before independence was declared. Once war was a reality, colonial leaders instinctively looked abroad for help. England's rival, France, also took a keen interest in events in America, dispatching an agent to Philadelphia in August 1775 to size up the prospects for rebellion. The Americans were not certain how Europe might respond to a revolution. John Adams of Massachusetts once speculated, with the moral self-righteousness that typified American attitudes toward European diplomacy, that it might take generous bribes, a gift for intrigue, and contact with "some of the Misses and Courtezans in

6. Fred Anderson, *The War That Made America* (New York, 2005).
7. Ibid., xxiii, 228.

keeping of the statesmen in France" to secure foreign assistance.[8] About the time French envoy Julien-Alexandre Ochard de Bonvouloir arrived in December, the Continental Congress appointed a Committee of Secret Correspondence to explore the possibility of foreign aid. The committee sounded out Bonvouloir on French willingness to sell war supplies. Encouraged by the response, it sent Connecticut merchant Silas Deane to France to arrange for the purchase of arms and other equipment. Three days before Deane arrived in France, Congress approved a Declaration of Independence designed to bring the American colonies into a union that could establish ties with other nations.[9] Whatever place the Declaration has since assumed in the folklore of American nationhood, its immediate and urgent purpose was to make clear to Europeans, especially the French, the colonies' commitment to independence.[10]

Although their behavior at times suggests otherwise, the Americans were not naive provincials. Their worldview was shaped by experiences as the most important colony of the British Empire, particularly in the most recent war. Colonial leaders were also familiar with European writings on diplomacy and commerce. Americans often expressed moral indignation at the depravity of the European balance-of-power system, but they observed it closely, understood its workings, and sought to exploit it. They turned for assistance to a vengeful France recently humiliated by England and presumably eager to weaken its rival by helping its colony gain independence. Painfully aware of their need for foreign aid, they were also profoundly wary of political commitments to European nations. Conveniently forgetting their own role in provoking the Seven Years' War, they worried that such entanglements would drag them into the wars that seemed constantly to wrack Europe. They feared that, as in 1763, their interests would be ignored in the peacemaking. Americans had followed debates in England on the value of connections with Continental powers. They adapted to their own use the arguments of those Britons who urged avoiding European conflicts and retaining maximum freedom of action. "It is the true interest of America to steer clear of European contentions," Paine advised in *Common Sense*.[11]

---

8. Jack N. Rakove, *The Beginnings of National Politics: An Interpretive History of the Continental Congress* (New York, 1997), 93.

9. Peter S. Onuf, "The Declaration of Independence for Diplomatic Historians," *Diplomatic History* 22 (Winter 1998), 71.

10. William Earl Weeks, *Building the Continental Empire: American Expansion from the Revolution to the Civil War* (Chicago, 1996), 10–11.

11. Gilbert, *Beginnings*, 32–43. The Paine quote is from p. 43.

Americans also agreed that their ties with Europe should be mainly commercial. Through their experience in the British Empire, they had embraced freedom of trade before the publication of Adam Smith's classic *Wealth of Nations* in 1776. They saw the opportunity to trade with all nations on an equal basis as being in their best interests and indeed essential for their economic well-being. Independence would permit them to "shake hands with the world—live at peace with the world—and trade to any market," according to Paine.[12] The enticement of trade would secure European support against Britain. Drawing upon French and Scottish Enlightenment philosophers, some Americans believed that replacement of the corrupt, oppressive, and warlike systems of mercantilism and power politics would produce a more peaceful world. The free interchange of goods would demonstrate that growth in the wealth of one nation would bring an increase for all. The interests of nations were therefore compatible rather than in conflict. The civilizing effect of free trade and the greater understanding among peoples that would come from increased contact would promote harmony among nations.

Keenly aware of their present weakness, the American revolutionaries envisioned future greatness. They embraced views dating back to John Winthrop and the founders of the Massachusetts Bay Colony of a city upon a hill that would serve as a beacon to peoples across the world. They saw themselves conducting a unique experiment in self-government that foreshadowed a new era in world politics. As a young man, John Adams of Massachusetts proclaimed the founding of the American colonies as "the opening of a grand scheme and design in Providence for the elimination of the ignorant, and the emancipation of the slavish part of mankind all over the earth." Americans had gloried in the triumph of the British Empire in 1763. When that empire, in their view, had failed them, they were called into being, in the words of patriot Ezra Stiles, to "rescue & reinthrone the hoary venerable head of the most glorious empire on earth." They believed they were establishing an empire without a metropolis, based on "consent, not coercion," that could serve as an "asylum for mankind," as Paine put it, and inspire others to break the shackles of despotism. Through free trade and enlightened diplomacy they would create a new world order.[13]

Even while Deane was sailing to France in pursuit of money and urgently needed supplies, another committee appointed by Congress was drafting a treaty to be offered to European nations embracing these first

---

12. Fitzsimons, "Paine's New World Order," 576.
13. Peter S. Onuf, *Jefferson's Empire: The Language of American Nationhood* (Charlottesville, Va., 2000), 2, 25, 57; Gilbert, *Beginnings*, 55.

precepts of American foreign policy. The so-called Model Treaty, or Plan of 1776, was written largely by John Adams. It would guide treaty-making for years to come. In crafting the terms, Adams and his colleagues agreed as a fundamental principle that the nation must avoid any commitments that would entangle it in future European wars. Indeed, Adams specifically recommended that in dealing with France no *political* connections should be formed. America must not submit to French authority or form military ties; it should receive no French troops. France would be asked to renounce claims to territory in North America. In return, the Americans would agree not to oppose French reconquest of the West Indies and would not use an Anglo-French war to come to terms with England. Both signatories would agree in the event of a general war not to make a separate peace without notifying the other six months in advance.

The lure to entice France and other Europeans to support the rebellious colonies would be commerce. Since trade with America was a key element of Britain's power, its rivals would not pass up the opportunity to capture it. The Model Treaty thus proposed that trade should not be encumbered by tariffs or other restrictions. Looking to the time when as a neutral nation they might seek to trade with nations at war, Americans also proposed a set of principles advocated by leading neutral nations and proponents of free trade. Neutrals should be free in wartime to trade with all belligerents in all goods except contraband. Contraband should be defined narrowly. Free ships would make free goods; that is to say, cargo aboard ships not at war should be free from confiscation. The Model Treaty was breathtaking in some of its assumptions and principles. Congress approved it in September 1776 and elected Thomas Jefferson of Virginia (who declined to serve) and elder statesman Benjamin Franklin of Philadelphia to join Deane in assisting with its negotiation and bringing France into the war. The Americans thus entered European diplomacy as heralds of a new age.[14]

Not surprisingly, the French were also nervous about close connections. The architect of French policy toward the American Revolution was the secretary of state for foreign affairs, Charles Gravier, comte de Vergennes. An aristocrat and career diplomat, Vergennes had spent so much time abroad—more than thirty years in posts across Europe—that a colleague dismissed him as a "foreigner become Minister."[15] He was well versed in

14. Gilbert, *Beginnings*, 56.
15. Orville T. Murphy, "The View from Versailles: Charles Gravier Comte de Vergennes's Perceptions of the American Revolution," in Ronald Hoffman and Peter J. Albert, eds., *Diplomacy and Revolution: The Franco-American Alliance of 1778* (Charlottesville, Va., 1981), 110.

international politics, cautious by nature, and hardworking. Jefferson said of him that "it is impossible to have a clearer, better argued head." Vergennes's chief concern was to regain French preeminence in Europe.[16] He saw obvious advantages in helping the Americans. But he also saw dangers. France could not be certain of their commitment to achieve independence or their ability to do so. He worried they might reconcile with Britain and join forces to attack the French West Indies. He recognized that overt aid to the Americans would give Britain cause for a war France was not prepared to fight. French policy therefore was to keep the rebels fighting by "feeding their courage" and offering "hope of efficacious assistance" while avoiding steps that might provoke war with Britain. The French government through what would now be called a covert operation provided limited, clandestine aid to the rebels. It set up a fictitious trading company headed by Pierre-Augustin Caron de Beaumarchais, a colorful aristocrat and playwright whose comedies like *The Barber of Seville* poked fun at his own class, and loaned it funds to purchase military supplies from government warehouses to sell the Americans on credit.

Ninety percent of the gunpowder used by the colonists during the first years of the war came from Europe, and foreign aid was thus indispensable from the outset. By the end of 1776, however, it was increasingly apparent that secret, limited aid might not be enough. Early military operations were disappointing, even calamitous. From the outset, Americans believed that other peoples shared their aspirations. Naively assuming that the residents of Canada, many of them French Catholics, would rally to the cause, they invaded Britain's northernmost province in September 1775. Expecting Canada to fall like "easy prey," in George Washington's words, they also grossly underestimated what was required for the task. Nine months later, on the eve of the Declaration of Independence, the disheartened and defeated invaders limped home in disgrace.[17] In the meantime, Washington had abandoned New York. His army was demoralized, depleted in numbers, short of food, clothing, and arms, and suffering from desertion and disease. Early military reverses hurt American credit in Europe. Designed to attract foreign support, the Declaration of Independence drew little notice in Europe.[18]

---

16. William Howard Adams, *The Paris Years of Thomas Jefferson* (New Haven, Conn., 1997), 185; Murphy, "View from Versailles," 110.
17. Richard W. Van Alstyne, *Empire and Independence: The International History of the American Revolution* (New York, 1965), 104–5.
18. Ibid., 100; Jonathan R. Dull, *A Diplomatic History of the American Revolution* (New Haven, Conn., 1997), 185.

From the time he landed in Paris, the energetic but often indiscreet Deane compromised his own mission. He cut deals that benefited the rebel cause—and from which he profited handsomely, provoking later charges of malfeasance and a nasty spat in Congress. He was surrounded by spies, and his employment of the notorious British agent Edward Bancroft produced an intelligence windfall for London.[19] He recruited French officers to serve in the Continental Army and even plotted to replace Washington as commander. He endorsed sabotage operations against British ports, provoking angry protests to France. Even more dangerously, he and his irascible colleague Arthur Lee made the French increasingly uneasy about supporting the Americans. When Franklin landed in France in December 1776, the Revolution was teetering at home; America's first diplomatic mission was doing as much harm as good.

Franklin's mission to Paris is one of the most extraordinary episodes in the history of American diplomacy, important, if not indeed decisive, to the outcome of the Revolution. The eminent scientist, journalist, politician, and homespun philosopher was already an international celebrity when he landed in France. Establishing himself in a comfortable house with a well-stocked wine cellar in a suburb of Paris, he made himself the toast of the city. A steady flow of visitors requested audiences and favors such as commissions in the American army. Through clever packaging, he presented himself to French society as the very embodiment of America's revolution, a model of republican simplicity and virtue. He wore a tattered coat and sometimes a fur hat that he despised. He refused to powder his hair. His countenance appeared on snuffboxes, rings, medals, and bracelets, even (it was said) on an envious King Louis XVI's chamber pot. His face was as familiar to the French, he told his daughter, as "that of the moon."[20] He was compared to Plato and Aristotle. No social gathering was complete without him. To his special delight, women of all ages fawned over "*mon cher papa*," as one of his favorites called him. A master showman, publicist, and propagandist, Franklin played his role to the hilt. He shrewdly perceived how the French viewed him and used it to further America's cause.[21]

With independence hanging in the balance, Franklin's mission was as daunting as that undertaken by any U.S. diplomat at any time. Seventy years old when he landed, he suffered the agony of gout. In addition to

19. Rakove, *Beginnings*, 249.
20. Gordon S. Wood, *The Americanization of Benjamin Franklin* (New York, 2004), 177.
21. Ibid., 180.

his diplomatic responsibilities, he bore the laborious and time-consuming responsibilities of a consul. The British were enraged with the mere presence in Paris of that "old veteran in mischief," and repeatedly complained to the comte de Vergennes about his machinations.[22] His first goal was to get additional money from the French, a task this apostle of self-reliance must have found unsavory at best. He was also to draw France into a war for which it was not yet ready and for which he had little to offer in return. He went months without word from Philadelphia. Most war news came from British sources or American visitors. He was burdened with the presence in Paris of a flock of rival U.S. diplomats including the near paranoid Lee and the imperious and prickly Adams, both of whom constantly fretted about his indolence and Francophilia. The French capital was a veritable den of espionage and intrigue.

With all this, he succeeded brilliantly. The most cosmopolitan of the founders, he had an instinctive feel for what motivated other nations. He patiently endured French caution about entering the war. A master of what a later age would call "spin," he managed to put the worst of American defeats in a positive light. By displaying his affection for things French and not appearing too radical, he made the American Revolution seem less threatening, more palatable, and even fashionable to the court. He won such trust from his French hosts that they insisted he remain when his rivals and would-be replacements sought to have him recalled. He secured loan after loan from Vergennes, sometimes through tactics that verged on extortion. He repeatedly reminded the French that some Americans sought reconciliation with Britain. In January 1778, he conspicuously met with a British emissary to nudge France toward intervention.

That step came on February 6, 1778, when France and the United States agreed to a "perpetual" alliance. By this time, France was better prepared for war and a bellicose spirit was rising in the country. British, French, and Spanish naval mobilization in the Caribbean raised the possibility that war might engulf the West Indies. A major U.S. victory at Saratoga in upstate New York in October 1777 clinched the decision to intervene. British general John Burgoyne's drive down the Hudson Valley was designed to cut off the northeastern colonies, thereby ending the rebellion. The capture of Burgoyne's entire army at Saratoga destroyed such dreams, bolstered sagging American spirits, and spurred peace senti-

---

22. Stacy Schiff, *A Great Improvisation: Franklin, France, and the Birth of America* (New York, 2005), 68.

ments in Britain. It was celebrated in France as a victory for French arms. Beaumarchais was so eager to spread the news that his speeding carriage overturned in the streets of Paris. Franklin's friend Madame Brillon composed a march to "cheer up General Burgoyne and his men, as they head off to captivity."[23] Above all, Saratoga provided a convincing and long-sought indication that the Americans could succeed with external assistance, thus easing a French commitment to war.[24]

Negotiations for the treaty proceeded quickly and without major problems. For the Americans, desperation led pragmatism to win out over ideals. They had long since abandoned their scruples about political connections and their naive belief that trade alone would gain French support. The two nations readily agreed not to conclude a separate peace without each other's consent. Each guaranteed the possessions of the other in North America for the present and forever, a unique requirement for a wartime alliance. For the Americans, the indispensable feature of the agreement was a French promise to fight until their independence had been achieved. The United States gave France a free hand in taking British possessions in the West Indies. The two nations also concluded a commercial agreement, which, while not as liberal as the Model Treaty, did put trade on a most-favored-nation basis, a considerable advance beyond the mercantilist principles that governed most such pacts. Americans wildly celebrated their good fortune. Franklin outdid himself in his enthusiasm for his adopted country. Even the normally suspicious Adams declared the alliance a "rock upon which we may safely build."[25]

Like all alliances, the arrangement with France was a marriage of expedience, and the two sides brought to their new relationship long-standing prejudices and sharply different perspectives. French diplomats and military officers were not generally sympathetic to the idea of revolution. They saw the United States, like the small nations of Europe, as an object to be manipulated to their own ends. In the best tradition of European statecraft, French diplomats used bribery and other forms of pressure to ensure that the Continental Congress served their nation's interests. French officers in the United States protested that upon their arrival the Americans stopped fighting.[26] For their part, Americans complained that French aid was inadequate and French troops did not fight

23. Ibid., 110–11.
24. Dull, *Diplomatic History*, 89–96, and Van Alstyne, *Empire and Independence*, 131–33, give less significance to Saratoga in the origins of the alliance.
25. Van Alstyne, *Empire and Independence*, 163.
26. Murphy, "View from Versailles," 133.

aggressively. They worried that France did not support their war aims. Among Americans, moreover, until 1763 at least, France had been the mortal enemy. As an absolute monarchy and Catholic to boot, in the eyes of many it was the epitome of evil. Americans inherited from the British deep-seated prejudices, viewing their new allies as small and effeminate, "pale, ugly specimens who lived exclusively on frogs and snails." Some expressed surprise to find French soldiers and sailors "as large & as likely men as can be produced by any other nation." Riots broke out in Boston between French and American sailors. In New York, French troops engaged in looting. To avoid such conflict, French officers often isolated their forces from American civilians, sometimes keeping them on board ships for weeks.[27]

Whatever the problems, the significance of the alliance for the outcome of the Revolution cannot be overstated.[28] The timing was perfect. The news arrived in the United States just after the landing of a British peace commission prepared to concede everything but the word *independence*. The alliance killed a compromise peace by ensuring major external assistance in a war for unqualified independence. Congress celebrated by feting the newly arrived French minister, Conrad Alexandre Gerard, the first diplomat formally accredited to the United States, with food and drink sent by the British commissioners to lubricate the wheels of diplomacy. The French alliance ensured additional money and supplies not only from France but also from other European nations. In all, the United States secured $9 million in foreign military aid without which it would have been difficult to sustain the Revolution. Americans carried French weapons and were paid with money that came from France.[29] The French fleet and French troops played a vital role in the decisive battle of Yorktown.

For a steep price—the promise of assistance in the recapture of Gibraltar—France persuaded Spain to enter the conflict. Spain also provided economic and military aid to the United States and drove the British from the Gulf Coast region of North America. A threatened Franco-Spanish invasion of England in 1779 caused panic, making it difficult for the British government to reinforce its navy and troops in North America. The Dutch would also eventually join the allied coalition. An

27. William C. Stinchcombe, "Americans Celebrate the Birth of the Dauphin," in Hoffman and Albert, *Diplomacy and Revolution*, 44–47.
28. Wood, *Franklin*, 191.
29. Alexander DeConde, "The French Alliance in Historical Speculation," in Hoffman and Albert, *Diplomacy and Revolution*, 18.

ill-fated British campaign against Dutch colonial outposts in Africa, Asia, and the Caribbean diverted attention and precious resources from the American theater. In 1780, Russia's Catherine the Great formed an armed neutrality, a group of nations including Sweden, Denmark, Austria, Prussia, Portugal, and the Kingdom of Naples, who joined together to protect by force, if necessary, neutral shipping from British depredations, helping ensure a flow of supplies to the United States. The Americans were so enthused about the principles of Catherine's program that as a present belligerent but possibly future neutral they tried to join. The French alliance transformed a localized rebellion in North America into a global war that strained even Britain's vast resources and greatly benefited the Americans.[30]

Even with such support, the war went badly. A French ploy to end the conflict quickly by blockading New York and forcing the surrender of the British army failed miserably. Seeking to exploit widespread Loyalist sentiment, Britain in 1779 shifted to a southern strategy, taking Savannah and later Charleston. British success in the South forced Congress to abandon its scruples against foreign troops, evoking urgent pleas that France send military forces along with its navy. It would be the summer of 1780 before they arrived, however, and in the meantime the U.S. war effort hit a low point. Troops in New Jersey and Pennsylvania revolted. The army was in "extreme distress," in Vergennes's words, and he warned French naval commanders not to land forces if the American war effort seemed about to collapse.[31] Chronic money problems required another huge infusion of French funds. By this time, France was also in dire straits militarily. French policymakers briefly contemplated a truce that would have left Britain in control of the southern states.

From Canada to the Floridas, the American Revolution also raged on the western frontier, and here too the war went badly. At the outbreak, the colonists hoped for Native American neutrality. Britain actively sought the Indians' assistance. Perceiving the Americans as the greatest threat to their existence and Britain as the most likely source of arms and protection, most tribes turned to the latter, infuriating the embattled Americans. Adams denounced the Indians as "blood Hounds"; Washington called them "beasts of prey."[32] The Americans seized the opportunities

---

30. Ibid., 17–18; Dull, *Diplomatic History*, 163.
31. Murphy, "View from Versailles," 144; Dull, *Diplomatic History*, 107.
32. James M. Merrell, "Declarations of Independence: Indian-White Relations in the New Nation," in Jack P. Greene, ed., *The American Revolution: Its Character and Limits* (New York, 1987), 198–99.

created by Indian affiliation with Britain to wage a war of extirpation, where possible driving the Indians further west and solidifying claims to their lands. Even some tribes who collaborated with the Americans suffered at their hands during and after the revolution. "Civilization or death to all American Savages" was the toast offered at a Fourth of July celebration before an American army marched against the Iroquois in 1779.[33]

This important and often neglected phase of the Revolutionary War began before the Declaration of Independence. In 1774, the governor of Virginia sent an expedition into Shawnee territory in the Ohio Valley, fought a major battle at Point Pleasant on the Ohio River, and forced the Indians to cede extensive land. Three years later, to divert American attention from a British offensive in upstate New York, the British commander at Detroit dispatched Indian raiding parties to attack settlements in Kentucky. Over the next two years, sporadic fighting occurred across the Ohio frontier. The state of Virginia, which had extensive land claims in the region, dispatched George Rogers Clark to attack the British and their Indian allies. In 1778, Clark took forts at Kaskaskia, Cahokia, and Vincennes. The British retook Vincennes the following year. Clark took it back one more time, but he could not establish firm control of the region. Settlements in Kentucky—the "dark and bloody ground"—came under attack the next two years.

The Americans opened a second front in the war against the Indians in western New York. The Iroquois Confederacy split, some tribes siding with the British, others with the Americans. When Indians working with Loyalists conducted raids across upstate New York in 1778, threatening food supplies vital to his army, Washington diverted substantial resources and some of his best troops to the theater with instructions that the Iroquois should be not "merely *overrun* but *destroyed*." In one of the best-planned operations of the war, the Americans inflicted heavy losses on the Iroquois and pushed the frontier westward. But they did not achieve their larger aim of crippling Indian power and stabilizing the region. "The nests are destroyed," one American warned, "but the birds are still on the wing."[34] The Iroquois became more dependent on the British and more angry with the Americans. During the remainder of the war, they exacted vengeance along the northern frontier.

The Americans fared best in the South. Although threatened by the westward advance of the Georgia colony, the Creeks clung to their long-

33. Ibid., 198.
34. Barbara Graymont, *The Iroquois in the American Revolution* (Syracuse, N.Y., 1972), 220.

standing tradition of neutrality in wars among whites. They also learned valuable lessons from their neighbors, the Cherokees. Having suffered huge losses in the Seven Years' War, the Cherokees welcomed Britain's post-1763 efforts to stop the migration of colonists into the trans-Appalachian West. Out of gratitude for British support and encouraged by British agents, they rose up against the colonists in May 1776. Their timing could not have been worse. Britain had few troops in the southern states at this time. The Americans seized the chance to eliminate a major threat and strengthen their claims to western lands. Georgia and the Carolinas mobilized nearly five thousand men and launched a three-pronged campaign against the Cherokees, destroying some fifty villages, killing and scalping men *and* women, selling some Indians into slavery, and driving others into the mountains. A 1780 punitive expedition did further damage. The Cherokees would in time re-create themselves and develop a flourishing culture, but the war of American independence cost them much of their land and their way of life.[35]

Adoption in March 1781 of a form of government—the Articles of Confederation—marked a major accomplishment of the war years, but it did not come easily and proved at best an imperfect instrument for waging war and negotiating peace. Discussion of formal union began in the summer of 1776. Pressures to act intensified in the fall of 1777 when Congress, faced with rising inflation, requested that the states furnish additional funds, stop issuing paper money, and impose price controls. Foreign policy exigencies proved equally important. Optimistic after Saratoga that an alliance with France would be reality, Congress believed that agreement on a constitution would affirm the stability of the new government and its commitment to independence, strengthening its position with other nations. Much like the Declaration of Independence, the Articles of Confederation were designed to secure foreign support.[36]

It took nearly four years to complete a process initiated to meet immediate demands. Congress moved expeditiously, approving a draft on November 15, 1777. The states were forbidden from negotiating with other nations. They could not make agreements with each other or maintain an army or navy without the consent of Congress. On the other hand, the Confederation government could not levy taxes or regulate commerce. It could not make treaties that infringed on the legislative rights of any state.

35. Theda Perdue, *The Cherokee* (New York, 1989), 35–36; Allen R. Millett and Peter Maslowski, *For the Common Defense: A Military History of the United States of America* (New York, 1984), 74.
36. Rakove, *Beginnings*, 179.

Affirming the principle of state sovereignty, the articles left with the states any powers not "expressly delegated" to the national government. The Congress rejected numerous amendments proposed by the states, but the process took time, and ratification was delayed until March 1781. By that point, many of the deficiencies of the new instrument had been exposed. Congress addressed a most obvious shortcoming, the lack of executive machinery, by creating in 1781 departments for war, finance, and foreign affairs headed by individuals who were not among its members. Robert R. Livingston of New York was named secretary of foreign affairs. Even then, many national leaders believed that the Articles of Confederation were obsolete by the time they had been approved.[37]

II

A sudden and dramatic reversal of military fortunes in late 1781 led to negotiations to end the American war. Countering Britain's southern strategy, the United States and France shifted sizeable military forces to Virginia. The French fleet was deployed to the Chesapeake Bay, where the allies in October trapped and forced the surrender of a major British army under the ill-fated Lord Charles Cornwallis on a narrow peninsula along the York River. The victory at Yorktown may have spared the allies from disaster.[38] Although Britain still held Charleston and Savannah, Cornwallis's defeat thwarted the southern strategy. It gave a huge boost to faltering American morale and revived French enthusiasm for the war. Yorktown undermined popular support for the war in Britain and, along with the soaring cost of the conflict, caused the fall of the ministry of Lord North and the emergence of a government intent on negotiating with the United States. The war continued for two more years, but after Yorktown attention shifted to the challenging task of peacemaking.

Victory at Yorktown did not give the United States the upper hand in the peace negotiations, however. Washington's army remained short of food, supplies, arms, and ammunition. Britain retained control of some southern states, where fighting still raged. In fact, after Yorktown, the American theater became a sideshow in the global war. In negotiations involving four major nations and numerous lesser ones and a war that stretched from the Gulf of Mexico to South Asia, events in far-flung areas often had a major impact. British setbacks in the Caribbean combined

37. Ibid., 190.
38. Dull, *Diplomatic History*, 120.

with Yorktown to encourage peace sentiment in England. French naval defeats in the West Indies in the spring of 1782 made Paris more amenable to separate U.S. negotiations with Great Britain.

For the United States, of course, recognition of its independence was the essential condition for peace.[39] Independence was the reason the war had been fought, and it formed the indispensable principle of the first statement of war aims drafted in 1779. Congress had hesitated even to raise such issues for fear of exacerbating sectional tensions in wartime. At France's insistence (primarily as a way of bringing U.S. goals into line with its own), the Americans finally did so, and the results made plain the ambitions of the new nation. The territory of the independent republic should extend to the Mississippi River, land that, except for Clark's victories, the United States had not conquered and did not occupy, and to the 31st parallel, the existing border between Georgia and the Floridas. Americans claimed Britain's right acquired from France in 1763 to navigate the Mississippi from its source to the sea.[40] They also sought Nova Scotia. New England's fishing industry was valued at nearly $2 million and employed ten thousand men, and access to North Atlantic fisheries comprised a vital war aim.[41] In his private and unofficial discussions with British diplomats, Franklin went further. Outraged by the atrocities committed by an enemy he denounced as "the worst and wickedest Nation upon Earth," he urged Britons to "recover the Affections" of their former colonies with a generous settlement including the cession of Canada and the Floridas to the United States.[42]

In June 1781, again under French pressure and when the war was going badly, Congress significantly modified the instructions to its diplomats in Europe. Reflecting America's dependence on France, the influence of— and bribes provided by—Gerard and his successor, the comte de la Luzerne, and a widespread fear that French support might be lost, the new instructions affirmed that independence should no longer be a precondition to negotiations. The boundaries proposed in 1779 were also deemed not essential. The commissioners could agree to a treaty with Spain that did not provide for access to the Mississippi. In a truly extraordinary provision, Congress instructed the commissioners to place themselves

---

39. Gregg L. Lint, "Preparing for Peace: The Objectives of the United States, France, and Spain in the War of the American Revolution," in Ronald Hoffman and Peter J. Albert, eds., *Peacemakers: The Treaty of 1783* (Charlottesville, Va., 1986), 32–33.
40. Ibid., 33–35.
41. Richard B. Morris, *The Forging of the Union, 1781–1789* (New York, 1987), 140.
42. Edmund S. Morgan, *Benjamin Franklin* (New Haven, Conn., 2002), 275–76.

under French direction, to "undertake nothing . . . without their knowledge and concurrence; and ultimately to govern yourselves by their advice and opinion."[43] When the military situation changed dramatically after Yorktown, Congress discussed modifying these highly restrictive
instructions but did nothing. Fortunately for the United States, its diplomats in Europe ignored them and acted on the basis of the 1779 draft.[44]

French and Spanish war aims complicated the work of the American
peace commissioners. France and especially Spain had gone to war to
avenge the humiliation of 1763, weaken their major rival by detaching
Britain's most valuable colonies, and restore the global balance of power.
France was committed by treaty to American independence, but not to
the boundaries Americans sought. Indeed, at various points in the war it
was prepared to accept a partition that would have left the southern
colonies in Britain's possession. A weaker United States, Vergennes and
his advisers reasoned, would be more dependent on France. France did
not seek to regain Canada, but it preferred continued British dominance
there to keep an independent United States in check. It also sought access to the North Atlantic fisheries.

France's ties with Spain through their 1779 alliance further jeopardized
the achievement of U.S. war aims. Although it provided vital assistance to
the United States, Spain never consented to a formal alliance or committed itself to American independence. Because France had promised to
fight until Spain recovered Gibraltar, America's major war aim could be
held hostage by events in the Mediterranean. Spain also sought to recover
the Floridas from Britain. Even more than France, it preferred to keep
the United States weak and hemmed in as close to the Appalachians and
as far north as possible. Spain saw no reason to grant the United States access to the Mississippi.

Ironically, but not surprisingly, given the strange workings of international politics, the United States found its interests more in line with
those of its enemy, Great Britain, than its ally, France, and France's ally,
Spain. To be sure, Britons acquiesced in American independence only
grudgingly. As late as 1782, well after Yorktown, top officials insisted on
negotiating on the basis of the *uti possidetis*, the territory actually held at
the time, which would have left Britain in control at least of the south-
ernmost American states. King George III contemplated negotiating with

---

43. Bradford Perkins, "The Peace of Paris: Patterns and Legacies," in Hoffman and Albert,
    Peacemakers, 196.
44. Lint, "Preparing for Peace," 49–50.

the states individually, a classic divide-and-conquer ploy. The British government would have concluded a separate peace with France if expedient. Even after Lord North resigned in March 1782 and a new government took power, there was talk of an "Irish solution," an autonomous America within the British Empire.[45]

Gradually, top British officials and especially William Petty Fitzmaurice, the earl of Shelburne, shifted to a more conciliatory approach. Conservative, aloof, and secretive, known for his duplicity, Shelburne was called "the Jesuit of Berkeley Square." He was persuaded to adopt a more accommodating approach by his friend Richard Oswald, a seventy-six-year-old acquaintance and admirer of Franklin. Oswald owned property in the West Indies, West Florida, and the southern colonies. He had lived six years in Virginia. He and Shelburne, in the latter's words, *"decidedly tho reluctantly"* concluded that Britain's essential aim should be to separate the United States from France. Independence was acceptable if it could accomplish that.[46] They hoped that an America free of France through a shared history, language, and culture would gravitate back toward Britain's influence and become its best customer.[47]

Given the different parties involved and the conflicts and confluences of interests, the peace negotiations were extremely complicated. They resembled, historian Jonathan Dull has written, a "circus of many rings," with all the performers walking a tightrope.[48] Military action on land or sea even in distant parts of the globe could tip the balance one way or the other. Europe and America formed a very small world in the 1780s. The key players knew and indeed in some cases were related to each other. Diplomats moved back and forth between London and Paris with relative ease. At one point, two competing British cabinet ministers had representatives in Paris talking to the Americans. In the latter stages, Franklin's fellow commissioners John Adams and John Jay went off in directions that might have been disastrous.

With North's resignation, an unwieldy government headed by Lord Rockingham took power in England. Two men were nominally responsible

45. Esmond Wright, "The British Objectives, 1780–1783: 'If Not Dominion Then Trade,'" in Hoffman and Albert, *Peacemakers*, 8–10.
46. Shelburne to Oswald, July 27, 1782, in Mary A. Giunta, ed., *Documents of the Emerging Nation: U.S. Foreign Relations, 1775–1782* (Wilmington, Del., 1998), 91.
47. Perkins, "Peace of Paris," 198; Wright, "British Objectives," 10–15; Charles R. Ritcheson, *Aftermath of Revolution: British Policy Toward the United States* (New York, 1969), 74, 79, 82.
48. Van Alstyne, *Empire and Independence*, 215; Jonathan R. Dull, "Vergennes, Rayneval, and the Diplomacy of Trust," in Hoffman and Albert, *Peacemakers*, 105.

for negotiations with the Americans, the Whig Charles James Fox, secretary of state for foreign affairs, who favored immediate independence, and the more cautious Shelburne, secretary of state for home and colonial affairs. Before North's resignation, Franklin, through an especially effusive letter of thanks to Shelburne for a gift of gooseberry bushes sent to a friend in France, had hinted that the Americans might negotiate a separate peace. Shelburne agreed that negotiations could begin in France. Not yet in full control, however, he refused to accept independence except as part of a broader settlement. Franklin again pleaded for British generosity, hinting that in return the United States might help end Britain's wars with France and Spain by threatening a separate peace.

The two sides got past the first major hurdle in July 1782. Shelburne maneuvered Fox out of the negotiations and then out of the cabinet. Rockingham died shortly after, making Shelburne head of the cabinet and giving him control over the negotiations. By this time, Shelburne had resigned himself to full American independence. He named Oswald to negotiate with Franklin. Reflecting the new nation's importance in the balance of power, he instructed his envoy that "if America is to be independent, she must be so of the whole world. No secret, tacit, or ostensible connections with France." Shelburne went along with Franklin's ploy not because of the strength of the American's bargaining position but rather because he was eager for peace with France and Spain and agreed with Franklin that peace with the United States could help end the European war. Oswald accepted in principle Franklin's "necessary" terms: complete and unqualified independence, favorable boundaries, and access to the fisheries.[49]

This left numerous thorny matters unresolved. Britain demanded compensation for property confiscated from those Americans who had remained loyal to the Crown. Americans insisted upon access to the Mississippi. Franklin was furious with Britain's initial reluctance to concede independence and the atrocities he claimed its troops had committed. The fact that his estranged son, William, was a Loyalist gave him a deeply personal reason to oppose for this group the sort of generosity he repeatedly asked of Britain. He exclaimed regarding the Mississippi that "a Neighbour might as well ask me to sell my street Door" as to "sell a Drop of its Waters."[50] Initial discussions produced little progress.

From this point, John Jay, and to a lesser extent Adams, replaced Franklin as the primary negotiators. Both men were profoundly suspicious

49. Dull, *Diplomatic History*, 146.
50. Morgan, *Franklin*, 287–88.

of Britain—and even more of France. Their approach to the negotiations differed sharply from their elder colleague. From the moment he had arrived in Europe in 1778, Adams had raised a ruckus. "Always an honest Man, often a Wise one, but sometimes in some things out of his Senses," Franklin had said of Adams, and in terms of the younger man's service in Paris, the criticism was understated.[51] Adams repeatedly complained of "the old Conjurer's" indolence, his "continued Discipation," and his subservience to France. He even accused Franklin of conspiring to get him aboard a ship that was captured by the British. Like other Americans, Adams inherited from the British a deep dislike for France, an "ambitious and faithless nation," he once snarled.[52] His staunch republican ideology bred suspicion of all men of power. Adams railed against the "Count and the Doctor." He insisted that France was determined to "keep us poor. Depress us. Keep us weak."[53] A descendant of French Protestants, Jay came by his suspicions naturally. They were heightened and his disposition soured by the three frustrating and largely fruitless years he spent in Madrid seeking to persuade Spain to ally with the United States. Adams's and Jay's suspiciousness and their often self-righteous, moralistic demeanor, one suspects, were also born of the anxieties afflicting these neophytes in the settled world of European diplomacy. They protested the immorality of that system, but, given their suspicions, they had no qualms about breaking the terms of their treaty with France and negotiating separately with Britain. Jay arrived in Paris in May 1782, but he was bedridden with influenza for several months. When he recovered and Franklin became deathly ill with kidney stones, he turned his worries on the British. Because Oswald's commission did not mention the United States by name and therefore did not explicitly recognize American independence, Jay broke off talks with England.

Within several weeks even more suspicious of France and Spain, Jay abruptly changed course. The trip of one of Vergennes's top advisers to Britain persuaded him that some nefarious Anglo-French plot was afoot. With the consent of Franklin and the enthusiastic support of Adams, he dropped his demand for prior recognition of U.S. independence at about the time Shelburne was prepared to grant it. He sent word to London that the United States would abandon the alliance with France if a separate peace could be arranged. Oswald's commission was revised to include

51. Wood, *Franklin*, 195.
52. James H. Hutson, "The American Negotiators: The Diplomacy of Jealousy," in Hoffman and Albert, *Peacemakers*, 54.
53. Ibid., 61–62.

the name of the United States, thus extending formal recognition of independence. It was a curious and costly victory for the Americans. In the hiatus caused by Jay's breaking off of the discussions, the British lifted Spain's siege of Gibraltar, leaving them in a stronger negotiating position and less eager to end the European war. When the talks resumed, Jay compounded his earlier mistake by conceding on the fisheries. He also devised a harebrained scheme to encourage America's enemy, Britain, to attack its backer, Spain, and retake Pensacola. The proposal undoubtedly reflected Jay's passionate hatred for Spain and perhaps his Anglophilia. Had the British gone along, their position on the Gulf Coast would have been greatly strengthened, threatening the safety of a new and vulnerable republic.[54]

Despite Jay's dubious maneuvers, a peace settlement was patched together in October and November of 1782. Adams and Jay argued interminably over countless issues—"the greatest quibblers I have ever seen," one British diplomat complained.[55] In the end, they got much of what they wanted and far more than their 1781 instructions called for. Britain agreed to recognize U.S. independence and withdraw its troops from U.S. territory, the essential concessions. Although many complicated details remained to be worked out, the boundary settlement was remarkably generous given the military situation when the war ended: the Mississippi River in the west; the Floridas in the south; and Canada to the north. Britain extended to the United States its rights to navigate the Mississippi, a concession that without Spain's assent was of limited value. The fisheries were one of the most difficult issues, and the United States could secure only the "liberty," not the right, to fish off Newfoundland and the Gulf of St. Lawrence. Other troublesome issues were "resolved" with vague statements that would cause prolonged and bitter disputes. Creditors in each nation were to meet no legal obstacles to the repayment of debts. Congress would recommend to the states the restitution of Loyalist property confiscated during the war.

The American negotiators have often been given the credit for this favorable outcome. They shrewdly played the Europeans against each other, it has been argued, exploiting their rivalries, wisely breaking congressional instructions, and properly deserting an unreliable France to defend their nation's interests and maximize its gains. Such an interpretation is open to question. The Americans, probably from their own

54. Dull, *Diplomatic History*, 149.
55. Hutson, "American Negotiators," 53.

insecurities, were anxiety-ridden in dealing with ally and enemy alike.[56] Jay's excessive nervousness about England and then his separate approach to that country not only broke faith with a supportive if not entirely reliable ally but also delayed negotiations for several months. It eased pressure on Shelburne to make concessions and left the United States vulnerable to a possible Shelburne-Vergennes deal at its expense. Jay and Adams had reason to question Vergennes's trustworthiness, but they should have informed him of the terms before springing the signed treaty upon him. Ultimately, the favorable settlement owed much less to America's military prowess and diplomatic skill than to luck and chance: Shelburne's desperate need for peace to salvage his deteriorating political position and his determination to settle quickly with the United States and seek reconciliation through generosity.[57]

News of the preliminary treaty evoked strikingly different reactions among the various parties. Finalization of the terms required a broader European settlement, which would not come until early 1783, but war-weary Americans greeted news of the peace with relief and enthusiasm. At the same time, some members of Congress, encouraged by the ardently pro-French Livingston, sought to rebuke the commissioners for violating their instructions and jeopardizing the French alliance. The move failed, but Franklin was sufficiently offended to muse that the biblical blessings supposedly accorded to peacemakers must be reserved for the next life. Britons naturally recoiled at Shelburne's generosity, and the architect of the peace treaty fell from power in early 1783. His departure and British anger at defeat ensured that the generous trade treaty he had contemplated would not become reality. Vergennes was at least mildly annoyed at the Americans' independence, complaining that if it were a guide to the future "we shall be but poorly payed for all we have done for the United States." He was shocked at British generosity—the "concessions exceed all that I should have thought possible."[58] He was also relieved that the Americans had freed him of obligations to fight until Spain achieved its war aims and thereby helped him secure the quick peace he needed to address European issues. It was Franklin's task to repair the damage done by Jay and Adams (with his consent, of course) and

56. Samuel Flagg Bemis, *The Diplomacy of the American Revolution* (Bloomington, Ind., 1957), 255–56, and Richard B. Morris, *The Peacemakers: The Great Powers and American Independence* (New York, 1965), 459, praise Adams and Jay. Perkins, "Peace of Paris," 201, and Dull, *Diplomatic History,* 146–51, are more critical.

57. Perkins, "Peace of Paris," 220–21; Dull, *Diplomatic History,* 149–51.

58. Perkins, "Peace of Paris," 215.

also to secure additional funds without which, Livingston implored him, "we are inevitably ruined."[59] He begged Vergennes's forgiveness for the Americans "neglecting a Point of *bienseance*." Adding a clever twist, he confided that the British "flatter themselves" that they had divided the two allies. The best way to disabuse them of this notion would be for the United States and France to keep "this little misunderstanding" a "perfect Secret."[60] The old doctor even had the audacity to ask for yet another loan. Already heavily invested in his unfaithful allies and hopeful of salvaging something, Vergennes saw little choice but to provide the Americans an additional six million livres.

The treaties ending the wars of the American Revolution had great significance for the people and nations involved. Most Native Americans had sided with Britain, but the peace treaty ignored them and assigned to the United States lands they regarded as theirs. "Thunder Struck" when they heard the news, they issued their own declarations of independence, proclaiming, in the words of the Six Nations, that they were a "free People subject to no Power upon Earth."[61] For France, an ostensible winner, the war cost an estimated one billion livres, bankrupting the treasury and sparking a revolution that would have momentous consequences in America as well as in Europe. Britain lost a major part of its empire but, ironically, emerged stronger. Its economy quickly recovered, and with the industrial revolution flourished as never before.[62] The treaty sealed U.S. independence. The extensive boundaries provided the springboard for continental empire. Americans would quickly learn, however, that securing the peace could be even more difficult than winning the war.

III

Peace brought scant stability. Debt weighed upon nation and citizens alike. War had ravaged parts of the country. Slaves had been carried off, traditional markets closed, and inflation unleashed. Shortly after the war, the nation plunged into its first full-fledged depression. The economy improved slowly over the next five years, but a Congress lacking real authority could not set economic policies. Wartime unity gave way to snarling rivalry over western lands. Attendance at the Congress was so erratic that there was seldom a quorum. The shift of its meeting place from

59. Morgan, *Franklin*, 289.
60. Franklin to Vergennes, December 17, 1782, in Giunta, *Documents*, 124–25.
61. Merrell, "Declarations," 197.
62. Dull, *Diplomatic History*, 161.

Philadelphia to Princeton and then to Annapolis, Trenton, and New York City symbolized the instability of the institution and the nation itself.[63]

Challenges from abroad posed greater threats. The rebelling colonies had exploited European rivalries to secure economic and military aid from France and Spain and a generous peace treaty from Britain. Once the war ended, divisions among the major powers receded along with opportunities for the United States. The Europeans did not formally coordinate their postwar approaches, but their policies were generally in tandem. They believed that the United States, like republics before it, would collapse of its own weight. The sheer size of the country worked against it, according to Britain's Lord Sheffield. The "authority of Congress can never be maintained over those distant and boundless regions." Some Britons even comforted themselves that their generosity at the peace table would hasten America's downfall; the time often estimated was five years.[64] A French observer speculated that the whole "edifice would infallibly collapse if the weakness of its various parts did not assure its continuance by making them weigh less strongly the ones over the others."[65]

Europeans were not disposed to help the new nation's survival. To keep it weak and dependent, they imposed harsh trade restrictions and rebuffed appeals for concessions. Britain and Spain blocked the United States from taking control of territory awarded in the 1783 treaty. Lacking the means to retaliate and divided among themselves on foreign policy priorities, Americans were powerless to resist European pressures. More than anything else, their inability to effectively address crucial foreign policy problems persuaded many leaders that a stronger central government was essential to the nation's survival.

One area of progress was in the administration of foreign affairs. Livingston had repeatedly complained of inadequate authority and congressional interference. He resigned before the peace treaty was ratified. Congress responded by strengthening the position of the secretary for foreign affairs. John Jay assumed the office in December 1784 and held it until a new government took power in 1789, providing needed continuity. An able administrator, he insisted that his office have full responsibility for the nation's diplomacy. Remarkably, he also conditioned his acceptance on

63. Rakove, *Beginnings*, 342.
64. Peter S. Onuf, "Anarchy and the Crisis of the Union," in Herman Belz, Ronald Hoffman, and Peter J. Albert, eds., *To Form a More Perfect Union* (Charlottesville, Va., 1992), 280.
65. Luis Guillaume Otto to Vergennes, October 1, 1785, in Giunta, *Documents*, 178.

Congress settling in New York.[66] Assisted by four clerks and several part-time translators, he worked out of two rooms in a tavern near Congress's meeting place. He did not achieve his major foreign policy goals, but he managed his department efficiently. Interestingly, a secret act of Congress authorized him to open and examine any letters going through the post office that might contain information endangering the "safety or interest of the United States." He appears not to have used this authority.[67]

Americans and Europeans confronted each other across a sizeable divide, the product of experience and ideology clearly reflected in diplomatic protocol. Upon arriving as U.S. envoy in England, John Adams quickly wearied of affairs at the Court of St. James's. Good republican—and New Englander—that he was, he complained to Jay after an audience with George III that the "essence of things are lost in Ceremony in every Court of Europe." But he responded pragmatically. The United States must "submit to what we cannot alter," he added resignedly. "Patience is the only Remedy."[68] Troubled by the meddling of French diplomats in the United States during the Revolution, Francis Dana, minister to Russia in 1785, urged that the United States abandon diplomacy altogether, warning that "our interests will be more injured by the residence of foreign Ministers among us, than they can be promoted by our Ministers abroad."[69] Americans were much too worldly and practical to go that far, but they did incorporate their republicanism into their protocol and sought to shield themselves from foreign influence. Foreign diplomats were required to make the first visit to newly arriving members of Congress, a sharp departure from European practice. Congressmen made sure never to meet with the envoys by themselves. The "discretion and reserve" with which Americans treated representatives of other countries, a French diplomat complained, "appears to be copied from the Senators of Venice." The "outrageous circumspection" with which Congressmen behaved "renders them sad and silent." Like Adams, the Frenchman saw no choice but to adapt. "Congress insists on the new etiquette," French diplomat Louis Guillaume Otto sighed, "and the foreign Ministers will be obliged to submit to it or to renounce all connection with Members of Congress."[70]

The most pressing issue facing the United States during the Confederation period was commerce. Americans took pride in their indepen-

---

66. Walter Stahr, *John Jay, Founding Father* (New York and London, 2005), 197.
67. Morris, *Forging of the Union*, 194–95; David Patterson, "The Department of State: The Formative Years, 1775–1800," *Prologue* 21 (Winter 1989), 317.
68. Adams to Jay, June 2, 1785, in Giunta, *Documents*, 151.
69. Rakove, *Beginnings*, 347.
70. Otto to Vergennes, October 1, 1785, in Giunta, *Documents*, 178–79.

dence, but they recognized that economically they remained part of a larger trading community. "The fortune of every citizen is interested in the fate of commerce," a congressional committee reported in 1784, "for it is the constant source of industry and wealth; and the value of our produce and our land must ever rise or fall in proportion to the prosperous or adverse state of our trade."[71] In a world of empires, the republic had to find ways to survive. Americans had often protested the burdens imposed by the Navigation Acts, but they had also benefited from membership in the British Empire. They hoped to retain the advantages without suffering the drawbacks. They assumed that their trade was so important that other nations would accept their terms. In fact, the Europeans and especially Britain set the conditions. And the competition among regions, states, and individuals prevented Congress from agreeing on a unified trade policy.[72]

Shelburne's fall from power brought a dramatic shift in British commercial policy. The change toward a hard line reflected persisting anger with the colonies' rebellion, their victory in the war, and what many Britons believed were overly generous peace terms. Despite Adam Smith's fervent advocacy of free trade, the Navigation Acts remained central to British economic thinking. British shipping interests especially feared American postwar competition. The influential Sheffield insisted that since the Americans had left the empire they must be treated as foreigners. This "tribune of shipbuilders and shipowners" argued that America's dependence on British credit and its passion for British manufactures would force trade back into traditional channels. London could fix the terms. On July 2, 1783, ironically the seventh anniversary of Congress's initial resolution for independence, Parliament issued an order in council excluding U.S. ships from the West Indies trade. British policymakers hoped that the rest of the empire could replace the Americans in established trade channels. That did not happen, but the 1783 order devastated New England's fishing and shipping industries. Britain also exploited U.S. removal of wartime trade restrictions and Congress's inability to agree on a tariff to flood the U.S. market with manufactured goods. It restricted the export of any items that would help Americans create their own manufactures. Britain's harsh measures contributed significantly to the depression that caused ruin across the nation.[73]

71. Adams, *Jefferson*, 160.
72. Merrill Jensen, *The New Nation: A History of the United States During the Confederation, 1781–1789* (New York, 1950), 156.
73. Morris, *Forging of the Union*, 130–32.

John Adams assumed the position of minister to England in June 1785 with instructions to press for the elimination of trade restrictions and secure an equitable commercial treaty. Adams sought to hit the British where it hurt, repeatedly warning that the effect of their trade restrictions was to "incapacitate our Merchants to make Remittances to theirs." He carried on a "Sprightly Dialogue" with Prime Minister William Pitt the Younger on trade and other matters and attributed British commercial restrictions to jealousy.[74] After six months, he admitted that he was a "cypher" and that the British were determined to reduce the United States to economic bondage.[75] Minister to France Thomas Jefferson, who joined Adams in London in 1786, flatly labeled the British "our enemies," complaining that they were "more bitterly hostile to us at present than at any point of the late war." British officials responded to American appeals, he added, by "harping a little on the old String, the insufficiency of the powers of Congress to treat and to compel Compliance with the Treaties."[76] Adams occasionally threatened a Navigation Act discriminating against British imports, but he knew, as did Jay, that such a measure could not be enacted or enforced by a government operating under a constitution that left powers over commerce to the states.

The United States fared little better with other major European powers. Americans hoped that the enticement of their bounteous trade, long circumscribed by British regulations, would lure Spain and France into generous commercial treaties. Spain did open some ports to the United States. Spanish products entered American ports on a de facto most-favored-nation basis. But Spain refused a commercial treaty without U.S. concessions in other areas. More important, once the war ended, Spain closed the ports of Havana and New Orleans to U.S. products and denied Americans access to the Mississippi River.

Of all the European nations, France was the most open to U.S. trade, but this channel failed to meet expectations. Jefferson succeeded the estimable Franklin as minister to France in 1784, "an excellent school of humility," he later mused, and ardently promoted expanded trade with France.[77] The Virginian's cosmopolitan tastes, catholic interests, and aristocratic manners made him a worthy successor and also a hit at court. He believed that if the United States shifted its trade to the French West Indies and opened its ports to French products, British dominance of U.S. commerce could be

74. Giunta, *Documents*, 161.
75. Morris, *Forging of the Union*, 205.
76. Adams, *Jefferson*, 200.
77. Gaye Wilson, "Doctor Franklin," *Monticello* 16 (Winter 2005), 1.

broken. With his customary attention to detail, Jefferson studied possible items of exchange, urging the French to convert to American whale oil for their lamps and American rice farmers to grow varieties the French preferred. French officials, Vergennes included, went to some lengths to encourage trade, dispatching consuls to most American states and opening four ports to U.S. products. Responding to domestic and colonial interest groups, the French also closed off the French West Indies to major U.S. exports such as sugar and cotton and imposed tariffs on imports of American tobacco. Jefferson pushed for concessions. "If France wishes us to drink her wine," he insisted, "she must let her Islanders eat our bread."[78] But the barriers to trade were greater than the concessions on each side. The French lacked the capital to provide the credits American merchants needed to import their products. France refused to adapt products to American tastes and could not produce others in quantities needed to satisfy American demands. Despite strong efforts from both countries, the trade remained limited to small quantities of luxury goods, wine, and brandy.

The so-called Barbary pirates posed another impediment to commerce. For years, the North African states of Morocco, Algiers, Tunis, and Tripoli had earned a lucrative take by plundering European ships, ransoming or enslaving captive sailors, and extorting from seafaring nations handsome annual fees for safe passage through the Mediterranean. It "was written in their Koran," a Tripolitan diplomat instructed Adams and Jefferson, "that all nations who should not have acknowledged their authority were sinners, that it was their right and duty to make war upon them wherever they could be found, and that every [Muslim] who should be slain in battle was sure to go to paradise."[79]

The Europeans generally found it cheaper to pay than to subdue the pirates by force. As part of the empire, Americans had British protection, and they earned significant profits selling flour, fish, and timber to Mediterranean ports. Jay sought unsuccessfully to get protection for American ships and seamen written into the peace treaty. Once independent, the Americans had to fend for themselves, and the trade was hampered by attacks from the Barbary States. In late 1783, Morocco and Algiers seized three ships and held the crews for ransom. "Our sufferings are beyond our expressing or your conception," an enslaved captive reported to Jefferson.[80] Congress put up $80,000 to free the captives and buy a

78. Adams, Jefferson, 166.
79. Stahr, Jay, 218.
80. Richard O'Bryen to Jefferson, August 24, 1785, in Giunta, Documents, 229.

treaty, a princely sum given the state of the U.S. treasury but not nearly enough to satisfy the captors. Like the Europeans, Adams believed it cheaper to pay than to fight. Jefferson became "obsessed" with the pirates, preferring to cut "to pieces piecemeal" this "pettifogging nest of robbers."[81] In truth, Congress had neither the money nor will to do either. It appealed to the states for funds with no results. Diplomat Thomas Barclay managed to negotiate without tribute a treaty with the emperor of Morocco, mainly because that ruler disliked the British. Otherwise, problems with the Mediterranean trade were left for another day.

The new nation enjoyed some successes during the Confederation period. The small concessions made by some European states were quite extraordinary in terms of eighteenth-century commercial policies.[82] The United States negotiated agreements with Sweden and Prussia based on the liberal principles of the 1776 Model Treaty. Enterprising merchants actively sought out new markets. In August 1784, after a voyage of six months, the *Empress of China* became the first American ship to reach the port of Canton, where it exchanged with Chinese merchants pelts and "green gold," the fabled root ginseng believed to restore the virility of old men, for tea, spices, porcelain, and silk. The voyage earned a profit of 25 percent, and the ship's return to New York in May 1785 excited for the first time what would become perennial hopes among U.S. merchants of capturing the presumably rich China market. At first unable to distinguish Americans from the British, Chinese merchants were also enthused by the prospect of trade with these "*New People*" upon seeing from a map the size of this new country.[83] American shippers continued to perfect the fine art of evading European trade restrictions. Especially in the West Indies, they employed various clever schemes to get around the British orders in council, developing a flourishing illicit traffic that even the brilliant young naval officer Horatio Nelson could not stop. Commerce increased steadily during these years, and the United States eased out of the depression, but trade never attained the heights Americans had hoped. To many leaders, the answer was a stronger federal government with authority to regulate commerce and retaliate against those nations who discriminated against the United States.

A second major postwar problem was the windfall the nation acquired from England in the 1783 treaty, the millions of acres of sparsely settled land between the Appalachian Mountains and the Mississippi River. This

81. Adams, *Jefferson*, 202–3.
82. Jensen, *New Nation*, 169.
83. Samuel Shaw to Jay, May 19, 1785, in Giunta, *Documents*, 242.

bounty made the United States an instant great power, but taking control of it and administering it posed enormous challenges. Many of the states held conflicting titles to western lands; Congress's authority was at best uncertain. Already forced westward by the advance of colonial settlements, Native Americans also claimed land in the trans-Appalachian West and were determined to fight for it. They gained support from the British, who hung on to forts granted the United States in the 1783 treaty, and from the Spanish in the Southwest. The problem was complicated when Americans after independence poured westward. The population of Kentucky, according to one estimate, totaled but 150 men in 1775. Fifteen years later, it exceeded 73,000 people. The "seeds of a great people are daily planting beyond the mountains," Jay observed in 1785.[84]

Among the major accomplishments of the Confederation government were the establishment of federal authority over these lands and creation of mechanisms for settling and governing the new territory. The issue of federal versus state control was resolved during the war when the states ceded their land claims to the national government as a condition for adoption of the Articles of Confederation. Virginia had proposed in 1780 that the lands acquired by the national government should be "formed into distinct republican states, which shall become members of the federal union, and have the same rights of sovereignty, freedom, and independence, as the other states."[85] Fearful of the proliferation of thinly populated and weak states with loose bonds to the Confederation, Congress in the Northwest Ordinance of 1787, its most important achievement, put settlement and economic development before statehood. The ordinance did not permit immediate admission to the Union but placed the new settlements under what Virginian James Monroe admitted were "Colonial principles." It did guarantee for those in the territories the fundamental rights and liberties of American citizens and eventual acceptance into the United States on an equal basis with the other states. It became the means by which territory beyond the Mississippi would be incorporated into the Union.[86]

It was one thing to *plan* for governing and incorporating this territory, quite another to control it, and here the Confederation government was far less successful. Continued rapid settlement of the West and effective use of the land required protection from Indians and Europeans and

---

84. Jensen, *New Nation*, 114.
85. Morris, *Forging of the Union*, 227.
86. Peter S. Onuf, *Statehood and Union: A History of the Northwest Ordinance* (Bloomington, Ind., 1987), 44–66. The Monroe quote is from p. 49. Also Morris, *Forging of the Union*, 229.

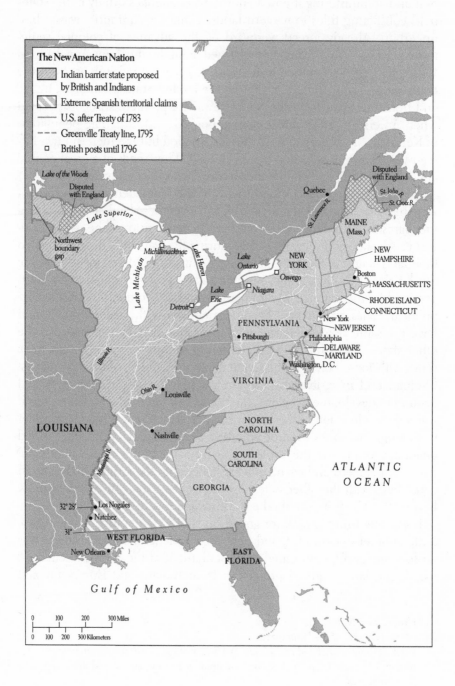

The New American Nation

- ▨ Indian barrier state proposed by British and Indians
- ▤ Extreme Spanish territorial claims
- —— U.S. after Treaty of 1783
- --- Greenville Treaty line, 1795
- ▫ British posts until 1796

Lake of the Woods

Disputed with England

Lake Superior

Northwest boundary gap

Quebec

Disputed with England

St. John R.

St. Croix R.

St. Lawrence R.

MAINE
(Mass.)

NEW
HAMPSHIRE

Michilimackinac

Lake Michigan

Lake Huron

Lake Ontario

NEW
YORK

Oswego

Niagara

Lake Erie

Detroit

Boston

MASSACHUSETTS

RHODE ISLAND

CONNECTICUT

New York

NEW JERSEY

Illinois R.

PENNSYLVANIA

Pittsburgh

Philadelphia

DELAWARE

MARYLAND

Washington, D.C.

Ohio R.

Louisville

VIRGINIA

LOUISIANA

Nashville

NORTH
CAROLINA

SOUTH
CAROLINA

Mississippi R.

GEORGIA

ATLANTIC
OCEAN

32° 28'

Los Nogales

Natchez

31°

WEST FLORIDA

New Orleans

EAST
FLORIDA

Gulf of Mexico

0   100   200   300 Miles

0   100   200   300 Kilometers

access to markets. The government could provide neither, encouraging among settlers in the western territories rampant disaffection and even secessionist sentiment.

The state and national governments first addressed the Indian "problem" with a massive land grab. Americans rationalized that since most of the Indians had sided with the British they had lost the war and therefore their claim to western lands. The state of New York took 5.5 million acres from the Oneida tribe, Pennsylvania a huge chunk from the Iroquois. Federal negotiators dispensed with the elaborate rituals that had marked earlier negotiations between presumably sovereign entities and instead treated the Indians as a conquered people. The British had not told the Indians of their territorial concessions to the Americans. The Iroquois came to negotiations at Fort Stanwix in October 1784 believing that the lands of the Six Nations belonged to them. Displaying copies of the 1783 treaty awarding the territory to the United States, federal negotiators informed them: "You are a subdued people. . . . We shall now, therefore declare to you the condition, on which alone you can be received into the peace and protection of the United States." In the Treaty of Fort Stanwix, the Iroquois surrendered claims to the Ohio country.[87] Federal agents negotiated similar treaties with the Cherokees in the South and acquired most Wyandot, Delaware, Ojibwa, and Ottawa claims to the Northwest.

Such heavy-handed tactics provoked Indian resistance. Native American leaders countered that, unlike the British, they had not been defeated in the war. Neither had they consented to the treaty. Britain had "no right Whatever to grant away to the United States of America, their Rights or properties."[88] Leaders such as the Mohawk Joseph Brant and the Creek Alexander McGillivray, both educated in white schools and familiar with white ways, found willing allies in Britain and Spain. Brant secured British backing to build a confederacy of northern Indians to resist American expansion. The Creeks had long considered themselves an independent nation. They were stunned that the British had given away their territory without consulting them. McGillivray tried to pull the Creeks together into a unified nation to defend their independence against the United States. In a 1784 treaty negotiated at Pensacola, he gained Spanish recognition of Creek independence and promises of guns and gunpowder. For

87. Merrell, "Declarations," 201; Graymont, *Iroquois*, 278–79.
88. Merrell, "Declarations," 202.

the next three years, Creek warriors drove back settlers on western lands in Georgia and Tennessee.[89] By the late 1780s, the United States faced a full-fledged Indian war across the western frontier.

The threat of war pushed Congress into making the pragmatic adjustment from pursuing a policy of confrontation to treating the Indians more equitably. Americans were also sensitive to their historical reputation. Certain that they were a chosen people creating a new form of government and setting higher standards of behavior among nations, they feared that if they did not treat Native Americans equitably, as Secretary of War Henry Knox put it, "the disinterested part of mankind and posterity will be apt to class the efforts of our Conduct and that of the Spanish in Mexico and Peru together."[90] American negotiators reverted to native ritual and custom in the negotiations, admitted that the British had no right to give away Indian lands, and even offered to compensate Indians for territory taken in earlier treaties. The Northwest Ordinance provided that Indians should be dealt with in the "utmost good faith" and that "their land and property shall never be taken from them without their consent."[91] Under Knox's direction, Confederation leaders also set out to Americanize the natives, conferring on them the blessings of "civilization" and eventually absorbing them into American society. The goal was the same; the methods changed to salve America's conscience and preserve its reputation. The new approach produced policies that would be followed far into the future. But it did not resolve the immediate problem of quelling Indian resistance.

Equally serious threats came from the British and Spanish, and the Confederation's inability to deal effectively with these problems provided some of the most compelling arguments for a stronger national government. In the Northwest, the British refused to evacuate a string of frontier posts at Detroit, Niagara, and other points along the Great Lakes and used their presence on territory awarded the United States in the treaty to abet Indian resistance to American settlement of the Northwest. British diplomats insisted that they had not upheld their treaty obligations because the United States had not carried out provisions relating to payment of debts owed British creditors and compensation for Loyalist property confiscated during the war. In truth, Britain had refused to vacate the posts as a matter of policy, deliberately using the treaty provision that called for their departure "with all convenient speed" as a rationale to

89. Michael D. Green, The Creeks (New York, 1990), 41–44.
90. Merrell, "Declarations," 205.
91. Ibid., 204.

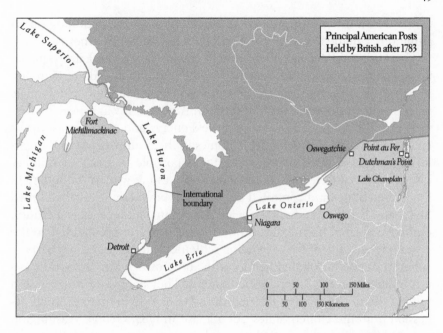

reap maximum profits from the lucrative fur trade. Whenever Americans protested their retention of the posts, however, British officials hurled back at them charges of their own non-compliance.

The Confederation government could not get the British off its territory. Negotiations accomplished nothing; it could not force them to leave. Jay tried hard to meet British objections, but in the case of debts and treatment of Loyalists, the real power resided with the states. They were not inclined to fulfill, and in some cases actively obstructed, the vague promises made to creditors and Loyalists. The United States also sought French support. Nervous about U.S. obligations under the 1778 alliance, Jay at first explored the possibilities of extrication, only to be informed that "those who have once been the allies of France are her allies always."[92] Unable to wriggle free of the alliance, he sought to use it, appealing for French support in getting Britain to abide by its treaty obligations. France refused to meddle in Anglo-American affairs. In any event, French policy after the Revolution was "to have the United States remain in its present state" and not "acquire a force and power" that it "would probably be very easy to abuse."[93] Some French officials, including the

92. DeConde, "French Alliance," 28.
93. Morris, *Forging of the Union*, 209.

comte de Moustier, minister to the United States, were dreaming up an ambitious scheme to restore the French empire to North America.

The United States fared worse with Spain. Of all the European nations, Spain was the most threatened by the new nation and therefore the most hostile. A declining power, Spain was in poor condition to defend its once proud empires in North and South America. It was especially nervous about the Americans, whose restless energy and expansionist thrust endangered its weakly defended colonies in the Southwest. Spain sought to hem in the United States as tightly as possible by treaty or military force. It refused to recognize the Mississippi as the western boundary of the United States and contested the southern boundary set by the United States and Britain in 1783. It rejected American claims to free navigation of the Mississippi from its headwaters to the sea, a crippling blow to the economic viability of the expanding settlements in the Southwest. Spanish officials also negotiated treaties with and provided arms to Southwestern Indians to resist American settlement. They conspired with western settlers and rascals such as the notorious James Wilkinson to promote secession from the United States. After a visit in 1784, George Washington reported that "the western settlers stand as it were upon a pivot; the touch of a feather would turn them any way."[94]

Jay and Spain's special envoy Don Diego de Gardoqui set out in 1785 to resolve these differences. Fearing that the rapid population growth in the American West might threaten its holdings, Spain sought a treaty as a shield against an expanding United States. It hoped to exploit northeastern distrust of the West to achieve its goal.[95] The government authorized Gardoqui to accept the boundary for East Florida specified in the 1783 Anglo-American treaty, but to reject 31° north for West Florida. He was to insist on Spain's "exclusive right" to navigate the Mississippi and seek a western boundary for the United States well east of that river and in some areas as far north as the Ohio River.[96] In return for acceptance of Spain's essential demands, he could offer a commercial treaty and an alliance guaranteeing the two nations' possessions in North America. A congressional committee informed Jay, on the other hand, that an acceptable treaty must include full access to the Mississippi and the borders set forth in the 1783 peace agreement. The secretary was given some flexibility on boundaries, but he could conclude no agreement without consulting Congress.

94. Jensen, New Nation, 171.
95. Francisco Rendon to Don Jose de Galvez, February 12, 1785, in Giunta, Documents, 197.
96. Conde de Floridablanca to Don Diego Gardoqui, October 2, 1784, ibid., 190.

The Jay-Gardoqui talks took place in the United States, lasted for more than a year, and eventually produced the outlines of a deal. Gardoqui had first met Jay in Spain. Viewing him as self-centered, "resolved to make a fortune," and, most important, dominated by his socialite wife, the Spanish envoy concluded that "a little management" and a "few timely gifts" would win over Mrs. Jay and hence her husband. "Notwithstanding my age, I am acting the gallant," he cheerily advised Madrid, "and accompany Madame to the official entertainments and dances because she likes it."[97] In the best traditions of European diplomacy, he also presented Jay the gift of a handsome Spanish horse, which the secretary accepted only with Congress's approval.

Such extracurricular exertions could not overcome the standoff on the Mississippi. As Spain had hoped, Jay eventually concluded that Gardoqui would not give way on that issue and decided on an "expedient" that waived U.S. access to the river for twenty-five years. In return, Spain would grant the United States a generous commercial treaty, and the two nations would guarantee each other's North American territories. Jay did not discuss the terms with Congress, as he had been instructed—yet another manifestation of his independent cast of mind—although he did consult with individual legislators. A negative response from Virginian Monroe, who had drafted his original instructions, failed to deter him. In May 1786, he offered the agreement to Congress.

Jay's proposal exposed sharp sectional differences and sparked open talk of secession. The onetime Hispanophobe insisted that since Spain was the only European power willing to negotiate, the United States should conclude an agreement. He defended the terms on the basis of the commercial benefits: full reciprocity; the establishment of consulates; Spain's commitment to buy specified American products with much-needed hard currency; full access to the ports of metropolitan Spain. "We gain much, and sacrifice or give up nothing," he claimed. Concession on the Mississippi was "not *at present* important," he added, and "a forbearance to use it while we do not want it, is no great sacrifice."[98] Regarding a concession on the Florida boundary, he argued that it was better to "yield a few acres than to part in ill-humour."[99]

Southerners thought otherwise. They minimized the value of Spain's commercial concessions and maximized the importance of the Mississippi. "The use of the Mississippi is given by nature to our western country,"

97. Jensen, *New Nation*, 172.
98. Stahr, *Jay*, 215.
99. Morris, *Forging of the Union*, 241.

Virginia's James Madison proclaimed, "and no power on earth can take it from them."[100] Failure to gain access to the river would splinter the West from the East. Lurking behind heated southern opposition was the hope that the addition of new states beneath the Ohio River would enlarge their power in the national government. Jay's proposal required them to abandon their expansionist aims for the benefit of northern commerce. Monroe accused him of a "long train of intrigue" to secure congressional approval.[101] Westerners vowed to raise an army of ten thousand men, attack Spanish possessions, and even separate from the United States.[102] To "make us vassals to the merciless Spaniards is a grievance not to be borne," one spokesman thundered.[103] Northern delegates tried to mollify their southern brethren by holding out for the 31st parallel as a Florida boundary. But when seven northern states voted to revise Jay's instructions, southerners questioned the viability of the national government. "If seven states can carry a treaty . . . , it follows, of course, that a Confederate compact is no more than a rope of sand, and if a more efficient Government is not obtained a dissolution of the Union must take place."[104] It took nine states to ratify, and Jay reluctantly concluded that a "treaty disagreeable to one-half the nation had better not be made for it would be violated." Gardoqui went home empty-handed. The debate over the abortive treaty produced the sharpest sectional divisions yet. Southerners began to suspect that the deadlock threatened the unity of the new nation.[105]

IV

An emerging sense of crisis among leaders of a nationalist bent produced in 1786 urgent calls for changing the Articles of Confederation or scrapping them altogether. The government seemed incapable of relieving the nation's commercial woes. As early as 1784, some delegates had considered asking the states to give Congress power to discriminate against British imports, but the lack of a quorum forestalled action. A congressional committee proposed in early 1785 an amendment to the Articles giving Congress power to regulate commerce. The proposal was debated but never approved, partly from southern fear of northern commercial interests, also because of a more generalized concern about expanded

100. Jensen, New Nation, 173.
101. Stahr, Jay, 216.
102. Otto to comte de Montmorin, March 5, 1787, in Giunta, Documents, 210–11.
103. Jensen, New Nation, 173.
104. Morris, Forging of the Union, 243.
105. Rakove, Beginnings, 350.

federal power.[106] Although some regions had begun to recover from the postwar depression, commercial problems crippled key sectors of the U.S. economy such as shipbuilding and whaling.[107] Americans deeply resented the indignities heaped upon them by other nations, especially the British.

The situation in the West seemed to nationalists equally menacing. Britain defiantly clung to the Great Lakes forts and continued to exploit the fur trade. From the Canadian border to the Floridas, the United States faced the danger of Indian warfare. Indian attacks killed as many as 1,500 Kentuckians between 1783 and 1790. Two hundred Virginians died in October 1786 alone. In that same year, seven thousand Creeks threatened Savannah on the Georgia coast.[108] The national government was no more effective in dealing with the Indian menace than with commercial problems. It lacked an army and the money to raise one. Its inability to secure access to the Mississippi raised further concerns about its weakness. Jay's apparent willingness to bargain away what southerners considered their birthright threatened dissolution of the Union. The crisis of 1786 posed fundamental questions about whether Congress had the power and backing to defend U.S. interests in a hostile world or even whether it could agree upon those interests that must be protected.[109]

Foreign policy concerns drove nationalist demands to revise the nation's form of government. By 1786, leaders were deeply concerned with the dignity, honor, and respectability of their country. In declaring themselves independent and winning their freedom from Great Britain, Americans were acutely conscious that they were conducting a novel experiment in self-government that could serve as an example to the rest of the world. Their nation's weakness in the face of foreign humiliation threatened that experiment and was therefore especially difficult to accept. Nationalists thus concluded that they must have a government strong enough to command respect abroad. Adams insisted that until the national government could prevent the states from undermining the 1783 treaty it would be impossible to negotiate with England. "Of all the nations on earth," Jefferson protested from Paris, the British "require to be treated with the most hauteur. They require to be kicked into common

106. Ibid., 346–47.
107. Frederick W. Marks III, "Power, Pride, and the Purse: Diplomatic Origins of the Constitution," *Diplomatic History* 11 (Fall 1987), 311–12.
108. Ibid., 310.
109. Rakove, *Beginnings*, 350.

good manners." The young New York firebrand Alexander Hamilton lamented that the nation was at "almost the last stage of national humiliation."[110] "Is respectability in the eyes of foreign powers a safeguard against foreign encroachments?" he later asked in the *Federalist Papers*. "The imbecility of our government forbids them to treat with us," he answered.[111]

Over the next two years, the nationalists translated their concerns into action. In January 1786, Virginia proposed a convention to be held in Annapolis, Maryland, to deal with commercial issues. Only five states sent representatives—the host state, ironically, was not one of them—but Hamilton used the meeting to enlarge the discussions to other weaknesses of the federal system. The resolution emerging from Annapolis in September described the condition of the union as "delicate and critical" and called upon the states to send delegates to another meeting in Philadelphia to "derive such further provisions as shall appear to be necessary to render the constitution of the Federal Government adequate to the exigencies of the Union."[112] Congress gave lukewarm endorsement limited to revising the Articles of Confederation.

A taxpayers' revolt in western Massachusetts led by revolutionary war veteran Daniel Shays just as representatives were preparing to go to Philadelphia provided another boost to the nationalist cause. State military forces raised for the occasion easily suppressed the uprising, but the events confirmed in the minds of nationalists and the propertied classes fears of chaos and even dissolution of the Union. Shays's Rebellion also had foreign policy implications since the rebels had reportedly discussed with the British possible separation from the Union.[113] It strengthened belief in the need for a strong national government that could regulate the militia, maintain order, and hold the Union together. "We are fast verging to anarchy and confusion," Washington warned Madison in November 1786.[114]

The fear of anarchy, although exaggerated, was widely shared and had international implications. Jefferson in Paris worried that signs of chaos would weaken the United States in the eyes of Europeans sympathetic to

110. Jonathan R. Dull, "Two Republics in a Hostile World: The United States and the Netherlands in the 1780s," in Greene, *Revolution*, 158.
111. Daniel G. Lang, *Foreign Policy in the Early Republic: The Law of Nations and the Balance of Power* (Baton Rouge, La., 1985), 81.
112. Morris, *Forging of the Union*, 257.
113. Marks, "Diplomatic Origins," 312–13.
114. Morris, *Forging of the Union*, 266.

the Revolution. He and other Americans also viewed events at home in terms of what was happening in Europe. The "partition" of rebellious Poland by outside powers and the plight of the fledgling Dutch republic, divided internally and threatened from within and without, were ever-present reminders of the fragility of the American experiment.[115] Nationalists viewed the American Revolution as a "new chapter in the law of nations" and often comforted themselves that their republic was "immune to the savage enmities of the Old World." By 1786, they feared that the independence of the individual states might lead to the Europeanization of America, its breakup into quarreling entities resembling the European state system. Such a condition could lead to European intervention or the reimposition of despotism. Indeed, Shays's Rebellion and separatist sentiment in Vermont seemed to some nationalists a "stalking horse for counterrevolutionary conspiracy."[116]

The Constitutional Convention met in Philadelphia from May 25 to September 17, 1787. Jefferson hailed it as an "assembly of demigods." A French diplomat agreed that "we will never have seen, even in Europe, an assembly more respectable for the talents, knowledge, disinterestedness, and patriotism of those who compose it."[117] In 1787, the king of Prussia intervened militarily to crush rebellion in the Netherlands and restore monarchy. The specter of Holland's misfortune clouded the meeting in Philadelphia until it ended.[118] The discussions were dominated by nationalists, but debates were often heated. Crucial differences between large and small states over representation in the legislature were resolved by the "Great Compromise," which provided for equal representation in the upper house, the Senate, and proportional representation in the House of Representatives. The constitution also provided for a president to be elected every four years and a federal judiciary.

Foreign policy issues played a major role in calling the convention and would be important in the deliberations themselves. The fundamental question of the foreign policy powers to be assigned to each branch of government created ambiguities that have vexed the republic ever since. On one issue—commerce—there was little debate. Under the Confederation, the states could not agree on a uniform commercial policy. Other nations had exploited the differences. The need for a unified

115. Lawrence S. Kaplan, "Jefferson and the Constitution: The View from Paris, 1786–89," *Diplomatic History* 11 (Fall 1987), 323.
116. Onuf, "Anarchy," 272–74, 281–82.
117. Kaplan, "Jefferson," 322; Morris, *Forging of the Union*, 269.
118. Kaplan, "Jefferson," 334.

federal policy "has been so often enforced and descanted upon," a New York newspaper observed, "that the whole subject appears to be worn threadbare."[119] The need for federal authority to regulate commerce was the major reason the convention had been called. All plans proposed in Philadelphia gave the national government that power. A Committee of Detail assigned to Congress "the exclusive power of regulating Trade and levying imposts." Some nervous Deep South states pushed for a two-thirds vote to approve commercial legislation. Madison led the opposition, arguing that "we are laying the foundation of a great empire" and should "take a permanent view of the subject." The great issue, he insisted, was "the necessity of securing the West India trade to this country." The proposal was defeated, but the southerners extracted concessions in the form of provisions preventing any interference with the slave trade before 1808 and prohibiting export duties.[120]

The several branches shared power on other key foreign policy questions such as the making of treaties and diplomatic appointments. Early in the convention, delegates generally agreed that the Senate should be primarily responsible for foreign affairs. They naturally worried that an executive with too much power might replicate the monarchy from which they had just escaped. If presidential powers extended to war and peace, South Carolinian Charles Pinckney warned, it "would render the executive a monarchy of the worst kind, to wit an elected one."[121] Since Congress had executive powers under the Articles, it seemed natural to many of the delegates to leave them there. The smaller Senate, composed of more experienced and presumably wiser members, would be better able to deal with foreign policy issues than the popularly elected House. Thus late in the deliberations, when such issues were finally addressed, the power to make treaties and appoint diplomats was given to the Senate.

Ultimately, such powers were shared with the executive. Some delegates believed that the president could act as a check on the Senate and might better serve "as the general Guardian of the national interest."[122] Others felt that a single individual could operate more effectively than a larger legislative body and maintain the secrecy sometimes necessary in

119. Jacques J. Gorlin, "Foreign Trade and the Constitution," in Robert A. Goldwin and Robert A. Licht, eds., *Foreign Policy and the Constitution* (Washington, 1990), 57.
120. Morris, *Forging of the Union*, 284–85.
121. Jack N. Rakove, "Making Foreign Policy: The View from 1787," in Goldwin and Licht, *Constitution*, 6.
122. Ibid., 13.

handling foreign policy issues. The large states objected to what New York's Rufus King called "the vicious principle of representation," which made them equal with the small. Others disliked the fact that senators were elected by the state legislatures. Madison thus pushed for the president to act on these matters with the "advice and consent" of the Senate. The most controversial proposal was to require a two-thirds vote for approving treaties. The large states objected that a minority of small states could block a treaty. Madison sought to make peace treaties easier to approve by requiring a simple majority, but the two-thirds clause stuck, giving a minority a potent weapon that would be used often in the future.[123]

The constitutional provision that has caused the greatest controversy— the power to make war—was similarly shared yet, ironically, seems to have provoked little discussion in Philadelphia. Some delegates preferred to give the power to the president. Others, not surprisingly, feared granting such power to one person, proposing that it stay with the legislature and even with the Senate. Reflecting the spirit of compromise that marked the proceedings, Madison urged assigning to the president as commander in chief the power to "repel sudden attacks" when Congress could not act but giving Congress the power to declare war. This ambiguous compromise left the president an opening to employ military force without securing a declaration, one of the most persistent and difficult issues to emerge from the Constitution.

Submission of the document to the states for ratification set off a spirited debate, and foreign policy was central to the discussion. Indeed, the debate over the Constitution was the first in a series of recurring debates over the goals of U.S. foreign policy and the nation's proper role in the world. Those nationalists who shrewdly called themselves Federalists insisted that the weaknesses so blatantly manifest in the Articles of Confederation must be corrected if the United States was to survive and prosper in a hostile world. Those who came to be known as Antifederalists minimized external dangers and warned of the threat to American liberties from a more powerful national government and more active involvement in world affairs.

Federalists saw signs of national decline everywhere.[124] Foreign troops remained on America's soil; ships in its ports flew other flags while U.S. vessels rotted at their moorings. Congress could not enforce treaties. Unpaid debts had destroyed U.S. credit abroad. The lack of respect with which the nation was treated provided the most compelling sign of U.S.

123. Ibid., 9–13.
124. Norman A. Graebner, "Isolationism and Antifederalism: The Ratification Debates," *Diplomatic History* 11 (Fall 1987), 337.

weakness. "At the peace . . . America held a most elevated rank among the powers of the earth," a Pennsylvanian lamented, "but how are the mighty fallen! disgraced have we rendered ourselves abroad and ruined at home."[125] The nation's weakness made it "a prey to the nations of the earth," a defender of the Constitution declaimed. "What is there to prevent an Algerine pirate from landing on your coast, and carrying away your citizens into slavery?" a North Carolinian asked with obvious hyperbole. "You have not a single sloop of war."[126] Federalists insisted that the nation's prosperity hinged on a thriving commerce and thus on access to foreign markets. They wanted the United States to take its rightful place among the world's great nations. A constitution that strengthened national power would enable the nation to address its most important foreign policy problems and command respect abroad. It would "raise us from the lowest degree of contempt, into which we are now plunged," a Massachusetts newspaper proclaimed, "to an honorable, and consequently equal station among nations."[127] Some Federalists even championed the Constitution as an "inspirational instrument to the Old World," an essential means to extend to other nations the American model of republican union.[128]

Antifederalists took a more sanguine view of the nation's condition, a more limited view of its role in the world. They accused their foes of seeking to terrify the people by concocting "imaginary danger" and of overpromising the benefits of a new constitution. Anticipating arguments that would run throughout future foreign policy debates, they insisted that the United States because of its distance from Europe and the barrier provided by the Atlantic Ocean enjoyed unprecedented security. Should a European nation be so foolish as to attack, it would fight at a distinct disadvantage. Because of the European balance of power, other nations would come to America's aid. The United States could best exploit its geographical advantage by focusing on problems at home and providing the world "an example of a great people, who in their civil institutions hold chiefly in view, the attainment of virtue, and happiness among themselves."[129] It should not seek to influence European politics or intrude in disputes beyond its borders. Southern Antifederalists took issue with the Constitution itself. They feared that assigning to a bare majority

125. Ibid.
126. Ibid., 339.
127. Ibid., 340.
128. Onuf, "Anarchy," 300, 303.
129. Graebner, "Isolationism," 345.

the power to regulate commerce would benefit northern merchants at their expense. Opponents from all regions expressed concern over giving Congress unlimited power to tax. A standing army would burden the citizens economically, a Virginian warned; it "must sooner or later, establish a tyranny, not inferiour to the triumvirate . . . of Rome."[130]

Ratification took place between December 1787 and the summer of 1788. Convention leaders wisely decided not to submit the document to Congress or the state legislatures but rather to state conventions created expressly for that purpose. As a matter of expediency, they sent the draft constitution to Congress in the fall of 1787. That body—soon to be voted out of existence—approved its submission to the states. In many states, the debate provoked frantic political maneuvering and bitter debate. Virginia and New York were vital, and their approval solidified the Union, although New York's endorsement came after the necessary nine states had already ratified, putting the Constitution into effect. More than anything else, the commitment of the Constitution's sponsors to add a Bill of Rights ensured its approval. A new constitution "had been extorted from the grinding necessity of a reluctant nation," the young diplomat John Quincy Adams concluded without exaggeration.[131]

Whatever its ambiguities and defects, the Constitution corrected where foreign affairs were concerned the most glaring deficiencies of the Articles of Confederation. It gave the new national government clear authority to handle trade and foreign policy matters and responsibility to protect the nation's security and advance its global interests. These changes came none too soon. In 1789, France was swept by revolution. Three years later, war broke out in Europe, providing for the United States a challenge as great as the Revolution and its aftermath.

130. Ibid., 340.
131. Morris, *Forging of the Union*, 317.

2

"None Who Can Make Us Afraid"

The New Republic in a Hostile World, 1789–1801

George Washington's 1796 musings about a United States so powerful that none could "make us afraid" reflected the fear that gripped the nation throughout the turbulent 1790s, a time of dire threats from without and bitter divisions within. They also put into words the first president's vision of an American empire invulnerable to such dangers. If the United States could avoid war for a generation, he reasoned, the growth in population and resources combined with its favorable geographic location would enable it "in a just cause, to bid defiance to any power on earth."[1] Washington and his successor, John Adams, set important precedents in the management of foreign and national security policy. Conciliatory at the brink of war, they managed to avert hostilities with and wring important concessions from both England and France. They consolidated control of the western territories awarded in the 1783 peace treaty with Britain, laying a firm foundation for what Washington called the "future Grandeur of this rising Empire."[2] The Federalists' conduct of U.S. foreign policy significantly shaped the new nation's institutions and political culture. Through skillful diplomacy and great good fortune, the United States emerged from a tumultuous decade much stronger than at the start.

I

During the first years under its new Constitution, the United States faced challenges in foreign relations unsurpassed in gravity until the mid-twentieth century. In 1792, Europe erupted in a war that for more than two decades would convulse much of the world in bitter ideological and military struggle. Americans agreed as a first principle of foreign policy that they must stay out of such wars, but neutrality afforded little shelter. Europe "intruded" on America "in every way," historian Lawrence Kap-

---

1. Quoted in Burton Ira Kaufman, *Washington's Farewell Address: The View from the 20th Century* (Chicago, 1969), 183.
2. Ibid., 184.

lan has written, "inspiring fear of reconquest by the mother country, offering opportunity along sparsely settled borderlands, arousing uncertainties over the alliance with a great power."[3] The new nation depended on trade with Europe. The major belligerents attempted to use the United States as an instrument of their grand strategies and respected its neutrality only when expedient. The war also set loose profound divisions within the United States, and the internal strife in turn threatened America's ability to remain impartial toward the belligerents. Nor did the United States, while claiming neutrality, seek to insulate itself from the conflict. Rather, like small nations through history, it sought to exploit great-power rivalries to its own advantage. Sometimes brash and self-righteous in its demeanor toward the outside world, assertive in claiming its rights and aggressive in pursuing its goals, the nation throughout the 1790s was constantly embroiled in conflict. At times its very survival seemed at stake.

The United States in 1789 remained weak and vulnerable. When Washington assumed office, he presided over fewer than four million people, most of them concentrated along the Atlantic seaboard. The United States claimed vast territory in the West, and settlement had expanded rapidly in the Confederation period, but Spain still blocked access to the Mississippi River. The isolated frontier communities had only loose ties to the federal union. British and Spanish agents intrigued to detach them from the United States while encouraging the Indians to resist American expansion. Economically, the United States remained in a quasi-colonial status, a producer of raw materials dependent on European credits, markets, and manufactured goods. Washington and some of his top advisers believed that military power was essential to uphold the authority of the new government, maintain domestic order, and support the nation's diplomacy. But their efforts to create a military establishment were hampered by finances and an anti-militarist tradition deeply rooted in the colonial era. On the eve of war in Europe, the United States had no navy. Its regular army totaled fewer than five hundred men.

The Constitution at least partially corrected the structural weaknesses that had hampered the Confederation's conduct of foreign policy. It conferred on the central government authority to regulate commerce and conduct relations with other nations. Although powers were somewhat ambiguously divided between the executive and legislative branches,

3. Lawrence S. Kaplan, "Thomas Jefferson: The Idealist as Realist," in Frank Merli and Theodore A. Wilson, eds., *Makers of American Diplomacy from Benjamin Franklin to Alfred Thayer Mahan* (New York, 1974), 56.

Washington sure-handedly established the principle of presidential direction of foreign policy.

The first president created a Department of State to handle the day-to-day management of foreign relations, as well as domestic matters not under the War and Treasury departments. His fellow Virginian Thomas Jefferson assumed the office of secretary, assisted by a staff of four with an annual budget of $8,000 (including his salary). The other cabinet officers, particularly the secretaries of war and treasury, inevitably ventured into foreign policy. Washington made it a practice to submit important questions to his entire cabinet, resolving the issue himself where major divisions occurred. In keeping with ideals of republican simplicity—and to save money—the administration did not appoint anyone to the rank of ambassador. That "may be the custom of the old world," Jefferson informed the emperor of Morocco, "but it is not ours."[4] The "foreign service" consisted of a minister to France, chargés d'affaires in England, Spain, and Portugal, and an agent at Amsterdam. In 1790, the United States opened its first consulate in Bordeaux, a major source of arms, ammunition, and wine during the Revolution. That same year, it appointed twelve consuls and also named six foreigners as vice-consuls since there were not enough qualified Americans to fill the posts.[5]

A keen awareness of the nation's present weakness in no way clouded visions of its future greatness. The new government formulated ambitious objectives and pursued them doggedly. Conscious of the unusual fertility of the land and productivity of the people and viewing commerce as the natural basis for national wealth and power, American leaders worked vigorously to break down barriers that kept the new nation out of foreign markets. They moved quickly to gain control of the trans-Appalachian West, encouraging emigration and employing diplomatic pressure and military force to eliminate Native Americans and foreigners who stood in the way. Even in its infancy, the United States looked beyond existing boundaries, casting covetous eyes upon Spanish Florida and Louisiana (and even British Canada). Perceiving that in time a restless population that was doubling in size every twenty-two years would give it an advantage over foreign challengers, the Washington administration accepted the need for patience. But it prepared for the future by encouraging settlement of contested territory. Rationalizing their covetousness with the

4. Quoted in James A. Field Jr., *America and the Mediterranean World, 1776–1882* (Princeton, N.J., 1969), 40.
5. David S. Patterson, "The Department of State: The Formative Years, 1775–1800," *Prologue* 21 (Winter 1989), 323–24.

doctrine that superior institutions and ideology entitled them to whatever land they could use, Americans began to think in terms of an empire stretching from Atlantic to Pacific long before the population of existing boundaries was completed.[6]

The most urgent problem facing the new government was the threat of Indian war in the West. The "condition of the Indians to the United States is perhaps unlike that of any other two people in existence," Chief Justice John Marshall would later write, and clashing interests as well as incompatible concepts of sovereignty provoked conflict between them.[7] Most of the tribes scattered through the trans-Appalachian West lived in communal settlements but roamed widely across the land as hunters. American frontier society, on the other hand, was anchored in agriculture, private property, and land ownership, and Americans conveniently rationalized that the Indians had sacrificed claim to the land by not using it properly. The Indians only grudgingly conceded U.S. sovereignty. Increasingly aware that they could not hold back American settlers, they sought to contain them in specified areas by banding together in loose confederations, signing treaties with the United States, seeking assistance from Britain or Spain, or attacking exposed frontier settlements. Following precedents set by the colonial governments, the United States had implicitly granted the Indians a measure of sovereignty and accorded them the status of independent nations through negotiations replete with elaborate ceremony and the signing of treaties. As a way of asserting federal authority for Indian affairs over the states, the Washington administration would do likewise. From its birth, however, the United States had vehemently—and contradictorily—insisted that the Indians were under its sovereignty and that Indian affairs were therefore internal matters. The various land ordinances enacted by the Confederation presumed U.S. sovereignty in the West and sought to provide for orderly and peaceful settlement. But the onrush of settlers and their steady encroachment on Indian lands provoked retaliatory attacks and preemptive strikes.

The Washington administration desperately sought to avoid war. With limited funds in the treasury and no army, the infant government was painfully aware that it could not afford and might not win such a war. At this time, Americans in the more settled, seacoast areas accepted the Enlightenment view that all mankind was of one species and capable of

6. Albert K. Weinberg, *Manifest Destiny: A Study of Nationalist Expansionism in American History* (Chicago, 1963), 72–81.
7. Quoted in Francis Paul Prucha, *American Indian Treaties: The History of a Political Anomaly* (Berkeley, Calif., 1991), 1.

improvement. In addition, Washington and Secretary of War Henry Knox insisted that the United States, a bold experiment in republicanism closely watched by the whole world, must be true to its principles in dealing with the Indians. For the short term, the administration sought to avert war by diplomacy, building on the treaties negotiated under the Confederation to keep Indians and settlers apart and achieve cheap and peaceful expansion. For the long term, Knox promoted a policy of expansion with honor that would make available to the Indians the blessings of American civilization in return for their lands, a form of pacification through deculturation and assimilation.[8]

Washington's diplomacy achieved short-term results in the Southwest. The powerful Creeks had traditionally preserved their independence by playing European nations against each other. Eager to bind the autonomous groups that composed the tribe into a tighter union under his leadership and to fend off onrushing American settlers, the redoubtable half-breed Alexander McGillivray journeyed to New York in 1790 and amidst pomp and ceremony, including an audience with the Great Father himself (Washington), agreed to a treaty. In return for three million acres of land, the United States recognized the independence of the Creeks, promised to protect them from the incursions of its citizens, and agreed to boundaries. A seemingly innocent provision afforded a potentially powerful instrument for expansion with honor. "That the Creek nation may be led to a greater degree of civilization, and to become herdsmen and cultivators, instead of remaining in a state of hunters," the treaty solemnly affirmed, "the United States will from time to time furnish gratuitously the said nation with useful domestic animals and implements of husbandry."[9] The United States also provided an annuity of $1,500. The bestowing of such gifts would help civilize the Indians and, in Knox's words, have the "salutary effect of attaching them to the interests of the United States."[10] A secret protocol gave McGillivray control of trade and made him an agent of the United States with the rank of brigadier general and an annuity of $1,200.

8. Robert Berkhofer Jr., *The White Man's Indian: American Images of the Indian from Columbus to the Present* (New York, 1978), 142–44; Reginald Horsman, *Race and Manifest Destiny* (Cambridge, Mass., 1981), 104–6.
9. Michael D. Green, *The Creeks* (New York, 1990), 43–46; Prucha, *Indian Treaties*, 79–84.
10. David Nichols, "The Transformation of Indian Civilization Policy," unpublished paper in possession of author, 8–10.

In the short run, each party viewed the treaty as a success. It boosted the prestige of the new U.S. government, lured the Creeks from Spain, and averted conflict with the most powerful southwestern tribe. It appeared to the Creeks to recognize their sovereignty and protect them from American settlers, buying McGillivray time to develop tribal unity and strength. In fact, the state of Georgia did not respect the treaty and the United States would not or could not force it to do so. Boundaries were not drawn, and settlers continued to encroach on Creek lands. To entice McGillivray away from the United States, Spanish agents doubled the pension provided by Washington. The Creek leader died in 1793, his dream of union unrealized, conditions in the Southwest still unsettled.[11]

The Northwest was far more explosive. The Confederation government had signed treaties with Indians north of the Ohio River, but some tribes had refused to go along, and those who had were dissatisfied. With British encouragement, the Indians sought to create a buffer state in the Northwest. As settlers poured into the area, tensions increased. Frontier people generally viewed the Indians as inferior savages and expendable and preferred to eliminate rather than pacify them. Eventually, their view prevailed.

Eager to avoid war and uphold American honor, the Washington administration capitulated to pressure from land speculators and settlers in Kentucky and elsewhere along the frontier. The administration continued to negotiate with the Indians, but it approached them in a high-handed manner that made success unlikely: "This is the last offer that can be made," Knox warned the northwestern tribes. "If you do not embrace it now, your doom must be sealed forever."[12] By backing its diplomacy with force, moreover, the administration blundered into the war it hoped to avoid. In 1790, to "strike terror into the minds of the Indians," Washington and Knox sent fifteen hundred men under Josiah Harmar deep into present-day Ohio and Indiana. Returning to its base after plundering Indian villages near the Maumee River, Harmar's force was ambushed and suffered heavy losses. To recoup its prestige among its own citizens and the Indians with whom it sought to negotiate, the administration escalated the conflict in 1791, sending fourteen hundred men under Gen.

---

11. Green, *Creeks*, 46; Lawrence S. Kaplan, *Thomas Jefferson: Westward the Course of Empire* (Wilmington, Del., 1999), 82.
12. Richard H. Kohn, *Eagle and Sword: The Beginnings of the Military Establishment in America* (New York, 1975), 112; Horsman, *Race and Manifest Destiny*, 111–14.

Arthur St. Clair into Indian country north of Cincinnati. St. Clair's small and ill-prepared force was annihilated, losing nine hundred men in what has been called the worst defeat ever suffered by an American army.[13] On the eve of war in Europe, the United States' position in the Northwest was more precarious than before, its prestige shattered.

The terrifying reality of slave revolt in the Caribbean and specter of slave rebellion at home further heightened American insecurity in the early 1790s. Inspired by the rhetoric of the French Revolution, slaves in the French colony of Saint-Domingue (the western third of the island of Hispaniola, present-day Haiti) rebelled against their masters in August 1791. At the height of the struggle, as many as one hundred thousand blacks faced forty thousand whites and mulattoes. The fury stirred by racial antagonism and the legacy of slavery produced a peculiarly savage conflict. Marching into battle playing African music and flying banners

13. Allan R. Millett and Peter Maslowski, *For the Common Defense: A Military History of the United States of America* (New York, 1984), 92.

with the slogan DEATH TO ALL WHITES, the rebels burned plantations and massacred planter families.[14]

Americans' enthusiasm for revolution stopped well short of violent slave revolt, of course, and they viewed events in the West Indies with foreboding. Trade with Saint-Domingue was important, the exports of $3 million in 1790 more than twice those to metropolitan France. Friendship with France also encouraged sympathy for the planters. Some Americans worried that Britain might exploit the conflict on Saint-Domingue to enlarge its presence in the region. But the U.S. response to the revolution derived mainly from racial fears. At this time, attitudes toward slavery remained somewhat flexible, but those who favored emancipation saw it taking place gradually and peacefully. The shock of violent revolt on nearby islands provoked fears of a descent into "chaos and negroism" and the certainty, as Secretary of the Treasury Alexander Hamilton put it, of "calamitous" results. Southerners like Jefferson harbored morbid dread that revolt would extend to the United States, setting off a frenzy of violence that could only end in the "extermination of one or the other race." State legislatures voted funds to help the planters on Saint-Domingue suppress the rebellion. Stretching executive authority, the Washington administration advanced France $726 million in debt payments and sold arms to the planters.[15]

Such efforts were unavailing. The rebel victory in June 1793 sent shock waves to the North. Defeated French planters fled to the United States, bringing tales of massacre that spread panic throughout the South. While Jefferson privately fretted about the "bloody scenes" Americans would "wade through" in the future, southern states tightened slave codes and began to develop a positive defense of the "peculiar institution."[16] Nervousness on the northwestern frontier was exceeded by the horror of slave revolt in the South.

II

Republican ideology looked upon political parties as disruptive, even evil, but partisan politics intruded into foreign policy early in Washington's first term, a development that the president himself never fully accepted and that, throughout the 1790s, significantly influenced and vastly complicated the new government's dealings with the outside world. The struggle

14. Tim Matthewson, "George Washington's Policy Toward the Haitian Revolution," *Diplomatic History* 3 (Summer 1979), 324–28.
15. Ibid.
16. Jefferson to James Monroe, July 14, 1793, in Julian P. Boyd, ed., *The Papers of Thomas Jefferson*, vol. 26 (Princeton, N.J., 1995), 503.

centered around the dynamic personalities of Jefferson and Hamilton, but it reflected much deeper divisions within U.S. society. It assumed a level of special intensity because the participants shared with equal fervor the conviction of revolutionaries that each step they took might determine the destiny of the new nation.[17] In addition, in a new nation any domestic or foreign policy decision could establish a lasting precedent.[18]

Tall, loose-jointed, somewhat awkward in manner and appearance, Jefferson was the embodiment of the southern landed gentry, an aristocrat by birth, an intellectual by temperament, a scholarly and retiring individual who hated open conflict but could be a fierce infighter. Small of stature, born out of wedlock in the West Indies, Hamilton struggled to obtain the social status Jefferson acquired by birth. Handsome and charming, a man of prodigious intellect and boundless energy, he was driven by insatiable ambitions and a compulsion to dominate. Jefferson represented the predominantly agricultural interests of the South and West. Optimistic by nature, a child of the Enlightenment, he had faith in popular government—at least the elitist form practiced in Virginia—viewed agriculture and commerce as the proper bases for national wealth, and was almost morbidly suspicious of the northeastern moneyed groups who prospered through speculation. To Hamilton, order was more important than liberty. A brilliant financier, he believed that political power should reside with those who had the largest stake in society. He attached himself to the financial elite Jefferson so distrusted. The dispute became deeply personal. Hamilton viewed Jefferson as devious and scheming. Jefferson was offended by Hamilton's arrogance and transparent ambition. He especially resented that the secretary of the treasury seemed to have Washington's ear.[19]

The Hamilton-Jefferson foreign policy struggle has often been portrayed in terms of a realist/idealist dichotomy, with Hamilton cast as the realist, more European than American in his thinking, coldly rational and keenly sensitive to the national interest and the limits of power, Jefferson as the archetypical American idealist, intent on spreading the

17. Stanley Elkins and Eric McKitrick, *The Age of Federalism: The Early American Republic, 1788–1800* (New York, 1993), 4, 77. Classic accounts of the origins of American political parties from very different perspectives are Joseph Charles, *The Origins of the American Party System: Three Essays* (New York, 1961) and Lance Banning, *The Jeffersonian Persuasion: Evolution of a Party Ideology* (Ithaca, N.Y., 1978).
18. Joseph J. Ellis, *American Sphinx: The Character of Thomas Jefferson* (New York, 1997), 121.
19. Ibid., 25–26, 136–37, 146; Kaplan, *Jefferson*, 73–74, 78.

nation's principles even at costs it could not afford. Such a construct, although useful, imposes a modern frame of reference on eighteenth-century ideas and practices and does not do justice to the complexity of the diplomacy of the two men or the conflict between them.[20]

Both shared the long-range goal of a strong nation, independent of the great powers of Europe, but they approached it from quite different perspectives, advocating coherent systems of political economy in which foreign and domestic policies were inextricably linked with sharply conflicting visions of what America should be. Hamilton was the more patient. He preferred to build national power and *then* "dictate the terms of the connection between the old world and the new."[21] Modeling his system on that of England, he sought to establish a strong government and stable economy that would attract investment capital and promote manufactures. Through expansion of the home market he hoped in time to get around Britain's commercial restrictions and even challenge its supremacy, but for the moment he would acquiesce. His economic program hinged on revenues from trade with England, and he opposed anything that threatened it. Horrified at the excesses of the French Revolution, he condemned Jefferson's "womanish attachment" to France and increasingly saw England as a bastion of stable governing principles. More accurate than Jefferson and Madison in his assessment of American weakness and therefore more willing to make concessions to Britain, he pursued peace with a zeal that compromised American pride and honor and engaged in machinations that could have undermined American interests. His lust for power could be both reckless and destructive.

Deeply committed to perfecting the republican triumph of the Revolution, Jefferson and his compatriot James Madison, the intellectual force behind republicanism and leader in the House of Representatives, envisioned a youthful, vigorous, predominantly agricultural society composed of virtuous yeoman farmers. Their vision required the opening of foreign markets to absorb the produce of American farms and westward expansion

---

20. For example, Paul Varg, *Foreign Policies of the Founding Fathers* (New York, 1970) and more recently Robert W. Tucker and David Hendrickson, *Empire of Liberty: The Statecraft of Thomas Jefferson* (New York, 1990) and Walter Russell Mead, *Special Providence: American Foreign Policy and How It Changed the World* (New York, 2001). A persuasive critique, at least for Jefferson, is Lawrence S. Kaplan, "Jefferson as Idealist-Realist," in *"Entangling Alliances with None": American Foreign Policy in the Age of Jefferson* (Kent, Ohio, 1987), 3–23.
21. Quoted in Michael H. Hunt, *Ideology and U.S. Foreign Policy* (New Haven, Conn., 1987), 24.

to ensure the availability of sufficient land to sustain a burgeoning population. Britain stood as the major barrier to their dreams—it had "bound us in manacles, and very nearly defeated the object of our independence," Madison declaimed. Still, they were confident that a youthful, dynamic America could prevail over an England they saw as hopelessly corrupt and fundamentally rotten. Confirmed Anglophobes, they were certain from the experience with non-importation in the Revolutionary era that dependence on American necessities would force Britain to bend to economic pressure. They hoped to divert U.S. commerce to France. Although committed to free trade in theory, they proposed harsh discriminatory duties to force Britain to sign a commercial treaty.[22]

Jefferson and Madison were indeed idealists who dreamed of a world of like-minded republics. They were also internationalists with an abiding faith in progress who accepted, for the moment at least, the existing balance-of-power system and hoped to make it more peaceful and orderly through the negotiation of treaties promoting free trade and international law.[23] Jefferson especially admired France and things French. He welcomed the French Revolution and urged closer ties with the new government. As a French diplomat pointed out, however, his liking for France stemmed in part from his detestation for England, and, in any event, Americans in general were "the sworn enemy of all the European peoples."[24] He was also a tough-minded diplomatist, who advocated playing the European powers against each other to extract concessions. Jefferson and Madison saw Hamilton's policies as abject surrender to England. They viewed the secretary of the treasury and his cronies as tools "of British interests seeking to restore monarchy to America," an "enormous invisible conspiracy against the national welfare."[25] In diplomacy, Jefferson was more independent than Hamilton and could be shrewdly manipulative, but his commitment to principle and his tendency to overestimate American power at times clouded his vision and limited his effectiveness.

The battle was joined when the new government took office. Conflict first broke out over Hamilton's bold initiative to centralize federal power and create a moneyed interest by funding the national debt and assuming

22. See especially Drew R. McCoy, *The Elusive Republic: Political Economy in Jeffersonian America* (Chapel Hill, N.C., 1980), 146–52.
23. Peter Onuf and Nicholas Onuf, *Federal Union, Modern World: The Law of Nations in an Age of Revolution* (New York, 1994), 92–105.
24. Ellis, *American Sphinx*, 124–25.
25. Kaplan, "Idealist as Realist," 71.

state debts, but it quickly extended to foreign affairs. In 1789, an Anglo-Spanish dispute over British fur-trading settlements at Nootka Sound on Vancouver Island in the Pacific Northwest threatened war. Jefferson urged U.S. support for the side that offered the most in return. Hamilton did not openly dissent. Certain that American interests would best be served by siding with Great Britain, however, he confided in British secret agent George Beckwith (the secretary of the treasury was referred to as No. 7 in coded dispatches) that Jefferson's position did not represent U.S. policy. The differences became irrelevant when the threat of war receded, but they widened over commercial policy. Jefferson and Madison pushed for discriminatory duties against British commerce. Hamilton openly used his influence to block their passage in the Senate.[26]

Because of the sharp divisions within its own councils and primarily because of its continued weakness, the new government was little more successful than its predecessor in resolving the nation's major diplomatic problems. Britain in 1792 finally opened formal diplomatic relations, but Jefferson could not secure a commercial agreement or force implementation of the treaty of 1783. The United States was a relatively minor concern to Britain at this point. Content with the status quo, London did not take seriously Jefferson's threats of discrimination, in part because British officials correctly surmised that economic warfare would hurt America more than their own country, in part because of Hamilton's private assurances. In any event, Jefferson's bombastic rhetoric and uncompromising negotiating position left little room for compromise. The secretary of state fared no better with France and Spain. The French government refused even to negotiate a new commercial treaty and imposed discriminatory duties on tobacco and other American imports. Ignoring Jefferson's slightly veiled threats of war, Spain refused commercial concessions and would not discuss the disputed southern boundary and access to the Mississippi. On the eve of war in Europe, the position of the United States seemed anything but promising.

III

The outbreak of war in 1792 offered enticing opportunities to attain long-standing goals but posed new and ominous dangers to the independence and even survival of the republic. The Wars of the French Revolution and Napoleon differed dramatically from the chessboard engagements of the age of limited war. The French Revolution injected ideology and

26. Kaplan, *Jefferson*, 73.

nationalism into traditional European power struggles, making the conflict more intense and all-consuming. Declaring war on Austria in August 1792, France launched a crusade to preserve revolutionary principles at home and extend them across the European continent. Alarmed by developments in Europe, England in February 1793 joined the Continental allies to block the spread of French power *and* the contaminating influence of French radicalism. Monarchical wars gave way to wars of nations; limited war to total war. The belligerents mobilized their entire populations not simply to defeat but to destroy their enemies, creating mass armies that fought with a new patriotic zeal. The conflict spread across the globe. Britain, as always, sought to strangle its adversary by controlling the seas. As with earlier imperial conflicts, colonies formed an integral part of the grand strategies of the belligerents. The war expanded to the Mediterranean, South Asia, and the Western Hemisphere.[27]

These wars of new ferocity and scope left the United States little margin for safety. The great powers of Europe viewed the new nation as little more than a pawn—albeit a potentially useful one—in their struggle for survival. Perceiving the United States as weak and unreliable, neither wanted it as an ally. Each preferred a benevolent neutrality that offered access to naval stores and foodstuffs, shipping as needed, and the use of U.S. ports and territory as bases for commerce raiding and attacks on enemy colonies. They sought to deny their enemy what they wanted for themselves. They were openly contemptuous of America's wish to retain commercial ties with both sides and insulate itself against the war. They blatantly interfered in U.S. politics and employed bribery, intimidation, and the threat of force to achieve their aims.

Americans had long agreed they must abstain from Europe's wars, and the new nation's still fragile position in 1793 underscored the urgency of neutrality. Individuals as different as Hamilton and Jefferson could readily agree, moreover, that to become too closely attached to either power could result in a loss of freedom of action, even independence. Sensitive to the balance-of-power system and their role in it, Americans also quickly perceived that, as in the Revolution, they might exploit European conflict to their own advantage. They also recognized that war would significantly increase demands for their products and might open ports previously closed. As a neutral the United States could trade with all nations, Jeffer-

27. John Lynn, "Revolution in Warfare During the Age of the French Revolution," in Robert A. Doughty et al., *Warfare in the Western World*, vol. 1 (New York, 1996), 173–93.

son observed with more than a touch of self-righteousness, and the "new world will fatten on the follies of the old."[28]

To proclaim neutrality was one thing, to implement it quite another. The United States was tied by treaty to France and by Hamilton's economic system to Britain, posing major threats to neutrality. Establishing a workable policy was also difficult because as a newly independent nation the United States lacked a body of precedent for dealing with the complex issues that arose. International law in the eighteenth century generally upheld the right of neutrals to trade with belligerents in non-contraband supplies and the sanctity of their territory from belligerent use for military purposes. It was codified only in bilateral treaties, however, which were routinely ignored in times of crisis. Within the general agreement on principles, there was considerable divergence in application. Following the practice of the small, seafaring nations of northern Europe, the United States interpreted neutral rights as broadly as possible. By contrast, Britain relied on sea power as its chief military instrument and interpreted such rights restrictively. Lacking a merchant marine and dependent on neutral carriers, the French accepted America's principles when it was useful, but when the United States veered in the direction of Britain, they reacted strongly. In the absence of courts to enforce international law and especially in the context of total war, power was the final arbiter. From 1793 to 1812, the United States could not maintain a neutrality acceptable to both sides. Whatever it did or refrained from doing, it provoked reprisals from one belligerent or the other.

Growing internal divisions also complicated implementation of a neutrality policy. Still sympathetic to France and seeing in the war an opportunity to free his country from commercial bondage to Britain, Jefferson persuaded himself that the United States could have both neutrality and the alliance with France. Increasingly alarmed by the radicalism of the French Revolution and more than ever persuaded that America's security and his own economic system demanded friendship with Britain, Hamilton leaned in the other direction, grandly indifferent to the consequences for France.[29]

The conflict surfaced when England and France went to war in 1793. In April, Washington requested his cabinet's advice on the issuance of a declaration of neutrality and the more prickly question of U.S. obligations

28. Jefferson to Edward Rutledge, July 4, 1790, in Boyd, *Papers of Jefferson*, vol. 16 (Princeton, N.J., 1961), 600–601.
29. Kaplan, "Idealist as Realist," 71–72.

under the 1778 alliance. Hoping to extract concessions from England, Jefferson urged delaying a statement of neutrality. Hamilton favored an immediate and unequivocal declaration, ostensibly to make America's position clear, in fact to avoid any grounds for conflict with London. The French alliance bound the signatories to guarantee each other's possessions in the Western Hemisphere and to admit privateers and prizes to their ports while denying such rights to their enemies. Acceptance of these obligations meant compromising U.S. neutrality; rejection risked antagonizing France. Hamilton advocated what amounted to unilateral abrogation of the alliance, arguing that the change in government in France rendered it void. Jefferson upheld the sanctity of treaties, claiming that they were negotiated by nations, not governments, and could not be scrapped at whim, but he was motivated as much by a desire to avoid offense to France as by respect for principle. He contended on a practical level that France would not ask the United States to fulfill its obligations, a prediction far off the mark. Washington eventually sided with Hamilton on the issuance of a declaration of neutrality and with Jefferson on the status of the French alliance, a compromise that satisfied neither of the antagonists but established the basis for a reasonably impartial neutrality.[30]

France and its newly appointed minister to the United States, Edmond Charles Genet, challenged the policy at the start. The Girondin government was certain that people across the world—particularly Americans—shared its revolutionary zeal and would assist its crusade to extend republicanism. Genet was instructed to conclude with the United States an "intimate concert" to "promote the Extension of the Empire of Liberty," holding out the prospect of "liberating" Spanish America and opening the Mississippi. Failing this, he was to act on his own to liberate Canada, the Floridas, and Louisiana, and was empowered to issue commissions to Americans to participate. He was also to obtain a $3 million advance payment on America's debt to France. While these matters were under negotiation, he was to secure the opening of U.S. ports to outfit French privateers and bring in enemy prizes. The instructions, if implemented, would have made the United States a de facto ally against England.[31]

The new minister's unsuitability for his position exceeded his chimerical instructions. A gifted linguist and musician, handsome, witty and

---

30. Kaplan, *Jefferson*, 94–98.
31. The standard account is Harry Ammon, *The Genet Mission* (New York, 1973), but see also Elkins and McKitrick, *Age of Federalism*, 330–54.

charming, he was also a flamboyant and volatile individual who had already been thrown out of Catherine the Great's Russia for diplomatic indiscretions. Inflamed with the crusading zeal of the Girondins, he poorly understood the nation to which he was accredited, assuming mistakenly that popular sympathy for France entailed a willingness to risk war with England and that in the United States, as in his country, control of foreign relations resided with the legislature.

From the moment he came ashore, Genet was the proverbial bull in the china shop. Landing in Charleston, South Carolina, where he was widely feted by the governor and local citizenry, he commissioned four privateers that soon brought prizes into U.S. ports. The lavish entertainment he enjoyed along the land route to Philadelphia confirmed his belief that Americans supported his mission, a conclusion reinforced by early meetings with Jefferson. Hoping to persuade Genet to proceed cautiously lest he give Hamilton reason to adopt blatantly anti-French policies, the secretary of state took the minister into his confidence and spoke candidly, even indiscreetly, about U.S. politics, encouraging the Frenchman's illusions and ardor.

In fact, the two nations were on a collision course. After long and sometimes bitter debates and frequently over Jefferson's objections, the cabinet had hammered out a neutrality policy that construed American obligations under the French alliance as narrowly as possible. The United States denied France the right to outfit privateers or sell enemy prizes in its ports and ordered the release of prizes already brought in. It flatly rejected Genet's offer of a new commercial treaty, as well as his request for an advance payment on the debt, and ordered the arrest of Americans who had enlisted for service on French privateers.

The U.S. policies violated the spirit, if not the letter, of the alliance, giving Genet grounds for protest, but his blatant defiance of American orders undercut his cause. He responded intemperately to Jefferson's official statements, insisting that they did not reflect the will of the American people. Ignoring U.S. instructions, he commissioned a privateer, *La Petite Democrate*, under the government's nose in Philadelphia and began organizing expeditions to attack Louisiana by sea and land, the latter to be manned primarily by Kentuckians headed by revolutionary war hero George Rogers Clark. In defiance of Jefferson's request to delay sailing of the ship and while the cabinet was heatedly debating whether to forcibly stop its departure, he ordered *La Petite Democrate* out of reach of shore batteries and eventually to sea. Responding to repeated official protests, he threatened to take his case to the nation over the head of its president.

Genet's actions sparked a full-fledged, frequently nasty debate in the country at large. Supporters of France and its minister accused the government of pro-British sympathies and monarchical tendencies, calling them "Anglomen" and "monocrats." Those who defended the government denounced the opposition as tools of France and radical revolutionaries. The outlines of political parties began to take form. Jeffersonians took the name Republicans, Hamiltonians became Federalists. Political dialogue was impassioned, street brawls were not uncommon, and old friendships were severed. Newspapers aligned with Hamilton or Jefferson and frequently encouraged by them waged virulent war, debating the basic principles of government while indulging in name-calling and calumny from which even the demigod Washington was not immune. Discussions in the cabinet reflected the increasingly bitter mood of the nation, provoking a harried and thin-skinned president (the first of many holders of the office, in this regard) to explode that "*by god* he had rather be in his grave than in his present situation."[32]

The Genet affair ended in anticlimax and irony. By July 1793, the administration felt compelled to ask for his recall, even Jefferson agreeing that the appointment had been "calamitous" and confiding in Madison that he saw the "necessity of quitting a wreck which could not but sink all who cling to it."[33] Hamilton and Knox sought to do it in a way that would discredit the French minister and his American supporters. Washington wisely sided with Jefferson, seeking to do so without alienating France. By the time the United States asked for his recall, the Girondins had been replaced by the Jacobins, who, though more radical at home, did not share their predecessors' zeal for a global crusade. Suffering disastrous defeats on land and sea and in desperate need of American food, the new government readily acceded, denouncing Genet's "giddiness." In one of those bizarre twists that marked the politics of the French Revolution, it accused him of complicity in an English plot. Had he returned home, he would likely have been guillotined. Aware of what awaited him, Genet requested, and as a humanitarian gesture was granted, asylum in the United States.[34] He lived out his life as a gentleman farmer and unsuccessful amateur scientist in New York, becoming an American citizen in 1804 and marrying the daughter of New York governor George Clinton.

32. Quoted in Elkins and McKitrick, *Age of Federalism*, 361.
33. Ellis, *American Sphinx*, 127.
34. Eugene R. Sheridan, "The Recall of Edmond Charles Genet: A Study in Transatlantic Politics and Diplomacy," *Diplomatic History* 18 (Fall 1994), 463–88.

Genet's shenanigans were generally counterproductive. The escape of *La Petite Democrate* did not provoke British reprisals; the minister's grand scheme for the liberation of Louisiana quickly collapsed from shortage of funds and lack of American support. On the other hand, the cautious and at least mildly pro-British definition of neutral obligations set forth piecemeal by the Washington administration was enacted into law in 1794, forming the basis for U.S. neutrality policies into the twentieth century. Frustration with Genet contributed to Jefferson's decision to leave office in late 1793, removing from the cabinet a voice sympathetic to France and eventually contributing to a tilt in policy toward Britain.

More than anything else, the Genet mission exposed the fragility of American neutrality, the extent to which the European powers would go to undermine it, and the depth of internal conflict on foreign policy. It marked the beginning, rather than the end, of a twenty-year effort to steer clear of the European war while profiting from it, and it divided Americans into two deeply antagonistic factions.

IV

Even while the Genet affair occupied center stage, the United States and Britain edged toward war. Still sometimes portrayed by Americans as the ruthless aggression of an arrogant great power against an innocent and vulnerable nation, the crisis of 1794 was considerably more complex in its origins. It provides, in fact, a classic example of the way in which conflicts of interest, exacerbated by intense nationalism on one side, a lack of attention on the other, and the ill-advised actions of poorly informed and sometimes panicky officials miles from the seat of government can create conditions for war even when the governments themselves have reason to avoid it. In this instance, war was averted, but only narrowly and only because both nations and especially the United States found compelling reason for restraint.

By early 1794, the long-simmering conflict along the Great Lakes threatened a clash of arms. Increasingly concerned with the explosive frontier, the British after St. Clair's defeat devised a "compromise" that would have set aside specified lands for the Indians in territory claimed by the United States. By this time, however, neither of the other parties was inclined to negotiate. Buoyed by their victory, the Indians demanded lands from the Canadian border to the Ohio River and murdered under flags of truce several U.S. agents sent to treat with them. Americans never understood the pride and suspicion with which the Indians viewed them. They would concede only limited territory to people Hamilton dismissed as "vagrants." Even after a humiliating defeat, they patronized the victors. They blamed the British for the tribes' exorbitant claims and violently protested their interference in what they viewed a purely internal matter.[35]

In the absence of a settlement, tensions flared. When nervous British officials in Canada learned that the United States was preparing another military expedition to be commanded by General "Mad Anthony" Wayne of Revolutionary War fame, they feared attacks on their frontier posts. Without London's approval, they incited the Indians to resist American advances. As a "defensive" measure, they sent troops to the Maumee River near present-day Detroit. What the British viewed as defensive, Americans regarded as further evidence of British perfidy and provocation. As Wayne moved north and British forces south, there was much loose talk of war.

Conflicts over issues of neutrality posed even more difficult problems. From its birth as a nation, the United States had claimed the right to trade with belligerents in non-contraband and defined contraband narrowly to include only specifically military items such as arms and ammunition. It also endorsed the principle that free ships make free goods, meaning that the private property of belligerents aboard neutral ships was immune from seizure. The United States insisted that these "rights" had sanction in international law and incorporated them into treaties with several European countries. But they served the national interest as well. Desperately in need of U.S. foodstuffs, France purchased large quantities of grain and permitted American ships to transport supplies from its West Indian colonies to its home ports, a right generally denied under mercantilist doctrine. Hundreds of American ships swarmed into the Caribbean and across the Atlantic to "fatten on the follies" of the Old World.

Americans' quest for profits ran afoul of Britain's grand strategy. Recognizing France's dependence on external sources of food, the British government set out to starve its enemy into submission, blockading French ports, broadening contraband to include food, and ordering the seizure of American ships carrying grain to France. The British did not want to drive the United States into the arms of France and thus agreed to purchase confiscated grain at fair prices. Preoccupied with the European war, increasingly alarmed at the burgeoning American trade with France, and badly misjudging the Washington administration's handling of Genet, they implemented their strategy in a high-handed and often brutal manner that threatened to provoke war. Without any warning and frequently exceeding their instructions, overzealous British officials in the West

35. Kohn, *Eagle and Sword*, 146, 155–57; Elkins and McKitrick, *Age of Federalism*, 436–38.

Indies seized 250 ships. Egged on by a system that permitted the captors personally to profit from such plunder, ship captains boarded American vessels, stripped them of their sails, and tore down their colors. Hastily assembled kangaroo courts condemned ships and cargoes. Captains and crews were confined, often without provisions. Some Americans were impressed into the Royal Navy; others died in captivity. Britain justified its efforts to curtail trade with France through its so-called Rule of 1756 declaring that trade illegal in time of peace was illegal in time of war. British officials later admitted, however, that the ship seizures of 1794 far exceeded the bounds of this rule.[36]

London's actions stirred powerful resentment in the United States. What seemed to Britons essential acts of war appeared to Americans a threat to their prosperity and a grievous affront to their dignity as an independent nation. Angry mobs in seaport cities attacked British sailors. In Charleston, a crowd tore down a statue of William Pitt the Elder that had survived the Revolution. Congress assembled in early 1794 in a mood of outrage. Madison's proposals in the House of Representatives for discrimination against British commerce failed in the Senate by the single vote of Vice President John Adams. Even Federalists spoke of war. An angry Congress proceeded to impose a temporary embargo on all foreign shipping and to discuss even more drastic measures such as repudiation of debts owed Britain and creation of a navy to defend American shipping.

The crisis of early 1794 posed a dilemma for the Washington administration. Most top officials regarded a British victory as essential to the preservation of stable government in Europe and hence to the well-being of the United States. On the other hand, they appreciated and indeed shared the rising public anger toward Britain and perceived that their political foes might use it to discredit them. Acquiescence in British highhandedness was unthinkable. Should Madison's quest for economic retaliation succeed, on the other hand, it might provoke a disastrous war. Without precedent to guide him, Washington took the initiative in addressing the crisis, agreeing to Hamilton's proposal to send a special mission to London to negotiate a settlement that might avert war and silence the opposition. Chief Justice John Jay, an experienced diplomat and staunch Federalist, was selected for the mission.[37]

36. Joseph M. Fewster, "The Jay Treaty and British Ship Seizures: The Martinique Cases," *William and Mary Quarterly* 45 (July 1988), 426–52.
37. The classic accounts are Samuel Flagg Bemis, *Jay's Treaty: A Study in Commerce and Diplomacy* (rev. ed., New Haven, Conn., 1962) and Jerald A. Combs, *The Jay Treaty: Political Battleground of the Founding Fathers* (Berkeley, Calif., 1970).

Washington and his advisers perceived that an agreement might be costly. As was customary in a time when communications were slow and uncertain, Jay was given wide latitude. The only explicit requirements were that he agree to nothing that violated the French treaty of 1778 and that he secure access to trade with the British West Indies, both regarded as essential to appease the domestic opposition. He was also instructed to seek compensation for the recent seizures of vessels and cargoes, to settle issues left from the 1783 treaty, particularly British retention of the Northwest posts, and to conclude a commercial treaty that would resolve sticky questions of neutral rights. The administration appears not to have expected major concessions on matters concerning neutrality. It hoped rather to win enough in other areas to make concessions to the British palatable to its critics.

The British too were in a conciliatory mood, although within distinct limits. Preoccupied with events in Europe and with a political crisis at home, officials were caught off guard by the furious American reaction to ship seizures in the West Indies. Their military position on the Continent precarious, they had no need for war with the United States. Even before Jay arrived in London, they revoked the harsh orders that had led to the West Indian ship seizures. The government received Jay cordially. Its chief negotiator, Lord Grenville, sought to establish an effective working relationship with him. British leaders were prepared to make concessions to avoid conflict with the United States. To have given in on neutral rights would have denied them a vital weapon against France at a critical time, however, and on such issues they stood firm.

The settlement worked out during six months of sporadic and tedious but generally cordial negotiations reflected these influences. The British willingly abandoned an untenable position, agreeing to evacuate the Northwest posts. The treaty was silent on their relations with the Indians. To the annoyance of southern planters, it said nothing about compensation for slaves carried off during the Revolution. A boundary dispute in the Northeast and the question of pre-Revolutionary debts owed by Americans to British creditors were referred to mixed arbitral commissions.[38]

In view of its long-standing opposition to commercial concessions of any sort, Britain was surprisingly liberal in this area. In fact, the home island and especially the colonies depended on trade with the United States. The British Isles were opened to Americans on a most-favored-nation basis. American ships were permitted into British India with virtu-

38. The negotiations are discussed in Bemis, *Jay's Treaty*, 318–73, and from the British perspective in Charles R. Ritcheson, *Aftermath of Revolution: British Policy Toward the United States, 1783–1795* (New York, 1971), 318–59.

ally no restrictions and also gained access to the much-coveted West Indian trade, although vessels were restricted to less than seventy tons and the Americans were forbidden to reexport certain products including even such items produced in the United States. On balance, for a nation still committed to mercantilist principles, the concessions were generous.

As Hamilton and Jay had feared, Britain stood firm on neutral rights. Grenville readily agreed to compensate the United States for ships and cargoes seized in the West Indies but would go no further. Jay conceded the substance, if not the principle, of British definitions of contraband and the Rule of 1756. For all practical purposes, he scrapped the principle of free ships and free goods and agreed to admit British privateers and prizes to American ports, a direct violation of the 1778 treaty.

Critics then and later have argued that Jay gave up more than was necessary and secured less than he should have in return. He was too eager for a settlement, they claim, and refused to hold out, bargain, or exploit his strengths and British weaknesses. Some scholars have also contended that Hamilton undercut Jay's position by confiding in the British minister to Washington, George Hammond, that the United States would not join a group of nations then forming an armed neutrality to defend their shipping against Britain.[39] As in earlier cases, Hamilton's machinations cannot be condoned, but, in this instance, their practical effects appear limited. The armed neutrality lacked support from major European neutrals such as Russia. In any event, the United States had little to contribute or gain from it. Hamilton's assurances reached London only after the negotiations were all but concluded and told the British little they did not know. Jay was indeed anxious for a settlement. He might have gained a bit more by dragging out the negotiations. But on neutral rights Britain could not be moved. Their backs to the wall on the Continent and in the Caribbean, London officials could not relinquish their most effective weapon. Without an army or navy and standing to lose huge revenues from war with England, the United States could not make them do so.

Although desperate for peace, Hamilton and Washington were themselves keenly disappointed with the terms. For a time, the president hesitated to submit the document to the Senate, but he eventually rationalized that a bad treaty was better than none at all. He sent Jay's handiwork to the upper house without any recommendation, but he was so concerned with possible public reaction that he insisted it be considered in

39. Bemis argues this in *Jay's Treaty*, 337–40. For persuasive rebuttals, see Elkins and McKitrick, *Age of Federalism*, 410, and Bradford Perkins, *The First Rapprochement: England and the United States, 1795–1805* (Berkeley, Calif., 1967), 42–43.

secret. The Senate approved the treaty by the barest majority, 20–10, and then only after the article on West Indian trade was excised because the limits on tonnage effectively eliminated American ships from the trans-Atlantic trade.

No other treaty in U.S. history has aroused such hostile public reaction or provoked such passionate debate, even though, ironically, the Jay Treaty brought the United States important concessions and served its interests well. The explanation must be sought not only in rampant political partisanship but also in ideology and the insecurities of a new and fragile nation.[40] The treaty provoked such anger because it touched Americans in areas where they were most sensitive. The mere fact of negotiations with Britain was difficult for many to accept. To some Americans, Jay's concessions smacked of subservience. Moreover, to an extent that was not true in Europe, foreign policy in the United States was subject to debate by a public whose understanding of the issues and mechanisms was neither sophisticated nor nuanced, that sought clear-cut and definitive solutions, and defined outcomes in terms of victory and defeat. By the very nature of diplomacy, such high expectations were bound to be disappointed and the results to be received with something less than enthusiasm. American insecurity thus manifested itself in a frenzy of anger and an outpouring of patriotic fervor.

When the text of the treaty was published by a Republican newspaper less than a week after approval by the Senate, popular indignation swept the land. The aura of secrecy that had shrouded the treaty and its disclosure on the eve of emotional July 4 celebrations heightened the intensity of the reaction. Even in Federalist strongholds, the document and its author were publicly condemned. In towns and villages across the country, incensed citizens lowered flags to half mast and hangmen ceremoniously destroyed copies of the treaty. Burning effigies of that "damned arch traitor Jay" lit the night. The British minister was publicly insulted by a hostile crowd. When Hamilton took the stump in New York to defend the treaty, he was struck by a stone. Once again, the venerable Washington came under attack, irate critics labeling him a dupe and a fool and even accusing him of misusing public funds.

Outraged by the terms of the treaty and smelling political blood, Republican leaders fanned the popular indignation. Southerners and westerners, suspicious of Jay since his negotiations with Spain a decade earlier, saw their worst fears confirmed in the obnoxious document. Failure to

40. Elkins and McKitrick, *Age of Federalism*, 416.

deal with the issue of confiscated slaves and submission of the debt controversy to an arbitral commission touched southern interests directly.
From the Republican point of view, the commercial treaty and the cave-
in on neutral rights totally undermined the principles essential for a truly
independent status for the United States. By prohibiting interference in
Anglo-American trade for ten years, it surrendered the instrument—
commercial discrimination—needed to attain that end. It represented a
humiliating capitulation to the archenemy Britain and a slap in the face
to France. Madison and Jefferson saw treaties as a means to reform the
balance-of-power system and international law. To them, the Jay Treaty
represented an abject retreat to the old ways. It was "unworthy [of] the
voluntary acceptance of an Independent people," Madison fumed.[41] Jefferson was more outspoken, denouncing the treaty as a "monument of
folly and venality," an "infamous act," nothing more than a "treaty of alliance between England and the anglomen of this country against the
legislature and people of the United States." Those who had been "Sam-
sons in the field and Solomons in the council," he privately exclaimed,
"have had their heads shorn by the harlot England."[42]

The treaty survived the storm. Hamilton, now a private citizen, joined
Jay in mounting a vigorous and generally effective defense of their handiwork. Despite their compunctions about mobilizing a presumably ignorant
public, the Federalists effectively rallied popular support, highlighting
the concessions made by Britain and emphasizing that, whatever its deficiencies, the treaty preserved peace with the nation whose friendship
was essential to U.S. prosperity and well-being.[43] Perhaps persuaded by
Hamilton and Jay, Washington overcame persistent reservations about
ratifying the treaty. The bitter personal attacks on him by foes of the treaty
probably contributed to his decision. A harried president finally signed
the Jay Treaty in August 1795.

Defeated in the Senate and by the executive, the Republicans
mounted a bitter rearguard effort that would delay implementation of the
treaty for almost a year and raise important constitutional questions. Insisting that the House also had the power to approve treaties, a position
Jefferson himself had explicitly rejected some years earlier, the

41. Onuf and Onuf, *Federal Union*, 161.
42. Tucker and Hendrickson, *Empire of Liberty*, 67; Jefferson to Philip Mazzei, April 14,
    1796, in Paul Leicester Ford, ed., *The Writings of Thomas Jefferson* (10 vols., New York,
    1892–99), 7:72–78.
43. Todd Estes, "Shaping the Politics of Public Opinion: Federalists and the Jay Treaty
    Debate," *Journal of the Early Republic* 20 (Fall 2000), 393–422.

Republican-controlled lower chamber demanded that the president submit to it all documents relating to negotiation of the treaty. Washington refused, setting an important precedent on executive privilege. The House quickly approved a resolution reaffirming its right to pass on any treaty requiring implementing legislation. Some Republicans shied away from direct confrontation with the president, however, and in April 1796 the House appropriated funds to implement the treaty by a narrow margin of three votes, setting a precedent that has never been challenged.

Remarkable and fortuitous economic and diplomatic gains facilitated public acceptance of the treaty. There is no better balm for wounded pride than prosperity. As a neutral carrier for both sides, the United States enjoyed a major economic boom in the aftermath of the treaty. Exports more then tripled between 1792 and 1796. "The affairs of Europe rain riches on us," one American exulted, "and it is as much as we can do to find dishes to catch the golden shower."[44]

While Jay was negotiating in London and the treaty was being debated at home, Wayne settled the future of the Northwest on U.S. terms. Following the St. Clair debacle, he gathered an imposing army eventually numbering 3,500 men and prepared his campaign with the utmost care. In August 1794, he routed a small force of Indians at Fallen Timbers near British-held Fort Miami. Despite earlier inciting them to battle, the British refused to back the Indians or even allow them into the fort when Wayne had them on the run. After a tense standoff outside the fort where, perhaps miraculously, neither Britons nor Americans fired a shot, Wayne systematically plundered Indian storehouses and burned villages in the Ohio country. In August 1795, he imposed on the defeated and dispirited tribes the Treaty of Greenville that confined them to a narrow strip of land along Lake Erie. It was certainly not expansion with honor, but in the eyes of most Americans the ends justified the means. Wayne's campaign crippled the hold of Indians and British in the Old Northwest, restoring the prestige of the American government and strengthening its hold on the Ohio country. Removal of the British was the last step in completing the process Wayne had begun, a point defenders of the Jay Treaty hammered home in speech after speech.[45]

An unanticipated and quite astounding diplomatic windfall from the Jay Treaty also eased its acceptance. A declining power, Spain found itself in a precarious position between the major European belligerents. Allied

---

44. Quoted in Elkins and McKitrick, *Age of Federalism*, 441.
45. Kohn, *Eagle and Sword*, 156–57, 182.

for a time with Britain, it changed sides when the advance of a French army into the Iberian peninsula threatened its very survival. Fearing British reprisals and suspecting—incorrectly, as it turned out—that the Jay Treaty portended an Anglo-American alliance that might bring combined expeditions against Spanish America, a panicky Madrid government moved quickly to appease the United States. The U.S. minister, Thomas Pinckney, was astute enough to seize the opportunity. In the Treaty of San Lorenzo, signed in October 1795 and sometimes called Pinckney's Treaty, Spain recognized the boundary claimed by the United States since 1783. It also granted the long-coveted access to the Mississippi and for three years the right to deposit goods at New Orleans for storage and transshipment without duties. Resolving at virtually no cost to the United States issues that had plagued Spanish-American relations and threatened the allegiance of the West, Pinckney's Treaty pacified the restless westerners and made the Jay Treaty more palatable.[46]

From the vantage point of more than two hundred years, the verdict on Jay's Treaty is unambiguous. Jay was dealt a weak hand and might have played it better. In seeking and pushing the treaty, Hamilton and Jay acted for blatantly partisan and self-serving reasons, promoting their grand design for foreign relations and domestic development. Their dire warnings of war may have been exaggerated. The most likely alternative to the treaty was a continued state of crisis and conflict that could have led to war. On the other hand, Republican ranting was also driven by partisanship and was certainly overstated. Diplomacy by its very nature requires concessions, a point Americans even then were inclined to forget. The circumstances of 1794 left little choice but to sacrifice on neutral rights. Jay secured concessions Jefferson could not get that turned out to be very important over the long run. Most important, Britain recognized U.S. independence in a way it had not in 1783. Rarely has a treaty so bad on the face of it produced such positive results. It initiated a period of sustained prosperity that in turn promoted stability and strength. It bound the Northwest and Southwest to a still very fragile federal union. It bought for a new and still weak nation that most priceless commodity—time.

V

Whatever its long-term benefits, the treaty afforded the United States no immediate respite. Conflict with France dominated the remainder of the decade, provoking a sustained diplomatic crisis, blatant French interference

46. The standard account is Samuel Flagg Bemis, *Pinckney's Treaty: America's Advantage from Europe's Distress, 1783–1800* (rev. ed., New Haven, Conn., 1960).

in American internal affairs, and an undeclared naval war. The war scare of 1798 heightened already bitter divisions at home. Federalist exploitation of the rage against France for partisan advantage provoked fierce Republican reaction that could not be silenced through repression. Suspicions on each side ran wild, Federalists claiming that Republicans were joining with France to bring the excesses of the French Revolution to America, Republicans insisting that the Federalists, allied with Britain, were seeking to destroy republicanism at home. The war scare also set the Federalists squabbling among themselves, producing cabinet intrigues and rumors of plots akin to coups.

Absorbed with the European war and its own internal politics, France viewed the United States as a nuisance and possible source of exploitation rather than a major concern. The Directory then in power represented the low point of the revolution, unpopular, divided against itself, and rife with corruption. French policy toward the United States, if indeed it could be called that, reflected the whim of the moment, a need for food, a lust for money. The French naturally protested the Jay Treaty, claiming they had been "betrayed and despoiled with impunity." But the treaty was as much pretext as cause for attacks on the United States that were reckless to the point of stupidity. Flushed with victories on the Continent, France arrogantly toyed with the United States and plundered its shipping, outraging a profoundly insecure people whose nerves were already frayed from years of mistreatment at the hands of the great powers.[47]

Following the Jay Treaty, France retaliated against the United States. Genet's successors, Joseph Fauchet and Pierre Adet, lobbied vigorously to defeat the treaty in the Senate and House, offering bribes to some congressmen. Failing, they tried intimidation to mitigate its effects. Proclaiming that the treaty of 1778 was no longer in effect and hinting ominously at a severance of diplomatic relations, they insisted that U.S. concessions to Britain compelled them to scrap the principle of free ships, free goods. They seized more than three hundred American ships in 1795 alone. Hoping to exploit popular anger with Jay's Treaty, they used the threat of war to secure the election of a more friendly government. Adet interfered in the election of 1796 in a way not since duplicated by a foreign representative by warning that war could be avoided only by the election of Jefferson. A furious Washington denounced French treatment of the United States as "outrageous beyond conception."[48]

---

47. Elkins and McKitrick, *Age of Federalism*, 506, 511, 538.
48. Alexander DeConde, *Entangling Alliance: Politics and Diplomacy Under George Washington* (Durham, N.C., 1958), 488.

French meddling provoked a sharp presidential response in the form of Washington's Farewell Address. Drafted partly by Hamilton, the president's statement was at one level a highly partisan political document timed to promote the Federalist cause in the approaching election. Washington's fervid warnings against the "insidious wiles of foreign influence" and "passionate attachments" to "permanent alliances" with other nations unmistakably alluded to the French connection and Adet's intrigues. They were designed, at least in part, to discredit the Republicans.[49]

At another level, the Farewell Address was a political testament, based on recent experience, in which the retiring president set forth principles to guide the nation in its formative years. Washington's admonitions against partisanship reflected his sincere and deep-seated fears of the perils of factionalism at a delicate stage in the national development. His references to alliances set forth a view common among Americans that their nation, founded on exceptional principles and favored by geography, could best achieve its destiny by preserving its freedom of action. Although it would later be used as a justification for isolationism, the Farewell Address was *not* an isolationist document. The word *isolationism* did not become fixed in the American political lexicon until the twentieth century. No one in the 1790s could have seriously entertained the notion of freedom from foreign involvement.[50] Washington vigorously advocated commercial expansion. He also conceded that "temporary alliances" might be required in "extraordinary emergencies." Influenced by experience dating to the colonial period, he stressed the importance of an independent course free of emotional attachments and wherever possible binding political commitments to other nations. When the country had grown strong and the interior was tied closely to the Union, it would be able to fend off any threat, a blueprint for future empire.[51]

For whatever reason, Americans heeded Washington's warnings, and France's efforts to swing the election of 1796 backfired. The Federalists took the high ground of principle and nationalism, charging their opponents with serving a foreign power. Although it is impossible to weigh with any precision the impact of Adet's interference, it likely contributed to the Federalist victory. Despite a split between those Federalists supporting Vice President John Adams and those, including Hamilton, who

49. The text of the Farewell Address and various interpretations of it can be conveniently found in Kaufman, *Washington's Farewell Address.*
50. Kaplan, *Entangling Alliances,* 94.
51. Fred Anderson, *The War That Made America: A Short History of the French and Indian War* (New York, 2005), 163.

preferred Thomas Pinckney, Adams won seventy-one electoral votes to sixty-eight for Jefferson. At a time when the runner-up automatically became vice president, the nation experienced the anomaly of its two top officials representing bitterly contending parties.

Failing to "revolutionize" the U.S. government, France sought to punish the upstart nation for its independence. Proclaiming that it would treat neutrals as neutrals allowed England to treat them, Paris officially sanctioned what had been going on for months, authorizing naval commanders and privateers to seize ships carrying British property. They quickly equaled the haul of 1795. Atrocities sometimes accompanied the seizures—one American ship captain was tortured with thumbscrews until he declared his cargo British property and liable for seizure. By 1797, French raiders boldly attacked U.S. ships off the coast of Long Island and Philadelphia. France also refused to receive the newly appointed U.S. minister, Charles C. Pinckney, insisting that an envoy would not be accredited until the United States redressed its grievances.[52]

In seeking to intimidate the United States, France badly misjudged the mood of the nation and the character of its new president. Sixty-one years old, vain, thin-skinned, and impulsive, John Adams was also a man of keen intelligence and considerable learning. In many ways, he was the most stubbornly independent of the Founders. Pessimistic in his view of human nature and conservative in his politics, he had been skeptical of the French Revolution from the outset.[53] A staunch nationalist, he reacted indignantly to French high-handedness. And some of his advisers would have welcomed war. In awe of his predecessor, he retained not only the cabinet system but also Washington's cabinet: the querulous and narrow-minded Timothy Pickering as secretary of state and Oliver Wolcott, the mediocre Hamilton confidant, as secretary of the treasury. Adams never shared the pro-British sympathies of his colleagues. Short and plump, by his own admission "but an Ordinary Man," he lacked his illustrious predecessor's commanding presence. Unsure of himself in the presidency and deeply angered by France, he tolerated his advisers' virulently anti-French policies to the brink of war.

Adams's initial approach to France combined a willingness to employ force with an openness to negotiations. Shortly after taking office, he revived long-dormant plans to build a navy to protect U.S. shipping. Still

52. Alexander DeConde, The Quasi-War: The Politics and Diplomacy of the Undeclared War with France, 1797–1801 (New York, 1966), 124–25.

53. Joseph J. Ellis, Passionate Sage: The Character and Legacy of John Adams (New York, 2001).

hoping to avert war, he emulated Washington's 1794 approach to England by dispatching to France a special peace mission composed of John Marshall, Elbridge Gerry, and Charles C. Pinckney. He instructed his commissioners to ask compensation for the seizures of ships and cargoes, secure release from the articles of the 1778 treaty binding the United States to defend the French West Indies, and win French acceptance of the Jay Treaty. They were authorized to offer little in return.

Given American terms, a settlement would have been difficult under any circumstances, but the timing was especially inopportune. Revolutionary France was at the peak of its power. Napoleon Bonaparte had won great victories on the Continent. Britain was isolated and vulnerable. France was willing to settle with the United States, but it saw no need for haste. In need of money and accustomed to manipulating the small states of Europe through a "vast network of international plunder," the Directory set out to extort what it could from the United States. Its minister of foreign relations, the notorious Charles Maurice de Talleyrand-Périgord, an aristocrat, former Roman Catholic bishop, and notorious womanizer, had lived in exile in the United States and had little respect for Americans. Certain that the new nation "merited no more consideration than Genoa or Geneva," he preferred at least for the moment a condition he described as "half friendly, half hostile," which permitted France to enrich itself by looting U.S. ships.[54] A master of survival in the hurly-burly of French politics, conniving, above all venal, Talleyrand also hoped to enrich himself at American expense. He treated Adams's commissioners as representatives of a European vassal state. When the delegation arrived in France, it was told by mysterious agents identified only as X, Y, and Z that negotiations would proceed more smoothly if the United States paid a bribe of $250,000 and loaned France $12 million.[55]

The so-called XYZ mission failed not because France insulted American honor but because the U.S. diplomats concluded that no settlement was attainable. Pinckney's much publicized response—"No, no, not a sixpence"—did not reflect the initial view of the commissioners. They were prepared to pay a small douceur if persuaded that negotiations could succeed. Although doubtful the U.S. treasury could sustain a loan of the magnitude requested, they considered asking for new instructions if they could convince France to stop attacking American ships. Eventually,

54. William Stinchcombe, *The XYZ Affair* (Westport, Conn., 1981), 35.
55. Stinchcombe's *XYZ Affair* is the standard account.

however, it became clear that Talleyrand had no intention of easing the pressure or compensating their country for earlier losses. Certain that their mission was hopeless, Pinckney and Marshall returned home, playing for all it was worth the role of aggrieved republicans whose honor had been insulted by a decadent old world.

The XYZ Affair set off a near hysterical reaction in the United States, providing an outlet for tensions built up over years of conflict with the Europeans. Adams was so incensed with the treatment of his diplomats that he began drafting a war message. Publication of correspondence relating to the mission unleashed a storm of patriotic indignation. Angry crowds burned Talleyrand in effigy and attacked supposed French sympathizers. Memorials of support for the president poured in from across the country. The once popular tricolor cockade gave way to the more traditional black cockade, French songs to American. Frenzied public gatherings sang new patriotic songs such as "Hail Columbia" and "Adams and Liberty" and drank toasts to the popular slogan "Millions for defense but not one cent for tribute." Militia rolls swelled. Old men joined patriotic patrols, while little boys played war against imaginary French soldiers. Exulting in the "most magical effects" of the XYZ furor on public attitudes, Federalists fanned the flames by disseminating rumors of French plans to invade the United States, incite slave uprisings in the South, and burn Philadelphia and massacre its women and children. Basking in the glow of unaccustomed popularity, Adams stoked the martial spirit. "The finger of destiny writes on the wall the word: 'War,' " he told one cheering audience.[56]

The president eventually settled for a policy of "qualified hostility." Some Republicans challenged the war fever—Jefferson sarcastically talked of the "XYZ dish cooked up by Marshall" to help the Federalists expand their power.[57] With only a narrow majority in the House, Adams feared that a premature declaration might fail. Moreover, he learned from reliable sources that France did not want war, giving him pause. Although he remained willing to consider war, he determined to respond forcibly to French provocations without seeking a declaration. A firm American posture might persuade France to negotiate on more favorable terms or provoke the United States to declare war. Continued conflict might eventually goad Congress into acting.

56. Adams quoted in DeConde, *Quasi-War*, 81; Thomas M. Ray, " 'Not One Cent for Tribute': The Public Addresses and American Popular Reaction to the XYZ Affair, 1798–1799," *Journal of the Early Republic* 3 (Winter 1983), 389–411.
57. Kaplan, *Jefferson*, 118.

Adams thus pushed through Congress a series of measures that led to the so-called Quasi-War with France. The 1778 treaty was unilaterally abrogated, an embargo placed on trade with France. Secretary of State Pickering reversed Washington's policy toward Saint-Domingue, cutting a deal with the independent black republic to restore trade and employing warships to help solidify its power.[58] Congress approved the creation of a separate Department of the Navy, authorized the government to construct, purchase, or borrow a fleet of warships, approved the arming of merchant vessels and the commissioning of privateers, and permitted U.S. ships to attack armed French vessels anywhere on the high seas. Over the next two years, the United States and France waged an undeclared naval war, much of it in the Caribbean and West Indies, the center of U.S. trade with Europe and the focal point of British and French attacks on American shipping. Supported by a fleet of armed merchantmen, the infant U.S. Navy drove French warships from American coastal waters, convoyed merchant ships into the West Indies, and successfully fought numerous battles with French warships. Americans cheered with especial nationalist fervor the victory of Capt. Thomas Truxtun's *Constellation* over *Insurgente*, reputedly the fastest warship in the French navy.[59]

Adams's more belligerent advisers saw in the conflict with France a splendid opportunity to achieve larger objectives. The war scare provided a pretext for the standing army Federalists had long sought. In the summer of 1798, Congress authorized an army of fifty thousand men to be commanded by Washington in the event of hostilities. Federalists in the cabinet and Senate also sought to rid the nation of recent immigrants from France and other countries who were viewed as potential subversives—and even worse as Republican political fodder—enacting laws making it more difficult to acquire American citizenship and permitting the deportation of aliens deemed dangerous to public safety. Striking directly at the opposition, the Federalists passed several vaguely worded and blatantly repressive Sedition Acts that made it a federal crime to interfere with the operation of the government or publish any "false, scandalous and malicious writings" against its officials. Egged on by Hamilton, some extremists fantasized about an alliance with England and joint military operations against the Floridas, Louisiana, and French colonies in the West Indies.[60]

58. Tim Matthewson, "Jefferson and Haiti," *Journal of Southern History* 61 (May 1995), 215.
59. The standard account is DeConde, *Quasi-War*.
60. Kohn, *Eagle and Sword*, 219–55; Paul Douglas Newman, "The Federalists' Cold War: The Fries Rebellion, National Security, and the State, 1787–1800," *Pennsylvania History* 67 (Winter 2000), 63–104.

The war scare of 1798 waned as quickly as it had waxed. When the hostile U.S. reaction made clear the extent of his miscalculations, Talleyrand shifted direction. French officials feared driving the United States into the arms of England, solidifying the power of the Federalists, and denying France access to vital products. Already negotiating with Spain an agreement to regain Louisiana as part of a larger design to restore French power in North America, nervous officials perceived that war with the United States would invite an assault on Louisiana and destroy France's dreams of empire before implementation had begun. The demonstrated ability of the United States to defend its commerce reduced the profits from plunder, rendering the "half friendly, half hostile" policy counterproductive. As early as the summer of 1798, Talleyrand began sending out signals of reconciliation. His message grew stronger by the end of the year.

As belligerent as anyone at the outset, Adams in time broke with his more extreme colleagues. Gerry, who had remained in Paris, the Quaker George Logan, then on an unofficial and unauthorized peace mission in France, Adams's son John Quincy, and other U.S. diplomats in Europe all reported unmistakable signs of French interest in negotiations. Adams had never taken seriously the threat of a French invasion of the United States. Lord Nelson's destruction of the French fleet at Aboukir Bay in Egypt in October 1798 rendered it a practical impossibility. There was "no more prospect of seeing a French army here, than there is in Heaven," the president snarled.[61]

Within the United States, peace sentiment grew. In the absence of formal hostilities, the war fever dissipated, turning to apathy and then protest against the high taxes and repressive measures adopted by the government. Adams gradually recognized, moreover, that Hamilton was behind the more aggressive measures proposed by his cabinet. He suspected, not without reason, that the ambitious New Yorker might be conspiring to gain control of the government. The president was enraged when his cabinet, Federalist senators, and Washington pressured him to appoint Hamilton inspector general of the army, a post everyone recognized, in view of Washington's age and increasing infirmity, was tantamount to actual command. Adams thus decided in early 1799 to send another peace mission to France.

The decision set off a struggle that sundered Adams's administration and in time destroyed his party. Still eager for war—or at least the threat of war—and stunned by Adams's decision, extreme Federalists resisted. A

---

61. Quoted in Elkins and McKitrick, *Age of Federalism,* 606.

group of senators vowed to block the nomination of an envoy to France, provoking an enraged president to threaten resignation—which would have left the government in the hands of the despised Jefferson. Adams eventually agreed to enlarge the delegation to three persons. While the president was in Massachusetts tending his ill wife, Pickering, Wolcott, and Secretary of War James McHenry continued to obstruct his policy, delaying issuing instructions to the commissioners and trying to persuade them to resign. There was even talk of something akin to a palace coup, in which Hamilton would have been a major participant, with the cabinet taking control from the president. Returning to the temporary capital at Trenton at the urging of loyal cabinet members, Adams was stunned to find the inspector general conferring with some of his advisers. Without consulting the cabinet, he ordered the delegation to leave for France at once. Upon learning that Pickering and McHenry were plotting with Hamilton to unseat him in the election, Adams forced McHenry to resign. Pickering refused resignation on grounds that he needed the salary to support his large family. Adams was compelled to fire him, making him the only secretary of state to leave office in this manner. The president denounced Hamilton as "the greatest intriguant in the world—a man devoid of every moral principle—and a bastard."[62]

A settlement would not come easily. The instructions Pickering drafted for the delegation asked a great deal: formal release from the treaty of 1778; compensation for seizures of American ships and property (estimated at $20 million); and French acceptance of the Jay Treaty. From France's standpoint, the Americans asked everything and offered nothing. French officials desperately wanted to regain exclusive right to bring privateers and prizes into American ports and insisted that they would compensate the United States for damages only if the treaties remained in effect. The negotiations quickly deadlocked, causing an agitated and impatient Adams to reconsider a declaration of war.

Both sides found reason to compromise. Napoleon by late 1800 had assumed near dictatorial powers and was busy promoting schemes to end the European war on favorable terms and restore the French empire to North America. The reacquisition of Louisiana was nearing fruition. The United States had to be pacified at least until France could take control of its new territory. Napoleon was also encouraging European neutrals to arm against Britain. He saw an opportunity to loosen Anglo-American ties and win over the neutrals by demonstrating his commitment to liberal

62. Quoted in Page Smith, *John Adams* (2 vols., New York, 1962), 2:1027–28.

maritime principles. Sensing that France was daily growing stronger in Europe and further delay might be costly, the U.S. delegation departed from its instructions and agreed to compromise. The Convention of 1800 restored diplomatic relations, tacitly terminated the alliance of 1778, postponed (forever as it turned out) further consideration of treaties and financial claims, and included a statement of neutral rights that did not conflict with Jay's Treaty. To impress Europe with his achievement, Napoleon staged an elaborate signing ceremony at Mortefontaine on October 3, 1800, complete with sumptuous banquets, rounds of toasts, fireworks and booming cannon, and plays and concerts.[63]

Although unpopular in the United States, the convention was eventually approved. Americans' expectations continued to exceed their nation's power. As with the Jay Treaty, critics protested that the commissioners had paid too much for peace. Jefferson complained of "bungling negotiations."[64] Extreme Federalists complained of further humiliation at the hands of France. Upon first submission to the Senate, the convention failed to receive a two-thirds majority. The prospect of continued hostilities with France provoked sober second thoughts, however. Many senators concluded that the United States could not do better and might do worse. Adams quickly resubmitted the agreement. It was narrowly approved with an amendment striking out the provisions calling for further discussion of treaties and indemnities. The document was ratified by his successor, Thomas Jefferson, in December 1801.

The Convention of 1800 represented a giant step toward an independent U.S. foreign policy. To be sure, the commissioners abandoned substantial, if inflated, financial claims against France. As with the Jay Treaty, however, when viewed from the longer perspective, the advantages far outweighed the shortcomings. The convention ended five years of conflict with France and eliminated, at least temporarily, the threat of a war the United States could ill afford. It stopped French plunder of American commerce and secured the release of ships. France recognized the independence of the United States as it had not before and tacitly accepted the Anglo-American connection set forth in Jay's Treaty. Most important, although it could not be fully appreciated at the time, the United States freed itself from the alliance of 1778, a source of tension with France and domestic discord since the outbreak of the European war. Continuation

---

63. The Mortefontaine negotiations and celebrations are covered in DeConde, *Quasi-War*, 223–58.
64. Kaplan, *Jefferson*, 123.

of that conflict until 1815 perpetuated the threat to the United States, but severance of ties with France rendered its situation much less complicated. The nation would not be a party to another "entangling alliance" until the mid-twentieth century.

If the price for peace and freedom of action was relatively low for the nation, it was high for its principal author and his party. Adams's belated commitment to negotiations with France irreparably divided his party, sealing his defeat in the election of 1800 and contributing to the demise of Federalism. At least in retrospect, he insisted that the price was worth paying. "I desire no other inscription over my gravestone," he later wrote, "than: 'Here lies John Adams, who took upon himself the responsibility for peace with France in the year 1800,' "[65]

Despite their partisanship and occasional excess, the Federalists skillfully guided the United States through a perilous era. Displaying opportunism and pragmatism in time of crisis, they exploited the European war to America's advantage while scrupulously avoiding the full-scale involvement that would have been disastrous at this stage of the nation's growth. Insisting on its rights to trade with both major belligerents, the United States suffered heavy losses in shipping but achieved major gains in foreign trade. Exports increased from $20 million in 1792 to more than $94 million in 1801, imports from $23 million in 1790 to $110 million in 1801, and the reexport trade jumped from $1 million in 1792 to nearly $50 million in 1800. This prosperity was based on unusual conditions, to be sure, but it provided a foundation for future economic growth. The removal of British troops from U.S. soil, along with Spanish recognition of the southern boundary and granting of access to the Mississippi, eased the foreign threat to frontier communities, curbed secessionist impulses among westerners, and facilitated incorporation of the West into the Union. By the end of the decade, moreover, restless Americans had begun to filter into Spanish Florida and Louisiana, preparing the way for future acquisition. Federalists gained a measure of international respect for the United States not forthcoming in the 1780s. They secured release from the French alliance, making possible a truly independent foreign policy. Few decades in U.S. history have been as dangerous and yet as rich in accomplishment.

The Federalists also bequeathed an enduring legacy of practice and doctrine. Inheriting a distrust of executive or legislative control of foreign policy, the Founders created a mixed constitutional arrangement with

65. Quoted in DeConde, *Quasi-War*, 339.

little basis in historical experience. Without precedent to guide him, Washington molded the vagaries of the Constitution into a workable system. The result was not a democratic foreign policy in any real sense of the word. Constitutional ambiguities would lead to executive abuses of power and intense executive-legislative conflict. But the system subjected foreign policy to the popular will to a greater degree than in other governments to that time. The Washington administration also put into practice a body of doctrine that neatly assimilated the American experience and accurately reflected popular aspirations. Based on the premise of American exceptionalism, it called for independence from Europe and looked to the day when the American empire would rival the Old World in size and strength. Significantly, although Jefferson hailed what he called the "revolution of 1800," he did not repudiate the Federalist heritage. Rather, he and his successors refined it into a foreign policy of independence and expansion that would guide the nation for years to come.

3

"Purified, as by Fire"

Republicanism Imperiled and Reaffirmed, 1801–1815

No one personifies better than Thomas Jefferson the essential elements of a distinctively American approach to foreign policy. "He thought of America the way we like to think of ourselves," Robert Tucker and David Hendrickson have written, "and saw its significance as we still do, in terms larger than itself." Like his countrymen at the time and since, Jefferson drew a sharp distinction between the "high moral purpose" that animated America and the "low motives of power and expediency that drove others." He disclaimed ambition for the United States, and when engaged in disputes with other nations often took the high ground of moral principle. In theory, at least, he rejected the mechanisms of traditional European diplomacy. Viewing war as the foremost enemy of liberty, he claimed to spurn force as an instrument of diplomacy, preferring, as he put it, the "Quaker system." After the buffeting of the 1790s, he yearned for disengagement from Europe, speaking of "divorce" from Britain and France and even a China-like isolation from the outside world. "The promise of Jefferson's statecraft," Tucker and Hendrickson conclude, "was thus of a new diplomacy, based on the confidence of a free and virtuous people, that would secure ends founded on the natural and universal rights of man, by means that escaped war and its corruptions."[1]

Jefferson was also a "practical idealist" (often more practical than idealistic), and in this too he set an enduring tone for his nation's foreign policy. His invocation of principle masked grandiose ambitions. Republican ideology rested on the twin pillars of commercial and landed expansion, each of which required contact and on occasion provoked conflict with the outside world, rendering Jefferson's dream of economic engagement and political separation a chimera. Whether he came to recognize this is unclear. What is clear is his willingness to put aside his scruples to

1. Robert W. Tucker and David C. Hendrickson, *Empire of Liberty: The Statecraft of Thomas Jefferson* (New York, 1992), 6, 19.

achieve his goals. He sought to exploit the European system to America's advantage, all the while proclaiming his nation's moral superiority. He was willing, at times, to employ devious and even duplicitous means to achieve ends he considered noble or simply necessary.

Jefferson's successes and failures were of epic proportions, also typifying those of his nation. His ideological fervor and self-confidence gave a steely strength to his diplomacy. Through skillful maneuvering and extraordinary good fortune, he secured for the United States in his first term the great windfall of the vast Louisiana territory. As so often happens, success gave rise to a near-fatal hubris. His subsequent efforts to "conquer without war" in the bitter struggle with England over neutral rights failed miserably. He refused to compromise his principles or to fight for them, pushing his confidant and successor James Madison toward a war they both dreaded and that could have been disastrous. The United States survived, however, and that alone seemed to vindicate its policies and confirm in the eyes of its leaders and people the strength of its principles and institutions.[2]

I

Jefferson took office under unusually favorable circumstances. By the end of 1800, the European combatants had bludgeoned each other to a draw. Napoleon's defeat of Austria solidified French control of the Continent and left England without allies, but British dominance of the seas stood in the way of a complete French victory. Each side felt compelled to regroup. After a year of negotiations, the Peace of Amiens (March 1802) formally ended the war. The treaty left most of the central issues unresolved and would last less than a year. But it gave Jefferson precious breathing space to effect the transfer of power, what he called "the revolution of 1800," consolidate his position, and calm the divisions that had sundered the nation during Adams's last years in office.

Although much stronger and more secure in 1801 than when Washington had assumed the presidency, the United States remained weak by European standards. The population had doubled since 1776, exceeding by the turn of the century five million people (approximately one-fifth slaves) and reinforcing visions of future power and greatness, but it was

2. Lawrence S. Kaplan, "Thomas Jefferson: The Idealist as Realist," in Frank J. Merli and Theodore A. Wilson, eds., *Makers of American Diplomacy: From Benjamin Franklin to Alfred Thayer Mahan* (New York, 1974), 53–79; Peter Onuf and Nicholas Onuf, *Federal Union, Modern World: The Law of Nations in an Age of Revolution* (New York, 1994), 174–75.

still scattered in largely isolated communities over a great expanse of land. Admission of Vermont, Tennessee, and Kentucky as states and the organization of territories in Indiana and Mississippi consolidated the domain of the original union. The ties between western settlements and the seaboard remained tenuous, however, and disunionist schemes and foreign intrigue persisted through the War of 1812. The United States had fattened on the European wars. Agriculture and commerce flourished. But prosperity hinged on war-induced foreign trade, making it highly vulnerable to external forces. The new capital in Washington, graced by a few pretentious buildings but otherwise a "place with a few bad houses, extensive swamps, hanging on the skirts of a too thinly peopled, weak and barren country," symbolized the grand aspirations and continuing backwardness of the new republic.[3]

In spite of his radical preelection image, Jefferson retained the instruments and followed the basic thrust of his predecessors' foreign policy. A champion of state power and congressional prerogatives in the Federalist era, in office he greatly enlarged the power of the central government and through personal persuasion and party discipline exercised firm control of Congress. He retained the cabinet system inherited from Washington. Having observed firsthand Adams's problems, he kept his own cabinet on a close rein, a system his secretary of state, Madison, found entirely acceptable. Anti-militarist in his philosophy and determined to slash government expenditures, Jefferson eagerly seized the occasion of peace in Europe to drastically scale back the army and navy. Adhering to republican doctrine, he shifted the focus of military policy from the regular army to the militia and from an oceangoing navy to small gunboats designed for harbor defense. But he maintained the basic military structure created by the Federalists. He even added to it by establishing the U.S. Military Academy at West Point to train an officer corps.[4]

The allure France once held for Jefferson waned with Napoleon's rise to power, and the third president was even more determined than his predecessors to pursue an independent foreign policy. His inaugural commitment to "peace, commerce, and honest friendship with all nations—entangling alliances with none" echoed in less qualified terms the sentiments of Washington's Farewell Address and reaffirmed to skeptics his

3. Quoted in Merrill D. Peterson, *Thomas Jefferson and the New Nation* (New York, 1970), 653.
4. Forrest McDonald, *The Presidency of Thomas Jefferson* (Lawrence, Kans., 1976), 43–44.

independence of spirit. Viewing separation from the "cankers" and "sores" of European society and the "madmen" and "tyrants" of European politics as essential to the purity of American institutions, he scrupulously avoided any foreign ties, which, like the French alliance, might compromise America's freedom of action, inflame its domestic politics, or contaminate its councils. He refused to associate the United States with a league of armed European neutrals committed to defending freedom of the seas, even though it supported principles Americans agreed with. Jefferson was in no sense an isolationist, however, and his diplomacy was flexible and pragmatic. A shrewd observer of world affairs, he understood the workings of the European system of politics and was quick to exploit it. He was prepared to depart from principle to advance American interests, even to the point of contemplating an alliance with England during the Louisiana crisis.[5]

While following the paths staked out by his predecessors, Jefferson also introduced important changes in style and substance. Confirmed in his Americanism and republicanism, he integrated them into his diplomacy and even flaunted them. He had long viewed professional diplomats and diplomacy as the "pest of the peace of the world," and he reduced U.S. representation abroad to the essential minimum. Eschewing the pomp and display of the courts of Washington and Adams, he dressed plainly—slovenly, critics said—and opened the doors of the presidential mansion on equal terms to visitors of high station and low. His personal warmth and glittering conversation, along with the simplicity and studied casualness of his style, charmed some European visitors. His disdain for protocol scandalized other members of the small and generally unhappy diplomatic community in Washington. Outraged when received by the president in a tattered bathrobe and slippers and forced at a presidential dinner to conform to "pell-mell" seating arrangements respecting no rank, the British minister to Washington, Anthony Merry, bitterly protested the affront suffered at the president's table. Jefferson no doubt privately chuckled at the arrogant Englishman's discomfiture, but his subsequent codification of republican practices into established procedures betrayed a larger purpose. By adapting the new nation's forms to its principles, he hoped to establish a uniquely American style in diplomacy.[6]

Republican ideology influenced Jefferson's foreign policy in more important ways. In his view, the preservation of the principles of the Ameri-

5. Ibid., 54. For Jefferson's flexibility, see especially Kaplan, "Idealist as Realist," 58–59.
6. McDonald, *Jefferson*, 39, 54–55; Dumas Malone, *Jefferson the President: First Term, 1801–1815* (Boston, 1970), 379–92.

can Revolution at home was inextricably linked to the nation's foreign policy. Genuine political and economic freedom required a population of independent landowners engaged in productive enterprises, as distinct from the stockjobbers and manipulators who held power in England and the wage-labor class they dominated. A republican population demanded, in turn, access to foreign markets to ensure continued outlets for America's agricultural surpluses and the availability of sufficient land to provide an economic basis for freedom for a rapidly expanding people. Commercial and territorial expansion were therefore indispensable to the preservation of republican institutions, and thus essential ingredients of Republican foreign policy.[7]

Despite its relative weakness, moreover, Jefferson believed that the United States could achieve its goals. Persuaded that the virtue of its people and the nature of its institutions were more important measures of a nation's strength than military or even economic power, he viewed the United States as the "strongest government on earth." He clung doggedly to the belief that Europe depended on the "necessities" produced by the United States, while Americans could do without the "superfluities" manufactured by Europe, giving them a potentially powerful weapon in the form of trade restrictions. Certain of America's strength, Jefferson was less inclined than the Federalists to accommodate other nations in times of crisis. Philosophically, he tended toward pacifism—"peace is my passion," he proclaimed—but he was not above using force to uphold principles he believed in. In dealings with the Barbary States of North Africa, Spain, and France during the Louisiana crisis, and Britain and France in conflicts over neutral rights, he was more belligerent and assertive than his predecessors. Certain that the United States was a "chosen country," the "world's best hope," he was less inclined to respect foreign holdings in North America. He was aggressively expansionist.[8] If Washington and the Federalists charted the basic course of U.S. foreign policy, Jefferson and the Republicans infused into it a peculiarly American spirit and style.

II

Jefferson's assertiveness is manifest in his handling of the Tripolitan War, America's first foreign war and the first of numerous intrusions into a region that, more than two centuries later, remained terra incognita for

7. Drew McCoy, *The Elusive Republic: Political Economy in Jeffersonian America* (Chapel Hill, N.C., 1980), 188–201.
8. Peterson, *Jefferson*, 657, 665.

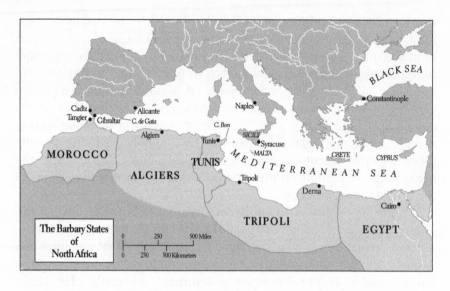

The Barbary States of North Africa

most Americans. Raiders from the Barbary States continued to prey on American shipping in the 1790s; Algiers captured eleven ships and more than a hundred sailors in 1793 alone. An irate Congress voted the next year to create a navy to defend U.S. commerce, but crises with Britain and France forced a bow to expediency. Concluding that it would cost less to pay than to fight, Washington and Adams ransomed the release of prisoners. They concluded treaties with Morocco, Algiers, and Tripoli at a cost of more than $1 million that protected U.S. trade in return for annual payments of money or the provision of ships, gunpowder, and naval supplies. As a gesture to local sensibilities, the treaty with Tripoli even explicitly avowed that the United States was "not, in any sense, founded on the Christian religion."[9]

Never comfortable with what he considered extortion, Jefferson reversed Federalist policy. Like most Westerners, he viewed the Islamic states as hopelessly despotic and oppressive. The actions of these "lawless pirates" violated his standards of civilized behavior and his commitment to free trade. He was certain that appeasement encouraged more outrageous demands. As minister to France and secretary of state he had advocated the use of force to uphold U.S. honor and keep vital shipping lanes

9. James A. Field Jr., *America and the Mediterranean World, 1776–1882* (Princeton, N.J., 1969), 32–43; Robert J. Allison, *The Crescent Obscured: The United States and the Muslim World, 1776–1815* (New York, 1995), 17–24.

open. "I think it is to our interest to punish the first insult," he insisted, "because an insult unpunished is the parent of many others."[10]

Upon assuming office, Jefferson found ample reason for reprisal. Annoyed that the United States had not sent its tribute on time and in the amount promised, the dey of Algiers commandeered an American ship, the *George Washington*, and compelled its humiliated captain to undertake a personal tribute mission for him to Turkey. Upset that he was receiving less booty than Algiers and therefore presumably was viewed as inferior, the pasha of Tripoli raised his demands and ceremoniously declared war on the United States by hacking down the flag at the U.S. consulate. The United States was "too high-minded to endure the degradation of others," Jefferson declaimed. Tripoli's demands were "unfounded either in right or compact," and the "style of the demand admitted but one answer."[11] Eager to prove to North Africans—and Europeans—that the United States would meet force with force, he dispatched four ships to the Mediterranean to "protect our commerce and chastise their insolence" by "sinking, burning, or destroying their ships and Vessels." Setting a major precedent in terms of executive authority, he did not seek congressional authorization to commit forces abroad, reasoning that war already existed by act of Tripoli.[12]

The Tripolitan War lasted from 1801 to 1805. Torn between his desire to punish his foes on the one hand and hold down federal expenditures on the other, Jefferson kept the conflict strictly limited and did not provide sufficient forces to patrol a fifteen-hundred-mile coast and "chastise the insolent." His naval commanders faced horrendous logistical problems and consequently displayed understandable caution, provoking an angry president to complain of a "two year sleep." Indecisiveness turned to near disaster in 1803 when the frigate *Philadelphia* ran aground off Tripoli and its captain and crew were held for $3 million ransom.[13]

His hands freed by the easing of the Louisiana crisis, Jefferson in late 1803 sharply escalated the war. He attempted unsuccessfully to organize an international naval force to curb piracy in the Mediterranean. He dispatched every available ship to the region. In what British naval hero Horatio Lord Nelson called "the most bold and daring act of the age," U.S. sailors slipped through the pasha's heavy defenses without the loss of a

10. Dumas Malone, *Jefferson and the Rights of Man* (Boston, 1951), 27.
11. Allison, *Crescent Obscured*, 24.
12. David A. Carson, "Jefferson, Congress and the Question of Leadership in the Tripolitan War," *Virginia Magazine of History and Biography* 94 (1986), 411–12.
13. Field, *Mediterranean World*, 50–51.

single life and burned the *Philadelphia*. The navy blockaded the coast off Tripoli and bombarded the city itself. In an early example of what would come to be called "mission creep," Jefferson and Madison approved the first U.S. attempt to replace a hostile foreign government. Madison conceded that to "intermeddle in the domestic contests of other countries" violated American principles, but, he reasoned, "it cannot be unfair, in the prosecution of a just war" to exploit "the enmity and pretenses of others against a common foe."[14] With authorization from Washington, the U.S. consul at Tunis, William Eaton, plotted with the pasha's exiled brother to overthrow the government of Tripoli. Assembling a motley force of eight U.S. Marines and some four hundred Greek and Arab adventurers, he marched five hundred miles across the desert and "liberated" Derna, the second most important city of Tripoli.[15]

The war ended in 1805 on terms less than satisfactory to some Americans. Facing serious embarrassment, even possible military defeat and deposition, the pasha agreed to a commercial treaty without tribute, although he did manage to extort $60,000 to ransom the hostages and secured U.S. agreement to the continued exile of his brother. Some Americans vigorously protested the ransom, insisting that the United States could have dictated terms. Eaton bitterly complained of the abandonment of the unfortunate pretender. By this time, however, the war was costing more than $1 million per year, provoking growing concern from a frugal president and Congress. The pasha's frequent warnings that, having killed his father and brother, he would have no scruples about a "few infidels" evoked concern for the hostages. Despite persistent grumbling, the treaty was approved.[16]

The Tripolitan War has been dismissed as unimportant, and in strictly practical terms it was.[17] It cost far more than the price of tribute. It did not end American difficulties with the Barbary States. When the threat of war with Britain forced U.S. withdrawal from the region in 1807, Algiers, Tunis, and Tripoli resumed harassment of U.S. shipping. Only after the War of 1812 was the United States, by another show of force, able to secure free passage of the Mediterranean.

14. James R. Sofka, "The Jeffersonian Idea of National Security: Commerce, the Atlantic Balance of Power, and the Barbary War, 1786–1805," *Diplomatic History* 21 (Fall 1997), 540.
15. Field, *Mediterranean World*, 52–54; McDonald, *Jefferson*, 78.
16. Field, *Mediterranean World*, 52–53; Dumas Malone, *Jefferson the President: Second Term, 1805–1809* (Boston, 1974), 40.
17. McDonald, *Jefferson*, 76.

To consider the war in such narrow terms badly misses the point. It had enormous psychological and ideological significance for the United States. The effective use of force stimulated the self-pride of the new nation; the exploits of the U.S. Navy and Marines on the "shores of Tripoli" formed an important part of its patriotic folklore. Coming at the same time as the acquisition of Louisiana, it gave Americans a renewed sense of mission and destiny. For some, it became a morality play. They perceived Islamic despotism as the most backward form of governance, depriving people of liberty and the fruits of their labor, restraining progress, and breeding lethargy, misery, poverty and ignorance. They exulted that republican ideals had given them the courage and strength to defeat the "plundering vassals of the tyrannical bashaw," striking a blow for liberty *and* Christianity. Americans had proven themselves, in the words of a contemporary nationalist poet, "a race of beings! of equal spirit to the first of nations." Proud that they rather than the Europeans had taken the lead in chastising the Barbary pirates, Americans were confirmed in their view of themselves as the agents of a new order of justice and freedom. Jefferson even speculated that his nation's success might encourage the European powers to emancipate themselves from that "degrading yoke."[18]

III

Jefferson's expansionism represents the fullest expression of his nationalism and republicanism. He shared with others of his generation a keen sense of America's exceptionalism and destiny. "A chosen country," he hailed it in his eloquent first inaugural address, "kindly separated by nature and a wide ocean from the exterminating havoc of one quarter of the globe" with "room enough for our descendants to the thousandth and thousandth generation." He was among the first to envision the extension of the nation's institutions to the Pacific Ocean. "However our present interests may restrain us . . . ," he wrote in 1801, "it is impossible not to look forward to distant times when our rapid multiplication will . . . cover the whole northern if not the southern continent with people speaking the same language, governed in similar forms, and by similar laws."[19] His vision of that "union" was vague, in some ways paradoxical, almost ethereal. He did not foresee the incorporation of this territory into a single political entity. Certain that geography and distance

18. Allison, *Crescent Obscured,* 46–54, 189, 193, 204; Jefferson to John Taylor, March 29, 1805, in Paul Leicester Ford, ed., *The Writings of Thomas Jefferson* (10 vols., New York, 1892–99), 4:574.

19. Jefferson to Monroe, November 24, 1801, in Ford, *Writings* 8:105.

would inhibit unity and that small, self-governing republics were best suited to preserve individual liberties, he saw rather a series of "distinct but bordering establishments" bound by "relations of blood [and] affection." Formal ties would not be required because such like-minded states, in contrast to Europe, would not be hostile to each other. As president, Jefferson perceived the immediate limits to U.S. expansion, but he was also alert to opportunities to reduce foreign influence on the continent. He used every available instrument, including the threat of war, to enlarge his "empire for liberty."[20]

A chance to do so to an extent he could not possibly have imagined came with the Louisiana crisis of 1802–3 and the acquisition of a vast new territory. This greatest achievement of Jefferson's presidency is often and rightly regarded as a diplomatic windfall—the result of accident, luck, and the whim of Napoleon Bonaparte—but it also owed much to design. Americans had coveted Louisiana and especially the crucial port of New Orleans since the colonial era. Through commercial and agricultural penetration, the United States had acquired significant influence there by the end of the century. The American presence in Louisiana, combined with Jefferson's shrewd and sometimes belligerent diplomacy, played a part in Napoleon's decision to sell to the United States territory he never occupied.

Throughout the last half of the eighteenth century, Louisiana was a pawn on the chessboard of European politics. Originally claimed by Spain but explored and settled by France, this enormous, uncharted region stretched from the source of the Mississippi to its mouth on the Gulf of Mexico and westward along its tributaries to the Rockies. Scattered Indian tribes, with whom Europeans and Americans carried on a lively and lucrative trade in furs, roamed its vast distances. Under French administration, it was sparsely settled and weakly defended. Having lost Canada to Britain in the Seven Years' War, France in 1763 ceded New Orleans and Louisiana west of the Mississippi to Spain, which acquired it mainly to keep it from British hands. Dreams of an American empire died hard in France, however, and for the rest of the century some officials pressed for reacquisition of Louisiana.

Americans also had designs on the Spanish colony. The United States early mastered the arts of infiltration and subversion and first employed with Spanish Louisiana the tactics later successfully used in the Floridas, Texas, California, and Hawaii. As early as the Revolution, restless frontiersmen began to filter into Louisiana. The reliance of trans-

---

20. Peter S. Onuf, *Jefferson's Empire: The Language of American Nationhood* (Charlottesville, Va., 2000), 118–19.

Appalachian settlers on the Mississippi River and New Orleans quickened interest in the region. Spain's refusal to grant access to the river provoked talk of secession or a war of conquest. Pinckney's Treaty temporarily eased the problem and sharply expanded American influence in Spanish territory. Flatboats loaded with foodstuffs, tobacco, and whiskey and skillfully maneuvered by the wild river men—the "half-horse, half-alligators" of popular legend—floated down the Mississippi in droves. By the end of the century, the United States dominated commerce at the port of New Orleans. Encouraged at times by their own government, at times by the Spanish, who saw them as a buffer against a possible British invasion from Canada, and often acting on their own, American settlers continued to drift into Louisiana. Although living on foreign soil, they retained allegiance to the United States and displayed open contempt for their nominal rulers. In some areas, they composed a majority of the population, in others an unassimilable minority compared by increasingly nervous Spanish officials to the "Goths at the gates of Rome."[21] Some even ventured illegally into upper Louisiana west of the Mississippi River. By the time Jefferson took office, Americans were actually taking control of territory under nominal European jurisdiction.[22]

As long as Louisiana remained in the hands of "feeble" Spain, Americans were content to be patient, and Jefferson was certain that in time the United States would acquire it "piece by piece." Should it be taken by a stronger power, however, a "profound reconsideration" of U.S. policy would be necessary.[23] Jefferson's fears were soon realized. Upon becoming First Consul in 1799, Napoleon took up long dormant schemes to restore French grandeur in North America. Persuaded that an empire composed of the Floridas, Louisiana, and the Caribbean sugar islands would enrich his treasury, enhance his prestige, undermine British trade, and give him leverage against the United States, he set out to relieve Spain of its colonies. In the secret Treaty of San Ildefonso (October 1800), Spain relinquished costly and increasingly vulnerable Louisiana for a piece of European territory, but it refused to give up the Floridas and extracted from Napoleon a pledge not to transfer his new possession to a third party. Once peace was established in Europe in 1801, Napoleon dispatched a military expedition to regain control of rebellious Saint-Domingue. His next move was to occupy New Orleans.

21. Alexander DeConde, *This Affair of Louisiana* (New York, 1976), 64.
22. Stephen E. Ambrose, *Undaunted Courage: Meriwether Lewis, Thomas Jefferson, and the Opening of the American West* (New York, 1996), 56.
23. Malone, *First Term*, 250.

Bonaparte's maneuvers sent shock waves across the Atlantic. Rumors of French acquisition of Louisiana began to reach America as early as the spring of 1801. Subsequent confirmation of the retrocession provoked an immediate and nervous response. "This little event of France possessing herself of Louisiana . . . ," Jefferson wrote a friend in April 1802, "is the embryo of a tornado which will burst on the countries on both sides of the Atlantic and involve in its effects their highest destinies."[24] Through unofficial emissaries, he dispatched stern warnings to France. "There is on the globe one single spot, the possessor of which is our natural and habitual enemy," he admonished. Should France take possession of New Orleans, the United States would have no choice but to "marry" itself to the "British fleet and nation" and use the outbreak of war in Europe as an excuse to take Louisiana by force.[25] To threaten war over territory to which the United States had no claim and that had been exchanged in a perfectly legal manner was, to say the least, extraordinary. Given Jefferson's history of Anglophobia, the prospect of an alliance with Britain was perhaps even more so. Justifying his position on the dubious grounds that "natural law" entitled Americans to security and the free navigation of rivers adjoining their territory, he softened the threat by suggesting that France could avert war by ceding New Orleans to the United States.

Sudden revocation in October 1802 of Americans' rights to deposit goods at New Orleans for transshipment to other ports without duty inflamed an already tense situation. Spain had delayed executing the treaty. Spanish officials in New Orleans sought to curb the rampant and costly American smuggling, but most Americans saw the sinister hand of Bonaparte behind what they viewed as a pretext for French seizure of the port. Westerners demanded war. To embarrass the administration and fulfill their old expansionist designs, Federalists joined forces. "It belongs of right to the United States to regulate the future destiny of North America," one Federalist newspaper declared. Anxious to undercut the opposition and resolve the crisis without war, Jefferson combined continued threats with diplomacy. He reiterated earlier warnings that French occupation of Louisiana could bring war and backed them by mobilizing forces along the frontier. Under the guise of a "scientific expedition," he ordered Meriwether Lewis and William Clark to reconnoiter upper Louisiana and the Missouri River valley, in part to gain intelligence about Spanish military power. In January 1803, he dispatched to Paris as his

24. Jefferson to Pierre Samuel DuPont, April 25, 1802, quoted in DeConde, *Louisiana*, 114–15.
25. Jefferson to Robert R. Livingston, April 18, 1802, in Ford, *Writings* 8:143–47.

special envoy James Monroe, a man respected in the West, authorizing him to purchase New Orleans and the Floridas (which he mistakenly assumed had also been transferred to France). If that failed, Monroe was to proceed to London to discuss an alliance. "On the event of this mission, depends the future destinies of this republic," Monroe himself exclaimed. Toasts drunk to the departing envoy revealed the bellicose mood of the nation: "Peace, if peace is honorable; war, if war is necessary."[26]

Jefferson's fears for Louisiana even prompted him to abandon—temporarily—efforts to subvert the rebellion on Saint-Domingue. Shortly after taking office, he had reversed Adams's policy toward the rebellious French colony. Labeling the rebels "cannibals" and fearing that the "combustion" they had sparked might spread to North America, he quietly suspended relations with the government of charismatic rebel leader Toussaint L'Ouverture and agreed to support French efforts to regain the colony. The threat of a French empire in North America gave Jefferson pause, however. Southern slaveholders fretted that a prolonged racial war on the sugar island posed a greater threat to slavery in the United States and that, once in control of Louisiana, the French might seek to abolish slavery there. The ever agile Jefferson shifted gears once again, withholding aid promised France and initiating a lively trade with Toussaint's forces including arms and ammunition. "St. Domingo delays their taking possession of Louisiana," Jefferson exulted, "and they are in the last distress for money for current purposes."[27]

By the time Monroe arrived in Paris in late winter 1803, a sequence of calamitous events in Europe and the Caribbean—fortuitous for the United States—pulled the props from beneath Napoleon's scheme for empire. Spanish officials procrastinated until late 1802 executing the treaty, delaying French plans to take possession of Louisiana and allowing time for U.S. hostility to build. They also refused to relinquish the Floridas, without which, Napoleon realized, Louisiana was indefensible. The First Consul had dispatched to Saint-Domingue in 1802 one of the largest expeditionary forces ever sent to the New World. His brother-in-law, Gen. Victor LeClerc, enjoyed early military successes. He tricked Toussaint into surrendering under the false pretense that blacks would be given their freedom. The rebel leader was instead sent to France and thrown into prison,

26. Quoted in Joseph J. Ellis, *American Sphinx: The Character of Thomas Jefferson* (New York, 1997), 206.
27. Tim Matthewson, "Jefferson and Haiti," *Journal of Southern History* 61 (May 1995), 217–29; Donald R. Hickey, "America's Response to the Slave Revolt in Haiti," *Journal of the Early Republic* 2 (Winter 1982), 368–69.

where he subsequently died. Even without Toussaint, blacks fiercely resisted French rule—the women "die with incredible fanaticism; they laugh at
death," LeClerc lamented.[28] Yellow fever decimated French forces. In all,
some twenty-four thousand French troops died in the futile effort to reconquer Saint-Domingue, denying Napoleon the centerpiece of his projected
empire. The expedition to take control of Louisiana was icebound in Holland. "Damn sugar, damn coffee, damn colonies," a frustrated Napoleon
blurted out in a moment of rage. By this time, the resumption of war with
England was imminent. Desperate for money and angry at Spain, he ignored the Treaty of San Ildefonso and sold the United States all of
Louisiana instead of simply New Orleans for funds to underwrite war
against England. His precise motives will never be known. Events in Europe and the Caribbean were certainly most important. But Jefferson's
threats appear to have made an impression. Napoleon probably reasoned
that it would be better to secure much-needed cash and U.S. goodwill than
risk losing by force a territory he did not control and could not defend. After some haggling, the two nations agreed on a price of $15 million.[29]

Having acquired far more than he had sought, Jefferson quickly
cleared away obstacles to possession of his empire for liberty. Troubled
that the Constitution did not explicitly authorize acquisition of new
lands, he considered an amendment remedying the omission. But when
told that Napoleon might be having second thoughts about the transaction, he waved aside his scruples and presented the treaty to Congress
without reference to the constitutional issue. A few die-hard Federalists
complained of paying an exorbitant price for a vast wasteland, poorly
masking their fears that the purchase would solidify Republican control
of the government. But the treaty was generally popular, and Congress
quickly approved it. When Spain protested the illegality of the transfer
and threatened to block it, Jefferson mobilized troops along the frontier
and vowed to seize Louisiana *and* the Floridas, leaving hapless Spain little choice but to acquiesce.

Governing the new territory caused more serious problems. Deeming
the Creoles and Indians unfit for self-government, Jefferson readily abandoned his principles of representative government, delaying full admission to the Union until the natives had served an apprenticeship and the
American population had increased. Only after vigorous protest from the

28. Quoted in Matthewson, "Jefferson and Haiti," 230.
29. DeConde, *Louisiana*, 147–75.

inhabitants did he speed up the timetable, in 1805 creating a representative assembly.[30]

In a move fraught with great portent for the future of the republic, Congress allowed national security concerns to thwart efforts to limit slavery in the Louisiana territory. Taking a modest step toward gradual abolition, Congress in 1804 prohibited the international and domestic slave trade in Louisiana. White Louisianans, some of them refugees from Caribbean sugar islands eager to replicate what they had left behind, warned they would not accept U.S. rule unless slavery was protected. They even threatened to approach Napoleon. Many Americans feared that the republic was dangerously overextended. The inhabitants of Louisiana, in their view, were not ready for self-government; "a more ignorant and depraved race of civilized men did not exist," Treasury Secretary Albert Gallatin observed. Without assurances about slavery, they would be susceptible to foreign, especially French, influence and prime candidates for disunionist schemes. To ensure U.S. control of the new territory, it was also deemed essential to encourage emigration of Americans there, and bans on slavery could hinder that process. Southerners increasingly feared that the rapid growth of the slave population in their states posed the threat of rebellions like the one on Saint-Domingue. Diffusion of the existing slave population through emigration into the new territories provided a safety valve. Responding to these multiple pressures, Congress in 1805 refused to renew its ban on the domestic slave trade in Louisiana or take measures to check the expansion of slavery, laying the foundation for the crisis of the Union a half century later.[31]

By any standard, the Louisiana Purchase was a monumental achievement. The nation acquired 828,000 square miles, doubling its territory at a cost of roughly three cents per acre, one of history's greatest real estate steals. Control of the Mississippi would tie the West firmly to the Union, enhance U.S. security, and provide enormous commercial advantages. Napoleon's sale of Louisiana all but eliminated a French return to North America, leaving the Floridas hopelessly vulnerable and Texas exposed. The United States' acquisition of Louisiana established a precedent for expansion and empire and gave substance to the idea that would later be called Manifest Destiny. This stunning achievement increased the self-confidence of the nation and reinforced an already deeply entrenched

30. Ibid., 210–11.
31. John Craig Hammond, " 'They Are Very Much Interested in Obtaining an Unlimited Slavery': Rethinking the Expansion of Slavery in the Louisiana Purchase Territories," *Journal of the Early Republic* 23 (Fall 2003), 353–80.

The Louisiana Purchase

U.S. states in 1804
U.S. territories in 1804
Louisiana Purchase

PACIFIC OCEAN

BRITISH TERRITORY

Lake of the Woods
Lake Superior
Lake Huron
Lake Michigan
Lake Ontario
Lake Erie

R. St. Lawrence

MAINE (Mass.)
NEW HAMPSHIRE
MASSACHUSETTS
RHODE ISLAND
CONNECTICUT
VERMONT
NEW YORK
NEW JERSEY
DELAWARE
MARYLAND
PENNSYLVANIA
VIRGINIA
OHIO
NORTH CAROLINA
SOUTH CAROLINA
GEORGIA
KENTUCKY
TENNESSEE

INDIANA TERRITORY

Illinois R.
Ohio R.
Mississippi R.

MISSISSIPPI TERRITORY

SPANISH FLORIDA

ATLANTIC OCEAN

Gulf of Mexico

LOUISIANA PURCHASE

Fort Mandan
Missouri R.
Platte R.

SPANISH TERRITORY

Columbia R.
Snake R.
Rio Grande
Colorado R.

MEXICO

0   100   200   300 Miles
0 100 200 300 Kilometers

sense of destiny. For Republicans, it assumed special significance. By making available the land necessary for continued expansion of agriculture, ensuring commercial growth, and easing the European threat, thus seemingly eliminating the need for a large military establishment, the purchase appeared to ensure the preservation of the essentially republican character of American society. All of this was accomplished without the use of force—"truth and reason have been more powerful than the sword," a pro-administration newspaper exulted—thus vindicating republican statecraft.[32]

His appetite whetted and self-confidence inflated beyond reason, Jefferson set out to relieve Spain of the Floridas. Americans had long viewed that land as essential to their security and prosperity. Rapidly expanding settlements in the Mississippi territory required access to the port of Mobile. The commerce of the Gulf Coast promised great riches. Resting astride the Gulf of Mexico, the Floridas, as Napoleon had perceived, were vital to the defense of Louisiana. In Spanish hands, they represented a nuisance rather than a threat, but Jefferson was tempted by Spain's weakness and harbored near paranoid fears these lands might be seized by Britain. Americans now insisted that the Floridas were manifestly useless to Spain and interpreted the ever adaptable and useful laws of nature as entitling them to a water boundary on the South.

Displaying an obsessiveness not easy to comprehend, Jefferson used every conceivable means to attain his object. Permitting his wishes to drive his claims, he argued with more force than logic that since Louisiana under French control had extended to the Perdido River, including a sizeable chunk of West Florida, the United States was entitled to the same boundary, a position Spain quickly and rightly dismissed. Confident that if he "pushed Spain strongly with one hand, holding out a price in the other, we shall certainly obtain the Floridas and in all good time," he employed the same bullying tactics used with France. He combined offers to purchase the Floridas with only slightly veiled threats to seize them by force. He concentrated troops along the Spanish frontier and secured congressional passage of the Mobile Act, a vague document that appeared unilaterally to assert U.S. jurisdiction over much of West Florida. Again rebuffed, he swallowed his republican scruples and responded positively to hints from Paris that for a price Napoleon would intercede with the stubborn Spain.[33]

32. Quoted in Tucker and Hendrickson, *Empire of Liberty*, 89.
33. DeConde, *Louisiana*, 214–15; Jefferson to John Breckinridge, August 12, 1803, in Ford, *Writings* 10:5n.

Jefferson's lust for Florida, along with pressures from southern slavehold-ers, also prompted abandonment of his brief and altogether expedient flir-tation with the rebellion on Saint-Domingue. On January 1, 1804, victorious rebels proclaimed the independent republic of Haiti and began systemati-cally killing French citizens who remained on the island. These events sent a chill through already nervous American slaveholders. At the very time the cotton gin was infusing new life into the institution of slavery in the United States, Haiti appeared a major threat. It was demonized and used as an ar-gument against emancipation. A Georgia senator even insisted that "the government of that unfortunate island must be destroyed." Still not ready to concede defeat, France demanded that the United States cease its "shame-ful" and "scandalous" trade with the rebels. The administration went well beyond that modest request, in effect denying the very existence of the new country. It refused to recognize the new republic or even to use the word *Haiti*. Fearing, as Jefferson's son-in-law put it, that trade with the island could result in "the immediate and horrible destruction of the fairest part of America," and hoping to curry French support on Florida, the United States imposed a trade embargo. For reasons of race and diplomatic expe-diency, it conceded to the British the wealth of the sugar island trade and moral leadership in its own hemisphere. As a result of persisting slaveholder opposition, the first republic in the Western Hemisphere outside the United States went unrecognized by Washington until 1862.[34]

Jefferson's Florida diplomacy reveals him at his worst. His lust for land trumped his concern for principle and obscured his usually clear vision. Having lost Louisiana as a result of French duplicity, Spain was not in a generous mood. It was determined to hold on to its last bit of leverage against an expansive America. Timing is crucial in international negotia-tion. In this instance, the twists and turns of European politics worked against the United States. At the outset, Napoleon eagerly played Wash-ington against Madrid to see what he could get, but when Spain and France joined forces in 1805 he supported his ally. In the meantime, the revelation of a possible bribe to France provoked intense opposition from old-school Republicans such as Virginian John Randolph, who de-nounced this "base prostration of the national character," weakening Jef-ferson's hand. A frustrated president would voice righteous indignation at Spanish "perfidy and injustice," but he was unable to secure the object of his ambitions.[35]

34. Matthewson, "Jefferson and Haiti," 234–39; Hickey, "Slave Revolt," 374–76; Tim Matthewson, "Jefferson and the Nonrecognition of Haiti," *Proceedings of the Ameri-can Philosophical Society* 140 (March 1996), 22–47.
35. Malone, *Second Term*, 73; Ford, *Writings* 9:381–82.

Jefferson's successor, James Madison, shared his fixation with the Floridas and evinced a willingness to use the presence of Americans there and the exigencies of the European war to take them. Drawn to West Florida by cheap and fertile land and easy access to the Gulf, American settlers made up a majority of the population by 1810. They resented Spanish rule—such as it was—and especially the duties they paid to use Spanish ports. Encouraged by Washington to form a "convention" should Spanish authority collapse, a collection of gentleman planters, hooligans, and fugitives from Spanish *and* American justice seized the fort at Baton Rouge. With no money in hand but a flag already designed, they proclaimed the independent republic of West Florida and requested annexation by the United States. By not waiting for the end of Spanish rule to declare independence, the rebels moved much further and faster than Madison intended. Fearful, on the other hand, that France or Britain might seize the territory, he acted preemptively to back up America's contested claim. Refusing to negotiate with the rebels, whose legitimacy he questioned, he ordered the occupation of West Florida to the Perdido River.[36] In 1811, he asserted U.S. jurisdiction over the province; the following year, he incorporated it into the state of Louisiana. Using the possibility of a British invasion as a pretext, Madison completed the conquest of Spanish West Florida in 1813 by annexing Mobile.

The administration's actions in East Florida in 1812 represent an embarrassing episode in early national history, a failed attempt to take by force territory to which the United States had little claim. Fearing the collapse of Spanish rule, Madison in 1810 dispatched Georgia adventurer George Mathews to inform the residents of East Florida that if they were to separate from Spain they would be welcomed into the United States. The following year, he secured from Congress authorization to use force to prevent a foreign takeover of East Florida, instructing Mathews in such an eventuality to occupy the province or negotiate with the locals. Mathews subsequently sought authority to foment revolution there. The administration's nonresponse was interpreted by him—and has been seen by some historians—as tantamount to silent complicity in the scheme. Others persuasively argue that this was standard operating procedure and did not imply consent. Whatever the case, the overzealous Mathews organized a group of local "Patriots" who seized Amelia Island off the Georgia coast and laid siege to St. Augustine. Complaining that Mathews's "extravagance" had put the

---

36. Thomas P. Abernethy, *The South in the New Nation, 1789–1819* (Baton Rouge, La., 1961), 340–66; J.C.A. Stagg, "James Madison and George Mathews: The East Florida Revolution of 1812 Reconsidered," *Diplomatic History* 30 (January 2006), 29–31.

administration in "the most distressing dilemma," Madison disavowed his reckless agent. On the verge of war with Britain, however, and more than ever concerned about the threat to East Florida, he authorized the Patriots to hold on to territory they had taken.[37] Furious with his abandonment, Mathews started home to expose the administration's complicity. In a rare bit of good luck during his embattled presidency, Madison was spared further embarrassment when Mathews died en route.[38]

While consolidating his Louisiana prize and pressing Spain on the Floridas, Jefferson had taken the first steps toward an American empire on the Pacific. During the height of the Louisiana crisis, he instructed his aide Meriwether Lewis to explore what was then Spanish territory. To the Spanish, he justified the mission in scientific and "literary" terms; to Congress, he spoke of exploiting the lucrative fur trade, "civilizing" the Indians, and finding the fabled water route to the Pacific. By the time Lewis and William Clark got under way, Louisiana belonged to the United States and Jefferson's vision had expanded to acquiring all of the West. He instructed the explorers to bring the Indians into the U.S. orbit, wrest the fur trade from Britain, and lay claim to the Pacific Northwest.[39]

One of the great adventures of all times, Lewis and Clark's dramatic and arduous journey to the Columbia River and back covered more than seven thousand miles and took more than two years. Confident that Indians, in contrast to blacks, were "noble savages" who could be civilized, Jefferson contemplated keeping the West as a vast reservation where those already settled and tribes transplanted from the East could be civilized and in time assimilated. Using the combination of threats and bribes that had long stamped American Indian policy, Lewis and Clark parleyed with tribes along the way, urging them to accept U.S. sovereignty, make peace among themselves, and welcome American traders. This initial approach to the Plains Indians had mixed results for the United States and largely negative results for the Indians. Representatives of some tribes actually visited Washington; some trade ties were established. Lewis and Clark did not seek to befriend the hostile Sioux and Blackfeet, however, and they were unable to make peace among the other tribes. Most important for the long run, reports from the expedition excited trappers and eventually settlers to head West, in time re-creating there and with the same results the wars of extermination already under way to the east.[40]

37. Stagg, "Madison and Mathews," 32–55.
38. Robert Allen Rutland, *The Presidency of James Madison* (Lawrence, Kans., 1990), 92.
39. Peterson, *Jefferson*, 762–64.
40. Ambrose, *Undaunted Courage*, 140–395.

The Lewis and Clark Expedition, 1803–1806

— Pittsburgh to Camp Wood (1803)
— Camp Wood to Pacific and return (1804–6)

Return Route Variations (1806)

...... Lewis and Clark
— — — Lewis
- - - - Clark

0   100   200   300 Miles
0 100 200 300 Kilometers

The explorers discovered no water route to the Pacific—dashing long-standing geographical assumptions—and their reports underlined the formidable barriers to settling the trans-Mississippi West. The expedition did produce priceless geographical and scientific discoveries, however, and it greatly facilitated U.S. expansion to the Pacific. Encouraged by Jefferson's offer of "every reasonable [government] patronage," the New York merchant John Jacob Astor immediately set out to capture the fur trade by constructing a series of posts from the Missouri River to the Columbia. In 1811, he established a fort at the mouth of the Columbia, laying the first substantial American claim to the Oregon territory. During the War of 1812, Astor loaned a near bankrupt United States $2.5 million in return for promises to defend Astoria it could not keep. The advance to the Pacific was delayed by geography and war, but Jefferson's vision of continental empire was eagerly taken up by his successors.[41]

IV

At best an armed truce, the Peace of Amiens broke down in 1803, and the European war entered an even more bitter phase, a desperate struggle for survival not to be resolved until Napoleon's defeat at Waterloo in 1815. During much of this time, the major combatants were locked in a stand-off, France dominating the continent of Europe, Britain ruling the seas. Combining with devastating effectiveness his genius for battlefield maneuver and the new military concept of mass armies imbued with patriotic zeal, Napoleon routed Austria and Prussia and quickly brought Russia to terms. The master of Europe, he sought next to subdue that despised "nation of shopkeepers" through his Continental System, a network of blockades set forth in his Berlin and Milan decrees and designed to strangle the British economy. In the meantime, Lord Nelson in 1805 destroyed the French fleet at Trafalgar, giving Britain uncontested control of the sea and permitting it to position and support forces anywhere along the coast of Europe. Unable to get at each other through conventional means, the powers resorted to new and all-inclusive forms of economic warfare, blithely ignoring the screams of neutrals.[42]

As in the 1790s, the United States became entangled in the struggle, but this time it did not escape direct involvement. Unlike Hamilton and

41. Peterson, *Jefferson*, 904; John M. Belohlavek, "Economic Interest Groups and the Formation of Foreign Policy in the Early Republic," *Journal of the Early Republic* 14 (Winter 1994), 480–81.

42. Robert Doughty, Ira Gruber, et al., *Warfare in the Modern World*, vol. 1, *Military Operations from 1600 to 1871* (Lexington, Mass., 1996), 212–34.

Washington in 1794, Jefferson refused to sacrifice American commerce or acquiesce in the British maritime system. His visceral dislike for England made such steps unpalatable if not impossible. He persisted in trying to exploit European rivalries, and for a time hesitated to jeopardize his quest for the Floridas by antagonizing Napoleon. True to republican ideology, he continued to believe that economic weapons would compel the Europeans to accept his terms. Unfortunately for Jefferson, the conflict had reached a level of intensity where the major belligerents were no longer subject to manipulation and threats. Neither would appease America. As the European war had brought Jefferson the twin windfalls of prosperity and Louisiana in his first term, so also it was the source of his unremitting misfortune in the second. Caught between what he angrily called the "tyrant of the ocean" and the "scourge of the land," he and his successor, Madison, reeled from crisis to crisis between 1805 and 1812.[43] Relations with France remained tense, but Britain's control of the seas impinged more directly on U.S. interests, provoking a sustained and particularly bitter dispute that eventually brought war.

The resumption of war in Europe brought to the forefront the volatile issue of the carrying trade. When France and Spain opened their colonies to American shipping in the 1790s, Britain had invoked the Rule of 1756, declaring that trade illegal in time of peace was also illegal in war. As part of the larger rapprochement following the Jay Treaty, the two nations had reached an unwritten compromise. American shippers had skirted British regulations by what was called the "broken voyage," picking up wares in French or Spanish colonies, returning to U.S. ports and observing normal customs procedures, then reexporting the cargoes to Europe. Eager to preserve U.S. friendship and certain that the awkwardness and expense of the procedure would limit the size of the trade, London had accepted the broken voyage. In the case of the ship *Polly* (1800), an admiralty court had even sanctioned its legality.[44]

When war resumed, Americans jumped back into the carrying trade with a vengeance, and as profits soared they became less and less scrupulous about observing the niceties of the broken voyage. Acts of Congress permitted merchants to recover much of the import duties on reexported items. Some shippers paid no duties at all. In many cases, they did not even bother to unload the cargoes. In a life-and-death situation, the carrying

---

43. Peterson, *Jefferson*, 916.
44. These issues are discussed in depth in Bradford Perkins, *Prologue to War: England and the United States* (Berkeley, Calif., 1961), 75–95, and Paul A. Varg, *Foreign Policies of the Founding Fathers* (Baltimore, Md., 1970), 172–79.

trade threatened to deprive Britain of the presumed advantages of control of the seas. In the 1805 *Essex* case, admiralty courts held that the final destination of the cargo determined the nature of the voyage, thus rendering the broken voyage illegal. Even before this, Britain had begun to seize American ships and confiscate cargoes. British measures jeopardized a trade that by 1805 exceeded $60 million, comprised nearly two-thirds of U.S. exports, and had become the basis of American prosperity. Some Americans conceded that this commerce was unnatural and temporary and therefore not worth the risk of war. But Jefferson viewed it as a way to make up an unfavorable balance of trade with Britain. He insisted that its loss would leave the United States vulnerable to British pressure and might force undesirable changes in the domestic economy. Many Americans denounced what seemed an obvious attempt to impoverish their country.

An even more difficult issue, the British practice of impressing sailors, allegedly deserters, from U.S. ships stemmed at least indirectly from proliferation of the carrying trade. Where impressment was concerned, the two nations took conflicting legal positions on the most basic of issues. Britain adhered to the doctrine of "indefeasible allegiance," the principle that a person born under its flag could not legally change citizenship. The United States permitted and even encouraged such changes by making naturalization easy and conferring full citizenship on those naturalized. Under the laws of each nation, therefore, an individual could be a citizen of both at the same time. The United States did not dispute Britain's right to search its merchant vessels for deserters in British ports. Britain did not claim the right to search men-of-war anywhere or U.S. merchant vessels in neutral ports. But the United States advanced the position—not then accepted by any other nation—that Britain could not search its merchant vessels on the high seas, a claim the British flatly rejected.

The issue touched vital interests and deep-seated emotions on both sides. Britain's survival depended on the Royal Navy, which, in turn, required an ample supply of seamen. Manpower was chronically short, a problem made worse by wholesale desertion to U.S. ships. As the carrying trade grew after 1803, the American merchant marine expanded enormously in size. Thousands of British sailors eagerly fled to ships where working conditions were far better and pay as much as five times higher. Some U.S. ship captains openly enticed sailors from the Royal Navy. The ease with which legal or forged citizenship papers could be acquired facilitated the practice. Albert Gallatin admitted that half of the sailors employed in the U.S. merchant marine were English—even according to

American definitions of citizenship. To the great annoyance of London, U.S. courts frequently refused to turn over deserters. Britain found this intolerable at a time of crisis and adamantly upheld its right to recover deserters.

Each side handled the issue in ways that exacerbated their differences. Had Britain exercised some discretion in implementing impressment, conflict might have been mitigated, but responsibility rested with officers of the Royal Navy, for whom restraint was not a desirable or even acceptable personality trait. Operating far from home and desperate for seamen, they cared little about American sensitivities. British ships hovered off the U.S. coastline, imposing a virtual blockade of many ports, a practice that galled an independent and insecure people. Ship captains often did not bother to investigate whether men taken were in fact deserters or even British citizens. Between three thousand and six thousand innocent Americans were pressed into British service from 1803 to 1812. On occasion, overzealous captains exceeded bounds recognized by both nations, stopping and searching U.S. naval vessels or merchant vessels in American waters. Americans thus viewed impressment as an affront to the dignity of a free nation and a gross assault on human rights. They also perceived that to surrender on the issue could wreck the merchant marine upon which their prosperity depended. The rigid position assumed by the United States left Britain no means to recover the thousands of sailors who deserted.

Attitudes and emotions on both sides of the Atlantic made already difficult conflicts of interest impossible to resolve. Engaged in a desperate struggle against Napoleonic tyranny, the British saw themselves defending the liberties of the "free world." They deeply resented U.S. interference with what they regarded as essential measures of war. They dismissed America's insistence on neutral rights as Francophilia in disguise or the product of a grasping desire to profit at the expense of a nation fighting for its life. Outraged Britons expressed open contempt for the Americans, "less popular and esteemed among us than the base and bigotted Portugeze, or the ferocious and ignorant Russians," a leading journal of opinion exclaimed. They minimized the threat of retaliation from "a nation three thousand miles off—scarcely held together by the weakest government in the world."[45]

Americans from Jefferson down failed to comprehend the extent to which the European war dominated British policy, attributing the harsh

45. Perkins, *Prologue*, 7; Onuf and Onuf, *Federal Union*, 213–15.

maritime measures to sheer vengeance or greed. The residue of Anglo-phobia left from the Revolution deepened as the crisis intensified. Out-raged by British insults to their honor, Americans insisted on demands London could not possibly meet, placing the two nations on a collision course.

An incident off the coast of Virginia in June 1807 brought the two na-tions to the brink of war. The frigate USS *Chesapeake* had taken on board a number of British deserters, some of whom had flaunted their new sta-tus before their former officers on the streets of Norfolk. Infuriated, the British naval commander in America, Adm. Sir George Berkeley, ordered tough measures. When the *Chesapeake* passed into international waters en route to its station in the Mediterranean, HMS *Leopard* opened fire. The outmanned, unprepared, and totally unsuspecting American ship struck colors virtually without a fight. The British took four men, one a deserter, the others impressed Americans who had fled British service.[46] American anger exceeded that provoked by the XYZ Affair. Mass meet-ings in seaboard cities denounced the outrage and demanded satisfac-tion. Mobs attacked British sailors. In Philadelphia, angry citizens nearly destroyed a British ship. "This country has never been in such a state of excitement since the battle of Lexington," Jefferson declared.[47]

Unlike Adams a decade earlier, the president did not fan the martial spirit. He closed American ports to Royal Navy ships and demanded not merely reparation but British abandonment of impressment. But he would go no further. Recognizing that the nation was unprepared to fight, fearing for the large number of U.S. ships at sea, and still hoping for a diplomatic solution, he contented himself with quiet preparations for a war that seemed likely if not inevitable. Jefferson's hesitant and even con-tradictory response prolonged the crisis without providing any means to resolve it. In the absence of presidential direction, the war fever quickly dissipated, making it difficult to ready the nation's defenses. The tough line with Britain precluded a diplomatic solution. Jefferson's quiet public response and the apparent acquiescence of the nation reinforced British certainty of American weakness.

Alone in Europe at this point, and faring poorly in the war, London was in no mood to compromise. The navy demonstrated its disdain for neutrality by bombarding Copenhagen and seizing the entire Danish fleet. The government recalled Berkeley but refused even to consider the

46. Spencer C. Tucker and Frank T. Reuter, "The *Chesapeake-Leopard* Affair," *Naval History* (March/April 1996), 40–44.
47. Peterson, *Jefferson*, 876.

larger issue of impressment. Foreign Minister George Canning provocatively blamed the *Chesapeake-Leopard* incident on the United States. A new order in council of November 1807 required ships bound for Europe to pass first through Britain and secure a license. The French responded by announcing that ships abiding by British regulations would be seized. Any ships now attempting to trade across the Atlantic were liable to seizure by one power or the other.[48]

Unwilling to compromise and unable to fight, Jefferson fell back on an embargo of American commerce. Publicly, he justified the step in terms of immediate, practical needs. It would keep ships and sailors "out of harm's way" and insulate the United States from belligerents who had reverted to the "vandalism of the fifth century." His private motives were more complex. Unless he could disabuse Europeans of the notion that the United States was wedded to "Quaker principles," he reasoned, it would be subject to the "plunder of all nations."[49] He and Madison had long agreed that European dependence on American necessities gave the United States the means to force them to respect its "rights." For Americans to do without the "superfluities and poisons" provided by Europe, on the other hand, would encourage domestic manufactures, thus promoting the independent and virtuous republic of which he and Madison dreamed. Jefferson hoped that his experiment in "peaceable coercion" might even offer an alternative to war to peace-loving peoples across the world and force the European powers to alter their methods of warfare. He seems to have perceived the pitfalls of a long-term embargo, but he depended on Europe's vulnerability and his own people's tolerance for sacrifice to ensure the success of his policy.[50]

Jefferson miscalculated on both counts. The embargo had no effect in France and indeed played into Napoleon's hands by depriving Britain of trade with the United States and increasing Anglo-American antagonism. Openly mocking America, Napoleon appointed himself an enforcer, ordering seizure of U.S. ships entering European ports. During its first year, the embargo caused a slight rise in prices and some unemployment in England, but little more. The timing was unfortunate. The unusually large trade of 1806 left British warehouses bulging with American goods. Revolution in Spain's Latin American colonies opened new markets to offset the loss of American buyers. The short-term pain was not sufficient

48. Burton I. Spivak, *Jefferson's English Crisis: Commerce, Embargo, and the Republican Revolution* (Charlottesville, Va., 1979), 99–102.
49. Ibid., 103.
50. McCoy, *Elusive Republic*, 218–19.

to compel a shaky British ministry, engaged in a war for survival, to capitulate to the United States. By the time England had begun to feel the pinch, support for "peaceable coercion" had dissipated in the United States.

Jefferson's greatest miscalculation was of his own people's willingness to endure economic hardship for the sake of principle. Accustomed to fat profits and intolerant of government interference, fiercely individualistic Americans evaded the law at will and resisted the stern measures used to enforce it. At the outset, loopholes made evasion easy. The coastal trade was essential for the seaboard cities. Ships licensed to trade among American ports transferred cargoes to British vessels waiting at sea or, claiming to be blown off course, slipped away to the West Indies or Canada's maritime provinces. Posting bond made no difference since profits obtained from illicit trade far exceeded the amount required. When the administration tightened the loopholes, merchants resorted to outright smuggling, a practice Americans had long since perfected. Hundreds of ships escaped the detection of overworked port officials. Large quantities of American foodstuffs, potash, and lumber went into Canada overland, by boat, or even by sled in winter. On occasion, wares were placed on hillsides and rolled north across the border! The British encouraged evasion by offering top prices and protecting smugglers from law enforcers. From the Great Lakes to the Atlantic, distinct borderland societies had emerged where people on each side were linked through business, friendship, and family ties. These communities were closer to each other than to their governments. Defiance verged on insurrection. Smuggled goods seized as evidence mysteriously disappeared. Federal agents were bribed or intimidated, or themselves joined in the plunder. Juries refused to convict smugglers.[51]

Jefferson sought to "legalize all *means* which may be necessary to attain its *end*," using the military to enforce the law, declaring the borderlands in a state of rebellion, and ordering out the militia.[52] The passage in January 1809 of additional enforcement measures sharply circumscribing individual liberties did not stop smuggling and provoked near-rebellion in New England. Angry crowds revived songs of protest from the revolution. Speakers compared Jefferson—unfavorably—to George III. The Massachusetts and Connecticut legislatures declared the embargo not legally binding. There was open talk of secession. Outside New England, the opposition was scattered and muted, but the obvious failure of the em-

51. Reginald C. Stuart, *United States Expansion and British North America, 1775–1871* (Chapel Hill, N.C., 1988), 42–52.
52. Tucker and Hendrickson, *Empire of Liberty,* 224.

bargo abroad and the hardships it imposed at home brought growing demands for repeal.[53]

Jefferson's failures of leadership contributed to the inglorious end of his experiment. He never adequately explained the purposes of the embargo, leaving the field to critics who accused him of oppressing and impoverishing his own people for the benefit of Napoleon. He could not fathom the nature or the depth of the opposition, dismissing his critics as die-hard Federalists, Anglophiles, or plain "rascals." Throughout 1808, friends begged him to reassess his policy. Stung by the bitter personal attacks, at times seemingly paralyzed by indecision, he clung stubbornly to the embargo and resorted to even more rigorous enforcement. After Madison was elected to succeed him, he virtually abdicated to a confused, divided, and sometimes panicky Congress. Jefferson and Madison had hoped to sustain the embargo until summer and then, if it had still not succeeded, couple repeal with steps toward war. Frightened by the specter of rebellion in New England, Congress moved repeal to March and rejected any moves toward war. To save face, the legislators approved a lame substitute, the Non-Intercourse Act, which resumed trade with all nations but Britain and France and offered to restore it with either of the belligerents who lifted its obnoxious decrees. Fittingly, the embargo expired the day Jefferson left office, having produced tragically ironic results. Designed as a substitute for the war that would undermine republican ideals, it produced a form of warfare at home. A president profoundly committed to individual freedom became trapped into imposing repressive measures that starkly violated his most basic convictions about civil liberties.[54]

V

Between 1809 and 1812, two nations with every reason to avoid conflict drifted inexorably into a war that could have been disastrous for either, providing a textbook example of how not to conduct diplomacy.

The United States clung stubbornly to the futile course set by Jefferson. Madison inherited a policy in shambles, a divided party, and an increasingly unruly Congress—Senate "malcontents" even blocked his appointment of the able Gallatin as secretary of state.[55] A small and retiring individual, lacking Jefferson's commanding presence and enormous prestige, Madison tended to defer in situations that demanded firm leadership. Faithful to principle to the point of folly, he refused concessions on

53. Peterson, *Jefferson*, 913–14.
54. McDonald, *Jefferson*, 139.
55. Rutland, *Madison*, 16–17.

neutral "rights." Equally fearful of the threat war posed to republican institutions, he hesitated to accept it even as a last resort. He retained faith in "peaceable coercion" long after its limits had become palpable. Thus Non-Intercourse was followed in May 1810 by Macon's Bill No. 2, which opened trade with Britain and France but indicated that if either dropped its restrictions the United States would impose an embargo on the other. Eager for peace to the point of gullibility, Madison leaped at French and British proposals when he ought to have been cautious. He accepted at face value the wily Napoleon's announcement, hedged with conditions, that he had repealed the Berlin and Milan decrees and reimposed non-intercourse on England. This ill-considered move soured relations with Britain while Napoleon used escape clauses to harass American shipping. Even when Madison finally concluded that war was inevitable, he moved in such a slow and circuitous fashion that friends and foes on both sides of the Atlantic were uncertain where he was heading.[56]

British diplomacy was also flawed. The European war reached its climactic stages during these years. Absorbed with the Peninsular War in Spain and Portugal and Napoleon's invasion of Russia, British officials gave little attention to America. Certain that the United States would not go to war, they also refused concessions. Although clearly in the wrong on the *Chesapeake* affair, they showed "contemptuous indifference" by taking four years to apologize.[57] Ironically, just when Madison and Congress were moving toward war, British manufacturing interests were lobbying to revoke the restrictive orders in council. But the London government accepted compromise as hesitantly as Madison accepted war. The direction of its policy was no more clear.[58]

In crises, diplomats can make a difference, but here the diplomats made things worse. Viewing the United States as a secondary theater, Britain made a series of unfortunate appointments to the Washington post. The youthful, inexperienced, and overeager David Erskine submitted to the Americans an agreement his government rejected, infuriating both capitals. Erskine was replaced by the arrogant, obnoxious, and blustering Francis James Jackson, already notorious—and given the sobriquet "Copenhagen"—for his prominent role in the destruction inflicted on neutral Denmark. Jackson confidently informed London that the United States would not fight: "Dogs that bark don't bite."[59] He made no effort to

---

56. Ibid., 64; J.C.A. Stagg, *Mr. Madison's War* (Princeton, N.J., 1983), 116.
57. George F. G. Stanley, *The War of 1812: Land Operations* (Ottawa, 1983), 21.
58. Rutland, *Madison*, 96.
59. Ibid., 44–45.

disguise his contempt for America and Americans, describing Madison as a "plain and rather mean-looking man" and his wife, the gracious and charming Dolley, as "fat and forty, but not fair." His demeanor provoked so much hostility in such a short time that Madison demanded his recall. London complied but delayed replacing him for months, leaving a vacuum at a critical time. Even after his recall, Jackson hung around longer, provoking more ire from outraged Americans. "Base and Insolent in the Extreme," furious citizens called him, "a miscreant so vile." Even the mild-mannered Madison described him as "mean" and "insolent." His replacement, the playboy Augustus John Foster, was less openly obnoxious if no less arrogant. But he listened to Federalist friends rather than trying to sense the changing mood in Washington, underscoring London's belief that America would not fight and reinforcing its complacency.[60]

During the last critical months, the United States had no ministers in key European capitals. John Armstrong left Paris and William Pinkney left London in 1811, Armstrong apparently to avoid being tainted with Madison's weak policies and to promote his own presidential ambitions, Pinkney out of sheer frustration with the impossibility of his assignment. "The Prime of my Life is passing away in barren Toil and Anxiety," the financially strapped diplomat lamented.[61] The U.S. chargé in London, the hapless Jonathan Russell, did not sense and thus could not inform Washington of subtle shifts in British policy.

The threat of Indian warfare on the frontier, which Americans also conveniently blamed on Britain, added to an already long list of grievances. In fact, the problem was self-inflicted. Disease, alcohol, commerce, and the relentless pressure of U.S. expansion placed the traditional culture of northwestern Indians under full assault. Some acquiesced, accepting American annuities and supplies and missionary efforts to turn them into farmers. Some found escape in whiskey. Others resisted. They found a leader in a Shawnee and former drunkard who, after claiming in 1805 to have a vision, took the name Tenskwatawa and initiated a revivalist movement to save Native American culture. Fusing traditional ways with Western ideas, including some borrowed from Christianity, the man also called "the Prophet" urged Indians to put aside the evil habits of the "Long Knives" and return to their ancient traditions. As Jefferson and Madison negotiated more treaties taking more Indian lands, Tenskwatawa's message fell on increasingly receptive ears, especially

60. For sample attacks on Jackson, see J.C.A. Stagg, ed., *The Papers of James Madison*, Presidential Series, vol. 2 (Charlottesville, Va., 1992), 27, 123, 263.
61. Pinkney to Madison, August 13, 1810, in Stagg, *Madison Papers* 2:478–82.

among the young. He attracted as many as three thousand followers and in 1808 established a village called Prophetstown in Indiana. Building on Tenskwatawa's revivalist movement, his half-brother, the redoubtable Tecumseh, set out to unite southern and northwestern tribes to resist further land cessions. Following in the footsteps of Mohawk visionary Joseph Brant, he traveled from the Great Lakes to the Mississippi territory in the daunting and ultimately futile task of bringing together disparate tribes into a pan-Indian confederation. "They have driven us from the sea to the lakes," Tecumseh warned in 1809. "We can go no farther."[62]

Americans viewed these developments with growing alarm. Neither understanding nor respecting Indian culture, they failed to perceive that Tenskwatawa's movement was the natural response of a people overwhelmed by change. They were inclined then—as historians have been since—to dismiss him as a charlatan and fanatic.[63] The British in fact responded with notable caution to Indian unrest, but Americans could not concede the legitimacy of Indian grievances without admitting their own guilt. They blamed the agitation on the British. From the relative security of Washington, Jefferson and Madison counted on American benevolence to solve the problem. As was often the case, however, the commander on the scene took a quite different approach. Certain that Indians understood only force, Governor William Henry Harrison sought to drive the Prophet from the Indiana territory. If he did not conspire to provoke an Indian attack, the result was the same. When Harrison established position outside Prophetstown, claiming to wish to parley, the Prophet ordered an attack. In the battle of Tippecanoe, November 7, 1811, each side suffered heavy losses. The Americans claimed victory, and indeed Harrison did destroy Prophetstown and discredit the Prophet as a leader. Formerly settled in one place, the Indians now scattered. Violence erupted across the frontier.[64] Americans increasingly feared a general Indian war, for which they blamed the British.

By the summer of 1812, anger and frustration reached the breaking point. Neither diplomacy nor economic retaliation had wrenched concessions from England. Americans from Madison down increasingly accepted the necessity for war. Madison appears to have reached such a conclusion as soon as late 1811, but his halting and ineffectual efforts to mobilize Congress failed.[65] A sizeable bloc of congressmen, the so-called

62. R. David Edmunds, *The Shawnee Prophet* (Lincoln, Neb., 1983), 34–79; the Tecumseh quote is from R. David Edmunds, *Tecumseh and the Quest for Indian Leadership* (New York, 1984), 131. See also John Sugden, *Tecumseh: A Life* (New York, 1998).

63. Edmunds, *Prophet*, 187–92.

64. Edmunds, *Tecumseh*, 159–60; Stagg, *Madison's War*, 189–92.

65. Rutland, *Madison*, 86; Stagg, *Madison's War*, 189–90.

War Hawks, were already committed to fight, but the rest were badly divided. The Federalist minority blamed the impasse on the Republicans. One group of Republicans opposed both war and acquiescence; another wavered uncertainly. Persuaded by May that no settlement was likely, and with the approaching election putting a premium on action of some kind, Madison submitted a war message to Congress. It was approved on June 17 without enthusiasm and by the closest vote of any declaration of war in U.S. history (79–49 in the House; 19–13 in the Senate).

Ironically, at the very time Americans were drifting toward war, Britain was lurching toward concessions. Years of trade restrictions had finally worked significant hardships, especially among the rising manufacturing class, producing growing pressures for changes in policy. In 1812, the Admiralty ordered the navy to avoid clashes with U.S. ships and stay clear of the coast. In late June, the ministry revoked the orders in council for one year. But each step was taken on an ad hoc basis without publicity or explanation of the larger forces that drove it. At a time when it could take as long as twelve weeks to exchange dispatches across the Atlantic, word of changes in policy on one side did not arrive in time to influence the other. The British found out about the American decision for war long after they had revoked the orders. The Americans did not learn about revocation of the orders until August, two months after declaring war.[66]

It has often been speculated that faster communication in 1812 might have averted an unnecessary war, but this may assume too much. The new British ministry, while more conciliatory, was not prepared to go as far as Madison wished. On several occasions after war began, the belligerents or outside powers such as Russia attempted to promote an armistice. Each effort failed because of persisting deadlock on impressment. Revocation of the orders in council was only temporary, not enough to satisfy the United States. In any event, had he known of them, Madison might have interpreted British concessions as a sign of weakness and pushed ahead with war.[67]

At least on the American side, the question of war or peace by 1812 transcended disagreements on specific issues. For many Americans, war provided an opportunity to fulfill long-standing expansionist designs on Florida and Canada. Southern War Hawks such as Kentucky's Henry Clay and Tennessee's Felix Grundy had their eyes firmly fixed on East Florida. Vast in size, weakly defended, its population small and presumed of dubious loyalty to the Crown, Canada also seemed irresistibly ripe for

66. Donald R. Hickey, *The War of 1812: A Forgotten Conflict* (Urbana, Ill., 1989), 42.
67. Stagg, *Madison's War*, 118–19.

the plucking. "I verily believe," Clay boasted to Madison, "that the militia of Kentucky are alone competent to place Upper Canada at your feet."[68] More important, Canada was the one place where mighty Britain seemed vulnerable. Its conquest would plug a major leak in the embargo and eliminate an alternative means of supply for the British West Indies, thus making U.S. trade restrictions more effective and giving the United States a way to wring concessions from Britain. Eliminating their primary means of support would help quell the Indian menace and open the Northwest to American expansion. In a broader sense, the elimination of British power from North America would enhance U.S. security.[69] Whether or not American expansion was essentially defensive, the conquest of Canada served urgent national needs. Manifest Destiny would be the "rallying cry of the next generation," Robert Rutland has written, "but as a political force it was first unleashed by the War Hawks of 1812."[70]

The vote of 1812 was along strict party lines, and for Republicans, by this time, war also seemed the only means to defend honor, principle, and party. Republicans in all sections felt a deep sense of humiliation at having endured for so long affronts to American sovereignty. The United States was being treated as though the war of independence had never occurred. Some form of redemption was essential to restore its self-respect. "By war, we should be purified, as by fire," Massachusetts Republican Elbridge Gerry told Madison.[71] For many Republicans, it was not only a matter of honor but also one of defending their principles and indeed their embattled party. Republican political economy depended on the right to export. By 1812, in the face of crippling threats from abroad, war seemed the only way to preserve the ideals of republican political economy.[72] Viewing the American Revolution as a unique experiment in constructing a society based on principles of individual liberty and their party as the guarantor of those principles, Republicans saw that experiment as imperiled by the great powers abroad and Federalists at home. If the government could not withstand that dual challenge, it would surely collapse, demonstrating the invalidity of republican principles. Republicans accepted war as the only way to preserve the party and the heritage of the

68. Quoted in Rutland, Madison, 95.
69. Reginald Horsman, "On to Canada: Manifest Destiny and United States Strategy in the War of 1812," Michigan Historical Review 13 (Fall 1987), 1–24, and "The War of 1812 Revisited," Diplomatic History 15 (Winter 1991), 122–23.
70. Rutland, Madison, 96.
71. Quoted in Hickey, War of 1812, 28; Roger Brown, The Republic in Peril: 1812 (New York, 1971) develops the theme of embattled Republicanism.
72. McCoy, Elusive Republic, 235; Brown, Republic in Peril, 182–86.

Revolution. Younger Americans who had not participated in the Revolution felt this with particular keenness. They must show "the World," War Hawk John C. Calhoun of South Carolina proclaimed, "that we have not only inherited the liberty which our Fathers gave us, but also the will and power to maintain it."[73]

VI

Madison accepted war in 1812 in the confidence that it would be relatively short, inexpensive, and bloodless—more talk than fight—and that the United States could achieve its objectives without great difficulty. In fact, the War of 1812 lasted two and a half years and cost more than two thousand American lives and $1.6 billion.[74] For Britain, the war was a military and diplomatic sideshow to the main performance in Europe; for the United States, it became a struggle for survival.

The Americans hoped to conquer Canada quickly and use it to extract concessions from Britain on neutral rights and Indian issues. Fearing that delay would permit Britain to reinforce its colony, Madison rejected London's proposals for a truce and urged vigorous prosecution of the war. "The sword once drawn, full justice must be done," Jefferson thundered from Monticello. " 'Indemnification for the past and security for the Future,' should be painted on our banners."[75]

As in previous crises, the aims of Republican strategy exceeded the means available to attain them. Canada *was* poorly defended and Britain *was* preoccupied with Europe, but the United States could not exploit these advantages. As a result of Republican frugality, the army had languished. Preparedness measures belatedly enacted by Congress after the declaration did little to rectify the deficiencies. The Madison administration attempted the unique experiment of sending an army to war without any staff organization. At the outset, the army consisted of but seven thousand men (more officers than soldiers), poorly trained and equipped and led by superannuated and incompetent commanders. The desertion rate was so high (often justified by lack of food and pay) that Madison pardoned deserters to fill rolls. Liberal dispensation of liquor and handsome

73. Quoted in Merrill D. Peterson, *The Great Triumvirate* (New York, 1987), 4. The generational concept is developed in Steven Watts, *The Republic Reborn: Politics, Diplomacy, and Warfare in the Early Republic, 1783–1830* (Baltimore, Md., 1987).
74. Rutland, *Madison*, 105. American battle deaths are numbered at 2,260. British and Canadian casualties have been estimated at 8,744, American at 7,738. Hickey, *War of 1812*, 302–3; Stanley, *War of 1812*, 433–34.
75. Dumas Malone, *The Sage of Monticello* (Boston, 1981), 105.

bounties failed to secure enough enlistments. The vaunted militia turned out to be disorganized and even cowardly. Some units simply refused to cross the border into Canada.[76]

Inadequately manned and poorly conceived, the much talked-about "holiday campaign" into Canada met disaster. British regulars supported by Tecumseh's Indians repulsed an invasion of Detroit in July 1812, removing any threat to Canada and leaving the American Northwest vulnerable. A later assault by the Niagara River met a similar fate. Its dreams of easy success quickly dashed, the United States found itself on the defensive.

During the first year and a half of the war, neither belligerent could gain the upper hand. Dismissed by some Royal Navy officers as a few ships "manned by a handful of bastards and out laws," the U.S. Navy acquitted itself honorably in individual encounters with British men-of-war. American privateers inflicted costly losses on enemy merchant shipping.[77] But the Royal Navy enforced a tight blockade of the U.S. coast, exacerbating economic problems. Raiding parties wreaked havoc among the seaboard population. On the Canadian frontier, U.S. Navy forces under Oliver Hazard Perry won a major victory on Lake Erie in September 1813. In October, Harrison inflicted a crushing defeat on the British and Indians at the battle of the Thames on the north shore of Lake Erie. The two victories, combined with Tecumseh's death in battle, eased the threat to the Old Northwest and even permitted a modest American incursion into Canada. In the meantime, a two-pronged U.S. invasion of Montreal was repulsed.

The fighting was not at all like the quaint eighteenth-century war Madison had foreseen. Action at the Thames was as savage as that in the especially brutal Peninsular War in Spain and Portugal. According to a British sailor who had seen both, the fire at Lake Erie made Trafalgar seem a "mere fleabite by comparison."[78] The Kentucky militia dressed in war paint and carried—and used—scalping knives. A British soldier described them as "wretches . . . capable of the greatest villainies." When Americans complained that British use of Indians led to atrocities, the British retorted that, after all, the Americans used Kentuckians.[79]

In 1814, America's position worsened measurably. Instead of relieving the nation's problems, the stalemated war compounded them. At least until Vietnam, the War of 1812 was easily the most unpopular conflict in

76. Stagg, *Madison's War*, 160–76.
77. Hickey, *War of 1812*, 135.
78. Quoted in ibid., 216.
79. Stanley, *War of 1812*, 208.

U.S. history, and Madison encountered enormous difficulties mobilizing his people. The British blockade denied the United States access to war materials from abroad. Creating domestic industries virtually from scratch posed nearly insuperable problems. Unable to find buyers for its bonds and reluctant for political reasons to raise taxes, the government faced near bankruptcy by 1814. The smuggling initiated during the embargo persisted in wartime in the form of trading with the enemy. "Self, the great ruling principle [is] more powerful with Yankees than any people I ever saw," sneered one British officer.[80] Many parts of the nation were decidedly apathetic toward the war. Open disaffection in Federalist New England was far more serious. Governors refused to order the militia beyond state borders. Congressmen attempted to block administration war measures. Extremists talked openly of seceding and creating an independent nation tied closely to England.

Developments abroad were even more ominous. Napoleon abdicated in April, and the imminent end of war in Europe permitted Britain to shift resources to North America. To exact revenge upon the United States, protect Canada, and improve its strategic position and bargaining power, Britain devised a three-pronged offensive: a diversionary strike in the Chesapeake Bay area, an invasion by Lake Champlain to isolate the disaffected northeastern states, and an attack on New Orleans to gain control of the Mississippi Valley. "Chastise the savages," thundered the London *Times*.[81]

To add to Madison's difficulties, formal Anglo-American peace negotiations were scheduled to begin just as the British launched their offensive. By the time the peace commissioners actually assembled in August 1814 in the British-controlled Flemish town of Ghent, Britain had gained the edge militarily. Its harsh demands reflected its change in fortunes. To repay their allies and protect Canada from the United States, the British demanded creation of an Indian buffer state comprising 250,000 square miles (about 15 percent of U.S. territory) between the Ohio River and the Great Lakes. They also insisted upon unrestricted access to the Mississippi, a northeastern boundary giving Canada a sizeable chunk of Maine, banishment of U.S. vessels from the Great Lakes, and exclusion of Americans from fishing grounds off Nova Scotia. London aimed to reverse major results of the 1783 Treaty of Paris.

In this supreme crisis, diplomacy salvaged for the United States what could not be won on the battlefield. Madison had already abandoned

80. Quoted in Hickey, *War of 1812*, 216.
81. Ibid., 182.

demands that Britain accept his position on neutral rights and impressment. The end of the European war seemed to make such issues irrelevant. Britain would relent only to the extent of a settlement on the basis of the *uti possidetis*, meaning that territory held at the time the war ended would go to the occupant. The U.S. delegation, headed by Clay, Gallatin, and John Quincy Adams, was perhaps the ablest ever put together by the nation. A master of card games—at Ghent he was often stumbling to bed about the time Adams was rising to pray—Clay sensed that the British were bluffing and persuaded his colleagues to stall. The delegation thus ignored Washington's instructions to break off the negotiations.[82]

Clay's high-stakes gamble paid off handsomely. In the last months of 1814, the U.S. position changed dramatically. In one of the most significant battles of the war, U.S. Navy forces under Capt. Thomas Macdonough destroyed an enemy fleet on Lake Champlain (September 11, 1814), giving the United States control of the lake and thwarting Britain's northeastern campaign. The British expedition into the Chesapeake Bay enjoyed initial success. Militia defending the makeshift capital at Bladensburg ran so fast they could not be captured. British forces entered and burned Washington, one of the most humiliating events in the nation's history.[83] The looting was left to American hooligans. But while poet Francis Scott Key watched and pondered and wrote what would later become the national anthem, a British attack on the vital commercial city of Baltimore was repulsed. The invaders retreated to their ships.

Luck once more smiled on the United States. The imminent breakdown of peace negotiations at Vienna and political turmoil in France threatened resumption of the European War. Faced with abandoning its inflated war aims in America or fighting an extended and costly war in which, according to the prime minister, Britain was "not likely to attain any glory or renown at all commensurate to the inconvenience it will occasion," London chose the better part of valor.[84] The negotiators signed a treaty on Christmas Eve. The next day they celebrated with beef, plum pudding, and toasts to the unlikely duo of George III and James Madison.

Dismissed as the "Treaty of Omissions" by a cynical French diplomat, the peace of Ghent accurately reflected the stalemate on the battlefield. It said nothing about impressment and other issues over which the United States had gone to war. Britain scrapped its vindictive and expansive war

82. Rutland, *Madison*, 170.
83. Ibid., 159–65.
84. Ibid., 177.

aims for the *status quo ante bellum*. The treaty fixed the northern boundary of the United States from the Lake of the Woods to the Rocky Mountains at the 49th parallel and referred the disputed northeastern boundary to arbitration. The U.S. delegation was itself bitterly divided on British demands regarding the Mississippi River and fisheries. The New Englander Adams was willing to trade British access to the Mississippi for the fisheries; Clay vehemently opposed sacrificing western interests. Not for the first time mediating among his contentious colleagues, the Swiss-born Gallatin proposed deferring these issues for future discussion, a wise decision as it turned out. The British went along.

Despite its inconclusive outcome, the War of 1812 had a huge impact on the future of North America. The United States had gone to war in 1812—as in 1775—confident of the dubious loyalty of British North Americans and even hopeful they might rally to appeals to throw off British "tyranny and oppression." Ironically, U.S. efforts to relieve Britain of its provinces and the bitter fighting along the border helped stimulate in Canada's disparate population a sense of cohesion and even nascent nationalism. The former Loyalists of Upper Canada, in particular, took enormous pride in repulsing the Yankee invaders, fueling an anti-Americanism that persisted into the future. The war gave Canadians a sense of their own distinct history and helped create a "national idea."[85]

The War of 1812 also sealed the tragic fate of Native Americans—the ultimate losers of a stalemated conflict. The Battle of the Thames opened the Northwest for U.S. expansion. The death of Tecumseh dashed fragile dreams of an Indian confederacy. In the South, conflict between those Creeks who sought accommodation with the United States and those who chose resistance exploded in July 1813 into war. The Americans invaded the Creek nation from three directions, destroying villages and inflicting heavy losses. At Horseshoe Bend in March 1814, Andrew Jackson's militia crushed the Creeks and their Cherokee allies, killing close to a thousand braves, causing even that hardened Indian fighter to admit that "the carnage was dreadfull." In all, some three thousand Creeks were killed, 15 percent of the population. "My people are no more!" the half-breed Creek leader William Weatherford lamented.[86] In the subsequent Treaty of Fort Jackson, imposed on accommodationist Creeks over bitter objections, the Indians surrendered without any compensation twenty-five million acres, roughly half their land, and forswore any future contact with the British and Spanish. The Treaty of Ghent was to restore the

85. Stanley, *War of 1812*, 411–12.
86. Quoted in Hickey, *War of 1812*, 151.

status quo ante bellum in Indian affairs and might have been interpreted as nullifying the earlier Treaty of Fort Jackson, but in fact both were ratified the same day. As a result of the War of 1812, foreign nations would never intercede with the Indians again, depriving them of what little leverage they had. The Indians would never again threaten U.S. expansion. From this point, the United States imposed its will on them. Councils were no longer matters of sovereign nations negotiating on the basis of rough equality. By the force of events, if not of law and equity, Indian affairs became a matter of domestic policy rather than foreign relations for the United States. The War of 1812 opened the way for removal of the Indians and their destruction as a people.[87]

Although the United States had achieved none of its aims and barely averted disaster, the war marked a major step in its development. With peace in Europe, the issues that had led to war lost their significance. It would be another fifty years—and with the roles reversed—before questions of neutral rights would resurface. The United States had survived a major challenge without external assistance, demonstrating to a skeptical Europe that hopes of its imminent collapse were unfounded. Henceforth, Europeans would treat the new nation with greater respect.

Probably most important was the impact on the national psyche. From 1783 to 1814, Europeans had subjected the United States to repeated indignities and challenged its existence as an independent nation. At home, Federalists questioned the validity of the government's principles and defied its authority. Many Republicans themselves began to doubt whether a government such as theirs could survive in a hostile world. The nation's demonstrated ability to withstand the test of war eased growing self doubts. Twenty-six Federalist delegates from the New England states had assembled at Hartford, Connecticut, in December 1814 to consider demands to be made to the national government. The news from Ghent and New Orleans rendered the Hartford Convention irrelevant and made it the butt of national ridicule. The Federalist party was discredited, never to recover. The Republican party emerged from the war more firmly entrenched, its prestige greatly increased. National unity was enhanced. "They are more Americans," Gallatin observed of his adopted countrymen, "they feel and act more as a nation."[88] Through that remarkable process by which memory becomes history, the repeated embarrassments

87. Michael D. Green, *The Creeks* (New York, 1990), 50–53; Francis Paul Prucha, *American Indian Treaties: The History of a Political Anomaly* (Berkeley, 1994), 129–32.
88. Quoted in Rutland, *Madison*, 188.

and near disaster that had marked the war were forgotten. Victories over the world's greatest power avenged old wrongs and restored national self-confidence. In particular, the decisive victory of Jackson's strange assortment of frontiersmen, pirates, free blacks, Creoles, and Indians over eight thousand seasoned British veterans in the monthlong Battle of New Orleans was seen as confirming the superiority of virtuous republican militiamen over European conscripts. Americans learned of New Orleans and the Treaty of Ghent at about the same time, and this sudden turn of events had a huge psychological impact. "Never did a country occupy more lofty ground," Massachusetts Republican and Supreme Court Justice Joseph Story exclaimed with unrestrained hyperbole. "We have stood the contest single-handed against the conqueror of Europe."[89] "What is our present situation?" Clay asked in jubilation. "Respectability and character abroad—security and confidence at home. . . . Our character and Constitution are placed on a solid basis, never to be shaken."[90] The War of 1812 thus "passed into history not as a futile and costly struggle in which the United States barely escaped dismemberment and disunion, but as a glorious triumph in which the nation had single-handedly defeated the conqueror of Napoleon and the Mistress of the Seas."[91] Now resting on a firm foundation, the United States was poised for conquest of the continent.

89. Quoted in ibid., 189.
90. Perkins, *Prologue to War*, 435.
91. Hickey, *War of 1812*, 299–309.

4

"Leave the Rest to Us"

The Assertive Republic, 1815–1837

During a tense exchange on January 27, 1821, Secretary of State John Quincy Adams and the British minister to the United States, Stratford Canning, debated the future of North America. Emphasizing the extravagance of Britain's worldwide pretensions, Adams pointedly remarked: "I do not know what you claim nor what you do not claim. You claim India; you claim Africa; you claim—" "Perhaps," Canning sarcastically interjected, "a piece of the moon." Adams conceded he knew of no British interest in acquiring the moon, but, he went on to say, "there is not a spot on *this* habitable globe that I could affirm you do not claim." When he dismissed Britain's title to the Oregon country, implying doubts about all its holdings in North America, an alarmed Canning inquired whether the United States questioned his nation's position in Canada. No, Adams retorted. "Keep what is yours and leave the rest of the continent to us."[1]

That a U.S. diplomat should address a representative of the world's most powerful nation in such tones suggests how far the United States had come since 1789 when Britain refused even to send a minister to its former colony. Adams's statement also expressed the spirit of the age and affirmed its central foreign policy objective. Through individual initiative and government action, Americans after the War of 1812 became even more assertive in foreign policy. They challenged the European commercial system and sought to break down trade barriers. Above all, they poised themselves to take control of North America and seized every opportunity to remove any obstacle. Indeed, only to the powerful British would they concede the right to "keep what is yours." They gave Spaniards, Indians, and Mexicans no such consideration.

I

The quest for continental empire took place in an international setting highly favorable to the United States. Through the balance-of-power

---

1. Quoted in Samuel Flagg Bemis, *John Quincy Adams and the Foundations of American Foreign Policy* (New York, 1973), 491–92.

system, the Europeans maintained a precarious stability for nearly a century after Waterloo. The absence of a major war eased the threat of foreign intervention that had imperiled the very existence of the United States during its early years. Europe's imperial urge did not slacken, and from 1800 to 1878 the amount of territory under its control almost doubled.[2] But the focus shifted from the Americas to Asia and Africa. The Europeans accorded the United States a newfound, if still grudging, respect. Britain and, to a lesser extent, France clung to vague hopes of containing U.S. expansion but exerted little effort to do so. Periodic European crises distracted them from North America. The vulnerability of Canada and growing importance of U.S. raw materials and markets to Britain's industrial revolution constrained its interference. While Americans continued to fret nervously about the English menace, the Royal Navy protected the hemisphere from outside intervention, freeing the United States from alliances and a large military establishment. The nation enjoyed a rare period of "free" security in which to develop without major external threats.[3]

Revolutions in South America during and after the Napoleonic wars provided opportunities and posed dangers for the United States. Sentiment for independence had long simmered on the continent. When Napoleon took control of Spain and Portugal in 1808, rebellion erupted. A new republic emerged in Buenos Aires. Revolutionary leaders Simón Bolívar and Francisco de Miranda led revolts in Colombia and Venezuela, forming a short-lived republic of New Granada. After 1815, revolutions broke out in Chile, Mexico, Brazil, Gran Colombia, and Central America. Many North Americans sympathized with the revolutions. Speaker of the House Henry Clay hailed the "glorious spectacle of eighteen millions of peoples, struggling to burst their chains and to be free."[4] Some saw opportunities for a lucrative trade. Preoccupied with its own crises and eager to gain Spanish territory, the United States remained neutral, but in a way that favored the rebellious colonies. Madison and Monroe cautiously

2. Paul Kennedy, *The Rise and Fall of the Great Powers* (New York, 1987), 150, 160; Stephen Pelz, "Changing International Systems, the World Balance of Power, and the United States, 1776–1976," *Diplomatic History* 15 (Winter 1991), 51–63.

3. Charles Sellers, *The Market Revolution: Jacksonian America* (New York, 1991), 93; for U.S. nervousness about British territorial and commercial expansion, see Kinley J. Brauer, "The United States and British Imperial Expansion, 1815–1860," *Diplomatic History* 12 (Winter 1988), 19–37.

4. Quoted in Kyle Longley, *In the Eagle's Shadow: The United States and Latin America* (Wheeling, Ill., 2002), 38.

withheld recognition. United States officials feared Spain might attempt to recover its colonies or Britain might seek to acquire them, threatening another round of European intervention.

After 1815, the United States surged to the level of a second-rank power. By 1840, much of the territory extending to the Mississippi River had been settled; the original thirteen states had doubled to twenty-six. As the result of immigration and a high birth rate—what nationalists exuberantly labeled "the American multiplication table"—a population that had doubled between 1789 and 1815 doubled again between 1820 and 1840. Despite major depressions in 1819 and 1837, the nation experienced phenomenal economic growth. An enterprising merchant marine monopolized the coastal trade and challenged Britain's preeminence in international commerce. Wheat and corn production proliferated in the Northwest. Cotton supplanted tobacco as the South's staple crop and the nation's top export. The cotton boom resuscitated a moribund institution of slavery and added pressures for territorial expansion. Indeed, slavery and expansion merged in the prolonged political crisis over admission of Missouri to the Union in 1819—Thomas Jefferson's "fire bell in the night" that raised in a more ominous form the old threat of disunion. The crisis was resolved and disunion perhaps thwarted by the Missouri Compromise of 1820 that admitted Maine as a free state and Missouri as a slave state and prohibited slavery in the Louisiana Purchase territory north of 36° 30'.

Between 1820 and 1840, the U.S. economy began to mature. Construction of roads and canals brought scattered communities together and, along with the steamboat, shrank distances. These innovations dramatically transformed the predominantly agricultural, subsistence economy of Jefferson's time. Americans increasingly prided themselves on political separation from Europe, but the United States was an integral part of an Atlantic-centered international economy. European capital and technology fueled U.S. economic growth. Particularly in agriculture, the nation produced far more than could be consumed at home. Commerce with Europe remained essential to its prosperity.[5]

Purposeful leaders actively employing the organized power of the national government pushed this process along. Republican ideology was tempered by the exigencies of war. Shortages of critical items forced even Jefferson to concede the necessity of manufactures. Clay went further, promoting an "American System" that aimed at national self-sufficiency by developing domestic manufactures and expanding the home market through such Federalist devices as protective tariffs, a national bank, and federally financed internal improvements. Some Republicans clung to the Jeffersonian vision of a virtuous republic of small farmers. But with the market revolution, new National Republicans dreamed of national wealth and power based on commercial and territorial expansion. Like Clay, they adopted a neo-mercantilist approach that sought to expand

5. See especially Daniel Walker Howe, *What Hath God Wrought: The Transformation of America, 1815–1848* (New York, 2007), 46–48.

exports of agricultural and raw materials and protect domestic manufactures through tariffs.[6]

The War of 1812 gave a tremendous boost to nationalism. Americans entered the postwar era more optimistic than ever. Their faith in themselves and their nation's destiny knew few bounds. Their boastful pride in their own institutions often annoyed visitors. "A foreigner will gladly agree to praise much in their country," the perceptive Frenchman Alexis de Tocqueville complained, "but he would like to be allowed to criticize something and that he is absolutely refused." "I love national glory," one congressman exulted.[7] American horizons broadened. Even the optimistic Jefferson could envision nothing more than a series of independent republics in North America. His successor as the architect of U.S. expansion, John Quincy Adams, foresaw a single nation stretching from Atlantic to Pacific. As secretary of state and president he worked tirelessly to realize this destiny.

The quality of American statecraft remained high in the postwar era. Most policymakers had acquired practical experience in the school of diplomatic hard knocks. Cosmopolitan representatives of a still provincial republic, they generally acquitted themselves with distinction. The last—usually viewed as the least—of the Virginia Dynasty, James Monroe was an experienced and capable diplomatist. Described by contemporaries as a "plain man" with "good heart and amiable disposition," he was industrious, a shrewd judge of people and problems, and excelled at getting strong-willed men to work together.[8]

Monroe's secretary of state, John Quincy Adams, towered above his contemporaries and is generally regarded among the most effective of all those who have held the office. The son of a diplomat and president, Adams brought to his post a wealth of experience and extraordinary skills. He knew six European languages. His seventeen years abroad gave him unparalleled knowledge of the workings of European diplomacy. A man of prodigious industry, he oversaw, with the assistance of eight clerks, the workings of the State Department, writing most dispatches himself and creating a filing system that would be used until 1915. He regularly rose before dawn to pray. His early morning swims in the Potomac, clad only in green goggles and a skullcap, were the stuff of Washington legend. Short, stout, and balding, with a wandering eye—his frequent adversary

6. Ibid., 270–76, 283.
7. Sellers, *Market Revolution*, 76.
8. Noble E. Cunningham Jr., *The Presidency of James Monroe* (Lawrence, Kans., 1996), 187.

Stratford Canning called him "Squinty"—Adams could be cold and aus-
tere. Throughout his life, he struggled to live up to the high expectations
set by his illustrious parents, John and Abigail. Haunted by self-doubt and
fears of failure, he drove himself relentlessly. He was proud that his foes
found him an "unsocial savage." Through force of intellect and mastery
of detail he was a diplomat of enormous skill.[9]

Adams was also an ardent expansionist whose vision of American destiny was well ahead of his time. A profoundly religious man, he saw the
United States as the instrument of God's will and himself as the agent of
both. Sensitive to the needs of the shipping and mercantile interests of his
native New England, he viewed free trade as the basis for a new global
economic order. He fought doggedly to break down mercantilist barriers.
His vision extended literally to the ends of the earth. He relished in 1820
the possibility of a confrontation with Britain over newly discovered Graham Land on the northwest coast of Antarctica, a region he conceded
was "something between Rock and Iceberg."[10]

The focus of Adams's attention was North America. As early as 1811, he
had foreseen a time when all of the continent would be "one nation,
speaking one language, professing one general system of religious and political principles, and accustomed to one general tenor of social usage
and customs." That the United States in time should acquire Canada and
Texas, he believed, was "as much the law of nature as that the Mississippi
should flow to the sea." He told the cabinet in 1822 that "the world should
become familiarized with the idea of considering our proper dominion to
be the entire continent of North America." As secretary of state, he took
giant steps toward achieving that goal. As president from 1825 to 1829,
he—with his own secretary of state, Clay—continued to pursue it.[11]

Monroe introduced important modifications to U.S. diplomatic practice. In keeping with republican principles, he instructed his envoys to
"respectfully but decisively" decline the gifts that were the lubricant of
European diplomacy. Adams recommended that individuals who had
served abroad for more than six years should return home to be "new
tempered."[12] At the same time, Monroe had suffered numerous slights at

9. Bemis, Adams, 255–57, 262–77; William Earl Weeks, John Quincy Adams and Ameri-
    can Global Empire (Lexington, Ky., 1992), 9–17, 52–61.
10. Cunningham, Monroe, 119.
11. Walter LaFeber, ed., John Quincy Adams and American Continental Empire
    (Chicago, 1965), 36; Dexter Perkins, A History of the Monroe Doctrine (rev. ed.,
    Boston, 1963), 28.
12. Bemis, Adams, 264.

the hands of the great powers during his own diplomatic career, and he was eager to command their respect. Persuaded that Jefferson's pell-mell "protocol" had lowered American prestige among Europeans, he reverted to the more formal practice of Washington, receiving foreign envoys by appointment and in full diplomatic dress. U.S. diplomats wore a "uniform," a blue cloth coat with silk lining and gold or silver embroidery, and a plumed hat. When Monroe took office, the capital still showed scars of the British invasion. When he left, the city's appearance and social life had begun to rival European capitals, achieving a "splendour which is really astonishing," according to one American participant. As much as Jefferson's style had symbolized the republican simplicity of an earlier era, Monroe's marked the rise of the United States to new wealth and power.[13]

The formulation of policy changed little under Monroe and Adams. Monroe employed Washington's cabinet system, submitting major foreign policy issues for the full consideration of department heads. The demise of Federalism after 1815 left only one party for the next decade, but foreign policy remained an area of heated political battle. The so-called Era of Good Feelings was anything but. Throughout the administrations of Monroe and Adams, ambitious cabinet members exploited foreign policy issues to gain an edge on potential rivals. As the economy expanded and diversified, interest groups pushed their demands on the government. In the 1820s, foreign policy, like everything else, became locked in the bitter sectional struggle over slavery. By 1824, partisan politics was back with a vengeance as the followers of war hero Andrew Jackson challenged the Republican ascendancy.

II

Monroe's and Adams's administrations set commercial expansion as a paramount goal and employed numerous distinctly unrepublican measures to achieve it. Abandoning Jefferson's disdain for diplomats, they expanded the number of U.S. missions abroad. Between 1820 and 1830, they almost doubled the number of consuls, many of them assigned to the newly independent governments of Latin America. These men performed numerous and sometimes difficult tasks, looking after the interests of U.S. citizens and especially merchants, negotiating trade treaties, and seeking out commercial opportunities. When fire devastated Ha-

13. Cunningham, *Monroe*, 133–37; Robert Ralph Davis Jr., "Diplomatic Plumage: American Court Dress in the Early National Period," *American Quarterly* 20, no. 1 (1968), 170–71.

vana, Cuba, in 1826, for example, consul Thomas Rodney alerted Americans to the newly created market for building materials.[14] The National Republicans also put aside traditional fears of the navy, maintaining a sizeable fleet after the War of 1812 and employing it to protect and promote U.S. commerce. Squadrons of small, fast warships were posted to the Mediterranean, the West Indies, Africa, and the Pacific, where they defended U.S. shipping from pirates and privateers, policed the illegal slave trade, and looked for new commercial opportunities. While sailing the Pacific station during the 1820s, Thomas ap Catesby Jones, commander of the USS *Peacock*, negotiated trade treaties with Tahiti and the Hawaiian Islands.[15]

Monroe and Adams also pushed to secure payment of claims from the spoliation of American commerce, not simply for the money but also as a matter of principle. Payment of such claims would at least imply endorsement of the U.S. position on free trade and neutral rights. The United States pressed France for payment of more than $6 million for seizure of ships and cargoes under Napoleonic decrees and sought additional claims against smaller European states acting under French authority. It tried to collect money from Russia and, during Adams's presidency in particular, from the Latin American governments, most of the claims arising from privateering and other alleged violations of neutral rights by governments or rebels or in disputes between governments during the wars of independence. United States diplomats vigorously defended the nation's interests. Before demanding his passports (a diplomatic practice indicating extreme displeasure that often preceded the breaking of relations), the colorful consul to Rio de Janeiro, Condy Raguet, exclaimed that if U.S. ships wanted to break Brazil's blockade of the Rio de la Plata they would not ask permission and would be stopped only "by force of balls."[16]

Monroe and Adams used reciprocity as a major weapon of commercial expansion. In its last days, the Madison administration launched an all-out attack on the restrictive trading policies of the European powers. Responding to the president's call to secure for the United States a "just

14. Peter T. Dalleo, "Thomas Kean Rodney: U.S. Consul in Cuba: The Havana Years, 1825–1829," *Delaware History* 22 (Spring/Summer 1987): 204–18; David W. McFadden, "John Quincy Adams, American Commercial Diplomacy, and Russia, 1809–1825," *New England Quarterly* 66 (December 1993), 620–22.

15. John H. Schroeder, *Shaping a Maritime Empire: The Commercial and Diplomatic Role of the American Navy, 1829–1861* (Westport, Conn., 1985), 15–18.

16. Mary W. M. Hargreaves, *The Presidency of John Quincy Adams* (Lawrence, Kans., 1985), 73.

proportion of the navigation of the world," Congress in 1815 enacted reciprocity legislation that legalized the program of discrimination Jefferson and Madison had advocated since 1789. Passed in a mood of exuberant nationalism, the measure made the abolition of discriminatory duties and shipping charges contingent on similar concessions from other countries. Reciprocity was designed to strengthen the hands of U.S. diplomats in negotiations with European powers. As opposed to the most-favored-nation principle, the basis for earlier treaties, it provided, in Clay's words, a "plain and familiar rule" for the two signatories, uncomplicated by deals with other nations, thus reducing the chances for misunderstanding and conflict.[17] Reciprocity also made clear U.S. willingness to retaliate. Americans and Europeans increasingly recognized, moreover—the latter sometimes to their chagrin—that reciprocity did not always operate equally on all parties. Such was the superiority of the U.S. merchant marine and mercantile skill that often, as a diplomat pointed out, American shippers could secure a monopoly of trade "whenever anything like fair and equal terms [are] extended to us."[18] Through the 1820s, the United States used reciprocity to break down European commercial restrictions and gain access on favorable terms to newly opened markets in Latin America and elsewhere across the world.

For the effort expended, the Monroe-Adams trade offensive produced limited results. The United States settled a small claims dispute with Russia, but not much else. Negotiations with France provoked a nasty diplomatic spat. The United States pushed these claims with great vigor, at one point even discussing naval retaliation. Their treasury exhausted from years of war, the French perceived that if they paid the United States other claimants would get in line. Thus they stalled, reminding U.S. officials that loans made by French citizens during the American Revolution remained unpaid. The issue persisted into the Jackson administration, poisoning relations between onetime allies.[19]

In all, Monroe and Adams concluded twelve commercial agreements. They managed to secure reciprocity with Britain in direct commerce, giving the United States a huge advantage in the North Atlantic carrying trade. They concluded a most-favored-nation treaty with Russia in 1824 and reciprocity agreements with several smaller European nations. On the other hand, U.S. support for the Greek revolution thwarted negotia-

17. Quoted in ibid., 76.
18. Quoted in Paul A. Varg, *United States Foreign Relations, 1820–1860* (East Lansing, Mich., 1979), 75.
19. Hargreaves, *Adams*, 70–72.

tions with Turkey. Once again, discussions with France were especially frustrating. The United States attempted to batter down France's commercial restrictions by imposing discriminatory duties, provoking a brief but bitter trade war. A limited commercial treaty negotiated in 1822 left most major issues unresolved.[20]

Adams and Clay entertained high hopes for trade with Latin America and invested great energy in negotiations with that region, but they achieved little. For reasons of race and politics, more than economics, southerners continued to block trade with Haiti. Raguet's provocative behavior killed a treaty with Brazil, and no treaties were negotiated with Buenos Aires, Chile, or Peru. Minister Joel Poinsett's blatant meddling in Mexican politics, as well as major differences on issues of reciprocity, limited the treaty negotiated in 1826 to most-favored-nation status. It was not ratified until much later. Clay did conclude a treaty with the Central American Federation, a political grouping of the region's five states, something he viewed as his greatest accomplishment as secretary of state and a model for a new world trading system. The federation collapsed within a short time, however, and Clay's dreams died with it.[21]

Most frustrating was U.S. inability to open the British West Indies. Since the Revolution, Americans had sought access to the lucrative triangular trade with Britain's island colonies. London clung stubbornly to restrictive policies. In the commercial convention of 1815, Britain limited American imports to a small number of specified goods and required that they come in British ships. With large numbers of its own vessels rotting at the docks, the United States retaliated. A Navigation Act of 1817 limited imports from the West Indies to U.S. ships. The following year, Congress closed America's ports to ships from any colony where its ships were excluded. Seeking to get at the West Indies through Canada, the United States in 1820 imposed virtual non-intercourse on Britain's North American colonies. The issue took on growing emotional significance. Americans protested British efforts to gain "ascendancy over every nation in every market of the world."[22] Britons feared for their merchant marine and fretted about U.S. penetration of the empire. Even the normally conciliatory prime minister Lord Castlereagh insisted he would let the West Indies starve rather than abandon the colonial system.

Mainly because of U.S. intransigence, the conflict stalemated. Under pressure from West Indian planters and the emerging industrial class,

20. Ibid., 68, 72, 85–86.
21. Ibid., 77–84.
22. Quoted in Varg, *United States Foreign Relations*, 63.

Britain in 1822 opened a number of West Indian ports with only modest duties. Three years later, it offered to crack the door still wider if the United States would drop duties on British ships entering its ports. As secretary of state and president, Adams stubbornly persisted in trying to end the British imperial preference system, perhaps with the notion, as one of his New England constituents put it, that with full reciprocity the United States could "successfully compete with any nation on earth."[23] Even the British free trader William Huskinson denounced the U.S. position as a "pretension unheard of in the commercial relations of independent states."[24] When the United States refused to remove its duties, the British closed their West Indian ports. At this point, the issue became entangled in presidential politics. Jackson's supporters in Congress frustrated the administration's efforts to reopen negotiations, leaving Adams no choice but to reimpose restrictions on Britain. The Jacksonians ridiculed "Our diplomatic President," who, they claimed, had destroyed "colonial intercourse with Great Britain."[25] By this time the West Indian trade had declined in practical importance, but it remained a major symbol of the clash of empires. Neither would give in.

III

Although much stronger after the War of 1812, the United States still faced threats around its periphery. The European political situation was potentially explosive. The Latin American revolutions brought dangers as well as possible advantages. The world's greatest power remained in Canada with a long border contested at various points. Americans continued to fear British intrusion in the Pacific Northwest and Central America. The boundaries of the vast Louisiana territory were hotly disputed. For years, Spain had refused to recognize the legality of the purchase. Even after conceding on that issue, it sought to confine the United States east of the Mississippi. The United States claimed at times from the Louisiana acquisition the Floridas, Texas, and even the Oregon territory. Madison had returned East Florida to Spain in 1813. Spain's continued presence there, along with hostile Indian tribes, menaced the southern United States. In 1815, Americans still viewed the outside world with trepidation. While postponing some disputes in hopes that delay would work to their benefit, U.S. leaders continued to pursue security through expan-

---

23. Quoted in Hargreaves, *Adams*, 97.
24. Quoted in George Dangerfield, *The Awakening of American Nationalism, 1815–1828* (New York, 1965), 157.
25. Robert Remini, *Henry Clay: Statesman for the Union* (New York, 1991), 309.

sion. In the case of Spain, Monroe and Adams enjoyed predictable success, negotiating at gunpoint a treaty securing not only the Floridas but also Spanish claims to the Pacific Northwest.

The War of 1812 underscored the importance of the Floridas, reinforced U.S. covetousness, and strengthened the nation's already advantageous position. Britain's wartime invasion of West Florida, its alliances with southwestern Indians, and its rumored plans to incite slave revolts in the southern United States all highlighted how essential it was to gain a land often likened to a pistol pointed at the nation's heart. Spain was further weakened by the Napoleonic wars. Americans believed that the long-sought territory might be detached with relative ease.[26]

Even when the outcome is obvious, negotiations can be difficult. The terms on which the Floridas would come to the United States were important to both nations. Spain was prepared to abandon a colony it could not defend, but it hoped to protect its territories in Texas and California against the onrushing Americans and naively counted on British support. When negotiations began in early 1818, the able Spanish minister Don Luis de Onis proposed setting the western boundary of the United States at the Mississippi River. He also sought a U.S. pledge not to recognize the new Latin American republics. Monroe and Adams insisted on a line following the Colorado River into what is now northern Texas and from there north along the 104th parallel to the Rocky Mountains. The United States was willing to delay Latin American recognition, perceiving that doing so might complicate acquisition of the Floridas or even encourage European intervention to restore monarchical governments. On the other hand, a public pledge of non-recognition would antagonize new nations with whom the United States hoped to establish a thriving commerce and anger people like Clay who sympathized with the Latin Americans. The negotiations quickly deadlocked.[27]

At this point, the United States began to apply not so subtle pressure against the hapless Madrid government. Under Spain's lax administration, the Floridas had become a volatile no-man's-land, a center for international intrigue and illicit commercial activities, a refuge for those fleeing oppression—and justice. The area had more than its share of pirates, renegades, and outlaws, as U.S. officials charged, but it also attracted other people, many with legitimate grievances against the United States.

26. William Earl Weeks, *Building the Continental Empire: American Expansion from the Revolution to the Civil War* (Chicago, 1996), 32–34.
27. Weeks, *Adams*, 71–80.

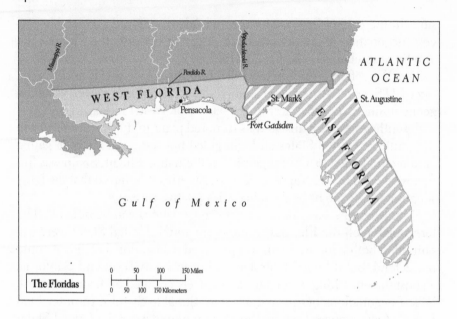

Latin American rebels used Atlantic and Gulf Coast ports to stage military operations against Spanish forces. Fugitive slaves sought escape from bondage. After the 1814 Treaty of Fort Jackson, Creeks expelled from their lands fled into the Floridas, some hoping to exact retribution against the United States. Outraged when the United States purchased from the Creeks lands they claimed and then forcibly removed them, the Seminoles launched a bloody war. Conflict thus raged along the Florida border. Americans drew a picture of outlaws attacking innocent settlers. In reality, all parties contributed to the melee.[28]

Under intense pressure from nervous settlers in the Southwest and land speculators who feared for their investments, the Monroe administration mounted military expeditions to quell the violence that could also be used as leverage in negotiations with Spain. In December 1817, the president authorized seizure of Amelia Island from Latin American rebels whose presence threatened eventual U.S. control. Shortly after, he authorized Gen. Andrew Jackson to invade Florida and "pacify" the Seminoles.

The nature of Jackson's instructions aroused bitter controversy. In a letter to Monroe, the general indicated that if given the go-ahead he

28. Ibid., 142.

could seize Florida within sixty days. When his behavior later provoked outrage at home and abroad, he insisted that he had received this authority. Monroe adamantly denied giving Jackson such orders, leaving critics to charge that the general had acted impetuously and illegally. Although Monroe seems not to have sent the requested signal, he did give the general "full powers to conduct the war in the manner he may judge best." The president had long favored forcibly dislodging Spain from Florida. He knew Jackson well enough to predict what he might do when unleashed. Thus, although he never sent explicit instructions, he gave the general virtual carte blanche and left himself free to disavow Jackson if he went too far.[29]

Whatever his instructions, this "Napoleon de bois," as the Spanish called him, moved with a decisiveness that likely shocked Monroe. A lifelong Indian fighter whose code of pacification was "An eye for an eye, a toothe for a toothe, a scalp for a scalp," Jackson hated Spaniards even more than native peoples. He had long believed that U.S. security demanded that the "Wolf be struck in his den." Indeed, he preferred simply to take the Floridas.[30] With a force of some three thousand regulars and state militia along with several thousand Creek allies, he plunged across the border. Unable to bring the Seminoles to battle, he destroyed their villages and seized livestock and stores of food, crippling their resistance. Claiming to act on the "immutable principle of self-defense," he occupied Spanish forts at St. Marks and Pensacola. At St. Marks, he captured a kindly Scots trader named Alexander Arbuthnot, whose principal offense was to have befriended the Seminoles, and a British soldier of fortune, Richard Armbrister, who was assisting Seminole resistance to the United States. Jackson had long believed that such troublemakers "must feel the keenness of the scalping knife which they excite." He vowed to deal with them "with the greatest rigor known to civilized Warfare."[31] Accusing the two men of "wickedness, corruption, and barbarity at which the heart sickens," he tried and executed them on the spot. Arbuthnot was hanged from the yardarm of his own ship, appropriately named *The*

29. Ibid., 109; Sellers, *Market Revolution*, 98.
30. Jackson to George Graham, December 17, 1817, in Harold D. Moser, ed., *The Papers of Andrew Jackson*, vol. 2 (Knoxville, Tenn., 1994), 161.
31. Jackson to Graham, April 22, 1817, ibid., 111–12. See also David Heidler and Jeanne Heidler, *Old Hickory's War: Andrew Jackson's Quest for Empire* (Mechanicsburg, Pa., 1996).

Chance. The hastily assembled military court at first shied away from a death sentence for Armbrister. Jackson restored it. This trial of two British subjects before an American military court on Spanish territory was an unparalleled example of frontier justice in action. "I have destroyed the babylon of the South," Jackson excitedly wrote his wife. With reinforcements, he informed Washington, he could take St. Augustine and "I will insure you cuba in a few days."[32]

Jackson's escapade provoked loud outcries. Spain demanded his punishment, indemnity, and the restoration of seized property. Angry British citizens urged reprisals for the execution of Arbuthnot and Armbrister. Clay proposed that Jackson be punished for violating domestic and international law. Panicky cabinet members pressed Monroe to disavow his general.

In fact, Monroe and especially Adams skillfully exploited what Adams called the "Jackson magic" to pry a favorable treaty from Spain. Adams correctly surmised that Spanish protests were mostly bluff. To permit them to retreat with honor, Monroe agreed to return the captured forts. But the United States also demanded that Spain strike a deal quickly or risk losing everything for nothing in return. The United States also threatened to recognize the Latin American nations. In a series of powerful state papers, Adams vigorously defended Jackson's conduct on grounds that Spain's inability to maintain order compelled the United States to do so. He warned the British that if they expected their citizens to escape the fate of Arbuthnot and Armbrister they must prevent them from engaging in acts hostile to the United States. Adams's spirited defense of Jackson played fast and loose with the facts and provided a classic example, repeated often in the nation's history, of justifying an act of aggression in terms of morality, national mission, and destiny. It marked an expedient act on the part of a man known for commitment to principle. It facilitated the expansion of slavery and Indian removal, two evils Adams would spend his later life fighting.[33] It also had the desired effect, breaking the back of domestic opposition, forestalling British intervention, and persuading Spain to come to terms.

The two nations reached a settlement in February 1819. Monroe abandoned his demand for Texas, perceiving that its acquisition would exacerbate an already dangerous domestic crisis over slavery in the Missouri territory. Instead, on Adams's suggestion, the United States asked for Span-

---

32. Jackson to Rachel Jackson, June 2, 1818, ibid., 212–13; to James Monroe, June 2, 1818, ibid., 215.
33. Weeks, *Adams*, 139.

ish claims to the Pacific Northwest, territory also claimed by Britain and Russia. Onis at first hesitated. But in the face of U.S. adamancy and without British support, he backed down. The so-called Transcontinental Treaty left Texas in the hands of Spain but acquired for the United States unchallenged title to all of the Floridas and Spanish claims to the Pacific Northwest. The United States agreed to pay some $5 million U.S. citizens insisted they were owed by the Spanish government. The heartland of the United States was at last secure against foreign threat. A weak U.S. claim to the Pacific Northwest was greatly strengthened against a stronger British claim by acquiring Spanish interests, the most valid of the three. Even before Americans became accustomed to thinking of a republic west of the Mississippi, Adams had secured Spanish recognition of a nation extending to the Pacific and made a first move toward gaining a share of East Asian commerce.[34] Taking justifiable pride in his handiwork, he hailed in his diary a "great epocha in our history" and offered "fervent gratitude to the Giver of all Good."[35] He might also have thanked Andrew Jackson.

The United States also aggressively challenged British and Russian pretensions in the Pacific Northwest. Anglo-American relations improved markedly after the War of 1812. Recognizing a growing commonality of economic and political interests, the former enemies negotiated a limited trade agreement, began the difficult process of fixing a Canadian boundary, and, through the Rush-Bagot agreement of 1817 providing for reduction of armaments on the Great Lakes, averted a potentially dangerous naval arms race. The ever alert Adams also pried from Britain acceptance of the *alternat*, a diplomatic practice providing that the names of the two nations would be alternated when used together in the text of treaties, a symbolic achievement of no small importance.[36]

While moving toward rapprochement, the established imperial power and its upstart competitor also vied for preeminence in the Pacific Northwest. Many observers dismissed the mountainous Oregon country with its rocky, windblown coastline as bleak and inhospitable. Others, Adams included, saw the ports of Puget Sound and the prevalence of sea otters as keys to capturing the fabled East Asian trade. At the insistence of merchant prince John Jacob Astor, the United States after the War of 1812 reasserted claims to the mouth of the Columbia River abandoned during

34. Ibid., 178.
35. Quoted in Bemis, *Adams*, 338–39.
36. The standard account of the postwar Anglo-American rapprochement is Bradford Perkins, *Castlereagh and Adams: England and the United States, 1812–1823* (Berkeley, Calif., 1964). For the importance of the *alternat*, see Bemis, *Adams*, 225–27.

The Transcontinental Treaty Line of 1819

From the mouth of the Sabine River to latitude 32 degrees, thence north to the Red River and along its course, turning north at the 100th meridian to the Arkansas River and following it to its source, thence north to the 42nd parallel and due west along it to the Pacific Ocean.

ATLANTIC OCEAN

Gulf of Mexico

PACIFIC OCEAN

(CANADA)

(MEXICO)

Lake Ontario

Lake Erie

Lake Huron

Lake Michigan

Lake Superior

Lake of the Woods

St. Lawrence R.

Ohio R.

Mississippi R.

Missouri R.

Platte R.

Arkansas R.

Red R.

Trinity R.

Colorado R.

Sabine R.

Colorado R.

Perdido R.

Rio Grande

Colorado R.

Snake R.

Columbia R.

Multnomah R.

Transcontinental Treaty Line of 1819

| 0 | 100 | 200 | 300 Miles |
| 0 | 200 | 300 Kilometers |

the war. The aggressive Adams also sought to further U.S. interests by extending the boundary with Canada along the 49th parallel to the Pacific, a move that would have left Puget Sound, the Columbia River basin, and the Oregon country in U.S. hands. Britain would not go this far. Nor did it wish to confront the United States. In the Anglo-American Convention of 1818, the two nations agreed to leave the Oregon country open to both countries for ten years, tacitly accepting the legitimacy of U.S. claims. Persuaded that America was poised to extend its "civilization and laws to the western confines of the continent," Secretary of War and then ardent nationalist John C. Calhoun in 1817 drew up plans to locate a string of forts extending to the mouth of the Yellowstone River. Again under the guise of a scientific and literary expedition, the administration in 1819 dispatched Stephen Long to survey the Great Plains and Rocky Mountain regions. He was also to seize control of the fur trade and chip away at British influence.[37]

Anglo-American rivalry quickened after 1818. The Hudson's Bay Company bought out the old Northwest Company and under the watchful eye of the Royal Navy began systematically exploiting the area south of the Columbia River, hoping to discourage Americans from settling there. Astor's plans never reached fruition. Although Adams hesitated to challenge Britain directly, members of Congress such as Dr. John Floyd of Virginia and Thomas Hart Benton of Missouri increasingly warned of a British menace and urged settlement of the Oregon country. Congressional pressures were driving the United States toward a confrontation with Britain when Russia added a third side to the triangle.[38]

IV

Russia's challenge in the Northwest, along with a revolution in Greece and the threat of European intervention to restore monarchical governments in Latin America, brought forth in December 1823 what came to be known as the Monroe Doctrine, one of the most significant and iconic statements of the principles of U.S. foreign policy and a ringing affirmation of U.S. preeminence in the Western Hemisphere and especially North America.[39]

37. Weeks, *Adams*, 122–23; Sellers, *Market Revolution*, 92; Cunningham, *Monroe*, 86–88.
38. Norman A. Graebner, *Empire on the Pacific: A Study in Continental Expansion* (rev. ed., Claremont, Calif., 1983), 37; Howard Jones and Donald Rakestraw, *Prologue to Manifest Destiny: Anglo-American Relations in the 1840s* (Wilmington, Del., 1997), 159.
39. The classic study is Dexter Perkins, *The Monroe Doctrine, 1823–1826* (Cambridge, Mass., 1927).

Tsar Alexander's ukase (imperial edict) of 1821 is often viewed as a typical expression of Russia's age-old propensity for aggrandizement, but it was considerably less. On the basis of explorations, Russia claimed the Pacific coast of North America. The tsar had given the Russian-American Company a trade monopoly as far south as 55° north. The company established scattered trading posts along the Alaskan coast, but it lacked government support and faced growing U.S. competition. New England traders and poachers took most of the region's sea otters and began supplying the indigenous population with guns and whiskey. Further alarmed by talk of American settlements in the northwest, the Russian-American Company secured Alexander's assistance. Apparently without much thought, he issued on September 4, 1821, another ukase granting Russians exclusive rights for trading, whaling, and fishing in the area of Alaska and the Bering Sea and south along the coast to 51° (far south of Russia's main settlement near the present site of Sitka, Alaska). Under threat of confiscation and capture, the ukase also forbade foreign ships from approaching within 100 Italian miles (115 English miles) of Russian claims.[40]

The ukase aroused grave concern in the United States. Russia's territorial aspirations posed no direct threat, since the United States had never claimed above 49°. The hostile reaction reflected more U.S. pretensions than those of Russia. But the coastal restrictions challenged the principle of freedom of the seas and threatened one of the most profitable enterprises of Adams's New England constituents. Congressmen agitated for settlement of the Columbia basin and urged Monroe to defend U.S. interests. The tsar at precisely this time was arbitrating an Anglo-American dispute over slaves carried away during the War of 1812, so Monroe and Adams proceeded cautiously. At the first opportunity, however, Adams informed the Russian minister "that we should contest the right of Russia to *any* territorial establishment on this continent, and that we should assume distinctly the principle that the American continents are no longer subjects for any new colonial establishments."[41]

The outbreak of revolution in Greece posed the equally significant and not entirely unrelated issue of America's commitment to republican principles and the role it should play in supporting liberation movements abroad. In the spring of 1821, the Greeks revolted against Turkish rule. Early the following year, various resistance groups coalesced, issued an

40. Normal E. Saul, *Distant Friends: The United States and Russia, 1763–1867* (Lawrence, Kans., 1991), 96–98.
41. Bemis, *Adams,* 368.

American-style declaration of independence, and appealed to the world—and especially the "fellow-citizens of Penn, of Washington, and of Franklin"—for assistance.

Widely acknowledged as the birthplace of modern democracy, Greece became the cause célèbre of the era. "Greek fever" took hold in the United States. Americans viewed the revolution as an offspring of their own and the Turks as the worst form of barbarians and infidels. Pro-Greek rallies were staged in numerous towns and cities; speakers called for contributions and volunteers. In one of the most famous exhortations, Harvard professor Edward Everett enjoined Americans to fulfill "the great and glorious part which this country is to act, in the political regeneration of the world."[42]

The issue divided the U.S. government. Always the skeptic, Adams dismissed the Greek infatuation as "all sentiment" and feared that support for the rebels would jeopardize trade negotiations with Turkey. On the other hand, minister to France Gallatin urged employment of the U.S. Navy's Mediterranean squadron against the Turks. Former president Madison advocated a public declaration in favor of Greek independence. Congressmen Clay and Daniel Webster of Massachusetts used their famed eloquence to press for the dispatch of an official agent to Greece. Clay indignantly protested that U.S. support for liberty was being compromised by a "miserable invoice of figs and opium." Monroe was leaning toward recognition when a more pressing challenge led the administration to take a public stand on the several issues it confronted.[43]

The possibility of European intervention to suppress the Latin American revolutions was the most serious threat to face the United States since the War of 1812. Following the Napoleonic wars, Tsar Alexander had taken the lead in mobilizing the Continental powers to check the forces of revolution. A religious fanatic whose propensity for prayer was said to have caused calluses on his knees, Alexander later became obsessed with a fear of revolution and increasingly associated opposition with godliness. For reasons of state, he refused to help the Turks suppress the Greeks. At the Congress of Verona in November 1822, however, he secured an allied commitment to restore the fallen monarchy in Spain. French troops subsequently accomplished this mission. With the

42. James A. Field Jr., *America and the Mediterranean World, 1776–1882* (Princeton, N.J., 1969), 122.

43. Remini, *Clay*, 222–25; Hargreaves, *Adams*, 118.

Spanish monarchy restored, talk swept Europe of an allied move to re-store Spain's Latin American colonies or establish in Latin America inde-pendent monarchies.[44]

The United States had responded cautiously to the Latin American revolutions. Adams was delighted with the further dissolution of Europe-an colonialism and hoped eventually to secure trade advantages from an independent Latin America. At the same time, he believed that the Spanish and Catholic influence was too strong to permit the growth of republicanism among the new nations. He did not share the enthusiasm of Clay and others who foresaw a group of Latin American nations that were closely tied to the United States and that might build institutions resembling those of the North Americans. Nor did he wish to antagonize Spain as long as the Florida question was unresolved and the *threat* of recognition gave him leverage with Onis. Over the protests of Clay and others, the administration withheld recognition until 1822 and sought to implement an "impartial neutrality." Clay's position was popular, how-ever, and clandestine organizations in East Coast ports provided arms, supplies, and mercenaries for the rebels. Loopholes in the neutrality laws permitted the fitting-out in U.S. ports of privateers that preyed on Spanish shipping.[45]

Whatever its attitudes toward Latin America, the United States could only view with alarm the possibility of European intervention. The threat revived memories of those early years when the omnipresent reality of for-eign intrusion endangered the very survival of the new republic. It could foreclose commercial opportunities that now seemed open in the hemi-sphere.

Curiously, in light of past antagonisms, it was the old Yankeephobe British foreign secretary George Canning who brought the issue of Eu-ropean intervention to the forefront. During conversations with a shocked U.S. minister Richard Rush in the summer of 1823, Canning proposed a joint statement opposing European intervention to restore the Spanish colonies and disavowing American and British designs on the new nations. The motives for this quite extraordinary proposal re-main a matter of speculation. Canning may already have committed himself to recognition of the Latin American nations and was seeking U.S. support against critics at home and abroad. Many Americans,

44. Perkins, *Monroe Doctrine*, 22–24, 34.
45. Arthur P. Whitaker, *The United States and the Independence of Latin America, 1800–1830* (New York, 1964), 217.

Adams included, suspected a clever British trick to keep Cuba out of U.S. hands.[46]

Whatever the case, Canning's "great flirtation" set off a prolonged debate in Washington. As was his custom, Monroe consulted with his illustrious Virginia predecessors before going to his cabinet. Jefferson and Madison swallowed their Anglophobia and counseled going along with Canning. Persuaded that European intervention was likely if not certain, Calhoun agreed.[47] Adams disagreed, and on most issues he prevailed. He astutely and correctly minimized the likelihood of European intervention. As secretary of state and a presidential aspirant, he may have feared that joining with Britain would leave him vulnerable to charges of being too cozy with an old enemy.[48] He was also alert to the advantages of acting alone. Acceptance of Canning's proposal might for the short run jeopardize chances of getting Cuba or Texas. An independent stance might advance prospects of trade with Latin American nations. "It would be more candid, as well as more dignified," he advised the cabinet, "to avow our principles explicitly to Russia and France than to come in as a cockboat in the wake of the British man-of-war."[49] Reaffirming his long-held view that U.S. political interests lay primarily on the North American continent and warning against an unnecessary affront to the European powers, Adams talked Monroe out of recognizing Greece. The president overruled his secretary of state only on the form the statement should take, including it in his annual message to Congress rather than the diplomatic dispatches Adams would have preferred (as that would have given him more credit).

What much later came to be called the Monroe Doctrine, in whose formulation Adams played the crucial role, was contained in separate parts of the president's December 2, 1823, message to Congress. Asserting the doctrine of the two spheres, which had some precedent in European treaties, he sharply distinguished between the political systems of the Old World and the New and affirmed that the two should not impinge on

46. See, for example, William W. Kaufmann, *British Policy and Latin America* (New Haven, Conn., 1951), 142–53.
47. Jefferson to Monroe, October 24, 1823, in Paul Leicester Ford, ed., *The Works of Thomas Jefferson* (New York, 1904), 12:318–21; Madison to Monroe, October 30, November 1, 1823, in Stanislaus Murray Hamilton, ed., *The Writings of James Monroe* (7 vols., New York, 1898–1903), 6:394–95.
48. Ernest R. May advances this argument in *The Making of the Monroe Doctrine* (Cambridge, Mass., 1976). For a persuasive rebuttal, see Harry Ammon, "Monroe Doctrine: Domestic Politics or National Decision," *Diplomatic History* 5 (Winter 1981), 53–70.
49. Quoted in Bemis, *Adams*, 385.

each other. He went on to enunciate a "non-colonization principle," a bold and pretentious public reiteration of the position Adams had taken privately with the Russian and British ministers: The American continents "by the free and independent conditions which they have assumed and maintain, are henceforth not to be considered as subjects of colonizations by any European power." Monroe went on to affirm that generally, and in the specific case of Greece, the United States would not interfere in the "internal affairs" of Europe. On the most pressing issue, he set forth a non-intervention principle, warning the Holy Allies and France that the United States would regard as "dangerous" to its "peace and safety" any European effort to "extend their system to any portion of the hemisphere."[50]

Monroe's statement raised as many questions as it answered. It left unclear whether the non-colonization principle applied with equal weight to all of North and South America and what—if anything—the United States might do to defend the independence of Latin America. The Greek issue was settled when Congress subsequently tabled a resolution calling for recognition, but Monroe's statement did not close the door entirely to U.S. involvement in Europe. It did not even represent a definitive exposition of U.S. policy. The administration, Adams included, was prepared to consider an Anglo-American alliance should the threat of European intervention materialize.[51]

The immediate response gave little indication that Monroe's pronunciations would assume the status of holy writ. Americans lustily cheered and then largely forgot the ringing reaffirmation of America's independence from Europe. European reaction ranged from outright hostility to incredulity at the pretentiousness of such strong words from such a weak nation. That high priest of the old order, Austria's Prince Metternich, privately denounced the statement as a "new act of revolt" and warned that it would "set altar against altar" and give "new strength to the apostles of sedition and reanimate the courage of every conspirator."[52] When Canning realized that he had been outmaneuvered, he released a statement given him by the French government making clear that Britain had been responsible for deterring European intervention. Many Latin Americans

50. Seventh Annual Message, December 2, 1823, in James D. Richardson, ed., A Compilation of the Messages and Papers of the Presidents of the United States (20 vols., Washington, 1897–1916), 2:776–789.
51. Gale W. McGee, "The Monroe Doctrine—A Stopgap Measure," Mississippi Valley Historical Review 38 (September 1951), 233–50.
52. Perkins, Monroe Doctrine, 73–75. Metternich is quoted on pp. 55–57.

had minimized the threat of European intervention from the outset. Those who took it seriously perceived that Britain, not the United States, had headed it off. Latin American leaders were eager to ascertain whether Monroe's apparent offer of support had substance, but they also feared a North American threat to their independence. The practical effects of the "doctrine" were also limited. Indeed, for many years, the United States stood by while Britain violated—and enforced—its key provisions.

The Monroe "doctrine" was by no means a hollow statement. It neatly encapsulated and gave public expression to goals Monroe and Adams had pursued aggressively since 1817. That it was issued at all reflected America's ambitions in the Pacific Northwest and its renewed concerns for its security. That it was done separately from Britain reflected the nation's keen interest in acquiring Texas and Cuba and its commercial aspirations in Latin America. It expressed the spirit of the age and provided a ringing, if still premature, statement of U.S. preeminence in the hemisphere. It publicly reaffirmed the continental vision Adams had already privately shared with the British and Russians: "Keep what is yours but leave the rest of the continent to us."

Monroe, Adams, and Clay continued to pursue this vision, pushing relentlessly against foreign positions in the Northwest and Southwest. Adams's vigorous protests against the ukase and Monroe's message were heard in St. Petersburg. This time listening to his foreign policy advisers rather than the Russian-American Company, the tsar made major concessions in treaties of 1824 and 1825, dividing Russian and United States "possessions" at 54° 40', opening the ports and coasts of the Russian Pacific to U.S. ships, and leaving the unsettled stretches of the Pacific Northwest open to American traders as long as they did not sell firearms and whiskey to the indigenous peoples.[53]

Chosen president by the House of Representatives after a hotly disputed 1824 election, Adams immediately ratcheted up the pressure on Britain. He sent the veteran diplomat Gallatin to London with instructions to extend the boundary along the 49th parallel to the Pacific. Still determined to protect British interests in the Oregon country, Canning insisted on the Columbia River as a boundary. When it was evident that neither nation would back down, they agreed in 1827 to leave the territory open indefinitely to the citizens of each. Adams found it expedient to delay rather than risk conflict at a time when the U.S. position was still weak.

53. Saul, *Distant Friends*, 101–3.

The United States also tried to roll back Mexico's boundaries in the Southwest. Clay had bitterly attacked Monroe and Adams for abandoning Texas in 1819. As Adams's secretary of state, he lamented that the Texas border "approached our great western Mart [New Orleans], nearer than could be wished."[54] With the president's blessings, he pushed the newly independent and still fragile government of Mexico to part with territory into which large numbers of U.S. citizens were already flocking. He authorized his minister to Mexico, South Carolinian Joel Poinsett, to negotiate a boundary at the Brazos River or even the Rio Grande, arguing, with transparently self-serving logic, that the detachment of Texas would leave the capital, Mexico City, closer to the nation's center, making it easier to administer. Not surprisingly, Mexico rejected Poinsett's overtures and Clay's logic. An outspoken champion of U.S.-style republicanism, the ebullient diplomat (better known for giving his name to a brightly colored Christmas flower native to Central America) was instructed by Clay to represent to Mexicans the "very great advantages" of the (North) American system. Poinsett took his instructions much too seriously, openly expressing his disdain for Mexican institutions and aligning himself with the political opposition. The triumph of the group he backed changed nothing. The new government resisted the meddlesome minister's offers of $1 million for the Rio Grande boundary and in 1829 requested his recall. As with Britain in the Northwest, Adams and Clay refused to press the matter, certain that in time Texas would fall into U.S. hands.[55]

V

Implicit in the Monroe Doctrine was a commitment to the extension of the ideology and institutions of the United States, a key issue throughout much of the mid-1820s. The Greek and Latin American revolutions made it a practical and tangible matter. The marquis de Lafayette had dedicated his life to liberal causes. His triumphal pilgrimage across the United States in 1825 evoked an orgy of speeches and celebrations, reminding Americans of the glories of their revolution and stimulating sympathy for the cause of liberty elsewhere. The fiftieth anniversary of the Declaration of Independence on July 4, 1826, also brought forth talk of a rededication to freedom. The remarkable, coincidental deaths of Thomas

54. James E. Lewis Jr., *John Quincy Adams: Policymaker for the Union* (Wilmington, Del., 2001), 103.
55. Hargreaves, *Adams*, 116–17; Karl M. Schmitt, *Mexico and the United States, 1821–1973: Conflict and Coexistence* (New York, 1974), 35–41.

Jefferson and John Adams on that very day seemed to President John Quincy Adams a "visible and palpable" sign of "Divine favor," a reminder of America's special role in the world.[56]

Much of the initiative for the extension of American ideals came from individuals, and the impetus was mainly religious. Inspired by the American Revolution and by a revival that swept the nation in the 1820s (the Second Great Awakening), troubled by the rampant materialism that accompanied frenzied economic growth, a small group of New England missionaries set out to evangelize the world. Originating primarily in the seaport communities and often backed by leading merchants, they saw religion, patriotism, and commerce working hand in hand. They were committed to the view of Congregationalist minister Samuel Hopkins that the spread of Christianity would bring about "the most happy state of public society that can be enjoyed on earth."[57] In the beginning, American evangelicals worked with the British. The first missionary traveled to India in 1812. In the 1820s, they struck out on their own. They did not seek or expect government support. Certain that the millennium was at hand—the estimated date was 1866—they brought to their work a special urgency and believed the task could be done in a generation. A mission went to Latin America in 1823 to survey the prospects of liberating that continent from Catholicism and monarchy. "If one part of this new national family should fall back under a monarchical system, the event must threaten, if not bring down evils, on the part remaining."[58] Two African American Baptist ministers were among the first Americans to go to Africa. The major thrust was the Middle East. An intrepid group of missionaries left for Jerusalem in 1819 to liberate the birthplace of Christianity from "nominal" Christians, "Islamic fanaticism," and "Catholic superstition." Plunged into the deadly maelstrom of Middle Eastern religion and politics, the mission moved on to Beirut and barely survived. But it established the foundation for a worldwide movement that would play an important role in U.S. foreign relations before the end of the century.[59]

The concept of mission assumed a major place in the foreign policy of Adams and Clay. The zealous, romantic Kentuckian had always

---

56. Hargreaves, *Adams*, 114–15.
57. Quoted in Field, *Mediterranean World*, 92.
58. Quoted in Hargreaves, *Adams*, 114.
59. Field, *Mediterranean World*, 68–101; Ussama Makdisi, "Reclaiming the Land of the Bible: Missionaries, Secularism, and Evangelical Modernity," *American Historical Review* 102 (June 1997), 680–90.

championed the cause of freedom, often to the discomfiture of Monroe and Adams. As secretary of state, Adams had rebuffed Clay's proposals to support the Greek and Latin American revolutions—the United States should be the "well-wisher to the freedom and independence of all . . . , the champion and vindicator only of her own," he proclaimed in an oft-quoted July 4, 1821, oration responding to Clay.[60] But as president he moved in that direction. Shortly after Lafayette's visit, he dispatched a secret agent to offer U.S. sympathy to the Greeks and assess their ability to "sustain an independent Government." Whether Adams saw this as preliminary to recognition is unclear. It became irrelevant. The agent died en route. In April 1826, the Greeks suffered a crushing defeat, seemingly answering the question he was sent to ask. Adams nonetheless expressed sympathy for them in subsequent speeches. He hailed the outbreak of war between Russia and Turkey in 1828 as offering them renewed hope.[61]

Closer to home, Adams and Clay sought to encourage republicanism in Latin America. For years, Clay had ardently championed Latin American independence. As secretary of state, he aspired to commit hemispheric nations to a loose association based on U.S. political and commercial principles. Although skeptical, Adams too came to envision the United States providing leadership to the hemisphere in those "very fundamental maxims which we from our cradle at first proclaimed and partially succeeded to introduce into the code of national law." The two men feared that the Latin American republics might fall back under European sway or as independent nations compete with each other and the United States in ways that threatened U.S. interests. The best solution seemed to be to reshape them according to North American republican principles and institutions.[62]

There is a fine line between encouraging change in countries and interfering in their internal affairs, and Adams, Clay, and their diplomats often crossed it. Raguet publicly expressed contempt for Brazil's monarchy and the corruption and immorality that, he claimed, inevitably accompanied it. Poinsett used the Freemasons' organization to foment opposition to the government of Mexico. The U.S. chargé actively intruded in a debate among Chileans over the principles of government.[63] During the

---

60. Adams's July 4, 1821, speech to the House of Representatives may be conveniently found at www.millercenter.virginia.edu/academic/americanpresidents/jqadams.
61. Hargreaves, *Adams*, 119–21.
62. Ibid., 127; Lewis, *Adams*, 87–88.
63. Hargreaves, *Adams*, 128.

revolutions against Spain, North Americans hailed Simón Bolívar as the George Washington of Latin America. But his advocacy of a presidency for life for Bolivia and Colombia aroused suspicions of British influence and fears of a turn toward monarchy. Clay privately enjoined the Liberator to choose the "true glory of our immortal Washington, to the ignoble fame of the destroyers of liberty." The U.S. chargé in Peru denounced Bolívar as a usurper and "madman" and backed his opponents. Minister to Colombia William Henry Harrison openly consorted with Bolívar's enemies and was asked to leave. An admirer of the United States, the Liberator observed that this rich and powerful northern neighbor "seemed destined by Providence to plague America with torments in the name of freedom."[64]

Adams and Clay never permitted the cause of freedom to interfere with more important interests. They were willing to recognize the Brazilian monarchy as long as Brazil's ports were open to U.S. trade. When the threat of European intervention caused Latin American leaders to ask how the United States might respond, they got only vague responses. Monroe's statement had not conveyed "any pledge or obligation the performance of which foreign nations have a right to demand," Clay asserted. The United States flatly rejected proposals by Colombia and Brazil for alliances. When wars or rumors of war among the Latin nations themselves threatened Hemispheric stability, Clay and Adams stuck to a policy of "strict and impartial neutrality."[65]

With Haiti and Cuba, race, commerce, and expediency dictated support for the status quo. Clay was inclined to recognize Haiti, but southerners like Calhoun fretted about "social relations" with a black diplomat and the participation of his children "in the society of our daughters and sons." Adams opposed recognition as long as the black republic granted exclusive trade privileges to France and showed "little respect" for "races other than African."[66] The United States preferred the certainties of continued Spanish control of Cuba to the risks of independence. Its rule threatened throughout the 1820s by rebellion from within and a possible British takeover or Mexican or Colombian invasion from without, Spain maintained at best a precarious hold on its island colony. United States

64. Ibid., 127; David Bushnell, "Simon Bolivar and the United States: A Study in Ambivalence," *Air University Review* 37 (July–August 1986), 106–12.
65. Hargreaves, *Adams*, 129–31.
66. Sellers, *Market Revolution*, 273; Remini, *Clay*, 299; Lars Schoultz, *Beneath the United States: A History of U.S. Policy Toward Latin America* (Cambridge, Mass., 1998), 80–81.

officials, on the other hand, saw Cuba as a natural appendage of their country, certain, as Adams put it, that, like an "apple severed by the tempest from its native tree," Cuba, once separated from Spain, could "gravitate only towards the North American union." For the moment, they were content with the status quo. A premature move to acquire Cuba might provoke British intervention. The "moral condition, and discordant character" of Cuba's predominantly black population raised the specter of the "most shocking excess" of the Haitian revolution. Clay and Adams thus rebuffed schemes proposed by Cuban planters for U.S. annexation and rejected British proposals for a multilateral pledge of self-denial. They warned off Mexico and Colombia, proclaiming that if Cuba was to become a dependency of any nation "it is impossible not to allow that the law of its position proclaims that it should be attached to the United States." They did nothing to encourage Cuban independence, preferring the status quo as long as the island was open to U.S. trade.[67]

Adams and Clay's efforts to promote closer relations with hemispheric neighbors through participation in an inter-American conference in Panama became hopelessly entangled in the bitter partisan politics that afflicted their last years in office. Bolívar conceived the idea of an inter-American congress to build closer ties among the new nations to help fend off European intervention and perhaps also support his own ambitions for Hemispheric leadership. Some Latin American leaders saw inviting the United States as a means to secure the pledges of support Washington had been unwilling to give on a bilateral basis. Adams and Clay were not prepared to go this far, but they were willing to participate, Clay to further his dreams of an American System, Adams, who critics sneered had caught the "Spanish American fever" from his secretary of state, to promote U.S. commerce and demonstrate goodwill. Their missionary impulse was manifest in Clay's instructions to the delegates. They were not to proselytize actively, but they should be ready to respond to questions about the U.S. system of government and the "manifold blessings" enjoyed by the people under it.[68]

The Panama Congress became a political lightning rod, drawing increasingly bitter attacks from the followers of presidential aspirants former secretary of the treasury William Crawford, Vice President Calhoun, and especially Andrew Jackson. Critics ominously warned that participation would violate Washington's strictures against alliances and sell out U.S. freedom of action to a "stupendous Confederacy, in which the

67. Hargreaves, Adams, 140–46; Remini, Clay, 301–3.
68. Quoted in Hargreaves, Adams, 157.

United States have but a single vote." Southerners protested association with nations whose economies were competitive, expressed concern that the congress might seek to abolish slavery, and objected to association with Haitian diplomats. A Georgia senator issued dire warnings against meeting with "the emancipated slave, his hands yet reeking in the blood of his masters." The acerbic Virginia congressman John Randolph of Roanoke declaimed against a "Kentucky cuckoo's egg, laid in a Spanish-American nest." Condemning the political "bargain" that had allegedly given Adams the presidency and made Clay secretary of state, he sneered at the union of the "Puritan with the black-leg," a "coalition of Blifil and Black George" (the reference to especially unsavory characters from Henry Fielding's novel *Tom Jones*). Randolph's charges provoked a duel with Clay more comical than life-threatening, the only casualty of which was the Virginian's greatcoat.[69]

United States participation never materialized. A hostile Senate delayed for months voting on Adams' nominees. By the time they were finally approved, one refused to go to Panama during the "sickly season," and the other died before receiving his instructions. When the congress finally assembled in June 1826 after repeated delays, no U.S. representative was present. After a series of sessions, it adjourned with no plans to reconvene. Adams gamely persisted, appointing a new representative, but the congress never met formally again. The Senate refused even to publish the administration's instructions to its delegates, writing a fitting epitaph to a comedy of errors. For the first time but by no means the last, a major foreign policy initiative fell victim to partisan politics.[70]

The Panama Congress fiasco typified the travails of Adams's presidency. Perhaps the nation's most successful secretary of state, he met frustration and failure in its highest office.[71] Although he brought to the White House the most limited mandate, he set ambitious goals. He and Clay achieved some important accomplishments, especially in the construction of roads and canals and the passage of a highly controversial protective tariff in 1828. In most areas, they failed. Outraged at losing an election in which they had won a plurality of the popular vote, Jackson and his supporters built a vibrant political organization and obstructed administration initiatives. Caught off guard by the opposition, Adams often seemed incapable of asserting effective leadership. Perhaps like Jefferson and also from hubris, he too overreached, refusing to bend from

69. Ibid., 147–148; Remini, *Clay*, 292–95.
70. Remini, *Clay*, 300–301.
71. Lewis, *Adams*, 99.

principle in trade negotiations with England and badly misjudging the willingness of weak nations such as Mexico to succumb to U.S. pressure.

This said, the era of Monroe and Adams was rich in foreign policy accomplishment. Through the Transcontinental Treaty, the United States secured its southern border, gained uncontested control of the Mississippi, and established a foothold in the Pacific Northwest. The threat of European intervention diminished appreciably. Britain was still the major power in the Western Hemisphere, but the United States in a relatively short time emerged as a formidable rival, already larger than all the European states except for Russia. Still threatened by manifold dangers in 1817, the U.S. continental empire was firmly established by 1824. Well might Adams observe in his last months as secretary of state that never had there been "a period of more tranquility at home and abroad since our existence as a nation than that which prevails now."[72]

VI

The election of Andrew Jackson in 1828 provoked alarm among some Americans and many Europeans, especially in the realm of foreign policy. The first westerner to capture the White House, Jackson, unlike his predecessors, had not served abroad or as secretary of state. His record as a soldier, especially in the invasion of Florida, raised legitimate concerns that he would be impulsive, even reckless, in the exercise of power.

Jackson introduced important institutional changes. His cabinet met sparingly and rarely discussed foreign policy. He went through four secretaries of state in eight years, much of the time assuming for himself the primary role in policymaking. He instituted the first major reform of the State Department, creating eight bureaus and elevating the chief clerk to a status roughly equivalent to a modern undersecretary. He expanded the consular service and sought to reform it by paying salaries, thus reducing the likelihood of corruption, only to have a penurious Congress reject his proposal and try to reduce U.S. representation abroad. With much fanfare, he institutionalized the principle of rotation in office—a spoils system, critics called it. He used the diplomatic service for political ends. Ministers William Cabell Rives, Louis McLane, Martin Van Buren, and James Buchanan distinguished themselves in European capitals, but they were among the major exceptions to a generally weak group of diplomatic appointments. The eccentric John Randolph—sent to St. Peters-

72. Ibid., 95; Weeks, *Continental Empire*, 58–59.

burg to get him out of Washington—left after twenty-nine days, finding the Russian weather unbearably cold even in August. Jackson crony and world-class scoundrel Anthony Butler was the worst of a sorry lot of appointments to Latin America.[73]

In keeping with the democratic spirit of the day, Jackson altered the dress of the diplomatic corps. His Democratic Party followers accused Monroe and Adams of trying to "ape the splendors . . . of the monarchical governments"; Jackson himself thought the fancy diplomatic uniform "extremely ostentatious" and too expensive. He introduced an outfit more in keeping with "pure republican principles," a plain black coat with gold stars on the collar and a three-cornered hat.[74]

Jackson's changes were more of style and method than substance. Cadaverous in appearance with strikingly gray hair that stood on end, chronically ill, still bearing the scars from numerous military campaigns and carrying in his body two bullets from duels, the rough-hewn but surprisingly sophisticated hero of New Orleans embodied the spirit of the new republic. His rhetoric harked back to the republican virtues of a simpler time, but he was both the product and an ardent promoter of an emerging capitalist society. Domestic struggles such as the nullification controversy and the bank war occupied center stage during Jackson's presidency. There were no major foreign policy crises. At the same time, Jackson saw foreign policy as essential to domestic well-being and gave it high priority. He was less concerned with promoting republicanism abroad than with commanding respect for the United States. He readily embraced the global destiny of a rising nation. More than his predecessors, he sought to project U.S. power into distant areas. He energetically pursued the major goals set by Monroe, Adams, and the despised Clay: to expand and protect the commerce upon which America's prosperity depended; to eliminate or at least roll back alien settlements that threatened its security or blocked its expansion.[75]

Jackson's methods represented a combination of frontier bluster and frontier practicality. In his first inaugural, he vowed to "ask nothing but what is right, permit nothing that is wrong." He did not live up to this high standard, but he did establish a style distinctly his own. Like Monroe and Adams, he had been profoundly influenced by the menacing and

73. Donald B. Cole, *The Presidency of Andrew Jackson* (Lawrence, Kans., 1993), 41–42, 93, 241–42; John M. Belohlavek, *"Let the Eagle Soar!" The Foreign Policy of Andrew Jackson* (Lincoln, Neb., 1985), 34–36.

74. Davis, "Diplomatic Plumage," 171–72.

75. Belohlavek, *Eagle*, 92–106.

sometimes humiliating experiences of the republic's infancy. He was extremely sensitive to insults to the national honor and threats to national security. He claimed to stand on principle. He insisted that other nations be made to "sorely feel" the consequences of their actions; he was quick to threaten or use force if he thought his nation wronged. In actual negotiations, however, he was conciliatory and flexible. If, on occasion, he raised relatively minor issues to the level of crises, he also solved by compromise problems that had frustrated Adams, a man renowned for diplomatic skill. His gracious manner and folksy charm won over foreigners who expected to find him offensive.[76]

Like Monroe and Adams before him, Jackson gave high priority to expanding U.S. trade. A product of the southwestern frontier, he recognized the essentiality of markets for American exports. Despite the efforts of his predecessors, commerce had stagnated in the 1820s, and surpluses of cotton, tobacco, grain, and fish threatened the continued expansion of agriculture, commerce, and manufacturing. He thus moved vigorously to resolve unsettled claims disputes, break down old trade barriers, and open new markets.[77]

Jackson perceived that securing payments of outstanding claims would bind grateful merchants to him, stimulate the economy, and facilitate new trade agreements. Through patient negotiation and the timely deployment of naval power, he extracted $2 million from the Kingdom of Naples. The threat of a trade war helped secure $650,000 from Denmark. Settlement of the long-standing French claims dispute represented a major success of his first administration and reveals much about his methods of operation. He attached great importance to the negotiations, believing that other nations would view failure as a sign of weakness. Informed by minister Rives that France would not pay unless "made to believe that their interests . . . require it," Jackson took a firm position. But after months of laborious negotiations, when the fragile new government of Louis Philippe offered to settle for $5 million, he readily assented, conceding that, although less than U.S. demands, the sum was fair. The United States promised to pay 1,500,000 francs to satisfy French claims from the American Revolution.[78]

76. Walter Russell Mead, *Special Providence: American Foreign Policy and How It Changed the World* (New York, 2001) uses Jackson to represent a belligerent strain in U.S. foreign policy. Arthur Schlesinger Jr. depicts a gentler, more diplomatic Jackson in *New York Review of Books* (May 15, 2003), 19.

77. Cole, *Jackson*, 121–23.

78. Belohlavek, *Eagle*, 92–106.

Jackson almost undid his success by pressing too hard for payment. Without bothering to determine when the first installment was due or notify the French government, he ordered a draft on the French treasury. It was returned unpaid, and the Chamber of Deputies subsequently rejected appropriations for the settlement. At this point, an angry Jackson impulsively threatened to seize French property. "I know them French," he reportedly exclaimed. "They won't pay unless they are made to."[79] The Chamber appropriated the funds but refused to pay until Jackson apologized. The dispute quickly escalated. The French recalled their minister from Washington, asked Rives to leave Paris, and sent naval forces to the West Indies. Jackson drafted a bellicose message and ordered the navy to prepare for war. A totally unnecessary conflict over a relatively trivial sum was averted when a suddenly conciliatory Jackson in his December 1835 message to Congress refused to apologize but insisted he meant no offense. Paris viewed the apology that was not an apology as sufficient and paid the claims.[80]

Jackson also broke the long-standing and often bitter deadlock over access to the British West Indies. The departure of Adams and the death of Canning in 1827 greatly facilitated settlement of an apparently intractable issue. More interested in markets than shipping, Jackson's southern and western constituents exploited Adams's blunders in the 1828 campaign. To prove his mettle as a diplomat, Jackson sought to succeed where his predecessor had failed. British planters and industrialists had long pressed the government to resolve the issue. At least for the moment, instability on the Continent made good relations with the United States especially important.[81]

The two nations thus inched toward resolving an issue that had vexed relations since the American Revolution. Persuaded that Adams's rigidity had frustrated earlier negotiations, Jackson abandoned his predecessor's insistence that Britain give up imperial preference. He continued to talk tough, at one point threatening to cut off trade with "Canady." But when advised by McLane in 1830 that the issue might be settled more easily by action than negotiation, he removed the retaliatory measures prohibiting entry into U.S. ports of ships from the British West Indies. London responded by opening the West Indies to direct trade. An issue that had grown in symbolic importance while declining in practical significance

79. Quoted in Marvin R. Zahniser, *Uncertain Friendship: American-French Relations Through the Cold War* (New York, 1975), 102.
80. Cole, *Jackson*, 126–27.
81. Ibid., 124–25.

was at last settled, removing a major impediment to amicable relations. Britons especially had feared accession of the allegedly Anglophobic Jackson, executioner of Arbuthnot and Armbrister. His demeanor in these negotiations won him an esteem in London given none of his predecessors and evoked a determination, in the words of King William IV, to "keep well with the United States."[82]

Jackson also energetically pursued new trade agreements. James Buchanan's dismal later performance as president has obscured his considerable skill as minister to Russia. He endured the St. Petersburg weather and the constant surveillance placed on foreigners. He ingratiated himself at court through his storytelling and dancing, even his flattery of the tsar. He negotiated a treaty providing for reciprocity in direct trade and access to the Black Sea.[83]

The United States also managed to achieve the treaty with Turkey that had eluded it for thirty years. Destruction of the Turkish navy by a combined European fleet at Navarino in 1827 convinced the sultan that closer relations with the United States would be useful. In return for a "separate and secret" U.S. promise to assist in rebuilding its navy, Turkey agreed to establish diplomatic and consular relations, trade on a most-favored-nation basis and admit American ships to the Black Sea. Although the Senate rejected the secret article, Americans without official sanction helped design ships and train sailors for the Turkish navy. The commercial treaty did not live up to expectations, only the exchange of rum and cotton goods in Smyrna for opium, fruit, and nuts turning out to be significant, but it established, along with the missionaries in Beirut, a basis for U.S. involvement in the Middle East.[84]

Jackson eagerly sought out trade with Asia. In January 1832, he appointed New England merchant and veteran sailor Edmund Roberts as a special agent to negotiate treaties with Muscat, Siam (Thailand), and Cochin China (southern Vietnam). To keep his mission secret, Roberts was given "ostensible employment" as clerk to the commander of the sloop *Peacock*. This first encounter between the United States and Vietnam was not a happy one. The ship landed near present-day Qui Nhon in January 1833. The discussions that followed constituted a classic cross-cultural exercise in futility. Low-level Vietnamese officials raised what Roberts called "impertinent queries," namely, whether the visitors had brought the obligatory pres-

82. Quoted in Charles R. Ritcheson, "Van Buren's Mission to London, 1831–1832," *International History Review* 8 (May 1986), 198–211.
83. Belohlavek, *Eagle*, 84–88; Saul, *Distant Friends*, 121–22.
84. Field, *Mediterranean World*, 141–53; Belohlavek, *Eagle*, 128–38.

ents for the king. Himself an imperious figure and like most Americans of the time strongly nationalistic, Roberts staunchly refused to use the "servile forms of address" the Vietnamese demanded in dealing with the emperor. They would accept nothing less, insisting that since the U.S. president was elected he was obviously inferior to a king. Roberts took a strong dislike to his hosts, describing them as untrustworthy and "without exception the most filthy people in the world." Most important, he refused to submit to "any species of degradation"—notably the elaborate ritual known as the ko-tow—to "gain commercial advantage." After a month of unproductive discussions, the *Peacock* sailed away.

Roberts's frustrations with Vietnam persisted. The *Peacock* went on to insular Southeast Asia, where he negotiated treaties with the rulers of Siam and Muscat, the former a model of commercial liberality. Jackson was so pleased that he asked his envoy to go back to Cochin China and then proceed to Japan, pragmatically imploring him, this time, to conform to local custom "however absurd." Wined and dined by rulers across the world, the venturesome Roberts had survived shipwrecks, pirates, and disease. This time his luck ran out. He contracted cholera en route. His ship landed at Da Nang in May 1836, but after a week of futile discussions, this time hampered by his illness, he sailed to Macao, where he died before completing his mission. The emperor Ming-Mang summed up the experience with a poem:

> We did not oppose their coming,
> We did not pursue them on their departure,
> We behaved according to the manners of a civilized nation
> What good would it do for us to complain of foreign barbarians.[85]

Building on Adams and Clay's foundation, Jackson negotiated ten commercial treaties in all. Exports nearly doubled during his two terms. Much of the increase was with Europe, still the major U.S. market, but the new treaties established a foundation for future commercial interests in the Middle East and East Asia.

Far more than his predecessors, Jackson thought in global terms, and he was committed to extending American influence into remote areas. He endorsed a plan for exploring the South Pole, agreeing, with its promoter, that it was important to show the flag "to every portion of the

85. Robert Hopkins Miller, *The United States and Vietnam, 1787–1941* (Washington, 1990), 32–40. Also Ronald Spector, "The American Image of Southeast Asia, 1790–1865: A Preliminary Assessment," *Journal of Southeast Asian Studies* III (September 1972), 299–305, and Belohlavek, *Eagle*, 162–77.

globe, to give to civilized and savage man a just impression of the power we possess."[86]

He upgraded the navy and used it to defend the nation's commercial interests and uphold its honor. For years, Americans had fished and sealed in the gray and icy South Atlantic and dried sealskins on the shores of the barren Falkland/Malvinas Islands. In the early 1820s, the new republic of Buenos Aires laid claim to the islands, established a tiny settlement of gauchos and ex-convicts, and restricted foreigners from fishing and sealing. When U.S. sailors in 1831 violated the orders, local authorities seized three American ships. Recently arrived in the area, the powerful USS *Lexington* proceeded to the Falkland/Malvinas under general instructions to protect U.S. commercial interests. Exceeding more specific orders issued by a diplomat in Buenos Aires without standing or instructions, and flying the French flag for purposes of deception, Capt. Silas Duncan neutralized Argentine defenses, declared the islands without government, placed the settlers under arrest, and took several hostages. Far from disavowing Duncan's actions, Jackson endorsed them. The new U.S. minister in Buenos Aires defended the captain to the point of demanding his passport to return home.[87]

A more serious incident occurred in 1831 along the "pepper coast" of present-day Indonesia. Malayan pirates attacked an American merchantman (ironically named *The Friendship*) in the West Sumatran port of Quallah Battoo, killing several sailors, taking $12,000 in specie and $8,000 in opium, and adding insult to injury by taunting the captain and his crew: "Who is greater now, Malay or American?" Outraged by this affront and persuaded that the "piratical perpetrators" were in "such a state of society that the usual course of proceedings between civilized nations could not be perused," Jackson dispatched the fifty-gun USS *Potomac* to the East Indies, instructed Capt. John Downes to demand indemnity and restitution of the stolen property, and authorized him to use force if no satisfaction was obtained. Arriving at the scene in early 1832, the impulsive captain decided to shoot first and talk later. He landed marines on Quallah Battoo, plundered the port, and burned the town, killing as many as two hundred Malays, women and children included. Annoyed that Downes had exceeded his orders, Jackson assigned him to finish his

---

86. Schroeder, *Maritime Empire*, 34.

87. Christian J. Maisch, "Falkland/Malvinas Islands Clash of 1831–1832," *Diplomatic History* 24 (Spring 2000), 185–210. Jackson's gunboat diplomacy is vigorously defended in Craig Evan Klafter, "United States Involvement in the Falklands Islands Crisis of 1831–1833," *Journal of the Early Republic* 4 (Winter 1984), 395–420.

career as an inspector of lighthouses. But he publicly defended the captain, condemning the Malays as a "band of lawless pirates" and admitting that his purpose was to "inflict a chastisement as would deter them from like aggressions."[88]

Jackson's gunboat diplomacy reveals much about U.S. foreign policy in the 1830s. It makes clear the nation's contempt for "lesser" peoples, its determination to command respect as a great power, and its conviction that military force could be used to alter the behavior of others. Jackson's political foes denounced him for being trigger-happy and bloodthirsty, and for usurping a war-making power rightly belonging to Congress. His defenders, in turn, dismissed as "unmanly" the notion that the president could not chastise "pirates" without an act of Congress. Americans in general applauded his actions as a "necessary lesson to be taught ignorant savages who would violate the rights of a young republic with a world destiny to fulfill."[89] The United States was justified in defending its interests, but in each case naval officers exceeded their orders and, in Sumatra in particular, inflicted destruction far out of proportion to the losses suffered. Moreover, the lessons administered seem to have been lost on their intended students. Numerous incidents along the pepper coast made clear that Downes's reprisals had not deterred "like aggression." In an ironic twist, Duncan's escapade left the Falkland/Malvinas vacant. When Britain filled the vacuum by seizing the islands in early 1833, Argentina asked for U.S. support under the Monroe Doctrine. It was one thing, of course, to take on Argentina, quite another Great Britain, and the United States did nothing. Jackson's action—and subsequent inaction— confirmed Latin American and especially Argentine suspicions of the United States. His gunboat diplomacy put the United States very much in the mainstream of Western imperialism rather than outside of it, as Americans have boasted, belying the nation's claims of its exceptionalism.

Like Monroe and Adams, Jackson moved vigorously to eliminate obstacles to U.S. expansion on the North American continent. This involved, on the one hand, removal of the Indians to unoccupied land west of the Mississippi, and on the other, efforts to acquire Texas from Mexico through purchase or negotiation. Jackson's inaugural pledge to ask nothing "not clearly right" and "permit nothing that is wrong," did not apply in these cases.

88. Belohlavek, Eagle, 152–62.
89. Schroeder, Maritime Empire, 28; Belohlavek, Eagle, 162.

Defeat in the War of 1812 had crippled Indian resistance to white expansion, and in its aftermath the United States moved to solve the Indian "problem." It was a solution devised by whites for Native Americans. Indians "neither are, in fact, nor ought to be considered as independent nations," Calhoun observed in 1818. "Our views of their interest, and not their own, ought to govern them."[90] That view came to center on removal. Monroe endorsed the policy as early as 1817. The cotton boom in the South and discovery of gold in Georgia prompted land-hungry settlers in Georgia, Alabama, and Mississippi to agitate for removing the southeastern Indians west of the Mississippi. Ironically, the main targets of removal, the so-called Five Civilized Tribes, had taken the greatest strides toward assimilation, but by this time that concept had fallen into disrepute. Some Americans viewed the degeneracy that "civilization" had brought to Indians as evidence that assimilation had failed. Most fell back on the blatantly racist and entirely expedient position that Indians were an inferior people beyond redemption. Even Clay, whose views were relatively humane, affirmed that the Indians "were not an improvable breed, and their disappearance from the human family will be no great loss to the world."[91]

In this atmosphere, drastic change in Indian policy was inevitable. Jackson was elected by states eager for removal. He had concluded that the Indians could not remain—it was impossible for separate peoples to coexist within a nation. Thus, even though the United States had signed numerous treaties with the various tribes, he rejected outright their claim to sovereignty. He rationalized removal as a way of saving Indian civilization—the only alternative to annihilation—although he must have foreseen that in time the same pressures might drive them from the lands to which they were being removed.[92]

One of the great tragedies of U.S. history thus unfolded during the Jackson years. Violating earlier treaty obligations, Congress passed in 1830 by a very thin margin a bill for removal. In theory, it was voluntary. Jackson insisted that he would not forcibly remove those Indians who submitted to state law, but state officials ignored his qualification and applied the law to Indians in a discriminatory and oppressive manner. Removal was accomplished by force, bribery, fraud, and the grossest exploitation. Jackson himself warned recalcitrant chiefs, if they rejected removal, not

90. Robert L. Meriwether et al., *The Papers of John C. Calhoun* (28 vols., Columbia, S.C., 1959–2003), 3:350.
91. Reginald Horsman, *Race and Manifest Destiny* (Cambridge, Mass., 1981), 198.
92. Cole, *Jackson*, 67–74.

to call upon their "great father hereafter to relieve you of your troubles." When his old adversaries, the Creeks and Cherokees, resisted and sued the United States, he made clear he must leave those "poor deluded" tribes "to their fate and annihilation."[93]

Jackson's claims that his policy toward his "red children" was "just and humane" ring hollow. Removal may indeed have been inevitable, but he might have done more to protect the rights of those who chose to remain and make the process of removal more humane. The government acquired 100 million acres of Indian land for $70 million plus 30 million acres in the West. Amidst horrific suffering, more than forty-six thousand Indians were forced from their ancestral lands into the wilderness across the Mississippi. The human losses were incalculable. Members of the tribes were divided against themselves. Efforts to remove the Seminoles sparked a war that lasted seven years and cost millions of dollars and thousands of lives. The cold winter of 1831–32, a cholera epidemic, and Congress's refusal to appropriate adequate funds added to the misery of those removed. The Cherokees resisted longest. They were herded into prison camps and eventually removed by force, resulting under Jackson's successor, Martin Van Buren, in the infamous "Trail of Tears." Jackson's removal policy spelled the doom of the American Indian. "What is history but the obituary of nations," one pro-removal congressman sighed.[94]

With no more scruples but much less success, the administration also attempted to push back the frontiers of Mexico. Like other southerners, Jackson viewed the exclusion of Texas from the treaty with Spain as a huge mistake. He feared leaving a foreign power in control of the lower branches of the Mississippi. He rationalized that national security and good relations with Mexico required a natural boundary. The "god of the universe had intended this great valley to belong to one nation," he exclaimed. "I shall keep my eye on this object, and the first propitious moment make the attempt to *regain* the Territory as far south and west as the great Desert."[95]

Jackson was not terribly troubled about the means employed. In August 1829, he empowered Poinsett to offer as much as $5 million for a boundary at the Rio Grande. The minister had already been discredited by his interference in Mexican politics. When Mexico demanded his recall, Jackson made a bad situation worse by replacing him with an old pal, Colonel Anthony Butler of Mississippi. A wheeler-dealer and notorious

93. Robert V. Remini, *Andrew Jackson and the Course of American Freedom, 1822–1832* (New York, 1981), 270, 272.
94. Horsman, *Race*, 202.
95. Remini, *Jackson*, 202, 218.

rascal, Butler also speculated in Texas lands. Jackson probably encouraged his aggressiveness and unscrupulousness by advising him that "I scarcely ever knew a Spaniard who was not the slave of avarice, and . . . this weakness may be worth a great deal to us in this case."[96]

Upon arriving at his post, Butler made obvious his contempt for the Mexicans and his determination to get Texas by fair means or foul. Alternately pushy and indolent, happily ignorant of and insensitive to his hosts, Butler completely misread his opposite number in negotiations, the clever and sophisticated secretary of foreign affairs, Lucas Alaman, who had no intention of selling Texas. Certain of success, Butler promised his chief that he would get what he wanted or "forfeit my head." He tried first to purchase the coveted territory. That failing, he urged Jackson to occupy strategic parts of Texas and then open negotiations. When Jackson rejected that proposal, he suggested in an uncoded communication the bribery of that "vile hypocrite and most unprincipled man," the Mexican leader Antonio Lopez de Santa Anna. This was too much even for Jackson. "A. Butler. What a scamp!" the president snarled as he ordered his minister recalled. Without Texas, still in possession of his head, and not content with the damage already done, Butler tarried for two years, among other things, challenging the Mexican secretary of war to a duel and threatening to cane and whip him in public. He is also alleged to have molested Mexican women. When ordered to leave the country, he had the effrontery—as well as the good sense—to request an armed guard to escort him to the border.[97]

The Butler mission represents the low point of Jacksonian diplomacy. The president sent perhaps the worst possible person on a mission of great delicacy, encouraged his bad behavior by sharing his own negative assessment of Mexicans, and refused to recall his agent when his conduct demanded it. Butler could not accomplish his mission. His arrogance and crudeness further poisoned Mexican-American relations, already strained by Poinsett's meddling, creating an atmosphere of anger and distrust conducive to war.

In the meantime, a revolution among Americans in Texas created a new set of problems—and opportunities. The United States did not incite the revolution; nor did the Jackson administration do anything to stop it. The president proclaimed U.S. neutrality but did not rigorously enforce

96. Belohlavek, *Eagle*, 225.
97. Quinton C. Lamar, "A Diplomatic Disaster: The Mexican Mission of Anthony Butler, 1829–1834," *Americas* 45 (July 1988), 1–18; Joe Gibson, " 'A. Butler: What a Scamp!' " *Journal of the West* 2 (1972), 235–47.

it. When the Texans won independence after the April 1836 Battle of San Jacinto and asked for recognition and annexation, Jackson demurred, fearing that the explosive issue of the expansion of slavery would tear apart his Democratic Party and cost his chosen successor, Van Buren, the election. Even after Van Buren had won, the ailing, outgoing president declined to act decisively, passing the buck to Congress. After an equally hesitant legislature finally enacted a resolution favoring recognition in March 1837, Jackson in one of his last acts recognized the Republic of Texas, leaving annexation for another day.

Despite his dedication to empire and his considerable foreign policy achievements, Jackson failed to complete a central task of continental expansion left undone by Monroe and Adams. In this case, the exigencies of politics won out over his commitment to expansionist goals. The annexation of Texas would form perhaps the defining event in the era of Manifest Destiny, helping to provoke a war with Mexico that in turn would round off U.S. continental expansion and inflame internal divisions that would lead to Civil War.

5

A Dose of Arsenic

Slavery, Expansion, and the Road to Disunion, 1837–1861

"The United States will conquer Mexico," philosopher Ralph Waldo Emerson predicted at the outbreak of war in May 1846, "but it will be as the man swallows the arsenic, which brings him down in turn. Mexico will poison us."[1] Emerson correctly predicted that America's first major foreign war would have disastrous consequences, but he was wrong about what they would be. The assumptions of Anglo-Saxon superiority he shared with his countrymen caused him to fear that absorption of Mexico's alien people would sully the purity of America's population and the strength of its institutions. In fact, it was the cancer of slavery within U.S. society that, when linked with disposition of the territory taken from Mexico, poisoned the body politic, provoking the irrepressible crisis that eventually sundered the Union.

Indeed, throughout the 1840s and 1850s, slavery and expansion marched hand in hand. Certain of the superiority of their institutions and greatness of their nation, a bumptious people continued to push out against the weak restraints that bound them. Through negotiation and conquest, they more than doubled the nation's territory by 1848. By the time of the Mexican-American War, however, the future of the South's "peculiar institution" had provoked passionate controversy. Even before the war, slavery had become for southerners the driving force behind expansionism and for abolitionists the reason to oppose acquisition of new territory. The conquest of vast new lands in the war with Mexico brought to the fore the pressing question of whether new slave states would be created, the issue that would tear the Union apart. Fears of the further extension of slavery and absorption of alien races, in turn, stymied southern efforts in the 1850s to acquire additional territory in the Caribbean and Central America. In foreign

1. William H. Gilman et al., *Journals of Ralph Waldo Emerson* (14 vols., Cambridge, Mass., 1960–78), 9:430–31.

policy, as in domestic affairs, slavery dominated the politics of the antebellum era.

I

The mid-nineteenth century marked a transitional stage between the post-Napoleonic international system and the disequilibrium leading to World War I. The European great powers sustained a general peace interrupted only by limited, regional wars. England solidified its position as hegemonic power. The Royal Navy controlled the seas; by 1860, Britain produced 20 percent of the world's manufactures and dominated global finance. The industrial revolution generated drastic economic changes that would produce profound political and social dislocations. Revolutions in France and Central Europe in 1848 shook the established order momentarily and threatened general war. The two nations that prevented war at this point, Britain and Russia, fought with each other in 1854. The Crimean War, in turn, stirred "revisionist" ambitions across Europe and heightened British isolationism, helping to initiate in the 1850s a period of mounting instability. While avoiding a major war, the European powers used the "firepower gap" created by new technology to further encroach on the non-Western world. The opening of China and Japan to Western influence, in particular, had enormous long-range implications for world politics.[2]

America's global position changed significantly. The United States took steps toward becoming a Pacific power, asserting its interests in Hawaii, participating in the quasi-colonial system the European powers imposed on China, and taking the lead in opening Japan. Its relations with Europe were more important and more complex. Economically, the United States was an integral part of the Atlantic trading community. Politically, it remained a distant and apparently disinterested observer of European internal politics and external maneuvering. Americans took European interest in the Western Hemisphere most seriously. Still nominally committed to containing U.S. expansion, Britain and France dabbled in Texas and California. The British quietly expanded in Central America. In fact, the powers were preoccupied with internal problems and continental rivalries, and European ambitions in the Western Hemisphere were receding. Nevertheless, U.S. politicians used the European threat to generate support for expansion. Increasingly paranoid slaveholders saw

2. Paul Kennedy, *The Rise and Fall of the Great Powers* (New York, 1987), 150; Stephen Pelz, "Changing International Systems, the World Balance of Power, and the United States, 1776–1976," *Diplomatic History* 12 (Winter 1988), 57–58.

the sinister force of abolitionism behind the appearance of every British gunboat and the machinations of every British diplomat.

The 1840s and 1850s brought headlong growth for the United States. As a result of a continued high birth rate and the massive immigration of Germans and Irish Catholics, the population nearly doubled again, reaching 31.5 million by 1860. Eight new states were admitted, bringing the total to thirty-three. Described with wonderment by foreign visitors as a "people in motion," Americans began spilling out into Texas and Oregon even before the region between the Mississippi River and Rocky Mountains was settled. Technology helped bind this vast territory together. By 1840, the United States had twice as much railroad track as all of Europe. Soon, there was talk of a transcontinental railroad. The invention of the telegraph and the rise of the penny press provided means to disseminate more information faster to a larger reading public, making it possible, in the words of publisher James Gordon Bennett, "to blend into one homogeneous mass . . . the whole population of the Republic." The antebellum era was the age of U.S. maritime greatness. Sleek clipper ships still ruled the seas, but in 1840 steamboat service was initiated to England, cutting the trip to ten days and quickening the pace of diplomacy.[3]

The economy grew exponentially after the Panic of 1837. Freed from dependence on Britain through development of a home market, America was no longer a colonial economy. In agriculture, cotton was still king, but western farmers with the aid of new technology launched a second agricultural revolution, challenging Russia as the world's leading producer of food. Mining and manufacturing became vital segments of an increasingly diversified economy. The United States was self-sufficient in most areas, but exports could make the difference between prosperity and recession; U.S. exports, mostly cotton, swelled from an average of $70 million during 1815–20 to $249 million in the decade before the Civil War.[4]

American approaches to the world appeared contradictory. On the one hand, technology was shrinking the globe. The United States was becoming part of the broader world community. Major metropolitan newspapers assigned correspondents to London and Paris. The government dispatched expeditions to explore Antarctica and the Pacific, the interior of Africa and South America, and the exotic Middle East. Curious readers devoured their reports. On their own initiative, merchants and mis-

3. William Earl Weeks, *Building the Continental Empire: American Expansion from the Revolution to the Civil War* (Chicago, 1996), 85.
4. Kinley J. Brauer, "The United States and British Imperial Expansion, 1815–1860," *Diplomatic History* 12 (Winter 1988), 36–37.

sionaries in growing numbers went forth to spread the gospel of Americanism. Each group looked beyond its immediate objectives to the larger goal of uplifting other peoples. "One should not forget," *New York Tribune* London correspondent Karl Marx wrote, "that America is the youngest and most vigorous exponent of Western Civilization."[5]

Americans observed the outside world with great fascination. They longed "to see distant lands," observed writer James Fenimore Cooper, to view the "peculiarities of nations" and the differences "between strangers and ourselves."[6] Some promoted development in other countries. The father of artist James McNeill Whistler oversaw the building of a railroad between Moscow and St. Petersburg. Growing numbers traveled abroad, many to Europe. These tourists carried their patriotism with them and found in the perceived inferiority of other nations confirmation of their own greatness. Those dissatisfied with America should tour the Old World, a Tennessean wrote, and they would "return home with national ideas, national love and national fidelity."[7]

On the other hand, U.S. policymakers and diplomats, once an experienced and cosmopolitan lot, were increasingly parochial, sometimes amateurish—and often proud of it. The presidential domination of foreign policy institutionalized by Jackson persisted under Polk. Of the chief executives who served in these years, only James Buchanan had diplomatic experience. Reflecting an emerging world role, the secretary of state had a staff of forty-three people by the 1850s; twenty-seven diplomats and eighty-eight consuls were posted abroad. Reforms limited consular appointments to U.S. citizens and restricted their ability to engage in private business.[8] The diplomatic corps was composed more and more of politicians and merchants. Some served with distinction; others made Anthony Butler look good.

Americans wore their republicanism on their sleeves and even enshrined it in protocol. Polk displayed "American arrogance" toward diplomats who addressed him in a language other than English and dismissed as "ridiculous" the repeated ceremonial visits of the Russian minister to announce such trivia as the marriage of the tsar's son.[9] Secretary of State William

5. Quoted in Larry Gara, *The Presidency of Franklin Pierce* (Lawrence, Kans., 1991), 129.
6. Quoted in Robert W. Johannsen, *To the Halls of the Montezumas: The Mexican War in the American Imagination* (New York, 1987), 144–45.
7. Quoted in Edwin T. Greninger, "Tennesseans Abroad in 1851–1852," *Tennessee Historical Quarterly* 49 (Summer 1990), 81–82. See also Reginald C. Stuart, *United States Expansionism and British North America* (Chapel Hill, N.C., 1988), 148–66.
8. Gara, *Pierce*, 57–59.
9. Paul H. Bergeron, *The Presidency of James K. Polk* (Lawrence, Kans., 1987), 218–19.

Marcy's "dress circular" of 1853 went well beyond Jackson's republicanism by requiring diplomats to appear in court in plain black evening clothes, the "simple dress of an American citizen." Parisians scornfully dubbed the U.S. minister "the Black Crow." Americans applauded. The person who represented his nation abroad should "look like an American, talk like an American, and be an American example," the *New York Post* proclaimed.[10] New World ways some times rubbed off on Old World diplomats. Russian Eduard Stoeckl married an American and during his time in Washington served in a fire company where, in his words, he "run wid de lantern."[11]

II

The catchphrase "Manifest Destiny" summed up the expansionist thrust of the pre–Civil War era. Coined in 1845 by the Democratic Party journalist John L. O'Sullivan to justify annexation of Texas, Oregon, and California, the phrase meant, simply defined, that God had willed the expansion of the United States to the Pacific Ocean—or beyond. The concept expressed the exuberant nationalism and brash arrogance of the era. Divine sanction, in the eyes of many Americans, gave them a superior claim to any rival and lent an air of inevitability to their expansion. Manifest Destiny pulled together into a potent ideology notions dating to the origins of the republic with implications extending beyond the continent: that the American people and their institutions were uniquely virtuous, thus imposing on them a God-given mission to remake the world in their own image.[12]

Many Americans have accepted the rhetoric of Manifest Destiny at face value, seeing their nation's continental expansion as inevitable and altruistic, a result of the irresistible force generated by a virtuous people. Once viewed as a great national movement, an expression of American optimism and idealism, and the driving force behind expansion in the 1840s, Manifest Destiny's meaning and significance have been considerably qualified in recent years.[13]

---

10. Quoted in Ralph Davis Jr., "Diplomatic Plumage: American Court Dress in the Early National Period," *American Quarterly* 20, no. 2 (1968), 175–79; Gara, *Pierce*, 58–59.
11. Norman E. Saul, *Distant Friends: The United States and Russia, 1763–1867* (Lawrence, Kans., 1991), 253.
12. Weeks, *Continental Empire*, 59–62.
13. The classic study, an intellectual history, remains Albert K. Weinberg, *Manifest Destiny: A Study of Nationalist Expansionism in American History* (Baltimore, Md., 1935). Other major works include Frederick Merk, *Manifest Destiny and Mission in American History: A Reinterpretation* (New York, 1966), Thomas R. Hietala, *Manifest Design: Anxious Aggrandizement in Jacksonian America* (Ithaca, N.Y., 1985), and Anders Stephanson, *Manifest Destiny—American Expansion and the Empire of Right* (New York, 1995).

For some Americans, no doubt, the rhetoric expressed idealistic sentiments. The acquisition of new lands and the admission of new peoples to the Union extended the blessings of liberty. Territorial expansion provided a haven for those fleeing oppression in other lands. Some Americans even believed that their nation had an obligation to uplift and regenerate "backward" peoples like Mexicans.

More often than not, Manifest Destiny covered and attempted to legitimate selfish motives. Southerners sought new land to perpetuate an economic and social system based on cotton and slavery and new slave states to preserve their power in Congress. People from all sections interested in the export trade coveted the magnificent ports of the Oregon country and California as jumping-off points to capture the rich commerce of East Asia. Restless, land-hungry westerners sought territory for its own sake. Some Americans argued that if the United States did not take Texas and California, the British and French would. At least, they might try to sustain independent republics that could threaten the security of the United States.

Manifest Destiny was also heavily tinged with racism. At the time of the Revolution and for years after, some Americans had sincerely believed that they could teach other peoples to share in the blessings of republicanism. The nation's remarkable success increasingly turned optimism into arrogance, however, and repeated clashes with Indians and Mexicans created a need to justify the exploitation of weaker people. "Scientific" theories of superior and inferior races thus emerged in the nineteenth century to rationalize U.S. expansion. Inferior races did not use the land properly and impeded progress, it was argued. They must give way before superior races, some, like African Americans, doomed to perpetual subservience, others, like Indians, to assimilation or extinction.[14]

Manifest Destiny was a sectional rather than national phenomenon, its support strongest in the Northeast and Northwest and weakest in the South, which supported only the annexation of Texas. It was also highly partisan. A second American party system emerged in the 1840s with the rise of two distinct political entities, roughly equal in strength, that set the agenda for national politics and took well-defined positions on major issues. The lineal descendants of Jefferson's Republicans, the Democrats rallied around the policies of the charismatic hero Andrew Jackson. The Whigs, a direct offshoot of the National Republicans along with some disaffected Democrats, formed in opposition to what its followers saw as the

14. Reginald Horsman, *Race and Manifest Destiny* (Cambridge, Mass., 1981), 301.

dangerous consolidation of executive power by "King Andrew I." Henry Clay was the leading national figure.[15]

The two parties differed sharply on the crucial issue of expansion. Looking backward to an idyllic agricultural society, the Democrats, like Jefferson, fervently believed that preservation of traditional republican values depended on commercial and territorial expansion. The Panic of 1837 and a growing surplus in agricultural production aroused their anxieties. Deeply alarmed by the rise of industrialization, urbanization, and class conflict in the Northeast, the very evils Jefferson had warned about, they saw expansion as a solution to the problems of modernization. The availability of new land in the West and acquisition of new markets for farm products would preserve the essentially agricultural economy upon which republicanism depended. An expanding frontier would protect Americans against poverty, concentration of population, exhaustion of the land, and the wage slavery of industrial capitalism. A sprawling national domain would preserve liberty rather than threaten it. Fortuitously, new technology like the railroad and telegraph that annihilated distance would permit administration of a vast empire. Expansion was fundamental to the American character, the Democrats insisted. The very process of the westward movement produced those special qualities that made Americans exceptional.[16]

More cautious and conservative, Whigs harbored deep fears of uncontrolled expansion. Change must be orderly, they insisted; the existing Union must be consolidated before the nation acquired more territory. The more rapidly and extensively the Union grew, the more difficult it would be to govern and the more it would be imperiled. The East might be left desolate and depopulated and sectional tensions increased. Whigs welcomed industrialism. In contrast to the Democrats, who promoted an activist role for government in external matters, they believed government's major task was to promote economic growth and disperse prosperity and capital in a way that would avert internal conflict, improve the lot of the individual, and enrich society. Government should promote the interests of the entire nation to ensure harmony and balance, ease sectional

15. Richard P. McCormick, *The Second American Party System* (Chapel Hill, N.C., 1966); Ronald P. Formisano, *The Birth of Mass Political Parties, Michigan, 1827–1861* (Princeton, N.J., 1971); Michael F. Holt, *Rise and Fall of the American Whig Party: Jacksonian Politics and the Onset of the American Civil War* (New York, 1999).
16. Michael A. Morrison, "Westward the Curse of Empire: Texas Annexation and the American Whig Party," *Journal of the Early Republic* 10 (Summer 1990), 226–29; Hietala, *Manifest Design*, 95–131, 196.

and class tensions, and promote peace. Like the Democrats, the Whigs talked of extending freedom, but their approach was passive rather than active. "The eyes of the world are upon us," Edward Everett asserted, "and our example will probably be decisive of the cause of human liberty."[17]

The increasingly inflammatory debate over slavery heightened conflict over expansion. As early as the 1830s, abolitionists began to attack slaveholder domination of the political system, creating one of the first pressure groups to influence U.S. foreign policy. The still volatile issue of Haiti became their cause célèbre. Abolitionists such as Lydia Maria Child and their frequent supporter John Quincy Adams condemned those who opposed recognition of the black republic because a "colored ambassador would be so disagreeable to our prejudice." They pleaded for recognition as a matter of principle and for trade. They pushed for opening of the British market for corn and wheat to spur prosperity in the Northwest, breaking the stranglehold of the "slavocracy" on the national government. Urging the United States to join Britain in an international effort to police the slave trade and abolish slavery, they passionately opposed the acquisition of new slave states.[18]

Increasingly paranoid slaveholders, on the other side, warned that a vast abolitionist conspiracy threatened their peculiar institution and indeed the nation. Haiti also had huge symbolic importance for them, the bloodshed, political chaos, and economic distress there portending the inevitable results of emancipation elsewhere. They saw abolitionism as an international movement centered in London whose philanthropic pretensions covered sinister imperialist designs. By abolishing slavery, the British could undercut southern production of staples, destroy the U.S. economy, and dominate world commerce and manufacturing. They denounced British high-handedness in policing the slave trade. They mongered among themselves morbid rumors of nefarious British plots to foment revolution among slaves in Cuba, incite Mexicans and Indians against the United States, and invade the South with armies of free blacks. They conjured graphic images of entire white populations being

17. Morrison, "Westward," 230–33; Norma Lois Peterson, *The Presidencies of William Henry Harrison and John Tyler* (Lawrence, Kans., 1989), 138. See also Major Wilson, *Space, Time, and Freedom: The Quest for Nationality and the Irrepressible Conflict* (Westport, Conn., 1974).
18. Edward P. Crapol, "The Foreign Policy of Anti-slavery, 1833–1846," in Lloyd C. Gardner, ed., *Redefining the Past: Essays in Diplomatic History in Honor of William Appleman Williams* (Corvallis, Ore., 1986), 88–102.

murdered except for the young and beautiful women reserved for "African lust." They condemned the federal government for not defending their rights from "foreign wrongs." They spoke openly of taking up the burden of defending slavery and even of secession. They ardently promoted the addition of new slave states. Pandering to the racial fears of northern Democrats, they suggested that extension of slavery into areas like Texas would draw the black population southward, even into Central America, ending the institution by natural processes and sparing the northern states and Upper South concentrations of free blacks.[19]

American expansionism in the 1840s was neither providential nor innocent. It resulted from design, rather than destiny, a carefully calculated effort by purposeful Democratic leaders to attain specific objectives that served mainly U.S. interests. The rhetoric of Manifest Destiny was nationalistic, idealistic, and self-confident, but it covered deep and sometimes morbid fears for America's security against internal decay and external danger. Expansionism showed scant regard for the "inferior" peoples who stood in the way. When combined with the volatile issue of slavery, it fueled increasingly bitter sectional and partisan conflict.[20]

III

Manifest Destiny had limits, most notably along the northern border with British Canada. Anglophobia and respect for Britain coexisted uneasily during the antebellum years. Americans still viewed the former mother country as the major threat to their security and prosperity and resented its refusal to pay them proper respect. At election time, U.S. politicians habitually twisted the lion's tail to whip up popular support. Upper-class Americans, on the other hand, admired British accomplishments and institutions. Responsible citizens understood the importance of economic ties between the two nations. A healthy respect for British power and a growing sense of Anglo-Saxon unity and common purpose—their "peculiar and sacred relations to the cause of civilization and freedom," O'Sullivan called it—produced very different attitudes and approaches toward Britain and Mexico. Americans continued to regard Canada as a base

---

19. Hietala, *Manifest Design*, 30–32. For a sampling of slaveholder fear mongering, see Edmund P. Gaines to Calhoun, May 5, 1844, in Clyde Wilson, ed., *The Papers of John C. Calhoun*, vol. 18 (Columbia, S.C., 1989), 440–44, Calhoun to Ana Maria Calhoun Clemson, May 16, 1844, ibid., 469, Calhoun to William King, August 12, 1844, ibid., vol. 19 (Columbia, S.C., 1990), 574–75, Robert M. Harrison to Calhoun, August 12, 1844, ibid., 634–36, and Wilson introduction to ibid., xiii–xviii.
20. Hietala, *Manifest Design*, passim.

from which Britain could strike the United States, but they increasingly doubted it would be used. They also came to accept the presence of their northern neighbor and evinced a willingness to live in peace with it. Even the zealot O'Sullivan conceded that Manifest Destiny stopped at the Canadian border. He viewed Canadians as possible junior partners in the process of Manifest Destiny but did not press for annexation when the opportunity presented itself, envisioning a peaceful evolution toward a possible merger at some unspecified future time.[21]

Rebellions in Canada in 1837–38 raised the threat of a third Anglo-American war, but they evoked from most Americans a generally restrained response. At the outset, to be sure, some saw the Canadian uprisings, along with events in Texas, as part of the onward march of republicanism. Along the border, some Americans offered the rebels sanctuary and support. Incidents such as the burning of the American ship *Caroline* by Canadian soldiers on U.S. territory in December 1837 inflamed tensions. As it became clear that the rebellions were something less than republican in origin and intent, tempers cooled. Borderland communities where legal and illegal trade flourished feared the potential costs of war. President Martin Van Buren declared U.S. neutrality and after the *Caroline* incident dispatched War of 1812 hero Gen. Winfield Scott to enforce it. Traveling the border country by sled in frigid temperatures, often alone, Scott zealously executed his orders, expressing outrage at the destruction of the *Caroline* and promising to defend U.S. territory from British attack but warning his countrymen against provocative actions. On one occasion, he admonished hotheads that "except it be over my body, you shall *not* pass this line." Another time, as a preemptive measure, he bought out from under rebel supporters a ship he suspected was to be used for hostile activities. Scott's intervention helped ease tensions along the border. In terms of Manifest Destiny, Americans continued to believe that Canadians would opt for republicanism, but they respected the principle of self-determination rather than seeking to impose their views by force.[22]

Conflict over the long-disputed boundary between Maine and New Brunswick also produced Anglo-American hostility—and restraint. Local

21. Stuart, *United States Expansionism*, 85–99.
22. Ibid., 126–47; Howard Jones and Donald A. Rakestraw, *Prologue to Manifest Destiny: Anglo-American Relations in the 1840s* (Wilmington, Del., 1997), 21–41; Scott Kaufman and John A. Soares Jr., " 'Sagacious Beyond Praise'? Winfield Scott and Anglo-American-Canadian Border Diplomacy, 1837–1860," *Diplomatic History* 30 (January 2006), 58–66.

interests on both sides posed insuperable obstacles to settlement. For years, Maine had frustrated federal efforts to negotiate. Washington did nothing when the state government or its citizens defied federal law or international agreements. When Canadian lumberjacks cut timber in the disputed Aroostook River valley in late 1838, tempers flared, sparking threats of war. The tireless and peripatetic Scott hastened to Maine to reassure its citizens and encourage local officials to compromise. As with the Canadian rebellions, cooler heads prevailed. The so-called Aroostook War amounted to little more than a barroom brawl, the major casualties bloody noses and broken arms. But territorial dispute continued to threaten the peace.[23]

Conflict over the slave trade added a more volatile dimension to Anglo-American tension. In the 1830s, Britain launched an all-out crusade against that brutal and nefarious traffic in human beings. The United States outlawed the international slave trade in 1808 but, because of southern resistance, did little to stop it. Alone among nations, it refused to participate in multilateral efforts. Slave traders thus used the U.S. flag to cover their activities. The War of 1812 still fresh in their minds and highly sensitive to affronts to their honor, Americans South *and* North loudly protested when British ships began stopping and searching vessels flying the Stars and Stripes. An incident in November 1841 raised a simmering dispute to the level of crisis. Led by a cook named Madison Washington, slaves aboard the *Creole* en route from Virginia to New Orleans mutinied, took over the ship, killed a slave trader, and sailed to the Bahamas. Under pressure from the local population, British authorities released all 135 of the slaves because they landed on free territory. Furious with British interference with the domestic slave trade and more than ever convinced of a sinister plot to destroy slavery in the United States, southerners demanded restoration of their property and reparations. But the United States had no extradition treaty with Britain and could do nothing to back its citizens' claims.[24]

The Webster-Ashburton Treaty of 1842 solved several burning issues and confirmed the limits of Manifest Destiny. By this time, both sides sought to ease tensions. An avowed Anglophile, Secretary of State Daniel Webster viewed commerce with England as essential to U.S. prosperity. The new British government of Sir Robert Peel was friendly toward the United States and sought respite from tension to pursue domestic reform

23. Jones and Rakestraw, *Prologue*, 8–11, Kaufman and Soares, "Scott," 66–71.
24. Jones and Rakestraw, *Prologue*, 81–89.

and address more urgent European problems. By sending a special mission to the United States, Peel struck a responsive chord among insecure Americans—"an unusual piece of condescension" for "haughty" England, New Yorker Philip Hone conceded.[25] The appointment of Alexander Baring, Lord Ashburton, to carry out the mission confirmed London's good intentions. Head of one of the world's leading banking houses, Ashburton was married to an American, owned land in Maine, and had extensive investments in the United States. He believed that good relations were essential to the "moral improvement and the progressive civilization of the world." Ashburton steeled himself for the rigors of life in the "colonies" by bringing with him three secretaries, five servants, and three horses and a carriage. He and Webster entertained lavishly. Old friends, they agreed to dispense with the usual conventions of diplomacy and work informally. Webster even invited representatives of Maine and Massachusetts to join the discussions, causing Ashburton to marvel how "this Mass of ungovernable and unmanageable anarchy" functioned as well as it did.[26]

The novice diplomats used unconventional methods to resolve major differences. On the most difficult issue, the Maine–New Brunswick boundary, they worked out a compromise that satisfied hotheads on neither side and then used devious means to sell it. Each conveniently employed different maps to prove to skeptical constituents their side had got the better of the deal—or at least avoided losing more. Webster had more difficulty negotiating with Maine than with his British counterpart. He used $12,000 from a secret presidential slush fund to propagandize his fellow New Englanders to accept the treaty. This knot untied, the two men with relative ease set a boundary between Lake Superior and the Lake of the Woods. They defused the still-sensitive *Caroline* issue and agreed on an extradition treaty to help deal with matters like the *Creole*. Resolution of differences on the slave trade was most difficult. Eventually, the treaty provided for a joint squadron, but the United States, predictably, did not uphold the arrangement. The Webster-Ashburton Treaty testified to Anglo-American good sense when that quality seemed in short supply. It confirmed U.S. acceptance of the sharing of North America with British Canadians. It resolved numerous problems that might have provoked war and set the two nations on a course toward eventual rapprochement. The

25. Quoted in ibid., 105.
26. Ibid., 114.

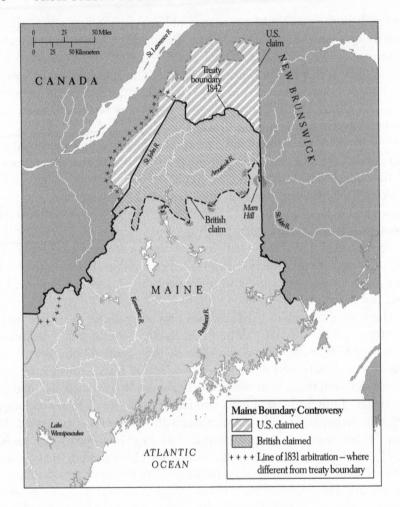

threat of war eased in the Northeast, the United States could turn its attention to the Pacific Northwest and the Southwest.[27]

Oregon was a major exception to the budding Anglo-American accord. The joint occupation had outlived its usefulness by the mid-1840s. The

27. Charles S. Campbell, *From Revolution to Rapprochement: The United States and Great Britain, 1783–1900* (New York, 1974), 62; Stuart, *United States Expansionism*, 101–2; Jones and Rakestraw, *Prologue*, 149. The standard account is Howard Jones, *To the Webster-Ashburton Treaty: A Study in Anglo-American Relations, 1783–1843* (Chapel Hill, N.C., 1977). See also Francis M. Carroll, *A Good and Wise Measure; The Search for the Canadian-American Boundary, 1783–1842* (Toronto, 2001).

Pacific Northwest became the focal point of a dangerous conflict sparked largely by bungling diplomacy and exacerbated by domestic politics in both countries and especially by the intrusion of national honor. The Oregon crisis brought out old suspicions and hatreds, nearly provoking an unnecessary and costly war.

In the 1840s, a long-dormant conflict in the Pacific Northwest sprang to life. British interests remained essentially commercial and quickened with the opening of China through the 1842 Treaty of Nanking. The ports of Oregon and Mexican California were perfectly situated for exploiting the commerce of East Asia, and merchants and sea captains pressed the government to take possession. Americans too saw links with the fabled commerce of the Orient, but their major interest in Oregon had shifted to settlement. Missionaries first went there to proselytize the Indians but established the permanent settlements that provided the basis for U.S. occupation. Driven from their homes by the depression of 1837 and enticed west by tales of lush farm lands, thousands of restless Americans followed in making the rugged, costly, and hazardous two-thousand-mile, six-month trek from St. Louis across the Oregon Trail. The return of the Great United States Exploring Expedition in June 1842 after an eighty-seven-thousand-mile voyage around the world stirred the American imagination and drew special attention to Oregon, "a storehouse of wealth in its forests, furs and fisheries," a veritable Eden on the Pacific.[28] Oregon "fever" became an epidemic. By 1845, some five thousand Americans lived in the region and established a government to which even the once mighty Hudson's Bay Company paid taxes. They talked of admission to the Union, a direct challenge to the 1827 agreement with Britain. The "same causes which impelled our population . . . to the valley of the Mississippi, will impel them onward with accumulating force . . . into the valley of the Columbia," Secretary of State John C. Calhoun informed the British minister in 1844. The "whole region . . . is destined to be peopled by us."[29]

Along with Texas, Oregon became a volatile issue in the hotly contested presidential campaign of 1844. Western expansionists advanced outrageous claims all the way to 54° 40', the line negotiated with Russia in 1824 but far beyond the point ever contested with Britain. The bombastic Senator Thomas Hart Benton of Missouri even threatened war, proclaiming that "30–40,000 rifles are our best negotiators." Expansionist

28. Peterson, *Harrison and Tyler*, 136–37.
29. Calhoun to Pakenham, September 3, 1844, in Wilson, *Calhoun Papers* 19:705.

Democrats tried to link Texas with Oregon, trading southern votes for Oregon with western votes for Texas. The Democratic platform thus affirmed a "clear and unquestionable" claim to all of Oregon. The dark horse candidate, ardent expansionist James K. Polk of Tennessee, campaigned on the dubious slogan of the "re-annexation of Texas" and "reoccupation of Oregon."[30]

A crisis erupted within months after Polk took office. The forty-nine-year-old Tennessean was short, thin, and somewhat drab in appearance with a sad look, deep piercing eyes, and a sour disposition. Vain and driven, he set lofty expansionist goals for his administration, and by pledging not to seek reelection he placed self-imposed limits on his ability to achieve them. He was introverted, humorless, and a workaholic. His shrewdness and ability to size up friends and rivals had served him well in the rough-and-tumble of backcountry politics, and he had an especially keen eye for detail. But he could be cold and aloof. Parochial and highly nationalistic, he was impatient with the niceties of diplomacy and lacked understanding of and sensitivity to other nations and peoples.[31]

Polk's initial efforts to strike a deal provoked a crisis. Despite his menacing rhetoric, he realized that the United States had never claimed beyond the 49th parallel. Thus while continuing publicly to claim all of Oregon, he professed himself bound by the acts of his predecessors. He privately offered a "generous" settlement at the 49th parallel with free ports on the southern tip of Vancouver Island. An experienced and skillful diplomat, British minister Richard Pakenham might have overlooked Polk's posturing, but he too let nationalist pride interfere with diplomacy. Infuriated by Polk's pretensions of generosity, he refused to refer the proposal to London. The Foreign Office subsequently disapproved Pakenham's action, but the damage was done. Stung by the rejection of proposals he believed generous, Polk was probably relieved that Pakenham had taken him off the hook. He defiantly withdrew the "compromise," rejected British proposals for arbitration, reasserted claims to all of Oregon, and asked Congress to abrogate the joint occupation provision of the 1827 treaty. The "only way to treat John Bull is to look him straight in the eye," the tough-talking Tennessean later informed a delegation of congressmen.[32]

30. The "reannexation" of Texas suggested, wrongly, that Texas had once belonged to the United States but had been carelessly squandered in the 1819 treaty with Spain.
31. Bergeron, *Polk*, 45; Hietala, *Manifest Design*, 249.
32. Jones and Rakestraw, *Prologue*, 235. Daniel Walker Howe, *What Hath God Wrought: The Transformation of America, 1815–1845* (New York, 2007), 715–22, argues that Polk took a hard line on Oregon to gain northern Democrats' support for a tough stance with Mexico.

Polk's ill-conceived effort to stare down the world's greatest power nearly backfired. In the United States, at least momentarily, the breakdown of diplomacy left the field to the hotheads. "54-40 or fight," they shouted, and O'Sullivan coined the phrase that marked an era, proclaiming that the U.S. title to Oregon was "by the right of our manifest destiny to overspread and to possess the whole of the continent which Providence has given us for the development of the great experiment of Liberty." Conveniently forgetting his earlier willingness to compromise, Massachusetts congressman John Quincy Adams now found sanction in the Book of Genesis for possession of all of Oregon.[33]

Its future imperiled by domestic disputes over trade policy, the Peel government wanted to settle the Oregon issue, but not at the price of national honor. American pretensions aroused fury in London. Foreign Minister Lord Aberdeen retorted in Polk's own phrase that British rights to Oregon were "clear and unquestionable." Peel proclaimed that "we are resolved—and we are prepared—to maintain them."[34] Responding directly to Adams, the *Times* of London sneered that a "democracy intoxicated with what it mistakes for religion is the most formidable apparition which can startle the world."[35] Hotheads pressed for war. The army and navy prepared for action. Some zealots welcomed war with the United States as a heaven-sent opportunity to eliminate slavery. Whigs stood poised to exploit any sign of Tory weakness. In early 1846, the government emphasized that its patience was wearing thin. Revelation of plans to send as many as thirty warships to Canada underscored the warning.

The two nations steadied themselves in mid-1846 just as they teetered on the brink of war. Polk perceived that his bluster had angered rather than intimidated the British and that more of the same might lead to war. Congressional debates in early 1846 made clear that despite the political bombast a war for *all* of Oregon would not have broad support. Also on the verge of war with Mexico, the United States was not prepared to fight one enemy, much less two. Polk thus set out to ease the crisis he had helped to provoke by putting forth terms he might have offered earlier. Shortly after Congress passed the resolution giving notice of abrogation of the 1827 treaty, he quietly informed London of his willingness to compromise. Reports from Oregon that American settlers were firmly entrenched and that Britain should cut its losses reinforced Peel's eagerness

33. Ibid., 240.
34. Ibid, 206.
35. Quoted in David M. Pletcher, *The Diplomacy of Annexation: Texas, Oregon, and the Mexican War* (Columbia, Mo., 1973), 339.

for a settlement. London thus responded with terms nearly identical to those earlier outlined by the United States. Ever cautious, Polk took the extraordinary step of securing Senate approval before proceeding. Already at war with Mexico, the United States approved the treaty as drafted in London, a mere nine days passing between its delivery to the State Department and ratification. "Now we can thrash Mexico into decency at our leisure," the *New York Herald* exclaimed.[36]

The Oregon settlement accorded reasonably well with the specific interests of each signatory. It extended the boundary along the 49th parallel from the Rockies to the coast, leaving Vancouver Island in British hands and Juan de Fuca Strait open to both countries. Against Polk's wishes, it also permitted the Hudson's Bay Company to navigate the Columbia River. The United States had no settlements north of the 49th parallel and had never claimed that area before the 1840s. Despite the sometimes heated rhetoric, few Americans thought all of Oregon worth a war. Britain had long sought a boundary at the Columbia River, but the fur trade in the disputed area was virtually exhausted. Possession of Vancouver Island and access to Juan de Fuca Strait adequately met its maritime needs.

In each nation, other crises put a premium on settlement. The war with Mexico and Britain's refusal to interfere there made peace both urgent and expedient for the United States. Strained relations with France, problems in Ireland, and an impending political crisis at home made a settlement with the United States desirable, if not absolutely essential, for the British. Both sides recognized the importance of commercial ties and a common culture and heritage. In the United States, respect for British power and a reluctance on racial grounds to fight with Anglo-Saxon brethren made war unthinkable. Most important, both sides realized the foolishness of war. Often praised for his diplomacy, Polk deserves credit mainly for the good sense to extricate the nation from a crisis he had helped provoke.[37]

The Oregon treaty freed the United States to turn its attention southward. It also provided the much-coveted outlet on the Pacific as well as clear title to a rich expanse of territory including all of the future states of Washington, Oregon, Idaho, and parts of Montana and Wyoming. Along with the Webster-Ashburton Treaty, it eased a conflict that had been a fact of life since the Revolution. Americans generally agreed that their "Manifest Destiny" did not include Canada. Having contained U.S. expansion in the North, Britain increasingly learned to live with the upstart repub-

36. Ibid., 414.
37. Ibid., 402–17; Howe, *What Hath God Wrought*, 718–22.

The Oregon Question,
1818–1846

1824 Russian-American Line
54° 40'

CONTINENTAL DIVIDE

Fraser R.

OREGON

BRITISH
POSSESSIONS

Gulf of Georgia

VANCOUVER ISLAND

Juan de Fuca
Strait

1846 Oregon Treaty Line

1818 Convention Line
49°

Gray's Harbor

Cape Disappointment

Fort Nisqually

Missouri R.

Astoria

Fort Vancouver
Columbia R.

TERRITORY

UNITED
STATES

Willamette R.

PACIFIC OCEAN

Snake R.

1819 Adams-Onis Line
42°

MEXICO

Great
Salt Lake

0   50   100   150 Miles

0   50   100   150 Kilometers

lic. Conflict would continue, but only during the American Civil War would it assume dangerous proportions. Increasingly, the two nations would find that more united than divided them. Despite the rhetoric of Manifest Destiny, the United States and Britain had reached an agreement on the sharing of North America.[38]

IV

"No instance of aggrandizement or lust for territory has stained our annals," O'Sullivan boasted in 1844, expressing one of the nation's most cherished and durable myths.[39] Dubious when it was written, O'Sullivan's affirmation soon proved completely wrong. The Mexican-American conflict of 1846–48 was in large part a war of lust and aggrandizement. The United States had long coveted Texas. In the 1840s, California and New Mexico also became objects of its desire. With characteristic single-mindedness, Polk set his sights on all of them. He employed the same bullying approach used with the British, this time without backing off, provoking a war that would have momentous consequences for both nations.

The United States government did not orchestrate a clever conspiracy to steal Texas, as Mexicans charged, but the result was the same. Lured to the "New El Dorado" by the promise of cheap cotton land, thirty-five thousand Americans with five thousand slaves had spilled into Texas by 1835. Alarmed by an immigration it once welcomed, the newly independent government of Mexico sought to impose its authority over the newcomers and abolish slavery. To defend their rights—and slaves—the Texans took up arms. After a crushing defeat at the Alamo, the subject of much patriotic folklore, they won a decisive victory at San Jacinto in April 1836.

An independent Texas presented enticing opportunities and vexing problems. Americans had taken a keen interest in the revolution. Despite nominal neutrality—and in marked contrast to the strict enforcement of neutrality laws along the Canadian border—they assisted the rebels with money, arms, and volunteers. Many Americans and Texans assumed that the "sister republic" would join the United States. From the outset, however, Texas got entangled with the explosive issue of slavery. Politicians handled it gingerly. Jackson refused to recognize the new nation until his successor, Van Buren, was safely elected. Eager for reelection, Van Buren warily turned aside Texas proposals for annexation.

38. Stuart, *United States Expansionism*, 104–5.
39. Hietala, *Manifest Design*, 193.

By 1844, Texas had become the focal point of rumors, plots and coun-terplots, diplomatic intrigue, and bitter political conflict. Many Texans fa-vored annexation, others preferred independence, some straddled the fence. Although unwilling to risk war with the United States, Britain and France sought an independent Texas and urged Mexico to recognize the new nation to keep it out of U.S. hands. Alarmist southerners fed each other's fears with lurid tales of sinister British schemes to abolish slavery in Texas, incite a slave revolt in Cuba, and strike a "fatal blow" against slavery in the United States, provoking a race war "of the most deadly and desolating character." In the eyes of some southerners, Britain's real aim was to throw an "Iron Chain" around the United States to gain "com-mand of the commerce, navigation and manufactures of the world" and to reduce its former colonies to economic "vassalage."[40]

For Americans of all political persuasions, the Union's future de-pended on the absorption of Texas. Whigs protested that annexation would violate principles Americans had long believed in and might pro-voke war with Mexico.[41] Abolitionists warned of a slaveholders' conspiracy to retain control of the government and perpetuate the evils of human bondage.[42] On the annexation of Texas "hinges the very existence of our Southern Institutions," South Carolinian James Gadsden warned Cal-houn, "and if we of the South now prove recreant, we will or must [be] content to be Heawers of wood and Drawers of Water for our Northern Brethren."[43]

In 1844, with an independent Texas a distinct possibility, the Virginian and slaveholder John Tyler, who had become president in 1841 on the death of William Henry Harrison, took up the challenge Jackson and Van Buren had skirted. A staunch Jeffersonian, Tyler is often dismissed as an advocate of states' rights who sought to acquire Texas mainly to protect the institution of slavery. In fact, he was a strong nationalist who pushed a broad agenda of commercial and territorial expansion in hopes of uniting the nation, fulfilling its God-given destiny, and gaining reelection.[44] Seeking to win over the Democrats or rally a party of his own, he pressed

40. Robert Paquette, "The Everett–Del Monte Connection: A Study in the International Politics of Slavery," *Diplomatic History* 11 (Winter 1987), 1–22; Edmund P. Gaines to Calhoun, May 5, 1844, in Wilson, *Calhoun Papers* 18:440–441, and Calhoun to William King, August 12, 1844, ibid. 19:568, 578.
41. Morrison, "Westward the Curse," 235.
42. Crapol, "Anti-slavery," 84–87, 89–91.
43. Gadsden to Calhoun, May 3, 1844, in Wilson, *Calhoun Papers* 18:84–85.
44. Edward P. Crapol, "John Tyler and the Pursuit of National Destiny," *Journal of the Early Republic* 17 (Fall 1997), 476–79.

vigorously for annexation of Texas. A treaty might have passed the Senate in 1844 had not Calhoun stiffened the opposition by publicly defending slavery. Once the 1844 election was over, lame duck Tyler again proposed admission. Instead of a treaty of annexation, which would have required a two-thirds vote in the Senate, he sought a joint resolution for admission as a state, requiring only a simple majority, on the questionable constitutional grounds that new states could be admitted by act of Congress. The resolution passed after heated debate and drawn-out maneuvering, winning in the Senate by a mere two votes. Texas agreed to the proposals, initiating the process of annexation.[45]

Mexico considered annexation an act of war. Born in 1821, the nation had great expectations because of its size and wealth in natural resources but had suffered economic devastation during its war of independence. The flight of capital abroad in its early years reduced it to bankruptcy. It was also afflicted by profound class, religious, and political divisions. The central government exercised at best nominal authority over the vast outer provinces. Political instability was a way of life. Rival Masonic lodges contended for power, ironic in a predominantly Catholic country. Coup followed coup, sixteen presidents serving between 1837 and 1851. The "volcanic genius" Antonio Lopez de Santa Anna embodied the chaos of Mexican political life. Brilliant but erratic, skilled at mobilizing the population but bored with the details of governance, he served eleven times as president. A master conspirator, he switched sides with alacrity and was said even to intrigue against himself. Noted for his flamboyance, he buried with full military honors the leg he had lost in battle. When he was later repudiated, his enemies dug up the leg and ceremoniously dragged it through the streets.[46]

Too proud to surrender Texas but too weak and divided to regain it by force, Mexicans justifiably (and correctly) feared that acquiescence in annexation could initiate a domino effect that would cost them additional territory. In their view, the United States had encouraged its citizens to infiltrate Texas, incited and supported their revolution, and then moved to absorb the renegade state. They denounced U.S. actions as "the most scandalous violation of the law of nations," the "most direct spoliation, which has been seen for ages."[47] When the annexation resolution passed Congress, Mexico severed diplomatic relations.

45. Peterson, *Harrison and Tyler*, 176–80, 256–58.
46. Enrique Krauze, *Mexico, Biography of Power: A History of Modern Mexico* (New York, 1997), 99–135, 142.
47. J. M. de Bocaneara to Ben Green, June 6, 15, 1844, in Wilson, *Calhoun Papers* 19:67, 79.

A dispute over the Texas boundary exacerbated Mexican-American conflict. Under Spanish and Mexican rule, the province had never extended south of the Nueces River; Texas had never established its authority or even a settlement beyond that point. On the basis of nothing more than an act of its own congress and the fact that Mexican forces withdrew south of the Rio Grande after San Jacinto, Texas had claimed territory to the Rio Grande. Despite the dubious claim and the uncertain value of the barren land, Polk firmly supported the Texans. He ordered Gen. Zachary Taylor to the area to deter a possible Mexican attack and subsequently instructed him to take a position as close to the Rio Grande as "prudence will dictate."[48]

Polk also set out to acquire California. Only six thousand Mexicans lived there. Mexico had stationed in its northernmost province an army of fewer than six hundred men to control a huge territory. In October 1842, acting on rumors of war with Mexico, Cmdre. Thomas ap Catesby Jones sailed into Monterey, captured the local authorities, and raised the U.S. flag. When he learned there was no war, he lowered the flag, held a banquet of apology for his captives, and sailed away.[49] Americans were increasingly drawn to California. Sea captains and explorers spoke with wonderment of the lush farmland and salubrious climate of this land of unlimited bounty and "perpetual spring," "one of the finest countries in the world," in the words of consul Thomas Larkin. The "safe and capacious harbors which dot her western shore," an Alabama congressman added, "invite to their bosoms the rich commerce of the East."[50] American emigration to California grew steadily, raising the possibility of a replay of the Texas game. Signs of British interest increased the allure of California and the sense of urgency in Washington. Polk early committed himself to its acquisition, alerted Americans in the area to the possibility of war, and ordered his agents to discourage foreign acquisition.

Polk also wielded a "diplomatic club" against Mexico in the millions of dollars in claims held by U.S. citizens against its people and government. Many of the claims were inflated, some were patently unjust, and most derived from profiteering at Mexico's expense. They were based on the new international "law" imposed by the leading capitalist powers that secured for their citizens the same property rights in other countries they

48. Bergeron, Polk, 58–63.
49. Peterson, Harrison and Tyler, 139.
50. Larkin to Calhoun, August 18, 1844, in Wilson, Calhoun Papers 19:606–7; Hietala, Manifest Design, 87.

had at home.[51] A commission had scaled the claims back to $2.5 million. Mexico made a few payments before a bankrupt treasury forced suspension in 1843. Americans charged Mexico with bad faith. Mexico denounced the claims as a "tribute" it was "obliged to pay in recognition of U.S. strength."[52]

Polk's approach to Mexico was dictated by the overtly racist attitudes he shared with most of his countrymen. Certain of Anglo-Saxon superiority, Americans scorned Mexicans as a mixed breed, even below free blacks and Indians, "an imbecile, pusillanimous race of men . . . unfit to control the destinies of that beautiful country," a "rascally perfidious race," a "band of pirates and robbers."[53] Indeed, they found no difficulty justifying as part of God's will the taking of fertile land from an "idle, thriftless people." They assumed that Mexico could be bullied into submission or, if foolish enough to fight, easily defeated. "Let its bark be treated with contempt, and its little bite, if it should attempt it, [be] quickly brushed aside with a single stroke of the paw," O'Sullivan exclaimed.[54] Some Americans even assumed that Mexicans would welcome them as liberators from their own depraved government.

Given the intractability of the issues and the attitudes on both sides, a settlement would have been difficult under any circumstances, but Polk's heavy-handed diplomacy ensured war. There is no evidence to confirm charges that he plotted to provoke Mexico into firing the first shot.[55] He seems rather to have hoped that by bribery and intimidation he could get what he wanted without war and to have expected that if war did come, it would be short, easy, and inexpensive. His sense of urgency heightened in the fall of 1845 by new and exaggerated reports of British designs on California, he tightened the noose. In December 1845, he revived the Monroe Doctrine, warning Britain and France against trying to block U.S. expansion. He deployed naval units off the Mexican port of Veracruz and ordered Taylor to the Rio Grande. He sent agents to Santa Fe to bribe provincial authorities of the New Mexico territory and persuade its residents of the benefits of U.S. rule. He dispatched secret orders to the navy's

51. Charles G. Sellers, *The Market Revolution: Jacksonian America, 1815–1846* (New York, 1991), 420.
52. Gene M. Brack, *Mexico Views Manifest Destiny, 1821–1846: An Essay on the Origins of the Mexican War* (Albuquerque, N.M., 1975), 95.
53. Horsman, *Race and Manifest Destiny*, 210; Hietala, *Manifest Design*, 156.
54. Quoted in Hietala, *Manifest Design*, 154.
55. The major "revisionist" study is Glenn W. Price, *Origins of the War with Mexico: The Polk-Stockton Intrigue* (Austin, Tex., 1967).

Pacific squadron and Larkin that should war break out or Britain move overtly to take California they should occupy the major ports and encourage the local population to revolt. He may also have secretly ordered the adventurer—and notorious troublemaker—John Charles Frémont to go to California. In any event, Frémont in the spring of 1846 turned abruptly south from an expedition in Oregon and began fomenting revolution in California.[56]

Having encircled Mexico with U.S. military power and begun to chip away at its outlying provinces, Polk set out to force a deal. Mistakenly concluding that Mexico had agreed to receive an envoy, he sent Louisianan John Slidell to Mexico City. The president's instructions make clear the sort of "negotiations" he sought. Slidell was to restore good relations with Mexico while demanding that it surrender on the Rio Grande boundary and relinquish California, no mean task. The United States would pay Mexico $30 million and absorb the claims of its citizens.

The predictable failure of Slidell's mission led directly to war. Mexico had agreed only to receive a commissioner to discuss resumption of diplomatic relations. Slidell's mere presence destabilized an already shaky government. When he moved on to the capital, violating the explicit instructions of Mexican officials, his mission was doomed.[57] After Mexico refused to receive him, he advised Polk that the United States should not deal further with them until it had "given them a good drubbing."[58] Polk concurred. After learning of Slidell's return, he began drafting a war message. In the meantime, Taylor took a provocative position just north of the Rio Grande, his artillery trained on the town of Matamoros. Before the war message could be completed, Washington learned that Mexican troops had attacked one of Taylor's patrols. American blood had been shed on American soil, Polk exclaimed with exaggeration. The administration quickly secured its declaration of war.

The Mexican-American War resulted from U.S. impatience and aggressiveness and Mexican weakness. Polk and many of his countrymen were determined to have Texas to the Rio Grande and all of California on their own terms. They might have waited for the apples to fall from the tree, to borrow John Quincy Adams's Cuban metaphor, but patience was not among their virtues. Polk appears not to have set out to provoke Mexico into what could be used as a war of conquest. Rather, contemptuous

56. Bergeron, *Polk*, 73–74.
57. Sellers, *Market Revolution*, 421.
58. Quoted in Norman A. Graebner, "The Mexican War: A Study in Causation," *Pacific Historical Review* 49 (August 1980), 418.

of his presumably inferior adversaries, he assumed he could bully them into giving him what he wanted. Mexico's weakness and internal divisions encouraged his aggressiveness. A stronger or more united Mexico might have deterred the United States or acquiesced in the annexation of Texas to avoid war, as the British minister and former Mexican foreign minister Lucas Alaman urged. By this time, however, Yankeephobia was rampant. Mexicans deeply resented the theft of Texas and obvious U.S. designs on California. They viewed the United States as the "Russian threat" of the New World. Incensed by the racist views of their northern neighbors, they feared cultural extinction. Newspapers warned that if the North Americans were not stopped in Texas, Protestantism would be imposed on the Mexican people and they would be "sold as beasts."[59] Fear, anger, and pride made it impossible to acquiesce in U.S. aggression. Mexico chose war over surrender.

Polk's strategy for fighting Mexico reflected the racist assumptions that got him into war. Certain that an inferior people would be no match for Americans, he envisioned a war of three to four months. The United States would secure control of Mexico's northern provinces and use them to force acceptance of the Rio Grande boundary and cession of California and New Mexico.

In a strictly military sense, Polk's estimate proved on the mark. Using artillery with devastating effect, Taylor drove Mexican attackers back across the Rio Grande. Over the next ten months, he defeated larger armies at Monterrey and Buena Vista, fueling popular excitement, making himself a national hero, and gaining control of much of northern Mexico. In the meantime, Cmdre. Robert Stockton and Frémont backed the so-called Bear Flag Revolt of Americans around Sacramento and proclaimed California part of the United States. Colonel Stephen Kearney's forces took New Mexico without resistance. To facilitate negotiations, Polk permitted the exiled Santa Anna to go back to Mexico where, in return, he was to arrange a settlement.

War is never as simple as its planners envision, however, and despite smashing military successes, Polk could not impose peace. Mexico turned out to be an "ugly enemy," in Daniel Webster's words. "She will not fight—& will not treat."[60] Despite crushing defeats, the Mexicans refused to negotiate on U.S. terms. They mounted a costly and frustrating guerrilla war against the invaders, "hardly . . . a legitimate system of war-

---

59. Brack, Mexico Views, 82, 99. A recent excellent analysis is Timothy Henderson, A Glorious Defeat: Mexico and Its War with the United States (New York, 2007).
60. Pletcher, Diplomacy of Annexation, 461.

fare," Americans snarled, additional evidence (if any was needed) of Mexican debasement.[61] Santa Anna did Polk's deviousness one better, using the United States to get home and then mobilizing fierce opposition to the invaders. "The United States may triumph," a Mexican newspaper proclaimed defiantly, "but its prize, like that of the vulture, will lie in a lake of blood."[62]

The United States by mid-1847 faced the grim prospect of a long and costly war. Annoyed that Taylor had not moved more decisively and alarmed that the general's martial exploits could make him a formidable political rival, the fiercely partisan Polk shifted his strategy southward, designing a combined army-navy assault against Veracruz, the strongest fortress in the Western Hemisphere, to be led by Gen. Winfield Scott and followed by an overland advance on Mexico City. Demonstrating the emerging professionalism of U.S. forces, Scott in March 1847 launched the first large-scale amphibious operation in the nation's history. After a siege of several weeks, he took Veracruz. In April, he defeated the ubiquitous Santa Anna at Cerro Gordo and began a slow, bloody advance to Mexico City. In August, five miles from the city, he agreed to an armistice.

Even this smashing success did not end the conflict. Fearing Scott as a potential political rival, Polk denied him the role of peacemaker, dispatching a minor figure, State Department clerk Nicholas Trist, to negotiate with Mexico. Shortly after his arrival, Trist fell into a childish and nasty spat with Scott that left the two refusing to speak to each other. The untimely feud may have botched an opportunity to end the war. More important, despite the imminent threat to their capital, the Mexicans stubbornly held out, insisting that the United States give up all occupied territory, accept the Nueces boundary, and pay the costs of the war. Santa Anna used the armistice to strengthen the defenses of the capital. With the breakdown of negotiations, Polk angrily recalled Trist, terminated the armistice, and ordered Scott to march on Mexico City.

The Mexican-American War was the nation's first major military intervention abroad and its first experience with occupying another country. Americans brought to this venture the ethos of the age, clearly defined notions of their own superiority, and the conviction that they were "pioneers of civilization," as contemporary historian William H. Prescott put it, bringing to a benighted people the blessings of republicanism. Given

61. Hietala, *Manifest Design*, 158.
62. Pletcher, *Diplomacy of Annexation*, 493.

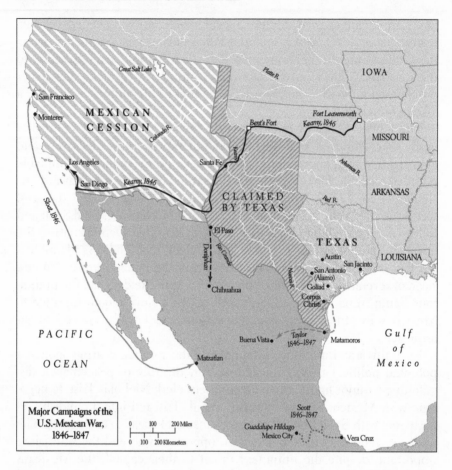

Major Campaigns of the U.S.-Mexican War, 1846–1847

the crushing impediment of racism they also brought with them, and the difficulties of living in a different climate and sometimes hostile environment, U.S. forces comported themselves reasonably well. There were atrocities, to be sure, and the Polk administration imposed a heavy burden on a defeated people by forcing them to pay taxes to finance the occupation. As a matter of military expediency, however, and to behave as they felt citizens of a republic should, the Americans tried to conciliate the population in most areas they moved through. Little was done to impose republicanism, and the impact of U.S. intervention on Mexico appears to have been slight. The areas occupied were briefly Americanized and some elements of American culture survived in Mexico, but the mixing of peoples was at best superficial and the gap between them remained wide. Ironically, the impact of intervention may have been greater on the occupiers, manifesting itself in such things as men's fashions and hairstyles and the incorporation of Spanish words and phrases into the language and as U.S. place names. The experience of fighting in a foreign land exposed Americans to a foreign culture, challenging their parochialism and contributing to the growth of national self-awareness.[63]

The war bitterly divided the United States. Citizens responded to its outbreak with an enthusiasm that bordered on hysteria. The prospect of fighting in an exotic foreign land appealed to their romantic spirit and sense of adventure. War provided a diversion from the mounting sectional conflict and served as an antidote for the materialism of the age. In the eyes of some, it was a test for the republican experiment, a way to bring the nation back to its first principles. "Ho, for the Halls of the Montezumas" was the battle cry, and the call for volunteers produced such a response that thousands had to be turned away. This was the first U.S. war to rest on a popular base. Stirring reports of battles provided to avid readers through the penny press by correspondents on the scene stimulated great popular excitement.[64]

Like most U.S. wars, this conflict also provoked opposition. Religious leaders, intellectuals, and some politicians denounced it as "illegal, unrighteous, and damnable" and accused Polk of violating "every principle of international law and moral justice."[65] Abolitionists claimed that this "piratical war" was being waged "solely for the detestable and horrible purpose of extending and perpetuating American slavery."[66] Whigs sought to exploit "Mr. Polk's War." The young congressman Abraham Lincoln introduced his famous "spot resolution," demanding to know precisely where Polk believed American blood had been shed on American soil. Senator Tom Corwin of Ohio declared that if he were a Mexican he would greet the invaders "with bloody hands" and welcome them to "hospitable graves." Polk's own Democratic Party was increasingly divided, the followers of both Calhoun and Van Buren opposing him. The opposition to the Mexican War was not as crippling as that during the War of 1812. Anti-war forces were weakened by the extremism of people such as Corwin and by their own ambivalence. Many who fervently opposed the war saw no choice but to support U.S. troops in the field. Opponents of the war also recognized that the nation as a whole supported

63. Johannsen, *Halls of the Montezumas*, 32–33, 50, 171–73, 205; Howe, *What Hath God Wrought*, 789–90, 797–98.
64. Johannsen, *Halls of the Montezumas*, 10, 12–13, 16, 25.
65. Graebner, "Mexican War," 405.
66. John H. Schroeder, *Mr. Polk's War: American Opposition and Dissent, 1846–1848* (Madison, Wisc., 1973), 99.

the war. Remembering the fate of the Federalists, Whigs in Congress tempered their opposition. In any event, they lacked the votes to block administration measures. Until after the Whigs won control of the House of Representatives in the 1846 elections, they could do little more than protest and make life difficult for Polk.[67]

Pinched economically from the growing cost of the war and frustrated that an unbroken string of military successes had not produced peace, Americans by 1848 grew impatient. Divisions in both parties sharpened. When the Wilmot Proviso, banning slavery in any territory acquired from Mexico, was introduced in Congress in August 1846, it brought that explosive issue to the surface. Outraged by Mexico's continued defiance and excited by tales of vast mineral wealth, "All Mexico" Democrats pushed for annexation of the entire country. At the other extreme, critics urged Polk's impeachment "as an indemnity to the American people for the loss of 15,000 lives . . . in Mexico."[68]

A peace settlement emerged almost by accident. After two weeks of heavy fighting, Scott's army forced the surrender of the heavily defended capital. "I believe if we were to plant our batteries in Hell the damned Yankees would take them from us," a stunned Santa Anna remarked after the fall of the supposedly impregnable fortress of Chapultepec.[69] Fearing a drawn-out war, Trist ignored Polk's orders to come home. Acting without authority, he negotiated a treaty that met the president's original demands. Mexico recognized the Rio Grande boundary and ceded upper California and New Mexico. The United States was to pay $15 million plus U.S. claims against Mexico.

Outraged by Trist's disobedience, Polk would have liked to take more territory to punish Mexico for its insolence. Ironically, the very racism that drove the United States into Mexico limited its conquests. "We can no more amalgamate with her people than with negroes," the former president's nephew and namesake Andrew Jackson Donelson observed. "The Spanish blood will not mix well with the Yankee," Prescott added.[70] Concern about the absorption of an alien population and the prospect of peace took the steam out of the All Mexico movement. Facing sharpening divisions at home, Polk felt compelled to accept the treaty negotiated by that "impudent and unqualified scoundrel." Some Whigs opposed it because it

67. Ibid., 72–73, 160–63; Johannsen, *Halls of the Montezumas*, 275–79.
68. Schroeder, *Mr. Polk's War*, 143.
69. Robert A. Doughty et al., *Warfare in the Western World* (2 vols., Lexington, Mass., 1996), 1:321.
70. Hietala, *Manifest Design*, 163; Johannsen, *Halls of the Montezumas*, 299.

gave the United States too much territory, others because the price was too high. In the final analysis, peace seemed preferable to more bloodshed. The treaty passed the Senate on March 10, 1848, by a bipartisan vote of 36 to 14. The Treaty of Guadalupe Hidalgo, in Philip Hone's apt phrase, was "negotiated by an unauthorized agent, with an unacknowledged government, submitted by an accidental president to a dissatisfied Senate."[71]

For Trist, the diplomat who had taken peace into his own hands, the reward was abuse from a vindictive boss. He was fired from his State Department post and not paid for his service until some twenty-five years later, shortly before his death.

For Mexico, the war was a devastating blow to the optimism that had marked its birth, perhaps the supreme tragedy in its history. When Santa Anna was shown maps of his country making clear for the first time the enormity of its losses, he wept openly. Mexico plunged deeper into debt. With half its territory gone, war raging in Yucatán, agrarian revolts sweeping the heartland, and Indian unrest in the north, the nation seemed near falling apart. Military defeat brought despair to leadership groups. Liberals questioned Mexico's capacity for nationhood. Conservatives concluded that republicanism was tantamount to anarchy and that they should look to Europe for models, even to monarchy. It was the "most unjust war in history," Alaman lamented, "provoked by the ambition not of an absolute monarchy but of a republic that claims to be at the forefront of nineteenth century civilization."[72]

For the United States, the war brought a vast bounty, adding 529,000 square miles to the national domain, coveted outlets on the Pacific, and the unanticipated boon of California gold. If Texas is added, the booty totals about 1.2 million square miles, one-third of the nation's present territory. All of this for thirteen thousand dead, an estimated $97 million in war costs, and the $15 million paid Mexico. North Americans saw the war as a great event in their own and indeed in world history. Success against Mexico demonstrated, Polk insisted, the "capacity of republican governments to prosecute successfully a just and necessary foreign war with all the vigor usually attributed to more arbitrary forms of government."[73] For a people still unsure of their bold experiment, the war confirmed their faith in republicanism and seemed to earn them new respect abroad. Some Americans even saw the European revolutions of 1848 as extensions

71. Quoted in K. Jack Bauer, *The Mexican War, 1846–1848* (New York, 1974), 399.
72. Krauze, *Mexico*, 143, 147–49; Johannsen, *Halls of the Montezumas*, 301.
73. Bergeron, *Polk*, 110.

of the great test between monarchy and republicanism that began on the battlefields of Mexico. "The whole civilized world resounds with American opinions and American principles," declared Speaker of the House of Representatives Robert Winthrop in a victory oration on July 4, 1848.[74]

The celebration of victory obscured only momentarily the war's darker consequences. It aroused among Latin Americans growing fear of what was already commonly labeled the "colossus of the North." Most important, acquisition of the vast new territory opened a veritable Pandora's box of troubles at home. From the Wilmot Proviso to Fort Sumter, the explosive issue of extending slavery into the territories dominated the political landscape,

---

74. Johannsen, *Halls of the Montezumas*, 5.

setting off a bitter and ultimately irreconcilable conflict. Polk's victory thus came at a huge price, setting the nation on the road to civil war.[75]

V

Rising with each word to new heights of exuberance, Secretary of State Daniel Webster proclaimed in 1851 that it was America's destiny to "command the oceans, both oceans, all the oceans."[76] Some of the same forces that drove the United States across the continent in the 1840s propelled it into the Pacific and East Asia. Trade, of course, was a major factor. The Panic of 1837 and growing concern with surplus agricultural productivity heightened the importance of finding new markets. Whigs like Webster saw commercial expansion as essential to domestic well-being and international stability. Democrats viewed it as essential to sustain the agricultural production that would safeguard the nation from the threats of manufacturing, economic distress, and monopoly. The lure of East Asian trade played a crucial role in the quest for Oregon and California; their acquisition, in turn, quickened interest in the Pacific and East Asia. "By our recent acquisitions in the Pacific," Secretary of the Treasury Robert Walker proclaimed in 1848, "Asia has suddenly become our neighbor, with a placid intervening ocean inviting our steamships upon the trade of a commerce greater than all of Europe combined."[77] It was no accident that in the 1840s the United States began to formulate a clear-cut policy for the Pacific region.

The Pacific Ocean was a focal point of international rivalry in the mid-nineteenth century, the United States an active participant. American merchants entered the China trade before 1800. From the first years of the century, sea captains and traders sailed up and down the west coast of the American continents and far out into the Pacific. Americans dominated the whaling industry, pursuing their lucrative prey from the Arctic Ocean to Antarctica and California to the Tasman Sea. Americans were the first to set foot on Antarctica. During its dramatic four-year voyage around the world, the Great United States Exploring Expedition, commanded by Capt. Charles Wilkes, charted the islands, harbors, and coast lines of the Pacific. The U.S. Navy assumed a constabulary role, supporting enterprising Americans in far-flung areas. United States citizens on

75. Sellers, *Market Revolution*, 425.
76. Quoted in Kenneth E. Shewmaker, "Forging the 'Great Chain': Daniel Webster and the Origins of American Foreign Policy Toward East Asia and the Pacific, 1841–1852," *Proceedings of the American Philosophical Society* 129 (September 1985), 250–51.
77. Walter LaFeber, *The Clash: U.S.-Japanese Relations Throughout History* (New York, 1997), 11.

their own initiative carved out interests and pushed the government to defend them.[78]

This was especially true in Hawaii, where Americans predominated by midcentury. Missionaries and merchants began flocking there as early as 1820 and by the 1840s played a major role in the life of the islands. United States trade far surpassed that of the nearest rival, Great Britain. New England Congregationalist missionaries established schools and printing presses and enjoyed unusually large conversion rates. As in other areas, Western disease ravaged the indigenous population and Western culture assaulted local customs. But the missionaries also helped Hawaii manage the jolt of Westernization without entirely giving in. Americans assisted Hawaiian rulers in adapting Western forms of governance and in protecting their sovereignty. On the advice of missionary William Richards, King Kamehameha II mounted a diplomatic offensive in the 1840s to spare his people from falling under European domination, pushing Hawaii toward the U.S. orbit.[79]

A result was the so-called Tyler Doctrine of 1842, the end of official indifference toward Hawaii. Protestant missionaries had also persuaded the Hawaiians to discriminate against French Catholics. When the French government threatened to retaliate, a nervous and opportunistic Kamehameha sought from the United States, Britain, and France a tripartite guarantee of Hawaiian independence. To get action from Washington, Richards even hinted at Hawaii's willingness to accept a British protectorate. Webster and the "Pacific-minded" Tyler perceived Hawaii's importance as the "Malta of the Pacific," a vital link in the "great chain" connecting the United States with East Asia. Unwilling to take on risky commitments, they rejected a tripartite guarantee and refused even to recognize Hawaii's sovereignty. The Tyler Doctrine did, however, claim special U.S. interests in Hawaii based on proximity and trade. It made clear that if other powers threatened Hawaii's independence the United States would be justified in "making a decided remonstrance." Seeking to protect U.S. interests at minimum cost, the doctrine claimed Hawaii as a U.S. sphere of influence and firmly supported its independence, establishing a policy that would last until annexation.[80]

78. Arthur Power Dudden, *The American Pacific: From the Old China Trade to the Present* (New York, 1992), 11–17; William Stanton, *The Great United States Exploring Expedition of 1838–1842* (Berkeley, Calif., 1975); Nathaniel Philbrick, *Sea of Glory: America's Voyage of Discovery, the U.S. Exploring Expedition, 1838–1842* (New York, 2003).
79. Dudden, *American Pacific*, 56–57.
80. Shewmaker, "Great Chain," 231–33.

As secretary of state under Millard Fillmore, Webster in 1851 went a step further. Under the Tyler Doctrine, U.S. interests expanded significantly. Hawaii resembled a "Pacific New England" in culture and institutions.[81] The development of oceangoing steam navigation increased its importance as a possible coaling station. Again threatened by French gunboat diplomacy, Kamehameha II in 1851 signed a secret document transferring sovereignty to the United States in the event of war. Webster and Fillmore steered clear of annexation and warned missionaries against provoking conflict with France. At the same time, in a strongly worded message of July 14, 1851, the secretary of state asserted that the United States would accept no infringement on Hawaiian sovereignty and would use force if necessary. Webster's willingness to go this far reflected the increased importance of Hawaii due to the acquisition of Oregon and California and rising U.S. interest in East Asia. His threats infuriated the French, but extracted from them a clear statement respecting Hawaiian sovereignty.[82]

The United States' concern for Hawaii was tied to the opening of China. Until the 1840s, East Asia remained largely closed to the West because of policies rigorously enforced by both China and Japan. China's isolationist policy reflected a set of highly ethnocentric ideas that viewed the Celestial Kingdom as the center of the universe and other peoples as "barbarians." The notion of equal relations among sovereign states had no place in this scheme of things. Ties with other nations were permitted only on a "tributary" basis. Foreign representatives had to pay tribute to the emperor through various rituals including the elaborate series of prostrations known as the ko-tow. In the 1790s, China began to permit limited trade—to make available to the barbarians necessities such as tea and rhubarb, its officials said—but it was restricted in volume and tightly regulated by Chinese merchants. Japanese exclusion was less ideological but more rigid. Viewing outsiders and especially missionaries as threats to internal stability, they kept out all but a handful of Dutch traders, who operated only on an island in Nagasaki harbor. Indeed, the Japanese so feared contamination that they prohibited their own people from going abroad and forbade those who did so from returning.[83]

81. Ibid., 239.
82. Ibid., 239–43.
83. Ssu-Yu Teng and John K. Fairbank, *China's Response to the West: A Documentary Survey, 1839–1923* (New York, 1954), 17–19; Edwin O. Reischauer, *The United States and Japan* (rev. ed., New York, 1957), 5–11.

By the 1840s, the European powers had far outstripped the isolated Asians in economic and military power. Eager for expanded trade and outlets for missionary activity, they challenged Chinese and Japanese restrictions. In the United States, producers of cotton and tobacco fancied huge profits from access to China's millions. Some Americans even envisioned their country as an entrepôt for a global trade in which European goods would be imported, transshipped across the continent, and then sent from San Francisco to East Asian ports by steamship.

The missionary impulse reinforced commercial drives. The 1840s was a period of intense religious ferment in the United States, and numerous Protestant sects stepped up evangelizing activities around the world. China and Japan, which seemed particularly decadent and barbaric, offered perhaps the greatest challenge. The Chinese empire was "so vast, so populous, and so idolatrous," one missionary exclaimed, "that it cannot be mentioned by Christians without exciting statements of the deepest concern." The handful of American missionaries already in China questioned its rulers' right to make "a large part of the earth's surface . . . impassable." They also emphasized China's weakness and pressed for its opening—by force if necessary.[84]

Britain took the lead. To redress a balance of trade chronically favoring China, Western merchants, Americans included, had taken to the illegal and profitable sale of opium. Chinese officials objected on economic grounds and also because of the baneful effects on their people. When they attempted to stop the trade, the British responded with force and used their trouncing of China in the so-called Opium War as leverage to pry it open. The Treaty of Nanking (1842), imposed on China by the British, marked the end of Chinese exclusion, putting into effect a system of blatantly discriminatory unequal treaties that reversed China's traditional way of dealing with other nations. The Chinese opened five ports to trade with Britain, eliminated some of the more obnoxious regulations imposed on British merchants, and opened their tariff to negotiation. They also ceded Hong Kong and agreed to a practice called extraterritoriality by which British citizens in China were tried under their own law rather than Chinese.

Through what came to be known as hitchhiking imperialism, the United States took advantage of British gains. Shortly after the Treaty of Nanking, Tyler sent Massachusetts merchant Caleb Cushing to negotiate

84. Murray A. Rubinstein, "The Wars They Wanted: American Missionaries' Use of the *Chinese Repository* Before the Opium War," *American Neptune* 48 (Fall 1988), 277–82.

with China. The two nations approached each other across a yawning geographical and cultural chasm. Contemptuous of Chinese pretensions of superiority, the administration instructed its delegation to take with them a globe (if one could be found) so that "the celestials may see that they are not the Central Kingdom." Cushing was to use religion as an excuse not to perform the ko-tow.[85] Chinese viewed the United States as "the most remote and least civilized" of Western nations—an "isolated place outside the pale." Their chief negotiator instructed the emperor to use a "simple and direct style" so his meaning would be clear. Hoping to play the barbarians against each other, the Chinese were willing to deal. In the Treaty of Wang-hsia (1844), they granted the United States the same commercial concessions as Britain. Most important, they agreed to a most-favored-nation clause that would automatically concede to the United States terms given any other nation.[86]

During the 1850s, the West made further inroads, implementing an increasingly exploitative form of quasi-colonialism. Capitalizing on China's prolonged and bloody civil war—the so-called Taiping Rebellion lasted fifteen years and took as many as forty million lives—and rewarding its intransigence and insults with high-handedness, the Europeans negotiated at gunpoint treaties that opened additional ports, permitted navigation into the interior, forced toleration of missionaries, legalized the opium trade, and, by fixing a maximum tariff of 5 percent, deprived China of control over its own economy.

Americans then and later fancied themselves different from the Europeans in dealing with China, and to some extent they were. Until the end of the century, at least, the United States remained a minor player. Trade with China increased significantly but remained only a small portion of China's commerce with the West. American missionaries were few in number and small in impact. "Our preaching is listened to by a few, laughed at by many, and disregarded by most," one missionary lamented.[87] Americans generally refrained from the use of force. Some, like minister John Ward, sent to ratify the 1858 treaties of Tientsin, observed Chinese conventions; Ward even rode in a mule cart traditionally

85. Kenneth E. Shewmaker, ed., *The Papers of Daniel Webster: Diplomatic Papers* (Hanover, N.H., 1983), 1:907–10; Webster to Caleb Cushing, May 8, 1843, ibid., 922–26.
86. Warren I. Cohen, *America's Response to China: An Interpretive History of Sino-American Relations* (New York, 1974), 14.
87. Michael H. Hunt, *The Making of a Special Relationship: The United States and China to 1914* (New York, 1983), 26.

deserved for tributaries, earning the contempt of his European counterparts and praise from his countrymen for Yankee practicality.[88]

The differences were more of form than substance. The United States sometimes participated in gunboat diplomacy and regularly used the most-favored-nation clause to secure concessions extorted by the Europeans at cannon's mouth. Like the Europeans, Americans generally looked down on the Chinese—one diplomat described a "china-man" as "surely the most grotesque animal."[89] Some Chinese perceived a subtle difference and tried to exploit it, but in general they made little distinction. "The English barbarians' craftiness is manifold, their proud tyranny is uncontrollable," one Chinese official observed. "Americans do nothing but follow in their direction."[90]

The United States took the lead in opening Japan. Encouraged by Britain's success in China and viewing Japan as a vital coaling station en route to the Celestial Kingdom, the last link in Webster's "great chain," Fillmore in 1852 named Cmdre. Matthew Perry to head a mission to Japan. Regarding the Japanese as a "weak and semi-barbarous people," Perry decided to deal forcibly with them. In July 1853, he steamed defiantly into Edo (later Tokyo) Bay with a fleet of four very large, black-hulled ships, sixty-one guns, and a crew of nearly one thousand men. He maneuvered his ships closer to the city than any foreigner had previously gone. Japanese initially responded to the "burning ships" with panic, then by official stalling. Fearing they might simply wait until his provisions were exhausted, Perry, after preliminary discussions with low-level officials, sailed to China, informing them he would return the following year to negotiate.

Perry came back in March 1854 with a larger fleet, threatening this time that if Japan did not treat with him it might suffer the fate of Mexico. Instructed by the State Department to "do everything to impress" the Japanese "with a just sense of the power and greatness" of the United States, he brought with him large quantities of champagne and vintage Kentucky bourbon to grease the wheels of diplomacy, a pair of Sam Colt's six-shooters and a scale model train to display U.S. technological advancement, and a history of the Mexican War to validate its military superiority. He employed Chinese coolies and African Americans in his

88. William M. Gabard, "John Eliot Ward: A Georgia Elitist in the Celestial Empire, 1858–1860," *Studies in the Social Sciences* 22 (June 1983), 56–60.
89. Hunt, *Special Relationship*, 35.
90. Earl Swisher, China's *Management of the American Barbarians* (New Haven, Conn., 1951), 46.

entourage in ways that highlighted the power of whites over peoples of color. He used uniforms, pageants, and music—even a blackface minstrel show—as manifestations of Western cultural supremacy. Perry's reluctant hosts most likely negotiated in spite of rather than because of his forceful demeanor and cultural symbols. Aware of the West's technological advances, they disagreed whether to resist or accommodate with and learn about this new threat. Alarmed by developments in China, they decided to deal with the United States rather than Britain and make limited concessions rather than have more exploitative agreements forced on them. Thus in the Treaty of Kanagawa, they opened two relatively isolated and inaccessible ports and agreed to provide refuge to crews of wrecked U.S. ships. The treaty got the Americans a foot in the door.[91]

It remained for Townsend Harris, a diplomat of undistinguished credentials with no force at his disposal, to establish the foundation for Japan's relations with the West for the remainder of the century. Arriving in 1856 as the first U.S. consul, he was shunted to the small and inaccessible village of Shimoda by a government that would have preferred he stay home. He was forced to share a run-down temple with rats, bats, and enormous spiders. Sometimes going months without word from Washington, Harris rightly considered himself the "most isolated American official in the world." Frustrated by Japanese obstructionism, he also came to admire the Japanese people and appreciate their culture, perhaps through the influence of a mistress, assigned him by the government, who may have been the inspiration for Giacomo Puccini's opera Madama Butterfly. Confident that with patience the West could elevate Japan to "our standards of civilization," Harris stubbornly persisted, repeatedly warning his hosts that it would be better to deal peaceably with the United States than risk China's fate at the hands of the Europeans. Eventually, he prevailed. In 1858, the Japanese agreed to permit trade, opened five new ports, established diplomatic relations, and accepted extraterritoriality. Within a decade, Harris's treaty would cause a revolution in Japan, but the immediate result was more resistance. As the first U.S. minister to the country, he faced continued obstruction and what his British counterpart called the "perpetual menace of massacre"—seven foreign diplomats were killed in eighteen months (including Harris's translator), some of them hacked to pieces by gangs of sword-wielding assassins. Ironically, as other nations arrived in Japan, U.S. influence waned. By 1861, when Harris left, it was, as in China, a junior

91. Jeffrey A. Keith, " 'An Entirely Peaceful Spirit of Conquest': Commodore Matthew Galbraith Perry's Cultural Diplomacy, 1852–1854" (M.A. thesis, University of Kentucky, 2006).

partner to the British.[92] Although a secondary power in East Asia, the United States established significant interests and framed a coherent policy based on the principle of equality of commercial opportunity, laying the foundation for a more active and influential role in the future.

VI

"The American destiny did not seem so manifest in the 1850s," historian Reginald Stuart has written.[93] During these years, Americans remained an aggressive, acquisitive, competitive breed certain of their own righteousness and the evil of their foes.[94] Victorious in war, having more than doubled the size of their nation, they began to see themselves as an emerging world power, even a rival to Britain. Expansionist sentiment remained alive. Some Democrats viewed an aggressive foreign policy as a way to divert the nation from growing internal divisions and hold an embattled Union together. Combining ardent nationalism with blatant racism, the Young America movement in the name of promoting republicanism hoped to project the nation's power abroad. Southerners sought salvation through expansion. They deemed the acquisition of new slave states essential to maintain a balance of power in the Senate. The expansion of slavery would also disperse the black population and thereby help solve the nation's race problem. "The safety of the South is to be found only in the extension of its peculiar institutions," DeBow's Review exclaimed, "and the security of the Union in the safety of the South."[95]

In the heyday of the so-called filibusters, U.S. expansion turned southward and assumed even more aggressive forms. The name "filibuster" originated through the French and Spanish languages from a Dutch word meaning pirate or freebooter. By no means unique to the United States, these patently illegal, privately organized and funded military expeditions against foreign territory became a staple of American life in the 1850s. The leadership included such well-known adventurers as the charismatic Venezuelan and former Spanish army officer Narciso López, Mexican War hero and Mississippi governor John Quitman, and, most prominently, the onetime physician and would-be ruler of Nicaragua, William Walker. The ranks drew from discharged Mexican War soldiers,

---

92. LaFeber, Clash, 18–23; Jack M. Hammersmith, Spoilsmen in a "Flowery Fairland": The Development of the U.S. Legation in Japan, 1859–1906 (Kent, Ohio, 1998), 1–25.
93. Stuart, United States Expansionism, 96.
94. Elbert B. Smith, The Presidencies of Zachary Taylor and Millard Fillmore (Lawrence, Kans., 1988), 18.
95. Gara, Pierce, 150.

restless young men who sought companionship, adventure, and military glory, the urban unemployed, including recent immigrants and refugees from failed European revolutions, southerners who hoped to expand slavery, and Freemasons who aspired to expand liberty—and constrict Catholicism. Celebrated in the popular press, stage productions, and song, the filibusters captured the romantic spirit of the age. Mexico was the target of countless attacks, most designed to detach its northern provinces. Cuba and Canada also drew attention. There were expeditions against Honduras, Nicaragua, and even Ecuador. A planned "invasion" of Hawaii was aborted. British officials, not without reason, fretted about a possible attack on Ireland. Americans joked about expeditions to the North Pole.[96]

In contrast to the previous decade, expansionism produced few results in the 1850s. The Franklin Pierce administration through the 1853 Gadsden Purchase extorted from Santa Anna, once again in power and out of pocket, thirty-nine million additional acres of Mexican territory to secure a southern route for the transcontinental railroad. It also seized—for its rich deposits of guano, widely used as fertilizer—Parker Island in the South Pacific, the first non-contiguous territory acquired.[97] But there were no other annexations. Brash self-confidence was tempered by escalating sectional divisions. The Compromise of 1850, which admitted California as a free state, exacerbated rather than resolved internal conflict. From the agony of "Bleeding Kansas" to the firing on Fort Sumter, the nation tore itself apart over the extension of slavery. Southern determination to expand the peculiar institution into new areas aroused passionate opposition in the North. Northern frustration of southern designs in turn provoked secessionist sentiment in the South. Expansionism thus tore the nation apart instead of pulling it together, making a mockery of the grand pretensions of Manifest Destiny.

For all the excitement they generated, the filibusters achieved nothing. Private citizens found it difficult to raise the necessary funds and organize and execute complex, often seaborne military operations. Though the Pierce and Buchanan administrations privately sympathized with filibusters' goals, they dutifully enforced the neutrality laws, deterring, hampering, and sometimes stopping expansionist schemes. In no case did local populations rise up to welcome the American invaders as liberators,

96. Robert E. May, *Manifest Destiny's Underworld: Filibustering in Antebellum America* (Chapel Hill, N.C., 2002), 1–116.
97. Gara, *Pierce*, 129–32, 147–48.

as the filibusters so naively expected. Once in country, the outsiders suffered from cholera and other deadly diseases. Many who sought adventure were wounded or killed in battle. Some were captured and executed. Aside from Walker in Nicaragua, none of the expansionist plots brought even short-term success.[98]

In terms of promoting republican principles abroad, the United States remained properly cautious. The nation by this time was firmly established as the center of world democratic revolution. European reformers conceded the Old World's preeminence in things aesthetic but praised America's political freedoms, religious tolerance, lack of poverty, and technological prowess. They looked to the New World for inspiration and support. Americans in turn hailed the European revolutions of 1848 as extensions of their own. As always preeminently concerned about slavery, southerners feared precedents that might be turned against them. "If we sanction interference, we will be the first who will be interfered with," a New Orleans newspaper warned.[99] But others enthusiastically endorsed the European revolutions and even urged active support of them.

Americans responded with special fervor to Hungary's rebellion against Austria's rule. The flamboyant Hungarian leader Louis Kossuth consciously modeled his declaration of independence after that of the United States and became a folk hero. Some Americans even urged active support for the "Noble Magyar." The U.S. government handled Kossuth with great care. Adhering to a long-standing convention of European diplomacy, President Zachary Taylor refused recognition until certain that the Hungarians could sustain an independent government on their own. When Austria, with Russian assistance, crushed the revolution, Webster dismissed the oppressor as "but a patch on the earth's surface" and made clear America's sympathy for people seeking self-determination.[100] The United States helped Kossuth get out of a Turkish prison and welcomed him to its shores. Fillmore openly sympathized with the Hungarian struggle. Webster exclaimed that he would "rejoice to see our American model upon the lower Danube and on the mountains of Hungary." But the United States offered no more than verbal support. Turning aside Kossuth's request for aid, Fillmore cautiously proclaimed America's true

98. May, *Filibustering*, 117–248.

99. Quoted in Joseph A. Fry, *Dixie Looks Abroad: The South and U.S. Foreign Relations, 1789–1973* (Baton Rouge, La., 2002), 67. Also Jozsef Gellen, "The American Experiment and Reform-Age Hungary, 1828–1848," in Jacques Portes, ed., *Europe and America: Criss-Crossing Perspectives, 1788–1848* (Paris, 1987), 131–48.

100. Smith, *Taylor/Fillmore*, 231.

mission was "to teach by example and show by our success, moderation, and justice the blessings of self-government and the advantages of our free institutions."[101]

The United States spurned opportunities for new annexations, even when offered on a silver platter. In the case of Yucatán, race proved the sticking point. This strategic peninsula, gateway to the Gulf of Mexico, erupted into the unusually brutal Caste War in 1847, Indians rising in revolt against their Spanish rulers. Some Americans wanted to save the embattled whites from extermination. Others warned that the British might seek control of a strategic area. The United States did mount a show of force in support of Yucatán's rulers in early 1848, but it turned back their proposals for annexation. Americans grew increasingly disenchanted with the Yucatán whites, who seemed "cowardly" and unworthy of their race. More important, they were not inclined to risk contamination by absorbing the "uncivilized, perfidious" Indians, who, Calhoun said, "were too ignorant to appreciate liberty, or exercise the rights if conferred."[102] Similarly, Pierce rebuffed Hawaiian proposals for annexation conditioned on the islands' admission as a state and the granting of full citizenship to their people.[103]

Persistent efforts to acquire Cuba ran afoul of the explosive slavery issue. Slaveholders saw the creation of new slave states there as a means to redress a congressional balance that had tipped against them. They feared that Britain might acquire Cuba and abolish slavery or push the Spanish toward abolition. They especially worried about what they ominously labeled "Africanization," a Cuban slave revolt as in Haiti that might spread the horrors of race war to the United States. Cuba took on added strategic significance with talk of a canal across the Central American isthmus.

Throughout the 1850s, Cuba was the object of various schemes for acquisition. Administrations from Polk to Buchanan tried to purchase it from Spain. Between 1849 and 1851, Narciso López launched four filibustering expeditions, appealing to southerners to "advance the cause of civilization and humanity"—and to seize the island "while the present condition of her slaves is untouched."[104] The pro-southern Pierce and

101. Ibid., 230–33.
102. Mark J. White, "The Case of the Yucatecan Request: American Foreign Policy at the Close of the Mexican War," *Mid-America* 72 (October 1990), 177, 184, 189.
103. Gara, *Pierce*, 147.
104. Cristobal Madam to William Preston, November 2, 1849, William Preston Papers, Special Collections, University of Kentucky Library, Box 46. My thanks to Dr. Randolph Hollingsworth for bringing these documents to my attention.

Buchanan administrations assigned high priority to acquisition. Pierre Soulé, minister to Spain and a diplomat notoriously lacking in diplomatic skills, made Cuba a personal obsession and tried to get it by fair means and mostly foul. He connived with Spanish rebels to overthrow the monarchy in hopes of getting a more compliant government, all the while shamelessly flattering the queen to do his bidding. In 1854, he and other pro-southern U.S. diplomats in Europe issued the so-called Ostend Manifesto (actually released at Aix-la-Chapelle without approval of Washington and hence without official standing), claiming that Cuba was essential to the United States and the institution of slavery. Should Spain refuse to sell it, the United States "by every law human and divine" would be "justified in wresting it from Spain."[105] When Britain and France seemed likely to go to war in 1859, southerners urged exploiting the opportunity to take Cuba. England could be kept quiet by maintaining a "defiant attitude toward France."[106]

All efforts failed. Spanish officials stubbornly insisted that they would rather see Cuba beneath the ocean than as part of the United States. Taylor and Fillmore scrupulously applied the neutrality laws, limiting U.S. support for López's ill-fated expeditions. The popular uprisings the adventurer counted on never materialized. On his last mission, he and some of his motley band of "freedom fighters," Americans included, were captured and executed. The Ostend Manifesto was too much even for the sympathetic Pierce, who saw no choice but to repudiate his reckless appointees. Cuba became as emotional an issue for opponents of slavery as for southerners. Free Soilers who staunchly opposed the extension of slavery blocked Buchanan's efforts to appropriate funds for its purchase. Some southerners expressed skepticism about acquiring a territory filled with alien races. The failure to acquire Cuba turned others toward secession.

Central America drew more U.S. attention than Cuba. Some North Americans had long viewed the region as an outlet for slavery and a possible solution to the nation's race problem. The establishment of trading interests in Asia, the acquisition of California and Oregon, and the gold rush of 1849 heightened interest in a passage across the isthmus. Henry Clay had dreamed of a canal to shorten the distance between Atlantic and Pacific. By the 1850s, Clay's dream had become a national priority. "Central America is destined to occupy an influential position in the fam-

---

105. Gara, *Pierce*, 150–55; "The Ostend Manifesto," October 18, 1854, in Ruhl Bartlett, ed., *The Record of American Diplomacy* (New York, 1950), 240–42.
106. Preston to James Buchanan, May 8, 1859, Preston Papers, Box 46.

ily of nations," the *New York Times* proclaimed in 1854, "if her advantages of location, climate and soil are availed of by a race of 'Northmen' who shall supplant the tainted, mongrel and decaying race which now occupies the region."[107]

Central America in the 1850s was a uniquely volatile region. Bolívar's federation had long since collapsed, giving way to five separate, insecure, and combative nations. Disputes between the countries over boundaries and resources were exceeded by the conflict within them. The chronic instability and sudden importance of the region drew foreign entrepreneurs, adventurers, and filibusters. Britain had long-standing strategic and economic interests in the area. As the United States began to assert itself, Anglo-American tensions escalated sharply. The 1850 Clayton-Bulwer Treaty, providing for joint construction and control of a canal, was negotiated to ease tensions, but its vague language actually sparked new conflicts.

From the late 1840s, the United States steadily expanded its role in Central America. In separate treaties with Colombia and Nicaragua, it acquired rights to build an isthmian canal. The treaty with Colombia gave it a virtual protectorate over the northernmost province of Panama. North Americans bought up Central America's lands and exploited its mines. Entrepreneurs such as the swashbuckling Cornelius Vanderbilt constructed land and water routes across the isthmus. In 1855, Americans completed a forty-eight-mile railroad across Panama, a triumph of Yankee skill and the "marvel" of an age full of remarkable technological advances.[108]

Whatever benefits they brought to Central America, the "Northmen" hailed by the *New York Times* were also meddlesome and aggressive. Even in the golden age of gunboat diplomacy, minister to Nicaragua Solon Borland gave diplomats a bad name. A physician turned politician, former senator from Arkansas, and avowed expansionist, Borland's self-proclaimed "greatest ambition" was to "see the State of Nicaragua forming a bright star in the flag of the United States." He managed to convert a relatively trivial incident into a near war with Britain. Seeking to protect a U.S. citizen wanted for murder, he claimed diplomatic immunity when local officials tried to arrest the accused and himself for interfering. When struck in the face with a randomly thrown bottle, he demanded a

107. Quoted in Thomas M. Leonard, *Central America and the United States: The Search for Stability* (Athens, Ga., 1991), 22.
108. Gara, *Pierce*, 145.

formal apology. A U.S. Navy vessel was sent to collect reparations for damage to American property and the treatment of Borland. When officials predictably rejected U.S. demands, the captain, exceeding his instructions, bombarded the British-controlled port of Greytown and sent marines ashore to burn what was left, doing an estimated $3 million damage. Some Americans protested this grossly excessive use of force. Experienced in such matters, the British denounced it as an unparalleled outrage and might have retaliated had they not been tied down by the Crimean War. Embarrassed but unwilling to apologize, the Pierce administration clumsily tried to shift blame elsewhere.[109]

The notorious William Walker put Borland to shame. Also a former physician—and lawyer, journalist and gold rusher—the hundred-pound "grey-eyed man of destiny" plunged headlong into the maelstrom of Nicaraguan politics. Attaching himself to the faction out of power, he and a band of adventurers he called "the Immortals" landed in Nicaragua in June 1855, imposed peace on the group holding power, and established a puppet government giving Walker control. Walker subsequently "won" the presidency through sham elections, reinstituted slavery, and established English as a second language. An overt racist who dismissed the local elite as "drivelers," he dreamed of creating a Central American union, based on slavery and run by white men, with himself as head and closely tied to the southern states. In time, he overextended himself. Otherwise unable to cooperate, the Central American nations banded together in what is still proudly called the "National War" to throw out the Yankee intruder. They received crucial support from Vanderbilt, whose interests Walker had challenged, and from the British, who saw him as an instrument of U.S. designs. Walker managed to escape and returned to New Orleans a hero. The U.S. Navy foiled a second expedition in 1859. The following year, on yet a third try to regain power, he was captured in Honduras, tried, and executed.[110]

United States intervention in Central America had significant results. No new territory was annexed, but U.S. interests and involvement expanded significantly. The nation acquired rights to the major canal routes, increased its political influence, and established a naval presence. North American companies controlled the existing routes across the isthmus. Most important, as the United States established its preeminence,

---

109. James M. Woods, "Expansionism as Diplomacy: The Career of Solon Borland in Central America, 1853–1854," *Americas* 40 (January 1984), 410–15.
110. Leonard, *Central America*, 22–30; John H. Coatsworth, *Central America and the United States: The Clients and the Colossus* (New York, 1994), 27–29.

Britain began to withdraw. Preoccupied with events in Europe, officials refused, as Lord John Russell put it, to permit the "miserable States in Central America" to provoke a needless war. They may even have developed a certain admiration for their offspring as an imperialist "chip off the old block."[111] They rationalized that U.S. control might be expedient politically and profitable economically. Britain thus initiated a gradual withdrawal from a region it had once dominated.[112]

For Central Americans, U.S. intrusion was at best a mixed blessing. The United States contributed to their economic development. Central Americans on occasion exploited the U.S. presence to their advantage. But North American racism and expansionism left a bitter legacy. Following the Walker affair, Costa Rica and Nicaragua declared themselves under the protection of Britain, France, and Sardinia against the "barbarians of the United States."[113] While Walker has remained an object of amusement for later generations of Americans, and has even been hailed as a "valiant idealist," his intervention in Nicaragua remains a major event in Central American history, a stark symbol of the ambitions and aggressiveness of the colossus to the north.[114]

The Buchanan presidency typifies the contradictions of U.S. expansionism in the 1850s. An experienced and successful diplomat, Buchanan, like his mentor Polk, was his own secretary of state. Indecisive and even timid in dealing with the nation's increasingly urgent domestic problems, he was belligerent with other nations and pursued numerous expansionist schemes. Like Polk, he looked John Bull straight in the eye. He defended Walker beyond the point of propriety. He dispatched a naval force of nineteen ships to avenge tiny Paraguay's killing of a single U.S. seaman. To secure payment for dubious financial claims against Mexico, he asked Congress for authority to detach its northern provinces and then to invade. He vigorously pursued the acquisition of Cuba. Anticipating twentieth-century chief executives, he sought and nearly secured from Congress a resolution giving him a blank check to use military force in Latin America. Caught up in the secession crisis, a preoccupied Congress wisely rejected Buchanan's wilder schemes, sealing the fate of expansion.[115]

---

111. Quoted in Paul A. Varg, *United States Foreign Relations, 1820–1860* (East Lansing, Mich., 1979), 230.
112. Elbert B. Smith, *The Presidency of James Buchanan* (Lawrence, Kans., 1975), 71.
113. Quoted in ibid., 73.
114. Coatsworth, *Central America*, 27; Albert Z. Carr, *The World and William Walker* (New York, 1963).
115. Smith, *Buchanan*, 69–80.

DURING THE AGE OF MANIFEST DESTINY, the United States greatly expanded its territory and acquired vast riches in natural resources, swelling national pride and laying the foundation for its future status as the world's greatest power. Popular myth to the contrary, foreign policy was central to the national experience in the antebellum era. Even in the 1850s, when little territory was added, Americans continued to operate across the globe. The United States expanded its involvement and interests in places like East Asia and Central America.

In terms of solving the nation's immediate problems, expansion did not live up to its billing. The Asian market did not meet expectations and did not absorb the nation's agricultural surplus. Commercial and territorial expansion did not head off industrialization and urbanization, as the Jeffersonians had hoped. The expansionism of the 1850s had generally negative results. To be sure, U.S. government aggressiveness, along with the filibusters, helped spur British withdrawal from Central America, a region deemed increasingly important to the United States. The "Yankees" were such "ingenious Rogues," Prime Minister Lord Palmerston complained, that they would get their way in Central America through the "indirect agency" of people like Walker—"Texas all over again." British withdrawal in turn ensured eventual U.S. dominance of the region. On the other hand, the filibuster expeditions provoked staunch opposition in Mexico and Cuba to the sale of territory to the United States. Along with relentless U.S. efforts to purchase territory to the south, the filibusters aroused fear and hatred of the United States in Central and indeed South America. Even Chileans feared that the "Yankee nation" was awaiting a chance to "devour them." Some Latins turned to Europe for protection against their rapacious northern neighbor. At least for the short term, filibustering slowed U.S. commercial expansion in Central America.[116]

Most important, expansion exacerbated rather than solved the nation's most urgent problem. Southern efforts to preserve their way of life through expansion aroused growing opposition in the North. Northern frustration of their designs sapped southern confidence in their ability to survive within the federal union, sparking secessionist sentiment. The emergence by 1856 of the Republican Party, a political alignment committed to stopping the expansion of slavery, suggested the extent to which Manifest Destiny had become a sectional issue. Rejection by leaders on both sides of the 1860 Crittenden Compromise, which would have ex-

116. Robert M. May, "Agents of Manifest Destiny," unpublished paper in possession of author, and *Manifest Destiny*, 240, 246–47.

tended the Missouri Compromise line to the Pacific—and possibly beyond—made clear the issue could not be resolved. Foreign policy was important to the calculations on each side. Southerners feared their loss of control of U.S. foreign policy doomed them to inferior status in the Union. For Republicans, on the other hand, slavery prevented the United States from achieving its higher global mission. It "deprives our republican example of its just influence in the world," Abraham Lincoln asserted in 1854; it "enables the enemies of free institutions to taunt us as hypocrites."[117] The irrepressible conflict over expansion and slavery led straight to Fort Sumter. The nation had swallowed Emerson's dose of arsenic.

117. Weeks, *Continental Empire*, 163; Fry, *Dixie*, 72–74.

6

"Last Best Hope"

The Union, the Confederacy, and Civil War Diplomacy, 1861–1877

The American Civil War was an event of great international importance.[1] Union and Confederate leaders recognized that their success or failure might swing on actions taken or not taken by the European great powers. European leaders, in turn, saw enticing opportunities and grave threats in the conflagration across the Atlantic. For Europeans, the Civil War also had momentous ideological implications. Conservatives welcomed the breakup of the Union, which some had long predicted, hoping that it would eliminate the menace of U.S.-style democracy throughout the world. Along with President Abraham Lincoln, on the other hand, liberals viewed the Union as the "last best hope of earth," agreeing that upon its survival hinged the future of republicanism for "the whole family of man."[2] The triumph of the Union, as Lincoln seems to have understood, ensured that within a short time the United States would emerge as a major world power.

I

The Civil War was part of a worldwide mid-nineteenth-century flowering of nation-building, a broader effort on the part of peoples across the globe to affirm, often through force of arms, their national identity. In Europe, Hungarians and Poles rose up in unsuccessful revolts against Austria and Russia. Modern nations took shape in Italy and Germany through military conquest. After a short war, the Swiss formed a federal union binding together cantons previously divided by religion. The Taiping "rebellion" raged for years in China at gruesome cost; the 1868 Meiji Restoration converted Japan from a feudal entity into a modern nation-state. The quest for

---

1. Robert E. May, ed., *The Union, the Confederacy and the Atlantic Rim* (Lafayette, Ind., 1995), 1–2.
2. James M. McPherson, " 'The Whole Family of Man': Lincoln and the Last Best Hope Abroad," in ibid., 136–38.

national identity extended to North America. With indirect U.S. support, Mexicans frustrated France's attempt to reestablish an American empire. The threat of U.S. annexation during the Civil War forced Britain to shore up Canada's vulnerability, leading in 1867 to creation of a united nation under a federal constitution with a centralized government.

The war also had enormous global implications. In the United States before 1861, union was an incomplete concept, especially in the South. The Civil War can thus be seen as an effort to establish a nation still not completely formed. Like similar struggles elsewhere, this was accomplished by force of arms. The Union victory also marked a turning of the tide internationally in favor of nationalism, solidifying a worldwide trend toward nation-states. More important, the Civil War fused nationalism with liberalism, giving significant moral purpose to nationalism, assuring that popular government could survive, and renewing hope among liberals across the world.[3] The steamship, telegraph, and trade brought nations closer at the same time nationalism was highlighting differences and provoking conflict. Other nations closely watched the U.S. internal struggle. Americans were more aware of events elsewhere because of increased immigration, faster and cheaper communication, growing literacy, and mass-circulation newspapers.[4]

Still clinging to dreams of imperial glory in the Western Hemisphere, Europeans attempted to exploit America's absorption in its domestic struggles. Spain invaded Santo Domingo in March 1861. In the spring of 1863, France's Napoleon III sent troops into Mexico. Europe itself was wracked with conflict during these years, however, putting a premium on caution in its handling of the American war. Crises erupted in 1862 from the Italian *Risorgimento* and Austria's conflict with Prussia. In 1863, the Polish rebellion against Russia threatened a general European war. By dividing the great powers against each other, these events rendered less likely any form of intervention in U.S. affairs. By increasing problems for France in Europe, German and Italian unification influenced Napoleon's eventual withdrawal from Mexico.[5]

3. Carl N. Degler, "One Among Many: The United States and National Unification," in Carl J. Guarneri, *America Compared* (New York, 1997), 335–52; David M. Potter, "Civil War," in C. Vann Woodward, ed., *The Comparative Approach to American History* (New York, 1968), 138–45.

4. Norman E. Saul, *Distant Friends: The United States and Russia, 1763–1867* (Lawrence, Kans., 1991), 329.

5. Paul Kennedy, *The Rise and Fall of the Great Powers* (New York, 1987), 187–93; D. P. Crook, *Diplomacy During the American Civil War* (New York, 1975), 21, 99, 107, 121, 155, 180–83.

For both Union and Confederacy, diplomacy was vital. Should the Europeans recognize the belligerency and eventually the independence of the South, offer economic and military aid, perhaps even send military forces, they could ensure its survival and ultimate independence. Their neutrality and refusal to intervene, on the other hand, would help the Union, perhaps even seal Confederate doom. Americans on both sides remembered, in this regard, that French intervention in 1778 had ensured the success of their revolution.[6]

Confederate diplomacy was founded on naïveté and illusion. Facing a huge disadvantage in such essential sinews of war as population, natural resources, and industrial capacity, the South might have looked abroad to make up the deficiency. In fact, southerners were strangely ambivalent toward the outside world. They believed themselves sophisticated and in touch with European elites. But they were quite out of tune with the prevailing currents of liberal nationalism in Europe.[7] Certain of their rectitude and invincibility, they badly misread European attitudes toward their cause and their own need for outside assistance. Especially in the Confederacy's first years, they undervalued the importance of diplomacy. President Jefferson Davis appointed incompetents to the vital position of secretary of state. He and his advisers did not actively seek foreign recognition and aid. If recognition was not forthcoming, some leaders arrogantly reasoned, so what? The "sovereign State of Mississippi can do a great deal better without England than England can do without her," its governor boldly—and recklessly—proclaimed.[8]

For years, southerners had fancied that they held a trump card. King Cotton, it was called, and it was based on the fundamental—and ultimately flawed—assumption that Europe in general and Britain in particular so depended on southern cotton that they had to ensure its continued import. In theory, at least, it made sense. When the Civil War broke out, about one-fifth of the population of Great Britain made a living from the manufacture of cotton, 80 percent of which came from the American South. France imported 90 percent of its cotton from the South; its textile factories employed 250,000 people. Should the cotton supply be cut off, the theory went, the European powers would be reduced to economic ruin and threatened with revolution. Southerners thus concluded that if

6. Gary W. Gallagher, The Confederate War (Cambridge, Mass., 1997), 145.
7. Emory M. Thomas, The Confederate Nation, 1861–1865 (New York, 1979), 167–68.
8. Henry Blumenthal, "Confederate Diplomacy: Popular Notions and International Rivalries," Journal of Southern History 32 (May 1966), 153; Joseph A. Fry, Dixie Looks Abroad: The South and U.S. Foreign Relations, 1789–1973 (Baton Rouge, LA., 2002), 75–78.

the Union attempted a blockade, which they fully anticipated, Britain and France would have to intervene to ensure their own survival. To underscore the point, they burned some 2.5 million bales at the start of the war.[9]

The architect of Union diplomatic strategy and the individual mainly responsible for its implementation was Secretary of State William Henry Seward. Seward was in many ways a strange person: "I am an enigma even to myself," he once remarked. A man of enormous energy, sloppy in appearance, he was also a genial host, a lover of fine cigars and brandy, a great raconteur, a person of such magnetism, Henry Adams once said, that he could "charm a cow to statesmanship." A man of considerable vision and sophistication, he was also earthy and a total political animal. He was brash, impulsive, and hot-tempered, given to bluster and threats. But he was most dangerous, associates said, "when he pretends to agree a good deal with you."[10]

More than a bit vainglorious, he fancied himself at the outset a prime minister to the younger and less experienced Lincoln, and he concocted schemes that bordered on the bizarre. For example, on April Fools' Day, 1861 (appropriately), he proposed that the crisis of secession might be averted if the United States declared war on France and Spain simultaneously. This "wrap the world in fire" proposal had the presumed advantage of holding the Union together by instigating a foreign war. Lincoln had the good sense to reject it.

After this inauspicious beginning, Seward matured and went on to conduct Union diplomacy with distinction, maneuvering astutely through a series of crises. Employing a policy of controlled anger, he repeatedly emphasized to European powers the dangers of sticking their noses in America's troubles. More than once, he demonstrated that rarest and most essential of diplomatic skills, talking tough enough to satisfy his domestic constituency and give an adversary pause while compromising when the situation demanded it. He carefully cultivated a madman image, encouraging other nations to believe him reckless. He often reminded Britain and France of the dangers of intervention in U.S. affairs, warning that a Union victory would mean a high price to pay later on. He became a fervent spokesman for the Union and the republican principles

9. Fry, Dixie, 76–77.
10. Howard Jones, Union in Peril: The Crisis over British Intervention in the Civil War (Chapel Hill, N.C., 1992), 7, 11, 88. On Seward, see also Gordon H. Warren, "William Henry Seward," in Frank J. Merli and Theodore A. Wilson, Makers of American Diplomacy: From Benjamin Franklin to Alfred Thayer Mahan (New York, l974), 195–219.

upon which it was founded. Once remembered for little more than the purchase of Alaska, which, of course, was labeled his "folly," Seward now ranks among the nation's best secretaries of state.

Lincoln proved a perfect complement to his brilliant and sometimes volatile adviser. The president brought no diplomatic experience to the White House. He had traveled only to Canada, knew no foreign languages, and even by nineteenth-century-American standards would be considered provincial. But he appointed able people to key positions. He was a master at managing the strong men who worked with him. A natural-born politician, he had an instinctive feel for the diplomatic art. Rivals for the presidency, he and Seward formed what Lincoln's personal secretary John Hay called an "official connection hallowed by a friendship so absolute and sincere," a true rarity in government. Lincoln found relief from the pressures of war in Seward's convivial Lafayette Square parlor. For the most part, he left the secretary of state free to do his job, only occasionally reining in his excesses. Above all, Lincoln was the quintessentially American practical idealist. As the war wore on, he eloquently voiced the importance of a Union victory for the worldwide cause of freedom and shrewdly maneuvered between sometimes conflicting domestic and foreign pressures to realize the ideals he preached.[11]

At the start of the Civil War, only tsarist Russia, among the European powers, stood squarely with the Union. This curious entente between autocratic Russia and the world's leading democracy was deeply rooted in recent history. In the 1840s, the two nations had followed non-conflicting expansionist courses. Each saw the other as a potential check against Britain. Americans played an important role in Russia's economic development, especially in transportation and communications. The two nations developed a remarkable cultural affinity. During the Crimean War, the United States became "considerably Russified," in Secretary of State William Marcy's words, maintaining a benevolent neutrality that verged on the alliance Americans professed to abhor. The United States sold Russia large quantities of coal, cotton, and war supplies. American volunteers fought with Russia; U.S. doctors served with its army. Contacts between the two nations increased after the war, and the rise of abolitionism in both countries in the 1850s provided another important link.[12]

11. Hay is quoted in Doris Kearns Goodwin, *Team of Rivals: The Political Genius of Abraham Lincoln* (New York, 2005), 745. On Lincoln, see Howard Jones, *Abraham Lincoln and a New Birth of Freedom: The Union and Slavery in the Diplomacy of the Civil War* (Lincoln, Neb., 1999) and Jan Morris, *Lincoln: A Foreigner's Quest* (New York, 2000).
12. Saul, *Distant Friends*, 166–237, 398–99; the quotation is from p. 201.

Russians feared with the outbreak of the Civil War that the United States would not be able to balance Britain during a period of instability in Europe. They were determined to repay U.S. support during the Crimean War. Tsar Alexander welcomed to St. Petersburg in June 1861 the Union minister, Cassius Clay of Kentucky, hailing two nations "bound together by a common sympathy in the common cause of emancipation." Throughout four years of bloody warfare in America and turbulence in Europe, his country never wavered from that position.[13]

The other major powers, France and England, were sharply divided on the American Civil War. In England, the rising forces of liberalism despised slavery and saw the United States as a beacon of democracy in a conservative world. Despite reservations about slavery, more conservative Britons and indeed the European ruling classes generally considered the breakup of the "American colossus" as "good riddance of a night mare."[14] They felt some kinship with the stability, order, and gentility of the southern social system, in contrast to the money-grubbing plutocracy and dangerous mobocracy that, in their eyes, characterized the Union.

Those Europeans responsible for the conduct of diplomacy, balance-of-power politicians in the great age of European realpolitik, saw advantages in a divided America as opposed to a *United* States. Some Britons, in particular, concluded that Canada and other vital interests in the Western Hemisphere might be more secure with a balance of power in North America instead of U.S. hegemony. Seeking to emulate his famous uncle and fire French national pride through foreign adventurism, Napoleon III thoroughly despised the United States and saw the Monroe Doctrine as a major obstacle to his grand scheme for restoring national glory and containing republicanism by rebuilding in America a French empire centered upon Mexico.

Finally, to some Europeans, the principle of self-determination, as manifested in southern secessionism, had an appealing ring. The staunchly pro-Confederate *Times* of London, undoubtedly with a twinkle in its journalistic eye, found an "exact analogy between the government in Washington and the Government of George III, and the South and the Thirteen Revolted Provinces."[15] Misjudging U.S. determination to restore the Union and taking Lincoln's early caution on slavery at face

---

13. Ibid., 312–25; the quotation is from p. 305.
14. *Times* of London, quoted in McPherson, "Whole Family," 136. The authoritative study of British opinion is R.J.M. Blackett, *Divided Hearts: Britain and the American Civil War* (Baton Rouge, La., 2001).
15. November 7, 1861.

value, some British leaders viewed the war as a "meaningless bloodbath." They hoped for peace, and saw separation as an acceptable means to that end.

Although sympathetic to the South and the idea of secession, European leaders were not disposed to intrude. The adventurism that had raised southern hopes of support in fact had left France overextended. A newly cautious Napoleon increasingly deferred to British leadership. British leaders saw advantages in separation and felt some urge to end the war on humanitarian grounds, but they refused to take risks. They listened to Seward's warnings and carefully avoided steps that might provoke war with the United States. They recognized the importance of U.S. trade to their economy and refused to jeopardize it. Much like the United States in the Napoleonic era, they wanted to avoid entanglement *and* trade with both sides. Neutrality was thus the obvious choice. They sought to steer a delicate course between the two belligerents while protecting their interests and keeping their own people from involving their nation in war. Above all, they sought to stay out of the war and ensure that France did the same.

II

The combatants themselves provoked the first international crisis of the Civil War. The Lincoln administration adamantly insisted that it faced nothing more than an insurrection, but it employed means appropriate for full-scale war. Seeking to strangle the Confederacy at birth, it proclaimed a blockade, even though, technically, a blockade was an act of war, and, practically, it did not have enough ships to seal off a three-thousand-mile coastline. The Confederacy sent three commissioners to Europe seeking recognition. Using precedents set by the United States, it authorized the employment of privateers—the "militia of the sea"—as an "efficient and admirable instrument of defensive warfare." The Union threatened to treat privateers as pirates.[16]

Britain responded on May 13, 1861, by proclaiming its neutrality. To some extent the declaration reflected rising hostility toward the United States. The British resented the protective tariff passed by the Republican Congress in 1861 and the Union blockade. They may have moved too fast. They announced their neutrality without consulting Washington. Union leaders considered the move at best premature, at worst outright hostile.

16. Davis message to Second Provisional Congress, April 29, 1861, in James D. Richardson, ed., *The Messages and Papers of Jefferson Davis and the Confederacy* (2 vols., New York, 1966), 1:75.

Still, the actions taken by the combatants, especially the blockade, left lit-tle choice. British leaders saw the rebellion for what it was—a war. They cleverly harked back to precedents set by George Washington in 1793.

The British correctly insisted that they were not taking sides, but their actions appeared to favor the South. The declaration of neutrality auto-matically conceded belligerent status to the Confederacy. It was seen in both North and South (incorrectly as it turned out) as a precursor to recognition of independence and perhaps even aid. Foreign Secretary Lord John Russell further angered the Union by receiving the Confeder-ate commissioners informally and announcing that Britain and France would act in concert in issues dealing with the war.

"God damn them!" Seward roared in response. His famous Dispatch No. 10 of May 21, 1861, although toned down by Lincoln, still threatened a break in relations if Britain continued to meet with southern represen-tatives and otherwise moved closer to recognizing Confederate indepen-dence.[17] He demanded respect for the Union blockade. When the British and French ministers visited him together, he insisted on seeing them separately. The U.S. minister to England, Charles Francis Adams, under-scored the secretary's warnings. Arriving at his post just as the neutrality crisis erupted, Adams went out of his way to avoid antagonizing his hosts by appearing at court in the traditional stockings and lace rather than the black republican garb required by Marcy's 1853 dress circular. Echoing Seward's warnings, he threatened to depart before beginning his mission if Britain gave further comfort to the enemy.

Taking heed of Union protests and warnings, the British maintained a proper neutrality, offending both sides but increasingly leaning toward the Union. Recognizing the future value of precedents set by Washing-ton, they did not challenge the blockade, despite its questionable legality. To the consternation of southerners, Russell did not receive the Confed-erate commissioners again. Britain refused to admit privateers to its ports, depriving the Confederacy of the presumed advantages of its "militia of the sea." British leaders did not want to appear to be supporting slavery. They were well aware of the long-run threat of diminishing cotton im-ports, but because of large crops in 1860 their warehouses were full and they could accept the short-term loss rather than provoke the Union. For the moment, they adopted a wait-and-see demeanor, letting the Ameri-can dust settle before they acted. Sometimes in diplomacy the "wisest

17. Phillip S. Paludan, *The Presidency of Abraham Lincoln* (Lawrence, Kans., 1994), 89–90.

strategy was to do nothing," Russell explained. "They who in quarrels in-
terpose, will often get a bloody nose," Prime Minister Lord Palmerston,
the consummate realist, pointedly reminded his colleagues.[18] Even the
Confederate victory at First Bull Run in July 1861, which momentarily
encouraged the South and demoralized the North, failed to budge
Britain from its strategy. Now the Confederacy protested British "truck-
ling" to Seward's "arrogant demands" and acceptance of the "so-called
blockade."

This changed suddenly in November 1861 when an incident at sea
brought the United States and Britain to the verge of war. The *Trent* affair
was the handiwork of the brilliant and eccentric Capt. Charles Wilkes.
An accomplished scientist as well as naval officer, Wilkes had headed the
Great United States Exploring Expedition on its worldwide journey in
the 1840s.[19] Arrogant, overbearing, as paranoid as the legendary Capt.
William Bligh, he was also impulsive and ambitious—he once promoted
himself to captain while at sea and ostentatiously donned the uniform he
had packed for the occasion. His actions in 1861 made clear the way an
impetuous individual could provoke a major crisis.[20] Learning that recently appointed southern diplomats James Mason and John Slidell were
aboard the British ship *Trent* en route from Havana to Europe via St.
Thomas, Wilkes, on his own authority, stopped and boarded the neutral
ship. Taking upon himself the role of international lawyer and prize court
judge, he captured Mason and Slidell. Without searching the ship or taking it to prize court, he sent it on its way. In fact, the neutral vessel was
carrying southern dispatches, generally recognized as contraband, but by
not following the proper rules of search and seizure Wilkes rendered his
actions illegal.

The capture of Mason and Slidell reversed the traditional roles of
America and Britain in maritime disputes and provoked anger across the
Atlantic. Britons were furious; there was much loose talk of war.[21] The
cabinet was understandably outraged and demanded that the United
States disavow Wilkes's actions, release Mason and Slidell, and apologize.
The dying Prince Albert, Queen Victoria's closest adviser, softened the
tone of the cabinet's ultimatum, giving diplomacy a chance to work, but

18. Jones, *Union in Peril*, 50.
19. William Stanton, *The Great United States Exploring Expedition of 1838–1842* (Berke-
    ley, Calif., 1975).
20. Geoffrey S. Smith, "Charles Wilkes and the Growth of American Naval Diplomacy,"
    in Merli and Wilson, *Makers of American Diplomacy*, 152.
21. Jones, *Union in Peril*, 87.

British leaders were still prepared to break relations, the last step before war. The nation began to mobilize and took steps to fortify Canadian defenses. France backed Britain and even proposed joint intervention in the Civil War, a step London quickly and wisely rejected. All "the world is disgusted by the insolence of the American Republic," Russell exclaimed.[22]

The U.S. reaction was mixed. To a nation starved for victories, the capture of the two Confederate diplomats was welcome news, especially since Mason and Slidell had been among the most rabid of southern disunionists. Northerners hailed Wilkes's audacity. Some hotheads responded to British war fever with bellicose talk of their own. Others recognized that Wilkes had violated the nation's traditional stand for freedom of the seas. In time, moreover, even the hottest of heads perceived the difficulty of defeating Britain and the Confederacy at once and recognized that a war with Britain might ensure southern independence. At first complacent, Lincoln and Seward gradually recognized the hornet's nest Wilkes had stirred. Near-panic in financial circles encouraged their desire for compromise. In this instance, Lincoln continued to talk tough to his domestic audience while letting Seward arrange a face-saving compromise. The secretary readily assented to British demands to give up the two diplomats. Since they were contraband, he insisted, their seizure had been legal, but Wilkes's failure to follow the rules forced their release. He also justified his action in terms of America's long-standing support for freedom of the seas and its opposition to impressment.

The *Trent* affair was both ominous and useful, forcing the United States and Britain at an early stage to confront the risks and possible costs of war. By eliminating a very real threat of conflict with Britain, it left the Union free to concentrate on defeating the Confederacy. But it did not end the possibility of recognition of southern independence or British intervention. And British leaders appear to have concluded from the experience that the best way to deal with the United States was to take a hard line.[23]

III

Following the *Trent* crisis, while Union and Confederate armies settled into their bloody struggle, diplomats from both sides competed for advantages that might determine the outcome of the war. Southern diplomacy

22. Ibid., 87.
23. Paludan, *Lincoln*, 93; Crook, *Diplomacy*, 57–60; Jones, *Union in Peril*, 98–99.

could never quite rise above its considerable limits. Communications posed especially difficult problems. The blockade and lack of access to a cable made it extremely difficult to issue instructions and receive dispatches. Confederate officials often had to get news from the northern press. Dispatches were lost or captured and sometimes appeared in Union newspapers.[24] In dealing with Caribbean countries, southerners had to explain away their aggressive past, something they tried to do—with only limited success—by noting that they had sought additional territory only to preserve a "balance of power in a Government from whose dominant majority they feared oppression and injury."[25] The Confederacy faced a huge challenge in persuading Britain and France to do things that threatened war with the Union. Most important, it could never overcome the stigma of slavery.

Ironically, although the Confederacy inherited through the national Democratic Party a corps of experienced diplomats, it made notably poor appointments. The first commissioners sent to England were an undistinguished group not well suited to a difficult assignment. William Lowndes Yancey, their spokesman, defended slavery with such passion that he quickly made himself unpopular in England.[26] Slidell and Mason were both seasoned diplomats, but they were not especially effective. Mason was an intelligent individual, but his boorish behavior, his errant aim with tobacco juice, and his reputation as an apologist for slavery limited his efforts in England. Slidell was astute and experienced and presumably had an affinity with the French through his background in Louisiana and fluency in the language, but he never grasped what motivated French officials or how the government operated. Historian Charles Roland has wryly observed that the two did more good for their cause while incarcerated in a northern prison than when they actually took their posts. Mexican recognition could have been a huge boon to the Confederacy, but John Pickett of Kentucky was as bad a choice for that country as Joel Poinsett and Anthony Butler. Like those two notorious predecessors, he blustered and threatened and displayed open contempt for the Mexican nation and people. His personal behavior was reprehensible—he was jailed for assaulting another American in Mexico City and eventually bribed his way out. In all, southern diplomats were a provincial lot who, even by the

24. Crook, *Diplomacy*, 80; Richardson, *Davis Messages* 2:326, documents a case where it took five months to receive a dispatch from Paris.
25. R.M.T. Hunter to William L. Yancey, Pierre A. Rost, and A. Dudley Mann, August 24, 1861, in Richardson, *Davis Messages* 2:74.
26. Charles P. Roland, *The Confederacy* (Chicago, 1960), 102.

standards of the time, evinced enormous insensitivity to foreign cultures. They were much less astute than their Union counterparts when dealing with world affairs.[27]

Southern foreign policy was poorly conceived. Confederate leaders did not give diplomacy high priority or adequate attention at the outset. By the time they recognized its importance, it was too late. Confident of victory, they did not seek alliances or even foreign assistance. Inexplicably, the Confederacy did not try to establish ties with Russia despite its size and the importance of cotton exports. It did not appoint a mission until late 1862; the commissioner never made it to St. Petersburg.[28] The South perceived the importance of an alliance with Mexico to secure access to the outside world through its ports, but it pursued this important goal in a bumbling way. Much in the mode of Butler, Pickett tried to bribe Mexico into recognition. That failing, like Poinsett, he backed the political opposition. When Mason met unofficially with Russell, he did not press the case for recognition and aid, perhaps the South's only hope for survival, letting Britain off the hook.

Even where it achieved some success, southern diplomacy was hemmed in by sharp limitations. Displaying a rare shrewdness born perhaps of necessity, the Confederacy negotiated in 1861 treaties with the Five Civilized Tribes living in Indian Territory in Oklahoma, even pledging that the Indians would not be "troubled or molested" by individuals or the states. The key provision for the Indians was the protection offered against the Union; in return, they vowed fealty to the South and even promised to fight. When the Confederacy could no longer provide such protection, however, and this came as early as the spring of 1862, the alliance disintegrated. The Indians were not inclined to assist a Confederacy that could do nothing for them.[29]

Confederate propaganda also revealed limitations. The key figure was Henry Hotze, a Swiss-born Mobile journalist who in May 1862 launched on his own the *Index*, a weekly newspaper propounding the southern point of view. In time, the Richmond government began to subsidize Hotze's work. It also sponsored a propaganda effort in France. Late in 1863, the Confederacy promoted the founding of a Society to Promote the Cessation of Hostilities, a pro-southern organization that used fact sheets, handbills, and lectures to sway British opinion toward recognition. Confederate propaganda evinced some sophistication, revealing a growing

27. May, *Union, Confederacy*, 12; Roland, *Confederacy*, 103–6.
28. Saul, *Distant Friends*, 335–36.
29. Thomas, *Confederate Nation*, 188–89.

maturity in southern foreign relations. Propagandists shrewdly concentrated on the hardest-hit areas of Britain, where they presumed their message would be best received. They admitted, however, that they could not get their point of view across even in these areas because of fierce working-class opposition to slavery.[30]

The South continued to rely on King Cotton. The voluntary embargo requested by the Confederate government was remarkably effective, far more so than Jefferson's leak-plagued efforts before 1812, making clear the power of southern nationalism. By the spring of 1862, the shortage of cotton began to have significant effects in Europe. Baron Rothschild spoke of a "whole continent in convulsion." Many British mills closed in 1862, prices skyrocketed, and unemployment steadily increased.

Whatever its effects, the cotton embargo did not live up to the faith placed in it. Economic sanctions take time to work, and time was not on the Confederacy's side. It was also a matter of strategy. The South tried to use the embargo as a "lever" to force European recognition. It might have done better to bargain shipments of cotton in return for recognition and assistance. The British blamed the South rather than the Union for the shortages. The virtual embargo of cotton undermined its value as a diplomatic weapon.[31]

Timing also worked against King Cotton. When war broke out in 1861, England had a huge surplus in its warehouses, in large part because of a bumper crop in 1860 and record imports. There was also a surplus of manufactured cotton goods, so much so, in fact, that many factory owners had shut down or drastically cut back production to keep prices from plummeting. Despite the effectiveness of the voluntary embargo, greed could not be eliminated, and some cotton made it through the embargoes and the Union blockade. Later in the war, the loss of southern cotton was offset by new sources in Egypt and British India. As the Union began to occupy parts of the South, it made sure to get as much cotton as possible to England.

Other factors limited the presumed clout of King Cotton. However important southern cotton may have been to its economy, Britain also had vital economic ties to the North. Bad crops at home during the war forced it to turn to the United States for grain. King Wheat thus proved as important as King Cotton. British citizens had also invested heavily in U.S. canals, railroads, and banks, and these sizeable investments might be

30. Ibid., 177–79; R.J.M. Blackett, "Pressure from Without: African Americans, British Public Opinion, and Civil War Diplomacy," in May, *Union, Confederacy*, 80–90.
31. Blumenthal, "Confederate Diplomacy," 170.

threatened if Britain moved too close to the Confederacy. Finally, and perhaps ironically, the Civil War stimulated an economic boom in England in various industries, more than compensating for the loss of cotton. King Cotton may have worked as well as economic sanctions ever have, but it was still not enough. Not for the first time or the last did a nation, or in this case an aspirant nation, fall victim to the chimera of what Jefferson called "peaceable coercion."

The central task of northern diplomacy was easier, of course: to keep the British and French on the cautious path toward which they were already predisposed rather than persuade them to take drastic steps. A new political party, the Republicans had no reservoir of diplomatic experience to draw on, but their diplomats in key positions performed effectively, in some cases remarkably so. Seward matured quickly. He worked diligently to maintain the harmony in Anglo-American relations that followed the *Trent* affair. He attempted to use Union military success to deter any European move toward intervention and to turn cotton against the South by opening captured southern ports to European ships as a gesture of goodwill.[32] Although ignorant of the language and unschooled in diplomacy, William Dayton of New Jersey proved a competent minister in Paris, establishing good relations with Napoleon III and working hard to head off French intervention.[33] Nominally minister to Belgium, the wealthy Henry Sanford of Connecticut did much more. Imaginative, indefatigable, often meddlesome in the eyes of colleagues, Sanford was a one-man diplomatic wrecking crew, organizing a number of Union propaganda initiatives, establishing an "octopus-like" secret service network of private investigators and paid informants to track Confederate activities on the Continent, and overseeing and sometimes funding with his own money preemptive purchases to keep crucial war supplies out of Confederate hands. A colleague referred to Sanford without exaggeration as a "Legation on Wheels."[34]

Cassius Clay of Kentucky earned both notoriety and a measure of distinction in Russia. Clay was one of those anti-slavery radicals Charles Francis Adams labeled "the noisy jackasses," and his militance worried Lincoln. He was sent to St. Petersburg because, it was said, he could do no harm there and—more important—it would get him out of Washington. Clay wore a dazzling array of Bowie knives and brought to his post

32. Crook, *Diplomacy*, 72–73.
33. *Dictionary of American Biography* (26 vols., New York, 1934–61), 3:167.
34. Joseph A. Fry, *Henry S. Sanford: Diplomacy and Business in Nineteenth-Century America* (Reno, Nev., 1982), 35–65.

his notoriously thin skin and propensity for the duel. His "pigeon wing" dancing provided amusement at court. Despite his characteristically eccentric behavior—maybe in part because of it—he proved a good choice. He came to admire the Russian people and to see Russia as "our sincere friend" and "most powerful ally." A surprisingly sophisticated diplomatist with a keen understanding of balance of power politics, he did nothing to harm the existing friendship. In many ways, he actively promoted it.[35]

Charles Francis Adams in London was even more effective—and much more significant. Like his illustrious father—and indeed grandfather—he also was a "bulldog among spaniels," relentless, tireless in bringing to British attention alleged violations of neutrality and warning of the pitfalls of intervention. Less combative than his distinguished forebears, characterized even by Russell as "calm and judicious," he also employed friendly persuasion to mitigate and reinforce Seward's threats. Adams is generally viewed as one of the most skillful diplomats to have served his nation, a person who made a difference during a critical period.

From expediency, the Union shelved its expansionist ambitions for the duration. Lincoln was in the Whig mold, believing that America's mission could best be carried out by demonstrating "before an admiring world . . . the capacity of a people to govern themselves."[36] Seward, in contrast, was an avowed expansionist, whose vision of empire exceeded that of John Quincy Adams. But he understood that such ambitions must be put aside to deal with the emergency. Early in the war, Lincoln and Seward toyed with colonization schemes as a means to address domestic problems and expand U.S. influence abroad. The dispatch of freed slaves into Central America and Mexico, they reasoned, would not only ease racial tensions at home but also help ensure U.S. control over raw materials, harbors, and transit facilities in a vital area. The national security argument gained force as Europeans intervened in Mexico and Central America, In 1862, Congress appropriated funds for a colonization program. African Americans and abolitionists bitterly opposed the idea, however. When Central Americans expressed fears of "Africanization" and especially of the intrusion of a nation that had already revealed its true colors "in the aggression of Walker," Seward and Lincoln backed off.[37]

35. Saul, *Distant Friends*, 317–19.
36. Paludan, *Lincoln*, 88–89.
37. Thomas Schoonover, "Miscontrued Mission: Expansionism and Black Colonization in Mexico and Central America During the American Civil War," *Pacific Historical Review* 44 (November 1980), 607–20.

In large part to promote U.S. diplomatic objectives, Lincoln slowly and with the utmost caution seized the moral high ground. The United States recognized Haiti and Liberia in 1862. Still wary of measures long urged by abolitionists and opposed by southerners, the president took the unusual step of asking Congress to endorse the move. The first U.S. representative to Haiti held the relatively lowly rank of commissioner. Also in 1862, the United States and Britain agreed to a treaty providing for mutual searches to end the slave trade. "If I have done nothing else worthy of self-congratulation," Seward boasted, "I deem this treaty worthy to have lived for."[38] In February 1863, the first American was executed for participation in that illegal activity. At least compared to the days when southerners controlled Congress, U.S. diplomacy was becoming increasingly color-blind.[39]

The issue of slavery had huge domestic and international implications, and Lincoln handled it with special care. As a young man, he had come to view the institution as morally wrong, but he accepted its protection by the Constitution. He had staunchly opposed the expansion of slavery but, like his idol Henry Clay, looked upon colonization as a possible solution to America's racial problems. The 1854 Kansas-Nebraska Act pushed him toward a harder line. Claiming to be "thunderstruck and stunned" by a measure that infused new life into a moribund institution, he opposed the further expansion of slavery with great moral force. He insisted that the demise of this "monstrous injustice" was essential to preserve the United States as a beacon of freedom throughout the world. When the war began, he was sufficiently concerned about the loyalty of border states such as Kentucky, Missouri, and Maryland and the support of moderates North and South to downplay slavery, focusing instead on preserving the Union. By July 1862, in the face of battlefield defeat and possible European intervention, he concluded that emancipation was a military necessity. Freeing the slaves in territory held by the Confederacy could undermine the southern war effort. It might fend off British and French intervention. It would preserve and indeed perfect the Union by securing the promises of freedom enunciated in the Declaration of Independence. "I shall not surrender the game leaving any available card unplayed," Lincoln affirmed.[40] On Seward's advice, to avoid the appearance of desperation, he delayed any move until the Union achieved some battlefield success.

Like the Confederacy, the Union waged an active propaganda war across the Atlantic. Seward sent former New York Evening Post editor

38. Crook, Diplomacy, 68–69.
39. Paludan, Lincoln, 133–34.
40. Quoted in Jones, Lincoln, 87.

John Bigelow to influence the French press favorably toward the Union. Bigelow and Republican politico Thurlow Weed carefully cultivated European journalists and sent letters to the editors of major newspapers. Sanford provided material to friendly newspapers across Europe and used his slush fund to hire European journalists to write favorable articles. African Americans played an important part. Fugitive slaves and freed slaves including Jefferson Davis's former coachman, Andrew Jackson, gave speeches discussing the horrors of slavery as they had experienced it to generate support for the Union and opposition to the Confederacy. Speeches in the mill areas in particular helped to focus the debate on the issue of freedom when it could have turned narrowly on cotton. Southern sympathizers, it was said, "breathed a sigh of relief" when Jackson returned to the United States at the end of 1863.[41]

IV

The summer and fall of 1862 were the closest the American Civil War came to becoming a world war, "the very crisis of our fate," in the anxious words of Charles Francis Adams.[42] While Union and Confederate armies slugged it out in the Mississippi Valley and especially across the bloody corridor between Richmond and Washington, the European great powers and especially Great Britain teetered on the brink of intervention. Cotton provides a partial explanation. By the summer of 1862, one-half of Britain's textile workers were unemployed, one-third of its mills had closed, and stocks were dwindling. The trans-Atlantic trade, vital to Britain's economy, suffered severe dislocation. Government revenues declined. Nervous manufacturers pressed the cabinet to do something. The economic crisis was even more severe in France. "We are nearly out of cotton, and cotton *we must have*," the French foreign minister told Sanford in April.[43]

For many Europeans, ending the war for geopolitical *and* humanitarian reasons became increasingly urgent. The longer the conflict dragged on, the greater its impact on the Old World, the more Europeans sought to end it before the conflagration spread. For Victorians, the carnage produced in America by the harnessing of modern technology to warfare came as a profound shock, provoking growing cries to stop what Britons labeled this "bloody and purposeless war," this "suicidal frenzy."[44] Gen-

41. Blackett, *Divided Hearts*, 189.
42. Crook, *Diplomacy*, 93.
43. Jones, *Union in Peril*, 156.
44. Ibid., 145, 150.

eral George McClellan's failure to take Richmond in the Peninsular Campaign of 1862 and his adversary Robert E. Lee's dazzling maneuvers persuaded many Europeans that the Union could not win. The war might go on indefinitely. As Lee's armies moved north in August 1862 for what might be a knockout blow, Europeans anticipated that another Union defeat might provide the occasion for intervention.

Although increasingly disposed to do something, British leaders remained cautious. Seward's warnings that the Civil War could become a "war of the world" could not be ignored. There was little inclination to risk war with the Union by challenging the blockade until Confederate independence, as Palmerston put it, was "a Truth and a Fact."[45] By the late summer of 1862, however, British leaders were increasingly disposed to mediate the American struggle as a way to end the bloodletting, ease Europe's economic problems, and perhaps even destroy slavery by stopping its expansion. Still failing to perceive Lincoln's steadfast determination to preserve the Union, British leaders assumed that European mediation would lead to an armistice, the end of the blockade, and the acceptance of two separate governments.

A Union military victory in the fall of 1862 gave Lincoln the opportunity to take the initiative on emancipation. Lee's advancing armies met Union forces at Antietam Creek near Sharpsburg, Maryland, on September 17. In the most gruesome day of the war, the two sides together lost five thousand killed and suffered twenty-four thousand casualties. The battle was at best a draw, but Lee's retreat back into Virginia permitted the Union to claim victory. Antietam stopped the Confederate offensive into the North and provided a much-needed boost to Union morale. Five days later, Lincoln issued a preliminary Emancipation Proclamation. The order did not go into effect until January 1, 1863. Reflecting the president's persisting concern for the border states, it applied only to areas held by the Confederacy. Prosaic in tone, it disappointed abolitionists. On the other hand, it further bolstered northern spirits and spurred black enlistments in the Union army. In his annual message to Congress, December 1, 1862, Lincoln remained cautious on slavery, again speaking of colonization and compensated emancipation. He also eloquently took the moral high ground. Warning that the "dogmas of the quiet past are inadequate to the stormy present" and calling upon Americans to "think anew and act anew," he insisted that only by eradicating slavery could the United States be true to its principles. "In *giving* freedom to the slaves,"

45. Ibid., 128.

he proclaimed, "we *assure* freedom to the *free*." He cast emancipation in global terms. At a time when republicanism appeared to be losing out across the world and the threat of European intervention still loomed over America, he insisted that the nation must eliminate the blot of slavery to ensure that it remained "the last best hope of earth."[46] The Emancipation Proclamation represented a crucial point in the war. It set in motion the process of ending slavery. It shifted U.S. war aims from mere preservation of the Union to its betterment by making the nation faithful to the ideals enunciated in its Declaration of Independence.[47]

Often cited as eliminating the threat of foreign intervention, Antietam and the Emancipation Proclamation for the short term actually increased pressures on Britain and France to do something. The bloodbath in Maryland and the absence of a decisive victory merely confirmed for European statesmen that the two combatants, without external intervention, might fight on indefinitely at horrendous cost. Lincoln had issued his Emancipation Proclamation in part to gain foreign support for the Union cause, but many Britons initially saw it as an act of desperation. Viewing emancipation through the prism of mid-nineteenth-century Anglo-Saxon racism, they also feared it might unleash slave insurrections throughout the South and even set off a race war that could spread beyond the United States. British leaders thus grew more inclined to intervene. Russell discussed with France the possibility of a joint intervention aimed at an armistice. Should the Union reject such proposals, they agreed, southern independence might be recognized. Liberal leader William Evart Gladstone's dramatic October 7, 1862, speech proclaiming that southern leaders had "made an army; they are making, it appears a navy; and they have made what is more than either, they have made a nation," seemed to portend recognition of Confederate independence.

Caution once again prevailed. Gladstone's speech was not authorized. It did not reflect the views of the government or even a pro-southern view on his part. Its main concern was to end the carnage. It evoked a negative reaction throughout England and forced the cabinet to examine the consequences of intervention. Russell was most inclined to act, but the more prudent eventually won the day. Seward's strong words helped persuade British leaders that neither side would accept compromise. Intervention posed varied and considerable dangers, especially the threat of war with the United States. It thus seemed better, as Secretary of War Cornewall Lewis

---

46. James D. Richardson, ed., *A Compilation of the Messages and Papers of the Presidents of the United States* (20 vols., Washington, 1897–1916), 8:3343–44.

47. Jones, *Lincoln*, 146.

quoted Hamlet, to "endure the ills we have, Than to fly to others we know not of." To this point, France had been more inclined toward intervention than Britain, but a crisis in Italy and turmoil within the French government drew attention away from America at a critical point, rendered Napoleon more cautious, and divided France and Britain. The Yankeephobic but ever careful Palmerston agreed that with Lee retreating into Virginia "the Pugilists must fight a few more Rounds before the Bystanders can decide that the State Should be divided between them."[48] As is so often the case at times of momentous decision, doing nothing seemed the best course.[49]

Another crisis followed in October, largely the work of France's Napoleon III. The French emperor's interventionism was motivated partly by the demand for cotton, but its roots went much deeper. Gaining power through elections after the 1848 revolution, the ambitious and mercurial Napoleon in time assumed the title of emperor and set out to emulate his more illustrious uncle and namesake by restoring France's imperial glory. He challenged British dominance in the Mediterranean and South Asia. He schemed to attain the American empire pursued fleetingly by his uncle. Taking advantage of Mexico's civil strife and chronic indebtedness, he hoped to establish there a base to promote French economic and political power in the Americas. He contemplated a canal across the Central American isthmus. He saw French hegemony in Mexico as a bulwark against U.S. expansion and a springboard to restore monarchy to other Latin American states, thereby heading off the "degradation of the Latin race on the other side of the ocean," in the words of one of his advisers, and containing the advance of republicanism.

Napoleon sent French troops into Mexico in late 1861, ostensibly to collect debts, in fact to establish an imperial foothold. An independent Confederacy would provide an invaluable buffer against the United States, he reasoned. He was increasingly inclined to recognize the Richmond government to further his grand design. Frustrated by British indecisiveness, Napoleon in October 1862 proposed joint French, British, and Russian mediation calling for a six-month armistice and the lifting of the Union blockade. Should the Lincoln administration say no, he told Slidell, the powers might recognize southern independence, perhaps even provide military assistance to force an end to hostilities. Early November 1862 thus became the most perilous time for the Union.[50]

48. Jones, *Union in Peril*, 193.
49. Crook, *Diplomacy*, 100.
50. Jones, *Lincoln*, 16, 56, 59, 70–71, 131–32, 163–66.

Again after advancing to the brink of intervention, the Europeans drew back. Russia was eager to end the war but unwilling to antagonize Washington. Its opposition helped kill Napoleon's proposal. Russell was inclined to act, but his colleagues remained cautious. Lewis remained the major voice of restraint, warning that Britain should wait until southern independence was firmly established or the North concluded from events on the battlefield that it could not win. Napoleon would not act without British support. His proposal died. Although it was not clear at the time, any possibility of European intervention expired with it.

Refusing to give up entirely, Napoleon through the instrumentation of a meddlesome and inept British member of Parliament made one last attempt in the summer of 1863. Determined to get cotton and to protect his Mexican venture by ensuring a balance of power in North America, he offered assurances to the pro-Confederate J. A. Roebuck that he would work with Britain toward recognition of the South. The bumbling Roebuck proved a poor choice. His indiscreet statement that the French feared being double-crossed by England infuriated the British, deepening their already considerable—and well-founded—suspicions of Napoleon. He further discredited himself by overstating French eagerness to act. His bitter attacks on the United States as a "mongrelised" democracy and the "great bully of the world" antagonized Union sympathizers and aroused concerns even among southern enthusiasts of the pitfalls of intervention. Once disposed to do something to stop the bloodletting, most British leaders had concluded that no outside power could stop the war except at great risk and cost to itself. British support was simply not forthcoming. Slidell could not persuade Napoleon to organize the Continental powers to act without Britain. A failed intervention could do more damage to his Mexican ambitions than none at all. Napoleon thus concluded that it would be better to do nothing and hope that the Confederacy could somehow secure its independence.[51]

A crisis over Poland in the summer of 1863 ended already dim prospects of European intervention. When the Poles rose up against Russia early in the year, France, Britain, and Austria demanded a settlement on the basis of amnesty and Polish independence. The apparent European support for the concept of self-determination seemed to offer hope to the Confederacy, but appearances were deceptive. The threat of war in Europe diverted attention from North America during an especially critical time. Napoleon could not resist meddling in the Polish crisis. His actions

51. Crook, *Diplomacy*, 139–42.

aroused British and Russian suspicions, closing the option of concerted action in America. Most important, European support for self-determination proved weak. When Russia rejected the powers' proposal and forcibly suppressed the revolt, they did nothing. National interest took precedence over concern for the Poles and commitment to an ideal.[52]

The Polish crisis also cemented the emerging entente between the Union and Russia, providing yet another reason for European caution. The United States had traditionally given verbal support to self-determination. Thousands of Poles had fled to America after failed rebellions in the 1830s and 1840s; twenty-five hundred Poles fought for the Union in the Civil War. The Lincoln administration might also have traded support for the Poles for a French pledge of non-intervention. But when caught between its ideals and self-interest, the Union behaved like the Europeans. U.S. officials were pleased, Adams noted, that the Polish crisis had "done something to take continental pressure from us." For reasons of expediency, Seward rebuffed a French proposal to join in protest, expressing contentment to leave the Poles to the tender mercies of the tsar. The Russian-American convergence on Poland reinforced European fears of an "unholy alliance" between the two rising powers that might, French writer Alexis de Tocqueville and others speculated, produce a major shift in the balance of power. This specter increased great-power reluctance to act either in Central Europe or in America.[53]

While Europe fretted about a Russian-American alliance, the appearance of a Russian "fleet" of six warships in New York harbor in September 1863 created a sensation in America—and abroad. At the time, grateful Americans hailed the visit as an overt display of Russian support for their cause, sharply contrasting it with British and French perfidy. More cynical contemporaries and subsequent historians argued that the Russians acted out of self-interest: to keep their fleet from being bottled up in Baltic ports if war broke out over Poland. In fact, Russian motives appear to have been even more complex. The fleet was conducting a normal training exercise and would have left port that summer without the threat of war. Russian officers wanted to observe the new ironclad warfare taking place in America and to demonstrate their country's rising naval capability. They also carried double crews in hopes of purchasing additional ships from the United States. Once the threat of war in Europe eased, they could achieve these practical aims while solidifying already strong ties with the United States.

52. Ibid., 121–24, 144–46.
53. Saul, *Distant Friends*, 338, 351–52.

Whatever the reasons, the Russian "invasion" of New York was a significant time in the Civil War. For two months, three thousand Russian visitors attended parades, balls, and dinners, while U.S. bands played "God Save the Tsar" and toastmasters hailed Lincoln and Alexander II. The visit boosted northern morale and had a negative impact in the South. It aroused further European concern of an alliance, eliminating any possibility of intervention in North America.[54]

To a large degree, as Horace Greeley suggested at the time, the Union was spared foreign intervention by the "unprincipled egotism that is the soul of European diplomacy."[55] Although they quickly recognized southern belligerency, the powers cautiously withheld recognition until the Confederacy proved it could stand on its own. In the wake of southern battlefield success in 1862, they edged warily toward intervention. But the Union victory at Antietam and the more decisive victories at Vicksburg and Gettysburg in the summer of 1863 eliminated any real prospect that the Confederacy could survive. Every time they began seriously to consider acting, the British concluded that the possible gains of war with the Union would not be worth the risks. For all his bluster and meddlesomeness, Napoleon followed London's lead. The Union was also lucky that the Civil War took place when Europe was as unstable as at any time since Waterloo. The distractions caused by its internal conflict and the resulting great power divisions rendered intervention less likely.

Ideology as well as realpolitik accounted for European non-involvement. The American Civil War aroused passionate feelings in Europe. The British and French governments, although far from democratic, could not ignore domestic opinion. Slavery, of course, was the crucial issue. British philosopher John Stuart Mill warned that Confederate success would be a "victory for the powers of evil which would give courage to the enemies of progress and damp the spirits of its friends all over the civilized world." As long as the North fought merely for union, foreigners saw little difference between the two combatants. But Lincoln's Emancipation Proclamation in time evoked a powerful pro-Union reaction in Britain, especially among liberals and the working class, that drowned out voices favorable to the Confederacy and influenced, if it did not determine, the government's policy. His firm stand against slavery also made it easier for onetime British proponents of intervention to rationalize inaction. A French citizen bluntly informed Slidell that "as long as you

54. Ibid., 399–52.
55. Crook, Diplomacy, 186.

maintain and are maintained by slavery, we cannot offer you an alliance. On the contrary, we believe and expect you will fail."[56]

V

The Civil War was also fought on the high seas, and here too the great powers, especially Britain, became involved, with traditional roles reversed. Union attacks on neutral shipping caused outrage in Britain, threatening war by the side door. British shipbuilders constructed for the Confederacy commerce raiders that devastated the U.S. merchant marine, provoking threats of war from Seward and Adams. As with the *Trent*, caution and good sense prevailed. Seward spoke loudly but acted quietly to mitigate conflict with England. The British permitted the Union to stretch belligerent rights in ways possibly useful in a future war.

Union interference with British shipping became a major problem by 1863. A thriving trade had developed in which cotton was exchanged for contraband. Neutral ships deposited goods bound for the Confederacy at ports in the Bahamas, Bermuda, and Cuba. There they were loaded aboard blockade runners, often shipped to Matamoros, Mexico, and then overland to the Confederacy. To cut down or eliminate this trade, Union warships harassed neutral shipping between Havana and Matamoros. Assigned to the region with his Flying Squadron, the indomitable Wilkes hovered off West Indian ports, establishing a virtual blockade of Nassau and Bermuda, plundering neutral shipping, and, as with the *Trent*, interpreting international law to suit himself. To justify its actions, Washington hurled back at the British the once despised doctrine of continuous voyage, even exceeding British precedent by declaring that overland trade to an enemy port made goods liable to seizure. Britain screamed about freedom of the seas and illegal search and seizure and denounced that "ill-informed and violent naval officer" Wilkes.[57]

Both sides exercised restraint. Without abandoning measures it considered essential, the Union took steps to mitigate conflict with England. It transferred the abrasive Wilkes where he could do less damage and commanded U.S. naval officers to observe proper rules of search and seizure. While going through the motions of backing its shipowners, the British government acquiesced in American actions and court rulings and ordered warships in the West Indies not to interfere with Union seizure of ships outside territorial waters.

56. McPherson, "Whole Family," 141–43; Jones, *Lincoln*, 154–57.
57. Smith, "Wilkes," 156.

In time, Britain also acceded to Union demands to stop private ship-builders from constructing ships for the Confederacy. The shipbuilding program was one of the few major successes of Confederate diplomacy. Early in the war, Confederate agent James Bulloch arranged to have built in Britain a small fleet of fast, propeller-driven cruisers to prey on enemy shipping. Commerce raiding, it was reasoned, could hamper Union logistics, drive up shipping and insurance costs, and force trade to neutral carriers. The first products of this program, the *Florida* and *Alabama*, went to sea in 1862. Since the two ships left port without armament, they did not violate British neutrality laws. The *Florida* steamed to Nassau in the spring of 1862, where it was armed and began to attack Union ships. Over loud Union protests, the *Alabama* also slipped out of port, sailed to the Azores, and acquired armaments. During its nearly two years at sea, it destroyed or captured sixty northern ships. Meanwhile, Bulloch contracted with British shipbuilders for more commerce raiders and also frigates and ironclad rams to break the blockade.[58]

In a very real sense, the Confederacy was the victim of its success. As the *Alabama*'s tally mounted, Union protests grew louder. The Confederate raiders caused alarm up and down the eastern seaboard. Insurance rates skyrocketed, and trade moved to neutral carriers. Union officials especially feared that the ironclad rams could shatter the flimsy wooden ships manning the blockade. The United States, of course, had been among the foremost neutral profiteers during the Napoleonic wars, but as a belligerent it saw things quite differently. Union officials demanded that the British government stop building ships for the Confederacy, threatening to unleash privateers against British shipping and seek reparations for damages. *New York Herald* editor James Gordon Bennett thundered that the United States would seize Canada in return for Britain's "villainous treachery" and hold it until "full and satisfactory retribution be made."[59]

The British gradually acceded to Union demands. From the outset, Foreign Office lawyers had urged that the ships be detained, but the ministry had adhered to the more narrow requirements of domestic law. In time, it came around. Union agents snooped around British shipyards and hired private investigators to confirm that the ships were intended for the Confederacy. Adams issued stern warnings, at times even threatening war. As the tide of battle turned against the South and the likelihood of European intervention diminished, the British government grew more cautious. Adams's warnings had an impact. Perhaps more important,

58. Thomas, *Confederate Nation*, 182–83.
59. Crook, *Diplomacy*, 116.

Britons grew increasingly concerned about setting precedents that the United States or some other neutral might use in some future war to build ships for their enemies, depriving them of their historic advantage of control of the seas.

Thus in the spring and summer of 1863, the government acted to prevent additional vessels from getting to sea. In April, officials seized the *Alexandra* on suspicion of intent, indicating a major shift in position. More important, in the summer of 1863, Britain first detained, then seized, and eventually purchased to spare the shipbuilder financial loss the first of the Laird rams, a ship ostensibly built for the pasha of Egypt. With understandable familial pride and exaggeration, Minister Adams's son Henry called it a "second Vicksburg . . . the crowning stroke of our diplomacy."[60]

For the Confederacy, it was the last straw. An embattled Jefferson Davis bitterly protested the bias of British neutrality, complaining that while taking measures hostile to the Confederacy, Britain, in defiance of the law of nations, permitted thousands of its Irish subjects to come to America in its ships and fight for the Union. Without these "armies from foreign countries," he claimed, the "invaders would ere this have been driven from our soil." In August 1863, Mason left the increasingly hostile environs of London for Paris. The Richmond government expelled British consular officials.[61]

Davis's tone suggested his government's desperation, and in early 1865, almost as an afterthought, the Confederacy tried one last diplomatic gambit to secure foreign recognition. Suffering military defeat on all fronts, with Atlanta having fallen and Gen. Ulysses S. Grant advancing on Richmond, Davis authorized Louisiana congressman Duncan Kenner to travel secretly to Europe and propose emancipation of the slaves in return for recognition. It was too little, too late. Kenner slipped through the blockade, but the Europeans were not buying. Napoleon affirmed what was already manifest—France would follow England's lead. Britain indicated that under no circumstances would it recognize the South. The mission made clear the extent to which a Confederacy on the verge of defeat would go to somehow salvage its independence. It confirmed once again Europe's unwillingness to intrude.

The Confederate surrender at Appomattox on April 9, 1865, saved the Union and destroyed slavery, resolving by force of arms the two great

60. Ibid., 152.
61. Davis messages, December 7, 1863, and November 7, 1864, in Richardson, *Davis Messages* 1:356, 487.

issues that had divided Americans throughout the nineteenth century. By establishing that the United States would indeed be united with a free-labor economic system, it answered the great question of American nationhood. It ensured that the nation would become a great power.[62] The Union's survival of the bloody test of war gave a tremendous boost to national pride and brought a resurgence of self-confidence and optimism. Americans marveled at their power, the largest army in the world, a navy of 671 ships, and a huge industrial base. "We shall be the greatest power on earth," Gen. Joseph Hooker exulted.[63] European monarchs had exploited America's internal conflict to reintrude in the Western Hemisphere, but they were soon in full flight. Spain withdrew from the Dominican Republic as the war ended; France and Russia were not far behind. "One by one they have retreated . . . ," Massachusetts senator Charles Sumner proclaimed, "all giving way to the absorbing Unity declared in the national motto, E pluribus unum." Expressing ideas many Americans fervently shared, Sumner foresaw a not too distant time when through stages "republican principles under the primacy of the United States must embrace the whole continent."[64]

The Civil War also restored faith in the viability of those principles and certainty in the future destiny of the republic. The Union victory affirmed as Lincoln had so eloquently proclaimed in his Gettysburg Address that "government of the people, by the people, for the people" would not "perish from this earth." The abolition of slavery purified American republicanism, producing a "new birth of freedom." Lincoln's assassination just five days after Appomattox added the force of martyrdom to the cause he had so nobly espoused and so diligently pursued. Americans thus emerged from the war with their traditional faith in the superiority of their ideals and institutions revivified. On April 21, 1865, Grant privately hailed a United States "that is now beginning to loom far above all other countries, modern or ancient. What a spectacle it will be to see a country able . . . to put half a Million soldiers in the field. . . . That Nation, united," he added, "will have a strength which will enable it to dictate to all others, [to] *conform to justice and right.*"[65]

62. Crook, *Diplomacy*, 9.
63. Morris, *Lincoln*, 198.
64. Charles S. Campbell, *The Transformation of American Foreign Relations, 1865–1900* (New York, 1976), 20.
65. To Julia Grant Dent, April 21, 1865, in John Simon, ed., *The Papers of U.S. Grant*, vol. 14 (Carbondale, Ill., 1985), 428–29. My thanks to Charles Bracelen Flood for bringing this document to my attention.

VI

The outburst of nationalism and rebirth of Manifest Destiny that accompanied the Union victory did not set loose a new wave of expansionism. Some Republican leaders clung to Whiggish views that America had enough land. Further expansion would hinder effective governance. The nation could best promote its ideals through example. War-weariness certainly played a part, as did a huge war debt and the enormous problems of Reconstruction: reunification of a defeated but still defiant South and consolidation of the vast western territory acquired before the war. The especially bitter struggle between Lincoln's successor, Vice President Andrew Johnson of Tennessee, and the Radical Republicans over reconstruction policy spilled over into foreign policy issues. In the case of Mexico, Central America, and the Caribbean, Americans remained reluctant to acquire territory populated by alien races. Thus, although opportunities presented themselves, Seward's purchase of Alaska was the only major acquisition during Reconstruction.[66]

This does not mean that expansionist sentiment did not exist or that foreign policy was not important in these years. On the contrary, the Civil War in many ways confirmed the importance of foreign policy to the survival of the republic. An expansionist vision persisted, especially in the persons of Seward and his successor, Hamilton Fish. If there were few new acquisitions, Seward and Fish nonetheless resumed the push to the Caribbean and Pacific initiated in the 1840s and 1850s, charting the course of a new empire and taking the first steps toward its realization. Those historians who view the postwar years as a great hiatus between two eras of expansion miss the essential continuity of America's outward thrust.

Toward its southern and northern neighbors, Mexico and Canada, the United States demonstrated remarkable restraint during and immediately after the war, accepting as permanent the boundaries carved out in the antebellum period. In furtherance of Napoleon's grand design, French troops occupied Mexico City in June 1863. Later that year, Napoleon installed as ruler of Mexico the well-meaning but dull-witted Archduke Maximilian, brother of Emperor Franz Josef of Austria. Maximilian and his equally naive wife, Carlotta, undertook with enthusiasm the "holy work" of saving Mexicans from their own fecklessness, stabilizing the country, and fending off the march of republicanism in the Western Hemisphere.[67]

---

66. Crook, *Diplomacy*, 178; Reginald C. Stuart, *United States Expansionism and British North America, 1775–1871* (Chapel Hill, N.C., 1988), 220.
67. Jones, *Lincoln*, 181–82.

Civil War combatants perceived the dangers and opportunities of these developments to their respective causes and dealt with them accordingly. Despite its professed commitment to the principle of self-determination, the Confederacy sought to accommodate the new Mexican government to curry favor with Napoleon and perhaps gain recognition. Fearful of antagonizing the Union, Napoleon politely rebuffed southern overtures. Seward responded with a policy of "cautious moderation." He had refused to recognize the puppet government and warned that at some future point the United States might remove it by force. On the other hand, he also declined to assist the Mexican resistance forces of Benito Juarez. The United States would practice in regard to Mexico "the non-intervention which they require all foreign powers to observe in regard to the United States," he informed the Europeans.[68] To keep Napoleon off balance, he left uncertain what the United States might do in the future.

As the Civil War ended, pressures mounted to do something. Congress and the press denounced foreign intervention. "Defenders of the Monroe Doctrine" organizations sprang up across the country. Defying the neutrality laws, Americans began to provide sizeable clandestine assistance to Juarez.[69] Before replacing Lincoln, Vice President Johnson had talked of war with Mexico as "recreation" for Union soldiers.[70] "Now for Mexico!" General Grant shouted on the day after Appomattox. Like Johnson, Grant and other generals saw a Mexican operation as a means to keep a large and increasingly restive army occupied. Warning that the establishment of a monarchical government in Mexico was an "act of hostility" against the United States and might provide a haven for Confederates leading to a "long, expensive and bloody war," Grant proposed to Johnson possible military action or at least disposing of America's huge arms surplus by selling weapons to Mexican resistance forces.[71]

Bogged down in a struggle with Congress over intractable Reconstruction problems, Johnson left diplomacy in the capable hands of Seward. The secretary of state dealt with Mexico in a way that belied his carefully cultivated reputation for recklessness. He saw a needless war as a threat to an already embattled administration and to his lingering presidential am-

68. Stephen J. Vallone, " 'Weakness Offers Temptation': William H. Seward and the Reassertion of the Monroe Doctrine," *Diplomatic History* 19 (Fall 1995), 585.

69. Karl M. Schmitt, *Mexico and the United States, 1821–1973: Conflict and Coexistence* (New York, 1974), 86.

70. Albert Castel, *The Presidency of Andrew Johnson* (Lawrence, Kans., 1979), 39–42.

71. Ibid.; Grant to Johnson, June 19, 1965, July 15, 1865, in LeRoy P. Graf and Ralph W. Haskins, *The Papers of Andrew Johnson*, vol. 8 (Knoxville, Tenn., 1989), 257–58, 410.

bitions. Grant positioned fifty thousand troops along the Rio Grande. Their commander, the dashing cavalryman Gen. Philip Sheridan, declared substantial stocks of weapons surplus and placed them along the border after informing Mexicans of their location. But Seward blocked Grant's more aggressive proposals, contenting himself with ratcheting up diplomatic pressure on Napoleon and Austria. In November 1865, he warned that failure to remove European troops could mean war. He sent Gen. John Schofield to Paris with instructions to "get his legs under Napoleon's mahogany and tell him he must get out of Mexico."[72] When Austria appeared on the verge of sending troops to back Maximilian, Seward warned he would consider it an act of war and the United States could not remain a "silent or neutral spectator." Aware that Austria was already deeply entangled in a crisis with Prussia, Seward exploited its vulnerability. His warning signaled France to speed its exit. Seward may also have hoped through diplomatic firmness to salvage a faltering administration.[73]

Pressure from the United States was not the only or perhaps even the most important reason for Napoleon's retreat. Juarez's forces waged deadly guerrilla warfare against the invaders. The inept Maximilian could never rally Mexican support, and his power did not extend beyond the presence of French troops. Increasingly absorbed with European problems, the unpredictable Napoleon quickly lost interest in Mexico and began to search for a way out without appearing to capitulate to the United States. Lacking French support and facing a crisis in Europe, Austria declined to test the sincerity of Seward's threats. Both governments left the hapless Maximilian to his own devices. He was thrown out of office and executed by a Mexican firing squad in June 1867. Without giving in to the more belligerent voices inside and outside of the government, Seward served notice on the Europeans that the temporary suspension of the Monroe Doctrine as a result of the Civil War had ended.[74]

A hotbed of intrigue and conflict during and immediately after the Civil War, Canada was also a potentially explosive issue. Easy access across the border made the northern neighbor a refuge for draft dodgers, bounty jumpers, and anti-war Copperheads, and therefore a source of great resentment to staunch Unionists. Canada also served as a base for Confederate guerrillas, including the legendary John Hunt Morgan. After 1864, the Confederate government mounted a desperate last-ditch effort

72. Vallone, "Monroe Doctrine," 588.
73. Ibid., 599.
74. Ibid.

to open a second front in Canada by embroiling the Union in conflict with Great Britain. A series of cross-border raids was designed to harass Union territory and provoke conflict with Canada. The attacks amounted to little more than pinpricks and at times verged on comic opera, except for a raid into the Vermont town of St. Albans by Kentuckians in October 1864. The raiders robbed a bank, shot up, looted, and burned the town, and then fled back across the border. Local authorities and federal troops pursued them, threatening a clash. Canada's refusal to extradite the raiders or make prompt restitution infuriated the Union. Americans naturally resented the use of Canadian soil for hostile purposes and threatened to gain restitution by seizing it after the war or taking it in compensation for claims for damage done by the *Alabama*. Sensitive to Canada's vulnerability, the British took Union threats seriously, fearing that a victorious— or defeated—Union might seek revenge by attacking Canada.

Tensions persisted after Appomattox. Hotheads demanded cession of Canada as payment for the *Alabama* claims and other alleged British breaches of neutrality. Rebellions in Canada's western provinces and annexationist sentiment on the British Columbia frontier after the U.S. purchase of Alaska created opportunities for American troublemakers and aroused nervousness in Canada. The most divisive postwar issue was a series of raids into Canada by the so-called Fenians, Irish expatriates, some of them Union veterans, operating from bases in the United States. Neither Johnson nor Seward at first took the Fenians seriously. They may have taken secret pleasure at Canada's discomfiture now that the incursionist shoe was on the other foot. Their failure to enforce the neutrality laws swiftly and effectively caused anger and resentment in Canada.

Despite persisting provocations, officials on both sides kept tensions in check. The British were determined to prevent border conflicts from getting out of control. Canadian officials made serious if not always effective efforts to enforce neutrality laws, and after initial hesitation offered restitution for the St. Albans raid. A New Yorker, Seward knew and understood the cross border neighbors and gave no encouragement to those who urged supporting rebellions in Canada or even annexation as compensation. Grant and Fish acted more effectively than Johnson and Seward to enforce the neutrality laws and curb the Fenians.

Partly in response to the perceived American threat, Britain created a federal union in Canada through the British North American Act of 1867. Most U.S. citizens quietly acquiesced, even though the word *dominion* in the new dependency's title gave some republican souls pause. Just as the British in 1776 had been certain that the new United States was not a viable entity, so also Americans believed that the new dominion of Canada would collapse. They accepted as an article of faith what has been called the convergence theory, the belief that because U.S. ideology, trade, and culture were so important to a people so similar to themselves the two nations would converge and Canada would join the United States. Dominion status was a transitional stage. There was no need to push for annexation.[75]

The 1871 Treaty of Washington helped ease escalating post–Civil War tensions and laid the basis for a growing Anglo-American accord. The treaty is most often noted for its agreement to arbitrate the especially contentious *Alabama* claims dispute and for its resolution of long-standing spats over U.S.-Canadian boundaries and access to fisheries. It evoked from both sides quite extraordinary concessions, a British apology for damages done by the Confederate raiders and eventual U.S. abandonment of its exorbitant "indirect" claims against Britain for Civil War damages, the latter occasioned in large measure by a desperate U.S. need for British capital to finance its enormous war debt.[76] A complex three-sided negotiation between the United States, Britain, and the Dominion of Canada, the Treaty of Washington also had major implications for North America. Much of the time was spent on Canadian issues. The result was tacit U.S. recognition of Canada's new status.[77]

Seward's moderation toward Mexico and Canada reflected his acceptance of the convergence theory, an integral part of his larger concept of America's destiny. Historians have vigorously debated whether his expansionism was opportunistic and ad hoc or reflected a larger design.[78] The distinct pattern of his goals and the purposefulness of his actions strongly suggest the latter. But there is no debating that he was the key figure in mid-nineteenth-century expansion, the link between the Manifest Destiny movement of the 1840s and the overseas expansionism of the 1890s. In terms of his vision of the nation's destiny, he was the logical successor to Jefferson and John Quincy Adams, the latter of whom he referred to as a "patron, a guide, a counsellor, and a friend."[79] His horizons extended well beyond the continentalism of his illustrious predecessors to the Caribbean and the Pacific.

75. Stuart, *United States Expansionism*, xi, 216–17.
76. Jay Sexton, "The Funded Loan and the *Alabama* Claims," *Diplomatic History* 27 (September 2003), 449–78.
77. Stuart, *United States Expansionism*, 252.
78. See Castel, *Johnson* for the former, Ernest N. Paolino, *The Foundations of American Expansionism: William Henry Seward and U.S. Foreign Policy* (Ithaca, N.Y., 1973) for the latter.
79. Walter LaFeber, *The New Empire: An Interpretation of American Expansionism* (Ithaca, N.Y., 1973), 25.

Like the expansionists of the 1840s, Seward fused commercial with territorial objectives and moved a step beyond them in promoting the acquisition of overseas territory. He added to Henry Clay's views on economic development specific new concerns arising out of the nation's industrial growth and technological advancement. He strongly endorsed the Republican program of economic development: a national banking system; federal support for internal improvements such as a transcontinental railroad and cable to bind western territories to the Union; and a tariff to protect nascent industries. He added a vigorous commitment to promote investments and markets abroad. Moving beyond his Whig roots, he conceived various expansionist schemes to establish bases and coaling stations for a steam-powered navy in the Caribbean and Pacific. This naval power would in turn protect existing markets and help add new ones. Seward thus also provides a crucial link between U.S. foreign policy in the nineteenth century and in the twentieth.

Never satisfied with a "small policy," in Henry Adams's words, the secretary of state pursued multifarious projects to fulfill his expansive vision of nation's destiny. The seat of empire was moving steadily westward, he believed, and the struggle for world power would occur in Asia. He saw no need for colonies or wars of conquest. Territory would accrue to the United States by natural processes and should be acquired, as Andrew Johnson put it, "peacefully and lawfully, while neither doing nor menacing injury to other states."[80] Seward's vision extended from the Caribbean and the Gulf of Mexico to the North Pole to East Asia (what he referred to, ethnocentrically, as the "Far West"). He had long envisioned the Caribbean as an American domain. The difficulty of chasing Confederate raiders "from our own distant shores" during the Civil War underscored the urgency of U.S. control. In January 1866, ostensibly for reasons of health, he toured the area in search of locations for naval bases and coaling stations in the Caribbean and Gulf of Mexico. He negotiated treaties for acquisition of the Virgin Islands and Danish West Indies and for a naval base at Samana Bay in the Dominican Republic. He contemplated acquisition of Cuba, Puerto Rico, Haiti, and Tiger Island off the coast of Honduras. Laying the groundwork for fulfillment of a dream dating back to Clay, he negotiated with Colombia a treaty for the right-of-way to build a canal across the isthmus of Panama. His vision extended to the North Atlantic, where he eyed the purchase of Iceland and Greenland, and to the Pacific, where he looked into acquisition of the Hawaiian and Fiji

---

80. Annual message, December 3, 1867, in Graf and Haskins, *Johnson Papers* 13:304.

islands, proposed a naval base on the island of Formosa, and initiated preparations for an expedition to open the "hermit kingdom" of Korea to trade and Western influence. His cabinet colleague and sometime foe Secretary of the Navy Gideon Welles called him a "monomaniac" on expansion. If he could live another thirty years, Seward once boasted, he would gain for the United States "possession of the American continent and the control of the world."[81]

Seward's reach exceeded the nation's grasp, or at least the vision of his contemporaries. Some of his schemes fell victim to events abroad or forces of nature. The Colombian Senate refused to ratify the canal treaty; a revolution in Santo Domingo doomed the Samana Bay deal. A hurricane that devastated the Danish West Indies and the opposition of General Grant helped thwart acquisition of those islands. Some of his projects died from lack of interest or support. Most ran afoul of the tempestuous politics of the time. While Seward was busily trying to expand the nation's horizons, Johnson was paralyzed by the conflict within his own party that led to his impeachment. A hostile Senate tabled a treaty for reciprocity with Hawaii and scuttled other Seward projects. "How sadly domestic disturbances of ours demoralize the national ambition," the secretary lamented in October 1868.[82]

Seward's tangible accomplishments were limited but significant. The navy took Midway Island in the Pacific in 1867 under an 1850s "Guano Law" that permitted acquisition of uninhabited Pacific islands. Strategists were disappointed when it proved unsuitable for a deepwater port. Only many years later would its strategic importance be realized as an airstrip.

Far more important was the windfall purchase of Alaska in the same year. Seward had long viewed this Russian possession as a potentially vital way station toward domination of the East Asian trade. Devastating Confederate attacks on Union shipping in the Aleutian Islands in 1865 had reinforced his certainty of its strategic significance in the north Pacific. Alaska was also seen as a way to pressure Canada to join the United States. For Russia, in the meantime, this vast frozen territory had become a financial and strategic liability. Some Russians feared with good reason that an expansive United States would simply take Alaska and reasoned that they had best get something while they could. The Russian-American Company's hold was weakening. Letting go was made easier since Russia was gaining new, more defensible, territory in Central and East Asia. Some Russians also believed that the sale of Alaska would be a

81. Castel, *Johnson*, 144–45; Warren, "Seward," 215.
82. Castel, *Johnson*, 205.

good way to solidify friendship with the United States, a proper ending for a period of good relations.[83]

Scorned by many at the time, the purchase became Seward's greatest triumph. Eager for something to offset the administration's domestic failures, he jumped at the chance to purchase Alaska. The price of $7.2 million was $2 million more than he wanted to pay and $2 million more than the Russians originally sought, but the secretary was in a hurry to consummate the deal; he and Russian minister Eduard Stoeckl worked until 4:00 A.M. to draw up a treaty. Critics dismissed Alaska as a "sucked orange," "Seward's folly," or Johnson's "polar bear garden." Editor Horace Greeley called it "Walrussia." Foes of the purchase accused Johnson and Seward of trying to deflect attention from failures at home. Seward lobbied furiously and effectively, however, emphasizing the land's commercial and strategic potential and the importance of obliging good friends like the Russians. Congress was in full revolt against Johnson by this time, and the House of Representatives out of pique threatened not to appropriate funds. While complaining about the "wholly exceptional" difficulties of conducting diplomacy in the American democratic system, Stoeckl, who stood to profit handsomely from the deal, bribed key congressmen. At the time of its purchase, the main product of "Seward's icebox" was indeed ice, sold in large quantities to the bustling communities along the West Coast. More quickly than anyone might have imagined, the secretary's vision was vindicated, his prize acquisition, like California earlier, bringing the added bonus of gold.[84]

Like Seward, Grant's secretary of state, Hamilton Fish, was a New Yorker. In contrast to his flamboyant predecessor, the wealthy and socially prominent Fish was dignified and stodgy. Where Seward had coveted his cabinet post as a stepping-stone to the presidency, Fish dismissed it as one "for which I have little taste and less fitness." Taste and fitness notwithstanding, he ranks among the nation's better secretaries of state, in large part because of his settlement of the *Alabama* claims dispute with Britain. Unimaginative and somewhat rigid in his thinking, he was a person of good judgment and distinguished himself in an administration not noted for the integrity or accomplishments of its top officials. He served longer than any other individual who held the post in the nineteenth century.

83. Saul, *Distant Friends*, 396.
84. Ronald J. Jensen, *The Alaska Purchase and Russian-American Relations* (Seattle, 1975), 81–85, 94.

Along with Johnson's successor, war hero General Grant, who instinctively sought to project American power abroad, Fish was a spiritual heir to Seward's expansionism.[85] In Latin America, Fish and Grant sought to replace European influence with that of the United States. The secretary of state envisioned a time, as he put it, when "America shall be wholly American," when the "prominent position" of the United States on the continent would entitle it to a "leading voice" and impose on it "duties of right and of honor regarding American questions, whether these questions affected emancipated colonies, or colonies still subject to European domination."[86] To expand U.S. influence, they tied to the Monroe Doctrine the no-transfer principle first enunciated by Jefferson in 1808, proclaiming unequivocally that "hereafter no territory on this continent shall be regarded as subject to transfer to a European power."[87] They anticipated that the erosion of European power would lead to increased U.S. trade and political influence. They pushed ahead with plans for an isthmian canal. When Colombia blocked yet another treaty, Grant ordered surveys of alternate canal routes, producing a recommendation to build across Nicaragua that would be accepted policy until the turn of the century.

The islands of Hispaniola and Cuba had long been of special concern to Americans. Seward had cast a covetous eye on Samana Bay, a magnificent natural harbor in the Dominican Republic that could guard the eastern approaches to a canal and protect U.S. commercial and strategic interests in the Caribbean. In the Dominican Republic, as elsewhere, internal rivalries created opportunities for U.S. expansion, and the object of American desires took the initiative. With Spain gone, contending factions could no longer play the Europeans against the United States and thus could only seek from Americans the money and guns to remain in power and deter the threat of a hostile Haiti. Between 1869 and 1873, various Dominican factions developed proposals for the lease of Samana Bay, a U.S. protectorate over the Dominican Republic, and even formal annexation. A fraudulent plebiscite was conducted to demonstrate popular support for joining the United States.[88]

85. James B. Chapin, "Hamilton Fish and American Expansion," in Merli and Wilson, *Makers of American Diplomacy*, 225; Campbell, *Transformation*, 25, 50.

86. Chapin, "Fish," 245.

87. LaFeber, *New Empire*, 36–37.

88. Louis Martinez-Fernandez, "Caudillos, Annexationism, and the Rivalry Between Empires in the Dominican Republic, 1844–1874," *Diplomatic History* 17 (Fall 1993), 595–96.

Despite support for annexation on both sides, the scheme faltered. Prodded by cronies with investments in the Dominican Republic, Grant was especially eager to oblige Dominican annexationists or at least acquire Samana Bay. He gave the issue top priority in his scandal-ridden administration. In 1869, the two countries actually agreed to a treaty incorporating the Dominican Republic as a territory. Grant lobbied vigorously for Senate approval, but he met massive and unrelenting opposition. Haiti bitterly opposed a U.S. presence next door, and its minister to the United States spent $20,000 to defeat the treaty. In the United States, expansion into the Caribbean had acquired a bad name among Republicans from Democratic exploits in the 1850s. Many Americans opposed the incorporation of territory with a large non-white population. "Beware of the tropics," warned soldier, diplomat, journalist, and Missouri senator Carl Schurz. "Do not trifle with that which may poison the future of this great nation."[89] On the other hand, some idealists opposed absorbing tropical territory they claimed nature had set aside for darker-skinned people. Much of the opposition, including that from the formidable Senator Sumner, was personal and political. Undeterred by the defeat of annexation, Grant pushed for the lease of Samana Bay to private U.S. interests. He might have succeeded had not a revolution in the Dominican Republic in 1873 led to revocation of the offer.[90]

As always, Cuba posed especially complex challenges. The Spanish colony had been a major object of prewar expansionists, many of them seeking to protect the institution of slavery. Yet another rebellion against Spanish rule in 1868 brought it back to the forefront. Americans were deeply divided. Still infused with idealistic zeal, some Republicans urged continuation of the "noble work" of the Civil War by abolishing slavery in Cuba. African American leaders like Frederick Douglass went further, advocating aid for the Cuban rebels, the abolition of slavery in Cuba, and even its annexation. Harking back to America's traditional sense of mission, other Republicans urged extending Lincoln's "new birth of freedom" by eliminating one of the last bastions of European imperialism in the Western Hemisphere. Spain's brutal treatment of the rebels gave moral urgency to the pleas of interventionists. On the other hand, conservative Republicans opposed the taking of territory inhabited by mixed races and especially worried that acquisition of tropical lands would "degrade" the American people and their institutions. Some former Whigs

89. Lars Schoultz, *Beneath the United States: A History of U.S. Policy Toward Latin America* (Cambridge, Mass., 1998), 83.
90. Campbell, *Transformation*, 50–52; Martinez-Fernandez, "Caudillos," 592–97.

insisted that the United States should continue to adhere to non-interventionism. Its ideals could best be spread by example.[91]

Grant and Fish approached the Cuban rebellion with great caution. Although Americans were eager to remove Spain from the Western Hemisphere, the Civil War remained fresh in their minds, and they were unwilling to risk war to abolish slavery or free Cuba. Fish refused to recognize Cuban belligerency, arguing that it could hurt their cause by expanding Spain's right of search. Premature recognition, he also perceived, would undercut the U.S. position in the ongoing dispute with Britain over the *Alabama* claims. Even when Spanish officials in 1873 seized the *Virginius*, an arms-running ship flying the American flag, and shot the captain, thirty-six of the crew, and sixteen passengers, the administration responded calmly. The ship was falsely registered in the United States and carrying arms to rebels and therefore liable to seizure.

United States officials were also leery of the consequences of Cuban independence. They doubted Cubans' capacity for self-government and feared that chaos might engulf the island, threatening U.S. economic and strategic interests. There was little support for annexation. The staunchly conservative Fish viewed Cubans as inferior even to African Americans and unfit to be U.S. citizens. He would have preferred an autonomous Cuba under informal U.S. economic and political control. A lawyer himself and a devotee of the emerging specialty of international law, Fish followed British Liberal Party leader Gladstone in advocating multilateral solutions to world problems. To resolve an issue that caused much turmoil in Congress, he proposed in late 1875 a six-nation approach to Spain to end the fighting. The European powers were then embroiled in a crisis in the Balkans and declined the overture, but Fish's ploy was quite extraordinary in its deviation from traditional American unilateralism. After ten years of brutal fighting in which as many as a hundred thousand people were killed, the Cuban rebellion fizzled out. Moving in the direction Fish preferred, U.S. investors took advantage of bankrupt and desperate Cuban and Spanish planters to buy up their property, considerably expanding America's economic stake and preparing the way for a very different outcome in 1898.[92]

Grant and Fish enjoyed greater success in the Pacific. As in the Caribbean, the Civil War highlighted the value of naval bases in the Pacific.

---

91. Jay Sexton, "The United States, the Cuban Rebellion, and the Multilateral Initiative of 1875," *Diplomatic History* 30 (June 2006), 339–48.

92. Ibid., 353–65; Louis A. Pérez, *Cuba Between Empires, 1878–1902* (Pittsburgh, 1983), 62–64; LaFeber, *New Empire*, 37–38.

Completion of the transcontinental railroad in 1869 raised hopes for vastly expanded commerce with Asia. Trans-Pacific steamship lines looked for stopping-off places en route to the Orient. Hawaii seemed an ideal midpoint and Pearl Harbor a potentially vital naval base to guard western approaches to a canal and protect the western coast of the United States. With the British and other European nations lopping off Pacific islands one by one, pressures developed for the United States to do the same.[93]

As in the Dominican Republic, much of the impetus for closer U.S.-Hawaiian ties came from forces outside Washington, in this case Americans with business interests and political clout in the islands.[94] The Civil War also had a huge impact in Hawaii. Confederate raiders destroyed the whaling business. The Union blockade increased demands for raw sugar, encouraging enterprising Americans to expand sugar cultivation. After the war, American entrepreneurs in Hawaii sought an expanded U.S. naval presence to defend a thriving commerce and a protected U.S. market for their sugar. They insinuated themselves with the Hawaiian government to achieve their goals. At one time or another, American sugar planters served as Hawaii's foreign minister and minister to Washington. They made up the delegation that negotiated the treaty. Talk of possible annexation found little support in Washington. "The indisposition to consider important questions of the future in the Cabinet is wonderful," Fish complained. "A matter must be imminent to engage attention—indifference and reticence—alas!"[95] Proposals for a naval base at Pearl Harbor also aroused opposition among native Hawaiians. Eventually, to win U.S. support for the free entry of sugar into the U.S. market, American sugar planters sent to Washington to negotiate a reciprocity treaty agreed that Hawaii would not grant such trade terms or naval bases to any other nation, thus limiting Hawaii's sovereignty in return for a secure market for their commodity. The idea, as the American who served as Hawaii's minister to the United States put it, was to "make Hawaii an American colony with the same laws and institutions as our own."[96] To seal the deal, Hawaii's King Kalakaua visited the United States in 1874, the first reigning monarch to do so.

93. Campbell, *Transformation*, 72.
94. Barry Rigby, "The Origins of American Expansion in Hawaii and Samoa," *International History Review* 10 (May 1988), 222.
95. Campbell, *Transformation*, 67–68.
96. Rigby, "Hawaii and Samoa," 226.

As Fish observed, the 1873 reciprocity treaty bound Hawaii to the United States with "hoops of steel." It set off a period of frantic development for Hawaii's sugar plantations, increasing the islands' dependence on U.S. capital and the U.S. market. The demand for cheap labor to work the plantations led to a huge influx of Asians. Hawaiians now controlled only 15 percent of the land and 2 percent of the capital and were relegated to a "dispossessed minority." These demographic changes in turn aroused U.S. fears of Asian control. It was only a short step to annexation.[97]

The United States' interest in Samoa also originated from local forces. Again, the Civil War played a role, the worldwide demand for raw cotton fueling a land rush on that remote South Pacific island that drew attention to its other advantages. About halfway between Hawaii and Australia, Samoa and particularly the harbor of Pago Pago—"the most perfectly landlocked harbor that exists in the Pacific Ocean"—attracted the attention of New York shipping interests. These shippers encouraged Commander Richard Meade of the Pacific squadron to claim the harbor for the United States. Meade dutifully obliged, but a contentious Senate in 1873 scrapped his treaty. Undeterred, Grant dispatched an agent to inquire about a naval base. A treaty was subsequently negotiated giving the United States the right to a base at Pago Pago and obliging it to use its good offices should Samoa encounter problems with third-party countries. Remarkably, the Senate approved this treaty in 1878, Samoa's first treaty with a foreign nation, perhaps reflecting Grant's departure from office or that body's appreciation of the growing importance of the Pacific. That treaty provided the basis for expanded U.S. involvement in the 1880s and subsequent annexation.[98] The treaties with Hawaii and Samoa mark major steps in the establishment of the United States as a Pacific power. They make clear the persistence of expansionist forces during the Civil War and Reconstruction.

THE YEAR 1877 MARKED AN END to the Civil War era. The political compromise worked out in March resolved the deadlocked Hayes-Tilden presidential election of 1876 by keeping the Republicans in the White House in return for restoration of home rule in the South. That year also marked the end of an epoch in U.S. foreign policy. The sections would continue to disagree on foreign policy issues, sometimes heatedly, but the

97. Ibid., 225–27.
98. Campbell, *Transformation*, 76.

Union victory definitively settled the fundamental question of American nationhood. Postwar non-intervention in Mexico and acquiescence in the Dominion of Canada fixed the boundaries of the continental United States. The Civil War and the Thirteenth Amendment abolished slavery. The major issues on which U.S. foreign policy had focused throughout much of the nineteenth century were resolved. Over the next three decades, the nation would be dramatically transformed through immigration, urbanization, and industrialization. It would take its place among the world's great powers. Continental expansion would give way to overseas expansion.

7

"A Good Enough England"

Foreign Relations in the Gilded Age, 1877–1893

By 1882, many Americans insisted that their country must control an isthmian canal, and when Great Britain showed no willingness to scrap the 1850 Clayton-Bulwer Treaty, providing for joint ownership and operation, the ever brash *New York Herald* offered its trans-Atlantic cousin some gratuitous advice. If Britain felt compelled to impose its designs on other peoples, the *Herald* opined, it should "take another turn" at the Boers, the Zulus, or the Afghans. "She need not bother with this side of the sea. We are a good enough England for this hemisphere."[1]

The newspaper's boast was more than a bit inflated when rendered, but by the 1890s it would approximate reality. During the so-called Gilded Age, a reunited and increasingly industrialized America lurched in fits and starts toward great power status. Absorbed in domestic problems and less concerned with external threats than at any time in their nation's history, Gilded Age Americans elevated traditional doctrines of non-entanglement to holy writ. At the same time, they were more than ever drawn to far-flung areas in search of adventure, opportunity, commerce, and "heathen" souls to be saved. Conscious of their rising power, they were more disposed to intervene in their own hemisphere and indeed beyond. During these years, such intrusions were often clumsy and counterproductive. Expansionist initiatives were frequently thwarted by a hostile Congress or junked by incoming administrations. By the turbulent 1890s, however, an increasingly powerful and anxiety-ridden United States began to assert its claims more vociferously and back them with action. Especially under the aggressive and sometimes bellicose leadership of President Benjamin Harrison and Secretary of State James G. Blaine, the United States between 1889 and 1893 moved decisively to strengthen its position at the expense of potential rivals in the Pacific Basin region and the Caribbean. At least for the Western Hemisphere, it was a "good enough England" indeed.

1. Quoted in Milton Plesur, *America's Outward Thrust: Approaches to Foreign Affairs, 1865–1890* (DeKalb, Ill., 1971), 176.

I

The world of the late nineteenth century was a turbulent place of rapid—and, to contemporaries, often bewildering—change. The railroad, steamship, and telegraph shrank distances dramatically, providing the means, contemporaries believed, to "erase ignorance and isolation, erode away the misunderstandings between peoples, and facilitate the getting and distribution of the new plenty."[2] People, goods, and capital moved freely across international boundaries in this first rush of what is now called "globalization," connecting disparate areas through an intricate network of commerce and investments. "The world is a city!" French banking magnate Carl Meyer von Rothschild approvingly exclaimed in 1875.[3]

Technological advances also made the world more dangerous. The transportation revolution permitted more rapid movement of larger military forces over larger areas, enabling the Western imperial powers to administer colonial holdings from greater distances. After almost a decade of false starts and frustrations such as fires, breaks in the line, and storms at sea, the United States and Britain in 1866 were linked by cable. Such ties soon extended to continental Europe and East Asia. The cost of sending telegraph messages initially limited the cable's utility in diplomacy, but its wider use over time speeded up communications, accelerating the pace of diplomatic activity, giving diplomatic crises a new urgency, and shifting control from diplomats on the scene to Washington.[4] The era also brought innovations in printing that, when combined with rising literacy rates in the Western industrialized countries, produced a rapt audience for exciting events in other places, creating both opportunities for mobilization of disparate peoples and popular pressures on those who wielded power. Above all, as the American Civil War so grimly demonstrated, the harnessing of modern technology to the once genteel "art" of war created enormous and still not fully appreciated powers of destruction.

The ethos of the age stressed competition and struggle, adding to the turbulence that marked the international system. Published in 1859,

2. David Healy, U.S. Expansionism: The Imperialist Surge in the 1890s (Madison, Wisc., 1970), 13.
3. Nicholas Kristoff, "At This Rate We'll Be Global in Another Hundred Years," New York Times, May 23, 1999.
4. James A. Field Jr., "American Imperialism: The Worst Chapter in Almost Any Book," American Historical Review 83 (June 1978), 661; David Paull Nickles, "Telegraph Diplomats: The United States' Relations with France, 1848 and 1870," Technology and Culture 40 (January 1999), 1–25.

Charles Darwin's *Origin of Species* theorized that plant and animal life had evolved through an ongoing competition in which only the "fittest" flourished; the weak fell by the wayside. As popularized and applied to international politics, Darwin's ideas emphasized a struggle among nations and survival of the strongest, encouraging peoples already inclined toward the pursuit of power and wealth to compete more aggressively for the world's resources and use force to achieve their goals. "Nations, like men, will shrink and decline when they fail to grasp firmly the opportunities for success and use them to the utmost," Alabama senator John Tyler Morgan grimly proclaimed.[5]

Britain remained the number-one power in a still Europe-centered world. The empire on which the sun never set encompassed by century's end some twelve million square miles of territory and nearly one-fourth of the world's population, the largest the world had ever seen. London also maintained a precarious industrial and commercial supremacy, but its strengths had increasingly become its weakness. Its vast holdings and commitments compelled it to struggle merely to hang on to its existing position.[6]

Newcomers to the great game of international politics increasingly challenged Britain and the other traditional powers, rattling the post-1815 equilibrium. Although still weak by European standards, a newly unified Italy posed a regional danger to declining powers such as France and Austria-Hungary. The main threat to the existing order came from Germany, which emerged with stunning speed. By late century, it had surpassed France and was beginning to challenge Britain in industry and commerce. Germany was the first power to realize the military potential of the modern nation-state. Its crushing of Austria in 1866 and even more shocking defeat of France in 1871 marked its coming of age. Through artful diplomacy, the "Iron Chancellor," Otto von Bismarck, managed to expand his nation's interests without arraying the other powers against him. The Germany of Wilhelm II (1888–1918) was more aggressive and less clever, arousing growing fears in Europe, Britain, and even the United States.

In the 1880s and 1890s, the Europeans again took their competition on the road. Colonies had fallen out of fashion at midcentury, but in the eighties they once again became sought after as sources of power

5. Joseph A. Fry, *John Tyler Morgan and the Search for Southern Autonomy* (Knoxville, Tenn., 1992), 74.
6. Paul Kennedy, *The Rise and Fall of the Great Powers: Economic Change and Military Conflict from 1500 to 2000* (New York, 1987), 176–77.

and wealth, setting off a new and furious scramble for political and economic advantages in unclaimed areas across the globe. Now joined by the Germans and Italians, the British and French competed for colonies in the Middle East, North and sub-Saharan Africa, and East and Southeast Asia and even, to the alarm of Americans, made gestures in the direction of Latin America. Between 1870 and 1900, Britain added more than four million square miles to its imperial holdings, France more than three and a half million, and Germany one million. The new rush for empire further destabilized an already unsettled world.[7]

Even as Europe expanded into new areas, its centuries-old preeminence was under challenge from emerging powers. Russia's vast size and wealth of resources were more than offset by its administrative and political weakness, but its enormous potential made its Continental rivals uneasy. Emulating the Europeans, Japan after the Meiji Restoration of 1868 set out to modernize, industrialize, and build a Western-style military apparatus. The Japanese remained well behind the Europeans to the turn of the century, but their remarkable advance in a short time gained notice. Their defeat of hapless China in the so-called Pigtail War of 1894–95 marked their advent as a rising power in East Asia.

No nation surpassed the United States in economic growth, and nothing was more decisive for the future of the international system than America's emergence as a world power. Powerful and prosperous, with relatively greater individual liberties, at least for white men, than any other nation, the United States after the Civil War continued to attract millions of people searching for opportunity. Before the war, most immigrants had come from northern and western Europe; after, they came mainly from southern and eastern Europe. These millions of so-called new immigrants dramatically altered the makeup of the nation, provoked rising domestic tensions, and had profound implications for the future of U.S. foreign relations. Hordes of immigrants combined with continued high birth rates to push the population of the United States to more than seventy-five million people by 1900, second only to Russia among the world's leading nations.

Consolidation proceeded apace. The South was slowly and at times painfully reintegrated—often at the expense of African Americans on whose behalf the Civil War had presumably been fought. Railroads and the telegraph bound the vast territory acquired before the Civil War. Six

7. Healy, U.S. Expansionism, 11–13.

new states entered the Union between 1889 and 1893, the most in any four-year period, bringing the total to forty-four.

During the last third of the nineteenth century, at the expense of Native Americans, the United States solidified its hold on the trans-Mississippi West. The discovery of gold and silver, the 1862 Homestead Act offering cheap land to settlers, and the completion of a network of western railroads sparked yet another mass migration after the Civil War. Americans settled more land between 1870 and 1900 than in all their previous history. The population of the last frontier beyond the Mississippi more than quadrupled. As before, the mass influx of white settlers sparked conflict with Indians native to the region and some tribes removed from the East. As in the East, the government sought to deal with the problem by confining the Indians to reservations on generally undesirable lands. It was left to the U.S. Army to implement a policy the fiercely independent western Indians despised and resisted by force. For nearly a quarter century, the western tribes waged relentless guerrilla warfare against the frontier army, fighting nearly one thousand mostly small engagements. As on earlier frontiers, the outcome was a foregone conclusion. The army used its mobility, firepower, superior numbers, and ruthless attacks on winter encampments to cripple resistance. Even more important was the massive influx of settlers whose crops and cattle destroyed the grass and wildlife, especially the buffalo, that provided the basis of Indian society, forcing them to the reservation—or death.[8]

The United States' Indian policy changed markedly during this last stage of forced displacement to western reservations. At one time treated as independent nations, by the 1830s they were viewed as what Chief Justice John Marshall called "a domestic dependent nation," what amounted to protectorate status. Treaties continued to provide a measure of self-rule, but in 1871 the government stopped making agreements with the Indians, and the Supreme Court empowered Congress legally to nullify earlier commitments. After this point, Indians were treated as dependent peoples, indeed colonial subjects. George Washington and Henry Knox's well-intentioned ideal of civilization with honor gave way to an attitude of civilization or else. Rather than enticing the Indian to white man's ways with trinkets, tools, and Bibles, the government imposed civilization on them by requiring them to use the English language, accept Christianity, hold private property, and adopt subsistence agriculture. Agents were sent to the reservations to

8. Allan R. Millett and Peter Maslowski, *For the Common Defense: A Military History of the United States of America* (New York, 1984), 236–41.

implement the new policies. The Bill of Rights did not apply. Indians could not even leave the reservation without permission. There was a direct line between the handling of Native Americans in the Gilded Age and the acquisition of overseas empire in the 1890s. "The ties between the Indian and foreign policy . . . were not so much broken as transformed," historian Michael Hunt has concluded. "The rationale used to justify the defeat and dispossession of one people would in the future serve to sanction claims to American superiority and dominion over other people."[9]

The Union's triumph in the Civil War positioned the nation to exploit its enormous economic assets: rich land; a wealth of natural resources; a growing and energetic population; the absence of foreign threat or other obstacles to growth. Possessing numerous advantages and few disadvantages, the United States transformed itself at near miraculous pace. Agricultural and industrial production soared. By 1900, the United States surpassed even Britain in manufacturing output. The nation began to pour its agricultural and industrial products across the world while maintaining a high tariff to protect its own industries from foreign competition. American "hyperproductivity," along with recurrent and increasingly serious economic crises, fed rising fears among elites that the home market could not absorb a mounting surplus, the so-called glut thesis, provoking agitation for the acquisition of new markets abroad and a more active foreign policy. Only in military power did the United States lag behind the Europeans, but even here the gap was closing by the turn of the century. In any event, America's smaller military expenditures provided an advantage obscured in an age where the trappings of power often masked its essentials. The costs of maintaining an empire in fact could be a source of weakness rather than strength. The rapid expansion of two new powers caused Europeans increasingly to fret about a world order dominated by a crude and backward Russia and a rich and vulgar America. The explosive growth of the United States—an "entire rival continent"—provoked the first of repeated European warnings about the Americanization of the world.[10]

9. Michael H. Hunt, *Ideology and U.S. Foreign Policy* (New Haven, Conn., 1987), 55. The connection between the Plains Indians and 1890s imperialism is explicated at length in Walter L. Williams, "United States Indian Policy and the Debate over Philippine Annexation: Implications for the Origins of American Imperialism," *Journal of American History* 66 (March 1980), 810–31.

10. Kennedy, *Great Powers*, 242–45.

II

Once dismissed by internationalist historians as an isolationist backwater and the nadir of statesmanship, Gilded Age diplomacy has been rehabilitated in recent years. Revisionist writers have found in the post–Civil War era the roots of the modern American empire. Drab and colorless the diplomatists may have been, it is argued, but they were hardworking and dedicated public servants who pursued the national interest with dogged determination. Concerned with the economic crisis produced by mounting agricultural and industrial surpluses, they were especially energetic in searching out foreign markets. They developed the rationale and began to create the instruments for the acquisition of overseas territory in the 1890s.[11]

Foreign relations have thus been brought back into the mainstream of Gilded Age history and the Gilded Age into the mainstream of U.S. foreign relations. To be sure, as critics have pointed out, "the era was marked by uncoordinated diplomacy, amateurish emissaries, shallow rhetoric, and much public and congressional indifference."[12] There was strong opposition to international involvement and especially commitment. Anti-imperialists defeated numerous expansionist initiatives. There was no master plan for empire. Still, diplomacy was much more important, active, systematic, and deliberate than previously allowed. During this period, the ideology and instruments that provided the basis for America's global involvement in the twentieth century took form. The Gilded Age was a transition period between the continental empire of Jefferson and Adams and the insular empire of the early twentieth century.[13]

Attitudes toward the outside world were paradoxical. For the first time in its short history, the new nation did not face a major external threat. Its position in North America was firmly established. Europe was retreating from the Western Hemisphere. The relative stability on the Continent spared the danger of a general European war. America's headlong economic growth and consolidation of the Union absorbed the energies and attention of its people after the Civil War. Under these circumstances, world events naturally receded in the scale of national priorities. Americans did not think of themselves as isolationists—indeed, the term *isolationism* was just beginning to creep into the national political vocabulary

11. Walter LaFeber, *The New Empire: An Interpretation of American Expansion, 1860–1898* (Ithaca, N.Y., 1963), 39–149; Joseph A. Fry, "Phases of Empire: Late Nineteenth Century U.S. Foreign Relations," in Charles W. Calhoun, ed., *The Gilded Age: Essays on the Origins of Modern America* (Wilmington, Del., 1996), 261–72.

12. Justus D. Doenecke, *The Presidencies of James A. Garfield and Chester A. Arthur* (Lawrence, Kans., 1981), 55.

13. Fry, "Phases of Empire," 283.

by the end of the century. But the nation's leaders did speak in reverential tones of the foreign policy principles bequeathed by Washington, Jefferson, and Monroe. Our "traditional rule of noninterference in the affairs of foreign nations has proved of great value in past times and ought to be strictly observed," President Rutherford B. Hayes proclaimed in 1877, a mantra ritualistically repeated by his Gilded Age successors.[14] Some ultra-nationalists even echoed in less qualified terms Jefferson's dream of scrapping an unrepublican and allegedly unnecessary diplomatic corps.

In the Gilded Age, as before and after, of course, Americans were anything but isolated from the outside world. From the beginning of the republic, U.S. foreign relations had been driven as much by private citizens as by government, and in these years, a society bursting with energy sent Americans abroad in varied roles.[15] The growing ease of travel, increased wealth, and the emergence of a tourism industry produced an explosion of overseas travel after the Civil War. By the end of the century, the State Department issued thirty thousand passports each year. Children of the elite took a Grand Tour modeled on that long practiced by the British aristocracy. Students flooded prestigious European universities. Immigrants returned home for visits. Some critics worried that foreign travel might taint the purity of the American character; the rude behavior of some of these travelers eternally stereotyped Americans to their European hosts. Visitors from the United States still found through exposure to foreign cultures confirmation of the virtues of their own society. After an extended stay in Europe, a young Harvard graduate and future ambassador to Germany and Britain in 1888 "bade adieu . . . to the 'effete despotisms of the old world.' " A year later, humorist Mark Twain boasted that "there is today only one real civilization in the world."[16] Nevertheless, the burst of tourism helped broaden America's perspectives and break down its parochialism. The experience of foreign travel significantly shaped the views of those who made up the nation's foreign policy elite in the twentieth century.[17]

---

14. Inaugural Address, March 5, 1877, in James D. Richardson, ed., *A Compilation of the Messages and Papers of the Presidents of the United States* (20 vols., Washington, 1897–1916), 10:4397.

15. Field, "Worst Chapter," 659.

16. Quoted in Jeffrey J. Matthews, *Alanson B. Houghton: Ambassador of the New Era* (Wilmington, Del., 2004), 24; Manfred Putz, "Mark Twain and the Idea of American Superiority at the End of the Nineteenth Century," in Serge Ricard, ed., *An American Empire: Expansionist Cultures and Politics* (Aix-en-Provence, 1990), 215–35.

17. Plesur, *Outward Thrust*, 103–8.

Often on their own, sometimes with public sponsorship, Americans took part in multifarious activities in distant lands. The charting of North America completed, adventurers set off to explore the new frontier in Alaska. The government sponsored expeditions into the Arctic region. Private groups explored the Holy Land and the rain forests of South America.

The Gilded Age also saw the first organized and officially sponsored efforts to export Yankee know-how, especially in Japan. As part of its effort to beat the West by joining it, the Japanese government recruited some three thousand foreign experts (*oyatoi*) to facilitate its rush toward modernization. Japanese leaders were not drawn to American democracy, preferring the German system of government. They relied mainly on Europeans to build a Western-style military establishment, although Japanese students did enroll at the U.S. Naval Academy and a U.S. citizen directed Japan's first naval school. Americans also assisted the Japanese in mastering Western diplomatic protocol and international law as a means to free them from the burdens of the Western-imposed unequal treaties. Americans played their most important role in education and agriculture. They helped establish a system of public education modeled loosely on that recently instituted in the United States. Experts from U.S. colleges, sponsored by the commissioner of agriculture, disseminated the latest methods of dairy farming and growing corn and wheat. Specialists from the Massachusetts agriculture college sought to extend the land grant model to Japan by helping establish at Sapporo an experimental farm and agricultural school that would become the University of Hokkaido. Americans brought to Japan such things as the McIntosh apple and Concord grapes. As expatriates seeking recreation, they introduced the Japanese to baseball, helping to start teams that in time would compete with Americans residing in that country. To the dismay of British observers, baseball by the end of the century had become more popular in Japan than cricket.[18]

Born earlier in the century, the Protestant missionary movement exploded after the Civil War. The number of foreign missions jumped from eighteen in 1870 to ninety in 1890. In China alone, the number of missionaries increased from 81 in 1858 to 1,296 in 1889. The missionaries fanned out across the world, from Catholic South America to the Muslim

18. William L. Neumann, *America Encounters Japan: From Perry to MacArthur* (New York, 1963), 72–86; Sayuri Guthrie-Shimizu, "For Love of the Game: Baseball in Early U.S.-Japanese Encounters and the Rise of a Transnational Sporting Fraternity," *Diplomatic History* 28 (November 2004), 637–62.

Middle East. They were especially active in "pagan" China and Japan and even began to establish an American presence in Africa.

The role and impact of American missionaries have been subjects of much controversy. Persuaded that God had blessed them with modern technology to facilitate their evangelizing of the world and fervently committed to "bring light to heathen lands," they brought to their task a self-righteous arrogance that would make them an easy target for critics in later centuries. In some areas, they were the advance guard for American commercial penetration. While spreading their gospel, they were often guilty of the worst kind of cultural imperialism. They invariably ran afoul of local customs and provoked nationalist opposition that, in places like Japan, sharply limited their influence. On the other hand, they stimulated American philanthropy. They opposed the introduction of opium into treaty ports in China and took the unpopular position of opposing exclusion of Chinese immigrants in debates that raged across the United States in these years. For better or worse, they introduced the modernization process into lands where they served. They were among the leading agents of the internationalization of America. They brought distant areas to the attention of a sometimes parochial nation and shaped popular attitudes toward other peoples. Their appeals for support and protection sometimes forced the government to act in areas where its role had been nonexistent.[19]

Missionary work provided opportunities abroad for Americans whose roles were constricted at home. African American missionaries sought converts in Africa while promoting colonization schemes with distinctly imperialist overtones. Increasingly frustrated with their place in U.S. society, ministers such as Alexander Crummell and Henry McLeod Turner advocated missionary work in Africa *and* "back to Africa" colonization schemes like those Henry Clay and Abraham Lincoln had once endorsed. They sought through return to the continent from which their race had come escape from their growing oppression in the United States and a means to establish their American national identity. While hailing Africa's higher morality, they shared with European colonialists a belief that the "dark continent" was in need of a civilizing mission and brought to their task a sense of their own superiority. Some even rationalized that slavery had been part of a divinely inspired master plan to prepare African Americans to regenerate a backward Africa. In the 1890s, Turner pro-

19. Plesur, *Outward Thrust*, 75–86; Michael H. Hunt, *The Making of a Special Relationship: The United States and China to 1914* (New York, 1983), 24–32, 154–65.

moted missions in Liberia and Sierra Leone as bases for his larger colonization project. Crummell went to Liberia as a missionary and proposed a U.S. protectorate over the nation founded by freed American slaves. These early pan-African schemes got little support from the African American middle class—the churches were dubious precisely because they smacked too much of earlier colonization plans. "We have no business in Africa," a bishop protested.[20] An indifferent U.S. government provided no backing. The only results were to provide intellectual justification for and indirect encouragement to European colonialism of Africa.[21]

Missionary work and other international charitable activities offered outlets and opportunities for women still denied full equality at home. By 1890, wives of male missionaries or groups of unwed women operating on their own made up roughly 60 percent of the total number. Their contributions were unique. Their approach to missionary work was more personal than that of men, resembling the sort of nurturing work they did in the domestic sphere at home. In China, women more often than men identified with and expressed concern for the powerlessness of the local population in dealing with the West. Dominated by their husbands, they protested the way outsiders dominated Chinese. By standing up for China, they stood up for themselves. In doing so, they took an important step toward their own liberation. Paradoxically, although empathizing with the Chinese, by promoting Westernization they exercised authority over them.[22]

Women also took a leading role in late-century international relief programs. When famine struck Russia in 1891, women at the local and national level under the leadership of legendary Civil War nurse and American Red Cross president Clara Barton organized a massive campaign to get corn and flour to the victims. Congress refused to appropriate funds, so the entire effort had to be privately financed. The women managed to secure some free transportation from the railroads and steamship companies. Some women traveled to Russia with the food to ensure that good meals were prepared for recipients. Critics groused that the autocratic tsarist government had inflicted the disaster on its own people, but the organizers appealed to the nation's humanitarian instincts, traditional

20. Quoted in James T. Campbell, *Surge of Zion: The African Methodist Episcopal Church in the United States and South Africa* (Chapel Hill, N.C., 1998), 88–99.
21. Tunde Andeleke, *UnAfrican Americans: Nineteenth-Century Black Nationalists and the Civilizing Mission* (Lexington, Ky., 1998), especially 111–39.
22. Jane Hunter, "Women Missionaries and Cultural Conquest," in Dennis Merrill and Thomas G. Paterson, *Major Problems in American Foreign Relations*, vol. 1, *To 1920* (Boston, 2005), 383–92.

Russian-American friendship, and Russia's timely support during the Civil War. Americans helped feed as many as 125,000 people in one of their first major overseas relief efforts. Women's involvement in the famine relief campaigns expanded their area of influence by pushing them into the traditionally male-dominated realm of international relations.[23]

In an era and nation where business reigned supreme, no segment of American society was more active abroad. It would be wrong, of course, to exaggerate the commitment of U.S. business to overseas expansion. Preoccupied with production for the home market, many businessmen were among the last to appreciate the importance of foreign markets. Congress was sometimes indifferent. The Republican devotion to a protective tariff hampered foreign trade. Americans were rank amateurs at overseas marketing, and the dumping of inferior and even dangerous products sometimes deservedly gave them a bad name.

Still, after the Civil War, U.S. business became more involved internationally. Government and business sponsored participation in expositions and world fairs to attract immigrant laborers and foreign capital and peddle their wares. For the first time, the nation had surplus capital to export. American entrepreneurs exploited mines and built railroads in other countries, especially in such friendly environs for foreign investors as Porfirio Diaz's Mexico. With the backing of J. P. Morgan & Co., James Scrymers linked the United States to much of South America by cable. United States companies dominated Russian markets in such diverse areas as farm machinery and life insurance. No firm exceeded John D. Rockefeller's Standard Oil in the breadth of its overseas operations. From the outset, Rockefeller set out aggressively to capture "the utmost market in all lands." Assisted by U.S. consuls who even bought lamps with their own funds and distributed them to create demand, his oil and kerosene found a huge market in a rapidly industrializing Europe. According to a Standard Oil representative, the corporation "forced its way into more nooks and corners of civilized and uncivilized countries than any other product in business history emanating from a single source." Throughout East Asia, Standard Oil's blue tin cans were a mainstay of the local economies, used to make tile roofs, opium cups, and hibachis. As late as the 1940s, "Rockefeller lamps" were status symbols in Vietnam.[24]

23. Shannon Smith, "From Relief to Revolution: American Women and the Russian-American Relationship, 1890–1917," *Diplomatic History* 19 (Fall 1995), 601–6.
24. Plesur, *Outward Thrust*, 14–22; Normal Saul, *Concord and Conflict: The United States and Russia, 1867–1914* (Lawrence, Kans., 1996), 276–81; Daniel Yergin, *The Prize: The Epic Quest for Oil, Money, and Power* (New York, 1991), 50–57.

America's Gilded Age foreign policies reflected these crosscurrents. Statesmen devoted relatively little time to foreign policy because there was no need to do so and because domestic issues were generally more pressing. "The President has rarely leisure to give close or continuous attention to foreign policy," Englishman James Bryce observed.[25] Most leaders understandably hesitated to take on major commitments abroad. As far as Europe was concerned, they absolutely refused to do so. What has been called "old paradigm" foreign policy generally consisted of improvised and ad hoc responses to developments abroad.[26]

But that was only one side of the picture. Many younger Americans, especially offspring of the elite, shared a growing sense of the nation's rising power and status in the world. Some warned of dangers in a changing international situation and urged reconsideration of traditional foreign policy principles. Some saw domestic imperatives as demanding more active policies. There was no master plan or grand design, to be sure, but many Americans agreed upon the need to expand foreign markets and increase U.S. influence in the Western Hemisphere and the Pacific. Some even expressed interest in acquiring territory.

In an era when political parties were fragmented and nearly equal in strength and when domestic issues held center stage, party positions on foreign policy were not sharply drawn. Republicans and Democrats agreed that the United States should abstain from involvement in Europe's politics, alliances, and wars. Most Americans supported expanding their nation's influence in the Western Hemisphere.

Composed of diverse regional and socioeconomic interests, the Democratic Party remained true to its Jeffersonian roots in supporting laissez-faire, limited government, and public frugality. Most Democrats advocated free trade and opposed protectionism. Some like Alabama's Morgan kept alive the expansionism of southern Democrats in the 1850s, advocating aggressive pursuit of foreign markets, a large modern navy, and construction of an isthmian canal to help free the South from "foreign" oppression at the hands of British creditors and northern reconstructionists. Morgan even endorsed the acquisition of overseas territory to boost the South's political power and provide a haven for colonized blacks. The great majority of southerners, on the other hand, opposed policies that might result in the absorption of non-white peoples, strengthening of the federal government, and competition with their agricultural products.

25. Quoted in John A. Garraty, *The New Commonwealth, 1877–1890* (New York, 1968), 283n.
26. Robert L. Beisner, *From the Old Diplomacy to the New, 1865–1900* (2nd ed., 1986), 37.

Most Democrats viewed commercial and territorial expansion as contrary to American traditions and principles. Some like Georgia's James Blount saw colonial acquisitions as all too reminiscent of the North's imposition of outside rule on the defeated South.[27]

The Republican Party had in many ways outlived the anti-slavery platform that brought it into being. Most Republicans still believed in a strong central government and subsidizing economic growth through a protective tariff. Some clung to cautious Whiggish notions opposing expansion. Others followed Seward in pushing for a more assertive foreign policy, a large navy, and a canal. The party was changing from its Whig roots to outright support of expansion and even imperialism.

Because the times did not demand it (and probably would not have permitted it), no Jefferson, John Quincy Adams, or Seward arose among Gilded Age diplomatists, and efforts on the part of historians to make one of James G. Blaine remain unconvincing. Secretaries of State William Evarts (1877–81), Frederick Frelinghuysen (1881–85), and Thomas Bayard (1885–89) were in most matters cautious. They managed American diplomacy without bravado but with quiet competence.[28] President Grover Cleveland, a Democrat, was stubborn, unimaginative, and insular in his thinking, but he was not afraid to make tough foreign policy decisions. He displayed on occasion an admirable tendency to do the right thing for the right reason, injecting an element of morality into an area of endeavor and political climate where it was normally absent.

Blaine served at the beginning of the 1880s and 1890s and was far and away the most colorful, controversial, and important of the lot. Charming, energetic, and hugely ambitious—"When I want a thing, I want it dreadfully," he once said—the "Plumed Knight" was a total political animal and a rabidly partisan Republican.[29] Intense, suspicious, and given to intrigue, he was often linked with the corruption that marked the age. If he *was* involved, he was too clever to get caught. As secretary of state, he was much more inclined to project American power abroad than the lawyers who preceded and followed him. He pursued with characteristic energy the expansion of U.S. trade and influence in the Western Hemisphere and the Pacific. He shared with earlier generations of Americans a sense of the nation's greatness and destiny. He developed a vision of em-

27. Fry, *Morgan*, 48, 74–75; Tennant S. McWilliams, "James H. Blount, the South, and Hawaiian Annexation," *Pacific Historical Review* 57 (February 1988), 39.
28. Doenecke, *Garfield and Arthur*, 142; Richard E. Welch Jr., *The Presidencies of Grover Cleveland* (Lawrence, Kans., 1988), 161.
29. Doenecke, *Garfield and Arthur*, 14.

pire that included U.S. preeminence in the hemisphere, commercial domination of the Pacific, an American-owned canal, and even the acquisition of Hawaii, Cuba, and Puerto Rico. Especially in his first term as secretary of state, "Jingo Jim," as he was called, could be impulsive, heavy-handed, and insensitive to other peoples. His diplomacy was also sometimes marked by demagoguery.[30] He was denied greatness in part because of such deficiencies in his leadership but even more because his tangible accomplishments were few and because the times did not provide the sort of foreign policy challenges faced by his more illustrious predecessors. At the same time, his "blueprint" for U.S. expansion and his mentoring of such future leaders as William McKinley and John Hay establish him as a major link between antebellum expansionism and late nineteenth-century U.S. imperialism.[31]

The instruments of Gilded Age foreign policy reflected more the nation's insular past than its global future. The State Department escaped the worst abuses of the era of spoilsmen, but its staff of eighty-one people remained small for an incipient world power. Work hours were a leisurely 9:00 A.M. to 4:00 P.M.; the pace was very slow.[32] State's methods of operation dated to John Quincy Adams. Much of the work was done by a single person, the legendary Alvey Adee, a bureaucrat par excellence who served nearly forty years as second assistant secretary of state. The State Department's institutional memory and a master of diplomatic practice, Adee drafted most of its instructions and dispatches. "Why there isn't a kitten born in a palace anywhere on earth that I don't have to write a letter of congratulation to the peripatetic tomcat that might have been its sire," Theodore Roosevelt would later joke, "and old Adee does that for me!"[33]

The rank of ambassador was still considered too pretentious for a republic, and U.S. diplomats were often outranked by representatives of much smaller nations. All were political appointees. Some such as James Russell Lowell in England and Andrew Dickson White in Germany distinguished themselves. Most of the "foreign service" consisted of "second-rate personnel frequently forced to live in third-rate surroundings," provoking John Hay to compare the diplomatic vocation to the " 'Catholic Church, calculated only for celibates.' "[34] In places like Japan, because of

30. Ibid., 74.
31. Edward P. Crapol, *James G. Blaine: Architect of Empire* (Wilmington, Del., 2000), xiv, 137–46.
32. Doenecke, *Garfield and Arthur*, 56–57.
33. Peter Bridges, "An Appreciation of Alvey Adee," *American Diplomacy* Web site, www .unc.edu/depts/diplomat/archives_roll/2001_10-12/bridges_adee/bridges_adee.html.
34. Doenecke, *Garfield and Arthur*, 56–57.

recurrent attacks on foreigners and devastating fires, diplomatic service could be life-threatening. A remarkable informality and ease of movement characterized the diplomatic community. Ebenezar Don Carlos Bassett became the first U.S. minister to Haiti and the first African American to hold a diplomatic position. When his term expired, he entered the Haitian foreign service and subsequently became consul-general in the United States.[35] The number of consulates had grown to two hundred by this time, supplemented by four hundred agencies in less important areas. Some consulates provided respectable pay; most compensated scant money with an exotic place to live.[36]

The state of the military reflected the mood of a nation without major external threat and still suffering from the fallout of a long and bloody war. The mighty army that had defeated the Confederacy was demobilized. A tiny remnant scattered in posts across the West occupied itself with eliminating Indian resistance. The once proud U.S. Navy was also scuttled, by the 1870s ranking below the "fleets" of Paraguay and Turkey. "The mention of our Navy only excites a smile," a shipbuilder snarled. "We have not six ships that would be kept at sea in war by any maritime power," the future high priest of sea power Capt. Alfred Thayer Mahan protested.[37]

Even in the Gilded Age, however, there were signs of the institutional changes that would mark America's rise to world power. Substantive reform of the State Department awaited the twentieth century, but the consular service was upgraded and focused toward finding markets. The army sought to improve the quality of its enlisted personnel and better educate its officers, created an intelligence arm, and in 1885 conducted its first large-scale maneuvers. The real focus of Gilded Age reform was the navy. Spurred by aggressive and sometimes alarmist naval officers and by a war scare with Chile, the Chester A. Arthur administration in the early 1880s initiated major efforts to build a modern fleet, establishing a Naval War College and the Office of Naval Intelligence and commissioning three new armor-plated cruisers to protect merchant ships in remote areas. Cleveland continued the naval building program. Modernization was well under way by the 1890s.

35. Wanda Faye Jackson, "The Diplomatic Relationship Between the United States and Haiti, 1862–1900" (Ph.D. dissertation, University of Kentucky, 1999), 49–50.
36. Ari Hoogenboom, *The Presidency of Rutherford B. Hayes* (Lawrence, Kans., 1988), 105, 108.
37. Doenecke, *Garfield and Arthur*, 146.

Symbolic of an emerging nation—if still way ahead of the upgrading of the agencies it housed—was the completion in 1888 of the State, War, Navy Building just west of the White House. Built at a cost of more than $10 million, this masterpiece of Victorian excess had a total floor area of ten acres and almost two miles of corridors. Some Americans boasted that it was the largest and finest office building in the world. At the very least, a Washington newspaper proclaimed, it was the "finest in the United States, and in every way worthy . . . [of] the uses to which it is to be devoted."[38]

III

Immigration strikingly reshaped U.S. society in the late nineteenth century, and some of the most complex problems for Gilded Age diplomacy stemmed from the increasing number, size, and diversity of ethnic groups in the United States. The pattern of immigration during the Gilded Age shifted from northern to eastern and southern Europe and Asia, bringing to U.S. shores millions of so-called new immigrants much less familiar in terms of their ethnicity, language, religion, and culture. The presence of immigrants from exotic races provoked growing internal tensions and in different ways sparked conflict with other countries. The harsh treatment of the new ethnic groups by bigoted Americans provoked diplomatic crises with the nations of their origin. The involvement of immigrants or naturalized Americans with revolutions in their homelands brought the United States into conflict with the threatened governments. Anticipating one of the major problems of twentieth-century foreign relations, some ethnic groups sought to get the U.S. government to defend their compatriots from oppression. The emergence of such problems in the Gilded Age highlighted the uniqueness of the American political system, the changing nature of U.S. foreign relations, and the nation's increasingly close connections with the outside world.

An old standby, the Irish problem, flared up anew in the late nineteenth century. Naturalized Americans played an increasingly prominent role in the ongoing Irish rebellion against British rule. The United States became a leading source of arms and explosives for Irish terrorists. The British Parliament sought to contain the flare-up in 1881 with a Coercion Act that permitted detention without trial of suspected revolutionaries. Some U.S. citizens were imprisoned under the act and appealed to Washington for help. The British also pressed Washington to shut down the Irish-American newspapers that encouraged arms shipments. A notorious

38. Lee Burke, *Homes of the Department of State* (Washington, 1977), 43–47.

Anglophobe, Blaine at first demanded release of the Americans. His successor, the usually calm Frelinghuysen, stood firmly for freedom of the press. Long-standing tensions in Anglo-American relations and Britain's traditional role as a whipping boy of U.S. politics created the potential for a crisis.

Sanity eventually prevailed. Some of the arrested Americans turned out to be shady characters, not the sort of persons causes célèbres are made of. It became increasingly obvious that they were using U.S. citizenship to protect themselves from British law. Blaine dismissed one who had falsified passport information as "a pestiferous fellow" who "deserved what he got."[39] Generally, he came to regard the agitators as "the scum of Europe." Some Americans continued to protest the treatment of their fellow citizens and the government's apparent indifference. "Oh, that we only had as much protection given to a live American citizen as . . . a dead Cincinnati hog!" a Brooklyn congressmen protested, an obvious reference to the simultaneous dispute with Britain and other European countries over U.S. exports of pork.[40] Most Americans sympathized with Irish nationalism, but not to the point of sparking a crisis with Britain. The increasingly overt and brazen activities of Irish nationalists in the United States and the explosion of bombs in the House of Commons and several English railroad stations provoked a backlash in America. Protest subsided. The Arthur administration took forceful measures to reduce illegal arms shipments. The British adamantly refused to modify the Coercion Law, but in time for reasons of their own released some Americans. The crisis eased, but similar disputes would recur in various forms as the Irish question festered over the next century.[41]

The problem of Chinese immigrants in the United States was more complex. Lured to America to perform backbreaking work in western mines and on the transcontinental railroad, the Chinese played an instrumental role in developing the nation. But their growing numbers, pronounced cultural differences, resistance to assimilation, and willingness to work for cheap wages provoked a vicious nativist backlash. Chinese were beaten, lynched, and brutally murdered, giving rise to the saying that a doomed person did not have a "Chinaman's chance." There was also rising agitation, especially in the West, for the exclusion of Chinese immigrants. China had once been indifferent to the treatment of its nationals abroad, but American actions were so egregious that it could not

39. Doenecke, *Garfield and Arthur*, 70.
40. Ibid, 138.
41. Ibid, 70–71, 138–39.

but express outrage. It must have wondered too at the pretenses of people who claimed to have established a superior civilization. Because of the unequal treaties, China was not even sovereign in its own territory. It could do little but protest. While Westerners enjoyed the protection of extraterritoriality in China, the Chinese government could not safeguard the lives of its citizens who were victimized in America.

The United States settled the issue on its own terms. Congress in 1879 passed a bill limiting the number of Chinese who could come into the country on any ship. As anti-Chinese as he was anti-British, then-Senator Blaine defended the legislation as a blow for the "civilization of Christ" against the "civilization of Confucius."[42] Arguing that the bill violated U.S. treaty obligations, Hayes courageously vetoed it. Recognizing the political strength of the agitators, however, the government negotiated a new treaty with China permitting the United States to limit or suspend but not to "absolutely prohibit" Chinese immigration. Congress immediately suspended immigration for twenty years, provoking an Arthur veto. The legislators responded with a new bill suspending Chinese immigration for ten years, the first such exclusion in U.S. history. More exclusionist laws followed. With no choice but to acquiesce, the Chinese in 1894 agreed to a new treaty that "absolutely prohibited" the immigration of Chinese laborers for ten years. Diplomatic relations worsened during the 1890s.[43]

The brutal mob killing of eleven Italians in New Orleans provoked an 1891 mini-crisis with Italy. A sharp rise in the number of Italian immigrants and an increase in gang warfare caused rising tensions in that tradition-bound southern city. The murder of a popular young police superintendent, allegedly by Italians with connections to a sinister "mafia," set off popular outrage. When the first group of those charged was found not guilty—a "thunderbolt of surprise," screamed the *Times-Picayune*—an angry mob including some of the city's leading citizens descended upon the jail, gunned down eight of the accused inside the walls, and removed and lynched three more from nearby tree limbs and lampposts. A dishonored and furious Italian government denounced this "atrocious deed," demanded protection for Italians in the United States, and insisted upon reparations. Belying his nickname "Jingo Jim," an ill and preoccupied Blaine at first responded complacently. Rising to the occasion as the dispute heated up, he retorted in notably undiplomatic language that some

42. Crapol, *Blaine*, 57.
43. Warren I. Cohen, *America's Response to China: An Interpretative History of Sino-American Relations* (New York, 1971), 35–38; Hoogenboom, *Hayes*, 177–84.

of the victims were U.S. citizens, explained that the federal government could not impose its will on the state of Louisiana, and expressed to Italy's minister his indifference what Italians might think about U.S. institutions. "You may do as you choose," he snarled in conclusion. Italy recalled its minister from Washington. Both nations strutted and blustered, and there was talk of war. After months of irresolution, Italy finally backed away from its threats, Harrison expressed regret for the killings, and the Italian minister returned to Washington. The perpetrators went unpunished, but an indemnity of $25,000 was eventually paid to the families of three of the victims. In the United States, the affair stoked a sharp rise in anti-immigrant sentiment leading to pressure for additional exclusionist legislation. Sea power advocates used the threat of war and the alleged vulnerability of U.S. ports even to the Italian fleet to drum up support for a larger navy.[44]

Quite different and much more significant was an increasingly assertive American response to the treatment of Jews in Russia. Russian anti-Semitism was deeply rooted. It grew much worse in the 1880s when famine ravaged the country and Jews were scapegoated for mounting revolutionary activities and assassination of the tsar. The issue involved the United States in several ways. American Jews traveling to Russia on business suffered various kinds of discrimination and appealed to their government for help. In addition, as their treatment in Russia became unbearable, thousands of Jews fled to a seemingly welcoming United States and through public protests called attention to the plight of those left behind. Americans were reading more about events abroad and beginning to sense that, as an emerging power, their country might exert some influence over other societies. Some began to view Russia's treatment of Jews as an outrage against humanity. Immigration officials and relief societies were overwhelmed by floods of immigrants and pleaded for surcease. Some Americans, including Secretary of State Walter Gresham, privately accused Russia of conspiring to undermine American society by "forcing upon our shores a numerous class of immigrants destitute of resources and unfitted in many important respects for absorption into our body politic."[45]

44. Homer E. Socolofsky and Allan B. Spetter, *The Presidency of Benjamin Harrison* (Lawrence, Kans., 1987), 152–54; Campbell, *Transformation*, 166–68; David A. Smith, "From the Mississippi to the Mediterranean: The 1891 New Orleans Lynching and its Effects on United States Diplomacy and the American Navy," *Southern Historian* 19 (Spring 1988), 60–85.
45. Saul, *Concord and Conflict*, 397.

The "Jewish Question" assumed growing importance in U.S. foreign relations. The State Department managed to protect the interests of most American Jews through quiet and persistent diplomacy. While affirming U.S. reluctance "officiously and offensively to intermeddle," diplomats also appealed to the Russian government in the most carefully phrased language and on the grounds of its own self-interest to cause the mistreatment of "these unfortunate fellow beings to cease."[46] Russian officials retorted that the United States had effectively dealt with problems posed by Chinese immigrants. If the influx of Jews grew too burdensome, they too could be excluded. Heightened Russian repression stimulated further Jewish emigration to the United States. The St. Petersburg government opened a new area of conflict by refusing to issue visas to American Jews. Along with Russian-speaking journalist and lecturer George Kennan's inflammatory mid-1880s expose of the horrific conditions in Siberian prisons, the ongoing dispute over treatment of Jews soured traditional Russian-American friendship and provoked some Americans to call for revolution in Russia. The issue was as important as any other in getting the American public involved in the "new foreign policy" of the 1890s. It was the first of numerous cases where pressure from ethnic groups and humanitarian concerns pushed the United States to challenge other governments, even friendly ones, on issues of human rights.[47]

IV

The U.S. economy was the marvel of the world in the late nineteenth century. The gross national product quadrupled from $9 billion during 1869–73 to $37 billion between 1897 and 1901. Production soared. Steel output increased from 77,000 tons in 1870 to 11,270,000 in 1900. Wheat and corn production doubled. The quality of American products, their low prices, and improved transportation produced a surge in trade. Exports jumped from $234 million in 1865 to $1.5 billion in 1900. In 1876, the centennial year, exports for the first time began regularly to surpass imports. As a result of rampant industrialization, exports of manufactured goods started to catch up with traditionally dominant agricultural products and would pass them in 1913. Britain was the major consumer of U.S. exports, followed by Germany and France—in all, Europe absorbed close to 80 percent of the total by the late 1880s. Closer to home, Canada and

46. Ibid., 249; John Lewis Gaddis, *Russia, the Soviet Union, and the United States: An Interpretive History* (2nd ed., New York, 1990), 29.
47. Saul, *Concord and Conflict*, 235–40; Gaddis, *Russia, The Soviet Union, and the United States*, 26–31.

Cuba were the major purchasers. For the first time, Americans had capital to invest elsewhere. By the end of the century, the nation was second only to Britain as an economic power. Americans hailed their rising prowess in the most exuberant terms. It is "our manifest destiny to rise to the first rank among the manufacturing nations," one enthusiast proclaimed. We have sent "coals to Newcastle, cotton to Manchester, cutlery to Sheffield, potatoes to Ireland, champagne to France, watches to Switzerland," boasted another.[48]

Some Americans increasingly feared that their blessing could become their curse. A severe depression in 1873 wreaked devastation across the land, raising concerns among some businessmen and government leaders that producing more than could be absorbed at home threatened economic stability. Exports still represented only about 7 percent of the gross national product, but they came to be seen as the key to economic well-being. "The house we live in has got too small," economist David Wells warned. Without an expansion of foreign markets, "we are certain to be smothered in our own grease."[49] Gilded Age politicians and businessmen thus set out to protect existing foreign markets and find new ones. The government began to play a more important role in this process. Such efforts were not always determined or systematic. Most businesses continued to focus on the domestic market. Devotion to protectionism inhibited the negotiation of new trade agreements and overturned existing ones. The results thus did not match up to the rhetoric.[50] At the same time, a growing concern for foreign markets spurred the United States to project its influence into new areas and even participate in an international conference, use old weapons with new vigor, and take a tough line with the European powers on vital trade issues.

The search for markets took Americans to distant shores. As early as 1867, Cdr. Robert W. Shufeldt had sought to emulate Perry by opening Korea, the "Hermit Kingdom," but he was twice rebuffed. Finally, in 1882, with the help of Chinese intermediaries, he negotiated the Treaty of Chemulpo, providing for trade on a most-favored-nation basis, the establishment of diplomatic relations, and, as in earlier treaties with China and Japan, extraterritoriality. The Chinese hoped to use the United States to strengthen their own control over a neighboring country, but the

48. David M. Pletcher, "Rhetoric and Results: A Pragmatic View of American Economic Expansionism, 1865–1898," *Diplomatic History* 5 (Spring 1981), 94–95; Campbell, *Transformation*, 85–86.
49. Pletcher, "Economic Expansionism," 95.
50. Ibid., 103–5.

Americans insisted, in Frelinghuysen's words, that "Corea is an independent, sovereign power." Seeking to exploit the United States to secure its independence, Korea agreed to an exchange of missions. A group of Koreans visited the Brooklyn Navy Yard and the U.S. Military Academy at West Point. A U.S. naval officer served as adviser to the Korean court. The Yankees quickly learned that Seoul was an especially precarious place to work. Minister Lucius Foote helped arrange a settlement between pro-Chinese and Japanese factions, but the result was to reduce U.S. influence. In any event, the United States quickly contented itself with being a minor player in a country torn by rivalries between larger and nearby nations. Trade was negligible.[51]

Some Americans also looked to the Congo River basin of West Africa for markets. A series of reports in the *New York Herald* first drew notice to the region. The newspaper in 1869 sent Scottish-born adventurer Henry M. Stanley to the Congo to find the long-missing medical missionary David Livingstone, who had gained international notoriety by "discovering" the Zambezi River and Victoria Falls. Stanley's 1871 encounter with his fellow Scotsman near Lake Tanganyika in present-day Tanzania, immortalized in the oft-quoted greeting "Dr. Livingstone, I presume," caused a worldwide sensation, attracting more attention to Africa. After a triumphant return to the United States, the intrepid explorer ranged deep into the Congo region, extolling its commercial possibilities. Some timely lobbying by Civil War diplomat and entrepreneur Henry Sanford, at this time serving as an agent for Belgium's King Leopold II, further promoted the Congo as a market for U.S. products. President Arthur himself spoke of "covering those unclad millions with our domestic cottons," calculating that "but three yards per capita would make an enormous aggregate for our cotton mills."[52]

The lure of African markets caused the United States in 1884 to break long-standing precedent by participating in an international conference held in Berlin to deal with the Congo region. The U.S. delegates were instructed to promote freedom of trade and steer clear of European entanglements—no mean task. The result was far less than America's Congo publicists had hoped. The conference solemnly declared itself in favor of free trade, but it also recognized Leopold's African International Association as the governing body. The association turned out to be a thinly veiled cover for exclusive trading arrangements and the most brutal

51. Doenecke, *Garfield and Arthur*, 153–56.
52. Quoted in Campbell, *Transformation*, 100–102.

exploitation of Africans. In any event, Republicans and Democrats denounced the agreement as an "entangling alliance." Cleveland took office in March 1885 just as the act was negotiated and, as with several other expansionist measures, refused to submit it to the Senate. The "noble dream" produced negligible results.[53]

Republican efforts to use reciprocity treaties to expand foreign trade met a similar fate. Monroe and Adams had employed the device earlier in the century to challenge mercantilist trade barriers. More recently, Hamilton Fish through reciprocity had bound Hawaii economically to the United States. At a time when Europeans threatened to shut America out of foreign markets, reciprocity had a special attraction. It seemed an ideal means to secure new outlets for U.S. products when free trade was impossible and retaliation dangerous while still permitting some protection. In dealing with less developed nations, it had special advantages. It could gain free entry for foreign raw materials and markets for U.S. manufactured goods. As the Hawaiian example had shown, it established a means of control without resort to colonial rule.

Reciprocity was the "linchpin" of Arthur and Frelinghuysen's foreign trade policy. They especially targeted Latin America, a "natural mart of supply and demand," in Arthur's words, hoping to tie Latin economies to the United States, weaken European influence, and promote larger U.S. political aims. They attached special importance to a treaty with Mexico, naming former president U.S. Grant as a negotiator and working out an agreement that exchanged American manufactured goods for Mexican foods and raw materials. Diplomat John W. Foster bludgeoned Spain into agreements for Cuba and Puerto Rico that eliminated virtually all barriers to trade. The Cuban deal, Foster boasted, was "the most perfect reciprocity treaty our Government has ever made," giving the United States "an almost complete commercial monopoly" and thus "annexing Cuba in the most desirable way."[54] Foster negotiated an even more favorable agreement with Santo Domingo making the U.S. dollar the unit of currency in bilateral trade.

The Arthur trade offensive met insuperable obstacles at home. The tariff was the most contentious political issue of the age. Democrats who preferred broad and general tariff reductions and Republicans who supported protection both opposed reciprocity. The tariff brought to the fore the competing interests of farmers, manufacturers, and consumers, and any specific proposal could draw fire from a range of groups. Critics of the

53. Doenecke, Garfield and Arthur, 162.
54. Ibid., 176.

Mexican treaty complained it would subsidize foreign investors and favor railroad interests. American cigar makers and sugar interests fought the Cuban treaty. In any event, the Arthur treaties were completed as Cleveland took office. A throwback to Jefferson and Jackson, he doubted the validity of the "glut thesis" and sought to reduce tariffs to lower consumer prices and eliminate special privileges for business. Viewing reciprocity as a "conspiratorial device to prevent passage of a general tariff reduction act," he scrapped the treaties negotiated by his predecessor.[55]

The so-called Pork War with Europe exemplified America's concern with markets and its growing assertiveness and produced better results. A horrible famine on the Continent in 1879 proved a bonanza for the United States, leading to massive exports of agricultural products and full recovery from the Panic of 1873. Alarmed at the flood of American imports, European nations began to limit and then ban them. American meats were probably no less safe than European, but rumors of disease were used to justify what was economically and politically expedient. The British consul bemoaned the fate of one poor victim who found worms "in his flesh by the millions, being scraped and squeezed from the pores of his skin." Britain limited imports of U.S. pork and beef. France and Germany banned all imports even though America's meats had been certified safe by the French Academy of Medicine and its pork was reputedly safer than German.

The European measures provoked fury in the United States. Outraged farmers and producers urged retaliation by banning imports of French and German wines. The *Chicago Tribune* denounced the "rule or ruin" policies of the European aristocracy. The *New York Herald* urged "avenging the American hog."[56] Responding to domestic pressures, Blaine protested vigorously, but he also proposed that all meat products be inspected before exportation and offered to lower tariffs if the Europeans would rescind their bans. Arthur and Frelinghuysen also handled the matter cautiously. Arthur created an independent commission to study American meat-producing methods. He endorsed "equitable retaliation" but refused to act, fearing that a trade war might hurt the United States more than Europe. Their stopgap measures avoided a dangerous conflict while keeping some European markets open.[57]

A more assertive United States in 1890 launched all-out war on European restrictions. The issue was of more than passing political importance.

55. Welch, *Cleveland*, 85.
56. Campbell, *Transformation*, 103.
57. Doenecke, *Garfield and Arthur*, 67–69, 136–38.

"It does not comport with the self-respect and dignity of this government to longer tolerate such a policy," Secretary of Agriculture Jeremiah Rusk advised President Benjamin Harrison. The United States established mechanisms to inspect meat to be exported, thus presumably removing the rationale for European bans. The Harrison administration also threatened to ban imports of German sugar and French wines (known, in some cases, to be adulterated), and Congress in 1890 provided the means to retaliate. When the German government proposed lifting the ban if the United States agreed not to shut off imports of German sugar, Blaine urged acceptance, but a determined Harrison demurred, making clear his readiness to retaliate. In the face of this determination, Germany lifted its ban in return for American promises to keep sugar on the free list. Other European nations followed suit. Exports of U.S. meat products doubled between May 1891 and May 1892.[58]

V

In areas of traditional concern such as the Western Hemisphere and the Pacific basin, the United States during the Gilded Age mounted a concerted effort to expand its influence. Americans harbored vague and generally unfounded fears that Europeans might use their strong existing position to extend their colonizing tendencies to the Western Hemisphere. Certain of the superiority of their institutions and conscious of their rising power, they increasingly claimed that their rightful place was at the head of the American nations. They believed they could assist their southern neighbors to be more stable and orderly. For reasons of both economics and security, they sought to roll back European influence and increase their own.

Part of the work was done by individuals without direction or even encouragement from government. Following the devastation of the Ten Years' War, U.S. entrepreneurs bought up sugar estates, mines, and ranches in Cuba. By the 1890s, they dominated the island's economy. Exploiting the generous subsidies and tax breaks offered foreign investors by dictator Porfirio Diaz, Americans came to view Mexico as a "second India, Cuba, Brazil, Italy, and Troy all rolled into one." U.S. capital poured across the border into railroads, mines, and oil, totaling $500 million by 1900, transforming Mexico into a virtual satellite of the United States, and causing growing alarm among Mexican nationalists.[59] Some Central

58. Socolofsky and Spetter, Harrison, 132–36.
59. Enrique Krauze, Mexico, Biography of Power: A History of Modern Mexico (New York, 1997), 6; Karl M. Schmitt, Mexico and the United States, 1821–1973 (New York, 1974), 101–5.

American rulers also welcomed U.S. capital as a means to modernize their economies, boost their nations' wealth, and uplift their people. They too granted generous concessions, permitting North Americans to buy up mines and plantations, control great wealth, and wield enormous power.[60]

For the first time, the United States came out openly and insistently for an American-owned and -controlled isthmian canal. From the outset, some Americans had demanded that they must build and operate such a canal. The 1850 Clayton-Bulwer Treaty had provoked bitter opposition on precisely such grounds. By the 1880s, a canal had assumed greater importance to the United States. Central American nations sought to exploit its anxieties. Nicaraguan overtures to British bankers and Colombia's deal with Ferdinand de Lesseps, builder of the Suez Canal, to construct a canal across Panama, stunned a complacent Washington into action. Former Union general Ambrose Burnside pronounced a French-built canal "dangerous to our peace and safety"; Congress responded with a flurry of resolutions. In terms of commerce and security, the normally laconic Rutherford B. Hayes declared, a canal would be "virtually a part of the coast line of the United States." The "true policy" of the United States must be "either a canal under American control, or no canal." Hayes did not stop the de Lesseps venture, but he did secure from the French government an affirmation that it was a private venture without official support.[61]

Hayes's successors went further. Blaine and Frelinghuysen stood firmly for an American-owned and -controlled canal and made sporadic efforts to modify or abrogate the Clayton-Bulwer Treaty. Blaine called an isthmian canal as much a "channel of communication" between the East and West coasts of the United States as "our own transcontinental railroad." It was "strictly and solely . . . an American question, to be dealt with and decided by the American governments." Rejecting such claims, the British firmly retorted that any Central American canal concerned "the whole civilized world."[62] To counter de Lesseps, Frelinghuysen negotiated a treaty with Nicaragua permitting the United States to build and operate a canal in return for a promise to defend that nation's sovereignty. The treaty was one-sided, the New York Times explained, because the "will of a mighty nation of 55,000,000 of homogenous, progressive and

60. Thomas M. Leonard, *Central America and the United States: The Search for Stability* (Athens, Ga., 1991), 42–44.
61. Hoogenboom, *Hayes*, 189–90.
62. Doenecke, *Garfield and Arthur*, 66–67.

patriotic people is of course irresistible when it runs counter to the wishes of feeble and unstable governments like Central and South America."[63] As with so many other Arthur-Frelinghuysen initiatives, the incoming Cleveland administration junked the treaty because it viewed the commitment to Nicaragua as an entangling alliance.

To reduce foreign influence in the hemisphere and increase its own, the United States claimed for itself a new leadership role and initiated a habit of "paternalistic meddling" that would persist far into the future. Blaine was the ringleader in both areas. His efforts reflected his assertive personality but also his conviction that exposure to the United States would have a positive "moral influence" and raise "the standard of . . . civilization" of peoples he regarded as congenitally quarrelsome and contentious, thus eliminating any excuses for European intrusion.[64] He first intervened in a boundary dispute between Mexico and Guatemala in 1881, foolishly encouraging Guatemala, which had the weaker claim, and thereby delaying a settlement. His intervention in the War of the Pacific the same year was even more clumsy in execution and harmful in results. Spying Britain's sinister hand behind Chile's efforts to gain territory disputed with Peru, he dispatched two singularly inept diplomats to the scene. One got involved in a shady scheme from which he stood to profit handsomely. Together, the two undercut each other's efforts and alienated both sides, Peru counting on U.S. support that was not forthcoming, Chile correctly viewing the United States as thwarting its ambitions. The British minister dismissed the U.S. intervention as "pretentious incapacity." Frelinghuysen liquidated it as quickly as possible. But it left a deep legacy of suspicion and anger on the west coast of South America.[65]

The pace of U.S. overseas activity quickened from 1889 to 1893 under the aggressive leadership of President Benjamin Harrison and Secretary of State Blaine. Defeated by Cleveland for the presidency in 1884, Blaine declined to run four years later. The Republicans nominated instead the Indiana lawyer, U.S. senator, and grandson of President William Henry Harrison. As a Senate mentor, Blaine had helped convert the Indianan to expansionism. The cold, aloof president and his dynamic, charismatic adviser never formed a close working relationship; their collaboration was often beset with rivalry and tension. But the two pursued an activist, sometimes belligerent foreign policy that jump-started a decade of expansionism, energetically reasserting U.S. leadership of the hemisphere,

---

63. Leonard, *United States and Central America*, 39–40.
64. Schoultz, *Beneath the United States*, 94.
65. Ibid., 94–97; Doenecke, *Garfield and Arthur*, 57–62.

pushing reciprocity with renewed vigor, escalating a minor crisis with Chile to the point of war, aggressively pursuing naval bases in the Caribbean and Pacific, and even giving the green light to a coup d'état in Hawaii. Small of stature with a high-pitched voice, "Little Ben" was especially bellicose and on several occasions had to be restrained by the man known as "Jingo Jim."[66]

Under Blaine's direction, the United States in 1889 hosted the first inter-American conference since the ill-fated Panama Congress of 1826. Concerned that interhemispheric conflict might invite European intervention, the secretary of state had first proposed such a meeting in 1881 so that the hemisphere nations could find ways to prevent war among themselves. The invitations were canceled after Garfield's assassination, partly to spite Blaine. Appropriately, the Plumed Knight was back in office when the conference finally convened in 1889. By this time, the focus had shifted to trade issues. The delegates were immediately whisked off on a six-week, six-thousand-mile tour of U.S. industrial centers, a crude brand of huckstering that annoyed some Latin visitors. Blaine's ambitious agenda for the six-month conference included such things as arbitration of disputes, a customs union, and copyright agreements. It produced little except the resolve to meet again and establishment of a bureaucracy based in Washington that would evolve into the Pan-American Union. Blaine's efforts brought few immediate, tangible gains, but they made clear U.S. determination to assume hemispheric leadership and initiated "the modern era of an institutionalized hemispheric community."[67]

Given broad authority by a measure Blaine had included in the tariff bill of 1890 to negotiate agreements without congressional oversight, the Harrison administration also mounted a new drive for reciprocal trade treaties in Latin America. Food and raw materials would be permitted to enter duty free, but if other nations did not respond with similar generosity the United States would reimpose duties. The administration used the first treaty with Brazil to pressure Spain into new agreements with Cuba and Puerto Rico. Of the former, steel magnate Andrew Carnegie observed, Cuba "hereafter will be of as little good to Spain as Canada is to Britain."[68] As with many other Republican initiatives, however, the Democrats' return to power in 1893 and passage of the Wilson-Gorman

66. Crapol, *Blaine*, 107–8, 112.
67. Schoultz, *Beneath the United States*, 283, 318; Socolofsky and Spetter, *Harrison*, 117–18.
68. Socolofsky and Spetter, *Harrison*, 119–23.

tariff in 1894 undercut Harrison's efforts, leaving little to show for two decades of effort.

The Harrison administration's assertiveness was most blatantly manifested in its handling of a minor dispute with Chile. During a drunken brawl in a seedy part of Valparaiso in late 1891, two sailors from the USS *Baltimore* were killed, seventeen wounded, and thirty-six jailed. The incident quickly escalated. As nationalistic as Americans, Chileans saw themselves as a rival to the United States for hemispheric leadership. Relations between the two nations had been strained since Blaine's ill-conceived intrusion into the War of the Pacific and worsened in 1889 when the United States openly interfered in Chile's internal politics. The *Baltimore's* captain insisted that his sailors had been "properly drunk," the victims of an unprovoked attack. Blaine was ill, and therefore not involved in the negotiations. A notably bellicose Harrison far exceeded traditional U.S. practice by demanding not only an apology but also "prompt and full" reparation. Still furious at the United States for its earlier meddling, Chile at first denied the charges and accused Washington of lying, but it subsequently expressed "very sincere regret for the unfortunate events." Unappeased and very much in keeping with the mood of the time, Harrison exclaimed that "we must protect those who in foreign ports display the flag or wear its colors." He continued to demand a "suitable apology" and reparation and threatened to break relations. As the two nations edged toward an especially foolish war, Chile blinked first, offering an apology and $75,000 in reparations. Belying his reputation for bellicosity, Blaine persuaded Harrison to accept. To Adm. Bancroft Gherardi, the incident made clear that the United States was "no longer to be trifled with."[69]

Harrison and Blaine employed economic and diplomatic pressure and gunboat diplomacy in a futile effort to secure naval bases in the Caribbean. The more U.S. leaders talked of a canal, the greater the perceived need for bases to protect it. Haiti's Môle St. Nicolas was especially attractive, and Blaine exerted strong pressure against a government threatened by revolution to acquire it. When that government balked, the United States permitted arms shipments to the rebels, hoping that its generosity would be repaid. After the rebels took power, the administration dispatched the distinguished African American leader Frederick Douglass, himself an ardent expansionist, to negotiate with Haiti. When those negotiations stalled, Blaine sent Admiral Gherardi to take over; when he also failed to budge Haitian leaders, the United States conducted a naval

69. Schoultz, *Beneath the United States*, 102–6; Socolofsky and Spetter, *Harrison*, 146–51.

demonstration off its shores. Haiti refused to be cowed. Santo Domingo was no more obliging. The United States' efforts to use the leverage provided by a reciprocity treaty to acquire Samana Bay produced nothing. Blaine resigned in June 1892 and died the following year without realizing his dream of a Caribbean naval base. To the end, he remained confident that the United States would acquire Cuba and Puerto Rico within a generation.[70]

The Harrison administration also sought to strengthen the U.S. position in the Pacific basin. Through a bizarre set of circumstances, not at all atypical for this turbulent era, the United States assumed a quite remarkable role on Samoa. Shortly after the 1878 treaty, the U.S. consul had signed an agreement neutralizing the town of Apia and establishing a multilateral governing body composed of himself and the British and German consuls. The agreement was never submitted to the Senate, but it operated anyway, "an unprecedented collaboration with European countries on a distant South Sea archipelago."[71] Such cooperation soon embroiled the United States in a mini-crisis with Germany. When German naval officers seized Apia in 1885 and then asserted their intention to take control of Samoa, the Cleveland administration balked. On his own, the U.S. consul launched a preemptive strike by declaring an American protectorate over all Samoa. An embarrassed secretary of state Bayard beat a hasty retreat, disavowing the overzealous consul and temporarily easing tensions. In 1887, however, Germany sent warships to Samoa and deported the pro-American king. Claiming sanctimoniously that the United States' "first allegiance" was to the "rights of the natives in Samoa," Cleveland and Bayard also sent warships. Already annoyed with Germany over the Pork War, the American press expressed outrage. Congress appropriated funds to defend U.S. interests on that distant isle.[72]

The Samoan crisis eased as quickly as it had flared up. The master diplomatist Bismarck did not want war with the United States over a faraway Pacific island and invited America and Britain to discuss the issue at a conference in Berlin. A timely hurricane, along with tidal waves, struck Apia in March 1889, sinking or disabling all German and U.S. warships and killing 150 men. This act of God diverted attention from the great power conflict, removed the instruments of war, and cooled tempers. The Berlin conference later that year, in which the United States was a full participant, quickly reached an agreement declaring Samoa independent

70. Crapol, *Blaine*, 129–30.
71. Campbell, *Transformation*, 77.
72. Ibid., 80–81.

but establishing a complex mechanism for what was in effect a tripartite agreement dividing power among the great powers while leaving Samoa nominally autonomous. At Blaine's insistence, the United States retained control over the superb harbor of Pago Pago. Some Americans cheered that their secretary of state had stood up to Germany's Iron Chancellor. For the first time in its history, the United States was formally committed to govern an overseas people. It was also a participant in an entangling agreement with two European nations in an area where it had scant interests.[73]

In Hawaii, Blaine and Harrison almost pulled off a replay of the methods used to secure Florida, Texas, and California. The reciprocity treaty of 1875 had done its job. By the 1880s, Hawaii was a virtual satellite of the United States, and any foreign challenge met a firm rebuff. When the British and French sought to defend their dwindling interests by insisting on most-favored-nation status, the Senate Foreign Relations Committee proclaimed Hawaii a part of "the physical and political geography of the United States." Blaine called it part of an "American Zollverein," the name given to a contemporaneous German customs union. In 1884, the two nations renewed the treaty for an additional seven years. Even Cleveland went along, although he opposed reciprocity in principle, insisting that Hawaii was essential to U.S. commerce in the Pacific.[74] Because of opposition from domestic sugar producers, Senate approval came only after three years and after an amendment giving the United States exclusive right to a naval base at Pearl Harbor. The British consul correctly predicted that the base agreement would "lead to the loss of Hawaiian independence."[75] Indeed, upon taking power in 1889, Blaine and Harrison negotiated with the American serving as Hawaiian minister to the United States an agreement making Hawaii a U.S. protectorate. The king resisted the provision permitting the United States to use military force to protect Hawaii's independence. The idea died—momentarily.

An abortive move to annex Hawaii made clear the lengths the Harrison administration would go to achieve its expansionist aims. The McKinley tariff of 1890 deprived Hawaiian sugar of its privileged position and spread economic distress on the islands. Along with the determined efforts of the new Queen Liliuokalani to regain the royal powers squandered to the Americans by her late brother and to restore "Hawaii for the Hawaiians," it threatened the economic well-being and political power of U.S.

73. Ibid., 83.
74. Doenecke, *Garfield and Arthur,* 177; Welch, *Cleveland,* 169.
75. Campbell, *Transformation,* 71.

planters. In early 1892, the Americans formed a secret "Annexation Club," sounded out U.S. minister to Hawaii John L. Stevens, an old friend and business partner of Blaine, and instigated a plot to overthrow the queen. Harrison carefully maintained what would later be called plausible deniability. Neither he nor Blaine encouraged Stevens's actions, but they presumably agreed with the plan and did nothing to stop it. Indeed, in June 1892, the administration assured a Stevens crony that if the Hawaiian people applied for annexation the United States could not say no. When the queen proclaimed a new constitution, the conspirators made their move. In January 1893, on orders from Stevens, the USS *Boston* landed sailors to preserve order, a step crucial to the outcome. The plotters seized power in a bloodless takeover. Stevens declared the new government under U.S. protection. "The Hawaiian pear is now fully ripe and this is the golden hour for the United States to pluck it," he advised the State Department.[76] Hawaiian representatives hustled to Washington, where, with embarrassing speed, a treaty of annexation was negotiated, signed, and submitted to the Senate. Disclaiming responsibility for the coup, Harrison nevertheless denounced the queen as "effete," warned that the United States must act decisively lest the ripe pear fall into the waiting lap of some rival nation, and urged annexation. Like other expansionist moves, this effort to acquire Hawaii would die—at least temporarily—at the hands of a second Cleveland administration, but it made quite clear the new commitment to expansionist goals and the willingness to use extraordinary means to achieve them. One hundred years later, without acknowledging United States responsibility, Congress would pass a bill formally apologizing to the people of Hawaii for the overthrow of its government.[77]

FOREIGN POLICY WAS NOT A HIGH NATIONAL PRIORITY in the Gilded Age. There was no threat to the nation's security. The Pork War was the closest thing to a real crisis; the overblown war scares with Italy and Chile, so typical of an age of flag-waving nationalism, patriotic posturing, and inflated concern with honor, were not far behind. Gilded Age diplomatists have been dismissed for not being "internationalists," but there was no need for them to be nor any reason to expect that of them. Dull and plodding they may have seemed, sometimes clumsy in the execution of policies, but they took their jobs seriously. They began to develop the

76. Quoted in Crapol, *Blaine*, 128.
77. Ibid., 125–26.

accoutrements of national power. Although the results would not be seen until later, they vigorously pursued new outlets for trade. They defended the nation's interests. They had no master plan or fixed agenda, but the goals they pursued and the decisions they made reflected their commitment to the extension of American power.[78] They achieved few tangible results, but in the Caribbean and the Pacific, areas of greatest U.S. interest, they shored up the nation's already strong position. They provided a springboard for another burst of expansionism in the 1890s.

78. Crapol in Joseph A. Fry, "From Open Door to World Systems: Economic Interpretations of Late Nineteenth-Century American Foreign Relations," *Pacific Historical Review* 65 (May 1996), 302.

8

The War of 1898, the New Empire, and the Dawn of the American Century, 1893–1901

The great transformation in U.S. foreign relations that began in the Gilded Age culminated in the 1890s. During that tumultuous decade, the pace of diplomatic activity quickened. Americans took greater notice of events abroad and more vigorously asserted themselves in defense of perceived interests. The war with Spain in 1898 and the acquisition of overseas colonies have often been viewed as accidents of history, departures from tradition, "the great aberration," in historian Samuel Flagg Bemis's words, "empire by default," according to a more recent writer.[1] In fact, the United States in going to war with Spain acted much more purposefully than such interpretations allow. To be sure, the nation broke precedent by acquiring overseas colonies with no intention of admitting them as states. At the same time, in its aims, its methods, and the rhetoric used to justify it, the expansionism of the 1890s followed logically from earlier patterns, built on established precedents, and gave structure to the blueprint drawn up by James G. Blaine in the previous decade.

I

During the 1890s, Americans became acutely conscious of their emerging power. "We are sixty-five million of people, the most advanced and powerful on earth," a senator observed in 1893 with pride and more than a touch of exaggeration.[2] "We are a Nation—with the biggest kind of N," Kentucky journalist Henry Watterson added, "a great imperial Republic destined to exercise a controlling influence upon the actions of mankind and to affect the future of the world."[3]

1. Samuel Flagg Bemis, A *Diplomatic History of the United States* (5th ed., New York, 1965), 463; Ivan Musicant, *Empire by Default: The Spanish-American War and the Dawn of the American Century* (New York, 1998).
2. Robert L. Beisner, *From the Old Diplomacy to the New, 1865–1900* (2nd ed., Arlington Heights, Ill., 1986), 78.
3. David Healy, *U.S. Expansionism: The Imperialist Urge in the 1890s* (Madison, Wisc., 1970), 46.

Acknowledgment of this new position came in various forms. In 1892, the Europeans upgraded their ministers in Washington to the rank of ambassador, tacitly recognizing America's status as a major power.[4] One year later, Congress without debate scrapped its republican inhibitions and the practices of a century by creating that rank within the U.S. foreign service, a move of more than symbolic importance. United States diplomats had long bristled at the lack of precedence accorded them in foreign courts because of their lowly rank of minister. They viewed the snubs and shabby treatment as an affront to the prestige of a rising power. An ambassador also had better access to sovereigns and prime ministers, it was argued, and could therefore negotiate more easily and effectively.[5]

The Columbian Exposition in Chicago in 1893 both symbolized and celebrated the nation's coming of age. Organized to commemorate the four-hundredth anniversary of Columbus's "discovery" of America, it was used by U.S. officials to promote trade with Latin America.[6] Its futuristic exhibits took a peek at life in the twentieth century. It displayed high culture and low, the latter including Buffalo Bill's Wild West Show, the first Ferris wheel, and the exotic performances of belly-dancer Little Egypt. It highlighted American technology and the mass culture that would be the nation's major export in the next century. Above all, it was a patriotic celebration of U.S. achievements, past, present, and to come. Frenchman Paul de Bourget was "struck dumb . . . with wonderment" by what he saw, "this wonderfully new country" in "advance of the age."[7]

Wonder and pride were increasingly tempered by fear and foreboding. During the 1890s, Americans experienced internal shocks and perceived external threats that caused profound anxieties and spurred them to intensified diplomatic activity, greater assertiveness, and overseas expansion. Ironically, just a month after the opening of the Columbian Exposition, the most severe economic crisis in its history stunned the nation. Triggered by the failure of a British banking house, the Panic of 1893 wreaked devastation across the land, causing some fifteen thousand business failures in that year alone and 17 percent unemployment. The

---

4. Paul Kennedy, *The Rise and Fall of the Great Powers: Economic Change and Military Conflict from 1500 to 2000* (New York, 1987), 194.
5. Warren Frederick Ilchman, *Professional Diplomacy in the United States: An Administrative History* (Chicago, 1961), 71–72.
6. Frank A. Cassell, "The Columbian Exposition of 1893 and United States Diplomacy in Latin America," *Mid-America: A Historical Review* 67 (October 1985), 109–24.
7. Robert Muccigrosso, *Celebrating the New World: Chicago's Columbian Exposition of 1893* (Chicago, 1998), 179, 193; Emily S. Rosenberg, *Spreading the American Dream: American Economic and Cultural Expansion, 1890–1945* (New York, 1982), 3.

depression shook the nation to its core, eroding optimism and raising serious doubts about the new industrial system.[8]

Social and political concerns combined with a malfunctioning economy to produce confusion about the present and anxiety for the future.[9] Close to a half million immigrants arrived in the United States each year in the 1880s. The ethnic makeup of these newcomers—Italians, Poles, Greeks, Jews, Hungarians—was even more unsettling to old-stock Americans than their numbers, threatening a homogenous social order. The sprawling, ugly cities they populated produced fears for the survival of a simpler, agrarian America.

Democracy itself seemed in jeopardy. At first enthusiastically hailed for their productive capacity, giant corporations such as Standard Oil, Carnegie Steel, and the Pennsylvania Railroad, and the huge banking houses such as J. P. Morgan and Co. that financed them, became increasingly suspect because of the allegedly corrupt and exploitative practices used by the so-called robber barons to build them, the enormous power they wielded, and their threat to individual enterprise. At the Chicago exposition, historian Frederick Jackson Turner presented a paper attributing American democracy to the availability of a western frontier. Coming at a time when demographers were claiming (incorrectly, as it turned out) that the continental frontier had closed, Turner's writings aroused concerns that the nation's fundamental values were in jeopardy. Such fears produced a "social malaise" that gripped the United States through much of the decade.[10]

The crisis was evidenced in various ways. The growing militancy of labor—there were 1,400 strikes in the year 1894 alone—and the use of force to suppress it produced a threat to social order that frightened solid middle-class citizens. The violence that accompanied the 1892 Homestead "massacre" in Pennsylvania, where private security forces battled workers, and the Pullman strike in Illinois two yeas later in which thirteen strikers were killed was particularly unsettling. The march on Washington of Jacob Coxey's "army" of unemployed in the spring of 1894 to demand federal relief and the Populist "revolt" of embattled southern and western farmers proposing major political and economic reforms portended a radical upheaval that might alter basic institutions.

The nation also appeared threatened from abroad. The uneasy equilibrium that had prevailed in Europe since Waterloo seemed increasingly

8. Charles S. Campbell, *The Transformation of American Foreign Relations, 1865–1900* (New York, 1976), 142.
9. Beisner, *Old Diplomacy to the New*, 74.
10. Ibid., 74–76.

endangered. The worldwide imperialist surge quickened in the 1890s. The partition of Africa neared completion. Following Japan's defeat of China in their 1894–95 war, the European powers turned to East Asia, joining their Asian newcomer in marking out spheres of influence, threatening to eliminate what remained of the helpless Middle Kingdom's sovereignty, perhaps shutting it off to American trade. Some Europeans spoke of closing ranks against a rising U.S. commercial menace. Some nations raised tariffs. Britain's threat to impose imperial preference in its vast colonial holdings portended a further shrinkage of markets deemed more essential than ever in years of depression.[11]

The gloom and anxiety of the 1890s produced a mood conducive to war and expansion. They triggered a noisy nationalism and spread-eagle patriotism, manifested in the stirring marches of John Philip Sousa and outwardly emotional displays of reverence for the flag. The word *jingoism* was coined in Britain in the 1870s. Xenophobia flourished in the United States in the 1890s in nativist attacks upon immigrants at home and verbal blasts against nations that affronted U.S. honor. For some Americans, a belligerent foreign policy offered a release for pent-up aggressions and diversion from domestic difficulties. It could "knock on the head . . . the matters which have embarrassed us at home," Massachusetts senator Henry Cabot Lodge averred.[12]

The social malaise also aroused concern about issues of manhood. The depression robbed many American men of the means to support their families. A rising generation that had not fought in the Civil War and remembered only its glories increasingly feared that industrialism, urbanization, and immigration, along with widening divisions of class and race, were sapping American males of the manly virtues deemed essential for good governance. The emergence of a militant women's movement demanding political participation further threatened men's traditional role in U.S. politics. For some jingoes, a more assertive foreign policy, war, and even the acquisition of colonies would reaffirm their manhood, restore lost pride and virility, and legitimize their traditional place in the political system. "War is healthy to a nation," an Illinois congressman proclaimed. "War is a bad thing, no doubt," Lodge added, "but there are far worse things both for nations and for men," among which he would have included dishonor and a failure vigorously to defend the nation's interests.[13]

11. Ibid., 77; Campbell, *Transformation*, 146.
12. Healy, *U.S. Expansionism*, 108.
13. Kristin L. Hoganson, *Fighting for American Manhood: How Gender Politics Provoked the Spanish-American and Philippine-American Wars* (New Haven, Conn., 1998), 35–40.

Changes at home and abroad convinced some Americans of the need to reexamine long-standing foreign policy assumptions. The further shrinkage of distances, the advent of menacing weapons, the emergence of new powers such as Germany and Japan, and the surge of imperialist activity persuaded some military leaders that the United States no longer enjoyed freedom from foreign threat. Isolated from civilian society, increasingly professionalized, their own interests appearing to be happily aligned with those of the nation, they pushed for a reexamination of national defense policy and the building of a modern military machine. They promoted the novel idea (for Americans, at least) that even in time of peace a nation must prepare for war. Army officers added Germany and Japan to the nation's list of potential enemies and warned of emerging threats from European imperialism, commercial rivalries, and foreign challenges to an American-controlled canal. They began to push for an expanded, more professional regular army based on European models.[14]

Advocates for the new navy offered more compelling arguments and achieved greater results. The most fervent and influential late nineteenth-century advocate of sea power was Capt. Alfred Thayer Mahan, son of an early superintendent of West Point. A mediocre sailor who detested sea duty, the younger Mahan salvaged a flagging career by accepting the post of senior lecturer at the new Naval War College. While putting together a course in naval history, he wrote his classic *The Influence of Seapower upon History* (1890). Mahan argued that the United States must abandon its defensive, "continentalist" strategy based on harbor defense and commerce raiding for a more outward-looking approach. Britain had achieved great-power status by controlling the seas and dominating global commerce. So too, he contended, the United States must compete aggressively for world trade, build a large merchant marine, acquire colonies for raw materials, markets, and naval bases, and construct a modern battleship fleet, "the arm of offensive power, which alone enables a country to extend its influence outward." Such moves would ensure U.S. prosperity by keeping sea lanes open in time of war and peace. A skilled publicist as well as an influential strategic thinker, Mahan won worldwide acclaim in the 1890s; his book became an international best seller. At home, a naval renaissance was already under way. Mahan's ideas provided a persuasive rationale for the new battleship navy and a more aggressive U.S. foreign policy.[15]

14. Beisner, *Old Diplomacy to the New*, 79; Allen R. Millett and Peter Maslowski, *For the Common Defense: A Military History of the United States of America* (New York, 1984), 255–58.
15. Russell F. Weigley, *The American Way of War: A History of United States Military Strategy and Policy* (New York, 1977), 78.

Some civilians also called for an activist foreign policy, even for abandoning long-standing strictures against alliances and inhibitions against overseas expansion. Such policies had done well enough "when we were an embryo nation," a senator observed, but the mere fact that the United States had become a major power now demanded their abandonment.[16] As a rising great power, the United States had interests that must be defended. It must assume the responsibility for its own welfare and for world order that went with its new status. "The mission of this country is not merely to pose but to act . . . ," former attorney general and secretary of state Richard Olney proclaimed in 1898, "to forego no fitting opportunity to further the progress of civilization."[17]

Since Jefferson's time, Americans had sought to deal with pressing internal difficulties through expansion, and in the 1890s they increasingly looked outward for solutions to domestic problems. With the disappearance of the frontier, it was argued, new outlets must be found abroad for America's energy and enterprise. In a world driven by Darwinian struggle where only the strongest survived, the United States must compete aggressively. The Panic of 1893 marked the coming of age of the "glut thesis." America's traditional interest in foreign trade now became almost an obsession. Businessmen increasingly looked to Washington for assistance.[18] Many Americans agreed that to compete effectively in world markets the United States needed an isthmian canal and island bases to protect it. In the tense atmosphere of the 1890s, some advocates of the so-called large policy even urged acquisition of colonies.

The idea of overseas empire ran up against the nation's tradition of anticolonialism, and in the 1890s, as so often before, Americans heatedly debated the means by which they could best fulfill their providential destiny. A rising elite keenly interested in foreign policy followed closely similar debates on empire in Britain and adapted their arguments to the United States.[19] Some continued to insist that the nation should focus on perfecting its domestic institutions to provide an example to others. But as Americans became more conscious of their rising power, others insisted they had a God-given obligation to spread the blessings of their superior institutions to less fortunate peoples across the world. God was "preparing in our civilization the die with which to stamp nations," Congregationalist

16. Beisner, *Old Diplomacy to the New*, 78.
17. Ibid., 84.
18. Ibid., 77; also Walter LaFeber, *The New Empire: An Interpretation of American Expansion, 1866–1898* (Ithaca, N.Y., 1967), especially 190–97.
19. Ernest R. May, *American Imperialism: A Speculative Essay* (rev. ed., Chicago, 1991).

minister Josiah Strong proclaimed, and was "preparing mankind to receive our impress."[20]

Racism and popular notions of Anglo-Saxonism and the white man's burden helped justify the imposition of U.S. rule on "backward" populations. Even while the United States and Britain continued to tangle over various issues, Americans hailed the blood ties and common heritage of the English-speaking peoples. According to Anglo-Saxonist ideas, Americans and Britons stood together at the top of a hierarchy of races, superior in intellect, industry, and morality. Some Americans took pride in the glory of the British Empire while predicting that in time they would supplant it. The United States was bound to become "a greater England with a nobler destiny," proclaimed Indiana senator and staunch expansionist Albert Jeremiah Beveridge.[21] Convictions of Anglo-Saxonism helped rationalize harsh measures toward lesser races. While disfranchising and segregating African Americans at home, some Americans promoted the idea of extending civilization to lesser peoples abroad. Recent experiences with Native Americans provided handy precedents. Expansionists thus easily reconciled imperialism with traditional principles. The economic penetration or even colonization of less developed areas would allegedly benefit those peoples by bringing them the advantages of U.S. institutions. Arguing for the Americanization and eventual annexation of Cuba, expansionist James Harrison Wilson put it all together: "Let us take this course because it is noble and just and right, and besides because it will pay."[22]

The new mood was early manifest in the assertive diplomacy of President Benjamin Harrison and Secretary of State James G. Blaine. In response to attacks on American missionaries, Harrison joined other great powers in seeking to coerce the Chinese government to respect the rights of foreigners. He also ordered the construction of specially designed gunboats to show the flag in Chinese waters. The bullying of Haiti and Santo Domingo in a futile quest for a Caribbean naval base, the bellicose handling of minor incidents with Italy and Chile, and the abortive 1893 move to annex Hawaii all indicated a distinct shift in the tone of U.S. policy and the adoption of new and more aggressive methods.

A second Grover Cleveland administration (1893–97) killed the Republican effort to acquire Hawaii. Anti-expansionist and anti-annexation, Cleveland had a strong sense of right and wrong in such matters. He

20. Quoted in Healy, U.S. Expansionism, 38.
21. Michael H. Hunt, Ideology and U.S. Foreign Policy (New Haven, Conn., 1987), 77–81.
22. Healy, U.S. Expansionism, 95.

recalled the treaty of annexation from the Senate and dispatched James Blount of Georgia on a secret fact-finding mission to Hawaii. Blount also opposed overseas expansion both in principle and on racial grounds. "We have nothing in common with those people," he once exclaimed of Venezuelans. He ignored the new Hawaiian government's frenzied warnings that Japan was waiting to seize the islands if the United States demurred. He concluded, correctly, that most Hawaiians opposed annexation and that the change of government had been engineered by Americans to protect their own profits. His report firmly opposed annexation.[23] Facing a divided Congress and a nation absorbed in economic crisis, Cleveland was inclined to restore Queen Liliuokalani to power, but he also worried about the fate of the rebels. The queen had threatened to have their heads—and their property. Unable to get from either side the assurances he sought and unwilling to decide himself, he tossed the issue back to Congress. After months of debate, the legislators could agree only on the desirability of recognizing the existing Hawaiian government. Cleveland reluctantly went along.[24]

Even the normally cautious and anti-expansionist Cleveland was not immune to the spirit of the age. In January 1894, his administration injected U.S. power into an internal struggle in Brazil. Suspecting (probably incorrectly) that Britain sought to use the conflict to enhance its position in that important Latin American nation, Cleveland dispatched five ships of the new navy, the most imposing fleet the nation had ever sent to sea, to break a rebel blockade and protect U.S. ships and exports. When the navy moved on to show the flag elsewhere, private interests took on the task of gunboat diplomacy. With Cleveland's acquiescence or tacit support, the colorful industrialist, shipbuilder, and arms merchant Charles Flint equipped merchant and passenger ships with the most up-to-date weapons, including a "dynamite gun" that could fire a 980-pound projectile. He dispatched his "fleet" to the coast of Brazil. The mere threat of the notorious dynamite gun helped cow the rebels and keep the government in power, solidifying U.S. influence in Brazil. In November 1894, Brazilians laid the cornerstone to a monument in Rio de Janeiro to James Monroe and his doctrine.[25]

23. Tennant S. McWilliams, "James H. Blount, the South, and Hawaiian Annexation," *Pacific Historical Review* 57 (February 1988), 25–46.
24. Richard E. Welch Jr., *The Presidencies of Grover Cleveland* (Lawrence, Kans., 1988), 171–75.
25. Steven C. Topik, *Trade and Gunboats: The United States and Brazil in the Age of Empire* (Stanford, Calif., 1996), 120–76.

The following year, the Cleveland administration intruded in a boundary dispute between Britain and Venezuela over British Guiana, rendering a new and more expansive interpretation of that doctrine. The dispute had dragged on for years. Venezuela numerous times sought to draw the United States into it by speaking of violations of Monroe's statement. Each time, Washington had politely declined, and it is not entirely clear why Cleveland now took up a challenge his predecessors had sensibly resisted. He had a soft spot for the underdog. He may have been moved by his fervent anti-imperialism. He was undoubtedly responding to domestic pressures, stirred up in part by the lobbying of a shady former U.S. diplomat now working for Venezuela. Britain appeared particularly aggressive in the hemisphere, and the United States was increasingly sensitive to its position. Some Americans feared the British might use the dispute to secure control of the Orinoco River and close it to trade. More generally, Cleveland responded to the broad threat of a surging European imperialism and the fear that the Europeans might turn their attention to Latin America, thus directly threatening U.S. interests. He determined to use the dispute to assert U.S. preeminence in the Western Hemisphere.[26]

Significantly, Richard Olney replaced Walter Gresham as secretary of state at this point. Not known for tact or finesse—as attorney general, Olney had just forcibly suppressed the Pullman strike—he quickly set the tone for U.S. intrusion. In what Cleveland called his "twenty-inch gun" (new Dreadnought battleships were equipped with twelve-inch guns), Olney's July 20, 1895, note insisted in prosecutor's language that the Monroe Doctrine justified U.S. intervention and pressed Britain to arbitrate. More important, it claimed hegemonic power. Today "the United States is practically sovereign on this continent," he proclaimed, "and its fiat is law upon the subjects to which it confines its interposition." The *New York World* spoke excitedly of the "blaze" that swept the nation after Olney's message.[27]

Even more surprising than the fact of U.S. intrusion and the force of Olney's blast was Britain's eventual acquiescence. At first shocked that the United States should take such an extravagant stand on a "subject so comparatively small," Prime Minister Lord Salisbury delayed four months before replying. He then lectured an upstart nation on how to behave in a grown-up world, rejecting its claims and telling it to mind its

26. Welch, *Cleveland*, 187–90; Beisner, *Old Diplomacy to the New*, 112–15. See also LaFeber, *New Empire*, 243–50.
27. Robert C. Hilderbrand, *Power and the People: Executive Management of Public Opinion in Foreign Affairs, 1877–1921* (Chapel Hill, N.C., 1981), 8.

own business. Now "mad clean through," as he put it, Cleveland responded in kind. On both sides, as so often in the nineteenth century, talk of war abounded. Once again, U.S. timing was excellent. Britain was distracted by crises in the Middle East, East Asia, and especially South Africa, where war loomed with the Boers. As before, the threat of war evoked from both nations ties of kinship that grew stronger throughout the century. London proposed, then quickly dropped over U.S. objections, a conference to define the meaning of the Monroe Doctrine, a significant concession. It also tacitly conceded the U.S. definition of the Monroe Doctrine and its hegemony in the hemisphere.[28]

The larger principle more or less settled, the two nations, not surprisingly, resolved their differences at the expense of Venezuela. Neither Anglo-Saxon country had much respect for the third party, "a mongrel state," Thomas Bayard, then serving in London as the first U.S. ambassador, exclaimed dismissively. They were not about to leave questions of war and peace in its hands. Britain agreed to arbitrate once the United States accepted its conditions for arbitration. The two nations then imposed on an outraged Venezuela a treaty providing for arbitration and giving it no representation on the commission. Britain got much of what it wanted except for a strip of land controlling the Orinoco River, precisely what Washington sought to keep from it. Venezuela got very little. Despite Olney's bombast, the United States secured British recognition of its expanded interpretation of the Monroe Doctrine and a larger share of the trade of northern South America. Olney's blast further announced to the world and especially to Britain that the United States was prepared to establish its place among the great powers, whatever Europeans might think. It elevated the Monroe Doctrine to near holy writ at home and marked the end of British efforts to contest U.S. preeminence in the Caribbean.[29]

From 1895 to 1898, the expansionist program was clearly articulated and well publicized and gained numerous adherents. In the 1896 election campaign between Republican William McKinley of Ohio and Democrat William Jennings Bryan of Nebraska, domestic issues, especially Bryan's pet program, the coinage of silver, held center stage. But the Republican platform set forth a full-fledged expansionist agenda: European withdrawal from the hemisphere; a voluntary union of English-speaking

28. Lars Schoultz, *Beneath the United States: A History of U.S. Policy Toward Latin America* (Cambridge, Mass., 1998), 119.
29. Ibid., 124; Welch, *Cleveland*, 192; Campbell, *Transformation*, 221; LaFeber, *New Empire*, 278–83.

peoples in North America, meaning Canada; construction of a U.S.-controlled isthmian canal; acquisition of the Virgin Islands; annexation of Hawaii; and independence for Cuba. The War of 1898 provided an opportunity to implement much of this agenda—and more.[30]

II

What was once called the Spanish-American War was the pivotal event of a pivotal decade, bringing the "large policy" to fruition and marking the United States as a world power. Few events in U.S. history have been as encrusted in myth and indeed trivialized. The very title is a misnomer, of course, since it omits Cuba and the Philippines, both key players in the conflict. Despite four decades of "revisionist" scholarship, popular writing continues to attribute the war to a sensationalist "yellow press," which allegedly whipped into martial frenzy an ignorant public that in turn drove weak leaders into an unnecessary war.[31] The war itself has been reduced to comic opera, its consequences dismissed as an aberration. Such treatment undermines the notion of war by design, allowing Americans to cling to the idea of their own noble purposes and sparing them responsibility for a war they came to see as unnecessary and imperialist results they came to regard as unsavory.[32] Such interpretations also ignore the extent to which the war and its consequences represented a logical culmination of major trends in nineteenth-century U.S. foreign policy. It was less a case of the United States coming upon greatness almost inadvertently than of it pursuing its destiny deliberately and purposefully.[33]

The war grew out of a revolution in Cuba that was itself in many ways a product of the island's geographical proximity to and economic dependence on the United States. As with the Hawaiian revolution, U.S. tariff policies played a key role. The 1890 reciprocity treaty with Spain sparked an economic boom on the island. But the 1894 Wilson-Gorman tariff, by depriving Cuban sugar of its privileged position in the U.S. market, inflicted economic devastation and stirred widespread political

30. Joseph A. Fry, "Phases of Empire: Late Nineteenth-Century U.S. Foreign Relations," in Charles W. Calhoun, ed., *The Gilded Age: Essays on the Origins of Modern America* (Wilmington, Del., 1996), 277.

31. *New York Times*, February 15, 1998.

32. Louis A. Pérez, "The Meaning of the *Maine*: Causation and the Historiography of the Spanish-American War," *Pacific Historical Review* 58 (August 1989), 319–21.

33. Ernest R. May, *Imperial Democracy: The Emergence of America as a Great Power* (New York, 1973), 270, and the commentary in Thomas G. Paterson, "United States Intervention in Cuba, 1898: Interpretations of the Spanish-American-Cuban-Filipino War," *History Teacher* 29 (May 1996), 345.

unrest. Revolutionary sentiment had long smoldered. In 1895, exiles such as the poet, novelist, and patriot leader José Martí returned from the United States to foment rebellion. Concerned about possible U.S. designs on Cuba, Martí, Máximo Gómez, and Antonio Maceo sought a quick victory through scorched earth policies—"abominable devastation," they called it—seeking to turn Cuba into a desert and by doing so drive Spain from the island. Spanish general Valeriano "Butcher" Weyler retaliated with his brutal *"reconcentrado"* policies, herding peasants into fortified areas where they could be controlled. The results were catastrophic: Ninety-five thousand people died from disease and malnutrition. On the other side, weather, disease, and Cuban arms took a fearsome toll on young and poorly prepared Spanish forces, an estimated thirty-five thousand of them killed each year. The rebels used the machete with especially terrifying effect, littering the sugar and pineapple fields with the heads of Spanish soldiers.[34]

From the outset, this brutal insurgent war had an enormous impact in the United States. Since Jefferson's day, Cuba's economic and strategic importance had made it an object of U.S. attention. Like Florida, Texas, and Hawaii, the island was Americanized in the late nineteenth century. The Cuban elite was increasingly educated in the United States. By the end of the century, the United States dominated Cuba economically. Exports to the United States increased from 42 percent of the total in 1859 to 87 percent in 1897. United States investments have been estimated at $50 million, trade at $100 million. The war threatened American-owned sugar estates, mines, and ranches and the safety of U.S. citizens. A junta located mainly in Florida and New York and led by Cuban expatriates, some of them U.S. citizens, lobbied tirelessly for *Cuba Libre*, sold war bonds in the United States, and smuggled weapons onto the island. Cubans naturalized as U.S. citizens returned to fight. Not surprisingly, Cubans had mixed feelings about U.S. assistance. Some conservative leaders lacked confidence in their peoples' ability to govern themselves and feared chaos if the African, former slave population took power. They were amenable to U.S. tutelage—even annexation—to maintain their positions and property. Others like Martí, Gómez, and Maceo, while eager for American backing, feared that military intervention might lead to U.S. domination. "To change masters is not to be free," Martí warned.[35]

34. Alistair Hennessey, "The Origins of the Cuban Revolt," in Angel Smith and Emma Dávila-Cox, eds., *The Crisis of 1898: Colonial Redistribution and Nationalist Mobilization* (New York, 1998), 81–88.
35. Louis A. Pérez Jr., *Cuba Between Empires, 1878–1902* (Pittsburgh, 1983), 94.

The "yellow press" (so named for the "Yellow Kid," a popular cartoon character that appeared in its newly colored pages) helped make Cuba a cause célèbre in the United States. The mass-circulation newspaper came into its own in the 1890s. The New York dailies of William Randolph Hearst and Joseph Pulitzer engaged in a fierce, head-to-head competition with few restraints and fewer scruples about the truth. They eagerly disseminated stories furnished by the junta. Talented artists such as Frederic Remington and writers such as Richard Harding Davis portrayed the revolution as a simple morality play featuring the oppression of freedom-loving Cubans by evil Spaniards.[36] The yellow press undoubtedly contributed to a war spirit, but Americans in areas where it did not circulate also strongly sympathized with Cuba. The Dubuque, Iowa, *Times*, for example, appealed to "men in whose breast the fire of patriotism burns" for the "annihilation of the Spanish dogs."[37] The press did not create the differences between Cuba, Spain, and the United States that proved insoluble. War likely would have occurred without its agitation.

Sympathy for Cuba and outrage with Spain produced demands for intervention and war. Anxieties in the country at large fed a martial fever. Businessmen worried that the Cuban problem might delay recovery from the depression. Some Americans, like the Cuban Creoles, feared that an insurgent victory would threaten U.S. investments and trade. The rising furor quickly took on political ramifications. Divided Democrats sought to reunite their party over the Cuban issue and embarrass the Republicans; Republicans tried to head off the opposition. Elites increasingly agreed that the United States must act. National pride, a resurgent sense of destiny, and a conviction that the United States as a rising world power must take responsibility for world events in its area of influence gave an increasing urgency to the Cuban crisis.[38]

From the time he took office in 1897, President William McKinley was absorbed in the Cuban problem. Once caricatured as a weakling, the puppet of big business, McKinley has received his due in recent years. His retiring demeanor and refusal to promote himself concealed strength of character and resoluteness of purpose. A plain, down-home man of simple tastes, McKinley had extraordinary political skills. His greatest asset was his understanding of people and his ability to deal with them. Accessible, kindly, and a good listener, he was a master of the art of leading by indirection, letting others seem to persuade him of positions he had

36. Schoultz, *Beneath the United States*, 131.
37. Hilderbrand, *Power and the People*, 23.
38. Lewis L. Gould, *The Presidency of William McKinley* (Lawrence, Kans., 1980), 63.

already taken, appearing to follow while actually leading. "He had a way of handling men," his secretary of war Elihu Root observed, "so that they thought his ideas were their own."[39] He entered the presidency with a clearly defined agenda, including the expansionist planks of the Republican platform. In many ways the first modern president, he used the instruments of his office as no one had since Lincoln, dominating his cabinet, controlling Congress, and skillfully employing the press to build political support for his policies.[40]

For two years, McKinley patiently negotiated with Spain while holding off domestic pressures for war. Reversing America's long-standing acceptance of Spanish sovereignty, he sought by steadily increasing diplomatic pressure to end Weyler's brutal measures and drive Spain from Cuba without war. For a time, he appeared to succeed. The Madrid government recalled Weyler and promised Cuban autonomy. But his success was illusory. By this time, Spain was willing to concede some measure of self-government. But the insurgents, having spent much blood and treasure, would accept nothing less than complete independence. Spanish officials feared that to abandon the "ever faithful isle," the last remnant of their once glorious American empire, would bring down the government and perhaps the monarchy. They tried to hold off the United States by a policy of "procrastination and dissimulation," deluding themselves that somehow things would work out.[41]

Two incidents in early 1898 brought the two nations to the brink of war. On February 9, Hearst's New York World published a letter written by Enrique Dupuy de Lôme, Spanish minister in Washington, to friends in Cuba describing McKinley as weak and a bidder for the crowd and speaking cynically of Spain's promises of reforms in Cuba. It was a private letter, of course, and Americans themselves had publicly said much worse things about McKinley. But in the supercharged atmosphere of 1898, this "Worst Insult to the United States in Its History," as one newspaper hyperbolically headlined it, provoked popular outrage. More important, de Lôme's cynical comments about reforms caused McKinley to doubt Spain's good faith.[42]

39. Hilderbrand, Power and the People, 18, 40.
40. Ibid., 10–11; Gould, McKinley, 56; Joseph A. Fry, "William McKinley and the Coming of the Spanish-American War: A Study of the Besmirching and Redemption of an Historical Image," Diplomatic History 3 (Winter 1979) 77–97.
41. Gould, McKinley, 61–62.
42. H. Wayne Morgan, America's Road to Empire: The War with Spain and Overseas Expansion (New York, 1965), 41–43.

Less than a week later, the battleship USS *Maine* mysteriously exploded in Havana harbor, killing 266 American sailors. The catastrophe almost certainly resulted from an internal explosion, but Americans pinned responsibility elsewhere. "Remember the *Maine*, to hell with Spain" became a popular rallying cry. Without bothering to examine the facts, the press blamed the explosion on Spain. Theater audiences wept, stamped their feet, and cheered when patriotic songs were played. Jingoes wrapped themselves in flags and demanded war. When McKinley pleaded for restraint, he was burned in effigy. Congress threatened to take matters into its own hands and recognize the Cuban rebels or even declare war.[43]

McKinley's last-ditch efforts to achieve his aims without war failed. Phrasing his demands in the language of diplomacy to leave room for maneuver, he insisted that Spain must get out of Cuba or face war. In Spain also, opposition to concessions grew. The Spanish resented being blamed for the *Maine*. The threat of U.S. intervention in Cuba provoked among students, middle-class urbanites, and even some working-class people a surge of patriotism not unlike that in the United States. A jingoist spirit marked bullfights and fiestas. Street demonstrations rocked major Iberian cities. In Málaga, angry mobs threw rocks at the U.S. consulate amidst shouts of *"Viva España! Muerte a los Yanques! Abajo el armisticio!"* As in the United States, the press incited popular outrage.[44] Fearing for its survival and even for the monarchy, the government recognized that it could not win a war with the United States and feared disastrous consequences. In keeping with the spirit of the era, however, it preferred the honor of war to the ignominy of surrender. It offered last-minute concessions to buy time but refused to surrender on the fundamental issue.

Since he left scant written record, it is difficult to determine why McKinley finally decided upon war. He was understandably sensitive to the mounting political pressures and stung by charges of spinelessness. But he appears to have found other, more compelling reasons to act. Historians disagree sharply on the state of the insurgency, some arguing that the rebels were close to victory, others that the war had ground into a bloody stalemate.[45]

43. Hyman G. Rickover, *How the Battleship* Maine *Was Destroyed* (Washington, 1976). For the reaction, see May, *Imperial Democracy,* 139–47.

44. John L. Offner, *An Unwanted War: The Diplomacy of the United States and Spain over Cuba, 1895–1898* (Chapel Hill, N.C., 1992), 191; Angel Smith, "The People and the Nation: Nationalist Mobilization and the Crisis of 1895–98 in Spain," in Smith and Dávila-Cox, *Crisis of 1898,* 164.

45. Offner, *Unwanted War,* 227–28; Pérez, *Cuba Between Empires,* 177–78; Louis A. Pérez Jr., *The War of 1898: The United States and Cuba in History and Historiography* (Chapel Hill, N.C., 1998), 89.

McKinley found either prospect unacceptable. An insurgent triumph threatened American property and investments as well as ultimate U.S. control of Cuba. Memories of another Caribbean revolution a century earlier had not died, and in the eyes of some Americans Cuba raised the grim specter of a second Haiti. Continued stalemate risked more destruction on the island and an unsettled situation at home. It was therefore not so much the case of an aroused public forcing a weak president into an unnecessary war as of McKinley choosing war to defend vital U.S. interests and remove "a constant menace to our peace" in an area "right at our door."[46]

The ambiguous manner in which the administration went to war belied its steadfastness of purpose. True to form, the president did not ask Congress for a declaration. Rather, he let the legislators take the initiative, the only instance in U.S. history in which that has happened. He sought "a neutral intervention" that would leave him maximum freedom of action in Cuba. His supporters in Congress warned that it would be a "grave mistake" to recognize a "people of whom we know practically nothing." They affirmed that the president must be in a position to "insist upon such a government as will be of practical advantage to the United States." McKinley successfully headed off those zealots who sought to couple intervention with recognition of Cuban independence. But he could not thwart the so-called Teller Amendment providing that the United States would not annex Cuba once the war ended. The amendment derived from various forces, those who opposed annexing territory containing large numbers of blacks and Catholics, those who sincerely supported Cuban independence, and representatives of the domestic sugar business, including sponsor Senator Henry Teller of Colorado, who feared Cuban competition. McKinley did not like the amendment, but he acquiesced. Cubans remained suspicious, warning that the Americans were a "people who do not work for nothing."[47]

III

By modern military standards, the War of 1898 did not amount to much. On the U.S. side, the last vestiges of nineteenth-century voluntarism and amateurism collided with an incipient twentieth-century military professionalism, creating confusion, mismanagement, and indeed, at times, comic opera. Volunteers responded in such numbers that they could not be absorbed by a sclerotic military bureaucracy. Large numbers of troops languished in squalid camps where they fought each other and eventu-

46. Gould, McKinley, 85.
47. Pérez, Cuba Between Empires, 188–89.

Advance on Santiago de Cuba

— Shafter's advance

El Caney
Kettle Hill
San Juan Hill
Santiago de Cuba
Santiago Bay
San Juan R.
Sevilla
Las Guásimas
Siboney
Daiquirí
CARIBBEAN SEA

3 Miles
0 1 2 3
0 1 2 3 Kilometers

ATLANTIC OCEAN

PUERTO RICO
San Juan
Guánica

HAITI
DOMINICAN REPUBLIC
Port-au-Prince
Santo Domingo
Miles

CARIBBEAN SEA

Sampson
Santiago de Cuba
Toral
Cervera (from Spain)
Sampson
Shafter

JAMAICA

BAHAMA ISLANDS

CUBA

ISLE OF PINES

Havana
Shafter (from Norfolk)

FLORIDA (U.S.)
Tampa
Key West
Shafter

GULF OF MEXICO

0 50 100 150 200 Miles
0 50 100 150 200 Kilometers

War of 1898, Caribbean Theater

—— American forces
--- Spanish forces

ally drifted home. Americans arrived in Cuba's tropical summer sun in woolen uniforms left over from the Civil War. They were fed a form of canned beef variously described as "embalmed" and "nauseating." The U.S. commander, Gen. William Shafter, weighed more than three hundred pounds and resembled a "floating tent." Mounting his horse required a complicated system of ropes and pulleys, a feat of real engineering ingenuity.

Despite ineptitude and mismanagement, victory came easily, causing journalist Richard Harding Davis to observe that God looked after drunkards, babies, and Americans. With McKinley's approval, Assistant Secretary of the Navy Theodore Roosevelt had ordered Adm. George Dewey's fleet to steam to the Philippines. In a smashing victory that set the tone for and came to symbolize the war, Dewey's six new warships crushed the decrepit Spanish squadron in Manila Bay, setting off wild celebrations at home, sealing the doom of Spain's empire in the Philippines, and creating an opportunity for and enthusiasm about expansionism. Victory in Cuba did not come so easily. United States forces landed near Santiago without resistance, the result of luck as much as design. But they met stubborn Spanish resistance while advancing inland and in taking the city suffered heavy losses from Spanish fire and especially disease. Exhausted from three years of fighting Cubans, Spanish forces had no desire to take on fresh U.S. troops. Food shortages, mounting debt, political disarray, and a conspicuous lack of support from the European great powers sapped Spain's enthusiasm for war.[48] It took less than four months for U.S. forces to conquer Cuba (just as disease began to decimate the invading force). Victory cost a mere 345 killed in action, 5,000 lost to illness, and an estimated $250 million.

The ease and decisiveness of the victory intoxicated Americans, stoking an already overheated chauvinism. "It was a splendid little war," Ambassador John Hay chortled from London (giving the conflict an enduring label), "begun with the highest motives, carried on with magnificent intelligence and spirit, favored by that fortune which loves the brave." "No war in history has accomplished so much in so short a time with so little loss," concurred the U.S. ambassador to France. The ease of victory confirmed the rising view that the nation stood on the brink of greatness.[49]

48. A good military history is David F. Trask, *The War with Spain in 1898* (New York, 1981).
49. Walter Millis, *The Martial Spirit* (New York, 1931), 340; Morgan, *Road to Empire*, 83.

In the national mythology, the acquisition of empire from a war often dismissed with caricature has been viewed as accidental or aberrational, an ad hoc response to situations that had not been anticipated. In fact, the administration conducted the war with a clarity and resoluteness of purpose that belied its comic opera qualities. The first modern commander in chief, McKinley created a War Room on the second floor of the White House and used fifteen telephone lines and the telegraph to coordinate the Washington bureaucracy and maintain direct contact with U.S. forces in Cuba.[50] More important, he used the war to advance America's status as a world power and achieve its expansionist objectives. He set out to remove Spain from the Western Hemisphere, completing a process begun one hundred years earlier. Moving with characteristic stealth, he kept rebel forces in Cuba and the Philippines at arm's length to ensure maximum U.S. control and freedom of choice. Until the war ended, he asserted, "we must keep all we get; when the war is over we must keep what we want."[51]

McKinley used the exigencies of war to fulfill the old aim of annexing Hawaii. Upon taking office, he had declared annexation but a matter of time—not a new departure, he correctly affirmed, but a "consummation."[52] "We need Hawaii as much as in its day we needed California. It was Manifest Destiny," he stated on another occasion.[53] A perceived threat from Japan underscored the urgency. Hawaii had encouraged the immigration of Japanese workers to meet a labor shortage, but by the mid-1890s an influx once welcomed had aroused concern. When the government sought to restrict further immigration, a Japan puffed up by victory over China vigorously protested and dispatched a warship to back up its words. McKinley sent a new treaty of annexation to the Senate in June 1897, provoking yet another Japanese protest and a mini war scare (one U.S. naval officer actually predicted a Japanese surprise attack on the Hawaiian Islands). Advocates of annexation insisted that the United States must "act NOW to preserve the results of its past policy, and to prevent the dominancy of Hawaii by a foreign people."[54] The anti-imperialist opposition had the votes to forestall a two-thirds majority. The administration thus followed John Tyler's 1844 precedent by seeking a joint

50. Gould, McKinley, 93.
51. Ibid., 101.
52. Ibid., 49.
53. María Dolores Elizalde, "1898: The Coordinates of the Spanish Crisis in the Pacific," in Smith and Dávila-Cox, Crisis of 1898, 191.
54. Campbell, Transformation, 237.

resolution. In any event, by early 1898 the emerging crisis with Spain put a premium on caution.

What had once been a deterrent soon spurred action. Relentlessly pursuing annexation, Hawaii's pro-American government opened its ports and resources to the United States instead of proclaiming neutrality. The war made obvious Hawaii's strategic importance. Worries about German and Japanese expansion in the Pacific reinforced the point. Hawaii assumed a major role in supplying U.S. troops in the Philippines. McKinley even talked of annexing it under presidential war powers. Shortly after the outbreak of war, he submitted to Congress a resolution for annexation. Legislators declared Hawaii a "naval and military necessity," the "key to the Pacific"; not to annex would be "national folly," one exclaimed. The resolution passed in July by sizeable majorities. The *haole* (non-Hawaiian) ruling classes cheered. Some native Hawaiians lamented that "Annexation is Rotten Bananas." One group issued a futile protest against "annexation . . . without reference to the consent of the people of the Hawaiian Islands." The Women's Patriotic League sewed hatbands declaring "*Ku'u Hae Aloha*"(I Love My Flag).[55]

While fighting in Cuba, the United States also moved swiftly to take Puerto Rico before the war ended. Named "wealthy port" by its first Spanish governor, the island occupied a commanding position between the two ocean passages. It was called the "Malta of the Caribbean" because it could guard an isthmian canal and the Pacific coast as that Mediterranean island protected Egypt. In contrast to Cuba, the United States had little trade with and few investments in Puerto Rico. But Blaine had put it on his list of necessary acquisitions, mainly as a base to guard a canal. By preventing the United States from taking Cuba, the Teller Amendment probably increased the importance of Puerto Rico. Once the United States was at war with Spain, Puerto Rico provided another chance to remove European influence from the hemisphere. From his debarkation point in Texas, Rough Rider and ardent expansionist Theodore Roosevelt urged his imperialist cohort Senator Lodge to "prevent any talk of peace until we get Porto Rico and the Philippines as well as secure the independence of Cuba."[56] Once war began, some businessmen recommended taking Puerto Rico for its commercial and strategic value. Protestant missionaries expressed interest in opening the island—

55. Ibid., 295; Mehmed Ali, "Ho'ohui'aina Palaka Mai'a: Remembering Hawaiian Annexation One Hundred Years Ago," *Journal of Hawaiian History* 32 (1998), 141–54.
56. Healy, *U.S. Expansionism*, 112.

already heavily Roman Catholic—to the "Gospel of the Lord Jesus Christ."[57] By late June, if not earlier, the administration was committed to its acquisition, ostensibly as payment for a costly intervention.

The main U.S. concern was to seize Puerto Rico before Spain sued for peace. On July 7, the White House ordered Gen. Nelson A. Miles to proceed to Puerto Rico as soon as victory in Cuba was secured. Miles landed at Guánica on July 25 without significant opposition—indeed, the invaders were greeted with shouts of "*viva*" and given provisions. Puerto Rico was relatively peaceful and prosperous. Its people enjoyed a large measure of autonomy under Spain. They looked favorably upon the United States; many were prepared to accept its tutelage. Thus even after the invaders made clear they intended to take possession of the island, they encountered only sporadic and scattered opposition and suffered few casualties. United States forces characterized the invasion as a "picnic." The only shortage was of American flags for the Puerto Ricans to wave.[58] The occupation was completed just in time. On August 7, Spain asked for peace terms. It had hoped to hang on to Puerto Rico, but the United States insisted upon taking the island in lieu of "pecuniary indemnity."[59]

The island land grab extended to the Pacific. Increased great-power interest in East Asia heightened the importance of the numerous islands scattered along Pacific sea routes. Prior to 1898, Germany, Great Britain, and the United States were already engaged in a lively competition. To secure a coaling station for ships en route to the southwest Pacific, McKinley on June 3 ordered the navy to seize one of the Mariana Islands strategically positioned between Hawaii and the Philippines. Three U.S. ships subsequently stopped at Guam. In a scene worthy of a Gilbert and Sullivan operetta, they announced their arrival by firing their guns. Not knowing the two nations were at war, the Spanish garrison apologized for not being able to answer what they thought was an American salute because they had no ammunition. Spanish defenders were taken prisoner and the island seized. With Guam and the Philippines, the United States saw the need for a cable station to better communicate with its distant possessions. Wake Atoll, a tiny piece of uninhabited land in the central Pacific, seemed suitable. Although Germany had strong claims, U.S. naval officers seized Wake for the United States in January 1899. Mainly

57. Julius W. Pratt, *Expansionists of 1898* (Chicago, 1964), 274, 277, 287.
58. Millis, *Martial Spirit*, 335–38; Emma Dávila-Cox, "Puerto Rico in the Hispanic-Cuban-American War: Re-assessing 'the Picnic,' " in Smith and Dávila-Cox, *Crisis of 1898*, 115–18.
59. Pratt, *Expansionists of 1898*, 330.

eager to solidify its claims to Samoa, Germany did not contest the U.S. claim. As it turned out, Wake Island did not prove feasible for a cable relay station. The United States did nothing more to establish its sovereignty.[60]

McKinley moved with more circumspection on the Philippines. It remains unclear exactly when he decided to annex the islands. He first hinted they might be left in Spanish hands; the United States would settle for a port. He later suggested that the issue might be negotiated. Even before he received official confirmation of Dewey's victory, however, he dispatched twenty thousand soldiers to establish U.S. authority in the Philippines. Permitting missionary and business expansionists to persuade him of what he may already have believed, he apparently decided as early as the summer of 1898 to take all the islands. Moving with customary indirection, he helped shape the outcome he sought. He used extended speaking tours through the Middle West and South to mobilize public opinion. He stacked the peace commission with expansionists. He made a conscious decision appear the result of fate and destiny, proclaiming by the time negotiations began that he could see "but one plain path of duty—the acceptance of the archipelago." In December 1898, his negotiators thus imposed on a reluctant but hapless Spain the Treaty of Paris, calling for the cession of Cuba, Puerto Rico, and the Philippines. The United States awarded Spain a booby prize of $20 million.[61]

Dealing with insurgent forces in Cuba and the Philippines proved more complex and costly. Americans took to Cuba genuine enthusiasm for a noble cause, "the first war of its kind," a fictional soldier averred. "We are coming with Old Glory," a popular song proclaimed.[62] Their idealism barely outlasted their initial encounters with Cuban rebels. Viewing *Cuba Libre* through the idealized prism of their own revolution, Americans were not prepared for what they encountered. They had no sense of what a guerrilla army three years in the field might look like. They brought with their weapons and knapsacks the heavy burden of deeply entrenched racism. The Cubans thus appeared to them "ragged and half-starved," a "wretched mongrel lot," "utter tatterdemalions." From a military standpoint, they seemed useless, not worthy allies. Their participation was quickly limited to support roles, the sort of menial tasks

60. Thomas Schoonover, *Uncle Sam's War of 1898 and the Origins of Globalization* (Lexington, Ky., 2003), 89; Dirk Spennerman, "The United States Annexation of Wake Atoll, Central Pacific Ocean," *Journal of Pacific History* 33 (September 1998), 239–47.
61. Trask, *War with Spain*, 441–42.
62. Pérez, *War of 1898*, 24.

African Americans were expected to perform at home. The proud rebels' rejection of such assignments reinforced negative stereotypes. Indeed, Americans came to look more favorably upon the once despised Spanish soldiers, viewing them as a source of order, a safeguard for property, and a protection against a possible race war.[63]

Popular perceptions nicely complemented the nation's political goals. Cuba in fact had made significant progress toward self-government in the last days of Spanish rule, but this was lost on the invaders. The ragtag Cubans were no more fit for self-government than "gunpowder is for hell," General Shafter thundered, and from the moment they landed Americans set out to establish complete control regardless of the Teller Amendment.[64] The United States ignored the provisional government already in place and refused to recognize the insurgents or army. It did not consult Cubans regarding peace aims or negotiations and did not permit them even a ceremonial role in the surrender at Santiago or the overall surrender of the island. They were required to recognize the military authority of the United States, which, to their consternation, refused any commitment for future independence.

The United States handled the Philippines in much the same way. There as in Cuba, Americans encountered revolution, the first anti-colonial revolt in the Pacific region, a middle-class uprising launched in 1896 by well-educated, relatively prosperous Filipinos such as the twenty-nine-year-old Emilio Aguinaldo. Seeing the exiled Aguinaldo as possibly useful in undermining Spanish authority, U.S. officials had helped him get home, perhaps deluding him into believing they would not stay. Once there, he declared the islands independent, established a "provisional dictatorship" with himself as head, and even designed a red, white, and blue flag. Americans on the scene conceded that Aguinaldo's group included "men of education and ability" but also conveniently concluded that it did not have broad popular support and could not sustain itself against European predators. McKinley gave no more than fleeting thought to independence and rejected a U.S. protectorate. He instructed the U.S. military to compel the rebels to accept its authority. The United States refused to recognize Aguinaldo's government, as with the Cubans, keeping it at arm's length. In December 1898, McKinley proclaimed a military government. He vowed to respect the rights of Filipinos but made no promises of self-government. On the scene, tensions mounted

63. Pérez, *Cuba Between Empires*, 197–201; Pérez, *War of 1898*, 94–95.
64. Pérez, *Cuba Between Empires*, 218.

between U.S. occupation forces and the thirty thousand Filipinos besieging Manila.[65]

From the late summer of 1898 until after the election of 1900, one of those periodic great debates over the nation's role in the world raged in the United States. The central issue was the Philippines. Defenders of annexation pointed to obvious strategic and commercial advantages, fine harbors for naval bases, a "key to the wealth of the Orient." The islands would themselves provide important markets and in addition furnish a vital outpost from which to capture a share of the fabled China market. The imperialists easily rationalized the subjugation of alien peoples. Indeed, they argued, the United States by virtue of its superior institutions had an obligation to rescue lesser peoples from barbarism and ignorance and bring them the blessings of Anglo-Saxon civilization. As McKinley allegedly put it to a delegation of visiting churchmen, there seemed nothing to do but to "educate the Filipinos, and uplift them and civilize them and Christianize them, and by God's grace do the very best we could by them."[66] If America were to abandon the islands after rescuing them from Spain, they might be snapped up by another nation—Germany had displayed more than passing interest. They could fall victim to their own incapacity for self-government. The United States could not in good conscience escape the responsibilities thrust upon it. "My countrymen," McKinley proclaimed in October 1898, "the currents of destiny flow through the hearts of the people. . . . Who will divert them? Who will stop them?"[67]

An anti-imperialist movement including some of the nation's political and intellectual leaders challenged the expansionist argument on every count. Political independents, the anti-imperialists eloquently warned that expansion would compromise America's ideals and its special mission in the world.[68] The acquisition of overseas territory with no prospect for statehood violated the Constitution. More important, it undermined the republican principles upon which the nation was founded. The United States could not join the Old World in exploiting other peoples without betraying its anti-colonial tradition. The acquisition of overseas empire would require a large standing army and higher taxes. It would

65. Brian Linn, *The Philippine War, 1899–1902* (Lawrence, Kans., 2000), 42–46.
66. May, *Imperial Democracy*, 252–53.
67. Gould, *McKinley*, 136–37.
68. Robert L. Beisner, *Twelve Against Empire: The Anti-Imperialists, 1898–1900* (New York, 1968), 17.

compel U.S. involvement in the dangerous power politics of East Asia and the Pacific.

At the outbreak of war in 1898, the philosopher William James marveled at how the nation could "puke up its ancient soul . . . in five minutes without a wink of squeamishness." He denounced as "snivelling," "loathsome" cant talk of uplifting the Filipinos. The U.S. Army was at that time suppressing an insurrection with military force, and that, he argued, was the only education the people could expect. "God damn the U.S. for its vile conduct in the Philippines," he exploded.[69] Industrialist Andrew Carnegie, contending that the islands would drain the United States economically, offered to buy their independence with a personal check for $20 million. Other anti-imperialists warned that any gains from new markets would be offset by harmful competition with American farmers. Some argued that the United States already had sufficient territory. "We do not want any more States until we can civilize Kansas," sneered journalist E. L. Godkin.[70] Many anti-imperialists objected on grounds of race. "Pitchfork Ben" Tilman of South Carolina vehemently opposed injecting into the "body politic of the United States . . . that vitiated blood, that debased and ignorant people."[71] The nation already had a "black elephant" in the South, the *New York World* proclaimed. Did it "really need a white elephant in the Philippines, a leper elephant in Hawaii, a brown elephant in Porto Rico and perhaps a yellow elephant in Cuba?"[72]

The anti-imperialists may have made the stronger case over the long run, but the immediate outcome was not determined by logic or force of argument. The administration had the advantage of the initiative, of offering something positive to a people still heady from military triumphs. Many Americans found seductive the February 1899 appeal of British poet Rudyard Kipling to take up the "white man's burden," first published just days before the Senate took up the issue of annexation. The Republicans also had a solid majority in the Senate. A remarkably heterogeneous group, the anti-imperialists were divided among themselves and lacked effective leadership. They had to "blow cold upon the hot excitement," as James put it.[73] In an early example of foreign policy

69. Ibid., 44, 48.
70. H. W. Brands, *The Reckless Decade: America in the 1890s* (New York, 1998), 330.
71. Stanley Karnow, *In Our Image: America's Empire in the Philippines* (New York, 1989), 137.
72. Beisner, *Twelve Against Empire*, 219.
73. Ibid., 228.

bipartisanship, William Jennings Bryan, the titular leader of the Democratic opposition, vitiated the anti-imperialist cause and infuriated its leaders by instructing his followers to vote for the peace treaty with Spain, which provided for annexation of the Philippines, in order to end the war. The Philippines could be dealt with later. The outbreak of war in the Philippines on the eve of the Senate vote solidified support for the treaty. In what Lodge called "the hardest, closest fight I have ever known," the Senate approved the treaty 57–21 in February 1899, a bare one vote more than necessary, and a result facilitated by the defection of eleven Democrats.[74] McKinley was easily reelected in 1900 in a campaign in which imperialism was no more than a peripheral issue.

IV

As the great debate droned on in the United States, the McKinley administration set about consolidating control over the new empire. The president vowed that the Teller pledge would be "sacredly kept," but he also insisted that the "new Cuba" must be bound to the United States by "ties of singular intimacy and strength." Many Americans believed that annexation was a matter of time and that, as with Texas, California, and Hawaii, it would evolve through natural processes—"annexation by acclamation," one official labeled it. Some indeed thought that the way the United States implemented the occupation would contribute to this outcome. "It is better to have the favors of a lady by her consent, after judicious courtship," Secretary of War Elihu Root observed, "than to ravish her."[75] The United States established close ties with Cuban men of property and standing—"our friends," Root called them—many of them expatriates, some U.S. citizens. It created an army closely tied to the United States. It carried out good works. The occupation government imposed ordinances making it easy for outsiders to acquire land, built railroads, and at least indirectly encouraged the emigration of Americans. "Little by little the whole island is passing into the hands of American citizens," a Louisiana journal exclaimed in 1903, "the shortest and surest way to obtain its annexation to the United States."[76]

The expected outcome did not materialize, and other means had to be found to establish the ties McKinley sought. Except for a small minority

74. Healy, U.S. Expansionism, 227.
75. Pérez, Cuba Between Empires, 279.
76. Carmen Diana Deere, "Here Come the Yankees: The Rise and Decline of United States Colonies in Cuba," Hispanic American Historical Review 78 (November 1998), 734.

of pro-Americans, sentiment for annexation did not develop in Cuba. Nationalism remained strong and indeed intensified under the occupation. The first elections did not go as Americans wanted; some officials continued to fear that Cubans of African descent might plunge the nation into a "Hayti No. 2." The outbreak of war in the Philippines in early 1899 aroused similar fears for Cuba.

Eager to get out but determined to maintain control of a nominally independent Cuba, the United States settled on the so-called Platt Amendment to create and sustain a protectorate. Drafted by Root and attached to a military appropriation bill approved by Congress in March 1901, it forbade Cuba from entering into any treaty that would impair its independence, granting concessions to any foreign power, or contracting a public debt in excess of its ability to pay. It explicitly empowered the United States to intervene in Cuba's internal affairs and provided two sites for U.S. naval bases. "There is, of course, little or no independence left Cuba under the Platt Amendment," military governor Gen. Leonard Wood candidly conceded.[77] When Cubans resisted this obvious infringement on their sovereignty with street demonstrations, marches, rallies, and petitions, the United States demanded that they incorporate the amendment into their constitution or face an indefinite occupation. It passed by a single vote. "It is either Annexation or a Republic with an Amendment," one Cuban lamented; "I prefer the latter." "Cuba is dead; we are enslaved forever," a patriot protested.[78]

A 1903 reciprocity treaty provided an economic counterpart to the Platt Amendment. The war left Cuba a wasteland. In its aftermath, the United States set out to construct a neo-colonial economic structure built around sugar and tobacco as major cash crops and tied closely to the U.S. market. Without prodding from their government, Americans stepped in to buy up the sugar estates from fleeing Spaniards and destitute Cubans. Using Hawaii as a model, U.S. officials saw in free trade a means to promote annexation by "natural voluntary and progressive steps honorable alike to both parties." Reciprocity would allegedly revive the sugar industry, solidify the position of Cuba's propertied classes, and promote close ties to the United States. It would deepen Cuba's dependence on one crop and one market. The arrangement naturally provoked complaints from U.S. cane and beet growers. Cuban nationalists protested that it would substitute the United

77. Ibid.
78. Pérez, *Cuba Between Empires*, 327; Ramon Ruiz, *Cuba: The Making of a Revolution* (Amherst, Mass., 1968), 33.

States for "our old mother country." Approved in 1903, the agreement provided the basis for Cuban-American economic relations for more than a half century. The War of 1898 thus ended with Cuba as a protectorate of the United States. Not surprisingly, it remained for Cubans a "brooding preoccupation." While Americans remembered the war as something they had done *for* Cubans and expected Cuba to show gratitude, Cubans saw it as something done *to* them. The betrayal of 1898 provided the basis for another Cuban revolution at midcentury.[79]

The acquisition of a Pacific empire elevated the expansionist dream of an isthmian canal to an urgent priority. Defense of Hawaii and the Philippines required easier access to the Pacific, a point highlighted during the war when the battleship *Oregon* required sixty-eight days to steam from Puget Sound to Cuba. A canal would also give the United States a competitive edge in Pacific and East Asian markets. The availability of long-sought naval bases in the Caribbean now provided the means to defend it. Thus after the war with Spain, the McKinley administration pressed Britain to abrogate the Clayton-Bulwer Treaty. The threat of congressional legislation directing the United States to build a canal without reference to the 1850 treaty pushed the British into negotiations. When the Senate vehemently objected to a treaty giving the United States authority to build and operate but not to fortify a canal, the State Department insisted on reopening negotiations. Preoccupied with European issues and its own imperial war in South Africa and eager for good relations with Washington, London conceded the United States in a treaty finally concluded in November 1901 exclusive right to build, operate, and fortify a canal, an unmistakable sign of acceptance of U.S. preeminence in the Caribbean. The way was clear for initiation of a project that would be carried forward with great gusto by McKinley's successor, Theodore Roosevelt.[80]

Pacification of the Philippines proved much more difficult and costly. McKinley spoke eloquently of "benevolent assimilation" and insisted that "our priceless principles undergo no change under a tropical sun. They go with the flag."[81] But he also ordered the imposition of unchallenged U.S. authority. The United States soon found itself at war with Aguinaldo's in-

---

79. Pérez, *War of 1898*, 125; Louis A. Pérez Jr., "Incurring a Debt of Gratitude: 1898 and the Moral Sources of U.S. Hegemony in Cuba," *American Historical Review* 104 (April 1999), 358, 381.
80. Schoultz, *Beneath the United States*, 161; Walter LaFeber, *The Panama Canal: The Crisis in Historical Perspective* (New York, 1979), 18.
81. Linn, *Philippine War*, 30.

surgents. The Filipinos naively expected to gain recognition of their independence and then counted on the U.S. Senate to defeat the peace treaty. Many Americans viewed the Filipinos with contempt. Tensions increased along their adjoining lines around Manila until an incident in February 1899 provoked war. Americans called it the "Philippine Insurrection," thus branding the enemy as rebels against duly constituted authority. The Filipinos viewed it as a war for independence fought by a legitimate government against an outside oppressor. It became an especially brutal war, hatreds on both sides fueled by nationalism, race, and a tropical sun. It provoked enormous controversy in the United States for a time and then was largely forgotten until obvious if often overdrawn parallels with the war in Vietnam revived interest in the 1960s.

The army of occupation and U.S. civilian officials took seriously McKinley's charge of "benevolent assimilation," seeking to defuse resistance through enlightened colonial policies. The military developed a "pacification" program to win Filipino support, building roads and bridges, establishing schools, tackling the twin scourges of smallpox and leprosy with public health facilities, and distributing food where it was most needed. They began to restructure the Spanish legal system, reform the tax structure, and establish local governments. McKinley sent fellow Ohioan William Howard Taft to the Philippines in 1900 to implement his policies. Taft shared the general American skepticism of Filipino capacity for self-government, but he also accepted McKinley's earnest sense of obligation to America's "little brown brothers." He launched a "policy of attraction," drawing to the United States upper-class *ilustrados* to govern the islands under colonial tutelage. They helped establish a Filipino political party with its own newspaper and American-style patronage. The United States' colonial policies drained support from Aguinaldo while sparing the nation some of the cost and stigma of direct imperialism. At the same time, U.S. officials on the scene reinforced ties with the old elite from the Spanish era, ensuring that it would remain in power long after they left. They began the process of Americanization of the islands.[82]

In time, U.S. forces also suppressed the insurgency, no mean feat in an archipelago of seven thousand islands, covering an area of half a million square miles, with a population of seven million people. American volunteers and regulars fought well and maintained generally high morale against an often elusive enemy under difficult conditions, suffocating heat and humidity, drenching monsoon rains, impenetrable jungles, and

82. Karnow, *In Our Image*, 171–77.

rugged mountains. After a period of trial and error, the army developed an effective counterinsurgency strategy. Its civic action programs helped win some Filipino support and weaken the insurgency. Later in the war, it added a "policy of chastisement," waging fierce and often brutal campaigns against pockets of resistance. The United States did not commit genocide in the Philippines; atrocities were neither authorized nor condoned. Under the pressures of guerrilla warfare in the tropics, however, brutal measures were employed. Americans came to view the war in racial terms, a conflict of "civilization," in Roosevelt's words, against the "black chaos of savagery and barbarism." The U.S. troops often applied to their Filipino enemy racial epithets such as "nigger," "dusky fellow," "black devil," or "goo-goo" (the last a word of uncertain origin and the basis for "gook" as used by GIs in the Korean and Vietnam wars). The war also gave rise to the word *boondock*, derived from the Tagalog *bonduk*, meaning remote, which to soldiers had dark and sinister connotations.[83] To secure information about the guerrillas, U.S. troops used the notorious "water cure," allegedly learned from Filipinos who worked with them, in which a bamboo tube was thrust into the mouth of a captive and dirty water—"the filthier the better"—was poured down his "unwilling throat." In Batangas, late in the war, Americans resorted to tactics not unlike those employed by the despised Weyler in Cuba, forcing the resettlement of the population into protected areas to isolate the guerrillas from those who served as their sources of supply. Following the "Batangiga massacre" in which forty-eight Americans were killed, Gen. Jacob Smith ordered that the island of Samar be turned into a "howling wilderness." Although not typical of the war, these events were used to discredit it and came to stamp it. They aroused outrage at home, provoked congressional hearings that lasted from January to June 1902, and revived a moribund anti-imperialist movement.[84]

Americans too often ascribe the outcome of world events to what they themselves do or fail to do, but in the Philippine War the insurgents contributed mightily to their own defeat. Aguinaldo and his top field commander, a pharmacist, military buff, and admirer of Napoleon, foolishly adopted a conventional war strategy, suffering irreplaceable losses in early frontal assaults against U.S. troops before belatedly resorting to guerrilla

83. Linn, *Philippine War*, 223; for a more critical view, see Paul A. Kramer, "Race-Making and Colonial Violence in the U.S. Empire," *Diplomatic History* 30 (April 2006), 169–210.
84. Kramer, "Race-Making," 189, 197, 201–3.

tactics. By the time they changed, the war may have been lost.[85] Although the Filipinos fought bravely—the bolo-men sometimes with the machetes for which they were named—they lacked modern weapons and skilled leadership. Given the difficulties of geography, they could never establish centralized organization and command. Split into factions, they were vulnerable to U.S. divide-and-conquer tactics. Aguinaldo and other insurgent leaders came from the rural gentry and never identified with the peasantry or developed programs to appeal to them. In some areas, the guerrillas alienated the population by seizing food and destroying property—some Filipinos, ironically, found their needs better met by Americans.[86] The insurgents placed far too much hope in the election of Bryan in 1900 and found his defeat hugely demoralizing. The capture of Aguinaldo in March 1901 in a daring raid by Filipino Scouts allied with the United States and posing as rebel reinforcements came at a time when the insurgents were already reeling from military defeats. If not the turning point in the war, it helped break the back of the rebellion, although fighting persisted in remote areas for years.

On July 4, 1902, new president Theodore Roosevelt chose to declare the war ended and U.S. rule confirmed. Victory came at a cost of more than 4,000 U.S. dead and 2,800 wounded, a casualty rate of 5.5 percent, among the highest of any of the American wars. The cost through 1902 was around $600 million. The United States estimated 20,000 Filipinos killed in action and as many as 200,000 civilians killed from war-related causes. At home, the war brought disillusionment with the nation's imperial mission.

V

The United States had taken an interest in the Philippines in part from concern about its stake in China, and it is no coincidence that acquisition of the islands almost immediately led to a more active role on the Asian mainland. By the late 1890s, China had become a focal point of intense imperial rivalries. For a half century, the European powers—joined by the United States—had steadily encroached on its sovereignty. Following the Sino-Japanese war of 1894–95, the great powers exploited China's palpable weakness to stake out spheres of influence giving them exclusive

85. Glenn Anthony May, "Why the Filipinos Fired High: Popular Participation in the Philippine Revolution and the Philippine-American War," *Biblion* 7 (Spring 1999), 87–104.
86. Linn, *Philippine War*, 197.

concessions over trade, mining, and railroads. Germany initiated the process called "slicing the Chinese melon" in 1897. Using the killing of two German missionaries as a pretext, it secured from the hapless imperial government a naval base at Qing Dao along with mining and railroad concessions on the Shandong peninsula. Russia followed by acquiring bases and railroad concessions on the Liaodong peninsula. Britain secured leases to Hong Kong and Kowloon, France concessions in southern China. The powers threatened to reduce the once proud Middle Kingdom to a conglomeration of virtual colonies.[87]

The U.S. government had shown little interest in China during the Gilded Age, but in the 1890s pressures mounted for greater involvement. Trade and investments enjoyed a boomlet, once again stirring hopes of a bounteous China market. The threat of partition after the Sino-Japanese War produced pressures from the business community to protect the market for U.S. exports. By this time, missionaries had increased dramatically in numbers and penetrated the interior of China. As certain of the rectitude of their cause as the Chinese were of the superiority of their civilization, the missionaries promoted an ideology very much at odds with Confucianism and undermined the power of local elites. Scapegoats in Chinese eyes for growing Western influence, the missionaries were increasingly subjected to violent attacks and appealed to their government to defend them against the barbaric forces that threatened their civilizing mission. Missionaries, along with the "China hands," a small group of diplomats who became self-appointed agents for bringing China into the mainstream of Western civilization, constituted a so-called Open Door constituency that sought to make the United States responsible for preventing further assaults on China's sovereignty and reforming it for its own betterment. Some influential Americans indeed came to view China as the next frontier for U.S. influence, the pivot on which a twentieth-century clash of civilizations might hinge.[88]

These pressure groups were pushing for an active role in China at precisely the point when the United States was becoming more sensitive to its rising power and prestige in the world. For years, the U.S. government had resisted appeals from missionaries for protection, reasoning that it could hardly ask the Chinese government to take care of Americans when it did not protect Chinese and when its exclusionist policies in-

87. Schoonover, War of 1898, 68–77.
88. Michael H. Hunt, The Making of a Special Relationship: The United States and China to 1914 (New York, 1983), 143–68.

curred their wrath. Secretary of State Olney initiated the change. Acting as assertively with China as with the British in Latin America, he proclaimed in 1895 that the United States must "leave no doubt in the mind of the Chinese government or the people in the interior" that it is an "effective factor for securing due right for Americans resident in China."[89] To support his strong words, he beefed up the U.S. naval presence in Chinese waters. The United States in the 1890s "dramatically broadened" the definition of missionary "rights" and made clear its intent to defend them.[90]

Once the Spanish crisis had ended, the McKinley administration also took a stand in defense of U.S. trade in China. The task fell to newly appointed Secretary of State John Hay. At one time Lincoln's private secretary, the dapper, witty, and multitalented Hay had worked in business and journalism and was also an accomplished poet, novelist, and biographer. He had served in diplomatic posts in Vienna, Paris, Madrid, and London before returning to Washington. Independently wealthy, urbane, and extraordinarily well connected, the Indianan was a shrewd politician. Like many Republicans, he had once opposed expansion, but he gave way in the 1890s to what he called a "cosmic tendency."[91] Pressured by China hands like W. W. Rockhill, Hay concluded that a statement of the U.S. position on freedom of trade in China would appease American businessmen and possibly earn some goodwill among the Chinese that might benefit the United States commercially. It would convince expansionists the United States was prepared to live up to its responsibilities as an Asian power. In addition, according to one State Department operative, it could be a "trump card for the Administration and crush all the life out of the anti-imperialist agitation."[92] Thus in September 1899, Hay issued the first Open Door Note, a circular letter urging the great powers involved in China not to discriminate against the commerce of other nations within their spheres of influence.

The following year, the United States joined Japan and the Europeans in a military intervention in China. Simmering anti-foreign agitation fed by bad harvests, floods, plague, and unemployment boiled over in the

89. Warren I. Cohen, *America's Response to China: An Interpretative History of Sino-American Relations* (New York, 1971), 54.
90. Hunt, *Special Relationship*, 162.
91. Foster Rhea Dulles, "John Hay," in Norman A. Graebner, ed., *An Uncertain Tradition: American Secretaries of State in the Twentieth Century* (New York, 1961), 22–27.
92. A. Whitney Griswold, *The Far Eastern Policy of the United States* (rev. ed., New Haven, Conn., 1962), 71.

summer of 1900 into the Boxer Rebellion, so named because its leaders practiced a form of martial arts called spirit boxing. Blaming foreigners for the ills that afflicted their country, the "Righteous and Harmonious Fists" sought to eliminate the evil. They bore placards urging the killing of foreigners. Certain that their animistic rituals made them invincible—even against bullets—they fought with swords and lances. Armed bands of Boxers numbering as high as 140,000 burned and pillaged across North China, eventually killing two hundred missionaries and an estimated two thousand Chinese converts to Christianity. With the complicity of the empress dowager, the Boxers moved on Beijing. In June 1900, joined by troops of the imperial army, they killed two diplomats—a German and a Japanese—and besieged the foreign legations, leaving some 533 foreigners cut off from the outside world. Often dismissed as fanatical and reactionary, the uprising, as one sensitive and empathetic China hand presciently warned, was also "today's hint to the future," the first shot of a sustained nationalist challenge to the humiliation inflicted on a proud people by the West.[93]

The great powers responded forcibly. After a first military assault failed to relieve the siege of the legations, they assembled at Tianjin an eight-nation force of some fifty thousand troops and on July 7 took the city. In August 1900, while the world watched, the multilateral force fought its way over eighty miles in suffocating heat and against sometimes stubborn opposition to Beijing. After some hesitation, McKinley dispatched A China Relief Expedition of 6,300 troops from the Philippines to assist in relieving the siege, setting an important precedent by intervening militarily far from home without seeking congressional approval.[94] Although collaboration among the various powers was poor—each nation's military force sought to grab the glory—the troops relieved the siege, in the process exacting fierce retribution against the Chinese through killing, raping, and looting. Although late in arriving, the Germans were especially vicious. Kaiser Wilhelm II enjoined his troops to act in the mode of Attila's Huns and "make the name of Germany become known in such a manner in China, that no Chinese will ever again dare look askance at a German."[95] The kaiser's statement and the Germans' brutal behavior gave them a name that would follow them into World War I. In a protocol

93. Hunt, Special Relationship, 187.
94. Walter LaFeber, "The 'Lion in the Path': The U.S. Emergence as a World Power," Political Science Quarterly 101, no. 5 (1986), 714.
95. Peter Fleming, The Siege of Peking (London, 1959), 135–36.

of September 1901, the powers demanded punishment of government officials who had supported the Boxers, imposed on China an indemnity of more than $300 million, and secured the right to station additional troops on Chinese soil.

While acting with the great powers, the United States was also quite sensitive to its own interests and sought some degree of independence. An unspoken reason for sending U.S. troops was to help protect China from further foreign encroachments. McKinley ordered the Americans to act separately from the powers when they could and cooperate when they must. He insisted that they treat the Chinese firmly but fairly. In general, U.S. troops comported themselves well. The United States sought to use its influence to prevent the conflict from spreading beyond northern China and the peace settlement from resulting in partition. Even while the foreign troops were gathering for the expedition to relieve the siege, Hay in July 1900 issued another statement, this one nothing more than an affirmation of U.S. policy. This second Open Door Note made clear the United States' intention to protect the lives and property of its citizens in China, its commitment to lifting the siege of Beijing, and its determination to protect "all legitimate interests." It expressed concern about the "virtual anarchy" in Beijing and hope that it would not spread elsewhere. The words that drew the most attention then and since affirmed that the policy of the United States was to promote "permanent safety and peace to China, preserve Chinese territorial and administrative entity . . . and safeguard for the world the principle of equal and impartial trade with all parts of the Chinese empire."[96]

The Open Door Notes have produced as much mythology as anything in the history of U.S. foreign relations. Although he knew better, Hay encouraged and happily accepted popular praise for America's bold and altruistic defense of China from the rapacious powers. These contemporary accolades evolved into the enduring myth that the United States in a singular act of beneficence at a critical point in China's history saved it from further plunder by the European powers and Japan. More recently, historians have found in the Open Door Notes a driving force behind much of twentieth-century U.S. foreign policy. Scholar-diplomat George F. Kennan dismissed them as typical of the idealism and legalism that he insisted had characterized the American approach to diplomacy, a meaningless statement in defense of a dubious cause—the independence of

96. The text is in Ruhl Bartlett, ed., *The Record of American Diplomacy* (New York, 1950), 413.

China—which had the baneful effect of inflating in the eyes of Americans the importance of their interests in China and their ability to dictate events there.[97] Historian William Appleman Williams and the so-called Wisconsin School have portrayed the notes as an aggressive first move to capture the China market that laid the foundation for U.S. policy in much of the world in the twentieth century.[98]

As historian Michael Hunt has observed, the original Open Door Notes, while important, amounted to much less than has been attributed to them. The United States by issuing the notes was looking out for its own interests; any benefit to China was incidental. McKinley and Hay had little concern for China. Hay was contemptuous even of those Chinese who sought to befriend the United States and did not bother to consult them before acting on their behalf. To the great anger of the Chinese, he did not challenge the despised unequal treaties. The United States took for itself $25 million of the huge indemnity imposed upon China. It participated in forcing the Chinese to accept permanent stationing of Western military forces between Beijing and the sea, additional evidence of China's impotence, and increased its own military forces there.[99] It did not even rule out the acquisition of its own sphere of influence. "May we not want a slice, if it is to be divided?" the ever alert McKinley inquired.[100]

The notes had little immediate impact for China or the United States. The United States, in Hunt's words, had taken a "token nod at the future possibility of the China market," but it did little subsequently to promote trade with China. The first note did not even address the important issue of investments in spheres of influence.[101] The powers' response to the first note was qualified and evasive, something Hay for political expediency managed to twist into "final and definitive." The second time, a wiser secretary of state did not ask for a response. The notes did less to save China from partition than the fact that the Europeans and Japan for their own reasons chose not to push for it. The Open Door Notes satisfied the need for action at home and threatened no one abroad. Their issuance did signal the beginning of an independent U.S. role in East Asian politics, a

97. George F. Kennan, *American Diplomacy, 1900–1950* (New York, 1952), 23–37.
98. William A. Williams, *The Tragedy of American Diplomacy* (rev. ed., New York, 1988), 49–57; Thomas J. McCormick, *China Market: America's Quest for Informal Empire, 1893–1901* (Chicago, 1967).
99. Cohen, *America's Response to China,* 59.
100. Hunt, *Special Relationship,* 182.
101. Ibid., 152–54.

course fraught with difficulties and destined to occupy a central place in twentieth-century American foreign policy.

ALTHOUGH SHORT IN DURATION and relatively low in cost—at least for the victor—the War of 1898 had significant consequences. For Cuba, Puerto Rico, and the Philippines, it exchanged one colonial master for another and brought changes in the form of external control. Spaniards viewed it as "the Disaster," a defeat that raised basic questions not simply about the political system but also about the nation and its people. The "question for us . . . the only and exclusive question," a popular magazine observed, "is one of life and death, . . . of whether we can continue to exist as a nation or not." "Everything is broken in this unhappy country," a Madrid newspaper added, "all is fiction, all decadence, all ruins."[102] Although the Disaster did not spark a revolution or even major political changes, it accentuated the class and regional divisions that would lead to the Spanish Civil War.

"No war ever transformed us quite as the war with Spain transformed us," Woodrow Wilson, then president of Princeton University, wrote in 1902.[103] "The nation has stepped forth into the open arena of the world." Wilson's statement was filled with the hyperbole that marked many contemporary assessments, but it contained more than a grain of truth. As a result of the war with Spain, the United States became a full-fledged member of the imperial club, assuming a protectorate over Cuba and taking Hawaii, Puerto Rico, and the Philippines as outright colonies. Its acquisitions in the Pacific made it a major player, if not the dominant power, in that region. With the Open Door Notes and the China Relief Expedition, it became an active participant in the volatile politics of East Asia. The War of 1898 reinforced Americans' sense of their rising greatness and reaffirmed their traditional convictions of national destiny. It sealed the post–Civil War reconciliation of the Union. By 1898, the South had come to terms with its defeat in the Civil War and eagerly accepted the conflict with Spain to prove its loyalty. The North came to recognize the nobility of Confederate sacrifice. Certain that the Civil War had reaffirmed America's mission in the world, former Union and Confederate soldiers eagerly took up the cause of *Cuba Libre*.[104]

102. Sebastian Balfour, "The Impact of War within Spain: Continuity or Crisis?" in Smith and Dávila-Cox, *Crisis of 1898*, 102.
103. "The Ideals of America," *The Atlantic Monthly*, December, 1902. www.theatlantic.com/issues/o2dec/wilson.htm.
104. Gaines Foster, "Coming to Terms with Defeat: Post–Vietnam War America and the Post–Civil War South," *Virginia Quarterly Review* 66 (Winter 1990), 27.

The War of 1898 did not produce a realignment in the global balance of power, but it did mark the onset of a new era in world politics. The revolutions in Cuba and the Philippines and the conflicts that followed set the tone for a sustained struggle between colonizers and colonized, one of the major phenomena of the twentieth century. The war brought the end of the Spanish empire and sealed the demise of Spain as a major power. It represented both symbolically and tangibly America's emergence as a world power. The War of 1898 drew European attention as few other events of the decade. Europeans erred in believing that the United States would immediately become a major player in world politics. It possessed the capability, but not yet the will, to act on a global basis. They correctly recognized, however, that it had emerged from war as the seventh great power.[105] Indeed, although it was by no means clear at the time, the War of 1898 also marked the beginning of what would come to be called the American Century.

William McKinley presided over and in many ways guided these changes in U.S. foreign policy. More a practical politician than a thinker, he did not articulate a new vision of America's role in the world. Rather, he took full advantage of the opportunities provided by the War of 1898, responding to and helping to popularize the expansionist doctrines of duty, dollars, and destiny. He fashioned an overseas empire, rooted U.S. influence more deeply in the Caribbean and Pacific Basin, and began to stake out an independent role in East Asia. In his last months in office, he pushed for economic reciprocity and greater world involvement. Speaking at an exposition in Buffalo on September 5, 1901, he warned his countrymen that with the speed of modern communications American "isolation was no longer possible or desirable."[106] A week later, he was dead, the victim of an assassin's bullet. His successor, Theodore Roosevelt, his polar opposite in personality and leadership style, would take up the challenge.

105. Kennedy, *Great Powers*, 248; May, *Imperial Democracy*, 221, 239, 264–65.
106. James D. Richardson, ed., *A Compilation of the Messages and Papers of the Presidents of the United States* (20 vols., Washington, 1897–1916), 15:662.

9

"Bursting with Good Intentions"

The United States in World Affairs, 1901–1913

Contrary to European predictions, the United States did not become a major player in world politics immediately after the War of 1898. An avowed Anglophile, President Theodore Roosevelt flirted with the idea of an alliance with Great Britain, but he knew that such an arrangement was not feasible because of the relative security the nation continued to enjoy and its long-standing aversion to foreign entanglements. The brief flurry of enthusiasm for empire barely outlasted the war with Spain. The need to consolidate territory already acquired consumed great energy and resources. The Philippine War soured many Americans on colonies. Once an enthusiast for empire, Roosevelt himself would admit by 1907 that the Philippines was America's Achilles' heel. While busy solidifying its position in such traditional areas of influence as the Caribbean and the Pacific Basin, the United States did not acquire new colonies or involve itself in the frantic jockeying for alliances that stamped European politics before World War I. It was a great power but not yet a participant in the great-power system.[1]

The United States between 1901 and 1913 did take a much more active role in the world. Brimming over with optimism and exuberance, their traditional certainty of their virtue now combined with a newfound power and status, Americans firmly believed that their ideals and institutions were the way of the future. Private individuals and organizations, often working with government, took a major role in meeting natural disasters across the world. Americans assumed leadership in promoting world peace. They began to press their own government and others to protect human rights in countries where they were threatened. The perfect exemplar of the nation's mood in the new century, Roosevelt promoted what he called "civilization" through such diverse ventures as building the Panama Canal, managing the nation's imperial holdings in the Philippines and the Caribbean, and even mediating great-power disputes and wars. "We are

---

1. Paul Kennedy, *The Rise and Fall of the Great Powers* (New York, 1987), 248.

bursting today with good intentions," journalist E. L. Godkin proclaimed in 1899.[2]

I

"What a playball has this planet of ours become," novelist Jack London exclaimed at the turn of the century. "Steam has made its parts accessible. . . . The telegraph annihilates space and time."[3] Indeed, the world had shrunk appreciably by the year 1900. Steamships crossed the Atlantic in less than a week—"giant ferryboats" traversing the "straits of New York," Americans called them.[4] Cable joined much of the globe. Passports were unnecessary in many areas; people moved easily from one country to another to visit or work. The revolutions in technology and transportation permitted large-scale trade and international investments. Commerce and capital moved with relative freedom across national borders. This early globalization of capitalism led some enthusiasts to proclaim a new era of world peace. Applying modern ideas to Enlightenment theories, British businessman Norman Angell in his 1910 best seller *The Great Illusion* proclaimed capitalism an inherently peaceful system that rendered unnecessary formal empires based on possession of territory and thus might eliminate great-power rivalries and make war unthinkable because of the potential cost to winners as well as losers.

Angell also recognized the destructive capacity of modern nation-states, which, in fact, along with the expansion of capitalism and technological and geopolitical changes, was opening the way to history's bloodiest century. The early 1900s represented the high-water mark of imperialism. In 1901, the great powers maintained 140 colonies, protectorates, and dependencies covering two-thirds of the earth's surface and one-third of the world's population. "No land is occupied that is not stolen," humorist Mark Twain quipped after a global tour in the 1890s.[5] The rise of Germany, Japan, and the United States and the demise of the Spanish empire upset the existing order and aroused uncertainty and fear among the established powers, manifested in heated colonial rivalries, a spiraling arms race, and shifting alliances. In a diplomatic revolution of mammoth

---

2. Pedro A. Cabán, *Constructing a Colonial People: Puerto Rico and the United States, 1898–1932* (Boulder, Colo., 1999), 109.
3. Judy Crichton, *America 1900: The Turning Point* (New York, 1998), 5.
4. Ibid., 70.
5. Mark Twain, *Following the Equator* (New York, 1897), quotation taken from *Mark Twain: A Film Directed by Ken Burns* (PBS, 2002), part 2.

proportions, traditional enemies Britain and France joined to face the emerging threat of Germany. Britain's accommodation with its ancient rival Russia in turn aroused German fear of encirclement. The increasing rigidity of alliances and the escalating arms race raised the possibility that a crisis in the most remote part of the world could plunge Europe into conflagration.

The Russo-Japanese War of 1904–5 further jostled an already wobbly international system. Revelations of Russia's stunning weakness gave Germany a fleeting edge in great-power rivalries, adding anxiety in Britain and France. The surprisingly easy victory of an Asian nation over Europeans assaulted the theories of racial supremacy that undergirded a Eurocentric world order and excited hope among Asians groaning under imperialism. It was "like a strange new world opening up," Vietnamese patriot Phan Boi Chau recorded. "We have become increasingly enthusiastic and intense in our commitment to our ideals."[6]

The years 1900 to 1912 also witnessed the first stirring of the revolutions that would rock the twentieth century. The war with Japan helped spark an abortive revolution in Russia in 1905, a forerunner of the more radical upheaval to come. Republicans overthrew the decaying Manchu regime in China in 1911, setting off nearly four decades of internal strife and agitation against foreign domination. Revolutions also erupted in Mexico and Iran. In all these early twentieth-century upheavals, peasants, industrial workers, the petty bourgeoisie, and provincial elites challenged established governments while meeting the threats posed by foreign powers and each other. Their success was limited, but they hinted at the shakiness of the established order and the turmoil ahead.[7]

In terms of size and population, the United States was clearly a great power. Between 1900 and 1912, the last of the original forty-eight states were admitted to the union, completing the organization of the continental United States. The territory of the mainland exceeded three million square miles; the new overseas empire covered 125,000 square miles extending halfway across the world. A still rapidly expanding population surpassed seventy-seven million in 1901 and was becoming daily more diverse. Almost eight million immigrants entered the United States during the Roosevelt presidency alone. By 1910, America's twelve largest cities

6. Robert J. McMahon, ed., *Major Problems in the History of the Vietnam War* (New York, 1990), 31–32.
7. Richard H. Collin, "Symbiosis Versus Hegemony: New Directions in the Foreign Relations Historiography of Theodore Roosevelt and William Howard Taft," *Diplomatic History* 19 (Summer 1995), 493.

had populations one-third foreign born. New York, it was said, "had more Italians than Naples, more Germans than Hamburg, twice as many Irish as Dublin, and more Jews than the whole of western Europe."[8] The influx of these new immigrants inflamed nativist passions and significantly influenced U.S. foreign relations.

Economically, the United States was first among equals. Per capita income was the highest in the world, although the average concealed gross and growing disparities between rich and poor. Agricultural and industrial productivity soared; the national wealth doubled between 1900 and 1912. A favorable balance of trade permitted a dramatic rise in foreign investments—from $700 million in 1897 to $3.5 billion by 1914. A once yawning gap between what Americans owed abroad and were owed closed by that same year, eliciting predictions that New York would soon be the center of world finance. "London and Berlin are standing in perfectly abject terror," novelist Henry James observed in 1901, "watching Pierpont Morgan's nose flaming over the waves, and approaching horribly nearer their bank vaults."[9] The consolidation of industry that began in the late nineteenth century continued apace in the early twentieth. More and more corporations fell under the control of the great New York banking houses.

The nation's political life centered around adaptations to these changes. The Progressive movement comprised an almost bewildering mélange of sometimes conflicting groups. What they shared was a faith in progress and a conviction that problems could be solved by professional expertise. The progressives set out to deal with the disorders of the 1890s by applying modern problem-solving techniques. They put great stock in bureaucracy and saw government as the essential instrument of order and progress.[10]

The American mood at the turn of the century was one of unbounded optimism and unalloyed exuberance. The return of prosperity salved the wounds opened in the 1890s. Americans again marveled at their productivity and gloried in their material well-being. The defeat of Spain filled the nation with pride. "There is not a man here who does not feel four hundred percent bigger in 1900 . . . ," New York senator Chauncey Depew observed, "[now] that he is a citizen of a country that has become a world power."[11] Americans, and indeed some Europeans, more than ever

8. Lewis L. Gould, *The Presidency of Theodore Roosevelt* (Lawrence, Kans., 1991), 36.
9. Jean Strouse, *Morgan: American Financier* (New York, 1999), 412.
10. Emily S. Rosenberg, *Spreading the American Dream: American Economic and Cultural Expansion, 1896–1945* (New York, 1982), 42.
11. Crichton, *America 1900*, 10.

believed that their way of doing things would prevail across the world. Woodrow Wilson told a 1906 audience that the great vitality of the United States would thrust it into new frontiers beyond Alaska and the Philippines: "Soon . . . the shores of Asia and then Autocratic Europe shall hear us knocking at their back door, demanding admittance for American ideas, customs and arts."[12] The first generation of historians of U.S. foreign policy shared this excitement for the nation's new role in the world. Archibald Cary Coolidge hailed the emergence of his country as one of those nations "directly interested in all parts of the world and whose voices must be heard."[13]

The internationalization of America and the Americanization of the world was under way by 1900. Another spurt in tourism manifested the nation's emerging internationalism. The growing ease and luxury and declining cost of travel increased the number of Americans going to Europe from 100,000 in 1885 to nearly 250,000 by 1914. Americans proudly referred to themselves as the "world's wanderers" and boasted that in the "century of travel, Americans are the nation of travelers." Some tourists approached Europe much like their ancestors, their experiences abroad confirming their Americanness. Others viewed travel as a way to broaden their horizons and spread American values and influence. Some hoped to liberalize and Americanize the Old World—even to improve French hygiene by flaunting the newest brand of American-made soap. Some saw travel as a way to promote peace, reasoning that the better people got to know each other the more difficult it would be to go to war. Most saw increased travel as a manifestation of their nation's power and influence. "To be a world power was to travel," it was said, "and to travel was to be a world power." Whatever the rationalization, travel influenced Americans' views of other nations and of their own place in the world. It shaped the culture from which twentieth-century policymakers and an elite keenly interested in foreign policy would emerge. In the spirit of the age, it led to calls for a more professional foreign service, even for improved foreign language skills.[14]

12. Speech, March 22, 1906, in Arthur S. Link, ed., *The Papers of Woodrow Wilson* (69 vols., Princeton, N.J., 1966–94), 16:341.
13. Archibald Cary Coolidge, *The United States as a World Power* (New York, 1912), 7. See also John H. Latané, *America as a World Power* (New York, 1907), Carl Russell Fish, *American Diplomacy* (New York, 1919), and Albert Bushnell Hart, *The Foundations of American Foreign Policy* (New York, 1901).
14. Christopher Endy, "Travel and World Power: Americans in Europe, 1890–1917," *Diplomatic History* 22 (Fall 1998), 565–94.

Once scorned by Europeans for its cultural backwardness, the United States by the turn of the century had assumed an important role in the international cultural establishment. American artists and writers took advantage of French encouragement of the arts; wealthy Americans sponsored such artists as Picasso, Matisse, and Cézanne. Henry James and James McNeill Whistler were among England's cultural elite. Americans bought and collected foreign art. J. P. Morgan acquired so many treasures that Europeans began to impose limits on art exports. Charles Freer's gift of Asian art spurred the creation of the first national gallery.[15]

In terms of its technological and manufacturing feats, the United States was widely recognized as *the* world power by 1900. At the Paris Universal Exposition that year, a huge dome topped by an oversized eagle towering above everything else marked the U.S. pavilion. It contained six thousand exhibits, second only to France, displaying everything from steam engines to meats. "It seems almost incredible," reveled a *Munsey's Magazine* writer, "that we should be sending cutlery to Sheffield, pig iron to Birmingham, silks to France, watch cases to Switzerland . . . or building sixty locomotives for British railways."[16] Europeans expressed fascination with U.S. methods of mass production and especially Frederick Taylor's principles of scientific business management. Some urged their emulation. Others warned that to copy U.S. techniques would lead to shoddy products. Europeans also feared the mass consumption and democracy that were presumably the inevitable by-products of mass production and would, they fretted, undermine their high culture and threaten their elites. British journalist William Stead's 1901 best seller *The Americanization of the World* sounded an alarm bell that would echo repeatedly throughout the century.[17]

United States citizens, sometimes working with the government, eagerly took up the cause of humanitarian relief for peoples stricken by natural disaster. The wealth generated by the industrial revolution created a strong sense of noblesse oblige. Many citizens also agreed that their nation's status as a world power entailed global responsibilities. Modern communications brought to their attention disasters in far-flung areas; modern transportation made it possible to provide timely assistance. San Franciscans in the wake of their own horrendous earthquake in 1906

15. Collin, "Symbiosis," 483–84.
16. Crichton, *America 1900*, 30.
17. Volker Berghahn, "Philanthropy and Diplomacy in the 'American Century,' " *Diplomatic History* 23 (Summer 1999), 393–96; Richard Pells, *Not Like Us: How Europeans Have Loved, Hated, and Transformed American Culture Since World War II* (New York, 1997), 7.

contributed $10,000 to victims of a similar disaster in Chile. Dr. Louis Klopsch of the *Christian Herald*, called the "twentieth-century captain of philanthropy," used his paper to collect contributions for famine relief in China and Scandinavia. In 1902, Roosevelt set aside $500,000 for victims of an earthquake on the islands of Martinique and St. Vincent. In 1907 and 1909, sailors from U.S. Navy ships helped with earthquake relief in Jamaica and Messina, Italy. Reorganized in 1905 under a congressional charter giving it status as a semiofficial government agency, the American Red Cross took the lead in many emergency operations. America's "habit of giving" saved countless lives and provided hope across the world. United States aid provoked some criticism, even from recipients, but also earned praise. According to the empress dowager of China, America was "known as the one foreign nation that is really a friend and whose people though barbarians, are really kind."[18]

The United States' rise to world power led to increased citizen activism on foreign policy issues. Americans agitated for reform of and even revolution against the oppressive tsarist government of Russia, in 1911 pressuring Congress into abrogating the commercial treaty of 1832. They took up the cause of world peace. In 1910, steel magnate Andrew Carnegie established the first foundation with an "explicit international orientation." Funded with $10 million of U.S. Steel stock, the Carnegie Endowment for International Peace sought to promote peace through law, international exchanges, and research.[19]

Increased citizen activism led to growing interest in and involvement with foreign policy issues on the part of American women. The realm of diplomacy, like that of politics, remained an exclusive male preserve, but women moved easily from agitation for suffrage and temperance at home into causes abroad. Philanthropy was more open to female participation than the political system. Reformer Alice Stone Blackwell took a leading role in efforts to promote revolution in Russia, even advocating a form of terrorism.[20] Women had early taken up the cause of world peace, urging arbitration of the controversy with Britain in 1895 lest men "deluge the world in blood for a strip of land in Venezuela." After the turn of the century, they campaigned for disarmament and international arbitration of disputes and to publicize their cause designated May 15 as "Peace Day."

18. Merle Curti, *American Philanthropy Abroad* (New Brunswick, N.J., 1963), 216–17, 222–23; Berghahn, "Philanthropy," 397–98.
19. Berghahn, "Philanthropy," 397–98.
20. Shannon Smith, "From Relief to Revolution: American Women and the Russian-American Relationship, 1890–1917," *Diplomatic History* 19 (Fall 1995), 607–15.

In promoting peace, they took a position at odds with their male counter-parts, singling out what they saw as misguided and dangerous notions of manliness. Deploring modern industrialism, which they viewed as the tri-umph of male values, they fought against military appropriations, the sale of real and toy guns, and even the sport of boxing.[21]

In an age of internationalization, even African Americans, the most oppressed of American minorities, looked abroad. Leading educational in-stitutions like Hampton Institute in Virginia and Tuskegee Institute in Alabama, each committed to uplifting African Americans by teaching self-help, industrial arts, and Christian morality, sought to project their values abroad. Samuel Armstrong, the founder of Hampton, envisioned a "Gir-dle Around the World" and encouraged Hawaiians, Africans, Cubans, even Japanese minority groups to come to Hampton, learn its ways, and return home to uplift their peoples by introducing a "little Hampton" there. Booker T. Washington sought to spread his Tuskegee model to Africa by bringing students to the Alabama school and dispatching Tuskegee stu-dents to Togo, Sudan, Liberia, and South Africa. Like elites at home, the colonial authorities in Africa found Washington's ideas and programs con-genial as ways to help manage the "natives" and make them more produc-tive workers.[22] As on domestic issues, the more radical W.E.B. DuBois, a founder of the National Association for the Advancement of Colored Peo-ple, took issue with the Tuskegee-Hampton approach. Linking discrimina-tion against African Americans at home with the exploitation of black people, especially Africans, abroad, he vigorously advocated an end to racial oppression at home and imperialism abroad.[23]

II

Although thrust into office by an assassin's bullet, Theodore Roosevelt perfectly fitted early twentieth-century America. He had traveled through Europe and the Middle East as a young man, broadening his horizons and expanding his views of other peoples and nations. An avid reader and prolific writer, he was abreast of the major intellectual currents of his day

21. Judith Papachristou, "American Women and Foreign Policy, 1898–1905," *Diplomatic History* 14 (Fall 1990), 493–509.

22. Jeanne Zeidler, "Samuel Chapman Armstrong's Vision: Hampton's Girdle Around the World," paper presented at the Pacific Coast Branch, American Historical Associ-ation, August 1995; Michael O. West, "The Tuskegee Model of Development in Africa: Another Dimension of the African/African American Connection, *Diplomatic History* 16 (Summer 1992), 371–87.

23. Tunde Adeleke, *Nineteenth-Century Black Nationalists and the Civilizing Mission* (Lexington, Ky., 1998), 137–139.

and had close ties to the international literary and political elite. From his early years, he had taken a keen interest in world affairs. He was a driving force behind, as well as an active participant in, the "large policy" of the 1890s. In his first address to Congress, in December 1901, he preached the gospel of international noblesse oblige: "Whether we desire it or not, we must henceforth recognize that we have international duties no less than international rights."[24]

The youngest president to this time, Roosevelt brought to the office a flamboyant style that neatly reflected the America of his time. A "steam engine in trousers," he was called, "an avalanche that the sound of your voice might loosen," and his youthful exuberance and frenetic energy mirrored the pent-up vitality of his emerging nation. Henry James labeled him "Theodore Rex" and described him as "the mere monstrous embodiment of unprecedented and monstrous noise."[25] A supreme egoist—his memoir of the war with Spain should have been titled "Alone in Cuba," one wit observed—he loved to be the center of attention. At the beginning of the age of mass media, he and his attractive family made excellent copy, fascinating and captivating the public and making TR, as he was called, the first politician to attain celebrity status. Building on precedents set by McKinley, he mastered the art of press relations and especially the press release to monopolize the news.[26]

Unlike his predecessors at least back to John Quincy Adams, he demonstrated a particular zest and flair for diplomacy, placing himself at the center of policymaking and setting precedents for executive dominance that became a hallmark of twentieth-century U.S. foreign policy. He reveled in intimate exchanges at the top level and in the stealth and secrecy that were part of the process. He disdained the "pink tea" protocol of formal diplomacy. He delighted in vigorous walks and horseback rides that left the stuffed shirts panting in the rear. He often short-circuited regular channels, using personal friends such as British ambassador Cecil Spring-Rice and his French and German counterparts, Jules Jusserand and Speck von Sternburg, the famous "tennis cabinet," as sources of information and diplomatic intermediaries.

Roosevelt was not a free agent in making foreign policy. In the days before scientific polling, it was impossible to determine what the public

24. Gould, Roosevelt, 13.
25. Jacob Heilbrun, "Larger than Life," New York Times Book Review (December 30, 2001), 7.
26. Robert C. Hilderbrand, Power and the People: Executive Management of Public Opinion in Foreign Affairs, 1877–1921 (Chapel Hill, N.C., 1981), 53–55.

thought and how public opinion affected policy. The press could provoke excitement on specific issues as with Cuba in the mid-1890s, especially in the metropolitan areas on the two coasts. When the nation was not threatened from abroad, however, the mass public, especially in the rural Midwest and South, showed little interest in foreign policy. Americans firmly believed that their country should not join alliances or assume commitments that could lead to war. Congress to some extent reflected popular attitudes and set additional barriers to presidential freedom of action. Partisan politics could play a crucial role. Especially at a time when presidents were steadily expanding their power, Congress jealously guarded its prerogatives.

Roosevelt believed that America's new role required a strong executive. He often lamented that "this people of ours simply does not understand how things are outside our boundaries." He understood that Americans would not support some of the things he wished to do in foreign policy. Borrowing from the "social control" theories of sociologist Edward Ross, he saw his role as managing and manipulating a presumably ignorant or indifferent public and Congress to do what he deemed right and necessary.[27] On occasion, he used the "bully pulpit" to educate the nation about things he believed in its best interest. More often, he stretched presidential powers as far as he could without provoking outright rebellion. He frequently operated in secrecy to keep the public and Congress from knowing what he was up to. During most of his presidency, he enjoyed comfortable majorities in Congress. But in his second term he encountered stubborn opposition from fiercely partisan southern Democrats who feared he might use expanded presidential powers to challenge their racial policies and Republicans who worried about the direction of his domestic programs and his accumulation of power. Numerous times, when thwarted by congressional opposition, he used executive agreements to implement his policies. Building on precedents set by McKinley, he established a firm basis for what would later be called the imperial presidency.[28]

TR was not above using foreign policy for partisan political advantage. In 1904, on the eve of the Republican nominating convention, he instructed Secretary of State John Hay to make public the ringing ultimatum "Perdicaris Alive or Raisuli Dead," purportedly to force the release of an American held hostage by a local chieftain in Morocco. The ostensibly bold threat set off wild cheers at the convention and has been hailed since as an example of

27. Ibid.; Walter LaFeber, "The 'Lion in the Path': The U.S. Emergence as a World Power," *Political Science Quarterly* 101, no. 5 (1986), 716–18.
28. Joseph A. Fry, *Dixie Looks Abroad: The South and U.S. Foreign Relations, 1789–1973* (Baton Rouge, La., 2002), 134–37.

the virtues of tough talk in diplomacy. In fact, Perdicaris was not a U.S. citizen. Roosevelt had no intention of using force to retrieve him. Most important, his release had already been secured by diplomacy before the telegram was sent. "It is curious how a concise impropriety hits the public," Hay chortled.[29] Although Americans were sometimes uneasy with TR's activism, they delighted in his growing international notoriety and the importance it signified for their young nation. They guffawed when he uttered such outrageous statements as "If I ever see another king, I will bite him."

A quintessentially American figure and a legitimate American hero, Roosevelt has been a subject of controversy. Especially during periods when interventionism has been out of fashion, he has been denounced as a heavy-handed imperialist, insensitive to the nationalism of people he considered backward. During the Cold War years, on the other hand, he was widely praised as a realist, more European than American in his thinking, a shrewd and skillful diplomatist who understood power politics, appreciated the central role America must play in the world, and vigorously defended its interests.

Roosevelt understood power and its limits, to be sure, but he was no Bismarck. On the contrary, he was quintessentially American in his conviction that power must be used for altruistic purposes. He was very much a person of his times. Cosmopolitan in his views, he hailed the advance of Western and especially Anglo-Saxon civilization as a world movement, the key to peace and progress. He believed his most important task was to guide his nation into the mainstream of world history. He viewed "barbaric" peoples as the major threat to civilization and thus had no difficulty rationalizing the use of force to keep them in line. "Warlike intervention by the civilized powers would contribute directly to the peace of the world," he reasoned, and could also spread American virtues and thereby promote the advance of civilization.[30] He was less clear how to keep peace among the so-called civilized nations. Pure power politics ran counter to the morality that was such an essential part of his makeup. In any event, he recognized that Americans' traditional aversion to intervention in European matters limited his freedom of action. The more appropriate role for the United States was as a civilizing power carrying out its moral obligations to maintain peace.[31]

29. Gould, *Roosevelt*, 136.
30. Frank Ninkovich, "Theodore Roosevelt: Civilization as Ideology," *Diplomatic History* 10 (Summer 1986), 233.
31. Ibid.; Serge Ricard, "Theodore Roosevelt and the Diplomacy of Righteousness," *Theodore Roosevelt Association Journal* 12 (Winter 1986), 3–4.

Almost as important, if much less visible, was Elihu Root, who served Roosevelt ably as secretary of war and of state. A classic workaholic, Root rose to the top echelons of New York corporate law and the Republican Party by virtue of a prodigious memory, mastery of detail, and the clarity and force of his argument. A staunch conservative, he profoundly distrusted democracy. He sought to promote order through the extension of law, the application of knowledge, and the use of government. He shared Roosevelt's internationalism and was especially committed to promoting an open and prosperous world economy. He was more cautious in the exercise of power than his sometimes impulsive boss. For entirely practical reasons, he was also more sensitive to the feelings of other nations, especially potential trading partners. A man of great charm and wit—when the 325-pound Taft sent him a long report of a grueling horseback ride in the Philippines' heat, he responded tersely: "How's the horse?"—he sometimes smoothed over his boss's rough edges. He was a consummate state-builder who used his understanding of power and his formidable persuasiveness to build a strong national government.[32] He was the organization man in the organizational society, "the spring in the machine," as Henry Adams put it.[33] He founded the eastern foreign policy establishment, that informal network connecting Wall Street, Washington, the large foundations, and the prestigious social clubs, which directed U.S. foreign policy through much of the twentieth century.[34]

Roosevelt and Root devoted much attention to modernizing the instruments of national power. Their reforms were part of a worldwide trend toward professionalization of military and diplomatic services based on the notion that modern war and diplomacy required specialized training and highly skilled personnel. They believed that, as an emerging great power in a world filled with tension, the United States must have well-trained public servants to defend its interests, promote its commerce, and carry out its civilizing mission. The call to public service was also a way to combat the selfishness and decadence that threatened the nation from within.

Learning from the chaos that accompanied mobilization for war in 1898, Root had begun to reform the army when Roosevelt took office. Generally acknowledged as the father of the modern U.S. Army, he

---

32. Richard Hume Werking, *The Master Architects: Building the United States Foreign Service, 1890–1913* (Lexington, Ky., 1977), 93.
33. Walter LaFeber, "Technology and U.S. Foreign Relations," *Diplomatic History* 24 (Winter 2000), 7.
34. George Mowry, *The Era of Theodore Roosevelt, 1900–1912* (New York, 1958), 43, 121; Walter Isaacson and Evan Thomas, *The Wise Men: Six Friends and the World They Made* (New York, 1986), 28–29, 186–87, 244, 336.

initiated its conversion from a frontier constabulary to a modern military force and introduced the radical idea of military professionalism to a nation proud of its citizen-soldier tradition. He created the Army War College in 1903 to prepare senior officers for war. Attacking the army's antiquated and conflict-ridden bureaucracy and following European and especially German models, he secured congressional approval in 1903 for a general staff to better plan for and conduct war. By trading federal funds for increased federal control, he also initiated the difficult and politically sensitive process of building a national reserve force from state-run militias. The so-called Root Reforms aroused bitter opposition inside and outside the army. Although they did not go as far as Root and others would have liked, they represented a major step toward modernization.[35]

Much closer to the president's heart and more acceptable to the nation was the further expansion and upgrading of the navy. A disciple of Alfred Thayer Mahan and sea power, Roosevelt retained throughout his life a boyish enthusiasm for ships and the sea. An "adequate" navy, he declared, was the "cheapest and most effective peace insurance" a nation could buy. He brought to the task his special zeal and skill at public relations.[36] Under his guidance, the U.S. Navy completed the shift from harbor defense to a modern battleship fleet, expanding from eleven battleships in 1898 to thirty-six by 1913 and rising to third place behind Britain and Germany. Direct naval appropriations during Roosevelt's tenure exceeded $900 million; the fleet grew from 19,000 sailors to 44,500. As was his wont, Roosevelt intervened personally to improve the accuracy of naval gunners. His dispatch of the Great White Fleet on its world tour in 1907 was, to him, a crowning achievement. "Did you ever see such a fleet and such a day?" an unusually exuberant (even for him!) president crowed. "By George, isn't it magnificent?" The cruise exposed major technical problems with the fleet and a serious shortage of bases in crucial areas, but it represented a coming-out party of sorts for the modern U.S. Navy.[37]

Roosevelt and Root also initiated reform of the consular and diplomatic services. At a time when competition for markets was a national priority, changes in the consular service aroused little controversy. Some Americans continued to see little need for diplomats—consuls were quite enough—but they were increasingly shouted down by the

35. Gould, *Roosevelt*, 123; Allan R. Millett and Peter Maslowski, *For the Common Defense: A Military History of the United States of America* (New York, 1984), 299–319.
36. Gould, *Roosevelt*, 43.
37. Ibid., 263; Millett and Maslowski, *Common Defense*, 299–309.

voices of modernization. Diplomats as well as consuls could serve the demands of an expanding commerce. Greater foreign travel and commerce required more and better representation. Most important, as TR put it, was the "growth of our present weight in the councils of the world." The United States needed skilled professional diplomats to compete with other nations. To level the playing field, it must eliminate politics, patronage, and amateurism. "The nation is now too mature to continue in its foreign relations these temporary expedients natural to a people to whom domestic affairs are the sole concern," Roosevelt's successor, William Howard Taft, exclaimed.[38] TR took up the cause, and Root applied his considerable skills to institution-building. The unlikely combination of Massachusetts Republican senator Henry Cabot Lodge and Alabama Democratic senator John Tyler Morgan spearheaded reform in Congress.

To remove patronage and politics, consuls and diplomats were selected by examination, carefully evaluated, and promoted on the basis of performance. As a practical business matter, the consular service was restricted to U.S. citizens. Consuls were paid better salaries and forbidden to do business on the side. Emphasis was placed on language skills. As secretary of state, Root shook the hidebound State Department from top to bottom. There was talk of specialized training for diplomats. Universities from New York to California began to create courses and programs—the Harvard Business School actually began as a venue for public service training. Following European models, geographical divisions were established in the State Department to provide the sort of expertise needed to deal with specialized problems.[39] Diplomats rotated between Washington and the field. Some of the changes were undone when Democrat Woodrow Wilson became president in 1913, but the process of reform was under way. To this point, U.S. diplomats had leased space for missions in other countries. Responding to the slogan "Better Embassies Mean Better Business," bankers, businessmen, and lawyers joined forces in 1909 to create improved working facilities for diplomats and consuls. In 1911, Congress authorized the State Department to buy land upon which to build new embassies.[40]

---

38. Warren Frederick Ilchman, *Professional Diplomacy in the United States, 1779–1939* (Chicago, 1961), 111.
39. Werking, *Master Architects*, 129.
40. Jane C. Loeffler, "The Architecture of Diplomacy," *Journal of the Society of Architecture Historians* 49 (September 1990), 251–55.

III

As the United States became more and more a nation of nations, ethnic groups played an increasingly important part in U.S. foreign relations. Some immigrant groups sought to use their rising power to influence policy on issues affecting the lands from which they had come, on occasion provoking conflict with these nations. More often, the persecution of immigrants by Americans sparked protest from the countries of their origin, threatening good relations, and with Japan raising the possibility of war.

Russia's persecution of Jews became an especially volatile issue in the early twentieth century. Large numbers of Jews had emigrated to the United States from Russia and eastern Europe. Like other immigrant groups, many sought to return to visit or stay. The Russian government viewed Jews as a major source of revolutionary activity and hence a threat to order. Fearing the return of Jews under protection of U.S. citizenship, it denied them visas. A new series of pogroms early in the century posed a more serious problem. As many as three hundred pogroms took place in the years 1903 through 1906, one of the worst at Kishinev, the capital of Bessarabia, where in April 1903, forty-seven Jews were killed, hundreds wounded, and thousands left homeless.[41]

American Jews vigorously protested. By this time, they comprised a populous and well-organized group and controlled several major New York banking houses. They represented a crucial voting bloc in major cities. Already angry over Russian travel restrictions, they expressed outrage at the pogroms. They conducted mass protests in New York and Chicago that drew support from human rights advocates such as social worker Jane Addams and journalist Carl Schurz. They flooded the government with petitions demanding action.[42]

The Roosevelt administration responded cautiously. The president and Hay to some degree shared the anti-Semitism that pervaded old-stock America and viewed the Jewish protest as an unwelcome intrusion from a minority group promoting narrow interests. They believed that protest was futile. On the other hand, they had little use for the tsar, shared Jewish anger at these "fiendish cruelties," and feared that the pogroms might provoke flight to the United States of "hordes of Jews . . . in unabsorbable

41. Norman E. Saul, *Concord and Conflict: The United States and Russia, 1867–1914* (Lawrence, Kans., 1996), 474–77.

42. Ibid.; Stuart E. Knee, "The Diplomacy of Neutrality: Theodore Roosevelt and the Russian Pogroms of 1903–1906," *Presidential Studies Quarterly* 19 (Winter 1989), 71–73.

numbers," something to "rank with the exodus from Egypt," Hay warned. With an election a year away, they recognized the value of doing something. They passed on to the Russian government a petition drafted by the protestors. To secure maximum political advantage, they released it to the press. This marked the first official U.S. protest against Russian anti-Semitism in a case where the nation's interests were not directly involved.[43]

Hay congratulated himself that the administration had at least laid the issue before the world, but the protest had little practical effect. The Russian government naturally bristled at U.S. intrusion and refused to accept the petition. Ambassador Artur Cassini pointedly retorted that the lynching of African Americans and beating of Chinese in the United States made it "unbecoming for Americans to criticize" Russia. A new wave of pogroms accompanied the outbreak of revolution in Russia in 1905, with an estimated 3,100 Jews killed in that year alone.[44]

"What inept asses they are, these Kalmucks!" Hay privately fumed, but the administration refused to do more, and Jewish protest mounted and took new forms. The powerful financier Jacob Schiff called for military intervention, and fifty thousand Jews marched in New York City. Schiff and other Jewish bankers blocked U.S. and European loans to Russia for its war with Japan and helped the Japanese secure funds, hoping that a Russian military defeat might provoke revolution and ultimately improve conditions for Jews. In 1906, the protestors formed the American Jewish Committee to orchestrate their actions. Increasingly, they focused on abrogation of the Russian-American commercial treaty of 1832, pointing out that it called for equal treatment for citizens of all countries and should be either honored or scrapped. Upon succeeding Roosevelt, Taft tried to head off congressional action by negotiating an agreement with Russia for joint abrogation. The Russians stubbornly refused. In December 1911, responding to Jewish pressures, the House of Representatives passed 300 to 1 a resolution favoring abrogation. Bowing to the inevitable, a reluctant Taft gave the required year's notice for termination of the treaty.[45]

American Jewish leaders hailed abrogation as a "great victory for human rights," but it was considerably less. It did little to help Russian Jews; by provoking an anti-American backlash, it may have worsened their condi-

---

43. Knee, "Neutrality," 73–74; Gould, *Roosevelt*, 89–90; John Lewis Gaddis, *Russia, the Soviet Union, and the United States: An Interpretive History* (2nd ed., New York, 1990), 42–43.
44. Knee, "Neutrality," 72–73.
45. Gaddis, *Russia*, 43–46; Saul, *Concord and Conflict*, 523–37, 567.

tion.[46] Russia raised tariffs on U.S. imports and imposed boycotts on some items, leading some Americans to protest that minority groups were exercising mischievous influence on U.S. foreign policy. The affair was of more than passing importance. The United States alone among the great powers spoke out against Russian treatment of Jews. The protest made clear the growing importance of ethnic groups in foreign policy. It brought into being one of the most powerful lobbies in twentieth-century America.

While American Jews protested human rights abuses in Russia, violations of human rights in the United States set off loud protests in China and Japan. The Chinese had ample reason for anger. After extended debate, Congress in 1904 bowed to exclusionist pressure and made permanent late nineteenth-century restrictions imposed on Chinese immigration. In the meantime, the Bureau of Immigration interpreted exclusionist laws in an arbitrary and intimidating manner.[47] Bureau officials interrogated, harassed, and humiliated Chinese seeking admission to the United States and used the most whimsical reasons to keep them out. State and local laws blatantly discriminated against the ninety thousand Chinese already in the United States, reducing them to the "status of dogs," one Chinese American complained. The Bureau of Immigration seemed intent on driving them all from the country.[48] Even Chinese exhibitors at the 1904 Louisiana Purchase Exposition in St. Louis were subjected to discriminatory regulations and restrictions.[49]

Mounting Chinese anger exploded in 1905 in a boycott of U.S. goods. Centered in the treaty ports, the boycott was one of the first visible signs of an emerging nationalist sentiment among a proud people subjected to foreign domination and insult. Chinese Americans helped instigate the boycott and supported it with contributions of money. Inspired by Japan's war against Russia, gentry, students, women, and intellectuals struck out in whatever ways seemed most available. They singled out the United States because of its gross abuses of human rights and because it appeared least likely to exact harsh retribution. They displayed anti-American posters and sang anti-American songs. They destroyed American property, even such prized personal possessions as record players. A Cantonese student denied access to the United States took his own life on the

46. Alexander DeConde, *Ethnicity, Race and American Foreign Policy* (Boston, 1992), 71.
47. Michael H. Hunt, *The Making of a Special Relationship: The United States and China to 1914* (New York, 1983), 228.
48. Delber McKee, "The Chinese Boycott of 1905–1906 Reconsidered: The Role of Chinese-Americans," *Pacific Historical Review* 55 (May 1986), 171.
49. Hunt, *Special Relationship*, 228–34.

steps of the U.S. consulate. "My chair coolies are hooted in the street and I would not be surprised if my servants left me," a beleaguered U.S. consul whined. The Chinese government did not officially support the protestors, but it acquiesced in and approved what they did. The Open Door constituency begged the government to do something.[50]

Roosevelt handled the boycott with political acumen and dexterity. A person who admired strength in people and nations, he deplored Chinese weakness—one of his major terms of opprobrium was "Chinaman." In the 1890s, he had backed exclusion on racial and economic grounds. He sensed the new winds blowing in China, however, and he recognized the blatant injustice in U.S. policies. To quiet U.S. China hands and the Chinese, he vaguely called for changes in the law on the grounds that "we cannot expect to receive equity unless we do equity." He also promised to implement existing laws more equitably and pressed the immigration bureau to mend its ways. But he would not take risks to ensure equity, and he recognized that his power to sway Congress and the states was limited. He assured exclusionists that he would continue to oppose the admission of Chinese laborers: "We have one race problem on our hands and we don't want another." When the boycott spread and five Americans were killed in an unrelated incident, he demanded an end to the protest and beefed up U.S. military forces in and around China.[51]

The incident faded without tangible result. The boycott fizzled from its own weakness rather than Roosevelt's threats. The boycotters disagreed on what they were trying to do and overestimated the capacity of economic pressure to influence U.S. policies. The boycott was mainly important as an early manifestation of the rising nationalism that would soon erupt in revolution. In the United States, little changed. Exclusionists continued to control the Congress. The bureau temporarily softened its methods and ended its efforts to drive Chinese from the United States. Americans continued to treat Chinese badly. In its death throes, the Chinese government could do little more than feebly protest.

The United States sought to appease the Chinese by remitting the indemnity imposed after the Boxer Rebellion. Often viewed as an act of generosity, remission was in fact an act of calculated self-interest. For Roosevelt, it provided a substitute for Congress's refusal to modify the exclusion laws. For those merchants and missionaries who sought to extend U.S. influence and trade in China, it offered a means to palliate the justi-

50. Delber McKee, "The Boxer Indemnity Remission: A Damage Control Device," *Society for Historians of American Foreign Relations Newsletter* 23 (March 1992), 10.
51. Hunt, *Special Relationship*, 243.

fiably righteous indignation of the Chinese. It could also be "used to make China do some of the things we want," State Department official Huntington Wilson observed. Alarmed at the number of Chinese going to Japan to study, diplomats also saw remission as a "cultural investment." "The Chinese who acquires his education in this country," diplomat Charles Denby observed, "goes back predisposed toward America and American goods." The United States thus forbade the funds from being used for economic development, insisting rather upon the establishment of an American school in China and creation of a program to send Chinese to study in the United States.[52]

A similar conflict with Japan provoked in 1907 a sustained war scare. Ironically, the restrictions placed on Chinese immigration and a continued demand for cheap labor led to a dramatic influx of Japanese workers, mostly from Hawaii. This sudden appearance of "hordes" of immigrants from a nation that had just thrashed a European power provoked working-class resentment against those who would "labor for less than a white man can live on" and wild fears of the "Orientalization of the Pacific Coast." Ostensibly to solve a shortage of school space caused by the recent catastrophic earthquake, in fact to avoid racial "contamination," the San Francisco School Board in October 1906 placed Chinese, Korean, and Japanese children in segregated schools.[53]

This ill-considered order provoked conflict with a nation that could do more than boycott U.S. goods. The Japanese government was not inclined to go to war over a relatively minor issue, but it could not but view the order as an insult and felt compelled to respond to the protests of its own people. Tokyo underestimated the depth of Californians' fears. Viewing U.S. politics through the prism of its own political culture, it also overestimated Washington's ability to control state and local governments. The Japanese thus sharply protested the segregation order.[54]

Roosevelt badly mishandled this issue. He shared to some degree the racial prejudices of the Californians, although he greatly respected what the Japanese had accomplished and admired their discipline and patriotism. He recognized, too, the threat they posed to the Philippines and Hawaii. He also at first underestimated the depth of anti-Japanese sentiment in California. Privately, he raged at the "idiots" who had proclaimed the order and employed racist terms to denounce racist actions—as "foolish

52. McKee, "Indemnity," 13: Hunt, Special Relationship, 270.
53. Walter LaFeber, The Clash: U.S. Japanese Relations Through History (New York, 1997), 88.
54. Charles E. Neu, The Troubled Encounter: The United States and Japan (New York, 1975), 48–49.

as if conceived by the mind of a Hottentot," he declaimed. Publicly, he denounced the segregation order as a "wicked absurdity." But he could not persuade the Californians to rescind it. "Not even the big stick is enough to compel the people of California to do a thing which they have a fixed determination not to do," the *Sacramento Union* thundered.[55] He compounded his problems with a hasty and ill-conceived effort to charm the Japanese into accepting a treaty providing for the mutual exclusion of laborers. They naturally took offense at the obviously one-sided nature of the treaty and the patronizing manner in which it was presented.[56]

Having won over neither Californians nor Japanese, a chastened Roosevelt set out to cobble together a settlement. He secured from Congress legislation banning immigration from Hawaii, Canada, and Mexico, thus stopping the major source of Japanese immigration without singling them out by name. He used the leverage thus gained to prevent the California legislature from passing discriminatory legislation and to persuade the San Franciscans to revoke their obnoxious order. As part of what came to be known as the "Gentleman's Agreement," Japan agreed to restrict the emigration of laborers to the United States.

In the short run, the crisis persisted. Japanese immigration actually increased following the Gentleman's Agreement, fanning tensions on the West Coast. Anti-Japanese riots in California further provoked Japan. Hotheads in both countries warned ominously of "yellow perils" and "white perils." Some commentators compared the warlike atmosphere to 1898. Roosevelt seems to have overestimated at this stage Tokyo's inclination toward war. He also exploited the crisis to promote his beloved navy and to indulge his boylike zest for playing war. He persuaded Congress to authorize four new battleships and pressed the navy to develop War Plan Orange, the first time Japan had officially been declared a potential enemy. His master stroke, as he saw it, was to send the fleet on a world cruise that included a stop in Japan. He hoped through this blatant show of force to publicize the importance of the navy, build political capital in California, and give pause to the Japanese.

Fortunately for Roosevelt, what could have resulted in disaster ended without incident. The Japanese cut the flow of laborers, fulfilling their part of the Gentleman's Agreement and taking the steam out of the agitation in California. The world cruise exposed the deficiencies of the Great White Fleet more than its power, but the Japanese warmly received the sailors. Crowds sang "The Star-Spangled Banner" in English and waved

55. Gould, *Roosevelt*, 258.
56. Neu, *Troubled Encounter*, 51.

American flags. United States sailors played baseball against Japanese teams. Although agitators in both countries continued to talk of war and the immigration issue would not go away, Roosevelt left office without further crisis.[57]

IV

In the first decade of the twentieth century, Americans took an active role in promoting world peace. The American peace movement was part of a larger Western phenomenon. One hundred and thirty new non-governmental organizations dedicated to various international causes sprouted up in the early 1900s, many of which would play an important role in years to come. Like their European counterparts, U.S. peace advocates believed that a shrinking world, frightening advances in military technology, and the escalating costs of weapons gave a special urgency to their cause. Optimistic about humankind and confident of progress, they hoped that the growth of capitalism and democracy would make war less likely. They also worried about rising tensions in Europe and sought to take steps to reduce the chances of conflict. Conservative in politics, these "practical" peace reformers equated peace with order and respect for the law. They believed the United States must work closely with other "civilized" nations, especially Great Britain, and that their cause could best be furthered by the extension of Anglo-Saxon principles, especially the codification of international law and arbitration. They saw no contradiction between working for peace and maintaining military strength.[58]

The organized peace movement flourished in the United States early in the century. Some groups sponsored international friendship and understanding among schoolchildren and college students. The World Peace Foundation focused on research and education. Solid citizens such as Root and steelmaker Carnegie gave the movement respectability and resources. Like others of his era, Carnegie believed that the wealthy must assume responsibility for making a better world. Peace became one of his passions. His Endowment built up the international relations sections of Carnegie-funded libraries. It promoted peaceful resolution of disputes. Its charter reflected the optimism of the era. Once war had been eliminated, it declared, the Endowment could move on to the "next most degrading remaining evil or evils."[59]

57. James R. Reckner, *Teddy Roosevelt's Great White Fleet* (Annapolis, Md., 1982).
58. Charles DeBenedetti, *The Peace Reform in American History* (Bloomington, Ind., 1984), 65–68, 79–83.
59. Curti, *Philanthropy*, 198.

Firm internationalists, the peace seekers believed that understanding and cooperation among nations were essential for world peace. They were also firmly ethnocentric. In their view, the world could best be regenerated by the spread of American values, principles, and institutions. They worked within precisely defined limits. Certain that their nation's security was not threatened by war in Asia or Europe, they did not consider breaking with tradition by joining alliances or involving the United States in world politics. Acting as "enlightened bystanders," they had no sense that achievement of their goal might require drastic measures.

They fastened rather on cautious, legalistic means such as arbitration. Arbitration was a natural for U.S. peace advocates. The U.S. practice of submitting disputes to arbitration dated to the 1794 Jay Treaty with England. Arbitration fitted within the Anglo-American tradition of extending legal concepts to international relations. It perfectly suited those peace advocates who desired to take practical steps without compromising U.S. freedom of action.

The peace advocates won the ear of policymakers, but they never determined how to take effective steps without compromising national sovereignty. With Roosevelt's blessing, Hay negotiated in 1904–5 with all the major European nations and Japan eleven bilateral treaties providing arbitration of all disputes that did not involve questions of national honor or vital interests—glaring exceptions. Already embroiled with the activist TR over numerous issues, a contentious Senate insisted that it must approve each case in which the United States went to arbitration. Dismissing the amended treaties as a "sham," Roosevelt refused to sign them.[60] A more accommodating and cautious Root tried to pick up the pieces, conciliating the Senate and then negotiating twenty-four bilateral arbitration treaties with all the major powers except Russia and Germany. The Root treaties were easily approved and won their author a Nobel Peace Prize. They were so restrictive as to be of dubious value.[61]

American peace advocates and policymakers also supported the idea of regular great-power meetings to discuss matters of war and peace. Such efforts had the advantage of being multilateral rather than bilateral. They could deal with a broad spectrum of issues. The tsar had proposed the first "peace" conference, which met at The Hague in May 1899. Befitting its new world status, the United States took an active role. Male and female peace enthusiasts from across the world also flocked to The Hague,

60. Gould, *Roosevelt*, 149.
61. Hilderbrand, *Power and the People*, 86–87; Richard W. Leopold, *The Growth of American Foreign Policy: A History* (New York, 1962), 284–90.

where they held "fringe" meetings and, in the words of the U.S. delegate, submitted "queer letters and crankish proposals." The Quakers were "out in full force," he complained. Military figures such as Mahan and British admiral Sir John Fisher attended as delegates. The conference has been aptly characterized as a noble undertaking with limited results. It did "outlaw" several weapons, took steps to ensure better treatment of prisoners of war, thus seeking to render war more humane if not eliminating it, and agreed on a multilateral arbitration treaty. But it accomplished nothing in disarmament beyond an innocuous statement that the reduction of military budgets was "extremely desirable for the increase of the material and moral welfare of mankind." It did not even approve a U.S. proposal for a court of neutral nations to arbitrate disputes.[62]

Roosevelt proposed a second Hague conference to push for arbitration and reductions in armaments, but he politely allowed the tsar to issue formal invitations. Forty-four nations gathered in the summer of 1907. The conferees did not address such crucial issues as neutral rights and accomplished nothing in arms reduction. Finley Peter Dunne's fictional newspaper humorist, Mr. Dooley, acidly observed that they spent most of the time discussing "how future wars should be conducted in th' best inthrests iv peace."[63] The delegates also rejected Root's proposal for a permanent world court. They initiated the practice of attaching reservations to their signatures, a method already used by U.S. senators. The main result was acceptance of Carnegie's proposal for the construction of a "peace palace" at The Hague.[64]

Ironically, it was the warmonger of 1898 and hero of San Juan Hill who gave practical expression to the burgeoning peace sentiment by helping to end the Russo-Japanese War and prevent war between France and Germany. Much has been made of Roosevelt's realpolitik, and power politics undoubtedly entered into his unprecedented intrusions in world affairs. Other factors were more important. Like the peace advocates, he felt that the United States must work actively to promote peace. "We have become a great nation . . . and we must behave as beseems a people with such responsibilities."[65] As one of the "civilized" nations, the United States had a moral duty to preserve peace.[66] TR also loved to be at the

---

62. Saul, *Concord*, 440–44; Geoffrey Best, "Peace Conferences and the Century of Total War," *International Affairs* 75, no. 3 (1999), 623, 631.
63. Leopold, *American Foreign Policy*, 292.
64. Saul, *Concord*, 522.
65. Gould, *Roosevelt*, 173.
66. Ninkovich, "Roosevelt," 241.

center of things, and such interventions gave him a bigger stage to perform on. As much as he complained about the pretensions of foreign heads of states and the intractability of diplomacy, he reveled in the intrigue and secrecy and the manipulation of people and nations. He also believed that his intercession could further vital U.S. interests.

The outbreak of war between Russia and Japan in 1904 provided the first opportunity for the onetime warrior to play the role of peacemaker. Since Japan's rise to world power, the two nations had competed for influence and markets in northeast Asia. Rivalry erupted into military conflict in February when Japan suddenly terminated six months of negotiations and launched a surprise attack on the Russian fleet at Port Arthur in southern Manchuria.

Roosevelt moved slowly toward mediation. At first, he and Root cheered Japanese successes—and even the way they began the war! TR feared Russian advances in East Asia; he profoundly disliked their autocratic form of government and branded the tsar "a preposterous little creature."[67] Although he shared the racism of his contemporaries, he respected Japanese economic and military prowess, even conceding that they would be a "desirable addition" to "our civilized society." He hoped to thwart a possible threat to the Philippines and Hawaii by deflecting Japan's expansion toward the Asian mainland. The Japanese, he crowed, were "playing our game." As they drove from victory to victory over shockingly inept Russian forces, however, he began to fear they might get the "big head." It would be best if the two nations fought to a draw, exhausting each other in the process. At the outset, he concentrated on preventing the war from becoming another occasion for plundering China. Later, he decided that it must be stopped before Japan could gain too great an edge and offered his good offices.[68]

With difficulty, he got the combatants to the conference table. Each Russian military disaster seemed to render the tsar less amenable to compromise. Surprised with the ease of their success, the Japanese began to push for total victory. Roosevelt privately railed at the stubbornness and delusions of each. The Russians were capable of "literally fathomless mendacity"; Japan was an "oriental nation, and the individual standard of truthfulness is low."[69] His persistence paid off. Japan's destruction of the Russian fleet at Tsushima in May 1905 forced the tsar to negotiate. Japan's

67. Gould, Roosevelt, 182.
68. Howard K. Beale, Theodore Roosevelt and the Rise of America to World Power (New York, 1962), 236–39.
69. H. W. Brands, TR: The Last Romantic (New York, 1997), 534.

military success came at the cost of financial ruin; its leaders also found reason to talk. In the summer of 1905, the two nations agreed to attend a peace conference.

The meeting opened at the navy yard in Portsmouth, New Hampshire, August 9, 1905. Its location in the United States was without precedent. Roosevelt played a major role. He did not attend, but he watched closely from his Long Island home and exerted influence through tennis cabinet intermediaries such as von Sternburg and Jusserand, and even Kaiser Wilhelm II. In a preconference gathering at his Oyster Bay estate, he displayed diplomatic finesse by ordering a stand-up buffet dinner to avoid touchy protocol questions of seating and by delivering an admirably tactful toast. Privately, he vented his frustration: the Russians were "soddenly stupid, corrupt, treacherous, and incompetent," the Japanese "entirely selfish." It was difficult to be patient, he told friends, when "what I really want to do is to give utterance to whoops of rage and jump up and knock their heads together."[70] To free itself of financial dependence on U.S. bankers, Japan sought a large indemnity and the retention of Manchurian territory it had taken. Despite its enormous losses, Russia refused concessions—"not an inch of ground, not a kopek of compensation."[71] "The Japanese ask too much," Roosevelt complained, "but the Russians are ten times worse than the Japs because they are so stupid." Russian stubbornness paid off. Chief negotiator Count Sergei Witte made peace possible by ignoring the tsar's objections to ceding half of Sakhalin. Recognizing that their financial plight prevented them from resuming the war, the Japanese agreed to Roosevelt's pleas for compromise. The September 1905 Treaty of Portsmouth provided no indemnity. Japan secured Port Arthur, southern Sakhalin, and Russian recognition of its sphere of influence in Korea. Manchuria was left open to both powers.[72]

Roosevelt quickly discovered the curses as well as blessings that befall the peacemakers. Americans cheered this new evidence of their nation's benign influence in the world and exulted that their president's big stick could be used to impose peace. TR won the 1906 Nobel Peace Prize, the first American to be so honored. As with most such compromises, neither of the signatories was happy. Russians denounced Witte as "Count Half-Sakhalin." Russian-American relations, already strained over the Jewish issue, were further poisoned. Unable to grasp why their smashing military

70. Beale, *Rise to World Power*, 265.
71. Saul, *Concord*, 504.
72. Eugene Trani, *The Treaty of Portsmouth: An Adventure in American Diplomacy* (Lexington, Ky., 1969).

victories had not won a bigger diplomatic payoff, Japanese found in the United States a handy scapegoat. Mourning crepe was hung from government buildings. In September 1905, during anti-peace riots, mobs surrounded the U.S. legation in Tokyo.[73]

Even before the Portsmouth conference, Roosevelt had begun to shore up the U.S. position in the Philippines. While inspiring Asians, Japan's stunning military success worried some Americans. United States officials, Roosevelt included, increasingly recognized that its naval prowess threatened the Philippines and even Hawaii, where the Japanese population continued to grow. Now painfully aware of the vulnerability of islands once touted as the nation's outer defenses, Roosevelt in July 1905 dispatched to Tokyo his protégé and favorite troubleshooter, Taft. The president's flamboyant and outspoken daughter Alice also went along and dominated the headlines. Meanwhile, Taft held secret discussions with Prime Minister Taro Katsura. In the resulting agreement, the United States gave Japan a free hand in Korea, violating the U.S.-Korea treaty of 1882; Katsura disavowed any Japanese aspirations toward the Philippines or Hawaii. Approved by the president, the so-called Taft-Katsura agreement remained secret until unearthed in his papers nearly two decades later. When Korea in November 1905 called upon the United States to live up to its treaty obligations, TR demurred, privately commenting that the Koreans could do nothing to defend themselves.[74]

The rise in tensions following the Treaty of Portsmouth, the concurrent crisis over Japanese immigration, fueled by reckless talk of yellow and white perils, and the growing possibility of conflict over Manchuria created pressures for further initiatives. In late November 1908, Root and Japanese ambassador Takahira Kogoro negotiated another secret agreement pledging respect for the status quo in the Pacific region, thus tacitly conceding Japan's preeminent interests in southern Manchuria. When Root proposed that the Senate might at least be informed of the understanding, Roosevelt, now a lame duck, responded curtly: "Why invite the expression of views with which we may not agree?"[75]

Roosevelt's role in averting war between France and Germany was less direct but still important. French efforts to create an exclusive sphere of influence in Morocco threatened existing German interests. Germany naturally objected and by threatening war hoped to drive a wedge between France and its new ally, Great Britain. Engaging in a histrionic display so typical of

73. Saul, Concord, 505; LaFeber, Clash, 84.
74. Gould, Roosevelt, 185.
75. LaFeber, Clash, 92.

the era, the kaiser made a dramatic, saber-rattling speech aboard a warship at Tangier, at the same time calling for an international conference to discuss the issue. Privately, he appealed to the United States to intercede.

Roosevelt moved cautiously. Some "civilized" nation should uphold order in Morocco, he reasoned, and France seemed a logical candidate. He did not want to alienate France or Britain, with whom he sympathized and sought to maintain close ties. "We have other fish to fry," he also noted, "no real interests in Morocco." Ultimately, the threat of a "world conflagration" drove him to act. In doing so, he broke precedent even more sharply than in the Russo-Japanese War, implicitly altering the Monroe Doctrine by asserting the right of the United States to intervene in European matters that affected its security.[76] He nudged both sides toward the peace table. He helped resolve haggling over the agenda by persuading France and Germany to go "with no program." Largely through a major gaffe on the part of von Sternburg, he extracted a crucial German promise to accept the settlement he might work out.

The conference opened in January 1906 in Algeciras, Spain. Roosevelt played a less conspicuous role than at Portsmouth, but he exerted important and at times decisive influence. As before, he closely watched the proceedings and worked through trusted personal intermediaries. He took a consistently pro-French position while effusively flattering the kaiser. When Wilhelm backed himself into a corner from which there appeared no face-saving exit, TR threatened to publish Germany's inadvertent pledge to compromise. Faced with this dismal prospect, the kaiser gave in and then had to swallow Roosevelt's fulsome praise for his "epoch-making political success" and "masterly policy." France got most of what it wanted; the kaiser got Roosevelt's praise. War was averted, achieving the president's short-term aim; Germany was isolated and angry.[77]

V

During the first years of the new century, U.S. officials devoted much effort to managing the empire taken from Spain in 1898. They brought to the task a keen sensitivity to their new world role and the importance of what they were doing. They imparted to their work the zeal for social engineering that marked the Progressive Era. Forms of governance and relationships with the United States varied markedly in the new possessions. In all cases, Americans believed in their exceptionalism. They were

76. Serge Ricard, "Theodore Roosevelt: Principles and Practices of a Foreign Policy," *Theodore Roosevelt Association Journal* 28 (Fall/Winter 1992), 4.
77. Beale, *Rise to World Power*, 331.

doing the "world's work," Roosevelt boasted, bringing to their new wards the blessings of civilization rather than exploiting them. Whatever the intentions, of course, U.S. policies were exploitative. It was not simply a matter of Americans taking advantage of helpless victims. Local elites, often Creoles who shared the racist assumptions of their new colonial masters, collaborated with the imperial power to advance their personal interests and maintain their privileged position.

At first overlooked in imperial calculations, Puerto Rico came to assume exaggerated importance in American eyes. It would provide bases to guard the canal. It could serve as a transit point for the growth of U.S. trade and investment in Latin America. The expansion of sugar production would reduce dependence on Europe for a vital consumer product. As Americans optimistically set out to educate Puerto Ricans to "our way of looking at things," they reasoned that if they did their job well they could "win the hearts" of other Latin Americans and "weld together" the civilizations of the two continents.[78]

The United States carved out a unique status for its new Caribbean possession. Racist attitudes toward Puerto Ricans made incorporation and self-government equally unthinkable. The island's dense population made colonization by Americans impractical. The Foraker Act of 1900 established Puerto Rico as an unincorporated territory, a possession of the United States but not part of it, the United States' first legally established overseas colonial government. The Supreme Court in the 1901 Insular Cases ruled that the United States could govern the island without the consent of the people for an unspecified period. The Constitution "follows the flag," Root declared sardonically, "but doesn't quite catch up with it."[79] The United States also kept Puerto Rico at a distance economically, imposing a tariff on most of its imports. The new scheme of governance—what Root called "patrician tutelage"—took away much of the autonomy Spain had conceded in 1897. The vote was limited to literate male property owners, disfranchising 75 percent of the male population. An executive council composed of five Americans appointed by the president worked closely with local elites and wielded such power that Puerto Ricans compared it to the "Olympian Jupiter."[80]

The occupation government and colonial administration set out to Americanize the island, hoping in the process to create a model of order

78. Cabán, Colonial People, 124.
79. Ibid., 90–91.
80. Gervasio Luis García, " 'I Am the Other': Puerto Rico in the Eyes of North Americans, 1898," Journal of American History 87 (June 2000), 40–41.

and stability.[81] They built roads to attract investment and facilitate economic development. They implemented sanitation and public health programs to ensure a healthy workforce and permit "white American officials" to "escape death in doing their duty." They rewrote the legal code. United States officials viewed Puerto Ricans as morally deficient and lazy— "where a man can lie in a hammock, pick a banana with one hand, and dig a sweet potato with one foot," Gov. Charles Allen explained, "the incentive to idleness is easy to yield to." Viewing the local population as "plastic" and capable of being molded, they reconstructed the educational system to instill into Puerto Ricans that "indomitable thrift and industry which have always marked the pathway of the Anglo-Saxon."[82] English replaced Spanish as the language of instruction. Classes promoted such values as honesty, hard work, and equality before the law. In the mode of Tuskegee Institute, Puerto Ricans were taught manual and technical skills to make them productive workers. Through high tariffs and incentives, the island was integrated into the U.S. economic system, transforming a reasonably diverse agricultural economy into one based on large-scale sugar production. Experts like Jacob H. Hollander of Johns Hopkins University reformed the tax code and made tax collection more efficient. United States officials even sought to Anglicize the name of the island by changing the spelling to "Porto Rico," a move *National Geographic* magazine adamantly rejected.[83]

The new name never quite caught on, and proconsuls could not undo centuries of Spanish rule and remake the United States' new colonial subjects into North Americans. The roads and public health programs improved the quality of life and laid a basis for economic expansion. Educational programs were at best a qualified success. Efforts to force-feed the English language hindered instruction in other areas. Puerto Ricans clung to Spanish; illiteracy rates remained high. Despite vigorous efforts to Americanize the islanders, nationalist sentiment remained alive. Puerto Ricans challenged government dictates and agitated for greater self-government.

Even more than in Puerto Rico, the United States in the Philippines set out with missionary zeal to replicate its institutions. Idealistic young Americans went forth to educate the "natives." Colonial officials built

81. Cabán, *Colonial People*, 105.
82. Wolfgang Binder, "The Tropical Garden and the Mahanesque Resting Place in the Caribbean: Remarks on the Early Incorporation of Puerto Rico by the United States of America," in Serge Ricard, ed., *An American Empire: Expansionist Cultures and Policies, 1881–1917* (Aix-en-Provence, 1990), 100.
83. García, "Puerto Rico," 49–50.

roads and railroads, modernized port facilities at Manila, and through public health programs contained the deadly diseases of malaria and cholera. Experts stabilized the Philippine currency and reformed the legal system. Through what was called reciprocal free trade, the United States sought to foster a mutually beneficial economic development. Beginning with reforms at the local levels, U.S. officials instructed their new wards in democratic politics as a basis for eventual self-government. "We are doing God's work here," Governor General Taft exulted.[84]

As in Puerto Rico, the results were no better than mixed. To its credit, the United States avoided the worst exploitation of European imperialism. Congress imposed restrictions that prevented Americans from taking over huge chunks of land. Literacy and life expectancy levels rose markedly; an honest judiciary and efficient tax system were put into place. The use of English gave scattered islanders with a bewildering diversity of dialects a lingua franca, even if an alien one. Upper-class Filipinos aped American manners. The masses took to baseball and Sousa marches. As journalist Stanley Karnow has observed, however, the "Filipinos became Americanized without becoming Americans."[85] Racism further tainted an already unequal and distant relationship between master and subject. Suffrage was limited to property owners, and no more than 3 percent of the population voted. Behind the facade of democracy, an oligarchy of wealthy Filipino collaborators dominated politics and society and exploited their own people. Reciprocal free trade tied the two economies together, making the Philippines vulnerable to the booms and busts of the U.S. business cycle, stimulating uneven economic growth, and widening an already huge gap between rich and poor. Whatever the United States' intentions, the result was a colonial relationship.[86]

In terms of long-term ties, the United States set the Philippines on a very different course from Puerto Rico. From the outset, U.S. rule had been rationalized in terms of noble intentions. The Schurmann Commission of 1899 recommended eventual independence for the islands, and the United States could not easily scrap promises to prepare them for self-government. Some Filipinos were ambivalent. Those who benefited from the colonial relationship recognized the economic perils that might accompany independence and feared Japan. The elite nevertheless ritualistically clamored for independence, finding eager listeners

84. Stanley Karnow, *In Our Image: America's Empire in the Philippines* (New York, 1989), 228.
85. Ibid., 204–9.
86. Ibid., 209.

among traditionally anti-imperialist Democrats in the United States. When the Democrats won the presidency in 1912, the Wilson adminis- tration introduced a program of "Filipinization," giving Filipinos more seats on the governing executive council and larger roles in the bureau- cracy. In 1916, Congress passed the Jones Act, committing the United States to independence as soon as the Filipinos could establish a "stable government." The pledge was vaguely worded, to be sure, but it was still unprecedented. No imperial nation to this point had promised indepen- dence or even autonomy.[87]

By the time TR took office, the United States was poised to fulfill the dream of a canal across the Central American isthmus. In late 1901, after extensive deliberation, a private commission recommended that it be built across Nicaragua, which was closer to the United States, had a more favorable climate, and posed fewer engineering challenges than the rival site in Panama. Within six months, the United States had shifted to Panama. Fearing the loss of its sizeable investment, the French company that had failed to build a canal across Panama and its redoubtable agent Philippe Bunau-Varilla reduced the price for its concession and mounted a frantic lobbying campaign. Its chief agent, the unscrupulous and pow- erful New York lawyer William Nelson Cromwell, spent lavishly and may have bribed key congressmen. The lobbyists even placed on the desks of senators as a warning against that route stamps portraying a Nicaraguan volcano belching forth tons of lava. Meanwhile, an engineering firm concluded that Panama's technical problems could be managed. Con- gress in June 1903 voted overwhelmingly for that route.[88]

Only Colombia now stood in the way. Although separated from Panama by a stretch of impenetrable jungle, Colombia had withstood countless revolutions to maintain its precarious hold over the isthmus. Having just suffered a long civil war, it desperately needed money and was sensitive to questions of its sovereignty. When Hay negotiated a treaty giving Colombia $10 million with annual payments of $250,000 and the United States a one-hundred-year lease over a six-mile strip of land, Colombian politicians understandably balked. They did not want to lose the treaty, but they feared giving away so much for so little. For reasons noble and petty, they hoped by holding out to get a better deal.

Colombian rejection of the treaty set in motion powerful forces. Pana- manians eager for independence and U.S. largesse plotted yet another

87. Ibid, 247.
88. Walter LaFeber, *The Panama Canal: The Crisis in Historical Perspective* (New York, 1979), 19–28.

revolt. They were encouraged by the indefatigable Bunau-Varilla, who feared going home empty-handed and sought to manipulate the political situation to salvage his clients' investment. Outraged at Colombia's "obstruction," Roosevelt and Hay made no effort to understand its legitimate concerns or to exploit its continuing interest. They were not to be deterred by a pipsqueak nation. Roosevelt privately denounced the Colombians as "contemptible little creatures," "jack rabbits," and "homicidal corruptionists." He did not instigate the rebellion—he knew he did not have to. He and Hay dealt with Bunau-Varilla discreetly. But they made clear they would not obstruct a revolt, and their timely dispatch of warships to the isthmus prevented Colombia from landing troops to suppress the uprising. A stray jackass and a "Chinaman" were the lone casualties in a relatively bloodless revolution. The United States recognized the new government with unseemly haste.[89]

Having contrived to secure appointment as envoy to the United States, the opportunistic Bunau-Varilla moved swiftly to consummate the deal. Even before the revolution, he had drafted a declaration of independence and constitution for Panama. His wife had designed a flag (later rejected because it too closely resembled Old Glory). Determined to complete the transaction before real Panamanians could get to Washington, he negotiated a treaty drafted by Hay with his assistance and far more favorable to the United States than the one Colombia had rejected. The United States got complete sovereignty in perpetuity over a zone ten miles wide. Panama gained the same payment promised Colombia. More important for the short run, it got a U.S. promise of protection for its newly won independence. Bunau-Varilla signed the treaty a mere four hours before the Panamanians stepped from the train in Washington. Nervous about its future and dependent on the United States, Panama approved the treaty without seeing it.[90]

Colombia, obviously, was the big loser. Panama got nominal independence and a modest stipend, but at the cost of a sizeable chunk of its territory, its most precious national asset, and the mixed blessings of a U.S. protectorate. Panamanian gratitude soon turned to resentment against a deal Hay conceded was "vastly advantageous" for the United States, "not so advantageous" for Panama. TR vigorously defended his actions, and some scholars have exonerated him.[91] Even by the low standards of his

89. Gould, *Roosevelt*, 95–97.
90. John Major, "Who Wrote the Hay–Bunau-Varilla Convention?" *Diplomatic History* 8 (Spring 1984), 115–23.
91. Collin, "Symbiosis Versus Hegemony," 477–79.

day, his insensitive and impulsive behavior toward Colombia is hard to defend. Root summed it up best. Following an impassioned Rooseveltian defense before the cabinet, the secretary of war retorted in the sexual allusions he seemed to favor: "You have shown that you have been accused of seduction and you have conclusively proven that you were guilty of rape."[92] Although journalists criticized the president and Congress investigated, Americans generally agreed that the noble ends justified the dubious means. Even before completion of the project in 1914, the canal became a symbol of national pride. The United States succeeded where Europe had failed. It wiped out yellow fever and surmounted enormous engineering challenges. The canal symbolized for Americans their ingenuity and resourcefulness rather than imperialism; "the greatest engineering wonder of the ages," it was hailed, "a distinctively American triumph." Its symbolic importance in turn gave them a special attachment to it that make subsequent adjustments difficult.[93]

"The inevitable result of our building the canal," Root observed in 1905, "must be to require us to police the surrounding premises." In fact, the United States had long claimed the Caribbean as its exclusive preserve. In 1892, Harrison and Blaine arranged with U.S. bankers to get the Dominican Republic's debts out of the hands of European creditors. The Platt Amendment had imposed a protectorate on Cuba. Before the first dirt was shoveled in Panama, breakdown of the Harrison-Blaine deal and the threat of foreign intervention in the Dominican Republic led to the assertion through the so-called Roosevelt Corollary to the Monroe Doctrine of broad U.S. police powers in the hemisphere.[94]

The corollary developed out of a prolonged crisis in Venezuela that for nervous U.S. officials highlighted the threat of European and especially German intervention. Since independence, Latin American nations had contracted sizeable foreign debts, and private citizens of the Western nations mounted growing claims against Latin governments. Some claims were legitimate, some spurious, most inflated, but in the heyday of gunboat diplomacy governments were not disposed to discriminate and often backed their citizens with force. Latin Americans sought to turn European concepts of international law to their favor. The so-called Calvo Doctrine

92. Howard Jones, *The Course of American Diplomacy* (New York, 1985), 248.
93. J. Michael Hogan, "Theodore Roosevelt and the Heroes of Panama," *Presidential Studies Quarterly* 19 (Winter 1989), 79, 86, 89.
94. LaFeber, *Panama Canal*, 53–54; Cyrus Veeser, "Inventing Dollar Diplomacy: The Gilded Age Origins of the Roosevelt Corollary to the Monroe Doctrine," *Diplomatic History* 27 (June 2003), 301–26.

asserted that investors and creditors were entitled to no special rights just because they were foreigners. The Drago Doctrine boldly claimed that the forcible recovery of loans violated the principle of sovereign equality among nations. Neither the Europeans nor the United States recognized such heretical notions. "We do not guarantee any state against punishment if it misconducts itself," Roosevelt proclaimed.[95]

Venezuelan indebtedness provoked a crisis in 1902. Falling back on the Calvo and Drago doctrines, the feisty and defiant dictator Cipriano Castro defaulted on loans held by British creditors and insisted that claimants must seek justice through Venezuelan courts. The great powers informed the United States in late 1902 that they would collect the debts—by force if necessary. Roosevelt gave them a green light, although he did warn, in view of the melon carving in China, that punishment must not "take the form of the acquisition of territory by any non-American power." The Europeans demanded that Venezuela pay. When Castro refused, they seized the dilapidated vessels that constituted his "navy," blockaded Venezuela's ports, and even bombarded Puerto Cabello. Other claimants—including the United States—now lined up to profit from Anglo-German aggressiveness.[96]

Roosevelt later claimed that by issuing a stern ultimatum he had forced the Germans to arbitrate, but resolution of the crisis appears to have been more complicated. Castro originally proposed U.S. arbitration, a shrewd ploy to exploit growing U.S. concern with European intervention. Roosevelt *was* increasingly troubled by German belligerence. The United States *did* have a strong naval force in the area, including Adm. George Dewey's flagship. But no evidence has ever been discovered of a presidential ultimatum. Recent research concludes, on the contrary, that although the Germans behaved with their usual heavy-handedness, in general they followed Britain's lead. The British, in turn, went out of their way to avoid undermining their relations with the United States.[97] Both nations accepted arbitration to extricate themselves from an untenable situation and stay on good terms with the United States.

The Venezuelan episode persuaded administration officials to take steps to head off future European interventions. Britain and Germany encouraged the United States to take the lead in policing its hemisphere. In May 1904—ironically, or perhaps appropriately, at a dinner celebrating

95. Lars Schoultz, *Beneath the United States: A History of U.S. Policy Toward Latin America* (Cambridge, Mass., 1998), 180.

96. Nancy Mitchell, "The Height of the German Challenge: The Venezuela Blockade, 1902–1903," *Diplomatic History* 20 (Spring 1996), 190.

97. Ibid., 200.

the anniversary of Cuba's "independence"—Root delivered the statement that would become the Roosevelt Corollary to the Monroe Doctrine. "Any country whose people conduct themselves well can count on our hearty friendliness," he pledged. But "brutal wrongdoing, or an impotence which results in a general loosening of the ties of civilized society, may finally require intervention by some civilized society, and in the Western Hemisphere the United States cannot ignore this duty."[98] Roosevelt's corollary thus upheld the original intent of the Monroe Doctrine by reversing one of its key provisions and explicitly giving the United States the right of intervention. It cleared up any ambiguity as to who controlled the region.

The administration first applied the corollary in the Dominican Republic. Even before Root's May 1904 statement, that beleaguered Caribbean nation had begun to come apart. A massive influx of U.S. investments and the conversion to an export economy had hopelessly destabilized Dominican life. The nation was deeply in debt to European and U.S. creditors, the victim of an incredibly complex set of sordid deals between its own often unscrupulous leaders and foreign loan sharks. It could not pay. It verged on anarchy, the result of bitter conflicts among groups an American with typical disdain dismissed as "political brigands . . . little better than savages."[99] Dictator Carlos Morales flirted with saving himself from internal foes and external creditors by inviting a long-term U.S. protectorate. Dominican default on a stopgap debt arrangement and the Hague Court's award to Britain and Germany, seemingly rewarding their aggressiveness in Venezuela, threatened by late 1904 another European intervention in the Caribbean. Safely reelected, Roosevelt decided to act.[100]

The United States developed for the Dominican Republic what has aptly been called a "neo-colonial substitute."[101] Roosevelt had no interest in annexation or even the protectorate proposed by Morales. He sought less drastic means that would help stabilize the Dominican Republic economically and politically and give the United States some control without formal responsibility. With two warships providing a "powerful moral effect on the rash and ignorant elements," a U.S. diplomat with a naval officer at his side negotiated a treaty (first proposed by Morales) giving the

98. Gould, *Roosevelt*, 175; the corollary itself is in *Congressional Record* 39 (December 6, 1904), part 1, 19.
99. Schoultz, *Beneath the United States*, 183, 188.
100. Collin, "Symbiosis Versus Hegemony," 488–89.
101. Emily S. Rosenberg and Norman L. Rosenberg, "From Colonialism to Professionalism: The Public Private Dynamic in United States Financial Advising, 1898–1929," *Journal of American History* 74 (June 1987), 61.

United States control of the customs house and providing that 45 percent of the receipts should go to domestic needs, the rest to foreign creditors. When a now thoroughly contentious Senate refused to consider the treaty, Roosevelt used the threat of foreign intervention to proceed with an informal arrangement under an executive agreement. In 1907, the Senate approved a modified treaty.[102]

The Dominican experiment brought together diplomats, financial experts, and bankers in best Progressive Era fashion to employ "scientific" methods to promote stability and modernization. The U.S. government served as midwife, bringing in economist Hollander, who had already revamped Puerto Rico's finances, to scale back the Dominican debt, improve tax collection, and limit expenditures. Through government intercession, U.S. bankers offered Dominican bonds at high prices. To get the loan, the Dominican Republic accepted a receivership. The key was U.S. control of the customs houses, which would ensure regular payments to foreign creditors and the availability of funds for domestic needs. By removing the major prize and the means for competing factions to buy arms, it would also reduce the likelihood of revolution. Stabilization of the economy would encourage U.S. investment, which in turn would promote economic development.[103] The arrangement brought dramatic short-term improvement and became the model for de facto protectorates elsewhere in the Caribbean and Central America and even in Africa.

William Howard Taft and his secretary of state, Philander Knox, formalized TR's ad hoc arrangements into policy. The enormous Taft and the diminutive (5' 5" tall) Knox, a corporate lawyer with the sobriquet "Little Phil," made an odd couple in appearance. Taft had a very hard presidential act to follow. It did not help that the onetime friends became bitter enemies before he took office. A capable diplomatic troubleshooter, Taft, by his own admission, had an "indisposition to labor as hard as I might" and a "disposition to procrastinate."[104] He lacked Roosevelt's gift for public relations. Relations with Congress, already bad when Roosevelt left office, deteriorated sharply under his successor. Knox was cold, aloof, and impeccably dressed, a socialite and an avid golfer—he once affirmed that he would not let "anything so unimportant as China" interfere with his golf game. He worked short hours and took long Palm Beach vacations. While setting the broad contours of policy, he left the details to his

102. Schoultz, *Beneath the United States*, 185–188.
103. Rosenberg and Rosenberg, "Colonialism to Professionalism," 62–63; Emily S. Rosenberg, "Revisiting Dollar Diplomacy: Narratives of Money and Manliness," *Diplomatic History* 22 (Spring 1998), 159–68.
104. Hilderbrand, *Power and the People*, 76.

subordinates, mainly his abrasive and short-tempered assistant secretary of state, Francis Huntington Wilson.[105]

Taft and Knox adopted the Dominican model to develop a policy called "dollar diplomacy," which they applied mainly in Central America. They sought to eliminate European political and economic influence and through U.S. advisers promote political stability, fiscal responsibility, and economic development in a strategically important area, the "substitution of dollars for bullets," in Wilson's words.[106] United States bankers would float loans to be used to pay off European creditors. The loans in turn would provide the leverage for U.S. experts to modernize the backward economies left over from Spanish rule by imposing the gold standard based on the dollar, updating the tax structure and improving tax collection, efficiently and fairly managing the customs houses, and reforming budgets and tariffs. Taft and Knox first sought to implement dollar diplomacy by treaty. When the Senate balked and some Central American countries said no, they turned to what has been called "colonialism by contract," agreements worked out between private U.S. interests and foreign governments under the watchful eye of the State Department.[107] Knox called the policy "benevolent supervision." One U.S. official insisted that the region must be made safe for investment and trade so that economic development could be "carried out without annoyance or molestation from the natives."[108]

These ambitious efforts to implement dollar diplomacy in Central America produced few agreements, little stability, and numerous military interventions. Part of the problem was attitude. Knox and Wilson had little regard for Central Americans—"rotten little countries," the latter called them.[109] They provoked staunch nationalist opposition. Guatemala and Costa Rica flatly rejected U.S. proposals, the latter turning to Europe to refinance its debt. Honduras's finance minister took flight rather than sign an agreement; its congress, under death threat from nationalist mobs, refused to make the country an "administrative dependency of the United States."[110] When diplomacy failed, private interests took over. "Sam the

105. Walter Scholes, "Philander Knox, 1909–1913," in Norman A. Graebner, ed., *An Uncertain Tradition: American Secretaries of State in the Twentieth Century* (New York, 1961), 59–60.
106. Schoultz, *Beneath the United States*, 208.
107. Rosenberg and Rosenberg, "Colonialism to Professionalism," 65–67; Rosenberg, "Dollar Diplomacy," 166–168.
108. Cabán, *Colonial People*, 103–4.
109. Schoultz, *Beneath the United States*, 209.
110. Ibid., 214.

Banana Man" Zemurray, the legendary entrepreneur who had already begun converting Honduras into a "banana republic," helped finance a rebellion led by an African American soldier of fortune and supported by a U.S. warship. Upon taking power, a pro-U.S. government showed its gratitude by granting favors to Zemurray, who in turn negotiated a loan to help the new president pay off his debts.[111] In the Dominican Republic itself, the much ballyhooed 1907 agreement broke down five years later amidst political upheaval. When rebels seized control of several customs houses, Taft sent in the Marines to put down the revolution, force out the president, and hold a new election. The U.S. military intervention of 1912 was the prelude to a much larger and longer intervention four years later.

Efforts to "stabilize" Nicaragua through dollar diplomacy also required U.S. military power. The independent and highly nationalist dictator José Santos Zelaya demonstrated his displeasure with the U.S. selection of Panama as the canal site by hinting that he might negotiate with a European nation. He also aspired to dominate Central America. When Zelaya threatened to invade El Salvador in 1909, the United States expressed strong disapproval, and U.S. investors encouraged a rebellion. When two Americans assisting the rebels were captured and executed, the United States broke relations and vowed to apprehend and prosecute Zelaya. The dictator fled to Mexico. After another change of government, the United States negotiated a Dominican-like treaty with Adolfo Díaz, formerly a bookkeeper with a U.S. mining company. By this time, the U.S. Senate was in full rebellion. The treaty never got out of the Foreign Relations Committee.

More deals and another revolution led to military intervention. Once it was clear the Senate would not approve the treaty, Taft, emulating TR, oversaw the negotiation of a private arrangement by which U.S. bankers gave the Díaz government cash in return for control of the National Bank of Nicaragua and 51 percent ownership of its railroads, initiatives that tied Nicaragua firmly to the U.S. economy and gave a huge boost to trade.[112] The United States sent 2,700 marines to put down a 1912 rebellion. It left a "legation guard" of several hundred marines to symbolize its presence. In a treaty negotiated just before Taft left office, it gave Nicaragua $3 million for a naval base and canal rights. The treaty was not ratified until 1916.

111. Walter LaFeber, *Inevitable Revolutions: The United States in Central America* (New York, 1984), 44; Lester D. Langley, *The Banana Wars: An Inner History of American Empire, 1900–1934* (Lexington, Ky., 1983), 133–34.
112. Schoultz, *Beneath the United States*, 217.

The Taft administration also tried dollar diplomacy in Liberia. By 1908, this West African nation founded in the nineteenth century by colonization societies and freed slaves was deeply in debt to British creditors, torn by internal rebellion, and embroiled in border disputes with neighboring British and French colonies. A U.S. commission warned that failure to solve Liberia's problems could result in its being colonized by Europeans and "speedily disappear[ing] from the map." It recommended use of the Dominican model with a U.S. Army officer assuming responsibility for building a military force to protect its frontiers. Taft approved the proposal to help America's "ward." A loan was arranged and a warship sent to contain the rebellion. When Congress blocked the Nicaraguan treaty, the administration worked out a private contract for Liberia under State Department supervision. The arrangement did not succeed. The U.S. receiver general and the Frontier Force were "unpopular and inept." The loss of trade from World War I plunged Liberia into deeper economic doldrums.[113]

In applying dollar diplomacy in East Asia, the Taft administration broke sharply with its predecessor. Roosevelt had little sympathy for China and no use for the Open Door policy. His major concern was protecting a vulnerable Philippines against Japan. Egged on by Willard Straight, a former consul general at Mukden and staunch partisan of China, Taft and Knox came to see China and especially Manchuria as a ripe field for U.S. trade and investment and an independent and friendly China as important to the United States. Deeply suspicious of Japan—"a Jap is first of all a Jap," Taft once proclaimed, "and would be glad to aggrandize himself at the expense of anybody"—they sought to use private U.S. capital to thwart Japanese expansion and bolster the independence of China.[114] They found eager accomplices in Beijing and among Chinese officials in Manchuria who saw the United States as a useful counterweight against Russia and Japan.

A bold move to promote American investments in Chinese railroads proved counterproductive. United States officials correctly recognized that control of the railroads was the key to political and economic power. Taft personally interceded with the Chinese to secure for the United States an equal share of an international loan to fund the construction of a railroad in southern China. Chinese officials went along but refused to push other nations to agree. The powers eventually accepted U.S. participation, but the

---

113. Emily S. Rosenberg, "The Invisible Protectorate: The United States in Liberia, 1909–1940," *Diplomatic History* 9 (Summer 1985), 191–99.
114. Hunt, *Special Relationship*, 210.

arrangement was never completed. At about the same time, the embattled Chinese governor general of Manchuria, with the support of Beijing, devised a plan to secure U.S. funding for a trans-Manchurian railroad to counter the growing power of Russia and Japan. Knox eagerly agreed and took the scheme a giant step further by proposing the internationalization of all railroads in Manchuria, a quite unprecedented venture and an obvious attempt to check Japanese influence.[115] As naive as it was ambitious, the scheme totally misfired. Hoping to divide Russia and Japan, Knox and Taft drove them together. In a July 1910 pact, they divided Manchuria into spheres of influence and agreed to cooperate to maintain the status quo. Knox's scheme depended on support from the other powers, but Britain refused to offend its new Asian ally, Japan, and France would not antagonize its ally Russia.

Undaunted, the dollar diplomats launched one last effort in East Asia. Claiming it their "moral duty" to help China, Knox finally persuaded hardheaded U.S. bankers to put up $2 million as part of an international consortium to promote economic development. He then elbowed his way into the consortium. Before the deal was consummated, revolution broke out in China. The new Chinese government sought better terms. Wary of the revolution, the great powers and indeed the United States delayed recognition for months. U.S. bankers left out of the consortium screamed in protest. By the time the deal was finally concluded in early 1913, the Taft administration was on its way out.[116]

FILLED WITH GOOD INTENTIONS, Americans took a much more active role in the world after 1901. Even in the implementation of colonial policies, they saw themselves charting a new course. Theodore Roosevelt embodied the American spirit of his era. He served in a time of peace when the United States was not threatened and there was no major crisis. He exemplified the best and worst of his country's tradition. Recognizing that the nation's new position brought responsibilities as well as benefits and that international involvement served its interests, Roosevelt took unprecedented initiatives, in the process demonstrating the president's capacity to be a world leader. He began to modernize the instruments of U.S. power. He recognized that the combination of "practical efficiency" and idealism was both necessary and rare.[117] His practical idealism helped end a war in East Asia and prevent war in Europe, each of which

115. LaFeber, Clash, 95.
116. Robert D. Schulzinger, U.S. Diplomacy Since 1900 (5th ed., New York, 2002), 42–43.
117. Gould, Roosevelt, 298.

served U.S. needs. Recognizing limited U.S. interests in China and Korea and the vulnerability of the Philippines and even Hawaii, he was the consummate pragmatist in East Asia, refusing to take on commitments he could not uphold.

In Central America and the Caribbean, on the other hand, Roosevelt and Taft displayed the narrowness of vision and disdain for other peoples that had afflicted U.S. foreign policy from the birth of the republic. To be sure, Roosevelt launched what his predecessors had long dreamed of, the construction of an isthmian canal, by any standard a huge achievement. And some measure of U.S. influence in the region was inevitable. But the arrogant way he dealt with Colombia and its offspring Panama and the heavy-handed interventions under the Roosevelt Corollary and dollar diplomacy changed forever the way the United States was viewed in its own hemisphere. As implemented by Roosevelt and Taft, "benevolent supervision" was not benevolent for those supervised. The attempt to impose American ideas, institutions, and values upon different cultures was arrogant and offensive—and did not work. Rampant U.S. economic intervention destabilized a region where Americans professedly sought order. The almost reflexive military interventions further damaged U.S. long-term interests and left an enduring and understandable legacy of suspicion among Latin Americans of the "Colossus of the North." "A wealthy country," Latin poet Rubén Darío put it, "joining the cult of Mammon to the cult of Hercules; while Liberty, lighting the path to easy conquest, raises her torch in New York."[118]

Revolutions in China, Mexico, and Russia and the outbreak of war in Europe would pose even sterner challenges for Woodrow Wilson and the foreign policy of the new world power.

118. Rubén Darío, "To Roosevelt," in Dennis Merrill and Thomas G. Paterson, eds., *Major Problems in American Foreign Relations*, vol. 1, *To 1920* (6th ed., Boston, 2005), 405.

10

"A New Age"

Wilson, the Great War, and the Quest for a New World Order, 1913–1921

It was called the Great War, and its costs were horrific, its consequences profound. Between August 1914 and November 1918, the European powers fought it out across a blood-soaked continent. Harnessing modern technology to the ancient art of war, they created a ruthlessly efficient killing machine that left as many as ten million soldiers and civilians dead, countless others wounded and disfigured. The war inflicted huge economic and psychological damage on people and societies; it shattered once mighty empires. It coincided with and in important ways shaped the outbreak of revolutionary challenges to the established economic and political order. Together, the forces of war and revolution unleashed during the second decade of the twentieth century set off an era of conflict that would last nearly until the century's end.

Woodrow Wilson once declared that it would be an "irony of fate" if his presidency focused on foreign policy.[1] Indeed, it seems more than a twist of fate if not quite predestination that placed him in the White House during this tumultuous era. He brought to the office an especially keen sense of his own calling to lead the nation and of America's destiny to reshape a war-torn world. From his first days as chief executive, he confronted revolutions in Mexico, China, and later Russia. Initially content to follow the traditional path of U.S. neutrality in Europe's wars, in the face of Germany's U-boat attacks he eventually—and reluctantly—concluded that intervention was necessary to defend his nation's rights and honor and assure for himself and the United States a voice in the peacemaking. Once at war, he gave urgent and eloquent expression to a liberal peace program that fully reflected American ideals dating to the beginning of the republic. He enjoined Americans to assume a leadership position in world affairs. Committing himself and his nation to little short of revolutionizing the international system, he learned through bitter experience that the world was less malleable than he had assumed. He met frustration abroad and bitter defeat at home, a failure that took

1. Arthur S. Link, *Woodrow Wilson and the Progressive Era, 1910–1917* (New York, 1954), 81.

the form of grand tragedy when a new and even more destructive war broke out less than two decades hence. Yet the ideas he set forth have continued to influence U.S. foreign policy throughout the twentieth century and beyond.

I

Wilson towers above the landscape of modern American foreign policy like no other individual, the dominant personality, the seminal figure. Born in the South shortly before the Civil War, the son of a Presbyterian minister, from his youth he assiduously prepared himself for leadership—"I have a passion of interpreting great thoughts to the world," he wrote even as a young man.[2] After studying law, he earned a doctorate in history and political science at Johns Hopkins University. He became a "public intellectual" before the phrase was coined, establishing a national reputation through his writing and speeches as a keen student of U.S. history and government. Drawn to the world of action, he shifted to university administration and then to politics, as president of Princeton University and subsequently governor of New Jersey demonstrating brilliant leadership in implementing sweeping reform programs against entrenched opposition. Much has been made of his moralism. Like many of his contemporaries, he was a deeply religious man. Religion gave a special fervor to his sense of personal and national destiny. He was also a practical person who quickly grasped the workings of complex institutions and learned how to use them to achieve his goals. Somewhat forbidding of countenance, with high cheekbones, a firm jaw, and stern eyes, he was a shy and private man who could come across as cold and arrogant. Yet among friends he was capable of great warmth; among those he loved, great passion. He was an accomplished and entertaining mimic. His practiced eloquence with the written and spoken word gave him a capacity to sway people matched by few U.S. leaders. Those who worked with him sometimes complained that his absorption in a single matter limited his capacity to deal with other issues. His greatest flaws were his difficulty working with strong people and, once his mind was made up, a reluctance to hear dissenting views.[3]

Wilson prevailed in 1912 mainly because Republicans were split between party regulars who supported Taft and progressives who backed the increasingly radical Bull Moose candidate Theodore Roosevelt. Socialist Eugene

2. Thomas J. Knock, *To End All Wars: Woodrow Wilson and the Quest for a New World Order* (New York, 1992), 13.
3. Kendrick A. Clements, *The Presidency of Woodrow Wilson* (Lawrence, Kans., 1992), 1–14.

V. Debs won 6 percent of the vote in this most radical election in U.S. history. Wilson came to power fully committed to his New Freedom reform program that sought to restore equality of opportunity and democracy through tariff and banking reform and curbing the power of big business.[4]

He also brought to the presidency firm convictions about America's role in the world. He fervently believed that foreign policy should serve broad human concerns rather than narrow selfish interests. He recognized business's need for new markets and investments abroad, but he saw no inherent conflict between America's ideals and its pursuit of self-interest, believing, in biographer Kendrick Clements's phrase, that the United States "would do well by doing good."[5] He shared in full measure and indeed found religious justification for the traditional American belief that providence had singled out his nation to show other peoples "how they shall walk in the paths of liberty."[6] He had watched with fascination his nation's emergence as a world power, and he perceived that this new status put it in a position to promote its ideals. He shared the optimism and goals of the organized peace movement. At first opposed to taking the Philippines, he went along on grounds that nations like the United States and Britain that were "organically" disposed toward democracy should educate other peoples for self-government.[7] An admirer of conservative British political philosopher Edmund Burke, he feared disorder and violent change. As at home, he viewed powerful economic interests as obstacles to equal opportunity and democratic progress in other countries.[8]

Wilson's views were influenced by Col. Edward M. House (the title was honorific), a wealthy Texas politico who without official position remained his alter ego and closest adviser until the last years of his presidency. Small of stature, quiet and self-effacing, House was a shrewd judge of people and a skilled behind-the-scenes operator. His aspirations were revealed in his anonymously published novel, *Philip Dru: Administrator*, the tale of a Kentuckian and West Point graduate who after corralling the special interests at home launched a crusade with Britain against Germany and Japan for disarmament and the removal of trade barriers.[9]

4. H. W. Brands, "Woodrow Wilson and the Irony of Fate," *Diplomatic History* 28 (September 2004), 503–12.
5. Clements, *Wilson Presidency*, 93.
6. Knock, *End All Wars*, 11.
7. Woodrow Wilson, "A Political Essay," October 1, 1900, in Arthur S. Link, ed., *The Papers of Woodrow Wilson* (69 vols., 1966–94), 12:17–18.
8. Knock, *End All Wars*, 7–8.
9. Lloyd C. Gardner, *Safe for Democracy: The Anglo-American Response to Revolution, 1913–1923* (New York, 1987), 43–44.

Wilson's genuine and deeply felt aspirations to build a better world suffered from a certain culture-blindness. He lacked experience in diplomacy and hence an appreciation of its limits. He had not traveled widely outside the United States and knew little of other peoples and cultures beyond Britain, which he greatly admired. Especially in his first years in office, he had difficulty seeing that well-intended efforts to spread U.S. values might be viewed as interference at best, coercion at worst. His vision was further narrowed by the terrible burden of racism, common among the elite of his generation, which limited his capacity to understand and respect people of different colors. Above all, he was blinded by his certainty of America's goodness and destiny. "A new age has come which no man may forecast," he wrote in 1901. "But the past is the key to it; and the past of America lies at the center of modern history."[10]

As a scholar, Wilson had written that the power of the president in foreign policy was "very absolute," and he practiced what he had preached, expanding presidential authority even beyond TR's precedents. He was fascinated by the challenge of leading a great nation in tumultuous times. Early in his presidency, he wrote excitedly to a friend about the "thick bundle of despatches" he confronted each afternoon, a "miscellany of just about every sort of problem that can arise in the foreign affairs of a nation in a time of general questioning and difficulty." He distrusted and even had contempt for the State Department, complaining on one occasion that dispatches written there were not in "good and understandable English." Like the professor he had been, he corrected and returned them for resubmission. He composed much diplomatic correspondence on his own typewriter and handled some major issues without consulting either the State Department or his cabinet.[11]

Wilson's early forays into the world of diplomacy suggest much about the ideas and ideals he brought to office. His naming of William Jennings Bryan as secretary of state was politic in light of the Great Commoner's stature in the Democratic Party and crucial role in the 1912 campaign. It followed a long tradition of appointing the party leader to that important post. Bryan had traveled widely, including an around-the-world jaunt in 1906. In this respect, at least, he was better qualified than Wilson to shape U.S. foreign policy. Even more than Wilson, Bryan believed that Christian principles should animate foreign policy. A longtime temperance

10. Knock, *End All Wars*, 14.
11. Frederick S. Calhoun, *Power and Principle: Armed Intervention in Wilson's Foreign Policy* (Kent, Ohio, 1986), 13, 17; House Diary, December 18, 1914, *Wilson Papers* 27:415; Wilson to Mary Ellen Hulbert, April 4, 1915, ibid. 32:476.

advocate, he set the diplomatic community abuzz by refusing to serve alcohol at official functions (the Russian ambassador claimed not to have
tasted water for years and to have survived one event only by loading up
on claret before he arrived).[12] Wilson and Bryan negotiated a treaty with
Colombia apologizing and offering monetary compensation for the U.S.
role in the Panamanian revolution. This well-intentioned and truly remarkable move quite naturally provoked cries of rage from the Rough
Rider, Theodore Roosevelt, and sufficient opposition in the Senate that it
was not ratified. It won warm applause in Latin America. In a major
speech at Mobile, Alabama, in October 1913, Wilson explicitly disavowed
U.S. economic imperialism and gunboat diplomacy in Latin America,
linking the exploitative interests that victimized other peoples to the
bankers and corporate interests he was fighting at home and promising to
replace those old "degrading policies" with a new policy of "sympathy
and friendship."[13]

As war enveloped Europe, Wilson and Bryan sought to implement
ideas long advocated by the peace movement. Bryan's agreement to serve
had been conditioned on freedom to pursue "cooling off treaties." During
1913–14, ironically as Europe was rushing headlong toward war, he negotiated with twenty nations—Britain and France included—treaties designed to prevent such crises from escalating to military conflict. When
diplomacy failed, nations would submit their disputes for study by an international commission and refrain from war until its work was completed. Dismissed by critics then and since as useless or worse, the treaties
were indeed shot through with exceptions and qualifications. Bryan nevertheless considered them the crowning achievement of his career. Wilson
took them more seriously after the Great War began, even concluding
that they might have prevented it. The Bryan treaties marked Wilson's
initial move toward an internationalist foreign policy.[14]

The quest for a Pan-American Pact reveals in microcosm Wilson's larger
designs and the obstacles they encountered abroad. Originally proposed
by Bryan in late 1913, the idea was embraced by the president after the outbreak of war in Europe. Viewing it as a means to preserve peace following
the war, he rewrote it on his own typewriter. It called for mutual guarantees among hemispheric nations of political independence and territorial
integrity "under republican government" and for member governments to

12. Michael Kazin, A Godly Hero: The Life of William Jennings Bryan (New York, 2006),
    216–19.
13. Mobile Speech, October 27, 1913, Wilson Papers 28:448–52.
14. Knock, End All Wars, 22.

take control of the production and distribution of arms and munitions. He later linked the pact with U.S. efforts to expand trade in Latin America. Presented first to Argentina, Brazil, and Chile, it drew suspicion. Chile especially feared that its consent would affect its ongoing border dispute with Peru. More important, politicians were alarmed by the huge expansion of U.S. trade and feared that, despite his soothing words, Wilson no less than his predecessors wished to dominate the hemisphere economically and might use the provision calling for republican government to impose U.S. values. Chilean objections delayed consideration of the treaty; U.S. military intervention in Mexico doomed it. It became the basis of Wilson's later proposals for a League of Nations[15]

II

From the outset, Wilson grappled with the complex issues raised by revolution. These early twentieth-century upheavals erupted first in East Asia and Latin America. Although they shared the aim of overthrowing established orders, they were as diverse as the nations in which they occurred. In China, reformers inspired by Japan and the West sought to replace a monarchical, feudal order with a modern nation-state. In Mexico, middle- and lower-class revolutionaries challenged the power of entrenched economic and political interests and the Catholic Church. In each case, nationalists sought to eliminate or at least curb the power of foreign interests that had undermined their country's sovereignty and economic independence.

Wilson's response to these revolutions revealed his good intentions and the difficulties of their implementation. Traditionally, the United States had sympathized with revolutions at least in principle, but when they turned violent or radical or threatened U.S. interests, it had called for order or sought to channel them in moderate directions.[16] With China and Mexico, Wilson plainly sympathized with the forces of revolution. He understood better than most Americans the way in which they expressed the desire of people for economic and political progress. Even in Central America, he hoped to seize the opportunity to improve the lot of the peoples involved. Wilson's "ethnocentric humanitarianism" failed to recognize that in seeking to direct the future of these nations he limited their ability to work out their own destiny. His presumptuous interference overlooked their own national pride and aspirations.[17]

15. Ibid., 39–45, 83–84.
16. Michael H. Hunt, *Ideology and U.S. Foreign Policy* (New Haven, Conn., 1987), 106–8.
17. Calhoun, *Power and Principle*, 23–24.

After a decade of agitation, nationalist reformers in late 1911 overthrew the moribund Qing regime. Upon taking office, Wilson responded enthusiastically and optimistically to the Chinese Revolution. True to his reformist instincts and taking his cues mainly from missionaries, he concluded that China was "plastic" in the hands of "strong and capable Westerners." He and Bryan believed that the United States should serve as a "friend and exemplar" in moving China toward Christianity and democracy. They also agreed that "men of pronounced Christian character" should be sent there.[18] Wilson took bold steps to help China. In March 1913, without consulting the State Department, he withdrew the United States from the international bankers' consortium formed by Taft and Knox to underwrite loans to China. Certain that the Europeans preferred a weak and divided China, a week later and without consulting them he recognized strongman Yüan Shih-k'ai's Republic of China. The open door, he proclaimed, was a "door of friendship and mutual advantage . . . the only door we care to enter."[19]

Wilson's gestures did nothing to alter the harsh realities in China. In its early stages, the revolution brought little substantive change. The masses were not involved. Leaders sought to advance their own power rather than build a modern state. Reformers fought with each other; Yüan's government was shaky at best. The powers sought to exploit China's weakness to expand their influence. Continued U.S. involvement in the consortium might have helped check Japanese and European ambitions. Wilson's well-intentioned withdrawal thus did as much harm as good. He subsequently rejected China's request for loans, making clear the limits of American support.

The outbreak of war in Europe exposed even more starkly the limits of U.S. helpfulness. "When there is a fire in a jeweler's shop the neighbours cannot be expected to refrain from helping themselves," a Japanese diplomat candidly admitted.[20] Japan immediately joined the Allies and took advantage of Europe's preoccupation to drive the Germans from Shandong province. In early 1915, Tokyo presented the embattled Chinese government with its Twenty-One Demands, which sought mainly to legitimize gains made at Germany's expense and expand Japanese influence in Manchuria and along the coast. Even more intrusively, Tokyo demanded that China accept Japanese "advisers" and share responsibility for maintaining order in key areas.

18. Michael H. Hunt, The Making of a Special Relationship: The United States and China to 1914 (New York, 1983), 218–19.
19. Wilson statement, March 18, 1913, Wilson Papers 27:194.
20. Clements, Wilson Presidency, 108.

The Chinese sought U.S. support in resisting Japan. Some nationalists saw the United States as little different than other imperial powers; others admired and hoped to emulate it. Still others viewed it as the least menacing of the powers and hoped to use it to counter more aggressive nations. Yüan hired an American to promote his cause and used missionaries and diplomats to gain support from Washington. Working through the U.S. minister, he appealed to the United States to hold off Japanese pressures.

Although deeply concerned with Japanese actions, Wilson and his advisers were not inclined to intercede. State Department counselor Robert Lansing concluded that it would be "quixotic in the extreme to allow the question of China's territorial integrity to entangle the United States in international difficulties."[21] True to his pacifist principles, Bryan gave higher priority to avoiding war with Japan than to upholding the independence of China. He made clear the United States would do nothing. Preoccupied with the European war and the death of his beloved wife, Ellen, Wilson at first did not dissent. He continued to sympathize with China, however, informing Bryan that "we should be as active as the circumstances permit" in championing its "sovereign rights."[22] Wilson's firmer stance combined with British protests and divisions within the Tokyo government led Japan to moderate its demands.

Wilson continued to take limited measures to help China. In 1916, he encouraged private bankers to extend loans, both to preserve U.S. economic interests and to counter Japanese influence. Soon after, he retreated from his 1913 position by authorizing a new international consortium of bankers to provide loans, even agreeing to help them collect if the Chinese defaulted. Alarmed by America's more assertive stance, Japan sent a special emissary to Washington in the summer of 1917. Kikujiro Ishii's discussions with Lansing, who was by this time secretary of state, revealed major differences, but the two nations eventually got around them by agreeing that Japan's geographical propinquity gave it special but not paramount interests in China. In a secret protocol, the United States again pushed for the open door. The two nations agreed not to exploit the war to gain exclusive privileges. Wilson's position revealed his continuing concern for the Chinese Revolution and Japanese intrusion but made clear to both nations his unwillingness to act.[23]

21. Warren I. Cohen, *America's Response to China: An Interpretative History of Sino-American Relations* (New York, 1971), 92.
22. Wilson to Bryan, April 14, 1915, *Wilson Papers* 32:521.
23. Cohen, *Response to China*, 96.

Closer to home, the United States had no such compunctions. In Central America and the Caribbean, revolution was an established part of the political process, its aims, at least in U.S. eyes, less about democracy and progress than power and spoils. The growing U.S. economic and diplomatic presence had further destabilized an already volatile region while the opening of the Panama Canal and the outbreak of war in Europe heightened U.S. anxiety about the area. The United States had vital interests there. It also had the power and was willing to use it to contain revolutions and maintain hegemony over small, weak states whose people were deemed inferior. "We are, in spite of ourselves, the guardians of order and justice and decency on this Continent," a Wilson confidant wrote in 1913. "[We] are providentially, naturally, and inescapably, charged with maintenance of humanity's interest here."[24]

During the campaign and the early days of his presidency, Wilson had denounced Taft's dollar diplomacy and military interventionism and spoken eloquently of treating Latin American nations "on terms of equality and honor."[25] He and Bryan genuinely hoped to guide these peoples— "our political children," Bryan called them—to democracy and freedom. They sought to understand their interests even when they conflicted with those of the United States. However they packaged it, the two men ended up behaving much like their predecessors. Wilson deemed it "reprehensible" to permit foreign nations to secure financial control of "these weak and unfortunate republics." But he endorsed a form of dollar diplomacy to control their finances.[26] He and Bryan looked upon them with the same sort of paternalism with which they regarded African Americans at home. They assumed that U.S. help would be welcomed. When it was not, they fell back on diplomatic pressure and military force.[27]

The result was a period of military interventionism exceeding that of Roosevelt and Taft. During its two terms in office, the administration sent troops to Cuba once, Panama twice, and Honduras five times. Wilson and Bryan added Nicaragua to an already long list of protectorates. Despite his anti-imperialist record, Bryan sought to end a long period of instability there with a treaty like the Platt Amendment that would have given the United States the right to intervene. When the Senate rejected this provision, the administration negotiated a treaty giving the United States exclusive rights to the Nicaraguan canal route, a preemptive move

24. William Bayard Hale to Wilson, July 9, 1913, *Wilson Papers* 28:33.
25. Mobile Speech, October 27, 1913, ibid. 28:448–52.
26. House Diary, October 30, 1913, ibid. 28:476.
27. Kazin, *Godly Hero*, 228–30.

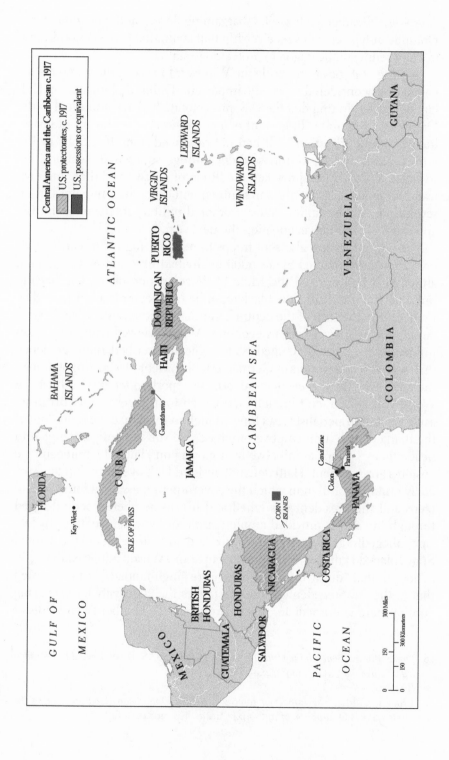

Central America and the Caribbean c.1917

U.S. protectorates, c. 1917

U.S. possessions or equivalent

ATLANTIC OCEAN

GULF OF MEXICO

FLORIDA

Key West

BAHAMA ISLANDS

ISLE OF PINES

CUBA

Guantánamo

JAMAICA

HAITI

DOMINICAN REPUBLIC

PUERTO RICO

VIRGIN ISLANDS

LEEWARD ISLANDS

CARIBBEAN SEA

WINDWARD ISLANDS

MEXICO

BRITISH HONDURAS

GUATEMALA

HONDURAS

SALVADOR

NICARAGUA

CORN ISLANDS

COSTA RICA

PANAMA

Colon

Canal Zone

Panamá

PACIFIC OCEAN

COLOMBIA

VENEZUELA

GUYANA

300 Miles

0   150

0   150   300 Kilometers

depriving Nicaragua of a vital bargaining lever, and providing for a Dominican-type customs receivership that facilitated U.S. economic control and reduced Nicaragua to protectorate status.[28]

Because of its position astride the Windward Passage, the island of Hispaniola was considered especially important. Dollar diplomat Jacob Hollander boasted in 1914 that the U.S. protectorate had accomplished in the Dominican Republic "little short of a revolution . . . in the arts of peace, industry and civilization."[29] It had not produced stability. Efforts by the United States in 1913 to impose order through supervised elections, the so-called Wilson Plan, provoked the threat of a new revolution and civil war. Dominicans ignored Bryan's subsequent order for a moratorium on revolution. All else failing, Wilson ordered military intervention in 1915 and full-scale military occupation the next year.[30]

The administration also sent troops to neighboring Haiti. Partly by its own choice, the United States traditionally had little influence in Haiti, although it had coveted the Môle St. Nicolas, one of the Caribbean's finest ports. Historically, the black republic had been most influenced by France; after the turn of the century, German merchants and bankers secured growing power over its economy. Wilson viewed rising European influence as "sinister." United States officials ascribed more credence than warranted to rumors of German establishment of a coaling station at the mole and to the even more bizarre report—*after* the outbreak of World War I—of a joint French-German customs receivership. Bryan set aside his anti-imperialist views long enough to try to take the mole "out of the market" with a preemptive purchase. He subsequently attempted to head off any European initiative by imposing on Haiti a Dominican-type customs arrangement. Haiti defiantly resisted U.S. overtures, but an especially brutal revolution in which the government massacred some 167 citizens and the president was killed and his dismembered body dragged through the streets provided ample reason for U.S. intervention. In July 1915, allegedly as a strategic measure and to restore order, the United States placed Haiti under military occupation. Wilson admitted that U.S. actions in that "dusky little republic" were "highhanded," but he insisted that in the "unprecedented" circumstances the "necessity for exercising control there is immediate, urgent, imperative." The better elements of

28. Lars Schoultz, *Beneath the United States: A History of U.S. Policy Toward Latin America* (Cambridge, Mass., 1998), 224–29.

29. Ibid., 229.

30. Bruce J. Calder, *The Impact of Intervention: The Dominican Republic During the United States Occupation of 1916–1924* (Austin, Tex., 1984), 6–19.

the country would understand, he hoped, that the United States was there to help, not subordinate, the people.[31]

Whatever Wilson's intentions, the military occupations on Hispaniola represent major blots on the U.S. record. The United States imposed at the point of a gun the stability it so desperately sought, but at great cost to the local peoples and to its own ideals. In the Dominican Republic, the U.S. Marines fought a nasty five-year war against stubborn guerrillas in the eastern part of the country, often applying brutal methods against those they contemptuously labeled "spigs." Using models developed in Puerto Rico and the Philippines, U.S. proconsuls implemented technocratic progressive reforms, building roads and developing public health and sanitation programs. The reforms benefited mainly elites and foreigners. Little changed as a result, and when the marines withdrew in 1924, life quickly reverted to normal. The Americans bequeathed to Dominicans a keen interest in baseball. The domineering presence of outsiders certain of their superiority also created a nascent sense of Dominican nationalism. Perhaps the main result of the occupation, an unintended consequence, was that the Guardia Nacional established to assist in upholding order would become the means by which Rafael Trujillo maintained a brutal dictatorship for thirty-one years.[32]

In Haiti, the marines also encountered stubborn resistance, making it impossible for Wilson to remove them when he was so inclined in 1919. The United States systematically eliminated German economic interests and gained even tighter control over Haiti's finances and customs than it had of the Dominican Republic's. But it could not attract much investment capital, and the country remained impoverished. There was no pretense of democracy: Secretary of the Navy Josephus Daniels was jokingly called "Josephus the First—King of Haiti." The U.S. financial adviser employed the threat of not paying the salaries of Haitian officials to gain veto power over legislation. The racism of occupying forces was even more acute where the people were stereotyped like African Americans—"the same happy, idle, irresponsible people we know," as a marine colonel put it. United States officials imposed the Jim Crow style of segregation already in place in the American South. They promoted a Tuskegee-type educational system emphasizing technical education and manual labor. Once the marines left, as in the Dominican Republic, the roads (built with forced labor) fell into disrepair and public health programs languished. The blatant

31. Wilson to Edith Bolling Galt, August 15, 1915, *Wilson Papers* 34:209; Hans Schmidt, *The United States Occupation of Haiti, 1915–1934* (New Brunswick, N.J., 1985), 12–63.
32. Calder, *Impact of Intervention*, 238–47.

racism of the occupation forces pushed a local elite in search of its identity to look back to its African roots.[33]

Wilson's problems in Central America paled compared to the challenges posed by Mexico. The most profound social movement in Latin American history, the Mexican Revolution was extremely complex, a rebellion of middle and lower classes against a deeply entrenched old order and the foreigners who dominated the nation's economy followed by an extended civil war. It would be six years before the situation stabilized. The ongoing struggle created major difficulties for Wilson. His well-intentioned if misguided meddling produced two military interventions in three years and nearly caused an unnecessary and possibly disastrous war. The best that can be said is that he kept the interventions under tight control and learned from his Mexican misadventures something of the limits of America's appeal to other nations and its power to effect change there.

For thirty-one years, Porfirio Díaz had maintained an open door for foreign investors. Under his welcoming policies, outsiders came to own three-fourths of all corporations and vast tracts of land—newspaper mogul William Randolph Hearst alone held some seven million hectares in northern Mexico. United States bankers held Mexican bonds. British and U.S. corporations controlled 90 percent of Mexico's mineral wealth and all its railroads and dominated its oil industry. Díaz hoped to promote modernization and economic development, but the progress came at enormous cost. Centralization of political control at the expense of local autonomy caused widespread unrest, especially in the northern provinces, provoking growing anger toward the regime and its foreign backers. Foreigners used Mexican lands to produce cash crops for export, disrupting the traditional economy and village culture and leaving many peasants landless. Mexican critics warned of a "peaceful invasion." Díaz's policies, they charged, made their nation a "mother to foreigners and a stepmother to her own children."[34] Mexico's economy was at the mercy of external forces, and a major recession in the United States helped trigger revolution. In 1910, middle and

---

33. Schmidt, *Haiti*, 74, 174–88; Emily S. Rosenberg, *Financial Missionaries to the World: The Politics and Culture of Dollar Diplomacy, 1900–1930* (Durham, N.C., 2003), 82–84.

34. Yves-Charles Grandjeat, "Capital Ventures and Dime Novels: U.S.-Mexican Relations during the Porifiriano," in Serge Richard, ed., *An American Empire: Expansionist Cultures and Policies, 1881–1917* (Aix-en-Provence, 1990), 137–49; William Schell Jr., "American Investment in Tropical Mexico: Rubber Plantations, Fraud, and Dollar Diplomacy," *Business History Review* 64 (Summer 1990), 219.

lower classes under the leadership of Francisco Madero rose up against the regime. In May 1911, they overthrew Díaz.

Counterrevolutions quickly followed. Madero instituted a parliamentary democracy but maintained the status quo economically, disappointing many of his backers. Díaz's supporters plotted to regain power. In his last years in office, Díaz had balanced rising U.S. power in Mexico by encouraging European and especially British economic and political influence. When Madero sustained this policy, U.S. businessmen who at first welcomed the revolution turned against him. They gained active support from Ambassador Henry Lane Wilson, a conservative career diplomat friendly to U.S. business interests and skeptical of the revolution. A heavy drinker, something of a loose cannon, and meddlesome in the worst tradition of Joel Poinsett and Anthony Butler, Wilson sought to undermine official support for Madero and sympathized with plots to get rid of him.General Victoriana Huerta overthrew the government in February 1913 and brutally murdered Madero and his vice president. Out of negligence and indifference, Ambassador Wilson bore some responsibility for this gruesome outcome. Madero's corpse was scarcely in the grave when his supporters launched a civil war against Huerta.[35]

In one of his first ventures in diplomacy, President Wilson set a new subjective standard for recognizing revolutionary governments. Responding to the French Revolution, Thomas Jefferson had established the precedent of recognizing any government formed by the will of the nation. The United States traditionally had recognized governments based simply on whether they held power and fulfilled their international obligations. With Mexico, Wilson introduced a moral and political test. Huerta was indeed a despicable character, crude, corrupt, cruel, "an ape-like man" who "may be said almost to subsist on alcohol," a presidential confidant reported.[36] Wilson was appalled by the murder of Madero and indignantly vowed that he would not "recognize a government of butchers." He also suspected Huerta's ties to U.S. and especially foreign businessmen. In view of the importance of the Panama Canal, he told the British ambassador, it was vital for Central American nations to have "fairly decent rulers." He "wanted to teach those countries a lesson by insisting on the removal of Huerta."[37] He hoped, in his own pretentious and oft-quoted words, to teach U.S. neighbors to "elect good men." Aware that

35. Karl M. Schmitt, *Mexico and the United States, 1821–1973: Conflict and Co-existence* (New York, 1974), 116–26.
36. William Bayard Hale report, July 9, 1913, *Wilson Papers* 28:31.
37. British Embassy in Washington to Sir Edward Grey, October 14, 1913, ibid., 543.

recognition might cripple the opposition, he withheld it in hopes of bringing to power a more respectable government. In so doing, he created yet another instrument to influence the internal politics of Latin American nations.[38]

Wilson also dispatched two trusted personal emissaries to Mexico to push for a change of government. Neither was up to the task. William Bayard Hale was a journalist and close friend; John Lind, a Minnesota politician. Neither spoke Spanish or knew anything about Mexico; Lind indeed considered Mexicans "more like children than men" and claimed they had "no standards politically."[39] Their mission—to counsel Mexico "for her own good," in Wilson's patronizing words—was a fool's errand. They were to persuade Huerta to hold elections in which he would not run and all parties would abide by the result. The president authorized Lind to threaten the stick of military intervention and dangle the carrot of loans before those Mexican leaders who went along.

Predictably, the ploy failed. The crafty Huerta dodged, feinted, and parried. At first flatly rejecting proposals he deemed "hardly admissible even in a treaty of peace after a victory," he then appeared to acquiesce, promising to give up the presidency and hold elections in late October.[40] After a series of military defeats, however, he arrested most of the congress and in what amounted to a coup d'état established a dictatorship. Huerta's opposition responded no more positively to U.S. interference. Constitutionalist "First Chief" Venustiano Carranza expressed resentment at Wilson's intrusion and angrily insisted that he would not participate in a U.S.-sponsored election.

Admitting to a "sneaking admiration" for Huerta's "indomitable, dogged determination," Wilson stepped up the pressure.[41] He blamed the British for Huerta's intransigence and combined stern public warnings with soothing private explanations of U.S. policy. He seriously considered a blockade and declaration of war, again claiming it to be his "duty to force Huerta's retirement, peaceably if possible but forcibly if necessary."[42] Ultimately, he contented himself with measures short of war, warning the Europeans to stay out, sending a squadron of warships to Mexico's east coast, and lifting an arms embargo to help Carranza militarily.

38. Peter V. N. Henderson, "Woodrow Wilson, Victoriano Huerta, and the Recognition Issue in Mexico," Americas 41 (October 1984), 154, 173.
39. Schoultz, Beneath the United States, 243; Wilson to Bryan, September 19, 1913, Wilson Papers 28:293.
40. Schoultz, Beneath the United States, 243.
41. Wilson to Mary Ellen Hulbert, February 2, 1914, Wilson Papers 29:211.
42. Ibid., 245.

If Wilson was looking for a pretext for military intervention, he got it at Tampico in April 1914 when local officials mistakenly arrested and briefly detained a contingent of U.S. sailors who had gone ashore for provisions. The officials quickly released the captives and expressed regret, but the imperious U.S. admiral on the scene demanded a formal apology and a twenty-one-gun salute. A Gilbert and Sullivan incident escalated into full-scale crisis. Undoubtedly seeking to gain diplomatic leverage, Wilson fully backed his admiral. Huerta at first rejected U.S. demands. Sensing an opportunity for gainful mischief, he then cleverly proposed a simultaneous salute and next a reciprocal one. Wilson rejected both; Huerta rebuffed America's "unconditional demands."[43]

Seizing what he called a "psychological moment," Wilson ordered a military intervention at Veracruz to promote his broader goal of getting rid of Huerta.[44] He pitched his actions on grounds of defending national honor. He easily secured congressional authorization to use military forces, although some hotheads, including his future archenemy, Republican senator Henry Cabot Lodge of Massachusetts, preferred all-out war, military occupation of Mexico, and even a protectorate. To demonstrate his good intentions, the president recruited veterans from Philippine nation-building to show the Mexicans and others through the U.S. occupation the values of progressive government. "If Mexico understood that our motives were unselfish," Colonel House affirmed, "she should not object to our helping adjust her unruly household."[45]

It was a very big "if," of course. For the short term, at least, the intervention failed on all counts. Instead of welcoming the North Americans as liberators, Mexicans of varied political persuasions rallied to the banner of nationalism. In Veracruz, civilians, prisoners quickly released from jails, and soldiers acting on their own fiercely resisted the invasion. It took two days to subdue the city. More than two hundred Mexicans were killed, nineteen Americans. Across Mexico, newspapers cried out for "Vengeance! Vengeance! Vengeance!" against the "pigs of Yanquilandia." In several cities, angry mobs attacked U.S. consulates. Even Carranza demanded U.S. withdrawal.[46]

United States forces took control of the city in early May, remained there for seven months, and performed numerous good works—with

43. Link, *Progressive Era*, 122–23.
44. Clements, *Wilson Presidency*, 99.
45. Robert E. Quirk, *An Affair of Honor: Woodrow Wilson and the Occupation of Vera Cruz* (New York, 1962), 77.
46. Ibid., 107.

ephemeral results. The military government implemented progressive reforms to show Mexicans by "daily example" that the United States had
come "not to conquer them, but to help restore peace and order." Occupation troops built roads and drainage ditches; provided electric lighting
for streets and public buildings; reopened schools; cracked down on
youth crime, gambling, and prostitution; made tax and customs collection more equitable, efficient, and lucrative for the government; and developed sanitation and public health programs to transform a beautiful
but filthy city into "the cleanest town in the Republic of Mexico." As in
the Dominican Republic and Haiti, within weeks after the marines left it
was hard to tell that Americans had been in Veracruz.[47]

The intervention contributed only indirectly to the removal of Huerta.
At first, the dictator used the U.S. presence to rally nationalist support.
Shaken by Mexican resistance, saddened by the loss of life, and increasingly fearful of a Mexican quagmire, Wilson as a face-saving gesture accepted in July a proposal from Argentina, Brazil, and Chile to mediate.
While Wilson and Huerta's representatives quickly deadlocked in the
surreal and inconclusive talks at Niagara Falls, New York, the civil war intensified. Now able to secure arms, Carranza's forces steadily gained
ground and in mid-1914 forced Huerta to capitulate. Chastened by the
experience, Wilson confided to his secretary of war that there were "no
conceivable circumstances which would make it right for us to direct by
force or by threat of force the internal processes of a revolution as profound as that which occurred in France."[48] In November 1914, with Carranza firmly in power, the president removed the occupation forces.

A year of relative quiet followed. In Mexico itself, the civil war raged
on, rival factions under populist leaders Emiliano Zapata in the south
and Francisco "Pancho" Villa in the north challenging Carranza's fragile
government. To promote order and perhaps a government he could influence, Wilson tried to mediate among the warring factions, issuing at
least a veiled threat of military intervention if they refused. Carranza and
Zapata flatly rejected the overture. Villa's fortunes were obviously declining, and he appeared receptive, opening a brief—and fateful—flirtation
with the United States. Carranza continued to gain ground militarily,
however. Increasingly preoccupied with the European war, having just
weathered the first U-boat crisis with Germany, and fearful of growing
German intrigue in Mexico, Wilson did an abrupt about-face. Even

---

47. Ibid., 171; Jodi Pettazonni, "The Occupation of Veracruz, Mexico" (M.A. thesis, University of Kentucky, 2000), 57–79.
48. Wilson to Lindley M. Garrison, August 8, 1914, *Wilson Papers* 30:362.

though he considered Carranza a "fool" and never established the sort of paternalistic relationship he sought, he reluctantly recognized the first chief's government. He even permitted Carranza's troops to cross U.S. territory to attack the Villistas.[49]

Villa quickly responded. To the end of 1915, he had seemed among various Mexican leaders the most amenable to U.S. influence. A share-cropper and cattle rustler before becoming a rebel, the colorful leader was a strange mixture of rebel and caudillo.[50] At first viewed by Wilson and other Americans as a dedicated social reformer, a kind of Robin Hood, he sought to secure arms and money by showing restraint toward U.S. interests in areas he controlled. He refused even to protest the occupation of Veracruz. As his military and financial position worsened, however, he began to tax U.S. companies more heavily. Several major military defeats in late 1915 and Wilson's seeming betrayal caused him to suspect—incorrectly—that Carranza had made a sordid deal with Wilson to stay in power in return for making Mexico an American protectorate.[51]

Denouncing the "sale of our country by the traitor Carranza" and claiming that Mexicans had become "vassals of an evangelizing professor," Villa struck back.[52] He began to confiscate U.S. property, including Hearst's ranch. In January 1916, his troops stopped a train in northern Mexico and executed seventeen American engineers. Even more boldly, he decided to attack the Americans "in their own den" to let them know, he informed Zapata, that Mexico was a "tomb for thrones, crowns, and traitors."[53] On March 9, 1916, to shouts of "*Viva Villa*" and "*Viva México*," five hundred of his troops attacked the border town of Columbus, New Mexico. They were driven back by U.S. Army forces after a six-hour fight in which seventeen Americans and a hundred Mexicans were killed. Villa hoped to put Carranza in a bind. If the first chief permitted the Americans to retaliate by invading Mexico, he would be exposed as a U.S. stooge. Conflict between Carranza and the United States, on the other hand, might permit Villa, by defending the independence of his country, to promote his own political ambitions.[54]

49. Memorandum by Thomas Beaumont Hohler, October 21, 1915, ibid. 35:98.
50. Friedrich Katz, *The Secret War in Mexico* (Chicago, 1981), 145.
51. Friedrich Katz, "Pancho Villa and the Attack on Columbus, New Mexico," *American Historical Review* 83 (February 1978), 112–17.
52. Katz, *Secret War*, 307.
53. Ibid.
54. Katz, "Attack on Columbus," 101.

Wilson had little choice but to respond forcibly. He may have feared that Villa's actions would have a domino effect throughout Central America in a time of rising international tension. In the United States, hotheads who had demanded all-out intervention since 1914, including oilmen, Hearst, and Roman Catholic leaders, grew louder. This first attack on U.S. soil since 1814 provoked angry cries for revenge that took on greater significance in an election year. Wilson may also have seen a firm response to Villa's raid as a means to promote his plans for reasonable military preparedness and strengthen his hand in dealing with European belligerents. He quickly put together a "punitive expedition" of more than 5,800 men (eventually increased to more than 10,000), under the command of Gen. John J. Pershing, to invade Mexico, capture Villa, and destroy his forces. United States troops crossed the border on March 15.[55]

The expedition brought two close, yet distant, neighbors to the brink of an unwanted and potentially disastrous war. Pershing's forces eventually drove 350 miles into Mexico. Even with such modern equipment as reconnaissance aircraft and Harley-Davidson motorcycles, they never caught a glimpse of the elusive Villa or engaged his troops in battle. Complaining that he was looking for a "needle in a haystack," a frustrated Pershing urged occupation of part or all of Mexico. All the while Villa's army, now estimated at more than ten thousand men, used hit-and-run guerrilla tactics to harass U.S. forces and seize northern Mexican cities. On one occasion, Villa reentered the United States, striking the Texas town of Glen Springs.[56]

Although Wilson had promised "scrupulous respect" for Mexican sovereignty, as Pershing drove south tensions with Carranza's government inevitably increased. Mexican and U.S. forces first clashed at Parral. On June 20, a U.S. patrol engaged Mexican troops at Carrizal. Americans at first viewed the incident as an unprovoked attack and demanded war. Wilson responded by drafting a message for Congress requesting authority to occupy all Mexico. Now embroiled in yet another dangerous submarine crisis with Germany, he also mobilized the National Guard and dispatched thirty thousand troops to the Mexican border, the largest deployment of U.S. military forces since the Civil War.

Cooler heads ultimately prevailed. Peace organizations in the United States, including the Women's Peace Party, pushed Wilson for restraint,

---

55. Schoultz, *Beneath the United States*, 249; Linda Hall and Don Coerver, "Woodrow Wilson, Public Opinion, and the Punitive Expedition: A Re-assessment," *New Mexico Historical Review* 72 (April 1997), 171–94.
56. Calhoun, *Power and Principle*, 57.

and when they publicized evidence that Americans had fired first at Carrizal, he hesitated. Carranza's freeing of U.S. prisoners helped ease tensions. Wilson admitted shame over America's first conflict with Mexico in 1846 and had no desire for another "predatory war." He suspected that it would take more than five hundred thousand troops to "pacify" Mexico. He did not want one hand tied behind his back when war with Germany seemed possible if not indeed likely.[57] "My heart is for peace," he told activist Jane Addams. In a speech on June 30, 1916, he eloquently asked: "Do you think that any act of violence by a powerful nation like this against a weak and distracted neighbor would reflect distinction upon the annals of the United States?" The audience resoundingly answered "No!"[58] After six months of tortuous negotiations with Mexico, the punitive expedition withdrew in January 1917, just as Germany announced the resumption of U-boat warfare.

Wilson's firm but measured response helped get military preparedness legislation through Congress in 1916, strengthened his hand with Germany during yet another U-boat crisis, and aided his reelection in November. Mobilization of the National Guard and the training received by the army facilitated U.S. preparations for war the following year.[59] On the other hand, the failed effort to capture Villa left a deep residue of ill will in Mexico. Only recently dismissed as a loser, the elusive rebel joined the pantheon of national heroes as the "man who attacked the United States and got away with it."[60] Carranza moved closer to Germany, encouraging Berlin to explore with Mexico the possibility of an anti-American alliance.

Wilson's Mexican policy has been harshly and rightly criticized. More than most Americans, he accepted the legitimacy and grasped the dynamics of the Mexican Revolution. He deeply sympathized with the "submerged eighty-five percent of the people . . . who are struggling towards liberty."[61] At times, he seemed to comprehend the limits of U.S. military power to reshape Mexico in its own image and the necessity for Mexicans to solve their own problems. But he could not entirely shed his conviction that the American way was the right way and he could assist Mexico to find it. He could never fully understand that those Mexicans who shared his goals would consider unacceptable even modest U.S. efforts to influence their revolution. Conceding Wilson's good intentions, his actions were often

57. Wilson conversation with Newton Baker, May 12, 1916, *Wilson Papers* 37:36.
58. Knock, *End All Wars*, 82–83.
59. Hall and Coerver, "Punitive Expedition," 192–94.
60. Katz, "Attack on Columbus," 130.
61. Interview, April 27, 1914, *Wilson Papers* 29:516.

counterproductive. He averted greater disaster mainly because in 1914 and again in 1916 he resisted demands for occupation, even the establishment of a protectorate, and declined to prolong fruitless interventions.[62]

III

If Mexico, by Wilson's admission, was a thorn in his side, the Great War was far more, dominating his presidency and eventually destroying him, politically and even physically. On the surface, Europe seemed peaceful in the summer of 1914. In fact, a century of relative harmony was about to end. For years, the great powers felt increasingly threatened by each other, their fears and suspicions manifested in a complex and rigid system of alliances, an arms race intended to gain security through military and naval superiority, and war plans designed to secure an early advantage. Unstable domestic political environments in Germany and Russia cleared the path to war. When a Serbian nationalist assassinated the Austrian Archduke Franz Ferdinand and his wife, Sophie, in Sarajevo in June, what might have remained an isolated incident escalated to war. Its honor affronted, Austria-Hungary gained German support and set out to punish Serbia. Russia responded by mobilizing behind its Serbian ally, an act designed to deter Germany that instead provoked a declaration of war. Britain joined Russia's ally France in war against Germany. None of the great powers claimed to want war, but their actions produced that result. Expecting a short and decisive conflict, Europeans responded with relief and even celebration. Young men marched off to cheering crowds with no idea of the horrors that awaited them.[63]

The conflict that began in August 1914 defied all expectations. Technological advances in artillery and machine guns and an alliance system that encouraged nations facing defeat to hang on in expectation of outside support ensured that the war would *not* be short and decisive. The industrial revolution and the capacity of the modern nation-state to mobilize vast human and material resources produced unprecedented destructiveness and cost. Striking quickly, Germany drove to within thirty miles of Paris, reviving memories of its easy victory in 1870–71. This time French lines held. An Allied counteroffensive pushed the Germans back to France's eastern boundary, where they dug into heavily fortified entrenchments. By November 1914, opposing armies faced each other along a 475-mile front from the North Sea to the Swiss border. The combatants

62. Clements, *Wilson Presidency*, 103.
63. John Keegan, *The First World War* (New York, 2000), 48–74; Michael Howard, *The First World War* (London, 2003), 18–31.

had already incurred staggering costs—France's battle deaths alone exceeded three hundred thousand, and its losses from dead, wounded, or missing surpassed nine hundred thousand. Despite huge casualties on both sides, the lines would not move significantly until March 1917. These first months destroyed any illusions of a quick end and introduced the grim realities of modern combat.[64]

Conditioned by more than a century of non-involvement in Europe's quarrels, Americans were shocked by the guns of August. The outbreak of war "came to most of us as lightning out of a clear sky," one thoughtful commentator wrote. They also expressed relief to be remote from the conflict. "Again and ever I thank God for the Atlantic Ocean," the U.S. ambassador in Great Britain exclaimed.[65] Americans were not without their prejudices. More than one-third of the nation's citizens were foreign born or had one parent who was born abroad. A majority, including much of the elite, favored the Allies because of cultural ties and a belief that Britain and France stood for the right principles. German Americans, on the other hand, naturally supported the Central Powers, as did Irish Americans who despised Britain, and Jewish and Scandinavian Americans who hated Russia. "We have to be neutral," Wilson observed in 1914, "since otherwise our mixed populations would wage war on each other."[66]

Whatever their preferences, the great majority of Americans saw no direct stake in the struggle and applauded Wilson's proclamation that their country be "neutral in fact as well as in name . . . , impartial in thought as well as in action." Indeed, in terms of the nation's long tradition of non-involvement in Europe's wars, the seeming remoteness of the conflict, and the advantages of trading with both sides, neutrality appeared the obvious course. The president even wrote a brief message to be displayed in movie theaters urging audiences "in the interest of neutrality" not to express approval or disapproval when war scenes appeared on the screen. From the outset, Wilson also saw in the war a God-given opportunity for U.S. leadership toward a new world order. "Providence has deeper plans than we could possibly have laid ourselves," he wrote House in August 1914.[67]

As a neutral, the United States could provide relief assistance to wartorn areas, and its people responded generously. The American Red Cross

64. Keegan, *First World War*, 133.
65. Link, *Progressive Era*, 145; Ross Gregory, *The Origins of American Intervention in the First World War* (New York, 1971), 3.
66. Melvin Small, *Democracy and Diplomacy: The Impact of Domestic Politics on U.S. Foreign Policy, 1789–1994* (Baltimore, Md., 1996), 43.
67. Wilson to House, August 13, 1914, *Wilson Papers* 30:336.

shipped supplies worth $1.5 million to needy civilians; its hospital units cared for the wounded.[68] Belgian relief was one of the great humanitarian success stories of the war. Headed by mining engineer and humanitarian Herbert Hoover, the program found ingenious ways to get around the German occupation and the British blockade to save the people of Belgium. Admiringly called a "piratical state organized for benevolence," Hoover's Commission for Belgian Relief had its own flag and cut deals with belligerents to facilitate its work. It raised funds from citizens and governments across the world, $6 million from Americans in cash, more than $28 million in kind. The commission bought food from many countries, arranged for its shipment, and, with the help of forty thousand Belgian volunteers, got it distributed. It spent close to $1 billion, fed more than nine million people a day, and kept a nation from starving. Known as the "Napoleon of mercy" for his organizational and leadership skills, Hoover became an international celebrity.[69]

The implementation of neutrality policy posed much greater challenges. It had been very difficult a century earlier for a much weaker United States to remain disentangled from the Napoleonic wars. America's emergence as a major power made it all the more problematical. Emotional and cultural ties to the belligerents limited impartiality of thought. Wilson and most of his top advisers, except for Bryan, favored the Allies. The United States' latent military power made it a possibly decisive factor in the conflict. Most important, its close economic ties with Europe and especially the Allies severely restricted its ability to remain uninvolved. At the outbreak of war, exports to Europe totaled $900 million and funded the annual debt to European creditors. Some Americans saw war orders opening a further expansion of foreign trade. At the very least, maintaining existing levels was an essential national interest. That this might be incompatible with strict neutrality was not evident at the beginning of the war. It would become one of the great dilemmas of the U.S. response.

In reality, trade was so important to Europe and the United States itself that whatever Americans did or did not do would have an important impact on the war and the domestic economy. Attempts to trade with one set of belligerents could provoke reprisals from the other; trading with both, as in Jefferson and Madison's day, might result in retaliation from each. A willingness to abandon trade with Europe might have ensured U.S. neutrality, but it would also have entailed unacceptable sacrifices to

68. Merle Curti, *American Philanthropy Abroad* (New Brunswick, N.J., 1963), 230–31.
69. George H. Nash, "An American Epic: Herbert Hoover and Belgian Relief in World War I," *Prologue* (Spring 1989), 57–86.

a nation still reeling from an economic downturn. The United States could not remain unaffected, nor could it maintain an absolute, impartial neutrality.

Although legally and technically correct, Wilson's neutrality policy favored the Allies. Seeking to establish the "true spirit" of neutrality, Bryan, while the president was absent from Washington mourning the death of his wife, imposed a ban on loans to belligerents on the grounds that money was the worst kind of contraband. The consequences quickly became obvious. The Allies desperately needed to purchase supplies in the United States and soon ran out of cash. Bryan's strict neutrality thus threatened the Allied cause and U.S. commerce. Drawing a sharp distinction between public loans, by which U.S. citizens would finance the war with their savings, and credits that would permit Allied purchases and avoid "the clumsy and impractical method of cash payments," Wilson modified the ruling in October 1914.[70] In the next six months, U.S. bankers extended $80 million in credits to the Allies. A year later, the president lifted the ban on loans entirely. Wilson correctly argued that loans to belligerents had never been considered a violation of neutrality. The result, House candidly admitted in the spring of 1915, was that the United States was "bound up more or less" in Allied success.[71]

Far more difficult to explain, Wilson also acquiesced in Britain's blockade of northern Europe. Employing sea power in a manner sanctioned by its gloried naval tradition, Britain set out to strangle the enemy economically, seeking to keep neutral shipping from entering north European ports and threatening to seize contraband. British officials used precedents set by the Union in the Civil War. Sensitive to history, they also applied the blockade in ways that minimized friction with the United States. In marked contrast to Jefferson and Madison, Wilson acquiesced, an "astonishing concession" of neutral rights, in the words of a sympathetic biographer.[72] His position may have reflected his pro-Allied sympathies. More likely, he perceived that, in part because of the British blockade, U.S. trade with Germany was not important enough to make a fuss over. His acquiescence reflected a pragmatic response to a situation he realized the United States could not change. A historian himself, at the start of the war he appears mostly to have feared drifting into conflict with England over neutral rights like his fellow "Princeton man" James Madison a century before.[73]

70. Robert Lansing memorandum, October 23, 1914, *Wilson Papers* 31:219.
71. House to Wilson, May 25, 1915, ibid. 33:254.
72. Clements, *Wilson Presidency*, 120–21.
73. House Diary, September 30, 1914, *Wilson Papers* 31:109.

He worried that getting drawn into the war might compromise his role as a potential peacemaker. He informed Bryan in March 1915 that arguing with Britain over the blockade would be a "waste of time." The United States should simply assert its position on neutral rights and in "friendly language" inform London that it would be held responsible for violations.[74] Acceptance of the blockade tied the United States closer to the Allied cause. It also encouraged British infringements on U.S. neutral rights, leading to major problems in 1916.

By contrast, Wilson took a firm stand against the U-boat, Germany's answer to the British blockade. In February 1915, Berlin launched a submarine campaign around the British Isles and warned that neutral shipping might be affected. Wilson responded firmly but vaguely by holding the Germans to "strict accountability" for any damage done to Americans. A hint of future crises came in March 1915 when a U.S. citizen was killed in the sinking of the British freighter *Falaba*, an incident Wilson privately denounced as an "unquestionable violation of the just rules of international law with regard to unarmed vessels at sea."[75]

On May 7, 1915, a U-boat lurking off the southern coast of Ireland sent to the bottom in eighteen minutes the British luxury liner *Lusitania*, taking the lives of twelve hundred civilians, ninety-four of them children (including thirty-five babies), from injuries, hypothermia, and drowning. Bodies of victims floated up on the Irish coast for weeks. One hundred and twenty-eight U.S. citizens died. The sinking of the *Lusitania* had an enormous impact in the United States, becoming one of those signal moments about which people later remember where they were and what they were doing. It stunned the United States out of its complacency and brought the Great War home to its people for the first time. It propelled foreign policy to the forefront of American attention.[76] Some U.S. citizens expressed great moral outrage at this "murder on the high seas." Ex-president Theodore Roosevelt condemned German "piracy" and demanded war. After days of hesitation and a careful weighing of the alternatives, Wilson dispatched to Berlin a firm note reasserting the right of Americans to travel on passenger ships, condemning submarine warfare in the name of the "sacred principles of justice and humanity," and warning that further sinkings would be regarded as "deliberately unfriendly."[77]

---

74. Wilson to Bryan, March 25, 1915, ibid. 32:432–33.
75. Wilson to Bryan, April 3, 1915, ibid. 32:469.
76. John Milton Cooper Jr., "The Shock of Recognition: The Impact of World War I on America," *Virginia Quarterly Review* 76 (Autumn 2000), 557.
77. Gregory, *Origins of Intervention*, 63–64.

Wilson's strong stand derived from a rising fear of Germany and especially from concern for his own and his nation's credibility. Suspicion of Germany had grown steadily in the United States since the turn of the century, especially with regard to its hostile intentions in the Western Hemisphere. German atrocities in neutral Belgium, exaggerated by British propaganda, their crude and shocking efforts to bomb civilians from the air, and rumors, sometimes fed by top Berlin officials, of plans to foment rebellion within the United States provoked fear and anger among Americans, the president included. U-boat warfare further called into question basic German decency. The submarine had not been used extensively or effectively in warfare prior to 1915. This new and seemingly horrible weapon violated traditional rules of naval warfare that spared civilians. It killed innocent people—even neutrals—without warning. Britain could compensate U.S. merchants for property seized or destroyed, but lives taken by submarines could not be restored. Most Americans held to what Wilson called a "double wish." They did not want war, but neither did they want to remain silent in the face of such a brutal assault on human life. Republicans appeared ready to exploit the sinking of the *Lusitania* if the president did not uphold the nation's rights and honor. Wilson also did not want war, but he recognized that to do nothing would sacrifice principles he held dear and seriously damage his stature at home and abroad.[78]

Wilson's tough line on the *Lusitania* provoked crises in Washington and Berlin. Still committed to a strict neutrality, no matter the cost, Bryan insisted that Americans must be warned against traveling on belligerent ships. Protests against U-boat warfare must be matched by equally firm remonstrances against British violations of U.S. neutral rights. When Wilson rejected his arguments, the secretary resigned as an act of conscience, removing an important dissenting voice from the cabinet. The Germans also claimed that equity required U.S. protests against a blockade that starved European children. They insisted, correctly as it turned out, that the *Lusitania* had been carrying munitions. Chancellor Theobald von Bethmann-Hollweg nevertheless recognized that it was more important to keep the United States out of the war than to use submarines without restriction. When a U-boat sank the British ship *Arabic* in August, killing forty-four, two Americans included, Wilson extracted from Berlin a public pledge to refrain from attacks without warning on passenger vessels and a commitment to arbitrate the *Lusitania* and *Arabic* cases. The president weathered his first crisis with Germany, but only

78. Ibid., 60–63. The "double wish" is noted in John A. Thompson, *Woodrow Wilson* (London, 2002), 112.

because of decisions made in Berlin. He perceived that at some future date Germany could force on him a painful choice between upholding U.S. honor and going to war.[79]

After a respite of nearly a year, Wilson in the spring and summer of 1916 faced neutrality crises with both Germany and Britain. On March 24, 1916, a U-boat torpedoed the British channel packet *Sussex*, killing eighty passengers and injuring four Americans. Following a month's delay, the president and Robert Lansing, Bryan's successor as secretary of state, sternly responded that Germany must stop submarine warfare or the United States would break diplomatic relations, a step generally recognized as preliminary to war. After a brief debate, Berlin again found it expedient to accommodate the United States. Bethmann-Hollweg's *Sussex* pledge of early May promised no further surprise attacks on passenger liners. Wilson won a great victory, but in doing so he further narrowed his choices. Should German leaders decide that use of the U-boat was more important than keeping the United States out of war, he would face the grim choice of submission or breaking relations and possibly war. The United States' neutrality hung on a slender thread.[80]

In the meantime, tensions with Britain increased sharply. A crisis had been averted the previous year when London after declaring cotton contraband bought enough of the U.S. crop to sustain prices at an acceptable level. Britain's brutal suppression of the Irish Easter Rebellion in the spring of 1916 and especially the execution of its leaders inflamed American opinion, even among many people normally sympathetic to the Allies. In the summer of 1916, the Allies tightened restrictions against neutral ships and seized and opened mail on the high seas. In July, London blacklisted more than eighty U.S. businesses charged with trading with the Central Powers, thereby preventing Allied firms from dealing with them. Wilson privately fumed about Britain's "altogether indefensible" actions, threatened to take as firm a position with London as with Berlin, and denounced the blacklist as the "last straw." Meanwhile, U.S. bankers financed Britain at a level of about $10 million a day. Britain bought more than $83 million of U.S. goods per week, leaving the nation more closely than ever tied to the Allied cause.[81]

The neutrality crises provoked sweeping reassessments of the most basic principles of U.S. defense and foreign policies. In 1915–16, Americans

79. Ernest R. May, *The World War and American Isolation, 1914–1917* (Chicago, 1959), 225–27; Thompson, *Wilson*, 114–17.

80. Gregory, *Origins of Intervention*, 94–96; Thompson, *Wilson*, 121–22.

81. Wilson to House, May 16, 1916, *Wilson Papers* 37:57–58; July 24, 1916, ibid., 467.

heatedly debated the adequacy of their military preparedness, the first time since the 1790s that national security concerns had assumed such prominence in U.S. political discourse.[82] Preparedness advocates, many of them eastern Republicans representing the great financial and industrial interests, insisted that America's defenses were inadequate for a new and dangerous age. Claiming that military training would also Americanize new immigrants and toughen the nation's youth, they pushed for expansion of the army and navy. They promoted their cause with parades, books, and scare films such as *Battle Cry for Peace*, which portrayed in the most graphic fashion an invasion of New York City by enemy troops unnamed but easily identifiable as German by their spiked helmets.

On the other side, pacifists, social reformers, and southern and midwestern agrarians denounced preparedness as a scheme to fatten the pockets of big business and fasten militarism on the nation. They professed to favor "real defense against real dangers, but not a preposterous 'preparedness' against hypothetical dangers." They warned that the programs being considered would be a giant step toward war.[83] Popular songs such as "I Didn't Raise My Boy to Be a Soldier" expressed their sentiments. The divisions were reflected in Congress, where by early 1916 Wilson's proposals for "reasonable" increases in the armed services were mired in controversy.

Fearful that America might be drawn into war and facing reelection, Wilson in 1916 belatedly assumed leadership of a cause he had previously spurned, breaking one of the most difficult legislative logjams of his first term. To build support for his program, he went on a speaking tour of the Northeast and Middle West, seeking to educate the nation to the dangers posed by a world at war. To thunderous ovations, he called for increased military expenditures—even at one point for "incomparably the greatest navy in the world." Returning to Washington, he skillfully steered legislation through a divided Congress. "No man ought to say to any legislative body 'You must take my plan or none at all,'" he proclaimed on one occasion, a striking statement given the stand he would take on the League of Nations in 1919. The National Defense Act of June 1916 increased the regular army to 223,000 over a five-year period. It strengthened the National Guard to 450,000 men and tightened federal controls. A Naval Expansion Act established a three-year construction program including four dreadnought battleships and eight cruisers the first year. Ardent preparedness advocates such as Theodore Roosevelt dismissed Wilson's program as

82. Knock, *End All Wars*, 58.
83. Jane Addams et al to Wilson, October 29, 1915, *Wilson Papers* 35:134.

"flintlock legislation," measures more appropriate for the eighteenth century than for the twentieth. "The United States today becomes the most militaristic naval nation on earth," critics screamed from the other extreme. In fact, Wilson's compromise perfectly suited the national mood and significantly expanded U.S. military power. A remarkably progressive revenue act appeased leftist critics by shifting almost the entire burden to the wealthy with a surtax and estate tax.[84]

The Great War also sparked a debate over basic foreign policy principles that would rage until World War II and persist in modified form thereafter. Breaking with hallowed tradition, those who came to be called internationalists insisted that the American way of life could be preserved only through active, permanent involvement in world politics. Conservative internationalists such as former president William Howard Taft and senior statesman Elihu Root, mostly Republicans and upper-class men of influence, had long promoted international law and arbitration. In response to the war, they embraced still vague notions of collective security. Generally pro-Allied, they saw defeat of Germany as an essential first step toward a new world order. In June 1915, during the *Lusitania* crisis, Taft announced formation of a League to Enforce Peace to promote the creation of a world parliament, of which the United States would be a member, that would modify international law and use arbitration to resolve disputes. The conservatives also supported a buildup of U.S. military power and its use to protect the nation's vital interests. Progressive internationalists, on the other hand, fervently insisted that peace was essential to ensure advancement of domestic reforms they held dear: better working conditions for labor; social justice legislation; women's rights. Liberal reformers such as social worker Jane Addams and journalist Oswald Garrison Villard vigorously pushed for ending the Great War by negotiation, eliminating the arms race and economic causes of war, compulsory arbitration, the use of sanctions to deter and punish aggression, and establishing a "concert of nations" to replace the balance of power.[85]

In response to the new internationalism, a self-conscious isolationism began to take form, and the word *isolationism* became firmly implanted in the nation's political vocabulary. Previously, non-involvement in European politics and wars had been a given. But the threat posed by the Great War and the emergence of internationalist sentiment gave rise to an ideology of isolationism, promoted most fervently by Bryan, to

---

84. Knock, *End All Wars*, 90; George C. Herring Jr., "James Hay and the Preparedness Controversy," *Journal of Southern History* 30 (November 1964), 383–404.
85. Knock, *End All Wars*, 50–58.

preserve America's long-standing tradition of non-involvement as a way of safeguarding the nation's way of life.[86]

While Democratic Party zealots during the election campaign of 1916 vigorously pushed the slogan "He Kept Us Out of War," Wilson began to articulate an internationalist position and also the revolutionary concept that the United States should assume a leadership position in world affairs. In a June 1916 speech Colonel House described as a "land mark in history," he vowed U.S. willingness to "become a partner in any feasible association of nations" to maintain the peace.[87] "We are part of the world," he proclaimed in Omaha in early October; "nothing that concerns the whole world can be indifferent to us." The "great catastrophe" brought about by the war, he added later in the day, compelled Americans to recognize that they lived in a "new age" and must therefore operate "not according to the traditions of the past, but according to the necessities of the present and the prophecies of the future." The United States could no longer refuse to play the "great part in the world which was providentially cut out for her. . . . We have got to serve the world."[88]

Shortly after his narrow reelection victory over Republican Charles Evans Hughes, a gloomy Wilson, fearing that the United States might be dragged into war, redoubled his efforts to end the European struggle. Twice previously, he had sent House—"my second personality"—on peace missions to Europe. His hands strengthened by reelection, he began to promote a general peace agreement including a major role for the United States. In December 1916, he invited both sides to state their war aims and accept U.S. good offices in negotiating a settlement.

In a dramatic January 22, 1917, address to the Senate, Wilson sketched out his revolutionary ideas for a just peace and a new world order. To the belligerents, he eloquently appealed for a "peace without victory," the only way to ensure that the loser's quest for revenge did not spark another war. In terms of the postwar world, a "community of power" must replace the balance of power, the old order of militarism, and power politics. The equality of nations great and small must be recognized. No nation should impose its authority on another. A new world order must guarantee freedom of the seas, limit armaments, and ensure the right of all peoples to form their own government. Most important, Wilson advocated a "covenant" for an international organization to ensure that "no such catastrophe shall ever overwhelm us again." Speaking to his

86. Cooper, "Shock of Recognition," 579–81.
87. Knock, *End All Wars*, 77.
88. Wilson speeches, October 5, 1916, *Wilson Papers* 38:337–38, 347.

domestic audience, the president advanced the notion, still heretical to most Americans, that their nation must play a key role in making and sustaining the postwar settlement. Without its participation, he averred, no "covenant of cooperative peace" could "keep the future safe without war." He also stressed to his domestic audience that his proposals accorded with American traditions. The principles of "President Monroe" would become the "doctrine of the world." "These are American principles, American policies . . . ," he concluded in ringing phrases. "They are the principles of mankind and must prevail."[89]

Wilson's speech was "at once breathtaking in the audacity of its vision of a new world order," historian Robert Zieger has written, "and curiously detached from the bitter realities of Europe's battlefields."[90] His efforts to promote negotiations failed. His equating of Allied war aims with those of Germany outraged London and Paris. When the blatantly pro-Allied Lansing sought to repair the damage with an unauthorized public statement, he infuriated Wilson and aroused German suspicions. In any event, by early 1917, none of the belligerents would accept U.S. mediation or a compromise peace. Both sides had suffered horribly in the rat-infested, disease-ridden trenches of Europe—"this vast gruesome contest of systematized destruction," Wilson called it.[91] The battles of attrition of 1916 were especially appalling. Britain suffered four hundred thousand casualties in the Somme offensive, sixty thousand in a single day, with no change in its tactical position. Germans called the five-month struggle for Verdun "the sausage grinder"; the French labeled it "the furnace." It cost both sides nearly a million casualties. German and French killed at Verdun together exceeded the total dead for the American Civil War.[92] By the end of the year, both sides were exhausted.

As investments of blood and treasure mounted, attitudes hardened. In December 1916, David Lloyd George, who had vowed to fight to a "knock-out," assumed leadership of a coalition government in Britain and responded to Wilson's overture with a list of conditions unacceptable to the Central Powers. The Germans made clear they would state their war aims only at a general conference to which Wilson would not be invited. In the meantime, more ominously, German leaders finally acceded to the navy's argument that with one hundred U-boats now available an

---

89. "Peace Without Victory" speech, January 22, 1917, ibid. 40:533–39.
90. Robert H. Zieger, *America's Great War: World War I and the American Experience* (Lanham, Md., 2000), 48.
91. Knock, *End All Wars*, 107.
92. My thanks to Thomas Knock for sharing this information with me.

all-out submarine campaign could win the war before U.S. intervention had any effect. On January 31, Berlin announced the beginning of unrestricted submarine warfare.[93]

Wilson faced an awful dilemma. Stunned by these developments, he privately labeled Germany a "madman that should be curbed." But he was loath to go to war. He still believed that a compromise peace through which neither side emerged triumphant would be best calculated to promote a stable postwar world. It would be a "crime," he observed, for the United States to "involve itself in the war to such an extent as to make it impossible to save Europe afterward." In view of his earlier threats, he had no choice but to break relations with Germany, and he did so on February 3. Despite the urging of House and Lansing, he still refused to ask for a declaration of war. He continued to insist that he could have greater influence as a neutral mediator than as a belligerent. He recognized that his nation remained deeply divided and that many Americans opposed going to war. As late as February 25 he charged the war hawks in his cabinet with operating on the outdated principles of the "Code Duello."[94]

Events drove him to the fateful decision. The infamous Zimmermann Telegram, leaked to the United States by Britain in late February, revealed that Germany had offered Mexico an alliance in return for which it might "reconquer its former territories in Texas, New Mexico, and Arizona." The document fanned anti-German sentiment in America and increased Wilson's already pronounced distrust of Berlin.[95] In mid-March, U-boats sank three U.S. merchant vessels with the loss of fifteen American lives. For all practical purposes, Germany was at war with the United States. Reluctantly and most painfully, Wilson concluded that war could not be avoided. The Germans had repeatedly and brutally violated American rights on the high seas. A failure to respond after his previous threats would undermine his position abroad and open him to political attack at home. Wilson had long since concluded that the United States must play a central role in the peacemaking. Surrender on the U-boat issue would demonstrate its unworthiness for that role. Germany's own repeated violation of its promises and its intrigues as evidenced in the Zimmermann Telegram made clear to Wilson that it could not be trusted. Only through active intervention, he now rationalized, could U.S. influence be used to establish a just postwar order. War was unpalatable, but at least it would give the United States a voice at the peace table. Otherwise, he told

93. May, *World War*, 404–15.
94. Franklin Lane to W. Lane, February 5, 1917, *Wilson Papers* 41:282.
95. Katz, *Secret War*, 350–78.

Addams, he could only "call through a crack in the door."[96] Moving slowly to allow public opinion to coalesce behind him, Wilson concluded by late March that he must intervene in the war.

On April 2, 1917, the president appeared before packed chambers of Congress to ask for a declaration of war against Germany. In a thirty-six-minute speech, he condemned Germany's "cruel and unmanly" violation of American rights and branded its "wanton and wholesale destruction of the lives of non-combatants" as "warfare against mankind." The United States could not "choose the path of submission," he observed. It must accept the state of war that had "been thrust upon it." He concluded with soaring rhetoric that would echo through the ages. "It is a fearful thing to lead this great peaceful people into war," he conceded. But "the right is more precious than peace, and we shall fight for the things which we have always carried dearest to our hearts, for democracy, for the right of those who submit to authority to have a voice in their own Governments, for the rights and liberties of small nations, for a universal dominion of right by such a concert of free people as shall bring peace and safety to all nations and make the world itself at last free." As critics have repeatedly emphasized, Wilson set goals beyond the ability of any person or nation to achieve. Perhaps he felt such lofty aims were necessary to rally a still-divided nation to take action unprecedented in its history. He may have aimed so high to justify in his own mind the horrors he knew a war would bring. In any event, he set for himself and his nation an impossible task that would bring great disillusionment.[97]

IV

Germany's gamble to win the war before the United States intervened in force nearly succeeded. Adhering to the nation's long-standing tradition of non-entanglement and in order to retain maximum diplomatic freedom of action, Wilson and General Pershing insisted that Americans fight separately under their own command rather than being integrated into Allied armies. It took months to raise, equip, and train a U.S. army and then transport it to Europe. A token force of "doughboys" paraded in Paris on July 4, 1917, but it would be more than a year before the United States could throw even minimal weight into the fray. In the meantime, buoyed by promises of future U.S. help, France and Britain launched disastrous summer 1917 offensives. French defeats provoked mutinies that sapped the army's will to fight. Allied setbacks in the west combined with

96. Knock, *End All Wars*, 120.
97. "Wilson War Message," April 2, 1917, *Wilson Papers* 41:519–27.

the Bolshevik seizure of power in late 1917 and Russia's subsequent withdrawal from the war gave the Central Powers a momentary edge. Facing serious morale problems at home from the Allied blockade, Germany mounted an end-the-war offensive in the spring of 1918.

It was a transformative moment in the war.[98] The German army again drove close to Paris, but it could not break through Allied lines and suffered irreplaceable losses. The addition of 850,000 fresh U.S. troops made possible an Allied summer counteroffensive. More important, as the German high command conceded, huge numbers of Americans arriving at the front produced foreboding of defeat.[99]

Long before the fighting ended, Wilson had begun to fashion a liberal peace program to reshape the postwar world. The ideas he advanced were not original with him. Even before the founding of the nation, Americans believed they had a special destiny to redeem the world. Prior to 1914, European, British, and American thinkers had dreamed of reforming international politics, a task made urgent by the horrors of the Great War. But Wilson promoted these ideas with a special fervor and eloquence and made himself their leading spokesman. In the process, he formulated and articulated a set of principles that would bear his name—Wilsonianism—and would influence U.S. foreign policy and world politics for years to come.

In Wilson's view, the war provided that opportunity for world leadership for which Americans had been preparing themselves since the birth of the nation. The death and destruction visited upon Europe made clear the bankruptcy of the old order. Scientific and technological advances created the means to uplift the human race. The United States must therefore take the lead in building a better world. "We are participants, whether we would or not, in the life of the world," Wilson affirmed in 1916. Replacing traditional American unilateralism with a universalist view, he insisted that "the interests of all nations are our own also. We are partners with the rest. What affects mankind is inevitably our affair."[100]

Wilson insisted that a just and lasting peace must be constructed along American lines. He assumed the superiority of Western civilization and the continued dominance of the West. But he believed that European imperialism had exploited helpless peoples and generated explosive tensions among the great powers. Old World diplomacy had produced only "aggression, egotism, and war." Economic nationalism, with its tariff wars and exclusive, monopolistic trading arrangements, had exacerbated international

98. Keegan, *World War I*, 373.
99. Ibid., 410–11.
100. "Peace Without Victory" speech, January 27, 1917, *Wilson Papers* 40:539.

conflict. Wilson found equally abhorrent the radical notions of Bolshevik leader Vladimir Lenin, who had seized power in Russia in late 1917, that the international system could be freed of war only by a worldwide revolution that eliminated capitalism. He firmly believed in American exceptionalism. Only a world reformed along liberal-capitalist lines would serve the United States and the broader interests of mankind. Economic nationalism must give way to a commercial internationalism in which all nations had equal access to the markets and raw materials of the world, tariff barriers were eliminated, and freedom of the seas guaranteed. Colonial empires should eventually be dissolved and all peoples given the right to determine their own destiny. Power politics must be replaced by a new world order maintained by an organization of like-minded nations joined to resolve disputes and prevent aggression—"not a balance of power but a community of power."[101]

In a series of public statements, most notably in his Fourteen Points address of January 8, 1918, Wilson molded these broad principles into a peace program. Called by the *New York Herald* "one of the great documents in American history," the speech responded to Lenin's revelations of the Allied secret treaties dividing the spoils of war and his calls for an end to imperialism as well as a speech by Lloyd George setting out broad peace terms. Wilson sought to regain the initiative for the United States and rally Americans and Allied peoples behind his peace program. He called for "open covenants of peace, openly arrived at." He reiterated his commitment to arms limitations, freedom of the seas, and reduction of trade barriers. On colonial issues, to avoid alienating the Allies, he sought a middle ground between the old-style imperialism of the secret treaties and Lenin's call for an end to empire. He did not use the word *self-determination*, but he did insist that in dealing with colonial claims the "interests" of colonial peoples should be taken into account, a marked departure from the status quo. He also set forth broad principles for European territorial settlements—a sharp break from the U.S. tradition of non-involvement in European affairs. The peoples of the Austro-Hungarian and Ottoman empires should be assured "an absolutely unmolested opportunity of autonomous development." Belgium must be evacuated, territory formerly belonging to France restored. A "general association of nations" must be established to preserve the peace.[102]

101. N. Gordon Levin Jr., *Woodrow Wilson and World Politics: America's Response to War and Revolution* (New York, 1968), 61–64.
102. Fourteen Points address, January 8, 1918, *Wilson Papers* 40:534–39; Knock, *End All Wars*, 142–47.

Germany was the key, and here Wilson had to balance his desire for an early end to the war against the need to keep the alliance together and palliate the Allies and Republican war hawks at home. As a belligerent, he abandoned of necessity his "peace without victory" stance of 1917. He came to blame Germany more for the origins of the war and view German autocracy and militarism as threats to the peace. While continuing to seek "impartial justice," he concluded that Germany must be defeated and its government purged of autocratic and expansionist elements. A reformed Germany could be reintegrated into the community of nations.[103]

From the time the United States entered the war, Wilson worked tirelessly to achieve a peace along these lines. Recognizing their mutual dependence and hoping to establish a solid basis for postwar collaboration, he actively promoted cooperation with the Allies, pushing his military leaders to work closely with the British and French and agreeing to a unified command. American and Allied scientists shared information and collaborated in solving problems such as the U-boat, chemical warfare, camouflage, and signals.[104] Aware, on the other hand, of the Allied secret treaties and deferring to America's unilateralist tradition, he carefully maintained his freedom of action, making clear that his nation was fighting for its own reasons, refusing to join a formal alliance, and even referring to the United States as an "Associated" rather than "Allied" power. In the best tradition of the 1776 Model Treaty, he declined to appoint a *political* representative to the Allied Supreme War Council.[105]

The administration in late 1917 mounted a major overseas propaganda program, the first such effort in U.S. history.[106] Under the leadership of the zealous journalist George Creel, a Committee on Public Information (CPI) had already begun drumming up support for the war at home. Wilson soon extended the program abroad to counter German propaganda and educate world opinion about his peace principles. In the major cities of Europe and Latin America and in revolutionary Russia and China, hastily established CPI offices translated stories from the U.S. press for placement in local newspapers, distributed photographs and war posters,

103. Arthur S. Link, *Woodrow Wilson: Revolution, War and Peace* (Arlington Heights, Ill., 1979), 85; Thompson, *Wilson*, 157–60.

104. Calhoun, *Power and Principle*, 167–74; Roy MacLeod, "Secrets Among Friends: The Research Information Service and the Special Relationship in Allied Scientific Information and Intelligence," *Minerva: A Review of Science, Learning, and Policy* 37 (Autumn 1999), 201–33.

105. Link, *Revolution, War, and Peace*, 76–77; Calhoun, *Power and Principle*, 178–79.

106. Gregg Wolper, "Wilsonian Public Diplomacy: The Committee on Public Information in Spain," *Diplomatic History* 17 (Winter 1993), 17.

and in some areas showed films such as *America's Answer*, a depiction of the arrival of U.S. troops in France and their movement to the western front. Wilson's speeches were translated and widely distributed in books and pamphlets.[107] The CPI campaign won some support for the Allied cause and for Wilson's peace aims. It also raised hopes among peoples throughout the world. Abroad as at home, Wilson conceded to Creel, U.S. propaganda had "unconsciously spun a net for me from which there is no escape," high expectations that could lead to a "tragedy of disappointment."[108]

Wilson also had to contend with a Russia torn by war and revolution. He cheered the overthrow of the tsarist regime in March 1917, declaring the newly formed and moderate Provisional Government a "fit partner" for a "league of honor" and quickly recognizing it. He also sought to boost its prestige by sending to Petrograd a mission headed by Elihu Root. With characteristic American optimism and abysmal misunderstanding of what was happening, Root reported that the government could survive and even continue the war with limited U.S. assistance. Wilson promised $450 million in aid (of which $188 million was actually transferred) and dispatched transportation experts to keep the railroads going, a YMCA mission to boost army morale, and a Red Cross team to provide relief and, on the side, encourage the people to back the government and continue the war. Such well-intentioned gestures had little impact on a complex and fluid situation. Lenin's Bolsheviks overthrew the shaky Provisional Government in November, sparking a prolonged civil war. The new rulers in March 1918 negotiated a separate peace, allowing Germany to shift forces to the western front.[109]

After six months of relentless pressure from the Allies and much "sweating blood" on his part, Wilson in July 1918 reluctantly agreed to interventions in Siberia and North Russia.[110] The operations occurred under very confused circumstances; the motives behind them and Wilson's support for them remain elusive. In early 1918, the Allies began to advocate intervention in Siberia to keep the eastern port of Vladivostok open and vital supplies out of German hands. Subsequently, they pushed

107. Ibid., 17–34; James D. Stratt, "American Propaganda in Britain During World War I," *Prologue* 28 (Spring 1996), 17–33; Kazuyuki Matsuo, "American Propaganda in China: The U.S. Committee on Public Information, 1918–1919," *Journal of American-Canadian Studies* 14 (1996), 19–42.
108. Matsuo, "Propaganda," 21.
109. John Lewis Gaddis, *Russia, the Soviet Union, and the United States: An Interpretive History* (2nd ed., New York, 1990), 61–63.
110. Knock, *End All Wars*, 156.

for intervention at the northern ports of Murmansk and Archangel and urged support for a seventy-thousand-man Czech Legion committed to fighting the Central Powers—and also the Bolsheviks. Stunned and out-raged by Lenin's separate peace, Allied leaders desperately sought to sus-tain some kind of eastern front against Germany.

Wilson sympathized on this point. As much as he understood Bolshe-vism, moreover, he despised it. He never felt Lenin's regime represented the Russian people. He refused to recognize it. Following the November Revolution, the administration continued to channel funds and supplies to anti-Bolshevik forces through the Provisional Government embassy in Washington and reimbursed the British for their aid. But Wilson was keenly aware from his own travails in Mexico the limits of military force in solving complex political problems. He feared that interference in Russia, as in Mexico, might actually solidify Bolshevik control. In June 1918, precisely when German forces advanced to within artillery range of Paris, he acceded to Allied pressure. Wilson wanted to demonstrate that he was a "good ally," thus establishing a basis for postwar cooperation.[111] He also hoped that the twenty thousand U.S. troops he sent to Siberia would help thwart any Japanese ambitions in that region. When the Czech Legion reached Vladivostok in June, threw out the Bolshevik gov-ernment, and vowed to fight with the Allies, he saw the "shadow of a plan" for a viable eastern front and felt a moral obligation to aid the Czechs. If Russians rallied around their "slavic kinsmen" against the Bol-sheviks, so much the better, although he placed strict limits on the num-ber of U.S. troops and the ways they could be used. He convinced himself that limited and indirect Allied aid might inspire representatives of the "Real Russia" to rally against the Bolsheviks and would thus be an act of liberation rather than interference.[112] The United States did not inter-vene sufficiently to influence events in Russia. Its intervention did feed the myth among Soviet propagandists and some revisionist historians that Wilson had sought to overthrow the Bolshevik government.

The autumn of 1918, in historian Arthur Walworth's apt phrase, was "America's moment."[113] By the summer, the United States had more than a million troops in Europe, with another three million in training. At Château-Thierry in June, U.S. forces helped blunt the German drive

111. Calhoun, Power and Principle, 199–200.
112. David S. Fogelsong, America's Secret War Against Bolshevism: U.S. Intervention in the Russian Civil War (Chapel Hill, N.C., 1996), 190–91.
113. Arthur Walworth, America's Moment, 1918: American Diplomacy at the End of World War I (New York, 1977).

toward Paris. In the late summer and early fall, the doughboys played a key role in the Allied counteroffensive that forced the Germans back to the Hindenburg Line. The mere presence of huge numbers of fresh U.S. troops had a hugely demoralizing effect on an exhausted German army.[114] The United States thus determined the outcome of the war. And under Wilson's leadership, it was poised to shape the peace. Inspired by the president's vision of their nation's new role and by the chance for leadership and constructive achievement, Americans excitedly took up the challenge. As early as January 1918, preparing for the Fourteen Points address, House boasted of "remaking the map of the world" in two hours. A "remarkably productive morning!" he added.[115] Lansing's nephew Allen Dulles waxed eloquent about "pulchritudinous [American] youth" taking up the "greatest obligation and opportunity that a nation ever had. . . . We are called to put the world in order again."[116] The Americans would soon learn that huge expectations and intractable problems were an integral part of their new world role.

Negotiations for an armistice with Germany revealed the challenges that lay ahead and the conflict between Wilson's hopes for an enduring peace and his appeals for a crusade against German autocracy. Seeking to divide the Allies and salvage some semblance of victory, a dispirited Germany in early October approached Wilson directly for an armistice based on the Fourteen Points. A new parliamentary government sought to avoid the punitive terms favored by Britain and France and was prepared to make concessions.

Wilson's position was extremely delicate. He still believed that a fair peace was the best way to end the war. At home, however, he faced congressional elections that would affect his ability to negotiate a settlement and sell a League of Nations to his own people. His Republican foes vigorously pressed for a hard line against Germany. Wilson also recognized that the Allies wanted a victor's peace, sought territorial gains at Germany's expense, and preferred to leave the armistice to the military to ensure that Germany could not use a cease-fire to prepare for resumption of the war. He proceeded with great caution, exploring Germany's commitment to the Fourteen Points and its willingness to evacuate territory then held. He told a skeptical Democratic senator that he was thinking of "a hundred years hence." When advised that if he was too conciliatory he might be destroyed politically, he retorted that "I am willing if I can serve

114. Keegan, *First World War*, 410–14.
115. Knock, *End All Wars*, 142.
116. Peter Grose, *Gentleman Spy: The Life of Allen Dulles* (Boston, 1994), 35, 45.

my country to go into a cellar and read poetry for the remainder of my life."[117] Under pressure from the Allies and critics at home and eager to gain control of the peace process, he gradually toughened his stance, at one point even acceding to Allied occupation of German territory and insisting that Germany's "military masters and the monarchical autocrats" must go.[118] He sent House to deal with the Allies, instructing him only that he would know what to do.

The armistice emerging from these confused triangular discussions ended the fighting but also set the tone for what would follow. House confronted vengeful Allies who feigned ignorance of the Fourteen Points. After difficult negotiations, he secured their agreement in principle, but Britain reserved the right to interpret freedom of the seas, and France insisted that Germany must compensate the Allies for civilian and property losses. The military was to handle the armistice, opening the way for occupation of German territory. House claimed a "great diplomatic victory." Under the circumstances, he may have got as much as could be expected. But it was not what Wilson had envisioned, and it opened the way for more serious problems. The fundamental contradiction between Wilson's desire to join with the Allies in defeating Germany and mediate between the two sides made it difficult if not impossible for him to achieve his lofty goals.[119]

Greater challenges awaited in Paris, where the peace conference opened on January 12, 1919. In heading the U.S. delegation himself, Wilson broke precedent, becoming the first president to go to Europe while in office and personally to conduct major negotiations. He remained abroad for more than six months, with only a two-week interlude in the United States, suggesting the extent to which foreign relations now dominated his agenda. The president has often been criticized for this initial venture in summit diplomacy. To be sure, his deep personal involvement deprived him of the detachment that can be invaluable in negotiations and severely strained his already frail constitution. Given the urgency of the negotiations, his personality and leadership style, and the fact that British and French heads of government were leading their delegations, it is impossible to envision him acting any other way.[120]

117. Thompson, *Wilson*, 175–76.
118. Ibid., 177.
119. Klaus Schwabe, "U.S. Secret War Diplomacy, Intelligence, and the Coming of the German Revolution in 1918: The Role of Vice Consul James McNally," *Diplomatic History* 16 (Spring 1992), 200.
120. Thompson, *Wilson*, 212.

The peacemakers confronted monumental problems. Europe lay dev-astated, "a laboratory resting on a vast cemetery," Czech leader Thomas Masaryk observed.[121] Old boundaries were torn asunder, leaving in-tractable territorial problems. The German, Austro-Hungarian, and Ot-toman empires lay in ruins, raising hopes of nationhood for peoples throughout Central Europe, the Balkans, and the Middle East and leaving a powder keg of conflicting nationalist and ethnic aspirations. Anarchy prevailed in many areas. The threat of revolution hung like a storm cloud over Germany and Central Europe. A truly daunting agenda included dis-arming the losers, reviving European economies, confronting the Bolshe-vik challenge, and creating new states in Europe and the Middle East.

The passions set loose by four years of fighting further complicated the peacemaking. Excluded from the conference, the defeated Germans nervously awaited their fate, while among the victors a spirit of revenge prevailed. France had lost two million men, the most of any belligerent, suffered massive destruction to its territory, and was intent upon avenging its losses. Prime Minister Georges Clemenceau embodied his nation's spirit. "I had a wife, she abandoned me," he once snarled; "I had chil-dren, they turned against me; I had friends, they betrayed me. I have only my claws, and I use them."[122] The seventy-seven-year-old "Tiger" survived an assassin's bullet during the conference. He expressed open cynicism for the Fourteen Points. Britain too had suffered enormous losses, and al-though its government and its prime minister, the charming, shrewd, and hard-bitten Welshman David Lloyd George, supported much of Wilson's program, they could not go too far toward conciliating Germany without risking domestic political backlash. The Allies had sweeping imperial goals. On the other side, the war and Wilson's rhetoric raised hopes of freedom among nationalities and oppressed peoples across the world. Representatives of many different peoples—African Americans included—came to Paris in search of guarantees of racial equality. Chi-nese nationalists looked to the peace conference to end great-power dom-ination of their country. The young Vietnamese patriot Nguyen Tat Than (later to adopt the sobriquet Ho Chi Minh) rented a tuxedo to present a petition to the conference for his country's independence. Spokespersons for Haiti and the Dominican Republic appealed to Wilson in Paris for self-determination.[123]

121. Walworth, America's Moment, 1.
122. Quoted in "Fighting Men," National Interest 69 (Fall 2002), 129.
123. Erez Manela, The Wilsonian Moment: Self-Determination and the International Ori-gins of Anticolonial Nationalism (New York, 2007), 1–51.

In dealing with these formidable problems, Wilson was hampered by an inadequate advisory system and his own leadership style. He had never liked or trusted Lansing; during the long stay in Europe, his relationship with Colonel House suffered an irreparable break. The peace commission he chose to accompany him was not a distinguished group—ex-president Taft called them a "bunch of cheapskates"—and did not play a major role. At the president's direction, House in the fall of 1917 assembled a group of scholars to analyze postwar problems, a significant and innovative effort to bring scholarly expertise to bear on foreign policy issues. The so-called Inquiry employed 150 people and produced more than three thousand papers and reports. Its Red and Black Books were extensively used in resolving numerous specific issues, especially the territorial settlements that recast the maps of Europe and the Middle East. As Wilson relied even less on the State Department, the Inquiry's importance grew.[124]

Ultimately, as was his custom, Wilson depended mainly on himself. Especially after he broke with House, he was largely on his own. Most decisions were made in small groups, the Council of Four and the Council of Ten. The so-called Big Four met 140 times between January and May. The negotiations were arduous and tension-ridden, with frequent threats from various quarters, Wilson included, to bolt the conference. On one occasion, Clemenceau and Lloyd George came close to fisticuffs. After his February trip to the United States, Wilson also recognized that he would face stern opposition from Senate Republicans. He was sixty-three years old, in poor health, and the strain told on him. He became seriously ill in March, largely because he had pushed himself beyond normal limits. His illness may have affected his ability to function in the last stages of the conference. At times, he displayed odd behavior. He took a more hostile position than previously toward Germany; once, oddly, when Lloyd George sought to soften the Allied stand on a particular issue, he sided with Clemenceau.[125]

Wilson's triumphant arrival in Europe could not but have led him to overestimate the leverage he would have in dealing with his Allied counterparts. His ship, the *George Washington* (a captured and renamed German luxury liner), docked at Brest on December 13, 1918—the president considered thirteen his lucky number. Banners welcomed the "Champion

124. Jonathan M. Nielson, "The Scholar as Diplomat: American Historians at the Paris Peace Conference of 1919," *International History Review* 14 (May 1992), 228–51.

125. Thompson, *Wilson*, 212, minimizes the effects of Wilson's illness on the actual negotiations.

of the Rights of Man," the "Founder of the Society of Nations." The moaning sounds of bagpipes resounded amidst shouts of *"Vive l'Amérique! Vive Wilson!"* According to one observer, the president's reception in Paris, where crowds lined the Place de Concorde and the Champs-Elysées to view him, was "the most remarkable demonstration of enthusiasm and affection . . . that I have ever heard of, let alone seen."[126] This scene was replicated in London and Manchester, Rome, Genoa, Milan, and Turin. Hailed across the Continent almost as a messiah, Wilson, according to British economist and future critic John Maynard Keynes, "enjoyed a prestige and moral influence throughout the world unequaled in history."[127] The exuberant greeting misled him to believe that Allied peoples supported his aims regardless of where their leaders stood.

Wilson in other ways seems to have exaggerated his bargaining power. Early in the war, he had confidently predicted that the Allies would be "financially in our hands" and thus could be brought around "to our way of thinking." The Allies in fact owed more than $10 billion to the U.S. government and private bankers, but such leverage worked both ways. The U.S. economy came to depend on war orders from Britain and France. European debts provided useable leverage only if the United States was willing to forgive them, which was never an option.[128] At times, Wilson seemed to believe that the threat of a separate peace with Germany might force the Allies to go along with his proposals, but once the armistice had been arranged this weapon lost its potency. Wilson's negotiating position had been compromised before he arrived in Europe. Responding to pleas from fellow Democrats and seeking to build support for his peace plans, he made a blatantly partisan appeal for the election of a Democratic Congress. Republican victories in the 1918 elections weakened him in dealing with European leaders. His commitment above all to a League of Nations and his insistence on including its charter in the treaty gave his adversaries precious leverage over him. The United States emerged from the war relatively much stronger, but it was not powerful enough to impose its will on other nations. The Allies were in a position to ignore him when they so chose.[129]

Amidst these difficulties, Wilson sought to negotiate a lasting peace. Germany was the most difficult problem, and the terms eventually settled upon

---

126. Margaret Macmillan, *Paris 1919: Six Months That Changed the World* (New York, 2003), 15–16.
127. Manela, *Wilsonian Moment*, 45.
128. Clements, *Wilson Presidency*, 174; Thompson, *Wilson*, 191–93.
129. Macmillan, *Paris 1919*, xxx; Thompson, *Wilson*, 191–93.

represented a compromise between France's quest for vengeance and future security and Wilson's pleas for a just peace. Clemenceau ultimately yielded his demands for dismemberment of Germany and permanent occupation of parts of it. But the Allies agreed to fixed limits on German military power, temporary occupation of the Rhineland and the Saar Basin, and an Anglo-American pledge (quite unprecedented for the United States) to aid France in the event of German attack. Wilson refused Allied demands that Germany pay the entire cost of the war. Under enormous pressure from France and Britain, however, and in his anti-German phase, he went along with the notorious "war guilt clause," drafted by another Lansing nephew, future U.S. secretary of state John Foster Dulles, which placed responsibility on Germany for all the damages caused by the war. He reluctantly agreed that Germany should pay extensive reparations, the figure to be fixed by a separate commission. He made such concessions mainly because Clemenceau and Lloyd George repeatedly insisted that their people demanded them. He also needed to give them something to secure their support for changes Americans such as Taft insisted must be made in the League of Nations. When Lloyd George belatedly tried to soften the terms, Wilson stood firmly with Clemenceau, indicating his belief that Germany had earned a "hard peace."[130]

In disposing of the German and Ottoman empires, Wilson confronted stiff resistance from the Allies, who had made secret commitments to each other and Japan. To avert the seemingly inevitable land grab, he proposed that the former German and Ottoman colonies should be governed through "mandates," by which advanced nations operating under the aegis of the League of Nations would serve as trustees to prepare the colonial areas for independence. The European allies and Japan at first adamantly resisted but eventually went along, perhaps confident that mandates could be used to advance their aims. In the Middle East and Africa, the Allies snapped up former enemy colonies. The mandate system proved little more than annexation in disguise.

Wilson's most damaging concession politically was on the Chinese province of Shandong, which Japan had seized from Germany in 1914. Chinese nationalists demanded restoration of the birthplace of Confucius, "the cradle of Chinese civilization," they called it, a "dagger pointed at the heart of China."[131] Throughout the world, Shandong became an emotionally

---

130. Thompson, *Wilson*, 210; Macmillan, *Paris, 1919*, 459–83; Clements, *Wilson Presidency*, 179–82, 186.
131. Macmillan, *Paris 1919*, 334; Stephen G. Craft, "John Bassett Moore, Robert Lansing, and the Shandong Question," *Pacific Historical Review* 66 (May 1997), 239.

charged symbol of Wilson's failure to honor self-determination. Already angry that the Big Four had rejected their proposal for a clause on racial equality, the Japanese threatened to leave the conference and stay out of the League if they were not permitted to "carry out their obligations to China."[132] To secure their endorsement of the treaty, Wilson accepted their verbal assurances that Chinese sovereignty would be restored by 1922. It was the "best that could be accomplished out of a 'dirty past,' " he told his physician.[133] On the other hand, the president resisted Italy's demands for Fiume on the Adriatic and appealed to the Italian people over the heads of their leaders, provoking anti-American demonstrations across Italy and Prime Minister Vittorio Orlando's departure from Paris.

Redrawing the maps of Central Europe and the Balkans posed special problems. The term *self-determination* had never been defined with any clarity, and its practical application in regions of mixed nationalities and ethnic groups proved nightmarish. Wilson admitted that he had no idea what demons the concept would unleash. The peacemakers established a number of new independent nations, including Poland, to which Wilson was deeply committed, Yugoslavia, and Czechoslovakia, not only to satisfy nationalist aspirations but also to create buffers between Germany and Russia. They attempted to draw boundary lines on the basis of ethnic considerations and collaborated in containing a Communist revolution in Hungary. But large numbers of Germans still lived in some of the new states; some also included ethnic groups that despised each other. The settlements left old problems unresolved and created new ones, setting off conflicts that would vex international relations into the next century.[134]

Although it was not on the agenda, the Russian problem, in delegate Herbert Hoover's words, was "the Banquo's ghost sitting at every conference table."[135] Preoccupied with other issues, the Allies never developed a consistent policy toward revolutionary Russia. Efforts to arrange meetings with Bolshevik leaders failed, in part because of Big Four absorption in matters deemed more pressing. Russia's exclusion from the conference seriously weakened the settlement. The end of the war eliminated much of the rationale for the military interventions. Confronted with rising

132. Noriko Kawamura, "Wilsonian Idealism and Japanese Claims at the Paris Peace Conference," *Pacific Historical Review* 66 (November 1997), 524.

133. Knock, *End All Wars*, 250.

134. Macmillan, *Paris 1919*, 109–42, 207–70; Betty Miller Unterberger, "The United States and National Self-Determination: A Wilsonian Perspective," *Presidential Studies Quarterly* 26 (Fall 1996), 926–41.

135. Gaddis, *Russia, the Soviet Union, and the United States*, 78.

political opposition at home and declining morale and even the threat of mutiny among the troops, Wilson withdrew U.S. forces from North Russia in June 1919. Americans remained in Siberia for almost another year.

Wilson could never quite make up his mind what to do with Bolshevik Russia. He had learned from Mexico the limits of military intervention. He stubbornly rejected various Allied proposals, including one by British cabinet officer Winston Churchill, to eliminate the Bolshevik government through a full-fledged military effort—"trying to stop a revolutionary movement by troops in the field is like using a broom to hold back a great ocean," he snapped.[136] He distrusted opposition leader Adm. Alexander Kolchak and feared a return to traditional Russian autocracy. Yet, as in Mexico, he continued to delude himself that limited intervention was not intervention at all. He may have hoped that the Bolshevik government would collapse of its own weight. He persisted in sending clandestine military aid to opposition forces through the still-functioning Washington embassy of the Provisional Government. Persuaded that food was "the real thing" to combat Bolshevism, he also authorized the American Red Cross and Hoover's American Relief Administration to distribute food and other relief supplies to anti-Bolshevik forces in the Baltic region. The United States did just enough to anger the Bolsheviks but not nearly enough to achieve the aim of a non-Communist Russia.[137]

Committed above all to establishing a workable League of Nations, Wilson justified concessions on other issues to attain that goal. He also hoped that a strong League in time would modify the harsh terms of the treaty and resolve issues left unsettled. In designing an international organization, the president had to struggle with people like Lansing, who opposed any commitments, and with the French, who preferred to maintain the wartime alliance. He finally secured Allied agreement to a League composed of an Assembly of all nations and a Council made up of the five victorious powers and four other nations elected by the Assembly. It would be empowered to supervise the mandated territories, encourage peaceful resolution of disputes through arbitration and adjudication—the key peacekeeping provisions, in Wilson's mind—and employ economic and military sanctions against aggressors. The most controversial provision was a collective security mechanism that Wilson hoped would "disentangle all the alliances in the world." Article X provided that member nations would "respect and preserve as against external aggression the political integrity and existing political independence of all Members of the League."

136. Link, *Revolution, War, and Peace*, 96.
137. Fogelsong, *Secret War*, 187.

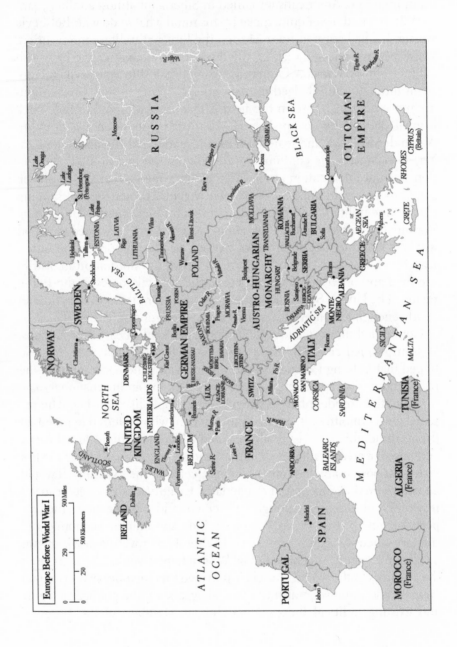

Europe Before World War I

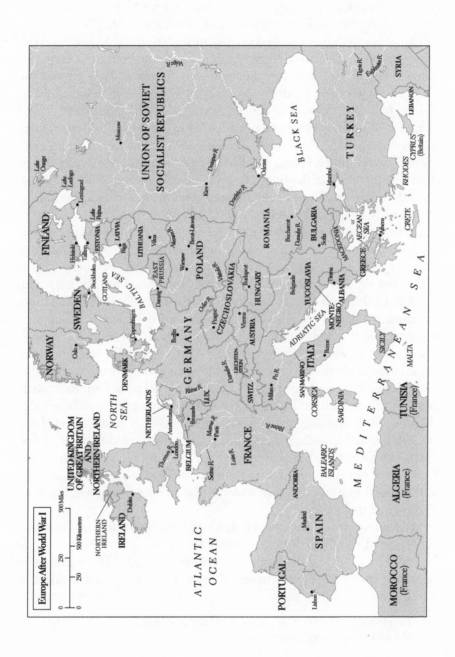

Europe After World War I

ATLANTIC OCEAN

NORWAY

SWEDEN

FINLAND

Lake Onega

Lake Ladoga

Leningrad

Helsinki
Tallinn

Lake Peipus

ESTONIA

LATVIA
Riga

LITHUANIA
Vilna

UNION OF SOVIET SOCIALIST REPUBLICS

Moscow

Volga R.

Dnieper R.

Kiev

Odessa

Dniester R.

BLACK SEA

TURKEY

Istanbul

Oslo

Stockholm

GOTLAND

BALTIC SEA

Copenhagen

DENMARK

EAST PRUSSIA

Danzig

Berlin

Warsaw

Vistula R.

POLAND

Niemen R.

Brest-Litovsk

ROMANIA

Bucharest
Danube R.

BULGARIA
Sofia

MACEDONIA

AEGEAN SEA

GREECE

Athens

RHODES

CYPRUS
(Britain)

CRETE

Odra R.

Prague
CZECHOSLOVAKIA

Vienna
AUSTRIA

Budapest
HUNGARY

Belgrade

YUGOSLAVIA

Tirana
ALBANIA

MONTE-
NEGRO

SYRIA

Tigris R.

Euphrates R.

LEBANON

ADRIATIC SEA

NORTH SEA

UNITED KINGDOM OF GREAT BRITAIN AND NORTHERN IRELAND

NORTHERN IRELAND

IRELAND

Dublin

NETHERLANDS

Amsterdam

GERMANY

Rhine R.

LIECHTEN-STEIN

Danube R.

SWITZ.

Milan

Po R.

ITALY

Rome

SAN MARINO

CORSICA

SARDINIA

SICILY

MALTA

MEDITERRANEAN SEA

Thames R.

London

Brussels
BELGIUM

LUX.

Marne R.
Paris

Seine R.

FRANCE

Loire R.

Rhône R.

ANDORRA

BALEARIC ISLANDS

SPAIN

Madrid

PORTUGAL

Lisbon

TUNISIA
(France)

ALGERIA
(France)

MOROCCO
(France)

500 Miles

250

0

500 Kilometers

250

0

Although painfully aware of the treaty's shortcomings, Wilson was pleased with his accomplishment. The League was a "living thing . . . ," he said, "a definite guarantee of peace . . . against the things which have just come near bringing the whole structure of civilization into ruin."[138]

The peace settlement evoked cries of protest from many quarters. Having never seen Allied armies or experienced occupation, most Germans deluded themselves that they had not been defeated. They viewed the treaty as vengeful and punitive and claimed to have been betrayed. Flags flew at half mast. Germans angrily protested a "shameful treaty," "the worst act of world piracy under the flag of hypocrisy."[139] Liberals across the world expressed shock and bitterness at Wilson's seeming abandonment of the Fourteen Points. Disillusioned American progressives shared dismay at the terms of the treaty. Bolting the conference, Wilson's young, idealistic adviser William Bullitt told reporters he was going to the Riviera to lie on the beach and watch the world go to hell.[140]

Disappointment was especially keen among colonial peoples. The peacemakers in Paris focused mainly on European issues. Wilson gave little attention to the application of self-determination elsewhere. Recognizing the explosive potential of the issue, he refused to take it up with the Allies. Although sharply qualified, his rhetoric of self-determination, disseminated across the world by modern communications techniques, inspired among peoples under colonial rule hopes for freedom. Nationalists adopted his words to legitimize their cry for independence. The struggle for independence became internationalized and Wilson its unwitting champion. Oppressed people across the world looked to Paris for realization of their aspirations. Failure of the peacemakers even to acknowledge their demands naturally sparked widespread disillusion and anger. Mass protests erupted in India, Egypt, Korea, and China, among other places. "So much for national self-determination," a young library assistant, Mao Zedong, protested. "I think it is really shameless!" Across the world, an anti-colonial movement began to form that in time would achieve what Wilson had spoken of.[141]

Wilson recognized the limits of his handiwork, but he felt, probably correctly, that it was the best that he could accomplish given the formidable obstacles he faced and the limits of his power. He hoped that a League in operation could remedy the treaty's defects. He signed the document in

138. Thompson, *Wilson*, 201; Link, *Revolution, War, and Peace*, 99.
139. Macmillan, *Paris 1919*, 463–65, 474.
140. Ibid., 80.
141. Cohen, *Response to China*, 97, 101; Manela, *Wilsonian Moment*, 194–95, 215–25.

the ornate Hall of Mirrors of the palace at Versailles, the very symbol of the old order he sought to displace, on June 28, 1919, the anniversary of the assassination in Sarajevo that had sparked the conflagration. Exhausted from his labors, still not recovered from a debilitating illness, he hastened home to secure ratification of the treaty. Speaking before Congress on July 10, he issued a ringing challenge: "Dare we reject it and break the heart of the world?"[142]

V

For the next eight months, the nation engaged in yet another great debate over its role in the world. The carnage of the war gave a special urgency to the discussions. They took place in a politically supercharged environment, against the backdrop of strikes and labor violence, race riots, and the notorious Red Scare, with a presidential election just a year away.

The struggle contained many interlocking elements. Wilson had stretched executive powers before and during the war. At one level, it represented a clash between competing branches of government. It was also an intensely personal feud between two men who despised each other. Senator Henry Cabot Lodge had disliked Wilson from the start. By 1915, he called the president, except for James Buchanan, "the most dangerous man that ever sat in the White House" and confided in Roosevelt that he "never expected to hate anyone in politics with the hatred I feel towards Wilson."[143] Lodge set out to defeat and humiliate his archenemy over the League issue. The president was determined not to let his foe thwart his great cause.

It was a fiercely partisan battle. There was no tradition in U.S. politics of bipartisanship on major foreign policy issues. On the contrary, since the Jay Treaty in 1794, parties had fought bitterly over such matters. Raised in the South during the Civil War and Reconstruction, Wilson was a dyed-in-the-wool Democrat. Republicans resented his success and were out to get him. They launched fierce partisan attacks on his internationalist proposals even before he went to Paris. The president's own actions helped to ensure greater opposition. He had done little during the war to build a bipartisan coalition behind his proposals. His appeal for the election of a Democratic Congress in 1918 gave them an opening they readily exploited. He had not taken a leading Republican with him to

142. John Milton Cooper Jr., *Breaking the Heart of the World: Woodrow Wilson and the Fight for the League of Nations* (New York, 2001), 8–9.
143. William C. Widenor, *Henry Cabot Lodge and the Search for an American Foreign Policy* (Berkeley, Calif., 1983), 173, 208.

Paris or consulted closely with the opposition in formulating his peace proposals.

The battle centered around what part the United States should play in the postwar world. It was not primarily a debate between isolationists and internationalists, as it has often been portrayed, although inflated rhetoric on both sides sometimes made it appear so. Rather, it focused on the extent and nature of the commitments the United States should assume. "Internationalism has come," Democratic Senate leader Gilbert Hitchcock observed, "and we must choose what form the internationalism is to take." The debate marked a "great historical moment," historian John Milton Cooper Jr. has concluded, and "elicited a breadth and depth of discussion" of fundamental foreign policy issues "that had not risen before and that remained unmatched since."[144]

By the time Wilson returned home, the lines had formed. Polls of newspaper editors and resolutions from state legislatures, the only measures of public opinion at the time, indicated strong support for the president's proposals, but opposition had developed. Progressive internationalists, Wilson's key allies in 1916, were profoundly disillusioned by his wartime acquiescence in the suppression of civil liberties. They were also angered by the "madness at Versailles," Wilson's seeming abandonment of the Fourteen Points and his support for a League that seemed better designed to uphold rather than reform the old order of world politics. Their ranks included some of the nation's leading intellectuals, who provided highly articulate arguments that other opponents used with devastating effect.[145] Ethnic groups poured out resentment against the treatment of their homelands: German Americans castigated the punitive treaty and the "League of Damnations"; Italian Americans denounced Wilson's opposition to Italy's territorial claims; Irish Americans attacked him for failing even to consider freedom for their homeland and warned that Article X would be used to suppress legitimate nationalist movements and keep U.S. money from being sent to Ireland.[146] Their passions still aflame from the fervor of the Great Crusade against autocratic Germany, nationalists warned in overblown rhetoric that Wilson's League would surrender U.S. sovereignty to a world body.

144. Cooper, *Breaking the Heart of the World*, 1, 4. The Hitchcock quote is from Thomas Knock, " 'Playing for a Hundred Years Hence': Woodrow Wilson's Internationalism and His Would-be Heirs," paper in possession of author. My thanks to Professor Knock for bringing this quote to my attention.

145. Knock, *End All Wars*, 242–43, 252–59.

146. Elizabeth McKillen, "The Corporatist Model, World War I, and the Public Debate over the League of Nations," *Diplomatic History* 15 (Spring 1991), 177–79.

The issue would be decided in the Senate, where a particularly complex array of forces was at work. The Republicans had a majority of only two. While most of them accepted involvement in some form of international organization—indeed, their party had pioneered such efforts—they were not disposed to accept Wilson's proposals uncritically or hand him a major victory on the eve of a presidential election. Many Republicans resented Wilson's aloofness and arrogance and distrusted what progressive senator George Norris branded his "anxiety for power."[147]

Most important, Republicans differed with the president on key substantive questions. Fourteen Republican senators, the so-called Irreconcilables, opposed entry into the League in any form. They represented different geographical regions and political philosophies and opposed Wilson for various reasons. Some, like Norris, felt the United States should use its influence to promote disarmament and help oppressed peoples. The Nebraskan had originally supported Wilson's peace efforts, but he became disillusioned by the terms of the treaty, particularly Shandong, which he condemned as the "disgraceful rape of an innocent people."[148] He feared the league would perpetuate the status quo and bind the United States to the reactionary great powers. Conservative nationalists like former secretary of state Philander Knox viewed the League as hopelessly utopian and argued that U.S. interests could best be protected by using military power in cooperation with friendly states. Staunch unilateralists like senators Hiram Johnson of California and William Borah of Idaho expressed horror at the thought of surrendering U.S. freedom of action to a world organization. "What we want," Borah asserted, "is . . . a free, untrammeled Nation, imbued again with the national spirit; not isolation but freedom to do as our own people think wise and just."[149]

Most Republicans accepted a League in some form. A group of mild reservationists, mostly from the Middle West and moderate in view and demeanor, sought only minor changes that would protect U.S. sovereignty and clarify and limit obligations under Article X. These Republicans provided the basis for a compromise, but they could not go too far for fear of undercutting their party's interests. A larger group of strong reservationists headed by Lodge raised searching questions about the League. Some doubted it would work: Nation-states could not be expected to transfer

147. Richard W. Lowitt, *George W. Norris: The Persistence of a Progressive, 1913–1933* (Urbana, Ill., 1971), 109.
148. Ibid., 116.
149. Ralph Stone, *The Irreconcilables: The Fight Against the League of Nations* (Lexington, Ky., 1970), 57.

sovereignty to an untested international organization and would not send troops to implement Article X unless their vital interests were threatened. Others warned that the League would involve the United States in disputes that were not its concern, undermine its preeminence in the Western Hemisphere, threaten control of domestic issues such as immigration and tariff policy, and take from Congress the power to declare war. While willing to endorse U.S. participation in a League, they wanted stronger reservations to protect its sovereignty and weaken obligations under Article X, which they viewed as an unacceptable departure from U.S. tradition.[150]

The opposition seized the initiative before Wilson returned from Paris. Amply financed by millionaire industrialists Henry Clay Frick and Andrew Mellon, the Irreconcilables launched a nationwide campaign, sending out thousands of pamphlets denouncing the "Evil Thing with a Holy Name" and making hundreds of speeches, many of them appealing to the racial and nationalist prejudices of Americans. Senator Joseph Medill McCormick of Illinois warned that Wilson's superstate would lead to "efficient and economical Japanese operating our street railways . . . Hindoo janitors in our offices and apartments . . . Chinese craftsmen driving rivets, joining timbers, laying bricks in the construction of our buildings." Borah claimed that through the League the United States would "give back to George V what it took away from George III."[151]

In the meantime, Foreign Relations Committee chairman Lodge stacked his committee with anti-League Republicans, including six Irreconcilables. His strategy was to stall, allowing opposition to build, and then secure defeat of the treaty or its approval with major reservations. Lodge consumed six weeks reading the massive document aloud to his committee. He invited large numbers of witnesses to testify, most of them hostile, including Lansing, who had broken with Wilson in Paris, and representatives of disgruntled ethnic groups.

Wilson was not uncompromising at the start of the fight. During his trip back from Europe in February, he had met with members of the foreign affairs committees of both houses of Congress, explained his proposals for a League of Nations, and attempted to address objections. While responding firmly to hard-core foes like Lodge, he sought to palliate moderates like Taft. Indeed, he had taken back to Paris for discussion with his counterparts proposals set forth by the former president. But there were limits beyond which he would not go, most notably the obligations under

---

150. Link, *Revolution, War, and Peace*, 109–12; Cooper, *Breaking the Heart of the World*, 129–31.
151. Stone, *Irreconcilables*, 82.

Article X. And at times he breathed defiance to his critics. In a dramatic meeting on August 19, the only time a congressional committee has ever subjected a president to direct questioning, the Foreign Relations Committee met with Wilson at the White House for three hours. The tone was civil, although some senators sought to extract from the president information that could be used against him. But the meeting changed no minds and produced no movement toward compromise.[152]

Facing possible defeat and persuaded—mistakenly—that an outpouring of popular support might move the recalcitrant senators, an already feeble Wilson, against the advice of his wife, Edith (whom he had married in 1915), and his personal physician, decided to take the fight to the nation. McKinley had done the same thing in 1898 to gain backing for the Treaty of Paris. In 1916, Wilson had used a similar trip to secure preparedness legislation. In September, at Columbus, Ohio, he launched a ten-thousand-mile swing through the West. He delivered forty-two speeches in twenty-one days, all without benefit of microphone, and made numerous other public appearances. Speaking to large and generally enthusiastic crowds, he passionately defended the League of Nations—"the only possible guarantee against war," he called it. The alternative, he warned, would be more foreign wars and a national security state that might threaten American democracy. He sought to ease fears about Article X, noting on one occasion that U.S. troops would not be sent to the Balkans or Central Europe—"If you want to put out a fire in Utah, you don't send to Oklahoma for the fire engine." Often, he touched the emotions of his listeners, singling out in the audience mothers of young men killed in battle. He appealed to Americans to accept the responsibilities of world leadership.[153]

By the time the president reached Pueblo, Colorado, on September 25, he was exhausted and suffering from severe headaches. After what turned out to be the last speech of the tour, he collapsed. Reluctantly admitting that he could not go on—"I just feel as if I am going to pieces"—he looked out the window of his train and began to weep. A week later, back in Washington, he suffered a massive stroke that left him partially blind and paralyzed on the left side.[154]

During the next two months, the treaty went down to defeat. The speaking tour had been a personal success in many ways, but it changed nothing in the Senate. Wilson could barely function. Although his wife and his physician shielded him from problems and hid from the government and

152. Thompson, *Wilson*, 223–24.
153. Thompson, *Wilson*, 227–32; Cooper, *Breaking the Heart of the World*, 158–197.
154. Cooper, *Breaking the Heart of the World*, 189.

the nation the extent of his incapacity, he could not provide leadership during the most critical stage of one of the most important political struggles in U.S. history. His illness may have made him less disposed to compromise.[155]

Ironically, although an overwhelming majority of senators favored a League in some form, friend and foe combined to keep the United States out. While Wilson was on tour, the Foreign Relations Committee submitted a majority report proposing forty-five amendments and four reservations. Democrats and mild reservationists defeated the amendments, but the votes were close, suggesting the difficulties ahead. In October, Lodge reported the treaty with fourteen reservations—the number was not coincidental! Ratification would depend on acceptance by three of the four Allied powers. The most significant reservations excluded the Monroe Doctrine and domestic issues from League jurisdiction, allowed member nations to withdraw, and severely restricted U.S. obligations under Article X. The United States would accept no obligation to defend the territorial integrity or political independence of any country. United States naval or military forces could not be deployed without the explicit approval of Congress. The reservation effectively gutted the key collective security provision. It exceeded what the mild reservationists wanted, but they went along rather than bolt the party on a crucial issue.[156]

The threat of defeat raised the possibility of some sort of compromise, but Wilson refused to go along. Hitchcock approached him on the eve of the vote and found him unmoveable. He insisted that Article X—what he had called the "king pin of the whole structure"—was essential to the concept of collective security. Without it, there would be no new world order, only a reversion to old-style power politics. He vowed that if the treaty passed with reservations, he would kill it by pocket veto. He seemed almost to welcome defeat. The onus would be squarely on Lodge and the Republicans. Believing that the public still supported him, Wilson speculated that the 1920 election could then be made a "great and solemn referendum" on a noble cause. At times during these weeks, he even toyed with running for a third term. He seemed to have lost touch with the political mood of the nation, even with reality.[157]

Wilson's adamancy sealed the fate of the treaty. Before packed chambers, on November 18 and 19, among the most dramatic days in the Senate's storied history, thirty-four Republicans and four Democrats voted for

155. Ibid., 199–208.
156. Thompson, *Wilson*, 234–35.
157. Ibid., 239–40.

the treaty *with* reservations. The remaining Democrats combined with the Irreconcilables for fifty-five votes against. In a second roll call shortly after, the Irreconcilables joined with the strong reservationists to defeat the treaty as Wilson had presented it, 38 for, 53 against.[158]

The shock of outright defeat generated pressures in Congress and the country for compromise, but they came to nothing. Wilson had begun to recover from the stroke, but his improvement did not bring a return to full leadership or a willingness to compromise. He saw his opponents as seeking to destroy his internationalist program. The qualified commitment they proposed was completely unacceptable to him. A young and healthy Wilson might have salvaged something of his brainchild, but the first stages of recuperation seem to have heightened his defiance. Denouncing the opposition as "nullifiers," he vowed he would "make no compromise or concession of any kind," leaving with Republicans "undivided responsibility" for the fate of the treaty. In a letter to Hitchcock released to the press on March 8, he insisted that any reservation that weakened Article X "cuts at the very heart and life of the Covenant itself," that any agreement that did not guarantee the independence of members was a "futile scrap of paper."[159] The mild reservationists pressed Lodge to compromise, but the Irreconcilables threatened to leave the party and the Massachusetts senator held firm. Some Democrats eventually broke with Wilson, preferring a modified treaty to none at all, but it was not enough. When the final vote was taken on March 19, 1920, the eight dissident Democrats and reservationist Republicans failed by a mere seven votes to get the two-thirds majority needed to pass the treaty with Lodge's reservations.[160]

At the time and since, blame has been variously cast for the outcome of 1919–20. Lodge and other Republicans have been charged with rabid partisanship and a deep-seated personal animus that fueled a determination to embarrass Wilson. It can be argued, on the other hand, that they were simply doing the job the political system assigned to the "loyal" opposition and that the Lodge reservations were necessary to protect national sovereignty. The Democrats have been criticized for standing firmly—and foolishly—with their ailing leader, instead of working with Republicans to gain a modified commitment to the League of Nations. Wilson himself has been accused of the "supreme infanticide," slaying his own brainchild through his stubborn refusal to deal with the opposition.

158. Cooper, *Breaking the Heart of the World*, 234.
159. Ibid., 346.
160. Ibid., 362–70.

There is much truth here also, although as his defenders have pointed out, he passionately believed that the treaty as he had crafted it was the only way to mend a broken world. There has also been much speculation about the way his mental and physical health influenced his actions of 1919–20, even a psychoanalytic study by no less than Sigmund Freud. The ultimate reason appears much more fundamental. Throughout his career and especially in the Great War, Wilson acted with rare boldness in seeking to reshape a war-torn world and educate Americans to a new leadership role. His aspirations are understandable given the gruesome destruction caused by the war. What he sought may indeed have been necessary to avert the disaster that lay ahead. Still, it is difficult to avoid the conclusion that he aimed too high. In Paris, his European counterparts took the Fourteen Points apart. Americans were simply not ready to undertake the huge break from tradition and assume the sort of commitments he asked of them.[161]

The defeat of Wilson's handiwork leaves haunting if ultimately unanswerable questions. The Wilson of 1919–20 believed that vital principles were at stake in the struggle with Lodge and that compromise would render the League of Nations all but useless. Would a more robust and healthy Wilson—the artful politician of his first term—have built more solid support for his proposals or found a middle ground that would have made possible Senate approval of the treaty and U.S. entry into the League of Nations? Could a modified League with U.S. participation have changed the history of the next two decades?

Whatever the answers to these questions, it is strikingly clear that the Great War and Woodrow Wilson transformed U.S. foreign policy dramatically. As a result of the war, the United States became a major player in world politics and economics. The more Europe indulged in self-destruction, the greater America's relative power. Americans still did not see themselves as threatened by events beyond their shores and hence remained unwilling to take on the sort of commitments Wilson asked of them. But they began to recognize their changing position in the international system. In trying to establish for his nation a leadership role,

---

161. Thomas A. Bailey, *Woodrow Wilson and the Great Betrayal* (Chicago, 1977), 277, coins the phrase "supreme act of infanticide." Thomas Knock's " 'Playing for a Hundred Years Hence' " emphasizes Wilson's commitment to principles and the importance of those principles. Sigmund Freud and William C. Bullitt coauthored a vindictive psychobiography entitled *Thomas Woodrow Wilson, Twenty-eighth President of the United States: A Psychological Study* (Boston, 1967). Thompson, *Wilson*, 241–42, offers a broader and more persuasive conclusion.

Wilson articulated a set of principles that in various forms would guide U.S. foreign policy for years to come. The venerable Elihu Root observed in 1922 that Americans had "learned more about international relations within the past eight years than they had learned in the preceding eighty years." And they were "only at the beginning of the task," he presciently added.[162]

162. Selig Adler, *The Isolationist Impulse: Its Twentieth-Century Reaction* (New York, 1957), 112.

11

Involvement Without Commitment, 1921–1931

Often dismissed as an isolationist backwater, the era of the 1920s in fact defies simple explanation. It lacks an overarching theme and a dominant, Wilson-like figure. United States foreign policy derived from numerous complex and sometimes conflicting pressures, producing a bundle of seeming contradictions. The United States was without question the world's top economic power, but it lacked commensurate military power and was not always inclined or able to use its economic might effectively. Republican officials went far beyond their predecessors in terms of involvement in world problems. The United States assumed a level of leadership quite unprecedented in its history. Still in the absence of a compelling external threat and in light of Wilson's recent experience, the Republican leaders did not defy the nation's long-standing tradition against "entangling" alliances and did not embrace collective security. Wherever possible, they used the private sector to implement solutions developed in Washington. The Republicans might, perhaps should, have done more, especially in the economic realm, but it would have been difficult for them to do so. And there is no guarantee that more decisive action could have averted the economic and political disasters that lay ahead. The 1920s must therefore be considered on their own terms. Involvement without commitment seems the best way to sum up the U.S. approach to the world during that period. The nation vigorously promoted its interests while scrupulously guarding against entanglements. This approach brought remarkable short-term successes that concealed major long-term failures.[1]

I

In a strange, almost surreal way, despite the massive bloodletting of 1914–18, the postwar world remained Eurocentric. To be sure, Western Europe was drastically weakened, but its potential challengers, the United

1. A good survey is Warren I. Cohen, *Empire Without Tears: America's Foreign Relations, 1921–1933* (New York, 1987). See also Brian J. C. McKercher, "Reaching for the Brass Ring: The Recent Historiography of Interwar American Foreign Relations," *Diplomatic History* 15 (Fall 1991), 565–98.

States and Japan, were focused on regional hegemony, and Russia was devastated by war and revolution. Thus during the 1920s, European issues continued to dominate the agenda of world politics. Britain and France maintained leadership roles through traditional diplomacy and the newly formed League of Nations. In a supreme irony, despite the war and Wilsonian rhetoric of self-determination, through the League mandate system the area under imperial control actually increased during the postwar years.

The appearances of Eurocentricity concealed fundamental changes in the international system that left Europe much weaker and less stable. The continent had suffered incalculable destruction. The final casualty list from assorted war-related causes may have been as high as sixty million people, nearly half of them in Russia, with France, Italy, and Germany also suffering huge losses. The economic costs have been estimated as high as $260 billion. Manufacturing and agricultural production dropped sharply in all European nations. The financing of the war through borrowing left massive indebtedness, shifting the center of world financial power from London to New York, undermining the foundations of the world economy, and eventually provoking an economic and political crisis of the first magnitude. The psychological and emotional costs were equally high. The war challenged Europeans' faith in progress and certainty of their own superiority. In part also as a result of the war, mass public opinion assumed a greater role in the diplomatic process, and Europe in the postwar era was riven by deep-seated and volatile passions. Much of the public in the Western democracies recoiled against the horrible suffering of the Great War, producing various forms of escapism. Others, especially those dissatisfied with the results, seethed with anger and lusted for revenge. Among mass publics throughout Europe, ideologies of the extreme right and left gained numerous adherents.

War always leaves difficult problems, and this was especially true in postwar Europe. Despite substantial physical destruction and territorial losses, Germany remained potentially a great power. The Versailles Treaty hemmed in the loser with various restrictions and saddled it with substantial reparations, leaving great resentment and frustration. For many Germans, the essential goal was to restore the fatherland to its rightful place in Europe, exactly what France most feared and sought desperately to prevent. The greatest changes came in eastern and central Europe where the Austro-Hungarian empire gave way to a number of newly independent nations. However admirable their intentions, the peacemakers could not make these new nations ethnically homogeneous, thus building into them inherent conflicts and weaknesses, creating vulnerable borders, and inviting great power interference.[2]

In the colonial areas, the Great War accelerated the nationalist revolts that after a second world war would initiate the process of decolonization. The wartime need for people and resources put huge strains on colonial populations and economies, disrupting normal patterns of life and producing need for repayment of sacrifices in blood and treasure. Wilsonian and Leninist rhetoric of self-determination encouraged local nationalisms, and the obvious weakening of the European powers spurred thoughts of revolt. Throughout Asia and the Middle East, nationalist groups formed to demand political and economic concessions. The colonial powers' brutal repression of postwar revolts exposed as sham their talk of justice, fueling rage that further boosted nationalism. The empires remained intact during the 1920s, but growing unrest there distracted European leaders from addressing European problems and caused divisions among the powers themselves.[3]

Technology continued to shrink the world and change the way people lived and nations interacted with each other. Global application of cable, telephone, and radio dramatically improved communications, providing new means to bring people together. In March 1926, the first news story was transmitted from London to New York by trans-Atlantic telephone— "space rolled up like a cloud," one newspaper proclaimed.[4] In the United States, especially, the automobile drastically altered popular lifestyles. By creating insatiable demands for oil and rubber, it also raised new economic and foreign policy concerns. Nothing struck the imagination of people worldwide like Charles Lindbergh's stunning nonstop flight from New York to Paris in 1927. The effect, the aviator himself observed, was "like a match lighting a bonfire." The wonders of modern communication quickly spread to the far corners of the globe news of the wonders of modern transportation, sparking wild celebrations and exuberant flights of rhetoric. An Indian periodical claimed that Lindbergh's triumph was "a matter of glory, not only for his countrymen, but the entire human race." The flight was widely viewed as a sign of progress, proving with what "proud contempt man can defy the adverse forces of nature." It was hailed for uniting "the hearts of all men everywhere." Less commented

2. Paul Kennedy, *The Rise and Fall of the Great Powers: Economic Change and Military Conflict from 1500 to 2000* (New York, 1987), 275–90; John Keegan, *The First World War* (New York, 1998), 421–27.
3. Raymond F. Betts, *Decolonization* (London, 1998), 4–18.
4. *St. Louis Post-Dispatch*, March 8, 1926.

on in the exultation of the moment was the potential military application of what would soon come to be called air power.[5]

The only nation except Japan to benefit from the Great War, the United States emerged unquestionably the world's greatest economic power. The population increased by 30 percent between 1900 and 1920 to more than 106 million people. The United States was the world's largest agricultural and manufacturing producer and during the 1920s, remarkably, produced more industrial output than the next six powers combined. The war solidified the nation's position as a creditor. It was the world's leading financial power and had a large supply of gold. Its productivity, wealth, and standard of living were the envy of people across the globe.

The Republicans would be sharply criticized after World War II for unilaterally disarming the United States during the 1920s, but in truth they maintained a military establishment entirely adequate for the times. The overriding fact in determining national security policies was the absence of any serious threat to U.S. security. Europe was exhausted from war, Japan in a cooperative mood, and Soviet Russia preoccupied with internal development. In this strategic context, the United States was properly content to maintain a small regular army of about 140,000 men to be supplemented in war by the mobilization of a reserve of citizen soldiers. The officer corps remained at twice the prewar level; army appropriations even during the Great Depression were more than double what they had been before 1914. Army leaders worked significant qualitative improvements, including the beginnings of armored forces and an air corps. The United States came out of the war with the world's largest navy, and sea-power enthusiasts hoped to maintain naval supremacy, but such a goal made no sense in an era of peace and security. The Republicans initiated significant disarmament and settled for parity with Great Britain in capital ships, while developing heavy cruisers and aircraft carriers. Post–World War II internationalists (mainly Democrats) criticized them for not maintaining adequate military power. In reality, it was quite appropriate for the United States during these years to be economically powerful and only moderately strong militarily.[6]

Far more important than America's military strength during the 1920s was what scholar Joseph Nye would later label its "soft power," the global influence deriving from its economic might, technological superiority, and cultural sway.[7] At the end of the war, the United States stood above

5. A. Scott Berg, Lindbergh (New York, 1998), 135–43.
6. Kennedy, Rise and Fall, 328–29; John Braeman, "Power and Diplomacy: The 1920s Reappraised," Review of Politics 44 (July 1982), 342–69.
7. Joseph S. Nye Jr., The Paradox of American Power (New York, 2002), 9–12.

the rest of the world, youthful, dynamic, and prosperous, the city on a hill Puritan leader John Winthrop had spoken of three hundred years earlier. Especially to war-weary Europeans seeking to make the transition to peace, America's values of optimism, pragmatism, and efficiency and its high standard of living appeared worthy of emulation. Long scorned by Europeans for its lack of high culture, the United States in the 1920s became a center for the global export of mass culture. Its artists and writers flooded Europe and became trendsetters for the decade. Its films took over European markets, establishing fashions, spreading the American way of life, and selling U.S. products. "Your movies and talkies have soaked the French mind in American life, methods, and manners . . . ," ambassador Jean Claudel observed, "bringing a new vision of power and a new tempo of life. . . . More and more we are following America." Such soft power naturally provoked resentment, especially among proud, aristocratic Europeans. But it also enabled the United States to pursue its foreign policy aims in Europe with minimal commitment.[8]

American attitudes toward the outside world were marked by turbulent crosscurrents during the 1920s. The patriotism drummed up for the Great Crusade produced powerful nativist and chauvinist sentiments that persisted well into the decade, leading to attacks on those branded "un-American" at home, suspicion of involvement abroad, and limits on immigration, especially of Orientals. Even among many of the elite who played an important role in the war and the peace negotiations, the experience reaffirmed old suspicions of Europe and convictions of U.S. superiority. "The more I learn to know the Old World, the stronger my love for America . . . ," Secretary of State Robert Lansing wrote from Paris in 1919. "The more I breathe the foulness of European intrigue, the sweeter and purer becomes the air of my native land."[9] His young nephew Allen Dulles expressed similar views. "Notwithstanding all the pious utterances of European statesman, the policy of most of these governments over here is just as devious as it was a hundred years ago," the future CIA director wrote his father.[10]

At the same time and paradoxically, the war and Wilsonianism boosted popular interest in the outside world. The 1920s brought another explosion of missionary activity abroad, as large numbers of Americans de-

8. Frank Costigliola, *Awkward Dominion: American Political, Economic, and Cultural Relations with Europe, 1919–1933* (Ithaca, N.Y., 1984), 20–22.
9. Stephen G. Craft, "John Bassett Moore, Robert Lansing, and the Shandong Question," *Pacific Historical Review* 66 (May 1997), 244.
10. Peter Grose, *Gentleman Spy: The Life of Allen Dulles* (Boston, 1994), 63.

parted for Asia, Africa, and Latin America to spread the Gospel and American values. The experience probably had more effect on developing their own worldliness than on serving the people they worked among. American volunteer groups set up schools and hospitals in areas as remote as Albania. Tourism skyrocketed in the 1920s, especially in Europe, where an estimated 251,000 travelers spent upwards of $300 million in 1929 alone. The flood of tourists helped to heal Europe's balance of payments problems; on occasion, Americans provoked such resentment abroad with their wealth and arrogant behavior that President Calvin Coolidge felt compelled to intervene.[11]

American universities gave growing attention to the study of world affairs. The number of international programs doubled between 1916 and 1921. Shortly after the war, Georgetown University, Johns Hopkins, and Tufts created separate schools of world politics. In 1921, a group of East Coast businessmen, bankers, lawyers, and academics, some closely connected to the government, organized the Council on Foreign Relations, a decidedly elitist group committed to promoting public interest in foreign policy issues and providing expert advice to government. With prominent names on its roster like statesmen Elihu Root and Henry Stimson and banker Thomas Lamont, the council held monthly black-tie dinners to discuss current issues and began publishing its signature journal, *Foreign Affairs*. It vigorously promoted internationalism and became a breeding ground for the "establishment" that would shape U.S. foreign policy through much of the twentieth century.[12]

African Americans, the most oppressed minority group in American society, also looked abroad. Leaders like Walter White, W.E.B. DuBois, and the singer Paul Robeson increasingly appreciated that the problems of people of color were international in scope and that global solutions might be necessary. White's association with the Pan-African Congress in 1921 revealed to him the international dimensions of issues of race and white supremacy, and the connections between racism and imperialism, white supremacy, and global capitalism. Some like Marcus Garvey sought foreign solutions to U.S. race problems by advocating a mass exodus of African Americans back to Africa. Others like DuBois pushed for considering the problems of people of color in their international dimension.[13]

11. Costigliola, *Awkward Dominion*, 171–73.
12. Cohen, *Empire Without Tears*, 2, 11; Robert D. Schulzinger, *The Wise Men of Foreign Affairs: The History of the Council on Foreign Relations* (New York, 1984), 5–30.
13. David Levering Lewis, *W.E.B. DuBois: The Fight for Equality and the American Century, 1919–1963* (New York, 2000), 37–84.

Traditionally, after wars Americans have rebelled against strong presidential leadership, and this was especially true after World War I. McKinley, Roosevelt, and Wilson had significantly expanded the presidency, and Americans neither wanted nor got that sort of leader in the 1920s. Warren Harding was a weak and amiable nonentity, precisely what party stalwarts sought. Ultimately, he was the tragic victim of the corruption of the men around him. He came to despise his job. It's "hell," he told a friend. "There is no other word to describe it."[14] A dour and flinty Vermonter, "Silent Cal" Coolidge reveled in presidential inactivity. Both came from provincial backgrounds and showed little interest in and much ignorance of the world. Harding had traveled extensively but apparently learned very little. Coolidge flaunted his provincialism, telling friends he did not need to go to Europe because he could learn what he needed at home. Elihu Root snarled that Coolidge did not have an international hair in his head; Coolidge admitted that his intellect was not a "gushing fountain."[15] Their inattention and lack of boldness may have been especially costly in terms of addressing crucial global economic issues. The best that can be said about them is that they had the good sense to leave the conduct of foreign policy in the generally capable hands of their secretaries of state.

During the 1920s, the secretaries of state resumed the preeminent role in policymaking they had played before McKinley and Roosevelt. The New York lawyer and unsuccessful presidential candidate Charles Evans Hughes was one of the ablest ever to hold the post. An indefatigable worker, utterly devoted to the job, he filled the sizeable void left by Harding and Coolidge and was perhaps the last secretary to personally manage U.S. foreign policy. Hughes ably presided over a department with a budget of $2 million and a staff of six hundred people. He won the loyalty of his aides with his dedication and warm, outgoing personality. Blessed with a brilliant mind, he was also politically astute. Keenly aware of Wilson's fate, he shied away from grand schemes and bold initiatives, but through careful study and preparation steered seventy-one treaties through a contentious Senate. In perfect keeping with the times, he sought a "maximum of security with a minimum of commitment."[16] His successor, Frank B.

14. Eugene P. Trani and David L. Wilson, *The Presidency of Warren G. Harding* (Lawrence, Kans., 1977), 172.

15. Robert H. Ferrell, *The Presidency of Calvin Coolidge* (Lawrence, Kans., 1998), 23.

16. John Chalmers Vinson, "Charles Evans Hughes, 1921–1925," in Norman A. Graebner, ed., *An Uncertain Tradition: American Secretaries of State in the Twentieth Century* (New York, 1961), 134; Waldo H. Heinrichs, *American Ambassador: Joseph C. Grew and the Development of the United States Diplomatic Tradition* (Boston, 1966), 105.

Kellogg, matched him only in dedication to and hours spent on the job. A Minnesota farm boy without formal education, Kellogg in best Horatio Alger fashion had become a prominent lawyer, Republican politician, and ambassador to Great Britain. Cautious to a fault, he was a classic workaholic who often became bogged down in minutiae and whose working habits produced the anxious, sometimes bad-tempered demeanor that earned him the nickname "Nervous Nellie." His major accomplishment, the Kellogg-Briand Pact outlawing war, won him a Nobel Peace Prize— and the derision of subsequent generations of internationalist pundits and historians.[17]

Developments in the diplomatic corps reflected the crosscurrents of the age. On the one side, the foreign service became increasingly professionalized, "a pretty good club," in the words of one of its members, of upper-class white males from the most prestigious prep schools and Ivy League universities who shared the same values, a taste for "old wines, proper English and Savile Row clothing," and a deep commitment to converting a traditionally amateur operation into a permanent profession. On the other side, the consuls and their business and congressional allies pushed for a higher status for the less effete, more "manly," and more typically American consular service to more effectively promote U.S. business abroad. After years of consular agitation, Congress forced the two services into an uneasy merger with the 1924 Rogers Act. Three years later, the apparent favoritism of the snobbish diplomats for themselves over the "hard-working" consuls provoked a backlash in Congress and the press that resuscitated the traditional American disdain for diplomacy and diplomats. One outraged critic insisted that the diplomats should be sent to consular posts "where they would do some real work." The result was a setback for professionalization of the foreign service and additional legislation to force closer integration with the consuls.[18]

The new world of the 1920s brought intrusions on the State Department's traditional domination of U.S. foreign policy. For his interference in this area as in others, Herbert Hoover was known as secretary of commerce and undersecretary of everything else. The Republican administrations eagerly farmed out key tasks to private experts such as industrialist Owen D. Young, Lamont, and Johns Hopkins economist Edwin Kemmerer. Private lobbying groups also exerted growing influence, especially the organized peace movement, which consisted of a variety of

17. Heinrichs, *Ambassador*, 109–10; L. Ethan Ellis, "Frank B. Kellogg, 1925–1929," in Graebner, *Uncertain Tradition*, 149–67.
18. Heinrichs, *Ambassador*, 101–25.

organizations—working sometimes together but often at cross-purposes—
and exerted powerful pressure for disarmament and the outlawing of war.[19]

Flushed with its "victory" over Wilson and in full rebellion against
three decades of executive domination, Congress was more assertive in
foreign policy in the 1920s than at any time since the Gilded Age. It mat-
tered not who was secretary of state, Senator Boies Penrose boasted,
"Congress—especially the Senate—will blaze the way in connection with
our foreign policies."[20] Penrose's rhetoric aside, of course, Congress was
not well suited to "blaze the way." As an institution, it was too big and unwieldy to actually frame and implement policies. Most legislators were interested mainly in domestic issues. They were divided on the basis of party,
and the two parties were sharply divided internally, limiting their ability
to agree on anything. Congressional influence was mainly negative. Vivid
memories of Wilson's humiliating defeat undoubtedly inhibited initiatives among executives not prone to activism in any event, leading Hughes
and Kellogg to frame cautious policies and carefully cultivate congressional support for them. On numerous occasions, Congress played an obstructionist role.[21]

A power unto themselves in the Congress were the so-called Peace Progressives, a small but tightly unified and vocal bloc that exerted an influence far disproportionate to its numbers. Composed mainly of midwestern
and western radicals, most of them Republicans, the Peace Progressives
kept up a drumfire of criticism of U.S. foreign policy throughout the 1920s.
Often wrongly dismissed as isolationists, they took a keen interest in foreign policy issues, articulated a global vision sharply opposed to that of
mainstream Republicans, and ardently promoted the use of U.S. influence to build a better world. Foes of big business in domestic policy, they
also objected to the overarching influence of business in foreign policy.
They were staunchly anti-imperialist and anti-militarist. They denounced
U.S. military intervention in the Caribbean and advocated support of nationalism in areas long dominated by outside powers. They urged recognition of the Soviet Union, not out of sympathy for Bolshevism but from the
belief that engagement with Communism would help reform it. They
worked closely with peace groups to push radical disarmament measures
and the outlawing of war. Led by Senator William Borah, the so-called
Lion of Idaho, a powerful figure of leonine countenance, stentorian voice,

19. Charles DeBenedetti, *The Peace Reform in American History* (Bloomington, Ind.,
    1980), 108–21.
20. Trani and Wilson, *Harding Presidency*, 115.
21. Ibid., 59–60; Ferrell, *Coolidge Presidency*, 42–43.

and indomitable will, they helped end the U.S. occupation of Nicaragua, cut off funds for naval construction, and avert war with Mexico.[22]

II

The business of America is business, Calvin Coolidge famously proclaimed, and indeed, in the absence of any compelling strategic threat, economic issues assumed primacy in the 1920s. Many business and political leaders recognized the growing interdependence of the world economy; some appreciated that America's new creditor status opened promising opportunities and imposed urgent responsibilities.[23] Americans voraciously devoured the world's resources. The United States consumed 60 percent of the world output of eight critical raw materials and 40 percent of ten others; by 1922, it used 70 percent of the world's rubber supply.[24] Industrialists and government officials naturally worried about the nation's growing dependence on foreign sources for vital raw materials such as rubber, silk, nitrates, and especially oil to fuel the burgeoning automobile business and keep the navy afloat. The United States still relied on foreign trade for a smaller share of its gross domestic product than any other major economic power, and the more nationalist business leaders believed that the economy would grow even if Germany and France were in recession. Many businessmen and political leaders continued to view overseas trade and investments as important to American prosperity, however. They also believed that the spread of liberal capitalism would help promote a stable and prosperous world order by improving living standards in other countries and eliminating the conditions that bred revolution. Some business leaders fervently believed that the expansion of American corporate culture could help modernize "backward" areas, thereby promoting prosperity and order as well as lining their own pockets with profits. Without international trade, the high priest of American capitalism, Herbert Hoover, warned, "not a single automobile would run; not a dynamo would turn; not a telephone, telegraph, or radio would operate." Commerce was "the life blood of modern civilization."[25]

22. Robert David Johnson, *The Peace Progressives and American Foreign Relations* (Cambridge, Mass., 1995).

23. Jeffrey J. Matthews, *Alanson B. Houghton, Ambassador of the New Era* (Lanham, Md., 2004), 48–49.

24. Michael J. Hogan, *Informal Entente: The Private Structure of Cooperation in Anglo-American Economic Diplomacy, 1918–1928* (Chicago, 1991), 187.

25. Melvyn P. Leffler, "Expansionist Impulses and Domestic Constraints, 1921–1932," in William H. Becker and Samuel F. Wells Jr., eds., *Economics and World Power: An Assessment of American Diplomacy Since 1789* (New York, 1984), 232–33.

More than at any time in the past, business and government worked hand in hand through informal cooperative arrangements to promote the general interest, often in ways that "blurred the lines between public and private sector operations."[26] Recognizing the importance of markets and investments, Congress passed in 1918 the Webb-Pomerene Act and in 1919 the Edge Act exempting exporters and bankers respectively from antitrust provisions and permitting them to combine to engage in foreign trade and lending, giving them more resources and limiting their risks. Hoover's Commerce Department energetically searched out and furnished to eager businessmen information about opportunities for foreign trade and investment. Consuls and diplomats vigorously promoted the Open Door policy to ensure equal access for American exporters, investors, and exploiters of foreign raw materials. Where expedient, the U.S. government also sanctioned exclusive arrangements between American and foreign businessmen to share markets and raw materials. Even in the crucial new areas of cable and radio operations in America's hemispheric area of influence, under the watchful eye of the State Department, U.S. and British businessmen worked out cooperative deals to avoid wasteful and costly competition.[27] In an age where any sort of political commitment was anathema, government also relied on unofficial agents, often businessmen, economists, or bankers, to negotiate or implement agreements with other nations or serve as financial consultants to other governments.[28]

The results, at least in terms of numbers, were impressive. After the recession of 1919–21, the U.S. economy boomed. Trade flourished; exports jumped from $3.8 billion in 1922 to $5.1 billion in 1929, and finished manufactured products expanded to 50 percent of total exports by the end of the decade. Automobile exports represented 10 percent of the total and assumed an increasingly critical place in the overall economy. Other major items included cash registers, typewriters, sewing machines, agricultural equipment, tires, and petroleum products. By 1929, the United States was the world's leading exporter, with Western Europe, Canada, and Japan the major recipients of its products. Despite the high rates imposed in the Fordney-McCumber tariff of 1922, imports also increased, from $3.1 billion in 1922 to $4.4 billion in 1929, oil and rubber being among the key items.[29]

26. Cohen, *Empire*, 19.
27. Hogan, *Informal Entente*, 105–58.
28. Emily S. Rosenberg, *Financial Missionaries to the World: The Politics and Culture of Dollar Diplomacy, 1900–1930* (Durham, N.C., 2003), 97–150.
29. Leffler, "Expansionist Impulses," 246; Cohen, *Empire*, 23–25.

Those who had traditionally looked to European and especially British bankers for capital after World War I of necessity turned to the United States. Investments in the form of loans rose to more than $15 billion by the end of the decade, most of them long-term loans to debtor nations. Private U.S. lenders poured huge sums of money into Latin America and Japan. American loans played a crucial role in stabilizing the war-shattered German economy. They helped create a favorable balance of trade and permitted other nations to buy U.S. products.[30]

Even more significant was the vast expansion of direct investments resulting in the construction of American factories abroad. Such investments rose to $4 billion in the 1920s, the first great age of the multinational corporations. These institutions would assume growing importance in the world economy and play crucial political roles in nations across the world. American businessmen were drawn overseas by proximity to markets, avoidance of high tariffs, and cheap labor. They often cut favorable deals with friendly local governments. The practice was most extensive in Europe, where investment more than doubled in the 1920s and more than 1,300 firms were established. Corporations such as Ford and General Motors dominated the automobile industry in Europe and Canada. Firms like General Electric and International Telephone and Telegraph took over utilities and communications services across the world; by 1930, GE had invested $500 million in eleven Latin American countries alone. International Business Machines and Remington Rand dominated the production and sales of office equipment. Oil companies built refineries and expanded marketing operations across the world. The notorious United Fruit Company bought up plantations and controlled railroad and port facilities throughout Central America and the Caribbean. Wealthier than most of the so-called banana republics in which it operated, it also wielded enormous political power.[31] By 1930, U.S. direct investment exceeded that of France, Holland, and Germany combined.

American multinational corporations also exploited crucial raw materials. Lured by the prospect of riches "beyond the dreams of avarice," the Guggenheim family, with government support, negotiated a highly favorable arrangement giving it control of the extraction of Chilean nitrate.[32] The government in its quest for independent supplies of desperately needed rubber also encouraged industrialist Harvey Firestone to lease

30. Cohen, *Empire*, 28–29.
31. Ibid., 36–40.
32. Thomas F. O'Brien, " 'Rich Beyond the Dreams of Avarice': The Guggenheims in Chile," *Business History Review* 63 (Spring 1989), 142.

Liberian lands on which rubber trees could be grown. It further supported Firestone by arranging a quasi-official loan that required U.S. "advisers," in the mode of the Central American republics, to assume responsibility for Liberian finances.[33] Alarmed by the prospects of an oil shortage, Americans, often with government backing, mounted a global drive for the precious commodity. The State Department pressed for an open door in the Middle East and declaimed against British and French deals dividing Mesopotamia. Eventually, with State Department backing, U.S. oilmen cut themselves in on the "Red Line Agreement," sharing with European firms the bountiful new resources discovered in Iraq. The government also supported oilmen's efforts to regain control of confiscated oil fields in Mexico and the Soviet Union or at least secure reasonable compensation. Additionally, Americans took full advantage of the cruel and venal dictator Gen. Juan Vicente Gómez's generosity with his country's natural resources to exploit the vast oil deposits discovered in Venezuela in the 1920s. The frenzy continued until the location of new oil fields in Texas turned the anticipated shortage into a glut.[34]

The rampant economic expansion of the 1920s brought unprecedented U.S. involvement in the world and fueled a short-term prosperity, but it did not always serve the broader national interests. Despite talk about economic interdependence and the value of foreign trade, the domestic market remained most important to the economy, and domestic priorities generally took precedence over foreign policy objectives. Throughout the decade, for example, the desire to maintain low taxes at home posed an insurmountable barrier to forgiving Allied war debts and reducing German reparations. Manufacturers' insistence on continued high tariffs to protect against an anticipated flood of European imports skewed the balance of trade in favor of the United States, making it difficult for other nations to buy its products. Loans made up some of the difference, but only as long as American bankers were able and willing to float them. Postwar U.S. economic policies thus provided no better than a rickety foundation for long-term international and domestic prosperity.[35]

Although Americans generally agreed on the goals of foreign economic policy, they often sharply disagreed on methods. Within the U.S. government, the Commerce and State departments fought bitterly for influence.

---

33. Emily S. Rosenberg, "The Invisible Protectorate: The United States, Liberia, and the Evolution of Neocolonialism, 1909–1940," *Diplomatic History* 9 (Summer 1985), 203–4.
34. Daniel Yergin, *The Prize: The Epic Quest for Oil, Money, and Power* (New York, 1991), 194–243.
35. Leffler, "Expansionist Impulses," 258–59, 264–65.

The business community was itself sharply divided, not only by rivalries among competing firms in the same industries but also between businesses that operated in the domestic and international markets and between producers and exporters. The result was a mishmash of sometimes contradictory policies rather than a coherent, closely integrated foreign economic policy.

For all the bold talk about business-government cooperation in foreign economic policy, the objectives of the two often conflicted. This was especially true in foreign lending, where efforts to ensure that private loans served the broader national interest often ran afoul of bureaucratic rivalry and business imperatives. Hoover believed that government should exercise some supervision over private loans to ensure their soundness, increase the possibility that they would actually contribute to economic development, and prevent them from being used in ways that threatened U.S. interests, by expanding armaments, for example. He encountered often bitter opposition from the State Department and bankers. Hughes sought to use loans for broader political purposes—to secure concessions from Mexico in oil negotiations, push Caribbean governments in desired directions, or promote China's economic development and territorial integrity. For obvious reasons, bankers sought mainly profit. As a result, government exercised loose supervision of loans but lacked real enforcement power. The result was at best mixed. Bankers refused loans to China urged by the State Department because they were deemed too risky, while skirting government restrictions and subsidizing Japanese imperialism in Manchuria. In the Caribbean, the loans the State Department encouraged to help achieve its political ends turned out to be unsound economically. Some loans were discouraged for frivolous reasons—rejection of loans to a Czech brewery in the era of Prohibition, for example—while others helped underwrite German rearmament. Businessmen squabbled among themselves on lending policy, exporters bitterly complaining that bankers were financing purchases by their foreign competitors. The result was a "sort of twilight zone" between government responsibility and laissez-faire that never really worked but was never really addressed or corrected.[36]

Rather than promoting modernization and stability in developing countries, the multinational corporations came to play complex and often destabilizing roles. In Cuba, for example, a General Electric subsidiary, American and Foreign Power Company (AFP), updated equipment and management methods, improved service, paid higher than local wages,

36. Hogan, *Informal Entente*, 103; Cohen, *Empire*, 34–35, 42–43.

and created incentives, including sponsoring athletic teams, to promote employee loyalty. It also developed close ties with local elites and intruded in Cuban politics, supporting leaders like the brutal Gerardo Machado who in turn protected it from regulation. The high rates charged by the U.S. utilities giant and its efforts to impose American corporate values provoked a Cuban backlash. Many management positions were given to North Americans, and Cuban workers were displaced. AFP's policies stirred up Cuban resistance in the form of strikes and consumer boycotts that took on the added dimension of nationalist opposition to outside oppression. Ironically, Cubans adapted some of the values of American corporate culture to their own ends, significantly shaping their own society and its ties with the United States.[37]

III

Economic expansion was inextricably linked with the achievement of major U.S. foreign policy goals during the 1920s. Republican policymakers were *not* ignorant of or indifferent to the outside world. On the contrary, the Great War highlighted for them in the most gruesome way the importance of events abroad to their nation's prosperity and security. Peace and order were vital for American commercial expansion, which in turn was important for prosperity. American trade, on the other hand, might help promote economic growth in other parts of the world, thus easing the discontents that spawned revolution. Anything but isolationist in their dealing with crucial postwar problems, Republican leaders involved the United States to an unprecedented extent in reconstructing postwar Europe and promoting stability in East Asia, even assuming the sort of leadership role the United States had not previously considered. The key, of course, was to do this without political entanglements. The Republicans thus relied heavily on economic measures to achieve their goals. They often used private bankers and businessmen as their instruments.

The League of Nations remained strictly taboo. After the debacle of 1919–20, few U.S. officials were bold—or foolish—enough to advocate League membership. Harding artfully straddled the issue during the 1920 campaign, but upon taking office he categorically resolved it: "A world super-government is contrary to everything we cherish and can have no sanction by our Republic," he proclaimed in his inaugural address.[38] Lingering opposition to the League in the Senate and lack of public

---

37. Thomas F. O'Brien, "The Revolutionary Mission: American Enterprise in Cuba," *American Historical Review* 98 (June 1993), 785.
38. Trani and Wilson, *Harding Presidency*, 142.

interest deterred Harding from pursuing his vague alternative proposal for an "association of nations." For a time, in a remarkable act of undiplomatic rudeness, the United States refused even to answer correspondence from the League, placing it in the State Department's dead letter file. Recognizing the political liability that Wilson's handiwork had become, his Democratic Party spurned the League in its 1924 platform.[39]

Although deemed a political albatross, the League issue would not die easily. During the 1920s, almost despite itself, the United States drew closer to the organization its president had once championed. Wilsonians continued to press for full membership. Peace advocates such as Frederick J. Libby of the National Council for the Prevention of War and James T. Shotwell of the Carnegie Endowment for Peace lobbied relentlessly and effectively for some kind of U.S. association with the world organization. Once the League was a going concern, the United States had little choice but to deal with it. From the early 1920s, diplomats began to correspond with League officials; U.S. representatives met unofficially with League commissions dealing with economic and social questions. The Republicans in time assigned some of their best people to Geneva, where they sat in on meetings concerning arms limitations and European reconstruction. From 1925 on, the United States had official representation. Obviously such limited involvement was not the equivalent of full membership, and the League's prestige and influence probably suffered accordingly. Yet to go this far represented a significant departure for a nation whose cardinal principle for 150 years had been avoiding Europe's "broils."[40]

Abstention from the World Court, the product of executive timidity and dilatoriness and Senate obstructionism, exposed the less savory side of Republican "internationalism." From the turn of the century, Republicans such as Root and William Howard Taft had promoted the expansion of international law. Harding, Coolidge, Hughes, and Kellogg all favored membership in the World Court. But the executive branch did not assign the issue high priority. Aware that mere discussion of joining the Court would raise the specter of League membership (which was not required), the politically sensitive Coolidge was prepared to "let it set."[41] While voting for U.S. membership in 1926, a still hyper-suspicious Senate loaded down its approval with conditions (some of them even drafted by American John Bassett Moore, a sitting judge on the Court), the most obnoxious of which would have prevented the Court from giving advisory opinions on matters

39. Cohen, *Empire*, 55.
40. Ibid., 57–58.
41. Ferrell, *Coolidge Presidency*, 157.

in which the United States claimed an interest. Such unilateralism—all too typical of America's approach to the world—obviously met strong opposition from other members. The eighty-four-year-old Root eventually helped redraft the Court protocol to meet Senate objections. In 1929, Hoover submitted it to the Senate. Bogged down in the Great Depression, however, he did not push it, and when it finally came up for consideration in 1935 it failed by seven votes. The United States never joined the World Court, a blunt reminder of the limits of Republican internationalism.[42]

By contrast, the United States assumed unprecedented and indispensable leadership in promoting international arms limitations. Reduction of armaments was an integral part of the Republicans' broader diplomatic and economic strategy. It would reduce government expenditures, permit a lowering of taxes, and promote the sort of peaceful and stable environment in which international trade and investment could flourish. After some initial hesitation, Harding and Hughes in 1921 jumped on an already speeding bandwagon. At a conference in Washington, the secretary of state pulled off a diplomatic tour de force, the first major international agreement on arms reduction ever negotiated.

By the time Harding took office, pressures for disarmament had mounted. Two years after the armistice, the United States, Great Britain, and Japan were planning major expansions of their already sizeable navies. In December, Peace Progressive and former Irreconcilable senator Borah proposed that the three nations reduce their navies by 50 percent over five years. The Borah Resolution struck a responsive chord among war-weary peoples in the United States and across the world. Arms reduction could permit much-needed tax relief and head off a looming arms race. Many commentators believed that the European arms race had been a major cause of the Great War, and disarmament could ease the threat of another devastating conflict. For some Americans, Borah perhaps included, U.S. leadership in arms reduction could compensate for refusal to join the League. Disarmament was a cause behind which virtually every individual and group could rally. The indefatigable Libby mounted a huge lobbying campaign. He was joined by other organizations in the burgeoning postwar peace movement, churches, and newly empowered women's groups such as the League of Women Voters and the Women's International League for Peace and Freedom. With this sort of popular backing, the Borah Resolution passed Congress easily in July 1921—ironically, as part of that year's Naval Appropriations Act.[43]

42. Ibid., 157–59; Cohen, *Empire*, 57–58.
43. Cohen, *Empire*, 46–49.

The great powers responded quickly. With characteristic vagueness, Harding had already endorsed arms reduction. Although Hughes was reluctant to appear to be following Congress's lead, he found the popular pressures irresistible and the need to address rising tensions in East Asia compelling. He thus issued an invitation for a conference to meet in Washington. Caught between popular pressures for disarmament and demands from his admirals to maintain Britain's traditional dominance of the seas, Prime Minister David Lloyd George found Hughes's proposal a convenient way out. He recognized, moreover, that the war-depleted British treasury could not match that of the United States in a long-term competition. The Foreign Office worried about the budding rivalry in East Asia. The Anglo-Japanese Alliance of 1902, long an irritant for the United States, was up for renewal. Lloyd George thus saw a chance to accommodate Washington and shed dangerous treaty obligations without alienating an important ally. The British therefore proposed a conference with a broader agenda to include all nations with interests in East Asia. The United States quickly assented.

The U.S. invitation to confer in Washington came as a "bolt from the sky" to Tokyo. Japanese leaders feared that the United States and Britain might be ganging up on them. Moderates seized the opportunity to promote cooperation with the West without sacrificing vital interests in Manchuria. Facing serious economic and political problems at home and dangerously overextended abroad, the government sought to contain its own military leaders and break out of the diplomatic isolation in which Japan found itself after World War I. Wasting no time, the wary but willing conferees agreed to meet in Washington in late 1921.[44]

Hughes handled the conference with consummate skill. He prepared with the utmost care, mastering the technicalities of complex weapons systems without getting bogged down in detail. He kept U.S. naval officers on board without letting them take control. Avoiding Wilson's mistakes, he made Massachusetts senator Henry Cabot Lodge part of the solution, thus preventing him from again becoming the problem. He developed a full-fledged plan for sizeable reductions in the tonnage of battleships, the ultimate weapon of the era, and kept his proposals secret until the conference opened. On November 11, 1921, Armistice Day, the delegates attended a moving ceremony at Arlington National Cemetery. The following day, in what journalist William Allen White called "the most intensely dramatic

44. Sadao Asada, "Between the Old Diplomacy and the New, 1918–1922: The Washington Conference and the Origins of Japanese Rapprochement," *Diplomatic History* 30 (April 2006), 214–15.

moment I have ever witnessed," Hughes unveiled his plan in what became known as his "bombshell speech" before a stunned audience at Washington's Constitution Hall. Addressing a packed house including prime ministers, admirals, the entire U.S. Congress, and some four hundred journalists from across the world, he insisted that competition in armaments "must stop!" He proceeded to call for the scrapping of sixty-six ships, including four British super-dreadnoughts authorized but not yet under construction and a Japanese battleship, the *Mutsu*, built in part with collections from schoolchildren. "Hughes sank in thirty-five minutes more ships than all of the admirals of the world have sunk in a cycle of centuries," an admiring journalist wrote. Caught completely off guard, a British admiral "turned several colors of the rainbow and behaved as if he were sitting on hot coals." The crowd rose to its feet in a "tornado of cheering."[45]

After nearly three months of arduous negotiations, the conferees in early 1922 reached a series of agreements dealing not only with arms limitation but also with some of the delicate political issues that had prompted the arms race. Hughes negotiated with Tokyo a separate agreement giving the United States cable rights on the Japanese island-mandate of Yap and an agreement with Britain and Japan ending their alliance. A Four-Power Treaty replaced the alliance and committed the parties to respect each other's possessions in the Pacific and consult in case of conflict among themselves or external threat from some other nation. Although later denounced as toothless and essentially meaningless, the agreement significantly eased tensions in the Pacific and facilitated major reductions in armaments.[46]

Following the broad outlines sketched by Hughes at the opening of the conference, a Five-Power Treaty dealt with capital ships. "For the first time in recorded history," historian Warren Cohen has written, "the Great Powers voluntarily surrendered their freedom to arm as they pleased."[47] The treaty established a ratio of 5:5:3 in battleship tonnage for the United States, Britain, and Japan; France and Italy accepted 1.67. It eliminated thirty U.S. ships built or under construction, twenty-two British, and fifteen Japanese. Britain accepted equality with the United States, no small concession. Japan grudgingly agreed to a position of inferiority, in part

---

45. The standard account is Thomas H. Buckley, *The United States and the Washington Conference, 1921–1922* (Knoxville, Tenn., 1970). A lively portrayal is Robert K. Massie, "The 1921 SALT Talks—And You Are There," *New York Times Magazine*, October 1, 1977), 38ff.
46. Cohen, *Empire*, 50–51.
47. Ibid., 52.

because it was permitted to keep the symbolically powerful *Mutsu* and also because of a vital clause in which the United States and Britain agreed to maintain the status quo in fortifications and bases in the Pacific and East Asia. In contrast to the United States and Britain, Japan only had to "defend" one ocean. Most important, its leadership recognized it could not win an arms race with the United States. Hughes negotiated effectively in part because Herbert Yardley, a talented U.S. cryptologist, broke Japan's diplomatic code and could reveal before each day's meeting the position its delegates would take and how far they could be pushed.[48]

A third agreement, the Nine-Power Treaty, attempted to stabilize great-power competition in China. The signatories refused to address the obnoxious unequal treaties, especially on tariff autonomy and extraterritoriality, another crushing blow to Chinese seeking to regain their nation's sovereignty. On Manchuria, Hughes reverted to Theodore Roosevelt's pragmatic approach and indeed used veteran diplomat and TR confidant Root to work behind the scenes with Japan. The Nine-Power Treaty thus resembled the Root-Takahira (1908) and Lansing-Ishii (1917) agreements, an ambiguous compromise implicitly recognizing Japan's special interests in Manchuria. Rather than pressing Japanese delegates on the still-sensitive issue of Shandong, Hughes encouraged private discussions with China, even holding the last meeting in his home. Japan voluntarily agreed to return the former German leasehold to China while retaining some railroad concessions, and did so later in the year. The Nine-Power Treaty itself was notably and unsurprisingly non-substantive, once again calling on the signatories not to interfere in China's internal affairs or to seek exclusive concessions and to respect China's sovereignty and territorial integrity. It sought to freeze the status quo rather than alleviate the inequities under which China suffered.[49]

The Washington agreements were much criticized after World War II. The United States alone adhered to the naval arms limitations, it was argued, leaving itself vulnerable to Japanese attack. The agreements lacked enforcement provisions and were therefore essentially worthless. Such arguments reflect ex post facto and ahistorical reasoning. The Senate would never have accepted the sort of enforcement clauses critics later insisted were necessary. As it was, a leery Senate microscopically examined the treaties for hidden commitments and approved the Four-Power Treaty by only four votes over the necessary two-thirds. To be sure, the

48. Walter LaFeber, *The Clash: U.S.-Japanese Relations Throughout History* (New York, 1997), 139–40; David Kahn letter to editor, *New York Times Book Review*, May 5, 2002.
49. Asada, "Old Diplomacy and the New," 223–28.

treaties were not without serious deficiencies. Russia and Germany were left out. The naval arms limitations did not go beyond capital ships, freeing nations to move in other directions. China would not forget yet another affront at the hands of the imperial powers. This said, the Washington treaties stabilized a dangerous arms race and dramatically eased great-power tensions. The United States gave up only ships and bases Congress would likely not have funded. By conceding Japan its long-sought due as a major power, they established a basis for cooperation in the Pacific and initiated a Japanese-American rapprochement. Most important, this first example of arms limitation eased the enormous burden of arms on people throughout the world, helping make possible recovery from a devastating war. In all, it was an enormously significant event, making clear the new role of the United States in the world.[50] The United States took the initiative in calling the conference and hosted it in Washington. Its secretary of state spearheaded the negotiations and achieved most of his nation's major objectives.

In European reconstruction, as in disarmament, the United States played a key role, although in this area it was not as eager or decisive in taking the lead. Republican leaders were not indifferent to Europe's post-war plight, as has often been charged. They recognized all too clearly the extent to which the war had shattered the European economic order; they were keenly aware of the importance of a stable, prosperous Europe to America's economic and political well-being. They also perceived that their nation's altered economic status required a more active role in resolving European problems, a harsh reality underscored by the recession of 1919–21. Some, like Hoover, even believed that the United States should employ its vast economic power and influence to save the world from "misery and disaster worse than the dark ages."[51] Here, however, formidable domestic political constraints blocked the way. As a consequence, Republican administrations relied on economic rather than political methods, and on unofficial and private emissaries to negotiate and implement solutions.

The problems were monumental. The war had wreaked massive physical and emotional destruction across the Continent, stoking the enmities that had provoked conflict in the first place. Angry at their defeat and the victor's peace imposed on them, Germans were not disposed to cooperate. Disappointed with Anglo-American refusals to provide firm security guarantees against a German resurgence, France sought to use economic pres-

50. Cohen, Empire, 54.
51. Costigliola, Awkward Dominion, 44.

sure to keep Germany at heel. Overshadowing everything else, and standing as insuperable obstacles to reconstruction, were the $33 billion in reparations Germany was required to pay the Allies and the $27 billion in war debts owed by the Allies, $10 billion to the United States. Viewing reparations as a means to keep Germany weak and under control, France demanded full payment. Germany adamantly retorted that the amount of reparations imposed on it far exceeded its ability to pay. The British linked the debts owed them with those they owed the United States, building a united European front on this issue. The Allies naturally claimed that since such debts had been incurred in a common cause—the United States had paid mainly in dollars, they in blood—they should be scaled back or canceled altogether. They linked war debts and reparations, insisting that they could not grant relief to Germany without relief themselves.[52]

It would take another devastating world war to demonstrate that economic generosity could be the height of political realism, and Americans in the 1920s could hardly be expected to see this. To be sure, some international businessmen and bankers and diplomats such as Alanson Houghton, former Corning Glass magnate and Harding's ambassador to Germany, perceived in terms of war debts and reparations that expediency would be the better part of wisdom. But most U.S. officials agreed with Harding that the dilemma for the United States was "how to assert a helpful influence abroad without sacrificing anything of importance to our people."[53] American leaders were intent on protecting the domestic market from a surge of postwar European imports. Congress enacted high tariffs in the early 1920s and maintained them throughout the decade, making it difficult for Europeans to sell in the United States. United States officials also refused to take any step that required higher taxes. Republican leaders generally sympathized with the need to adjust German reparations schedules and recognized that war debts posed a huge obstacle to European recovery. But they also perceived that the solutions put forth by the Europeans would require high taxes at home. They believed that the war debts gave them some leverage in pushing Europeans toward the sort of settlements they viewed as necessary for proper reconstruction. They publicly denied a link between reparations and war debts. Congress underscored the political delicacy of the war debts issue in 1922 by creating a World War Foreign Debts Commission and setting a standard of 4.25 percent interest to be paid over twenty-five years. Because

52. Cohen, *Empire*, 20–21, 90–91.
53. Melvyn P. Leffler, *The Elusive Quest: America's Pursuit of European Stability and French Security, 1919–1933* (Chapel Hill, N.C., 1979), 68.

of timid leadership, conflicts within the executive branch over what to do, and congressional constraints, the Harding administration refused to jump into the fray in 1921–22, closely guarding its freedom of action and permitting the situation in Europe to deteriorate dangerously.[54]

While Europe wallowed in torpor, conflict, and indecision, the United States gradually assumed leadership. Cooperating with private bankers on both sides of the Atlantic, British and U.S. officials worked out a debt settlement providing for payment over sixty-two years at a sliding scale of 3 to 3.5 percent interest. Some British leaders naturally complained, as Chancellor of the Exchequer Stanley Baldwin put it, that a tightfisted United States deserved a "replica of the golden calf." But most also conceded that such a settlement was essential for broader European recovery. Business and political leaders on both sides also recognized, as one American banker put it, that if the two countries could work together "the rest of the world would have a combination to whom they would have to pay attention." Congress acquiesced in a settlement more generous than it had mandated. The British passed on their savings to their debtors. The agreement set a precedent for further Anglo-American cooperation and facilitated subsequent settlement of the reparations problem.[55]

Hughes allowed the recalcitrant French and Germans to approach the brink of disaster before interceding. While rejecting U.S. efforts to reach a debt settlement, France continued to demand reparations from Germany. When Germany refused to pay, France and Belgium in January 1923 marched into the Ruhr, seized the coal mines, and extended the area of occupation. The Germans responded with passive resistance, putting huge strain on an already shaky French economy. The Ruhr occupation caused a deepening economic and political crisis in Germany—the mark fell to the lowest point ever reached by any currency to that time—raising the threat of a right-wing coup or, even worse in American eyes, a "Red Republic." The cost of the occupation drove the value of the franc down by more than 40 percent, making France amenable to U.S. pressure. Sovereignty was "dear to the hearts of the French people," banker Lamont shrewdly observed, "but the Franc was much dearer."[56]

With Europe on the verge of a major crisis, Hughes finally acted. The Ruhr occupation alarmed Americans as nothing to this point, even Senator Borah insisting that "bold and determined" action was required to avert "ut-

---

54. Hogan, *Informal Entente*, 51–52.
55. Costigliola, *Awkward Dominion*, 106–7; Hogan, *Informal Entente*, 51–53.
56. Hogan, *Informal Entente*, 69.

ter economic chaos."[57] Previously, Hughes had proposed that the reparations problem be turned over to a committee of experts to devise a workable and equitable solution. He now revived the proposal and applied intense pressure. With Hughes's backing, Lamont withheld a desperately needed loan until France agreed to liquidate the occupation and refer the issue to an independent commission. After nearly a year of crisis and with Europe on the verge of chaos, the two countries accepted Hughes's proposal.

The United States played a central role in resolving the tangle. The administration named Chicago banker Charles G. Dawes and Owen D. Young, a General Electric executive with close ties to the J. P. Morgan banking firm, to head its group of experts, closely monitored their work, and stepped in on occasion to mediate disputes. It was no easy task. A settlement had to be hard enough on Germany to satisfy Allied and particularly French concerns while soft enough to be acceptable to Berlin. The fast-talking and indefatigable Dawes—an "astounding human dynamo," one colleague called him—also had close connections to France from his wartime service in Paris and helped bring the French along.[58] Young devised a flexible and ingenious plan, ironically one that would bear Dawes's name, that became a means not only to solve the intractable reparations problem but also to promote German recovery. The plan scaled back the reparations figure and started with small payments that increased as the German economy improved. By requiring recipients to buy German products, it also helped kick-start German recovery. Germany was provided a loan of $200 million and required to undertake reforms U.S. businessmen considered essential. Responsibility for payment was assigned to an American, S. Parker Gilbert, who in the process gained substantial influence over German finances. Hoover exulted in the "disinterested statesmanship" carried out by private American citizens and labeled the Dawes Plan a "peace mission without parallel in international history."[59] Hughes strong-armed the Germans and still-recalcitrant French to go along. "Here is the American policy," he flatly informed French premier Raymond Poincaré. "If you turn this down, America is through."[60] The deal was settled at a conference in London in the summer of 1924. Despite the reservations of some bankers, the American portion of the loan was snapped up in minutes. "How magnificent!" Lamont crowed.[61]

57. Leffler, *Elusive Quest*, 42.
58. Ferrell, *Coolidge Presidency*, 147.
59. Hogan, *Informal Entente*, 77.
60. Costigliola, *Awkward Dominion*, 123.
61. Ibid., 124.

The United States also used its economic power to further the success of the October 1925 Locarno Conference, a political complement to the Dawes Plan. Recognizing that the reintegration of Germany into Europe through the reparations deal left France at a strategic and economic disadvantage, the United States sought to ease French security concerns. When negotiations for a European security pact stalled in the spring of 1925, Houghton, newly appointed U.S. ambassador to Great Britain, stepped in. Increasingly alarmed with the political instability in Germany and the Coolidge administration's timidity in addressing European issues, the ambassador, boldly acting on his own, issued during a May 1925 speech in London what came to be called the "peace ultimatum." If the Europeans did not move decisively, he warned, the United States might hold back further loans—American bankers were not interested in "speculative advances." Coolidge in time publicly backed his ambassador's position. Houghton played an important role in preliminary discussions leading to the conference. United States involvement thus abetted, if it did not determine, the agreements subsequently reached at Locarno. France, Belgium, and Germany consented to respect the boundaries drawn at Versailles, keep the Rhineland demilitarized, and refrain from attacking each other. Britain and Italy signed as guarantors. Germany also agreed to arbitrate with the new states of Eastern Europe its eastern boundaries. Locarno seemed to resolve major issues left over from Versailles and ease French security concerns at least a bit, providing some hope for European recovery and stability.[62]

The United States also secured war debt settlements with the Allies, but not without provoking ill will across the Atlantic. The ever cautious Coolidge administration walked a very fine line between its genuine concern for European recovery and fear of a taxpayer revolt. Continuing to skirt the terms set down by Congress in 1922, it established the principle of settling on the basis of a nation's capacity to pay and concluded a series of agreements more generous than that with the British. Seeking to woo Italian American voters and lure Italy from a united front with France, the administration negotiated with Benito Mussolini's government an especially generous settlement, a low interest rate canceling more than 75 percent of the debt.

France was a different matter altogether. Several members of the French parliament at one point proposed that the United States be given French Indochina in exchange for the debts, an ironic suggestion in terms of later history but a nonstarter on both sides. The French insisted more

62. Matthews, *Houghton*, 120–28.

adamantly than other Allies that their enormous sacrifices of blood and treasure entitled them to full cancellation. Economic and political chaos in France made it difficult even to initiate negotiations. A U.S. embargo on loans ultimately had the intended effect of forcing France to the bargaining table. French negotiators agreed to a settlement that would have canceled 52.8 percent of the debt. But French war veterans marched in protest, and angry citizens attacked American tourists—after they had completed their purchases, humorist Will Rogers sarcastically observed. Determined to stabilize the French economy without outside help and "to free ourselves of the yoke of Anglo-Saxon finance," Poincaré's government refused an American loan and began quietly paying off the debts without ratifying the agreement. More than any other issue, war debts poisoned U.S. postwar relations with the Allies. Proud Europeans deeply resented their new and humiliating dependence on the United States; even some Italians complained that the United States was trying to "enslave a whole continent." Viewing the debt settlements as generous, Americans took umbrage at French labeling of Uncle Sam as "Uncle Shylock."[63]

Despite these recriminations, the Republicans appeared to have accomplished much by 1926. The United States for the first time took the lead in addressing Europe's problems. It used its considerable economic leverage to settle the reparations issue, arrange debt agreements, and push the Europeans to stabilize their currencies on the basis of the gold standard. The policies seemed to have immediate, positive results. Near rock bottom just months before, the French and German economies rebounded. European production exceeded prewar levels. Exports increased sharply. As recovery continued, Americans reasoned, it would be easier to liquidate the debts. The reintegration of Germany into the European economy and the return of prosperity would provide a solid basis for prosperity, stability, and peace. All this had been accomplished, the Republicans could congratulate themselves, without political commitments or sacrifices on the part of the U.S. taxpayer.

Such assessments turned out to be premature, of course. Republican successes contained fundamental flaws.[64] Americans exaggerated their own role in European recovery and underestimated the additional sacrifices they had imposed on already burdened Europeans. They failed to see the limitations of their policies and the need for continued adjustments or to appreciate the full extent of the war's impact on Europe or the real depth of resentments it stirred. They did not see that the Dawes Plan

63. Costigliola, *Awkward Dominion*, 131–38; Leffler, *Elusive Quest*, 138–54.
64. Costigliola, *Awkward Dominion*, 216–17.

had advantaged Germany at France's expense and that Locarno was at best an imperfect palliative. The economic arrangements relied too heavily on U.S. loans, whose continued availability in turn depended on an unreliable source. It seems obvious in retrospect that a truly successful American policy would have required lower tariffs, cancellation of war debts, and a more restrictive policy on loans. This was by no means obvious at the time, however, and if it had been it would still have been politically very difficult to obtain.

The United States played a much less significant role in addressing the vast problems of postwar reconstruction and nation-building in Eastern and Central Europe. Wilson had helped create the newly independent states there, of course, and his rhetoric and the vital wartime assistance provided by the American Relief Administration raised expectations on both sides that could not be met. Americans hoped that the new states would follow a democratic model and become outlets for their investment capital and markets for their products. Eastern Europeans looked upon the United States mainly as "the nation with money" and hoped for protection and assistance without interference.[65] In reality, U.S. relations with Eastern Europe turned out to be a peripheral concern to each.[66] The United States saw even less reason to get politically involved there than in Western Europe. It scrupulously avoided the numerous, complex, and volatile issues that divided peoples and governments against each other. Trade and investment developed to only modest proportions. Czechoslovakia's relatively democratic government and stable economy made it a good risk, and it attracted $85 million in U.S. investments, second only to Germany in the region. Ford, General Motors, IBM, and National Cash Register found major markets for their products.[67] In contrast, the peoples who made up Yugoslavia were wary of foreign economic penetration, long a source of oppression, and their numerous, arcane rules governing trade—"the granite wall of stupid Serb unreason," one U.S. minister contemptuously labeled them—and their chaotic political and economic situation discouraged investors. The United States did negotiate with Yugoslavia a war debts settlement second only to its arrangement with Italy in terms of generosity. United States banks provided modest loans. Socony built an oil refinery in Croatia, Alcoa opened mines, and American Telephone and Telegraph

65. Neal Pease, *Poland, the United States, and the Stabilization of Europe, 1919–1933* (New York, 1986), 22.

66. Linda R. Killen, *Testing the Peripheries: U.S.-Yugoslav Economic Relations in the Interwar Years* (New York, 1994), vii.

67. Cary W. Blankenship, "Nationalization of Industry in Czechoslovakia in 1945" (Ph.D. dissertation, University of Kentucky, 2002), 95–98.

and International Telephone and Telegraph developed communications networks. But the most that can be concluded is that the United States played a role in the Yugoslavian economy.[68]

Poland was a special case and demonstrates quite clearly the limitations of U.S. policies in the 1920s. A large and vocal bloc of Polish American voters and Poland's extremely important and vulnerable geographical position between the jaws of what State Department official William Castle called the "nutcracker" of Russia and Germany made it an issue Americans could not ignore. Yet even as a problem, Poland was not taken that seriously. "Warsaw is so damned far away," the journalist Walter Lippmann observed.[69] Poland's hopes for U.S. security guarantees against its larger neighbors and for generous U.S. loans were not realized. The Harding and Coolidge administrations carefully avoided entanglement in its ongoing and potentially explosive border dispute with Germany. They hoped through expanded loans, investment, and trade to encourage in Poland a stability that in turn would help stabilize Eastern Europe. Yet while keeping a close eye on events, they relied on the private sector to develop and implement programs. With the "covert backing" of the Coolidge administration, Edwin Kemmerer, who had served as a "money doctor" for Central American nations, drew up an economic reform plan for Poland including the gold standard, a balanced budget, and stabilization loans. Subsequently, U.S. bankers granted Poland a credit of $20 million and a loan of $72 million. The Chicago banker Charles Dewey went to Warsaw as financial adviser. The results were meager. Dewey's performance made palpably clear the shortcomings of unofficial "experts." He knew little of Poland and less of international finance. Employing, in his own words, the booster "methods of the President of the Kiwanis Club," he waxed enthusiastic about Poland and developed a series of grandiose and totally unrealizable schemes for economic development, provoking his colleagues to dismiss him as "Pan Deweski." Poles, like other Eastern Europeans, looked suspiciously on foreign capital; Americans hesitated to invest in a nation seemingly so backward and vulnerable. In any event, the loans that were supposed to represent a beginning marked the end as U.S. capital shifted after 1927 to domestic markets and then dried up during the depression.[70]

68. Killen, *Testing the Peripheries*, 104, 117.

69. Pease, *Poland*, 167.

70. Neal R. Pease, "Charles Dewey as the First United States Financial Adviser to Poland, 1927–1930," *International History Review* 9 (February 1987), 85; Frank Costigliola, "American Foreign Policy and the 'Nut Cracker': The United States and Poland in the 1920s," *Pacific Historical Review* 48 (February 1979), 85–105; Rosenberg, *Financial Missionaries*, 176–84.

In dealing with Bolshevik Russia, the Republicans initiated a debate that would be repeated many times over in the twentieth century with mixed and inconclusive results: Is it better to try to change an obnoxious government by isolating it politically or "engaging" it economically? With Russia in the 1920s, the United States tried both. Drawing on precedents set with Huerta's Mexico, Wilson in 1917 had refused to recognize the revolutionary government. When Lenin took Russia out of the war in 1918, a policy of expediency hardened into dogma. The Bolshevik government had taken power by force, U.S. officials insisted, and did not represent the Russian people. It had refused to carry out its international obligations, especially the repayment of debts incurred by predecessor regimes. It was committed to overthrowing other governments. Americans hoped that non-recognition and the Allied military interventions would topple the hated Bolshevik government or cause it to collapse under its own weight.[71]

The regime did not collapse, of course—if anything, the Allied interventions helped solidify its hold on power—but the Republicans did not deviate from the position Wilson had staked out. Because it emphatically rejected their most fundamental tenets such as religion and private property, Communism was anathema to many Americans—"the most hideous and monstrous thing that the human mind has ever conceived," Robert Lansing averred, a "murderous tyranny," according to Hoover.[72] Antipathy to Communism remained a potent force throughout the 1920s. It was regularly fed by such bedrock institutions as the Roman Catholic Church, labor unions, and patriotic organizations such as the Daughters of the American Revolution. Russia's clumsy and generally ineffectual efforts to subvert other governments through the Communist International, or Comintern, reinforced American fears. A State Department already fervently anti-Communist closely monitored Comintern activities through its listening post in Riga, Latvia. The Comintern succeeded only in remote and insignificant Outer Mongolia, but its subversive activities in Europe and especially Latin America aroused exaggerated U.S. fears and provided a continued reason for non-recognition. Even in 1931, when the United States was the only major power still withholding recognition and the Japanese takeover of Manchuria suddenly brought a convergence of Soviet and American interests, the Hoover administration refused to reconsider the policy.[73]

71. John Lewis Gaddis, *Russia, The Soviet Union, and the United States: An Interpretive History* (2nd ed., New York, 1990), 93–95.
72. Ibid., 105; Douglas Little, "Antibolshevism and American Foreign Policy: The Diplomacy of Self-Delusion," *American Quarterly* 35 (Fall 1983), 379–81.
73. Gaddis, *Russia*, 94–97, 105–16; Little, "Self-Delusion," 376–90.

While seeking to isolate Russia through non-recognition, the United States also engaged it economically. Lenin and his successor, Joseph Stalin, recognized their desperate need for Western capital and technology and assumed that the United States, to meet its pressing needs for foreign markets, would provide it. Americans hoped that exposing the Russian people and perhaps even some of its leaders to the wonders of capitalism would persuade them to reject Communism. The result, ironically, was to assist in the preservation of the despised Soviet state.

Americans responded with characteristic generosity to a devastating Russian famine in 1921–22. The Communist regime hesitated to ask for outside assistance, but the need was desperate, and it hoped that famine relief might somehow lead to recognition and trade. Working through the American Relief Administration (ARA), a private agency with close ties to Washington, Hoover with typical energy organized a massive emergency relief program. In the war years, food had been openly used as a political weapon; Hoover this time explicitly disavowed political activities. Nevertheless, with the Soviet regime seemingly on the ropes, he hoped that this most vivid display of the contrast between the bounty of capitalism and the deprivation of Communism would cause Russians to reject a system imposed on them. For most of the nearly four hundred ARA workers in what they called Bololand (for Bolshevik), the only goal was to feed the hungry, especially the children. Encountering horrific conditions of hunger, disease, and death, even stories of cannibalism, they employed eighteen thousand Russians and established seventeen thousand relief stations from the Ukraine to Siberia. During its two years in operation, ARA, working with other non-governmental organizations such as the American Red Cross, provided more than half a million tons of food, clothing, and medicine at a cost of some $50 million in U.S. funds and an additional $11 million provided through Soviet shipments of gold to the United States. The ARA may have saved as many as ten million people from starvation. It earned the gratitude of many Russians, and shouts of "Arah" were often heard as its trucks went by. Disappointed that the relief effort did not lead to recognition, the Soviet government in time attacked ARA for dumping surplus food and for espionage and counterrevolutionary activities. In fact, as the government must have recognized but could not admit, America's efforts to undermine its authority through goodwill helped it survive a most critical period in its history.[74]

74. Costigliola, *Awkward Dominion*, 87–93; Benjamin D. Rhodes, "American Relief Operations at Nikolaiev, USSR, 1922–1923," *Historian* 51 (August 1989), 611–26; Bertrand M. Patenaude, *The Big Show in Bololand: The American Relief Expedition to Soviet Russia in the Famine of 1921* (Stanford, Calif., 2002).

Despite the absence of formal trade ties, American businesses, some-times with Washington's blessings, also cut numerous deals that helped promote economic development in Stalin's Russia. Lenin and Stalin rec-ognized their desperate need for U.S. capital, technology, and equipment and sought to limit the control of foreign capitalists by granting short-term concessions. For the Republican administrations, such contacts presented a dilemma. They did not want to help a hated regime. On the other hand, they were deeply committed to the expansion of American trade and in-vestments and reluctant to interfere with the operations of private busi-ness. Like GE's Young, they could also rationalize that U.S. aid might give the Communists "the very gun with which they will shoot themselves."[75]

In fact, because of Soviet restrictions and controls, especially limits on profits, American capitalists generally fared poorly in Russia. International Harvester lost over $41 million during the period of its concession. W. Averell Harriman, son of the railroad magnate and a future ambassador to the Soviet Union, ran an unprofitable manganese operation in the Cauca-sus. A major exception was the legendary Armand Hammer. In the richest of ironies, Lenin himself converted the eccentric physician and son of a Russian immigrant into an "entrepreneur who milked capital for his future businesses from the communist state." Hammer ran concessions in asbestos production and pencil manufacturing. The Soviets permitted him to take away his profits by buying and taking home priceless Russian works of art.[76]

Stalin relied heavily on American technical expertise in his First Five-Year Plan, adopted in 1928. More than two thousand U.S. engineers helped build automobile and tractor plants, construct steel mills, and de-velop mining operations. General Electric constructed a massive dam on the Dnieper. Arch-capitalist Henry Ford provided a foundation for the Russian automobile industry by building a huge automobile plant in Novgorod and selling the Russians two thousand vehicles. Despite vari-ous impediments, trade expanded significantly. The United States pro-vided about 25 percent of total Soviet imports, including such important items as cotton, tractors, and industrial and agricultural equipment. Overall, the import of American expertise, investment capital, and equip-ment helped to stabilize economic and thereby political conditions in the Soviet Union during a critical period.[77]

75. Costigliola, *Awkward Dominion*, 150.
76. James K. Libbey, *Russian-American Economic Relations, 1763–1999* (Gulf Breeze, Fla., 1999), 83–84.
77. Ibid., 73–99; Costigliola, *Awkward Dominion*, 157–162; Katherine A. S. Siegel, "Tech-nology and Trade: Russia's Pursuit of American Investment, 1917–1929," *Diplomatic History* 17 (Summer 1993), 378, 388.

In East Asia, the Republicans pursued similar goals with much the same methods and fewer results. Hughes hoped to create through the Washington treaties a firm basis for stability in the region. The agreements on naval armaments and the Pacific islands had eased Japanese-American tensions, and the reaffirmation of the Open Door principles appeared to establish great-power agreement in respect of Chinese sovereignty. "We are seeking to establish a *Pax Americana* maintained not by arms but by mutual respect and good will and the tranquilizing process of reason," the secretary proclaimed in 1923.[78] Typical of the era, dollars were to abet "the tranquilizing process of reason." American officials hoped that trade and loans would promote peace in an often turbulent area.

Timely and generous U.S. aid for the victims of a horrible 1923 earthquake in Japan helped build on the spirit of Japanese-American cooperation evinced at the Washington Conference. The disaster killed as many as two hundred thousand Japanese, left as many as two million homeless, and threatened countless others with starvation and disease. Americans provided $11.6 million in relief, and the Asiatic Fleet and the U.S. Army in the Philippines helped deliver and distribute emergency aid. Americans naturally hoped that their generosity would improve relations with Japan, often strained in the twentieth century. While some Tokyo officials sought to obscure the extent and importance of foreign aid, many Japanese responded in kind. The Americans have behaved "like the Americans of old," a Tokyo newspaper gratefully exclaimed. "They have been efficient, sentimental and generous in giving and forgetful of everything else in their zeal to help helpless sufferers."[79]

Gratitude is fleeting in international relations as in ordinary life, of course, and the goodwill earned by earthquake relief was more than destroyed by new and restrictive congressional immigration legislation the following year. The product of decades of agitation among old-stock Americans against the flood of "new" immigrants from Eastern and Southern Europe, West Coast hostility toward Orientals, and the especially virulent racism of the 1920s, the legislation created quotas sharply limiting the number of European immigrants. It took specific aim at the Japanese. Partly as the result of a well-intended but extremely unfortunate diplomatic gaffe, an amendment excluded Japanese immigrants altogether. Recognizing the seriousness of the exclusion proposal, U.S. officials encouraged the Japanese to protest. Tokyo dutifully warned of "grave consequences" should the amendment pass. Ironically, leaders of the

78. LaFeber, *Clash*, 144.
79. Merle Curti, *American Philanthropy Abroad* (New Brunswick, N.J., 1996), 345–46.

exclusionist bloc in Congress used the alleged Japanese "threat" to secure overwhelming support for their amendment. Hughes properly lamented that in a few minutes Congress had "spoiled the work of years and done a lasting injury." The legislation unilaterally abrogated Roosevelt's Gentleman's Agreement of 1907. It provoked an outburst of anti-Americanism in Japan. Protestors organized boycotts and tore down the flag at the U.S. embassy. One militant committed suicide. The misguided legislation shook Japan's policy of cooperation with the West to its foundation, giving ammunition to those who preferred a unilateral approach and encouraging a shift toward expansion on the East Asian mainland.[80]

Private economic diplomacy, a major instrument of Republican policy, also failed to promote U.S. goals in East Asia. In most cases, the bankers who were supposed to be the agents of Hughes's policy behaved like bankers rather than the diplomats Washington wanted them to be. The State Department hoped to use loans to promote economic development in China, thereby helping to protect its sovereignty as well as expand U.S. trade. But the major banking houses already had millions of dollars of unpaid Chinese loans on their books. Troubled by China's weakness and internal divisions, they naturally hesitated to put more money at risk. In contrast, State Department efforts to limit loans that Japan might use to expand its influence in Manchuria, Mongolia, and North China generally failed. On one occasion, when the Japanese protested, the State Department withdrew its objections. Bankers like Lamont found Japanese-controlled areas more stable, therefore a better risk, and devised means to "launder" funds to get around State Department objections. American loans played a significant role in Japan's quiet expansion on the Asian mainland in the 1920s.[81]

The major challenge to Hughes' design for peace and order in East Asia was Chinese nationalism. After the fall of Yüan Shih-k'ai's government in 1916, China descended into chaos and civil war. A nominal government at Peking controlled little of the country; local warlords prevailed, fighting among themselves, in most regions. The one thing the various factions agreed upon was hatred of the foreigner. In the mid-1920s, Sun Yat-sen's Kuomintang Party sought to establish itself as the leader of China. It gained vital support from the Soviet Union, which sacrificed some of its concessions under the unequal treaties and provided military and political assistance. Using nationalism to rally the people to its banner, the Kuom-

80. LaFeber, *Clash*, 144–46; William L. Neumann, *America Encounters Japan: From Perry to MacArthur* (New York, 1965), 176–79.
81. Cohen, *Empire*, 31–32, 38.

intang set off a period of nationalist agitation. A May 1925 incident in Shanghai led to an explosion of anti-imperialism across the country with attacks on foreign interests and demands for the removal of foreign military forces and ending the unequal treaties. A year later, when the Kuomintang under its new leader Chiang Kai-shek mounted its Northern Expedition and occupied Nanking, there were further attacks on foreigners and foreign property. Six foreigners were killed, including one American. A youthful Pearl Buck, later to be the interpreter of China to millions of Americans, escaped by hiding in a hut. "You Americans have drunk our blood for years and become rich," one protestor screamed.[82] British and U.S. gunboats eventually quelled the violence, but there was talk of war.

The United States at first responded hesitantly to these events. China was far away and by no means an area of major concern. Events there were impossibly confusing. The Coolidge administration initially followed the advice of diplomats who argued that concessions would only produce more demands and insisted that "order" must be restored before negotiations could begin. Americans were slow to comprehend the dynamic force of Chinese nationalism and the legitimacy of its demands. They feared Communist influence in the Kuomintang. They took a firmer position in response to the outburst at Nanking, joining the British and Japanese in demanding apologies, reparations, and punishment for the perpetrators.[83]

United States policy gradually shifted toward accommodation. In 1927, Chiang turned on his Communist allies, eliminating those who did not flee, moved on Beijing, and in a classic maneuver to play the barbarians against each other openly sought U.S. support. American officials had little faith in Chiang, whom they considered at best a warlord, at worst a militarist and potential dictator. They had no illusions that his group actually controlled the country. They were confounded by the turmoil. On the other hand, Kellogg began to develop a vague sense of the strength of Chinese nationalism and to conclude that the unequal treaties were outdated. Gunboat diplomacy was out of fashion in the 1920s; there was little inclination to uphold the treaties by force. "It is impossible to make war on four hundred million people," Kellogg wisely observed, "and in my judgment you cannot longer parcel out China in concessions or by spheres of commercial influence by armed force." Hoping to win over the Chinese, the United States was the first power to extend tariff autonomy

82. Akira Iriye, *Across the Pacific: An Inner History of American-East Asian Relations* (New York, 1967), 154–55.
83. Cohen, *Empire*, 81–82.

to China, hedging its bets by doing so on a most-favored-nation basis, which delayed actual implementation until 1933.[84] With the confusion and violence, no one considered terminating extraterritoriality. Under Kellogg, the United States broke with the powers, becoming the first nation to abandon even part of the unequal treaties.

IV

The Republicans significantly altered the means, if not the ends, of U.S. Latin American policies in the 1920s, shifting away from the gunboat diplomacy and military interventionism that had marked the previous twenty years. The elimination of any immediate foreign threat to the hemisphere as a result of World War I eased concerns about the security of the region. The excesses of Wilsonian interventionism had produced a backlash at home, raising demands for the liquidation of military occupations and abstention from future interventions. Muckraking journalists produced damning exposes of the torture and murder carried out by occupation forces in Haiti and the Dominican Republic. Throughout the 1920s, moreover, the so-called Peace Progressives in Congress, led by the indomitable Borah, insisted that the United States practice what it preached in terms of self-determination. The tone was set in the campaign of 1920. Making a case for entry into the League, Democratic vice presidential candidate Franklin D. Roosevelt confidently reassured the electorate that the United States could depend on the votes of the Central American republics. He then planted foot firmly in mouth by gratuitously boasting that he personally had written the constitution of Haiti. Harding seized the opening. Seeking to discredit his opponents and win African American votes, he condemned the "rape" of the Dominican Republic and Haiti and promised that his administration would not "cover with a veil of secrecy repeated acts of unwarranted interference in domestic affairs of the little republics of the Western Hemisphere."[85]

As in other areas, business interests had precedence in Latin America in the 1920s, providing another incentive for the velvet glove. Europe's economic exhaustion left the hemisphere open for U.S. economic expansion. In the aftermath of war, capital poured into Latin America in unprecedented quantities, and trade soared. Americans sought oil in Venezuela and Colombia to meet the needs of the automobile society, exploited critical raw materials, and took over utilities and banking.

---

84. Ferrell, *Coolidge Presidency*, 164.
85. Lars Schoultz, *Beneath the United States: A History of U.S. Policy Toward Latin America* (Cambridge, Mass., 1998), 255.

Gunboat diplomacy had given the United States a bad name in the hemisphere. It seemed important for the sake of business to repent for past sins and refrain from new ones.

At the same time, the Republicans could not go too far. Protection of property and investments more than ever required stable societies and responsible governments that would respect foreign business interests. Defense of the canal still demanded order in a notably volatile region. U.S officials—especially the "experts" in the State Department's Latin American division—still looked upon their southern neighbors as childlike and backward, hopelessly prone to violence, and inherently incapable of self-government. The Russian and Mexican revolutions aroused an exaggerated fear of Bolshevik influence in the hemisphere. Thus while scrapping direct military intervention, the Republicans sought new means of control to balance the need for a lighter touch with the continued requirement of order and protection of property rights.

A familiar device was to work through private financial agents, using loans to force reforms that would stabilize Latin economies and politics and in turn promote U.S. trade and investment. The first such arrangement, worked out by the peripatetic Kemmerer with Bolivia, provided for the direct involvement of the State Department and U.S. bankers and provoked protest at home and in Latin America. The Republicans then shifted to a less intrusive and blatantly exploitative model where Latin American countries would voluntarily seek help from private financial advisers. As applied first in Colombia and later in Chile, Bolivia, and Ecuador, the new arrangement called for bankers to lend money to Latin American governments that sought the help of a "private" financial adviser. Kemmerer would then draw up plans for financial and currency reform. Members of a nominally private mission would remain to supervise the program after he had gone on to the next stop. Thus was created the new profession of international financial advisers, a quasi-colonial substitute for traditional relationships. "Kemmerized" countries appeared to do well in the 1920s. They drew sizeable U.S. investments, and the State Department's hand was much less visible. On the other hand, these arrangements promoted dependency on U.S. foreign trade and capital and led to overborrowing, with disastrous long-term economic results, provoking a nationalist backlash in the very different milieu of the 1930s.[86]

86. Emily S. and Norman L. Rosenberg, "From Colonialism to Professionalism: The Public-Private Dynamic in United States Financial Advising, 1898–1929," *Journal of American History* 74 (June 1987), 71–82.

The United States also sought to win friends by conciliating the anger and wounded pride of its southern neighbors. Americans were eager to move into Colombian oil fields. With the old Rough Rider now snugly in the grave, the Republicans could do what they had kept Wilson from doing. Leaving out the apology that had helped defeat Wilson's 1913 treaty with Colombia, they approved a new pact providing "heart balm" of $25 million for the theft of Panama. Hughes went out of his way to show respect for his Latin counterparts. He sought to resurrect the spirit of Pan-Americanism first enunciated by Henry Clay and promoted by James G. Blaine, speaking eloquently of a "common sentiment that makes us neighbors in spirit." With varying degrees of success, he tried to assist in the resolution of border disputes that for years had plagued relations among the South American nations themselves. Although not a glad-hander by nature, he met with Latin American diplomats in his office, dined with them, and sought to make them feel like representatives of important nations.[87]

He also initiated a change in the interpretation of the Monroe Doctrine of considerable long-range significance. Without entirely disavowing the right of U.S. intervention, he set out in the doctrine's centennial year to separate the two. In a Rio de Janeiro speech celebrating one hundred years of Brazilian independence, he declared that we "assert no rights for ourselves that we do not accord to others." In several 1923 speeches, he limited intervention to the region near the canal and vowed it would be used only as a "last resort." "I utterly disclaim as unwarranted . . . ," he affirmed, "a claim on our part to supervise the affairs of our sister republics, to assert an overlordship, to consider the spread of our authority beyond our own domain as the aim of our policy, and to make our power the test of right in this hemisphere."[88]

As a major part of their new approach, Harding and Hughes began to liquidate the Central American protectorates created by Roosevelt, Taft, and Wilson. Certain that blacks were not capable of self-government and that a premature withdrawal would lead to barbarism, even cannibalism, the administration stopped short of pulling out of Haiti. Ignoring Borah's protests that the Haitians "may not be capable of self-government as we understand it, but it is their government," they contented themselves with reorganizing the occupation government and seeking to make it more responsible. They did, however, terminate military occupation of the Dominican Republic. The process had actually begun under Wilson but had run afoul of conflicts over the terms of

87. Trani and Wilson, Harding Presidency, 136–37.
88. Ibid.

withdrawal. Hughes unilaterally broke the deadlock. Troops were withdrawn in 1924. The United States maintained substantial leverage through its continued control of the customs house. Americans congratulated themselves on the improvements brought to the Dominican polity; normality returned soon after the marines left. The occupation had little positive impact.[89]

In the Dominican Republic, the United States stumbled onto a device that helped solve the problem of how to maintain stability without direct intervention. In the last stages of the occupation, U.S. officials created a domestic constabulary, the Guardia Nacional, to promote internal order. The aim was to establish an apolitical force that would provide security while the electoral process worked. In this way, Americans applied their own values and institutions to a very different political culture with quite different results. The Guardia Nacional quickly became politicized and in time assumed dominant power. One of its early leaders, the notorious Rafael Trujillo, used his position with the organization to assume absolute political control. For the next thirty years, he ran the country in the most brutal and authoritarian fashion while carefully respecting U.S. interests. "He may be a sonofabitch," Franklin Roosevelt is supposed to have remarked, "but at least he's our sonofabitch." The Dominican model enabled the United States to reconcile its conflicting interests in the Caribbean and Central America.[90]

The Republicans found extrication from Nicaragua much more difficult. They brought the marines home in August 1925, but Nicaragua immediately erupted in civil war. The Coolidge administration faced a dilemma. It did not want to reimpose a military government, but neither could it permit a nation so close to the canal to descend into anarchy. Coolidge and Kellogg saw Nicaragua as a "test case" for U.S. control in a vital region. State Department officials warned that by dabbling in Nicaragua, Mexico, acting at the instance of the Soviet Union, was seeking to "drive a 'hostile wedge' between the United States and the Panama Canal." In August 1926, the administration sent the marines back into Nicaragua. In April 1927, Coolidge dispatched New Yorker Henry Stimson to Nicaragua with instructions to "clean up that mess."[91]

89. Schoultz, *Beneath the United States*, 257–58; Trani and Wilson, *Harding Presidency*, 135.
90. Bruce J. Calder, *The Impact of Intervention: The Dominican Republic During the U.S. Occupation of 1916–1924* (Austin, Tex., 1984), 239; Schoultz, *Beneath the United States*, 257–60.
91. Schmitz, *Stimson*, 51; Ferrell, *Coolidge Presidency*, 135.

Stimson cleaned up only part of it. Viewing free elections as the solution to Nicaragua's political woes, he persuaded the combatants to lay down their arms and agree to U.S.-supervised elections. Under the able direction of Brig. Gen. Frank McCoy, the elections held in 1928 and 1930 were widely viewed as fair, but they did not bring peace to Nicaragua. The self-appointed "general" César Augusto Sandino rebelled against the U.S.-imposed settlement, fled to the rugged mountains of northwest Nicaragua, and for five years waged a brutal and effective guerrilla war against the marines, making himself a hero to anti-American Nicaraguans, other Latin Americans, and anti-imperialists in the United States. The marines pursued the guerrillas relentlessly and bombed villages suspected of harboring them, but they could not capture the elusive Sandino.[92]

Ultimately, a Dominican-type solution emerged in Nicaragua. Reintervention and the costly, nasty, and unsuccessful war against Sandino provoked widespread and noisy agitation in Congress and among activist citizens' groups to get out of Nicaragua once and for all, and the Peace Progressives managed to secure a cutoff of funds for further operations. Having trained a Guardia Nacional to maintain order, the marines left in early 1933 with Sandino still at large. Guardia leader Anastasio Somoza, who spoke fluent English and impressed Stimson as "very frank, friendly [and] likable," lured Sandino to Managua and arranged to have him gunned down on an airstrip. Within a short time and despite rules designed to prevent a military takeover, Somoza assumed control of the presidency and then the country, establishing a brutal dictatorship through which he and his family would rule with an iron hand and U.S. complicity until 1979.[93]

The Coolidge administration's peaceful resolution of a mid-1920s dispute with Mexico also demonstrated how the United States in a very different way could employ new methods to achieve old aims. Under President Venustiano Carranza and his successors, Álvaro Obregón and Plutarco Calles, the Mexican Revolution turned sharply to the left after 1917. The decidedly nationalist constitution of that year sought to regain for Mexico the land and natural resources generously dispensed to foreigners by Porfirio Díaz. Article 27 in particular specified that land and rights to subsoil deposits belonged to the Mexican people, threatening the vast holdings of Americans who owned more than 40 percent of Mexico's land and

92. Lester D. Langley, *The Banana Wars: An Inner History of American Empire, 1900-1934* (Lexington, Ky., 1983), 212–16.
93. Schmitz, *Stimson*, 57–60.

60 percent of its oil. The constitution also included a progressive statement on labor policy that alarmed American businessmen.[94]

These measures provoked a conflict that would fester for more than a decade and once more spark talk of war. Oilmen naturally feared the threat to their interests and insisted that concessions to Mexico might provoke attacks on U.S. property throughout the hemisphere. Harding and Hughes at first backed the oilmen, withholding recognition from Obregón, who took power in May 1920 after the assassination of Carranza. An empty sleeve gave graphic demonstration to Obregón's revolutionary credentials, but he also desperately needed U.S. recognition, money, and arms to stabilize his regime. He thus offered private assurances not to rigorously enforce Article 27, but Washington held out for a formal treaty. Eager to end the dispute so that Mexico could repay its substantial debts and contract new loans, banker Lamont in 1923 helped broker a deal, the so-called Bucarelli Agreement, excluding from the provisions of Article 27 those lands on which some "positive acts" had been taken toward development. Overriding Hughes on one of only several occasions, Harding insisted on acceptance, clearing the way for recognition and a loan. The United States displayed its gratitude by providing arms to Obregón and lending him aircraft and pilots to bomb rebel troops.[95]

Conflict erupted again in 1925 after Calles, a former teacher, shopkeeper, and bartender, known as "the Turk," replaced Obregon. The colorful Calles's base was in the trade unions, and he too sought to walk a high and thin tightrope between his more radical supporters and the United States. Calles promoted a new law limiting to fifty years possession of oil lands owned by foreigners prior to 1917. To display his nationalist credentials and distract attention from Mexico's economic problems, he also launched an attack on the powerful Catholic Church, causing a strike by Mexican clerics and a brutal civil war with the so-called Cristeros that would last three years, take seventy thousand lives, and inflict huge economic costs on Mexico.[96]

Calles's initiatives provoked a resumption of conflict with the United States. Oilmen once again screamed in outrage. Catholic organizations such as the Knights of Columbus protested the attack on the church. Ambassador James Sheffield, a worthy successor to the numerous other ugly Americans sent to Mexico, vigorously backed the oil companies. He

94. Cohen, Empire, 64.
95. Karl M. Schmitt, Mexico and the United States, 1821–1973 (New York, 1974), 163–65.
96. Ibid.

privately denounced Calles as a "murderer and assassin." He described Mexicans as greedy and ignorant because of their Indian blood. "Calomel [a nasty-tasting purgative] is more effective than pink lemonade when you have ills to cure," he advised the State Department. Sharing Sheffield's alarm at the specter of a "Bolshevik Mexico," Kellogg issued an ill-considered statement that Mexico was on trial before all the world. The situation was worsened by U.S. fears that Mexico was stirring up perennially embattled Nicaragua, thus challenging its control of the region. Preparing the way for possible military intervention, Kellogg ominously warned the Senate Foreign Relations Committee that Russian agents were active in Mexico. Calles meanwhile threatened to "light up the sky all the way to New Orleans" by setting fire to Mexico's oil wells.[97]

Once again, cooler heads prevailed, this time fortunately *before* the United States dispatched troops across the border. The talk of war was probably more ritualistic than earnest. In fact, neither side wanted conflict. The oilmen's influence was seriously compromised because of their involvement in the Teapot Dome scandal that had rocked the Harding administration. Bankers like Lamont and peace groups urged Coolidge to negotiate. The Senate dismissed Kellogg's ranting about Bolshevism as nonsense and called for arbitration.

Coolidge thus opted for negotiation. In September 1927, he and Calles opened the first long-distance connection between Washington and Mexico City, conducting a telephone "summit" that immediately eased tensions. Coolidge made an especially inspired choice by replacing Sheffield with his old college roommate, now a J. P. Morgan Company partner, Dwight Morrow. Morrow turned out to be a true rarity in the long and troubled history of Mexican-American relations, setting out above all to like the people he was assigned to deal with. According to French foreign minister Aristide Briand, Morrow was as "shrewd as a pocketful of mice." Eschewing calomel, the newly appointed diplomat adopted a shocking "pink lemonade" approach toward an old adversary.[98] He applauded Mexican food and culture and ventured into the marketplace to meet ordinary people. His clumsy efforts to speak Spanish won widespread praise. He changed the sign to read "United States Embassy" instead of "American Embassy," a small measure of enormous symbolic significance. To demonstrate his trust, he met with Calles with

97. Enrique Krauze, *Mexico—Biography of Power: A History of Modern Mexico*, *1810–1996* (New York, 1997), 418.
98. Richard W. Fanning, *Peace and Disarmament: Naval Rivalry and Arms Control*, *1922–1933* (Lexington, Ky., 1995), 116.

only a Mexican interpreter. He spoke to Washington over the telephone in full knowledge that the line was tapped. To the delight of an entire nation, he persuaded his future son-in-law, the world hero Charles Lindbergh, to fly directly from Washington to Mexico City, two-thirds the distance from New York to Paris, and the popular "ambassador of the air" received a wildly enthusiastic reception. Morrow eventually persuaded Calles to return to the essence of the Bucarelli Agreement. The oil companies were not appeased, but the ambassador's "Ham and Eggs" diplomacy had saved them from the more serious threat of seizure of their assets without compensation. Morrow also brought in a U.S. Catholic priest to mediate between Calles and the Mexican church, helping settle the *Cristero* revolt and ease Calles's domestic problems. It was the last time serious consideration was given to U.S. military intervention in Mexico. Without giving up anything, Morrow had shown what one person with a conciliatory approach could accomplish. The settlement was much more important to Calles than to Coolidge. Well might some Mexicans admonish: "God save us from friendship with the United States."[99]

The high-water mark of the Republican era came in August 1928 with the signing of the Kellogg-Briand Pact outlawing war as an instrument of national policy. This much maligned and frequently ridiculed agreement had a curious birth in France's unrelenting efforts to protect its security against a future German attack. Seeking to entice the United States into the French security system, at least by indirection, Foreign Minister Briand shrewdly capitalized on the surge of goodwill generated by Lindbergh's trans-Atlantic flight to propose through a quite extraordinary public letter to the American people a bilateral treaty outlawing war. Such a treaty, he reasoned, would tie the United States closely to France and perhaps serve as a deterrent to Germany. It would create a sort of negative alliance that, in the event of war with Germany, would permit France to exploit U.S. neutrality without fear of war.[100]

Furious with Briand's decidedly undiplomatic intrusion in U.S. politics, Coolidge and Kellogg would have preferred to ignore the overture. But in the best spirit of the 1920s, the peace movement organized a massive public relations campaign in support of outlawing war. Seeing little choice but to give in, Coolidge and Kellogg, with equal cleverness, one-upped Briand by proposing a multilateral agreement. Hoist on his own

99. Berg, *Lindbergh*, 172–73; Cline, *Mexico*, 210–13; Krauze, *Mexico*, 419.
100. Cohen, *Empire*, 59–62. The standard account is Robert H. Ferrell, *Peace in Their Time: The Origins of the Kellogg-Briand Pact* (New Haven, Conn., 1952).

petard, the foreign minister in turn had no choice but to go along, and a suddenly enthusiastic Kellogg vigorously pushed the agreement at home and abroad. Fittingly, after months of sometimes difficult negotiations, fifteen nations, including all the European great powers, signed an agreement renouncing war as an instrument of national policy. The U.S. Senate approved the treaty with but one dissenting vote. Few believed it would actually eliminate war, but many did hope that an important step had been taken toward promoting peace. Americans were especially pleased that their nation had taken the lead in this most worthy of causes. Conspicuously lacking in enforcement provisions, the Pact of Paris perfectly fitted the Republican approach of involvement without commitment, most often cited as its major flaw. A more important omission may have been the lack of provision for peaceful change.[101]

V

In March 1929, Herbert Hoover and Secretary of State Henry Stimson assumed responsibility for carrying forward the policies initiated by Harding and Hughes. Taking office at a time of optimism, they found their task complicated by their own uneasy working relationship and very soon by the economic crisis that began with a stock market crash eight months after their ascension to power. Out of necessity, Hoover and Stimson involved the United States in the increasingly serious European problems to an even greater degree than their Republican predecessors. They promoted with new resolve the seemingly tried and true solutions of the era. Such efforts proved insufficient. By 1931, the world was deeply mired in economic crisis. In Europe and East Asia, economic dislocation provoked political and military challenges not simply to the regional status quo but to the entire postwar structure of peace.

Hoover and Stimson appeared ideally qualified to sustain the momentum generated by their predecessors, but this extraordinarily experienced and unusually talented foreign policy "team" proved much less than the sum of its parts. Hoover had been a strong internationalist in the early 1920s, but his experience as secretary of commerce appears to have made him cautious.[102] Both men lacked political experience and a zest for politics—Hoover once scorned politicians as "reptiles." An engineer by training and skilled manager, Hoover conspicuously lacked leadership skills and was prone to analyze problems to death. He was also a pessimist,

101. Costigliola, *Awkward Dominion*, 191.
102. Clifford R. Levin, "Herbert Hoover, Internationalist, 1919–1933" *Prologue* 20 (Winter 1988), 249–67.

and working through an issue with him, Stimson once complained, was like "sitting in a bath of ink." An elitist through and through, the very embodiment of the eastern foreign policy "establishment" of Roosevelt and Root, Stimson, on the other hand, believed in the essentiality of strong executive leadership and, like his mentors, in the utility of force in diplomacy. He reveled in the nickname "Colonel" earned through war service and disparaged Hoover's "Quaker nature" and caution. When in doubt, he insisted, you "march toward the guns."[103] The two men respected each other and shared similar views on most major issues, but sharp differences in personality, style, and philosophy produced an awkward working relationship.

The economic crisis that began in 1929 would dominate and in time destroy the Hoover presidency. The full force of the Great Depression would not be felt until after 1931, but the stock market crash of late 1929 had immediate and profound economic consequences. In the United States, manufacturing dropped sharply, unemployment increased dramatically, and growing numbers of businesses and banks failed. As the crisis deepened, American corporations focused inward on the domestic market. Trade declined sharply. Overseas investment slowed and then ceased altogether. Banks stopped lending money abroad, and tourism ended. The dollars that had underpinned postwar economic recovery dried up, with ripple effects across the world. The depression exposed the flaws in Republican approaches to postwar problems. It dimmed U.S. prestige in Europe, weakening its ability to lead and Europe's willingness to follow. A confirmed internationalist on many issues through much of his distinguished career, Hoover himself turned inward, seeking the solution to the nation's economic problems mainly at home.

In the face of new and increasingly daunting challenges, Hoover and Stimson clung to familiar solutions. Even more than Hughes, the Quaker Hoover saw armaments as a major impediment to peace and prosperity. He thus brought a new fervor to an old issue. Post–Washington Conference efforts to extend limits to other classes of ships had failed. A follow-up conference at Geneva in 1927 had broken down over Anglo-American wrangling on cruisers, but one indication of a sharp deterioration in U.S.-British relations in the late 1920s. In the absence of agreement, the United States in early 1929 set out to build fifteen new cruisers, signifying the onset of a new arms race. The U.S. move scared Britain into accepting parity with the United States and led to a 1930 naval conference in London.

Hoover attached great importance to the conference, sending a high-level delegation including Stimson and Dwight Morrow and putting

103. Schmitz, *Stimson*, 79; Costigliola, *Awkward Dominion*, 225–27.

forth bold new proposals. The United States and Britain quickly reached agreement on cruisers, but they could never palliate French insistence on a broader security treaty. They accommodated only with great difficulty Japan's demands to increase its Washington ratios. After three months of arduous negotiations, the United States, Britain, and Japan signed an agreement for a 10:10:6 ratio on light cruisers while conceding Japan 10:10:7 on heavy cruisers and battleships and parity in submarines. The London accord restored some Anglo-American amity and resolved the long-troublesome cruiser issue, pleasing Hoover and Stimson. In fact, London marked a transitional phase in the netherworld between the 1920s and 1930s. The conferees saw dimly if at all that the future of naval warfare resided in aircraft carriers. The failure to satisfy France may have been more important over the long run than the three-power agreement. The moderate Japanese government went along only because it needed Western credits and wanted to continue its policy of cooperation. The treaty was immensely unpopular in Japan—"a beautiful gold lacquer lunch box containing gruel," one critic complained. Unbeknownst to the participants, the London Conference marked the end of cooperation and the beginning of an era of conflict.[104]

On economic issues, as well, Hoover and Stimson fell back on old solutions in the face of new and complex problems. In the United States, as elsewhere, a natural response to the onset of depression was to protect the nation's own economy by raising the tariff. Ignorant of or indifferent to the international implications of protection and most concerned with protecting the domestic market, Congress in the 1930 Hawley-Smoot tariff raised rates on average to 40 percent, a 7 percent jump over the highly protectionist tariff of 1922 and the highest rates in U.S. history. Like many American businessmen, Stimson recognized the potential damage of such a tariff to international trade. Although he refused to risk his own political capital on what he saw as a no-win issue, he pushed Hoover to veto the bill. The president was himself sensitive to the potential dangers, but he too saw the domestic market as the key to recovery and deluded himself that the flexible provisions in the 1930 tariff could be used to sustain trade. Hoover acquiesced. The results were catastrophic. The tariff provoked huge resentment abroad—the French considered it tantamount to a declaration of war—and ultimately retaliation, further drying up international trade.[105]

The old issues of war debts and reparations refused to go away. Even as Hoover took office, yet another committee of experts met in Paris to

104. Fanning, *Peace and Disarmament*, 128, 132.
105. Leffler, *Elusive Quest*, 195–202.

work out a final reparations settlement. Headed by veteran financial diplomat Owen D. Young, the committee also included American bankers Morgan and Lamont. The task was even more challenging than five years earlier. Europe's apparent economic recovery removed the sense of urgency that had brought about the Dawes settlement. The powers were as divided as ever. Germany continued to insist on major reductions, France on holding the line. The Hoover administration feared the Allies would use the negotiations to link reparations and war debts and believed that the Europeans should assume a greater burden of the settlement. Young summoned his considerable negotiating skills to devise an acceptable plan. He threatened to shut off credits to gain European acceptance. He used the intercession of no less than Root to bring Hoover and Stimson around. The Young Plan called for gradual and significant reductions in reparations payments while ensuring that the Allies got enough to meet their war debt obligations. To administer the arrangements, it established a Bank for International Settlements, which Young envisioned as the economic arm of the Kellogg-Briand Pact. This final settlement turned out to be anything but final. It was probably the best that could have been obtained under the circumstances, but its success hinged on continued foreign loans and German economic growth, two early victims of the global economic crisis. Reluctant converts, Hoover and Stimson gave the scheme no more than lukewarm support.[106]

A mounting economic crisis in Europe and especially in Germany in 1931 forced Hoover to launch a new and courageous initiative. A banking crisis that began in Austria and quickly spread to Germany and France threatened not only economic collapse in Western Europe but also political upheaval. In addition, the United States had invested huge sums of money in Germany, and a collapse could be disastrous. The situation had moved far beyond the old issues of reparations and war debts, but those twin scourges of the postwar era retained huge symbolic importance. Germany's announcement that it could no longer pay reparations forced the United States to act. After dawdling for days, Hoover finally accepted Stimson's pleas for decisive action. Without consulting the Allies, he announced in June 1931 a one-year moratorium on war debt payments conditional on Allied acceptance of a one-year moratorium on reparations. This boldest move yet proved too little, too late. Worldwide stock prices rose sharply, and U.S. exports increased. Annoyed at the administration's unilateral move and certain that it would be more beneficial to the

106. Ibid., 202–19; Costigliola, *Awkward Dominion*, 190–92.

United States, the French stalled approval. The economic surge quickly ended, and worse yet threatened.[107]

THE MYTHS REGARDING 1920s U.S. foreign policy refuse to go away. After its "two-year-Wilsonian internationalist binge," Arthur Schlesinger Jr. wrote in 1995, the United States returned to the "womb" of "familiar and soothing isolationism."[108] To be sure, the Harding and Coolidge administrations eschewed the sort of bold, imaginative steps on such crucial issues as war debts, reparations, and European security that would have been required to prevent the Great Depression and another world war. Some Americans, mostly businessmen and bankers involved in global operations, saw the need for such measures. But most did not, and it would have taken rare courage and exceptional political skills on the part of policymakers to implement them. At a time when the United States did not appear threatened and the nation, after Wilson's Great Crusade, had turned sharply inward, it is not surprising that such boldness did not emerge. Most Americans saw no compelling need to depart from their nation's long-standing tradition of non-entanglement in European politics.

To say that America in the 1920s returned to the womb of isolationism, however, is to grossly misread what actually happened. While scrupulously avoiding binding political commitments, the Republicans took unprecedented measures and managed significant accomplishments. Cautious they were. They were also non-ideological and commendably pragmatic in dealing with daunting international problems. They took the first baby steps toward ending the obnoxious unequal treaties and accommodating with Chinese nationalism. They began to liquidate the military occupations of Central American and Caribbean nations, reverted to Blaine-like efforts to set relations with hemispheric nations on a more equitable basis, and came to terms with the Mexican Revolution without sacrificing basic U.S. interests. Exploiting the worldwide postwar mood, Hughes pulled off achievements in naval arms limitation that look even more impressive after a century of frustrating efforts to contain the proliferation of increasingly menacing weapons of mass destruction. Within limits set by their own vision and powerful domestic political constraints, the Republicans assumed leadership in addressing issues of European economic recovery and political security. They recognized the growing interdependence of the world economy. They creatively

107. Robert H. Ferrell, *American Diplomacy in the Great Depression: Hoover-Stimson Foreign Policy* (New York, 1970), 114–16; Schmitz, *Stimson*, 83–89.
108. Arthur Schlesinger Jr., "Back to the Womb," *Foreign Affairs* 74 (July/August 1995), 3.

used the private sector to find solutions. To some extent, perhaps, they were victims of their early successes. The return of peace, relative stability, and prosperity to Europe in the mid-1920s seemed to validate rather than raise questions about the measures taken, removing any sense of urgency for new and bolder steps. Hoover and Stimson thus tweaked programs already in operation rather than devise new ones.

The Great Depression after 1931 would shatter late-1920s complacency. Along with World War II, it would change the world beyond recognition and eventually call forth from the United States the sort of bold measures postwar commentators believed necessary in 1921.

12

The Great Transformation

Depression, Isolationism, and War, 1931–1941

"Our international trade relations, though vastly important, are in point of time and necessity secondary to the establishment of a sound national economy," Franklin Delano Roosevelt proclaimed in his March 4, 1933, inaugural address. "I favour as a practical policy the putting of first things first."[1] Indeed, in this speech to a nation laid low by economic catastrophe, FDR focused exclusively on domestic programs and appealed to Americans' self-reliance. He devoted but one long, and notably vague, sentence to foreign policy—less than Grover Cleveland in 1885. A clear sign of the times, these observations about national priorities also distinguish the 1930s from the preceding decade. During the 1920s, the United States actively participated in resolving international problems. After 1931, involvement without commitment gave way to a pervasive and deeply emotional unilateralism along with congressional safeguards against intervention in war.

Only toward the end of that tumultuous decade, when the reality of war seemed about to touch the United States directly, did a reluctant nation, led by Roosevelt himself, shift course. The shockingly rapid fall of France to the Nazi blitzkrieg in June 1940 spurred a great transformation in attitudes toward what was now being called national security.[2] For the first time since the early republic, many Americans feared that in a world shrunken by air power their safety was threatened by events abroad and concluded that the defense of other nations was vital to their own. The flaming wreckage of the fleet at Pearl Harbor on December 7, 1941, provided a graphic visual image marking the end of one era and the beginning of another.

I

The major cause of the chaos that was the 1930s was the Great Depression, the economic crisis that gripped the world throughout much of the

---

1. www.bartleby.com/124/pres49.html.
2. The phrase is from Robert Endicott Osgood, *Ideals and Self-Interest in America's Foreign Relations: The Great Transformation of the Twentieth Century* (Chicago, 1964).

decade and provided a major stimulus for conflict and war. Faced with a sharp economic downturn after 1931, panicky governments across the world to save themselves took autarkic measures such as raising tariffs and manipulating currencies. In a tightly interconnected world economy, such tactics proved disastrous.[3] The collapse of a major Austrian bank in 1931 set off a banking crisis in Germany that in turn dealt a staggering blow to France. In the nineteenth and early twentieth centuries, Britain had stepped in to meet economic crises. In the early 1930s, economist Charles Kindelberger has tersely concluded, "the British couldn't and the United States wouldn't."[4] In September 1931, an embattled Britain abandoned the gold standard, which the United States had pushed it to adopt in the mid-1920s. Across the industrialized world, banks failed, production fell off drastically, and unemployment rose to unprecedented levels. World trade fell by one-third from 1928 to 1932. The international economy ground to a standstill.

Economic catastrophe set off seismic political shocks, rocking to its foundations the rickety structure of peace cobbled together by the great powers in the 1920s. To cope with a crisis unprecedented in its magnitude, governments abandoned cooperation. Their egocentric efforts to revive their own economies provoked further conflict among potential rivals and erstwhile allies. Even the causes of the depression became an issue of bitter debate, Europeans pointing at the United States, President Herbert Hoover, more accurately, blaming Europe. Economic crisis caused profound and pervasive political unrest. Amidst nervous and increasingly angry publics, extremism replaced moderation, caution gave way to adventurism. Fragile democracies in Spain and Germany gave way to fascist dictatorships. Japan abandoned cooperation with the Western powers for rearmament, militarism, and a quest for regional hegemony. At the very time when the postwar system came under grave challenge, the democracies were least inclined to uphold it. Absorbed in domestic crisis and still haunted by bitter memories of the Great War, they reduced armaments and sought protection through the chimera of appeasement. Divided within itself, at times seemingly on the verge of civil war, France passed to Britain responsibility for upholding the world order. Significantly weakened and without the will to maintain its traditional international position, overextended and unsure of the United States, Britain lurched from "agitation to agitation," in the words of

3. Robert S. McElvaine, *The Great Depression: America, 1929–1941* (New York, 1984), 34.
4. Charles P. Kindelberger, *The World in Depression, 1929–1939* (Berkeley, Calif., 1986), 294.

Prime Minister Ramsay MacDonald, without developing a comprehensive policy.[5]

The boxing aphorism "The bigger they are, the harder they fall" applies to the U.S. economy in the 1930s. The acknowledged world economic powerhouse in the 1920s, the United States was devastated by the depression. Because its economy was less regulated and therefore more volatile, it had fewer cushions against the shocks. After a brief upturn in 1930, it was driven to rock bottom by the European crisis. The gross national product fell by 50 percent between 1929 and 1932, manufacturing by 25 percent, construction by 78 percent, and investment by a stunning 98 percent. Unemployment soared to 25 percent. With growing hunger and homelessness, traditional American optimism gave way to despair. The internationalism that had competed with more conventional attitudes during the 1920s was replaced by a new isolationism.[6]

The major trends of international politics in the 1930s were graphically displayed during the Manchurian crisis of 1931–32, the first step on the road back to war. One and one-half times larger than Texas, strategically located between China, Japan, and Russia, Manchuria had been a focal point of great-power conflict in Northeast Asia from the start of the century. Underpopulated, fertile in agricultural output, and rich in raw materials and timber, it drew outside powers like a magnet, especially Japan, whose dreams of national glory required external resources. Manchuria had traditionally been part of China—indeed, the last dynasty had come from there. As Imperial China fell on hard times, however, the great powers increasingly intruded. Conflict over Manchuria helped provoke the 1905 Russo-Japanese War. In 1907 and again in 1910, the two nations divided it into spheres of influence. Shielded by these agreements, Japan established preeminent economic and political power in southern Manchuria.[7]

Revolutionary China began to challenge outside influence in Manchuria in the late 1920s. Chiang Kai-shek's control over China proper remained tenuous, at best, but he often used attacks on foreign interests to rally domestic support, and Manchuria seemed an especially inviting target. In 1929, Chiang launched a short and ultimately disastrous war against Soviet interests in north Manchuria. Unchastened by defeat, he followed with a less overtly provocative assault against Japan,

---

5. Paul Kennedy, *The Rise and Fall of the Great Powers* (New York, 1987), 333.
6. David M. Kennedy, *Freedom from Fear: The American People in Depression and War* (New York, 1999), 84–88.
7. Christopher G. Thorne, *The Limits of Foreign Policy: The West, the League, and the Far Eastern Crisis, 1931–1933* (New York, 1973), 32–35.

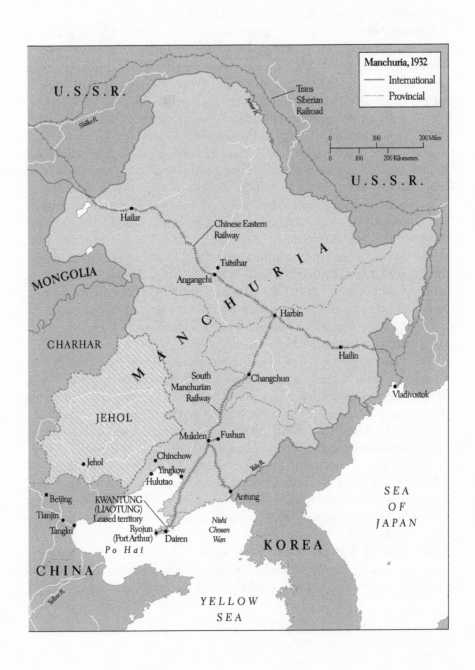

Manchuria, 1932
— International
—·— Provincial

U.S.S.R.

Shilka R.

Naur R.

Trans Siberian Railroad

U.S.S.R.

Hailar

Chinese Eastern Railway

MONGOLIA

Tsitsihar

Angangchi

M A N C H U R I A

Harbin

CHARHAR

Hailin

South Manchurian Railway

Changchun

Vladivostok

JEHOL

Mukden   Fushun

Jehol

Chinchow

Yalu R.

Yingkow

Hulutao

Beijing

KWANTUNG (LIAOTUNG) Leased territory

Antung

SEA OF JAPAN

Tianjin

Ryojun (Port Arthur)

Dairen

Nishi Chosen Wan

Tangku

Po Hai

KOREA

CHINA

Yellow R.

YELLOW SEA

0   100   200 Miles
0   100   200 Kilometers

encouraging Chinese to emigrate to Manchuria, pushing boycotts of Japanese goods, and urging local warlords to construct a railroad line parallel to the Japanese-controlled South Manchurian Railway.[8]

Chiang's challenge caused grave concern in Japan. The depression had brought economic catastrophe to the island nation, heightening Manchuria's economic importance. Japan relied on Manchuria for food, many vital raw materials, and about 40 percent of its trade. Although it sought to resolve the mounting difficulties with China by negotiation, even the moderate government then in power viewed Manchuria as essential. The elite officer corps of the Kwantung Army in Manchuria had its own plans. Alarmed at the Chinese challenge and Tokyo's meek response, fearful of losing a major foothold on the Asian mainland, the army saw an opportunity to solidify Japan's position—and its own—in Manchuria, perhaps seize control of the government from the moderates, and implement far-reaching expansionist plans in Asia. The Kwantung Army viewed the international situation as favorable for boldness. The Western powers were preoccupied with the mounting economic crisis; the Soviet Union seemed unlikely to do anything. Thus at Mukden in south Manchuria in September 1931, the army blew up a section of its own railroad, blamed the explosion on the Chinese, and, in a carefully planned and well-executed move, used that incident as pretext to wipe out Chinese resistance in Manchuria.[9]

The West responded much as the Kwantung Army had anticipated. China's appeals to the League of Nations, the United States, and Great Britain went unheard. At a low point of the depression, the European powers were absorbed in domestic problems, their leaders politically insecure and on the defensive.[10] Although Manchuria later took on enormous significance, at the time it seemed no more than marginally important. Indeed, conservative Europeans looked upon the Chinese as scheming and duplicitous and viewed Japan as a source of stability and a bulwark against Communism in northeast Asia. Those few Westerners who viewed with alarm what they saw as Japanese aggression refused to risk a tough stand.

Secretary of State Henry L. Stimson at first contented himself with watchful waiting, viewing the incident as a police action against Chinese dissidents, hoping that Tokyo could control the army, and fearing that a

8. Warren I. Cohen, *America's Response to China: An Interpretative History of Sino-American Relations* (New York, 1971), 124–25.

9. Thorne, *Limits*, 37–38.

10. Ibid., 78–80.

provocative U.S. response might rally the Japanese people to the army. Already at odds with Stimson over other issues, President Hoover adamantly opposed risk-taking. The United States did send a high-level diplomat to participate in Security Council discussions on Manchuria, a significant initiative in itself, but it would go no further. Encouraged by the U.S. response, the League passed a resolution reminding Japan *and* China of their responsibilities under the Kellogg-Briand Pact, calling for peaceful resolution of the dispute, and asking Japan to withdraw its troops. When this failed, it would do no more than accept Japan's proposal to send an investigatory commission to Manchuria.[11]

The crisis deepened in late 1931. The Kwantung Army expanded its operations well beyond Mukden, posing a threat to all Manchuria and even North China. The Tokyo government would not or could not stop the onslaught. Wilsonian concepts of collective security called for economic sanctions to stop aggression. Some Europeans and Americans, Stimson included, increasingly viewed Japanese actions as a threat to world order and were willing to go this far. Most Americans saw no vital interests in Manchuria, however, and few sympathized with China. Hoover privately ruminated that it might not be a "bad thing if Mr. Jap should go into Manchuria, for with two thorns in his side—China and the Bolsheviks—he would have enough to keep him busy for awhile." In any event, he adamantly opposed sanctions, which he dismissed as "sticking pins in tigers." He viewed going to war with Japan over Manchuria as "folly."[12] Without U.S. backing, the League refused to contemplate sanctions.

Determined to do something but without weapons at his disposal, Stimson in January 1932 resorted to the expedient that became known as the Stimson Doctrine (the first such pronouncement since Tyler). Now certain that Japanese aggression posed a threat to world order, he hoped to use *moral* sanctions to rally world opinion against Japan. A lawyer by profession, he believed it useful to brand outlaw behavior as such "by putting the situation morally in its right place."[13] Taking up an idea first proposed by Hoover, he informed Japan and China that the United States would not recognize territorial changes brought about by force and in violation of the Open Door policy and the Kellogg-Briand Pact. Stimson's doctrine remained a unilateral statement of U.S. policy. Fearing a Japanese threat to

---

11. Robert H. Ferrell, *American Diplomacy in the Great Depression: Hoover-Stimson Foreign Policy, 1929–1933* (New York, 1970), 138–43.
12. Justus D. Doenecke and John E. Wilz, *From Isolation to War, 1931–1941* (Arlington Heights, Ill., 1991), 35, 38; Thorne, *Limits*, 243.
13. Thorne, *Limits*, 245.

their Asian colonies, France and Britain responded ambiguously—and it took London four months to do that. The League gave no more than belated and qualified endorsement.

The Stimson Doctrine had no impact on Japan. By November, the Kwantung Army had moved almost four hundred miles north of Mukden, making clear its determination to take all of Manchuria. The moderate Japanese cabinet fell on December 31, 1931, leaving the government in the hands of men Stimson labeled "virtually mad dogs."[14] Shortly after, just as the secretary of state issued his doctrine, fighting extended to Shanghai, a major Chinese port city seven hundred miles south of Manchuria. When a Chinese boycott and mob violence threatened Japanese lives and property, the local Japanese commander dispatched forces to the scene. Eventually, seventy thousand Japanese troops entered Shanghai. Planes and naval vessels bombarded parts of the city, causing extensive civilian casualties and foreshadowing the carnage that would be inflicted on civilians over the next decade. Again, China appealed to the world for help.

Again, Stimson resorted to expedients. Japanese actions were increasingly difficult to justify in terms of defending established interests. The ferocity of the fighting and civilian casualties in Shanghai, widely reported in the Western press, provoked worldwide outrage. But there was only scattered support for strong action. The Western powers remained mired in the depression. The League awaited the report of its investigatory commission. Absorbed in economic problems and facing an election, Hoover did nothing more than beef up U.S. forces to protect the 3,500 Americans in Shanghai. Still persuaded that he must do something but certain that Britain and France would provide no more than "yellow-bellied" support, Stimson fell back on the Nine-Power Pact. In an open letter to Senate Foreign Relations Committee chairman William Borah, he charged Japan with violating that agreement, thereby releasing other signatories from their obligations under the Washington Treaties, a thinly veiled—and largely empty—threat that the United States might begin naval rearmament.[15]

By his own admission, Stimson was armed with nothing more than "spears of straw and swords of ice," and his statement did nothing to stop the Japanese conquest of Manchuria.[16] Japan did withdraw its troops from Shanghai—before Stimson released the Borah letter. In the meantime, it

14. David F. Schmitz, *Henry L. Stimson: The First Wise Man* (Wilmington, Del., 2001), 107.
15. Ibid., 110–11.
16. Ibid., 111.

solidified its control of Manchuria. Using as a figurehead the last Manchu emperor, the tragic "boy emperor," Henry Pu Yi, the Japanese created in March 1932 the puppet state of Manchukuo. The League commission's report placed some blame on China for provoking the Mukden incident but criticized Japan for using excessive force. It called for non-recognition of Manchukuo and proposed an autonomous Manchuria in which Japan's established rights would be respected. When the League adopted the report in early 1933, the Japanese walked out. Stopping in the United States en route home, delegate Yosuke Matsuoka complained that the West had taught Japan to play poker, gained most of the chips, and then declared the game immoral and changed to contract bridge.[17]

It has been conventional wisdom since the 1940s that a firm Western response in 1931 would have prevented World War II. The so-called Manchurian/Munich analogy, which preached the necessity of resistance to aggression at the outset, became a stock-in-trade of postwar U.S. foreign policy. To be sure, the paralyzing impact of the depression and the sharp divisions among the Western powers resulted in a weak response. Only the United States did anything, and as both the British and Chinese hastened to point out, Stimson's protests were "only words, words, words, and they amount to nothing if not backed by force."[18] But there is no certainty that a firmer response in Manchuria would have prevented subsequent Japanese and German aggression. Nor did the non-response necessarily ensure future war. Neither Japan nor Nazi Germany at this time had a master plan or explicit timetable for expansion. The plain hard truth is that the Western powers in 1931 lacked both the will and the means to stop Japan's conquest of Manchuria. However attractive economic sanctions may seem in retrospect, their track record through history does not inspire confidence. They generally succeed only when the major powers unite behind them, which was assuredly not the case in 1931–32. The Western democracies together could not have brought to bear enough military power to stop Japan. To have gone to war in 1931 might have been more disastrous than a decade later. The crisis was significant less for its destruction of an established order in East Asia than for the stark revelation that there had been no order in the first place. It highlighted the weakness of the League of Nations but did not bring its downfall. Above all, it demonstrated the limits of what diplomacy can do in some crisis situations. [19]

17. Doenecke, *Isolation to War*, 46.
18. Cohen, *America's Response to China*, 134; for the British, see Thorne, *Limits*, 247.
19. Thorne, *Limits*, especially 404–10.

II

Shortly after Japan left the League of Nations, ending the Manchurian crisis, and with the U.S. economy at a standstill, a despondent Hoover gave way to the ebullient Franklin Roosevelt. Raised to old money in the genteel surroundings of New York's Hudson Valley, FDR, as he came to be known, was a middling student at prestigious Groton Academy and Harvard. After a brief and undistinguished fling at the law, he followed his distant cousin Theodore by taking the post of assistant secretary of the navy in the Wilson administration. Stricken with a crippling and life-changing case of polio in the early 1920s, he found his niche in electoral politics, winning the governorship of New York and then soundly defeating the discredited Hoover in 1932.

Roosevelt dominated the tumultuous decade that followed as few presidents have dominated their eras, and only Wilson stands above him in importance in twentieth-century U.S. foreign policy. He was a man of dauntless optimism, a trait that served him and the nation well during years of economic crisis and war. Although he had few close personal friends, he was capable of great warmth and personal charm and possessed formidable political skills. Blessed with a resonant voice and a rare eloquence, he used the new medium of radio to singular advantage in informing, reassuring, and rallying a troubled nation. As a result of the noblesse oblige in which he was raised, religion, and perhaps his struggle with polio, he developed a deep sensitivity to the needs of the less fortunate. He had a rare ability in hard times to articulate the core values of freedom from want and fear. His influence, like that of Wilson, touched millions of people across the world.[20]

Roosevelt viewed himself as a practical idealist—"I dream dreams," he once said, "but I am an intensely practical man"—and his accomplishments were considerable, but his leadership was not without flaws. He could be frustratingly elusive and enigmatic, confounding contemporaries and historians alike. It remains extremely difficult at any given time to read his mind with any precision on any issue. A notoriously sloppy administrator who knowingly appointed conflicting personalities to competitive positions, he created a multiplicity of agencies with overlapping responsibilities, then watched with seeming glee as they engaged in bitter and at times enervating turf wars. Especially in the area of diplomacy, he

20. James MacGregor Burns's *Roosevelt: The Lion and the Fox* (New York, 1956) and *Roosevelt: The Soldier of Freedom* (New York, 1970) remain the most insightful FDR biographies. Robert Dallek, *Franklin D. Roosevelt and American Foreign Policy, 1932–1945* (New York, 1979) is the most comprehensive treatment of the subject.

made some bizarre and disastrous appointments. He could be bold and brilliantly improvisational. Yet through much of the 1930s, on vital issues of national security he could seem maddeningly timid, perhaps underestimating his powers of persuasion, not acting until events imposed decisions upon him.

Through the 1930s, the making of U.S. foreign policy remained a relatively simple process. The State Department continued to be the key player, although on major issues Roosevelt usually took control and in some areas his close friend Treasury Secretary Henry Morgenthau Jr. played an important role. True to form under FDR, State itself was deeply divided. The secretary, Cordell Hull, remained in office a record twelve years, but his influence was limited. A native of the rugged Cumberland region of Tennessee, "the judge," as he was called, was a political appointee, a veteran congressman, confirmed Wilsonian, and fervent advocate of free trade, useful to FDR mainly in keeping southern congressmen in line. Frailness of body and a benign countenance masked an iron will, a fiercely competitive spirit, and a raging temper. Hull's seething hatreds could set loose a volcanic eruption of profanity, made all the more colorful by a slight speech impediment. The undersecretary after 1937, Sumner Welles, was in many ways Hull's polar opposite. Born to wealth (and then married to more), Welles shared FDR's prep school and Ivy League pedigree. Suave, sophisticated, and snobbish, he was dapper in dress with finely tailored suits and an ivory-handled walking stick. No one "could possibly look so much like a career diplomat," a colleague observed, "bearing, gestures, the way his chin is carried, everything." The fierce rivalry between the two misfits burned throughout much of the Roosevelt era.[21]

During the long interregnum between Hoover's defeat and Roosevelt's inauguration (new presidents were then inaugurated in March), the United States approached the brink of despair. One-fourth of the workforce was unemployed; relief funds from state and local governments had been exhausted. Farmers had suffered economically since the Great War, and as prices plummeted still further in the 1930s mortgage foreclosures became commonplace. Shanty towns for the homeless—so-called Hoovervilles—took shape in most major cities. In early 1933, a series of bank failures produced runs on the banks by panicky citizens that in turn led to the declaration of banking "holidays" in many states to prevent further failures. While

---

21. David E. Lilienthal, *The Journals of David E. Lilienthal* (7 vols., New York, 1964–73), 2:564. Irwin F. Gellman, *Secret Affairs: Franklin Roosevelt, Cordell Hull, and Sumner Welles* (New York, 2002) gives full coverage to the Hull-Welles feud.

the economic situation deteriorated, Congress did nothing. Hoover stubbornly tried to secure from FDR a commitment to follow his discredited programs. The president-elect wisely refused but left little indication how he might deal with the nation's most serious crisis since the Civil War. The mood of the country was one of deep despondency. "We are in the doldrums," a journalist observed, "waiting not even hopefully for the wind which never comes."[22]

Conditions abroad were equally grim. Europe continued its economic plunge, and the leading nations could not agree how to stop it. A once "cosmopolitan world order had dissolved into various rivaling subunits," Paul Kennedy has written, "a sterling block, based upon British trade patterns . . . ; a gold block, led by France; a yen block dependent upon Japan . . . ; a U.S.-led dollar block (after Roosevelt also went off gold); and, completely detached from these convulsions, a USSR steadily building 'socialism in one country.' "[23] As always, Germany was especially volatile. In January 1933, in a move whose full significance was not clear at the time, the aged president, Paul von Hindenburg, asked National Socialist leader Adolf Hitler to assume the chancellorship. Hitler would subsequently assume full powers. By the end of the year, he would pull Germany out of the Geneva Disarmament Conference and the League of Nations.

As a vice presidential candidate in 1920, Roosevelt had campaigned vigorously for the League of Nations, but like the nation he too turned sharply inward under the burden of the Great Depression. In 1932, he explicitly spurned his mentor Wilson's handiwork and scoffed at the Hoover moratorium. After assuming the presidency, he further reduced in size an already small army. Like Theodore a naval enthusiast, he built the fleet up only to the limits set by the Washington and London conferences. As his inaugural address suggested, he firmly believed that the depression had domestic roots. He sought nationalist solutions, mainly through inflation.

FDR's handling of the World Economic Conference in London in the summer of 1933 reveals not only his "putting of first things first" but also a cavalier and feckless diplomatic style that would become something of a trademark and in this case would have baneful consequences. During the frantic first Hundred Days of the New Deal, Roosevelt deluged Congress with a flood of domestic legislation attacking the depression from various directions. To make sure international problems did not intrude on his domestic agenda, he delayed the long-proposed conference until June.

22. William E. Leuchtenburg, *Franklin D. Roosevelt and the New Deal* (New York, 1963), 26.
23. Kennedy, *Great Powers*, 283.

This painting by Benjamin West portrays the peacemakers of the American Revolution, from left to right John Jay, John Adams, Benjamin Franklin, Henry Laurens, and William Temple Franklin. British diplomats refused to sit for the painting, leaving it unfinished. *Library of Congress.*

Thomas Jefferson's idealism and hard-nosed practicality epitomized what would become a distinctively American approach to foreign policy. His expansionist vision and skillful diplomacy, along with a huge dose of good luck, secured the windfall of the Louisiana Purchase. *Library of Congress.*

A brilliant financier, Secretary of the Treasury Alexander Hamilton put the new nation on a sound economic footing. His bitter struggle with Secretary of State Thomas Jefferson in the early 1790s helped shape the foreign policy of the United States during its infancy. *Library of Congress.*

The so-called Barbary Wars were the nation's first foreign war. They evoked among Americans powerful nationalist sentiments tinged with anti-Muslim prejudices as demonstrated in this engraving of Stephen Decatur and Daniel Fraser in mortal conflict with the enemy. *U.S. Naval Historical Center.*

John Quincy Adams is generally regarded as the nation's greatest secretary of state. His shrewd diplomacy brought to the United States East and West Florida and Spanish claims to the Pacific Northwest. He was instrumental in formulating the Monroe Doctrine. *Library of Congress.*

This hand-colored lithograph made near the end of Andrew Jackson's presidency by N. Currier of Currier and Ives fame portrayed him in the heroic pose in which Americans pictured him. *Library of Congress.*

The removal of Native Americans to lands across the Mississippi in the 1830s brought forth great tragedy, as portrayed in this rendition of the infamous Trail of Tears that went with Cherokee removal to the West. *Woolaroc Museum, Bartlesville, Oklahoma.*

Col. Harney and U.S. dragoons pursue Mexicans at the Battle of Churubusco, August 20, 1847. The Mexican-American War reinforced in the minds of Americans the singular virtues of their republic. *Library of Congress.*

This Japanese print portrays a U.S. naval officer (not Perry) in the most fearsome manner. *Library of Congress.*

This portrait of Commodore Matthew C. Perry was produced around the time of his landmark voyage that led to the opening of Japan. *Library of Congress.*

A physician and lawyer, William Walker, the "grey-eyed man of destiny," was one of the 1850s' leading filibusterers. He got himself elected president of Nicaragua. Thrown out of office, he was executed in Honduras in 1860 on a third attempt to regain power. *Library of Congress.*

Abraham Lincoln, portrayed in this 1863 Alexander Gardner photograph, presided over a bloody war to preserve a Union free of slavery that could stand as the "last best hope" for freedom in the world. *Library of Congress.*

Lincoln's secretary of state, William Henry Seward, skillfully employed a combination of bluster and conciliation to defend Union interests during the Civil War. *Library of Congress.*

U.S. Navy Capt. Charles Wilkes's November 1861 seizure of two Confederate diplomats from the British mail packet *Trent* provoked the first diplomatic crisis of the Civil War. Seward's timely concessions smoothed Anglo-American relations at a crucial time. *Library of Congress.*

This portrait of the colorful James G. Blaine, the "Plumed Knight of Maine," hangs in the Department of State where he twice served as the nation's chief diplomat. An ardent expansionist, Blaine prepared the way for the U.S. overseas thrust in the 1890s. *Library of Congress.*

Chinese immigrants played an important part in the building of the United States, especially in the completion of the transcontinental railroad. They were also the object of bitter resentment among many Americans, resulting in restrictive Congressional legislation and anti-Chinese riots such as this one in Denver on October 31, 1880. *Library of Congress.*

Portrayed here in dress uniform, Emilio Aguinaldo led the Philippine rebellion against U.S. occupation forces. *Library of Congress.*

Filipino insurgents at prayer before surrendering to U.S. forces. *National Archives (photo no. 395-pi-1-50_wc0322).*

President Theodore Roosevelt once boasted that he took Panama while others debated the issue. A person who loved to be at the center of everything, TR is shown here in November 1906 operating a steam shovel at the Panama Canal construction site. *Theodore Roosevelt Collection, Harvard College Library.*

Roosevelt's chief diplomatic trouble shooter, William Howard Taft, is pictured here seated on an unfortunate water buffalo. Taft served as governor-general of America's new Philippines colony. *U.S. Army Military History Institute.*

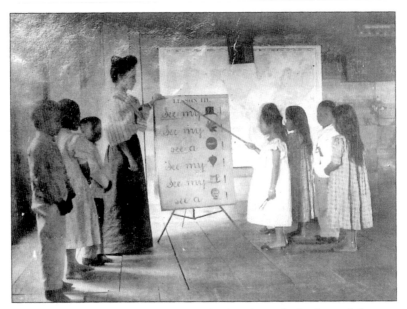

The United States was determined to be a good colonialist in the lands it took from Spain. An American is shown here conducting classes in schools established for Filipino children. *National Archives (photo no. 350-P-CA-5-1).*

Wilson received a hero's welcome in Paris and other European cities in early 1919, encouraging his belief that peoples everywhere sought the kind of peace he had so eloquently advocated. *Princeton University Library.*

The Council of Four (left to right, British prime minister David Lloyd George, Italian leader Vittorio Orlando, French premier Georges Clemenceau, and U.S. president Woodrow Wilson) did much of the work of drafting the controversial Treaty of Versailles that ended the First World War. *National Archives (photo no. 111-sc-055456_wc0722).*

U.S. Secretary of State Charles Evans Hughes signs the treaties resulting from the 1921–1922 conference held at Washington on arms limitations. The Washington treaties were Hughes's crowning achievement and one of the first successful international ventures at arms control. *Library of Congress.*

Banker Dwight Morrow was one of the nation's most effective diplomats and a sharp contrast to many of his predecessors who had served in Mexico. He is shown here with Mexican president Plutarco Calles and Secretary of Agriculture Luis Leon at the opening of a rural school. *Library of Congress.*

Bread and soup lines such as these in Chicago were common in most U.S. cities at the height of the Great Depression. The economic crisis caused Americans to turn inward and dominated the framing of U.S. foreign policy up to 1939. *Franklin D. Roosevelt Library.*

This poignant picture of a terrified Chinese baby left alone after the brutal Japanese bombing of a Shanghai railroad station in August 1937 provoked anger toward the perpetrators and sympathy for the Chinese. *National Archives (photo no. 208-aa-132n-2_ wc1131).*

The Japanese attack on the U.S. naval base at Pearl Harbor, December 7, 1941, shown here in graphic detail, galvanized a divided nation for war. It also shattered the longstanding assumption that the United States was safe from foreign attack, thus redefining the bases of U.S. national security. *Library of Congress.*

The Big Three first met in Teheran, Iran, in December 1943. They reached agreement on the timing and location of an Anglo-American second front in Western Europe. Their discussions also decisively influenced the contours of postwar settlements. *Library of Congress.*

A rare moment of levity between Generalissimo and Madame Chiang Kai-shek and U.S. general Joseph W. "Vinegar Joe" Stilwell. The Chiangs despised the general and he more than reciprocated, complicating U.S. efforts to develop a viable China policy during World War II. *National Archives (photo no. NA-111-SC-134627).*

President Harry S. Truman and his dapper secretary of state Dean Acheson worked together extraordinarily well. They were key figures in implementing the postwar revolution in U.S. foreign policy and the Cold War containment policy. *Courtesy of Harry S. Truman Library.*

This jeep, like all Marshall Plan aid, bears a label on the back affirming that it came from the United States. It is being sent to Southeast Asia in 1955 (probably to Vietnam) as part of the worldwide U.S. effort to contain communism. *Library of Congress.*

This 1948 photograph of U.S. Air Force C-47 transports lined up for unloading at Berlin's Templehof Airport makes clear the day-and-night effort that went in to supplying blockaded West Berlin by airlift. *Library of Congress.*

President Truman is shown here awarding Gen. Douglas MacArthur his fifth Distinguished Service Medal during their October 1950 Wake Island conference. The general gave assurances that victory was in sight in Korea. In 1951, following Chinese intervention, Truman relieved an insubordinate MacArthur of his command. *Library of Congress.*

Prime Minister Mohammad Mosaddeq during his fall 1951 trip to the United States sought to identify Iranian nationalism with the American Revolution by visiting the Liberty Bell in Philadelphia. In August 1953, he was overthrown by a U.S.-sponsored coup. *Department of State, Courtesy of Harry S. Truman Library.*

Encouraged in part by U.S. propaganda, the fall 1956 Hungarian rebellion was brutally suppressed by Soviet forces. In this picture, Soviet tanks have been immobilized by Hungarian student protestors. *AP Images.*

On a goodwill visit to Latin America in May 1958, Vice President Richard M. Nixon was attacked by anti-American mobs while driving through the streets of Caracas, Venezuela. The incident brought Latin America back to the forefront of U.S. foreign policy. The sign held up by protesters states: "Nixon, your government is responsible for the Guatemalan Tragedy." *Richard Nixon Presidential Library.*

A somber President John F. Kennedy talks with Soviet premier Nikita Khrushchev during their June 1961 Vienna summit. Their acrimonious discussions set off a period of Cold War tensions leading up to the Cuban missile crisis. *U.S. Department of State photograph, courtesy of John F. Kennedy Presidential Library.*

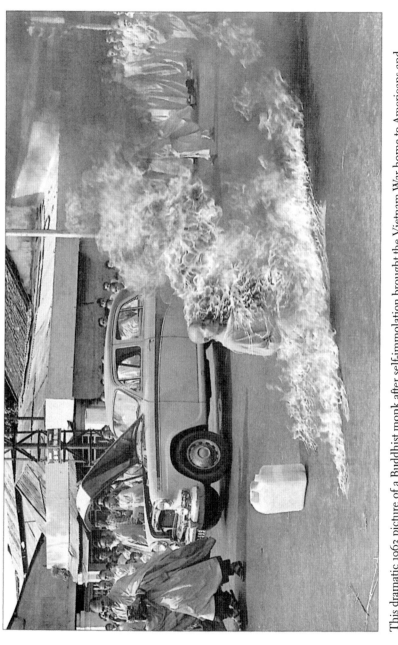

This dramatic 1963 picture of a Buddhist monk after self-immolation brought the Vietnam War home to Americans and contributed to the Kennedy administration's approval of a coup to overthrow South Vietnamese president Ngo Dinh Diem. *AP Images / Malcolm Browne.*

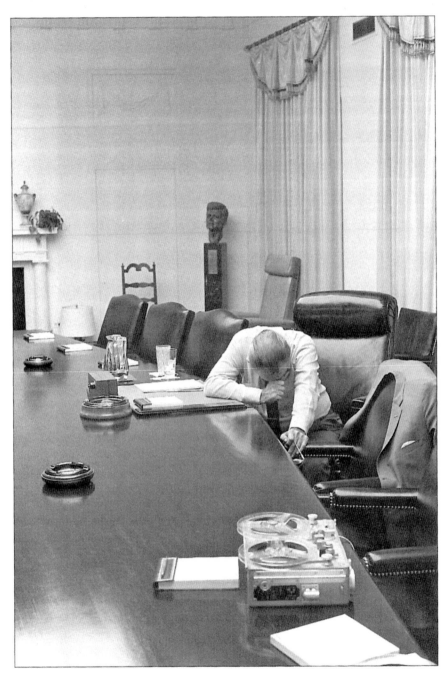

A distraught Lyndon Baines Johnson is shown here after listening to a tape recording describing an ambush, sent to him by his son-in-law from Vietnam. The war weighed heavily on LBJ and was instrumental in his decision not to seek renomination in 1968. *Lyndon Baines Johnson Presidential Library photo by Jack Kightlinger.*

Richard M. Nixon and Henry A. Kissinger discuss Vietnam in 1972. The two men pulled off extraordinary diplomatic feats but were eventually the victims of their own methods. *Richard Nixon Presidential Library.*

Leonid Brezhnev clamps his hand around Nixon's leg during a 1974 summit. This picture was taken during a weekend trip to Yalta on the Black Sea. The town was hastily renamed Oreanda to avoid political problems for Nixon. *Richard Nixon Presidential Library.*

President Richard M. Nixon and wife Pat at the Great Wall of China in February 1972. Nixon's much ballyhooed trip brought forth a diplomatic revolution and boosted his reelection prospects at home. *Richard Nixon Presidential Library.*

This picture displays the long lines that often formed at U.S. gasoline stations in the 1970s, in part a result of the 1973 Arab oil embargo. As in the 1930s, domestic economic woes exerted a powerful influence on U.S. foreign policy in this decade. *Library of Congress.*

China's diminutive vice-premier Deng Xiaoping tries on a cowboy hat during a Texas stop on his 1979 U.S. visit. Deng's tour symbolized the culmination of a dramatic reversal in Sino-American relations. *AP Images.*

Islamic fundamentalist cleric Ayatollah Khomeini, in the center of this picture, waves to exuberant followers following his return to Iran from exile. The Iranian revolution posed major challenges for the United States in the late 1970s and beyond. *AP Images/ Campion.*

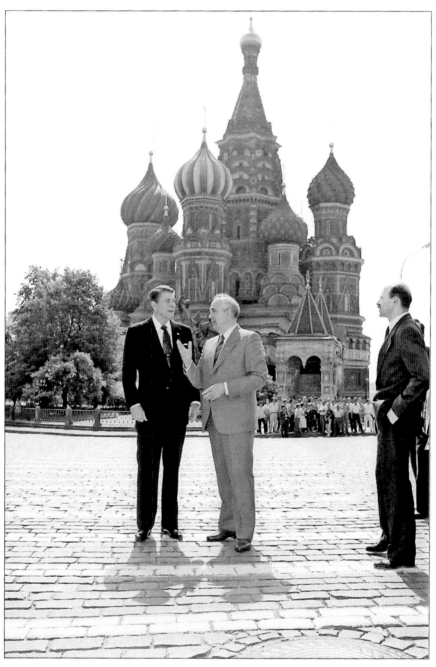

Friends by this time, U.S. president Ronald Reagan and Soviet general secretary Mikhail Gorbachev chat amiably in front of St. Basil's cathedral in Moscow's Red Square during their 1988 summit. The Cold War was nearing an end. *Ronald Reagan Presidential Library.*

On June 5, 1989, a lone Chinese man stands in front of a column of tanks dispatched to put down the pro-democracy rebellion led by students in Beijing's Tiananmen Square. AP *Images/Jeff Widener.*

Secretary of State Madeleine Albright and President Bill Clinton. The daughter of a diplomat, Albright was the nation's first woman secretary of state. She was so hawkish on the issue of Kosovo that the war came to be known as "Madeleine's War." *William J. Clinton Presidential Library.*

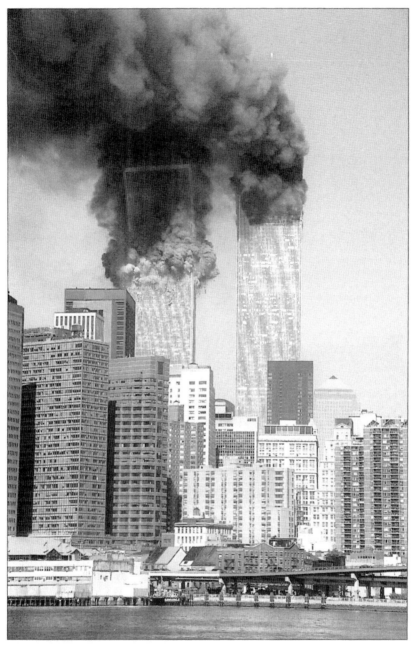

Smoke and flames billow from New York's World Trade Center twin towers on the morning of September 11, 2001, shortly after they were struck by airliners hijacked by terrorists. The one hundred story towers crumbled to the ground, leaving a massive pile of rubble and killing 2,603 people. Nine/eleven, as it came to be called, shocked Americans into the hard reality that even superpowers are vulnerable. *AP Images / Jim Collins.*

Standing on the deck of the aircraft carrier *Abraham Lincoln* on May 10, 2003, beneath a banner proclaiming "Mission Accomplished," President George W. Bush hailed the triumph of U.S. forces in Iraq. Even as he spoke, an insurgency was forming that would make a tragic mockery of the banner. *AP Images/ J. Scott Applewhite.*

He made sure that the still-divisive issue of World War I debts stayed off the agenda. He sent to the conference a bizarre assemblage of delegates ranging from the drunken isolationist Senator Key Pittman of Nevada to the Wilsonian internationalist and free trader Hull, virtually ensuring no agreement. As the conference was about to convene, he blithely sailed away for an extended vacation. And when the conferees finally agreed on a plan for international currency stabilization, he fired off to London his infamous "Bombshell Message"—appropriately dispatched from the cruiser USS *Indianapolis*—making clear his rejection of such schemes and his determination to find economic solutions at home. Roosevelt's salvo ended the conference without any agreement. Published on July 4, 1933, and hailed by some Americans as a second declaration of independence, it destroyed the last vestige of international cooperation in dealing with the worldwide depression.[24]

Roosevelt has been rightly criticized for his handling of the London conference. Economists disagree in assessing the conference itself, many concluding that currency stabilization would not have worked and that since the domestic market remained the key to U.S. prosperity FDR was right to focus on homegrown solutions. Scholars also agree, however, that he erred by encouraging the conferees to believe he supported their work and Hull to believe that he was committed to tariff reduction. His views toward the deliberations exposed facile national stereotypes: "When you sit around the table with a Britisher," he observed during the deliberations, "he usually gets 80% of the deal and you get what's left."[25] FDR later admitted that the rhetoric of his Bombshell Message was overblown and destructive, but at the time he boasted that it might persuade Americans that their country did not always lose in international negotiations. Whatever the economic consequences, of course, the failure of the conference and FDR's role in it had a devastating diplomatic impact, especially on relations with Britain.[26]

Roosevelt's personal imprint also marked another early foreign policy initiative: recognition of the Soviet Union. The policy of non-recognition had long since become outdated, of course, and the ever pragmatic FDR abandoned it because he believed it served no useful purpose. Hard-core anti-Communists such as patriotic organizations, the Roman Catholic Church, and some labor unions still passionately opposed recognition, but in the depths of the depression it was no longer a hot-button issue.

24. Kennedy, *Freedom from Fear*, 155–57; Leuchtenburg, *New Deal*, 200–201.
25. Kindelberger, *Depression*, 231.
26. Ibid., 230–31; Leuchtenburg, *New Deal*, 202–3.

Some Americans, FDR and many business leaders included, hoped that diplomatic relations would bring increased trade. Roosevelt may also have hoped that the mere act of recognition would give pause to expansionists in Germany and Japan.[27]

Properly wary of State Department hard-liners, Roosevelt centered negotiations in the White House, and over nine days in November 1933 he and Soviet foreign minister Maxim Litvinov hammered out a badly flawed agreement. FDR was sufficiently sensitive to his domestic critics to seek concessions in return for recognition—unusual if not indeed extraordinary in diplomatic practice. The agreement itself took a convoluted form: eleven letters and one memorandum addressing a range of issues. Unsurprisingly, given the vast gulf of culture and ideology that separated the two nations, the negotiations proved difficult. Roosevelt focused on securing diplomatic relations. He gained vague Soviet guarantees of religious freedom for Americans in the USSR and promises to stop Comintern propaganda in the United States. Unable to agree on the crucial issues of possible loans and debts owed by the prerevolutionary governments, the two sides settled for sloppy language that would cause much future wrangling.[28]

Establishment of diplomatic relations was the only tangible result of the Roosevelt-Litvinov agreements. FDR pleased the Soviets by naming their onetime advocate William C. Bullitt the first U.S. ambassador to Moscow. Bullitt set about his task with customary zeal, in his spare time seeking to teach the Russians baseball and the Red Army cavalry the decidedly unproletarian sport of polo. Plans to construct on the Moscow River a U.S. embassy modeled on Jefferson's Monticello evoked positive responses from FDR and Soviet dictator Joseph Stalin.[29] For both nations, the warm glow of expectations quickly gave way to disillusion. Stalin seems to have hoped for active U.S. cooperation in blocking Japan. When this did not happen and the Japanese threat appeared to wane, his interest in close relations slackened. From the U.S. standpoint, the Soviets did not live up to their commitments to stop propagandizing in the United States. Negotiations on loans quickly stalled, and Litvinov took vigorous exception to U.S. demands for payments of old debts. "No nation today pays its debts," an incredulous foreign minister insisted with

27. Edward M. Bennett, *Franklin D. Roosevelt and the Search for Security: American-Soviet Relations, 1933–1939* (Wilmington, Del., 1985), 1–16.
28. John Lewis Gaddis, *Russia, the Soviet Union, and the United States: An Interpretive History* (2nd ed., New York, 1990), 120–21.
29. David Mayers, *The Ambassadors and American Soviet Policy* (New York, 1995), 111–12.

more truth than diplomacy.[30] The anti-Semitic Bullitt found dealing with the Jewish Litvinov especially vexing, and life in the Soviet police state took its toll on American diplomats. Baseball and polo never caught on; there was no Monticello on the Moscow. Relations quickly soured. In 1936, a disenchanted Bullitt departed the Soviet Union a confirmed and virulent anti-Communist.[31]

The one sentence of FDR's inaugural address devoted to foreign policy included that memorable if also notably vague line "In the field of world policy I would dedicate this nation to the policy of the good neighbor." Meant to apply generally, it became identified with the Western Hemisphere and was one of Roosevelt's most important legacies. A product of self-interest and expediency along with a strong dose of idealism and more than a smattering of genuine goodwill, the Good Neighbor policy in its initial stage terminated existing military occupations and disavowed the U.S. right of military intervention without relinquishing its preeminent position in the hemisphere and dominant role in Central America and the Caribbean. In time, it extended beyond policy into the realm of cultural interchange.[32]

Hoover laid the foundations. Shortly after the 1928 election, the president-elect carried on the tradition of personal diplomacy begun by Charles Evans Hughes by taking a two-month goodwill tour of Latin America, where he publicly used the phrase "good neighbor." In office, he removed the marines from Nicaragua and promised to get them out of Haiti. He stopped short of publicly repudiating the Roosevelt Corollary to the Monroe Doctrine, but he explicitly disavowed intervention to protect U.S. investments. He adopted a new and more flexible policy toward recognition. He came very close to apologizing for the U.S. occupation of Haiti and Nicaragua. Building on Wilson's ideas, he sought through commercial and financial arrangements to promote stability in Latin America and thereby create in the Western Hemisphere a model for world peace. His unwillingness to adjust tariff and loan policies to the harsh realities of hard times doomed his economic program. His broader ambitions were subsumed when he became totally absorbed in and ultimately rendered impotent by the Great Depression.[33]

30. Gaddis, Russia, the Soviet Union, and the United States, 124.
31. Mayers, Ambassadors, 108–17.
32. Frederick B. Pike, FDR's Good Neighbor Policy: Sixty Years of Generally Gentle Chaos (Austin, Tex., 1995), 15.
33. Ferrell, Great Depression, 215–30; William O. Walker, "Crucible for Peace: Herbert Hoover, Modernization and Economic Growth in Latin America," Diplomatic History 30 (January 2006), 83–117.

With his usually keen eye for public relations, Roosevelt made the good neighbor phrase part of his political vocabulary and expanded the policy and the spirit, winning praise at home and respect throughout the hemisphere. In the absence of any immediate threat to the Americas and with trade expansion a high priority, it was expedient to conciliate peoples the United States had often demeaned. The rise of dictators in Central America produced stability and eliminated pressures for U.S. intervention. Roosevelt understood that because of its wealth and power the United States would be an object of resentment among many Latins, but he felt it "very important to remove any legitimate grounds of their criticism."[34] The sources of Good Neighborism went much deeper. As it turned away from Europe and Asia in the 1930s, the United States devoted greater attention to its own hemisphere. More important, the depression helped peoples of very different continents identify with each other in ways they had not before. Latin Americans could view their northern neighbors as victims of the same poverty and want they had long endured. As they lost faith in their own exceptionalism, North Americans were less inclined to impose their will and values on others. The easing in the United States during the 1930s of deep-seated racial and anti-Catholic prejudices also made possible greater acceptance of Latin Americans. There was much cross-fertilization of ideas among intellectuals on both continents. In the United States, Latin American and especially Mexican art came into vogue. Latin subjects and stars gained popularity in movie theaters.[35]

Scarcely had Roosevelt taken office before yet another revolution in Cuba put his good intentions to the test. The depression hit Cuba very hard, sparking an uprising by students, soldiers, and workers against President Gerardo "Butcher" Machado. When Machado responded with state-sponsored terror, FDR sent his friend Welles to Cuba as ambassador to handle the crisis. Welles helped unseat Machado, but two changes of government later the ambassador grew alarmed at the radical turn taken by the revolution. President Ramón Grau San Martin, a stubbornly independent physician and university professor, sought to institute sweeping reforms while workers went on strike and seized the sugar mills. The aristocratic Welles was appalled by the ascendancy of the rabble and worried about Communist influence among the workers. He viewed Grau as well-meaning but fuzzy-minded and hopelessly ineffectual. Although he sought to disguise it as a "temporary" and "strictly limited" intervention,

34. Lloyd C. Gardner, *Economic Aspects of New Deal Diplomacy* (Madison, Wisc., 1964), 51.
35. Pike, *Good Neighbor Policy*, 15–110.

he acted very much in the mode of his predecessors, on several occasions in the fall of 1933 appealing for U.S. troops to restore order and replace Grau with a more dependable government.[36]

In contrast to *his* predecessors, FDR refused, an important first step in the Good Neighbor process. Welles withheld recognition from Grau, a powerful weapon by itself. FDR authorized him to use political means to undermine the government and dispatched warships to display U.S. power. But he adamantly rejected repeated appeals for troops. He was influenced by his former Navy Department boss, Josephus Daniels, then ambassador to Mexico, who pooh-poohed Welles's fears of Communism and firmly advised against military intervention. More important, the United States was soon to meet with other hemispheric nations at Montevideo, where intervention was expected to be a key issue, and Roosevelt did not want to carry there the stigma of yet another Cuban intrusion. The urgent need for expanding trade with Latin America put a premium on the velvet glove approach. Ultimately, Welles achieved his goals without use of military force. With his encouragement, a group of army plotters headed by Fulgencio Batista overthrew the Grau government. In time, Batista established a dictatorship that, like Trujillo's in the Dominican Republic, produced order without U.S. occupation or military intervention.[37]

The issue of military intervention was at the top of the agenda of the Montevideo Conference in September 1933. That gathering was a landmark in that Kentuckian and University of Chicago professor Sophonisba Breckinridge became the first woman to represent the United States at an international conference. Following Hughes's precedent, Hull attended and used his down-home Tennessee political manner to cultivate the Latin delegates, popping in on gatherings to extend a warm handshake and "Howdy do" to sometimes startled diplomats, unpretentiously introducing himself as "Hull of the United States." When the Latin American nations sought from U.S. delegates a firm and unequivocal agreement that "no state has the right to intervene in the internal and external affairs of another," Hull strode boldly to the podium and proclaimed that "no government need fear any intervention on the part of the United States under the Roosevelt administration," winning warm applause from the assembled conferees.[38] The agreement that was subsequently signed

36. Lars Schoultz, *Beneath the United States: A History of U.S. Policy Toward Latin America* (Cambridge, Mass., 1998), 300.
37. Ibid., 301–3.
38. Irwin F. Gellman, *Good Neighbor Diplomacy: United States Policy in Latin America, 1933–1945* (Baltimore, 1979), 51.

modified the commitment to exclude treaty obligations. To appease still-uneasy neighbors, FDR shortly after the conference firmly declared that "the definite policy of the United States from now on is one opposed to armed intervention."[39]

The administration followed with tangible steps. A 1934 agreement with Cuba abrogated the obnoxious Platt Amendment, ending the first phase of the special U.S. relationship with that nation. That same year, the last marines departed Haiti. Two years later, a new agreement was negotiated assigning to Panama a larger share of canal revenues and eliminating the clause in the 1903 treaty giving the United States the right to intervene in its internal affairs.

As part of its shift to non-intervention, the United States in the 1930s also changed its policy on recognition. Washington had frequently withheld recognition to deter revolutions or eliminate governments that had taken power by military means, most recently, of course, in Cuba. A coup by Guardia Nacional commander Anastasio Somoza in Nicaragua in 1936 provided the test case for change. Some Latin American observers even at this point foresaw the sort of brutal dictatorship Somoza would impose. A U.S. diplomat lamented that creation of the Guardia Nacional had provided Nicaragua "with an instrument to blast constitutional procedure off the map," offering "one of the sorriest examples . . . of our inability to understand that we should not meddle in other people's affairs."[40] On the other hand, the United States had no enthusiasm for further interference in Nicaragua. Many Latin Americans watched closely to see what U.S. pledges of non-intervention really meant when put to the test. Like Stimson earlier, some U.S. officials concluded that at least a Somoza dictatorship could bring stability to a chronically troubled land. As with many other instances in the world of diplomacy, neither intervention nor non-intervention seemed entirely satisfactory. In this case, the United States chose to err on the side of inaction.

Hull also took the lead in implementing the economic arm of the Good Neighbor policy. A passionate advocate of free trade throughout his career, with Roosevelt's blessings he helped push through Congress in 1934 a Reciprocal Trade Agreements Act that gave the executive broad authority to negotiate with other nations a lowering of tariffs by up to 50 percent. Hull's pet project helped to eliminate the customarily fierce congressional battles over tariffs and the log-rolling that went with them. It

39. Schoultz, *Beneath the United States*, 304–5.
40. William Kamman, "U.S. Recognition of Anastasio Somoza, 1936," *Historian* 54 (Winter 1992), 273; Schoulz, *Beneath the United States*, 273.

has remained the basis for U.S. tariff policy since 1934.[41] Under his careful management, the agreements had special application for Latin America. In the case of Cuba and the Central American nations, they encouraged the export of U.S. finished goods and the import of agricultural products like coffee, sugar, and tobacco, thus solidifying a quasi-colonial relationship that stunted their economic development and increased their dependence on the United States. Along with the Export-Import Bank, which provided loans to other nations to purchase goods in the United States, the reciprocal trade agreements helped triple U.S. trade with Latin America between 1931 and 1941. They strengthened the dominant role of the United States in hemispheric commerce.

The Good Neighbor policy was far more than policies and programs; it was also deeply personal and closely identified with Franklin Roosevelt. His genuine affection for people carried over into his foreign policy, as did his ability to identify with what he would call the "common man," something that especially resonated in Latin America. Once as overbearing as cousin Theodore, FDR retained a certain condescension, but he had long since concluded that it was diplomatically expedient—and good politics—to cultivate friendship among the good neighbors. He went out of his way to demonstrate that Latin America counted through such occasions as Pan-American Day in U.S. schools. His commanding presence combined with his populist instincts appealed to Latin Americans, making him the most popular U.S. president ever within the hemisphere at large.[42] In 1934, he continued the new tradition of personal diplomacy by visiting South America, even showing up in Haiti, Panama, and Colombia. His arrival at an inter-American conference in Buenos Aires shortly after his overwhelming reelection in 1936 was nothing short of triumphal, a national holiday that drew huge enthusiastic crowds. The Latin American press hailed him as *"el gran democrata"* whose New Deal served as a model of the kind of reform Latin America needed.[43] Buenos Aires represented the capstone of the first phase of the Good Neighbor policy. In a markedly changed climate, FDR had introduced significant changes, most notably a formal end to military interventions and deliberate efforts to cultivate good will, without changing the essence of a patron-client relationship. As the world's attention shifted after 1936 toward the impending crises in East Asia and Western Europe, the Good Neighbor policy would increasingly focus on hemispheric defense.[44]

41. Gellman, *Good Neighbor Diplomacy*, 96.
42. Pike, *Good Neighbor Policy*, 134–37.
43. Leuchtenburg, *New Deal*, 209.
44. Gellman, *Good Neighbor Diplomacy*, 108.

III

As the threat of war mounted in the 1930s, Americans responded with a fierce determination to stay out. A minority of internationalists still favored collective security to prevent war, but most Americans preferred to concentrate on domestic issues, shun international cooperation, retain complete freedom of action, and avoid war at virtually any cost. The term *isolationism* has often—and mistakenly—been applied to all of U.S. history. It works best for the 1930s.[45] To be sure, the United States never sought to cut itself off completely as China and Japan had done before the nineteenth century. Americans took a keen interest in events abroad, maintained diplomatic contact with other nations, and sought to sustain a flourishing trade. But their passionate 1930s quest to insulate the nation from foreign entanglements and war fully merits the label isolationist.

Isolationists did not share the same ideology or belong to any organization.[46] They ran the political gamut from left to right. Such sentiment was strongest in the middle western states and among Republicans and Irish and German Americans, but it cut across regional, party, and ethnic lines. Isolationists did share certain basic assumptions. They did not make moral distinctions among other nations. European conflict in particular they viewed as simply another stage in a never-ending struggle for power and empire. When the United States was grappling with limited success to resolve the economic crisis at home, they had no illusions about their ability to solve others' problems. Like Americans since the middle of the nineteenth century, they believed that the crises building in Europe and East Asia did not threaten their security. Although they disagreed, often sharply, on domestic issues and in their willingness to sacrifice trade and neutral rights to avoid conflict, they shared a faith in unilateralism and a determination to stay out of war.

Such views sprang from varied sources. The United States since 1776 had made it a cardinal principle to avoid "entangling" alliances and Europe's wars. In this sense, Americans were simply adhering to tradition. But the Great Depression gave 1930s isolationism a special fervency. With breadlines lengthening and the economy at a standstill, most Americans agreed they should concentrate on combating the depression. Foreign policy fell to the bottom of the national scale of priorities. The depression also shattered the nation's self-confidence, standing on its head the Wilsonian notion that the United States had the answer to world problems. Bitter

45. Walter A. McDougall, *Promised Land, Crusader State: The American Encounter with the World Since 1776* (Boston, 1997), 39–40.
46. Manfred Jonas, *Isolationism in America, 1935–1941* (Ithaca, N.Y., 1966), 32–33.

conflicts over tariffs and Allied default on war debts exacerbated already strained relations with Britain and France, nations with whom cooperation would have been necessary to uphold the postwar order. Hostility toward the outside world increasingly marked the popular mood. "We do not like foreigners any more," Representative Maury Maverick of Texas snorted in 1935.[47]

Unpleasant memories of the Great War reinforced the effects of the depression. By the mid-1930s, Americans generally agreed that intervention had been a mistake. The United States had no real stake in the outcome of the war, it was argued; its vital interests were not threatened. Some "revisionist" historians charged that an innocent nation had been tricked into war by wily British propagandists. Others blamed Wilson and his pro-British advisers for not adhering to strict neutrality. More conspiratorially, still others argued that bankers and munitions makers—the "merchants of death" theory popularized by a Senate investigating committee headed by North Dakota's Gerald Nye—had pressed Wilson into abandoning neutrality by permitting a massive trade in war materials. When these investments were threatened by a German victory in 1917, it was alleged, these same selfish interests drove him to intervene. Americans generally agreed that their participation had neither ended the threat of war nor made the world safe for democracy.[48] Revisionist history provided compelling arguments to avoid repeating the same mistake and historical "lessons" to show how.

Above all, the threat of another war pushed Americans toward isolationism. From 1933 to 1937, Japan consolidated its gains in Manchuria and began to exert nonmilitary pressure on North China. In the spring of 1934, a Foreign Office official publicly proclaimed that Japan alone would maintain peace and order in East Asia. This so-called Amau Doctrine directly challenged Western interests in East Asia and raised the possibility of conflict. In Europe, Benito Mussolini sought to recapture Italy's lost glory by conquering Ethiopia. In a January 1935 plebiscite, the people of the Saar Basin dividing Germany and France voted to join the former. Several months later, Hitler announced that Germany would no longer adhere to the disarmament limits imposed by the Treaty of Versailles. As the threat of war increased in East Asia and Europe, the nation responded with near unanimity. "Ninety-nine Americans out of a hundred," the *Christian Century* proclaimed in January 1935, "would today regard as an

47. Doenecke, *Isolation to War*, 6.
48. Warren I. Cohen, *The American Revisionists: The Lessons of Intervention in World War I* (Chicago, 1967) is the standard account.

imbecile anyone who might suggest that, in the event of another European war, the United States should again participate in it."[49] Scientific surveys of public opinion were just coming into use, and a February 1937 poll indicated that a stunning 95 percent of Americans agreed that the nation should not participate in any future war.

Peace activism flourished. In its heyday, the organized peace movement had an estimated twelve million adherents and an income of more than $1 million. Protestant ministers, veterans, and women's groups led the opposition to war. Pacifists and anti-war internationalists joined forces in 1935 to form an Emergency Peace Campaign that held conferences and conducted study groups across the nation. Its No Foreign War Crusade opened on April 6, 1937, the twentieth anniversary of U.S. entry into World War I, with rallies in two thousand cities and on five hundred campuses. College students formed the vanguard of the antiwar opposition. In April 1935, 150,000 students on 130 campuses participated in anti-war protests; the following year the number increased to an estimated 500,000. Students lobbied to get the Reserve Officer Training Corps (ROTC) off campuses. They formed organizations such as Veterans of Future Wars, which, with tongue only partially in cheek, demanded an "adjusted service compensation" of $1,000 for men between the ages of eighteen and thirty-six so they could enjoy "the full benefit of their country's gratitude" *before* being killed in battle.[50]

This mood was quickly manifested in policy. In April 1934, Congress passed an act introduced by and named for arch-nationalist and hard-core isolationist Senator Hiram Johnson of California forbidding private loans to nations in default on war debt payments. The Johnson Act was popular at home but mischievous in its consequences. By declaring token payments illegal, it gave debtor nations a handy excuse not to pay. By restricting U.S. freedom of action, it would later impede an effective response to the emerging world crisis.[51] Spurred by the right-wing radio priest Father Charles Coughlin and Hearst newspapers, the Senate in January 1935 stunned an unwary and even complacent FDR by once again rejecting U.S. membership in the World Court, a result primarily of continuing hostility to the League of Nations and rising anti-foreignism. "To hell with Europe and the rest of those nations!" a Minnesota senator screamed.[52]

49. Jonas, *Isolationism*, 1.
50. Charles DeBenedetti, *The Peace Reform in American History* (Bloomington, Ind., 1980), 122–33.
51. B.J.C. McKercher, *Transition of Power: Britain's Loss of Global Preeminence to the United States* (Cambridge, Eng., 1999), 175–76.
52. Leuchtenburg, *New Deal*, 216; Kennedy, *Freedom from Fear*, 232–34.

The defeat left Roosevelt battle-scarred and notably cautious for the struggle ahead.

When German rearmament and Italy's October 1935 attack on Ethiopia transformed issues of war and peace from the abstract to the immediate, the United States sought legislative safeguards for its neutrality. Isolationists were prepared to sacrifice traditional neutral rights and freedom of the seas to keep the United States out of war. An internationalist minority believed that the best way to avoid war was to prevent it and saw neutrality as a means to that end. Working with the League and the Western democracies, they reasoned, the United States could employ its neutrality as a form of collective security to punish aggressors and assist their victims and thus either deter or contain war. Even Roosevelt believed that the United States needed legal safeguards to avoid being dragged willy-nilly into war as in 1917. In early 1935—unwisely as it turned out—he encouraged isolationist senators to introduce legislation.[53]

FDR's move backfired. He had hoped for a flexible measure that would permit him to discriminate between aggressor and victim, but the Senate legislation imposed a mandatory embargo on shipments of arms and loans to belligerents once a state of war was declared to exist. "You can't turn the American eagle into a turtle," the Foreign Policy Association howled, and Roosevelt sought to alter the legislation to suit his needs.[54] But the Italo-Ethiopian conflict heightened fears of war, and Senate leaders warned that if the president tried to buck the tide he would be "licked sure as hell."[55] FDR did secure a six-month limit on the legislation, and he may have hoped to modify it later. Preoccupied with the flurry of crucial domestic bills such as Social Security that constituted the so-called Second New Deal and in need of isolationist votes for key measures, he signed in August 1935 a restrictive neutrality law based squarely on perceived lessons from World War I. Once a state of war was determined to exist, a mandatory embargo would be imposed on arms sales to belligerents. Belligerent submarines were denied access to U.S. ports. Remembering the *Lusitania*, the first step on the road to World War I, Congress also instructed the president to warn Americans that they traveled on belligerent ships at their own risk. The following year radical isolationists tried to extend the embargo to all trade with belligerents, while FDR sought discretionary power to limit trade in critical raw materials and manufactured goods to prewar

53. Robert A. Divine, *The Reluctant Belligerent: American Entry into World War II* (2nd ed., New York, 1979), 19.

54. Ibid, 20.

55. Doenecke, *Isolation to War*, 57.

quotas, a device that in war would favor Britain and France at the expense of Germany. Again unwilling to risk his domestic programs and sensitive to the upcoming presidential election, Roosevelt in March 1936 grudgingly accepted a compromise extending the original act and adding an embargo on loans.[56]

Historical lessons are at best an imperfect guide to present actions, and, as with the War of 1812 and the Great War, it was much easier for the United States to proclaim a neutrality policy than to implement it. Americans continued to disagree, often heatedly, about the intent of their neutrality. Should it be strictly applied and designed mainly to keep the nation out of war? Or should it allow the president to support collective security by punishing aggressors and assisting victims? Such debates even tore apart pacificist internationalist groups like the Women's International League for Peace and Freedom.[57] Not surprisingly, some Americans took sides in the wars that erupted in the mid-1930s and pressed the government to implement a neutrality favorable to their cause. As in earlier wars, even constitutional safeguards could not shield the United States from influencing world events. Whatever it did or did not do, its actions could have significant results, sometimes in ways that Americans did not like. Amidst all the complexity and confusion, FDR struggled to curb aggression without risking war and provoking an isolationist backlash, using the restrictive Neutrality Acts ingeniously and sometimes deviously and seeking ways outside of neutrality to influence world events.

The Italo-Ethiopian War illustrates the problems. That war evoked an especially strong response among African Americans.[58] Ethiopia had a special symbolic importance for them because of its place in biblical lore and because it was one of the few areas of Africa not colonized by whites. Involving themselves for the first time in a high-profile foreign policy debate, they vigorously protested Italian aggression and demanded embargoes on trade with Italy, boycotted Italian American businesses in the United States, petitioned the U.S. Catholic hierarchy and the pope, organized mass rallies in major cities, raised funds for Ethiopia, and even in small numbers volunteered to fight in the war until warned that such service violated neutrality laws.[59] On the other side,

56. Divine, Reluctant Belligerent, 29.
57. Anne Marie Pois, "The U.S. Women's International League for Peace and Freedom and American Neutrality, 1935–1939," Peace and Change 14 (July 1989), 263–84.
58. Brenda Gayle Plummer, Rising Wind: Black Americans and U.S. Foreign Affairs (Chapel Hill, N.C., 1996), 37.
59. Ibid., 37–51.

Italian Americans generally backed Italy and protested when the government interpreted the Neutrality Act to favor Ethiopia.

Roosevelt struggled with limited success to implement U.S. neutrality in ways that would stop Italy and deter other aggressors. He invoked the Neutrality Act in recognition that it might hurt Italy more than Ethiopia and in hopes that an arms embargo would support League sanctions against Italy. The government also warned Americans against traveling on belligerent passenger ships, in an effort to hurt the Italian tourism industry. The administration subsequently imposed a "moral embargo," urging businesses to limit trade with Italy to prewar levels. When that failed, it threatened to publish the names of firms trading with Italy.[60]

Although a clever use of the Neutrality Act, these moves neither bucked up the League nor thwarted Italy. The League did declare Italy the aggressor and imposed limited sanctions. Largely because of British and French fear of war, however, vital items like oil were omitted from the restricted list. This huge loophole significantly mitigated the effects of the already ineffectual moral embargo. The sanctions annoyed Italy without stopping it. Collective security was further undermined when it was revealed that British foreign minister Sir Samuel Hoare and French prime minister Pierre Laval had worked out a plan that would have bought peace by giving two-thirds of Ethiopia to Italy. Undeterred by the weak Western response and using all the instruments of modern war including poison gas, Italy completed its conquest in eight months and then left the League of Nations. The absence of the United States from the League gave the Europeans a handy excuse for inaction; their weakness, in turn, confirmed American distrust and fed isolationist sentiments.[61]

The Spanish Civil War was equally complex, and the policies developed, for many Americans, were just as unsatisfactory. Right-wing rebels led by fascist Francisco Franco and assisted by Germany and Italy set out to topple militarily a democratic government supported by socialists, Communists, and anarchists, and backed by the Soviet Union, in an especially nasty civil conflict that captured the world's attention. The Spanish Civil War became for many Americans a cause célèbre, an epic struggle between good and evil. Most citizens, to be sure, remained uninformed and indifferent, but groups on each side of the political spectrum took up the cause with near fanatical zeal. Alarmed by the government's treatment of the Spanish church, American Catholics, an increasingly potent political lobby, rallied to Franco. Liberals and radicals, including writers, movie

60. Leuchtenburg, *New Deal*, 220.
61. Divine, *Reluctant Belligerent*, 27–28.

stars, journalists, intellectuals, and left-wing agitators, passionately supported the Loyalists. Some 450 Americans even formed an Abraham Lincoln Brigade to fight for the government. Thrown into battle in early 1937 without adequate preparation, they suffered horrific casualties in what many viewed a noble cause.[62]

The administration again cooperated with the Western democracies, at least indirectly, but its policies were unpopular at home and had harmful results abroad. Seeking to contain the Spanish Civil War, the British and French naively adopted a policy of non-intervention. The United States went along, refusing to invoke the Neutrality Acts, which, it claimed, did not apply to civil wars, and again proclaiming a moral embargo on the sale of war supplies to both factions. When exporters ignored it, Congress legislated an arms embargo against both sides. With Germany and Italy generously backing the rebels, the moral embargo worked against the Loyalists, which, as a recognized government, could normally expect to procure war supplies from abroad. This so-called malevolent neutrality was designed to keep the United States out of the war and appease American Catholics. It also reflected concern in government circles, especially in the top echelons of the State Department, that a Loyalist victory would lead to a Communist takeover of Spain that might have spillover effects elsewhere in Europe and threaten U.S. trade and investments. Some conservative diplomats termed the war a conflict of "Rebel versus Rabble," "between nationalism on the one hand, and Bolshevism naked and unadorned on the other."[63] On the other hand, liberals, even isolationists like Senator Nye, increasingly feared that the United States was abetting a fascist victory. The brutal bombing and shelling of civilians by German and Italian air squadrons at Guernica in April 1937, later immortalized in Pablo Picasso's stunning mural, caused international outrage, an act of "fiendish ferocity" according to one U.S. newspaper.[64] The administration nonetheless clung to its policy until Franco triumphed in the spring of 1939, in large part because Roosevelt was immobilized over opposition to his attempt to pack the Supreme Court with sympathetic justices and refused to risk another defeat. Franco later praised the United States for a "gesture we Nationalists will never forget"; FDR conceded a "great mistake."[65]

62. Ibid., 34.
63. Douglas Little, *Malevolent Neutrality: The United States, Great Britain, and the Origins of the Spanish Civil War* (Ithaca, N.Y., 1985), 241–42.
64. Quoted in Allen Guttmann, *The Wound in the Heart: America and the Spanish Civil War* (New York, 1962), 107.
65. Robert A. Divine, *The Illusion of Neutrality* (Chicago, 1962), 172, 228.

The difficulties of implementing neutrality produced in 1937 demands for revision of the legislation. Internationalists still opposed the mandatory arms and loans embargo and sought presidential discretion to support collective security. Increasingly concerned with the threat of war, some members of Congress wanted to close a large loophole by extending the embargo to all goods. Even isolationists like Borah protested the surrender of traditional neutral rights as "cowardly" and "sordid." Still others worried that a total embargo would damage the U.S. economy.

Financier and sometime presidential adviser Bernard Baruch, czar of industrial mobilization during World War I, came up with a clever solution. Insisting that the entanglements of loans and the risk of shipping war materials posed the greatest threats to neutrality, he proposed that the United States "sell to any belligerent anything except lethal weapons, but the terms are 'cash on the barrel-head and come and get it.'" Baruch's scheme offered the allure of peace without sacrificing prosperity. FDR favored cash and carry, recognizing that it could help Britain and France in the event of war. He sought discretionary authority to apply the principle. This time, remarkably, he succeeded. On May 1, 1937, while fishing in the Gulf of Mexico, he signed a measure that retained the embargo on arms and loans and prohibited Americans from traveling on belligerent ships. It also gave the president broad discretionary authority to apply cash-and-carry to trade with belligerents. This compromise permitted Americans to have their cake and eat it too, presumably minimizing the risk of war without abandoning U.S. trade altogether. The *New York Herald-Tribune* dismissed the 1937 legislation as "an act to preserve the United States from intervention in the War of 1914–'18."[66] In fact, by continuing to tie American hands in crucial areas it probably encouraged further aggression and ultimately helped bring on a war the nation could not avoid.

FDR also worked outside the Neutrality Acts in sometimes inscrutable ways in a futile effort to shape world events. He shared the determination of most Americans to stay out of war. The best way to do that, he believed, was to prevent war. He seems early to have concluded that Germany, Italy, and Japan threatened the peace. Recognizing the limits on his own freedom of action, he sought means to "put some steel in the British spine," even regaling British representatives with tales of his time spent in a German school when he had stood up to the local bully. Seeking to "get closer . . . with a view to preventing a war or shortening it if it should come," from 1934 to 1937 he floated various schemes to encourage British resistance to the Axis and build a basis for Anglo-American partnership.

66. Leuchtenburg, *New Deal*, 225.

He proposed exchanges of information on weapons and industrial mobilization. He approved the Royal Navy keeping in service overage destroyers beyond treaty limits and suggested exchanging sailors on navy ships. As early as 1934, he proposed "united action" to prevent or localize war. He later suggested expanding the doctrine of effective blockade to include land traffic, a means to isolate aggressors that would evolve into his quarantine speech. His major proposal was for an international peace conference to be held under U.S. auspices that would encourage participants to agree upon a set of principles. Should they refuse or agree and later break their promises, they could be branded as outlaws. FDR hoped in the process to educate Americans for the international role they must play.[67]

Such efforts produced no tangible results. The gap of distrust was too deep to be bridged by small gestures. Whatever FDR might say privately, the British viewed the Neutrality Acts as an insuperable impediment to cooperation with the United States and a sharp limit on the president's ability to keep commitments. They dismissed some of his proposals as "dangerously jejune" and "a little too naive and simplistic." His unorthodox style also caused problems. His proposals were often transmitted in oblique and elliptical fashion and shrouded in secrecy. On occasion, the British missed the signals. In any event, they feared the United States would "let us down or stab us in the back after having thrust us forward to our cost." The ascension of Neville Chamberlain to the prime ministership precisely when Roosevelt proposed an international conference was especially bad timing. Chamberlain trusted neither the United States nor Roosevelt. In any event, he was disposed to avoid war through negotiation. FDR's embarrassing defeat in the Court fight made the British even more wary of his ability to follow through on any commitments.[68]

Just two months after Roosevelt's signing of the 1937 Neutrality Act, war erupted in East Asia. An incident at the Marco Polo Bridge in Beijing on July 7, 1937, sparked fighting between Chinese and Japanese troops that quickly escalated into full-scale war. Unlike Mukden in 1931, the Japanese did not stage this incident. This time it was the civilian government in Tokyo that used the clash to eliminate the Kuomintang threat to Japan's hegemony over an area deemed vital to its security and prosperity.

67. Richard A. Harrison, "A Presidential Demarche: Franklin D. Roosevelt's Personal Diplomacy and Great Britain," *Diplomatic History* 5 (Summer 1981), 245–72, and "A Neutralization Plan for the Pacific: Roosevelt and Anglo-American Cooperation, 1934–1937," *Pacific Historical Review* 57 (February 1988), 47–72.
68. Ibid; McKercher, *Transition of Power*, 252.

The conflict soon fanned out over North China and spread south. Using modern weapons with ruthless precision, Japanese forces seized Shanghai, China's largest city. They followed with the notorious "rape of Nanking," six weeks of terror marked by rampant burning and looting, the mass execution of prisoners of war, and the merciless slaughter of civilians, women and children included. Countless women were brutally raped and forced into prostitution. In all, as many as three hundred thousand Chinese may have been killed.[69] Even these horrific methods could not bring China to heel. Chiang Kai-shek moved his government to Chungking in the hinterland. Bogged down in a more difficult struggle than anticipated, the Japanese fought on to terminate what they euphemistically called the "China Incident."

Reactions in the United States to the Sino-Japanese War varied. Many Americans still saw Japan as a bulwark against Soviet Russia and even against Chinese revolutionary nationalism. Some Americans valued a flourishing trade with Japan. On the other hand, many increasingly took sides. Missionaries who remained to help the Chinese reported the horrors of Japanese aggression; accounts of the rape of Nanking caused particular outrage. Warning that the United States must not be intimidated by "Al Capone nations," missionaries pushed for a "Christian boycott" of Japanese goods and stopping the sale of war materials to Japan. Novelist Pearl Buck and Time-Life mogul Henry Luce, both children of missionary parents, complemented their efforts. Millions of Americans read Pearl Buck's novel *The Good Earth*, first published in 1931, and identified with the Chinese peasants whose story it told. The movie version appeared in 1937. Luce's increasingly popular high-circulation magazines and March of Time newsreels also presented highly idealized pictures of China and Chiang Kai-shek, a recent convert to Christianity. Over time, such images swayed U.S. opinion against Japan and toward China. Whatever their sympathies, Americans in late 1937 staunchly opposed going to war.[70]

The official U.S. response to the Sino-Japanese War reflected the nation's ambivalence. As with Ethiopia and Spain, Roosevelt manipulated U.S. neutrality to influence events in ways that he—and most Americans—favored. Recognizing that cash-and-carry would benefit the Japanese and exploiting the absence of a declaration of war, he refused to invoke the Neutrality Acts. But he would go no further, and his subsequent actions were characteristically elusive. In October 1937 in Chicago, a stronghold

69. Iris Chang, *The Rape of Nanking: The Forgotten Holocaust of World War II* (New York, 1997).
70. Kennedy, *Freedom from Fear*, 401–2.

of isolationism, he briefly heartened internationalists with his famous speech calling for a quarantine of the contagion of aggression, at least hinting at sanctions. Apparently misreading a surprisingly positive national response or uncertain what to do once he received it, he quickly backtracked, affirming the next day that " 'sanctions' is a terrible word to use. They are out of the window." In dealing with the war in Asia, as with other issues, Americans and Europeans brought out the worst in each other. When a League-arranged meeting of the Nine-Power Pact signatories (without Japan) met in Brussels in November 1937, the mere hint of sanctions drew from Hull's State Department a strong disclaimer and call for adjournment. Briefly buoyed by FDR's quarantine speech, the Europeans were no more willing than the United States to risk sanctions. Once again, U.S. unreliability gave them a handy excuse to do nothing. "Hardly a people to go tiger shooting with," Chamberlain's sister sneered.[71]

Even the Japanese sinking of a U.S. Navy vessel failed to provoke the United States into action. On December 11, 1937, during the height of the rape of Nanking, Japanese aircraft bombed and strafed the USS *Panay,* a gunboat in the Yangtze River engaged in evacuating civilians. The pilots cruelly attacked survivors seeking to escape in lifeboats. The *Panay* was sunk; forty-three sailors and five civilians were injured, three Americans killed. FDR and other top officials were furious and contemplated a punitive response. But this shockingly brutal and unprovoked attack sparked little of the rage of the *Maine* or *Lusitania.* Indeed, Americans seemed to go out of their way to keep a war spirit from building. Some even demanded that U.S. ships be pulled out of China. Apparently as shocked as the United States, the Japanese government quickly apologized, promised indemnities for the families of the dead and injured, and provided assurances against future attacks. Even more telling, and revealing a different side of Japanese society, thousands of ordinary citizens, in keeping with an ancient custom, sent expressions of regret and small donations of money that were used to care for the graves of American sailors buried in Japan.[72]

As the Sino-Japanese War settled into a stalemate, the situation in Europe dramatically worsened. Continuing his step-by-step dismantling of the despised Versailles settlement, Hitler in March 1936 sent troops into the demilitarized zones of the Rhineland. He stepped up rearmament, ominously focusing on offensive weapons such as tanks, planes, and U-boats, and also

71. Doenecke, *Isolation to War,* 71.
72. Trevor K. Plante, " 'Two Japans': Japanese Expressions of Sympathy and Regret in the Wake of the *Panay* Incident," *Prologue* 33 (Summer 2001), 109–20.

began to form alliances, signing with Italy in October 1936 the Rome-Berlin Axis and with Japan the following month an Anti-Comintern Pact. Fulfilling a long-standing personal dream, the Austrian-born dictator in March 1938 through propaganda and intimidation, and again in violation of the Versailles treaty, forged a union with Austria, sealing the arrangement with a rigged plebiscite in which a resounding 99.75 percent of the voters approved the *Anschluss*.

Hitler's threats against Czechoslovakia provoked a full-fledged war scare in 1938, what has come to be known as the Munich crisis. Cynically taking up the Wilsonian banner of self-determination, he first demanded autonomy for the 1.5 million German speakers in the Sudeten region of western Czechoslovakia and then cession of the entire Sudetenland to Germany. Fearing that the loss of this mountainous region would deprive it of a natural barrier against a resurgent Germany, the Czech government balked. When troop and ship movements across Europe and even plans for the evacuation of Paris signaled the likelihood of war, Britain and France stepped in to resolve the dispute—at any cost. Accepting at face value Hitler's pledge that "this is the last territorial claim I have to make in Europe," they pushed for a negotiated settlement. When their representatives met with Italy and Germany at Munich in September 1938, they agreed in two short hours to turn over much of the Sudeten territory to Germany in exchange for a four-power guarantee of Czechoslovakia's new borders. The Czechs had little choice but to concede. For much of Europe, the fate of relatively few people and a small slice of territory seemed an acceptable price to avert war. The West relaxed and took comfort from Chamberlain's claims to have achieved "peace in our time." The words would take on a cruelly ironic ring the following year when Nazi troops stormed into Czechoslovakia.[73]

The United States' role in the crisis was secondary but still significant. Like Europeans, Americans feared the crisis might lead to war—"Munich hangs over our heads, like a thundercloud," journalist Heywood Broun observed.[74] They also fervently hoped it could be settled by negotiation, irrespective of the merits of the case. Roosevelt was of mixed mind. Privately he fretted about the sacrifice of principle and the danger of encouraging the appetite of aggressors. Without acknowledging that U.S. inaction had discouraged British and French firmness, he also privately

73. Sally Marks, "Munich: Hitler's Failure," in F. Kevin Simon, ed., *The David A. Sayre History Symposium Collected Lectures, 1985–1989* (Lexington, Ky., 1991), 150–57.
74. Barbara Farnham, "Roosevelt and the Munich Crisis—Insights from Prospect Theory," *Political Psychology* 13 (June 1992), 228n.

lamented that the Allies had left Czechoslovakia to "paddle its own ca-
noe" and predicted they would "wash the blood from their Judas Iscariot
hands."[75] At first, he contemplated the possibility of war with equanimity,
gratuitously advising a British diplomat in that contingency that the Allies
should pursue a defensive strategy and adding customarily vague and
qualified assurances of U.S. support. When war seemed imminent, however, he was moved to act. Still painfully aware that public opinion
sharply limited his freedom of action, he carefully avoided offers of mediation or arbitration. He actively promoted negotiations without taking a
position on the issues. He made clear to Britain and France—and
Hitler—that the United States "has no political involvements in Europe,
and will assume no obligations in the conduct of the present negotiation." When he learned that negotiations would take place, he tersely and
enthusiastically cabled Chamberlain: "Good Man." Like most Americans and Europeans, he was relieved by the Munich settlement and
shared Chamberlain's hopes for a "new order based on justice and on
law." The United States was not directly complicit in the Munich settlement, but it abetted the policies of Britain and France.[76]

From the outbreak of war in Europe into the next century, Munich
would be the synonym for appeasement, its inviolable lesson the folly of negotiating with aggressors. Like all historical events, its circumstances were
unique, its lessons of limited applicability. An angry and frustrated Hitler
viewed Munich not as victory but defeat. He had wanted war in 1938 but
was maneuvered into negotiations. Unable to wriggle out, he ultimately demurred from war because of the hesitance of his advisers and allies.[77] For
Britain and France, Munich, however unpalatable, was probably necessary. Both were weak militarily and in no position to fight. British public
opinion strongly opposed war, and the dominions were not willing to fight
for Czechoslovakia. The Western allies could not depend on the United
States or put much faith in Czech resistance. Munich bought them a year
to prepare for war. It was also made clear to the Western allies—belatedly to
be sure—the full extent of Hitler's ambition and deceitfulness.[78]

For all parties concerned, Munich was the turning point of the
pre–World War II era. Frustrated in 1938, Hitler made sure the next time

75. David Reynolds, *From Munich to Pearl Harbor: Roosevelt's America and the Origins of the Second World War* (Chicago, 2001), 42–48.
76. Farnham, "Roosevelt and the Munich Crisis," 208–20.
77. Gerhard Weinberg, *A World at Arms: A Global History of World War II* (New York, 1994), 27–28.
78. Donald Lammers, "Munich, 1938: A Crisis Nonpareil in British Foreign Policy," in Simon, *Sayre Lectures*, 167; McKercher, *Transition*, 252–57.

he got the war he wanted. Certain that the Western powers would not stop Hitler, Soviet dictator Joseph Stalin began to contemplate a deal with his archenemy. Having assumed they had bought peace at Munich, the British and French could not but be humiliated by Hitler's subsequent occupation of Czechoslovakia and invasion of Poland and felt compelled to act. In both Britain and France, Munich created a clarity that had not existed before.[79]

Munich was also a watershed for Roosevelt. Hitler's "truculent and unyielding" response to his appeals for equitable negotiations along with reports from U.S. diplomats in Europe persuaded him that the Nazi dictator could be neither trusted nor appeased.[80] He was a "wild man," the president mused, a "nut." Munich also convinced FDR that Hitler was responsible for Europe's drift toward war and might be bent on world domination. The president was no longer casually confident of a British and French victory in the event of war. The Italian prophet of air power, Giulio Douhet, had argued that by terrorizing civilian populations, bombing could win wars. The fear of German air power—put on such brutal display in Spain—paralyzed Europe during the Munich crisis. Roosevelt's exaggerated but very real concerns about German air superiority, in his own words, "completely reinvented our own international relations." For the first time since the days of the Monroe Doctrine, he concluded, the United States was vulnerable to foreign attack. Already alarmed by Germany's penetration of Latin America, he also feared that it might get air bases from which it could threaten the southern United States. "It's a very small world," he cautioned. The best way to prevent Germany and Italy from threatening the United States and keep the United States out of war, he reasoned, was to bolster Britain and France through air power. In the months after Munich, Roosevelt sought a policy of "unneutral rearmament" by securing massive increases in the production of aircraft and repealing the arms embargo to make them available to Britain and France.[81]

Once again, he failed to get the legislation he wanted. He had suffered a major political defeat in the 1937 Court fight, and his effort to save the New Deal by purging conservative Democrats in the 1938 elections backfired. Those legislators he sought to get rid of survived; the Republicans scored major gains. As a presumed lame duck, he was not in a strong position to move Congress. Now facing even greater opposition, he was loath to risk the prestige of his office on foreign policy legislation he badly

79. Gerhard Weinberg, "Munich After 50 Years," *Foreign Affairs* (Fall 1988), 167–73.
80. Farnham, "Roosevelt and the Munich Crisis," 216.
81. Reynolds, *Munich to Pearl Harbor*, 42–48.

needed. Remaining in the background, he entrusted the task to the ine-briated, infirm, and inept Senator Key Pittman, who predictably bungled it. Subsequent efforts to secure compromise legislation narrowly failed. In a last-ditch effort to salvage something, Roosevelt and Hull met with leg-islators at the White House on July 18. The secretary warned that the arms embargo "conferred gratuitous benefit on the probable aggressors." Ad-monishing that war in Europe was imminent, FDR averred that "I've fired my last shot. I think I ought to have another round in my belt." After a lengthy discussion and informal polling of the group, Vice President John Nance Garner advised the president, "Well, Captain, we may as well face the facts. You haven't got the votes, and that's all there is to it." It would take the harsh reality of war rather than the mere threat of it to push Congress and the nation beyond the position assumed in the mid-1930s.[82]

Roosevelt was similarly hamstrung in dealing with the tragic plight of German Jews. Upon taking power in 1933, the Nazi regime began system-atic persecution, imposing boycotts on businesses, proscribing Jews from certain jobs, and restricting their civil rights. Using as a pretext the shoot-ing of a German diplomat in Paris by a young German-Jewish refugee, it launched after Munich a full-scale campaign of terror. On November 9, 1938, while police did nothing, hooligans pillaged, looted, burned syna-gogues, and destroyed Jewish homes. A dozen Jews were killed, twenty thousand arrested, and much property destroyed. The shattered glass lit-tering the streets gave the name *Kristallnacht* (the night of broken glass) to the officially authorized rampage. To compound the injury, the govern-ment decreed that the damage be paid for by a tax levied on Jews. Reveal-ing its deeper intentions, it closed Jewish-owned stores and confiscated personal assets. In the wake of *Kristallnacht*, as many as 140,000 Jews sought to flee Germany.[83]

The Roosevelt administration could do little to help the victims of this forced diaspora. Although anti-Semitism remained a potent force in the United States, many Americans expressed outrage at Hitler's vicious as-sault and sympathy for its victims. FDR recalled his ambassador from Berlin for "consultation." He would not return. In numerous speeches, the president highlighted Hitler's treatment of Jews to make sharp moral distinctions between Nazi Germany and other states. But he could do nothing to stop the atrocities short of war. More poignantly, the United States was neither willing nor able to provide refuge for more than a

82. Doenecke, *Isolation to War*, 81; Leuchtenburg, *New Deal*, 292.
83. Kennedy, *Freedom from Fear*, 415–16.

handful of those fleeing Nazi persecution. The 1924 law permitted a total of only 150,000 immigrants a year, of which the Jewish quota was a small percentage. Germany permitted departing Jews to take only about four dollars with them, while U.S. law denied entry to those who might be a charge on the state, tightening the limits still further. Roosevelt stretched the law as best he could to admit more refugees. But the only real answer was a basic modification of policy, and at a time of continuing high unemployment there was little inclination to do that. Thousands of Jews were stranded at transit points across Europe. Some made it on ships to the Americas only to be denied permission to land. Returned to Europe, they fell under Hitler's sway again after the fall of France.[84]

IV

The war Hitler wanted at Munich came in 1939. In March, he scrapped the agreement negotiated there by invading Czechoslovakia. Mortified by this obvious contempt for their good-faith effort at accommodation, British and French leaders extended military commitments to Poland, Romania, Greece, and Turkey. Eager to act while he still had the military advantage and to avoid the mistakes of Napoleon and Kaiser Wilhelm, Hitler secured his eastern flank in late August by cutting a non-aggression deal with archenemy Stalin, adding a secret protocol that divided Eastern Europe into spheres of influence. Certain now that he had "the world in my pocket," he invaded Poland on September 1. Stunned by the Nazi-Soviet Pact, the Western allies declared war on Germany. It was now possible to speak of a Second World War.

Roosevelt's response differed sharply from Wilson's in 1914. In a radio address on September 3, he expressed hope that the United States could remain out of the war and vowed to do what he could to ensure that end. At the same time, he made clear that war in Europe could not but affect the United States. "When peace has been broken anywhere, peace of all countries everywhere is in danger," he averred, a statement that broke sharply with traditional U.S. thinking on national security. "I cannot ask that every American remain neutral in thought . . . ," he added, an oblique reference to Wilson's affirmation that Americans remain neutral in thought and deed. "Even a neutral cannot be asked to close his mind or conscience." On September 5, he dutifully invoked the Neutrality Acts, thereby shutting off the belligerents from access to war materials.[85]

---

84. A more critical analysis is David S. Wyman, *Paper Walls: America and the Refugee Crisis, 1938–1941* (Amherst, Mass., 1968).
85. Reynolds, *Munich to Pearl Harbor*, 63–64.

As always, Roosevelt accurately gauged the public mood. Many Americans were horrified by Hitler's persecution of the Jews, the full extent and ultimate aims of which were by no means clear at this point. They were shocked by his cynical disregard for an agreement presumably negotiated in good faith at Munich and angered by his sordid pact with Stalin. Germany's easy conquest of Czechoslovakia and Poland aroused vague but mounting concern that Hitler's ambitions and growing military power might threaten U.S. security and economic well-being. Thus while minority groups such as Irish, German, and Italian Americans harbored at least mild sympathies for the Axis, most Americans (84 percent in one poll) and especially the elites concerned about international issues favored an Allied victory. Still hopeful at the outbreak of war that this could be accomplished without direct U.S. intervention, they backed modest steps to aid the Allies while seeking to minimize the risks of war.

Roosevelt cleverly played on a mood he likely shared to secure the changes in the neutrality laws he had sought for months. Ingeniously—perhaps disingenuously—packaging his proposals as a "Peace Bill" to keep the United States out of war and insisting that he was reverting to traditional standards of neutrality, he warned that existing legislation permitted American ships to go into combat zones, where, as in 1917, they would be prey for enemy warships. Avoiding any hint that he was seeking to assist the Allies, he proposed to ban U.S. ships from war zones while also asking for repeal of the arms embargo. For the first time on a foreign policy issue, he put the full prestige of his office on the line and summoned all his considerable political skills. He called a special joint session of Congress and presented the legislation in person. His aides lobbied furiously to keep wobbly legislators in line and win over fence-sitters and Republican internationalists. The White House encouraged private citizens to organize nominally private groups to mount an intensive public campaign to win popular support and put pressure on Congress. Headed by legendary Kansas journalist William Allen White, the organization orchestrated speeches, radio addresses, rallies, and letter-writing campaigns. The measure naturally provoked powerful opposition from isolationists who saw through FDR's rhetoric and warned, correctly as it turned out, that aid to the Allies would lead to war. After nearly six weeks and more than a million words of often heated debate, Roosevelt in early November signed legislation repealing the arms embargo but extending cash-and-carry to all trade, still a major limitation on the president's ability to assist Britain and France. Nevertheless, it was another important turning point. The United States was again poised to be the arsenal of democracy. A measure promoted to keep the nation out of war provided the means to make it virtually a cobelligerent.[86]

The new relationship developed more slowly than Roosevelt had hoped in the fall and winter of 1939–40. After Hitler and Stalin partitioned Poland, and the Soviet Union swallowed up Estonia, Lithuania, and Latvia and invaded Finland, an extended lull followed. In this period of inaction and uncertainty known as the Phony War, the United States and Britain did not openly clash over neutrality issues as in 1914–17, but there were problems. Although cheered by repeal of the arms embargo, British officials objected to U.S. caution, insisting that, as in World War I, the Americans would fight to the last Briton and then step in to dictate the settlement. "God protect us from a German victory and an American peace" was a frequently heard complaint.[87] Roosevelt hoped that Allied purchases of war materials would stimulate U.S. rearmament and promote prosperity. Fearing a long war, the British husbanded their resources, especially cash. They placed small war-related orders. To the great irritation of Hull and the southern bloc in Congress, they cut back purchases of other items such as tobacco.

The next turning point came in the spring of 1940. In April, after six months of inactivity, Hitler unleashed blitzkrieg warfare in all its fury, employing air power, armor, ground forces, and fifth column subversion against Scandinavia, the neutral Low Countries of Western Europe, and France. The results stunned the world. Denmark capitulated without opposition; Norway fell within weeks. The Netherlands surrendered in four days, Belgium in less than a month. The greatest shock came in France. German forces skirted the supposedly impregnable Maginot Line. Exploiting the Allies' poor leadership and failure to coordinate forces, they sped down the Somme Valley and by late May reached the English Channel. The only flaw in the Nazi campaign was a delay that permitted the British miraculously to evacuate 220,000 of their own forces and an additional 120,000 French troops at Dunkirk. Enormous quantities of vital war materials were abandoned in France. In a ceremony rich with symbolism, a jubilant Hitler on June 22 accepted the French surrender in the same railway car in the Compiègne Forest where Germany had signed the armistice on November 11, 1918. In less than three months, Hitler had accomplished what Kaiser Wilhelm could not do in four years. Britain stood alone.

The fall of France had an enormous impact in the United States. It caught even well-informed Americans completely by surprise, and the

86. Ibid., 65–68.
87. Ibid., 73.

complacency that had marked the Phony War gave way to fear, even panic. For the first time since the early national period, Americans felt threatened by events abroad. Hitler's ruthless attacks on neutral nations, the collapse of France, and the speed, precision, and seemingly unchallengeable power of the Nazi war machine worked a great transformation in American attitudes toward the war and indeed toward foreign policy and national defense. A nation that had long taken its security for granted suddenly felt vulnerable.[88]

Roosevelt used the urgency created by these shocking events to push with a rare dispatch and certitude his policies of rearmament and aid to Britain. To build bipartisan backing, he brought into his cabinet Republican internationalists Henry L. Stimson and Chicago publisher Frank Knox to head the War and Navy departments, solidifying cabinet support for his policies and creating the closest thing the United States has had to a coalition government.[89] Resolving months of indecision and justifying his actions in terms of duty rather than ambition, he permitted his political stalwarts to arrange a "spontaneous" demonstration at the Democratic convention in favor of his tradition-shattering nomination for a third term. In a dramatic speech in Charlottesville, Virginia, in June 1940, he denounced Italy's intervention in the war, warned that the United States could not remain free in a world dominated by the "contemptuous, unpitying masters of other continents," and vowed to "extend to the opponents of force the material resources of this nation." He secured $10.5 billion from Congress for rearmament. He overrode War Department opposition to gain the release of substantial quantities of arms and ammunition to be sold to private companies and then through cash-and-carry to Britain.[90]

Roosevelt also took unprecedented steps to mobilize public support. The White House used the Federal Bureau of Investigation not only to monitor subversive groups but also, through such means as illegal wiretaps, to secure information about the activities of anti-interventionists, giving it a marked political advantage in a major foreign policy debate. The administration closely followed public opinion polls, sometimes shaping the responses by formulating the questions. To undermine Catholic opposition, Undersecretary of State Welles encouraged the U.S. hierarchy to deliver speeches supporting aid to Britain and then distributed the

88. Marvin R. Zahniser, "Rethinking the Significance of Disaster: The United States and the Fall of France," International History Review 14 (May 1992), 252–76.

89. Weinberg, World at Arms, 153.

90. Leuchtenburg, New Deal, 302; Divine, Reluctant Belligerent, 90.

speeches to the nationwide Catholic press.[91] Pressure groups organized around causes or specific issues had existed since the turn of the century, but for the first time in 1940–41 they played a central role in a debate on a vital issue. And for the first time they had intimate ties with government. In the spring of 1940, Roosevelt encouraged White to form the Committee to Defend America by Aiding the Allies (CDA) to educate the nation about the fascist threat and mobilize backing for aid to Britain. The Committee eventually had six hundred chapters and thousands of members. It held local and regional meetings, wrote newspaper and magazine articles, sponsored radio messages, and petitioned Congress. The extent of this ostensibly private group's ties with government was not known at the time. In fact, the administration often suggested what it should do and furnished inside information, making it appear that the government was responding to popular demand, a practice that raises serious questions about the democratic process.[92] Those internationalists who believed the fascist threat demanded an immediate declaration of war formed in June 1940 a splinter organization, the Century Group, named after the posh New York men's club where they met. Later reincarnated as the Fight for Freedom Committee, it supplanted the CDA as the major pressure group as the nation moved closer to war.[93]

Pressure groups also spearheaded the opposition. In July, Yale University students and midwestern businessmen formed the America First Committee. As the name suggests, America Firsters ardently opposed intervention—and aid to Britain, which, they argued, would inevitably lead to intervention. They saw the war not as a great ideological conflict but as another round in the endless struggle among Europeans for power and empire. The United States, they insisted, had no stake in that conflict. Some like aviator hero Charles Lindbergh preached accommodation with Hitler. Others minimized the German threat and advocated defense of the Western Hemisphere. America First was an unwieldy coalition of strange bedfellows, businessmen, old progressives and leftists,

91. Charles R. Gallagher, "Fighting Fascists in the Sunshine State: Bishop Joseph P. Hurley and American Interventionism in Florida, 1940–1941," paper presented at the Florida Historians' Conference, March 13, 1998. Steven Casey, *Cautious Crusade: Franklin D. Roosevelt, American Public Opinion, and the War Against Nazi Germany* (New York, 2001) is the fullest, most up-to-date analysis.

92. Melvin Small, *Democracy and Diplomacy: The Impact of Domestic Politics on U.S. Foreign Policy, 1789–1794* (Baltimore, Md., 1996), 70–71; Lise Namikas, "The Committee to Defend America and the Debate Between Internationalists and Interventionists, 1939–1941," *Historian* 61 (Summer 1999), 843–63.

93. Mark Chadwin, *The Hawks of World War II* (Chapel Hill, N.C., 1968).

and some strongly anti-Jewish groups. Many blamed Roosevelt's interventionist policies on a personal lust for power. These various groups created local and regional offices, organized rallies, sent out mailings, and propagandized Congress.[94]

The most important development in the fall of 1940 was the famous destroyers-bases deal in which the United States "gave" Britain fifty old destroyers in exchange for leases for U.S. naval bases on British possessions in the Western Hemisphere. Initiating a new period of cautious cooperation with the United States and what would become a special personal relationship with FDR, Britain's new prime minister, Winston Churchill, first raised the issue in May, warning of his nation's declining cash reserves and its desperate need for military equipment, especially for ships to meet an increasingly urgent German threat in the Atlantic. When Roosevelt deflected these requests, Churchill warned in July that "the whole fate of the war may be decided by this minor and easily remediable factor."[95] Although troubled by Churchill's reputation as a heavy drinker, FDR was encouraged by his firm leadership and was urged on by hawks in his cabinet and the Century Group. Increasingly optimistic that Britain could hold out, he nevertheless faced major obstacles. Alarmed by the president's earlier efforts to make arms available to Britain, Congress had forbidden such transfers unless the items in question had been declared by U.S. military leaders obsolete and of no value to the national defense.

Roosevelt ingeniously—some have argued illegally—got around the various obstacles. He encouraged White's group to stimulate debate, making it appear that the idea came from the public. He headed off possible domestic challenge by having top military leaders declare the ships obsolete. To sweeten the deal for Congress, the public, and the U.S. military, he persuaded a wary and reluctant but ultimately compliant Churchill to agree to ninety-nine-year leases for U.S. bases on eight British territories from Central America to Newfoundland and to pledge publicly that Britain would not surrender its fleet. Through Century Group intermediaries, he secured from his Republican opponent Wendell Willkie a private pledge not to make the arrangement a campaign issue. In his boldest—and most legally

94. Wayne Cole, *America First: The Battle Against Intervention, 1940–1941* (Madison, Wisc., 1953). For its failure in the South, see Joseph A. Fry, *Dixie Looks Abroad: The South and U.S. Foreign Relations, 1789–1973* (Baton Rouge, La., 2002), 204–5. The best study of the anti-interventionists is Justus D. Doenecke, *Storm on the Horizon: The Challenge to American Intervention, 1939–1941* (Lanham, Md., 2000.)

95. Reynolds, *Munich to Pearl Harbor*, 84.

questionable—move, he avoided Congress by using an executive order, citing a 1936 Supreme Court ruling that in foreign affairs the executive was "the sole organ of the federal government" and did not require congressional authority to act. The deal did not provide immediate tangible assistance either to Britain or the United States. It was months before the ships would be available for use or construction could begin on the bases. But it gave a powerful morale boost to embattled Britain at one of the most crucial periods in its history—"more precious than rubies," Churchill called the rusty destroyers. It stretched the president's constitutional authority beyond generally acknowledged bounds, establishing a precedent that would be used repeatedly in the next half century. It was, in Churchill's words, a "decidedly unneutral act," pushing the United States into a new phase of non-belligerency—not yet at war but closely tied to Britain—and a giant step closer to war.[96]

The election campaign of 1940 in a curious way may have set back policies both candidates preferred. Willkie generally agreed with Roosevelt's foreign policy; at first he faithfully adhered to his pledge not to challenge aid to Britain. As his campaign lagged, however, he let fly with charges that Roosevelt's handling of policies would lead the nation into war. The president responded with a typically Rooseveltian obfuscation that he likely later regretted. "I have said this before," he proclaimed in Boston, "but I shall say it again and again. Your boys are not going to be sent into any foreign wars," calculatingly omitting the phrase in the written speech "except in case of foreign attack." "That hypocritical son of a bitch!" Willkie exclaimed. "That's going to beat me."[97]

The war itself rather than FDR's shenanigans likely dictated Roosevelt's victory and unprecedented third term. Americans watched—and listened— in late 1940 as Britons heroically held out against furious German air attacks in the Battle of Britain. Radio played a vital role. "You burned the city of London in our houses and we felt the flames that burned it," poet Archibald MacLeish told legendary radio commentator Edward R. Murrow, who reported the Battle of Britain firsthand.[98] Britain's stubborn resistance created with Americans a shared identity and a growing belief that with U.S. aid it could survive. Polls indicated a sharp increase in Americans' support for aid to Britain even though they recognized it entailed greater risks of war. With war looming, Roosevelt's experience gave him a distinct edge over his contender.

96. Ibid., 85–87.
97. Kennedy, *Freedom from Fear*, 463.
98. Pike, *Good Neighbor Policy*, 235.

On December 8, 1940, while indulging in a postcampaign cruise aboard the USS *Tuscaloosa*, FDR received by seaplane an urgent letter from Churchill. Ambassador Lord Lothian had already bluntly informed American reporters: "Britain's broke. It's your money we want." Churchill spelled out the same message in more delicate language and greater detail. He stressed the "solid identity of interests" between the two nations fighting tyranny and highlighted the dangers of mounting shipping losses in the Atlantic. Above all, he warned, "the moment approaches when we shall no longer be able to pay cash for shipping and other supplies."[99]

Recognizing the urgency in Churchill's tone, Roosevelt responded with uncharacteristic dispatch. While at sea, he read the message over and over, contemplating a response. At a press conference on December 17, as though extemporizing, he floated a trial balloon, in best Rooseveltian fashion talking about getting rid of the "silly, foolish old dollar sign," noting that it would be better to lend or lease supplies to Britain than leave them in storage in the United States, and spinning a homey yarn about the man who lent his garden hose to a neighbor whose house was on fire, expecting nothing in return but to get the hose back.[100]

While his advisers formulated the details of the remarkable innovation that would be called lend-lease, FDR on December 29 enunciated what was much later labeled the Roosevelt Doctrine. In a radio address billed as a talk on "national security," he challenged head-on traditional views that the nation was not threatened by events abroad. In the starkest of terms, he portrayed a world divided between good and evil, warning that Axis tyranny endangered the basic freedoms Americans held most dear. The Western Hemisphere was threatened, he emphasized, by air power and subversion. As guardian of the Atlantic, Britain must be defended. There could be no negotiations with a "gang of outlaws," he insisted. Reiterating his desire to keep the United States out of war, he spoke of "an emergency as serious as war itself" and called upon the nation to become "the great arsenal of democracy."[101]

Fully aware that the destroyers-bases deal had stretched the Constitution to the limit—he is said to have feared impeachment—this time he went to Congress to get the extraordinary power he sought. Cleverly packaged as a "Bill to Promote the Defense of the United States," the legislation gave the

99. Churchill to FDR, December 7, 1940, in Warren F. Kimball, ed., *Churchill and Roosevelt: The Complete Correspondence* (3 vols., Princeton, N.J., 1984), 1:102–9.
100. Warren F. Kimball, *The Most Unsordid Act: Lend-Lease, 1941* (Baltimore, Md., 1969), 120–21.
101. Reynolds, *Munich to Pearl Harbor*, 106–7.

president unprecedented authority to "sell, transfer, exchange, lease, lend or otherwise dispose of" any "war material" to any nation whose defense was deemed vital to the defense of the United States." To give it a patriotic ring and counter anti-British sentiments from Irish Americans in House Majority Leader John McCormack's Boston district, it was even more artfully designated HR 1776, although that historic number was not due to be attached to the next piece of legislation.[102]

In FDR's words, the lend-lease bill was "argued in every newspaper, on every wave length—over every cracker barrel in all the land."[103] Recognizing that it had firm public backing and solid majorities in both houses, the administration took the high road, giving the opposition ample time to develop its arguments and for the most part staying above the fray. As before, it justified the grant of extraordinary powers to the president on grounds of national emergency. It continued to insist that aid to Britain was the best way to stay out of war. Its star witness, no less than Wendell Willkie, warned Americans that passage was the only "chance to defend liberty without themselves going to war." The opposition mounted a furious counterattack—the last gasp of 1930s isolationism—warning that expanded aid to Britain would necessitate convoys, which inevitably would lead to war, and protesting that the bill would confer dictatorial authority on an already too powerful president. At times the discussion got ugly, as when Montana senator Burton K. Wheeler called lend-lease the New Deal's Triple A foreign policy that would plow under every fourth American boy. After weeks of heated debate, the bill passed in early March 1941 by large and generally partisan majorities.[104]

Lend-lease did represent a huge step toward war. It skirted the cash-and-carry provisions of the Neutrality Acts as well as Johnson Act prohibitions against loans; it addressed directly the critical problem of the British dollar shortage. This "Declaration of Interdependence," as the London *Economist* called it, shed the last pretense of U.S. neutrality, opening the nation's warehouses to what was now a de facto ally and providing a mechanism for the first U.S. foreign aid program. It was not "the most unsordid act," as Churchill in a flight of rhetoric once called it (he of all people knew better).[105] Roosevelt deliberately left unstated what was

102. Kimball, *Most Unsordid Act*, 151–52.
103. George C. Herring Jr., "Experiment in Foreign Aid: Lend-Lease, 1941–1945," (doctoral dissertation, University of Virginia, 1965), 19.
104. Kimball, *Most Unsordid Act*, 195–229.
105. Warren F. Kimball, *The Juggler: Franklin D. Roosevelt as Wartime Statesman* (Princeton, 1991), 49–57, for State Department efforts to pry open British imperial trade in return for lend-lease.

expected in return, but within weeks after the bill passed it was clear that the supplies would not be an outright gift, and the State Department's dogged quest for bases and trade concessions in exchange alarmed top British officials. Given the woeful state of U.S. preparedness, lend-lease for the short term provided little help. But it offered reassurance that substantial assistance would soon be under way, a huge boost to British spirits. As the isolationist opposition had warned, it also brought to the forefront the issue of convoys. It would do no good to send supplies to Britain only to see them end up on the bottom of the ocean.

As was his custom, after a bold move Roosevelt reverted to caution. British shipping losses in the Battle of the Atlantic increased to perilous proportions in the spring of 1941, bringing urgent pleas from Churchill and some FDR advisers for convoys, but the president responded with half measures. He was ill much of the time, and not up to another political battle. Although the public increasingly accepted the risk of war, a solid majority still hoped to stay out. Opponents of lend-lease had warned that aid to Britain would inevitably lead to convoys, and the president recognized that any overt move in that direction would bring down their wrath on him. In any event, the U.S. Navy was far from ready at this point to assume convoy duties. Thus FDR moved by stealth and indirection. Even before lend-lease had passed Congress, he authorized top-secret joint planning exercises between U.S. and British military officials, one result of which was agreement, in the event of a two-front war, on a Europe-first strategy. In April, he stretched the U.S. defense perimeter to 26° west longitude, far out into the North Atlantic, and shifted twenty ships from the Pacific fleet. Avoiding any word or deed even hinting at convoys, he authorized U.S. ships to "patrol" this area, report to the British the presence of Axis vessels, and use force if they threatened American shipping. Disguising the significance of his move with another folksy history lesson, he compared the patrols to Old West scouts sent ahead of the wagon train to warn of possible ambush. Viewing Danish colony Greenland as a vital base for British and American shipping and vulnerable to a German takeover, he brought the frigid island under U.S. protection.[106]

Although it was not entirely clear at the time, FDR's stealthy moves represented a sharp extension of traditional U.S. concepts of national defense. Indeed, in 1940–41, Americans began to think and talk of national security in ways they had not since the early republic. Expansion of the defense zone deep into the western Atlantic marked a sharp break with

106. Reynolds, *Munich to Pearl Harbor*, 127–29.

tradition.[107] In a major speech on May 27, the president gave his listeners a geography lesson, warning ominously of Hitler's global ambitions and expressing special concern about the threat to island outposts such as Greenland, Iceland, and the Azores from which Nazi Germany might control the Atlantic and even mount air attacks against North and South America. He also outlined a crudely formed doctrine of preemption. With new military technologies, he warned, "if you hold your fire until you see the whites of his eyes, you will never know what hit you! Our Bunker Hill of tomorrow may be several thousand miles from Boston, Massachusetts." Although the speech won widespread praise, Roosevelt did not follow with new steps other than declaring a vague and indeterminate state of unlimited national emergency and beginning quiet, behind-the-scenes negotiations to bring Iceland under U.S. protection. By June 1941, he had extended the nation's defense perimeter well out into the North Atlantic.[108]

As the threat of war increased after 1939, U.S. officials increasingly feared for the security of the Western Hemisphere. German and Italian immigration into Latin America in the interwar years along with a German trade offensive Hull labeled "cut throat trouble breeding" aroused fears of an Axis fifth column.[109] Germany's stunning military victories in the spring of 1940 transformed concern into outright alarm. Inexperienced intelligence agents and private informants such as the Cuba-based novelist Ernest Hemingway deluged Washington with frightening reports of German influence. Partly from genuine fear, partly to build support for his policies, FDR in a series of 1941 Fireside Chats warned of the danger next door, one time even divulging the existence of a secret map—later proven bogus—demonstrating Hitler's plan to seize Latin America before attacking the United States. Exaggerated U.S. fears reflected the insecurity that gripped the nation after the fall of France and a distrust of Latin governments presumably too complacent or weak to defend themselves. Some Latin leaders suspected what they considered undue U.S. concern about their security; others saw a chance to exploit U.S. fears for economic and political gain.

Concern for hemispheric defense provided the decisive inducement for a remarkably conciliatory U.S. response to yet another oil dispute with

107. Waldo Heinrichs, *Threshold of War: Franklin D. Roosevelt and American Entry into World War II* (New York, 1988), 46.
108. Ibid., 90; Reynolds, *Munich to Pearl Harbor*, 126–30.
109. Max Paul Friedman, "Specter of a Nazi Threat: United States–Colombian Relations, 1939–1945," *Americas* 56 (April 2000), 577.

Mexico. When President Lázaro Cárdenas nationalized foreign-owned oil companies in 1938, Hull firmly reminded Mexico of its international obligations. Oilmen in the United States organized a boycott of Mexican oil. But when the dispute dragged on, Ambassador Josephus Daniels urged conciliation. "It is always noble in the strong to be generous, and generous, and generous," he told the president.[110] Roosevelt had little interest in backing the oil companies, members in good standing of that group he had branded "economic royalists." With Mexico seeking to sell oil to Germany and Italy, he saw urgent need for a generous settlement. After months of discussion, the two nations in November 1941 established a joint board to evaluate confiscated oil properties and set terms for payment. To sweeten the deal, the United States extended loans to Mexico.[111]

The administration developed a multifaceted effort to expand U.S. influence in the hemisphere. It negotiated arrangements for naval and air bases across Latin America. To counter German influence with Latin militaries and promote hemispheric military cooperation, it sent military advisory missions to numerous Latin American nations and invited their officers to study in U.S. military schools. The United States also expanded hemispheric trade by providing loans through the Export-Import Bank for the purchase of U.S. surplus commodities and to fund development projects such as a Brazilian steel mill. To the great annoyance of some hemispheric governments, U.S. officials compiled blacklists of firms and individuals suspected of ties with the Axis. Especially fearful that airliners might be used as bombers, the United States pressed Latin governments to eliminate German influence in commercial aviation. Under intense U.S. pressure, Brazil took control of German-owned airlines operating within its territory and got rid of all German personnel. In June 1940, with U.S. encouragement, Pan American Airways pulled off a virtual "coup" by firing en masse German pilots and mechanics employed by its Colombian subsidiary and replacing them with North Americans.[112]

United States officials also mounted a diplomatic offensive to promote hemispheric security. At a 1939 conference in Panama, the delegates created a "neutrality zone" extending from three hundred to one thousand miles around the hemisphere in which non-American nations were forbidden from committing hostile acts. At Havana the following year, in the

110. Kyle Longley, *In the Eagle's Shadow: The United States and Latin America* (Wheeling, Ill., 2002), 173.

111. Howard F. Cline, *The United States and Mexico* (New York, 1963), 229–48.

112. Erik Benson, "Flying Down to Rio: American Commercial Aviation, the Good Neighbor Policy, and World War II, 1939–1945," *Essays in Economic and Business History* 19 (2001), 61–73; Friedman, "Specter," 565.

atmosphere of panic after the fall of France, the United States sought to prevent Germany from seizing the territories of its European victims. The Act of Havana provided that any American republic (namely the United States) might step in and establish a provisional regime should a hemispheric territory be threatened by an outside power. The delegates also adopted a resolution providing that aggression against any American nation would be considered an attack on all.

The most innovative instrument of the administration's prewar diplomatic offensive was a vast expansion of the cultural programs created under the Good Neighbor policy. In August 1940, Roosevelt named Nelson Rockefeller, thirty-two-year-old grandson of the oil baron, to head the Office for the Coordination of Commercial and Cultural Relations Between the American Republics. Within a short time, the energetic Rockefeller created a remarkable range of programs to counter German influence and sell the North American way of life. His office distributed articles from U.S. newspapers and magazines and itself produced *En Guardia*, a magazine distributed throughout Latin America. It purchased advertising space in pro-U.S. newspapers to promote U.S. radio programs and blacklist stations carrying Nazi broadcasts. It sponsored art exhibitions and musical concerts. A tour of the east coast of Latin America by the outspoken anti-fascist maestro Arturo Toscanini and the NBC Symphony in 1940 met such a triumphal response that a U.S. diplomat hailed it as a "United States' 'fifth column.' "[113] The State Department later conceded, obviously with a touch of envy, that Rockefeller had pulled off "the greatest outpouring of propagandistic material by a state ever."[114]

As the United States edged closer to war with Germany in the summer of 1941, tensions with Japan increased sharply. The two nations held divergent visions for the future of East and Southeast Asia. Especially because of the vulnerability of resource-rich European colonies in Southeast Asia, the fall of France for each tightly linked the European war with that in Asia, making resolution of differences far more difficult. In addition, in attempting to influence their adversary's actions, they repeatedly misjudged each other, taking steps that produced results opposite from those intended. Two nations that did not want war and had every reason to avoid it moved inexorably in that direction.

113. Donald C. Meyer, "Toscanini and the Good Neighbor Policy: The NBC Orchestra's 1940 South American Tour," *American Music* 18 (Fall 2000), 238; Emily Rosenberg, *Spreading the American Dream: American Economic and Cultural Expansionism, 1890–1945* (New York, 1982), 207–9.
114. Peter H. Smith, *Talons of the Eagle: Dynamics of U.S.–Latin American Relations* (New York, 1996), 85.

China remained the most difficult issue. After early, decisive victories, Japan's war machine bogged down in the vast hinterland of China, unable to win the war and, because of the vast blood, treasure, and pride already invested, unwilling to liquidate it. Frustration brought increasingly harsh treatment of Chinese in occupied areas, provoking outrage in other countries. For many Americans, by the late 1930s China had become an important cause. The United States had modest economic interests there, and some businessmen still clung to dreams of a vast China market. Japanese aggression evoked widespread sympathy for the Chinese people. Lobbying groups like United China Relief depicted a valiant and overmatched China "holding the western ramparts for us and for the democratic way of life in the world."[115] Leading citizens like Stimson had long believed that because it depended on the United States for crucial resources, Japan was a prime target for economic pressure. As the war dragged on, there were growing demands for U.S. aid to China and sanctions against Japan. Roosevelt and Hull, to whom the president assigned major responsibility for East Asian matters, were more cautious. With Munich still fresh in their memories, they did not want to appear to be appeasing Japan. But with war in Europe looming and the nation grossly unprepared, they did not want to risk war either. Thus in July 1939, Hull indicated that the 1911 commercial treaty with Japan would be permitted to lapse in six months. When that happened in early 1940, he announced that trade would henceforth be on a day-to-day basis. The administration hoped to restrain Japan by keeping it guessing regarding U.S. intentions.[116]

A Japanese threat to resource-rich Southeast Asia led to the imposition of sanctions. Germany's lightning thrust through Western Europe in 1940 inextricably bound together heretofore separate wars on different continents. The defeat or preoccupation of the European colonial powers left French Indochina and the Dutch and British East Indies exposed. These colonies lay astride vital shipping lanes. They possessed a bounty of raw materials such as oil, rubber, tin, and tungsten that provided the sinews of modern war. Control of Southeast Asia offered Japan the means to tighten the noose around China and free itself from dependence on the west for vital resources. Thus, in the summer of 1940, Tokyo announced plans for a Greater East Asia Co-Prosperity Sphere, a wordy—and transparent—euphemism for economic and political hegemony in East and Southeast Asia. It compelled France to stop the flow of supplies to

115. T. Christopher Jespersen, *American Images of China, 1931–1949* (Stanford, Calif., 1996), 56.

116. Doenecke, *Isolation to War*, 120–21.

China through Indochina, and Britain to close the Burma Road. Shortly after, it demanded of France air bases and permission to station troops in northern Indochina.[117]

The prospect of Japanese encroachment on Southeast Asia in the fall of 1940 raised alarm bells in Washington. Loss of the region's resources could further cripple Britain's already reeling effort to resist Germany and hamper U.S. rearmament. Now secretary of war, Stimson, along with Treasury Secretary Morgenthau and other hawks in the cabinet and Congress, insisted that full-fledged sanctions would compel Japan to scale back its ambitions. Even ambassador to Japan Joseph Grew, who had opposed sanctions, now agreed upon the importance of sending a clear message to Tokyo. At a time when the United States was preoccupied with events in Europe, Roosevelt and Hull still refused to risk a complete break. The administration again adopted limited measures in hopes of checking further aggression without war, using legislation that permitted the president to hold back items vital for national defense to impose an embargo on aviation gasoline and high-grade scrap iron. Two months later, after Japan had moved into northern Indochina and amidst rumblings of a possible Japanese alliance with Germany, the embargo was expanded to include all scrap iron and steel.[118]

Japan and the United States now found themselves caught up in a tangle of miscalculations and conflicting aspirations. Even all-out sanctions have a bad track record historically, and a limited embargo did enough to alarm the Japanese without altering their behavior. Eager to capitalize on Germany's stunning military success and enticed by irresistible opportunities in Southeast Asia, Japan just days after the United States announced sanctions joined a Tripartite Pact with Italy and Germany, one article of which was plainly directed against the United States. Japanese leaders hoped to intimidate Washington into acquiescing in their grand design for Asia—"Only a *firm response* will prevent war." As with U.S. sanctions, the result was the opposite of what was intended. The pact linked Japan with America's de facto enemy Germany in what FDR called an "unholy alliance" out to "dominate and enslave the entire human race," thereby stiffening U.S. resolve.[119] In late 1940, the United States expanded the embargo to include iron ore, pig iron, copper, and brass, deliberately leaving oil as the ultimate bargaining

---

117. Divine, *Reluctant Belligerent*, 96–97.
118. Ibid., 98–99.
119. Peter Mauch, "Revisiting Nomura's Diplomacy: Ambassador Nomura's Role in the Japanese-American Negotiations, 1941," *Diplomatic History* 28 (June 2004), 358, 362.

instrument. Through major miscalculations on both sides, Japan and the United States were fixed on a collision course.

An effort to resolve differences in early 1941 only compounded them. Through two well-meaning but ill-informed American missionaries in Japan, word reached Washington in January that Japan wished to improve relations with the United States and would even make major concessions. Shortly after, a new Japanese ambassador, Adm. Kichisaburo Nomura, opened extended discussion with Hull, frequently meeting in the secretary's Washington apartment. Nomura had served as naval attaché in Washington during World War I and had a far more realistic assessment than many of his cohorts of the costs of war with the United States. He viewed the pursuit of expansion in Asia and accommodation with the United States as like "chasing rabbits in two different directions" and was committed to the latter.[120] Despite good intentions, his efforts were unavailing. He and Hull often talked past each other. They spoke without an interpreter, and Nomura's limited understanding of English at times misled him regarding the progress that had been made. Differing translations of documents added to the problems. Nomura led his superiors to believe Hull had approved a draft agreement far more generous than was the case. They thus sought additional concessions. When Nomura came back with a much tougher proposal, Hull felt betrayed; when the Japanese realized the real U.S. position, they were angered. This diplomatic imbroglio, the result of sometimes amateurish diplomacy and a language barrier, made clear the extent of the impasse and heightened an already substantial distrust on both sides.

Hitler's bold, indeed reckless, invasion of the Soviet Union on June 22, 1941, a massive assault sending 3.2 million men along a two-thousand-mile front, offered new opportunities for the United States—and new perils. By linking events on three continents, it helped clarify U.S. policies and bring the nation closer to war. The immediate effect, of course, was to ease pressures on Britain. Thus, despite his long-standing and often virulent opposition to Bolshevism, Churchill immediately offered to assist Moscow. "If Hitler invaded hell," the prime minister declared, "he would at least make a favourable reference to the Devil."[121] Roosevelt also welcomed the respite afforded Britain and feared the consequences of a Soviet collapse. But Soviet-American relations had deteriorated sharply since the brief thaw of 1933–34, and there was strong opposition to aiding

120. Ibid., 359.
121. Warren F. Kimball, *Forged in War: Churchill, Roosevelt, and the Second World War* (New York, 1999), 90–91.

Russia. After Stalin's bloody purges of dissidents, the Nazi-Soviet pact, and the rape of Poland, many Americans viewed him, in the words of *Time* magazine, as "a sort of unwashed Genghis Khan" with "blood dripping from his fingertips"; the only difference between Stalin and Hitler, some critics quipped, was the size of their respective mustaches.[122] Many of Roosevelt's top military advisers doubted that the Russians could withstand the Nazi onslaught and feared that equipment sent them would be wasted. From the outset, FDR seems to have believed that Soviet survival was the key to Germany's defeat, which, in turn, he saw as essential to U.S. security. Thus he agreed to assist the Soviet Union but offered only limited aid and required payment in return.

Following Germany's invasion of Russia, the United States and Britain drew closer to each other, and FDR moved closer to active participation in the Battle of the Atlantic. On July 1, the United States assumed responsibility for the protection of Iceland, a key refueling station for British and U.S. ships and the island outpost guarding the Denmark Strait, through which German ships passed into the western Atlantic. At about the same time, FDR authorized the navy to begin planning for convoys. In August, Roosevelt and Churchill met secretly in Argentia, Newfoundland, appropriately aboard vessels of war at a naval base turned over to the United States in return for the destroyers. At this first summit, amidst the paraphernalia of war and the pomp of Anglo-American unity—including a joint religious service in which "Onward, Christian Soldiers" was sung—they agreed on the Atlantic Charter, a broad statement of principles upon which the war would be fought. Roosevelt also committed the United States to assume responsibility for convoys in the western Atlantic on September 1.[123]

An incident in early September provided the pretext for implementing this promise, making the United States in effect a cobelligerent. Uneager for conflict with America while the war in Russia still raged, Hitler had ordered his U-boat commanders to exercise maximum restraint. On September 4, the destroyer USS *Greer*, en route to Iceland, was tracking a submarine and radioing its position via Washington and London to British aircraft on the scene. When the aircraft attacked with depth charges, the U-boat retaliated by firing torpedoes at the *Greer*. The torpedoes missed, but an opportunist FDR used an allegedly unprovoked attack to escalate

---

122. George C. Herring Jr., *Aid to Russia, 1941–1946: Strategy, Diplomacy, the Origins of the Cold War* (New York, 1973), 22.
123. Theodore Wilson, *The First Summit: Roosevelt and Churchill at Placentia Bay, 1941* (rev. ed., Lawrence, Kans., 1991).

the naval war. He concealed the extent to which the *Greer* had provoked the attack, thus leaving himself open to later—entirely justified—charges of deception. Rather, he cast the incident in terms of an imminent and urgent German threat to freedom of the seas. Denouncing the U-boats as "rattlesnakes," he insisted the navy must not wait until they struck before taking action to "crush them." He used the occasion to assume responsibility for convoys as far as Iceland and to announce a policy of "shoot on sight."[124] The U.S. Navy was now involved in an undeclared naval war in the Atlantic. In mid-October, a torpedo hit the destroyer *Kearney*, killing eleven seamen. Two weeks later, another torpedo sank the *Reuben James*, taking the lives of 115 sailors. Almost as an afterthought, Congress in mid-November repealed the major provisions of the Neutrality Acts.

Concern for the survival of the USSR also hardened the standoff with Japan.[125] Japanese leaders disagreed whether to move north against Soviet Russia or into Southeast Asia, but their first response to the Russo-German war was to secure from French colonial authorities the right to station troops in southern Indochina. For the United States and Britain, Russia and the Atlantic had priority over East Asia, but they recognized that a Japanese move in either direction would threaten these more vital interests. They thus sought to deter Japan through economic and military pressure without provoking war. In late July, the United States broke off the now desultory Hull-Nomura discussions. Aware that a Japanese military presence in southern Indochina directly threatened the Philippines, it beefed up the defense of islands whose independence it had pledged just seven years earlier. To bolster Chinese resistance, it sent a lend-lease mission to China and agreed to provide more than three hundred aircraft and to help train pilots. Japan's move into Indochina gave hawks in Roosevelt's cabinet the upper hand in the ongoing struggle over economic pressure. Still certain that full sanctions would force the Japanese to give in, they secured on July 25 an order to freeze Japanese assets in the United States and used the resulting licenses and controls to turn the oil spigot off and on as they chose. As actually implemented by hard-liners in the bureaucracy, the freezing order became a de facto embargo of all trade with Japan. With a mere eighteen months' oil supply in reserve, Japan had to regain access to U.S. sources or secure alternative supplies in Southeast Asia.[126]

By the late summer of 1941, the two nations had reached an impasse. Predictably, even a complete shut-off of trade refused to bend Japan to

124. Kennedy, *Freedom from Fear*, 498–99, provides a staunch defense of FDR's actions.
125. Heinrichs, *Threshold of War*, 92.
126. Doenecke, *Isolation to War*, 138–39.

America's will, but the oil embargo forced it to choose between concessions or war. Some leaders recognized that a long war with the United States could be disastrous, and this brought about frantic, if sharply constrained, efforts to reach a modus vivendi. From July until late November, each side issued various proposals that were dutifully discussed with no tangible result. The younger officers now driving Japanese policy were proud, aggressive inheritors of a samurai spirit that favored death over surrender. The government offered some concessions on Southeast Asia and the Tripartite Pact in return for restoration of U.S. trade, but it refused to withdraw from China.

Already on the verge of conflict with Germany and not prepared for a war on one front, much less on two, a more prudent United States might have pursued at least a temporary arrangement with Japan even at the expense of China. But U.S. officials remained adamant on that issue. Hull continued to handle most of the negotiations on the U.S. side, and he had come to doubt the sincerity of the Japanese—as "crooked as a barrel of fish hooks," he once labeled them. Welles viewed a settlement without China as like the play *Hamlet* without "the character of Hamlet."[127] For their own reasons, Churchill and Chiang Kai-shek denounced concessions to Japan as tantamount to appeasement that might demoralize the anti-Axis coalition at a critical point in the war. FDR was especially concerned about Russia, which was again reeling before the German advance. The discussions thus produced no breakthrough. The Japanese had already decided that if there was no settlement by November 30, they would go to war.

War came on December 7, 1941. In a desperate effort to solve their problems and, they hoped, intimidate the United States into acquiescing to their East Asian design, the Japanese mounted a bold attack by carrier aircraft against the U.S. naval and military bases at Pearl Harbor. They achieved complete surprise, catching the Americans asleep on a Sunday morning, with devastating results, killing 2,500 soldiers and sailors, destroying 152 of 230 aircraft, sinking five battleships, and damaging numerous other vessels.

Ever since that day of "infamy," Roosevelt haters, revisionists, and conspiracy theorists have charged that the president through MAGIC intercepts and other sources knew of the attack but withheld critical information to ensure its success, thereby pushing an unwilling nation into an unnecessary war. Like other conspiracy theories, this one will not go away.[128] Such

---

127. Mauch, "Nomura's Diplomacy," 375.
128. A statement of the conspiracy thesis can be found in John Toland, *Infamy: Pearl Harbor and Its Aftermath* (New York, 1982). The most persuasive account is Gordon W. Prange, *At Dawn We Slept: The Untold Story of Pearl Harbor* (New York, 1981).

charges ignore the skill of the enemy. The attack was brilliantly planned and executed. It benefited from good luck in the form of cloud cover that hid the fleet during part of its passage across the Pacific. On the United States side, there was a major intelligence failure. Americans had broken the Japanese diplomatic code. Those intercepts made clear an attack was coming but did not point to Pearl Harbor as the target. And they were not supplemented by human intelligence or other reliable sources of information. Most important was a failure of imagination. Americans knew an attack would soon take place, but they looked toward Southeast Asia and the Philippines, where the brunt of the Japanese assault did occur. Underestimating their adversary, they did not believe that Japan would even attempt such an audacious scheme, much less pull it off.[129]

A more telling, if less frequently offered, criticism is that the Roosevelt administration might have been more conciliatory toward Japan. Had it abandoned, at least temporarily, its determination to drive the Japanese from China and restored some trade, it might have delayed a two-front war when it was not yet ready to fight one major enemy. Having already learned what seemed the hard lessons of appeasement, U.S. officials rejected a course of expediency. Rather, they backed a proud nation into a position where its only choices were war or surrender.[130] Japan chose war, with fateful consequences for both nations. For the Japanese, ultimately, a brilliant tactical maneuver proved a catastrophic strategic blunder, rallying the United States as nothing else could have for a fight to the finish. Hitler solved Roosevelt's dilemma in the Atlantic. Although not bound to do so by the defensive clauses in the Tripartite Pact, he declared war four days later. After a long period of hesitation and indecision, the United States was at war.

THE YEARS FROM 1931 to 1941 brought major changes in U.S. foreign policy. Responding to the Great Depression and the threat of a new world war, Americans in the mid-1930s embraced isolationist attitudes and endorsed neutrality policies that in the event of war called for the sacrifice of traditional neutral rights for which the nation had fought in 1812 and 1917. The Munich Conference and especially the fall of France produced another reversal. Many anxious Americans now concluded that their values and interests were threatened by events abroad and that their

129. David Kahn, "Pearl Harbor as an Intelligence Failure," in Akira Iriye, *Pearl Harbor and the Coming of the Pacific War* (Boston, 1999), 158–68.
130. Paul W. Schroeder, *The Axis Alliance and Japanese-American Relations, 1941* (Ithaca, 1958), originally developed this argument. For a more recent statement, see Kennedy, *Freedom from Fear*, 513–14.

security required them to assist nations combating the Axis menace even at the risk of war.

Franklin Roosevelt took the lead in educating Americans to this new perspective on world affairs. He has been criticized for his timidity in responding to World War II and for underestimating his powers of persuasion. But he had vivid memories of Wilson's defeat and feared getting too far out in front of public opinion. He therefore moved with great caution, giving time for events to underscore the lessons he sought to teach and for U.S. rearmament to gain steam. Step by step between 1939 and 1941, he abandoned neutrality and, through aid to Britain and other nations fighting Hitler, took the United States to the brink of war. In orchestrating this great transformation, FDR stretched the powers of his office to unprecedented extents. At times, he was less than candid with the American people. He used dubious if not illegal means to spy on his political foes. He created the basis for what would be called the imperial presidency and for the Cold War national security state. By articulating the notions that America could be truly secure only in a world in which its values prevailed and that its way of life could best be defended by acting abroad, he set forth the intellectual underpinnings for an American globalism that would take form in World War II and flourish in the postwar years.[131]

131. Reynolds, *Munich to Pearl Harbor*, 4.

13

"Five Continents and Seven Seas"

World War II and the Rise of American Globalism, 1941–1945

"The problems which we face are so vast and so interrelated," Franklin Roosevelt explained to Ambassador Joseph Grew on January 21, 1941, "that any attempt even to state them compels one to think in terms of five continents and seven seas."[1] Thus, almost a year before Pearl Harbor, FDR came to appreciate the enormously transformative impact of World War II on U.S. foreign relations. Even prior to December 7, 1941, Americans had begun to reassess long-standing assumptions about the sources of their national security (a phrase just coming into use). While often obscuring the intent and significance of his actions, the president had taken major steps toward intervention in the European and Asian wars. What the fall of France did not accomplish in terms of reshaping American attitudes and institutions, Pearl Harbor did. The Japanese attack on Hawaii undermined as perhaps nothing else could have the cherished notion that America was secure from foreign threat. The ensuing war elevated foreign policy to the highest national priority for the first time since the early republic. By virtue of its size, its wealth, its largely untapped economic and military potential, and its distance from major war zones, the United States, along with Britain and the Soviet Union, assumed leadership of what came to be called the United Nations, a loose assemblage of some forty countries. During the war, it built a mammoth military establishment and funded a huge foreign aid program. It became involved in a host of complex and often intricately interconnected diplomatic, economic, political, and military problems across the world, requiring a sprawling foreign policy bureaucracy staffed by thousands of men and women engaged in all sorts of activities in places Americans could not previously have located on a map. This time, Americans took up the mantle of world leadership spurned in 1919. "We have tossed Washington's Farewell Address in to the discard," Michigan's isolationist senator Arthur Vandenberg lamented before Pearl Harbor. "We have thrown

1. Joseph C. Grew, *Turbulent Era: A Record of Forty Years in the U.S. Diplomatic Service* (2 vols., London, 1953), 2:1260.

ourselves squarely into the power politics and power wars of Europe, Asia, and Africa. We have taken the first step upon a course from which we can never hereafter retreat."[2]

I

The military situation in the months after Pearl Harbor was unremittingly grim. From January to March 1942, FDR speechwriter Robert Sherwood later recalled, Japan swept across the Pacific and Southeast Asia with such stunning speed that the "pins on the walls of map rooms in Washington and London were usually far out of date."[3] Singapore fell on February 15, "the greatest disaster to British arms which our history records," according to Prime Minister Winston Churchill.[4] By mid-March, Japanese forces had conquered Malaya, Java, and Borneo, landed on New Guinea, and occupied Rangoon. For weeks, U.S. and Filipino troops valiantly held off enemy invaders. Without food, clothing, and drugs, exhausted from disease and malnutrition, they fell back to Bataan and then Corregidor and finally surrendered on May 6. From Wake Island in the Central Pacific to the Bay of Bengal, Japan reigned supreme.

In Europe, Hitler had delivered on his promise of a "world in flames." Germany retained the upper hand in the Battle of the Atlantic through much of 1942, destroying eight million tons of shipping and threatening to sever the vital trans-Atlantic lifeline. The Axis controlled continental Europe. The Red Army had stopped the Wehrmacht short of Moscow and with the help of "General Winter" had mounted a counteroffensive, but Germany remained strong enough to launch a spring 1942 offensive that once again threatened Soviet defeat. Hitler sent armies into North Africa to seize the Suez Canal and cripple British power in the Middle East. Through Gen. Erwin Rommel's brilliant generalship, the Germans nearly succeeded in the early summer of 1942. Had Spain bowed to Hitler's pressure and entered the war, Germany could have controlled Gibraltar and the Mediterranean. At the height of their power, the Axis dominated one-third of the world's population and mineral resources. The Allies most feared in these perilous months an Axis linkup in the Indian Ocean and central Asia to defeat the USSR, secure the vast oil reserves of the Middle East, and end the war.

2. Arthur H. Vandenberg Jr., *The Private Papers of Senator Vandenberg* (Boston, 1952), 10.
3. Robert E. Sherwood, *Roosevelt and Hopkins: An Intimate History* (New York, 1948), 490.
4. Winston S. Churchill, *The Hinge of Fate* (Cambridge, Mass., 1950), 92.

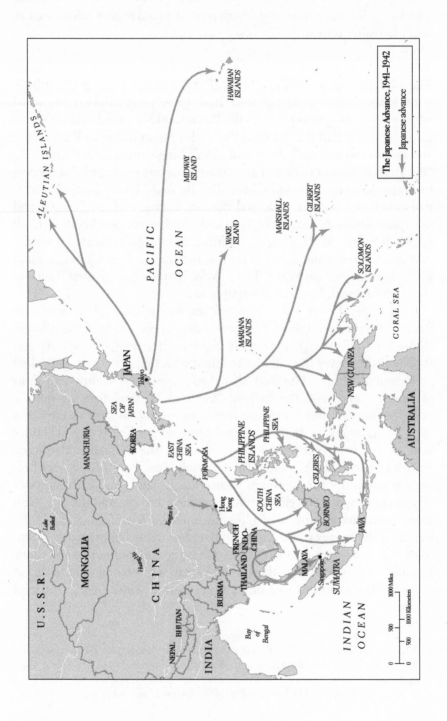

The Japanese Advance, 1941–1942

→ Japanese advance

Although nowhere near ready for a two-front war, the United States was much better prepared than in 1917. The National Guard was called to active duty, and a selective service system had been in place for more than a year, expanding the army from 174,000 in mid-1939 to nearly 1.5 million two years later. By 1945, the nation had more than 12.1 million men and women in uniform. In the months before Pearl Harbor, the army had trained with antiquated equipment and makeshift substitutes. American industry could not produce the supplies needed to rearm the United States and fill the plates of allies seated at what Churchill called "the hungry table." But Roosevelt had used the emergency of 1940–41 to set ambitious production goals, doubling the size of the combat fleet and producing 7,800 military aircraft. By removing any doubt about full U.S. involvement in the war, Pearl Harbor eliminated the last barrier to full mobilization. War production stimulated a stagnant economy, brought spare production into operation, and converted unemployment into an acute labor shortage. It would be 1943 before the miracle of U.S. war production was fully realized, but it was evident much sooner that Roosevelt's goals, seemingly fantastic at the time, would be far surpassed.

With the onset of global war, the making of foreign policy became more complex—and even more disorderly. The president's advisers were deeply divided both ideologically and on the basis of personality. Vice President Henry A. Wallace became the most vocal spokesman for a liberal internationalism that would extend the benefits of the New Deal to other peoples, provoking conservatives to denounce him and his "radical boys" as the "postwar spreaders of peace, plenty, and pulchritude."[5] The State Department receded further into the background, in part from FDR's disdain for that "haven for routineers and paper shufflers."[6] In addition, the escalating Hull-Welles feud nearly paralyzed the department until Hull's cronies forced the undersecretary's dismissal after revelations of a homosexual encounter. A crippled and demoralized department continued to shape trade policy and produced reams of paperwork on postwar issues, but the exhausted and increasingly dispirited Hull was not invited to the major Big Three conferences and did not even get minutes of the 1943 Casablanca meeting.

Others filled the vacuum. Elder statesman Henry Stimson presided over war production and played a key role in developing the atomic

5. Beatrice Bishop Berle and Travis Beal Jacobs, eds., *Navigating the Rapids, 1918–1971: From the Papers of Adolph A. Berle* (New York, 1973), 400.

6. Paul D. Mayle, *Eureka Summit* (Newark, Del., 1987), 37.

bomb. Secretary of the Treasury Henry Morgenthau Jr. exploited his position as FDR's Hudson Valley neighbor to frame postwar economic programs and encroach on State's turf in designing policies for China and postwar Germany. Dubbed by Churchill "Lord Root of the Matter" for his incisive mind and matter-of-fact approach to problem-solving, the cadaverous former social worker and New Deal relief administrator Harry Hopkins remained the president's alter ego until chronic illness and a mysterious parting of the ways with his boss reduced his influence. The indispensable person was Army Chief of Staff Gen. George C. Marshall. He "towers above everybody else in the strength of his character and in the wisdom and tactfulness of his handling of himself," Stimson observed with obvious admiration. Marshall brought stability to the chaos that was wartime Washington. An administrative genius, he was, in Churchill's words, the "true 'organizer of victory.'"[7]

To meet the rapidly expanding demands of a host of new global diplomatic and military problems, FDR created a huge foreign policy bureaucracy that would become a permanent fixture of American life. Even before Pearl Harbor, he concluded that the State Department could not cope with the exigencies of total war. Thus, as with New Deal domestic programs, he established emergency "alphabet soup" agencies. Some of them were given deceptively innocent names, perhaps reflecting the nation's continuing innocence, more likely to obscure their purpose. An Office of Facts and Figures, later the Office of War Information (OWI), was responsible for propaganda at home and abroad; The Coordinator of Information, precursor to the Office of Strategic Services (OSS)—and subsequently the Central Intelligence Agency (CIA)—was America's first independent intelligence agency.

These new agencies assumed various wartime tasks. OWI censored the press and churned out posters, magazines, comic books, films, and cartoons to undermine enemy morale and sell the war and U.S. war aims to allies and neutrals.[8] The Office of Lend-Lease Administration (OLLA) ran that essential wartime foreign aid program.[9] Wallace's Board of Economic Warfare (BEW) conducted preemptive purchasing to keep vital raw materials out of enemy hands and manipulated trade to further the war effort. The

7. Entry for December 16, 1943, Diary of Henry L. Stimson, microfilm edition; Forrest C. Pogue, *George C. Marshall: Organizer of Victory, 1943–1945* (New York, 1973), 585.
8. Allan M. Winkler, *The Politics of Propaganda: The Office of War Information, 1942–1945* (New Haven, Conn., 1978).
9. George C. Herring Jr., "Experiment in Foreign Aid: Lend-Lease, 1941–1945" (Ph.D. dissertation, University of Virginia, 1965), especially 129–64.

Office of Foreign Relief and Rehabilitation Operations (OFRRO) handled relief programs in liberated areas. Headed by a World War I Medal of Honor winner, the flamboyant Col. William "Wild Bill" Donovan, the OSS at its peak employed thirteen thousand people, as many as nine thousand overseas. Bearing a distinct Ivy League hue, it brought to Washington scholars such as historians Arthur M. Schlesinger Jr. and Sherman Kent, and even the Marxist philosopher Herbert Marcuse, to analyze the vast amounts of information collected on enemy capabilities and operations. Clandestine operatives such as the legendary Virginia Hall slipped into North Africa and Europe to prepare the way for Allied military operations and carried out black propaganda operations and "dirty tricks" in Axis-occupied areas and enemy territory. OSS agents in various guises worked with partisan and guerrilla groups in the Balkans and East Asia. In Bern, a Secret Intelligence unit headed by Allen Dulles established contact with opponents of Hitler and gathered information about the Nazi regime.[10]

The emergency agencies had a mixed record. BEW had more than two thousand representatives in Brazil, provoking the foreign minister half-jokingly to tell a U.S. diplomat that if more "ambassadors of good will" were sent to his nation "Brazil would be obliged to declare war on the United States."[11] In best Rooseveltian fashion, there was rampant overlap of responsibility and duplication of effort. A "coordinator" in wartime Washington, Wallace joked, "was only a man trying to keep all the balls in the air without losing his own."[12] Bitter turf battles set off what one official deplored as "another war."[13] The squabbles in Washington undoubtedly pleased a president who seemed to enjoy such things, but conflict in North Africa between civilian relief agencies grew so disruptive that the army had to take over. When an especially nasty feud between Wallace and conservative Secretary of Commerce Jesse Jones went public, the president relieved Wallace and combined the economic agencies into the Foreign Economic Administration. Despite their incessant squabbling, the agencies carried out essential wartime tasks. They were also a prolific breeding ground for postwar internationalism, providing a baptism by fire for such prominent postwar leaders as George W. Ball, Adlai E. Stevenson, and Dulles.

10. Central Intelligence Agency, *The Office of Strategic Services* (Washington, 2000).
11. Spruille Braden, *Diplomats and Demagogues: The Memoirs of Spruille Braden* (New York, 1971), 275.
12. John Morton Blum, *V Was for Victory: Politics and Culture During World War II* (New York, 1976), 45.
13. Fred I. Israel, ed., *The War Diary of Breckinridge Long: Selections from the Years 1939–1944* (Lincoln, Neb., 1966), 289–90.

World War II also thrust the military into a central role in formulating U.S. foreign policy. Traditionally, the armed forces had carried out policies designed by civilian leaders, but the nation's full-scale engagement in a total and global war and its involvement with a coalition pushed them into the realm of policymaking and diplomacy. Military ascendancy also resulted from Hull's rigid insistence on the artificial distinction between political and military matters and Roosevelt's growing dependence on his uniformed advisers. FDR initiated the process in 1939 by bringing them into the Executive Office of the President, thus bypassing the war and navy secretaries. In February 1942, he created the Joint Chiefs of Staff, composed of the service chiefs. In July, he named former chief of naval operations Adm. William Leahy his personal chief of staff with the primary duty of maintaining liaison between the White House and the Joint Chiefs. In this new role, the top brass formulated strategic plans. They accompanied the president to all his summit meetings, where they coordinated with Allied counterparts plans and operations. The emergence of the military into a key policymaking position brought enduring changes in civil-military relations and the formulation of national security policy.[14]

The military's new headquarters in Arlington, Virginia, symbolized its growing importance in the Washington power equation. Begun on September 11, 1941, and occupied in 1942, this five-sided monstrosity with its miles of baffling corridors—"vast, sprawling, almost intentionally ugly"—housed some thirty thousand employees in 7.5 million square feet of floor space. Roosevelt disliked the building's architecture and assumed at war's end it would be used for storage. In fact, it remained in full operation. The very word *Pentagon* in time came to represent throughout the world the enormous military power of the United States—and, in the eyes of domestic and foreign critics, the allegedly dominant and sinister influence of the military in American life.[15]

Responsibility ultimately rested in the firm hands of the commander in chief. By this time sixty years old, FDR was weary from the strains of eight demanding years in the White House and his long struggle with polio. But the new challenges of global war reinvigorated him. He retained the undaunted optimism that was such an essential part of his personality, as necessary in 1942 as a decade earlier. "I use the wrong end of the telescope," he wrote Justice Felix Frankfurter in March, "and it

---

14. Mark A. Stoler, *Allies and Adversaries: The Joint Chiefs of Staff, the Grand Alliance, and U.S. Strategy in World War II* (Chapel Hill, N.C., 2000), viii–ix, 64–65.
15. Pogue, *Organizer of Victory*, 38–39.

makes things easier to bear."[16] He inspired Americans and others with his lofty rhetoric. He reveled in the ceremonial aspects of his job as commander in chief and delighted in the formulation of grand strategy. Always inclined toward personal diplomacy, he took special pleasure in his direct contact with world leaders such as the sinister and Sphinx-like Joseph Stalin and the bulldog Churchill. His broad circle of personal contacts provided him invaluable information outside regular channels. His chaotic administrative style supposedly left him firmly in control, but as the problems of global warfare became more numerous, more diffuse, and more complex, it also produced serious policy snafus (an acronym that grew out of bureaucratic foul-ups in World War II and stood for "situation normal, all fucked up") and gave clever subordinates the opportunity for freelancing, sometimes with baleful results. Not surprisingly, he continued to rely on obfuscation and outright deceit. "You know I am a juggler," he confessed in the spring of 1942, "and I never let my right hand know what my left hand does. . . . I may have one policy for Europe and one diametrically opposite for North and South America. I may be entirely inconsistent, and furthermore I am perfectly willing to mislead and tell untruths if it will help win the war."[17]

Some critics claim that Roosevelt's wartime leadership lacked guiding principles, that he drifted from crisis to crisis without a clear sense of purpose or direction. Others insist that in fighting the evils of Nazism he was blind to the dangers of Communism. Still others contend that he and his military advisers focused too much on winning the war and gave insufficient attention to crucial political issues.

In truth, FDR was in many ways a brilliant commander in chief. He effectively juggled the many dimensions of the job. He skillfully managed the war effort and doggedly defended U.S. interests. Keenly aware of the dynamics of coalition warfare, he alone among Allied leaders had what he called a "world point of view."[18] He correctly gave highest priority to holding the alliance together and winning the war, essential given the desperate situation of 1942 and the vastly divergent interests and goals of the major Allies. At times he seemed to act on whim or to muddle through, but he had a coherent if not completely formulated or publicly

16. Max Freedman, ed., *Roosevelt and Frankfurter: Their Correspondence* (Boston, 1967), 692.

17. Warren F. Kimball, *The Juggler: Franklin Roosevelt as Wartime Statesman* (Princeton, N.J., 1991), 7.

18. FDR to WSC, July 29, 1942, in Warren F. Kimball, ed., *Churchill and Roosevelt: Their Complete Correspondence* (3 vols., Princeton, N.J., 1984), 1:545.

articulated view for the peace. Like Wilson, he firmly believed in the superiority of American values and institutions. He was also certain that postwar peace and stability depended on the extension of those principles across the world and that other peoples would accept them if given a chance. By providing a middle ground between the totalitarianism of left and right, the New Deal, in his view, pointed the way to the future, and he saw in the war an opportunity to promote world reform along those lines. At the same time, as Robert Sherwood observed, "the tragedy of Wilson was always somewhere within the rim of his consciousness."[19] He saw better than his mentor the limits of American power; he intuitively understood that diplomatic problems were not always susceptible to neat solutions. Roosevelt's pragmatic idealism, Warren Kimball has observed, thus "sought to accommodate the broad ideas of Woodrow Wilson to the practical realities of international relations."[20] Global war provided the ultimate test for his enormous political skills; the untimeliness of his death ensured for him an uncertain legacy.

II

"There is only one thing worse than fighting with allies," Churchill asserted on the eve of victory in World War II, "and that is fighting without them!"[21] Although an exercise in Churchillian hyperbole, the observation underscores a fundamental reality of coalition warfare: Alliances are marriages of convenience formed to meet immediate, often urgent needs. They contain built-in conflicts; their usefulness rarely extends beyond achievement of the purposes for which they were formed. Great Britain, the Soviet Union, and the United States were forced into partnership in the summer of 1941 by the mortal threat of Nazi Germany. They agreed that Hitler must be defeated. They collaborated effectively to that end. But they brought to the alliance deep-seated mutual suspicions. They disagreed sharply on how and for what goals the war should be fought.

Throughout their wartime partnership, the major Allies viewed each other with profound distrust. The Soviet leaders had gained power by conspiratorial means and were suspicious by nature. Indeed, there is ample evidence that at various points Stalin suffered from acute paranoia. Communist ideology taught hatred of capitalism and seemed validated by history: the Allied interventions of 1918–19 designed in the Soviet view to overthrow their fledgling government; the long period of diplomatic

19. Sherwood, *Roosevelt and Hopkins*, 227.
20. Kimball, *Juggler*, 64.
21. Quoted in Stoler, *Allies and Adversaries*, viii.

ostracism by the West; and the Munich agreement that left the Soviet Union exposed to Nazi power. They had no choice but to turn to the Western nations in June 1941 but remained wary of their allies. While traveling in the West, Foreign Minister V. M. Molotov slept with a revolver under his pillow. "Churchill is the kind who, if you don't watch him, will slip a kopek out of your pocket . . . ," Stalin told a Yugoslav Communist in 1944. "Roosevelt is not like that. He dips his hand in only for bigger coins."[22] Westerners reciprocated Soviet suspicions. Churchill brought to the alliance a well-earned reputation as a Bolshevik-hater, and many Britons shared his view. The deeply emotional antipathy of Americans toward Communism was reinforced in the 1930s by Stalin's bloody purges of top party officials, his sordid 1939 pact with Hitler, and the "rape" of Poland and Finland. They only grudgingly acquiesced in Roosevelt's 1941 efforts to assist the Soviet Union. They warmed to the Russian people and even "Uncle Joe" Stalin somewhat during the war, but old fears never entirely dissipated.[23]

During World War II, the United States and Britain achieved probably the closest collaboration by any allies in time of war. Top military leaders worked together through a Combined Chiefs of Staff. The nations shared economic resources. They even agreed to share vital information on such top-secret military projects as the atomic bomb (which was not given the Soviet Union), although in this area Britain repeatedly protested that its ally did not keep its promises. Roosevelt and Churchill established a rare camaraderie, communicating almost daily during much of the war. Yet these two extraordinarily close allies remained deeply suspicious of each other. An ancient strain of Anglophobia in American life manifested itself repeatedly during the war. Britons saw better than Americans, and naturally resented, that the seat of world power was passing to the trans-Atlantic upstart. The two nations fought bitterly over strategy and trade issues. Despite their genuine friendship, Roosevelt and Churchill suspected one another and clashed over sensitive questions like the future of the British Empire.[24]

22. Milovan Djilas, *Conversations with Stalin* (New York, 1962), 73–74.
23. George C. Herring, *Aid to Russia, 1941–1946: Strategy, Diplomacy, the Origins of the Cold War* (New York, 1973), 18–22, 94.
24. See, for example, Warren F. Kimball, *Forged in War: Churchill, Roosevelt, and the Second World War* (New York, 1997) and Christopher Thorne, *Allies of a Kind: The United States, Britain, and the War Against Japan* (New York, 1978). Kimball, "The Bomb and the Special Relationship," *Finest Hour: The Journal of Winston Churchill* 137 (Winter 2007–8), 37–42, details the problems with atomic collaboration.

The three Allies were deeply divided on grand strategy. With much of its territory occupied by the Wehrmacht, the Soviet Union desperately needed material aid and the immediate opening of a second front in Western Europe to ease pressure on the embattled Red Army. Some U.S. Army planners agreed with the Soviet approach, if not with its timing. But U.S. Navy leaders after the humiliation of Pearl Harbor pushed for all-out war against Japan, and they gained support from Gen. Douglas MacArthur and much of the American public. The British posed a major roadblock to Stalin's demands. They vividly recalled the slaughter of 1914–18 and perceived that an early second front would necessarily be made up mainly of British troops. Thus they opposed an invasion of Western Europe until the Allies had gained overwhelming preponderance over Germany. Britain and especially Churchill also promoted operations around the periphery of Hitler's Fortress Europe to protect their imperial interests in the Middle East, southern Europe, and South Asia. For Stalin, such operations, however useful, were not enough. The U.S. brass vigorously objected to what they considered pinprick operations to pull British imperial chestnuts out of the fire.[25]

The Allies also disagreed sharply over war aims. Even with the Red Army reeling in the summer of 1941, Stalin made clear his determination to retain the Baltic States and those parts of Poland acquired in his deal with Hitler. His larger aims, like the man himself, remain shrouded in mystery, probably shifting with the circumstances of war. Ideology undoubtedly shaped the Soviet worldview, but Stalin's goals seem to have originated more from Russian history.[26] He had no master plan for world conquest. Instead, he was a cautious expansionist, improvising and exploiting opportunities. At a minimum, the Kremlin sought to prevent Germany from repeating the devastation it had inflicted on Russia in the First World War and the early stages of the Second. Stalin also wanted a buffer zone in Eastern and Central Europe made up of what he called "friendly" governments, which meant governments he could control.[27] The British hoped to restore a balance of power in Europe, the traditional basis of their national security, which required maintaining France and even Germany as major powers. Despite an explosion of nationalism in the colonial areas during the war, Churchill and other Britons clung to

25. Stoler, *Allies and Adversaries*, 87–96.
26. Vladislav M. Zubok, "Stalin's Plans and Russian Archives," *Diplomatic History* 21 (Spring 1997), 296.
27. Ibid.; Melvyn P. Leffler, "Inside Enemy Archives: The Cold War Reopened," *Foreign Affairs* (July-August 1996), 124–25, and *A Preponderance of Power: National Security, the Truman Administration, and the Cold War* (Stanford, Calif., 1992), 49, 99, 102–3.

the empire. "I have not become the King's First Minister in order to preside over the liquidation of the British Empire," the prime minister once snarled.[28] The war aims of the United States were less tangible but no less deeply held. Political settlements should be based on the concept of self-determination of peoples; colonies should be readied for independence; an Open Door policy should govern the world economy; and a world organization should maintain the peace.

Unlike Wilson, who had insisted that the United States fight as an "associated" power, Roosevelt assumed leadership of the United Nations—indeed, he coined the term during Churchill's late 1941–early 1942 visit to Washington, delightedly wheeling into the prime minister's quarters and informing him while he bathed.[29] The challenges were formidable. The president had to resist domestic political and navy pressures to scrap the Germany-first strategy and avenge Pearl Harbor. He had to deflect demands from his top military advisers to push U.S. rearmament at the expense of the Allies' immediate and urgent material needs. He had to resolve strategic disputes among the Allies and avert or resolve incipient conflicts over war aims. Above all, he had to hold the alliance together and employ its resources in ways best calculated to defeat its enemies.

To avoid divisive and possibly fatal conflict over war aims—and also the unpleasant situations he so disliked—FDR insisted that political issues not be resolved—or even for the most part discussed—until the war had ended. Such a course held great risk. The momentum and direction of the armies would likely determine, possily to U.S. detriment, the shape of territorial settlements. Roosevelt was also criticized after the war for failing to extract major political concessions from both allies while they were most dependent on the United States. Such arguments do not hold up under close scrutiny. Stalin might well have acceded to U.S. demands in 1941 only to break agreements later if it suited him. In any event, in the dark days of 1941–42, to have extorted concessions at the point of a gun might have critically set back or destroyed the Allied war effort.

Roosevelt used lend-lease to hold the alliance together and also as an integral part of what historian David Kennedy has called his "arsenal of democracy strategy."[30] After Pearl Harbor, his military advisers insisted on top priority for precious supplies, arguing that if the United States was

28. Quoted in Kimball, *Juggler*, 136.
29. Berle and Jacobs, *Navigating the Rapids*, 394–95.
30. David M. Kennedy, *A Tale of Three Cities: How the United States Won World War II* (Melbourne, Australia, 2001), 6, 12.

ever to take the offensive, "we will have to stop sitting on our fannies giving out stuff in driblets all over the world."[31] Looking at the war from a broader perspective, FDR perceived that lend-lease could assure allies of U.S. good faith and increase the fighting capabilities of armies already in the field, thus keeping maximum pressure on the enemy while his nation mobilized. He was also shrewd enough to recognize that supplying Allied armies would produce victory with less cost in U.S. lives. He thus gave Allied claims equal, in some cases higher, priority than U.S. rearmament. He used supplies with an eye to psychological as well as military impact. After Britain's devastating defeat at Tobruk in the summer of 1942, he sent three hundred of the newest Sherman tanks, a huge morale booster. He gave aid to Russia top priority among all competing claims and exerted enormous effort to deliver the goods.[32] The administration rejected British proposals to pool resources. Nor did it ever completely do away with the "silly, foolish old dollar sign," and at Congress's insistence it kept detailed records of the cost of every item shipped. Under FDR's leadership, the United States provided more than $50 billion in supplies and services to fifty nations, roughly half of it to the British Empire, around one-fifth to the USSR. Aid to Britain alone included some 1,360 items, everything from aircraft to cigarettes to prefabricated housing for factory workers. Soviet leaders often complained about the paucity and slowness of U.S. lend-lease shipments, but at Yalta in February 1945 the normally laconic Stalin paid eloquent tribute to its "extraordinary contribution" to Allied victory.[33]

Above all else, the questions regarding the timing, location, and priority to be given military operations divided the Allies. For the United States, the first major issue was the importance to be assigned the Pacific war. After Pearl Harbor, MacArthur and the navy insisted that they must have substantial reinforcements merely to hold the line. Large and vocal segments of public opinion demanded vengeance against Japan. A major U.S. naval victory at the Battle of Midway in June 1942 helped stabilize lines in the Pacific. But Chief of Naval Operations Adm. Ernest King continued to push for limited offensives to exploit Japan's overextension. MacArthur—for once—agreed with the navy. When the depth of British

31. Richard W. Steele, *The First Offensive, 1942: Roosevelt, Marshall, and the Making of American Strategy* (Bloomington, Ind., 1973), 79.
32. Herring, *Aid to Russia*, 54–60.
33. *Foreign Relations of the United States: The Conferences at Malta and Yalta, 1945* (Washington, 1955), 768.

opposition to an immediate second front in Western Europe became clear, even General Marshall supported a shift to the Pacific.[34]

Roosevelt solved the issue in typical fashion. He diverted substantial supplies to MacArthur and King for limited offensives. As late as 1943, resources and manpower allocated to Europe and the Pacific were roughly equal, violating the spirit and letter of the Europe-first principle. In part, this outcome reflected the influence of King. A bad-tempered, ruthless infighter whose motto was "When the going gets rough they call on the sons of bitches," he secured Marshall's support by backing army proposals for the European theater.[35] In diverting resources to the Pacific, Roosevelt may also have been responding to domestic pressures. He certainly hoped to sustain the fighting spirit of forces there and to maintain maximum pressure on all fronts.

At the same time, he stuck with the principle that Germany was the major enemy and had first claim on resources for a major offensive. He rejected proposals to punish the British by shifting to the Pacific—that would be like "taking up your dishes and going away."[36] In 1943, when European operations began to take form and the Pacific theater demanded more and more, he put on the brakes, preventing the war against Japan from absorbing resources that would further delay cross-Channel operations. The result was a strategy that retained but modified the Germany-first principle. Europe kept top priority for a major offensive, but the United States committed itself to wage war vigorously on both fronts. This put enormous strain on relations with Britain and the USSR. MacArthur and King predictably complained they could not carry out assigned tasks. In the final analysis, however, it proved a viable strategy for a two-front war, bringing the defeat of Japan months after V-E Day.

Controversy over the time, place, and size of a second front in Europe strained the alliance to the breaking point between January 1942 and the Tehran Conference in late 1943. In part, the conflict derived from Soviet demands for an immediate Anglo-American invasion of Western Europe. But it was also a question of British versus U.S. military doctrines and the Mediterranean against Western Europe. Here too, Roosevelt made the major decisions. Again, they reflected political and psychological considerations and produced compromises, in this case, short-term commitment to the peripheral strategy, long-run commitment to a cross-Channel invasion.

34. Stoler, *Allies and Adversaries*, 79–86.
35. Pogue, *Organizer of Victory*, 7.
36. Stoler, *Allies and Adversaries*, 86.

The central question—and the most important and divisive issue among the Allies until late 1943—was whether to mobilize resources for an early strike across the English Channel or mount lesser offensives around the periphery of Hitler's Fortress Europe. Following principles deeply rooted in their respective military traditions, Marshall and the U.S. Army generally favored the former, the British the latter. Roosevelt in May 1942 made an ill-advised, if carefully qualified, commitment to Foreign Minister Molotov for an early second front, which the Russians appear not to have put much stock in. A month later, to the consternation of his own military advisers, he approved British proposals for Operation Torch, an immediate invasion of French North Africa. The decision arose from Britain's steadfast rejection of an immediate invasion of France. Since the British would provide the bulk of the troops for such an operation, FDR felt compelled to attack somewhere else. He was thinking of domestic politics; he desperately wanted to get U.S. troops into action against Germany in 1942. He also acted on the basis of immediate military and psychological concerns. Germany's summer offensive in Russia threatened a breakthrough into the Caucasus and Iran. Rommel's victory at Tobruk gave the Germans the upper hand in North Africa and threatened the union of two victorious German armies in an area of huge strategic importance. A U.S. offensive might tip the scales back toward the Allies.[37]

Roosevelt was also concerned about the immediate political and psychological needs of an ally. British morale was badly shaken by defeats in the Middle East and Southeast Asia. Churchill was in political trouble. A North African offensive might bolster flagging British spirits, end at least temporarily the raging controversy over the second front, and seal the Anglo-American alliance. Roosevelt recognized that it would not appease Stalin, whose complaints had become increasingly shrill. But he apparently reasoned that action somewhere would be better than further delay. He gambled that the Russian armies would survive and sought to compensate by stepping up crucial lend-lease deliveries.[38]

As U.S. military planners had feared, the invasion of North Africa in November 1942 was followed by agreement at an Anglo-American summit in Casablanca in January 1943 to invade Sicily and then Italy. Since operations in North Africa and the Pacific were absorbing increasing volumes of supplies, the British now argued that the Allies lacked sufficient resources to mount a successful invasion of France and insisted that they follow up victo-

37. Kimball, *Forged in War*, 143–55; Robert Dallek, *Franklin D. Roosevelt and American Foreign Policy, 1932–1945* (New York, 1979), 345–49.
38. Herring, *Aid to Russia*, 68–74.

ries in the Mediterranean. Divided among themselves, U.S. military planners were no match for their British counterparts. "We came, we listened, and we were conquered," one officer bitterly complained.[39] The harsh reality was that as long as the British resisted a cross-Channel attack and the United States lacked the means to do it alone, there was no other way to stay on the offensive. In any event, logistical limitations likely prevented a successful invasion of France prior to 1944. As a way of palliating Stalin's Russia, the "ghost in the attic" at Casablanca, in Kimball's apt words, Roosevelt and Churchill proclaimed that they would accept nothing less than the unconditional surrender of the Axis. The statement also reflected FDR's determination to avoid repeating the mistakes of World War I, as well as his firm belief that Germany had been "Prussianized" and needed a complete political makeover.[40]

These decisions had vital military and political consequences. The dispersion of resources, as Marshall and others repeatedly warned, delayed a cross-Channel attack until 1944. By giving the Germans time to strengthen their defenses in France, it made the task more costly. Repeated delays in the second front strained the alliance with Moscow in ways that could not be overcome by Roosevelt's soothing words, lend-lease diplomacy, or unconditional surrender. They probably encouraged Stalin to pursue the possibility of a separate peace with Germany in the spring and summer of 1943. It may be argued, on the other hand, that Roosevelt's decisions over the long run better served the Allied cause. Without a full-fledged British commitment, a cross-Channel attack in 1943 might have failed. Even if the British had been compelled to go along, an assault as early as the spring of 1943 ran huge risks. Defeat or stalemate in Western Europe, in the absence of operations elsewhere, could have had profound political and military consequences. The Torch and Casablanca decisions sealed the Anglo-American alliance at a critical point in the war. They permitted maximum use of British manpower and supplies, enabled the Allies to stay on the offensive, and kept pressure on the Germans. In time, they opened the Mediterranean to Allied shipping, knocked Italy out of the war, helped keep Turkey and Spain neutral, and strained German manpower and resources. They provided useful lessons for the cross-Channel attack. The peripheral approach was costly, but given the realities of 1942 and 1943 it seems the strategy most appropriate for coalition warfare.[41]

39. Stoler, *Allies and Adversaries*, 103.
40. Kimball, *Juggler*, 76–79.
41. Maurice Matloff, "Franklin Delano Roosevelt as War Leader," in Harry L. Coles, ed., *Total War and Cold War: Problems in Civilian Control of the Military* (Columbus, Ohio, 1962), 42–65, and Kent Roberts Greenfield, *American Strategy in World War II: A Reconsideration* (Baltimore, 1963), both provide valuable analyses of FDR as grand strategist.

What eventually made the Mediterranean strategy work was Roosevelt's unstinting commitment to a knockout blow across the Channel. He never lost sight of its military and political significance. And as the balance of power within the alliance shifted in mid-1943 and the United States, by virtue of its vast manpower and resources, became the dominant partner, grand strategy conformed more with the American—and Russian—than the British design.

When Roosevelt, Churchill, and Stalin met together for the first time at Tehran in early December 1943, the Allied military situation had improved dramatically. At Stalingrad in late 1942, the Red Army had turned back Hitler's drive into the Caucasus, inflicting huge losses on the Wehrmacht. In July 1943, the Soviets repulsed Germany's summer offensive against the Kursk salient in a titanic battle featuring thousands of tanks. The Reich never regained the initiative in the east. The Red Army by late 1943 had liberated much of Russia proper and was poised to drive across Eastern Europe to Berlin. The Western allies had wrapped up operations in North Africa and implemented successful, if costly, invasions of Sicily and Italy. Allied victory was assured; it was a matter of how long and at what cost.

Amidst much ceremony and pomp at Tehran, the Big Three, as they came to be called, began to discuss postwar issues and set Allied strategy for the rest of the war. The Americans found Stalin—whom one official aptly labeled a "murderous tyrant"—to be intelligent and a master of detail. The tone of the meetings was generally cordial and businesslike. Seeking to promote cooperation, FDR went out of his way to ingratiate himself with the Soviet dictator, meeting privately with him and even teasing a not-at-all amused Churchill in Stalin's presence. The conferees reached no firm political agreements. They spoke of dismembering Germany. Certain that the USSR would be the dominant power in Eastern Europe and that he could not keep U.S. troops in Europe after the war, FDR hinted to Stalin that he would not challenge Soviet domination of the Baltic States and preeminence in Poland, although he urged token concessions to quiet protest in the West. His refusal to make any commitments, on the other hand, and his failure to mention the atomic bomb project, which Stalin knew about, likely gave the suspicious Soviet leader pause.

The main decision was to confirm the cross-Channel attack. Churchill continued to promote operations in the Mediterranean. At one point, FDR appeared to agree with him. To the great relief of top U.S. military leaders, Stalin dismissed further Mediterranean operations as "diversions" and came down firmly behind an invasion of France. The conferees set the date for May 1944. Stalin agreed to time a major offensive with the invasion of France and to enter the war against Japan three months after the defeat of Germany. The discussions at Tehran decisively shaped the outcome of the war and the nature of the peace. Primarily through Roosevelt's leadership, the Allies had emerged from a period of defeat and grave internal tension and formed a successful grand strategy.[42]

III

Alliance diplomacy tells only part of the much larger story of U.S. foreign relations in World War II. In a total war fought across a global expanse, the United States mounted an unprecedented range of activities even in places where its prior involvement had been slight. In regions of traditional importance such as Latin America and China, it assumed a much larger role and greater responsibilities. In areas such as the Middle East and South Asia, it took a much keener interest and acquired new commitments. The overriding objective, of course, was defeating the Axis, but Americans in Washington and far from home were also alert to postwar economic and strategic advantage. Certain that greater U.S. involvement was essential for postwar peace and security and to improve the lot of other peoples, they found themselves entangled in intractable issues such as decolonization and the Jewish quest for a homeland in Palestine that would dominate the agenda of world politics for years to come. They plunged into complex local situations not easily susceptible to U.S. power and raised expectations difficult to meet. They early experienced the burdens and frustrations of world power.

Long before Pearl Harbor, the United States had moved to counter the Axis threat to the Western Hemisphere, and during the war the Roosevelt administration intensified its efforts to promote regional security. Building on the foundations of the Good Neighbor policy, U.S. officials continued to speak of a Western Hemisphere ideal and hold up the American "republics" as alternatives to fascism. Roosevelt even boosted the inter-American "system" as a model for postwar order in which great powers would maintain regional harmony and stability through wise leadership and by actively cultivating good relations among their neighbors, using police powers only when essential and then with equity and justice. The Good Neighbor policy was a "radical innovation," journalist Walter Lippmann proclaimed, a "true substitute for empire."[43]

---

42. Good short analyses of Teheran may be found in Kimball, *Forged in War*, 241–55, and David M. Kennedy, *Freedom from Fear: The American People in Depression and War* (New York, 1998), 674–85.
43. Kimball, *Juggler*, 107.

Thanks in part to the attention lavished on the hemisphere during the 1930s, the United States secured the active support of most Latin American nations after 1941. United States officials preferred that the other American "republics" merely break diplomatic relations with the Axis, since full belligerency would have compounded already daunting defense and supply problems. To curry U.S. favor—and secure economic aid—the Caribbean and Central American nations, most of them dictatorships, exceeded U.S. wishes by quickly declaring war. Mexico, Colombia, and Venezuela soon broke relations. "If ever a policy paid dividends," State Department official Adolf Berle crowed, "the Good Neighbor policy has."[44] The United States eventually got its way, but not as easily as Berle assumed. At a hastily convened meeting in Rio de Janeiro in January 1942, Chile and Argentina blocked a U.S.-sponsored resolution requiring the breaking of relations. The best that could be secured was an alternative recommending such a step, "a pretty miserable compromise," Hull fumed. Although most nations complied before the meeting ended, Hull remained outraged, conveniently blaming his rival Welles, who headed the U.S. delegation.[45]

Chile and especially Argentina held out for much of the war. With a deeply divided government and a long, indefensible coastline, Chile refused to break relations until early 1943. Far removed from the war zones, Argentina did not share U.S. preoccupation with the Axis threat. It had a large German and Italian population and Axis sympathizers within its officer corps. Traditionally, Argentines had looked more to Europe than to the United States. During the 1930s, they had repeatedly challenged U.S. leadership and resisted North American cultural hegemony. Engaged in an all-out war with enemies deemed the epitome of evil, U.S. leaders, on the other hand, had little patience with Argentina's independence, which they blamed on pro-Nazi sympathies rather than nationalism. Hull and Roosevelt resented Argentina's challenge to U.S. leadership. In Hull's mind, the dispute remained tied to the despised Welles and thus often took the form of a Tennessee mountain feud. A military takeover by Col. Juan Perón in 1944 heightened U.S. fears of fascism in Latin America. With Welles gone, Hull escalated the rhetorical warfare against Argentina and recalled his ambassador. Only Hull's retirement in late 1944 and Argentina's last-minute leap onto the Allied victory bandwagon brought a

44. Frederick B. Pike, *FDR's Good Neighbor Policy: Sixty Years of Generally Gentle Chaos* (Austin, Tex., 1995), 257.
45. Ibid., 257–61.

short-term resolution to the ongoing crisis. Argentina declared war just in time to secure an invitation to the 1945 United Nations conference at San Francisco.[46]

The United States mounted a multifaceted effort to eliminate Axis influence in the Western Hemisphere, build up defenses against the external threat, and promote hemispheric cooperation. The administration insisted that U.S. companies operating in Latin America fire German employees and cancel contracts with German agents. It blacklisted and imposed boycotts on Latin firms run by and employing Germans. With government support, U.S. businesses set out to replace the German and Italian firms driven out of business.[47] The United States sent FBI agents to assist local police in tracking subversives and create counterespionage services.[48] Nelson Rockefeller's Office of the Coordinator of Inter-American Affairs funded a program to combat diseases such as malaria, dysentery, and tuberculosis, especially in regions that produced critical raw materials or where U.S. troops might be stationed. Building on programs initiated by the Rockefeller Foundation, the Institute for Inter-American Affairs worked with local health ministries to improve sanitation and sewage, develop preventive medicine programs, and build hospitals and public health centers. This precursor to the Cold War Point Four program reflected the idealistic—as well as pragmatic—side of the wartime Good Neighbor policy. It won some goodwill for the United States in the hemisphere.[49]

With a $38 million budget by 1942, the CIAA also expanded the propaganda barrage set off before Pearl Harbor. It used various means to drive Axis influence off the radio and out of the newspapers and mounted an intensive, broad-based "Sell America" campaign. In cooperation with Latin governments, it used a blacklist of Axis films to secure for the United States a near monopoly on movies shown in Latin America. It arranged

46. Lars Schoultz, *Beneath the United States: A History of U.S. Policy Toward Latin America* (Cambridge, Mass., 1998), 312–13.

47. Max Paul Friedman, "There Goes the Neighborhood: Blacklisting Germans in Latin America and the Evanescence of the Good Neighbor Policy," *Diplomatic History* 27 (September 2003), 569–97; Graham D. Taylor, "The Axis Replacement Program: Economic Warfare and the Chemical Industry in Latin America," *Diplomatic History* 8 (Spring 1984), 145–64.

48. Gerald K. Haines, "Under the Eagle's Wing: The Franklin Roosevelt Administration Forges an American Hemisphere," *Diplomatic History* 1 (Fall 1977), 375.

49. Jimmie Irene Page, "A Study of the Institute of Inter-American Affairs as an Instrument of United States Diplomacy in Chile" (M.A. thesis, University of Kentucky, 1972); Luis Pena, "Fighting the Invisible Enemy and Enhancing the United States Image in Venezuela," *Maryland Historian* 15 (Fall–Winter 1984), 11–22.

for goodwill tours by Hollywood stars such as the swashbuckling Douglas Fairbanks Jr. and the glamorous Dorothy Lamour. Under the watchful eyes of CIAA censors, Hollywood films continued to present favorable images of North Americans to Latin America and of Latin Americans to the United States. Walt Disney's cartoon "Saludos Amigos" featured a humanized Chilean aircraft that courageously carried the mail over the Andes, and a colorful parrot, José Carioca, who outtalked and outwitted the clever and acerbic Donald Duck.[50]

The United States used military aid and advisory programs to eliminate European military influence and increase its own. Seeking to convert the Latin American military to U.S. weapons, the administration provided more than $300 million in military equipment. Lend-lease supplies helped equip Mexican and Brazilian units that actually fought in the war and provided assorted weapons to other hemispheric nations. In cases like tiny Ecuador, where military aid could not be justified, the U.S. Army creatively displayed its newest hardware in a "Hall of American Weapons" in the national military academy.[51] Fearing coups by pro-Axis military officers, the United States before Pearl Harbor began to use a carrot-and-stick approach to replacing Axis military advisers with its own. United States officials also hoped that close military ties would inculcate their own military values and thereby promote the Good Neighbor ideal and political stability. Responding to U.S. pressures, most Latin governments eased out European military missions. By Pearl Harbor, the United States had advisers in every Latin nation. Senior officers came to the United States on goodwill tours; Latin Americans attended U.S. military educational institutions, including the service academies—the sons of Nicaraguan dictator Anastasio Somoza and his Dominican counterpart, Rafael Trujillo, attended West Point.[52]

From the standpoint of U.S. interests, wartime policies succeeded splendidly. With Europe out of the picture, trade skyrocketed. The United States purchased huge quantities of critical raw materials, which, along with Export-Import Bank loans, helped stabilize Latin economies. At the height of the war, Latin America sent 50 percent of its exports to and received 60 percent of its imports from the United States. After 1942, active

50. Haines, "Eagle's Wing," 380–83.
51. George C. Herring, "The Most Unsordid Act Revisited: Lend-Lease, War Aims, and Results," paper presented at the Anglo-American-Soviet conference on World War II, Middelburg, Netherlands, June 1985, 17.
52. Mark T. Gilderhus, *The Second Century: U.S.-Latin American Relations Since 1889* (Wilmington, Del., 2000), 102; Eric Paul Roorda, *The Dictator Next Door* (Durham, N.C., 1998), 219–20.

military collaboration became less crucial. Latin America's main role was to furnish air and naval bases and provide raw materials. Indeed, the U.S. military spurned full-fledged cooperation because of the demands that might result. Still, Mexico provided an air squadron to fight in the Pacific. Even more important, 250,000 Mexicans served in the U.S. armed forces, and Mexico provided a majority of the more than three hundred thousand *braceros* workers who helped meet an acute labor shortage in the United States. Brazil sent forces to fight in Italy and made available bases for the United States on its protruding northeast corner—the "bulge" of Brazil—a critical stopping point for U.S. ships and aircraft en route to North Africa.[53] By war's end, the United States had achieved hegemony in the hemisphere without imposing its will by force.

In terms of advancing the Good Neighbor ideal, wartime policies were less successful. In an ethereal sense, so much of that spirit was tied to the charismatic persona of Franklin Roosevelt, and the spirit—and policy— barely survived his death. Once the Axis threat eased, Latin America became a lesser priority for the United States. Unfulfilled expectations led to disappointment and frustration. United States officials resented Latin displays of independence and sometimes complained that they received only a small return on their considerable investment. Latin Americans expressed disappointment at what they considered meager U.S. aid. Although they profited from wartime trade, Latin nations also suffered from chronic shortages and high inflation and worried about their growing economic dependence on the United States.[54]

Close contact between North Americans and Latin Americans often raised tensions. In implementing the blacklists, U.S. officials made clear they did not trust governments they considered inferior to effectively root out Axis influence. They acted unilaterally and with a heavy hand to counter a threat they grossly exaggerated. In targeting people and firms to be blacklisted, they often acted on hearsay and rumor. Latins deeply resented the infringements on their sovereignty. The Colombian foreign minister denounced the blacklist as "economic excommunication" and compared it to the Spanish Inquisition.[55] In the British Caribbean nations put under U.S. control by the 1940 destroyers-bases deal, the people originally welcomed the North American presence as a means to achieve

53. Schoultz, *Beneath the United States*, 313.
54. Kyle Longley, *In the Eagle's Shadow: The United States and Latin America* (Wheeling, Ill., 2002), 183–84; Gilderhus, *Second Century*, 104–5.
55. Friedman, "There Goes the Neighborhood," 582–83.

independence and prosperity. But the demeanor of superiority manifested by the occupiers and especially their efforts to impose racial segregation quickly brought disillusionment. "Maybe the American military
authorities have forgotten they are not in Alabama," a Guyanese complained.[56] Good Neighbor propaganda relentlessly promoted favorable
mutual images but worked no more than limited changes. While generally acceding to its wishes, Latin Americans continued to resent and fear
the United States; North Americans clung doggedly to old stereotypes.[57]

Despite the rhetoric of republicanism, U.S. wartime policies actually
strengthened dictatorships and heightened oppression in many countries.
Repressive governments exploited the counterespionage programs the
FBI helped establish in Brazil and Guatemala to stifle internal dissent.[58]
The refusal to intervene that was basic to the Good Neighbor policy
made it expedient to tolerate dictatorships in the name of order. Clever
tyrants like Trujillo hired professional lobbyists to promote their cause in
Washington and skillfully exploited the Axis threat and U.S. preference
for stability to increase their military power and enhance their personal
power. The military aid and advisory programs helped expand the military's power in Latin American politics. Sharing a common "military culture" that favored order at the expense of democracy, U.S. officers sometimes formed close connections with their Latin counterparts and helped
buffer dictators like Trujillo against internal foes and State Department
critics. Salvadorean dictator Maximiliano Martinez's bloody suppression
of a 1943 internal revolt made plain the tragic human consequences of a
"spoonful" of U.S. weapons—six tanks and five thousand old rifles.[59] Trujillo used U.S. military aircraft and rifles to terrorize his own people and
destabilize Central America. Friends of liberty in the region were "puzzled and discouraged," a State Department official reported, that the
United States while fighting dictators abroad was supporting them in the
hemisphere. The United States, Latin critics complained, had become a
"good neighbor of tyrants."[60]

Concern for the hemisphere also produced renewed interest and limited wartime commitments in Liberia, a country founded by freed Ameri-

56. Annette Palmer, "The United States in the British Caribbean, 1940–1945: Rum and
    Coca-Cola," *Americas* 43 (April 1987), 445.
57. Schoultz, *Beneath the United States*, 314–15.
58. Haines, "Eagle's Wing," 375.
59. Herring, "Most Unsordid Act Revisited," 18.
60. Philip Bonsal report, June 24, 1944, Papers of Edward R. Stettinius Jr., Manuscript Di-
    vision, University of Virginia Library; Haines, "Eagle's Wing," 377–78; Roorda, *Dic-
    tator Next Door*, 187.

can slaves. West Africa's proximity to the "bulge" on the east coast of Brazil and rising Nazi influence there brought Liberia to U.S. attention before Pearl Harbor. The loss of Southeast Asian rubber heightened the importance of the enormous Firestone plantations. The invasion of North Africa increased the value of the Brazil–West Africa air route. FDR's brief post-Casablanca visit to Liberia and his flight from there to Brazil gave presidential impetus to plans already under consideration in the government. During the war, the United States began to construct an airfield in Liberia and drew up plans for a modern port at Monrovia. To sweeten the deal, it provided Liberia a $1 million grant. To promote economic development, it dispatched technical missions to evaluate Liberia's mineral resources, increase its agricultural productivity, and improve medical facilities. Deeply concerned at the Amero-Liberian elite's exploitation of the native population, FDR was prepared to insist on reforms as a condition for further U.S. aid. He even contemplated some form of trusteeship to ensure the right kind of progress. His plans were incomplete when he died in April 1945.[61]

While solidifying its position close to home, the United States also took the first fateful steps toward entanglement in the Middle East, a complex and volatile region that would entice and frustrate Americans for the rest of the century and beyond. Some officials naively believed that the United States had earned the goodwill of Middle Eastern people, as Hull put it, from a "century of . . . missionary, education, and philanthropic efforts . . . never tarnished by any material motives or interests."[62] As Hull's remark suggests, the region was not entirely terra incognita to Americans. Missionaries had been there since the 1820s, working mainly with Christian minorities but also establishing schools and hospitals open to Muslims. Missionaries and educators founded Robert College in Turkey and the American University in Beirut. They spearheaded Near East Relief, which mounted a heroic effort to ease the vast human suffering from World War I and the breakup of the Ottoman Empire and has been called "one of the most notable chapters in the annals of American philanthropy abroad."[63] Good intentions notwithstanding, most Americans placed Arab and Jew alike near the bottom of their racial hierarchy, viewing them as backward, superstitious, and desperately in need of

61. Lloyd N. Beecher Jr., "The Second World War and U.S. Politico-Economic Expansionism: The Case of Liberia, 1938–1945," *Diplomatic History* 3 (Fall 1979), 391–412.
62. Gaddis Smith, *American Diplomacy During the Second World War* (2nd ed., New York, 1985), 96.
63. John A. DeNovo, *American Interests and Policies in the Middle East, 1900–1939* (Minneapolis, 1963), 387.

Westernization.[64] Material interests rather than ideals drove the wartime push into the Middle East. American merchants and businessmen had long been active in the region—in the twentieth century, oilmen especially so—and by 1940 U.S. firms had acquired oil concessions in Iraq, Kuwait, and Saudi Arabia. The growing importance of economic interests produced a diplomatic presence. The significance of Middle Eastern oil plus increasingly insistent demands on the part of Jewish-Americans for U.S. recognition of Zionist proposals for a Jewish homeland in Palestine brought together before World War II the conflicting forces that would dominate and bedevil U.S. Middle East policy to the present.

Early in the war, the United States deferred to the British. The Middle East had traditionally been a British sphere of influence, and as long as the region was in peril militarily Americans were not disposed to challenge their ally. When the British brutally suppressed a nationalist revolt in Egypt in February 1942, the Roosevelt administration said nothing.[65] It permitted Britain to distribute American lend-lease supplies to Middle Eastern nations. Even in Saudi Arabia, where U.S. oilmen hit a gusher in 1938, FDR allowed Churchill to take the lead. "This is a little far afield for us," he conceded to one of his advisers in 1941.[66]

United States policy changed dramatically in 1943. By this time the region was relatively secure, and the focus of war had shifted to new theaters, freeing Americans to challenge British colonialism. Exporters feared that Britain's domination of the region would close off vital postwar markets and insisted that the United States must liberate itself from British control. Critics like Roosevelt's personal emissary, the flamboyant and sometimes clownish former secretary of war Patrick Hurley—who also had close ties to U.S. oil interests—charged that Britain and the Soviet Union were using American supplies to curry favor with Middle Eastern nations. In response, the administration in 1943 took over distribution of lend-lease and marked all supplies with the U.S. flag and the words "Gift of the U.S.A." to make clear the source and thereby presumably gain full political benefit.[67]

The main reason for the shift can be summed up in one three-letter word: oil. With the loss of Southeast Asian supplies in early 1942, the im-

---

64. Douglas Little, *American Orientalism: The United States and the Middle East Since 1945* (Chapel Hill, N.C., 2004), 10.

65. Peter L. Hahn, *The United States, Great Britain, and Egypt, 1945–1946: Strategy and Diplomacy in the Early Cold War* (Chapel Hill, N.C., 1991), 18.

66. Little, *American Orientalism*, 48.

67. Herring, "Experiment in Foreign Aid," 348–52.

portance of Middle Eastern oil increased. World War II made quite clear that oil was the most precious commodity in modern warfare and the essential ingredient of national security and power. The U.S. war machine guzzled voracious quantities—the Fifth Fleet fighting in the Pacific consumed by itself 3.8 billion gallons of fuel in a single year. Government studies warned in alarmist—and, it would turn out, greatly exaggerated—tones that the nation could not meet its essential postwar needs from domestic sources. It must look abroad, and in "all the surveys of the situation," a State Department official recalled, "the pencil came to an awed pause at one point and place—the Middle East."[68]

The shift can be seen in policies toward individual nations. In Egypt, which had no oil, America's political and military presence remained limited, but its economic influence increased significantly. Minister Alexander Kirk railed against British imperialism and pushed for an Open Door policy.[69] United States investors and multinational corporations, working with conservative Egyptian elites and backed by Kirk, formed a sort of "New Deal coalition" that frustrated British neo-colonial schemes by establishing joint ventures for such projects as a huge chemical plant at Aswan on the Nile. The U.S. government helped fund the plan with a 1945 Export-Import Bank loan, marking the beginning of the retreat of British business from Egypt and the entry of U.S. firms such as Ford, Westinghouse, Kodak, and Coca-Cola.[70]

The United States pursued a much more vigorously independent course in Saudi Arabia. Hull described Saudi oil as "one of the world's greatest prizes." The country's strategic location between the Red Sea and the Persian Gulf offered logistical advantages for both the European and Pacific wars.[71] In April 1942, the Roosevelt administration opened a legation in Jidda and sent a technical mission to advise the government on irrigation. In February 1943, it made Saudi Arabia eligible for direct lend-lease aid. Two of King Ibn Saud's sons were invited to Washington and entertained lavishly at the White House. The United States extended a sizeable loan to the Arab kingdom and sent a military mission without consulting the British.

68. Daniel Yergin, The Prize: The Epic Quest for Oil, Money, and Power (New York, 1991), 396.
69. Hahn, United States, Great Britian, and Egypt, 18.
70. Robert Vitalis, "The 'New Deal' in Egypt: The Rise of Anglo-American Competition in World War II and the Fall of Neo-colonialism," Diplomatic History 20 (Spring 1996), 211–39.
71. Hull to Harold Ickes, November 13, 1943, Department of State, Foreign Relations of the United States, 1943, vol. 4 (Washington, 1964), 941.

The U.S. entry into Saudi Arabia set off a spirited—and for Saudi leaders lucrative—competition with Britain. The desert kingdom at this time had few resources and considerable needs. A man of great physical strength and an astute warrior-statesman, the fiercely independent Ibn Saud had used divide-and-conquer tactics to unite disparate tribes into the foundation of a modern state. He sought to exploit the Anglo-American rivalry to strengthen his nation and enhance his personal power. He submitted duplicate orders. When the two rivals tried to cooperate to curb his gargantuan appetite for military hardware and personal accoutrements, he hinted to each he might turn to the other. "Without arms or resources," he complained to nervous Americans, "Saudi Arabia must not reject the hand that measures its food and drink."[72] An aficionado of automobiles, he extorted luxury vehicles from both nations and still whined to Americans about the lack of spare parts and the slow delivery of an automobile promised his son.[73] In early 1944, Roosevelt and Churchill sought to calm rising tensions with mutual assurances about each other's stake in Middle Eastern oil. FDR averred that the United States was not casting "sheep's eyes" toward British holdings in Iran; extending the ovine metaphor, the prime minister responded that Britain would not "horn in" on U.S. interests in Saudi Arabia.[74] In Saudi Arabia, however, the competition continued and, reflecting the shifting balance of economic power, became increasingly one-sided. In early 1945, Churchill sent Ibn Saud a refurbished Rolls-Royce. FDR trumped him with a spanking new DC-3 aircraft and a crew for one year, the basis for Trans World Airlines' entry into Middle East air routes.[75] Saudi Arabia was the only nation for whom lend-lease was continued after the war. The United States solidified its control of Saudi oil and over strong British opposition developed plans to build an air base at Dhahran (completed in 1946) to protect those holdings.[76]

The wartime experience in Iran best exemplifies the illusions and frustrations of America's initial move into the Middle East. Iran possessed the region's largest known oil reserves, long dominated by the Anglo-Iranian

72. William Eddy to Hull, September 7, 1944, *Foreign Relations of the United States, 1944*, vol. 6 (Washington, 1967), 734–36.

73. James Moose to State Department, August 2, 1944, William Culbertson Papers, Manuscript Division, Library of Congress, Washington, DC.

74. FDR to WSC, March 3, 1944, WSC to FDR, March 4, 1944, in Kimball, *Churchill-Roosevelt Correspondence* 3:14, 17.

75. David Holden and Richard Johns, *The House of Saud* (New York, 1981), 139–40.

76. James L. Gormly, "Keeping the Door Open in Saudi Arabia: The United States and the Dhahran Airfield, 1945–1946," *Diplomatic History* 4 (Spring 1980), 189–205.

Oil Company. Threatened by the Nazis in 1941, it was jointly occupied by the British and Russians, who deposed the pro-German shah and installed his son, the twenty-two-year-old Muhammad Reza Shah Pahlavi, a retiring and in some ways tragic figure who would be a major player in postwar Middle Eastern history. Sharing British and Soviet concern about the Nazi threat, the United States acquiesced in the occupation. Iran had long survived by playing outside powers against each other. With the British and Russians working together, it turned to the United States as a buffer.

Washington responded sympathetically. United States officials recognized the strategic importance of Iran. Some also saw an opportunity for their nation to live up to its anti-colonial ideals by protecting Iran against the rapacious Europeans. FDR conceded on one occasion that he was "thrilled with the idea of using Iran as an example of what we could do by an unselfish American policy."[77] The United States thus charted an independent course, furnishing lend-lease supplies directly rather than through the British and dispatching a number of technical missions to provide the know-how to assist Iran toward independence and modernization. The United States alone, a State Department official observed, could "build up Iran to the point at which it will stand in need of neither British nor Russian assistance to maintain order in its own house."[78]

This ambitious and ill-conceived experiment in nation-building failed miserably. It operated on the naive assumption that limited advice and assistance from disinterested Americans would enable Iran to develop the stability and prosperity to fend off predators like the Soviet Union and Britain. The U.S. Army did construct a vital supply route from the Persian Gulf to the USSR, but that project brought little immediate benefit to Iran, and the carousing and cultural insensitivity of some of the thirty thousand GIs working on it offended local Muslim sensibilities. A mission directed by Col. H. Norman Schwarzkopf, who had won national notoriety as head of the New Jersey State Police during the kidnapping of aviator Charles Lindbergh's child, achieved a "small miracle" by converting a "once bedraggled" gendarmerie into a respectable rural police force. The other missions were understaffed and poorly prepared. Few of the Americans knew the language or anything about the country. They squabbled among themselves and with the U.S. Army, losing credibility

---

77. Mark Hamilton Lytle, *The Origins of the Iranian-American Alliance, 1941–1953* (New York, 1987), 59.
78. James A. Bill, *The Eagle and the Lion: The Tragedy of Iranian-American Relations* (New Haven, Conn., 1988), 19.

among their hosts. The most conspicuous failure was a finance mission headed by Arthur Millspaugh, who had enjoyed some success in Iran in a similar capacity in the 1920s. A poor administrator, he spoke no French or Farsi. He correctly pinpointed the problems to be addressed, but his proposed solutions and his imperious methods alienated those Iranians who profited most from the status quo and those nationalists eager for reform.[79] "The Iranian himself is the best person to manage his house," nationalist leader Mohammad Mosaddeq proclaimed.[80] The missions undermined the positive image the United States had brought to Iran in 1941. Iranians made them a scapegoat for the nation's problems. Designed to bolster Iran's independence, they destabilized its politics and aggravated tensions with Britain and the USSR.

The failure of the missions marked the end of the idealistic phase of U.S. policy in Iran. At Tehran in December 1943, Roosevelt persuaded Churchill and Stalin to agree to a declaration pledging support for Iran's independence. Bemoaning Soviet and British imperialism and the chaos that afflicted the American effort in Iran, the voluble Hurley urged a redoubled U.S. intervention headed by a strong-willed individual—no doubt himself. High State Department officials, on the other hand, denounced Hurley's proposal as a "classic case of imperial penetration," an "innocent indulgence in messianic globaloney."[81] Roosevelt seemed interested, but his attention quickly shifted to other matters and he rejected Hurley's proposal.

By this time U.S. policy in Iran was undergoing major change. The relentless push for concessions in Iran drove the major oil companies and the U.S. and British governments toward cooperative arrangements to stabilize international production and distribution. The Anglo-American Petroleum Agreement of 1944 infuriated small U.S. producers and was never approved by Congress, but it eased temporarily the fierce rivalry in Iran. More important, a Soviet move for an oil concession in northern Iran in 1944 increasingly brought two formerly bitter rivals together. Both British and U.S. diplomats viewed Moscow's ploy not as a response to U.S. efforts to gain oil concessions in Iran but as a power play to expand its influence into the Persian Gulf. If not yet working together, Britons and Americans increasingly agreed on the need to check the Soviet threat. No mere puppet, the Iranian government itself resolved the

79. Lytle, *Iranian-American Alliance*, 103–17.
80. Bill, *Eagle and Lion*, 26.
81. Lytle, *Iranian-American Alliance*, 60.

immediate crisis and protected its future interests by refusing to approve any oil concessions until the war ended.[82]

By 1943, that other inflammatory ingredient of an already volatile Middle Eastern mix had also come into play. The Zionist quest for a Jewish homeland in Palestine emerged late in the nineteenth century out of desperation—and hope—on the part of Europe's persecuted and dispossessed Jews. The idea gradually gained support among America's large and increasingly influential Jewish community. When World War I set off a bidding war between the Allies and the Central Powers for Jewish support, the Zionist dream first gained international recognition. The British-sponsored Balfour Resolution of 1917, perfunctorily supported by Woodrow Wilson, pledged carefully qualified backing for a Jewish homeland in Palestine. With the rise of a new wave of anti-Semitism in the 1930s, especially in Nazi Germany, immigration to Palestine soared, sparking violent resistance from native Arabs. Fearful on the eve of war of a dangerous conflict in a strategically critical area, Britain in 1939 issued a white paper drastically curtailing Jewish immigration to Palestine and then shutting it down after five years. The white paper solved little. Arabs doubted its assurances; Jews mobilized to fight it.[83]

The drive for a Jewish homeland became linked in wartime with the unfolding horror of Hitler's Final Solution. As early as the summer of 1942, word began to filter out of Europe of the establishment of death camps and the systematic killing of European Jews. The initial reports did not begin to capture the enormity of the atrocities, but many Americans, insulated from direct contact with the war, questioned them nonetheless. Even when the magnitude of the extermination began to emerge, the administration could do little. FDR publicly condemned the killing of Jews and vowed to conduct war criminal trials to hold the perpetrators accountable. To take the matter out of the hands of an unsympathetic State Department, he created in 1943 a War Refugees Board that enjoyed some success helping Hungarian Jews escape Nazi grasp. But the president refused, with the war still far from won, to challenge Congress by seeking to ease immigration restrictions. And the War Department rejected proposals to bomb the death camp at Auschwitz on grounds that it would accomplish little and divert crucial resources from "essential" military tasks. The pragmatic U.S. response to a great moral catastrophe is somehow unsatisfying. But it is far from clear that any of the courses proposed to deal

82. Yergin, *Prize*, 405–8; Lytle, *Iranian-American Alliance*, 120–22.
83. David Schoenbaum, *The United States and the State of Israel* (New York, 1993), 25.

with the Holocaust could have been effectively implemented or would have saved significant numbers of lives.[84]

As the magnitude of Hitler's atrocities began to emerge, Zionists stepped up their agitation for a homeland, and sympathy tinged with some measure of guilt brought growing support. Many Americans also saw large-scale immigration of Jews to Palestine as preferable to swelling their already sizeable numbers in the United States. At New York's Biltmore Hotel in May 1942, Palestinian Jewish leaders such as David Ben-Gurion and Chaim Weizmann inspired a gathering of Jewish-Americans to support unlimited immigration into Palestine and the creation of a "Jewish Commonwealth integrated into the structure of the new democratic world."[85] The Biltmore group mounted a massive and effective campaign to sway Congress and the American public.

Caught between Arab fears and Jewish demands, the Roosevelt administration handled a volatile issue like a ticking time bomb. The president had made Jewish-Americans an integral part of his New Deal coalition and relied on their electoral support. In the State Department and other federal agencies, on the other hand, there was virulent anti-Semitism. Most important, the question of a Jewish homeland threatened to upset the delicate political balance in a critical region. GIs had already come under fire in Palestine, and military leaders feared that Jewish agitation could spark further conflict in an important rear area. At a time when U.S. attention was focused on the Middle East to meet presumably urgent demands for oil, the Palestine issue threatened to upset the Arabs who controlled it. Ibn Saud prophetically warned Roosevelt in 1943 that if the Jews got their wish, "Palestine would forever remain a hot bed of troubles and disturbances."[86] FDR at times fantasized about going to the region after leaving the presidency and promoting economic development projects like the Tennessee Valley Authority. He expressed confidence that he could resolve the dispute in face-to-face conversations with Arab leaders. Characteristically, the administration dealt with the most pressing issues with pleas for restraint, platitudes, and vague assurances to

---

84. Dallek, *Roosevelt and American Foreign Policy*, 446–48; Kennedy, *Freedom from Fear*, 794–97. David S. Wyman, *The Abandonment of the Jews: America and the Holocaust, 1941–1945* (New York, 1998) provides a strong critique of U.S. policy. Michael C. Desch, "The Myth of the Abandonment: The Use and Abuse of the Holocaust Analogy," *Security Studies* 15 (January–March 2006), 16–23, offers a persuasive response.

85. Schoenbaum, *United States and Israel*, 25.

86. Matthew Wayne Coulter, "The Joint Anglo-American Statement on Palestine," *Historian* 54 (Spring 1992), 469.

both sides. A master of the latter, FDR, after assuring Ibn Saud in 1943 that he would do nothing without full consultation, concluded the following year—at election time—that Palestine should be for Jews alone.[87] During the campaign, while fending off a congressional resolution favoring a Jewish homeland, he promised to help Jewish leaders find ways to establish a state.

For Roosevelt, the last act in the unfolding drama came in February 1945 en route home from the Yalta Conference when he met Ibn Saud at Great Bitter Lake north of the Suez Canal. The king was transported there by a U.S. destroyer, traveling in a tent pitched on deck (U.S. sailors called it the "big top") with an entourage of forty-three attendants and eight live sheep to meet requirements of Muslim laws for preparing food. Much impressed with Ibn Saud, FDR labeled him a "great whale of a man" and left a wheelchair for the battle-scarred warrior's use. The president hoped to persuade the king to acquiesce in a Jewish homeland. What he got was adamant opposition to further Jewish settlement—even to the planting of trees in Palestine. "Amends should be made by the criminal, not by the innocent bystander," he told FDR, proposing instead a Jewish homeland in Germany. Taken aback, Roosevelt pledged in typical fashion that he would "do nothing to assist the Jews against the Arabs and would make no move hostile to the Arab people." His subsequent public statement that he had learned more from Ibn Saud in five minutes than from countless exchanges of letters struck fear in Zionists allayed only in part by subsequent soothing reassurances.[88] The Middle East took a backseat to more pressing issues in the last stages of the war. By virtue of its rising power and emerging interests, however, the United States had taken a keen interest in the region and through oil and Palestine had become caught up in a hopelessly intractable dispute.

A powerful undercurrent in the Middle East, the issue of colonialism dominated U.S. involvement with South and Southeast Asia. Held in check in the 1930s by brute force and token concessions, nationalists quickly saw in the war a chance to gain their freedom. They read carefully and literally the 1941 Atlantic Charter and found in it sanction for their cause. Japan's sweep through Southeast Asia in 1942 graphically exposed the weakness of colonial regimes. In some areas, the new rulers

---

87. Thomas M. Campbell and George C. Herring, eds., *The Diaries of Edward R. Stettinius, Jr., 1943–1946* (New York, 1975), 170, 174.
88. Holden and Johns, *House of Saud*, 137–40; Rachel Bronson, *Thicker than Oil: America's Uneasy Partnership with Saudi Arabia* (New York, 2006), 38–42.

imposed a more cruel and oppressive rule than the Europeans, but their cry of "Asia for Asians" resonated with local nationalists. Because of its power and its anti-colonial tradition, nationalist leaders looked to the United States for support. Like it or not, the Roosevelt administration found itself ensnared in the complex historical process of decolonization that would dominate world politics for years to come.

The colonial issue was among the most challenging of the myriad complex problems raised by the war. Many Americans were firmly committed to Wilson's dream of self-determination. African Americans in particular saw a direct connection between the oppression of peoples of color at home and abroad and pushed for an end to both.[89] The colonial issue became in the eyes of Americans and peoples across the world a test case for the nation's commitment to its war aims. At the same time, many U.S. officials doubted, usually on the basis of racial considerations, that colonial peoples were ready for self-government and feared that premature independence could lead to chaos. They also worried that to force the issue of independence during the war could undermine crucial allies like Britain and threaten Allied cooperation when the outcome of the war remained uncertain.

Roosevelt's handling of the issue is typically difficult to decipher. He often railed against European colonialism—Britain, he once snarled, echoing John Quincy Adams, "would take land anywhere in the world even if it were only a rock or sand bar."[90] At a Casablanca conference dinner, while Churchill chomped angrily on his cigar, FDR raised with the sultan of Morocco the possibility of independence. On the other hand, he shared the assumptions of his generation that most colonial peoples were unready for independence and would need guidance from the "advanced" nations. Critics have correctly noted that his often bold rhetoric was not matched by decisive actions. He refused to demand of the colonial nations forthright pledges of independence. As Kimball has emphasized, on the other hand, he was utterly Wilsonian, and correct, in his assessment that colonialism was morally reprehensible—and doomed. Ever the pragmatist, he refused to jeopardize the alliance by mounting a frontal assault on colonialism. At the same time, he kept the issue on the front burner, bringing it up often, using various means to nudge the colonial powers in the right direction, apparently hoping that what he called

89. Brenda Gayle Plummer, *Rising Wind: Black Americans and U.S. Foreign Affairs* (Chapel Hill, N.C., 1996), 87–100.
90. Campbell and Herring, *Stettinius Diaries*, 40.

the glare of "pitiless publicity" (turning Churchill's own words against him) would promote international support for independence.[91]

In the first years of the war, India was the most visible and emotional of decolonization issues, and it clearly reveals Roosevelt's approach. Under the leadership of the saintly Mahatma Gandhi, Indian nationalists had pushed the British toward self-government, and they seized the emergency of war to press for pledges of independence. Many British leaders, including the arch-imperialist Churchill, were not prepared to abandon the crown jewel of an empire on which it was once said the sun had never set. They in turn used military exigencies and the threat of communal warfare between Hindus and Muslims as excuses to delay, offering no more than vague promises of "dominion status" once the war had ended.[92]

India quickly became the major irritant in the Anglo-American partnership. Even before Pearl Harbor, the United States had given symbolic support to India's appeals for independence by establishing direct diplomatic relations with the colonial regime. It insisted that lend-lease aid be sent directly to the Indian government rather than through the British. At their first wartime meeting in January 1942, Roosevelt prodded Churchill to pledge support for eventual Indian independence. By his own account, the prime minister exploded, and the president never again raised the issue with him directly. But FDR continued to needle Churchill through third parties ranging from Hopkins to Chinese leader Chiang Kai-shek. He insisted that the government of India sign the United Nations Declaration. At various stops on a world tour taken at the president's behest, Wendell Willkie denounced imperialism. In China, he pressed the colonial powers to set a timetable for independence. Over and over, the president offered U.S. mediation between Britain and Gandhi's nationalists.

Such efforts deeply antagonized the British. Hopkins's initiative provoked a "string of cuss words that lasted two hours into the night"; Willkie's unwelcome intrusion brought forth Churchill's famous affirmation about the liquidation of the British Empire.[93] In India, the standoff hardened, and when nationalists demanded that Britain get out, the authorities responded by imprisoning Gandhi and other leaders. Britons suspected the United States of horning in on their imperial interests; Indians viewed it as an accessory to British imperialism. Critics at home and abroad attacked the Roosevelt administration for doing nothing. A

---

91. For the Casablanca encounter, see Kimball, Forged, 192–93; FDR's views on colonialism are discussed in Kimball, Juggler, 127–31; the "pitiless publicity" quote is from 145.
92. Ibid., 132–40.
93. Stimson Diary, April 22, 1942; Kimball, Juggler, 136.

high State Department official warned that if the United States appeared to be "more interested in the creation of sonorous phrases than in the implementation of the principles enunciated in those phrases, we can expect a harvest of hate and contempt the like of which our imperialistically minded ally has never known."[94]

Roosevelt responded in 1943 by sending career diplomat William Phillips to India as his personal representative, his furthest and final intrusion into an intractable issue. An Anglophile who looked down on "lesser" peoples, Phillips typified that group of upper-class professional diplomats who manned the State Department. Viewing him as "the best type of American gentleman," some British officials expected him to sympathize with their position. Once in India, however, he traveled widely and spoke to Indians as well as Britons. He found the British stubbornly uncompromising, the Indians divided on many issues but united in their demand for independence. Seeing firsthand the rising power of Indian nationalism, he pressed the British to make concessions. They rebuffed his interference and even forbade him to see Gandhi, then engaged in a much publicized hunger strike. Phillips eventually left India in frustration, and his generally unsuccessful mission typifies Roosevelt's approach to this difficult issue. The president refused to challenge Churchill directly and thereby threaten the alliance. On the other hand, he used Phillips to keep the colonial issue alive and pressure the British. Phillips's presence in India and his growing support for the cause helped regain the trust of Indians and permitted the United States to retain a nominal commitment to the ideal of self-determination.[95]

Frustrated in India, Roosevelt after 1943 shifted his attack on colonialism to French Indochina, in his view no doubt a more convenient and vulnerable target. His relentless verbal assault against French colonialism and his espousal of a trusteeship policy for Indochina manifested the then novel presumption that the United States should and could dictate solutions to global problems. It reveals much about Roosevelt's—and America's—larger views toward colonialism, nationalism, and the postwar world.

In 1943, FDR frequently expressed his wish not to permit the French to regain their Indochinese colonies, then under Japanese protectorate. His position and the adamancy with which he expressed it reflected his general dislike for the French, reinforced by their collapse in 1940, and his

---

94. Kenton J. Clymer, "The Education of William Phillips: Self-Determination and American Policy Toward India, 1942–1945," *Diplomatic History* 8 (Winter 1984), 29.
95. Ibid., 34.

particular contempt for the imperious Free French leader Charles de Gaulle. Unlike the British, the Dutch, and especially the Americans, FDR averred, France had brutally exploited the Indochinese and done nothing to prepare them for self-government. It had "milked" Indochina for one hundred years, he told the British ambassador. "The people . . . are entitled to something better than that."[96]

Roosevelt's determination to prevent a French return did not translate into support for Vietnamese independence. In part because the French had not been responsible colonizers, he believed, the Vietnamese were not ready to govern themselves. He knew little of the nationalist movement then building in Vietnam. Like most Americans, he paternalistically looked down upon the Vietnamese as childlike and in need of guidance before being given their freedom. He thus proposed the idea of trusteeship through which an advanced nation would help backward people evolve toward full independence. His model, not surprisingly, was U.S. rule in the Philippines, through which, in his view, a benevolent Western nation had prepared a colonial people for independence over a half century. There are "many minor children among the peoples of the world who need trustees," he observed in 1941, "just as there are many adult nations or peoples who must be led back into a spirit of good conduct."[97]

Roosevelt's trusteeship scheme provoked vigorous opposition abroad and at home. As a means to restore their lost glory, French citizens of all political persuasions were deeply and emotionally committed to reestablishing the empire in Indochina. To curry favor with an old ally and protect their own Southeast Asian colonies, the British backed the French. Churchill stonewalled Roosevelt on decolonization in general and the Indochina trusteeship in particular. Behind FDR's back, the British also facilitated a French return to Indochina by permitting French participation in the British-run Southeast Asia Command. Some conservative State Department officials preferred a French return to Indochina on condition the French committed themselves to eventual independence. Top military officers sought U.S. sovereignty over the Pacific islands held by Japan as mandates to permit "full control" over bases deemed vital to America's postwar security. They saw application of the trusteeship principle to liberated areas in general as a threat to U.S. security interests.[98]

96. Mark Philip Bradley, *Imagining Vietnam and America: The Making of Postcolonial Vietnam, 1919–1950* (Chapel Hill, N.C., 2000), 81.
97. Smith, *American Diplomacy*, 80.
98. Stimson Diary, April 17, 1945.

Roosevelt bent in the face of opposition, but he did not falter in his commitment to the idea of trusteeship for Indochina—and presumably other colonial areas as well. While admitting the need for U.S. bases in the Pacific, he adamantly insisted that sovereignty must rest with the islands themselves. Eventually and grudgingly bowing to Paris and London on Indochina, he conceded that France might be the trustee, but he insisted upon a firm and explicit French commitment to independence and accountability to international authority, presumably a new international organization. By permitting France to return, the compromise certainly weakened the trusteeship plan. On the other hand, as Kimball concludes, Roosevelt may have set a trap to force France in time to dissolve its empire in Indochina and elsewhere as well. FDR certainly underestimated French determination to return and Vietnamese determination to resist. But his instincts were right, and the result of his not following them more aggressively and his successors deviating sharply from them was thirty years of war in Indochina.[99]

Few wartime problems were more perplexing for the United States than what historian Herbert Feis called "the China tangle," where imperialism was also a key issue.[100] Japan's defeat seemed likely to end Western imperialism in China, but it was not clear what would follow. The United States and China differed sharply over how and for what purposes the war should be fought.

The two nations entered the alliance with high expectations. Chiang Kai-shek shared the intense nationalism of his generation and did not exempt the United States from those imperialist nations responsible for China's woes. But for Chiang Pearl Harbor was a godsend. The United States would now presumably take up the burden of liberating China. It would provide military and economic assistance to help eliminate rivals like Mao Zedong's Communists and solidify Nationalist control over a free China. By December 1941, Chiang had a well-lubricated influence machine operating in the United States including paid lobbyist and former New Deal insider Tommy "the Cork" Corcoran, China Defense Supplies, a purchasing agent staffed by well-connected Americans, and the powerful Time-Life publications of Henry Luce. With U.S. belligerency, Chiang's operatives sought to make China a full partner in the war.

Americans also had high expectations. Conditioned by forty years of the Open Door policy to see themselves as China's patron and more re-

99. Kimball, *Juggler*, 153–57.
100. Herbert Feis, *The China Tangle* (New York, 1965).

cently by Luce to view Chiang as a heroic and embattled defender of freedom against Japanese tyranny, they looked upon China as an important ally. Roosevelt sensed the power of Chinese nationalism and sought to contain it through the person of Chiang Kai-shek. He spoke of China as a fourth great power, a bastion of regional stability in East Asia after Japan's defeat, and a buffer against possible Soviet expansion. Like other Americans, he hoped a grateful China would support U.S. policies, "a faggot vote," Churchill sneered.[101] Shortly after Pearl Harbor, the administration moved to cement its ties to China by extending a loan of $500 million and dispatching Gen. Joseph Stilwell to Chungking as a military adviser.

Expectations on both sides were quickly shattered. Those Americans who came into contact with Chiang's China soon discovered that popular images bore little resemblance to reality. The Nationalist government was weak, divided internally, riddled with corruption, and lacking in popular support. The heroic leader depicted by Luce, a veritable Asian George Washington, sought mainly to preserve his own power. The largely conscript army was a slightly organized rabble, by no means ready to undertake operations against the Japanese. In any event, Chiang refused to risk it in combat, counting on the Americans to liberate China while he subdued his internal rivals.[102]

China was even more disappointed with the United States. Despite the president's rhetoric, China was not admitted to the Allied inner circle. It remained a second-class ally whose role was to keep Japanese troops busy until the European war was won. The wars in Europe and the Pacific continued to have top priority, and precious few supplies were allocated for China. Even when supplies were available, it took superhuman efforts to get them to Chungking. When the Japanese closed the Burma Road in 1942, supplies had to be shipped to the west coast of India, transshipped by rail across the breadth of the Indian subcontinent, and then flown over the perilous hump of the Himalayas to Chungking. Increasingly frustrated with the paucity of U.S. aid, Chiang issued only slightly veiled threats to quit the war. We are "on a raft with one sandwich between us, and the rescue ship is heading away from the scene," an equally frustrated Stilwell complained. "They are too busy elsewhere for small fry like us."[103]

101. Warren I. Cohen, *America's Response to China: An Interpretative History of Sino-American Relations* (New York, 1972), 162.
102. Michael Schaller, *The United States and China in the Twentieth Century* (New York, 1990), 74–80.
103. Theodore White, ed., *The Stilwell Papers* (New York, 1948), 171.

Stilwell and Chiang agreed on little else, and their relationship quickly soured. The acerbic general, appropriately nicknamed "Vinegar Joe," had served in China in the 1920s, knew the language, and had great affection for the people. He wanted to build an effective army to fight the Japanese, but his efforts to reform the army threatened Chiang's key power base, and the generalissimo naturally balked. Stilwell despised Chiang and filled the pages of his diary with venomous outbursts against a man he called in his more generous moments "the Peanut," at other times a "grasping, bigoted, ungrateful little rattlesnake."[104] He sought full control over U.S. aid to bend Chiang to his will.

To get around Stilwell and challenge China's low place in the Allied pecking order, Chiang sent his wife—the couple had been named *Time's* "Man and Wife of the Year" in 1937—to the United States in 1942 on a personal lobbying mission. The daughter of a wealthy, U.S.-educated Shanghai father, the diminutive, beautiful Mayling Soong, in Barbara Tuchman's words, "combined graduation from Wellesley College with the instinct for power of the Empress Dowager."[105] Her delicate stature only slightly obscured an iron will and a cruel streak. She lingered in the United States for six months. Privately, she railed against Stilwell. In speeches to huge and adoring throngs in major U.S. cities and especially in a remarkable February 1943 appearance before a joint session of Congress—the first Chinese and only the second woman to address that body—she openly challenged the Europe-first strategy and the low priority assigned aid to China. She received a four-minute standing ovation. Madame Chiang "enthralled and captivated Washington as few other official visitors have ever done," the *New York Herald-Tribune* enthused.[106]

Unwilling to alter the nation's strategic priorities, increasingly disillusioned with Chiang, and weary of "the missimo's" lobbying, FDR appeased his disgruntled ally with expedients.[107] As part of its broader assault on imperialism and to palliate Chiang, the United States in 1943 relinquished extraterritoriality, one of the most galling features of the unequal treaties imposed on China in the mid-nineteenth century. It also eliminated the immigration restrictions that had been a special irritant in Chinese-American relations since the 1880s. Roosevelt promised Chiang that territories taken from China by Japan since their war of 1895 would

104. Schaller, *United States and China*, 84.
105. Barbara W. Tuchman, *Stilwell and the American Experience in China, 1941–1945* (New York, 1971), 116.
106. February 19, 1943.
107. Stimson Diary, November 4, 1943.

be returned. He boosted China as one of his Four Policemen who would assume responsibility for regional stability after the war. He did not include Chiang in Big Three summit meetings, but he met privately with the generalissimo in Cairo en route to Tehran in late 1943. Over Stilwell's vociferous objections, he approved a proposal advanced by Gen. Claire Chennault, another U.S. adviser in Chungking, to launch a major bombing campaign against Japanese positions in China.

An already tattered alliance all but came apart in 1944. Chennault's aerial attacks had disastrous consequences, provoking a massive Japanese counteroffensive that produced huge Chinese losses and strengthened Japan's position in coastal China. The more Americans saw of the Nationalist government, in the meantime, the more they complained of corruption, greed, and venality, including the embezzlement of substantial funds by Chiang's family. In contrast, the Communists based in Yenan province projected an image of efficiency and order. Their suave spokesman, Zhou En-lai, told Americans what they wanted to hear, promising to take the fight to the Japanese. The Communists also staged a huge July 4 celebration in Yenan, and Mao assured U.S. visitors that the most conservative American businessman would find nothing objectionable in his program. A frustrated Roosevelt administration demanded that Chiang put Stilwell in full command of the army and mount operations against the Japanese. More ominously, the United States insisted on sending observers to Yenan. These moves shook to their foundations the Sino-American alliance and indeed Chiang's entire approach to the war.[108]

The generalissimo fended off the immediate U.S. threat. He grudgingly acquiesced in the sending of Americans to Yenan. After a series of incredibly complex moves and countermoves in an intricate diplomatic chess game, he finessed U.S. demands to put his troops into action. He wangled the appointment of the peripatetic Hurley as personal U.S. representative to his government and then used the new appointee to get rid of the despised Stilwell.[109]

Chiang's short-term successes backfired, contributing to a major shift in U.S. policy that would disastrously affect his long-run interests. His demonstrated unwillingness to fight combined with the success of General MacArthur's island-hopping campaign in the Pacific brought a top-level decision to avoid major military operations on the East Asian mainland. China would continue to be a peripheral player; its status as a

108. Dallek, *Roosevelt and American Foreign Policy*, 485–502.
109. Schaller, *United States and China*, 102–3.

second-class ally was confirmed. U.S. postwar visions also changed. The Yenan observers, who called themselves the Dixie Mission since they were in "rebel" territory, were welcomed by an orchestra and chorus performing Chinese classics and in turn hastily improvised a choral group to sing American "classics" such as "My Old Kentucky Home." They were impressed with the Communists' professionalism, efficiency, and apparent willingness to fight and viewed their hosts as "backsliders" from pure Marxist ideology. Some Americans concluded that Mao's forces would win a civil war and advocated U.S. support for them. Others feared that a Communist victory might bring Soviet control of and U.S. eviction from China.[110] Most conceded that Chiang's China could not act as regional policeman. To avert a looming civil war, the Roosevelt administration set out to bring the Nationalists and Communists into a coalition that would produce some semblance of order and maintain U.S. influence in a vital region after the defeat of Japan and the demise of Western imperialism.

Such a feat would have been difficult to pull off by the most skilled of diplomats in the best of circumstances, but in the hands of the inept and opinionated Hurley in the volatile climate of wartime China it was doomed from the start. As ignorant of China as of the Middle East, Hurley assumed his customary role of buffoon. He referred to Chiang and his wife as "Mr. And Mrs. Chek," to Mao as "Moose Dung," and to Zhou as "Joe N. Lie." On one occasion, upon landing at Communist headquarters, to the shock of all present, he let out a Cherokee war whoop. His Yenan hosts soon referred to him as "the Clown."[111] His antics concealed the hard edge to his diplomacy. A virulent anti-Communist and unabashed partisan of Chiang, he set out to construct a coalition with the Communists as junior partners. When U.S. diplomats on the scene questioned the wisdom of his approach, he branded them disloyal and demanded their recall. This first clumsy effort to avert civil war in China failed miserably by late 1944, sending FDR casting about for alternatives. It set the stage for civil war in China and the postwar Red Scare in the United States. The China tangle, in turn, presaged the host of complex political problems the United States would confront as the focus shifted from winning the war to securing the peace.

110. Frederick Kevin Simon, "The United States Observer Group in Yenan: A Venture in Sino-American Relations, 1944–1945" (M.A. thesis, University of Kentucky, 1977), chapter 2.
111. Schaller, *United States and China*, 103–4.

IV

In the year after the Tehran Conference, the Allies sealed the Axis fate. The Red Army had liberated all of Soviet territory by early 1944, and in the summer it mounted a massive offensive across Eastern and Central Europe timed to coincide with the Western allies' invasion of France. Following their successful D-Day landing at Normandy on June 6, the United States and Britain began the liberation of France and the drive toward Germany. Hitler's defeat was assured; the only questions were the time it would take and the costs that would be incurred. Allied forces also made significant progress against Japan. After reversing the tide of battle at Midway in the summer of 1942 and Guadalcanal later in the year, U.S. forces began an arduous and bloody advance across the islands of the South and Central Pacific to Japan. Following the air and naval battle of

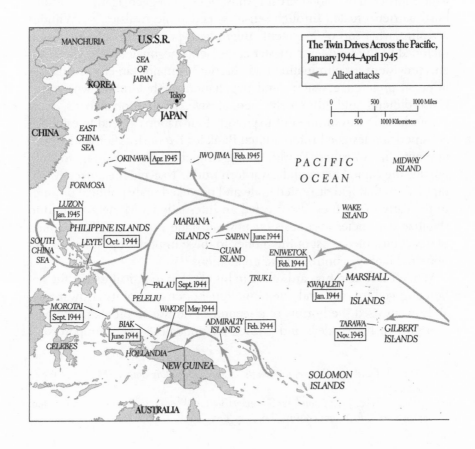

the Philippine Sea and the climactic battle of Leyte Gulf in October 1944, the greatest and last naval engagement of the war, the United States was poised to liberate the Philippines. In the meantime, new B-29 Super-fortress bombers, with vast range and a huge payload, mounted a devastating aerial campaign against the Japanese home islands.

With Axis defeat all but certain, the postwar issues that had been put on hold inevitably moved to the forefront. In the economic realm, Americans began planning early and used their economic clout to impose their will. Haunted by bitter memories of the Great Depression and fearing a postwar reprise, they set out to correct the problems they fervently believed had caused that catastrophe and the resulting war. As much as they squabbled among themselves, most U.S. officials—even Hull and Welles!—agreed that eliminating trade barriers was the key to postwar peace and prosperity. America's huge wartime productivity underscored the need for foreign markets once hostilities ended. "Commerce is the lifeblood of a free society," FDR proclaimed in 1944, and the "arteries" which carried that "blood stream" must not be "clogged again . . . by artificial barriers created through senseless economic rivalries."[112] Without revealing what sort of "payment" might be expected, the administration included in the lend-lease master agreements negotiated with all recipients provisions for eliminating trade barriers. A major target was Britain's imperial preference system, and negotiations with London were especially difficult and ultimately inconclusive. At Bretton Woods, New Hampshire, in the summer of 1944, forty-four nations agreed to establish an American-designed International Bank for Reconstruction and Development (the so-called World Bank), funded at $7.6 billion, to help provide the capital to rebuild a war-torn world. To avoid the currency manipulations that had disrupted trade and provoked nasty political disputes in the early 1930s, they also created an International Monetary Fund to stabilize currencies as a basis for postwar trade expansion. The United States contributed most of the money to these important postwar institutions and thereby controlled their operations.[113]

While FDR held his cards close to his chest on political issues, the nation engaged in a full and often emotional discussion of its postwar role. Wilsonians used the horrors of a second world war to proclaim vindication of their hero's ideas and pressed for unqualified U.S. support for a

---

112. Lloyd C. Gardner, *Economic Aspects of New Deal Diplomacy* (Madison, Wisc., 1964), 287.

113. Alfred E. Eckes Jr., *A Search for Solvency: Bretton Woods and the International Monetary System, 1941–1971* (Austin, Tex., 1975), 135–64.

reincarnated and reinvigorated League of Nations. In 1944, Hollywood produced a hit film entitled *Wilson* that portrayed its subject and his dreams as the tragic victims of personal and partisan squabbling. Responding to Luce's 1941 call for an "American Century," Vice President Wallace proclaimed the "century of the common man" and advocated a "people's revolution"—a global New Deal—to ensure that all peoples had "the privilege of drinking a quart of milk every day." Sumner Welles and contract bridge guru Ely Culbertson advocated an international police force; others proposed a world federation. Wendell Willkie's stirring account of his global tour, *One World*, stressed that the shrinkage of distances had brought peoples together and made peace indivisible. It enjoyed the highest sales of any book published in the United States to this time. Alarmed by the rampant idealism of Wallace and Willkie, Yale University political geographer Nicholas Spykman urged a realpolitik approach to the postwar world. Journalist and onetime Wilsonian Walter Lippmann's 1943 book, *U.S. Foreign Policy: Shield of the Republic*, echoed Spykman in calling for a foreign policy based on the balance of power. An instant best seller, it was excerpted in the *Reader's Digest* and, most remarkably, appeared in a cartoon version in the *Ladies' Home Journal*. Polls taken in 1942–43 indicated broad popular support for U.S. participation in an international organization. Congress jumped out ahead of the White House in late 1943 by approving separate resolutions to that effect.[114]

A newly empowered military establishment approached postwar planning with special urgency. In their view, the debacle at Pearl Harbor had occurred because the civilian leadership, rejecting their advice, had pursued provocative policies toward Japan not backed by force. Another war was certain, they insisted, and technological advances would leave no time for last-minute preparation. The nation must be able to deter aggression or overwhelm it at the outset. There was even discussion of preemptive war. Military leaders were deeply skeptical of international organization. In a "world in which people play for keeps," Admiral King asserted, "we have got to take care of ourselves."[115] They insisted on being included in postwar planning and urged that the nation maintain sufficient military power to deal with any threats. Air power was especially important, and the United States must have the bases to make it workable. They began to see at least dimly the major geopolitical consequences of the war—the

114. Robert A. Divine, *Second Chance: The Triumph of Internationalism in America During World War II* (New York, 1967), 78–81, 103–5, 124–27, 170–71, 177.
115. Stoler, *Allies and Adversaries*, 144.

decline of Britain and the rise of the Soviet Union. They did not yet view the USSR as a potential enemy. Indeed, their planning through most of 1944 called for maintaining the Grand Alliance. Britain and Russia would police postwar Europe. The United States would be responsible for the Western Hemisphere and the Pacific and must have the naval and air power and overseas bases to play that role.[116]

While U.S. planning proceeded, the postwar world began to take form. As Allied armies swept through enemy-occupied regions, they shaped political settlements in the areas they liberated. In Italy, for example, without consulting the Soviets and to the horror of American liberals, the United States and Britain cut a deal with the fascist Marshal Badoglio for an interim government. As the Red Army drove across Eastern and Central Europe in 1944, Stalin dictated the arrangements in Romania, Bulgaria, and Hungary. He did not initially impose Communist governments, but he did make sure that those placed in power would comply with his wishes.

The political destiny of Poland became the cause célèbre, a major reason for the breakdown of the Grand Alliance and the beginning of the Cold War. The Nazi invasion of Poland in 1939 had brought France and Britain into the war, and for Churchill and to some extent Roosevelt, Poland assumed a special moral and symbolic significance. FDR also repeatedly reminded Stalin of the large bloc of Polish American voters in the United States, whose numbers he considerably exaggerated, likely as a ploy to wrest cosmetic concessions to make the inevitable outcome in Poland look better. For Russians, on the other hand, Poland historically had been the avenue for invasion by Germany, and Stalin insisted that any postwar government be "friendly." The virulently anti-Soviet Polish government-in-exile in London lobbied relentlessly for British and American backing. Stalin formed a clique of Polish Communists who accompanied the Red Army on its westward advance. He callously used the August 1944 Warsaw Uprising to solidify its position. As Soviet forces approached the capital, the Polish underground, seeking to liberate the city on its own, rose up against Nazi occupation forces. Claiming that his exhausted armies had advanced beyond their supply lines, Stalin kept them on the outskirts of Warsaw while the Nazis brutally decimated the rebels. To the shock of his allies, the Soviet dictator refused Anglo-American requests to airdrop supplies to those he dismissed as "criminals" and "adventurists."[117]

---

116. Ibid., 61, 190–200; Michael Sherry, *Preparing for the Next War: America Plans for Postwar Defense, 1941–1945* (New Haven, Conn., 1977), 52–54.
117. W. Averell Harriman and Elie Abel, *Special Envoy to Churchill and Stalin 1941–1946* (New York, 1975), 338–49.

By late 1944, the brave new world Americans hoped for appeared in jeopardy. To the dismay of those few U.S. officials in the know, at an October meeting in Moscow code-named Tolstoy, Stalin and Churchill met before a warm fire in the Kremlin and after exchanging Polish jokes sketched out on paper a division of interest in Eastern and Central Europe: the Soviet Union preeminent in Bulgaria and Romania; Britain in Greece; influence to be shared in Yugoslavia and Hungary. "Let us burn the paper," Churchill said of what he later called a "naughty document," lest "it seemed we had disposed of these issues, so fateful to millions of people, in such an offhand manner." "No, you keep it," Stalin responded.[118] In early December 1944, British soldiers forcibly suppressed a left-wing uprising in Greece as a first step toward restoring the monarchy. Despite Roosevelt's plaintive appeals for delay, Stalin on December 31 recognized the Communist-led government he had installed in Poland.

These events caused great alarm in the United States. Both liberals and conservatives denounced British actions in Greece, warning that this war was going the same direction as the last. Polish Americans and the Catholic Church expressed grave concern about Poland. Those American officials privy to the Churchill-Stalin "deal" warned that the creation of spheres of influence would subvert essential U.S. war aims. Stunned by Stalin's handling of the Warsaw Uprising, diplomats including ambassador to Moscow W. Averell Harriman and his top aide, George F. Kennan, began to view the Soviet Union as the major threat to the peace and urged the president to stand up to Stalin, even threaten to cut off military aid unless he conformed to U.S. wishes. Some military planners such as Secretary of the Navy James Forrestal pinpointed the USSR as the new enemy upon which U.S. postwar foreign and national security policies should focus.[119]

The Allies also took conflicting positions on Germany. Thinking in traditional balance-of-power terms, Churchill saw the restoration of a de-Nazified Germany as an essential counterweight to rising Soviet might in Europe. Stalin had insisted upon a punitive peace including dismemberment and heavy reparations to help compensate for the devastation inflicted on Soviet territory during the war. Roosevelt claimed to be equally "bloodthirsty." Stereotypically viewing Germans as warlike, he insisted that they must be de-Nazified *and* de-Prussianized. On one occasion, speaking metaphorically, he remarked that it would be necessary to

118. Smith, *American Diplomacy*, 145.
119. Stoler, *Allies and Adversaries*, 215.

"castrate" them to keep them from reproducing their own kind.[120] In the fall of 1944, he endorsed the draconian Morgenthau Plan, crafted by his secretary of the treasury, which called for awarding slices of German territory to neighbors and reducing the rest to two partitioned agricultural states. Many top Roosevelt advisers expressed horror at a plan that would require long-term U.S. occupation and have huge economic consequences for postwar Europe. A leak to the press during FDR's reelection campaign caused a furor.

Although increasingly uneasy about the direction of the alliance, Roosevelt clung to the approach he had taken early in the war. He reneged on the Morgenthau Plan. He continued to insist that discussion of postwar issues be delayed until the next Big Three meeting. He did not want conflict over Eastern Europe and Greece to jeopardize postwar greatpower cooperation. Informed of the Churchill-Stalin spheres-of-influence deal, he let his allies know that there was no question in the world in which the United States did not have an interest. He was painfully aware that the Western allies needed Soviet help to end the war against Germany and defeat Japan at minimal cost. He also perceived that presence of the Red Army gave the Soviets the dominant position in Eastern Europe and there was little he could do about it.[121] He continued to wrestle with the dilemma of how to win Stalin's trust without making it appear to Americans that he had abandoned self-determination. On Eastern Europe, Kimball notes, he "evaded, avoided, and ignored specifics," hoping to "insulate the more important objective—long-term collaboration."[122] He continued to hope that by persuading Stalin the United States posed no threat he could get him to maintain an open sphere of influence that would protect vital Soviet interests but allow the free flow of information and trade and at least the semblance of basic freedom for the peoples involved. He hedged his bets by refusing to share with the Soviet leader information about work on the atomic bomb and by holding back commitments of postwar economic aid.[123]

Roosevelt discussed these issues with Churchill and Stalin for the last time at Yalta in the Crimea in early February 1945. The very name "Yalta" has served as a metaphor for the ebb and flow of tensions with the Soviet

120. Warren F. Kimball, *Swords or Ploughshares? The Morgenthau Plan for Defeated Nazi Germany* (New York, 1976), 96.
121. Campbell and Herring, *Stettinius Diaries*, 214.
122. Kimball, *Juggler*, 100.
123. Ibid., 102–69; Kimball, "Bomb and the Special Relationship," 39–41.

Union. For some U.S. participants, the conference seemed, in Hopkins's words, "the first great victory for the peace," a meeting where allies with divergent interests reached reasonable agreements to end the war and establish a basis for lasting peace.[124] Less than ten years later, in the tense atmosphere of the early Cold War, Yalta became synonymous with treason, fiercely partisan critics of FDR claiming that a dying president, duped by pro-Communist advisers, conceded Soviet control over Poland and Eastern Europe and sold out Chiang Kai-shek. A "great betrayal," it was labeled, "appeasement greater than Munich." Because a "sick man went to Yalta" and "gave away much of the world," Senator William Langer fumed, "our beloved country is facing ruin and destruction."[125]

The Yalta Conference cannot be understood without recognizing the historical context in which it took place. By the time the Big Three met at the former tsarist retreat in the Black Sea resort town, the Red Army had "liberated" much of Eastern and Central Europe and was poised to drive toward Berlin. Meanwhile, Germany's last-ditch December 1944 counteroffensive, leading to the Battle of the Bulge, slowed the U.S. advance. The end of the European war was in view, but much hard fighting lay ahead. Uncertain whether the atomic bomb would be available in time or indeed would work, U.S. military leaders agreed with FDR that Soviet entry into the war against Japan was essential to secure victory at acceptable cost. Although the Allies differed significantly on crucial postwar issues, Roosevelt still hoped for great-power cooperation. The trip for an already ill man was exhausting. The classic photographs of a drawn and haggard president adorned in that loose-fitting black cape graphically manifest the illness that would soon kill him. But there is no evidence that his mental faculties were in any way impaired. The conference provided many dramatic moments. There was ceremony galore, including sumptuous banquets with endless rounds of toasts. On the verge of victory in Europe, the Big Three saluted each other with lavish words of praise. At times, the tensions were palpable. When Churchill insisted that Poland was for Britain a matter of honor, Stalin shot back that for the USSR it was a matter of security. When Roosevelt suggested that elections in Poland should be as "pure" as Caesar's wife, the Soviet dictator retorted that "in fact she had her sins."[126]

124. Sherwood, *Roosevelt and Hopkins*, 870.
125. George C. Herring, "Yalta as Cold War Metaphor," in F. Kevin Simon, ed., *The David A. Sayre History Symposium: Collected Lectures, 1985–1989* (Lexington, Ky., 1991), 121.
126. John L. Snell et al, *The Meaning of Yalta: Big Three Diplomacy and the Balance of Power* (Baton Rouge, La., 1956), 105, 113.

Over five days of arduous negotiations, the Big Three hammered out broad agreements to end the war and establish the peace. The terms reflected the decisions made—or not made—at Tehran and, more important, the positions of the respective armies. Much to the satisfaction of Roosevelt, and of most Americans, Stalin agreed to take part in a United Nations organization essentially as the United States had designed it. In return for the restoration of Russia's pre-1905 position in East Asia, he agreed to enter the war against Japan three months after V-E Day, a promise that seemed to FDR and his military advisers—at this time—especially important. He also expressed "readiness" to conclude an alliance with China, a commitment Roosevelt hoped would affirm his support for Chiang Kai-shek and help avert civil war there. On the key issues involving German dismemberment and reparations, the Allies continued to disagree and deferred substantive decisions. On the even more divisive issues of Eastern Europe and Poland, they used diplomatic phraseology to gloss over numerous unsettled conflicts.[127] A vague and unworkable Declaration on Liberated Europe called for elections in areas liberated from the Germans. Roosevelt had hoped for at least token concessions on Poland, but Stalin remained obdurate. The Allies agreed to an equally vague statement that the existing Polish government—the one created by Stalin—should be reorganized on a "broader democratic basis." When Admiral Leahy protested that the agreement was so elastic it could be stretched from the Crimea to Washington without breaking, the president responded with resignation: "I know, Bill. But it's the best I could do for Poland at this time."[128]

In the weeks after Yalta, relations among the Allies soured. Efforts to implement the agreement on Poland foundered amidst charges and countercharges and reports from inside the country of intimidation and mass arrests. "Poland has lost her frontier," Churchill warned Roosevelt, referring to the earlier cession of territory to the USSR. "Is she now to lose her freedom?"[129] A clandestine effort by OSS operative Allen Dulles in Bern to arrange for the surrender of German troops in Italy aroused the darkest Soviet suspicions and provoked the most vitriolic exchange ever between FDR and Stalin. The Soviet dictator accused the United States, if not Roosevelt directly, of betrayal; the president ex-

127. Smith, *American Diplomacy*, 151.
128. Dallek, *Roosevelt and American Foreign Policy*, 515.
129. Quoted in Kimball, *Juggler*, 177.

pressed "bitter resentment" at the "vile misrepresentations" of Stalin's informants.[130]

On April 12, 1945, at Warm Springs, Georgia, Roosevelt died. It was a crucial event at an especially critical time in the Grand Alliance, but its precise significance is difficult to gauge. The argument that Roosevelt was moving toward taking a hard line with the Soviet Union is unpersuasive.[131] In his last weeks, he firmly resisted Churchill's call for such policies. He privately mused that the prime minister would like nothing better than Soviet-American conflict. His last comments to Churchill on the issue were in fact calm and characteristically upbeat. It seems doubtful, on the other hand, as has been argued, that the Yalta agreements provided a solid foundation for stable U.S.-Soviet postwar relations.[132] Did FDR still hope that his personal influence could bridge the widening gap of suspicion that separated the two nations? Or was he simply muddling through, as in 1940–41, letting events themselves clarify his course ("when I don't know how to move, I stay put," he explained it)?[133] We can never know for sure. To the end, the president was what Henry Wallace called "a waterman" who "looks in one direction and rows the other with the utmost skill."[134] Like Abraham Lincoln, he died before his work was complete, shrouding his legacy in uncertainty, leaving the haunting and unanswerable question of whether history might have turned out differently had he lived.

Like Wilson, FDR cast a long shadow over twentieth-century U.S. foreign policy. He perceived earlier than most other Americans the ways that technology had shrunk the world and the interconnectedness of global issues. In the frantic months before Pearl Harbor, he began to articulate a new U.S. national security policy and toward that end to create the

130. Stalin to FDR, April 3, 1945, FDR to Stalin, April 5, 1945, in Ministry of Foreign Affairs, USSR, *Correspondence Between the Chairman of the Council of Ministers of the USSR and the Presidents of the United States and the Prime Ministers of Great Britain During the Great Patriotic War of 1941–1945* (2 vols., New York, 1965), 2:205–8.

131. John Lewis Gaddis, *The United States and the Origins of the Cold War* (New York, 1972) and Alonzo L. Hamby, *Beyond the New Deal: Harry S. Truman and American Liberalism* (New York, 1973) make this argument.

132. Daniel Yergin, *Shattered Peace: The Origins of the Cold War and the National Security State* (New York, 1977) and Dianne Shaver Clemens, *Yalta* (New York, 1970) take this position.

133. Waldo Heinrichs, *Threshold of War: Franklin D. Roosevelt and American Entry into World War II* (New York, 1988), 46.

134. John Morton Blum, ed., *The Price of Vision: The Diary of Henry A. Wallace, 1942–1946* (Boston, 1973), 313.

trappings of an "imperial presidency." His wielding of presidential power, including looseness with the truth, infringement on civil liberties, and harassment of dissenters, is often justified in terms of the magnitude of the threat he faced. In the hands of his successors, it would be perverted to cover a multitude of sins. Within the Grand Alliance, he more than anyone else determined Allied strategies, which in turn decisively shaped postwar settlements. With a huge boost from Germany and Japan, he moved his nation away from its unilateralist tradition toward international cooperation. He defined and gave voice to U.S. war aims. Like Wilson, he believed that "Americanism" offered the best means to a peaceful and prosperous world. Yet while he presided over a vast accretion of U.S. power, he retained a keen sense of its limits. He understood better than most other Americans that diplomatic problems rarely had neat, definitive solutions. His vision of postwar allied cooperation tragically, if not surprisingly, proved an illusion. In large part because of that, the United Nations would prove an ineffectual instrument for maintaining the peace. Yet the ideals he so eloquently pronounced of basic human freedoms and international cooperation remain standards for today. More than any other twentieth-century U.S. leader, he projected a compelling image across the world. "The mere fact that he could make himself as much a personal friend of the little laborer in the Brazilian streets as he did of millions of Americans is a tribute to something more than politics," his adviser Adolf Berle commented on the day of his death. "The great secret was the tremendous well-spring of vital friendship which he somehow communicated far beyond the borders of his own country."[135]

One of the greatest flaws in his leadership was his refusal to confide in others the contours of his policies and aspirations, even as he understood them. His death thus left a gaping vacuum. Nowhere was this more the case than in his failure, even when he must have been increasingly cognizant of his own mortality, to educate Vice President Harry S. Truman. A border-state senator of middling reputation, the Missourian Truman was selected in 1944 as a compromise candidate in lieu of the incumbent, Wallace, anathema to Democratic Party conservatives, and the conservative James F. Byrnes of South Carolina, unacceptable to liberals. The vice president was not included in Roosevelt's inner circle after the inauguration. He knew little more about the deliberations at Yalta than could be read in the newspapers. He was not briefed on the atomic bomb. Well

135. Berle and Jacobs, *Navigating the Rapids*, 526–27.

might he exclaim upon learning of FDR's death: "I feel like I have been struck by a bolt of lightning."[136]

Truman was not without foreign policy views. During the 1930s, he had dutifully followed what appeared to be the national consensus by voting for the Neutrality Acts with few illusions they would keep the United States out of war. Like most Democrats, he was a confirmed Wilsonian. As the world moved toward war, he gravitated easily toward internationalism. He regularly voted for aid to Britain. Once war began, he assumed that the United States through the power of its ideals would be able to shape the new international order. Although he accepted the necessity of the wartime alliance, he despised Communism and thought Stalin as "untrustworthy as Hitler and [gangster] Al Capone."[137] He had little sense of the complexity of the issues dealt with at Yalta and the ambiguity of agreements concluded there.

Faced with rising tensions in the alliance and listening to FDR's more hard-line advisers, Truman, in the manner that would become his trademark, at first took a tough stance. On April 23, in a face-to-face meeting at the White House, he gave Soviet foreign minister Molotov (ironically then in Washington on a courtesy call en route to the United Nations conference at San Francisco) what he called "the one-two, right to the jaw," sternly insisting that the USSR abide by the Yalta agreements. When a startled Molotov protested that he had never been talked to like that before—dubious, knowing who his boss was—Truman curtly retorted: "Carry out your agreements and you won't get talked to like that." The president's ill-conceived tough talk masked profound inner doubts. "Did I do the right thing?" he asked a friend shortly after.[138] Two weeks later, in a singularly impolitic act that could not but stoke already rampant Soviet suspicions, the Truman administration on V-E Day summarily terminated lend-lease to the USSR, even turning back ships at sea. The move may have been necessary to meet congressional restrictions, as the administration insisted, but in the eyes of some of its proponents it was also intended to send a message to an ally in the process of becoming an adversary. It was handled without any consultation and in an unnecessarily crude and offensive manner.[139]

136. Alonzo L. Hamby, *Man of the People: A Life of Harry S. Truman* (New York, 1999), 293.
137. Ibid., 266–68.
138. Herring, *Aid to Russia*, 198–99.
139. Ibid., 203–11.

These first moves did not mark Truman's abandonment of FDR's efforts to cooperate with the Soviet Union.[140] In fact, through the first months of his presidency, the new president veered back and forth between confrontation and conciliation, between a Rooseveltian optimism that he could deal with Stalin and the conviction that a newly powerful nation with virtue on its side could have its way with tough talk. In mid-May, the administration reversed course on supply ships bound for the USSR and sought to work out arrangements for aid during the war against Japan. Truman dispatched to Moscow the desperately ill Hopkins, known to be as close to Stalin as any American. While there, Hopkins carefully explained the lend-lease imbroglio. He secured face-saving concessions that enabled the United States to recognize the Polish government. At this time, a colorful assemblage of 282 delegates representing fifty-two nations was meeting in San Francisco to draft a charter for the United Nations Organization. Hopkins also secured Stalin's intercession to break a deadlock over use of the veto power in the Security Council, permitting approval of the charter on June 25.[141]

Yet gradually, almost imperceptibly, attitudes toward the Soviet Union changed. Returning to Washington after FDR's death, Harriman ominously warned of a "barbarian invasion of Europe." He did not despair of accommodation with the USSR. But he insisted that it could be achieved only by taking a harder line, including the use of U.S. economic power as a bargaining weapon, a position many U.S. officials now endorsed.[142] Reports poured in from Eastern and Central Europe of the Soviets' use of heavy-handed, repressive measures to impose their will on local populations. The end of the European war on May 8, 1945, removed one major reason for remaining quiet in the face of Soviet violations of self-determination. The successful July 16 testing of an atomic weapon at Alamogordo, New Mexico, during the last Big Three conference at Potsdam outside Berlin eliminated yet another reason for conciliating an increasingly difficult ally. Soviet entry into the Pacific war was now deemed not just unnecessary but undesirable. Upon receiving word of the test, Stimson observed, Truman was "tremendously pepped up" and took on "an entirely new feeling of confidence." Faced with continued disputes over Eastern Europe and Germany, he and his new secretary of state,

140. Yergin, *Shattered Peace* and Gar Alperovitz, *Atomic Diplomacy—Hiroshima and Potsdam: The Use of the Atomic Bomb and the Confrontation with U.S. Power* (rev. ed., New York, 1985) contend that Truman reversed FDR's policy of cooperation.
141. Divine, *Second Chance*, 295–97.
142. Herring, *Aid to Russia*, 195–96.

James F. Byrnes, deferred agreements on major issues in hopes that use of the bomb against Japan, by demonstrating America's new power, would make the USSR "more manageable" in Eastern Europe.[143]

The dropping of atomic bombs on Hiroshima and Nagasaki in August 1945 remains among the most controversial actions in U.S. history. Truman and his advisers justified their decision in simple and clear-cut terms: The bombs were used to end the war quickly and spare the estimated half million to a million U.S. casualties that would be incurred in invading the Japanese home islands. Revisionist historians, on the other hand, have questioned whether the bomb was necessary to end the war. They accuse Truman of scrapping FDR's policy of cooperation and using the bomb mainly to bludgeon the Soviet Union into accepting America's postwar aims. The controversy has raged for more than a half century, producing exhaustive research, scrutiny of the most minute details, and voluminous writing. It goes to the very heart of what Americans believe about themselves and how other peoples view them.[144]

The official explanation for using the bomb raises numerous questions. Estimates of possible casualties from an invasion were grossly inflated. The actual numbers given to Truman in the summer of 1945 were 31,000 casualties, 25,000 deaths, in the first thirty days; other estimates for the first phase run as high as 150,000 to 175,000.[145] The president and his advisers perceived that Japan was on the verge of defeat. They saw options to end the war other than invasion or use of the bomb. They could blockade the Japanese home islands and continue the ferocious conventional bombing campaign launched in late 1944; they could modify the unconditional surrender policy to lure Japanese moderates into suing for peace. Stalin had reaffirmed to Hopkins his determination to enter the war. The shock effect of Soviet belligerency might force a Japanese surrender.

The administration rejected these alternatives. Blockade and bombing could require as long as a year and cost as much as an invasion. Some policymakers favored modifying the unconditional surrender policy to

143. Martin J. Sherwin, A World Destroyed: The Atomic Bomb and the Grand Alliance (New York, 1977), 223–24.
144. Excellent introductions to the ongoing controversy on the use of the atomic bomb are J. Samuel Walker, "The Decision to Use the Bomb: A Historiographical Update," in Michael J. Hogan, ed., Hiroshima in History (New York, 1996), 11–37, and "Recent Literature on Truman's Atomic Bomb Decision: A Search for Middle Ground," Diplomatic History 29 (April 2007), 311–34.
145. Richard B. Frank, Downfall: The End of the Japanese Empire (New York, 1999), 132–33, 139–48, 194–95, 243–45, 338–40.

facilitate peacemaking; others feared that a conciliatory approach might encourage diehards in the Japanese government and provoke a political backlash at home. Soviet entry might not compel a Japanese surrender. In any event, U.S. officials increasingly worried about Stalin's ambitions in East Asia and sought to end the conflict before the USSR could invade Manchuria and demand the spoils of war in Japan.

Dropping the bomb was thus an obvious choice for Truman, not even a decision in the usual sense of the word.[146] He had inherited from FDR a weapon built to be used and a military strategy that emphasized winning the war at the lowest cost in American lives. In this case, far from abandoning Roosevelt's policies, Truman embraced them. Even though the casualty estimates were much lower than he and his advisers later claimed, in their eyes even the smaller figures easily justified use of what the president himself admitted was "the most terrible weapon in the history of the world."[147] The bomb had been built at great cost to be used. Failure to employ it might have provoked popular outrage, even calls for impeachment.

The nation to be targeted removed any moral qualms about the bomb's use. At Pearl Harbor, Japan had inflicted physical devastation and humiliation on a proud nation. The ensuing conflict was especially vicious, a "war without mercy," according to historian John Dower, a fierce, unrelenting struggle between peoples of different races with deeply entrenched stereotypes of each other. Americans considered Japanese subhuman—Truman used the word "beast." The ferocity with which the "yellow vermin" defended remote Pacific islands, the suicide air attacks on U.S. Navy ships, and the atrocities inflicted on prisoners of war fueled fear, rage, and a thirst for revenge.[148] Given the mentality of total war and the peculiar brutality of the Pacific war, Americans did not hesitate to use any weapon to subdue a fiendish and fanatical foe.

The bomb was not employed primarily to intimidate the Soviets, as revisionists have argued, but it did offer important collateral benefits. Stimson early recognized the huge implications of nuclear weapons for international relations in general and Soviet-American relations in particular. On several occasions, he urged consultation with Stalin, possibly even trading atomic secrets for political concessions. Truman and Byrnes,

146. J. Samuel Walker, *Prompt and Utter Destruction: Truman and the Use of Atomic Bombs Against Japan* (Chapel Hill, N.C., 2004), 75.

147. Ibid., 60.

148. John W. Dower, *War Without Mercy: Race and Power in the Pacific War* (New York, 1986), 54, 142.

in contrast, believed such a powerful weapon could give them the upper hand in postwar negotiations with Stalin. It might end the war before the Soviets could make advances in East Asia.[149] Not surprisingly, Truman's calculatedly casual mention of the bomb at Potsdam caused Stalin to speed up his timetable for entering the Pacific war and accelerate his own nuclear project. Soviet-American jockeying for position in East Asia in the last days of the war against Japan and after fueled the tensions already aroused over European issues.[150]

Historians still vigorously debate whether the bombs or Soviet intervention were more important in Japan's decision to surrender, but there can be no doubt that the "double shock" of the two atomic bombs, along with the Soviet invasion of Manchuria, stunned Japan into surrender.[151] The destruction was catastrophic. At Hiroshima on August 6, an explosion equal to 12,500 tons of TNT created a huge fireball and a flash of light three thousand times brighter than the sun. "We were struck dumb at the sight," a U.S. pilot recalled. On the ground, it produced a horrific picture of destruction and human agony.[152] An area about five square miles was completely obliterated. An estimated 80,000 to 100,000 people (including twelve American prisoners of war) were killed instantly, another 40,000 later, and the entire toll 230,000. The less fortunate were burned beyond recognition or suffered a slow and excruciatingly painful death from radiation poisoning. The bomb dropped on Nagasaki August 9 killed 35,000 to 40,000. The bombs and Soviet intervention on August 8 sparked bitter debate between those Japanese who wanted to end the war and others who preferred to fight to the death. All the while, the United States continued to devastate Japan with conventional bombing. Finally, on August 14, even while some military leaders plotted a coup, Emperor Hirohito intervened. His influence carried the day. By giving strength to the peace forces, a cabinet minister later affirmed, the bombs and Soviet intervention were "gifts from heaven."[153] The United States' use of the bombs was inevitable, but the peculiar devastation they caused and their lasting effects leave haunting questions as to whether they were absolutely necessary and morally justifiable.

149. Ibid., 300; Walker, *Prompt and Utter Destruction*, 96.
150. Tsuyoshi Hasegawa, *Racing the Enemy: Stalin, Truman and the Surrender of Japan* (Cambridge, Mass., 2005), 154–65.
151. Frank, *Downfall*, 272, 293–94, stresses the bombs; Hasegawa's *Racing the Enemy* emphasizes Soviet intervention.
152. Walker, *Prompt and Utter Destruction*, 77.
153. Sadao Asado, "The 'Shock' of the Atomic Bomb and Japan's Decision to Surrender—A Reconsideration," *Pacific Historical Review* 67 (November 1998), 498.

THE SECOND WORLD WAR was a "massively transformative event," David Kennedy has written.[154] Globally, it shattered the old order, giving rise to a new international system. Those nations that had dominated world politics for years were either devastated by the war or, like Britain, financially and emotionally exhausted by the process of wreaking that destruction. The Soviet Union and especially the United States emerged the only nations capable of exerting great influence beyond their own borders. In part because of the circumstances of the war, in part because of the way it was fought, the United States alone among nations came out stronger than at the beginning. At war's end, it possessed the most powerful military establishment the world had ever known—plus the atomic bomb. An economy still stagnant in 1940 had shown incredible productive capacity. The U.S. homeland was scarcely touched by the war; civilian casualties were negligible. The nation's position in traditional areas of interest was stronger than ever. More important, its areas of interest had expanded exponentially. During the war, places formerly obscure to Americans became familiar.[155] Through various kinds of wartime service, millions of Americans were internationalized. Many leaders believed more fervently than ever that their nation had been called to world leadership. The war had demonstrated the "moral and practical bankruptcy of all forms of isolationism," Luce proclaimed in 1941. It was America's "manifest destiny" to be "the Good Samaritan of the entire world."[156] At war's end, the New Republic spoke for much of the nation's intellectual elite in calling Washington "the newly created World-Capital-on-the-Potomac" and proclaiming America's destiny to reorder a world destroyed.[157] On the day of victory, according to Churchill, the United States stood "at the summit of the world."

154. Kennedy, Three Cities, 2.
155. Lytle, Iranian-American Alliance, 1.
156. Walter LaFeber, ed., The Origins of the Cold War (New York, 1971), 28–30.
157. Richard H. Pells, The Liberal Mind in a Conservative Age (New York, 1985), 12–13.

14

"A Novel Burden Far from Our Shores"

Truman, the Cold War, and the Revolution in U.S. Foreign Policy, 1945–1953

With a touch of modesty—and no small hyperbole—former secretary of state Dean Acheson titled his 1969 memoir *Present at the Creation* and in the introduction called the Truman administration's task after World War II "just a bit less formidable than that described in the first chapter of Genesis." The challenge, Acheson remembered, was to create from the chaos left by war "half a world, a free half . . . without blowing the whole to pieces in the process." Acheson took understandable pride at "how much was done."[1] In fact, the results in terms of U.S. foreign policy were more revolutionary than even he allowed. Responding to the turmoil that was the new world "order" and to a perceived global threat from the Soviet Union, the Truman administration between 1945 and 1953 turned traditional U.S. foreign policy assumptions upside down. A country accustomed to free security succumbed to a rampant insecurity through which nations across the world suddenly took on huge significance. Unilateralism gave way to multilateralism. Through the policy of containment, the Truman administration undertook a host of international commitments, launched scores of programs, and mounted a peacetime military buildup that would have been unthinkable just ten years earlier. The age of American globalism was under way.

I

The Second World War shattered the international system beyond recognition. Across Europe, Asia, the Middle East, and North Africa, the greatest conflict ever waged left a broad swath of destruction and human misery. An estimated 60 million people were killed, more than 36 million of them Europeans. The Soviet Union lost as many as 24 million, 14 percent of its prewar population. In China, an estimated 1.3 million soldiers were dead,

---

1. Dean Acheson, *Present at the Creation: My Years in the State Department* (New York, 1969), xvi.

perhaps 15 million civilians. Japan lost almost 3 million people out of a prewar population of 70 million. Through much of the world, cities lay in ruins, factories demolished or idle, roads and bridges destroyed, fields unplowed. Food and water were in short supply if available at all, causing starvation, malnutrition, and disease. The war took an especially heavy toll on civilians. Millions of people were homeless—9 million in Japan alone. Hundreds of thousands of refugees and displaced persons roamed the continent of Europe. In Berlin, according to U.S. diplomat Robert Murphy, "the odor of death was everywhere," the canals "choked with bodies and refuse." Ambassador Arthur Bliss Lane described Warsaw as a "city of the dead." The war ended at Hiroshima and Nagasaki, of course, and the especially gruesome destruction of those cities marked in horrific fashion the end of one era and the beginning of another.[2]

The war produced a redistribution of power more sweeping than in any previous period of history. Among the leading nations in the multipolar prewar international system, Japan, Italy, and Germany were defeated and occupied. Exhausted and nearly bankrupt, once-dominant Britain was reduced to a second-rank power. Defeated at the outset of the war and liberated by its allies, France suffered even greater loss of status and power. The Eurocentric world largely through a process of self-destruction came to an inglorious end. A new bipolar system replaced the old. Only the United States and the Soviet Union emerged from the war capable of wielding significant influence beyond their borders.

Decolonization, the liquidation of colonial empires that had been an established feature of world politics for centuries, further upset the old order. The war graphically displayed the weakness of the ruling powers, giving a huge boost to already potent nationalist movements.[3] In the Middle East and in South and Southeast Asia at war's end, revolutions erupted against onetime colonial masters. For the most part the colonial powers acquiesced in independence, leading to the creation of more than a hundred new nations over the next three decades. The resulting instability shook the foundations of an already fragile international system and in the context of the Cold War provided a fertile breeding ground for Soviet-American conflict.

The war caused domestic political turmoil throughout much of the world. The discredited regimes of the 1930s vied with insurgent groups for

---

2. Thomas G. Paterson, *On Every Front: The Making of the Cold War* (New York, 1979), 1–21. The Murphy quote is from p. 3, Lane from p. 7. See also Tony Judt, *Postwar: A History of Europe Since 1945* (New York, 2005), 13–40, and John Dower, *Embracing Defeat: Japan in the Wake of World War II* (New York, 1999), 21–45.

3. Raymond F. Betts, *Decolonization* (London and New York, 1998), 26.

power; leftists challenged the more entrenched, conservative elites. In Poland, Greece, France, Yugoslavia, Korea, and China, to name a few, contending factions bitterly fought for power, causing instability and presenting opportunities for U.S. and Soviet intervention. In a broader sense, historian Thomas Paterson has written, the war "unhinged the world of stable politics, inherited wisdom, traditions, institutions, alliances, loyalties, commerce, and classes."[4]

Technology dramatically—and to contemporaries frighteningly—altered the postwar international system. Advances in transportation, especially aviation, drastically shrank distances. The world seemed more compact, more accessible—and more menacing. A people who historically had enjoyed relative freedom from danger portrayed these new threats in the most alarming way. "If you imagine two or three hundred Pearl Harbors occurring all over the United States," one official warned in 1944, "you will have a rough picture of what the next war might look like."[5] Add to this what Secretary of War Henry Stimson called "the most terrible weapon ever known in human history"—the atomic bomb—an enormously destabilizing element in the postwar years.[6] In this smaller and more menacing world, places and events that previously seemed unimportant suddenly took on great significance, drawing the attention, and often the intervention, of the two major powers.

Of all the world's nations, only the United States emerged stronger and richer at war's end. An economy recently devastated by depression soared to new heights from the demands of war. The gross national product almost tripled between 1939 and 1945. The nation's productive capacity doubled in wartime; the losses suffered by the rest of the world, the Soviet Union especially, made America's economic power relatively—and artificially—much greater. Economically, without question, the United States was the world's dominant power.[7] America's relative military power exceeded its economic strength. On V-J Day, the United States had 12.5 million people under arms, more than half of them overseas. Its navy exceeded the combined fleets of all other nations; its air force commanded the skies; it alone possessed atomic weapons. Washington took London's place as the capital of world finance and diplomacy. Not surprisingly, the new United Nations Organization was located in New York.

4. Paterson, *On Every Front*, 13; Charles S. Maier, ed., *The Cold War in Europe: Era of a Divided Continent* (New York, 1991), 3–17.
5. Paterson, *On Every Front*, 31.
6. Ibid., 29.
7. Paul Kennedy, *The Rise and Fall of the Great Powers* (New York, 1987), 358.

Americans faced the postwar years with both optimism and concern. They reveled in Allied victory and took enormous pride in their nation's awesome military power. They were cheered by the return of abundance. At the same time, they worried that postwar demobilization could bring a return of economic depression, even the rise of a new fascism. The war had exposed a horrible capacity for evil and destruction, highlighted by the Holocaust and the atomic bomb. Some Americans naturally feared that another conflict could exceed even the scale of World War II, perhaps destroy humankind. Despite their vast power, perhaps indeed because of it, some Americans worried about their nation's postwar security. Because of advances in technology, the United States could no longer depend on the oceans, allies like Britain, or hemispheric defense for its security. It could prevent future Pearl Harbors, Navy Secretary James Forrestal insisted, only by maintaining enough military power to make it "obvious that nobody can win a war against us."[8] The United States could no longer focus its attention on the Western Hemisphere, Gen. George C. Marshall warned. "We are now concerned with the peace of the entire world."[9] Other Americans recognized that their nation had a special opportunity—a new manifest destiny—to straighten out the mess made by the Europeans. "We have . . . the abundant means to bring our boldest dreams to pass—to create for ourselves whatever world we have the courage to desire," Librarian of Congress Archibald MacLeish exulted.[10]

Postwar periods generally bring major problems of readjustment, and World War II was no exception. Demobilization of millions of troops and reconversion of industry to civilian production brought hardship to many Americans. After decades of sacrifice and deprivation, a people eager once again to enjoy the fruits of abundance was frustrated and increasingly angered by recurrent strikes, shortages of consumer goods, and skyrocketing inflation. The Truman administration responded clumsily to these events and increasingly bore the brunt of public outrage. "To err is Truman" was a common witticism. For those who plaintively queried "What would FDR do if he were alive?" the jocular answer was sometimes "What would Truman do if he were alive?"[11] Languishing in the political wilderness since 1932, power-hungry Republicans sharpened

8. Michael S. Sherry, *Preparing for the Next War: America's Plans for Postwar Defense, 1941–1945* (New Haven, Conn., 1977), 200.
9. Ibid., 202.
10. Quoted in Alan Brinkley, "For Americans It Was a Very Good War," *New York Times Magazine* (May 7, 1995), 57.
11. James T. Patterson, *Grand Expectations: The United States, 1945–1974* (New York, 1996), 145.

their political knives and savored the prospects of regaining control of Congress and the White House.

Policymaking changed dramatically under Truman's very different leadership style. Understandably insecure in an office of huge responsibility in a time of stunning change, the new president was especially ill at ease in the unfamiliar world of foreign relations. Where FDR had been comfortable with the ambiguities of diplomacy, Truman saw a complex world in black-and-white terms. He shared the parochialism of most Americans of his generation, viewed people, races, and nations through the crudest of stereotypes, and sometimes used ethnic slurs. He assumed that American ways of doing things were the correct way and that the peace should be based on American principles. An avid student of history, he drew simple lessons from complicated events. He preferred blunt talk to the silky tones of diplomacy, but his toughness on occasion masked deep uncertainties and sometimes got him in trouble. His courage in facing huge challenges and his "buck stops here" decisiveness—a sharp contrast with his predecessor's annoying refusal to make commitments—have won him deserved praise. But decisiveness could also reflect his lack of experience and sometimes profound insecurity. An orderly administrator, again in marked contrast to FDR, he gave greater responsibility to his subordinates and insisted upon their loyalty.[12]

Given his lack of experience and knowledge, Truman at the outset had no choice but to turn to the experts. But he shared Roosevelt's disdain for State Department professionals—"the striped pants boys," he called them—and he profoundly distrusted the advisers he had inherited. To fill an enormous vacuum, he first turned to former South Carolina senator James F. Byrnes, FDR's "assistant president" for the home front. Truman may have felt a twinge of guilt at having taken the 1944 vice presidential nomination from the more prominent Byrnes. The secretary of state was next in line for the presidency, and he certainly felt the South Carolinian was better qualified than the earnest but out-of-his-depth incumbent Edward R. Stettinius Jr. Truman also mistakenly believed that because Byrnes had been at Yalta he could provide much-needed foreign policy expertise. Small of stature, possessed of a "characteristic Irish charm," according to a British diplomat, the new secretary of state was a skillful politician and master fixer—"conniving," Truman said of him admiringly.

12. For sharply conflicting assessments, see Alonzo L. Hamby, *Man of the People: A Life of Harry S. Truman* (New York, 1999), especially 640–41, and Arnold A. Offner, *Another Such Victory: President Truman and the Cold War, 1945–1953* (Stanford, Calif., 2000), especially 16, 18, 23, 457–58, 465, 470.

On the other hand, his background was as provincial as his new boss's, and he too lacked knowledge of and fixed ideas about foreign policy. But he was not without confidence, and with the apparent blessings of the president, he set out to run foreign policy as he had managed wartime domestic programs. His lone ranger approach quickly got him into trouble with the bureaucracy and the man who had appointed him.[13]

As with domestic issues, between V-J Day and the end of 1945 Truman and Byrnes responded hesitantly and uncertainly to the baffling new world bequeathed by war. Like many other Americans, they yearned for simpler times, what Warren Harding had called normalcy. The United States' power was at its pinnacle, but it brought uncertainty instead of security, and Americans felt threatened, as Byrnes put it, by events from "Korea to Timbuktoo."[14] They worried about instability in Western Europe and the strategically vital Mediterranean region. Not ready to scrap wartime cooperation with the USSR, they were increasingly alarmed by Soviet behavior. They especially feared that an aggressive Stalin might exploit global instability. Truman and Byrnes thus veered between tough talk and continued efforts to negotiate. By the end of the year, the administration had branded the onetime ally as an enemy.

As it had been central to the beginnings of Soviet-American conflict, so also Eastern Europe played a critical role in the postwar transformation of American attitudes toward the USSR. Haunted by memories of the depression and World War II, U.S. officials fervently believed that the Wilsonian principles of self-determination of peoples and an open world economy were essential for peace and prosperity. The United States had negligible economic interests in Eastern Europe, and U.S. officials understood poorly if at all the determination of some of its indigenous leaders to nationalize major industries. They saw the trend toward nationalization as a threat to capitalism and a healthy world economy and attributed it to the imposition of Communism from the outside. They vaguely understood Soviet concern for friendly governments but continued to call for free elections even where they might result in anti-Soviet regimes.

Those Americans who accepted some degree of Soviet influence called for Soviet restraint and for an open sphere that allowed access for Western capital and journalists. From across Eastern Europe, U.S. diplomats reported with alarm the political oppression imposed by Soviet proconsuls

13. Robert L. Messer, *The End of Alliance: James F. Byrnes, Roosevelt, Truman and the Origins of the Cold War* (Chapel Hill, N.C., 1982), 4–7, 31, 77–79.
14. Melvyn P. Leffler, *A Preponderance of Power: National Security, the Truman Administration, and the Cold War* (Stanford, Calif., 1992), 116.

backed by the Red Army, especially in the former Nazi satellites Romania and Bulgaria. Eastern Europe provided a litmus test of Soviet postwar behavior. It was seized upon by U.S. officials to raise fears about Stalin's aggressive methods and expansionist designs.[15]

As they looked out across an unsettled world, Americans saw other alarming signs. In the tense postwar atmosphere, they tended to ignore cases where the Soviet Union had kept its agreements and acted in a conciliatory manner and fastened on examples of uncooperative and threatening behavior. They viewed demands for a role in negotiating a peace treaty with Italy and for reparations not as a response to U.S. protests about Eastern Europe but as manifestations of Soviet designs on Western Europe and the Mediterranean region. Soviet requests for a trusteeship over Tripolitania in North Africa suggested the broadening scope of the USSR's ambitions. Over Western protests, it kept troops in Iran and Manchuria. The fiercely independent Yugoslav leader Tito's seizure of Trieste, fulfilling long-standing Serbian ambitions, was viewed in Washington as confirmation of Soviet expansionism.

The first clash of the postwar era took place at the Council of Foreign Ministers meeting in London in September 1945. Now in charge of U.S. diplomacy, Byrnes went abroad naively confident of success. A skilled political broker at home, he was certain that these same talents could produce solutions for international disputes. He also believed that the awesome power so dramatically manifested at Hiroshima and Nagasaki would enable him to dictate settlements. He crossed the Atlantic, in his own words, with the atom bomb in his hip pocket. He was quickly disillusioned. If anything, America's atomic monopoly complicated postwar negotiations by forcing the Soviets to demonstrate they could not be intimidated. Foreign Minister V. M. Molotov repeatedly joked about the bomb, on one occasion offering a drunken toast to its power. He refused to make concessions. While Byrnes and British foreign minister Ernest Bevin joined in acrimonious exchanges with their Soviet counterpart, the two sides remained deadlocked. Molotov refused Byrnes's demands to reorganize the governments of Romania and Bulgaria; the secretary withheld recognition. The British and Americans rejected Soviet efforts to exclude China and France from discussion of the Balkan treaties. To Byrnes's dismay, the conference broke up without resolving anything, the Russians protesting that the secretary of state, although reputedly a practical man,

15. Ibid., 49–54; Paterson, *On Every Front*, 43–47; Thomas G. Paterson, *Soviet-American Confrontation: Postwar Reconstruction and the Origins of the Cold War* (Baltimore, Md., 1973), 99–199.

"acted like a professor," Byrnes damning Molotov as a " 'semi-colon' figure [who] could not see the big picture." "The outlook is very dark," Byrnes gloomily confided to friends.[16]

Apparently more interested in achieving agreements than in their substance, Byrnes focused on the next Council of Foreign Ministers meeting, set for Moscow in December, where he hoped to get around the obstructionist Molotov and deal directly with Stalin. Once there, he failed to move his hosts on the Balkans, eventually agreeing to recognize the existing governments after token Soviet concessions. In other ways, the Moscow conference looked more like Yalta than London, with Byrnes's old-fashioned horse-trading based on sphere-of-influence principles producing significant results. The ministers resolved the procedural differences that had stymied negotiation of European peace treaties. The Soviets acquiesced in U.S. domination of occupation policy in Japan and its preeminent influence in China. They accepted without significant modification Byrnes's proposals for international control of atomic energy.[17]

Ironically, Byrnes's conciliatory diplomacy at Moscow marked a major turning point in the evolution of U.S. Cold War policies. The imperious secretary failed to keep his boss informed about what he was doing. When the Moscow deal proved a political liability, Truman turned on him with a vengeance. Byrnes's pragmatic—and generally realistic—efforts to resolve postwar issues proved out of fashion in a Washington increasingly caught up in Cold War anxieties. Critics seized upon his concessions to denounce any compromise with Moscow and push for a get-tough approach. The U.S. chargé d'affaires in Moscow, George F. Kennan, privately condemned Byrnes's Balkans concessions as adding "some fig leaves of democratic procedure to hide the nakedness of Stalinist dictatorship."[18] Truman's military chief of staff, the crusty, hard-core anti-Communist Adm. William Leahy, denounced the Moscow communiqué as an "appeasement document."[19] Journalists and politicians joined in the criticism. When Truman subsequently received a report condemning Soviet repression in the Balkans and warning of a Soviet threat to the eastern Mediterranean, he flew into a rage.

The president responded to Byrnes's Moscow diplomacy with what has been aptly called a "personal declaration of Cold War."[20] Angered at the secretary's independence—which at first he had encouraged—Truman

16. Messer, *End of Alliance*, 133–34.
17. Ibid., 137–55.
18. Ibid., 155.
19. Offner, *Another Such Victory*, 121.
20. Ibid., 124.

set out to reassert his control over foreign policy. Confused, indeed be-fuddled, over the emerging conflict with the Soviet Union and embattled on the home front, he found comfort in the certainty of a black-and-white assessment of Soviet intentions and a hard-line foreign policy consisting of tough talk and no concessions. In a private letter to Byrnes in early 1946, he affirmed he would not recognize the "police states" in Bulgaria and Romania until they radically reshaped their governments. He de-nounced Soviet "aggression" in Iran and warned of a threat to Turkey and the straits linking the Black Sea and the Mediterranean. There would be no compromise simply to achieve agreements. Stalin understood only an "iron fist" and "How many divisions have you?" the president concluded in ringing terms. "I'm tired [of] babying the Soviets."[21]

It remains impossible to determine with certainty what Stalin actually sought at this time, but Truman's assessment appears much too simplistic. The Soviet dictator was a cruel tyrant who presided over a brutal police state. Neurotic in his suspicions and fears, he slaughtered without mercy millions of his own people during his long and bloody rule. He ruthlessly promoted his own power and the security of his state. He was determined to secure friendly—which meant compliant—governments in the crucial buffer zone between the USSR and Germany and to guard against a re-newed German threat. He was also a clever opportunist who would ex-ploit any opening given him by enemies—or friends. But he was acutely aware of Soviet weakness. And he was no Communist ideologue. Espe-cially in the immediate postwar years, when he needed breathing space, he refrained from pushing revolution in a war-torn world. His diplomacy manifested a persistent streak of realism. He did not seek war. "He was de-vious yet cautious, opportunistic yet prudent, ideological yet pragmatic," historian Melvyn Leffler has written.[22] Some of his ploys were intended to secure confirmation of great-power status for the Soviet Union, others merely to gain a bargaining edge. Some commentators have claimed that this "battle-scarred tiger," as Kennan called him, was as skilled at outwit-ting foes as he was evil. In truth, he made repeated mistakes that brought about the very circumstances he desperately sought to avoid.[23]

Americans could not or would not see this in early 1946, and Truman's hard-nosed assessment of what was now presumed to be a distinct Soviet

21. Ibid., 121–24.
22. Leffler, *Preponderance of Power*, 102.
23. George F. Kennan, *Memoirs, 1925–1950* (Boston, 1967), 293; Judt, *Postwar*, 119–30; Vladislav Zubok and Constantine Pleshakov, *Inside the Kremlin's Cold War: From Stalin to Khrushchev* (Cambridge, Mass., 1996), 47–53.

threat seemed validated from every direction. In a February 9 "election" speech, Stalin warned of the renewed threat of capitalist encirclement and called for huge boosts in Soviet industrial production. The speech was probably designed to rally an exhausted people to further sacrifice. Even Truman conceded that Stalin, like U.S. politicians, might "demagogue a bit before elections." But many Americans read into the Soviet dictator's words the most ominous implications. The hawkish Forrestal found confirmation of his belief that U.S.-Soviet differences were irreconcilable. Liberal Supreme Court Justice William O. Douglas labeled the speech "The Declaration of World War III."[24]

Less than two weeks later, Kennan unleashed on the State Department his famous and influential "Long Telegram," an eight-thousand-word missive that assessed Soviet policies in the most gloomy and ominous fashion. The namesake of a distant relative who in the late nineteenth century had documented for enthralled U.S. audiences the horrors of the Siberian exile system, the younger Kennan was one of a handful of men trained after World War I as experts on Bolshevik Russia. Conservative in his tastes and politics and scholarly in demeanor, he developed a deep admiration for traditional Russian literature and culture and, from service in the Moscow embassy after 1933, an even deeper antipathy for the Soviet state. Frustrated during the war when the Roosevelt administration ignored his cautionary recommendations, he eagerly responded when Truman's State Department requested his views. "They had asked for it," he later wrote. "Now, by God, they would get it."[25] In highly alarmist tones, he delivered over the wires a lecture on Soviet behavior that decisively influenced the origins and nature of the Cold War.[26] He conceded that the Soviet Union was weaker than the United States and acknowledged that it did not want war. But he ignored its legitimate postwar fears, and by showing how Communist ideology reinforced traditional Russian expansionism and portraying the Soviet leadership in near pathological terms, he helped destroy what little remained of American eagerness to understand its onetime ally and negotiate differences. He warned of a "political force committed fanatically to the belief that with [the] US there can be no permanent modus vivendi, that it is desirable and necessary that the internal harmony of our society be disrupted, our traditional way of life

24. Offner, *Another Such Victory*, 128–29.
25. Kennan, *Memoirs*, 293.
26. Frank Costigliola, "Unceasing Pressure for Penetration: Gender, Pathology, and Emotion in George Kennan's Formation of the Cold War," *Journal of American History* 83 (March 1997), 1331.

be destroyed, the international authority of our state be broken, if Soviet power is to be secure." By thus demonizing the Kremlin, he confirmed the futility and even danger of further negotiations and prepared the way for a policy he would label containment. The Long Telegram was exquisitely timed; arriving in Washington just as policymakers were edging toward similar conclusions, it gave expert confirmation to their views. Forrestal circulated it throughout the government. Kennan was brought home to head the State Department's recently created Policy Planning Staff.[27]

The hard line was publicly affirmed in early March by wartime hero Sir Winston Churchill. In a speech in Truman's home state of Missouri, the former prime minister warned that from "Stettin in the Baltic to Trieste in the Adriatic an Iron Curtain has descended across the Continent," coining a phrase that would become a staple of Cold War rhetoric. Like Kennan, he conceded that the Soviets did not want war, but he insisted that they did want the "fruits of war and the indefinite expansion of their power and doctrines." Like Truman, he insisted that they responded only to force. He called for an Anglo-American "fraternal association," an extension of the wartime alliance, to meet a new and ominous threat. This proposal provoked a furor in the United States, causing Truman to disavow prior knowledge of the speech (which he had) and even to invite Stalin to visit the United States (an invitation he knew would be declined). But the Iron Curtain speech, delivered with typical eloquence by a leader who had been right about Hitler, confirmed the administration's assessment of Soviet behavior and the need for a firm response backed by military force.[28]

From March to September 1946, tough rhetoric was matched by increasingly tough action. After extended debate, Congress finally approved in the summer a $3.75 billion loan for Britain at low interest. To be sure, the United States drove a hard bargain with a financially exhausted ally, demanding an end to preferential arrangements that discriminated against U.S. trade and insisting on sterling convertibility within a year. The administration also agreed to cancel the United Kingdom's $20 billion lend-lease "debt," not generous enough to satisfy some Britons, but a vast improvement over the 1920s. In Congress, Republicans who wanted drastic budget cuts and knee-jerk Anglophobes vigorously opposed the loan. Setting a precedent that would be used repeatedly in the Cold War, U.S. of-

27. Robert L. Beisner, "Patterns of Peril: Dean Acheson Joins the Cold Warriors, 1945–1946," *Diplomatic History* 20 (Summer 1996), 338.
28. Offner, *Another Such Victory*, 135–38.

ficials employed anti-Soviet rhetoric to gain passage of the bill.[29] Not surprisingly, Truman and his advisers took no similar steps to assist the Soviet Union. Whether Stalin would have accepted a loan even if it were offered on generous terms is doubtful. If he had, Congress likely would not have approved it. And a loan, even if provided, might have made no difference. But the administration's lame explanation that a wartime Soviet request had been lost in a records transfer after V-J Day fooled no one. When U.S. officials finally got around to offering a loan, they attached conditions they must have known the USSR would not accept. A loan would not have prevented the Cold War, but its denial certainly increased Soviet-American tensions and reflected mistaken U.S. views of Soviet dependency on external assistance.[30]

The administration also took a tough stand on Iran in the summer of 1946—the first full-fledged Cold War crisis. To the growing alarm of U.S. officials, the Soviets left occupation forces in Iran after the March deadline for withdrawal, demanded an oil concession, and backed a separatist movement in the northern province of Azerbaijan. Stalin's motives cannot be precisely divined. He certainly sought an oil concession to match those already given Britain and the United States. Following Germany's defeat, he probably hoped to reassert Russian power in a traditional sphere of influence. Fearing increased British and U.S. influence, he may also have been seeking a buffer to protect precious Soviet oil reserves in nearby Baku. He may have had designs on Azerbaijan, or he may simply have been seeking a bargaining chip for concessions on oil. Whatever the case, Truman and his advisers viewed Soviet actions as further evidence of an expansionist threat to a region now deemed vital to U.S. national security. They encouraged Iranian resistance to Soviet demands and backed Iran's appeals at the newly organized United Nations for withdrawal of Soviet forces.[31]

A Soviet retreat reinforced the administration's faith in the get-tough approach. In fact, the crisis was defused largely through the shrewd diplomacy of Iranian prime minister Ahmad Qavam. The sixty-eight-year-old Persian statesman began a long political career at age twelve. Described by a British official—with perhaps unintended praise—as "sly, intriguing and unreliable," he had mastered the art of protecting Iranian interests by

29. Richard Paul Hedlund, "Congress and the British Loan, 1945–1946: A Congressional Study" (Ph.D. dissertation, University of Kentucky, 1976), 92–93, 101–3, 133, 144, 160–64, 181–84.
30. Offner, *Another Such Victory*, 132.
31. Ibid., 138–40.

playing outside powers against each other.[32] Qavam bolstered his bargaining position by enlisting U.S. support. He then cut a deal with the Soviets exchanging controlling interests in a joint oil company for a troop withdrawal. Once the troops were gone, he sent Iranian forces into Azerbaijan to crush the separatists. The Iranian parliament subsequently rejected the oil concession, leaving the USSR a victim of Persian chicanery.[33] The Americans interpreted Soviet withdrawal as a result primarily of their own tough talk—Truman later falsely claimed to have issued an ultimatum. Engaging in some double-dealing of their own, they formed ties at Qavam's expense with the young and more pliable Shah Reza Pahlavi and gave Iran $10 million in military aid.

The U.S. handling of atomic energy in the spring of 1946 gave further evidence, as Byrnes put it, that American opinion was "no longer disposed to make concessions on important matters."[34] Undersecretary of State Acheson, not yet a Cold Warrior, and old New Dealer David Lilienthal, working with scientists like J. Robert Oppenheimer, presented in March 1946 a remarkably internationalist proposal. The Acheson-Lilienthal plan would have established an international authority to control the extraction, refinement, and use of atomic materials. Plants would be made difficult to convert to military use and would be scattered so that no single nation could gain a dominant position. The plan was to be implemented in stages, during which time the United States would retain its monopoly. It sought security through international cooperation.

The Acheson-Lilienthal plan was out of fashion in Truman's Washington by the time it was completed. Already persuaded of the futility of cooperation with the Soviet Union, the president and other Americans were further alarmed by revelations of a Soviet spy ring seeking to steal atomic secrets in Canada. Congress toughened Truman's spine by imposing limits on international cooperation. By appointing elder statesman Bernard Baruch to head atomic negotiations, Truman sealed the demise of nuclear internationalism. A relentless self-promoter and ardent nationalist, the seventy-five-year-old financier was inalterably committed to U.S. control and believed that the United States must retain its monopoly until it got the treaty it wanted. He added tough provisions for inspections and penalties for violators—"sure and swift punishment," as he put it—neither subject to Soviet veto. Although he did not like Baruch, Truman went along,

32. James A. Bill, *The Eagle and the Lion: The Tragedy of American-Iranian Relations* (New Haven, Conn., 1988), 33–34.
33. Ibid., 37.
34. Messer, *End of Alliance*, 200.

affirming that "we should not under any circumstances throw away our gun until we are sure the rest of the world can't arm against us."[35] When Baruch presented his proposal to the UN in June 1946, the Soviets countered with an even more unrealistic plan calling for outlawing atomic weapons, terminating ongoing programs, and destroying existing stockpiles. The Security Council eventually approved the Baruch Plan, the Soviet Union and Poland abstaining, but as Soviet-American conflict intensified there was no chance of agreement. Congress passed an additional act prohibiting exchanges of atomic "secrets" in the absence of international control. The two nations pressed ahead with their atomic projects.

Given its economic potential and its pivotal role in Europe, Germany could not but be a crucial issue in the emerging Soviet-American conflict. During 1945–46, the former allies had attempted sporadically to negotiate a peace treaty, but their actions increasingly spoke louder than their words. Occupation commander Gen. Lucius Clay admitted that the Soviets had kept most of their agreements and that France had been far more obstructionist. But the Soviets' vengeful treatment of Germans, their promotion of leftist political parties in their occupation zone, their incessant demands for additional reparations, and their insistence on sharing the precious resources of the Ruhr industrial area reinforced already well formed U.S. suspicions. Fearing that an impoverished Germany would delay European recovery, the United States stopped reparations from its own zone and announced plans to merge the three Western occupation zones, provoking loud Soviet protests.

By September 1946, the former allies had reached an impasse that would leave Germany—and especially divided Berlin—a Cold War hot spot for the next quarter century. In a much publicized speech at the Stuttgart Opera House, Byrnes curried German favor by pledging that the United States would not seek vengeance against its former enemy and did not want Germany to become a pawn in the emerging inter-Allied struggle. He denounced at least by implication Soviet efforts to shape politics in their occupation zone, opposed additional reparations and reparations from current production, and denied Soviet access to the Ruhr. To assuage German fears that a frustrated United States might leave Europe, he emphatically vowed: "We will not shirk our duty. We are not withdrawing. We are here to stay." The Stuttgart speech represented an important turning point in the origins of the Cold War. It made clear U.S. abandonment of a punitive policy and commitment to a strong, democratic Germany.

35. Walter LaFeber, *America, Russia, and the Cold War, 1945–1996* (8th ed., New York, 1997), 42.

Although designed in part as a message to France, it also drew a clear line against presumed Soviet expansionism.[36]

A crisis over Turkey in the fall of 1946 provoked the first of numerous war scares. Following threats against Turkey and troop movements in the Balkans, Moscow in August demanded revision of the Montreux Convention governing the Dardanelles and the Bosporus, the straits providing access from the Black Sea to the Mediterranean. The proposals would have given the Soviet Union bases along the straits and joint control with Turkey over access. A Georgian by birth, Stalin came naturally by his hatred of Turkey; his demands reflected ancient Russian interest in the straits. There is no reason to believe that at this point he contemplated invading Turkey, but he was willing to indulge in brinkmanship. United States officials attributed to him more sinister designs. Relying on superficial historical knowledge and dubious analogy, Truman had long since concluded that Stalin sought to grab the straits as a springboard for further expansion. Recently devised U.S. war plans highlighted the essentiality of the straits to control of the Mediterranean. Newly converted to the hard line, Acheson portrayed Turkey as the "stopper in the neck of the bottle" and issued extravagant warnings of a Soviet threat to Greece, Turkey, and the Middle East, even India and China. If necessary, he concluded, the USSR must be checked by force.[37] Yugoslav downing of an unarmed U.S. C-47 transport overflying its territory heightened tensions. "We might as well find out whether the Russians were bent on world conquest now as in five or ten years," Truman affirmed.[38]

The United States firmly resisted revision of the Montreux Convention. The Truman administration emphatically rejected Soviet demands for joint control of the straits. Backing up its strong words, it pressed Britain to assist Greece and Turkey in fending off the Soviet threat, making clear it would fill the breach if necessary. It dispatched an armada of eight warships, including the legendary battleship *Missouri* and the newly christened aircraft carrier *Franklin D. Roosevelt*, to the Mediterranean. The Joint Chiefs of Staff developed the first war plan for conflict with the USSR. Even without Western backing, Turkey would have fiercely resisted Soviet demands. The crisis fizzled out amidst Soviet-Turkish disagreement over whether talks on the straits should include the United States and Britain. As with Iran, it ended in net strategic gain for the United States. The Soviets withdrew substantial forces from the Balkans. The

36. Messer, *End of Alliance*, 201–203.
37. Beisner, "Patterns of Peril," 46.
38. LaFeber, *Cold War*, 38.

United States established a new Mediterranean command of twelve war-ships, giving it naval supremacy in the region. The Turkish affair of late 1946 persuaded many U.S. officials that Stalin would not be content with a sphere of influence in Eastern Europe and reinforced their view that it was necessary to demonstrate a willingness to go to war.[39]

The Clifford-Elsey report of September 1946 codified in one eighty-two-page document ideas that had been circulating in Washington for weeks. In a fit of pique, Truman in July asked Clark Clifford and George Elsey, two young White House staffers, to document recent Soviet viola-tion of agreements. They produced much more, a lengthy assessment of Soviet intentions and capabilities phrased in the most ominous tones along with a clarion call for U.S. rearmament and the containment of So-viet expansionism. Their analysis borrowed heavily from Kennan's Long Telegram and drew ideas from hardliners like Leahy and Forrestal. It was phrased in the black-and-white terms Truman preferred. Ignoring cases where the Soviets had kept agreements and the ways in which U.S. ac-tions might have alarmed Moscow, the authors compiled a legal brief to justify actions most U.S. officials now agreed must be taken. The Soviets were committed to expansion and sought world domination, Clifford and Elsey insisted. They would use any means, including political subversion and military force, to achieve their goals. Soviet expansionism posed a grave threat to U.S. vital interests across the world. There was no point in further negotiation; it was futile and even dangerous to seek cooperation. The Soviets understood only tough talk and military power. The United States must therefore maintain a high state of military readiness, acquire overseas military bases, expand its nuclear arsenal, and be prepared to use force if necessary. It must assist "democratic" countries threatened by So-viet expansion. A failure to act resolutely, as with the Western democra-cies in the 1930s, would encourage further aggression. Considered too hot to release to the public or even circulate within the government, the re-port was kept locked in a White House safe until discovered many years later. It was the first major government attempt to analyze Soviet behavior and recommend a proper U.S. response.[40]

The firing of dissident Secretary of Commerce Henry Wallace just two weeks before delivery of the Clifford-Elsey report solidified the Cold War consensus. For years Wallace had been the torchbearer for American

---

39. Eduard Mark, "The War Scare of 1946 and Its Consequences," *Diplomatic History* 21 (Summer 1997), 383–415.

40. Leffler, *Preponderance of Power*, 131. The entire Clifford Report may be found in Arthur Krock, *Memoirs: Sixty Years on the Firing Line* (New York, 1968), 417–82.

liberals. After most other New Dealers had left office or jumped aboard the Cold War bandwagon, he kept the faith, privately and publicly pleading for cooperation with the Soviet Union and questioning the get-tough approach. On September 10, Wallace met with Truman to go over an upcoming speech. The two subsequently differed over what took place, Wallace claiming, and Truman denying, that the president had cleared the secretary's draft. That speech departed sharply from what had become the conventional wisdom, urging Americans to examine how their actions might appear to other nations. Like Kennan, Wallace harked back to Russian history to explain Soviet insecurity, but he drew very different conclusions, warning of their sensitivity to U.S. moves they viewed as provocative. He sharply criticized U.S. atomic policy and the get-tough approach. "The tougher we get, the tougher the Russians will get," he averred. The speech caused a furor and immediately put Truman on the spot. Indulging his penchant for writing letters he later—in most cases wisely—declined to mail, the president privately denounced Wallace as one of the "parlor pinks" and "soprano-voiced men" who constituted a "sabotage front for Uncle Joe Stalin."[41] Pressed by now hard-liner Byrnes, he demanded Wallace's resignation and got it. Wallace's firing removed from the executive branch the last dissenter from Cold War orthodoxy for many years to come.

II

Now fully agreed in their assessment of the danger and the urgency of a U.S. response, Truman and his advisers moved decisively after 1947 to take up what Acheson called "a novel burden far from our shores."[42] They revamped the national security bureaucracy. Focusing on the eastern Mediterranean and Western Europe, they developed large-scale and unprecedented economic aid programs to combat ongoing insurgencies and clear up breeding grounds of economic want in which they believed Communism flourished. They intervened politically in various parts of the world where U.S. influence had been slight. Most remarkably, they formed an alliance with the Western European nations that involved binding commitments to intervene militarily, the first such obligations since the French alliance of 1778. If it did not quite match up to the Book of Genesis, as Acheson claimed, it was nonetheless revolutionary in conception and consequences.

41. Paterson, *On Every Front*, 105–6.
42. James Chace, *Acheson: The Secretary of State Who Created the American World* (New York, 1998), 167.

The administration first addressed the personnel and institutional problems that had afflicted policymaking since the end of the war. The independent and unpredictable Byrnes resigned in late 1946, and Truman named the illustrious George C. Marshall to succeed him. The president had enormous regard for the general—"What I like about Marshall is he's a man," he once affirmed, the highest praise one gentleman of that era could lavish upon another.[43] A person of vast experience, good judgment, and towering prestige, Marshall could shield the State Department from partisan attack and could be counted upon to work closely with the president, areas where Byrnes had conspicuously failed. Indeed, under Marshall's firm leadership and orderly administrative style, the State Department enjoyed a rare period of preeminence in the making of U.S. foreign policy.

Marshall was only one—and by no means the most important—of those men who became the architects of postwar U.S. foreign policy. Kennan and Acheson played crucial roles as intellectual godfather and prime mover respectively. They were joined by such notables as Forrestal, John J. McCloy, W. Averell Harriman, Robert Lovett, and Paul Nitze. Known collectively as the American Establishment—also the Wise Men—this group came out of the tradition of public service founded by Elihu Root. Henry Stimson was their mentor and beau ideal. Mostly northeasterners, they had in common prep school and Ivy League educations and the gentleman's values inculcated there. Most of them rose to power through the great New York banking houses and law firms and belonged to the city's most prestigious social clubs. They drew from Root and Stimson a devotion to public service that transcended partisan politics, an unswerving loyalty to their presidents, a firm commitment to internationalism, and a passionate belief in the nation's destiny to reshape a war-torn world. Although they spoke of the "burdens" of world leadership, they went about their task with zest. Staunch Atlanticists who revered European traditions, like Root and Stimson they could be patronizing toward "lesser" peoples. Coming from the very nerve center of world capitalism, they were appalled by Marxist dogma and Soviet totalitarianism. They were generally pragmatic and realistic rather than ideological in resisting the Soviet Union. But they frequently exaggerated the Soviet threat to sell their programs. Sometimes, they were persuaded by their own rhetoric or became its political captives.[44]

43. Offner, *Another Such Victory*, 186.
44. Walter Isaacson and Evan Thomas, *The Wise Men: Six Friends and the World They Made* (New York, 1986), 25–35, 738–41.

Of all the Wise Men, none was more controversial and influential than Dean Gooderham Acheson. The son of British and Canadian parents, Acheson was educated at Groton, Yale, and Harvard Law School. After clerking with legendary Supreme Court Justice Louis Brandeis, he joined one of Washington's most prestigious law firms. He entered the State Department in 1941, working mainly on economic issues. A large man, aristocratic in bearing and haughty of demeanor, he cut quite a figure with his heavy eyebrows, carefully waxed guardsman's mustache (which one writer swore had a personality of its own), elegant suits, and Homburg hat.[45] He was brilliant of mind and suffered fools poorly. A clever wordsmith, he did not hesitate to turn his acerbic wit on adversaries, which sometimes got him into trouble with Congress. He was certain that his nation had the power and the proper values to grasp the reins of world leadership. The United States was the "locomotive at the head of mankind," as he once put it, and "the rest of the world is the caboose." Once he became a Cold Warrior, he focused his formidable intellect and estimable diplomatic skills on building what he called "situations of strength" to contain Communism. Although pilloried by the Republican right for being soft on Communism, as undersecretary (1945–47) and secretary of state (1949–53), he played a decisive role in shaping the Truman administration's Cold War policies. "He was not merely present at the creation," biographer James Chace has observed, "he was the prime architect of that creation."[46]

The first task of the Cold Warriors was to restructure the government for a new era of global involvement. The changes reflected a broad recognition that, as the world's most powerful nation with global responsibilities, the United States must better organize its institutions and mobilize its resources to wage the Cold War. But changes of this magnitude did not come easily. Truman's efforts to eliminate crippling interservice rivalries by unifying the armed services provoked a revolt by the navy's top brass and an extended struggle within the government. At one level, the battles were about parochial bureaucratic interests. They also reflected a deeper conflict between those who sought to centralize authority in the mode of the New Deal to promote efficiency and economy and protect civilian prerogatives and those traditionalists who saw decentralization and checks and balances as the best way to avert militarization and a garrison state.[47]

45. Robert L. Beisner, *Dean Acheson: A Life in the Cold War* (New York, 2006), 88.
46. Chace, *Acheson*, 442.
47. Michael J. Hogan, *A Cross of Iron: Harry S. Truman and the Origins of the National Security State, 1945–1954* (New York, 1998), 5–21.

The National Security Act of July 1947—what has been called the "Magna Charta of the national security state"—was an awkward compromise.[48] It created a cabinet-level, civilian secretary of defense to preside over separate departments of the army, navy, and air force. It institutionalized the wartime Joint Chiefs of Staff (JCS), established a National Security Council (NSC) in the White House to better coordinate policy-making, and provided for an independent Central Intelligence Agency (CIA) to replace the defunct OSS. The effects of this landmark legislation were not immediately apparent. Under Marshall, Acheson, and their Republican successor, John Foster Dulles, State would dominate policy-making for the next decade. The act as subsequently modified, however, revolutionized the making of U.S. foreign policy. It institutionalized the enhanced role assumed by the military during World War II. The NSC would in time usurp the central role of the State Department. The CIA, as Clifford later put it, became "a government within a government, which could evade oversight of its activities by drawing the cloak of secrecy about itself." With the addition of more players and more competing centers of power, the policy process became more complex and more conflict-ridden.[49]

Even before the National Security Act passed Congress, the administration had taken the first step in implementing a policy of containment: economic and military aid for Greece and Turkey under what came to be called the Truman Doctrine. The United States' attention was first drawn to the eastern Mediterranean during the 1946 Turkish crisis. The possibility of a British withdrawal from Greece in early 1947 brought decisive action. Since 1944, British occupation forces had been assisting the Greek monarchy's efforts to suppress a left-wing insurgency. This costly and futile effort drained already scarce resources. In February 1947, London informed the State Department it could no longer keep forces in Greece.

Britain's demarche came as little surprise to many U.S. officials, was welcomed in some quarters in Washington, and spurred the government to action. Stalin did not instigate the indigenous Greek insurgency and thus far had provided no more than moral support, a point vaguely perceived by some U.S. officials. To promote their own regional and geopolitical interests rather than ideological agendas, Communist governments in Yugoslavia, Albania, and Bulgaria had backed the Greek rebels. United States officials feared that if the insurgency succeeded, Stalin might

48. Ibid., 24, 65.
49. Clark Clifford with Richard Holbrooke, Counsel to the President: A Memoir (New York, 1991), 170; Offner, Another Such Victory, 192; Hogan, Cross of Iron, 65–68.

exploit it. A leftist victory could have a bandwagon effect on the already fragile political situations in France and Italy. The collapse of the Greek government, in American eyes, could shatter Western influence in one of the most critical regions of the world and leave other areas vulnerable to Soviet influence. With the zeal of a new convert, Acheson in a secret February 27 meeting with congressional leaders—he called it an "Armageddon"—warned ominously that "like apples in a barrel infected by a rotten one, the corruption of Greece would infect Iran and all the East" and even threaten Africa, Asia Minor, and Western Europe. Not since Rome and Carthage, he concluded, had the world seen such a polarization of power.[50]

Truman took a hard-sell approach to secure congressional support for an unprecedented program of $400 million in aid for Greece and Turkey. The Republicans had won smashing victories in the 1946 elections, regaining control of both houses of Congress and vowing to implement massive budget cuts. Americans feared the Soviet Union, but they were preoccupied with domestic problems, uninformed about the situation in Greece, and wary of intervention abroad. Republican Senate leader Arthur Vandenberg of Michigan urged the president to "scare the hell out of the country," and Truman heeded his advice. In a much publicized speech before a joint session of Congress on March 12, the president echoed Acheson's warnings of a world divided between freedom and totalitarianism. Avoiding direct reference to the USSR, he compared the threat to Greece with the crisis preceding World War II. He called upon the United States to "support free peoples who are resisting attempted subjugation by armed minorities or outside pressures." Failure to act could threaten the Middle East and Western Europe. "If we falter in our leadership," Truman concluded, "we may endanger the peace of the world—and we shall surely endanger the welfare of this nation."[51]

A program so novel was bound to spur opposition. Columnist Walter Lippmann protested the sweeping language of the doctrine, its seemingly indiscriminate commitment to global interventionism, and its apparent rejection of diplomacy—arguments that proved over time prescient— provoking a Washington dinner party spat with Acheson that almost ended in fisticuffs. Critics emphasized that the Greek government was a repressive monarchy rather than a democracy. Many Americans who sympathized with the purposes of the doctrine feared that unilateral U.S.

50. Chace, *Acheson*, 164–66.
51. *Public Papers of the Presidents of the United States, Harry S. Truman, 1947* (Washington, 1963), 176–80.

action would undermine the nascent UN, in which much hope had been invested. Others worried that aid to Greece could lead to direct U.S. military intervention in a messy civil war in a faraway land.[52]

As so often in the Cold War, the president's call to action, abetted by a massive public information campaign, carried the day. The threat seemed ominous, the need urgent. A Congress in open revolt on domestic issues but perhaps recalling all too vividly its obstruction of executive authority in the 1930s fell into line. In a statement rich with symbolism, Senator Henry Cabot Lodge Jr., grandson of Wilson's nemesis, averred that the choice was "whether we are going to repudiate the President and throw the flag on the ground and stamp on it."[53] Legislation for measures without precedent in U.S. foreign policy passed quickly and by sizeable, bipartisan majorities, 67–23 in the Senate, and 287–107 in the House. The era of Cold War interventionism was under way.

Under the Truman Doctrine, the United States plunged into the Greek Civil War, the first of many such forays. It was an especially savage conflict with atrocities on both sides in which even children became pawns, brought home by the brutal and still unexplained assassination of CBS newsman George Polk, an unsparing critic of the Greek government. United States advisers tolerated their client's mass political arrests and executions for fear of undermining it. They would not abide incompetence, however, and assumed such control in Athens that the head of the aid mission was known as "the Most Powerful Man in Greece."[54] When the counterinsurgency effort stalled in 1948, the administration rebuffed Greek appeals for U.S. combat troops, mainly because they were not available. It relied instead on massive military aid and a 450-man advisory group headed by World War II hero Gen. James Van Fleet. Van Fleet reorganized the Greek army and infused it with a fighting spirit. In late 1948, using the massive firepower provided by the United States, napalm included, the army launched a decisive offensive against rebel encampments. In November 1949, Truman claimed victory. Some Americans viewed Greece as a prototype for future interventions.[55]

Such claims must be qualified. In portraying the war in Greece as a struggle between Communism and freedom, U.S. officials misinterpreted

---

52. Howard Jones, "A New Kind of War": America's Global Strategy and the Civil War in Greece (New York, 1989), 45–61.
53. Offner, Another Such Victory, 204.
54. Ibid., 206.
55. Lawrence S. Wittner, American Intervention in Greece, 1943–1949 (New York, 1982) is sharply critical of U.S. involvement; Jones, "A New Kind of War" is more positive in its appraisal.

or misrepresented the conflict, ignoring the essentially domestic roots of the insurgency, blurring the authoritarian nature of the Greek government, and greatly exaggerating the Soviet role. Victory came at great cost: more than 100,000 killed, an estimated 5,000 executed, 800,000 refugees including 28,000 children, and atrocities on both sides. The United States focused narrowly on military success and did little to address the problems that had caused the rebellion in the first place. United States aid undoubtedly played an important role in the government's survival and may have deterred greater Soviet involvement. But the insurgents also made a fatal error by shifting prematurely to conventional warfare and thus exposing themselves to U.S. firepower. The crucial factor in the outcome was the role of the Communist nations. Stalin responded to the Truman Doctrine by briefly aiding the rebels, but he hedged his bets by refusing to recognize them and within six months had cut off assistance. More important, he insisted that Yugoslavia's Tito do the same, causing an irreparable split, the first fissure in the Communist "bloc." When Tito at first refused to give in, Stalin set out to destroy him through increased political and economic pressure. Ultimately, to save his regime, Tito went along. His subsequent shut-off of aid and closing of the border was the decisive event, depriving the Greek rebels of assistance and sanctuary and leaving them little choice but surrender. Here, as in similar cases, local circumstances were decisive. The United States thus achieved its primary goal in this first Cold War military intervention, but at high cost for the people involved and for reasons more complex than it conceded or perhaps recognized. Greece offered a dubious precedent for future interventions.[56]

"This is only the beginning," the president told his cabinet while discussing the Truman Doctrine in early 1947, and indeed one of the most creative and important ventures in the history of U.S. foreign policy quickly followed, the Marshall Plan for European economic recovery.[57] It was disturbingly clear by the spring of 1947 that the crisis in the eastern Mediterranean was but the tip of the iceberg. In contrast to 1919, the United States had responded generously to postwar Europe's needs, but $9 billion in aid brought little progress toward recovery. Production had stalled, trade languished, and Europeans lacked the dollars to purchase urgently needed American goods. Acute shortages of food and fuel were exacerbated by a crippling summer 1946 drought and a bitterly cold winter. Hunger and malnutrition were rampant. United States officials viewed Germany as the key to European recovery and concluded that it

56. Offner, *Another Such Victory*, 207–9.
57. Leffler, *A Preponderance of Power*, 147.

was essential to stop reparations and take the limits off German industrialization. Still facing enormous reconstruction problems themselves, the Soviets understandably rejected such proposals. Americans interpreted Soviet intransigence as a sinister design to drag Europe further down and exploit the chaos. Two years after the war, the continent remained, in Churchill's words, "a rubble heap, a charnel house, a breeding ground for pestilence and hate." Americans feared that the worsening economic crisis might produce Communist takeovers through the electoral systems in such crucial countries as France and Italy, an obvious and compelling threat to U.S. prosperity and security.[58]

Through the rest of 1947, U.S. officials hammered out the details of a major new aid program. They insisted that the Europeans take the initiative in planning but set firm guidelines for them to follow. The essential goal was to spark economic recovery and relieve the vast human suffering. But the administration also sought to use U.S. aid to check an alarming leftward drift in European politics. Communists were to be excluded from recipient governments and socialist tendencies in domestic planning curbed. Americans pushed for balanced budgets, convertible currencies, and guarantees for U.S. trade where dollars were used for purchases. They required Britain and France to accept a reindustrialized Germany and France to abandon plans to detach the Ruhr, in effect substituting for a unified Germany a combined Western zone integrated into the rest of Europe. To promote greater efficiency and check ancient and destructive tendencies toward narrow nationalism, they designed a "creative peace" that would integrate the Western European economies and Britain and promote multilateral trade. They pushed the Europeans to institute mixed, collaborative systems such as the United States had created through the New Deal, in the words of one cynical Briton, "an integrated Europe looking like the United States of America—God's own country."[59] Not eager for Soviet participation but anxious to avoid responsibility for the division of Europe, the administration invited Moscow to join but set terms it believed Stalin could not accept. Some Americans even hoped that a powerful, reintegrated Western Europe might help split off Eastern Europe from its Soviet masters.

The Marshall Plan was not an easy sell at home. The amount proposed— $25 billion—and the multiyear authorizations were without precedent.

58. Ibid., 188–92; Offner, *Another Such Victory*, 214–20.
59. Michael J. Hogan, *The Marshall Plan: America, Britain, and the Reconstruction of Western Europe, 1947–1952* (New York, 1987), 427, and "The Search for a 'Creative Peace': The United States, European Unity, and the Origins of the Marshall Plan," *Diplomatic History* 6 (Summer 1982), 267–85.

Many Americans fretted that such expenditures would fuel an already insidious inflation. Critics from the right loudly protested a U.S.-funded European New Deal, from the left a "Martial Plan" that would irreparably divide Europe. The administration shrewdly attached Marshall's name to the program to minimize partisan attacks, but in an election year it was impossible to avoid politics. Over vigorous administration objections, Republicans insisted that aid also go to Chiang Kai-shek's embattled government in China, then losing its civil war with the Communists. A Communist coup in Czechoslovakia in February 1948, along with the alleged suicide—possibly murder—of popular Czech foreign minister Jan Masaryk, evoked terrifying memories of Hitler's conquest of that same country a decade before, generating popular support for the program. With official backing, the Committee for the Marshall Plan, modeled on the prewar Committee to Defend America by Aiding the Allies, mounted a massive "public education" program. Composed of a bipartisan group of top leaders from business, labor, and academia, the committee sent out more than 1.25 million reprints of articles, organized petitions, sponsored radio broadcasts, and lobbied Congress. "There was never such propaganda in the whole history of the nation," one critic complained.[60] The administration also scaled back the amount and reluctantly agreed to assist Chiang. Congress passed the legislation in April 1948, a $6 billion appropriation in June.

The United States did not replicate itself among the economies of Western Europe, as some U.S. officials had hoped. The Europeans were dependent but by no means powerless. While welcoming America's aid and even advice, they resisted the imposition of its ways. The result was a mixed economic system similar to that of the United States but far from identical. The Americans could not establish the type of France they preferred.[61] While moving closer to Europe, Britain clung to its special relationship with the United States. It also held on to the pound sterling and even secured a U.S. commitment to back it. Western Europe and Britain were thus no more than "half-Americanized."[62]

European revisionist historians have correctly pointed out that the Marshall Plan was not by itself responsible for Europe's dramatic postwar recovery, as Americans often assume, but they err in suggesting that it was not even an important factor. In fact, U.S. aid, along with the massive

60. Michael Wala, "Selling the Marshall Plan at Home: The Committee for the Marshall Plan to Aid European Recovery," *Diplomatic History* 10 (Summer 1986), 264.
61. Irwin W. Wall, *The United States and the Making of Postwar France, 1945–1954* (New York, 1991), 299.
62. Hogan, *Marshall Plan*, 436.

spending by the United States and its allies for the Korean War, provided the indispensable margin that made possible European recovery.[63] Between 1948 and 1952, the Marshall Plan furnished $13 billion in economic assistance. United States funds performed a dazzling array of tasks, helping to rebuild Italy's Fiat automobile plant, modernizing mines in Turkey, and enabling Greek farmers to purchase Missouri mules. The Marshall Plan provided the capital and imports essential to European recovery without sparking inflation. The import of American methods helped improve Western European budgeting and economic planning. By 1952, industrial productivity shot up to more than 35 percent over 1938 levels, agricultural production by 11 percent. Aid from the United States helped stabilize currencies, liberalize and stimulate trade, and promote prosperity. It started the process of integration that led to the Common Market and ultimately the European Union. Where possible, Europeans had to use U.S. funds to purchase American supplies, boosting exports and promoting prosperity at home. For Europeans and Britons, the Marshall Plan provided a huge psychological boost and restored hope and optimism. It helped to resolve the German problem by promoting reindustrialization and integration into Europe in ways acceptable to France, thus mitigating a bitter conflict dating to the late nineteenth century. It also solidified the shaky European governments against Communism, thereby reducing opportunities for Soviet expansion into Western Europe. The Marshall Plan was the one of the United States' most successful twentieth-century initiatives.[64]

The United States did not rely exclusively on economic assistance to contain Communism in Western Europe. Exporters pushed the distribution of such things as films and Coca-Cola—"the essence of capitalism in every bottle"—to promote the American way of life, provoking in a dependent and therefore especially hypersensitive France charges of "Coca-colonization."[65] Claiming to be the "spearhead of the democratic world," the American Federation of Labor opened a European office in late 1945.[66] Sometimes working with the CIA and the State Department, it set out to combat radicalism in European trade unions. In France, the AFL and the International Ladies' Garment Workers

63. Ibid., 432. The revisionist argument may be found in Alan S. Milward, *The Reconstruction of Western Europe, 1945–1951* (Berkeley, Calif., 1984).
64. Hogan, *Marshall Plan*, 445; also Judt, *Postwar*, 97, and David Reynolds, "The European Response: Primacy of Politics," *Foreign Affairs* (May/June 1997), 180–82.
65. Wall, *Making of Postwar France*, 113, 125–26.
66. Edmund F. Wehrle, *Between a River and a Mountain: The AFL-CIO and the Vietnam War* (Ann Arbor, Mich., 2005), 23.

Union provided to conservative unions moral support, advice, and substantial money, some of it furnished by the U.S. government and corporations. The French accepted the money and rejected the advice. The AFL's influence remained limited. It had much greater success in Germany, where, with government support, it provided urgently needed funds and relief assistance to help conservative unions gain control of the West German labor movement.[67]

The Truman administration employed many of its new national security mechanisms, including a CIA covert operation, to prevent a Communist victory in the crucial Italian elections of 1948. The threat seemed immediate and urgent, and there was talk of a possible civil war and even Soviet and U.S. military intervention. The United States employed carrot and stick. Top officials publicly threatened to cut off aid should the Communists win. Immigration visas were denied to Communists, and U.S. party members were threatened with deportation, endangering the livelihood of numerous Italians who depended on support from relatives in the United States. The administration also provided generous interim aid before the Marshall Plan went into operation, gave Italy twenty-nine merchant ships, and furnished arms to the Christian Democratic government. With firm U.S. backing, the Vatican mobilized Catholics to vote and excommunicated some Communists. The Voice of America broadcast a steady stream of propaganda. Films such as the anti-Soviet satire *Ninotchka* were distributed to Italian viewers. Prominent Italian Americans such as boxer Rocky Graziano and leading entertainers such as Bing Crosby and Dinah Shore affirmed support for a democratic Italy. Italian Americans urged relatives in Italy to vote Christian Democratic. In its first major covert operation, the CIA channeled huge sums of money to the Christian Democrats for their newspaper and for electioneering purposes. The party won a resounding victory, saving Italy from Communism, bolstering other Western European governments, and boosting Truman's stature among Italian Americans in an election year. Having solidified their power, on the other hand, the Christian Democrats refused to institute reforms Americans deemed essential for Italian democracy. Success in Italy, the result of many factors, also produced inflated faith in the utility of covert operations, leading to other, more questionable ventures.[68]

67. Wall, *Postwar France*, 96–112; Carolyn Eisenberg, "Working-Class Politics and the Cold War: American Intervention in the German Labor Movement, 1945–1949," *Diplomatic History* 10 (Fall 1986), 283–306.
68. James Edward Miller, "Taking Off the Gloves: The United States and the Italian Elections of 1948," *Diplomatic History* 7 (Winter 1983), 35–55.

Early challenges to Soviet control of Eastern Europe were far less successful. A policy of containment implied U.S. acquiescence in Moscow's sphere of influence, but from the onset of the Cold War the Truman administration thought in terms of rollback. Kennan proposed in 1947 a radical program of political warfare using sabotage, guerrilla operations, and propaganda activities to stir up rebellion in Soviet bloc countries and perhaps even the USSR itself. At least, he reasoned, such operations might have nuisance value. A top-secret agency innocuously titled the Office of Policy Coordination took charge of Operation Rollback. It dropped refugees and displaced persons from Eastern European countries behind the Iron Curtain by plane and ship. The results were generally disastrous. Soviet agents infiltrated training camps and were well informed about the operations. Some of the infiltrators were betrayed by British spies. Most were easily captured, many executed. Kennan later conceded that Operation Rollback was "the greatest mistake I ever made."[69]

The dramatic U.S. initiatives of 1947–48 hardened the division of Europe. Stalin at first displayed interest in the Marshall Plan, sending Molotov to a meeting in Paris and permitting Eastern European leaders to attend. Once it was clear that the terms were unacceptable and even threatening, especially the revival of Germany and the possibility that Eastern Europe might be drawn into the western economic orbit, the Soviet dictator abruptly changed course. Increasingly certain that U.S. policies were designed to undermine Soviet influence in Eastern Europe, he rejected the Marshall Plan, abandoned further efforts to negotiate with the West, and cracked down on his sphere of influence. In the summer of 1947, the Soviet Union "negotiated" a series of bilateral trade treaties with Eastern European nations collectively known as the Molotov Plan. In September, representatives gathered in Poland and established the Communist Information Bureau (Cominform) to enforce ideological purity. In words strikingly similar to those of the Truman Doctrine, Stalin's representative Andrei Zhdanov spoke of a world divided into two camps. From this point, Stalin refused to tolerate diversity within his sphere, insisting upon pro-Soviet governments that tailored their policies to his specifications. Through rigged elections, Communists took over in Hungary in late 1947. The Czech coup followed in early 1948. An increasingly paranoid Stalin and his henchmen in the East European satellites used purges, show trials, forced labor, and exile to eliminate possible enemies and squelch dissent.[70] The Soviet crackdown

69. Peter Grose, *Operation Rollback: America's Secret War Behind the Iron Curtain* (New York, 2000), 98–99.
70. Judt, *Postwar*, 192.

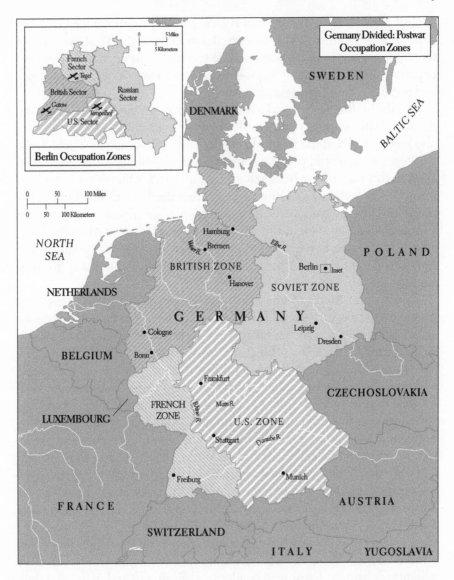

0   5 Miles
0   5 Kilometers

Germany Divided: Postwar
Occupation Zones

French
Sector
Tegel
British Sector
Gatow
Russian
Sector
Tempelhof
U.S. Sector

Berlin Occupation Zones

0   50   100 Miles
0   50   100 Kilometers

SWEDEN

BALTIC SEA

DENMARK

NORTH
SEA

POLAND

NETHERLANDS

Hamburg
Weser R.
Bremen
Elbe R.
BRITISH ZONE
Hanover
Berlin Inset
SOVIET ZONE

G E R M A N Y

Cologne
Leipzig
Dresden

BELGIUM   Bonn

Frankfurt

LUXEMBOURG

FRENCH
ZONE
Rhine R.
Main R.
U.S. ZONE

Stuttgart
Danube R.

Freiburg
Munich

FRANCE

AUSTRIA

SWITZERLAND

ITALY   YUGOSLAVIA

CZECHOSLOVAKIA

initiated forty years of brutal repression in Eastern Europe. The divided Europe that both sides had declaimed about rhetorically was becoming reality.

The most serious crisis of the early Cold War soon followed. Alarmed at the prospect of a reindustrialized West Germany under Allied control, Stalin launched a risky gamble to restore movement toward a unified Germany or drive the West from its Berlin enclave and solidify Soviet control over East Germany. When U.S. military commander Gen. Lucius Clay announced plans for currency reform in the Western occupation zones, a major step toward a West German state, nervous Soviet occupation authorities in July 1948 sealed access to the city by highway, rail, and water.

The Berlin Blockade posed a major challenge for the United States and its allies. They correctly perceived that Stalin did not want war, but they also recognized that the blockade created a volatile situation in which the slightest misstep could provoke conflict. Certain that the Allied position in West Berlin was militarily indefensible, some U.S. officials pondered the possibility of withdrawal. Others insisted that the United States could not abandon Berlin without undermining the confidence of Western Europeans—a "Munich of 1948," warned diplomat Robert Murphy.[71] Previously more open to negotiations with the Soviets than Washington, Clay now urged sending an armed convoy through East Germany to West Berlin.

Truman and Marshall chose a less risky course, "unprovocative" but "firm," in Marshall's words.[72] Drawing on Army Air Force experience carrying supplies over the Himalayas to China in World War II and a mini-airlift during a Soviet "baby-blockade" of West Berlin just months before, they turned to air power to maintain the Western position in Berlin and sustain its beleaguered people. It was the sort of thing Americans do best, a stroke of genius. The United States backed up the airlift by dispatching two squadrons of B-29 Superfortress bombers to Germany and Britain, signaling to the Soviets the danger of any escalation of the crisis. For eleven months in what was called Operation Vittles, fleets of C-47 Skytrain and C-54 Skymaster transports flew 250 missions a day around the clock, moving an average 2,500 tons of food, fuel, raw materials, and finished goods daily into Berlin to feed and heat two million people and maintain some semblance of a functioning economy. At the height of the blockade, planes landed every forty-five seconds. Some of the pilots who had bombed Berlin during the war now saved it. The Soviets also handled the situation delicately, refusing to challenge U.S. aircraft and, reflecting their contradictory goals, allowing huge gaps in the blockade that helped Berlin survive. Stalin's gamble proved a major blunder.[73] America won German

71. Offner, *Another Such Victory*, 256.
72. M. Steven Fish, "The Berlin Blockade of 1948–1948," in Alexander L. George, ed., *Avoiding War: Problems of Crisis Management* (Boulder, Colo., 1991), 204.
73. William Stivers, "The Incomplete Blockade: Soviet Zone Supply of West Berlin, 1948–1948," *Diplomatic History* 21 (Fall 1997), 596.

gratitude for its firm response, and Truman earned crucial accolades at home in an election year. German anger undermined already slim Soviet hopes of heading off Western plans for a divided nation. Recognizing that the blockade had been counterproductive, Stalin in the spring of 1949 backed down. Originally, he had insisted that he would not drop the blockade until the United States and its allies scrapped plans to rebuild West Germany. By the time he gave in, West Germany was near reality. A remarkable indication of Western military and economic power and political will, the Berlin airlift also sealed the division of Europe that would mark the Cold War.[74]

The Berlin Blockade also helped bring about the most radical U.S. step of the early postwar era, the North Atlantic Treaty Organization (NATO). Drawing upon their own historical experience in the Articles of Confederation, Americans in promoting the Marshall Plan urged the Western Europeans to find security through unification. The Czech coup underscored their importuning, and in April 1948 Britain joined four European nations in forming the Brussels Pact, a mutual defense treaty. For their part, the Europeans insisted that a U.S. defense commitment was the key to their political security and economic recovery. "Political and indeed spiritual forces must be mobilised in our defence," Bevin, a founder of the North Atlantic alliance, intoned.[75] Looking toward the Atlantic as well as the continent and fearing Soviet intimidation and subversion more than its military power, the ruddy, hard-drinking, fiercely anti-Communist former labor leader went further by seeking to bring the Scandinavian nations and the United States and Canada into a regional alliance. Some Americans like Kennan vigorously objected that the military emphasis of the discussions would harden the division of Europe, but the Berlin Blockade gave urgency to Bevin's warnings, leading to formal talks in Washington in July 1948, "the crucible in which NATO was formed."[76]

Over the next year, the alliance took shape. The most difficult issues were those of membership and the nature of the U.S. commitment. Western Europeans objected to Bevin's Atlantic focus, "a fabulous monster," French foreign minister Georges Bidault protested.[77] They bent to U.S. pressure, however, and Norway, Denmark, Iceland, and Canada, along

74. Martin Walker, *The Cold War—A History* (New York, 1993), 57.

75. Quoted in Lawrence S. Kaplan, *The United States and NATO: The Formative Years* (Lexington, Ky., 1984), 51.

76. Martin H. Folly, "Breaking the Vicious Circle: Britain, the United States, and the Genesis of the North Atlantic Treaty," *Diplomatic History* 12 (Winter 1988), 75.

77. Ibid., 76.

with Italy and Portugal, became charter members. The Europeans sought from the United States a binding pledge as in the Brussels Treaty requiring signatories to give member nations under attack "all military and other aid and assistance in their power." Wary of entanglement in Europe and especially of provoking a reaction from isolationist remnants in Congress, U.S. negotiators preferred a more restricted commitment. The participants eventually agreed that in response to an attack on a signatory, each member individually and acting with others should take "such actions as it deems necessary, including the use of armed force." The Treaty of Washington was signed in April 1949 with appropriate pomp and ceremony; the only discordant note, Acheson later recalled, was the Marine Band playing Cole Porter's "It Ain't Necessarily So," a tune that might have fed lingering European doubts about the sanctity of U.S. promises. By this time accustomed to radically new foreign policy measures, the Senate approved the treaty with little dissent in July 1949. What has been called the "American Revolution of 1949" was complete.[78] An alliance designed in the words of NATO's first secretary general, Lord Ismay, to "keep the Americans in, the Russians out, and the Germans down" would turn out to be one of the most enduring such arrangements in world history.[79]

III

By the late 1940s, the Cold War began to influence policies in other regions. In Latin America, the United States shifted from neglect to concern to active involvement centered around anti-Communism. The Good Neighbor spirit of the 1930s had reflected U.S. insularity during the depression. As the United States addressed a wide range of urgent global issues after the war, attention naturally shifted from the hemisphere. Unlike Cordell Hull and Sumner Welles, the Atlanticists who directed postwar policy had little interest in or knowledge of Latin America. Many held distinct prejudices about the peoples and cultures. While lavishing billions of dollars on Western Europe, the Truman administration responded to Latin American appeals for economic aid with proposals for limited technical assistance, loans, private capital, and increased trade. United States diplomats did expand and institutionalize the collective security arrangements created before Pearl Harbor. The 1947 Rio Pact was the first of the postwar regional military alliances authorized under Article 51 of the UN Charter and provided a model for NATO. By the spring 1948 inter-American meeting in Bogotá, the State Department had identified

78. Kaplan, NATO, 1.
79. Escott Reid, Time of Fear and Hope (Toronto, 1977), 63.

Communism as a potential danger to the hemisphere. Riots in the Colombian capital as the meeting took place—which U.S. officials incorrectly attributed to Communist influence—seemed to underscore the threat. The United States at Bogotá first began to mobilize anti-Communist sentiment in the hemisphere. The conferees created the Organization of American States to enforce regional security and passed an anti-Communist resolution sponsored by the U.S. delegation.[80]

Once more viewing the hemisphere as threatened by an alien ideology, the United States fell back on the reliance on dictators pioneered by Stimson in the 1920s. With U.S. support, democracy had flourished in Latin America during and immediately after the war, spawning reformist governments, a militant labor movement, left-wing political parties, and even a surge of Communist activity. Increasingly concerned about Communism elsewhere, U.S. officials believed that Latin America's "Hispano-Indian culture—or lack of it," as Acheson condescendingly labeled it, left the region especially susceptible to Communist penetration.[81] The United States thus acquiesced in and in some cases encouraged a movement on the part of conservative elites to turn back democracy. "We cannot be too dogmatic about the methods by which local communists are dealt with," Kennan observed.[82] Military dictators seized power in numerous countries. With U.S. sympathy and even support, they outlawed Communist parties, suppressed leftist organizations, and with AFL assistance drove out left-wing unions. To curry favor with Washington, Latin governments reduced or cut off trade with the Soviet Union and even severed diplomatic relations, which, ironically, had been established in wartime at Washington's behest. By 1950, U.S. officials viewed Latin America as an "arena for Cold War competition."[83]

The Cold War created dilemmas for the United States in faraway South Africa. Facing rising anger at the end of World War II on the part of their oppressed black populations, the minority white governments of southern Africa silenced dissent with brute force and dealt with their racial problems by imposing rigid and brutal systems of segregation called apartheid. The Truman administration confronted racial protests of its own at home, and African American leaders increasingly linked the evils

80. Mark T. Gilderhus, *The Second Century: U.S.–Latin American Relations Since 1889* (Wilmington, Del., 2000), 125–26.
81. Stephen G. Rabe, "The Elusive Conference: United States' Economic Relations with Latin America, 1945–1952," *Diplomatic History* 2 (Summer 1978), 293.
82. Gilderhus, *Second Century*, 135.
83. Ibid., 133.

of racial discrimination at home and colonialism abroad. United States officials also sought to take an enlightened position on racial issues to counter
increasingly shrill Communist propaganda and win the allegiance of
peoples of color across the world. The administration would have preferred to distance itself from South Africa's racial policies. Instead, as historian Thomas Borstelmann has pointed out, Cold War exigencies made
the United States a "reluctant uncle—a godparent—at the baptism of
apartheid."[84] United States leaders had long-standing ties with the South
African ruling class. South Africans shrewdly waved the anti-Communist
banner to win points with the United States. American corporations found
South Africa a lucrative place for exports and investments. But the most vital link was through strategic raw materials. Nuclear weapons were vital to
U.S. Cold War strategy, and uranium was essential for nuclear weapons,
"an absolute requirement of the very life of our nation," Nitze observed.
South Africa possessed large quantities of uranium. "Faced with the jugger-
naut of *apartheid* in a country of profound strategic importance to the
United States," Borstelmann concludes, the administration chose to "ally
itself closely with the world's leading apostles of racial discrimination."[85]

One place where Cold War imperatives did not rule was in the rapidly
escalating conflict between Arabs and Jews. The postwar situation in Palestine defied solution. Under a now defunct League of Nations mandate,
Britain exercised nominal control. But Zionists agitated more determinedly
for a Jewish state and with the moral force of the Holocaust behind them
pressed for rescission of the 1939 white paper to permit thousands of
refugees into Palestine. Terrorists such as Menachem Begin launched
deadly attacks against Arabs and British alike. Arabs girded to defend what
they considered their homeland. An Anglo-American study group in 1946
recommended the admission of one hundred thousand Jews to Palestine
and partition through the creation of a single state with separate Arab and
Jewish provinces. Others proposed a UN trusteeship. Britain tossed the hot
potato into the lap of the United Nations. Backed by the Soviet Union and
the United States—a rare moment of agreement—the world organization
in late 1947 approved partition by a bare two votes. As violence mounted,
the beleaguered British announced they would leave in May 1948. The
Jews vowed to create a provisional government.[86]

84. Thomas Borstelmann, *Apartheid's Reluctant Uncle: The United States and Southern
    Africa in the Early Cold War* (New York, 1993), 197.
85. Ibid., 193.
86. Peter L. Hahn, *Caught in the Middle East: U.S. Policy Toward the Arab-Israeli Con-
    flict, 1945–1961* (Chapel Hill, N.C., 2004), 44–49.

The Palestine issue posed a huge dilemma for the United States. Support for a Jewish state risked alienating those Arabs who sat on top of the world's richest oil deposits and controlled territory deemed strategically vital, perhaps driving them into the arms of the Soviet Union. Top diplomatic and military officials thus repeatedly urged the president not to endorse an independent Jewish state. The White House drew different conclusions. Truman brought to the presidency a strong sympathy for the underdog. Like others worldwide, he was horrified by grim postwar accounts of the Holocaust and troubled by the plight of thousands of Jewish refugees. Some of his advisers had close ties to Zionist groups. Facing an uphill struggle for election in 1948, the president could not but be sensitive to the Jewish vote, especially in key states like New York. Truman at first equivocated, backing a UN trusteeship but giving vague private assurances of support to prominent Jews.[87]

The issue came to a head in the spring of 1948. As Britain prepared to depart and Jews hurried to establish a government, debate raged in Washington. At a tense meeting on May 12, Clifford reported that a Jewish state was inevitable. Employing the Cold War arguments that usually prevailed, he warned that since the Soviet Union would likely recognize the new government, the United States should seek an edge by doing so first. The normally in-control Marshall exploded, dismissing Clifford's proposal as a "transparent dodge to win a few votes" and vowing that if it went through he, for one, would vote *against* Truman. Clifford fretted that Marshall's "righteous God-damned Baptist" arguments might sway the administration against recognition. Facing a grim domestic political situation, the president held firm. Through intermediaries, Clifford persuaded Marshall not to oppose recognition. When the announcement came three days later, the United States recognized the new government within eleven minutes. Truman acted on what he considered principle as well as political expediency. The move no doubt helped his stunning electoral upset over Republican Thomas Dewey in November. This essentially political act, taken against the advice of foreign policy experts, also infuriated the Arabs and represented the first step in building what would be the U.S.-Israeli special relationship. It sparked an Arab-Israeli war, the initial engagement in an ongoing struggle that would persist into the next century.[88]

By the beginning of Truman's second term, the Cold War had expanded to East Asia, a region that would command U.S. attention for the

---

87. Douglas Little, *American Orientalism: The United States and the Middle East Since 1945* (Chapel Hill, N.C., 2004), 80–85.
88. Ibid., 86–87.

next four years. Neither Truman nor Acheson knew much about that part of the world; what they knew tended to have a European bias. The United States became hopelessly ensnared in Chiang Kai-shek's losing cause in the epic Chinese civil war, blundered into hot war in Korea, and then foolishly provoked Chinese Communist intervention. Drawing a ring of containment from Korea to India, it laid the groundwork for long-term conflict with the new government in Beijing and a war in Vietnam.

A tangle the United States could never unravel during World War II, China posed even greater challenges after V-J Day. Japan's sudden surrender left that vast conflict-ridden nation in turmoil, and in August 1945, a civil war that had begun long before World War I entered its climactic phase. The nominal government headed by Chiang's Nationalists and isolated in the southwest corner of China and Mao Zedong's Communists, based in the north, immediately began jockeying for position. At U.S. urging, Stalin had recognized the Nationalists, but as the Red Army withdrew from Manchuria it facilitated Communist takeover of the positions vacated. Nervous about Soviet intentions, the United States saw little choice but to back Chiang. To block Communist gains and ensure his control, military officials ordered the Japanese to surrender only to the Nationalists, mounted a massive air and sea lift of half a million Nationalist troops to strategic locations ahead of the Communists, deployed fifty thousand U.S. Marines to guard railroads and major cities, and provided Chiang more than $1 billion in emergency military aid. Clashes between Communists and Nationalists in Manchuria and northern China and signs of Soviet support for the Chinese Communist Party (CCP) reinforced U.S. fears that conflict in China would provide opportunities for Soviet expansion, risking direct conflict with the United States. To head off a ruinous civil war and keep the USSR out of China, U.S. officials reverted to enticing the Communists into a coalition government in which Chiang would retain the upper hand.[89]

To implement this policy, Truman in late 1945 dispatched General Marshall to China on one of the most thankless missions ever undertaken by a U.S. diplomat. The task—shot through with contradictions—was to arrange a compromise between two warring parties while keeping a presumably reformed Nationalist government in power and checking Soviet and CCP influence. It was based on the naive assumptions that Chiang would reform his government and the two sides could reach meaningful agreements. Marshall had only limited leverage in the form of promises

---

89. Marc S. Gallichio, *The Cold War Begins in Asia: American East Asian Policy and the Fall of the Japanese Empire* (New York, 1988), 73–112.

of aid to each side. In the initial stages, he seemed to accomplish miracles. Called "the professor" by those Chinese he worked with, the illustrious general arranged a cease-fire and an end to troop movements. Even more remarkable, he sketched out the framework for a coalition government and integration of the armed forces. The Communists again spoke of promoting free enterprise and a "U.S. styled" democracy. Mao expressed interest in visiting Washington. It was a "stupendous accomplishment," the commander of U.S. forces in China, Gen. Albert C. Wedemeyer, exulted.[90]

Marshall's skill and prestige ultimately could not bridge the vast chasm separating the two Chinese parties. His departure from China at a critical point removed the tie that temporarily held them together. As the Soviets withdrew from Manchuria, Communist and Nationalist forces again vied for position, provoking armed clashes. After the general returned, the contradictions in his mission were blatantly exposed. The two sides regarded each other as deadly enemies and feared the implications of a coalition government.[91] Hotheads from both camps sabotaged negotiations. Confident of U.S. support, Chiang chose war over substantive concessions. The Communists perceived that Marshall was not in fact an impartial mediator and the United States was pursuing what delegate Zhou En-lai called a "double policy." Negotiations broke down, fighting resumed, and both sides vented their anger with the United States. In January 1947, after a year of frustration, Marshall came home to serve as secretary of state.[92]

Over the next three years, the Chinese civil war ground to a conclusion. The Nationalists began with a two-to-one advantage in manpower, three-to-one in firepower, but quickly squandered their edge. A corrupt and incompetent government provided a flimsy base upon which to wage a military campaign. Runaway inflation, malnutrition, and disease in Nationalist-occupied areas eroded already limited popular support. The army suffered from abysmal morale and what a U.S. officer called the "world's worst leadership."[93] Rather than attacking the enemy when it had the advantage, it stuck to its garrisons. The Communists skillfully exploited Nationalist lethargy, mobilizing the peasants and seizing the

90. Mark A. Stoler, George C. Marshall: Soldier-Statesman of the American Century (Boston, 1989), 148; Steven L. Levine, "A New Look at American Mediation in the Chinese Civil War: The Marshall Mission and Manchuria," Diplomatic History 3 (Fall 1979), 359.
91. Stoler, Marshall, 149.
92. Offner, Another Such Victory, 323–26.
93. Michael Schaller, The United States and China in the Twentieth Century (New York, 1990), 117.

initiative. When the tide of battle shifted in 1948, Nationalist armies simply melted away, surrendering en masse or fleeing the battlefield without their equipment. During four months of 1948, Chiang lost nearly 50 percent of his manpower and 75 percent of his weapons. In October alone, three hundred thousand Nationalists surrendered.

The Nationalist collapse began precisely when the Cold War in Europe was entering a crucial stage, posing difficult choices for the Truman administration. Having committed itself to contain Communism, should it use any means necessary to prevent a Communist victory in China? Should it at least make a good faith effort by continuing to support an embattled ally? Or, given the Nationalists' obvious deficiencies, should it cut its losses, abandon Chiang to his fate, and prepare for accommodation with the victors?

As it so often did when facing such choices, the administration took a cautious—in this case fateful—middle-of-the-road course. Truman and Marshall flatly rejected recommendations from some military advisers to send U.S. troops to save the Nationalists. China remained in their eyes a secondary theater. In any event, the troops were not available, and Marshall wisely questioned whether full-scale U.S. intervention could salvage the hapless Chiang. They declined even to send a military advisory group for fear of getting sucked deeper into a quagmire. On the other hand, although Truman viewed Chiang and his entourage as "thieves" and additional aid as "pouring sand in a rat hole," his administration refused to abandon them.[94] Chiang had vocal and deeply emotional support in the United States, especially from Henry Luce's Time-Life media empire and congressional Republicans who viewed Asia as the most important Cold War arena and China its key. Ill informed about China and zealous in their support of Chiang, they threatened to condition Marshall Plan aid to Europe on continued assistance to China. In any event, the president recognized that simply to abandon Chiang in an election year would give the opposition a whip to flog him with. United States officials also found a broader strategic rationale for continuing to aid the Nationalists. To drop Nationalist China at a critical juncture, they reasoned, would raise doubts about the credibility of U.S. commitments at home and especially in Europe, while continued aid might reassure Europeans of U.S. good faith. Miscalculating the rapidity of Chiang's collapse, they also hoped that limited aid might delay the international impact of his defeat until Europe was stabilized. In April 1948, the administration agreed to an additional $338 million in economic aid and $125 million in military aid,

94. Offner, *Another Such Victory*, 326.

hoping, in the words of one official, to "sweat it out and try to prevent the military situation from changing too drastically to the advantage of the communist forces."[95] It thus maintained its ties to a losing cause and compounded its error by not explaining to Americans why it had not done more. These decisions would have catastrophic consequences at home and abroad.

As the Cold War intensified in Europe and the Chinese civil war turned in favor of the Communists, attention shifted toward the erstwhile enemy, Japan. United States officials decided early in the war that Japanese society must be radically restructured, and they determined to act without interference from allies. Responsibility for the occupation fell upon Gen. Douglas MacArthur, Supreme Commander for Allied Powers (SCAP), who brought to the task a combination of imperial majesty, political populism, and missionary zeal. In the first years, the "blue-eyed shogun" and his entourage ruled Japan as "neo-colonial overlords," brooking little interference from Washington and civilians in Tokyo and issuing "edicts with imperious panache."[96] They took advantage of a shattered and compliant society to impose sweeping reforms designed to democratize Japan and thereby convert it into a "Switzerland of the Pacific."[97] While retaining the emperor, MacArthur modified his godlike status and allied him with the occupation. Americans drafted a new constitution creating a parliamentary democracy, established basic civil and legal rights, permitted women to vote and own property, demobilized the military, and renounced war. SCAP drew up plans for breaking up the great industrial combines (*zaibatsu*), encouraged labor unions, implemented land reform, recast the educational system, and even legalized the Communist Party. The occupation did not always energetically implement its plans, especially with the *zaibatsu*, and the conservative Japanese bureaucrats upon whom it relied managed to preserve continuity amidst drastic change. Still, the imposition of such profound reforms by an outside power was unprecedented. Satisfied with his handiwork, MacArthur in early 1947 proposed to negotiate a peace treaty.[98]

Washington thought otherwise. Alarmed by the Soviet threat in Europe and a possible Communist victory in China, U.S. officials feared that the economic stagnation and political disarray that accompanied

95. John H. Feaver, "The Chinese Aid Bill of 1948: Limited Assistance as a Cold War Strategy," *Diplomatic History* 5 (Spring 1981), 119.
96. Dower, *Embracing Defeat*, 27, 203–4.
97. Charles E. Neu, *Troubled Encounter: The United States and Japan* (New York, 1975), 204.
98. Dower, *Embracing Defeat*, 253–73.

MacArthur's reforms would produce chaos in Japan, leaving the United States isolated in East Asia. Thus, while launching the containment policy in Europe, they joined with conservative Japanese leaders in 1948 to effect a "reverse course" emphasizing economic reconstruction and political stability over reform. As in Germany, the United States removed limits on Japanese industrial growth, encouraged the regrowth of the *zaibatsu*, and stopped reparations. To meet the growing "dollar gap," U.S. officials promoted the expansion of Japanese exports—even to Southeast Asia, the center of the old Co-Prosperity Sphere. The reverse course curbed the growing power of labor unions and suppressed the radical groups that had formed early in MacArthur's tenure. With economic recovery now the "prime objective," Detroit banker and economic czar Joseph Dodge implemented an austerity program to control inflation, balance the budget, and boost exports. The reverse course imposed huge hardships on Japanese workers. The economy remained stagnant until the outbreak of war in Korea brought relief in the form of massive U.S. purchases.[99]

The reverse course in Japan was paralleled by a major shift in policies toward Southeast Asia. In both French Indochina and the Netherlands East Indies, the end of the war set off potent nationalist revolutions against colonial authority. Roosevelt's anti-colonialism had ebbed in his last months and passed altogether with his death and the rise of the Cold War. United States officials sympathized with nationalism in principle. On July 4, 1946, the Philippines was granted its independence, although the retention of military bases and close economic ties gave it a sort of neo-colonial status.[100] Americans doubted whether "backward" Asians were ready for independence. Focused in the immediate postwar years on the welfare of European allies and Japan, they took a hands-off approach that favored the colonial nations.

As Cold War tensions increased, however, the Truman administration attached growing importance to Southeast Asia. The triangular trade between the United States, Western Europe, and the Southeast Asian colonies was deemed vital to ease the dollar gap that retarded European economic recovery. Southeast Asia lay astride strategic water routes between the Pacific and the Middle East. Nervous about possible Communist gains there, U.S. officials threatened to terminate Marshall Plan aid to extract Dutch promises of independence for an anti-Communist nationalist group in Indonesia headed by Achmed Sukarno. "Money

99. Ibid., 525–555.
100. Stanley Karnow, *In Our Image: America's Empire in the Philippines* (New York, 1989), calls it "dependent independence" (323–26).

talked," a U.S. diplomat later observed.[101] Because of France's volatile politics and its crucial position in Europe, the Americans dealt with it much differently. In any event, the Vietnamese independence movement was headed by longtime Communist operative Ho Chi Minh. Primarily concerned with France and mistakenly viewing the fiercely nationalist Ho as a puppet of the Kremlin, the Truman administration with little enthusiasm and less optimism recognized in 1949 the French puppet government headed by the playboy emperor Bao Dai. In February 1950, it extended direct military aid to France for its war against Ho's Vietminh, a seemingly innocuous commitment with enormous unforeseen consequences.[102]

IV

The tumultuous years 1949 and 1950 were crucial in the evolution of U.S. Cold War policies in Asia and indeed globally. A series of stunning events sharply escalated Soviet-American tensions, aroused grave fears for U.S. security, and set off nasty internal debates that poisoned the political atmosphere. Responding to a crisis situation not unlike that of 1941, Truman administration officials globalized the containment policy, assumed manifold commitments in the worldwide struggle against Communism, and through National Security Council document number 68 embarked on full-scale, peacetime rearmament. With Truman's full confidence, Acheson, appointed secretary of state in January 1949, took the lead in implementing these radically new policies.

Soviet explosion of an atomic bomb in September 1949 spread dismay and anxiety across the country. Although not unexpected, it came sooner than most Americans had anticipated. It eliminated the U.S. nuclear monopoly, raised fears that Stalin might be emboldened to take greater risks, drastically heightened Americans' sense of their vulnerability, and in time produced a sweeping reassessment of Cold War strategy and the place of nuclear weapons in it.[103] In light of this shock, some Truman advisers, fearing a nuclear arms race, continued to press for international control of atomic energy. Others urged the production of a much more powerful hydrogen bomb to ensure that the United States maintained nuclear supremacy. Truman sided with the latter group, in February 1950 approving

101. Robert J. McMahon, *The Limits of Empire: The United States and Southeast Asia Since World War II* (New York, 1999), 33.
102. George C. Herring, *America's Longest War: The United States and Vietnam, 1950–1975* (4th ed., New York, 2001), 21–23.
103. Leffler, *Preponderance of Power*, 333.

production of a superbomb and significantly escalating an arms race that would continue for the next forty years and at times threaten to spiral out of control. "Can the Russians do it?" he asked at a crucial top-level meeting. When told the answer was yes, he quickly responded, "In that case we have no choice. We'll go ahead."[104]

The Communist triumph in China had an even more profound impact. For years, Americans had cherished the illusion that China was a special protégé who, with proper guidance, would become a modern democratic nation and close friend of the United States. The "loss" of China to Communism at a pivotal moment in the early Cold War had especially unsettling consequences. It extended to East Asia a conflict that had been centered in Europe. In one stroke, it seemed to shift the global balance of power against the United States. It created the appearance that Communism was on the move and the West on the defensive. It left frustrated and fearful Americans asking the portentous—and pretentious—question: Who lost China?

Vainly hoping for reason to prevail, Acheson released in August 1949 the richly documented "China White Paper" absolving the United States of blame for the Communist triumph. This "ominous result" was "beyond the control of the United States . . . ," the paper stoutly proclaimed. "It was the product of internal Chinese forces . . . which this country tried to influence but could not."[105] Such conclusions have stood the test of time, but they offered cold comfort to already rattled Americans in 1949. For right-wing Republicans, Chiang's most ardent supporters, who were deeply frustrated by Truman's shocking victory in 1948, the fall of China provided a political windfall. The administration had not taken the opposition into its confidence on China as with Europe. Republicans, joined by some Democrats, now charged that the administration had favored Europe at the expense of China and callously abandoned a faithful ally to its dreadful fate.

Revelations of Soviet espionage in the United States seemed to nervous Americans to explain otherwise unanswerable questions. Victim from a history of unbroken success of what British scholar D. W. Brogan called "the illusion of American omnipotence," the nation confronted failure at this critical time in its history by finding scapegoats at home.[106] Soviet spies had speeded Stalin's nuclear timetable by stealing U.S. secrets, it

104. Beisner, *Acheson*, 233; Gregg Herken, *Winning Weapon: The Atomic Bomb in the Cold War, 1945–1950* (New York, 1980), 304–22.
105. Department of State, *United States Relations with China: With Reference to the Period 1944–1949* (Washington, 1949), xvi.
106. D. W. Brogan, *The American Character* (New York, 1956), 207–8.

was alleged, a charge technically accurate, as it turned out, but grossly overstated. Repeating in a more susceptible milieu accusations first raised by Ambassador Patrick Hurley in 1945, critics like the ambitious young California congressman Richard M. Nixon charged that Communist sympathizers within the U.S. government had undermined support for Chiang, thus ensuring an eventual enemy triumph.[107] With the postwar Red Scare already under way, in February 1950, a heretofore obscure Republican senator from Wisconsin, Joseph R. McCarthy, in a major speech in Wheeling, West Virginia, claimed to have the names of some 206 Communists working in the State Department, accelerating the witch hunt that would bear his name. Stunned from their complacency, a people who through much of their history had enjoyed relatively cost-free security reacted with panic. A Cold War culture of near hysterical fear, paranoiac suspiciousness, and stifling conformity began to take shape. Militant anticommunism increasingly poisoned the political atmosphere at home and made negotiations with the Soviet Union unthinkable.

The war scare of 1949–50 had major consequences for U.S. policy in Asia. In December 1949, the Truman administration approved NSC-49 advocating that the United States "block further Communist expansion in Asia." With the fall of China, Japan emerged as the most important nation in East Asia, and U.S. officials urged the negotiation of a peace treaty and an end to the occupation. Southeast Asia took on even greater importance as a source of raw materials and markets for Japan and a means to close the Western European dollar gap. Reconciliation with Communist China may have been out of reach by this time. The anger provoked by the U.S. role in the Chinese civil war could not easily have been overcome. China's brutal treatment of American diplomats provoked outrage in the United States. Speaking metaphorically, Mao had vowed to "clean the house before entertaining guests." He would likely have contemplated ties with the United States only on terms the administration could never have accepted.[108] The pragmatic Acheson at times seemed open to eventual recognition of the People's Republic and often expressed hope that Mao might become an Asian Tito. But Truman despised the Chinese Communists and had little interest in accommodation. In any case, the events of 1949–50 created a domestic political climate that made suicidal any move toward reconciliation. Thus while trying to distance itself from Chiang, who had fled to Formosa, and promoting a wedge strategy

107. Schaller, *United States and China*, 118–21, 130–34.
108. The "lost opportunity" is debated in "Symposium: Rethinking the Lost Chance in China," *Diplomatic History* 21 (Winter 1997), 71–115.

it hoped might separate China from the Soviet Union, the administration shunned even the smallest step toward the Beijing regime. By late 1950, even this cautious policy was overtaken by events.[109]

The crisis atmosphere of 1949–50 produced most notably NSC-68, a sweeping restatement of U.S. national security policy and one of the most significant Cold War documents. In late 1949, Truman ordered a review of military policies in response to loss of the nuclear monopoly. Long frustrated by the staunch opposition of the president and Defense Secretary Louis Johnson to increased military spending, Acheson used the study, as he later put it, to "bludgeon the mass mind of 'top government'" into spending the money necessary for adequate defenses.[110] NSC-68 was drafted by Nitze, who had replaced Kennan as head of the Policy Planning Staff. A Wall Street investment banker, as intense in personality as his mentor James Forrestal, Nitze exceeded Acheson in his gloomy worldview. His study set forth an urgent statement of the national security ideology. It proclaimed the necessity of defending freedom across the world to save it at home. Written in the starkest black-and-white terms, it took a worst case view of Soviet capabilities and intentions. "Animated by a new fanatical faith," it warned, the USSR was seeking to "impose its absolute authority on the rest of the world." Soviet expansion had reached a point beyond which it must not be permitted to go. "Any substantial further extension of the area under the control of the Kremlin would raise the possibility that no coalition adequate to confront the Kremlin with greater strength could be assembled."[111]

In this context of a world divided into two hostile power blocs, a fragile balance of power, a zero-sum game in which any gain for Communism was automatically a loss for the "free world," NSC-68 outlined a dazzling array of measures—what Acheson labeled "total diplomacy"—to combat the Soviet threat.[112] It proposed shoring up Western Europe's defenses, filling the dollar gap, and extending containment to East Asia. It urged expanded military and economic assistance programs, covert operations, and psychological warfare. Above all, it pressed for a huge boost in defense spending to support a massive buildup of nuclear and conventional arms. The aim was to achieve military superiority and create what Acheson called "situations of strength." The ultimate goal was to win the Cold War by detaching Eastern Europe from the Soviet bloc and forcing a

109. Beisner, *Acheson*, 190–203.
110. Ibid., 238.
111. Department of State, *Foreign Relations of the United States, 1950: National Security Affairs, Foreign Economic Policy*, vol. 1 (Washington, 1977), 237–90.
112. Beisner, *Acheson*, 248.

change in the Soviet government itself. To rally a sometimes apathetic public to make the necessary sacrifices, NSC-68 proposed a public education program using plain, hard-hitting language—what former undersecretary of state Robert Lovett called "Hemingway sentences"—to make the threat, in Acheson's words, "clearer than truth."[113] Still refusing the sort of financial commitment Nitze proposed, Truman shelved the document in the spring of 1950. Events in Northeast Asia would soon put it back on the table.

In June, hot war broke out in Korea, a country far from the United States geographically but for years a focal point of East Asian rivalries. The product of fierce internal conflict among Koreans as well as the Cold War, the Korean "police action" lasted more than three years. It had profound global consequences, heightening Cold War tensions and producing expanded U.S. commitments in Europe and East Asia. It made possible full implementation of NSC-68, including a huge military buildup, economic mobilization, and a string of global commitments.

Much as in Germany, conflict in Korea arose from occupation zones hastily carved out at war's end. On the eve of Japan's surrender, lower-level U.S. Army officials working with *National Geographic* maps set the dividing line between American and Soviet occupation zones at the 38th parallel, conveniently leaving the capital, Seoul, and two-thirds of the population in U.S. hands. As with Germany, efforts to unify the country ran afoul of Cold War rivalries. Regimes emerged in each zone bearing the distinct imprint of the occupying power. The United States backed a conservative southern government headed by Syngman Rhee, a longtime exile, Princeton University graduate, and protégé of Woodrow Wilson. Seventy years old in 1945, Rhee was handsome, charming, and fiercely independent. His government was composed largely of wealthy landholders, some of whom had collaborated with the Japanese. In the north, the Soviets supported a leftist regime headed by the thirty-one-year-old Communist zealot Kim Il-Sung. Rhee and Kim were passionately committed to unifying Korea—on their own terms. Fighting raged across the peninsula between 1948 and 1950. Leftist guerrillas plotted to undermine Rhee, while armies from both zones waged sporadic warfare across the 38th parallel. As many as a hundred thousand Koreans were killed, thirty thousand in extended fighting on an island off the coast of South Korea.[114]

113. Ibid., 239; Chace, *Acheson*, 168.
114. Peter Lowe, *The Origins of the Korean War* (Essex, Eng., 1986) is a good survey. Bruce Cumings, in *The Origins of the Korean War*, vol. 1, *Liberation and the Emergence of Separate Regimes, 1945–1947* (Princeton, N.J., 1981), and vol. 2, *The Roaring of the Cataract, 1947–1950* (Princeton, N.J., 1990), offers a provocative revisionist interpretation.

Cold War rivalries made full-scale hostilities possible. Already spread thin, the United States worried that Rhee's ambitions might entangle it in a war it could not afford in an area of marginal significance. The Truman administration thus withdrew its military forces from Korea in 1949. In a much publicized January 1950 speech that accurately stated U.S. policy but said much more than it should have, Acheson left South Korea out of the U.S. "defensive perimeter." At the same time, after the fall of China, the administration increasingly perceived that for reasons of domestic politics it could not afford to lose additional Asian real estate to Communism. As Japan assumed greater importance in U.S. global strategy, Korea became an important buffer against China and the Soviet Union and a market for Japanese exports.[115]

Professing sleeplessness in his quest to unify Korea, the indefatigable Kim doggedly pursued Stalin's go-ahead for decisive action. Rebuffed numerous times, he finally extracted a qualified commitment in April 1950. Apparently persuaded by the Truman administration's refusal to rescue Chiang, its troop withdrawals from South Korea, and perhaps the Acheson speech that the United States would not respond, Stalin approved an invasion across the 38th parallel provided that Kim press for a quick victory. Kim had also hinted that he might turn to Mao, and Stalin did not want to appear to stand in the way of extending the revolution in East Asia. A unified Korea would solidify the Soviet position in Northeast Asia and put pressure on the United States in Japan. War in Korea, Stalin may also have reasoned, would tie Beijing closely to Moscow and eliminate any chance for rapprochement with the United States. The Soviet leader did caution Kim that "if you get kicked in the teeth. I shall not lift a finger." With Stalin's conditional blessing and ostensibly responding to South Korean provocations, Kim on June 25, 1950, dispatched a hundred thousand troops, backed by tanks, artillery, and aircraft, into South Korea.[116]

Although caught completely off guard, the Truman administration, to the shock of Stalin and his allies, responded promptly and after little debate. United States officials mistakenly believed that Moscow had instigated the attack as part of its grand design for world domination. They vividly recalled Manchuria and Munich and the Western non-response they believed had led to World War II. If they did nothing, they reasoned, nervous European allies would lose faith in their promises and the Communists would be emboldened to further aggression. The United Nations

115. Beisner, Acheson, 326–29.
116. Kathryn Weathersby, "To Attack or Not to Attack? Stalin, Kim Il Sung, and the Prelude to War," Cold War International History Bulletin 5 (1995), 1–9.

had been involved in creating South Korea, and U.S. officials also saw the North Korean invasion as a test for the fledgling world organization. Thus within days after the June 25 attack, the administration went to war. The president unwisely refused to seek congressional authorization for fear of setting a precedent that might bind his successors, suggesting the extent to which the Cold War had already shattered traditional attitudes on such issues. Taking advantage of Soviet absence from the Security Council, the administration secured UN backing for military action in Korea. It committed U.S. air, naval, and ground forces to the defense of embattled South Korea. In a significant move that dashed any hopes of reconciliation with China, it deployed the Seventh Fleet between Taiwan and mainland China. It stepped up aid to France for Indochina. In a broad band running from the Sea of Japan to the Gulf of Thailand, the United States extended across East Asia the containment policy already applied in Europe.[117]

In its first six months, the Korean War witnessed reversals of fortune seldom matched in the history of warfare. United States occupation troops hastily deployed from Japan and unready for battle could not stop the North Korean onslaught. By late summer, UN forces were isolated at Pusan on the southeast corner of Korea, very nearly being driven into the sea. At this point, UN commander General MacArthur devised a daring but perilous plan for an amphibious assault on the northwest port of Inchon to relieve pressure on the Pusan perimeter and catch overextended North Korean forces in a deadly pincer. The scheme was hazardous under the best circumstances. Tricky tides made the harbor navigable but one day a month and then only for a few hours, permitting alert defenders to predict the timing of an invasion. Perhaps to underscore his own brilliance if he succeeded, the imperious MacArthur termed the operation a 5,000-to-1 gamble and overrode the cautions of the Joint Chiefs.

A virtually unopposed landing succeeded smashingly. Now the suddenly victorious UN forces drove the North Koreans back across the 38th parallel. The United States might have stopped at this point, explored diplomatic options, even settled for the status quo ante bellum. But MacArthur's already ample ego was further swollen by a brilliant maneuver, and he was intent on rollback. Washington officials hesitated to take on "the sorcerer of Inchon." Caught up in the hubris, they too were seduced by the prospect of a major Cold War victory, especially on the eve of congressional elections. They arrogantly dismissed Chinese warnings

117. William Stueck, *The Korean War: An International History* (Princeton, N.J., 1995), 41–44; Beisner, *Acheson*, 333–37.

of intervention and rationalized that not to advance might be viewed as a sign of weakness. As UN forces plunged recklessly toward the Yalu River separating North Korea from Manchuria, MacArthur foolishly assured Truman of victory by Christmas. Hindered by ethnocentric blinders, Americans to a person could not see what later would seem so obvious.[118]

Chinese intervention in late November 1950 produced what MacArthur ruefully admitted was a new and different war. As Mao put it, China and Korea were "as close as the lips to the teeth," and the Chinese could not but view the advance of hostile troops to their border as a menace to their infant state and a test of their credibility.[119] Mao may have felt some obligation to the Korean Communists, who had provided vital support during the Chinese civil war. He also saw intervention as a way to enhance China's status by defeating the "arrogant" United States, sustain the revolutionary momentum generated during the civil war, and legitimize the position of the party within China.[120] Stalin sought to cover his own disastrous miscalculation by encouraging Chinese intervention and promising air support (which he later reneged on). The decision apparently provoked bitter debate in the Chinese Politburo, but Mao carried the day. Shortly after U.S. forces celebrated Thanksgiving near the Yalu, more than two hundred thousand Chinese troops entered the war.[121] MacArthur had foolishly exposed his armies by dividing them. In bitterly cold weather under horrendous conditions, UN forces fell back in what American troops labeled Operation Bugout, a headlong, ignominious, and frightfully costly retreat in bitterly cold weather that would end well south of the 38th parallel. Chinese and North Koreans now vowed to unify Korea.

After six months of armies racing up and down the peninsula, the war in 1951 settled into a bloody stalemate. Humiliated by defeat, a defiant MacArthur pressed for all-out war against China, insisting in conventional military terms that there was no substitute for victory. Constrained by allies and the United Nations, viewing Korea and indeed East Asia as a secondary Cold War theater, and fearful of a Soviet strike into Western Europe, the administration settled for a limited war to restore the *status quo ante bellum*. When MacArthur challenged the president by taking his case to Congress, Truman, fully supported by the Joint Chiefs of Staff,

118. Stueck, *Korean War*, 85–95.
119. Beisner, *Acheson*, 403.
120. Chen Jian, "In the Name of Revolution: China's Road to the Korean War Revisited," in William Stueck, ed., *The Korean War in World History* (Lexington, Ky., 2004), 93–96.
121. Stueck, *Korean War*, 97–125.

U.S.S.R.

CHINA

Farthest advance by
U.N. forces,
November, 1950

Chinese intervention,
October 1950

Yalu R.

•Chongju

NORTH
KOREA

SEA
OF
JAPAN

⊛ Pyongyang

Armistice Line,
July 27, 1953

Panmunjom

38th parallel

⊛ Seoul

Farthest advance by Chinese
and North Korean forces,
January 1951

Inchon•

Inchon landing,
September 15, 1950

SOUTH KOREA

Farthest advance by
North Korean forces,
September 1950

*Pusan
perimeter*

YELLOW

SEA

•Pusan

JAPAN

0   50   100 Miles
0   50   100 Kilometers

Korean War
1950–1953

CHEJU

happily relieved "Mr. Prima Donna, Brass Hat, Five Star MacArthur" of his command.[122] The general returned home to a hero's welcome, including a ticker-tape parade viewed by 7.5 million people in New York City and an emotional farewell speech to a joint session of Congress. Republicans sought to exploit the popular anger to discredit Truman. Flags flew at half mast, the president was burned in effigy, and there were calls for impeachment. In time, however, Americans grudgingly agreed with Gen. Omar Bradley that Korea was the "wrong war, at the wrong place, at the wrong time, and with the wrong enemy." In the meantime, MacArthur's replacement, Gen. Matthew Ridgway, stabilized the lines around the 38th parallel. Mao—his ambitions as rudely dashed as MacArthur's, his forces hopelessly overextended and suffering heavy casualties—also settled for limited war.[123]

The stalemate persisted beyond the end of the Truman administration. The Chinese periodically mobilized fresh manpower for new offensives, but they gained little ground. Ridgway developed "meat grinder" tactics to lure Chinese troops into the open and chew them up with artillery and aircraft. The fighting ground on mercilessly, increasingly reminiscent of World War I, the names given to major battle sites—Heartbreak Ridge, No-Name Ridge—suggestive of the cost and frustrations. Negotiations began in the summer of 1951, but they produced no more movement than military operations. The mere fact of negotiations among equals was sui generis for the United States, a nation accustomed to imposing peace terms on defeated enemies. The administration erred in assigning the task to military officers, a job they were ill suited for by temperament and experience. The U.S. negotiators found it especially difficult to deal with Chinese and Koreans, peoples they considered inferior, and Communists, whom they viewed as savages and criminals, in circumstances where they could not use without restriction the military power available to them. The talks quickly stalled over difficult substantive questions such as terms for a cease-fire and an armistice.[124] The most vexing issue proved to be repatriation of prisoners of war. China and North Korea adhered to the conventional position, endorsed by the 1949 Geneva Convention, of compulsory repatriation. For humanitarian reasons and to score Cold War debating points, Truman doggedly—and perhaps foolishly—insisted that POWs who did not wish to be repatriated need not be compelled to

122. Offner, *Another Such Victory*, 377.
123. Burton I. Kaufman, *The Korean War: Challenges in Crisis, Credibility, and Command* (New York, 1986), 144–79.
124. Rosemary J. Foot, *A Substitute for Victory: The Politics of Peacemaking at the Korean Armistice Talks* (Ithaca, N.Y., 1992), 1–19, 206–22.

do so. It would take 575 of the most tortuous meetings of the Cold War and a new Republican administration to end the Korean "police action" in July 1953.

The war left a bitter taste for Americans. The harsh climate, rugged terrain, and seemingly inscrutable people made Korea, for many U.S. soldiers, a "land that God forgot." The inconclusive nature of the combat, along with its deadliness, made the war especially difficult to fight. Accustomed to the verities of total war, many Americans bristled at the limits imposed by the nuclear age: a "stalemate—a frustration of desires—a compromise with principle—an acceptance of that which is unacceptable," one army officer complained. Positioned between World War II and Vietnam, two conflicts that touched the American psyche in very different ways, Korea became a forgotten war that Americans happily expunged from their memory.[125]

Yet this war that Americans preferred to forget had enormous consequences. For the Koreans, whose leaders' suicidal ambitions had sparked it, the results were catastrophic, an estimated three million dead, roughly 10 percent of the population, their country laid waste. The nation remained divided after the "peace" treaty, the South still occupied by foreign troops. For the major Communist nations, the war had mixed results. By holding its own against the United States, Mao's China achieved instant great-power status. China's dependence on the Soviet Union solidified their alliance for the short term, but that very dependence and sharp differences over the conduct of the war opened fissures in the Communist bloc that would widen in the coming decade. For Stalin, who had gambled on Kim's ability to win a quick victory, the Korean War was a major setback. The pressures he imposed on his East European allies to produce war materials created strains that would provoke uprisings that in turn threatened Soviet control over its vital buffer zone. Korea also produced Stalin's worst nightmare, a massive buildup of Western European defenses—including the first steps toward German rearmament—and U.S. mobilization for all-out war.[126]

As waged by the Truman administration, the Korean War became, in historian Walter LaFeber's apt phrase, "the war for both Asia and Europe."[127] In June 1950, Western Europe's defense structure was underfunded and shaky. With the impetus from the Korean War, NATO expanded to include

125. Creighton Abrams quoted in George C. Herring, "Limited War," in Stanley I. Kutler, ed., *Encyclopedia of the United States in the Twentieth Century* (3 vols., New York, 1996), 2:662; Joseph C. Goulden, *Korea: The Untold Story of the War* (New York, 1982), xv.
126. Zubok and Pleshakov, *Inside the Cold War*, 70.
127. LaFeber, *America, Russia, and the Cold War*, 99.

Greece and Turkey. Tito's renegade Communist government in Yugoslavia became a virtual associate member. Without seeking congressional assent, Truman in December 1950 sent four U.S. Army divisions to Europe, a move previously unthinkable, bringing the total of U.S. troops there to 180,000 and provoking a "great debate" at home over the commitment to Europe and the president's authority to send troops abroad. By the end of 1952, NATO had fifteen well-armed divisions. European defense spending swelled from 5 to 12 percent of the gross national product. A NATO command structure and headquarters had been created, and the U.S. commitment was strengthened by the enormously symbolic appointment of World War II hero Gen. Dwight Eisenhower as its first supreme commander. Rejecting Stalin's belated appeals for negotiations, the United States plunged ahead with integrating West Germany into its economic and political sphere and with plans for a European Defense Community to entice an extremely nervous France to accept German rearmament.[128] Although it could not have been seen at the time, in one of history's grand ironies, an immensely unpopular war in Northeast Asia had much to do with winning the Cold War in Europe.

Korea had profound consequences for U.S. policies in Asia. Chinese intervention and the humiliating defeat inflicted on American forces provoked added mutual hostility, destroying any chance for accommodation. It would be nearly thirty years before the nations would establish diplomatic relations. On the other hand, the exigencies of war pushed a previously wary United States into Taiwan's eager embrace, bringing forth in the summer of 1950 a U.S. military mission and $125 million in military aid. For the conservatives who ran Japan's government, the Korean War was a "gift of the gods."[129] United States military procurement pumped $2.3 billion into a lagging Japanese economy. Exports soared to 50 percent above prewar levels; the GNP increased by 10 percent. Over loud Soviet and Chinese protests, the United States incorporated its former enemy into its East Asian security orbit. The administration shrewdly named Republican John Foster Dulles to negotiate a peace treaty. The bumptious future secretary of state ran roughshod over Cold War enemies and allies alike, negotiating separate agreements that restored Japan's sovereignty over the home islands and provided for U.S. bases. The United States recognized Japan's "residual sovereignty" over Okinawa but ruled that island, with its vital nuclear bases, in what can only be called a neo-colonial fashion. Threats to block the treaty by California Republican William

128. Offner, *Another Such Victory*, 430–42.
129. Dower, *Embracing Defeat*, 541.

Knowland, widely known as "the senator from Formosa" for his passionate support of Chiang, led to additional provisions requiring Japan to agree to a treaty with Taiwan and accept restrictions on trade with China. Partly out of concern for Japan's export markets and despite sharp differences in goals and approach with France, the United States by 1952 was bearing much of the cost of France's war against Communist-led Vietminh rebels in Indochina.[130]

In the summer of 1950, to Acheson's delight, the administration took NSC-68 off the shelf. Following its guidelines, U.S. officials undertook full-scale mobilization for war in Korea—and for the long-term global struggle with the Soviet Union. Warning Congress that modern weaponry made the United States vulnerable to potential enemies as never before, Acheson likened it to the person who, on "the death of a parent, hears in a new way the roaring of the cataract."[131] The legislators heard the sound, and for the next three years military spending soared. Truman's defense budget of $53 billion for FY 1953 quadrupled that for 1949. It represented 60 percent of government expenditures and 12 percent of the GNP, compared to less than 33 and 5 percent respectively for FY 1950. The U.S. Army expanded by 50 percent to 3.5 million soldiers; U.S. Air Force air groups doubled to ninety-five. The military establishment's growing size enhanced its position in the new national security state.[132]

Between 1950 and 1952, the administration developed new weapons to wage the Cold War. Responding to the failure of U.S. intelligence to forecast the North Korean invasion of South Korea and Chinese intervention in the war, it created in October 1952 a new highly secret National Security Agency (NSA, or "No Such Agency," according to wags) to listen in on enemy communications and crack codes.[133] It institutionalized and expanded previously ad hoc foreign aid programs. Even before NSC-68, Congress approved the Mutual Defense Assistance Act, an important instrument in implementing the containment policy.[134] Designed mainly to boost European morale in the early days of NATO, the initial program authorized $1.3 billion to help equip nations involved in U.S. defense agreements. With the outbreak of war in Korea, the administration secured an additional

---

130. Walter LaFeber, *The Clash: U.S. Japanese Relations Throughout History* (New York, 1997), 288–95.
131. Offner, *Another Such Victory*, 383.
132. May, "U.S. Government," 273.
133. James Bamford, *Body of Secrets: Anatomy of the Ultra-Secret National Security Agency* (New York, 2001), 31.
134. Chester J. Pach Jr., *Arming the Free World: The Origins of the United States Military Assistance Program, 1945–1950* (Chapel Hill, N.C., 1991), 198.

$5 billion for a significantly expanded military aid program. In his 1949 inaugural address, Truman advanced a proposal, bold in conception if modest in scope, to provide economic and technical assistance to less developed nations to help stave off the poverty he and his advisers believed provided a fertile breeding ground for Communism. By the end of 1950, this so-called Point Four program had been extended to thirty-four nations; visitors from more than twenty countries were in the United States for training.[135]

Propaganda also became an essential part of Cold War strategy. As early as 1947, the administration had revived the wartime Voice of America to beam broadcasts into the Soviet Union. Persuaded that Europe was a "vast battleground of ideas," Congress through the 1948 Smith-Mundt Act created under the State Department the first peacetime information program. Director Edward Barrett, a protégé of OSS boss William Donovan, set out to "penetrate the iron curtain with our ideas." By 1950, broadcasts from thirty-six transmitters in twenty-five languages were estimated to reach three hundred million people.[136] Desperate Soviet efforts to jam the airwaves seemed to confirm the program's success. As in other areas, NSC-68 gave the propaganda war a boost. Truman had previously stressed the urgency of combating Communist propaganda with a "great campaign for truth." Former advertising executive and Connecticut senator William Benton called the Campaign for Truth a "Marshall Plan in the field of ideas." Although hampered by poor funding, bureaucratic warfare, and harassment from Senator McCarthy and his followers, the program flooded the world with films extolling the American way of life, provided material to newspapers, established student exchanges, and created information centers in sixty nations and 190 cities. Increasingly, it focused on Eastern Europe and the USSR with the avowed aim of rolling back Soviet power. Harvard and MIT scientists, working with the government through Project Troy (named for the Greek campaign that subverted the city-state of Troy), developed transmitters powerful enough to overcome Soviet jamming and leaflet-dropping balloons that penetrated the Iron Curtain by soaring above it.[137]

135. For the origins of Point Four, see Clifford, *Counsel to the President*, 247–53. Thomas G. Paterson, *Meeting the Communist Threat: Truman to Reagan* (rev. ed., New York, 1992), 147–58, provides a critique of the program.
136. Walter L. Hixson, *Parting the Curtain: Propaganda, Culture, and the Cold War, 1945–1961* (New York, 1998), 13; Derek Von Briesen, "The Campaign for Truth" (seminar paper, University of Kentucky, 1997), 5–10.
137. Allan A. Needell, "Truth Is Our Weapon: Project TROY, Political Warfare, and Government-Academic Relations in the National Security State," *Diplomatic History* 17 (Summer 1993), 399–401.

The administration also used front organizations. The government helped create and fund the ostensibly independent Committee for a Free Europe that used émigré broadcasters to beam through Radio Free Europe bare-knuckled propaganda denouncing the evils of Soviet imperialism, mocking Communism through satirical skits, and using American popular culture, especially jazz, to subvert East European youth.[138] In 1950, an increasingly influential and active CIA established in Paris the Congress for Cultural Freedom (CCF), another ostensibly independent group that waged a cultural Cold War by helping to organize and fund such events as art exhibits, literary symposia, and tours by the Yale Glee Club. The CCF distributed funds through such respectable front organizations as the Ford and Rockefeller Foundations and Time, Inc. (sometimes with their knowledge, sometimes without). It recruited former leftist intellectuals such as Sidney Hook and writers such as George Plimpton to write anti-Communist essays and publish literary journals. The agency came to be known as "the Good Ship Lollipop" by those few artists and intellectuals who knew of its support.[139]

THE NEW PROPAGANDA MACHINE scored some points abroad and helped mobilize domestic support for waging the Cold War, but it could not salvage the fortunes of its creators. In its last years, the Truman administration was shaken by domestic scandals, some touching very close to the White House. The Korean conflict took a huge toll in public war-weariness. The president's approval ratings plummeted. Having waved the banner of anti-Communism to gain support for their bold initiatives, U.S. officials could not contain the monster they had loosed. As the public mood soured in 1951 and 1952, McCarthy and his cohorts viciously and relentlessly attacked the president, Acheson, and even the once invulnerable Marshall, now secretary of defense, for being soft on Communism, sheltering Communists within the government, and not waging the Cold War with sufficient resolve. Truman did not seek reelection in 1952. Democratic nominee Adlai E. Stevenson of Illinois stood little chance against General Eisenhower, a moderate Republican and internationalist whose stature, charismatic smile, and vague promises to go to Korea (presumably to end the war) secured him an easy victory, ending twenty years of Democratic rule.

Despite leaving office in disrepute, the Truman administration bequeathed an extraordinary record of accomplishment in foreign affairs.

138. Hixson, *Parting the Curtain*, 59–65.
139. Frances Stonor Saunders, *The Cultural Cold War: The CIA and the World of Arts and Letters* (New York, 2000) discusses this project.

United States officials often misread and sometimes misrepresented Stalin's intentions. They exaggerated the Soviet threat. They unwisely rejected negotiations, leaving unanswered the question of whether the Cold War might have been ended earlier, its worldwide effects somehow mitigated. Still, their firm but measured responses to the challenges of postwar Europe produced creative initiatives such as the Marshall Plan and NATO. United States policies helped to ensure the economic and political recovery of Western Europe, purge it of self-destructive internecine hatreds, and produce firm ties to its trans-Atlantic partner.

Truman and Acheson were much less sure-handed and effective in Asia. Certainly U.S. officials implemented reforms that helped demilitarize and democratize Japan and integrate it into the Western trading community. But the administration could not disentangle itself from the mess in China, with huge consequences for U.S. foreign policy and domestic politics. Its actions and statements likely encouraged Stalin to give Kim the go-ahead to invade South Korea. The free hand given MacArthur after Inchon provoked a wider and much more destructive war. This said, the Communist side still suffered the greatest losses in the Korean War. The United States was perhaps least successful in dealing with problems posed by decolonization. Americans overestimated the economic and strategic significance of the periphery and its vulnerability to Soviet blandishments. Their concern for NATO allies made it difficult to accommodate the new forces of revolutionary nationalism. The extension of the containment policy to Southeast Asia put the United States on the wrong side of nationalist revolutions, laying the basis for war in Vietnam.

Successes and failures aside, the Truman administration in the short space of seven years carried out a veritable revolution in U.S. foreign policy. It altered the assumptions behind national security policies, launched a wide range of global programs and commitments, and built new institutions to manage the nation's burgeoning international activities. Perhaps most important, during the Truman years foreign policy became a central part of everyday life. As early as 1947, the doyen of the Establishment, Henry L. Stimson, would express in somewhat curious but telling words the change that had occurred: "Foreign affairs are now our most intimate domestic concern."[140]

---

140. David F. Schmitz, *Henry L. Stimson: The First Wise Man* (Wilmington, Del., 2001), xvi.

15

Coexistence and Crises, 1953–1961

On March 6, 1953, the Central Committee of the Soviet Communist Party announced with "profound sorrow" that Joseph Stalin was dead. Citizens of the USSR must have greeted the news with a mixture of relief and anxiety. Editorialists in the United States expressed undisguised joy at the demise of the "murderer of millions" but permitted themselves only a glimmer of hope. The great struggle of the century would continue, they averred. Stalin's successors could be as bad or worse. The world might be plunged into an "era of darkest uncertainty."[1] In fact, Stalin's death, along with the development of nuclear weapons with destructive capacity too awful to contemplate, changed the Cold War fundamentally in the 1950s. The conflict shifted to new battlegrounds, took new forms, and required new weapons. New leaders on both sides struggled to cope with a more complex and, in some ways, more menacing world.[2] While speaking of peaceful coexistence, they lurched from crisis to crisis. The end of the decade brought simultaneously major steps toward substantive negotiations and one of the most dangerous periods of the postwar era.

I

The Cold War remained the dominant fact of international life in the 1950s. It was still primarily a bipolar affair between the United States and the Soviet Union, with blocs massed around each of the central combatants. It resembled traditional power struggles between nation-states, but it was also a fierce ideological contest between two nations with diametrically opposed worldviews. The two sides saw each other as unremittingly hostile. They used every imaginable weapon: alliances; economic and military aid; espionage; covert operations including targeted assassinations; proxy wars; and an increasingly menacing arms race. The conflict extended across the world and even below the earth—the CIA dug a tunnel deep beneath East Berlin to better intercept Soviet bloc communications. With the advent of missiles and satellites in the late 1950s, the Cold War soared into space. The possession by each side of thermonuclear

---

1. *Denver Post* quoted in *New York Times*, March 7, 1953.
2. Kenneth Osgood, *Total Cold War: Eisenhower's Secret Propaganda Battles at Home and Abroad* (Lawrence, Kans., 2006), 75.

weapons and delivery systems capable of reaching the other's territory meant that any crisis risked escalation to a nuclear confrontation. Ironically, what Winston Churchill called the mutual balance of terror also provided a powerful deterrent to great-power war. The adversaries chose to wage the conflict largely through client states, diplomacy, propaganda, and threats of force. The challenge was to gain advantage without provoking a nuclear conflagration.[3]

The international system became more complex during this period. Fissures began to appear in Cold War alliances. Rebellions against Soviet rule broke out in East Germany, Poland, and Hungary. By the end of the decade, a long-simmering feud between the Soviet Union and China boiled to the surface. The Suez Crisis of 1956 provoked bitter conflict between the United States and its major allies, Britain and France.

During this heyday of decolonization, more than one hundred new nations came into being, creating a fertile breeding ground for great-power competition. The Cold War thus increasingly shifted to a battle for the allegiance of what a French demographer labeled the Third World. As with the United States in the Napoleonic era, some leading Third World nations sought to insulate themselves from great-power struggle and also exploit it through what came to be called neutralism, a refusal to take sides in the conflict that raged about them. India's Jawaharlal Nehru, Egypt's Gamal Abdel Nasser, and Yugoslavia's Josip Broz Tito assumed leadership of a budding neutralist movement that posed major challenges for the great powers. The advent of the Cold War to the Third World sometimes brought with it proxy wars causing massive physical destruction, loss of life, and disruption of domestic politics. While often victims of the Cold War, Third World leaders in seeking to exploit it for their own ends sometimes expanded, intensified, and prolonged the great-power conflict.[4]

Events in the Third World cannot be viewed solely through the prism of the Cold War.[5] To be sure, U.S. policymakers generally looked at issues this way, distorting their understanding of what was happening. They also perceived, however dimly, the equally or even more disturbing

---

3. Paul Gordon Lauren, Gordon A. Craig, and Alexander L. George, *Force and Statecraft: Diplomatic Challenges of Our Time* (4th ed., New York, 2007), 88–95.
4. Odd Arne Westad, "The New International History of the Cold War: Three (Possible) Paradigms," *Diplomatic History* 24 (Fall 2000), 551–65; Tony Smith, "New Bottles for New Wine: A Pericentric Framework for the Study of the Cold War," ibid., 567–91.
5. Matthew Connelly, "Taking Off the Cold War Lens: Visions of North-South Conflict During the Algerian War for Independence," *American Historical Review* 105 (June 2000), 739–69.

possibility that the non-white masses with or without the Soviet Union might align against the industrialized nations. East-West conflict could be augmented or possibly supplanted by North-South conflict. Some U.S. officials worried that pan-Arabist and Islamic movements might provoke a clash of civilizations. Race played an increasingly important role in world politics. In April 1955, at Bandung, Indonesia, delegates from twenty-nine nations gathered for the first worldwide meeting of peoples of color, raising fears among U.S. diplomats of a "rip-tide of nationalism" among Africans and Asians, even a new "yellow peril."[6]

By the mid-1950s, the Cold War had altered beyond recognition America's national security apparatus and global presence. In 1953, the defense budget exceeded $85 billion, constituted 12 percent of the gross national product, and consumed 60 percent of federal expenditures. Conscription was an established feature of postwar life; the nation had some 3.5 million men and women under arms. A State Department with five thousand prewar employees expanded to more than twenty thousand. Through a global network of alliances, the United States was committed to defend forty-two nations, a level of commitment, Paul Kennedy has observed, that would have made those arch-imperialists Louis XIV and Lord Palmerston a "little nervous."[7] More than a million U.S. military personnel manned more than eight hundred bases in a hundred countries. The Sixth Fleet patrolled the Mediterranean; the Seventh Fleet, the Pacific. The foreign aid budget averaged $5 billion per year between 1948 and 1953. Henry Stimson had snarled in the 1920s that gentlemen did not read each other's mail. In the intelligence agencies, gentlemen—and ladies—now regularly read each other's mail and listened in on telephone conversations and radio transmissions. The CIA illegally opened the mail of U.S. citizens corresponding with people in the USSR. To win the global competition for hearts and minds, Americans stationed abroad helped grow crops, build schools, train military personnel, and manipulate the outcome of elections. The wives of servicemen became unofficial ambassadors, sometimes repairing the public relations damage done by rowdy GIs and seeking to inculcate local women in the American way of life. Foreign governments hired U.S.

6. Thomas Borstelmann, *The Cold War and the Color Line: American Race Relations in the Global Arena* (Cambridge, Mass., 2001), 95; Jason Parker, "Cold War II: The Eisenhower Administration, the Bandung Conference, and the Reperiodization of the Postwar Era," *Diplomatic History* 30 (November 2006), 875; Matthew Jones, "A 'Segregated' Asia? Race, the Bandung Conference, and Pan Asianist Fears in American Thought and Policy, 1954–1955," *Diplomatic History* 29 (November 2005), 857.
7. Paul Kennedy, *The Rise and Fall of the Great Powers* (New York, 1987), 390.

public relations firms to boost their image and secure maximum economic and military assistance.[8]

As part of the Cold War quest for influence, the embassies built in other countries became political statements. The government recruited top architects such as Edward Durrell Stone and Walter Gropius to produce designs reflective of the nation's values and capable of boosting its prestige. The Cold War and modern architecture joined forces with sometimes stunning results. Designers sought to win goodwill from host nations by avoiding ostentatious display and where possible conforming with local architecture. Their buildings employed the glass curtain wall to stress openness and transparency, a sharp contrast with drab Soviet styles—a glass curtain juxtaposed against an Iron Curtain. They sought to capture the nation's spirit of freedom and adventure, self-confidence and prosperity. Stone's embassy in New Delhi achieved worldwide acclaim. Ironically, the structures built to symbolize the United States of the 1950s became easy targets for anti-American attacks in the next decade.[9]

The Cold War defined American domestic life in the 1950s. A huge spurt in population growth—the postwar baby boom—along with continued high demand for U.S. products abroad, fueled a period of sustained economic prosperity. What economist John Kenneth Galbraith called the "affluent society" produced a certain complacency and retreat from the reformist spirit of the New Deal. Abundance brought the fruition of American consumer culture.[10]

The Communist threat produced a mood of near hysterical fear, paranoiac suspiciousness, and stifling conformity. Top government officials—including the attorney general of the United States—ominously warned that the Communists were everywhere—"in factories, offices, butcher shops, on street corners, in private businesses . . . they were busy at work 'undermining your government, plotting to destroy your liberties, and feverishly trying, in whatever way they can, to aid the Soviet Union.'" Filmmakers, television producers, newspaper editors, and novelists spewed forth fearmongering products with such suggestive titles as *The Red Menace, I Was a Communist for the FBI*, and *I Married a Commmunist*. Federal and state

8. Ernest R. May, "The U.S. Government, a Legacy of the Cold War," *Diplomatic History* 16 (Spring 1992), 269–77; William G. Carleton, *The Revolution in American Foreign Policy: Its Global Range* (New York, 1965), 38–40.

9. *New York Times*, July 23, 2003; Jane C. Loeffler, "The Architecture of Diplomacy: Heyday of the United States Embassy-Building Program, 1954–1960," *Journal of the Society of Architecture Historians* 49 (September 1990), 251–78.

10. For the 1950s, see James T. Patterson, *Grand Expectations, The United States, 1945–1974* (New York, 1996), 311–74.

governments harassed, investigated, and deported real and suspected Communists and even encouraged citizens to spy on each other.[11] The danger posed by godless Communism spurred a religious revival. Church membership soared; religious motifs suffused the popular culture. President Dwight D. Eisenhower encouraged this phenomenon with outward displays of faith, the addition of "In God We Trust" to coins, and the inclusion of religious themes in his speeches. For Eisenhower, his secretary of state, John Foster Dulles, and other U.S. leaders, the Cold War was the equivalent of a holy war. Even the administration's national security statements affirmed that religious principles should inspire and direct U.S. domestic and foreign policies.[12]

Various segments of society joined in waging the Cold War. Universities welcomed government contracts for defense-related research and dispatched technical and agricultural missions to Third World countries to win friends for the United States. "Our colleges and universities must be regarded as bastions of our defense," Michigan State University president John Hannah exclaimed in 1961, "as essential to the preservation of our country and our way of life as supersonic bombers, nuclear-powered submarines and intercontinental ballistic missiles."[13] Private charitable organizations such as CARE and Catholic Relief Services willingly sacrificed their independence by accepting government funds and some measure of government supervision to expand their good works in priority areas.[14]

Race relations—the most divisive issue in American life in the 1950s—became inextricably entangled with the Cold War. The persistence of virulent racism in the United States and its most blatant manifestation in rigid, legalized segregation in the South gave the lie to U.S. claims for leadership of the "free" world and became a stock-in-trade of Communist propaganda. Diplomats from non-white countries encountered humiliating experiences in the United States, even in Washington, D.C., which

11. Stephen J. Whitfield, *The Culture of the Cold War* (2nd ed., Baltimore, 1996); Terry H. Anderson, *The Movement and the Sixties* (New York, 1996), 3–39.
12. Seth Jacobs, " 'Our System Demands the Supreme Being': The U.S. Religious Revival and the 'Diem Experiment,' 1954–1955," *Diplomatic History* 25 (Fall 2001), 596; Laura Szumanski Steel, "In the Name of the Father: The American Catholic Church and United States Foreign Policy During the Vietnam War" (Ph.D. dissertation, Temple University, 2005), chapter 1.
13. John Ernst, *Forging a Fateful Alliance: Michigan State University and the Vietnam War* (East Lansing, Mich., 1998), 6.
14. Delia Pergande, "Private Voluntary Aid in Vietnam: The Humanitarian Politics of Catholic Relief and CARE, 1954–1965" (Ph.D. dissertation, University of Kentucky, 1999), 18–24.

remained a very southern city and for diplomats of color a hardship post. Ambassador to the United Nations Henry Cabot Lodge Jr. labeled racial discrimination "our Achilles' heel before the world."[15] Even the Euro-centric Dean Acheson conceded that the United States must address the issue of racial injustice to deprive the Communists of "the most effective kind of ammunition for their propaganda warfare" and eliminate a "source of constant embarrassment to this government in the day-to-day conduct of its foreign relations."[16]

Dwight David Eisenhower in many ways epitomized the zeitgeist of the 1950s. A product of rural nineteenth-century America, he personified the values the nation clung to under external threat. Conservative in his politics, he was also moderate in his approach to life and avuncular in de-meanor. He brought to the presidency a lifetime of experience in the na-tional security matters that now held top priority. His leadership of Allied forces during World War II had "internationalized" him, setting him apart from the isolationist wing of the Republican Party. Though he was often dismissed as an intellectual lightweight and a political bumbler, his seem-ingly placid disposition and clumsy rhetoric concealed a clear mind, a firm grasp of issues, instinctive political skills, and a fierce temper. His casual attitude toward the use of nuclear weapons was balanced by his innate caution. His basic integrity won the trust of Americans and allies alike.

John Foster Dulles became the nation's chief diplomat almost as a mat-ter of inheritance. The grandson and namesake of late nineteenth-century secretary of state John W. Foster and nephew of Wilson's chief diplomat, Robert Lansing, he carried out his first diplomatic assignment at the age of thirty when he drafted the notorious reparations settlement at the Paris peace conference. As a partner in the powerful New York law firm of Sul-livan and Cromwell, he joined the world of corporate wealth and interna-tional finance. Like Woodrow Wilson the son of a Presbyterian minister, Dulles applied his intense religiosity to analyzing the tumultuous interna-tional politics of the 1930s and '40s. A great bear of a man, stern and un-smiling, he could appear brusque, even rude—"the only bull who carried his own China closet with him," Winston Churchill once snarled (and in-deed Dulles was a collector of rare china).[17] An indefatigable worker, as secretary of state he set a record by traveling more than a half million miles. Once viewed as the dominant force in policymaking in the Eisen-hower years, he and the president in fact formed an extraordinarily close

15. Borstelmann, *Cold War and the Color Line*, 76.
16. Quoted in *New Yorker*, May 3, 2004, 104.
17. Townsend Hoopes, "God and John Foster Dulles," *Foreign Policy* 13 (Winter 1973), 154.

partnership based on mutual respect in which the latter was plainly pre-eminent. Dulles's strident anti-Communist rhetoric and penchant for "brinkmanship" stamped him as an ideologue and crusader. He often served as a lightning rod for his boss. He was also a cool pragmatist with a sophisticated view of the world and ample tactical skills.[18]

The new administration restructured the mechanisms of policymaking. Confident in his own judgment on defense issues, Eisenhower kept his military advisers at arm's length. From extensive managerial experience in the army, he believed that careful staff work was essential for sound policy. He created the position of special assistant for national security affairs, a step with enormous long-range implications. He expanded attendance at NSC meetings and established separate planning and operations boards to facilitate decision-making and oversee implementation of policies. The full NSC met weekly, more often in times of crisis. In addition, the president met regularly, sometimes daily, in informal sessions over drinks with Dulles, often accompanied by his brother, CIA director Allen W. Dulles, and a kitchen cabinet of White House advisers.[19]

Especially in Eisenhower's first two years, Congress posed major challenges, ironically with Republicans giving the president the most headaches. Wisconsin senator Joseph R. McCarthy, now chairman of a Government Operations Committee, wreaked havoc through investigations of alleged Communist influence in the government. McCarthy's very success led directly to his failure. Televised hearings of his investigations of the army displayed to the nation the ridiculousness of some of his charges and the viciousness of his methods. Eisenhower eventually intervened to help check McCarthy. In December 1954, the Senate voted to censure him, ending his meteoric career in disgrace. The administration also fended off a constitutional amendment proposed and pushed doggedly by isolationist senator John Bricker of Ohio intended to thwart an alleged UN threat to U.S. sovereignty that would have sharply limited executive power in foreign policy. Eisenhower took a firm stand against the so-called Bricker Amendment and with crucial assistance from Texas Democratic senator Lyndon Baines Johnson secured its defeat. The Democrats regained control of Congress in 1954. Unwilling to challenge the president directly on major foreign policy issues, different groups of

18. Richard H. Immerman, *John Foster Dulles: Power, Piety, and Pragmatism* (Wilmington, Del., 1999), 46–51, and "Eisenhower and Dulles: Who Made the Decisions?" *Political Psychology* 1 (Autumn 1979), 21–38.
19. Immerman, *Dulles*, 48–51; David J. Rothkopf, *Running the World: The Inside Story of the NSC and the Architects of American Power* (New York, 2005), 65–70.

legislators used the power of the purse to chip away at foreign aid spending and push for a larger defense budget.[20]

Even before the administration could formulate a national security strategy, Stalin's death raised new and troublesome issues. More tyrannical than ever in his final years, the dictator suffered extreme paranoia and ruled by sheer terror. His successors, Lavrenty Beria and Georgi Malenkov, were products of the Stalinist system and loyal henchmen. Each had played a key role in building Soviet military power. Beria had run the nuclear program. Beria nearly matched Stalin's cruelty toward subordinates—"our Himmler," the dictator called him.[21] A shrewd and capable administrator, Malenkov was the more pragmatic of the two men. Both were technocrats rather than ideologues. Insecure at home, they saw themselves surrounded and threatened by U.S. bases. Soviet intelligence even warned that the United States might attempt to exploit the succession by starting a war. Against opposition from old-guard stalwarts like V. M. Molotov, Beria and Malenkov attempted to shift toward a less confrontational mode. At Stalin's funeral, Malenkov asserted that there was no "contested" issue that could not be resolved by "peaceful means." Fearing escalation of the Korean War, the new Soviet leaders talked to China about ending it. They sought to repair relations with Israel, Yugoslavia, and Greece. They warned that the emergence of new and more menacing nuclear weapons made war unthinkable and spoke of "peaceful coexistence." Hailing a "new breeze blowing on a tormented world," British prime minister Churchill urged Eisenhower to test the USSR's intentions by meeting with the new leaders.[22]

The administration responded coolly to Soviet overtures. Establishing a pattern that would be repeated time and again in Cold War presidential elections, Republicans in 1952 had blasted the Democrats for weakness, promising to combat Communism more vigorously, even to liberate "captive peoples." In light of its own belligerent rhetoric, the new administration could not jump into negotiations so soon after taking office. In any event, U.S. officials saw no real opportunity to ease tensions or negotiate substantive agreements. From Eisenhower down, they viewed the Soviet peace offensive, in the words of a State Department study, as a "treacherous stratagem of as yet indiscernible proportions" designed to undermine Western morale, expose divisions in the alliance, and hold

20. Robert David Johnson, *Congress and the Cold War* (New York, 2006), 57–87.
21. Vladislav Zubok and Constantine Pleshakov, *Inside the Kremlin's Cold War* (Cambridge, Mass., 1996), 139.
22. Ibid., 138–57; Osgood, *Total Cold War*, 56.

back Western rearmament.[23] Eisenhower responded with a major speech on April 16, warning of the dangers of war and vowing his personal commitment to peace. Pointing to numerous hot spots, he insisted that Soviet words must be matched by deeds. Mainly, he appealed to Americans and allies to rally behind U.S. leadership for victory in the Cold War.[24] Whether an opportunity for peace was missed, as diplomat Charles Bohlen later argued, can never be known for certain. Divisions within the Soviet leadership would have made major agreements at best difficult to achieve. The fact remains that the United States never tried.

Over the next six months, Eisenhower and his advisers formulated a grand strategy to fight the Cold War. Despite their 1952 attacks on the Democrats and promises of a "policy of boldness," the changes they initiated were more of means than ends. In office, the administration mollified the Republican right wing with fierce anti-Communist rhetoric. Dulles presided benignly over a purge of suspected leftists from the State Department, in the process ruining the lives of numerous dedicated public servants and eliminating much of its expertise on East Asia. For the most part, however, the administration's rhetoric was not matched by equally bold changes in policy. A fiscal conservative, Eisenhower was appalled by the enormous expenditures necessitated by NSC-68. Certain that the Cold War would last for many years, he feared that runaway defense spending could destroy the nation from within. He had no enthusiasm for further Korea-like military entanglements in peripheral areas. After an extended and painstaking review of options by several task forces, the administration settled on its New Look strategy. Despite Dulles's dismissal of European leaders as "shattered 'old people,'" it upheld the Democrats' commitment to collective security.[25] It sustained the principles of containment while altering the methods used. Superior military forces would be maintained to deter aggression. To permit substantial budget cuts without weakening the nation's defense posture, the New Look relied on nuclear weapons—"more bang for the buck," it was called. Dulles publicly outlined a concept of "massive retaliation" by which the United States would respond to aggression at times and places and with weapons of its own choosing, leaving open the use of nuclear weapons against the Soviet Union itself. Conventional forces would be cut dramatically. New alliances would be formed to deter and contain Communist expansion and provide manpower for regional or global conflicts.[26]

23. Osgood, *Total Cold War,* 62.
24. Ibid., 57–65.
25. Immerman, *Dulles,* 60.
26. Ibid., 81.

Eisenhower believed that a shooting war was unlikely and that the enemy would rely mainly on subversion to achieve its goals. NSC-162/2 of October 1953 thus put great emphasis on the importance of propaganda and psychological warfare, calling for the use of "feasible" political and economic pressures, propaganda, and covert operations to "create and exploit troublesome problems in the USSR, impair Soviet relations with Communist China, complicate control in the satellites, and retard the growth of the military and economic potential of the Soviet bloc." All weapons would be considered available for use. If the nation were to survive, a commission headed by World War II hero Gen. James Doolittle concluded in 1954, it must reconsider its long-standing concepts of fair play. "We must learn to subvert, sabotage, and destroy our enemies by more clever, more sophisticated, and more effective means than those used against us."[27] While sticking to established foreign policy goals, Eisenhower's New Look significantly altered the means to achieve them.

II

The strategy of massive retaliation was immediately put to the test in East and Southeast Asia. In its first two years, the Eisenhower administration contemplated or threatened the use of nuclear weapons in responding to crises in Korea, French Indochina, and the Taiwan Straits. In each case, Dulles claimed the strategy had worked. The reality is far more complicated.

Eisenhower managed to end the fighting in Korea, but his success owed as much to circumstances as to diplomatic proficiency. The president and Dulles did maneuver skillfully among their Communist enemies, allies who wanted to liquidate the war as quickly as possible, and South Korean president Syngman Rhee and the Republican right who clung to the chimera of victory. The administration later claimed that its threats to use nuclear weapons forced the Communists to settle. In fact, its warnings of nuclear escalation were notably vague—and may never have got to Beijing. The decisive event in the Korean settlement seems to have been Stalin's death. Problems of succession and rising unrest in Eastern Europe compelled the new Soviet leaders to seek a breathing space through the relaxation of tensions. Eisenhower had insisted that peace in Korea was an essential first step. Mao Zedong seems grudgingly to have concluded that any possible gain from continuing the war would not be worth the cost. Rhee almost sabotaged the negotiations by releasing thousands of

---

27. Quoted in Stephen E. Ambrose with Richard H. Immerman, *Ike's Spies: Eisenhower and the Espionage Establishment* (Garden City, N.Y., 1981), 188.

prisoners of war. He had to be appeased with promises of a U.S. mutual security pact, yet another entangling alliance. The Korean War officially ended in July 1953, but what amounted to an armed truce left a still bitterly divided nation and an international trouble spot that would outlast the Cold War.[28]

A crisis in Indochina the following year posed for the administration one of the sternest challenges in its eight years in office. By the spring of 1954, the outcome of France's eight-year war against the Communist-led Vietminh hinged on the fate of a fortress at Dien Bien Phu, in the remote northwest corner of Vietnam, where twelve thousand French troops were besieged by vastly superior enemy forces. Facing certain defeat, France in late March appealed to the United States to intervene. Eisenhower and Dulles sympathized with the plight of French forces if not with French goals. Above all, they feared the consequences of French defeat. The loss of additional Asian real estate a mere five years after the fall of China would invite attacks from Democrats and the Republican right wing. A Communist victory in Vietnam would threaten the rest of Southeast Asia with its crucial sea routes, vital natural resources, and markets essential for Japanese economic recovery. The consequences might extend to Europe, where a French defeat could spell the end of Allied plans for mutual defense. Eisenhower and Dulles seriously contemplated air and naval intervention, even the use of nuclear weapons. To underscore the importance of Vietnam, the president unveiled publicly on April 7 the famous domino theory, warning that if it should fall to Communism the rest of Southeast Asia might soon follow, with reverberations extending to the Middle East and Japan. But Congress refused to endorse intervention without the participation of Great Britain and French pledges of independence for Vietnam. Despite weeks of frantic shuttle diplomacy and urgent appeals for "United Action," Dulles could not secure the requisite pledges from either ally. Amidst angry recriminations among the Western nations, Dien Bien Phu fell on May 7, 1954, just as a conference already under way at Geneva began to consider the fate of French Indochina.[29]

The continued threat of U.S. military intervention—largely bluff— appears to have helped the administration at Geneva snatch some

28. Edward C. Keefer, "President Eisenhower and the End of the Korean War," *Diplomatic History* 10 (Summer 1986), 267–89; Roger Dingman, "Atomic Diplomacy During the Korean War," *International Security* 13 (Winter 1988–89), 79–91.

29. George C. Herring, *America's Longest War: The United States and Vietnam, 1950–1975* (4th ed., New York, 2002), 37–45; George C. Herring and Richard H. Immerman, "Eisenhower, Dulles, and Dienbienphu: 'The Day We Didn't Go to War' Revisited," *Journal of American History* 71 (September 1984), 343–63.

semblance of victory from near certain and total defeat. Dulles made a brief and stormy appearance, more scowling than usual, conducting himself, in the words of a biographer, with the "pinched distaste of a puritan in a house of ill repute," even reportedly turning his back when Chinese delegate Zhou En-lai extended a hand in greeting.[30] To deter possible Chinese intervention and influence the outcome of the conference, the United States kept alive the possibility of military involvement. The U.S. threat may have helped bring about a settlement. The Chinese and Soviets each had their own reasons for ending the war. They compelled reluctant Vietminh leaders to accept much less in the way of peace terms than they believed their battlefield success entitled them to. Following Cold War precedents badly applied in Germany and Korea, the Geneva Accords of July 21, 1954, divided Vietnam temporarily at the 17th parallel and set elections for 1956 to unify the country.[31]

Most observers believed that Ho Chi Minh's Vietminh would easily win the elections and unify the country, but the United States and the fiercely anti-Communist South Vietnamese leader Ngo Dinh Diem had other ideas. The "important thing," Dulles insisted, was "not to mourn the past but to seize the future opportunity to prevent the loss in Northern Vietnam from leading to the extension of communism throughout Southeast Asia and the Southwest Pacific."[32] Despite universally gloomy prospects for success in South Vietnam, the United States made a high-stakes gamble by committing itself firmly to the imperious Diem in late 1954 and standing by him when he almost lost power the following year. Violating the letter and spirit of the Geneva Accords, the United States backed Diem's refusal to participate in the national elections. Through a massive nation-building effort, it set out to construct in southern Vietnam an independent, non-Communist nation that could stand as a bulwark against further Communist expansion in a critical region. To further deter possible aggression, Dulles through extended negotiations in Manila in the fall of 1954 helped establish the Southeast Asia Treaty Organization (SEATO), an eight-nation alliance committed to defending the region from Communism.[33]

A 1954–55 crisis in the Taiwan Straits posed another major test for massive retaliation and had enormous long-term consequences for U.S.

30. Townsend Hoopes, *The Devil and John Foster Dulles* (Boston, 1973), 222.
31. Herring, *America's Longest War*, 45–51.
32. Ibid., 51.
33. David L. Anderson, *Trapped by Success: The Eisenhower Administration and Vietnam, 1953–1961* (New York, 1991), 121–99.

relations with Taiwan and China. The Chinese-American standoff provides a classic example of the way in which lack of direct communication, misperception, and miscalculation raised the threat of direct conflict during the Cold War, in this case for territory of no real value. In early September 1954, despite previous U.S. efforts at deterrence, the Chinese began shelling Quemoy and Matsu, tiny and strategically unimportant islands off the southeast coast of mainland China still under Nationalist control. Eisenhower and Dulles conceded that the islands were worthless. They did not want war. But neither did they wish to appear weak in the face of a Chinese challenge. They also recognized that Chiang Kai-shek might seek to exploit the crisis by sucking the United States into war with China. Mistakenly viewing the shelling as a prelude to Chinese seizure of the islands or even an attack on Taiwan, they experimented with a policy of deterrence through uncertainty, "keeping the enemy guessing," in Eisenhower's words, to head off aggression without getting more deeply entangled with Chiang. The policy had the opposite effect of what was intended, encouraging Mao's government in January 1955 to seize one of the Dachens, another set of offshore islands, in the belief that the United States would do nothing.[34]

The crisis quickly escalated to the brink of nuclear war. Mao sensed the danger of further moves and did nothing more. Again misperceiving Chinese intentions, the Eisenhower administration saw the Dachens seizure as a prelude to attacks on Quemoy, Matsu, or even Taiwan. The "Red Chinese appear to be completely reckless, arrogant, possibly overconfident, and completely indifferent to human life," the president warned.[35] To reassure Chiang and deter Mao, the administration signed a Mutual Defense Treaty with Taiwan (which did not include the offshore islands) and in January 1955 secured from Congress a Formosa Resolution giving the president blank-check authority to respond to Chinese "aggression." It considered preemptive military action, possibly even the use of nuclear weapons against Chinese forces on the islands. Believing war possible, if not likely, it set out, in Dulles's words, to "create a better climate for the use of atomic weapons."[36] Eisenhower raised the stakes and set off alarm bells at home and abroad by publicly suggesting on March 16, 1955, that

---

34. Gordon H. Chang and He Di, "The Absence of War in the U.S.-China Confrontation over Quemoy and Matsu in 1954–1955: Contingency, Luck, Deterrence?" *American Historical Review* 98 (December 1993), 1500–1524.

35. Ibid., 1514.

36. H. W. Brands Jr., "Testing Massive Retaliation: Credibility and Crisis Management in the Taiwan Strait," *International Security* 12 (Spring 1988), 142.

the United States might use nuclear weapons "as you use a bullet or any-thing else."[37] To persuade Chiang to abandon Quemoy and Matsu, the United States offered to blockade five hundred miles of the Chinese coast opposite Taiwan—an act of war—and place nuclear weapons on the is-land. Ironically, Chiang sabotaged this most risky escalation by refusing to give up the islands. Tension eased in April when Zhou En-lai at Ban-dung stunned the world with conciliatory gestures. Under pressure from nervous allies and an anxious public, the United States responded in kind. The two nations would soon initiate sporadic ambassadorial talks in Warsaw to help ease tensions.

Dulles later insisted—and some historians have supported his claim— that the Taiwan Straits crisis marked a victory for massive retaliation. To be sure, the United States avoided war and Taiwan was safe. But the Chinese focused attention on Taiwan, one of their principal aims in the first place, and also gained some Nationalist territory. Eisenhower's vague nuclear threats did not deter attacks on Quemoy, Matsu, or Taiwan—no such at-tacks were ever intended. The United States might have provoked a war over worthless real estate had it not been for Chiang's fortuitous obstinacy. The president's threats did little to establish U.S. credibility. In fact, they seem to have stiffened Chinese resolve and led Beijing to launch its own nuclear program. By provoking protests at home and among allies, they also raised serious questions about the viability of massive retaliation as the key element of New Look defense policy. More ominously for the long run, the crisis tightened U.S. ties with Chiang and produced more binding U.S. commitments to defend Taiwan, posing insuperable long-term obsta-cles to any reconciliation with the Beijing regime.[38]

The United States' credibility was also severely tested by crises in East-ern Europe. During the 1952 campaign, Dulles had rejected containment for an "explosive and dynamic" policy of "liberation" of captive peoples, and liberation at first became the cornerstone of the administration's poli-cies toward Eastern Europe. Eisenhower had seen the value of psycholog-ical warfare (psywar) as commander of Allied forces in Europe. He brought to the White House wartime propaganda adviser C. D. Jackson of Time-Life and endorsed his proposal to make psywar the "real guts" of U.S. policy for Eastern Europe. Jackson expanded and perfected programs initiated by the Truman administration. More and better leaflet-dropping

---

37. *Public Papers of the Presidents of the United States: Dwight D. Eisenhower, 1955* (Washington, 1959), 332.
38. Chang and He Di, "Absence of War," 1522–25; Brands, "Testing Massive Retaliation," 147–51.

balloons, thinly disguised as weather balloons, were sent out over the region—in all, sixty thousand balloons with three hundred thousand leaflets between 1951 and 1956. Radio Free Europe (RFE) and Radio Liberation overcame furious jamming to beam broadcasts into Eastern Europe and the Soviet Union itself. Such propaganda satirized Communist practices and mores, divulged the name of secret police operatives, and openly appealed to dissidents to revolt.[39]

Such psywar operations did not cause, but certainly encouraged, a series of revolts in Eastern Europe in the 1950s. Jackson had scarcely settled into office when harsh economic conditions in East Germany in June 1953 provoked protests in East Berlin that soon spread across the country, led to calls for a general strike, and eventually sparked widespread rioting. The uprising caught the United States completely off guard. Dulles and other U.S. officials hoped to exploit Soviet problems in East Germany. But they were distracted by Korea, where Rhee's release of prisoners of war imperiled the peace agreement. Attention was also focused on Western Europe, where they were attempting to beef up NATO defenses and begin West German rearmament. Eisenhower insisted that force could not be used. Neither Dulles nor anyone else could devise ways to exploit Soviet troubles. Moscow eventually suppressed the rebellion with twenty thousand troops and 350 tanks. All the United States could do was gain propaganda advantage through a relief program that provided five million food parcels—"Eisenhower Packages"—that fed one-third of East Germany's population. The East German crisis had a sobering effect on the concept of liberation, even Dulles concluding that forceful measures risked destruction of the free world. NSC-174 of December 1953 held to rollback as a long-term goal but tightly circumscribed it by affirming that the United States would not provoke war with the USSR and would seek to prevent "premature" uprisings in Eastern Europe.[40]

More serious crises erupted in Poland and Hungary three years later. In early 1955, the shrewd reformist Nikita Khrushchev, along with Nikolai Bulganin, took control of the Soviet government. A year later, in his famous keynote speech before a party congress, Khrushchev denounced Stalin's "crimes" and "cult of personality." The speech was not intended to be made public, but within weeks it appeared in newspapers around

39. Walter L. Hixson, *Parting the Curtain: Propaganda, Culture, and the Cold War, 1945–1961* (New York, 1997), 57–68.
40. Valur Ingimundarson, "The Eisenhower Administration, the Adenauer Government, and the Political Uses of the East German Uprising in 1953," *Diplomatic History* 20 (Summer 1996), 381–409.

the world. Designed to initiate a process of de-Stalinization in the Soviet Union and the satellites, it offered to Eastern Europeans hopes of liberalization and spurred uprisings in Poland and Hungary where old-line leaders clung desperately to power. The return of reformer Wyadislaw Gomulka raised fears in Moscow that Poland might break away from the Soviet bloc. Uninvited—and furious—Khrushchev and his entourage descended upon the Warsaw airport on October 19, 1956, backed by Red Army troops a hundred kilometers away. At a stormy session on the tarmac in tones loud enough to be heard by chauffeurs, Khrushchev threatened military intervention. The courageous Gomulka refused to talk with a "revolver on the table." Khrushchev eventually accepted Gomulka's pledges to retain close ties with Moscow and remain in the Warsaw Pact, the military alliance of seven Eastern European countries and the Soviet Union created in May 1955. "Finding a reason for an armed conflict would be easy," the Soviet leader conceded pragmatically, "but finding a way to put an end to such a conflict later on would be very hard."[41] While remaining faithful to the Soviet Union and exercising tight party control, Gomulka instituted modest reforms. Twenty-three years later, Poland made a relatively smooth transition to democracy.[42]

In Hungary, on the other hand, dissent grew into open rebellion, posing for Moscow a direct and menacing challenge. Khrushchev initially hoped for a Gomulka-type solution. But he lacked confidence in Hungarian leader Imre Nagy, and when the rebellion gained steam and Nagy promised a multiparty democracy, withdrawal from the Warsaw Pact, and an Austrian-like neutralism, an anxious Kremlin responded with brute force. With Britain and France attacking his new ally Egypt in the concurrent Suez Crisis and Hungary in open revolt, Khrushchev saw his credibility at stake. If the Soviet Union departed Hungary, he exclaimed, the "imperialists" will "perceive it as weakness on our part and will go on the offensive. . . . We have no other choice."[43] He used an estimated two hundred thousand troops and more than one thousand tanks to suppress the rebellion. The streets of Budapest ran red with blood for days. The city was left in rubble. As many as four thousand Hungarians were killed; another two hundred thousand fled to the West. Up to three hundred, Nagy included, were executed.

The reality of liberation posed a painful dilemma for those Americans who had so enthusiastically promoted it. Coming on the eve of the 1956

41. L. W. Gluchowski, "Poland 1956," *Cold War International History Project Bulletin* 5 (Spring 1995), 50.

42. Ibid., 50–51; Alexander Fursenko and Timothy Naftali, *Khrushchev's Cold War: The Inside Story of an American Adversary* (New York, 2006), 118–19.

43. Fursenko and Naftali, *Khrushchev's Cold War*, 130.

presidential election and in the midst of the Middle East crisis, Hungary raised especially difficult questions. Once again, the United States was caught by surprise. Although they too profoundly distrusted Nagy, Eisenhower and Dulles hoped for a solution like that in Poland. They carefully avoided provocative steps and even offered public assurances that the United States did not view an independent Hungary as a potential ally. At the same time, RFE broadcasts and the agitation of émigrés working under a CIA program led the rebels to count on U.S. support. Inaction thus created among Hungarians profound disillusionment. Again, however, the United States would do nothing more than seek propaganda gain by highlighting before world opinion Soviet repression. Ike lamented that the United States had "excited" Hungarians and was now "turning our backs on them." Dulles rationalized, rather pathetically, that "we always have been against violent revolution."[44] In fact, as far as Hungary was concerned, the policy of liberation was probably counterproductive. By casting doubts on Nagy's ability and loyalty and urging Hungary's withdrawal from the Warsaw Pact, RFE broadcasts may even have contributed to Soviet intervention and probably set back rather than speeded the process of freedom. Painfully aware of the fragility of the Communist bloc, Khrushchev more than ever saw the Cold War in zero-sum terms, ending any plans he may have had for reform in Eastern Europe.[45]

The bloody denouement in Hungary forced basic changes in U.S. propaganda toward Eastern Europe. Henceforth, the administration shied away from actively encouraging revolt in favor of more subtle forms of subversion through trade, travel, and culture. The aim was to break down the isolation of East Europeans and, by presenting positive images of life in the United States, increase their dissatisfaction with the regimes they lived under. The new approach involved expanded trade through loans and credits, exchange visits by students and professors, and information programs through books and specially designed newspapers and magazines. In Poland, the newly created U.S. Information Agency established an American bookstore and where possible set up libraries and reading rooms. The United States during the 1950s even initiated cultural exchanges with the Soviet Union itself.[46]

Music and especially jazz became powerful weapons in the new arsenal of liberation. In 1955, Voice of America (VOA) launched a nightly

44. *New York Times*, October 8, 2006.
45. Johanna Granville, " 'Caught with Jam on Our Fingers': Radio Free Europe and the Hungarian Uprising of 1956," *Diplomatic History* 29 (November 2005), 811; Immerman, *Dulles*, 153–54.
46. Hixson, *Parting the Curtain*, 87–119.

program, "Music USA," targeted especially at the youth of Eastern Europe and the USSR. Featuring mainly jazz, it was an instant sensation. Its disc jockey Willis Conover became one of the best known and most popular Americans on the Continent. "Music USA" reached an estimated thirty million people in the Soviet Union and Eastern Europe, a hundred million worldwide. It spawned numerous fan clubs and proved one of the most successful ventures in VOA history. Fighting the Cold War with "cool" music, Conover was said to be more powerful than a fleet of B-29 bombers, "the most famous American that virtually no American ever heard of."[47] Even those Americans who condemned the subversive effects of jazz at home welcomed the mischief it might cause abroad. The influence of the U.S. cultural offensive cannot be precisely measured, but over the long term it may have been considerable.[48]

In Western Europe, Eisenhower and Dulles brought to fruition policies initiated by Truman and Acheson. From the outset, relations with the major European allies were difficult at best. Dulles doubted the toughness of British and French leaders.[49] Since Soviet bombers could not reach the United States, London and Paris, on the other hand, feared that the new administration's nuclear bluster put them at risk. The relationship between Dulles and British foreign minister Anthony Eden was further complicated by a personality clash that evolved into intense personal hatred.

West Germany's independence and rearmament remained the most troublesome issues. Like its predecessors, the new administration saw NATO and collective security as the keys to European defense and German rearmament as indispensable to NATO. An alliance strengthened by an armed West Germany could meet the Soviet threat, while NATO would also keep in check a rearmed West Germany. Still haunted by bitter memories of two world wars, France naturally balked at the idea of a revived and rearmed Germany. French leaders proposed a European Defense Community (EDC) that would merge German forces into an integrated military organization, thereby precluding an independent German army and presumably giving France some control over German forces. But Britain's refusal to join EDC dimmed French enthusiasm. Weakened and divided by the war in Indochina and worried about Germany, a nervous and chronically unstable France slew its brainchild. "Too much inte-

47. New York Times, May 20, 1996.
48. Hixson, Parting the Curtain, 110–17; Reinhold Wagnleitner, Coca-Colonization and the Cold War: The Cultural Mission of the United States in Austria After the Cold War (Chapel Hill, N.C., 1994), 210–15.
49. Immerman, Dulles, 60.

gration, too little England," Prime Minister Pierre Mendes-France complained.[50] Even Dulles's threats of an "agonizing reappraisal" of U.S. policies failed to sway French leaders. In August 1954, the French parliament rejected EDC, a "dark day for Europe," German chancellor Konrad Adenauer moaned. "A grave event," Dulles concurred.[51]

French rejection of EDC stunned the allies into shockingly rapid resolution of their most nettlesome issue. Deeply committed to EDC, the United States, for one of the few times in the postwar era, took a backseat, permitting Churchill and Eden to devise an ingenious compromise, the so-called London Agreements, that retained some features of EDC while rearming West Germany within the framework of NATO. At a nine-power conference in September 1954, an obviously agitated but uncharacteristically silent Dulles deferred to Britain. The allies then achieved in a brief period what they had been unable to do before and produced a result that improved on the European Defense Community.[52] The conferees constructed a Western European Union on the foundation of the 1948 Brussels Treaty and expanded it to include Italy and West Germany. Its military forces were placed under NATO command. German rearmament was thus made more palatable by giving a U.S. commander control over the size and use of German forces. Adenauer also agreed not to produce warships, bombers, and atomic, biological, and chemical weapons. In return, the Western powers recognized West Germany's sovereignty. Exactly ten years after the end of war in Europe, the Allied occupation ended. The Truman program was completed. United States officials continued to pay lip service to unification, but they preferred a separate, rearmed West Germany tied to the West. The division of Europe was sealed for a generation. Western Europe settled into an unaccustomed period of stability, its once warring nations at peace with each other for the first time in decades, their internal politics fixed along centrist lines.[53] An unhappy Soviet Union responded to the European arrangements by forming its military counterpart to NATO, the Warsaw Pact.

German rearmament also led to the neutralization of Austria and a top-level summit meeting in Geneva. To improve its world position and gain breathing space for dealing with urgent domestic problems, the Soviet leadership set out to heal wounds opened by Stalin. A veritable globetrotter

50. Tony Judt, *Postwar: A History of Europe Since 1945* (New York, 2005), 245.
51. Rolf Steininger, "John Foster Dulles, the European Defense Community, and the German Question," in Richard H. Immerman, ed., *John Foster Dulles and the Diplomacy of the Cold War* (Princeton, N.J., 1990), 103.
52. Immerman, *Dulles*, 106.
53. Steininger, "Dulles," 104–7; Judt, *Postwar*, 242.

compared to his reclusive predecessor, the ebullient Khrushchev traveled to China, where with great ceremony he gave back Port Arthur and pushed for closer economic ties. He also flew to Belgrade to patch up relations with Tito. Fearing that Austria might go the way of Germany, he dropped a prior demand conditioning withdrawal of Red Army troops on German neutrality and asked simply for Austrian neutrality. The result was the Austrian State Treaty of May 1955. Having previously affirmed that Soviet withdrawal from Austria was the key to resolving other issues, Eisenhower had little choice but to succumb to Soviet appeals for a summit. To do otherwise, he conceded, would make him appear "senselessly stubborn in my attitude."[54]

The Geneva summit of May 1955 was significant mainly in that it took place, the first such meeting since the end of World War II. Unschooled in the conventions of great-power diplomacy, the Soviet leaders worried about how to behave and whether they would be treated as equals. Khrushchev's insecurities were magnified upon arrival by the fact that his plane was much smaller than Eisenhower's—"like an insect," he later barked.[55] Khrushchev and Bulganin clung desperately to hopes of somehow undoing West German ties to NATO. The Eisenhower administration was equally wary, fearing that the summit might disrupt hard-won Western unity, a fear underscored when the British proposed negotiations on German unification. Dulles had acquiesced only grudgingly to the idea of a summit and advised the president—known for his broad and winning grin—to appear stern and unsmiling. The administration made clear it would consider German unification only in the context of discussion of freedom in Eastern Europe and on condition that Germany remained tied to the West, terms that ensured no substantive negotiations. Bulganin sprang on the United States sweeping disarmament proposals that were difficult to reject without appearing to stand in the way of easing world tensions. Eisenhower countered by proposing mutual aerial surveillance—"Open Skies"—which the Soviets summarily dismissed as legalized spying. The two sides engaged in bizarre and surreal banter about the USSR joining NATO. Despite much brave rhetoric about the "spirit of Geneva," the conference adjourned without agreement. Eisenhower and Dulles believed they were moving in the right direction before the summit and did not want to be thrown off course. Khrushchev may have concluded that the Americans feared nuclear war as much as he and thus was tempted to initiate games of nuclear chicken.[56]

54. Immerman, *Dulles*, 135.
55. Fursenko and Naftali, *Khrushchev's Cold War*, 43.
56. William Taubman, *Khrushchev: The Man and His Era* (New York, 2003), 349–53.

III

Having cobbled together almost despite themselves a shaky equilibrium in Europe and East Asia, the Cold War combatants in the mid-1950s shifted to the Third World, where they competed vigorously for the allegiance of nations emerging from colonialism. The Middle East took center stage in this new phase of the Cold War and posed especially complex challenges. Throughout the region, revolutionary nationalists struggled to gain full independence and sought to exploit the Cold War to their advantage. Americans sympathized with nationalist aspirations. Eisenhower privately puzzled over why the United States could not "get some of the people in these down-trodden countries to like us instead of hating us," conveniently forgetting that skin color, America's own imperial past, and its close ties with the Western colonial powers tainted it in their eyes.[57] Khrushchev's late 1955 entrée into the Middle East through an arms deal and trade agreements with Egypt struck alarm bells in the West. Eisenhower and the men around him viewed Third World peoples as childlike, sometimes irresponsible, not ready for full independence, and especially vulnerable to clever propagandists like the Communists. The administration increasingly feared that Arab nationalism might veer to the left and that Allied obstructionism would facilitate that outcome. "We must have evolution, not revolution," Dulles averred.[58] The Arab-Israeli conflict, of course, added yet another volatile ingredient to an already explosive mix.

Eisenhower and Dulles significantly deepened U.S. involvement in the Middle East. They shared in full measure their predecessors' assessment of the region's importance for its military bases, lines of communication, and huge reservoirs of oil. They sought to promote stable, friendly governments capable of withstanding Communist-inspired subversion and willing to resist aggression. Exaggerating both the Soviet threat and Arab susceptibility to Moscow's influence, Eisenhower went much further than Truman, mounting covert operations to overthrow unfriendly governments, forging a regional anti-Communist alliance, attempting to mediate the Arab-Israeli dispute, and even employing military force. More often than not, the United States found itself hopelessly snarled in the raging conflicts between Arabs and Israelis, Arabs and Arabs, and Arab nationalism and the European colonial powers.

57. Quoted in Stephen Kinzer, *All the Shah's Men: An American Coup and the Roots of Middle Eastern Terrorism* (Hoboken, N.J., 2003), 158.
58. Peter L. Hahn, *Caught in the Middle East: U.S. Policy Toward the Arab-Israeli Conflict, 1945–1961* (Chapel Hill, N.C., 2004), 195.

Eisenhower's first major intrusion into the Middle East maelstrom came in 1953 in Iran, a focal point of U.S., British, and Soviet rivalry since 1941 and an early Cold War battleground. By the time the new administration took office, Iran once more had become the center of international attention when a bitter dispute over decolonization issues took on Cold War overtones. Long resentful of the Anglo-Iranian Oil Company's (AIOC) domination of their nation's most valuable resource and its shameful treatment of Iranian workers, nationalists in 1951 voted to take over the giant British corporation. They were led by newly elected prime minister Mohammad Mosaddeq, an enigmatic, eccentric, and immensely colorful figure. Nearly seventy years old, tall and balding, with an elongated, sharply protruding nose, the European-educated prime minister had a well-rehearsed flair for the dramatic. He often received visitors in his bedroom dressed in pajamas and burst into tears in the midst of conversation or speeches. He also had a xenophobic streak and a tendency toward political self-destruction. A traditional liberal, he was willing to cooperate with Communists when it suited his needs. Americans had little sympathy with British oil interests, but they also abhorred nationalization and hesitated to undermine a major ally. They increasingly feared that instability in the region along the Soviet Union's southern border might tempt Moscow's involvement. The Truman administration thus sought in vain to mediate the conflict. The crisis intensified in 1952 when Mosaddeq's government broke relations with Britain.[59]

Eisenhower quickly changed U.S. policy from mediation to intervention. As in other areas, Americans in Iran blurred distinctions between local nationalism and Communism. They suspected Mosaddeq of being a Communist or a tool of Communists. His clumsy efforts to exploit the Cold War by warning of a Communist takeover and even flirting with Iran's leftist Tudeh Party only confirmed their suspicions. They also viewed him as unreliable, unpredictable, and weak, even effeminate— Dulles called him "that madman"—and therefore an easy mark for wily Communists. Eisenhower had come to appreciate the value of covert operations in World War II as an inexpensive and relatively risk-free means to undermine untrustworthy governments. CIA director Dulles affirmed that when a country was vulnerable to a Communist takeover "we can't wait for an engraved invitation to come and give aid."[60] The United States thus

59. Mary Ann Heiss, *Empire and Nationhood: The United States, Great Britain, and Iranian Oil, 1950–1954* (New York, 1997), 107–34; Kenneth Pollack, *The Persian Puzzle: The Conflict Between Iran and America* (New York, 2005), 57–60.
60. Peter Grose, *Gentleman Spy: The Life of Allen Dulles* (Boston, 1994), 410.

joined with Britain in the spring of 1953 in a plot to replace Mosaddeq with the youthful and presumably more pliable Shah Reza Pahlavi, whom the prime minister had just removed from power. In what was called Project Ajax, CIA operative Kermit Roosevelt, a grandson of Rough Rider Teddy, hired local agitators to destabilize an already fragile Iranian political system and used satchels of cash to purchase the loyalty of key elements in the army. Partly as a result of the shah's irresolution—the CIA called him a "creature of indecision"—the scheme nearly backfired. It was salvaged by the persistence of Iranian dissidents, Roosevelt's refusal to obey orders to return home, and Mosaddeq's political miscalculations. In August, the prime minister was overthrown and replaced by the shah. The coup represented a major short-term victory for U.S. policy. The United States supplanted Britain as the dominant power in a pivotal Cold War nation and gained a grateful ally in the shah, and U.S. oil companies got a 40 percent interest in the international consortium that replaced AIOC. The coup also marked a major turning point in Iran's modern history, a retreat from at least the semblance of parliamentary government to what became a brutal dictatorship. The United States' hand was carefully concealed, but Iranian nationalists knew what had happened—and remembered. When a revolution toppled the shah twenty-five years later, it quickly turned radical and virulently anti-American.[61]

Subsequent forays into the Middle East did not produce even short-term gains. To counter any Soviet military threat to the region, Eisenhower and Dulles, in keeping with the New Look's emphasis on regional alliances, encouraged in 1954 formation of the Baghdad Pact among the "northern tier" nations of Turkey, Iran, Iraq, and Pakistan. To avoid provoking the Soviets, on the one hand, and encouraging Israel to ask for similar commitments, on the other, the United States remained out of the alliance. But it dispensed military aid to induce nations to join and maintained close ties with the pact's military bureaucracy. Whatever value the alliance may have had in containing the Soviets was more than offset by its inflammatory impact in an already troubled region. It divided Arab states against each other—even members of the alliance—raising tensions still further. Britain's active participation struck Arabs as imperialism in another guise, especially antagonizing Egypt and encouraging Nasser's arms deal with the USSR. The pact further exacerbated the Arab-Israeli conflict.[62]

61. *New York Times*, April 16, 2000; Pollack, *Persian Puzzle*, 64–71.
62. Douglas Little, *American Orientalism: The United States and the Middle East Since 1945* (Chapel Hill, N.C., 2004), 127–30; Hahn, *Caught in the Middle East*, 151–54.

Also in the interest of checking possible Soviet advances in the Middle East, the administration in 1955–56, working closely with the British, launched the first of countless futile U.S. efforts to resolve the intractable Arab-Israeli dispute. Certain that his administration's "lopsided" partiality toward Israel had doomed Truman's diplomacy, they tried to be impartial and pushed hard to complete negotiations before the U.S. presidential election of 1956 brought forth powerful Israeli political pressures. The gambit went nowhere. The Arab states viewed Israel as a "cancer" that must be removed. The signing of the Baghdad Pact just when the peace initiative was presented did great damage. The plan called for Israel to give up territory won in the 1948 war, an idea repulsive to its leaders. "The whole proposal smacks of Munich," snarled the Israeli ambassador to Washington, Abba Eban. The administration's timing was atrocious. Just when it sought to mediate, tensions between Arabs and Israelis rose to such dangerous levels that Eisenhower contemplated sending U.S. forces to the Middle East to prevent a conflagration. The more the United States pressed for peace, the more strained Arab-Israeli relations became.[63] To balance Soviet military aid to Egypt and appease domestic lobbyists, Eisenhower in the spring of 1956 approved a major arms deal for Israel.

All the deadly crosscurrents of a deeply troubled region came together in the Suez Crisis of 1956, an imbroglio that not only undermined U.S. policy in the Middle East but also opened deep fissures between the United States and its major European allies and handcuffed the administration in dealing with the simultaneous crisis in Hungary. The Suez Crisis originated in the broader struggle between Arab nationalism and European colonialism that heated up after Nasser's 1952 overthrow of the British puppet King Farouk. An admirer of Mosaddeq, the thirty-five-year-old army colonel was a master conspirator, compelling speaker, and fiery nationalist with ambitions for regional leadership and glory. The United States appreciated his suspicions of the colonial powers but worried about his neutralism. Dulles and Eisenhower at first sought to seduce him with promises of $400 million to assist with a pet project, the grandiose scheme for a mammoth dam at Aswan on the Nile River to produce hydroelectric power, control flooding, and promote Egyptian agriculture through irrigation.

The commitment to assist Nasser provoked an uproar in the United States. Southern congressmen seeking to protect vital cotton interests protested the use of economic aid to promote foreign competition. Supporters of Israel declaimed against assisting its mortal enemy. Militant

63. Hahn, *Caught in the Middle East*, 186.

anti-Communists bitterly opposed rewarding neutralism. When Nasser tried to blackmail the United States by recognizing the People's Republic of China and threatening to seek aid from Moscow, an outraged Dulles seized the opportunity to renege on an offer that had become a diplomatic and political liability. "Do nations which play both sides get better treatment than nations which are stalwart and work with us?" the secretary thundered.[64] Nasser in July 1956 stunned the world by using the U.S. action as an excuse to nationalize the British-run corporation that managed the Suez Canal, rationalizing that he needed the tolls to pay for his Aswan project and thus setting off a dangerous four-month crisis.

Nasser's bold move threatened Britain's oil supplies, jeopardized a vital lifeline to its interests in South and Southeast Asia, and struck directly at one of the proudest symbols of a once glorious empire. "The Egyptian has his thumb on our windpipe," Eden, now prime minister, exclaimed.[65] Denouncing Nasser as a "Moslem Mussolini" who must not be appeased and fearing that defeat at his hands could force Britain out of the Middle East, Eden rebuffed U.S. pleas for patience. He rejected—as did Nasser— Dulles's frantic last-minute proposals to form an international consortium to run the canal and pay Egypt equitable compensation. He formed with France, which feared Nasser's threat to its North African colonies, and Israel, which had numerous grievances against the Egyptian, a secret military plan calling for Israel to attack Egypt across the Sinai desert and provide a pretext for British and French military operations to recapture the canal and get rid of Nasser. On October 29, 1956, Israel attacked, seizing the Sinai and Gaza without significant opposition. When Nasser, as expected, rebuffed European demands for withdrawal, Britain and France launched air and naval attacks against Egypt. Before they could achieve their major objectives, Nasser one-upped them, blocking the canal by sinking more than fifty ships loaded with concrete, rocks, and even beer bottles. An attack justified on grounds of keeping the canal in operation had precisely the opposite effect.[66]

The Suez-Sinai War set off the most serious crisis in America's relations with its major Western allies since the 1930s and raised the possibility of war with the Soviet Union. Eden later claimed that Dulles had given him a green light for military operations. In fact, each nation completely misread the other's position, and Eisenhower and Dulles were kept in the dark

64. Immerman, *Dulles*, 149.
65. Peter L. Hahn, *The United States, Great Britain, and Egypt, 1945–1956: Strategy and Diplomacy in the Early Cold War* (Chapel Hill, N.C., 1991), 213.
66. Immerman, *Dulles*, 152.

about Allied military plans. The Americans had no use for Nasser. Dulles agreed with Britain that he should be "made to disgorge his theft."[67] But they were shocked that their allies had resorted to war on the eve of the U.S. presidential election and furious that they had taken action that inflamed Arab nationalism and risked major Soviet gains in a crucial region. The Anglo-French offensive also prevented them from taking full propaganda advantage of Soviet military intervention in Hungary. "Foster, you tell 'em goddamn it, we're going to apply sanctions, we're going to the United Nations, we're going to do everything that there is so we can stop this thing," Eisenhower raged.[68] The United States threatened sanctions against Israel. It refused to bolster British currency reserves and oil supplies—letting them "boil in their own oil," as the president put it, and permitting the pound sterling to plummet. Also caught off guard by Anglo-French military action, an equally enraged Khrushchev threatened—largely bluff—to unleash rockets against London and Paris. The Pentagon developed contingency plans for a general war for a cause the administration considered dubious. Desperate to repair damage with the Arabs and prevent Soviet intrusion into the Middle East, Dulles in a dramatic speech before the United Nations disassociated his nation from Britain, France, and Israel and proposed a cease-fire and withdrawal of all forces. He closed with a ringing attack on colonialism he said he would be proud to have as his epitaph. Britain and France gave in, in part from Soviet threats but mainly because U.S. pressures worsened an already serious economic situation in England, leaving them no choice.[69]

The Suez affair was one of the most complex and dangerous of Cold War crises. Walking a tightrope over numerous conflicting forces, Eisenhower and Dulles did manage to avert war with the Soviet Union and limit the damage to relations with the Arab states. On the other hand, America's relations with its major allies plunged to their lowest point in years. Washington and London each believed they had been double-crossed. The British and French resented their humiliation at the hands of their ally. Eden and Dulles's mutual hatred deepened—as "tortuous as a wounded snake, with much less excuse," an Eden still angry years later said of his by then deceased U.S. counterpart.[70] An already volatile Middle East was further destabilized. Nasser remained in power—a fact

67. Little, *American Orientalism*, 172.
68. Ibid., 176.
69. Ibid., 177; William Roger Louis, "Dulles, Suez, and the British," in Immerman, *Dulles and the Diplomacy of the Cold War*, 152–58; Hahn, *Caught in the Middle East*, 200–209.
70. Louis, "Suez," 158.

Dulles later privately lamented to the British. His noisy neutralism veered further eastward. Soviet premier Khrushchev mistakenly concluded that his rocket-rattling had carried the day—those "with the strongest nerves will be the winner," he boasted—thus emboldening him to further and even more reckless nuclear gambits.[71]

Amidst the wreckage of Suez and with an overwhelming electoral victory behind him, Eisenhower set out to craft a new strategy to protect U.S. interests in a vital region. He and Dulles backed off from mediation in the Arab-Israeli dispute, reasoning that with little hope of a settlement additional intrusion would only antagonize both sides. They rejoiced that European influence in the region was on the wane but feared the Soviets might fill the vacuum. They worried that Nasser and other Arab nationalists might create more instability that the Soviets could exploit. Presumably with Eisenhower's blessing, the CIA attempted unsuccessfully to overthrow the government of Syria, inflaming anti-U.S. sentiments in that country. It may have attempted to displace or even assassinate Nasser.[72]

But the main solutions were to bolster conservative, pro-Western governments in the region with economic and military assistance and deter Nasser and the Soviets with threats of military intervention. The administration lavished aid on Jordan and its boy king, Hussein. It put the greatest faith in Saudi Arabia and King Saud, son of the legendary Ibn Saud, some officials even hoping that as custodian of the holy places he might defuse Arab radicalism and isolate Nasser by becoming a sort of "Islamic pope." The modern U.S.-Saudi relationship took form during these years, but it did not have the effect Americans hoped for. Saud continued to rant against Israel and complain about the inadequacy of U.S. aid. Not a strong leader like his father, he drank heavily and became engaged in a bitter power struggle with his brother Faisal. By the end of the decade, the administration was exploring an accommodation with Nasser.[73]

To back up the threat of military intervention, Eisenhower and Dulles sought from Congress in early 1957 broad authority to send military forces to any nation threatened by a nation "controlled by International Communism." Democratic senator Hubert Humphrey of Minnesota warned of a "predated declaration of war," Oregon's Wayne Morse of a "chapter written in blood," but in tones reminiscent of Acheson in 1947 Eisenhower insisted that Soviet domination of the Middle East would "gravely

71. Taubman, *Khrushchev*, 359–60.
72. Douglas Little, "Mission Impossible: The CIA and the Cult of Covert Action in the Middle East," *Diplomatic History* 28 (November 2004), 674–81.
73. Nathan J. Citino, *From Arab Nationalism to OPEC* (Bloomington, Ind., 2002), 132–45.

endanger all the free world."[74] Ten years to the month after Truman requested aid to Greece and Turkey, Eisenhower secured from Congress $200 million in aid and blanket authority to intervene militarily in the Middle East. The so-called Eisenhower Doctrine took a giant step beyond its predecessor.

As before, it was easier to promulgate a doctrine than apply it. The administration continued to blur the distinction between indigenous conflicts and international Communism. As always, involvement in the Middle East brought a steep price and numerous trade-offs. Threatened by a radical nationalist rival, Jordan's pro-Western Hussein in the spring of 1957 used Cold War lingo to attract U.S. intervention. Eisenhower sent economic aid and in a modern act of gunboat diplomacy dispatched the Sixth Fleet to the eastern Mediterranean. Hussein remained in power, an apparent victory, but U.S. intervention heightened tension with Egypt and Israel and briefly threatened a general Middle Eastern war. A similar effort in Syria completely backfired. Soviet aid to the Syrian government provoked from Washington dire warnings of a Hitler-like threat to the Middle East. The United States again dispatched the Sixth Fleet to the region and tried to line up a coalition against Syria. But the CIA's bungled covert operation and U.S. indecision about intervention led potential allies to balk and in some cases even support Syria. When the dust settled, Egypt and Syria formed the United Arab Republic. Soviet influence grew.[75]

The United States sent troops to Lebanon under the Eisenhower Doctrine in the summer of 1958. Afflicted with deep-seated religious as well as ethnic and political divisions, Lebanon posed especially difficult challenges. When the Christian, pro-Western leader Camille Chamoun sought to extend his power, Muslim nationalists rebelled, and Chamoun appealed for U.S. aid. Eisenhower was wary of intervention, but the overthrow of the friendly Iraqi government at about the same time raised fears of a full-fledged Middle East crisis. Employing yet another analogy from the 1930s, the *New York Times* warned of a "Lebanese Anschluss."[76] The administration feared that Nasser, Israel, and the Soviets might exploit the turmoil. Eisenhower speculated that Lebanon might be "our last chance to do something."[77] After forcing Chamoun to step down, Eisenhower sent fourteen thousand marines to help stabilize Lebanon, the largest U.S.

74. Little, *Orientalism*, 132; Hahn, *Caught in the Middle East*, 225; Immerman, *Dulles*, 157.
75. Little, *Orientalism*, 132–36.
76. Hahn, *Caught in the Middle East*, 241.
77. Immerman, *Dulles*, 166.

amphibious operation since Inchon. Upon hitting the beach, the marines encountered vacationers rather than enemy soldiers. They remained until September and at least temporarily eased the crisis.

Short-term successes in Jordan and Lebanon could not obscure the perils and pitfalls of intervention in the Middle East. Eisenhower admitted that there was a "campaign of hatred against us" and the people were on "Nasser's side."[78] After extensive study, the NSC similarly concluded in late 1958 that the Eisenhower Doctrine was already outdated. By permitting itself to be "cast as Nasser's opponent," the United States had helped him become the "champion" of Arab nationalism. Interventionism had cost the United States Arab goodwill, further destabilized the region, and played into Soviet hands. The NSC recommended that the United States continue to defend the crucial northern tier states. It must distance itself still further from European colonialism. It must also seek ways to improve relations with Nasser and win Arab support. The administration tried to do these things, but it was not easy in a short time to repair the damage of six years of interventionism. Under Eisenhower's direction, the United States had plunged much more deeply into the politics of a turbulent region and assumed commitments difficult to shed. "U.S. leaders found themselves caught in the Middle East," historian Peter Hahn has concluded, "unable to relinquish the responsibilities that they had accepted even as those responsibilities became increasingly difficult to fulfill. And they were caught in the middle of the Arab-Israeli conflict, unable to resolve a dispute that would generate instability for years to come."[79]

While bringing the Cold War to nearby South Asia, the United States also encountered intractable local issues and sometimes unbridgeable cultural divides. Americans might well have empathized with India, which, after gaining independence from Britain in 1947, became the world's most populous democracy. But from the outset, the two peoples approached each other from markedly different perspectives. Indian culture was built on a sense of give-and-take Americans never quite understood. To Americans, on the other hand, Hinduism was backward looking and bred confusion, otherworldliness, and passivity.[80] Each nation had pretensions to moral superiority that rubbed the other the wrong way. Prime Minister Jawaharlal Nehru deeply resented U.S. pushiness and airs of

78. Little, *Orientalism*, 136.
79. Hahn, *Caught in the Middle East*, 293.
80. Andrew Rotter, "Religion and U.S. South Asian Relations," *Diplomatic History* 24 (Fall 2000), 602–8.

superiority. He claimed not to understand "why a man with such strong muscles should publicly demonstrate his muscles all the time."[81] Nehru's determination to remain neutral in the Cold War especially annoyed and alarmed Americans, raising fears that India might drift into the Communist "camp." India's frequent and shrill criticism of U.S. policies further riled leaders and citizens.

By contrast, American officials found much more to like in India's bitter rival Pakistan, the Muslim state carved out of the South Asian subcontinent in the partition that came with independence. Monotheistic Islam seemed much closer to Christianity. Pakistani leaders appeared much more vigorous, energetic, forthright, and warlike, in short more manly.[82] Unlike India and primarily for its own reasons—to build the military strength necessary to fend off its much larger neighbor—Pakistan expressed willingness to stand with the United States in the Cold War. "Pakistan is a country I would like to do everything for," Vice President Richard M. Nixon exclaimed. "The people have less complexes than the Indians. The Pakistanis are completely frank even when it hurts."[83] Not surprisingly, then, when the Eisenhower administration set out in 1953 to find allies, Pakistan stepped forward. It became a charter member of SEATO and the Baghdad Pact, making it, in the words of one wit, "America's most allied ally."[84] Large-scale economic and especially military aid programs quickly followed.

The alliance with Pakistan brought as many problems as benefits. Nehru hoped to keep the subcontinent free of the Cold War, but the United States brought it there. One major result, as Indians had predicted, was to provoke a profound anger against the United States, driving their country toward the Soviet Union. Nor did relations between the United States and Pakistan especially flourish under the alliances. It was never quite clear what role Pakistan would play in Middle East defense. Its incessant demands for the newest and most expensive military hardware annoyed and concerned top U.S. officials. Military aid from the United States enabled Pakistan's leaders to ignore major domestic problems and refuse to negotiate with India. In turn, Pakistan's leaders resented U.S. refusal to meet their demands and accused their ally of bad faith.[85]

81. Ilya V. Gaiduk, *Confronting Vietnam: Soviet Policy Toward the Indochina Conflict, 1954–1963* (Stanford, Calif., 2003), 63.
82. Rotter, "Religion," 609–10.
83. Robert J. McMahon, *The Cold War on the Periphery: The United States, India, and Pakistan* (New York, 1994), 171.
84. Ibid., 206.
85. Ibid., 189–205.

In the mid-1950s, the United States initiated a shift in its policies toward South Asia. Khrushchev's 1955 trip to the subcontinent followed by major commitments of aid for India alarmed U.S. officials. Some pundits speculated by this time that competition between China and India in terms of economic development might be the pivot on which world history turned. A 1957 economic crisis suggested that India could be losing. The United States thus became more receptive toward economic assistance for India. At the same time, Eisenhower had concluded that America's "tendency to rush out and seek allies was not very sensible," even a "terrible error."[86] The United States thus sought to contain military aid to Pakistan within reasonable bounds. To help stabilize South Asia, it set out to encourage negotiations between Pakistan and India on vexing issues such as the disputed territory of Kashmir.

The policy changes produced no more than modest gains and highlighted once more the difficulties of imposing Cold War frameworks on complex local situations. India happily accepted U.S. assistance, and relations improved somewhat in Eisenhower's last years. But it refused to negotiate with its archenemy. Pakistan deeply resented U.S. aid to India. While also refusing negotiations with its neighbor, it demanded more for itself. The United States could hardly refuse. Pakistan provided crucial posts for electronic eavesdropping on the Soviet Union. Bases at Peshawar and Lahore enabled high-flying U-2 spy aircraft to gather vital intelligence on Soviet military capabilities and missile installations. The 1958 coup in Iraq replaced a pro-American government with radical Arabs, making Pakistan more important for Middle East defense. Pakistan's shrewd and hard-nosed leader, Ayub Kahn, warned that U.S. bases put his country at risk, therefore necessitating F-104 fighters and Sidewinder missiles. The Eisenhower policy shift brought some balance to U.S. relations with South Asia and improved relations with India. But it did little to stabilize the subcontinent or resolve America's essential policy dilemmas there.[87]

In the raging Cold War competition for the allegiance of Third World nations, the United States found itself increasingly handicapped abroad by one of its most difficult problems at home—the denial of equal rights and opportunities for all its citizens and especially the segregation of African Americans in the South. Race relations at home intersected with foreign policy in various ways. African Americans now openly questioned their nation's claims to moral world leadership. "Advocacy of free elections in Europe by American officials is hypocrisy," the young minister

86. Ibid., 206.
87. Ibid., 258–71.

and civil rights leader Martin Luther King Jr. observed, "when free elections are not held in great sections of America."[88] African diplomats posted in Washington and at the United Nations ran up against discriminatory racial mores in the United States. Under fire for their handling of decolonization, Europeans turned the tables by pointing to the country's management of its own racial issues. Top officials increasingly recognized the contradiction. "We cannot talk equality to the peoples of Africa and Asia and practice inequality in the United States," Nixon warned the president upon returning from Africa in early 1957. "In the national interest, as well as for the moral issues involved, we must support the necessary steps which will assure orderly progress toward the elimination of discrimination in the United States."[89]

The Little Rock school desegregation crisis of September 1957 became a watershed issue for U.S. foreign policy. Eisenhower sent federal troops to the Arkansas capital with great reluctance. He was personally comfortable with segregation and had many friends among the southern elite. He believed social change could come only gradually and hesitated to intervene in what he considered a state matter. But Governor Orval Faubus's blatant defiance of Supreme Court school desegregation rulings left him no choice. More important, Little Rock had a huge worldwide impact. Scenes of federal troops escorting African American children to school while white foes of integration hurled ugly epithets of protest played in newspapers and especially on the powerful new medium of television across the world. Soviet and Chinese propagandists had a field day. Europeans still smarting from Suez crowed that America's handling of its own race problems hardly qualified it to lecture them. A Nigerian newspaper asserted that the United States "has no claim to be leader of Western democracies." The crisis in Arkansas was "ruining our foreign policy," Dulles warned the president; the impact in Asia and Africa "might be worse for us than Hungary was for the Russians."[90] Little Rock thus inextricably linked foreign and domestic issues. Americans, Eisenhower among them, concluded that the nation must effectively address its domestic issues to validate its claim to be leader of the free world.

Following Little Rock, the Eisenhower administration took modest steps to address a serious problem. It made symbolic gestures to improve its image among emerging nations. It supported a Haitian candidate for

88. Borstelmann, *Cold War and the Color Line*, 107.
89. Cary Fraser, "Crossing the Color Line in Little Rock: The Eisenhower Administration and the Dilemma of Race for U.S. Foreign Policy," *Diplomatic History* 24 (Spring 2000), 241.
90. Ibid., 247, 250.

president of the UN Trusteeship Council. In the late 1950s, decolonization hit Africa with a vengeance, and the United States supported more openly the independence and even neutralism of new nations there. The State Department established a Bureau of African Affairs, removing that continent's questions from the European divisions traditionally more sympathetic to the colonial powers. In October 1958, for the first time, the United States voted for a U.N. resolution condemning apartheid in South Africa. There were, of course, limits to how far the administration would go. Following the notorious 1960 Sharpeville massacre in South Africa in which police brutally killed sixty-nine protestors and wounded two hundred others, the State Department disavowed a U.S. diplomat who had issued a mild statement of protest. Most important, the administration recognized that it could no longer remain indifferent to the international implications of racial problems at home. Eisenhower and even more his successors plainly saw how important they had become to the nation's global position and pretensions.[91]

IV

Throughout its history, when facing a real or imagined foreign threat, the United States has taken a keener interest in the Western Hemisphere. The Cold War was no exception. During their first years, Eisenhower and Dulles continued with little change the Latin American policies they had inherited. They worried about Communism in the hemisphere, as elsewhere, but saw little reason for alarm or exceptional measures. Like Truman and Acheson, they rebuffed Latin American pleas for a hemispheric Marshall Plan, insisting that modest loans and private investment were the correct path to economic development. To sustain close ties with Latin American military leaders, they expanded their predecessors' military aid program. They mounted a major propaganda campaign featuring comic strips, cartoon books, and radio broadcasts warning the Latin American masses of the dangers of Communism. They continued the usual public relations measures of feting hemispheric leaders and celebrating Pan-Americanism—"you have to pat them a bit and make them think that you are fond of them," Dulles instructed the president.[92]

Continuing the practice dating to the 1920s, they accommodated the dictators who ruled thirteen of the twenty Latin American nations. Indeed, in their first years, they went much further, bestowing the Legion of

91. Ibid., 258–64; Borstelmann, *Cold War and the Color Line*, 122–28.
92. Stephen G. Rabe, "Dulles, Latin America, and Cold War Anticommunism," in Immerman, *Dulles and the Diplomacy of the Cold War*, 163.

Merit on such distasteful characters as dictators Marcus Pérez Jiménez of Venezuela and Manuel Odría of Peru and entertaining Nicaragua's brutal tyrant Anastasio Somoza and Paraguay's Alfredo Stroessner. During a goodwill tour in 1955, Nixon publicly embraced Cuban dictator Fulgencio Batista, whom he compared to Abraham Lincoln, and the Dominican Republic's Rafael Trujillo. At a time when anti-Communism was the highest priority, democracy and human rights took a backseat. In any event, as Nixon explained, "Spaniards had many talents, but government was not among them."[93]

The administration also followed through on a policy initiative devised by its predecessor by using covert operations in the summer of 1954 to topple the leftist government of Jacobo Árbenz in Guatemala. A handsome and charismatic politician, the popularly elected reformer sought to modernize his nation's economy by encouraging factories, establishing banks, and exploiting the nation's mineral resources. He launched a massive land reform program, expropriating thousands of acres for redistribution to peasants. In 1952, he seized four hundred thousand acres of land belonging to the mighty United Fruit Company, the U.S.-owned corporation that dominated Guatemala's economy. Closely connected with the U.S. government, "the Octopus," as it was known to Guatemalans, raised the specter of Communism and furiously lobbied the administration to do something. No less than the pioneer of public relations, Edward Bernays, who had originally peddled bananas as a cure for indigestion, put together a network of propaganda operatives to discredit Árbenz in Guatemala and brand him a Communist in the United States. In America, at least, UFCO preached to the choir. Although the CIA could find no direct ties with Moscow, the administration was already deeply suspicious of Árbenz. When his government took anti-U.S. positions in inter-American meetings and purchased arms from Czechoslovakia (because it could not buy them from the United States), it confirmed what most U.S. officials already suspected: Árbenz was a Communist and therefore a menace to the hemisphere.[94]

Implemented by the CIA in the summer of 1954 with a budget of $3 million, Operation PBSUCCESS lived up to its code name. The agency employed mercenaries from various Central American countries and established training camps in Florida, in Honduras, and on Somoza's estate

---

93. Ibid., 172.

94. Richard H. Immerman, *The CIA in Guatemala: The Foreign Policy of Intervention* (Austin, Tex., 1982) and Piero Gleijeses, *Shattered Hope: The Guatemalan Revolution and the United States, 1944–1954* (Princeton, N.J., 1991) are the standard monographs.

in Nicaragua. CIA-trained teams using psywar tactics showered Guatemala with broadcasts and leaflets fomenting rebellion. They sent "mourning cards" to Árbenz and other leaders, hinting at doom for any recipient, and warned Catholics that pictures of Lenin and Stalin would replace statues of the saints in their houses.[95] CIA propagandists exaggerated the strength of the uprising. On June 18, 1954, U.S.-picked rebel leader Castillo Armas "invaded" Guatemala with an "army" of about 150 men. A small "air force" of Cessnas and antiquated U.S. military aircraft "bombed" ammunition dumps and oil storage facilities in Guatemala City with such things as Molotov cocktails and blocks of dynamite attached to hand grenades. Wrongly persuaded that the United States would do anything to get rid of him, Árbenz, much like Mosaddeq, cracked under pressure, resigning on June 27 and fleeing into exile. Castillo Armas visited Washington shortly after and obeisantly inquired of Nixon: "Tell me what you want me to do and I will do it."[96]

The coup had significant consequences for all concerned. As in Iran, it succeeded despite numerous blunders in execution mainly because Árbenz, like Mosaddeq, lost his nerve. Top U.S. officials saw it as further confirmation of the ease with which hostile Third World governments could be eliminated. PBSUCCESS thus induced a great hubris in the agency and a certain complacency about Latin America and in time led to similar efforts in Cuba, British Guiana, and Chile. The coup produced a stable government friendly to U.S. interests, but for Guatemala it brought disaster. The overthrow of Árbenz shattered the political center and initiated a cycle of violence that would last for more than four decades. The CIA retained influence in Guatemala into the 1990s, assisting with a so-called counterinsurgency program that resulted in torture, political assassination, and the massacre of entire Mayan villages. Somewhere between one hundred thousand and two hundred thousand people were killed in what the agency's inspector general later conceded was "one of the saddest chapters of American relations with Latin America."[97]

A series of shocking events in the Eisenhower administration's last three years produced dramatic shifts in U.S. Latin American policy. The hemisphere itself underwent major changes. A recession in the United States caused a catastrophic drop in prices for Latin American exports, halting economic growth and leaving widespread human misery.

95. *New York Times*, July 6, 2003.
96. Ibid., November 30, 2003.
97. Ibid., March 17, 1999.

Economic problems brought political instability. Ten of the thirteen dictators fell from power. Economic and political unrest also provoked in the hemisphere rising anti-Americanism.

An attack on Nixon in Caracas in May 1958 brought home to North Americans in the most alarming fashion the seething discontent among their southern neighbors. Already concerned about the turmoil in Latin America, the administration sent the vice president back on another fact-finding mission and goodwill visit. He encountered some verbal protests in Montevideo, Uruguay, and his entourage was stoned in Lima, Peru, but in Caracas his life was threatened. En route to a ceremony at the tomb of the liberator Simón Bolívar, his motorcade was surrounded and stopped by an angry mob shouting anti-U. S. slogans. As the crowd closed in, the police fled. The mob broke the windows of cars in which the vice president and his wife were riding. For nearly fifteen minutes, they were trapped and seriously endangered. An alert and intrepid driver finally extricated them to the safety of the U.S. embassy. Nixon returned to Washington to a hero's welcome; eighty-five thousand people lined the route from National Airport into the city.[98] Some top officials at first dismissed the attacks as the work of Communist provocateurs, but CIA director Dulles insisted there was no evidence of Soviet involvement and conceded that there would be "trouble in Latin America even if there were no Communists."[99] The attack on Nixon stunned the administration into recognition of the surging unrest in Latin America, producing in time reassessments of basic policies.

The rise of Fidel Castro in Cuba and his drift toward the Soviet Union brought the Cold War into the U.S. backyard. Many Cubans admired the United States, imbibed its culture, baseball especially, and liked its people. But they also resented outside domination and blamed many of their problems on the United States. For nearly a quarter century, they had suffered under Fulgencio Batista's oppressive regime. The U.S. government encouraged tourism in the 1950s to help deal with the worldwide dollar gap, and Batista brought in mobster Meyer Lansky to clean up Havana's casinos. An estimated three hundred thousand Americans flocked to Cuba yearly, making it a playground for the rich and a source of wealth

---

98. Lars Schoultz, *Beneath the United States: A History of U.S. Policy Toward Latin America* (Cambridge, Mass., 1998), 351.

99. Rabe, "Latin America," in Immerman, *Dulles and the Diplomacy of the Cold War*, 181. The impact of the Nixon visit is analyzed in Marvin R. Zahniser and W. Michael Weis, "A Diplomatic Pearl Harbor? Richard Nixon's Goodwill Visit to Latin America in 1958," *Diplomatic History* 13 (Spring 1989), 163–90.

for U.S. organized crime.[100] The Platt Amendment had been abrogated in 1934, but its essence in terms of U.S. domination—what Castro called "Plattism"—lived on. Batista scrupulously accommodated Washington on major issues and granted favors, sometimes in return for bribes, to U.S. corporations like International Telephone and Telegraph. Reliant on the export of sugar, the Cuban economy remained an appendage of the United States.[101]

Castro boldly set out to change this. The son of a wealthy planter, well educated, a good enough pitcher that the New York baseball Giants once offered him a five-thousand-dollar signing bonus, the young rebel was also a fiery nationalist and admirer of José Martí, who had insisted that a genuine revolution must be a revolution against the United States. Still in his twenties, quixotic by nature, Castro launched premature uprisings in 1953 and 1956 that ended disastrously. Undaunted, he organized in the Sierra Maestra mountains of southeastern Cuba the guerrilla army that would drive Batista from power. He benefited from Batista's complacency, ineptitude, and cruelty, popular unrest due to high unemployment, and rising middle-class discontent. On January 1, 1959, a victorious Fidel rode triumphantly into Havana on a tank given Batista by the United States.[102]

As with China a decade earlier, Americans later played the blame game of who "lost" Cuba, some claiming that the Eisenhower administration should have seen Castro for what he was and nipped his movement in the bud, others insisting that it should have been more accepting of his revolution.[103] In truth, likely neither approach would have worked. There is no persuasive evidence that Castro entered Havana in January 1959 committed to a Marxist revolution. In any event, until this time the United States had been preoccupied with crises in the Middle East and elsewhere. It complacently assumed that Batista would prevail or, in the unlikely event Castro won out, as with previous Cuban leaders, he could not survive without U.S. backing. On the other hand, it is easy to exaggerate U.S. hostility. The United States was tainted by its long-standing support of Batista, to be sure, and it might have broken with him earlier. But it eventually cut off aid and pressed him to step down. Washington

100. Shelby Downing Lynn, "An American Playground: Eisenhower's Foreign Economic Policy of Tourism in Cuba and the Downfall of U.S.-Cuban Relations" (M.A. thesis, University of Kentucky, 2006), 15–36.

101. Thomas G. Paterson, *Contesting Castro: The United States and the Triumph of the Cuban Revolution* (New York, 1994), 15–65.

102. Ibid., 241–54.

103. Richard E. Welch Jr., *Response to Revolution: The United States and the Cuban Revolution, 1959–1961* (Chapel Hill, N.C., 1985).

was wary of Castro from the outset, but initially the bearded rebel in olive green combat fatigues was an object of fascination more than of hostility. Some Americans sympathized with his revolution. Eisenhower sent Philip Bonsal, an open-minded career diplomat, to Havana to work with Castro. In April 1959, when Washington welcomed him for an official visit, Nixon still hoped that the United States might "orient him in the right direction."[104] This, of course, was the rub. Castro was determined to free Cuba of U.S. domination and in time saw the Soviet Union as a means to that end. In the tension-ridden Cold War environment of 1959–60, any move in that direction was anathema to the United States.

The two sides soon fixed on a collision course. Castro aroused U.S. suspicions not long after taking power by legalizing the Communist Party and welcoming leftists to his government. He drove off moderates and conducted show trials and public executions of Batista supporters, provoking outrage in the United States. He began to expropriate land and nationalize basic industries and sought to purchase weapons from Soviet-bloc nations. On a second, highly publicized visit to the United States in late 1959 he denounced U.S. imperialism before the United Nations. Perhaps most ominously, he advocated a Nasser-like neutralism and called for revolution throughout Latin America. The United States maintained the arms embargo imposed on Batista and vigorously protested Castro's nationalization and expropriations. It increasingly feared that the contagion of Cuba's revolution might spread through Latin America. As tension heightened, Castro in early 1960 pursued a bold option not open to previous Cuban revolutionaries by seeking a trade deal with the Soviet Union. Eagerly seizing this rare opportunity to gain an ally at America's back door, Soviet leaders responded positively—"we felt like boys again," one official later told an American.[105] For Washington, Castro's move toward Moscow was the last straw. Labeling the Cuban a "madman," Eisenhower decided in March 1960 that he must go. Not wanting to overthrow him without an alternative available, the administration began to organize an opposition to prepare the way for a Guatemala-type operation.[106]

In response to this new challenge, the Eisenhower administration in its last months executed a reverse course in Latin America, mounting the most active approach to the hemisphere since the Good Neighbor policy. After years of coddling dictators, it publicly encouraged representative

---

104. Stephen G. Rabe, *Eisenhower and Latin America: The Foreign Policy of Anticommunism* (Chapel Hill, N.C., 1988), 124.
105. Dean Rusk as told to Richard Rusk, *As I Saw It* (New York, 1990), 245.
106. Paterson, *Contesting Castro*, 255–58.

government and actively supported moderate reformists such as Venezuela's Romulo Betancourt. It cut back and attempted to redirect the focus of the military aid programs that had drained resources desperately needed for development and helped keep brutal dictators in power. Belatedly conceding that economic deprivation provided a fertile breeding ground for Communism, it embraced aid programs it had once spurned. It acquiesced in commodity arrangements to help stabilize prices for Latin American exports such as coffee and raw materials. In the summer of 1960, it created a Social Progress Trust Fund of $500 million to promote medical, education, and land reform programs, not exactly the Marshall Plan Latin American leaders had pleaded for but a big step beyond earlier policies and a foundation for John F. Kennedy's Alliance for Progress.[107]

While seeking to improve relations with other Latin American nations, the United States set out to eliminate Castro. It launched full-scale economic warfare, including a virtual trade embargo, broke diplomatic relations, and sought to mobilize opposition to his regime among other Latin American nations. As in Guatemala, it mounted a propaganda campaign to incite rebellion in Cuba. It also began to organize political opposition among anti-Castro exiles and to arm and train an exile force for an invasion of Cuba. The CIA hatched a variety of plots to discredit and even assassinate Castro. Recognizing that the Batista-like and increasingly egomaniacal Rafael Trujillo posed the danger of another Castro in the Dominican Republic, the administration prepared a parallel set of actions to get rid of him.[108] After years of official U.S. indifference, Latin America, by virtue of Communism, Caracas, and Castro, was back at the top of the U.S. foreign policy agenda.

V

Cuba was not the only problem facing the Eisenhower administration in its last years. The world of the late 1950s was increasingly complex and infinitely more dangerous. Conflict between the Soviet Union and China, although still not out in the open, intensified at the end of the decade, complicating ties between the two Communist powers and their relations with the United States. The relentless advance of technology raised growing fears of a nuclear war no one might win. Eisenhower and Khrushchev saw the need to ease Cold War tensions, but their cautious moves in that direction confused as much as they clarified relations between the superpowers.

107. Rabe, *Eisenhower and Latin America*, 140–52.
108. Ibid., 134–69.

The Cold War had a gained momentum of its own. The two leaders' initial steps toward what would later be called detente ran afoul of hard-line critics in each nation, institutional and economic imperatives, and conflicts in other parts of the world. Taking control of U.S. foreign policy after Dulles's death in May 1959, Eisenhower responded prudently and with admirable restraint to the multiple challenges of his last years, but at times he appeared to be reacting to events rather than shaping them. On occasion, he seemed to be stumbling. Remembering their 1952 electoral defeat, Democrats attacked the administration for allowing the nation to fall behind technologically and responding ineffectually to the Communist menace. The administration left office in 1961 in much the same milieu in which it had come to power in 1953—with the roles of the two parties reversed.

Nothing fed public anxieties and the political turmoil of the late 1950s more than the rising threat of nuclear war and concerns, often politically inspired, that the United States was lagging behind the USSR in technology. Nuclear weapons had been the centerpiece of the administration's New Look defense strategy, and Dulles often boasted that massive retaliation had won major Cold War victories. But in the second term, the reliance on nuclear weapons drew fire from different directions. Critics questioned the wisdom of a grand strategy based on such weapons when the other side also possessed them. Europeans correctly feared they might bear the brunt of a Soviet response in the event of a nuclear exchange and could not but question U.S. dependence on nuclear weapons. The impact on Japanese fishermen of radioactive fallout from a U.S. nuclear explosion in the Pacific highlighted growing popular fears about the dangers. Nevil Shute's 1957 novel *On the Beach* told the grisly story of the destruction of the world by nuclear war. Organized by internationalists and liberal pacifists the same year, the Committee for a SANE Nuclear Policy (SANE) drew support from many celebrities and held rallies and protest marches demanding an end to atmospheric nuclear testing, steps toward nuclear disarmament, and international control of atomic energy. Intellectuals and political leaders across the world took up the cause.[109]

The New Look also provoked opposition from the other end of the political spectrum. Army officers and a growing body of civilian defense intellectuals increasingly warned that the reliance on nuclear weapons narrowed the nation's options to launching nuclear war or doing nothing. Especially as the Cold War shifted to the Third World, critics of massive retaliation called for building up conventional forces and developing capabilities for dealing with insurgencies. With total war threatening

109. Osgood, *Total Cold War*, 200.

nuclear annihilation, political scientist Robert Osgood insisted that limited war was the only rational alternative. Democratic senators Stuart Symington of Missouri, John F. Kennedy of Massachusetts, and Henry Jackson of Washington, arguing on the basis of badly flawed intelligence, warned that while relying on nuclear weapons the administration had allowed the United States to fall behind the Soviet Union in its means of delivering them. Charges of a "bomber gap" surfaced as early as 1954, accompanied by demands that the United States undertake a massive building program to outstrip the Soviets in nuclear weapons and develop invulnerable delivery systems.[110]

More than anything else, the *Sputnik* "crisis" shaped the American mood of the late 1950s. On October 4, 1957, with maximum fanfare and propaganda, the Soviet Union put into orbit with a huge R-7 intercontinental ballistic missile the world's first artificial satellite, a monumental scientific accomplishment. A month later, it orbited a much larger instrument carrying a live dog. The launch of *Sputnik I* and *Sputnik II* shook the United States to its core. The superiority of U.S. science was assumed to be the bedrock of the nation's security. What the *New York Daily News* called "Khrushchev's comet" appeared to undermine the basic principles of massive retaliation and the New Look—and add substance to Soviet rocket-rattling.[111] Much like Pearl Harbor, it created a sense of profound vulnerability, raising fears that turned to near panic. *Sputnik* even provoked questions among Americans and across the world whether the Soviet system might be superior to that of the United States, a huge problem in the ongoing global competition for hearts and minds. The explosion of an American rocket on its launch pad just weeks later ("Kaputnik," "Stayputnik," Americans nervously called it) added humiliation—and fear. The report of a blue-ribbon panel headed by H. Rowland Gaither Jr., presented to Eisenhower in November and leaked in part to the public, reinforced popular anxiety by painting a frightening picture of the inadequacy of the nation's defenses and calling for a Manhattan Project–like program for missile development and even the construction of fallout shelters. A call to arms much like NSC-68, the Gaither Report, according to the *Washington Post*, portrayed a "United States in the gravest danger in its history."[112] The *Sputnik* panic evoked calls from intellectuals for a refocus from the self-absorption in the era's consumer culture to a higher national purpose.

110. Robert E. Osgood, *Limited War: The Challenge for U.S. Policy* (Boston, 1957); Allan R. Millett and Peter Maslowski, *For the Common Defense: A Military History of the United States of America* (New York, 1984), 511–30.
111. Fursenko and Naftali, *Khrushchev's Cold War*, 151.
112. Chester J. Pach, *The Presidency of Dwight D. Eisenhower* (Lawrence, Kans., 1991), 173.

Eisenhower handled the *Sputnik* crisis with admirable calm and self-assurance. High-altitude U-2 spy planes flying over the USSR since 1956 provided up-to-date intelligence on Soviet military capabilities. The president knew—although he could not divulge it publicly—that while the Kremlin had scored a huge short-term propaganda victory, its missiles could not reach the United States. The USSR remained well behind in nuclear warheads, bombers, and even long-range missile technology. He had long feared that excessive military spending would require additional taxes, hold back capital accumulation, retard industrial growth, and risk a garrison state that could threaten American democracy. Through a series of speeches, he sought to reassure the nation that its defenses could deter any Soviet attack. He muted criticism by taking modest steps, a small increase in defense spending to calm public opinion and creation of the National Aeronautics and Space Administration (NASA) to promote space exploration. He supported feel-good and ultimately significant programs to advance U.S. education, especially in science, mathematics, engineering, and foreign languages—one of them revealingly entitled the National Defense Education Act. He ordered the construction of a super-secret underground bunker complex three stories deep and the size of two football fields adjacent to the posh Greenbrier Hotel in rural West Virginia where Congress could conduct the nation's business in the event of nuclear attack. But he firmly and courageously resisted the crash programs and massive spending called for by the military and panicky citizens. He would not commit billions of dollars to beat the Russians to the moon. His refusal to bend to popular pressures had a political cost, of course, permitting Democrats to continue to exploit charges of a defenseless America.[113]

While the nation agonized over *Sputnik*, the Cold War raged across the world. In distant Tibet, site of the mythical Shangri-La, fierce Khampa tribesmen, trained in Colorado by the CIA and parachuted back into their homeland, fought a "pinprick" war against Chinese occupation forces. The rebels gained valuable intelligence about China's nascent nuclear program. They also suffered horrendous losses—like "throwing meat into a tiger's mouth," one guerrilla conceded. The enterprise was generally counterproductive. The guerrillas did enough to annoy China but never threatened its control; U.S. support for them enabled the Chinese to use an external threat as an excuse to invade Tibet in 1959.[114]

113. Osgood, *Total Cold War*, 336–53.
114. "A Secret War on the Roof of the World," *Newsweek*, August 19, 1999, 34–35; John Kenneth Knaus, *Orphans of the Cold War: America and the Tibetan Struggle for Survival* (New York, 2002).

Certain that the mercurial Sukarno's neutralism exposed Indonesia to a possible Communist takeover, Eisenhower and Dulles in 1957 began covert support for rebel forces on the islands of Sumatra and Sulawesi. The CIA delivered arms by submarine and airdrop, and in 1958 U.S. and Taiwanese "volunteer" pilots began to provide air support. Unlike Mosaddeq and Árbenz, Sukarno hung tough and the Indonesian Army outfought the rebels. The U.S. hand was revealed in May 1958 when American pilot Allen Pope was shot down and captured. Eisenhower's claims that Pope was a soldier of fortune fooled no one. An embarrassed administration had to scrap an already faltering covert operation. The United States' involvement actually strengthened Sukarno and the Indonesian Communist Party. When the Soviets began large arms sales to Sukarno, the administration, to retain some influence in Indonesia, did the same. The debacle in Indonesia was an unnoted harbinger of things to come.[115]

Old Cold War hot spots flared up again in 1958. A second Taiwan Straits crisis erupted in August when China resumed shelling Quemoy and Matsu. Mao hoped to demonstrate his independence from Moscow and derail any Soviet tilt toward the United States. Thinking in conventional Cold War terms and fearing an all-out attack by Mao—or Chiang Kai-shek—Eisenhower and Dulles took a tough line. In his last go at brinkmanship, a gravely ill Dulles threatened war while the president briefly pondered using tactical nuclear weapons against Chinese airfields. Mao terrified Soviet diplomats by appearing to welcome a U.S. attack. Maneuvering skillfully amidst these conflicting forces, Eisenhower committed the United States to defending Quemoy and Matsu while leaving an opening for the Chinese. Having used the islands as a baton to make Khrushchev and Eisenhower dance, as he put it, Mao backed off. Sino-American ambassadorial talks resumed in Warsaw. Eisenhower's diplomacy provoked a backlash from some Democrats and European leaders who feared his actions might spark a war over worthless Asian real estate and from supporters of Taiwan who smelled appeasement.[116]

The United States encountered problems with allies as well as enemies. As Japan grew stronger economically and recovered from the trauma of defeat, sentiment increased for revision of the 1952 treaty. Japanese compared that pact to the unequal treaties of the past century. They resented the continued presence of more than two hundred thousand

---

115. Audrey R. Kahin and George McT. Kahin, *Subversion as Foreign Policy: The Secret Eisenhower and Dulles Debacle in Indonesia* (New York, 1995), 166–206.

116. Taubman, *Khrushchev*, 392; Robert A. Divine, *Eisenhower and the Cold War* (New York, 1981), 66–70.

U.S. "occupation" troops, highlighted by a much publicized 1957 incident in which a GI brutally shot a Japanese woman picking up shell casings on an American firing range. They feared the treaty might drag their nation into war with the Soviet Union or China. Vividly remembering Hiroshima and Nagasaki, they especially feared the presence of U.S. nuclear weapons on their territory. With typical, superheated Cold War rhetoric, Ambassador John Allison warned Washington that if relations were not soon put on a more equal basis Japan might slip away.[117]

Eisenhower moved expeditiously to stabilize relations with a crucial ally. In 1957, he authorized a major CIA covert operation to bolster conservative elements in Japanese politics. The agency bankrolled the Liberal Democratic Party (LDP) to the tune of $2 million to $10 million a year to influence elections for the legislature and secure political intelligence to discredit that party's foes. Such methods represented a blatant intrusion in Japanese politics and abetted the creation and perpetuation of a one-party "democracy."[118] The administration also opened discussions for a new security treaty. To facilitate the process, it voluntarily reduced by more than half the number of troops stationed in Japan and offered generous trade concessions. After months of sometimes difficult negotiations, the two nations in early 1960 concluded an agreement that made concessions to Japan but protected what the United States considered most important. Each side could terminate the treaty after ten years. The United States gave up the right to intervene militarily in Japan's internal affairs, but it could act to protect the security of Japan and the Far East, a vague provision that aroused great concern among Japanese. Japan renewed U.S. base rights, a crucial matter for Washington, but U.S. and Japanese forces could be employed only after consultation, a key issue for Japan. The delicate question of nuclear weapons was addressed in a separate, secret agreement, the existence of which has still not been officially acknowledged or the terms divulged, permitting the United States to move such weapons in and out of Japan.[119] The United States appears to have violated the spirit if not the letter of that agreement by keeping nuclear weapons on Iwo Jima and Chici Jima and housing bombs without cores and nuclear components on bases in Japan.[120] The treaty marked a major change in the Japanese-American relationship.

117. Michael Schaller, *Altered States: The United States and Japan Since the Occupation* (New York, 1997), 123.
118. *New York Times*, October 9, 1994.
119. Schaller, *Alerted States*, 139–41; Walter LaFeber, *The Clash: U.S.-Japanese Relations Throughout History* (New York, 1997), 319–20.
120. *New York Times*, December 12, 1999.

It also provoked a crisis in U.S.-Japanese relations. To be sure, Americans warmly welcomed Prime Minister Kishi Nobosuke to the United States in January 1960, and the Senate approved the treaty without fanfare. But in Japan it became an explosive political issue. The left bitterly protested the continued presence of foreign troops on Japanese soil and warned of being drawn into war with the Soviet Union or China. The Soviet shooting down of a Pakistan-based U.S. spy plane in May, followed by another round of Khrushchev nuclear threats, gave powerful ammunition to foes of the treaty. Thousands of Japanese took to the streets to protest the alliance and Eisenhower's scheduled June visit. For a while, both governments stood firm, but in the face of rising protest and violence the United States agreed to Kishi's request for postponement. The president authorized the CIA to take additional measures to firm up the position of the LDP and promote the treaty. The agency also funded right-wing hit groups to harass leftist protestors. Democrats complained of yet another embarrassing defeat. Editorialists deplored cancellation of Eisenhower's visit as a "serious challenge to American prestige and a threat to our entire position in Asia."[121]

In the meantime, Khrushchev triggered yet another crisis over that perennial Cold War flash point West Berlin. For the Soviet leadership, in the premier's colorful imagery, Berlin was a "bone in the throat," a "malignant tumor" that required "some surgery."[122] It provided an escape hatch for thousands of skilled workers who fled to the West, damaging the East German economy and embarrassing the USSR in a contest where symbols had become increasingly important. Khrushchev also perceived that Berlin was among his adversaries' most vulnerable positions—"the testicles of the West," he called it. "Every time I give them a yank, they holler."[123] Now more secure in the Kremlin hierarchy, the Soviet leader interpreted as a victory U.S. refusal in July 1958 to send troops to Iraq to uphold the pro-Western government, further bolstering his self-confidence and confirming his view that threats and pressure were the only language the West understood. Exhibiting both his "peasant logic" and his reckless, sometimes bizarre, diplomatic style—he compared it to playing chess in the dark—in November 1958 he squeezed hard by demanding that West Berlin be made a free city (a city governed autonomously under international agreement).[124] If the Western allies did not comply within six

---

121. Schaller, *Alerted States*, 159.
122. Taubman, *Khrushchev*, 396–97.
123. Pach, *Eisenhower Presidency*, 200.
124. Taubman, *Khrushchev*, 402.

months, he would conclude a separate peace with East Germany, terminating the World War II four-power arrangements and leaving the question of access to West Berlin in the hands of his East German ally. Khrushchev's confused and risky diplomacy was designed to scare the West into serious negotiations and wangle an invitation to visit the United States for a summit meeting. But his move was poorly thought out and characteristically impulsive. If it failed, he casually remarked to his son, "Then, we'll try something else."[125]

Eisenhower agreed that Berlin was a "can of worms." He also was eager to settle the volatile German question. But he could not appear to give in to Soviet threats. He rebuffed hawkish proposals from his military advisers but stood firm on Berlin. He ordered a quiet military buildup while calmly reassuring the nation. Khrushchev's ultimatum expired May 27, 1959—ironically, the day John Foster Dulles was buried—without any comment from Moscow. The crisis eased momentarily, but Berlin would remain the most explosive spot in world politics for the next few years.

Even as the Berlin crisis smoldered, the major powers inched toward the first Cold War agreement on nuclear weapons. Initial discussions emanating from the 1955 Geneva summit went nowhere. Eisenhower was at best lukewarm, believing that real disarmament would come only after the Cold War had been won. Nuclear testing was the most pressing issue, and the United States refused to deal with it except as part of a larger agreement that included on-site inspections, a provision the Kremlin seemed sure to reject. Moscow linked a ban on nuclear testing to a sweeping ban on all nuclear weapons, an offer the United States turned down because of its inferiority in conventional forces. The deadlock provided ample room for propaganda moves, and Moscow took full advantage. In late 1957, Bulganin proposed suspension of nuclear testing for two to three years along with a summit to discuss other disarmament issues. In January 1958, Khrushchev proclaimed Soviet intentions to cut conventional forces by three hundred thousand troops; two months later, he announced a unilateral suspension of nuclear testing.[126]

Within a year, both sides took dramatic steps forward. Even as he sought to exploit nuclear threats, Khrushchev increasingly saw the dangers of nuclear war. Keenly aware that military spending was holding back Soviet economic development, to which he was deeply committed, he sought

125. Ibid., 399.
126. Osgood, *Total Cold War*, 199–205; Martha Smith-Norris, "The Eisenhower Administration and the Nuclear Test Ban Talks, 1958–1960: Another Challenge to 'Revisionism,' " *Diplomatic History* 27 (September 2003), 509.

agreements that would enable him to divert precious resources to domestic needs. Eisenhower still dragged his feet. He did not trust the Soviets to abide by agreements that lacked the sort of inspections they were sure to reject. The Department of Defense and the Atomic Energy Commission adamantly insisted that testing was essential to U.S. national security. On the other hand, domestic and international pressures for test bans increased dramatically, and the president began to see other benefits. A test ban would be relatively easy to monitor, and Soviet acceptance of inspections might generate other intelligence to help guard against a surprise attack. A testing agreement might help check the spread of nuclear weapons to other nations, a growing concern in Moscow as well as Washington. After another uproar over the dangers of nuclear fallout, Eisenhower belatedly committed to suspending atmospheric testing and subsequently underground testing above the "threshold" of 4.75 on the Richter scale. "We have got to try to make some progress somewhere in the disarmament area," he exclaimed.[127] His stand helped get the Anglo-American-Soviet talks in motion. By early 1960, the major unresolved issue concerned the number of on-site inspections.[128]

Khrushchev's fall 1959 visit to the United States provided further hope for easing Cold War tensions. Eisenhower acceded to Khrushchev's wish to come to the United States reluctantly and mainly because a State Department official—without authorization—had extended an unconditional invitation. The affair was grand Cold War theater, a first-class media event before the phrase was coined. Barely five feet tall, portly, and balding, Khrushchev did not present an imposing figure. Limited in education, profoundly insecure, and determined to prove himself, the ebullient, bumptious, and unpredictable Soviet leader this time arrived in a humongous aircraft so high off the ground that the passengers had to exit from an emergency ramp. He showed poor taste in presenting his host a model of the latest Soviet space achievement. He bristled at tough questions from U.S. reporters about Hungary. "I do not have horns," he goaded a New York audience.[129] He complained that he was not permitted to visit Disneyland and protested—perhaps too much—the scanty apparel worn by actresses on the set of the movie *Can-Can*. He also displayed flashes of folksy charm. The two-week visit ended with private top-level talks at Camp David, the presidential retreat in the Maryland mountains. Ever nervous, Khrushchev worried that the hideaway named for Eisenhower's

127. Smith-Norris, "Nuclear Test Ban Talks," 535.
128. Osgood, *Total Cold War*, 206–10.
129. Fursenko and Naftali, *Khrushchev's Cold War*, 232.

grandson might be some kind of internment center. Perhaps surprisingly, the talks went smoothly. The Soviet premier came to see the president as someone he could work with. He withdrew his Berlin ultimatum—sort of—and Eisenhower vaguely agreed that the status of the city must change. Khrushchev also concluded that his grand scheme for improved relations was workable. The scheduling of a four-power summit for Paris in May 1960 followed by an Eisenhower visit to Moscow brought forth talk of a "spirit of Camp David" and worldwide hopes for peace.[130]

It was not to be. On May 1, two weeks before the summit was to begin and just as May Day celebrations were starting in Moscow, a Soviet surface-to-air missile shot down a U-2 spy plane over the village of Povarnia in the Ural Mountains. Both sides handled the incident badly. Eisenhower had long been uneasy about the U-2 flights, recognizing that they constituted an act of war. He consented to this particular flight only at the insistence of the military and the CIA and with assurances there would be no problems for the summit. For Khrushchev, the overflights had been especially humiliating. Still clinging to hopes for a productive summit, he blamed the hard-liners around Eisenhower. He hoped to capitalize on the triumph of shooting down the plane without destroying the summit, but he could not resist the temptation to overreach. He initially concealed that the pilot, Francis Gary Powers, had been taken alive and parts of the aircraft recovered, catching Washington in a lie when the usual explanations were issued of a weather plane straying off course. Eisenhower then compounded the problem by admitting to the spy flights without acknowledging that he had approved Powers's mission. Khrushchev's loud denunciation of the U.S. military for ordering the flight, perhaps intended to give Eisenhower a way out, instead forced the president to accept responsibility to make clear that he was in charge, thus undercutting Khrushchev's efforts to portray him as someone Moscow could deal with. Furious that Eisenhower had accepted responsibility, thus ruining his own scheme, an increasingly agitated Khrushchev once in Paris spewed forth a vitriolic, highly personal, forty-five-minute attack on the president. He demanded a formal apology and promises of no more violations of Soviet airspace. Publicly, the president struggled to contain his fury. Privately, he denounced Khrushchev as a "son-of-a-bitch" and refused even to speak his name.[131] He agreed to suspend the U-2 flights, no huge concession since spy satellites would soon take their place. But he refused to apologize, believing that Khrushchev would have to give way to save the

130. Ibid., 232–41; Taubman, *Khrushchev*, 419–41.
131. Pach, *Eisenhower Presidency*, 219.

summit. After days of frenzied efforts by British and French leaders to salvage something, the meeting broke up in anger. Whether the Paris meeting might have accomplished anything without the U-2 incident can never be known. The two sides still differed sharply on Berlin and disarmament. What is certain is that the "U-2 mess," as Eisenhower referred to it, destroyed the summit, cost the president and the United States heavily in prestige, ended any chance of substantive negotiations before the November elections, and left Berlin more dangerous than ever.[132]

The Cold War played an important part in the 1960 presidential campaign. The U-2 affair, Castro's move toward the USSR, the cancellation of Eisenhower's trip to Japan, and a summer crisis in the newly independent Congo all kept the nation's attention focused on foreign policy. Khrushchev's stormy autumn visit to the United States, complete with a fiery speech before the United Nations and the bizarre spectacle of the Soviet premier removing his shoe and pounding it furiously on the podium— amusing, had it not seemed so ominous—kept the Cold War threat very much alive for Americans. Following themes his party had exploited since *Sputnik*, Democratic candidate John Kennedy repeatedly criticized the Republicans for permitting the nation to fall behind militarily and suffer a huge loss of prestige in the world. He called for "new men to cope with new problems and new opportunities."[133] While touting his own proximity to power and foreign policy résumé, the Republican candidate, Vice President Nixon, questioned Kennedy's experience, maturity, and judgment. In the nation's first televised presidential debates and countless stump speeches, the candidates tangled over hot-button foreign policy issues. Kennedy questioned the wisdom of Nixon's commitment to defend Quemoy and Matsu, an entirely sensible stance but one the vice president cleverly twisted to depict his opponent as an appeaser. The Massachusetts senator blasted the Eisenhower administration for failing to prevent the rise of Castro. JFK won the election by a razor-thin margin, gaining a majority of neither the popular vote nor the states. He effectively hammered home his point about the nation's decline of prestige and played on Americans' fears of military weakness, but he nearly lost by mishandling foreign policy issues late in the campaign. What stands out in retrospect is the broad area of agreement between the two candidates, a clear reflection of the dominance of the Cold War consensus.[134]

132. Fursenko and Naftali, *Khrushchev's Cold War*, 287–91.
133. Robert A. Divine, *Foreign Policy and U.S. Presidential Elections, 1952–1960* (New York, 1974), 218.
134. Ibid., 283–87.

EISENHOWER'S STOCK HAS RISEN markedly in recent years. No longer dismissed as an intellectual lightweight and political babe-in-the-woods, he is generally recognized as a self-assured and prudent leader who understood politics and, having seen war firsthand, appreciated the limits of military power.[135] Despite frequent crises and the recurrent threat of war, he managed to keep the peace during his time in office. He worked out with the European allies and the Soviet Union the basis for a viable if by no means perfect settlement in Europe—Berlin, of course, the major exception—the foundation for what historian John Lewis Gaddis has called the "Long Peace."[136] He adjusted America's relations with its crucial East Asian ally Japan in the direction of a more equal partnership, not always easy for a hegemonic power to do. He avoided open-ended military commitments and took the first hesitant steps toward nuclear arms limitations. Even during the post-*Sputnik* hysteria, he remained calm and kept the military budget under some semblance of control. He perceived and feared the way the Cold War was reshaping the U.S. economy and in his farewell address warned of the rising power of a military-industrial complex.

As critics have pointed out, to stop there is to provide only a one-dimensional assessment of Eisenhower's foreign policy legacy.[137] Not surprisingly, given the New Look reliance on nuclear weapons, the U.S. nuclear arsenal grew to elephantine proportions during his presidency. By 1961, the United States had more than two thousand bombers, one hundred missiles, with many more on the planning board, and submarines capable of launching rockets with nuclear warheads. From 1958 to 1960 alone, the number of nuclear weapons increased from six thousand to eighteen thousand, overkill by any standard. Much like Truman and Acheson, Eisenhower failed most notably in dealing with Third World nationalism. He and his advisers persisted in viewing the new nations primarily in terms of the Cold War. They exaggerated the Soviet threat. They never fully appreciated the primal force of nationalism, the

135. Leading Eisenhower "revisionists" include Divine, *Eisenhower and the Cold War*, Fred I. Greenstein, *The Hidden-Hand Presidency: Eisenhower as Leader* (New York, 1982), and Stephen E. Ambrose, *Eisenhower*, vol. 2, *The President* (New York, 1984).

136. John Lewis Gaddis, *The Long Peace: An Inquiry into the History of the Cold War* (New York, 1987), 216–26, discusses the sources of Cold War stability.

137. Robert J. McMahon, "Eisenhower and Third World Nationalism: A Critique of the Revisionists," *Political Science Quarterly* 101, no. 3, 453–73; Stephen G. Rabe, "Eisenhower Revisionism: A Decade of Scholarship," *Diplomatic History* 17 (Winter 1993), 97–115.

new nations' entirely understandable hypersensitivity to outside influence, especially Western, and their neutralist tendencies. In the Middle East and South Asia, the administration exacerbated regional tensions and aroused sometimes fierce anti-Americanism. It tightened U.S. ties with right-wing dictatorships in South Korea and Taiwan, thus inhibiting its foreign policy flexibility and making adjustments with the People's Republic of China next to impossible. It avoided military intervention in Vietnam in 1954, but its subsequent political commitments to South Vietnam left difficult decisions about war for future leaders. Its rampant interventionism, including assassination plots against numerous Third World leaders and the overthrow of popularly elected governments, seemed necessary—and in some cases successful—at the time but violated long-standing U.S. principles and had baneful long-term consequences in terms of "blowback" for the peoples involved and for the United States. For the short term, with Cuba and Berlin unresolved and Americans increasingly anxious, the administration bequeathed its successor problems that would lead to the most dangerous period of the Cold War.

16

Gulliver's Troubles

Kennedy, Johnson, and the Limits of Power, 1961–1968

In his inaugural address, delivered on a blustery, bitterly cold day in January 1961, John F. Kennedy set forth in the starkest terms his nation's universalist approach to foreign policy in the heyday of the Cold War. The United States, he vowed, would "pay any price, bear any burden, meet any hardship, support any friend, oppose any foe, in order to assure the survival and success of liberty."[1] In practice, Kennedy found the world much less susceptible to U.S. influence than his soaring inaugural rhetoric proclaimed. By the time of his November 1963 assassination, he had begun to reassess some of the most basic Cold War assumptions. But it was his successor, Lyndon Baines Johnson, who would confront head-on the limits of U.S. power in a changing international system. LBJ's drastic 1965 escalation of the war in Vietnam produced no more than a stalemate. His withdrawal from the presidential race on March 31, 1968, just seven years after Kennedy's inauguration, the product in large part of simultaneous foreign policy crises in North Korea, the world economy, and Vietnam, made clear the inability of the nation to bear the burden as Kennedy had pledged. March 1968, in the words of authors Evan Thomas and Walter Isaacson, represented the "high-water mark of U.S. [postwar] hegemony."[2]

I

Kennedy was only forty-three years old when he assumed the presidency, and his accession marked the coming of age of the World War II generation. The son of a wealthy Boston Irish financier and former ambassador to England, the new president, a war hero himself, was strikingly handsome, bright, witty, charming, and ambitious. He attained no better than a lackluster record in the Senate and was looked upon—with good reason—as a playboy. Indeed, as president, he recklessly carried on dalliances with

---

1. JFK's inaugural address, January 20, 1961, may be conveniently found at www.bartleby.com124/pres56.html.
2. Walter Isaacson and Evan Thomas, *The Wise Men: Six Friends and the World They Made* (New York, 1986), 699.

secretaries, movie stars, and even a Mafia moll. As a senator, he did acquire some foreign policy expertise, taking a special interest in decolonization. He consciously styled his presidency after his illustrious Democratic predecessors Woodrow Wilson and Franklin Roosevelt. At home he committed himself to an extension of FDR's New Deal, the New Frontier, he called it. Like many of his generation, he was certain that foreign policy was the most exciting and urgent challenge a president faced. "I mean who gives a shit if the minimum wage is $1.15 or $1.25," he confided to kindred spirit (at least on that issue) Richard Nixon.[3]

In foreign policy, JFK sought to recapture the blend of idealism and pragmatism that had stamped FDR's leadership in World War II. He gathered about him a young, energetic corps of advisers from the top echelons of academia and business, self-confident, activist men—"action intellectuals," they were called—who shared his determination to "get the country moving again." The youthful and acerbic Harvard College dean and Henry Stimson protégé McGeorge Bundy was named national security adviser; World War II systems analysis "whiz kid" and Ford Motor Company boss Robert McNamara, secretary of defense. The president's younger brother, Attorney General Robert Kennedy, became his alter ego and closest adviser, even on foreign policy. In the aftermath of the Vietnam debacle, they would be labeled—with more than a touch of irony—the "best and the brightest."[4]

The dynamics of policymaking changed significantly. Appointment of the soft-spoken and retiring Georgian Dean Rusk as secretary of state suggested that the president, like FDR, planned to keep the reins of foreign policy tightly in his own hands. Kennedy quickly scrapped Eisenhower's formal, highly bureaucratized National Security Council structure in favor of a more freewheeling apparatus that left him at the center of decision-making and assured him the widest range of options. In the eyes of critics, the new system was disorderly, even chaotic, failed to ensure follow-up, and left major players uninformed. Under Bundy, an enlarged and reinvigorated NSC supplanted State as the key player in foreign affairs.[5]

The military's role became especially contentious. Civil-military relations deteriorated sharply in the Kennedy years, manifested in the popular culture through such films as *Seven Days in May* and *Dr. Strangelove*,

3. Robert Dallek, *An Unfinished Life: John F. Kennedy, 1917–1963* (New York, 2003), 370.
4. David Halberstam, *The Best and the Brightest* (New York, 1972).
5. David J. Rothkopf, *Running the World: The Inside Story of the National Security Council and the Architects of American Power* (New York, 2004), 84–85, 92–93.

which warned respectively of a military coup and a U.S.-initiated nuclear war brought about through a combination of military madness, standard operating procedures, and ingenuity. Youthful and insecure civilian leaders feared the growing power of the top brass, its ties to right-wing politicians, and its clout in Congress. They fretted about the Joint Chiefs' lack of political sophistication and their perceived eagerness to employ nuclear weapons. Military leaders such as the cigar-chomping Air Force Chief of Staff Gen. Curtis LeMay scarcely concealed their contempt for the inexperienced civilians in the White House, especially the Ivy League intellectuals—"the computer types," Gen. Thomas Powers snarled, who "don't know their ass from a hole in the ground."[6] From the outset, Kennedy struggled to keep the military in line without provoking open rebellion.

The New Frontiersmen accepted without question the basic assumptions of the containment policy. They perceived the tensions between Moscow and Beijing, but they still viewed Communism as monolithic and a mortal threat to the United States. They also believed, as Kennedy put it, that they must "move forward to meet Communism, rather than waiting for it to come to us and then reacting to it."[7] Coming of age during World War II, they feared another global conflagration. They were also exhilarated by the prospect of leading the nation through perilous times to the ultimate victory. They shared a Wilsonian view that destiny had singled out their nation and themselves to defend the democratic ideal. Reflecting the mood of the time, they believed they could do anything—hence the expansive rhetoric of Kennedy's inaugural address and his firm commitment to land an American on the moon. They also recognized the domestic political importance of foreign policy success. During the campaign, JFK had repeatedly charged the Republicans with indecisiveness and promised to regain the upper hand in the Cold War. Elected by a precariously narrow margin, he kept a wary eye on his domestic flank, ever sensitive to opposition charges of appeasement.

Like Eisenhower, Kennedy altered existing Cold War policies mainly in terms of the means to be employed. Although he quickly discovered that the missile gap actually favored the United States, JFK ordered an immediate and massive buildup of nuclear weapons, missile-firing submarines, and long-range missiles to establish clear superiority over the USSR. He also recognized that the frightful consequences of nuclear war

6. Quoted in John Lewis Gaddis, *Strategies of Containment: A Critical Appraisal of Postwar American National Security Policy* (New York, 1982), 251n.
7. Henry Fairlie, *The Kennedy Promise* (New York, 1973), 72.

limited the utility of nuclear weapons. Persuaded by Gen. Maxwell Taylor's book *The Uncertain Trumpet* that Eisenhower's reliance on nuclear weapons had left the United States muscle-bound in many Cold War situations, Kennedy expanded and modernized the nation's conventional forces to permit a "flexible response" to various kinds of threats. Certain that the emerging nations provided the principal battleground for Cold War competition, the administration sought ways to combat guerrilla warfare—"an international disease" the United States must learn to "destroy."[8] The president pushed the military to study counterinsurgency methods and create elite units to employ them. He took particular pride in the green beret worn by the army's Special Forces. He also felt that America must strike at the source of the disease. He pushed for economic and technical assistance programs to eliminate the conditions in which Communism flourished and channel revolutionary forces along democratic paths.

Throughout the campaign, Kennedy had ominously warned of the perils the nation faced, but he himself appears to have been unprepared for the magnitude of the problems. Khrushchev's threat to resolve the status of divided Berlin on his own terms held out the possibility of superpower confrontation. In January 1961, the Soviet premier delivered a seemingly militant speech pledging support for wars of national liberation. In fact, the statement defied Kremlin hard-liners and the Chinese by renouncing nuclear and conventional war. It may even have been intended to reassure the West. To the untutored ears of a new administration, it appeared a virtual declaration of war, and stepped-up Soviet aid to Castro's Cuba and insurgents in the Congo and Laos seemed to confirm the danger.[9] Such was the siege mentality that gripped the White House in early 1961 that the president on one occasion greeted his advisers by grimly asking, "What's gone against us today?"[10]

Cuba was the most vexing problem, and Kennedy early made a fateful decision. He had inherited CIA plans for a covert operation to overthrow Castro. Deferring to the presumed experts in the CIA and the military, the latter of whom had deep but unstated reservations about the workability of the plan, he did not closely scrutinize it. He and his advisers were not disposed to critique something that had been endorsed by one of the great military heroes of the century. The administration had dismantled an NSC organization that might have provided some institutional safeguards

8. Ibid., 132–64.
9. William Taubman, *Khrushchev: The Man and His Era* (New York, 2003), 486–87.
10. Walt Whitman Rostow, *The Diffusion of Power: An Essay on Recent History* (New York, 1972), 170.

against harebrained plots. Rusk did not voice his grave doubts, and Kennedy rebuffed those advisers who expressed skepticism. Despite misgivings himself, he approved the plan in hopes of gaining a major victory in his first months and because not to do so would leave him vulnerable to Republican attacks. To conceal the U.S. role, he refused to provide air support.

Appropriately code-named Bumpy Road, the operation produced what has been aptly called the "perfect failure."[11] Top CIA officials blamed JFK for the debacle for refusing to authorize air support, but the agency's own internal assessment, kept under tight wraps until 1998, told of a plan fatally flawed in conception and execution.[12] The CIA assumed, without any evidence, and incorrectly as it turned out, that a landing of Cuban exiles would trigger an internal insurgency that could topple Castro. Some CIA officials and the Joint Chiefs suppressed their reservations in the expectation that Kennedy, if things went badly, would do what was necessary to succeed, something he had no intention of doing. The plan quickly grew beyond the CIA's capacity to manage it, expanding from a small landing of guerrillas to a full-scale invasion force whose blown cover made plausible deniability an illusion. The exiles were poorly trained, disorganized, and divided among themselves. The air strikes that were to take out Castro's air force did not do so and tipped off the impending invasion. The site was shifted to the Bay of Pigs, an especially inhospitable spot for an amphibious landing. Without air support and asked to execute a withdrawal, the most difficult of military operations, the ragtag exile forces were sitting ducks for Castro's aircraft and well-prepared defenders. After three days of fighting, 140 were killed, 1,189 captured. The only answer to their final, tragic message—"We are out of ammo and fighting on the beach. Please send help"—came in the form of rescue teams who managed to pick up twenty-six survivors.[13]

For the new president, the phrase "Bay of Pigs" became a haunting synonym for humiliation. Kennedy accepted full responsibility—"victory has a hundred fathers and defeat is an orphan," he publicly affirmed—and his approval ratings shot up immediately. But he was shattered by the debacle and furious at the military and CIA for misleading him. He felt personally responsible for the fate of the nearly 1,200 Cubans held by Castro. At home, liberals attacked him for intervening in the internal affairs

11. Trumbull Higgins, *The Perfect Failure: Eisenhower, Kennedy, and the CIA at the Bay of Pigs* (New York, 1987).
12. *New York Times*, February 22, 1998.
13. Ibid.; Lawrence Freedman, *Kennedy's Wars: Berlin, Cuba, Laos, and Vietnam* (New York, 2000), 140–46.

of a sovereign state and jeopardizing the goodwill of other Latin American nations. Conservatives charged him with spinelessness.[14] The invasion took place on Khrushchev's birthday, provoking rage in the Kremlin. Anger changed to incredulity when Kennedy did not finish what he started—"Can he really be that indecisive?" the Soviet premier asked his son. Khrushchev concluded that Kennedy was weak and could be pushed around.[15] The president felt compelled to demonstrate his toughness.

The Bay of Pigs heightened the administration's determination to get rid of Castro. Fiercely competitive, the Kennedy brothers found defeat intolerable, especially at the hands of some one they viewed as a tinhorn dictator. They became obsessed with Castro, for them a cancer that had to be removed. Following the Bay of Pigs, they mounted a multifaceted effort to eliminate him that at times took the form of a personal vendetta. Since the revelation of these activities, attention has focused on the various, often bizarre plots to assassinate the Cuban leader (none apparently carried out) using such things as Mafia hit men, exploding cigars, or poison fountain pens. Such schemes are sensational and morally troubling, to be sure, but they represent a relatively small part of a much more comprehensive program. The United States tightened the economic screws by banning all Cuban imports and pushing its allies to do the same. It sought to isolate Cuba diplomatically within the hemisphere by securing its expulsion from the Organization of American States. Operation Mongoose, a covert operation aimed at Castro's removal was approved in November 1961, run out of the CIA, and monitored by a top-level group that included the attorney general. It developed into the agency's major covert operation; the CIA's Miami outpost, JMWAVE, became the largest in the world. Mongoose began slowly with contingency plans, intelligence gathering, and small-scale sabotage operations to destabilize Cuba. It intensified in the spring of 1962. The CIA and Pentagon concocted schemes for provoking U.S. military intervention, including the *Maine*-like explosion of a U.S. warship, the sinking of a boatload of refugees that could be blamed on Castro, and even holding Cuba responsible if a U.S. space mission failed. Mongoose proceeded in tandem with stepped-up planning for direct U.S. military intervention and massive spring 1962 military exercises in the South Atlantic and Caribbean involving some forty thousand troops and hundreds of ships and planes. There is no evidence that Kennedy had actually decided to intervene militarily in Cuba. Such an option was under consideration, however, and anti-Castro operations

14. James N. Giglio, *The Presidency of John F. Kennedy* (Lawrence, Kans., 1991), 58–59.
15. Taubman, *Khrushchev*, 493.

intensified in the fall of 1962 when the discovery of Soviet missiles in Cuba provoked a full-fledged crisis.[16]

After the Bay of Pigs, Kennedy suffered further frustrations. Incredibly, Laos was second only to Cuba as a foreign policy problem in the administration's early days. In an impossibly complicated and often desultory civil war in that distant, landlocked nation, leftist insurgents backed by North Vietnam and to a lesser extent the Soviet Union seemed on the verge of toppling a U.S.-backed government. Upon leaving office, Eisenhower had privately warned his successor that Laos was the "cork in the bottle" of Southeast Asia.[17] Kennedy initially took a tough stance. The Joint Chiefs proposed sending sixty thousand troops plus air cover and guaranteed victory if authorized to use nuclear weapons. Fearful of a replay of Korea in Laos, wary of military advice after the Bay of Pigs, and alarmed by the chiefs' seemingly casual attitude toward war with China and the use of nuclear weapons, Kennedy in late April rejected intervention. Concluding that a negotiated settlement was the best he could get, he agreed to participate in a conference at Geneva. The decision was eminently sensible. The significance of Laos was at best debatable; in any event, it was no place to fight. It was a logistical nightmare. In the eyes of Americans, its people appeared singularly unwarlike, "a bunch of homosexuals," Eisenhower sneered, a passive, indolent people, "a feeble lot," in the words of JFK's ambassador to Laos, Winthrop Brown. Kennedy himself wondered how he could explain sending troops to faraway Laos and not to nearby Cuba.[18] But the decision to negotiate after taking a firm position reinforced the appearance of weakness and left him vulnerable to hard-liners at home.

A stormy summit with Khrushchev at Vienna added to Kennedy's problems. Over the long term, the June discussions may have helped the two

16. *New York Times*, November 23, 1997; Thomas G. Paterson, "Spinning out of Control: Kennedy's War Against Cuba and the Missile Crisis," in Dennis Merrill and Thomas G. Paterson, eds., *Major Problems in American Foreign Relations*, vol. 2, *Since 1914* (6th ed., Boston, 2005), 401–13; James G. Hershberg, "Before the Missiles of October: Did Kennedy Plan a Military Strike Against Cuba?" *Diplomatic History* 14 (Spring 1990), 163–98.

17. Fred I. Greenstein and Richard H. Immerman, "What Did Eisenhower Tell Kennedy About Indochina? The Politics of Misperception," *Journal of American History* 79 (September 1992), 576.

18. Seth Jacobs, "No Place to Fight a War: Laos and the Evolution of U.S. Policy Toward Vietnam, 1954–1963," in Mark Philip Bradley and Marilyn B. Young, eds., *Making Sense of the Vietnam Wars: Local, National, and Transnational Perspectives* (New York, 2008), 49, 60; Noam Kochavi, "Limited Accommodation, Perpetual Conflict: Kennedy, China, and the Laos Crisis, 1961–1963," *Diplomatic History* 26 (Winter 2002), 108.

men understand each other, but the short-term results were disastrous. The president was in severe pain from various ailments and heavily medicated. Although he spent hours preparing, he was psychologically unready for the encounter. Ignoring the advice of experts, he engaged in fruitless ideological spats with Khrushchev. In substantive discussions, they agreed only on the need for peace in Laos, where neither had significant interests—or influence. They differed on terms for a nuclear test ban. Their discussions on the most pressing and dangerous issue, Berlin, were chilling. Certain that his younger and inexperienced adversary could be bullied, Khrushchev made clear that the status quo on Berlin was unacceptable. Kennedy insisted that the United States would not surrender its rights. Khrushchev renewed the six-month ultimatum and reiterated his threat of a separate peace. If the United States wanted war, he concluded, "let it begin now." "It will be a cold winter," a solemn president retorted.[19]

Kennedy came home severely shaken—Khrushchev "just beat hell out of me," he confided to a friend. Aides testified that for the next few months he was "imprisoned by Berlin." "If he thinks I'm inexperienced and have no guts . . . we won't get anywhere with him," the president said of Khrushchev.[20] Unlike the Bay of Pigs, this time he initiated a full-scale debate among his formal and informal advisers on what to do. Perhaps reliving 1948, hard-line former secretary of state Dean Acheson proposed a major military buildup, a declaration of national emergency, and, if the Soviets restricted access to West Berlin, an airlift and readiness to go to war. Cautious voices urged continued efforts to negotiate. As on so many issues, Kennedy came down in the middle. In a major speech on July 25, he hinted at a willingness to negotiate. But he also made clear U.S. determination to defend Western rights in Berlin and proposed a major military buildup. Stopping short of a declaration of national emergency, he announced another big jump in defense spending and an increase in draft calls, a reserve call-up, and extended enlistments to expand the armed forces. Most alarming, he pushed for a federal program to assist in the building of fallout shelters.

Kennedy's speech ratcheted up an already dangerous crisis by several notches. Khrushchev denounced it as a "preliminary declaration of war" and warned an American visitor with ties to the president that "we will meet war with war."[21] To underscore the seriousness of the crisis, he

19. Giglio, *Kennedy Presidency*, 74–78; Taubman, *Khrushchev*, 493–500.
20. Michael R. Beschloss, *The Crisis Years: Kennedy and Khrushchev, 1960–1963* (New York, 1991), 225.
21. Taubman, *Khrushchev*, 501–2.

decided to resume nuclear testing. His threats did nothing to resolve the immediate problem in East Berlin, where during July alone more than twenty-six thousand East Germans fled to the West. Picking up on discreet signals from Washington that the United States would not interfere in *East* Berlin, the Soviet Union and East Germany decided to stop the "hemorrhaging" by building a wall to seal off East Germany from West Berlin. Construction began without warning on Sunday, August 13, 1961, starting with barbed wire and then adding concrete blocks once it was clear the West would do nothing.

Ironically, what became one of the most conspicuous, ugly, and despised symbols of the Cold War was at first greeted by some Americans with a sense of relief. To be sure, some hotheads urged knocking the wall down before it was finished despite the obvious risk of war. In fact, few were willing to risk war and some actually accepted the wall as a way to ease tensions. Kremlinologists advised Kennedy that it was Khrushchev's way of defusing an increasingly explosive situation. Thus while dispatching Vice President Lyndon Johnson and former occupation commander Gen. Lucius Clay to West Berlin and sending troops through East Germany into the city to reaffirm the U.S. commitment, the administration acquiesced. "A wall is a hell of a lot better than a war," Kennedy privately mused.[22]

Although it brought the superpowers back from the brink, the wall did not resolve the fundamental issues. Following the summer crisis, Kennedy and Khrushchev initiated personal, backchannel communications—what presidential advisers dubbed a "Pen Pal Correspondence." Lower-level discussions on Berlin and other front-burner issues took place intermittently through the fall and into the winter of 1961–62. Khrushchev dropped his deadline; JFK made conciliatory public statements. As so often with the Cold War, however, hostility coexisted uneasily with conciliation. The Soviets conducted at least thirty atmospheric nuclear tests in the fall of 1961; the United States resumed underground testing. On one occasion in mid-October, U.S. and Soviet tanks faced off ominously at Checkpoint Charlie in Berlin. Soviet aircraft periodically harassed American planes in German air corridors. At times, Americans got the impression that Moscow had put Berlin on the shelf; on other occasions, it appeared still a top priority. In fact, it converged with Cuba in October 1962 to assume a central role in the most menacing of Cold War crises.[23]

22. Thomas Alan Schwartz, "Victories and Defeats in the Long Twilight Struggle: The United States and Western Europe in the 1960s," in Diane Kunz, ed., *The Diplomacy of the Crucial Decade* (New York, 1994), 124.
23. Taubman, *Khrushchev*, 537–41; Giglio, *Kennedy Presidency*, 85–88.

II

Great-power conflict dominated the first year of Kennedy's presidency, but the Third World was never far from his mind. The 1960s in many ways was the decade of the Third World. From 1960 to 1963, twenty-four new nations joined an already long list. Their emergence brought about what historian Raymond Betts has called a triangulation of world politics, a "large base of 'underdeveloped' nations . . . over which was a divided apex made up of the 'developed' (highly industrial) nations either siding with the United States or the Soviet Union."[24] The rise of the Third World dramatically changed the makeup of the United Nations and altered the balance of power in the General Assembly. In 1961, neutralist leaders Nehru, Nasser, Sukarno, Tito, and Kwame Nkrumah of Ghana convened in Belgrade the first Conference of Non-Aligned Countries with the declared intention of limiting the effects of the Cold War on the rest of the world. Revolutionaries like Castro, his confidant Ernesto "Che" Guevara, and the Congo's Patrice Lumumba inspired oppressed people everywhere and even became romanticized heroes for leftists in developed nations. There was talk of an "Afro-Asian bloc." The possibility of Third World nations acquiring nuclear weapons was especially troubling. The emphasis placed on the Third World by Cold War combatants bespoke their conviction that the outcome of that conflict could be decided by what happened there.

Kennedy set out to win the allegiance of the new nations. As a senator, he had questioned Dulles's hostility toward neutralism and the denial of aid to countries who disagreed with U.S. policies. He protested the overemphasis on military hardware at the expense of economic development. He embraced the argument of William Lederer and Eugene Burdick's 1958 best seller *The Ugly American* that the United States was losing the Third World because it assigned to those countries diplomats who could not speak the languages and isolated themselves in neo-colonial style in posh embassies. As president, Kennedy sought to expand economic assistance and to appoint ambassadors with language skills and area expertise. Paraphrasing Wilson, he spoke eloquently of making the world safe for diversity. His self-interested idealism established him as a hero to many Third World peoples.

Programs like Food for Peace and the Peace Corps put on full display Kennedy's concern for the Third World. Under the enlightened management of World War II bomber pilot, former history professor, and South Dakota progressive George McGovern, Food for Peace provided cheap

24. Raymond F. Betts, *Decolonization* (London, 1998), 42–43.

food and fiber from U.S. agricultural surpluses to be used as partial wages for workers building schools, hospitals, and roads in Third World countries. By 1963, it was feeding 92 million people per day, including 35 million children—"a twentieth century form of alchemy," Minnesota senator Hubert H. Humphrey exulted.[25] The more publicized Peace Corps provided a powerful and enduring example of Kennedy's practical idealism. During the 1960 campaign, he had taken up the idea of American youth going abroad to help other people. He named his dynamic brother-in-law Sargent Shriver, a business executive, to head the new program. More than forty-three nations requested volunteers the first four years; 2,816 Americans volunteered in the first year alone. The aim, obviously, was to win friends in Third World countries, a goal that served Cold War interests, but Shriver resisted State Department pressures to focus on trouble spots like Vietnam and went to great lengths to keep the CIA from using the Peace Corps to plant agents in other countries. The Peace Corps's impact on Third World development was negligible. Some volunteers lacked skills, others had little to do, and many ended up teaching English.[26] But its contributions in the realm of the spirit were enormous. It helped other peoples to understand the United States and Americans to understand them. It conveyed the hope and promise that represented the United States at its best. It confirmed the nation's values and traditional sense of mission.[27]

Translating an appreciation for Third World nationalism into policies for specific countries and regions, on the other hand, posed numerous practical difficulties and forced awkward compromises. South Asia was a case in point. JFK respected Prime Minister Nehru. He feared that to "lose" leading neutrals like India might cause the balance of power to "swing against us."[28] Early in his administration, he authorized a "tilt" toward India in hopes that it could be accomplished without jeopardizing relations with Pakistan. As with Eisenhower, the ploy failed. The

25. Thomas J. Knock, "Feeding the World and Thwarting the Communists: George McGovern and Food for Peace," in David F. Schmitz and T. Christopher Jespersen, eds., *Architects of the American Century: Individuals and Institutions in Twentieth-Century U.S. Foreign Policymaking* (Chicago, 2000), 98–120.

26. Elizabeth A. Cobbs, "Decolonization, the Cold War, and the Foreign Policy of the Peace Corps," *Diplomatic History* 20 (Winter 1996), 79–105; Giglio, *Kennedy Presidency*, 157.

27. Elizabeth Cobbs Hoffman, *All You Need Is Love: The Peace Corps and the Spirit of the 1960s* (Cambridge, Mass., 1998), 257.

28. Robert J. McMahon, *The Cold War on the Periphery: The United States, India, and Pakistan* (New York, 1994), 173.

administration exaggerated Chinese aims in South Asia, overestimated its threat to India and Pakistan, and underestimated the intractability of regional hatreds. The president could not establish a close relationship with the aloof and imperious Nehru. A Chinese military incursion into a remote border region of India in October 1962 forced India and the United States into an uneasy embrace, but infusions of U.S. military aid in addition to the massive economic assistance already provided purchased precious little influence in New Delhi. Military aid from the United States to India provoked outrage in Pakistan; Washington's efforts to appease its ally with additional weapons further destabilized an already volatile region. Attempts to ease Indo-Pakistani tensions through mediation got nowhere. In a blatant display of realpolitik, Pakistan drifted toward China. "History can be idiotic," ambassador to India John Kenneth Galbraith confided to his diary. "A staunch American ally against communism is negotiating with the Chinese Communists to the discontent of an erstwhile neutral."[29] At the time of Kennedy's death, his South Asian policy was in disarray.

Not surprisingly, the Middle East provided more difficult challenges and brought even more serious consequences. Kennedy sympathized with Arab nationalism. He respected and liked Dulles's nemesis, Nasser, and, as with Nehru, sought to seduce him through personal communication, development aid, and large quantities of desperately needed wheat. He hoped to convert the restless Egyptian to peaceful ways, ease Arab-Israeli tensions, and thereby minimize Soviet influence in a critical region. JFK's good intentions ran afoul of Nasser's regional ambitions, competing U.S. interests in the conservative Arab oil states, the power of the Israel lobby, and, of course, the Cold War. The president learned as others before him that, especially in the Middle East, it was impossible to have it both ways, much less all three.

A civil war in the obscure Red Sea kingdom of Yemen frustrated Kennedy's diplomacy. Angered by Syria's 1961 abandonment of the United Arab Republic, Nasser sent tanks, planes, and seventy thousand troops to support leftist rebels who had overthrown the Yemen monarchy. Fearful of Egyptian influence in a neighboring state, Saudi Arabia and Jordan backed conservative Arab counterrevolutionaries in what became a scaled-down, Middle East version of the Spanish Civil War. The United States initially recognized the Nasser-backed government, but the British expressed concern about their interests in nearby Aden. When Egypt threatened Saudi Arabia, U.S. oilmen dispatched dire warnings to Washington.

29. Ibid., 297.

Israel protested these new signs of Nasser's aggressiveness. After the Syrian and Iraqi governments were toppled in early 1963 by pro-Nasser forces and the Soviets sent modern tanks and bombers to Egypt, JFK backtracked. Carefully avoiding a complete break with Nasser, he threatened to cut off aid to Egypt, openly supported Jordan by dispatching the Sixth Fleet to the eastern Mediterranean, and ordered naval and air forces to Saudi Arabia. Nasser's intervention in Yemen undermined Kennedy's approach to Egypt, strengthened U.S. ties with the conservative Arab states, and opened the way for closer American-Israeli relations.[30]

Ironically, given the president's early efforts at evenhandedness, the modern U.S. alliance with Israel originated on his watch. The move toward Nasser provoked a powerful backlash from the Israel lobby and its congressional backers and a diplomatic blitz from Tel Aviv to secure from Washington state-of-the-art weapons and a security commitment. The State Department predictably opposed Israeli requests, and JFK was wary. But McNamara's Pentagon was a more powerful player in Kennedy's Washington than Rusk's State Department, and warnings that increased Soviet aid and West Germany's sale of missiles to Nasser had upset the Middle East arms balance brought the president around. In August 1962, he agreed to sell Israel Hawk surface-to-air missiles, a sharp departure from past U.S. policy that had banned sales of major weapons systems and a generally unrecognized landmark in the Israel–United States special relationship.[31] Increasingly alarmed by the prospect of nuclear proliferation to Third World countries, JFK attached high priority to preventing Israel from converting to weapons production its nuclear project at Dimona in the Negev Desert. Shortly before his death, in response to rising tensions in the Middle East and in return for vague—and as it turned out duplicitous—Israeli assurances regarding Dimona, he promised to assist Israel militarily should it be the victim of aggression, a giant step toward the alliance he and his predecessors had resisted. Instead of accommodating Arab nationalism and taking a more balanced approach in the region, JFK established the basis for the U.S.-Israeli special relationship.[32]

Kennedy made Africa a centerpiece of his anti-colonialism and gave that continent for the first time a high profile in U.S. foreign policy. He promoted African independence in numerous speeches. To get around the racism deeply entrenched in the U.S. government and the State

30. Warren Bass, *Support Any Friend: Kennedy's Middle East Policy* (New York, 2003), 98–143; Douglas Little, *American Orientalism: The United States and the Middle East Since 1945* (Chapel Hill, N.C., 2004), 183–85.
31. Bass, *Any Friend*, 145.
32. Ibid., 191–238; Little, *Orientalism*, 94–97.

Department's traditional European bias in dealing with Africa, he named former Michigan governor and civil rights activist G. Mennen Williams assistant secretary of state for African affairs and appointed ambassadors who knew the continent and sympathized with its people. He invited African leaders to the White House. Aware that segregation in the District of Columbia and surrounding states made Washington a hardship post for African diplomats, he pushed for desegregation along Route 40, a major east-west artery. His evolving stand in favor of civil rights for African Americans was influenced at least partly by a desire to show Third World leaders that U.S. freedom was color-blind.[33] He focused special attention on Ghana's Kwame Nkrumah, one of the most prominent African leaders, agreeing to fund a huge dam on the Volta River. Unlike Dulles with Nasser, he followed through on his commitment even after Nkrumah made anti-American speeches and sought aid from Moscow, although he did extract pledges that there would be no expropriation of U.S. property.[34]

As with the Middle East, JFK's support for African nationalism had sharply defined limits. On the most complex, volatile, and ultimately tragic of African issues, the Congo, he pursued a notably cautious approach. Brutally exploited by Belgium for nearly a century, the Congo was given independence in 1960 without preparation and in the expectation that the former colonists would retain dominant influence. Taking office just as the strife-torn Congo assumed crisis proportions, Kennedy declined to support nationalist leader Lumumba, the eloquent and charismatic former postal worker and beer salesman whom many Americans considered pro-Communist. He did not call for Lumumba's release when he was imprisoned by rivals or praise him after his brutal assassination. The president did oppose the secession of mineral-rich Katanga Province and its leader Moise Tshombe, who was backed by Europeans and southern American segregationists, an act of some political courage. But he left responsibility for holding the Congo together to the United Nations and refused to commit U.S. troops to the peacekeeping mission. He did welcome the ultimate UN victory. To the disgruntlement of some southern congressmen, he denied Tshombe a visa to the United States.[35]

Similar limits applied elsewhere in Africa. The administration spoke in favor of independence for the Portugese colony of Angola and provided

33. Thomas Borstelmann, *The Cold War and the Color Line: American Race Relations in the Global Arena* (Cambridge, Mass., 2001), 164–67.
34. Thomas J. Noer, "The New Frontier and African Neutralism: Kennedy, Nkrumah, and the Volta River Project," *Diplomatic History* 8 (Winter 1984), 61–79.
35. Borstelmann, *Cold War and the Color Line*, 149.

limited aid to pro-Western factions among the rebels. Portugal also secured U.S. military aid through NATO, however, and its use of American-provided napalm to suppress the rebellion provoked worldwide outrage. When the U.S. stand in favor of Angolan independence threatened renewal of the lease for its critical Azores air base, a badly divided administration backed off.[36] Similarly, while the United States verbally criticized South Africa's apartheid policies, it refused to support economic sanctions or an arms embargo. South Africa remained a major source of strategic minerals. Its gold helped stabilize the global economy. Its ports were important on the east-west passage, and the United States had just constructed a vital missile-tracking station near Pretoria. United States officials also feared destabilizing South Africa because the African National Congress (ANC) was allegedly controlled by Communists. The CIA appears to have played a role in helping the South African government locate and arrest ANC leader Nelson Mandela. When faced with what the State Department called "an embarrassing choice between security requirements and basic political principle," the United States opted for the former.[37]

Kennedy devoted more attention to Latin America than any other postwar president. He deliberately set out to recapture the spirit of FDR's Good Neighbor policy. He also concluded after the rise of Castro that Latin America was "the most dangerous area of the world" and that to safeguard its own security the United States must address the poverty and oppression that seemed a fertile breeding ground for Communism.[38] As president, he visited Latin America three times, drawing a million people in a triumphal 1962 appearance in Mexico City. He entertained hemispheric chiefs of state and diplomats, unlike so many of his predecessors dealing with them as equals and enjoying their company. He understood that the United States had committed wrongs in the hemisphere in the past, and he identified with the Latin American people. Because of his empathy, his style and charisma, and the tragic circumstances of his death, he is still revered in the hemisphere.[39]

Even before the Bay of Pigs, JFK demonstrated his commitment to Latin America. On March 13, 1961, with great fanfare, he announced the Alliance for Progress, the Marshall Plan–like aid program hemispheric leaders had been seeking since the 1940s, a "vast cooperative effort, unparalleled in magnitude and nobility of purpose," he proclaimed, "to satisfy

36. Giglio, *Kennedy Presidency*, 228–30.

37. Borstelmann, *Cold War and the Color Line*, 153–57.

38. Stephen G. Rabe, *The Most Dangerous Area of the World: John F. Kennedy Confronts Communist Revolution in Latin America* (Chapel Hill, N.C., 1999), 7.

39. Ibid., 1–2.

the basic needs of the American people for homes, work and land, health and schools."[40] In August, the administration pledged $1 billion for the first year and $20 billion for the next decade. Political democracy and fundamental reforms were to accompany economic development. The Alliance excited great hope in the hemisphere and at home. Like the Peace Corps, it seemed to epitomize the idealism of New Frontier foreign policy.

In fact, the administration's actions often belied its idealistic rhetoric and undercut its goals. JFK's overriding concern, at times an obsession, was to prevent another Cuba in the hemisphere. To achieve that aim, he interfered in Latin American politics on a scale unmatched since Wilson. United States officials would have liked to get rid of Jean Claude "Papa Doc" Duvalier, Haiti's reprehensible dictator, but they could not identify an acceptable alternative and acquiesced in his rule. The clever Duvalier even manipulated Washington into a generous aid package in return for Haiti's crucial vote to expel Cuba from the Organization of American States. The administration welcomed the assassination of the despicable Dominican dictator Rafael Trujillo in May 1961. But it viewed his eventual successor, the popularly elected Juan Bosch, as a fuzzy-headed intellectual, even what one diplomat called a "deep cover communist."[41] "There are three possibilities in descending order of preference," JFK opined, "a decent democratic regime, a continuation of the Trujillo regime, or a Castro regime. We ought to aim for the first, but we can't really renounce the second until we are sure we can avoid the third."[42] The United States thus stood by in September 1963 while Bosch was overthrown by the Dominican military.

The administration also undermined popularly elected leftist governments that did not follow its line on Cuba. Argentina and Brazil, the two largest hemispheric countries, struggled to pursue independent foreign policies, maintaining diplomatic relations and small trade with the Soviet Union while defying U.S. sanctions against Cuba. Even though Argentina's Arturo Frondizi enthusiastically backed the Alliance for Progress and actively cultivated U.S. support, the administration looked the other way when he was overthrown by the military in March 1962. Kennedy viewed Brazil's leftist leader João Goulart as unreliable. The CIA spent $5 million in a destabilization effort that helped lead to a military coup in 1964.[43] In Chile, it blatantly interfered in the electoral process, spending more than $2.5 million to replace the leftist Arturo

40. Giglio, *Kennedy Presidency*, 233.
41. Rabe, *Dangerous Area*, 46.
42. Ibid., 41.
43. Dallek, *Unfinished Life*, 522.

Alessandri with the more moderate and presumably more reliable Eduardo Frei. Frei was the type of Latin American leader the administration preferred. After his election in 1964, he achieved modest results under the Alliance for Progress. But the Kennedy covert operation also initiated a pattern of interference in Chilean politics that would have tragic results.

The most blatant and dubious intervention was in tiny British Guiana (now Guyana), which, remarkably, during the Kennedy years—and to its own misfortune—came to be viewed as crucial to U.S. security. On the verge of independence from Britain, this impoverished northern Latin American colony adjacent to Venezuela was headed by elected prime minister Cheddi Jagan, a U.S.-trained dentist and avowed Marxist. Jagan assured Kennedy privately in October 1961 that he would not permit a Soviet base in British Guiana. Unpersuaded, the administration with British complicity carried out in early 1962 a covert operation that included fomenting demonstrations, riots, and a general strike. In the summer of 1963, Kennedy pressured British prime minister Harold Macmillan to delay independence. The British reluctantly went along, instituting a new electoral process that would eliminate Jagan from office in 1964.[44] On November 18, 1963, four days before his assassination, JFK outlined what was to have been a Kennedy Doctrine, affirming that "every source at our command" must be used to "prevent the establishment of another Cuba in the hemisphere." It was a statement, McGeorge Bundy later conceded, that was "blanketed almost immediately by his death."[45]

The greatest failure of JFK's Latin American policy came in the area of its most expansive hopes. The Alliance for Progress built roads, schools, hospitals, and low-cost housing in many Latin American countries. It achieved striking results in Venezuela. Overall, however, the growth rate fell far short of the targeted 2.5 percent. Nor did the aid program accomplish much in terms of democratization and economic reform. In Washington, it suffered from weak leadership, bureaucratic torpor, and mismanagement. The United States eventually contributed $18 billion, but 70 percent was in loans instead of grants. It did not extend major trade concessions, and a sharp decline in prices for Latin American exports offset the benefits of U.S. assistance. Economic progress was also nullified by runaway population growth, a problem the administration dared not tackle because of the explosive politico-religious ramifications at home.

44. Department of State, *Foreign Relations of the United States, 1961–1963*, vol. 12 (Washington, 1996), 536–38, 607–9; *New York Times*, October 30, 1994.
45. *FRUS, 1961–1963* 12:351n.

The United States did not push Latin American governments on the crucial issue of land reform for fear of antagonizing entrenched elites, destabilizing recipient countries, or provoking U.S. corporations. The alliance floundered mainly because it set unrealistic goals: a fundamental restructuring of Latin American economics and politics in only ten years. Based on the impressive results achieved by the Marshall Plan in Europe and upon then fashionable academic models of development drawn from the U.S. experience, it ignored the idiosyncrasies of Latin American history and political culture. Perhaps the best that can be said is that it delayed by two decades the economic disaster that struck much of the continent in the 1980s.[46]

U.S. military aid in some ways subverted the Alliance for Progress. Typical of its broader concerns, the Kennedy administration emphasized strengthening Latin American internal security forces and training them in counterguerrilla methods to root out Castro-like insurgencies. It also drew on then voguish academic theories holding that enlightened military officers could be agents of development and even democratization in premodern societies. United States officials hoped that closer ties would inculcate Latin American military officers with democratic values and bring increased United States influence. The Kennedy administration expanded military aid by more than 50 percent to $77 million per year. In 1962 alone, more than nine thousand Latin American military personnel trained in such educational institutions as the School of the Americas at Fort Benning, Georgia. The results were not what had been hoped for. Between 1961 and 1963, military coups eliminated six elected governments. The U.S. aid program assisted the growth of military influence, and for the next two decades the military dominated hemispheric politics. Disillusioned with military aid, McNamara in 1965 recommended its termination. The State Department dissented, for fear, the secretary of defense reported without irony, of "alienating the military forces on whom the Alliance for Progress must depend to maintain stability in the area."[47] The program continued.

III

The most frightening of Cold War crises came in Latin America in October 1962. Khrushchev's reckless attempt to place offensive missiles in Cuba brought the United States and the USSR to the brink of war and the world to the edge of nuclear conflagration. It can never be known precisely what

46. Giglio, *Kennedy Presidency*, 233–36; Rabe, *Dangerous Area*, 148–49.
47. Rabe, *Dangerous Area*, 147.

moved the Soviet premier to initiate such a dangerous undertaking. He later insisted that he was protecting his Cuban ally from U.S. invasion, a claim that gains greater credence in light of what is now known about Operation Mongoose. Cuba *had* become very important to the Soviet leadership, and the threat of a U.S. invasion must have seemed to Moscow very real. Still, it remains difficult to believe that Khrushchev would have assumed such risk exclusively for the sake of a small ally in the enemy's sphere of influence. By placing medium- and intermediate-range missiles in Cuba, he could strike targets across the eastern and southern United States, and he certainly hoped to make up on the cheap the huge U.S. lead in long-range missiles. He may have hoped to use the Cuban missiles to force a favorable settlement on Berlin. His gambler's instinct likely tempted him to act, along with the lingering belief that Kennedy could be bullied. He wanted to show the United States how it felt to be surrounded by enemy missiles, to throw "a hedgehog at Uncle Sam's pants," as he put it. Thus in May 1962, he persuaded an understandably wary Castro to accept sixty medium- and intermediate-range missiles and a panoply of military equipment to support them. The missiles were carefully concealed on the decks of transport ships. The forty-two thousand troops sent to guard them—armed with tactical nuclear weapons—sweated out the long summer cruise below deck to avoid surveillance. In what proved a colossal miscalculation, Khrushchev persuaded himself that the weapons could be made operational before the United States detected them, forcing Kennedy to acquiesce.[48]

He was wrong on both counts. CIA analysts using information gleaned from the defector Col. Oleg Penkovsky and aerial photographs accurately identified the mysterious objects as medium- and intermediate-range missiles. McNamara may have been right in arguing that these weapons did not significantly alter the overall strategic balance. From Kennedy's standpoint this was irrelevant. Stunned by Khrushchev's bold ploy and boxed in by his own public statements that offensive weapons in Cuba were unacceptable, he feared that to do nothing in the face of this most blatant Soviet challenge would be political and diplomatic suicide. To fully assess his options, he formed an Executive Committee (ExComm) of top advisers that met regularly during the crisis. He never seriously considered negotiations to secure removal of the weapons. The Soviets had secretly placed them in Cuba and lied about what they were doing. To negotiate under such circumstances would be seen as weak. He also

48. Taubman, *Khrushchev*, 531–37; Alexansdr Fursenko and Timothy Naftali, *"One Hell of a Gamble": Khrushchev, Castro, Kennedy, 1958–1964* (New York, 1997), 166–83.

suspected that Moscow would drag out negotiations until the missiles were operational. The ornithological designations "hawk" and "dove" came into parlance during ExComm deliberations. Hawks such as the Joint Chiefs and Acheson pressed for air strikes against the missile sites followed by an invasion to make certain the weapons—and Castro—were removed. Doves questioned whether air strikes would destroy the sites, worried about the morality of a surprise attack against a small nation, rejected an invasion as too risky, and feared Soviet retaliation against Berlin. They urged a blockade of Cuba, to be called a quarantine, combined with pressures on Moscow to remove the missiles. Kennedy opted for this more cautious but still risky course. On Monday, October 22, he announced the quarantine and demanded removal of the missiles.[49]

His speech opened a week of harrowing moves and countermoves in this diplomatic chess game, played for the highest stakes. The United States went to the second highest state of defense readiness (DefCon 2) for the first time in the Cold War. The Strategic Air Command went to its highest alert, launching 550 B-52 bombers armed with nuclear warheads. Soviet technicians frantically worked on the missile sites, and by October 24 the medium-range weapons were near operational. United States warships took up station with standard operating procedures calling for firing a warning shot and, if that failed, disabling the rudder of the approaching ship. Soviet vessels with orders to return fire if fired upon moved ominously toward the quarantine line. Submarines from both sides silently plied the waters of the Caribbean. Harried officials worked under unimaginable pressures and went days without sleep; their nerves grew taut, their thought processes blurred. Attempting to micromanage the crisis to prevent a deadly mistake, even the famously detached Kennedy several times lost his cool. The first break occurred on October 24 when Soviet ships reversed course to avoid the quarantine. "We're eyeball to eyeball," the normally taciturn Rusk exclaimed, "and I think the other fella just blinked."[50]

Not quite. Only after yet another frightful scare was a crude settlement arranged. Apparently convinced on the basis of flawed intelligence that war was imminent, Khrushchev on October 25 dispatched to Washington a personal and highly emotional message warning of the "calamity" of

49. The classic study is Graham Allison, *Essence of Decision: Explaining the Cuban Missile Crisis* (Boston, 1971). For a very different approach, see Jutta Weldes, *Constructing National Interests: The United States and the Cuban Missile Crisis* (Minneapolis, 1999).

50. Giglio, *Kennedy Presidency*, 207.

war and offering to remove the missiles in return for a U.S. pledge not to invade Cuba. The next day, his fears eased, he sent another message that left U.S. officials shaking their heads in dismay.[51] More measured in tone, it upped the ante by also demanding removal of U.S. Jupiter missiles from Turkey. These weapons were obsolete, but getting rid of them raised numerous complications.[52] The anxiety level soared when a U-2 aircraft was shot down over Cuba. Kennedy's military advisers demanded retaliation. Preparations were being completed for an air strike to be followed by an invasion of Cuba. Unknown to the Americans, Castro was pushing Moscow to launch a first strike against the United States. On October 27, "Black Saturday," the administration shrewdly decided to ignore the second letter and accept the more favorable terms of the first. In the meantime, Robert Kennedy privately assured the Soviet ambassador that the Turkish missiles would be removed. Painfully aware of his military inferiority, Khrushchev, after hours of agonizing suspense, accepted the U.S. proposals.[53]

The missile crisis was the defining moment of the Kennedy presidency, and many observers have given him high marks. He was firm but restrained in responding to this most critical challenge, it is argued. He sought advice from different quarters. He left Khrushchev room for retreat. He did not gloat in the apparent U.S. victory.[54] The October confrontation is also the most studied of Cold War crises, and as more has been learned, the praise for Kennedy has been tempered. To be sure, Khrushchev bears primary responsibility for the confrontation. He deluded himself into thinking that he could get away with an incredibly rash move. But Kennedy's obsession with Cuba and the hostile actions carried out in Mongoose provided the occasion and rationale for Khrushchev's actions, a connection totally lost on U.S. officials at the time. Even while he rejected the more risky alternatives, Kennedy's initial response pushed the two nations to the verge of war. He did hold the hawks at bay and displayed skill in crisis management. But he would have been the first to admit that luck and chance helped determine the outcome. The United States came within hours of an invasion that could have had horrific consequences. The number of Soviet troops in Cuba far exceeded U.S. estimates, and they were armed with tactical nuclear weapons. An invasion could have

51. Taubman, Khrushchev, 568–70.
52. Philip Nash, The Other Missiles of October: Eisenhower, Kennedy, and the Jupiters 1957–1963 (Chapel Hill, N.C., 1997).
53. Freedman, Kennedy's Wars, 208–17.
54. Dallek, Unfinished Life, 571–74.

triggered nuclear war. "In the end," political scientist William Taubman concludes, Khrushchev and Kennedy "found the courage to pull back, leaving the other room to retreat . . . but not before the world came closer than it ever has to nuclear conflagration."[55]

The missile crisis had profound and in some ways paradoxical consequences. Kennedy's position at home was strengthened, at least for the short run. The Democrats bucked tradition by gaining seats in the Senate in the midterm elections. The president's personal popularity and approval rating soared. On the other side, Khrushchev's claims of victory rang hollow. Although he hung on for two more years, his power was reduced, his days numbered.[56]

Following the missile crisis, Moscow and Washington took the first groping steps toward what would be called detente. The Kennedy-Khrushchev confrontation had been highly personal, and the two leaders, after facing the nuclear abyss together, seem to have gained that empathy that comes from shared traumatic experience. In June 1963, they established a direct telegraphic link—the so-called hotline—to maintain close contact when required. The long-simmering Berlin problem began to lose its centrality. In one of his most noteworthy speeches, JFK at American University in June 1963 spoke the unspeakable, calling for a "genuine" peace, not a "Pax Americana enforced on the world by American weapons of war," observing that "enmities between individuals, as between nations, do not last forever," and urging Americans to reassess their attitudes toward the Soviet Union. Khrushchev called it the best speech since FDR and helped disseminate it by stopping the jamming of VOA broadcasts.[57] The two nations subsequently agreed on a limited test ban treaty, a first, highly circumscribed, but still significant step toward controlling nuclear weapons. The real loser of the missile crisis, Castro was enraged at being sold out by Khrushchev—"no cojones," he thundered. Recognizing the opportunity, JFK over the next year quietly explored the possibility of accommodation with Cuba.[58]

Kennedy's 1963 dovishness has fed speculation that had he lived he would have moved further to end the Cold War, but such arguments

55. Taubman, *Khrushchev*, 531–32. An older work that raises searching questions about JFK's skill at crisis management is James A. Nathan, "The Missile Crisis: His Finest Hour Now," *World Politics* 27 (January 1975), 256–81. More recent accounts that draw on Soviet sources include Fursenko and Naftali, *"One Hell of a Gamble"* and James G. Blight and David A. Welch, *On the Brink: Americans and Soviets Reexamine the Cuban Missile Crisis* (New York, 1989).

56. Giglio, *Kennedy Presidency*, 216; Taubman, *Khrushchev*, 581.

57. Dallek, *Unfinished Life*, 620–21; Giglio, *Kennedy Presidency*, 217.

58. Freedman, *Kennedy's Wars*, 240–44.

must be treated with caution. Old fears and suspicions died hard. If each side after October 1962 saw the urgency of change, each also felt limits to how far they could go. Hard-liners in each nation made deviation from Cold War certitudes risky, especially for Kennedy, who faced reelection in 1964. The one clear lesson many Soviet officials drew was not to get caught again in a position of military inferiority, and Moscow mounted a major effort to gain nuclear parity. Whether from politics or conviction, Kennedy's new dovishness only went so far. Shortly after American University, he made another speech, more publicized and better remembered, before shouting throngs in Berlin denouncing Communism and dismissing the idea of working with Communists. A speech to have been delivered in Dallas on November 22, 1963, bristled with boilerplate anti-Communism. While encouraging secret approaches toward Havana, he also publicly condemned Castro. In the spring of 1963, harassment of Cuba resumed. On the day of JFK's assassination, an agent delivered to a plant in the Havana regime a ballpoint pen with a hypodermic needle designed to poison the Cuban leader. Ever the political animal, Kennedy played both sides in the post-missile-crisis world, carefully keeping his options open.[59]

The major geopolitical result of the missile crisis was to accelerate the breakdown of bipolarity. By October 1962, the United States and its European allies were already sharply divided on economic and strategic issues. As the European economies recovered from World War II, the dollar gap that had plagued them in the era of the Marshall Plan gave way to a rising U.S. balance of payments deficit, a danger to the national security Kennedy considered second only to nuclear war. The president also feared that under the complex Bretton Woods arrangements to stabilize currencies with gold, the allies could employ their dollar surpluses to exhaust U.S. gold reserves. The Europeans increasingly doubted that the United States would use nuclear weapons to defend them and sought to acquire their own, a prospect that, especially in the case of West Germany, frightened Washington. Flexible response to them meant that the United States would defend Europe with conventional forces that they would provide. The Kennedy administration sought with little success to ease U.S. economic problems and resolve alliance differences by pushing tariff reduction, European unification, and such gimmicks as nuclear sharing through a Multilateral Force (MLF). It advanced the radical proposal of withdrawing large numbers of U.S. troops from Europe. It succeeded only in using the leverage provided by the 1961 Berlin crisis to persuade West Germany

59. Giglio, *Kennedy Presidency*, 218–20.

to purchase large quantities of U.S. military equipment to offset the spiraling cost of keeping American troops in Europe.[60]

The missile crisis widened and exposed these fissures. By first deciding what to do and then informing its allies, the United States confirmed European suspicions of how it would respond to a Soviet threat. France's Charles de Gaulle loyally supported Kennedy during the crisis, but he was more than ever persuaded that his nation must have its *force de frappe*. West German chancellor Konrad Adenauer fretted that Kennedy's post-missile-crisis moves toward the Soviet Union would mean the end of German unification. The Europeans soon took actions that shook the alliance to its core. De Gaulle vetoed British entry into the Common Market and rejected the MLF in favor of his own nuclear program. In a shocking reversal of long-standing trends, France signed a friendship treaty with West Germany, portending an independent European position in world affairs, even West German acquisition of nuclear weapons. With the U.S. balance of payments deficit soaring, Washington considered troop withdrawals. In late 1963, West Germany veered back toward the United States by continuing its offset purchases, but de Gaulle persisted in his independent path. He would soon challenge U.S. leadership in Europe and elsewhere.[61]

The myth of a Sino-Soviet "bloc" was also starkly exposed. The Chinese denounced Khrushchev's "adventurism" in provoking the missile crisis and "capitulationism" in ending it, and in late 1962 the long-hidden dispute between the two Communist powers burst out into the open. In time, the rift would open tempting opportunities for the United States, but at the outset Americans questioned how deep it ran and whether it was irreparable. Indeed, the growth of multipolarity after the missile crisis along with the first steps toward detente and growing nuclear proliferation made for a more complex and in some ways more dangerous world.

The major immediate effect was to heighten U.S.-Chinese tensions. In part because of its conflict with the USSR, Mao's regime seemed the more militant of the Communist powers, and its strident rhetoric bespoke an unbending commitment to world revolution. Indications that it would soon get the bomb heightened American fears, even leading to lower-level discussion in Washington and Moscow of a preemptive attack against China's

---

60. Frank Costigliola, "The Failed Design: Kennedy, de Gaulle, and the Struggle for Europe," *Diplomatic History* 8 (Summer 1984), 227–41; Francis J. Gavin, "The Gold Battle Within the Cold War: American Monetary Policy and the Defense of Europe," *Diplomatic History* 26 (Winter 2002), 70–78.

61. Costigliola, "Failed Design," 243–51; Gavin, "Gold Battle," 70–78.

nuclear facilities. United States officials took Beijing's rhetoric more seriously than they might have and exaggerated its ability to topple governments. For reasons of domestic politics as well as Cold War conviction, JFK
never seriously considered changes in the U.S. policy of containing and isolating China. Demonization of China had the effect of a self-fulfilling
prophecy. The Kennedy administration may also have used anti-Chinese
rhetoric to cover its domestic flank while seeking improved relations with
the USSR. Although ambassadorial talks would continue at Warsaw, China
would be for Washington Cold War Enemy No. 1. The focal point of conflict would be Southeast Asia in general and Vietnam in particular.[62]

Kennedy's handling of the last foreign policy crisis of his presidency reflected his post-missile-crisis ambivalence. By 1961, Eisenhower's nation-
building experiment in Vietnam was in tatters. Frustrated by President
Ngo Dinh Diem's refusal to hold the elections called for by the Geneva
Accords, former Vietminh remaining in the South began to re-create in
1957 the revolutionary networks used against France. They effectively exploited the rising rural opposition to Diem's oppressive methods—the
peasants were like a "mound of straw ready to be ignited," one insurgent
recalled.[63] After months of hesitation, North Vietnam in 1959 firmly committed itself to the rebellion, sending men and supplies southward along
what would be called the Ho Chi Minh Trail. In 1960, the insurgents coalesced into the National Liberation Front of South Vietnam (NLF) and
shifted from hit-and-run attacks to full-scale military operations. By year's
end, the U.S. ambassador warned Washington that unless Diem took
prompt and drastic steps to win the war and broaden his popular support
it should look for "alternative leadership."[64]

Although preoccupied with other issues and concerned about the obvious deficiencies in Diem's leadership, JFK in late 1961 sharply escalated
the U.S. commitment. Taking a cautious middle ground here as elsewhere, he rejected proposals to seek a negotiated settlement or to commit
U.S. combat troops. After Laos, the Bay of Pigs, and Berlin, however, he
felt compelled to do something, and he believed that the United States
must show it could counter Communist-inspired wars of national liberation. He increased the number of U.S. advisers from nine hundred when

---

62. Freedman, *Kennedy's Wars*, 250–55; Gordon H. Chang, *Friends and Enemies: The
    United States, China, and the Soviet Union, 1948–1972* (Stanford, Calif., 1990),
    242–47.
63. Quoted in George C. Herring, *America's Longest War: The United States and Viet-
    nam, 1950–1975* (3rd ed., New York, 1996), 75.
64. December 5, 1960, Department of State, *Foreign Relations of the United States,
    1958–1960*, vol. 1 (Washington, 1986), 707–11.

he took office to more than eleven thousand by the end of 1962. The "advisers" took an active role in combat and suffered casualties. Military aid doubled and included such modern hardware as armored personnel carriers and aircraft. Although increasingly concerned about Diem's ability to defeat the insurgency, the administration rejected as too risky proposals to condition expanded U.S. aid on major reforms. "Diem is Diem and the best we've got," JFK ruefully admitted.[65]

Kennedy's escalation failed to blunt the insurgency. The South Vietnamese army could not gain the initiative. The elusive guerrillas were difficult to locate and fought only when they had the upper hand. Skillfully blending intimidation with inducements such as land reform, they expanded their control of the South Vietnamese countryside. Diem resisted reforms and refused to broaden his government. The more embattled he became, the more he isolated himself in the presidential palace. As the U.S. presence became more intrusive, tensions between Americans and South Vietnamese increased.[66]

Vietnam became a full-fledged crisis in the summer of 1963 when the Catholic-dominated Saigon regime's harassment of South Vietnam's Buddhist majority provoked outright rebellion in the cities. The uprising drew international attention in June when an elderly monk immolated himself in front of large, shrieking crowds at a busy intersection in downtown Saigon. Pictures of the monk engulfed in flames appeared on television screens and in newspapers across the world. Diem's subsequent refusal to conciliate the Buddhists drove a bitterly divided administration to a fateful decision: He must go. With a green light from Washington, army generals on November 1, 1963, seized power. Diem and his brother Ngo Dinh Nhu fled to a Catholic church, where they were captured; they were later brutally murdered in the back of an armored personnel carrier. Kennedy found the murders especially distressing. More depressed than at any time since the Bay of Pigs, he realized that Vietnam had been his greatest foreign policy failure.[67]

Just three weeks later, JFK himself was assassinated in Dallas, and his sudden and shocking death had an enormous international impact, a symbol of his own magnetic personality and America's global position. He and his stylish wife, Jacqueline, had assumed a position akin to international royalty. The president drew huge and enthusiastic crowds in state visits to Mexico, Colombia, and even Venezuela, where Nixon had

65. Benjamin Bradlee, *Conversations with Kennedy* (New York, 1976), 59.
66. Herring, *America's Longest War*, 103–4.
67. Dallek, *Unfinished Life*, 684.

been so rudely treated in 1958. A trip to Europe in the summer of 1963 established him as an extraordinarily popular figure who attracted strong support for himself and his country.[68] Kennedy's assassination was perhaps "the first truly global instant of tragedy," historian Warren Bass has written.[69] Through the miracle of satellite transmission, the events of that awful weekend were beamed far and wide on television and evoked an outpouring of emotion. In the Middle East and Latin America, ordinary people stood in line for hours to sign condolence books at U.S. embassies. Europeans viewed him as *their* leader and felt a keen sense of personal loss. His life and the horror of his death symbolized for them what was good and bad about the United States.[70]

JFK's handling of Vietnam reflects the ambiguous and uncertain legacy of his thousand days in office. Some of his advisers, later echoed by scholars, have claimed that he planned after reelection in 1964 to extricate the United States from what he had concluded was a quagmire. Americans find such arguments comforting, but they rest more on conjecture than on evidence.[71] Kennedy had developed profound doubts about the prospects for success in South Vietnam. From the start of his presidency, he had adamantly opposed sending combat troops there. He had grown increasingly skeptical of his military advisers. On numerous issues, he had demonstrated flexibility. He had grown demonstrably in office. A good case can be made that when faced with the collapse of South Vietnam in 1964–65, he would have looked closely at diplomatic solutions.[72] But there is no persuasive evidence that he was committed to withdrawal. He had resisted negotiations as firmly as he had opposed combat troops. At his direction, the Defense Department had developed a plan for the phased withdrawal of U.S. troops by 1965, but it was contingent on progress in South Vietnam. In a speech to be given in Dallas on the day of his death, he conceded that Third World commitments could be "painful, risky, and costly," but, he added, "we dare not weary of the test."[73] As with Cuba and

68. Ibid., 623.
69. Bass, *Any Friend*, 240.
70. Rabe, *Most Dangerous Area*, 1–2; Bass, *Any Friend*, 240–45; Frank Costigliola, "Like Children in the Darkness: European Reaction to the Assassination of John F. Kennedy, *Journal of Popular Culture* 20 (Winter 1986), 120–21.
71. Dallek, *Unfinished Life*, 709–11. For a persuasive rebuttal, see Ronald Steel, "Would Kennedy Have Quit Vietnam?" *New York Times*, May 25, 2003.
72. Freedman, *Kennedy's Wars*, 400–413; Fredrik Logevall, *Choosing War: The Lost Chance for Peace and Escalation of the War in Vietnam* (Berkeley, Calif., 1999), 396–400.
73. Kennedy's November 22, 1963, address may be found at www.jfklibrary.org/His torical+Resources/Archives/Reference+Desk/Speeches/JFK/003POF03TradeMart 11221963htm.

broader Cold War issues, JFK appears not to have decided which way to go on Vietnam. Apparently convinced that the military situation was not going badly, he clung to hope that the problem might still resolve itself without drastic U.S. action.

In Vietnam, as elsewhere, Kennedy must be judged on the basis of what he did during his brief tenure in office. He and most of his advisers uncritically accepted the assumption that a non-Communist South Vietnam was vital to America's global interests. Their rhetoric in fact strengthened the hold of that assumption. That he never devoted his full attention to Vietnam seems clear. He reacted to crises and improvised responses on a day-to-day basis, seldom examining the implications of his actions. Although apparently troubled by growing doubts, he refused, even after the problems with Diem had reached a crisis point, to face the hard questions. His cautious middle course significantly enlarged the U.S. role in Vietnam. With the coup, the United States assumed direct responsibility for the Saigon government. Whatever his misgivings and ultimate intentions, JFK bequeathed to his successor a problem eminently more dangerous than the one he had inherited.

IV

French president de Gaulle once remarked that Lyndon Johnson was "the very portrait of America. He reveals the country to us as it is, rough and raw."[74] By any standard, LBJ was an extraordinary individual. A large man with oversize and eminently caricaturable features, he had ambitions the size of his native Texas, and insecurities to match. He was a driven man, single-minded, prodigiously energetic, at times overbearing, proud, and vain. In some ways, he fits political scientist Walter Russell Mead's Jacksonian diplomatic style, a product of the hinterland, parochial, strongly nationalistic, deeply concerned about honor and reputation, suspicious of other peoples and nations and especially of international institutions, committed to a strong national defense—particularly when it benefited Texas.[75] Like the Wilson of 1913, he would have preferred to focus on domestic reform. He lacked his predecessor's and successor's passion for foreign policy. He could be ill at ease with diplomacy and diplomats:

74. Thomas Alan Schwartz, *Lyndon Johnson and Europe: In the Shadow of Vietnam* (Cambridge, Mass., 2003), 237. The most up-to-date biographies are Robert Dallek, *Flawed Giant: Lyndon Johnson and His Times, 1961–1973* (New York, 1998) and the more insightful Randall B. Woods, *LBJ: Architect of American Ambition* (New York, 2006).

75. Walter Russell Mead, *Special Providence: American Foreign Policy and How It Changed the World* (New York, 2001), 218–63.

"Foreigners are not like the folks I am used to," he once commented only half-jokingly.[76] He had traveled abroad little before becoming vice president and was given to stereotyping other people. The Germans, he once said, were a "great people" but "stingy as hell."[77] He was capable of decidedly undiplomatic behavior, as when he plopped cowboy hats on visiting Japanese dignitaries or dressed down West German chancellor Ludwig Erhard in a way that appalled his aides. He was also extremely intelligent and knowledgeable about key issues. He had an uncanny ability to size up people. A strong streak of idealism drove him to do good in the world. Robert Kennedy, no shrinking violet himself, called his rival and sometimes bitter enemy "the most formidable human being I've ever met."[78]

Sensitive to charges that he lacked experience in foreign policy and determined to maintain continuity with Kennedy's policies, LBJ retained and relied heavily on his predecessor's advisers. He established especially close ties with McNamara and Rusk. Like their boss, both were workaholics. At least in the beginning, the president stood in awe of McNamara's brains, energy, and drive. "He's like a jackhammer," an admiring LBJ remarked. "He drills through granite rock until he's there." Johnson and Rusk shared southern roots, and both had been outcasts in Kennedy's "Camelot." They drew much closer during an increasingly embattled presidency. "Hardworking, bright, and loyal as a beagle" is the way LBJ praised his stolid and utterly reliable secretary of state.[79] Bundy and Johnson were never personally close, but the national security adviser had reshaped the NSC into the focal point of decision-making and was thus indispensable. LBJ preferred a more formal, orderly style to JFK's freewheeling approach. Much of the work was done by the "principals" in small, intimate White House lunches, usually on Tuesday, more suitable for frank discussions and less susceptible to leaks (except for the leaker in chief, LBJ himself).[80]

The Sino-Soviet split widened into an irreparable breach by the mid-1960s, solidifying the triangular nature of the Cold War. Like the United States, the USSR felt an urgent need to ease tensions and stabilize the great-power rivalry. The new collective leadership that sent Khrushchev into involuntary retirement in late 1964 also sought to appease an increasingly restless public with better living standards. Moscow thus toned down the rhetoric and opened itself to dialogue on some major issues. On

76. Dallek, Flawed Giant, 86.
77. Schwartz, Johnson, 154.
78. H. W. Brands, The Wages of Globalism: Lyndon Johnson and the Limits of American Power (New York, 1995), 25.
79. George C. Herring, LBJ and Vietnam: A Different Kind of War (Austin, Tex., 1994), 7.
80. Ibid., 6–9.

the other hand, old shibboleths died hard, and segments of the Soviet bureaucracy were vested in the Cold War. The new leaders mounted a huge defense buildup. Divided among themselves, without foreign policy experience, they moved both ways at once, hesitating to veer too far in any direction.[81]

Seeking to break out of its isolation, China won major victories in 1964 when France extended diplomatic recognition and the annual controversial vote on its admission to the United Nations ended in a tie. Beijing also joined the nuclear club with a successful test in October 1964. The Chinese took the more radical position in supporting Third World revolutions, especially in Africa. But the dominant fact of Chinese life after 1965 was the Great Cultural Revolution launched by Chairman Mao himself to reaffirm his control of the party and secure his historical legacy. Using the threat of superpower encirclement, he set off a veritable revolution at home, purging the bureaucracy of "revisionists," fomenting his Red Guard followers' revolutionary zeal, and using brute force to impose ideological purity. As many as half a million people died in the carnage that followed. The Great Cultural Revolution pushed China to the brink of civil war and its relations with the USSR to the edge of military conflict.[82]

LBJ and his advisers struggled to make sense of a sometimes baffling world. Following JFK's lead, they took further steps toward detente, seeking to "build bridges" to Eastern Europe by upgrading U.S. diplomatic representation, expanding trade, and developing cultural exchanges, partly in the hope that closer contact might undermine Communist ideology. In early 1967, LBJ even declared, in a not sufficiently recognized statement, that the U.S. goal was not to "continue the Cold War but to end it."[83] A bit of flexibility even crept into U.S. China policy. The administration used the Warsaw talks to make clear its limited goals in Vietnam as a way to avoid a repetition of China's entry into the Korean War. It stopped trying to block China's admission to the UN. Responding to popular pressures from

81. John Lewis Gaddis, *Russia, the Soviet Union, and the United States: An Interpretive History* (2nd ed., New York, 1990), 259–61; Vladislav Zubok and Constantine Pleshakov, *Inside the Kremlin's Cold War: From Stalin to Khrushchev* (Cambridge, Mass., 1996), 272–74.

82. Nancy Bernkopf Tucker, "Threats, Opportunities, and Frustrations in East Asia," in Warren I. Cohen and Nancy Bernkopf Tucker, eds., *Lyndon Johnson Confronts the World* (New York, 1994), 105–10; Arthur Waldron, "From Nonexistent to Almost Normal: U.S.-Chinese Relations in the 1960s," in Diane Kunz, ed., *The Diplomacy of the Crucial Decade: American Foreign Relations During the 1960s* (New York, 1994), 233–41.

83. Frank Costigliola, "Lyndon B. Johnson, Germany, and 'the End of the Cold War,' " in Cohen and Tucker, *Johnson*, 192–97. The quote is from p. 197.

intellectuals, business, and others urging diplomatic relations, it eased restrictions on trade and cultural exchanges and even authorized government officials to engage in informal contacts with the Chinese.

Old habits also died hard in Washington, however. LBJ saw his job mainly as following the policies he had inherited. In his first two years, he focused on getting elected in his own right and implementing Great Society reforms. His principal foreign policy concern was to avoid anything that smacked of weakness or defeat. He and his advisers believed that in an uncertain and still dangerous world it remained essential to display firmness and maintain U.S. credibility. China's nuclear test and its outright rejection of arms control talks seemed to underscore the threat it continued to pose. Its ostensible support for radical revolution confirmed the need to hold the line in Vietnam and elsewhere. In any event, the Cultural Revolution put on hold any movement toward rapprochement. U.S. leaders still believed that the nation must deter and contain its adversaries, uphold its commitments, and prove its reliability as world leader.[84]

In Latin America, the Cold War and especially its domestic political imperatives continued to dictate U.S. policies. LBJ shared in full measure Kennedy's obsession with Castro. He called off the assassination program and until early 1964 kept alive unofficial discussions of normalization. But he continued to fear a Castro threat to the hemisphere and especially worried about the domestic political consequences of another Cuba. In the summer of 1964, the administration pressured the OAS to isolate Cuba by cutting off trade and severing diplomatic ties. The specter of Cuba shaped U.S. policies on most hemispheric issues.[85]

The fate of the Alliance for Progress hinted at the direction Latin American policies would take under Johnson. Kennedy's disciples have unfairly blamed LBJ for the demise of one of his predecessor's pet projects. In fact, the alliance was moribund by November 1963, and JFK himself was deeply concerned at the lack of economic progress and the reversion toward dictatorships. As a Texan, the new president thought himself simpatico with Latin America and pledged to support the alliance. But his heart lay with the domestic reforms of his Great Society, and he understandably hesitated to favor a program that bore Kennedy's personal imprint. Under his deeply conservative assistant secretary of state for Latin American affairs, fellow Texan Thomas Mann, the emphasis shifted toward self-help,

84. Dallek, *Flawed Giant*, 84–90; Waldo Heinrichs, "Lyndon B. Johnson: Change and Continuity," in Cohen and Tucker, *Johnson*, 26–27; Brands, *Wages of Globalism*, 26–29.
85. William O. Walker, "The Struggle for the Americas: The Johnson Administration and Cuba," paper in possession of author.

private investment, and local control, which advantaged U.S. corporations and the entrenched local oligarchies the alliance had been aimed at. LBJ and his advisers generally preferred stability to the reform spirit of the early days of the Alliance for Progress.[86] Mann inadvertently proclaimed this approach in an off-the-record March 1964 statement that U.S. recognition policy should be guided by practical rather than moral considerations. This so-called Mann Doctrine was widely interpreted to mean that the administration would not look unfavorably on military governments.[87]

United States policy toward Brazil showcased the Mann Doctrine in action. Thanks in part to the CIA destabilization program launched under JFK, Brazil was in deep trouble economically by 1964. President Goulart appeared to be drifting further leftward, and U.S. ambassador Lincoln Gordon warned that this "incompetent, juvenile delinquent" might try to seize dictatorial powers which in turn could prompt a Communist takeover. Refusing to "stand around" and "watch Brazil dribble down the drain," U.S. officials informed dissident military officers they would not oppose a coup and if necessary would assist with military aid and a show of naval force.[88] When the insurrection began, however, Goulart fled to Venezuela, and the takeover, led by Gen. Humberto Castello Branco, proceeded smoothly. Acting Secretary of State George W. Ball at 3:00 A.M. on April 2 cabled the embassy effectively recognizing the new government. A "furious" LBJ subsequently chewed him out not for what he had done but for failing to inform the White House.[89] The administration rationalized that the Brazilian military had traditionally respected constitutional government. In fact, the new leaders promptly suspended basic rights. Brazil would remain under military government for ten years.

Johnson also faced a crisis in Panama in early 1964. It was a classic decolonization dispute, although most North Americans, blind to their colonial past, failed to see it that way. Panama had profited from the U.S.-built and -operated canal, but its people had long resented the 1903 treaty negotiated by Philippe Bunau-Varilla, the total U.S. sovereignty in the Canal Zone, and the wealth and display of the expatriate "Zonians" who lived in that imperial enclave. At a time when colonialism was waning worldwide, they pressed for a new treaty. The 1964 crisis erupted when Zonians at a local high school defied an agreement requiring Panama's

86. Rabe, *Most Dangerous Area*, 175–83; Walker, "Cuba," 60–61.
87. Department of State, *Foreign Relations of the United States, 1964–1968*, vol. 31 (Washington, 2004), 28–29.
88. Ibid., 418.
89. Ibid., 448.

flag to be flown alongside that of the United States. This largely symbolic but to Panamanians significant incident sparked rioting and then street battles in which twenty-four Panamanians and four U.S. soldiers were killed. President Roberto Chiari demanded a "complete revision of all treaties with the United States" and broke relations.[90]

In an election year, LBJ felt compelled to establish his foreign policy credentials. He conceded some merit in Panama's demands. He and his advisers saw the omnipresent hand of Castro behind the tumult in Panama and recognized the need for concessions to prevent it drifting leftward. But he also understood the emotional attachment of his countrymen to what they considered, in the words of his close friend and mentor Senator Richard Russell of Georgia, American "property" built with "American ingenuity and blood, sweat and sacrifices."[91] Viewing the crisis as a test of his personal strength as well as his diplomatic skills, Johnson feared any concessions that would make him appear weak. Over the next weeks, he put on full display the frenetic, consensus-seeking style that was his trademark. He parried U.S. senators on the left who sympathized with Panama and on the right who demanded toughness. He sent emissaries to calm the Zonians—and demand that they abide by the rules. Refusing to negotiate under threat, he rejected Chiari's demands for treaty revision. He also applied pressure—"squeeze their nuts just a little bit," as he crudely put it—by holding back economic aid and threatening to build a new sea-level canal elsewhere in Central America.[92] At the same time, he publicly agreed to discuss all issues dividing the two countries and privately hinted that treaty revision might result.[93] The two countries soon began serious negotiations and by 1967 had drafted an agreement making major concessions to Panama while preserving U.S. control of the canal. The issues that had provoked it were not resolved, but the 1964 crisis marked a turning point in U.S. policy toward Panama.[94]

Johnson's major Latin American challenge came in the Dominican Republic in the spring of 1965. United States officials had happily acquiesced in the overthrow of Juan Bosch and had been quite content with a reliable government headed by pro-U.S. businessman Donald Reid

90. Ibid., 779. A good recent analysis is Alan McPherson, "Courts of World Opinion: Trying the Panama Flag Riots of 1964," *Diplomatic History* 28 (January 2004), 83–112.

91. LBJ phone conversation with Russell, January 10, 1964, in Michael R. Beschloss, ed., *Taking Charge: The Johnson White House Tapes* (New York, 1997), 155.

92. *FRUS*, 1964–1968 31:836.

93. Brands, *Wages of Globalism*, 40–41.

94. Walter LaFeber, *The Panama Canal: The Crisis in Historical Perspective* (New York, 1979), 14–48.

Cabral. But Reid Cabral had little popular support, and a clumsy attempt to shore up his power in early 1965 provoked outright rebellion. Military officers loyal to Bosch responded by seeking to topple the government, plunging the nation into an especially confusing and bloody civil war. In a desperate act of self-preservation, the government begged Washington to send troops.

LBJ responded decisively. Top U.S. officials staunchly opposed the return of Bosch, "an idealist floating around on Cloud 9 type," Mann labeled him, fearing that his political ineptitude would give the "Castro types" the opening they needed. "How can we send troops 10,000 miles away [to Vietnam]," the president asked, "and let Castro take over right under our nose?"[95] At a crucial point in pushing key Great Society legislation through Congress, Johnson was not about to risk a foreign policy setback. Events in the Dominican Republic were truly bewildering. Bundy and McNamara repeatedly warned that the extent of Communist and Cuban influence could not be determined. Insisting that he had no choice and publicly justifying his actions in terms of saving American lives, the president on April 18 ordered the landing of five hundred marines from ships offshore. Within a week, more than twenty-three thousand U.S. troops were in the Dominican Republic.

As in Panama and Brazil, the United States achieved its immediate goal. American citizens were safely evacuated, U.S. forces restored order, and the diplomats eventually cobbled together an agreement providing for a provisional government and elections. There would be no Cuba in the Dominican Republic. Elected president in 1966, the authoritarian Joaquin Balaguer would dominate the country for the next twenty-five years. But LBJ paid a high price for his success. Complaining that the OAS was "taking a siesta" while the Dominican Republic was "on fire," he consulted it only to provide a veneer of legitimacy to his moves.[96] The essentially unilateral U.S. intervention awakened memories of gunboat diplomacy in the days of Teddy Roosevelt and Wilson. Combined with growing problems in the Alliance for Progress, it undercut much of the goodwill in Latin America generated in the Kennedy years. At home, as was his wont, LBJ responded with hyperbole to charges that he had overreacted. His claims of the threat to American lives and a Communist takeover proved questionable at best, widening what had already been labeled his "credibility gap." The Dominican intervention opened fissures

95. Department of State, *Foreign Relations of the United States, 1964–1968*, vol. 32, (Washington, 2005), 62, 65, 89, 100.
96. Ibid., 100.

in the Cold War consensus that would grow into a canyon over the next three years and raised further questions about the president's ability to handle tough foreign policy issues.[97]

After the Dominican crisis, U.S. relations with Latin America moved off center stage. The assassination of Che Guevara in Bolivia in 1966 and the failure of the revolution he tried to instigate there seemed to ease the threat of another Cuba. As Johnson became more and more absorbed in Vietnam, his interest in the hemisphere waned. United States officials blamed worsening relations on Latin Americans' self-centeredness and irresponsibility; Latin Americans, on U.S. obsession with security at the expense of economic progress and social justice. In April 1967, LBJ made a last-ditch effort to mend fences by attending a hemispheric meeting at Punta del Este. Some minor agreements were reached, and he pushed his advisers to meet the commitments. But no crisis pushed Latin America back to the top of the priority list. What JFK had called "the most dangerous area of the world" receded to the relative unimportance it had held before Nixon's 1958 trip to Venezuela.[98]

V

"I don't want to be known as a war president," LBJ insisted in the fateful summer of 1965, but the war in Vietnam that he launched with great reluctance and struggled to conclude would consume his presidency and define his historical reputation.[99] That "bitch of a war," as he called it, helped to destroy his Great Society, "the woman I really love."[100] It would dominate U.S. foreign policy into the next decade and shape attitudes toward military intervention abroad into the next century.

Johnson inherited a commitment already in peril. Kennedy and his advisers had hoped that Diem's overthrow would stabilize the Saigon government and invigorate the war against the insurgency. The opposite resulted. Buoyed by the coup, the NLF strengthened its hold in areas where it had a presence and expanded its influence into new parts of South Vietnam. Gambling that the United States would not intervene with full force, North Vietnam expanded the flow of men and supplies down the fabled Ho Chi Minh Trail, an elaborate, six-hundred-mile network of danger-filled roads and footpaths across the most difficult terrain.

97. Rabe, *Most Dangerous Area*, 191; Dallek, *Flawed Giant*, 266–67.
98. Mark T. Gilderhus, *The Second Century: U.S.-Latin American Relations Since 1889* (Wilmington, Del., 2000), 193–94.
99. Quoted in Brian VanDeMark, *Into the Quagmire: Lyndon Johnson and the Escalation of the Vietnam War* (New York, 1991), 178.
100. Doris Kearns, *Lyndon Johnson and the American Dream* (New York, 1976), 251.

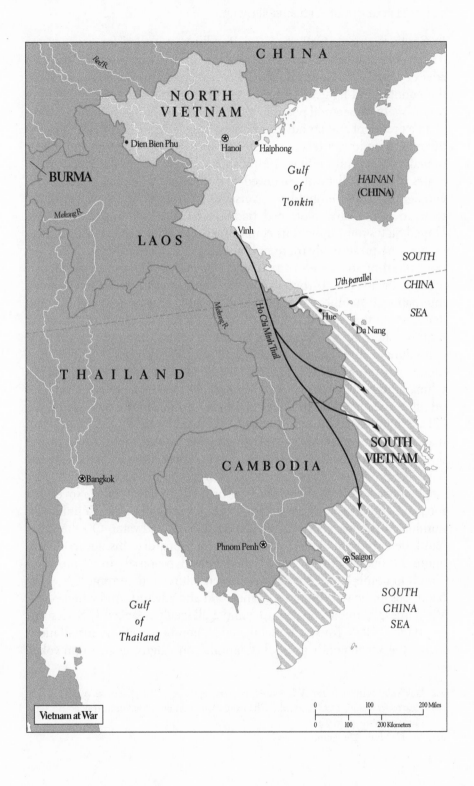

CHINA

NORTH VIETNAM

• Dien Bien Phu

⊗ Hanoi

• Haiphong

Red R.

BURMA

Mekong R.

LAOS

Gulf of Tonkin

HAINAN (CHINA)

• Vinh

17th parallel

SOUTH CHINA SEA

Mekong R.

Ho Chi Minh Trail

Hue

• Da Nang

THAILAND

SOUTH VIETNAM

⊗ Bangkok

CAMBODIA

Phnom Penh ⊗

⊗ Saigon

Gulf of Thailand

SOUTH CHINA SEA

| Vietnam at War |

0   100   200 Miles

0   100   200 Kilometers

In South Vietnam, Catholics and Buddhists struggled for power. One leader after another followed Diem—"government by turnstile," an LBJ adviser called it.[101] None could solidify his own control, much less govern the country and fight the insurgency. Throughout 1964, the collapse of South Vietnam seemed possible if not indeed likely.

The president and his advisers refused to accept this result. The domino theory was no longer taken as gospel by most regional experts, but it continued to creep into official justifications for escalating the war. United States officials still firmly believed that inaction in Vietnam would discourage allies and embolden adversaries. Curiously, the prospect of detente in some ways reinforced traditional Cold War imperatives. The United States must uphold its commitments and demonstrate its ability to contain the presumably more militant China and keep the Soviet Union from reverting to adventurism. The specter of China loomed ominously over Southeast Asia. Turbulence in the Third World appeared to threaten international stability; firmness in Vietnam, it was reasoned, would demonstrate that violent challenges to the status quo could not succeed. Johnson often expressed premonitions of disaster from an expanded U.S. commitment in Vietnam. He still felt compelled to act. He vividly remembered the political price the Democrats had paid for the "loss" of China in 1949. The fall of South Vietnam, he later explained, would have set off a "mean and destructive debate that would shatter my Presidency, kill my administration, and damage our democracy."[102] He was certain that conservatives would use any foreign policy failure to thwart his liberal domestic programs. "If I don't go in now and they show later that I should have," he predicted, "they'll push . . . Vietnam up my ass every time."[103]

The president moved cautiously at first. Facing election in November 1964, he could not appear to do nothing, especially after Republicans nominated the hawkish Arizona senator Barry Goldwater. On the other hand, he could not alarm the electorate or jeopardize his domestic programs by taking drastic steps. He deflected proposals from the Joint Chiefs to bomb North Vietnam and even China and commit U.S. combat troops to the war. But he sent more aid and advisers. And when North Vietnamese gunboats on August 2 and 4 allegedly attacked U.S. destroyers in the Gulf of Tonkin, he retaliated by bombing military installations across the seventeenth parallel. Claiming on August 4 an unprovoked

101. Jack Valenti in *Vietnam: A Television History*, episode 4, "LBJ Goes to War."
102. Kearns, *Johnson*, 252. Logevall, *Choosing War*, contends that Johnson could have chosen not to go to war.
103. VanDeMark, *Quagmire*, xv, 60.

attack on U.S. ships in international waters, an assertion later disputed and now known to be false, he rushed through a compliant Congress with near unanimous consent a Tonkin Gulf Resolution authorizing him to use "all necessary measures to repel any armed attack against the United States and to prevent further aggression." The president's decisive action helped seal a landslide victory over Goldwater in November. The Tonkin Gulf Resolution gave him authority to expand the war. But when doubts were later raised about the August 4 attack, legislators cried deceit, widening LBJ's credibility gap.[104]

The election over, the president during the first seven months of 1965 incrementally and often after hours of agonizing internal deliberations committed the United States to war. Chaos continued to reign in Saigon, and North Vietnam sent regular army units into the south. With South Vietnam facing near certain defeat, LBJ in February responded to NLF attacks on U.S. forces at Pleiku by ordering more retaliatory bombing raids against North Vietnam. This time, they regularized into the Rolling Thunder campaign of systematic, gradually expanding attacks moving steadily northward. The next month, he dispatched U.S. Marines to guard air bases, the first combat forces sent to Vietnam. After South Vietnamese units were mauled in a series of spring and early summer battles, U.S. military commander Gen. William C. Westmoreland urgently requested large increments of American combat forces. Following a searching analysis of the options, most likely with his mind already made up, Johnson in late July ordered the immediate dispatch of 175,000 U.S. troops, making what amounted to an open-ended commitment to save South Vietnam. Still deeply concerned about the Great Society, he cleverly disguised the significance of what he was doing. He repeatedly insisted that he was not changing U.S. policy.[105]

Over the next two years, LBJ steadily expanded the U.S. commitment. He rejected proposals to mobilize the reserves and rally public support for the war, fearing that such moves would threaten his domestic programs and take control of the war out of his hands. To avoid confrontation with the Soviet Union and especially China, he refused to authorize military operations outside of South Vietnam. He went out of his way to avoid Truman's mistakes in Korea by refusing to permit bombing near the Chinese border. Within those bounds, he drastically expanded American involvement—"all-out limited war," one official called it with no apparent

---

104. The authoritative account is Edwin E. Moise, *Tonkin Gulf and the Escalation of the Vietnam War* (Chapel Hill, N.C., 1996).

105. VanDeMark, *Into the Quagmire*, 153–214; Logevall, *Choosing War*, chapters 10 and 11.

sense of the paradox.[106] The bombing of North Vietnam grew from 63,000 tons in 1965 to 226,000 in 1967, inflicting an estimated $600 million of damage on a still primitive economy. By mid-1967, the United States had nearly 500,000 troops in South Vietnam. Westmoreland launched aggressive "search and destroy" operations against North Vietnamese and NLF regulars.

The United States could gain no more than a stalemate. The bombing did not cripple the enemy's will to resist or its capacity to support the NLF. The North Vietnamese dispersed and concealed their most vital resources; the USSR and China helped make up losses. An increasingly deadly air defense system took a growing toll in U.S. planes and pilots. On the ground, when U.S. forces engaged the enemy they usually prevailed. But an elusive foe fought only when conditions were in its favor and replaced and to some extent controlled its losses by melting into sanctuaries in Laos and Cambodia and across the 17th parallel.[107]

The one part of the war that really excited Johnson was the "battle . . . of crops and hearts and caring," but Americanization of the struggle proved counterproductive in terms of building a stable government that could provide a better life for "Vietnamese plain people."[108] Relegated to the sidelines, the South Vietnamese army did not receive the training or experience to assume later the burden of the fighting. Massive U.S. firepower devastated the South Vietnamese countryside, making refugees of as much as one-third of the population. The infusion of thousands of Americans and billions of dollars into a small country had a profoundly destabilizing effect on a fragile society. Corruption became a way of life. Tensions between Americans and South Vietnamese grew.[109]

As the war dragged on and its cost skyrocketed, opposition mounted at home. Frustrated with LBJ's limited war, conservative hawks demanded a knockout blow against North Vietnam to secure victory. On the other side, an extremely heterogeneous group of doves increasingly questioned the administration's policies. Radicals denounced the American ruling class's exploitation of helpless people to sustain a decadent capitalist system. Some anti-war liberals challenged the war's legality and morality. Others insisted that Vietnam was of no more than marginal significance to U.S. national security and was undermining relations with allies and holding back

106. Herring, *LBJ and Vietnam*, 184.
107. Herring, *America's Longest War*, 161–73.
108. Herring, *LBJ and Vietnam*, 67.
109. George C. Herring, " 'Peoples Quite Apart': Americans, South Vietnamese, and the War in Vietnam," *Diplomatic History* 14 (Winter 1990), 5–14.

detente with the USSR. The liberal critique broadened into an indictment of U.S. "globalism." The Johnson administration, Arkansas senator J. William Fulbright charged, had fallen victim to the "arrogance of power," that "fatal . . . over-extension of power and mission, which brought ruin to ancient Athens, to Napoleonic France, and to Nazi Germany."[110]

Opposition to the war took varied forms. Activists conducted teach-ins on college campuses and organized mass demonstrations in Washington and other cities. They openly encouraged resistance to the draft and sought to disrupt the war effort. In October 1967, some fifty thousand protestors marched on the Pentagon. Thousands of young Americans exploited legal loopholes, even mutilated themselves to avoid the draft; an estimated thirty thousand fled to Canada. A handful adopted the method of protest of South Vietnam's Buddhists, publicly immolating themselves, one young Quaker below McNamara's Pentagon office window, an act the secretary later conceded "devastated" him.[111]

The war's mounting costs were more important than the anti-war movement in generating public concern. Growing casualties, indications that more troops might be required, and LBJ's belated request for a tax increase combined in late 1967 to produce unmistakable signs of war-weariness. Polls showed a sharp decline in support for the war and the president's handling of it. The press increasingly questioned U.S. goals and methods. Members of Congress from both parties began to challenge LBJ's policies. Doubts arose even among his inner circle. The secretary of defense had been so closely identified with Vietnam that it had once been called "McNamara's War." In 1967, a tormented McNamara unsuccessfully urged the president to stop the bombing of North Vietnam, put a ceiling on U.S. ground troops, scale back war aims, and seek a negotiated settlement. By the end of the year, for many observers, the war had become the most visible symbol of a malaise that afflicted American society. Rioting in the cities, a spiraling crime rate, and noisy street demonstrations suggested that violence abroad set off violence at home. Divided against itself, the nation appeared on the verge of an internal crisis as severe as the Great Depression.[112]

---

110. Quoted in Thomas Powers, *Vietnam: The War at Home* (Boston, 1984), 118. The standard accounts of the anti-war movement are Charles DeBenedetti with Charles Chatfield, *An American Ordeal: The Antiwar Movement of the Vietnam Era* (Syracuse, N.Y., 1990), Terry Anderson, *The Movement and the Sixties* (New York, 1995), and Melvin Small, *Antiwarriors: The Vietnam War and the Battle for America's Hearts and Minds* (Wilmington, Del., 2002).

111. McNamara made the statement during a conference in Hanoi, June 1997.

112. Herring, *America's Longest War*, 191–99.

The United States' escalation of the war in Vietnam had a major impact on relations with adversaries and allies alike. It did not drive the Soviet Union and China back into each other's arms, as some pessimists had warned. Nor did it destroy detente. Negotiations with the USSR on such issues as arms control continued even as U.S. involvement in Vietnam deepened. By keeping the war limited and repeatedly making clear its intentions to Moscow and Beijing, the administration helped avert a great-power confrontation.[113] Still, the effects of escalation on relations with the Soviet Union were generally negative. Washington's naive hopes to exchange trade and improved relations for Soviet help in securing a favorable Vietnam peace settlement proved chimerical. Competing with China for leadership of the Communist world, Moscow could not appear indifferent to the fate of its ally, North Vietnam. In any event, having been sold out at Geneva in 1954, Hanoi was not about to entrust its fate to its allies. On the contrary, it brilliantly played them against each other to secure maximum aid while preserving its freedom of action. The USSR and China provided more than $2 billion in crucial supplies. Soviet bloc aid to North Vietnam in turn led Congress to reject Johnson's requests for most-favored-nation status for the USSR, an essential underpinning for detente.[114]

The first moves toward detente and expansion of the war in Vietnam also opened deep fissures in the Western alliance. Even as Soviet-American tensions eased, Johnson's advisers continued to view NATO as necessary to guarantee U.S. influence in Western Europe, especially with a recalcitrant France, and to keep West Germany "on a leash."[115] Losing the alliance would also mean "the loss of our diplomatic cards in dealing with the Russians," Vice President Hubert Humphrey candidly admitted.[116] The missile crisis had aroused European concerns about U.S. reliability. The easing of the Soviet threat seemed to reduce allied dependence on the United States. And the growing economic strength of Western Europe set off increased nationalism. At a minimum, the allies sought a partnership of equals. Determined to restore his nation to global prominence, de Gaulle entertained visions of a Europe closely tied to the USSR and free of the Anglo-Saxons. Heightened nationalism in Europe raised fears among nervous Americans of a revival of the forces that had provoked two world wars,

113. George C. Herring, "Fighting Without Allies: The International Dimensions of America's Failure in Vietnam," in Marc Jason Gilbert, ed., Why the North Won the Vietnam War (New York, 2002), 82–83.
114. Costigliola, "Johnson," 207.
115. Ibid., 117.
116. Ibid., 174.

making an alliance under U.S. control all the more important. Facing growing costs in Vietnam, Americans wanted the Europeans to pay more for their own defense.

The differences burst out into the open after 1963. The United States insisted that the defense of South Vietnam was essential to protect Western Europe. The Europeans were not persuaded, and in any event doubted U.S. ability to succeed there. Faced with growing anti-American protest among their own people, the allies staunchly resisted LBJ's appeals for troops, even, in the case of Britain, for the symbolic commitment of a "platoon of bagpipers."[117] As it grew stronger, West Germany pressed harder on reunification and acquiring nuclear weapons, setting off anxiety across the continent. Not surprisingly, the major challenge continued to come from de Gaulle. In 1964, he recognized China and especially infuriated Johnson by pushing for the neutralization of Vietnam. In February 1966, he withdrew from NATO and asked that its troops and headquarters be moved from France. He followed with an independent approach to Moscow. European refusal to support the United States in Vietnam and de Gaulle's challenge provoked forty-four senators in August 1966 to propose major cuts in U.S. forces in Europe.

Johnson and his advisers handled the European crisis adeptly. U.S. officials deeply resented the allies' refusal to support the war in Vietnam. "When the Russians invade Sussex," Rusk snapped at a British journalist, "don't expect us to come and help you."[118] But there was no retribution, and in 1966 LBJ provided crucial economic assistance to bolster the faltering pound sterling. Some U.S. officials privately railed at de Gaulle's "megalomania," but the president wisely refused to get into a "pissing match" with the French leader. "When a man asks you to leave his house, you don't argue," he remarked of the request to remove NATO troops, "you get your hat and go."[119] He also held off congressional pressures to withdraw troops from Europe. The administration even attempted to use detente to keep the alliance intact—and the United States in control—by encouraging West German approaches to the Soviet Union and Eastern Europe.[120]

The United States also narrowly averted—at least temporarily—a major crisis in the already shaky alliance. In early 1967, economically beleaguered Britain announced plans to reduce its overseas forces by one-third and threatened to remove its troops from Europe unless West Germany

117. Herring, "Without Allies," 79–80.
118. Ibid., 80.
119. Brands, *Wages of Globalism*, 94; Schwartz, *Johnson*, 105.
120. Costigliola, "Johnson," 196–97,

assumed the cost of supporting them. West Germany, in turn, threatened to curtail purchases of U.S. and British military equipment. After extended negotiations, Bonn consented to buy on a smaller scale. The United States and Britain agreed to "redeploy" troops from Germany to their home territories, keeping them under NATO command and ready to send back when needed. But Britain proceeded with cutbacks in July, and West Germany reduced its forces to 400,000 instead of building them up to 508,000 as originally planned.[121] The Western alliance was substantially weakened by France's defection and surging economic pressures.

The price of hegemony was starkly manifest in Asia and the Pacific. Detente and the Vietnam War sometimes disturbed America's Asian allies, but they also provided leverage to extort concessions from Washington. The mere hint of a change in U.S. China policy, along with Beijing's 1964 diplomatic successes and especially its nuclear test, deeply alarmed Taiwan's leaders. The United States quickly rebuffed Chiang Kai-shek's offers to take out China's nuclear program and launch a military offensive in southern China—the "Gimo and Madame eat-sleep-love-dream 'counterattack,' " the U.S. ambassador mused.[122] The administration also rejected his proposal for a regional military alliance and politely declined his offer of combat units for Vietnam. On the other hand, to palliate Chiang, the United States sent up-to-date military hardware, including fighter planes. The Nationalist leader skillfully exploited LBJ's absorption with Vietnam. Nationalist troops took part in CIA covert operations there. U.S. forces used Taiwan bases as staging areas for operations in Vietnam, and Taiwan earned huge profits from civilian contracts. The Vietnam War thus tightened U.S.-Taiwan ties.[123]

The war produced major strains in America's relations with its major East Asian ally, Japan. Japanese continued to press for the reversion of Okinawa. Minimizing the threat in Vietnam, they generally opposed the war and especially feared they might be sucked into it. U.S. officials were reluctant to give up the "Keystone of the Pacific," especially with war raging in Southeast Asia. Americans resented that Japan took advantage of the U.S. defense "umbrella" while contributing only minimally to its own security. As Japan's economy grew by leaps and bounds and the balance of trade shifted heavily in its favor, Americans pushed for greater access to its markets.[124]

121. Brands, *Wages of Globalism*, 108–9.
122. Gordon H. Chang, *Friends and Enemies: The United States, China, and the Soviet Union, 1948–1972* (Stanford, Calif., 1990), 227.
123. Tucker, "Threats," 111–15.
124. Ibid., 116–27.

LBJ's desperation for help in Vietnam forced repeated concessions to Japan. The son of a sake brewer and protégé of postwar leader Yoshida Shigeru, Prime Minister Eisaku Sato was a masterful politician and diplomat who adeptly maneuvered amidst a bewildering array of external and internal pressures. The two nations reached vague agreement on the reversion of Okinawa "within a few years," with the United States to retain basing rights.[125] Japan opened the door slightly to U.S. imports. Sato provided token support in Vietnam, mainly medical supplies and ships flying the U.S. flag for coastal transport in South Vietnam. Japan furnished bases for U.S. air operations. In the meantime, as one Japanese journalist observed, Japan, "like a magician, satisfied both its conscience and its purse."[126] Sato tolerated popular protests against the war. Vietnam helped Japan surpass the United States as the major economic power in the region. Japanese sold the U.S. armed forces an estimated $1 billion per year in everything from beer to body bags. Southeast Asia nations used vast U.S. expenditures to purchase Japanese consumer goods. Japan indeed may have been the only winner of the war in Vietnam.[127]

Other Pacific allies contributed troops for the war, but most drove a very hard bargain. Some shared with the United States concern about Chinese expansion in Southeast Asia. Some depended on U.S. security guarantees. Most seized the chance to extort concessions in return for modest numbers of troops. Only Australia provided sizeable forces at its own expense. New Zealand neatly balanced its concern not to offend the United States or inflame domestic critics of the war by sending a small artillery battery. South Korea provided about fifty thousand combat forces, but secured handsome subsidies, substantial additional military aid, and expanded security commitments. The Philippines' Ferdinand Marcos extracted maximum gain from a minimal investment. In addition to a small engineering unit, he offered to mobilize ten battalions of troops at U.S. expense, then kept them at home for his own self-protection. Recognizing that he had been had, LBJ warned an aide: "If you ever bring that man near me again, I'll have your head."[128]

125. Nicholas Evan Sarantakes, *Keystone: The American Occupation of Okinawa and U.S.-Japanese Relations* (College Station, Tex., 2000), 154–65.
126. Michael Schaller, "Altered States: The United States and Japan During the 1960s," in Kunz, *Crucial Decade*, 276.
127. Ibid., 263–79; Walter LaFeber, *The Clash: U.S.-Japanese Relations Throughout History* (New York, 1997), 339–47.
128. Stanley Karnow, *In Our Image: America's Empire in the Philippines* (New York, 1989), 377. For problems with the allies, see Herring, "Fighting Without Allies," 79–81.

VI

Even more than in Asia, in the ever volatile Middle East, the Johnson administration was subject to manipulation by a close friend with a powerful constituency in the United States and an ambitious foreign policy agenda. Following JFK's lead, Johnson took steps to further what was now called the special relationship. Like many Americans, he had long admired Israel's plucky defense of its territory. As a senator, he had faithfully supported the new nation. He appreciated the importance of the Jewish vote to the Democratic Party and the clout of the Israel lobby. His close friends among American Jews included several of his White House advisers. Indeed, his aide Harry McPherson once speculated that "some place in Lyndon Johnson's blood" there were a "great many Jewish corpuscles."[129]

As president, Johnson expanded the flow of weapons to Israel. He recognized the importance of Arab oil, of course, and he was increasingly angered by the opposition of Jewish intellectuals to the war in Vietnam. Like Kennedy, he worried about Israel's nuclear ambitions, and he refused repeated requests for F-4 fighter-bombers capable of carrying nuclear weapons. He preferred that arms be provided through third parties like West Germany than directly from the United States. But he was usually there for Israel, whether it be A-4 Skyhawk fighters, the first commitment of combat aircraft for Israel, M-48 tanks, or M-113 armored personnel carriers. Such weapons were deemed essential to counter Soviet shipments to Arabs and to placate Israel when the United States supplied moderate Arab states such as Jordan. United States officials also indulged in the wishful thinking that satisfying Israel's demands on conventional arms would sway it from seeking nuclear weapons. The administration tried to hinge military assistance on the right to inspect Israel's nuclear facilities, but the Israeli tail often wagged the superpower dog, and Tel Aviv stubbornly and successfully resisted U.S. conditions.[130]

The 1967 Middle East crisis, a classic example of the way escalation begets war, originated from the rekindling of the ever explosive Arab-Israeli dispute. Certain that Israel would soon acquire nuclear weapons, the radical Arabs stepped up their pressure. In February 1966, a Baathist regime seized power in Syria and, with Soviet backing, set out to "out-Nasir Nasir."[131]

129. Brands, *Wages of Globalism*, 187.
130. Little, *American Orientalism*, 97–99; Zach Levey, "The United States Skyhawk Sale to Israel, 1966: Strategic Exigencies of an Arms Deal," *Diplomatic History* 28 (April 2004), 255–76.
131. Douglas Little, "Choosing Sides: Lyndon Johnson and the Middle East," in Robert A. Divine, ed., *The Johnson Years*, vol. 3, *LBJ at Home and Abroad* (Lawrence, Kans., 1994), 173.

Syria's move spurred the Egyptian leader back into action lest he lose his position among the more militant Arabs. Nasser promptly demanded removal of a UN peacekeeping force stationed in the Sinai as a buffer between Egypt and Israel. Surprised when the UN complied, he massed troops along the Israeli border and threatened to close the Gulf of Sidra, Israel's lifeline to the outside world. In the meantime, the newly formed Palestine Liberation Organization (PLO) mounted deadly terrorist attacks against Israel from bases in the West Bank and the Golan Heights. Encircled and increasingly embattled, unsure of outside support, nervous Israelis feared for the existence of their state.

While frantically seeking to calm tensions on both sides, the United States appears to have given Israel the freedom to respond as it saw fit. United States officials recognized the perils of a Middle Eastern war, especially the possibility of a superpower confrontation at a time when they were bogged down in Vietnam. Even more, they feared further Soviet penetration of a vital region and a successful Arab war of liberation. Many openly sympathized with Israel. Choosing an analogy calculated to catch the president's ear, adviser John Roche referred to the "Israelis as Texas, and Nasser as Santa Ana."[132] The administration proposed an international naval force—the so-called Red Sea Regatta—to break Nasser's blockade but gained little support from Congress or key allies. The president at first tried to discourage Israel from firing the first shot, admonishing repeatedly—and suggestively—that "Israel will not be alone unless it decides to go it alone." But he also promised to use force to open the straits and in time conveyed signals through crony Abe Fortas and others that seemed to give Israel a green light to launch a preemptive strike. In any event, threatened on two sides and from within, and certain that the best defense was a good offense, Israel would probably have started the war anyway. Sensing that the best way to maximize its security was to strike first, Israel on June 5, 1967, launched a short and entirely one-sided conflict with enormous implications for the future of the Middle East.[133]

Israel's daring move paid huge military dividends. Striking without warning, U.S.-supplied Skyhawk jets bearing the Star of David insignia knocked out Egyptian and Jordanian air forces on the ground, destroying three hundred Egyptian planes in less than an hour and a half. Control of the air ensured smashing battlefield success. Using U.S.-provided tanks, Israel promptly seized Gaza, the Sinai, the West Bank, and East Jerusalem. The United States, privately pleased with the embarrassment suffered by

132. Ibid., 175.
133. Little, *American Orientalism*, 100–101.

Nasser and the USSR, firmly backed Israel. Mainly concerned with possible Soviet intervention, Washington sought to reassure Moscow that the United States had not been complicit in Israel's surprise attack. The Johnson administration also promoted a cease-fire in place, an arrangement that favored Israel.[134]

Israel's unprovoked and brutal attack on a U.S. Navy ship close to the Egyptian coast on the fourth day of the war made clear its willingness to defy its patron. The USS *Liberty* incident is still shrouded in mystery and has given rise to numerous conspiracy theories. It remains unclear exactly what the "ugliest, strangest looking ship in the U.S. Navy," as Adm. Thomas Moorer called it, was doing, why it was attacked, and who ordered the attack.[135] The slow-moving, unarmed, and unguarded electronic surveillance vessel was apparently not where it was supposed to be because of a communications foul-up. The Israelis may have tried to destroy it to prevent it from intercepting radio traffic reporting the massacre of Egyptian troops in the Sinai.[136] They may have been trying to hide from the prying ears of U.S. electronic espionage their preparations for attacking the Golan Heights.[137] On the afternoon of June 8, Israeli aircraft and then gunboats struck the *Liberty* with rockets, napalm, and torpedoes, killing 34 sailors, wounding 171. At first believing that Egypt or the Soviet Union was responsible, the United States dispatched aircraft from a nearby carrier. In the meantime, learning that Israel had attacked the ship and fearing escalation of the war, it recalled the planes. Israel naturally fell back on mistaken identity, a claim only the most gullible could believe. "Inconceivable," staunch friend of Israel Clark Clifford snorted. "Incomprehensible," Rusk concurred.[138] Israel apologized and paid an indemnity. United States officials accepted the apology without much further questioning.

Less than twenty-four hours later, Israeli forces attacked the Golan Heights and drove within forty miles of Damascus. They aimed, apparently, not only to strengthen their strategic position but also to eliminate the hostile Syrian government. The attack threatened the superpower confrontation U.S. officials most feared. Humiliated by the total defeat of two of its leading clients and ridiculed by the Chinese, Moscow promptly broke relations with Israel. Premier Alexei Kosygin warned LBJ in the first

---

134. A good military history is Michael B. Oren, *Six Days of War: June 1967 and the Making of the Modern Middle East* (New York, 2002).
135. John Omicinski, Gannett News Service, September 2, 2005.
136. James Bamford, *Body of Secrets* (New York, 2001), 203.
137. Little, *American Orientalism*, 241–42.
138. Department of State, *Foreign Relations of the United States, 1964–1968*, vol. 19 (Washington, 2004), 398–402.

use of their hotline that unless Israel was stopped the USSR might take action "which may bring us into a clash, which will lead to catastrophe." During a tense top-level meeting marked by hushed voices, LBJ ordered the Sixth Fleet from Crete to the eastern Mediterranean close to Syria. Tired of coddling Israel and angered by the *Liberty* attack, U.S. officials also insisted that it accept a cease-fire without delay.[139] The tough action—and Israel's achievement of its goals—produced results. The Soviet Union backed off, Israel backed down on June 11, and the crisis eased.

Israel's smashing victory had enormous consequences. In just 132 hours, it seized forty-two thousand square miles of territory, tripling the size of the country. Intoxicated with success, Israelis called it the Six-Day War, an unmistakable reference to the creation story in Genesis. Indeed, the war restored the dimensions of biblical Israel and soon led to occupation and settlement of the captured lands. For the Arabs, the war became known as the Disaster, a humiliation that made them even less inclined toward peace with Israel. Nasser's pan-Arab dreams were crushed. Arab nationalism would never recover from the debacle. Some Arab intellectuals turned to modernization and democracy; many others, to a revival of traditional Islam.[140] Although U.S. officials were pleased with Israel's success, the war caused major problems for them. The Israeli lobby now pressed for the full-fledged alliance that would further compromise America's position in a vital region. The Johnson administration feared that Israel's success would fuel its ambitions to acquire nuclear weapons and hang on to the conquered territories, moves that would further destabilize the Middle East. A humiliated USSR set out to rebuild its clients' shattered arsenals and recoup its influence. A Baathist coup by Saddam Hussein in Iraq in 1968 raised the possibility of a new Soviet client in an oil-rich state. Armed with Soviet weapons, Palestinian radicals mounted deadly attacks on Israeli positions in the West Bank and Israel itself.[141]

An administration already bogged down in Vietnam struggled with these intractable and dangerous problems. United States officials ignored demands for an alliance while maintaining close ties with Israel. The United States joined Britain in sponsoring UN Resolution 242, calling on Israel to relinquish territory in exchange for Arab acceptance of its existence, the so-called land-for-peace formula. It pressed Israel to negotiate and also to refrain from settling the occupied regions. It persisted in trying to keep Israel from going nuclear. When Israel refused to give assurances

139. Ibid., 409.
140. Oren, *Six Days*, 305–27.
141. Little, "Choosing Sides," 179–84.

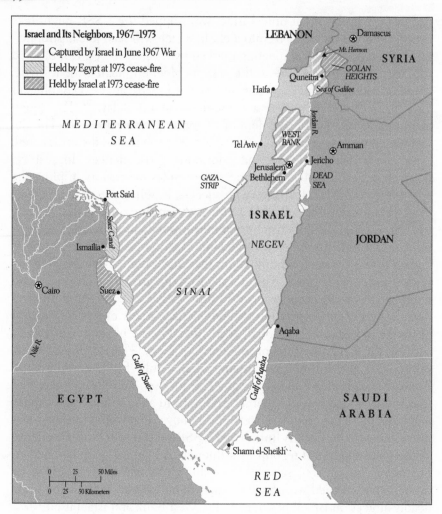

Israel and Its Neighbors, 1967–1973

▨ Captured by Israel in June 1967 War
▨ Held by Egypt at 1973 cease-fire
▨ Held by Israel at 1973 cease-fire

regarding nuclear weapons, LBJ rejected its requests for F-4 jets. The pattern of Israeli resistance to compromise was already set, however, and the president eventually gave in on the aircraft—a major escalation of the regional arms race—in return for meaningless assurances that Israel would not introduce nuclear weapons into the Middle East.[142]

To protect its broader interests, the United States adopted a "three pillars" approach, adding Saudi Arabia and Iran as the other two bulwarks of

142. Ibid., 181–83.

its regional strategy. After the Six-Day War, it cemented long-standing ties with these two oil-rich kingdoms with arms deals and other inducements. LBJ cultivated the shah of Iran with special care. Scrapping Kennedy's efforts to push reforms on a key ally, the president responded to the shah's endless complaints about the paucity of U.S. aid and his only slightly veiled threats to lean toward the USSR by lavishing military aid on him through numerous hastily concocted deals.[143] Such policies served U.S. short-term interests, but they did nothing to stanch Arab radicalism, and in Iran they would have fateful consequences.

VII

McNamara's replacement, Clark Clifford, remembered it as the most difficult year of his life, a year that seemed like five years; Rusk called it a "blur."[144] For the United States and the rest of the world, 1968 was a year quite unlike any other. In Western and Eastern Europe, loosely connected "networks of rebellion," composed mostly of young radicals inspired by Mao Zedong and Che Guevara, mounted major protests against the Vietnam War and U.S. imperialism, challenged their own governments, and sought an elusive third way between capitalism and Communism. The upheaval helped to bring down de Gaulle and provoke a Soviet invasion of Czechoslovakia. For Americans, 1968 was a year of unparalleled tragedy, marked by the assassination of civil rights leader Dr. Martin Luther King Jr. and presidential candidate Robert Kennedy within months of each other. It was a year of turmoil, with riots in Washington and other cities following King's death, the takeover of Columbia University by student radicals in April, and in August during the Democratic convention warfare in the streets of Chicago between police and anti-war protestors. The Johnson administration faced major foreign policy crises with North Korea, Vietnam, world gold markets, and Czechoslovakia. For the United States and the world, this halfway point between the end of World War II and the end of the Cold War was a watershed year.[145]

The year of crisis began on January 23 when North Korea seized the U.S. intelligence ship *Pueblo* in the Sea of Japan and imprisoned its officers and crew. In retrospect, the ill-fated voyage of the *Pueblo* seems a classic

---

143. James A. Bill, *The Eagle and the Lion: The Tragedy of American-Iranian Relations* (New Haven, Conn., 1988), 172.

144. Herring, *LBJ and Vietnam*, 165.

145. Carole Fink, Phillip Gassert, and Detlef Junker, eds., *1968: The World Transformed* (New York, 1998), 1–27.

example of Murphy's Law in action. The ship was woefully prepared for a dangerous mission, its crew inexperienced and ill trained, its skipper, Captain Lloyd Bucher, a submariner assigned to a onetime cargo vessel. Navy brass shrugged off the risks of electronic espionage off the coast of North Korea. When the ship was attacked, Bucher did not try to escape or fight. The crew did not destroy highly classified documents or its electronic gear, providing the enemy an intelligence windfall. LBJ wisely resisted demands to retaliate militarily. Underestimating North Korea's independence, he first sought to retrieve the ship and crew through the USSR. In fact, it took eleven months of patient and sometimes excruciating negotiations and a skillfully crafted apology to retrieve the sailors without their ship.[146]

A week after the *Pueblo* incident, North Vietnam and the NLF launched the biggest offensive of the war. Striking at Tet, the beginning of the lunar new year and the most festive of Vietnamese holidays, they shifted their attacks from the countryside to the previously secure urban areas of South Vietnam. In Saigon, the center of U.S. power, they hit the airport, the presidential palace, and, most dramatically, the U.S. embassy. Although caught off guard, U.S. and South Vietnamese forces repulsed the initial assaults, inflicted huge casualties, and retook lost ground. But the suddenness and magnitude of the offensive had a huge impact in the United States. Observing the events on nightly television news, a public that had been told the United States was winning the war was shocked and profoundly disillusioned. An "air of gloom" hung over White House discussions, one LBJ adviser later recalled; another likened the mood to that in 1861 after the first Battle of Bull Run.[147]

The choices open to policymakers all seemed bad. Top officials speculated that seizure of the *Pueblo* was part of a concerted Communist effort to open a "second front" to divert U.S. attention and resources from Vietnam. Some feared a second round of attacks in Vietnam or possibly even Berlin or the Middle East. Johnson's military advisers sought to use the crises to force mobilization of the reserves and a full military buildup. Their proposal to increase the armed forces by 206,000 troops especially alarmed civilian leaders. The estimated price tag of $10 billion imposed enormous economic and political burdens in an election year and when public anxiety about the war was already high.[148]

146. Mitchell Lerner, *The* Pueblo *Incident: A Spy Ship and the Failure of American Foreign Policy* (Lawrence, Kans., 2002), especially 5–23 and 231–37.
147. Herring, *America's Longest War*, 210.
148. George C. Herring, "Tet and the Crisis of Hegemony," in Fink et al., 1968, 39–41.

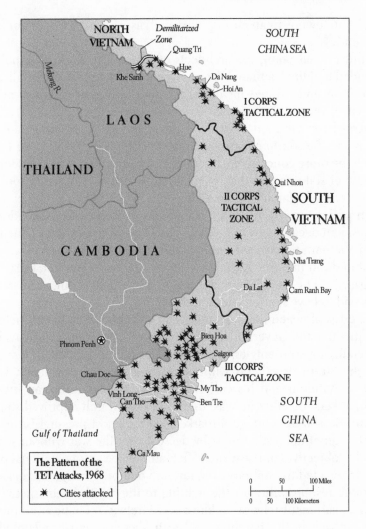

An economic crisis, itself partly caused by the war, significantly influenced policy deliberations. The war added costs as high as $3.6 billion per year to an economy already strained by domestic spending, causing inflation and a growing balance of payments deficit that weakened the dollar in international markets and threatened the world monetary structure. A financial crisis in Britain, leading to devaluation of the pound, caused huge losses from the gold pool. In March 1968, pressure on the dollar mounted and gold purchases reached new highs. At Washington's urging, the London gold market closed on March 14. The request for more troops was increasingly linked to the nation's economic woes. "The town is in an atmosphere of crisis," Dean Acheson confided to a friend.[149]

At this crucial point, the architects of major U.S. Cold War policies concluded that the Vietnam War was destroying the nation's overall security position and pressed for disengagement. Acheson, NSC-68 author Paul Nitze, veteran diplomat W. Averell Harriman, and Clifford, all key Truman advisers, formed a sort of cabal with dovish White House advisers such as McPherson to persuade Johnson to change course. "Our leader ought to be more concerned with areas that count," the imperious former secretary of state and hard-core Atlanticist insisted.[150] Acheson took the lead in a crucial March 26–27 meeting of the Wise Men, a group of senior foreign policy experts, including a number of former Truman advisers, the president occasionally consulted. The Wise Men generally concurred that in Vietnam the United States could "no longer do the job we have set out to do in the time we have left and we must begin to take steps to disengage." "The establishment bastards have bailed out," a dispirited LBJ is said to have snarled after the meeting.[151]

The crisis of hegemony was "resolved" in a manner both inconclusive and anticlimactic. Governments rarely deal with complex issues head-on, democratic governments especially so. The administration thus improvised short-term expedients without really addressing the larger issues raised by Acheson and his cohort. Under U.S. leadership, an international bankers' meeting in Washington in late March approved stopgap measures to stabilize the gold market. On the most pressing issue, LBJ sought to quiet domestic unrest by deescalating the war without scaling back U.S. objectives or reassessing Vietnam's place among national priorities. He rejected the military's request for additional troops and began to shift more responsibility for the fighting to the South Vietnamese. In a dramatic, nationally televised address on March 31, 1968, he announced a major cutback of the bombing of North Vietnam and proclaimed his willingness to undertake peace negotiations. In an announcement that stunned the nation, he revealed he would not be a candidate for another term as president. A war originally undertaken to sustain U.S. hegemony over the postwar international order was scaled back to maintain an economic and military system on the verge of collapse.[152]

149. Acheson to John Cowles, March 14, 1968, Dean G. Acheson Papers, Yale University Library, New Haven, Conn., box 7.
150. Isaacson and Thomas, *Wise Men*, 684.
151. Herring, *America's Longest War*, 225–26.
152. Herring, "Crisis of Hegemony," 44–48.

Not surprisingly, Johnson's hopes for a late-term peace went unrealized. Hanoi accepted his invitation to talk, and negotiations began in Paris in May, but they quickly deadlocked over such issues as the bombing of North Vietnam and the makeup of a new South Vietnamese government. In the summer of 1968, the Soviets helped broker a deal to get the talks off dead center. On October 31, a reluctant LBJ finally agreed to the total bombing halt Hanoi had long demanded. But the president's last-ditch effort to salvage negotiations and perhaps the presidential candidacy of Vice President Humphrey ran up against formidable forces. Fearing a last-minute peace deal that would sabotage their candidate's hopes, Richard Nixon's campaign officials, working through Harvard professor, sometimes LBJ consultant, and Republican foreign policy adviser Henry A. Kissinger and go-between Anna Chennault, widow of World War II China theater air commander Gen. Claire Chennault, urged South Vietnamese president Nguyen Van Thieu to block the rush toward peace. Thieu needed little persuading. Only after Nixon had been elected by a very thin margin and under enormous pressure from the Johnson administration did he agree to send delegates to Paris. Once there, the South Vietnamese raised procedural roadblocks that thwarted any remaining hope of a settlement.[153]

Frustrated in Vietnam, Johnson in his last months vigorously pursued detente with the USSR. He was deeply committed to arms control negotiations to ease the threat of nuclear war, redeem an administration tainted by Vietnam, and leave his mark on history. The process had begun with small but significant U.S.-Soviet agreements to reduce production of weapons-grade uranium (1964) and ban nuclear weapons in space (1966). Johnson's efforts to initiate negotiations on strategic arms limitations met a cautious response from Moscow. But France and China's emergence as nuclear powers and fears that West Germany might get nuclear weapons spurred serious non-proliferation negotiations. On July 1, 1968, the United States, Britain, and the Soviet Union signed a Nuclear Non-proliferation Treaty (NPT); signatories who possessed nuclear weapons agreed not to help others acquire them, and those who did not have them agreed not to purchase or develop them. More than one hundred nations eventually signed the NPT. By forestalling West German acquisition of nuclear weapons, it helped promote European stability. But France refused to sign, while agreeing to abide by the terms. China and aspiring nuclear powers Israel, India, Pakistan, and South Africa rejected the treaty. Despite its obvious flaws, LBJ hailed the NPT as one of his

153. Jeffrey Kimball, *Nixon's Vietnam War* (Lawrence, Kans., 1998), 56–62.

most important achievements.[154] The administration also seemed to achieve a breakthrough when the USSR in the summer of 1968 agreed to begin strategic arms negotiations. A Kosygin-Johnson summit was set for Leningrad in September.

The Soviet invasion of Czechoslovakia in August doomed the summit and arms control negotiations. Moscow had watched anxiously during the legendary Prague Spring of 1968 as Czech leaders responding to popular pressures promoted democratization while reiterating their fealty to the Warsaw Pact. Increasingly nervous about the spread of "anti-Soviet bacillus" into other Eastern bloc states and their own republics, and aware of the weakness of Czech troops along the German border, a reluctant Kremlin finally sent Warsaw Pact troops into Czechoslovakia.[155] Two weeks later, Brezhnev proclaimed a Soviet duty to intervene anywhere socialism was threatened, a statement Western journalists dubbed the Brezhnev Doctrine. The move caught Washington completely off guard. Vividly remembering Budapest in 1956 when the United States seemed to encourage revolt and then did nothing, U.S. officials went out of their way to avoid any appearance of interference, even to the point of toning down Radio Free Europe broadcasts. They continued naively to reckon that Moscow would not risk detente by intervening militarily. Ambassador to Washington Anatoly Dobrynin was assigned the unwelcome task of explaining the invasion to the president. To his surprise, a completely unsuspecting LBJ insisted on talking about the summit and in a bizarre scene offered his startled—and much relieved—guest a whiskey while regaling him with tales of Texas.[156]

When the harsh reality sank in, U.S. officials responded angrily. "The Cold War is not over," LBJ ruefully conceded, and Rusk complained of the Soviets "throwing a dead fish in the president's face."[157] Fearing that Moscow might also move against Romania or even Yugoslavia, the United States issued firm warnings. On the other hand, still eager for negotiations, it responded with no more than perfunctory protests and token retaliation. While canceling the summit, Johnson kept the door open for negotiations after a respectable interval, hoping, as he put it, that Soviet leaders might want to "take some of the polecat off them."[158] Indeed,

---

154. Hal Brands, "Progress Unseen: U.S. Arms Control Policy and the Origins of Détente, 1963–1968," *Diplomatic History* 30 (April 2006), 253–85.
155. Mark Kramer, "The Czechoslovak Crisis and the Brezhnev Doctrine," in Fink et al., *1968*, 121–51.
156. Schwartz, *Johnson*, 214–17.
157. Ibid., 217.
158. Ibid., 220.

until after he left office, he clung to hopes of a last-minute summit while demanding prior assurances of positive results on complex arms control issues. Moscow was understandably wary. President-elect Nixon made clear he would not honor the terms of an eleventh-hour deal.

Even without a summit, 1968 was a watershed year in the Cold War. The Czech crisis briefly set back superpower contacts, but it also furthered detente. The U.S. and USSR went to great lengths to avoid confrontation, even to the point of deploying forces along the Czech border in such a way as to minimize possibilities of a clash. At the "moment of truth," historian Vojtech Mastny concludes, both sides "showed a prudent disposition to underestimate their own strength and overestimate the strength of the adversary," making them less inclined to contemplate war. After 1968, neither side seriously considered war in Europe, thus stabilizing the region where the Cold War had begun and providing a solid basis for detente. Conservative American critics have grossly overestimated the impact of LBJ's inaction in the face of the invasion of Czechoslovakia. It did uphold the fragile status quo in Eastern Europe, to be sure, but it did not resolve Moscow's huge problems within the Warsaw Pact. Nor did it lead to tighter Soviet control over bloc nations. More important, perhaps, it made clear to the Kremlin the high cost of such actions. The year 1968 was thus an important landmark on the road to the end of the Cold War.[159]

The "global disruption" of that year produced other changes that marked the end of the postwar era. The U.S. non-response to the Soviet invasion of Czechoslovakia and its commitment to the NPT suggested to West German leaders that Washington would sacrifice German reunification to the interest of stability and order. Bonn thus embraced what would be called *Ostpolitik*, approaches to the USSR and Eastern Europe separate from the United States that provided an independent, European force for detente. Fearing that Moscow might intervene forcibly in East Asia, Chinese leaders clamped down on the Cultural Revolution and looked to the United States as a possible counter to the Soviet threat. When North Vietnam tilted toward the Soviet Union in 1968, China began to withdraw troops from Vietnam and invited Washington to reopen the Warsaw talks suspended the preceding year. These small steps opened the way for Nixon's dramatic moves toward normalization.[160]

159. Vojtech Mastny, "Was 1968 a Strategic Watershed in the Cold War?" *Diplomatic History* 29 (January 2005), 176.
160. Gottfried Niedhart, "Ostpolitik: The Role of the Federal Republic of Germany in the Process of Détente," in Fink et al., 1968, 173–92; Qiang Zhai, *China and the Vietnam Wars, 1950–1975* (Chapel Hill, N.C., 2000), 178–80.

The year 1968 also marked the beginning of the end of the postwar economic boom. The economic crisis of 1967–68, the most serious since the Great Depression, set off a prolonged malaise among the industrialized nations. The stopgap measures taken to deal with the March gold crisis eased the immediate problems, but they weakened the U.S. commitment to the Bretton Woods system of currency stabilization. The costs of what Paul Kennedy has called "imperial overstretch" also afflicted the USSR, creating additional incentives for both sides to find common ground, encouraging still greater independence among allies on both sides, and enabling the losers of World War II, Germany and Japan, to emerge as major players in the world economy. In the world economy, as in geopolitics, 1968 was a year of dramatic changes.[161]

LYNDON JOHNSON REGISTERED IMPORTANT ACCOMPLISHMENTS in foreign as well as domestic policy. Especially on arms control issues, his administration took steps toward detente with the USSR, establishing the conceptual framework upon which his successor would build. He moved cautiously in the right direction in dealing with China and Panama. As part of the Great Society, he scrapped the ultra-nationalistic and racially based national-origins immigration legislation of 1924, a system that had favored Northern and Western Europeans and, along with legalized segregation, embarrassed the United States in dealing with the non-white world. Condemning that law as "alien to the American dream," he secured passage in October 1965 of legislation that favored refugees from Communist countries and the Middle East, immigrants with special skills, and people related to U.S. citizens or resident aliens.[162] That landmark law opened the doors to a huge new influx of immigrants, the largest numbers from the Middle East, Asia, and especially Latin America, by century's end reconfiguring the nation's demographics.

Despite his achievements—and his wishes to the contrary—LBJ's presidency is still remembered mainly for Vietnam. A consummate pragmatist as a senator, in domestic politics, and on many foreign policy issues, he could not find in Vietnam that elusive middle ground that would have permitted disengagement without undermining his own and the nation's prestige. The war he took on with grave misgivings and struggled at great cost to end dominated his presidency and eventually drove him from office. It helped destroy the Great Society in which he had invested so

161. Carole Fink, Philipp Gassert, and Detlef Junker, "Introduction," in Fink et al., eds. 1968, 9.
162. Dallek, *Flawed Giant*, 226–27; Borstelmann, *Cold War*, 194–95.

much; it damaged the U.S. economy. In foreign policy, historian Nancy Tucker has written, "it intruded upon virtually every decision the administration made." It "strained friendships, aggravated animosities, and left a problematic legacy."[163] A war fought to uphold the nation's world position made the United States an international whipping boy. Its repercussions would last into the next century.

Vietnam was symptomatic of the larger foreign policy conundrum of an embattled presidency. Following long-established Cold War dictates, LBJ was committed to upholding a worldwide status quo in a time of sweeping change and as U.S. power operated under growing constraints. When Thieu blocked the administration's last-minute peace ploy in late 1968, Harry McPherson moaned that the "American Gulliver is tied down by the South Vietnamese Lilliputians."[164] In fact, during the Johnson years, "the American Gulliver" faced upstart Lilliputians all over the world. Despite major challenges in Panama and the Dominican Republic, LBJ held the line in Latin America, but he did so at the cost of much of the goodwill the United States had earned early in Kennedy's presidency. He kept the Western alliance together, but the defection of France and the growing independence of West Germany made it more an association of equals than one dominated by the United States. He paid a high price to allies to secure minimal support for the war in Vietnam. In the Six-Day War, where headstrong proxy Israel furthered major U.S. aims, the result was closer entanglement with Israel, greater reliance on Iran and Saudi Arabia, and deeper Soviet involvement in the Middle East. Johnson's abdication in March 1968, according to historian H. W. Brands, represented a "defeat for the policy of global containment," an implicit concession that "the job was more than America could handle."[165] The most urgent task for Richard Nixon and Henry Kissinger would be to devise new strategies to adapt to America's changed position in the world.

163. Nancy Tucker, "Lyndon Johnson: A Final Reckoning," in Cohen and Tucker, *Johnson*, 312–18.
164. Herring, *America's Longest War*, 265.
165. Brands, *Wages of Globalism*, 256–57.

17

Nixon, Kissinger, and the End of the Postwar Era, 1969–1974

It was an act without precedent in the annals of twentieth-century U.S. diplomacy: the odd couple of President Richard M. Nixon and National Security Adviser Henry A. Kissinger devising and implementing a foreign policy imaginative in concept and radical in some of its essential elements. The two men perceived the dramatic changes that had occurred since the end of World War II and set out to craft what Nixon called a "new approach to foreign policy to match a new era of international relations."[1] Keenly aware of the relative decline in U.S. power, they adapted by exploiting the rivalry between their two Communist adversaries, scaling back commitments, and using regional powers to promote world order. These self-styled realists operated in the manner of the great nineteenth-century European diplomatists they so admired. Shutting out the foreign policy bureaucracy, Congress, and indeed the nation, acting in secrecy and often with great dramatic flair, they pulled off in 1972—their year of triumph—breathtaking achievements, grandly staged summits in Moscow and more incredibly in Beijing, and the possibility of peace in Vietnam, helping to seal Nixon's smashing reelection victory in November.

Within less than two years, their Grand Design was in tatters, a disgraced Nixon forced to resign the office he had fought so doggedly to obtain. Brilliant in many respects, the Nixon-Kissinger scheme was fatally flawed in others. It assumed a level of cooperation and compliance on the part of other nations that simply did not exist. At home, moreover, in some very important ways, the two men swam against powerful currents. They insisted upon the primacy of foreign policy at a time when the nation, already in a postwar mode, was turning inward. They fancied themselves masters of realpolitik when Americans, recoiling from Vietnam, were rediscovering the idealistic strain in their foreign policy. They sought to expand the already broad parameters of what had been tagged the "imperial presidency" when Congress was out to recapture its place in the policymaking process surrendered during the Cold War and the nation was reacting against executive excess. More than anything else, Nixon

1. "U.S. Foreign Policy for the 1970s," February 18, 1970, Department of State, *Foreign Relations of the United States, 1969–1976*, vol. 1 (Washington, 2003), 196.

and Kissinger undermined their own plans by the methods they used. The ends justified the means, even when the latter conflicted with traditional American values. The secrecy they claimed essential to implement their bold ideas made enemies at home and antagonized allies abroad. They had no interest in or patience for—indeed placed themselves above—the painstaking work of building domestic support for their policies. When they encountered opposition, they sometimes responded with anger and vengefulness, resorting to illegal methods to discredit or silence their foes. Ultimately, they were snared by the web of intrigue, deceit, and reprisal they themselves had spun.[2]

I

By the time Nixon took office in January 1969, the contours of a new international system had become clear. The postwar years were over; a new and uncertain era was taking form. The Western European nations and Japan had recovered from the war economically and were challenging U.S. preeminence. The Western alliance was intact, but the allies acted more and more independently of the United States. Soviet leader Leonid Brezhnev's August 1968 invasion of Czechoslovakia by no means resolved Moscow's growing problems with the Warsaw Pact nations. More ominously for the Kremlin and significantly for the United States, the Soviet Union and its erstwhile ally China, after years of shouting, began shooting at each other. According to Soviet accounts, Chinese troops in early 1969 crossed their long East Asian border on nearly one hundred occasions, sparking fighting, casualties on both sides, and the threat of war. Soviet officials railed at those "squint-eyed bastards," shifted troops and planes to the east, contemplated nuclear attacks on Chinese forces, and floated discreet inquiries about how the United States might respond to a preemptive strike against China's fledgling nuclear capacity. The Chinese denounced what they now labeled their "#1 enemy." Mao Zedong urged the people to dig tunnels and store food.[3] The easing of the Cold War, rising Sino-Soviet tensions, and the chronic problems facing the multitude of new nations contributed to rampant instability in the Third World.

If a new international system presented opportunity as well as threat, the situation at home posed challenges as formidable as those faced by any incoming president since Franklin Roosevelt. The postwar economic

2. The metaphor is from William P. Bundy, *A Tangled Web: The Making of Foreign Policy in the Nixon Presidency* (New York, 1998).
3. Gordon H. Chang, *Friends and Enemies: The United States, China, and the Soviet Union, 1948–1972* (Stanford, Calif., 1990), 285–86; Michael Schaller, *The United States and China in the Twentieth Century* (New York, 1990), 176.

boom was ending by the time Nixon took office. Unemployment and inflation stoked by spending for the war in Vietnam increased during 1969. Economic growth slowed. At the end of the year, the nation was in recession for the first time in a decade. By the beginning of Nixon's second term, the economy had become a serious problem, soon exacerbated by skyrocketing fuel prices from an Arab oil embargo and afflicted by the new phenomenon of "stagflation," a simultaneous increase in unemployment and inflation that became the economic hallmark of the 1970s.

The most ominous problems in 1969 were political and especially social rather than economic, starkly symbolized by the violent protests and arrests at Nixon's inauguration parade. The nation was more divided than at any other time since its own Civil War. The rise of black power militance provoked a white backlash. A top-level commission appointed by Lyndon Johnson following riots in Detroit in 1967 ominously concluded that "our nation is moving toward two societies, one black, one white—separate and unequal."[4] Anti-war protests, the women's liberation movement, and the sexual revolution sparked deeply divisive culture wars that would rage into the next century. The rise of a counterculture—usually young, alienated rebels, often called hippies, who rejected the values of mainstream society—provoked an angry and fearful response from the middle-class Americans they disdained. A mushrooming crime rate and rising violence created the appearance of a nation coming apart at the seams. Within Nixon's first year, there were more than six hundred bombing incidents or attempts within the United States; the number more than doubled the next year. In an increasingly polarized society, with the left screaming revolution and the right demanding law and order, the center seemed to be crumbling.

The "team" that would devise new policies for a new era comprised an unlikely duo at best. As part of the Jewish diaspora of the 1930s, Henry Alfred Kissinger fled Nazi Germany as a youth and settled in New York City. After serving in the army, he earned a B.A. and Ph.D. in political science at Harvard, writing a dissertation on Castlereagh and Metternich, the architects of post-Napoleonic world order. As a faculty member at Harvard, he cultivated the international foreign policy elite, and his books on important issues brought him to the attention of establishment figures. He advised moderate Republican Nelson Rockefeller on foreign policy. As a consultant for the Kennedy and Johnson administrations, he participated in several Vietnam peace initiatives. During the 1968 campaign, he shamelessly played various sides against the middle. His owlish,

4. Terry Anderson, *The Sixties* (New York, 1999), 94.

professorial appearance and dry, self-effacing wit only partially obscured an enormous ego and a burning ambition to shape policies rather than write about them. His thick German accent and slow speech seemed to give authority to his pronouncements.[5]

Nixon grew up in a family of modest means in California. After a law degree from Duke University and service in the navy in World War II, where he earned a reputation as a shrewd—and successful—poker player, he entered politics, using McCarthyite methods before the senator from Wisconsin gave them a name and winning seats in the House and then the Senate. A surprise choice for vice president in 1952, he served loyally in that office. Narrowly defeated by JFK in 1960 and by Pat Brown for governor of California in 1962, he seemed politically dead, but he emerged, incongruously and seemingly miraculously, out of the chaos of 1968 to gain the office he had long coveted. Socially awkward and ill at ease with others and himself—"the oddest man I ever knew," one of his White House aides later recalled—Nixon had a keen analytical mind and was a perceptive observer of international affairs.[6] He appreciated Kissinger's help in 1968 and saw him as a useful link to moderate Republicans and the still potent eastern establishment. Kissinger had once declared Nixon unfit for the presidency but readily agreed to join his administration.

The middle-American politician and the German-born Harvard professor could hardly have been more different in background, but they shared a love of power and a zeal to mold a fluid world in ways that would establish their place in history. Loners and outsiders in their chosen professions, they were perhaps naturally drawn to each other. Both were insecure to the point of paranoia, and they waged constant warfare with their own inner demons. Not surprisingly, the two men never established a close personal relationship. Nixon tired of Kissinger's whining and frequent threats to resign. In his presence, Kissinger praised Nixon to the point of sycophancy; behind his back, he made snide remarks about the president's "meatball mind" and his drinking. When things went bad,

5. Kissinger's role in U.S. foreign policy is analyzed in Walter Isaacson, Kissinger: A Biography (New York, 1992), Jussi Hanhimäki, The Flawed Architect: Henry Kissinger and American Foreign Policy (New York, 2004), Robert Dallek, Nixon and Kissinger: Partners in Power (New York, 2007), and Jeremi Suri, Henry Kissinger and the American Century (2007).

6. There is no up-to-date biography of Nixon. Stephen E. Ambrose's Nixon: The Triumph of a Politician, 1962–1972 (New York, 1989) and Nixon: Ruin and Recovery, 1973–1990 (New York, 1991) cover the presidency in some detail. In addition to Dallek and Bundy, the most valuable analysis of Nixon's presidency is Melvin Small, The Presidency of Richard Nixon (Lawrence, Kans., 1999).

their relationship soured. But in their first years mutual suspicion was kept in check by mutual dependence, Kissinger using Nixon for access to power, Nixon relying on Kissinger to shape and implement his broad designs. Nixon especially had a reputation as a rigid ideologue, but in power the two men proved pragmatic and flexible. They shared an obsession with secrecy, a zest for intrigue, and a flair for the unexpected move. They also shared a certain disregard for democracy, equating dissent with treason and carrying to extremes the Cold War dogma that national security was too important to be left to an ignorant and indifferent public and a parochial and cumbersome Congress.[7]

From the outset, they took the foreign policy controls firmly and exclusively in their own hands. Reluctant to share power and certain that a hidebound bureaucracy could be an obstacle to the bold moves they hoped to implement, they restructured the machinery of government to put the National Security Council in control of policymaking and Kissinger in control of the NSC. They used new interdepartmental committees, chaired by the national security adviser, to shut out of the loop Secretary of Defense Melvin Laird and Secretary of State William Rogers, the latter an old friend of Nixon's, while keeping the departments busy compiling massive studies. They used backchannels to hide from their colleagues developments on crucial issues. The NSC more than doubled in size and nearly tripled in budget during the Nixon years. What had been created in 1947 as a coordinating mechanism became a little State Department. "It was a palace coup," author and former policymaker William Bundy observed, "entirely constitutional but at the same time revolutionary."[8]

Bureaucratic warfare is a way of life in Washington, but the Nixon administration created an atmosphere of oppressive secretiveness, paranoia, backbiting, and conspiracy that makes the word *Byzantine* seem tame by comparison. A notorious slave driver, Kissinger, it was said, treated his aides like mushrooms: They were "kept in the dark, got a lot of manure piled on them, and then got canned." Among his many character flaws, Nixon was incapable of giving orders and seeing that they were carried out. He preferred to operate alone and in secret, and his White House was a veritable den of conspiracy.[9] A frustrated Laird secured backchannel cables from friends in the National Security Agency; the Joint Chiefs of Staff employed a navy yeoman to purloin documents to keep them informed about what was going on in the White House.

7. Dallek, *Partners in Power*, 615–18.
8. Bundy, *Tangled Web*, 54–55.
9. Henry Kissinger, *White House Years* (Boston, 1979), 482.

By the time Nixon took office, the outlines for a fundamental re-orientation of U.S. foreign policy were already clear in his mind. Troubled by what he saw as a resurgence of isolationism in the United States in the wake of Vietnam, he was determined to find a way for his country to "stay in the world, not . . . get out of the world."[10] Ironically, for this old Cold Warrior, the essential goal was to facilitate an era of peaceful coexistence with the major Communist powers. After a "period of confrontation," he proclaimed in his inaugural address, "we are entering an era of negotiation."[11] This meant, on the one hand, the establishment of detente with the major adversary, the Soviet Union. The second step, obvious by this time but still bold in terms of long-standing domestic political constraints, was the normalization of relations with the People's Republic of China. "Taking the long view," he wrote in a much-quoted 1967 *Foreign Affairs* article, "we simply cannot afford to leave China forever outside the family of nations, there to nurture its fantasies, cherish its hates and threaten its neighbors."[12] Achievement of these goals would be the focus of foreign policy during Nixon's first term. They would be the polestars around which everything else would orbit.

II

The first task for Nixon and Kissinger was to end the war in Vietnam, a "bone in the nation's throat," in the words of one presidential adviser, a divisive force that had torn the country apart and blocked constructive approaches to domestic and foreign policy problems.[13] The two men also insisted that the war must be ended honorably, which meant to them no ignominious U.S. withdrawal and maintaining the South Vietnamese government intact. As a young congressman, Nixon had led the Republican attack on Truman for "losing" China. Like LBJ, he feared the domestic political backlash that might accompany the fall of South Vietnam to Communism. He worried that a disguised defeat or "elegant bugout" in Vietnam would destroy American self-confidence and breed a crippling isolationism at home.[14] Most important, he and Kissinger feared the international consequences of a precipitous withdrawal. Intent on restructuring relations with the Soviet Union and China, they believed they must extricate the United States from Vietnam in a manner that demonstrated its

---

10. *FRUS, 1969–1976* 1:191.
11. Ibid., 53–55.
12. Richard M. Nixon, "Asia After Vietnam," *Foreign Affairs* 46 (October 1967), 111.
13. William Safire, *Before the Fall: An Inside View of the Pre-Watergate White House* (New York, 1975), 121.
14. *FRUS, 1969–1976* 1:81,109.

resolve, upholding U.S. credibility with friend and foe alike. "However we got into Vietnam . . . ," Kissinger observed before taking office, "ending the war honorably is essential for the peace of the world. Any other solution may unloose forces that would complicate the prospects for international order."[15]

The two men believed they could compel North Vietnam to accept terms it had previously rejected. The USSR had expressed an interest in expanded trade and agreements to limit nuclear weapons, and the Americans believed this sort of "linkage" could be exploited to secure Soviet assistance getting North Vietnam to accept a "reasonable" settlement. Great-power diplomacy could be supplemented by military pressure. Like his predecessors going back to Truman, Kissinger insisted that a "fourth-rate power" like North Vietnam must have a "breaking point." Nixon believed that Eisenhower had gained peace in Korea in 1953 by hinting he might use nuclear weapons, and he concluded that similar warnings would intimidate the North Vietnamese. He counted on his reputation as a hard-liner to make the threats believable. He even sought to convey to foes the sense that he was capable of acting irrationally, the so-called madman theory. "We'll just slip the word to them that, 'for God's sake, you know Nixon's obsessed about Communism . . . and he has his hand on the nuclear button,' " he confided to his chief of staff during a walk on the beach in 1969.[16]

Like most people new to power, Nixon and Kissinger underestimated their adversaries and overestimated their ability to control events. Even had Moscow wanted to help Washington get out of Vietnam, it probably could not have done so. While competing with China for the allegiance of Third World nations, it could not appear too conciliatory toward the United States. The administration's efforts to tie Soviet-American negotiations to a peace settlement in Vietnam proved unavailing. In the summer of 1969, the United States put forth a new peace proposal and issued not so veiled warnings that if substantive negotiations did not begin by November 1, North Vietnam could expect "measures of great consequence and force." On Nixon's orders, Kissinger convened a top-level study group to draw up plans for an operation named Duck Hook calling for "savage, punishing blows" against North Vietnam up to and possibly including tactical nuclear weapons. Kissinger's study group eventually concluded that air strikes and a blockade might not wrench concessions

15. Henry A. Kissinger, "The Vietnam Negotiations," *Foreign Affairs* 47 (January 1969), 234.
16. H. R. Haldeman, *The Ends of Power* (New York, 1978), 83. The "madman theory" is analyzed in Jeffrey Kimball, *The Vietnam War Files: Uncovering the Secret History of Nixon-Era Strategy* (Lawrence, Kans., 2004), 15–20, 54–59.

from Hanoi or even limit its capacity to prosecute the war in South Vietnam. Nixon aides also warned that drastic escalation would reignite antiwar protests at home. Haunted throughout his career by the fear of failure, Nixon abandoned the plan for peace through coercion with the greatest reluctance and only after being persuaded that it would not work. As a limp substitute, he ordered for mid-October a Joint Chiefs of Staff Readiness Test in hopes that surveillance of Soviet ships heading for North Vietnam and putting Strategic Air Command bombers on high alert would send the appropriate messages. If Moscow picked up the signals, it did not respond as hoped. Hanoi was not intimidated.[17]

Unwilling simply to withdraw from Vietnam and unable to pressure North Vietnam into a settlement, Nixon fell back on what came to be called Vietnamization. After the Tet Offensive, Johnson had begun to shift the burden of the fighting to the South Vietnamese army, and Nixon made this the central element of his plan to achieve peace with honor. By beginning to withdraw U.S. troops and requiring the South Vietnamese to do more, he reasoned, he could pacify the home front. Indulging in some wishful thinking, he hoped also to persuade the North Vietnamese that they might do better negotiating with the United States now than with a much strengthened South Vietnam later. He succeeded at home at least for the short term. Major demonstrations took place across the United States in October and November 1969, drawing millions of people. But Nixon's troop withdrawals took much of the steam out of anti-war protests. Polls revealed strong public support for his policies. "We've got those liberal bastards on the run now," the president exulted, "and we're going to keep them on the run."[18]

Making Vietnamization work proved much more difficult. South Vietnamese found the very term insulting—a "U.S. Dollar and Vietnamese Blood Sharing Plan," they complained.[19] The United States poured into South Vietnam huge sums of money, vast quantities of weapons, and so many vehicles one congressman wondered whether the goal was to put "every South Vietnamese soldier behind the wheel."[20] Increased U.S. aid and improved training combined with a prolonged enemy stand-down to

17. William Burr and Jeffrey Kimball, "Nixon's Secret Nuclear Alert: Vietnam War Diplomacy and the Joint Chiefs of Staff Readiness Test, October 1969," *Cold War History* 3 (January 2003), 113–56.

18. Tad Szulc, *The Illusion of Peace* (New York, 1973), 158.

19. George C. Herring, " 'Peoples Quite Apart': Americans, South Vietnamese, and the War in Vietnam," *Diplomatic History* 14 (Winter 1990), 17–18.

20. George C. Herring, *America's Longest War: The United States and Vietnam, 1950–1975* (4th ed., New York, 2002), 284.

leave South Vietnam more secure than at any time since the war began. But huge problems remained. The Saigon government was riddled with corruption and could never win the support of the South Vietnamese people. On paper, the army appeared a formidable fighting force, but it relied heavily on U.S. air and logistic support. North Vietnamese negotiators posed the problem bluntly to Kissinger. If the United States could not win with a half million of its own men, how could it succeed when its "puppet troops" had to do the fighting? It was a question that troubled him, the national security adviser conceded.[21] He also feared that for Americans the troop withdrawals would be like salted peanuts: The more they got, the more they would want, in time leading to demands for unilateral withdrawal.[22] Nixon and Kissinger increasingly worried that the North Vietnamese would stall until the United States left and then deal with South Vietnam.

To improve the prospects of Vietnamization, Nixon in the spring of 1970 took the bold and fateful step of sending U.S. and South Vietnamese troops into Cambodia. For years, the North Vietnamese had exploited Cambodia's neutrality by using its territory for sanctuary. The U.S. military had repeatedly asked for and been denied authority to attack these safe havens. The overthrow of the neutralist Prince Sihanouk in March 1970 by a pro-U.S. faction headed by Lon Nol provided an opportunity difficult for Nixon to pass up. He realized that expansion of the war might have a "shattering effect" at home, but he accepted that risk.[23] He hoped that destruction of the sanctuaries would weaken North Vietnam's offensive capability, buy time for Vietnamization, and bolster a friendly government in Cambodia. By widening the war into previously off-limits Cambodia, he would also signal the enemy that, unlike Johnson, he would not be bound by restraints. In making the decision, Nixon put himself through an emotional wringer. Kissinger described him as "overwrought," "irritable," and "defiant."[24] Exhausted, at times quite agitated, he indulged in bizarre behavior. He pumped himself up by repeatedly watching the hit movie *Patton*, a stirring account of the legendary World War II hero. At times, he paced the Oval Office while smoking a corncob pipe in the mode of Gen. Douglas MacArthur. Kissinger had reservations about the move but went along, partly to outflank Laird and Rogers in the raging turf war that was Nixon's Washington.

21. Ibid., 287.
22. *FRUS, 1969–1976* 1:106.
23. Herring, *America's Longest War*, 290.
24. Jeffrey Kimball, *Nixon's Vietnam War* (Lawrence, Kans., 1998), 204–5.

The Cambodian "incursion" had disastrous results. To be sure, the U.S. military claimed success in terms of sanctuaries destroyed, weapons seized, and intelligence acquired, and the incursion may have bought some time for Vietnamization.[25] On the other hand, it enlarged the theater of operations at a time when U.S. forces were already stretched thin. It forced the North Vietnamese out of their sanctuaries and into the heartland of Cambodia, helping to spark in that unfortunate country a full-scale civil war that in time produced the Khmer Rouge genocide, one of the great human tragedies of recent history.

At home, the reaction exceeded Nixon's worst expectations—also in tragic ways. The Cambodian incursion revived an anti-war movement rendered moribund by Nixon's late 1969 moves. The unexpected expansion of a war the president had promised to wind down enraged his critics; his intemperate defense of his actions, including a statement indiscriminately branding protestors as "bums," added to the furor. Demonstrations erupted on campuses across the nation. The protest assumed new fury when four students at Kent State University in Ohio were killed in angry confrontations with the National Guard. More than a hundred thousand demonstrators gathered in Washington the first week of May to protest Cambodia and Kent State. Students at 350 colleges and universities went on strike; as many as five hundred schools were closed to avert further violence. Cambodia also provoked the most serious congressional challenge to presidential authority since the beginning of the war. Nixon had consulted with only a few hawkish legislators. Others were outraged at being kept in the dark and furious with the widening of the war. In a symbolic act of defiance, the Senate in June terminated the 1964 Tonkin Gulf Resolution. An amendment to cut off funds for operations in Cambodia after June 30 sponsored by Kentucky Republican John Sherman Cooper and Idaho Democrat Frank Church was approved by the Senate, although later rejected by the House.[26]

A thoroughly rattled president responded vindictively. There would be no more "screwing around" with congressional foes, he ordered his staff. "Having drawn the sword, don't take it out—stick it in hard."[27] He accused his critics of prolonging the war and warned that if "Congress undertakes to restrict me, Congress will have to assume the consequences."[28] He

25. John M. Shaw, *The Cambodia Campaign: The 1970 Offensive and America's Vietnam War* (Lawrence, Kans., 2005).
26. Herring, *America's Longest War*, 293–95.
27. Safire, *Before the Fall*, 190.
28. Henry Brandon, *The Retreat of American Power* (New York, 1974), 146–47.

ordered the military to do in secret whatever was necessary in Cambodia, regardless of Congress and the public. "Publicly, we say one thing," he indicated. "Actually, we do another."[29] He approved one of the most blatant assaults on individual freedom and privacy in U.S. history, the so-called Huston Plan, which authorized the intelligence services to open mail, use electronic surveillance, and even burglarize to spy on Americans. Although the agencies balked at the specific plan and Nixon later withdrew his approval, some of its methods were used in a futile effort to verify suspected links between American radicals and foreign governments. White House operatives also used part of the plan to stifle domestic dissent. The president's counterattack led straight to the abuses of power that produced the Watergate scandal and his downfall.[30]

Nixon's Cambodian incursion perpetuated the stalemate in Vietnam. Hanoi seemed content to wait until the president's position at home crumbled beneath him. Its negotiating position hardened. The military situation in Vietnam remained stable, but additional troop withdrawals to appease domestic critics left South Vietnam increasingly vulnerable. A second incursion into Laos in early 1971 without U.S. ground forces put on embarrassing display the South Vietnamese army's dependence on American support. At home, the trial of Lt. William Calley for the murder of more than five hundred Vietnamese civilians at My Lai in 1968 opened a short but bitter debate on U.S. war crimes. The leak by Daniel Ellsberg, a former Defense Department official, in June 1971 of a top-secret internal history of the war ordered by Robert McNamara, the so-called Pentagon Papers, appeared to confirm what antiwar critics had long been saying—that the government had repeatedly misled the public about what it was doing in Vietnam and the success attained. Public disillusion over the war reached an all-time high in the summer of 1971, a whopping 71 percent agreeing that the United States had erred sending troops to Vietnam, 58 percent viewing the war as "immoral." Kissinger worried that the administration might not be able to get through the year without "Congress giving the farm away."[31]

III

While struggling to end the Vietnam War, Nixon and Kissinger pushed ahead with their Grand Design—detente with the Soviet Union and rapprochement with the People's Republic of China. Detente did not, of course, originate with Nixon. Johnson had pursued negotiations with

29. Associated Press report, November 17, 2005.
30. Herring, *America's Longest War*, 295.
31. Vernon A. Walters, *Silent Missions* (New York, 1978), 516.

Moscow on such issues as arms control, attempted to "build bridges" to Eastern Europe, and even spoke boldly of ending the Cold War. His administration had accepted nuclear parity with the USSR and built its deterrence policy on the concept of mutual assured destruction (MAD), the surreal Cold War doctrine that sought to avert nuclear war by ensuring that each side had a second strike capability sufficiently terrifying to deter a first strike. Even earlier, France's Charles de Gaulle had pursued his own peculiarly European version of detente. And in 1963, West Berlin mayor Willy Brandt (later chancellor of West Germany) urged that Germany "break through the frozen front between East and West" through direct approaches to the USSR and Eastern Europe. Indeed, with their own countries in turmoil in 1968, leaders worldwide found compelling reasons to promote order in the international system.[32]

Nixon moved detente to the top of his foreign policy agenda. By the time he took office, the one-time ardent Cold Warrior viewed the Soviet Union as a "normal" world power more intent on maintaining its position than upsetting the international status quo and therefore a nation that could be negotiated with. He recognized that the relative decline in U.S. power required major adjustments in its relations with other nations and that Soviet needs and especially the Sino-Soviet conflict provided openings a skillful diplomatist might exploit. He perceived that his reputation as a hard-liner enabled him to do things other U.S. politicians could not—indeed, by making him appear statesmanlike they might even win him points at home. In pursuing detente, Nixon and Kissinger did not abandon containment. Rather, they hoped through negotiations on key issues to create linkages that would enable them to influence Soviet behavior in other areas. Through what Kissinger called the "subtle triangle of relations between Washington, Beijing, and Moscow," they sought to "improve the possibilities of accommodations with each as we increase our options with both."[33] They viewed detente not as an end in itself but rather, in Nixon's words, a means to "minimize confrontation in marginal areas and provide, at least, alternative possibilities in the major ones."[34] They hoped it would enable them to manage Soviet power and thus get the USSR to accept the emerging world order.[35]

32. Jeremi Suri, *Power and Protest: Global Revolution and the Rise of Détente* (Cambridge, Mass., 2003), 213–17.

33. Evelyn Goh, "Nixon, Kissinger, and the 'Soviet Card' in the U.S. Opening to China," *Diplomatic History* 29 (June 2005), 475.

34. Raymond Garthoff, *Détente and Confrontation: American-Soviet Relations from Nixon to Reagan* (Washington, 1985), 26.

35. Ibid., 33.

There were powerful specific incentives for improving relations with the Soviet Union. As chancellor of West Germany, Brandt was vigorously pursuing what he called *Ostpolitik* by making independent overtures to East Germany and the Soviet Union. Nixon and Kissinger shared Brandt's goals but feared the threat to NATO and America's world leadership and saw negotiations with Moscow as a way to maintain U.S. control. They regarded trade agreements with the USSR as a partial solution to America's economic problems. They hoped that expanded economic ties might give them leverage with Moscow on other issues and nudge the Soviet economy away from military spending toward the production of consumer goods. The nuclear arms race provided perhaps the most compelling inducement. Nixon and Kissinger feared that the Soviet Union having attained parity might seek superiority. Technology refused to stand still, and the development of primitive anti-ballistic missile (ABM) systems that could shoot down approaching enemy missiles and of multiple independently targeted reentry vehicles (MIRVs) that could spew forth numerous warheads toward different targets threatened to undermine MAD and set off an even more expensive and potentially more destructive phase of the competition.

For the Soviet Union, the move toward detente reflected rising confidence and growing anxiety, shared interests with the United States, and mutual misperceptions. Reducing the costs of the arms race and minimizing the risks of nuclear war were also among Moscow's most urgent priorities. The attainment of strategic parity gave Soviet leaders the self-confidence to begin negotiations. They were painfully aware by the late 1960s that their economy was sputtering, and they decided to address problems such as food shortages and technological backwardness through trade with the West rather than systemic reforms. They also hoped that expanded commerce would give the West a vested interest in friendly relations with the Soviet Union.[36] For the Soviets, detente might also help ease tensions in Europe, freeing them to focus on their increasingly dangerous eastern flank. Since 1917, the Soviet leadership while proclaiming a revolutionary ideology had craved acceptance as a world power, and detente seemed to offer such recognition. From their perspective (as well as the American), detente contained the seeds of future misunderstanding. They flatly rejected the concept of linkage, insisting that each issue must be considered on its own terms. They saw detente as a way to manage the United States in a world where it no longer had strategic superiority. For them,

36. James K. Libbey, *American-Russian Economic Relations, 1770s-1990s* (Claremont, Calif., 1989), 164–65.

detente and peaceful coexistence did not mean "forgoing the objective processes of historical development." Indeed, by matching U.S. nuclear power, they hoped to deny it the means to thwart revolutionary change.[37]

Nixon's inaugural address, hailing an "era of negotiation," sent powerful verbal signals to Moscow. In his first press conference, he accepted nuclear parity, a huge step, by committing to "sufficiency, not superiority."[38] Operating in the manner that would become their trademark, he and Kissinger worked outside regular bureaucratic channels. As with Vietnam, to be sure, experts negotiated on key issues through established mechanisms. In October 1969, the United States agreed to arms control talks in Helsinki and Vienna. But the real work was done through Kissinger's backchannel with Soviet ambassador to the United States, Anatoly Dobrynin. Beginning in early 1969, the two men met regularly, often daily and without note takers or interpreters. In 1972 alone, they spoke 130 times. They established a direct phone line between the White House and the Soviet embassy.[39]

Progress did not come easily. The United States expressed repeated disappointment at the lack of Soviet assistance in the Vietnam peace negotiations. As the administration simultaneously moved toward China, the Soviets voiced strong displeasure, on occasion threatening to break off negotiations. U-2 spy flights revealed in September 1970 construction of what appeared a submarine base at Cienfuegos on Cuba's southwest coast, threatening a mini-replay of the 1962 missile crisis. Kissinger and his aides viewed the project as a violation of Moscow's post-missile-crisis pledge not to put offensive forces in Cuba. The key proof, in the national security adviser's mind, was the appearance of a soccer field, presumably being built for Russian sailors. "These soccer fields could mean war," he ominously informed White House chief of staff Bob Haldeman. "Cubans play baseball. Russians play soccer."[40] Kissinger's excitable aide Gen. Alexander M. Haig Jr. spoke of a "reckless Soviet adventure."[41] Rather than go public, Nixon and Kissinger sensibly worked behind the scenes to head off a crisis. Soviet intentions remain unclear. In any event, they pulled down the suspected base before it was completed. The United States re-pledged not to invade Cuba. The flap made clear the extent to which lingering mutual suspicions could block progress on detente.

37. Garthoff, Détente, 37–53.
38. John Lewis Gaddis, Russia, The Soviet Union, and the United States: An Interpretive History (2nd ed., New York, 1990), 270.
39. Small, Nixon Presidency, 101.
40. Hanhimäki, Flawed Architect, 99.
41. Small, Nixon Presidency, 104.

The major roadblocks included the sheer complexity of the issues, the difficulty for each side to make concessions, and the enormity of the stakes. The USSR had already constructed ABM systems to protect Moscow. Johnson had committed the United States to a primitive system to defend against Chinese missiles. Based on expert advice, Nixon questioned the feasibility of ABMs and recognized that the cost would be astronomical. He was under great pressure from Congress not to proceed. But he saw an expanded ABM system as a potentially useful bargaining chip with Moscow and refused to be dictated to by increasingly contentious legislators. In a move part bluff, he endorsed a more advanced ABM system. Aware that MIRVs represented another major escalation of an already dangerous arms race, he ignored pleas from Congress to ban them and announced U.S. deployment. The key issues thus included a possible ban on MIRVs, how many ABMs should be allowed, and whether they should protect cities or missiles. In terms of offensive weapons, the United States in 1969 led the Soviet Union in long-range bombers and submarines capable of firing missiles while the USSR had more and larger intercontinental ballistic missiles (ICBMs). Each side naturally put forward proposals in its own favor. The issues were complex to the point of bafflement and impossible for non-experts to decipher—Nixon's eyes would regularly glaze over during detailed discussions. Leaders on both sides had powerful domestic constituencies to coerce or appease. Within the U.S. government, Kissinger conceded, there was a "babble of discordant voices."[42]

The Nixon-Kissinger modus operandi created additional problems for the United States—and sometimes for the USSR. Among U.S. negotiators, the left hand rarely knew what the right was doing. Confusion among American diplomats caused awkward moments with—and sometimes created splendid openings for—their Soviet counterparts. Kissinger's backchannel discussions undermined the morale of those involved in the regular negotiations and denied him much-needed technical advice, sometimes causing major blunders. Denouncing Kissinger's "duplicitous diplomacy," chief U.S. arms control negotiator Gerard Smith lamented that "at least in the USSR, the whole politburo was consulted."[43] A Soviet proposal in the formal sessions in early 1971 of terms close to those already discussed in "the channel" provoked a furor in the White House, Nixon fretting that the arms control negotiators rather than he might get credit for an agreement.

42. Garthoff, Détente, 137.
43. Isaacson, Kissinger, 327.

In the spring of 1971, after more than a year of wrangling, the two sides finally attained a "conceptual breakthrough." In the formal negotiations and "the channel," they had fought over whether to deal with ABMs and offensive weapons together or separately, and if the latter, which should come first. In May, they agreed to negotiate a separate ABM treaty and simultaneously to set vague and unspecified limits on offensive weapons, all to be consummated at a summit a year hence. Nixon was elated that an arms control agreement might be achieved on the eve of the presidential election. For Kissinger, the breakthrough was especially significant in confirming White House control of foreign policy.[44] The stage was set for a flurry of negotiations that would culminate in the ABM and SALT I agreements of 1972, the foundation stones of detente.

Meanwhile, Nixon and Kissinger inched cautiously toward normalizing relations with the People's Republic of China. United States elites, including much of the foreign policy establishment, had long argued that the policy of isolation and containment was outdated. Liberal Democrats such as Senator Edward Kennedy of Massachusetts had taken up the cause. A slowing economy revived century-old dreams of a potentially limitless Chinese market as a solution. Nixon and Kissinger saw geopolitical gains in the form of leverage with the Soviet Union and with North Vietnam in ending the war. Ever the political animal, Nixon relished the prospect of being the first American president to visit China, in part because of the exquisite irony given his reputation as a hard-core anti-Communist, also for the likely political advantage.[45]

China was moving in the same direction. Its leaders increasingly recognized that their national security required economic growth and modernization, which in turn demanded access to foreign ideas, technology, and imports. Easing of tensions with the United States would permit cuts in defense spending and afford access to trade and desperately needed technology. As tensions with the USSR escalated into border warfare, the United States appeared an increasingly useful counterweight. Despite its revolutionary ardor, China, much like the Soviet Union, desperately sought confirmation of its status as a world power. Recognition by the United States was an essential step toward that goal. Chinese moderates saw a rapprochement with the United States as a means to stabilize the nation's foreign relations and contain internal impulses toward radicalism.[46]

44. Hanhimäki, *Kissinger*, 129.
45. Small, *Nixon Presidency*, 119.
46. Ibid., 119–20; Schaller, *United States and China*, 176–77.

Thus for two and a half years, the erstwhile enemies carried out an elaborate, carefully choreographed diplomatic mating dance comprised of signals faint and strong, one step forward, two back. Early in Nixon's term, the Chinese spoke of peaceful coexistence and proposed reopening the Warsaw talks. Nixon signaled his interest through de Gaulle and Romanian dictator Nicolae Ceausescu. In July 1969, the United States eased restrictions on travel to China and reduced Seventh Fleet patrols in the Taiwan Straits. Most significantly, in early 1970 in Warsaw the two sides began to outline positions on such difficult issues as Taiwan and Vietnam.[47]

After twenty years of hostility and name-calling, the path to normalization was strewn with obstacles. In China, a hard-line faction headed by Lin Biao stubbornly opposed talks with the United States. Nixon had to worry about right-wing Republicans such as Arizona senator Barry Goldwater and California governor Ronald Reagan, bitter foes of Red China and staunch backers of Taiwan. The Vietnam War provided a huge barrier to normalization. Nixon's incursions into Cambodia in April 1970 and Laos in early 1971 provoked a renewed Chinese commitment to North Vietnam and loud protests from Beijing. Reverting to boilerplate Cold War rhetoric, Chinese leaders appealed to revolutionary forces everywhere to "unite and defeat the U.S. aggressors and all their running dogs."[48]

Both nations had set their course, however, and the pace quickened again in late 1970. The United States continued to withdraw forces from Vietnam while the Soviet Union expanded its deployments along the Chinese border. The course for Beijing seemed obvious. In December 1970, Mao Zedong invited to China American journalist Edgar Snow, author of a glowing 1938 account of the Chinese Communist movement, who was presumed, incorrectly, to have influence in Washington. Snow stood on the reviewing platform during a founder's day parade. In a conversation, the Great Helmsman confided his willingness to talk with Nixon "either as a tourist or as president."[49] United States officials completely missed the importance of these events until Snow published in *Life* four months later an account of his trip. Regardless, Nixon was increasingly eager to use reconciliation with China to isolate North Vietnam, and he too made important moves. In October, he became the first U.S. president to publicly use the term "People's Republic of China," a hugely symbolic step whose significance was not lost on Beijing. He sent

47. Schaller, *United States and China*, 180–82.
48. Ibid., 179.
49. Michael Schaller, *Altered States: The United States and Japan Since the Occupation* (New York, 1997), 226.

out additional feelers through Pakistan and Romania. In February 1971, he spoke publicly of drawing the PRC "into a constructive relationship with the world community" and pledged a willingness to respect its "legitimate national interests." In March 1971, the United States removed special passport restrictions imposed for travel to China, long viewed by the PRC as an affront to its sovereignty.[50]

This seemingly small step made possible what has come to be known as "Ping-Pong diplomacy," one of the most celebrated events on the road toward normalization. The U.S. table tennis team was competing in Japan in early 1971. Inadvertence sometimes plays a vital role in diplomacy. When an American player on his own initiative made friendly gestures toward a Chinese participant, Beijing mistakenly perceived another official signal and responded by inviting the U.S. team to China. The visit drew a horde of journalists and worldwide attention. Not surprisingly, the Americans lost to the acknowledged masters of the sport, but their trip represented a major breakthrough. "The Great Wall has come down," *Life* proclaimed. Prime Minister Zhou En-lai told the U.S. team that they had "opened the doors to friendly contacts."[51] In a move undoubtedly calculated to light a fire under the White House, a Chinese official proposed to a U.S. reporter the possibility of American dignitaries visiting China, including some prominent Democrats. Ping-Pong diplomacy opened the way to visits by students, scholars, and reporters. Nixon scrapped a long-standing trade embargo on China. Zhou followed by inviting a top-level U.S. official to visit for open-ended discussions.

That proved to be Kissinger, of course, and his July 1971 mission to Beijing was handled with all the mystery and intrigue of a classic cloak-and-dagger film. Uncertain about the outcome of the trip and wary of embarrassment, he and Nixon insisted on absolute secrecy. That, of course, also enabled them to keep the bureaucracy—especially the State Department and Rogers—completely in the dark. Typical of their strange relationship, Kissinger was not even honest with Nixon, encouraging his boss to believe that he might visit some city other than Beijing, thus allowing the president to fulfill his ambition to be the first to go to the capital.[52]

Flattering himself with the code name Polo after the venerable fourteenth-century Italian visitor to China, Kissinger set forth on an extended tour of Asia. While in Pakistan, he feigned illness, and a person

50. Bundy, *Tangled Web*, 165–67; Schaller, *United States and China*, 181.
51. Suri, *Power and Protest*, 240; Schaller, *United States and China*, 183.
52. James Mann, *About Face: A History of America's Curious Relationship with China from Nixon to Clinton* (New York, 1999), 31.

masquerading as the national security adviser was whisked off to a safe haven for "recuperation." At 4:00 A.M., July 9, he boarded a Pakistani aircraft for China—even the flight crew did not know the identity of their illustrious passenger. Informed that the Chinese retained bitter memories of John Foster Dulles's snub of Zhou at Geneva in 1954, Kissinger upon arrival warmly extended his hand. But it was the shrewd and silky Zhou who charmed his American visitor. "Urbane, infinitely patient, extraordinarily intelligent, subtle," Kissinger later flattered his host, "he moved through our discussions with an easy grace that penetrated to the essence of our new relationship."[53]

Kissinger's talks with the Chinese were far more substantive, and the United States conceded much more, than Nixon and Kissinger let on in their memoirs. The national security adviser did not respond when Zhou emphatically stated that Taiwan "is an inalienable part of Chinese territory" and even compared its relationship to China with that of Hawaii— and Long Island—to the United States. But he did pledge that the United States would not support independence for Taiwan or the newly flourishing Taiwan independence movements. "Good, these talks may now proceed," Zhou cooed in response. Kissinger subsequently pledged that the United States would not back Taiwanese military action against the mainland and indicated that recognition could come in Nixon's second term. He went to extraordinary lengths to ingratiate himself—and the United States—with his hosts and new friends, sharing intelligence gleaned from spy satellites about Soviet troop dispositions along the Chinese border. He also promised to inform the Chinese of the details of U.S. negotiations with the USSR that directly concerned them. Zhou skillfully deflected Kissinger's requests for assistance in ending the Vietnam War. About all the modern-day Marco Polo got was a much coveted Chinese invitation for Nixon to visit the following year—and the all-important (to Nixon) pledge not to permit any Democrats to come earlier.[54]

Nixon's July 15 bombshell announcement of Kissinger's trip and his upcoming visit to China had momentous consequences. Such a diplomatic volte-face could not but unnerve adversaries and allies alike. Kissinger took pains to give Dobrynin several hours' warning prior to the president's public statement that he would visit China before the Soviet Union, perhaps easing the jolt a bit. Nixon later dispatched Reagan on his maiden diplomatic voyage to reassure an understandably uneasy Taiwan. The news hit Japan with "typhoon force," the U.S. ambassador, himself in the

53. Ibid., 32.
54. Ibid., 30–36; New York Times, March 3, 2002.

dark until the last minute, observed. Nixon assigned the humiliated Rogers the thankless task of informing the Japanese, but because of a communications snafu Prime Minister Eisaku Sato got the word a mere three minutes before the president's speech. The Japanese were "upset as hell," it was said, and what came to be called the "Nixon shock" would contribute to the fall of Sato's government.[55] The diplomatic fallout continued into October when, with no more than perfunctory U.S. opposition, the United Nations voted to admit the People's Republic of China and expel Taiwan.

For Nixon, a rift with Japan, tensions with Taiwan, and a largely symbolic and expected defeat at the UN were small prices to pay for the larger diplomatic gains and especially for the presumed domestic political windfall. The president handled the Republican right with as much care as Dobrynin, instructing Kissinger to speak personally with Goldwater and Reagan. The announcement of Nixon's visit to China won near universal praise from Americans, however, forcing even liberal Democrats to grudgingly support a policy change they had pushed and a president they despised. A trip to Beijing in February provided something "good to hit the Democrats with at primary time," Nixon crowed.[56] Indeed, with summits set for Beijing and Moscow in 1972, the administration was poised to put into place the major elements of its Grand Design and launch a triumphal presidential campaign.

IV

As the "Nixon shock" makes clear, the administration's focus on Vietnam and detente gave a certain tunnel-vision quality to its foreign policies. That accurately reflected Nixon and Kissinger's assessment of what was really important in the world. It also indicated their concentration of control in the White House and inability to handle all the problems that fell in the lap of the world's greatest power. Sometimes, they pursued major goals without much regard for the impact on other nations. Often, they viewed events largely in terms of their connection to superpower relations. Thus, in dealing with the rest of the world the administration achieved no better than mixed results.[57]

As Soviet-American conflict eased and the Continent edged toward greater stability, European issues no longer seemed urgent. To be sure, Nixon did take a much publicized trip to Western Europe early in his

55. Schaller, *Altered States*, 228–29.
56. Ibid., 228.
57. Small, *Nixon Presidency*, 127.

presidency, during which he met with de Gaulle in a celebration of mutual admiration. At a NATO council meeting in Brussels, he pledged to "listen with new attentiveness" to America's European "partners," a promise he generally ignored. To the great annoyance of the Soviets, he subsequently visited Romania, Yugoslavia, and Poland. But in general, Europe did not occupy much of his and Kissinger's attention or loom especially large in their calculations.[58]

Even in the area of detente, the Europeans themselves led the way toward a reduction of tensions on the Continent. Brandt was the driving force. Like Kissinger a refugee from Nazi Germany, he grew up in Norway and embraced the Scandinavian middle way as a basis for his domestic and foreign policies. His *Ostpolitik* broke sharply with West Germany's traditional policy of isolating East Germany. Rather, it sought reunification by engagement with East Germany and extrication from superpower domination. To ease the way for other agreements, West Germany in 1969 signed the Nuclear Non-proliferation Treaty. During a spring 1970 visit to Moscow, Brandt's foreign minister, Egon Bahr, worked out principles that formed the essence of *Ostpolitik*. West Germany accepted the long-contested Oder-Neisse line as a boundary with Poland, promised to return the Sudetenland to Czechoslovakia, renounced the use of force to change boundaries, and agreed to establish relations with East Germany. The USSR agreed to support the reunification of Germany by peaceful means and discuss the status of West Berlin. These principles were subsequently incorporated into treaties with the Soviet Union, Czechoslovakia, and Poland. The treaties ratified and legalized the status quo in Eastern Europe. They formed the basis for the European settlement that had eluded the great powers after World War II. Ironically, the German issue changed from being a key point of Cold War conflict to a basis for detente.[59] In December 1970, placing a wreath on a memorial to victims massacred by the Nazis at the Warsaw ghetto, Brandt fell to his knees in a gesture of penitence hailed by *Time* as a "turning point in the history of Europe—and of the world."[60] That magazine named him Man of the Year in 1970. The next year he won the Nobel Peace Prize.

Brandt's diplomacy sparked movement in other areas. Since V-E Day, the status of West Berlin had been among the most explosive Cold War issues. The USSR wanted the West out of West Berlin, an isolated enclave

58. Ibid., 148–49.
59. Hanhimäki, *Flawed Architect*, 86.
60. Bundy, *Tangled Web*, 178.

within East Germany, or, failing that, only the most limited ties between West Berlin and West Germany. The West sought Soviet guarantees of access to West Berlin. Reflecting the interlocking nature of *Ostpolitik*, the August 1970 Soviet–West German Treaty smoothed the way for a September 1971 four-power agreement guaranteeing Western access to West Berlin in return for pledges that it would not be incorporated into West Germany. The treaty eliminated a dangerous problem. It facilitated negotiations on other issues and ultimately for progress on Soviet-American detente. Under Moscow's leadership, the Warsaw Pact, mainly to secure Western acceptance of the status quo in Eastern Europe, had long pressed for a broad East-West conference on European security. Fearing that Congress might unilaterally reduce U.S. forces in Western Europe, NATO had urged negotiations with its Eastern European counterpart on mutual and balanced force reductions in Europe. In 1972, the two sides agreed to begin discussions.[61]

Nixon and Kissinger viewed these momentous developments with ambivalence and more than a touch of envy. They could not openly oppose Brandt's pursuit of goals they nominally supported. When West German conservatives enlisted the support of Cold Warriors like Dean Acheson to protest the "mad race to Moscow," the president gently deflected them. But Kissinger, even more than Nixon, developed a deep dislike for Brandt and Bahr and distrusted *Ostpolitik*, which he considered "fuzzy-minded and dangerous," a "God-send for the Soviets." He worried that it might seduce American liberals and open rifts in NATO the Soviets could exploit, thereby neutralizing U.S. gains from the China initiative.[62] Vain and insecure, the two men could not but have been profoundly jealous of Brandt's achievements and worldwide recognition. They sought with little success to control and co-opt him. They did play a key role in the Berlin negotiations, typically by shutting out the State Department and working through Dobrynin and another backchannel with the U.S. ambassador to West Germany. Kissinger then delayed completion of the agreement to make it appear that his China trip had determined the outcome. Nixon claimed credit for a "major achievement."[63]

International economic issues also bedeviled America's relations with its major allies and further highlighted its fall from postwar hegemony. By 1970, the nation was mired in recession, marked by a drop in the gross national product and rise in unemployment and inflation. Most alarming,

61. Garthoff, *Détente*, 116–21.
62. Bundy, *Tangled Web*, 116; *FRUS, 1969–1976* 1:290.
63. Garthoff, *Détente*, 120, n. 30.

for the first time since 1895 the United States ran a trade deficit. During the Cold War, U.S. foreign economic policy had been driven by national security demands. Massive spending on foreign aid, European defense, and more recently the Vietnam War fueled a growing balance of payments deficit, damaging U.S. competitiveness in world trade. America's share of world exports dropped by almost 3 percent after 1960, a result of declining productivity and the undervaluation of European and Japanese currencies in relation to the dollar. The allies had amassed large gold holdings, and U.S. economists worried that they might start buying more gold at the undervalued price of $35 per ounce. The crisis came in the summer of 1971. The U.S. balance of payments deficit for the first six months, if used as a basis for calculating the entire year, would have totaled $22 billion. The trade deficit for the third quarter exceeded $800 million. When Germany proposed to devalue the mark and Britain on August 12 asked to draw $3 billion in gold, the administration moved into action. On Friday the thirteenth, Nixon convened his economic advisers for a secret meeting at Camp David described by one aide as the "most important weekend in economics" since FDR closed the banks in 1933.[64]

Over the next three days, the administration developed a bold and comprehensive program, a historical watershed, to address the nation's economic woes. The prime mover was former Texas governor and LBJ protégé John Connally, as dominant at this time on the economic front as Kissinger on the diplomatic. Nixon had become enthralled with the former Democrat, naming him secretary of the treasury in 1971, assigning him responsibility for economic policies, and even anointing him as his successor. A large and handsome man, charming—and intimidating—in the mode of his mentor, Connally was also a strong economic nationalist. "My view's that the foreigners are out to screw us," he once observed, "and therefore it's our job to screw them first."[65] At the Camp David meeting, about which even Kissinger was not kept informed, Connally took the "big bold approach." Tagged the New Economic Policy (until someone discovered that Lenin had once used the same label), his program imposed temporary freezes on wages, prices, and profits, lifted an excise tax to make automobiles more competitive, and enacted cuts in federal spending. Facing a trade deficit and gold drain, the administration acted unilaterally and on the principle that the United States no longer had the luxury of its

64. Bundy, *Tangled Web*, 261–64; Schaller, *Altered States*, 234; Francis J. Gavin, *Gold, Dollars, and Power: The Politics of International Monetary Relations* (Chapel Hill, N.C., 2004), 193–94.
65. Small, *Nixon Presidency*, 208.

postwar generosity. The administration imposed a 10 percent surcharge on imports. In a sharp break from Bretton Woods, it "closed the gold window" by refusing to honor requests to convert gold into dollars, thus abandoning the gold standard to devalue the dollar without formally admitting to devaluation and giving U.S. exports a competitive edge.[66]

At home, the Connally program won broad public support, sparking a jump in Nixon's approval ratings and the largest one-day surge in stock market prices to that time, ultimately bringing a respite from economic bad news and helping Nixon's reelection campaign. The Europeans and Japanese got little more warning on the economic gambit than on the China initiative. They bitterly protested the surcharge on imports and the administration's monetary moves. At a November follow-up meeting at Washington's Smithsonian Institution, Connally boasted that he took the role of "bully boy on the manicured playing fields of international finance."[67] The United States dropped the surcharge in return for allied agreements to eliminate specified trade restrictions. Connally also cajoled the allies into accepting a devaluation of the dollar versus their own currencies, giving a short-term stimulus to U.S. trade and keeping the alliance together. Over the longer haul, U.S. unilateralism left scars that took years to heal. The end of Bretton Woods spurred economic regionalism and prolonged currency instability. But there was no turning back. When the allies in 1973 urged the United States once again to assume responsibility for stabilizing international currencies, then Secretary of the Treasury and free market advocate George Shultz responded curtly, "Santa Claus is dead."[68]

Relations between the United States and Japan dipped to their lowest point since World War II during the Nixon years. As the Vietnam War dragged on, Japanese increasingly feared that their close ties with the United States would drag them into an unwanted war rather than protect them from some unspecified threat. Americans bristled at Japan's seeming ingratitude for past assistance and its lack of support on key issues. United States officials pressed Tokyo without much success to assume a larger role in regional defense, even join the nuclear club. American businesses began to view a once prostrate ally as a dangerous economic rival, spoke ominously of Japan, Inc., and, as in the 1930s, warned of Japanese ambitions to dominate the Pacific region, perhaps the world. Differences were compounded by the administration's ignorance of and indifference toward

---

66. Bundy, *Tangled Web*, 263–64.
67. Small, *Nixon Presidency*, 210.
68. Gavin, *Gold, Dollars, and Power*, 196; Joan Hoff, *Nixon Reconsidered* (New York, 1994), 143.

Japan. Kissinger was heard to dismiss the Japanese as "little Sony sales-men"; Nixon's attitudes were shaped by World War II.[69]

One of the most contentious issues was Okinawa. The Johnson admin-istration had got no further than broad agreement that Okinawa should revert to Japan with the United States retaining basing rights. Japanese and Okinawans continued to resent U.S. use of the island as a place to store nuclear weapons and as a base for operations in Vietnam. Some Americans believed they had paid in blood for the right to retain Oki-nawa. Military leaders identified it as an essential base. Nixon and Sato reached broad agreement on the future of Okinawa in late 1969. Under a treaty finally signed June 17, 1971, the United States agreed to reversion. Japan consented to U.S. retention of bases and their use for combat in the region. Responding to what the U.S. ambassador called Japan's "nuclear allergy," the United States pledged to remove its nuclear weapons. In a further agreement notable for its almost undecipherable diplomatic ver-biage, the two sides agreed to discuss in an emergency the possibility of the weapons' return provided that Japan's "particular sentiment" was taken into account. Transfer occurred in May 1972.[70]

Trade issues were not so easily settled. By the time Nixon took office, the United States was incurring an annual trade deficit with Japan of more than $1.3 billion. Because of domestic politics, the major problem was textiles; Japan sold more than fifty times what it bought. Southern states, notably South Carolina, depended heavily on the textile industry, and Nixon's "southern strategy" for holding power hinged on detaching southern whites from the Democratic Party. As hundreds of plants closed and thousands of textile workers lost their jobs, pressure mounted for a hard line. During the 1969 summit, Sato appeared to accept voluntary quotas on textile exports in return for the reversion of Okinawa, but the deal broke down. Other times, U.S. negotiators secured commitments only to have the Japanese renege or the legislature reject them. Nixon privately denounced the "Jap betrayal" and yearned to "stick it to Japan." The two sides seemed close to a full-fledged trade war.[71]

The Nixon shocks—*shokku* in Japanese—combined in the summer of 1971 to force a textile agreement. Announcement of Nixon's visit to China on July 15 left Sato's government reeling. Less than a month later, coinci-dentally but significantly on the anniversary of V-J Day, announcement of

69. Schaller, *Altered States*, 211–13; Walter LaFeber, *The Clash: U.S.-Japanese Relations Throughout History* (New York, 1997), 349–51.
70. Small, *Nixon Presidency*, 144–45.
71. Schaller, *Altered States*, 211, 224.

Connally's economic program—with the Japanese again getting only minutes prior notice—compounded the impact. Nixon conceded that the program was designed in part to give the Japanese "a jolt." The United States added threats to set import quotas under the Trading with the Enemy Act of 1917. In the wake of these twin shocks, Japan accepted voluntary restraints on textile exports, reduced its import quotas by more than half, and opened its markets to U.S. investors. The 1971 trade deal significantly improved Japanese-American relations and helped get Nixon through an election year.[72]

Nixon and Kissinger muddled through with America's major allies; with the Third World, they did not manage that. The major policy pronouncement—ostensibly—was the so-called Nixon Doctrine, announced by the president rather casually during a July 1969 press conference on Guam. The statement was not a doctrine in the sense that it comprised a set of principles carefully formulated to shape specific policies. Nixon's remarks had not even been vetted by Kissinger's staff. Originally aimed at East Asia and the Pacific, it presumably applied to Third World countries generally. It was an obvious complement to the policy of Vietnamization. Indeed, Nixon announced it along with the first troop withdrawals from Vietnam.[73]

The concepts were not new. Rather, they reflected Nixon's experience with New Look policies designed to avoid wars like Korea and ideas already broadly accepted in light of Vietnam to limit future U.S. entanglement in Third World conflicts. A sharp departure from John Kennedy's 1961 vow to "pay any price, bear any burden," the "doctrine" reflected a growing recognition that, as Nixon later put it, "America cannot—and will not—conceive *all* the plans, design *all* the programs, execute *all* the decisions, and undertake *all* the defense of the free nations."[74] On Guam, the president affirmed that the United States would uphold existing treaty commitments but would be very cautious in taking on new ones. It would protect those nations vital to U.S. security who were endangered by nuclear powers. It would provide military and economic assistance to nations threatened by insurgencies or external aggression, but they—the key point—must assume primary responsibility for their own defense. It also provided a basis for extending large-scale military aid to regional powers who would be responsible for stability in their areas. Originally tagged the Guam

72. Ibid., 231–41.
73. Small, *Nixon Presidency*, 63. A valuable analysis is Jeffrey Kimball, "The Nixon Doctrine: A Saga of Misunderstanding," *Presidential Studies Quarterly*, 36 (March 2006), 59–74.
74. Small, *Nixon Presidency*, 63; Bundy, *Tangled Web*, 68; FRUS, 1969–1976 1:92.

Doctrine by journalists, it was quickly renamed for Nixon by White House operatives who recognized its public relations value. It was applied inconsistently if at all and may have been more useful at home than in shaping foreign policy.[75]

The Nixon Doctrine reflected in part the lower priority the president and Kissinger assigned the Third World. Devotees of realpolitik, they respected power above all else, and they shared a certain disdain for Third World peoples and nations. "History has never been produced in the South," Kissinger lectured a Chilean diplomat. "The axis of history starts in Moscow, goes to Bonn, crosses over to Washington, and then goes to Tokyo."[76] Often quite sophisticated in their assessments of great-power politics, they could be naive and tunnel-visioned in assessing Third World conflicts. They were uninterested in local and regional disputes unless they were linked to great-power issues or, in Nixon's case, had implications for domestic politics.[77]

Latin America enjoyed priority in the Nixon scheme of power politics only by virtue of its proximity to the United States and the outsize and still looming presence of Fidel Castro. Nixon and Kissinger repeatedly stressed its unimportance. When a Chilean diplomat suggested that Kissinger knew nothing about Latin America, the national security adviser shot back, "No. And I don't care."[78] In discussing foreign aid, Nixon once referred to Latin America as a "disaster." While vowing to fight the "big battles" in foreign policy, he also made clear he preferred not to be bothered with hemispheric matters.[79] The one exception, of course, was Cuba, which had contributed to his electoral defeat in 1960. Like other policymakers of his era, he was obsessed with Castro. Kissinger once conceded that for the president Cuba was a "neuralgic problem."[80]

The Castro fixation played into the administration's otherwise inexplicable and morally repugnant interference in Chile between 1970 and 1973. During the Kennedy era, Chile and its moderate president, Eduardo Frei, had been a model of what the Alliance for Progress sought to encourage. Throughout the 1960s, as in other countries, the CIA funneled huge sums of money to friendly candidates in Chile and used psychological warfare to

75. Hanhimäki, *Flawed Architect*, 53–54.
76. Thomas Borstelmann, *The Cold War and the Color Line: American Race Relations in the Global Arena* (Cambridge, Mass., 2001), 233.
77. Small, *Nixon Presidency*, 144.
78. Mark T. Gilderhus, *The Second Century: U.S.-Latin American Relations Since 1889* (Wilmington, Del., 2000), 195.
79. *FRUS*, 1969–1976 1:101, 204–6.
80. Gilderhus, *Second Century*, 196.

discredit leftists. Washington was stunned, therefore, in 1970 when, despite major contributions of funds to acceptable candidates from International Telephone and Telegraph, Pepsi-Cola, and Anaconda Copper—and the CIA—avowed Marxist, socialist, and Castro friend Dr. Salvador Allende won a plurality of votes in a three-way election. Because none of the candidates received a majority, the outcome rested with the Chilean congress.

The prospect of an Allende victory sent shock waves through a previously preoccupied White House. Kissinger had once dismissed Chile as a "dagger pointed to the heart of Antarctica." But the election occurred simultaneously with the Cuban submarine crisis and another upheaval in the Middle East, and U.S. officials were deeply alarmed at the possibility of an Allende presidency. "There is a graveyard smell to Chile," ambassador Edward Korry reported from Santiago, "the smell of democracy in decomposition."[81] Nixon later justified his actions with a hyperbolic hemispheric domino theory, outrageous in its scope, passed on to him by an Italian businessman: "If Allende should win, and with Castro in Cuba, you will have in Latin America a red sandwich. And eventually it will all be red." The possible domestic political consequences seemed even more dangerous. Like other administrations back to Kennedy, Nixon lived in mortal terror of another Castro. "Chile could end up being the worst failure in our administration," a belatedly engaged Kissinger ominously warned a White House aide, " 'our Cuba' by 1972." "I don't see why we have to let a country go Marxist just because its people are irresponsible," he quipped on another occasion, perhaps expressing his innermost feelings about democracy.[82]

The administration thus authorized a major covert operation to thwart an Allende presidency. On September 16, Nixon allocated $10 million to the job, assigned the CIA exclusive responsibility, tasked it to "make the economy scream," and urged operatives to consider anything "your imagination can conjure."[83] The agency formulated a two-track program. Track I, its "Rube Goldberg gambit," named after the cartoonist famous for contriving the most intricate mechanisms to perform the most simple tasks, set up a complex, convoluted, and totally impractical scheme involving bribing Chile's legislators and undermining its constitution to bring Frei back as president. Track II called for a military coup or the assassination of Allende, along with the kidnapping of a top general who favored following constitutional processes. The murder of the general actually sparked a

81. *New York Times*, September 13, 1998.
82. Hanhimäki, *Flawed Architect*, 102, 104.
83. *New York Times*, September 13, 1998.

backlash in Chile. Both schemes failed. The Congress declared Allende president on October 24, 1970.

The Nixon administration proceeded to launch economic and psychological warfare against the Allende government. Egged on by large corporations threatened by the new government's nationalization program, the United States reduced once voluminous aid to a trickle. It denied credits to buy wheat, an especially important sanction in a time of worldwide grain shortages. An "invisible" blockade also included persuading the World Bank to prevent loans to Chile. The CIA provided funds for opposition newspapers and spread misinformation to undermine Allende. Continued U.S. military assistance sent an open invitation for a coup.

In September 1973, the Chilean military overthrew the government; Allende committed suicide or was murdered. No evidence has ever been produced to prove conclusively that the United States instigated or actively participated in the coup. Even without U.S. intrusion, Allende might have been overthrown. His frantic and ill-conceived efforts to nationalize basic industries and reshape the Chilean economy added to the nation's woes and provoked massive popular discontent. But there can be no doubt that U.S. intervention between 1970 and 1973 helped create the conditions in which the coup took place. Kissinger himself later admitted that while the United States had not done the job, "we helped them."[84] The administration recognized with unseemly haste the new government of Gen. Augusto Pinochet, an outspoken admirer of Spanish dictator Francisco Franco. It quickly restored economic aid. Pinochet adopted free market policies that favored U.S. corporations. He also instituted a brutal, authoritarian regime that executed as many as ten thousand dissidents and jailed many more. Kissinger may not merit the war-criminal stigma sometimes pinned on him, but the administration's overreaction to the Chilean election, its disdain for Chilean democracy, and its vicious assault on the Allende government make it in large measure responsible for what followed. Ironically, although neither Kissinger nor Nixon thought Latin America very significant, their actions there perhaps more than anywhere else blackened the reputations for statesmanship to which they attached such great importance.[85]

Their handling of a late 1971 crisis on the Indian subcontinent further reveals the moral—and geopolitical—bankruptcy of their approach to

84. Hanhimäki, *Flawed Architect*, 104.
85. Ibid., 104–5. The war criminal charge is set forth in Christopher Hitchens, *The Trial of Henry Kissinger* (London, 2001).

Third World issues. West Pakistan's brutal attempts to suppress an independence movement in the eastern section of a country whose two parts
were separated by a broad expanse of Indian territory produced rampant
atrocities and evoked worldwide condemnation. As many as ten million
refugees fled East Pakistan for India, creating a huge economic burden
for the New Delhi government and threatening its stability. India could
hardly resist a chance to profit at the expense of its mortal enemy. Its support for an independent Bangladesh threatened to provoke the third war
on the subcontinent since 1947. In late November, Indian troops crossed
into East Pakistan. Shortly after, fearing an Indian move into West Pakistan, President Yahya Khan, a dictator who had seized power in a coup
d'état, launched strikes against Indian air bases, invaded disputed territory in Kashmir, and called upon the United States to abide by its treaty
commitments.

The Nixon-Kissinger response was shaped by petty prejudices on the
one hand and contrived geopolitics on the other. Sharing a bias that had
afflicted their predecessors back to Truman, the two men generally disliked Indians, labeling them variously "slippery, treacherous people," "arrogant bastards," and "goddamn Indians." They especially disliked India's
prickly prime minister, Indira Gandhi, who, like her equally difficult father, Jawaharlal Nehru, often indulged in shrill criticism of the United
States. In their private conversations, which often resembled locker-room
talk and of which Nixon foolishly made a taped record, they referred to
Gandhi as "bitch," "whore," and "old witch."[86] The announcement of an
Indo-Soviet friendship treaty shortly before the war with Pakistan began, itself partly a response to the U.S. shift toward China, stirred their geopolitical fantasies. Viewing the situation not as a difficult regional problem but
as a menacing Cold War crisis, they concluded, without real evidence,
that India had hostile designs on West Pakistan and even that India and its
Soviet ally might seek regional hegemony.[87] By contrast, they liked Pakistani dictator Khan, desperately sought to keep him in office until their
China gambit was consummated, and even fancied balancing the presumed Soviet-Indian threat with a Sino-American-Pakistani alignment.

Thus, while claiming to be neutral, the administration secretly "tilted"
toward Pakistan. Conjuring a major international crisis out of an essentially local conflict, the anxious and sometimes near frantic leaders insisted that the entire U.S. international position was at stake. They could
not permit a loyal and useful ally to be destroyed. They must demonstrate

86. Dallek, *Partners*, 338; BBC News report, June 29, 2005.
87. Bundy, *Tangled Web*, 269.

to China, in the words of an NSC aide, that the United States was a "reliable country to deal with," and to all nations the president's toughness.[88] The administration provided arms to the Pakistanis, reaffirmed its commitment to Pakistan's sovereignty, and threatened to cancel the upcoming summit if the Soviets did not stop sending arms to India. Nixon ordered the aircraft carrier USS *Enterprise* and three escort vessels into the Bay of Bengal to reassure Pakistan and deter India. In the meantime, to protect the president's visit to China, the highest priority, Kissinger went to extraordinary lengths to keep the Chinese informed.

Nixon and Kissinger later insisted that their timely intervention had forced Moscow to back down and thwarted an Indian invasion of West Pakistan. In fact, there is little evidence to suggest that such threats existed. In Bundy's words, the U.S. response to the Indo-Pakistani war was "replete with error, misjudgment, emotionalism, and unnecessary risk-taking."[89] From a moral standpoint, the United States backed the wrong side. It also supported the losing side. Pakistan was forced to recognize the independence of Bangladesh. Moreover, when columnist Jack Anderson made public the administration's closely held tilt toward Pakistan (apparently leaked to him by a JCS spy, navy yeoman Charles Radford), an increasingly paranoid White House called into action the "plumbers" team it had assembled to plug leaks, a clear sign of the mindset that would produce the Watergate scandals.

Nixon's policies toward Africa paralleled those toward civil rights issues at home and reflected deeply held attitudes on race. The president shared the racial views of his generation and class. In the confines of the White House, he often used racial epithets such as "nigger," "jigaboo," and "jungle bunny." Recognizing that African Americans were closely tied to the Democratic Party, he all but ignored them as a voting bloc, pitching his campaigns toward southern whites. As vice president, he had taken progressive stands on civil rights. During his presidency, he advised his underlings to "do what the law requires and not *one bit* more."[90]

These views carried over into foreign policy. There "has never been an adequate black nation," he once observed, "and they are the only race of which this is true."[91] He paid little attention to Africa, its lack of significance in his mind made starkly manifest by his willingness to leave it to Rogers's State Department. When Biafra's secession from Nigeria set off

88. Small, *Nixon Presidency*, 107.
89. Bundy, *Tangled Web*, 288–89.
90. Borstelmann, *Cold War and the Color Line*, 233.
91. Ibid., 233.

a long and tragic civil war with enormous human suffering, the State Department backed Nigeria because it saw Biafra as a hopeless cause and hesitated to antagonize Nigeria, a major oil-producing state. Setting a precedent that would be followed into the next century, the administration also cast a blind eye toward strife-torn Burundi, where the minority Tutsis in 1972–73 murdered as many as 250,000 Hutus and drove another 100,000 into exile.

Like its predecessors, the administration also tolerated white minority regimes in southern Africa. United States officials conceded that such governments could not last indefinitely, but they believed, in the short-sighted words of National Security Study Memorandum 39, that "the only way that constructive change can come about is through them." In addition, the white regimes maintained stability in at least one part of Africa, a region where, not coincidentally, the United States had important trade ties and major investments. Thus, rather than pressuring them with sanctions, the administration chose to work with them. Trade with South Africa boomed. The United States, in defiance of UN sanctions, purchased large quantities of chrome from Rhodesia. The CIA reduced covert aid for black rebel groups in Portuguese Angola. With Africa, as in the Third World generally, Nixon and Kissinger displayed little interest in local conflicts unless they seemed tied to great-power issues.[92]

V

Despite the frustrations of his first years in office, Nixon enjoyed his moment of glory when it most counted—1972, an election year. In that dramatic twelve months, he made a path-breaking and much ballyhooed trip to China and followed it with a summit in Moscow, where enemies of nearly thirty years appeared to put the Cold War behind them.

Nixon's "week that changed the world" visit to China (February 21–27) was as much diplomatic pageantry as substance, largely by design. The president's handlers viewed the trip not only as a diplomatic breakthrough but also as an opportunity to boost his stature as world statesman. They also believed, as White House operative Chuck Colson observed hyperbolically, that "RN's election is in the hands of Peking." The administration persuaded the Chinese to permit U.S. construction of a satellite relay station in Beijing so that events could be broadcast live back home. "Nixon's Chinese Picture Show" was planned with all the care of a Hollywood spectacular. Events were scheduled for prime time in the United States. In assigning press passes, television was favored over the

92. Small, *Nixon Presidency*, 144.

more critical and analytical print media.[93] From Nixon's first appearance in China—alone on the tarmac extending a "handshake for peace" to Zhou—through countless banquets, and a presidential visit to the Great Wall, the trip was high drama. There were moments of incongruity: a Chinese military band in the age of rock and roll playing traditional American tunes such as "Oh Susannah" and "Home on the Range." Perhaps the greatest irony came on February 22, George Washington's birthday, when the onetime red-baiter Richard Nixon rose in the Great Hall of the People, a glass of lethal maotai in hand, to toast Mao Zedong with aphorisms drawn from the chairman's own sayings.[94]

The negotiations were conducted mostly with Zhou and—in another example of the White House's petty and secretive management style—entirely without Secretary of State Rogers. They produced important results. Before his departure, Nixon had sought unsuccessfully to get Chinese help on Vietnam. During their conversations, Zhou did provide oblique assurances that China would not intervene militarily, freeing Nixon's hands, if necessary, to escalate the war. The two nations agreed not to seek hegemony in Asia and to oppose any other nation's efforts to do so, an only slightly disguised allusion to the Soviet Union. The United States affirmed that it would continue to defend Japan but also promised to check any Japanese efforts to expand in Asia and to keep the Japanese from getting nuclear weapons. The touchiest issue, naturally, was Taiwan. In their Shanghai Communiqué, the two nations made separate and parallel statements. The United States agreed that Taiwan was part of China (a position the Chinese Nationalists agreed with) and went partway toward meeting China's demands for its withdrawal by promising that it would do so as tensions eased. China moved toward the U.S. position by expressing hope for a peaceful resolution of the Taiwan issue. Nixon also gave secret assurances that he would normalize relations in his second term. State Department officials were outraged when they learned that the communiqué had not mentioned the Taiwan defense treaty, warning that conservatives at home would be furious. Themselves enraged with State's insolence, Nixon and Kissinger conceded to the extent that Kissinger mentioned the treaty at a press conference.[95]

Nixon's China trip brought major payoffs. Conservatives naturally complained about the president consorting with the Antichrist and fretted about Taiwan; columnist William Buckley compared the smile on Zhou's

93. Tyler Powell, "Advertising and Designing Nixon's 'China Picture Show'" (Senior Thesis, University of Kentucky, 2000), 9, 17, 25, 27.
94. Isaacson, *Kissinger*, 402.
95. Mann, *About Face*, 45–59.

face to the way Stalin must have looked after Yalta. Not surprisingly, however, after all the publicity, the trip was immensely popular at home, winning bipartisan praise for the administration. There were immediate tangible results. The two nations established unofficial embassies through liaison offices in the capitals to conduct diplomatic business and promote trade. George H. W. Bush was named the first envoy. Commerce shot up, most of it U.S. grain exports to China. The expansion of travel and cultural exchange may have been more significant over the long haul. Nixon's bold move provided leverage against the USSR, helped ease tensions in East Asia, and reduced the threat of Sino-American conflict. For once, the actual results lived up to the hype spewed forth by the White House. The only untoward note was Nixon's gloomy, private postconference rumination, perhaps fueled by alcohol, over whether anyone would appreciate the significance of what had occurred.[96]

Indirectly, at least, Nixon's China trip also sparked a major escalation of the war in Vietnam. Increasingly nervous about U.S. approaches to China and the USSR and eager to exploit U.S. electoral politics and the vacuum created by Nixon's troop withdrawals, the North Vietnamese on March 30, 1972, launched a massive conventional invasion of South Vietnam. In its early stages, the so-called Easter Offensive succeeded smashingly. Again catching the United States and South Vietnam off guard, North Vietnamese forces advanced rapidly on three fronts, in the South driving within sixty miles of Saigon. Keenly aware of the implications for his foreign policy and especially for domestic politics, Nixon refused to stand by and allow South Vietnam to fall. Despite warnings from some anxious advisers that escalation might set off another outburst of domestic opposition or provoke Moscow to cancel the upcoming summit, he struck back with a vengeance. Aiming to cripple North Vietnam's capacity to make war, he ordered the most drastic U.S. escalation since 1965: a massive, sustained bombing campaign against North Vietnam itself; a naval blockade; and the mining of Haiphong, the nation's major harbor. Insisting that the United States could not have a "viable foreign policy" if it was "humiliated" in Vietnam, he ordered that Hanoi be "bombed to smithereens." "The "bastards have never been bombed like they're going to be bombed this time," he vowed.[97] Nixon's response blunted the North Vietnamese offensive. The ferocious fighting of the summer of 1972 raised the stalemate to yet another level of violence and on both sides in time created pressures for a settlement.

96. Ibid., 50–51; Small, *Nixon Presidency*, 124–25.
97. Herring, *America's Longest War*, 307; *Atlantic Monthly*, September 2004, 103.

Nixon's bold moves in Vietnam proved no more than a speed bump on the road to Moscow. On his third day in the USSR, in a session at Secretary General Leonid Brezhnev's dacha, Soviet leaders launched a three-hour tirade against America's "cruel" aggression in Vietnam, even comparing the United States to Nazi Germany. Following this obviously for-the-record outburst, the conferees adjourned to a bountiful and convivial dinner during which Brezhnev and Nixon jokingly agreed that Kissinger should be exiled to Siberia.[98]

The treaties concluded in Moscow laid the foundation for Soviet-American detente, establishing areas of agreement and a spirit of concord but also leaving ambiguities and differences that would cause later discord and spark bitter political controversy in the United States. As in Beijing, the State Department was shunted away from the main event; at one point, Kissinger even conspired with Brezhnev to spring an agreement on his unsuspecting rivals! The Cold War adversaries formalized a statement of "Basic Principles" to guide their future relations. Kissinger put much stock in the document, and Soviet leaders were especially pleased with phrases that recognized their superpower status. A statement that relations would be conducted on the "basis of peaceful coexistence" obscured only to the uninitiated Soviet determination to continue superpower competition. The two nations agreed not to exploit regional tensions, establish spheres of influence, or "engage in efforts to obtain unilateral advantage at the expense of the other." In fact, neither gave up efforts to do so. Each in time would accuse the other of violating the Moscow statement. The United States agreed to a Conference on Security and Cooperation in Europe, something important to the Soviets; the Kremlin in turn accepted the U.S. proposal to discuss mutual and balanced force reductions in Europe. Nixon and Brezhnev also discussed economic issues, facilitating major agreements later in the year.[99]

For both sides, the arms control agreements formed the keystone of this first detente summit. Most of the terms had been hammered out in preliminary talks in Helsinki and Vienna and via the Kissinger-Dobrynin backchannel. Foolishly, in order to claim full credit for themselves, Nixon and Kissinger left the experts cooling their heels in Helsinki while they handled the final, sometimes important, details in the frenzied, pressure cooker atmosphere of a summit. A treaty limiting anti-ballistic missile defense to two systems for each nation, one to protect the respective capitals, the other a major missile system, headed off a costly competition that could

98. Hanhimäki, *Flawed Architect*, 223–24.
99. Garthoff, *Détente*, 289–92.

have undercut MAD and the entire concept of deterrence. Hailed at the time as a significant achievement, the first Strategic Arms Limitation Agreement (SALT I) became the object of much future wrangling between the two nations and among Americans themselves. This five-year agreement put no limits on MIRVs, a major shortcoming. It fixed upper limits on offensive missiles at 1,600 for the USSR, 1,054 for the United States. It also restricted the number of submarines capable of launching missiles (SLBMs) and the improvement of missile systems already in existence. The two sides fought for hours over the number of SLBMs and the way they would be calculated and over the meaning of words such as *significant, light,* and *heavy.* Higher numbers for the Soviets on ICBMs and SLBMs obscured an overall U.S. lead in nuclear weapons, giving domestic foes ammunition to attack the agreement. Nixon and Kissinger's secretive, sometimes sloppy, and often slippery negotiating methods—Kissinger had a rare knack for smoothing over fundamental differences with clever words—and their determination to secure agreements at almost any cost resulted in some disadvantages for the United States, providing aggrieved lower-level officials a means to exact revenge against their egomaniacal bosses.[100]

Over the long haul, the payoff from the Moscow summit was not as great as Nixon and Kissinger had hoped for or even promised. Not surprisingly, in the glow of success, they oversold the benefits of detente at home with promises of a "generation of peace," paving the way for future disillusion. The political left would attack the arms control agreements for not going far enough, the right for conceding too much. Subsequent negotiations produced a major agreement extending to the USSR most-favored-nation status and Export-Import Bank credits in return for settling the long-standing post–World War II lend-lease debt. American businesses rushed to cut deals, and trade briefly flourished, but the commercial agreements never reached their full potential, in part because they got hopelessly snarled in domestic politics. United States–Soviet trade was also tainted in American eyes by what became known as the "Great Grain Robbery," a deal in which, Kissinger later conceded, the Communists outfoxed the capitalists. The administration went to great lengths to facilitate Soviet purchase of one-fourth of U.S. grain production at bargain prices. At a time of global crop failure, the sales caused shortages in the United States, recharging inflation and jacking up food prices. Angry consumers were not appeased by White House statements that Soviet-American trade contributed to detente.[101]

100. Isaacson, *Kissinger*, 429–36.
101. Small, *Nixon Presidency*, 114.

That said, the summit was still enormously significant. It was the first such meeting since Yalta to produce major concrete results. Interestingly, in time, it would suffer a fate not unlike that of its 1945 predecessor. It was important in terms of establishing a working relationship between the two powers and in tangible accomplishments, especially coming at the same time as the rapprochement with China.[102] Nixon exaggerated only slightly in telling Congress that "never before have two adversaries, so deeply divided by conflicting ideologies and political rivalries, been able to limit the armaments upon which their survival depends." For all its weaknesses, the SALT agreement represented, according to Kissinger biographer Walter Isaacson, "the most important insight of the nuclear age: that an unconstrained arms race was futile, costly, and dangerous."[103] At least for the short term, the summit was also extremely popular at home. Nixon's approval ratings shot up to 61 percent. Even the economy righted itself, the stock market hitting new highs and economic growth recording its highest rate since the boom year 1965. Nixon's reelection was all but assured.

When queried by exuberant colleagues on the return trip from Moscow what could be done for an encore, Kissinger replied without hesitation, "Make peace in Vietnam."[104] He almost pulled it off. The bloody fighting following the Easter Offensive gave the belligerents compelling reasons to settle. North Vietnam suffered enormously from Nixon's fierce countermeasures; its troops in the South were decimated by U.S. air power. It sought now mainly to get American forces out of South Vietnam in order to deal with the Saigon government alone. It counted on electoral pressures to force Nixon to compromise.

Nixon and Kissinger were indeed eager to end a war that had caused huge problems at home and abroad, but they disagreed on the timing. As victory over dovish Democratic nominee George McGovern seemed more and more likely, the president feared that a preelection settlement might be seen as a desperate ploy to win votes. Kissinger, on the other hand, believed that the United States would have greater leverage with Hanoi before rather than after the election. He therefore pushed ahead with negotiations. The United States had already agreed that North Vietnamese troops might remain in the south after a cease-fire, a major concession that would decisively influence the ultimate outcome of the war. By this time resigned to what Kissinger called a "decent interval" between U.S. withdrawal and a

102. Bundy, Tangled Web, 327; Isaacson, Kissinger, 436.
103. Isaacson, Kissinger, 436.
104. Ibid., 438.

South Vietnamese defeat, the administration dropped its insistence that President Nguyen Van Thieu remain in power, accepting a tripartite electoral commission that would arrange a political settlement following a cease-fire. By mid-October, Kissinger and his North Vietnamese counterpart, Le Duc Tho, had cobbled together the essentials of an agreement.[105]

Ironically, given his key role in the sordid 1968 preelection maneuvering that encouraged Thieu to obstruct Johnson's last-minute peace ploy, Kissinger in his haste to close the deal failed to anticipate a repeat performance. Fresh from his triumphs in Beijing and Moscow and now an international celebrity, the imperious and impatient American spent five tense days in Saigon employing what he called "shock tactics" to force Thieu into line. Furious at not being consulted and deeply resentful of Kissinger's arrogant and heavy-handed diplomacy, Thieu understandably refused to endorse an agreement he considered tantamount to national and personal "suicide." He demanded wholesale changes. To Kissinger's consternation, Nixon backed the South Vietnamese president. Now confident of an easy victory in November, the president was willing to wait until after the election and then demand that North Vietnam "settle or face the consequences of what we could do to them."[106]

Kissinger's carefully phrased election-eve statement that "peace is at hand" reassured U.S. voters and sealed Nixon's overwhelming victory over McGovern, but the president's support for Thieu ensured the breakdown of the October agreement. Kissinger's efforts to palliate Saigon by reopening issues presumably settled provoked North Vietnamese diplomats to do the same, causing negotiations to stall in late 1972 amidst great acrimony. Nixon responded by ordering the most intensive and devastating air attacks of the war. The so-called Christmas Bombing dumped more than thirty-six thousand tons of bombs on North Vietnam, more than during the entire period of 1969 to 1971. The bombing gave Hanoi incentive to resume negotiations. It also provoked a furious reaction in the United States and across the world, forcing Nixon to recognize that he must end the war before Congress reconvened and took control from his hands. The negotiations resumed in January 1973. After a week of tense and sometimes bitter exchanges, the United States and North Vietnam finally settled on an agreement not markedly different from the one concluded in October. United States military forces were out of South Vietnam by March 31, 1973. The agreement produced neither the peace nor the honor that Nixon had held out for.

105. Kimball, *Vietnam War Files*, 24–28.
106. Herring, *America's Longest War*, 311–13.

VI

Success is fleeting in politics and diplomacy, and pride, as the saying goes, comes before a fall. Nixon had hoped in a second term to build on the accomplishments of the first. Instead, the United States became deeply entangled in yet another dangerous war in the Middle East, provoking yet another crisis with the USSR. Detente came under fire at home. The tenuous Vietnam peace agreement fell apart. Most of all, the two men were victims of their own haunting insecurities and their modus operandi. A growing rivalry between them, provoked in part over who deserved credit for their successes, brought out the worst in each. Foolish, illegal, and, as it turned out, quite unnecessary measures taken by the president's political operatives to ensure his reelection and the administration's clumsy and bungled cover-up rendered Nixon increasingly powerless and drove him from office.

As always, the Middle East posed perplexing challenges for U.S. policymakers. The Six-Day War exacerbated the ongoing and seemingly unresolvable Arab-Israeli dispute. Even while assiduously cultivating detente with the Soviet Union, Nixon and Kissinger, like their predecessors, continued to fret about Soviet expansion in the Middle East. The problem of countering Soviet and radical Arab influence was magnified after 1969 by the further decline of Britain's political influence and military power in the region and by America's continuing preoccupation with Vietnam.

The solution was a variation of the Nixon Doctrine, what came to be called the "Twin Pillars" approach. It built on Johnson's post-1967 policy of relying on the friendly, conservative, oil-rich kingdoms of Saudi Arabia and Iran to defend U.S. interests. The Nixon Doctrine merely gave a new name to the old idea of furnishing weapons to friendly states to promote regional stability. With U.S. blessings, Saudi Arabia after 1969 used oil funds to more than double its military spending and brought together into the United Arab Emirates six tiny pro-Western and oil-rich Arab sheikdoms left vulnerable by Britain's departure.

Iran was the main U.S. bulwark of Middle East stability and the major beneficiary of the Nixon Doctrine. The shah dreamed of restoring the glories of ancient Persia, and Nixon's schemes suited him perfectly. Like Johnson, the president was captivated by the shah, naively viewing him, as did Kissinger, as "that rarest of leaders, an unconditional ally."[107] During a 1972 visit to Tehran, after explaining the Nixon Doctrine, the president

---

107. Kenneth Pollack, *The Persian Puzzle: The Conflict Between Iran and America* (New York, 205), 103.

leaned across the table and beseeched the shah: "Protect me." The administration opened America's vast arms bazaar to Iran, making the latest military hardware available (except, of course, nuclear weapons) and foolishly letting the shah decide how much was enough. While pushing oil prices as high as possible, the shah spent more than $16.2 billion over the next five years, the largest arms purchase to that time. Nixon praised the shah for "carrying burdens which otherwise we would have to assume," but Iran's short-term usefulness for U.S. interests obscured deeper and dangerous long-range problems.[108] The price the United States paid for its Middle East "pillar" was to refrain from criticism of the shah's oppression of his people and indifference to their basic needs. Iranians increasingly viewed him as America's lackey. Their hatred for him and the United States grew together, sparking the revolution in which both would be swept up.

The administration came to a third Middle East pillar by a circuitous route. Nixon was at best ambivalent toward Jews. He often used anti-Semitic epithets. He railed against the liberalism of American Jews and especially their presumed domination of the media. But he admired Israeli toughness. He recognized that in 1968 Jews had voted overwhelmingly for his opponent; he felt no debt to the Israel lobby. Indeed, in the beginning, he vowed an evenhandedness in the Middle East that made Israel's supporters exceedingly nervous. Certain that Israel would soon have a nuclear weapon, the administration at first took a hard line, threatening to hold back the F-4 fighters LBJ had promised. "This is one program on which the Israelis have persistently deceived us and may even have stolen from us," Kissinger warned Nixon in 1969, referring to fissionable material illegally acquired by Israel in 1965. In the face of Israel's continued resistance and its promises to keep quiet about its nuclear accomplishments, however, the administration acquiesced in its refusal to sign the Non-proliferation Treaty and stopped sending inspectors to Dimona.[109]

Concerned that Kissinger's Jewish background would handicap him in dealing with the Middle East and in any event hunting for bigger game, the president at first left that part of the world to Rogers. The State Department developed an impartial and comprehensive peace plan based on UN Resolution 242 requiring Israeli withdrawal from territories occupied during the Six-Day War and resolution of the problem of Palestinian

108. Douglas Little, *American Orientalism: The United States and the Middle East Since 1945* (Chapel Hill, N.C., 2004), 145.
109. *New York Times*, November 29, 2007; National Security Archive Update, April 28, 2006.

refugees by repatriation or resettlement in return for recognition and peace.

Not surprisingly, the Rogers Plan went nowhere. Nasser expressed vague interest, but Egyptian border raids against Israel spoke louder than his words. Israeli leaders predictably denounced it as a "disaster" and warned that any "government that would adopt and implement such a plan would be betraying its country." The Israel lobby descended upon Washington in full force in early 1970 to protest the Rogers Plan and demand shipment of the F-4s. Nixon dug in his heels on the fighter planes, but in an incredible example of the maneuvering and pettiness that afflicted the administration, he helped sabotage the State Department proposal, telling Kissinger to get word to new Israeli premier Golda Meir, then beginning a tour of the United States, that "wherever she goes, in all her speeches and press conferences, we want her to slam the hell out of Rogers and his plan."[110]

As always, the threat of Soviet gains brought a U.S. administration back to Middle Eastern basics. In the summer of 1970, Moscow sharply escalated the regional arms race, sending surface-to-air missiles and MIG-21 fighter jets to Egypt along with fifteen thousand military advisers and two hundred pilots to assist in their use. Nixon and Kissinger were alarmed at this move and became even more agitated when Nasser shifted his new military assets against Israeli positions in the Sinai. At this time of crisis in Cuba, Chile, and now the Middle East, the administration on September 1 released the long-withheld Phantom jets for delivery to Israel.

The payoff was quick and significant. A September 1970 crisis in Jordan endangered the tenuous Middle East peace and threatened yet another superpower confrontation. Palestine Liberation Organization leader Yasser Arafat had established a virtual Palestinian state within Jordan from which he conducted raids against Israel. In September, Arafat's hit squads several times tried to assassinate Jordan's pro-Western King Hussein and then hijacked four Western airliners, a form of terrorism that would assume major importance over the next decades. When Hussein imposed martial law, the Palestinians mounted a civil war against the king. Fearing escalation, Nixon warned the Soviets not to let their Syrian ally join the fight. The Kremlin seemed to concur, but Syrian tanks soon rumbled into Jordan. As always, interpreting the actions of a Soviet ally as a direct challenge from Moscow, Nixon, with Hussein's reluctant assent, asked Israel for the help of its air force along the Syria-Jordan border. The Israelis also readied their forces in the Golan Heights. The United States dispatched naval and

110. Small, *Nixon Presidency*, 129.

airborne forces into the area. Jordan more than took care of itself, as it turned out, repulsing the Syrians and driving the Palestinians beyond its borders in what became known as Black September.[111]

The Jordanian crisis brought the United States and Israel back to where they had begun, Israel now becoming the third pillar of U.S. Middle East strategy. "The President will never forget Israel's role in preventing the deterioration in Jordan," Kissinger informed an Israeli official in late September.[112] Nixon and Kissinger also demonstrated their gratitude in tangible ways. Adding the Middle East to their already bulging portfolio, they undermined persistent State Department efforts to push Israel toward political compromise and provided more and better aircraft. The two nations' intelligence agencies began active collaboration. Under the Nixon Doctrine, Israel became a "strategic asset."[113]

By the time of the next Middle East blowup, the administration had begun to crumble. Ironically, but not surprisingly given the personalities involved, it began with a falling-out between Kissinger and Nixon. The major reason—again no surprise—was jealousy. Adept at dealing with the media, Kissinger, the onetime Harvard professor, transformed himself in 1972 into not only a diplomatic superstar, the architect of the administration's smashing successes, but also an international celebrity who dated beautiful women such as actress Jill St. John, attended the toniest parties, and was even featured in *Playboy* magazine. Nixon at first found the "swinger" image amusing, but he quickly tired of it. He resented Kissinger's hogging the limelight. He watched with dismay as Kissinger got credit for the triumphs of 1972. His fury rose when the national security adviser appeared to blame him for the Christmas Bombing. He exploded when Kissinger, in ill-advised remarks to Italian journalist Oriana Fallaci, portrayed himself as a diplomatic Lone Ranger, a modern version of the western hero who rode into town by himself to take on the bad guys. When Nixon had to share *Time*'s Man of the Year award with his adviser, he was reportedly "white-lipped with anger."[114] Shortly after the election, the president decided that Kissinger must go. As it happened, no doubt to Nixon's consternation, the national security adviser remained—and was "promoted" to secretary of state in a summer 1973 shakeup largely because the Watergate imbroglio made him indispensable.

The scandal that brought the administration to its knees was unfolding even as Nixon celebrated his inauguration. What top officials initially

111. Ibid., 130–31.
112. Little, *Orientalism*, 106.
113. David Schoenbaum, *The United States and the State of Israel* (New York, 1993), 182.
114. Isaacson, *Kissinger*, 479.

dismissed as a "third-rate burglary attempt"—a June 1972 break-in at Democratic National Committee headquarters in Washington's posh Watergate hotel and apartment complex—grew in the summer of 1973 into a full-fledged exposé of presidential abuse of power. The burglars were tried and convicted in January 1973 just as the administration was setting an ambitious second-term agenda. Their ties to the president's reelection committee, efforts to silence them through payoffs, and the perjury of key witnesses were soon exposed. By March, White House counsel John Dean warned of a "cancer . . . close to the Presidency." In April, Nixon's top aides Bob Haldeman and John Erlichman were forced to resign in a failed effort to save the president himself. A Senate investigating committee and intrepid *Washington Post* reporters Carl Bernstein and Bob Woodward turned up sensational revelations of such things as the administration's failed cover-up, wiretapping of journalists and some of Kissinger's top advisers, payment of hush money to witnesses, and burglary of the office of "Pentagon Papers" leaker Daniel Ellsberg's psychiatrist. The televised hearings mesmerized the public. Tape recordings of White House conversations tied the president more closely to the Watergate affair and exposed the nation to a distinctly unpresidential persona: nervous, petty, profane, vindictive. As late as April, Nixon's approval ratings were still around 60 percent; by August, they had plummeted to 31 percent. His image was irreparably tarnished. As his congressional foes closed in for impeachment, most of his time and energy was devoted to his political survival.[115]

The Vietnam peace agreement was one of the first casualties. To the surprise of no one, war continued in Vietnam after peace had been proclaimed. South and North Vietnam both regularly violated the cease-fire to bolster their military positions in anticipation of a political settlement. Negotiations for a new government quickly deadlocked. Nixon had hoped to uphold the peace agreement by the threat or actual use of air power against North Vietnam, and he had made secret promises to Thieu along those lines. Kissinger journeyed to Paris in May to press for observance of the cease-fire. But he found himself without leverage. And the North Vietnamese pointedly accused him of trying to deceive the public on Vietnam "as you have done with Watergate."[116] Public opinion polls showed overwhelming popular opposition to military reintervention in any part of Indochina in any form. By this time, a Congress in full rebellion against a crippled president set out to end the war on its own. In late June, it ap-

115. Small, *Nixon Presidency*, 274–86.
116. Marvin and Bernard Kalb, *Kissinger* (Boston, 1974), 433.

proved an amendment requiring the immediate cessation of all military operations in and over Indochina. The House upheld Nixon's angry veto, but he was forced to accept a compromise extending the deadline to August 15. For the first time, Congress had acted decisively to stop the war. "It would be idle to say that the authority of the executive has not been impaired," Kissinger lamented with obvious understatement.[117] Later in the year, Congress passed over another veto the so-called War Powers Act, which required the president to inform the legislature within forty-eight hours of the deployment of U.S. military forces abroad and to withdraw them in sixty days in the absence of explicit congressional endorsement. The circumstances under which the debate took place, combined with Watergate and the vote terminating operations in Indochina, made virtually certain the end of direct U.S. military involvement in Vietnam.

By late 1973, detente, the crown jewel of the Grand Design, had also fallen on hard times. Nixon and Brezhnev met in the United States in the summer of 1973, but there were no tangible results. The United States refused to go along with a no-first-use agreement for nuclear weapons urged by Moscow. There was no progress on a SALT II agreement. More important, detente had come under growing fire at home. Nixon's military advisers had never been happy with the SALT negotiations. Inasmuch as they approved arms negotiations at all, they wanted nothing less than equality across the board. The Joint Chiefs of Staff found allies in James Schlesinger, who succeeded Laird as secretary of defense in July 1973, in old Cold Warrior Paul Nitze, a top arms control negotiator who resigned in protest against SALT, and among conservative Republicans and Democrats in Congress.[118]

A more formidable challenge came from Democratic senator Henry Jackson of Washington. Soviet persecution of Jews reopened in the 1970s an issue that had aroused great moral indignation among Americans early in the century. Liberal on domestic issues and a hard-line anti-Communist, the idealistic and ambitious Jackson developed his own form of linkage by conditioning approval of the Soviet trade agreement on freedom of Jews to emigrate from the USSR. His amendment, cosponsored by Republican representative Charles Vanik of Ohio, struck a responsive chord among Americans eager to recapture the moral high ground in the wake of Vietnam, winning broad popular and congressional support. Absorbed in great power politics, Nixon and Kissinger failed to grasp the significance of Jackson's move. They did not use detente to encourage Soviet concessions. Nor

117. Ibid., 434.
118. Small, *Nixon Presidency*, 116–17.

did they warn Moscow of dangers to the trade bill or lobby Congress for restraint. The Soviet leadership exacerbated matters by clamping an exit tax on those seeking to emigrate. The Jackson-Vanik amendment passed Congress in December 1973, the opening round in a congressional challenge to detente that would continue throughout the decade. The Kremlin responded by canceling the trade agreement. The debate over Jewish emigration marked the emergence onto the national political scene of human rights issues that would play a key role in U.S. foreign policy for years to come.[119]

The move toward normalization of relations with China also stalled. Kissinger and Nixon had played the Soviet card to cultivate closer ties with China, which, in turn, were to be used as leverage against the USSR, a delicate and dangerous game indeed. Especially anxious about the "new czars," Beijing had gone along to the point that in 1972 Kissinger could describe China with some exaggeration as a "tacit ally."[120] Relations cooled in the next two years. The United States was not sufficiently anti-Soviet to suit even Chinese moderates such as Zhou, who themselves were under growing fire from hard-liners. As the impact of Watergate grew, Nixon and Kissinger lost credibility in China. To get relations back on track, Kissinger in late 1973 proposed to Beijing a hotline and even satellite images to assist in targeting Soviet military installations. It soon became clear, however, that only a severance of all U.S. ties with Taiwan would bring closer relations, a step an already embattled administration was not about to take.[121]

Vietnam, Watergate, and detente became entangled with and were significantly influenced by a fourth Arab-Israeli war during Yom Kippur and Ramadan in 1973 that sparked yet another superpower close call. This time, the Arabs fired the first shot. Following Nasser's death in September 1970, the redoubtable Anwar Sadat took power in Egypt. More pragmatic than his predecessor, Sadat tilted toward the West, proposing a settlement with Israel based on land for peace and evicting fifteen thousand Soviet military advisers from Egypt. Sadat also repeatedly warned that if Israel did not respond positively to his overtures he would fight. When the Israelis declined, and the Nixon administration, preoccupied with triangular diplomacy and then Watergate, did not press them, Sadat made good on his threat. With financial assistance from Saudi Arabia, Egypt and

119. Noam Kochavi, "Insights Abandoned, Flexibility Lost: Kissinger, Soviet Jewish Emigration, and the Demise of Détente," *Diplomatic History* 29 (June 2005), 503–30.
120. Goh, "Soviet Card," 485–86.
121. Ibid., 499.

Syria launched a surprise attack on October 6, Yom Kippur. Catching Israel off guard, the Arabs scored huge victories. Israel lost a thousand troops the first day, five hundred tanks the first week.[122]

The U.S. response followed classic realpolitik lines and involved a gamble that might have backfired. The war came at an especially critical point in the Watergate scandal, and a beleaguered, depressed, and often inebriated Nixon was not an active player. Kissinger ran the show. He did not want Israel to lose the war. But he also reasoned that if Egypt and Syria made gains they could negotiate from a stronger position, increasing the possibility of a settlement. Thus when Israel pleaded with Washington for emergency resupply of equipment lost in the first days of the war, the administration hesitated. Kissinger blamed the delay on the Defense Department and used it to extract Israeli promises to accept a cease-fire and not to encourage American Jews to support Jackson-Vanik. Finally, nervous that a desperate Israel might resort to nuclear weapons, and determined to demonstrate that despite Vietnam the administration would back its allies and despite Watergate it could act decisively, Nixon interceded. "Get your ass out of here and tell those people to move," he ordered Kissinger.[123] During the second week of the war, the United States initiated a massive resupply effort, at times totaling a hundred tons per hour, eventually providing Israel with eleven thousand tons of equipment and ammunition. The infusion of U.S. military hardware enabled Israel to gain the initiative, reoccupy the Golan Heights, and advance into Egypt and Syria. The Arabs, Saudi Arabia included, responded with an oil embargo, causing huge economic problems for the United States and its allies and providing yet another indication of America's growing vulnerability.

The Israeli counteroffensive provoked the most dangerous superpower confrontation since the Six-Day War, a demonstration of the value and limits of detente. Facing defeat, the Arabs appealed for Soviet help. In the best spirit of detente, Brezhnev and Kissinger arranged a cease-fire agreement. Characteristically, however, with a wink and nod, Kissinger gave Israel a green light to delay observance of the cease-fire. An angry Sadat responded by asking the great powers to send troops to uphold the cease-fire they had negotiated. Brezhnev in stern tones warned that if the United States did not go along he would consider unilateral intervention. It seems clear now that he had no intention of doing so, but an edgy Washington mistakenly viewed the letter as an ultimatum and in any event did not want Soviet troops in the Middle East. With Nixon in bed, reportedly

122. Small, *Nixon Presidency*, 131–33.
123. Little, *Orientalism*, 242–43.

drunk, Kissinger presided over an emergency NSC meeting that beefed up U.S. naval power in the Mediterranean and moved military forces worldwide to DefCon 3, the alert preliminary to war. Kissinger later claimed to have orchestrated a "deliberate overreaction" to send the Soviets a message. His explanation may have been an after-the-fact rationalization for an alarmist response under stressful circumstances. In any event, Brezhnev responded calmly, and the superpower confrontation led to a cease-fire.[124]

From this point, Kissinger took the lead in Middle East peacemaking. Both sides had suffered horrendous losses in what turned out to be a "traumatic and fearsome experience." There had been no clear-cut victor, thus facilitating a settlement.[125] Despite assuring the Soviets he would keep them engaged, he deliberately excluded them, making himself the indispensable person. Using the enticement of additional military aid, he brought Israel into the process. He also won over Sadat, with whom he formed close personal ties. Engaging in what would be called "shuttle diplomacy," he flew back and forth among the Middle East capitals. He got Israel and Egypt to agree to armistice lines and Egypt to reestablish relations with the United States. In March 1974, he secured removal of the Arab oil embargo. Two months later, he brokered an agreement between Israel and Syria. It was a bravura performance, which earned Kissinger yet more accolades—*Newsweek*'s cover portrayed him wearing a Superman cape emblazoned with the label "Super-K." Kissinger made the United States the key player in the Middle East peace process and created the basis for later, more significant agreements. But his successes were not without costs. As U.S. influence in the Middle East grew, its ability to affect events elsewhere, most notably in Indochina, shrank. Kissinger's unilateralism achieved his essential aim of keeping the USSR out of the Middle East. But it also antagonized his Soviet counterparts, further undermined detente, and provided the Soviets a handy excuse to act unilaterally in other regions.[126]

The last hurrah of Nixon's diplomacy came in the summer of 1974 with a courageous but futile global grand tour. Throughout the Watergate proceedings, Nixon had continued to hope that foreign policy success would distract public attention from his domestic woes and demonstrate that he was indispensable. By this time, his presidency was in peril. He suffered

---

124. Hanhimäki, *Flawed Architect*, 313–17.
125. Bundy, *Tangled Web*, 442.
126. Hanhimäki, *Flawed Architect*, 325–31.

from a painful and life-threatening blood clot in one leg. Numerous times in his tempestuous career, Nixon had snatched victory from the jaws of defeat with some bold move. He undoubtedly hoped that his reception abroad would confirm his status as a world statesman, perhaps even salvage his presidency. The views of foreign leaders offered room for hope. Mao dismissed Watergate as a "fart in the wind."[127] Soviet officials "simply could not grasp," Dobrynin recalled, that the president could be prosecuted for "such a small matter." They blamed Watergate on a Zionist or anti-Soviet conspiracy.[128] Western European leaders also found Watergate hard to comprehend and would likely have preferred that Nixon remain in office.[129]

The first leg in the farewell globetrotting was the Middle East. In Egypt, huge crowds turned out to greet the nation's new friend. From there, he journeyed to Saudi Arabia, Syria, Israel, and Jordan, becoming the first U.S. president to visit Syria and Israel. Ironically, he was received more enthusiastically in Damascus than in Jerusalem, a reflection of U.S. evenhandedness since the October War. As a sop to Israel, he offered additional aid, including help with building a nuclear reactor for peaceful purposes. Nixon endured the journey despite at times intense pain, leading his physician to suggest that he might have a "death wish."[130]

After a stop back in the United States, the president traveled to Moscow in late June for a final meeting with Brezhnev. The visit included a three-day respite at a suburb of Yalta, hastily renamed Oreanda to spare Nixon political embarrassment from connection with another summit nearly thirty years earlier. Despite inflated U.S. hopes, the meeting produced only minor agreements, the limiting of ABMs to one for each nation rather than the two agreed upon in 1972 and assorted technical deals. There was no real progress on SALT II. In private conversations in the Crimea, Brezhnev pushed for a Soviet-American non-aggression pact, which, in the event of an attack on either signatory by an unnamed but obvious third party, bound the other to provide assistance, a nonstarter if ever there was one. By this time, however, detente had leveled off. Nixon returned home on July 3. His "last serious diplomatic moves had been gallant but hopeless efforts," Bundy has concluded, "typical of this last phase of his presidency when he was grasping at straws, hoping in vain for a

127. Ibid., 338.
128. Bundy, *Tangled Web*, 463–64.
129. Ibid, 463.
130. Small, *Nixon Presidency*, 293.

miracle."[131] A little more than a month later, facing certain impeachment and likely conviction, he resigned the presidency.

NIXON AND KISSINGER DESERVE FULL CREDIT for their important achievements. The politician and the professor had a keen grasp of the way the world was changing and a shrewd sense in terms of great-power politics of how to adapt. Kennedy and Johnson had initiated detente, to be sure, but Nixon and Kissinger took major strides forward, developing crude guidelines for cooperation with the Soviet Union and completing major strategic arms and trade agreements. Liberals and conservatives attacked detente at the time. Conservatives and neo-conservatives have denounced it since as a deal with the devil—what was needed with the USSR, they allege, was not negotiations and concessions but tough talk and diplomatic and economic pressures. In fact, despite its flaws, detente initiated processes that made possible the ending of the Cold War. It slowed a runaway arms race. It expanded the cultural exchanges that eventually helped discredit and weaken the Communist system. The opening to China was long overdue and inevitable, but Nixon and Kissinger seized the moment to start the process and carried it off with consummate diplomatic skill. Following the October War, Kissinger initiated a Middle East negotiating process that brought some progress toward peace, if not peace itself.

These significant accomplishments must be weighed against huge and glaring failures. Ironically, while taking steps to ease Cold War tensions, the two men imposed a rigid Cold War mindset on essentially local and regional problems in Latin America and South Asia. Their rampant interference in Chilean elections and their role in displacing the democratically chosen Allende violated hemispheric non-interference pledges and contributed to an era of bloody repression in Chile. Unabashed support for Pakistan and the elevation of the Indo-Pakistani dispute into a conflict with earthshaking global implications could have had disastrous consequences. Above all, there was Vietnam. Nixon and Kissinger developed Vietnam policies from badly flawed assumptions and with means entirely inadequate to the ends they sought. The height of realism is recognizing when to cut one's losses. They did that only grudgingly and after four more years of war, with more than twenty thousand American lives lost, and hundreds of thousands of Vietnamese. They accepted without close scrutiny the dubious belief that America's credibility as a great power depended upon achieving its goals in Vietnam. They naively

131. Bundy, *Tangled Web*, 469.

assumed that while scaling back U.S. power they could achieve the goal their predecessors could not, an independent, non-Communist South Vietnam. They were doomed to fail. Their stubborn persistence heightened divisions at home. The methods they used to deal with rising domestic dissent trampled on the Constitution and led directly to Watergate and the demise of the Nixon presidency. Their often bizarre behavior, the product of profound insecurities and revealed to the world in the Nixon tapes, at times raises serious questions about their fitness for office. Ultimately, they produced the very result they sought to avoid, massive popular disillusionment with global involvement and a marked turning inward. This, rather than a generation of peace, was their principal legacy.

18

Foreign Policy in an Age of Dissonance, 1974–1981

"This is not the alliance as it once seemed," the venerable London *Economist* fretted in a somber article entitled "The Fading of America" printed just days before the fall of Saigon in April 1975. The *Economist* found solace in its belief that Europe remained important to the United States while Vietnam had always been "at the farthest stretch of the American arm." But obvious changes in the national mood on the eve of defeat in war still raised fears that "the pulling in of burned American fingers could affect Europe too."[1]

The *Economist* correctly detected major shifts in the American temper and rightly traced them to the Vietnam War, but the changes went much deeper than it allowed or likely understood. Old dangers seemed to be receding in the 1970s, new ones rising, the world less easy to comprehend. At home, Americans suffered the most serious and prolonged economic crisis since the Great Depression. National priorities underwent their most dramatic shift since Pearl Harbor. Where a crude consensus had prevailed through much of the Cold War, dissonance was the hallmark of a very different decade. Bitter debates over Vietnam and the cultural revolution at home had opened deep fissures in the body politic. While liberal doves challenged Cold War verities from the left, conservatives and neo-conservatives attacked the realpolitik of Nixon and Kissinger from the right. The illusion of American omnipotence first exposed by the fall of China and the Korean War was graphically manifested again in the 1970s. A people accustomed to having their way in the face of recurrent failure felt frustrated and impotent and vented their fury on their tormenters—and their leaders. To complicate matters still further, a newly emboldened Congress in the aftermath of Vietnam and Watergate challenged more than three decades of presidential dominance in foreign policy. Against this backdrop of division and disarray, Gerald Ford and Jimmy Carter struggled to implement foreign policy after Nixon's resignation. Ford tried to perpetuate detente and ended up presiding over its demise; Carter sought to escape the Cold War and became its captive.

1. "The Fading of America," *Economist*, April 4. 1975, 12.

I

U.S. foreign policy experienced greater domestic shocks in the 1970s than at any other time since the 1930s. By easing the most obvious threats to the nation's security, Nixon's agreements with the Soviet Union and steps toward reconciliation with China cut away at support for continued Cold War sacrifices and commitments. As the Vietnam War dragged on, costs skyrocketed, and the domestic debate raged, Americans grew increasingly wary of overseas entanglements. Polls taken shortly before the fall of Saigon produced the stunning revelation that a majority was willing to send troops abroad only to defend Canada. "Vietnam has left a rancid aftertaste that clings to almost every mention of direct military intervention," the columnist David Broder observed in March 1975.[2]

Spiraling economic problems reinforced already strong tendencies to turn inward. Cold War expenditures had sustained a period of unprecedented economic expansion, but by the early 1970s that bubble had burst. Competition in world markets from a resurgent Western Europe and Japan hindered economic growth, especially in key areas such as steel and automobiles. The Vietnam War triggered runaway inflation—in July 1974 alone prices rose 3.7 percent, the second largest monthly jump since 1946. The 1973 Arab oil embargo—an "economic Pearl Harbor"—triggered an energy crisis marked by soaring prices for gasoline and fuel oil.[3] Inflation had customarily meant high employment, but the 1970s brought the new phenomenon called "stagflation." While lines at gas stations lengthened and inflation rose, unemployment mounted. A once vibrant economy plunged into full-fledged recession. The five issues that most concerned Americans in 1965 all involved foreign policy; nine years later, the top three were domestic.[4]

As it turned inward, the nation also shifted to the right politically. Conservatism seemed dead after the Goldwater debacle of 1964, but from the depths of defeat the movement's leaders over the next decade led a remarkable resurgence. They preached to an increasingly receptive audience; polls taken in the early 1970s revealed that Americans as a whole had become more conservative. The change reflected postwar affluence and a vast expansion of the middle class. It also represented a reaction against the social, cultural, and political radicalism of the 1960s, a gut response on the part of those Nixon labeled the Silent Majority to the

2. George C. Herring, *America's Longest War: The United States and Vietnam, 1950–1975* (4th ed., New York, 2002), 349.

3. Yanek Mieczkowski, *Gerald Ford and the Challenges of the 1970s* (Lexington, Ky., 2005), 5.

4. Ibid., 2–3, 148–56.

perceived excesses of the anti-war movement, the counterculture, black power, feminism, and gay rights. The Supreme Court's 1973 decision legalizing abortion infuriated Roman Catholics and evangelical Protestants, spurring the rise of a religious right that would assume growing political importance. Conservatives blamed the Great Society for the nation's economic woes and railed against high taxes, big government, and social engineering. In foreign policy, they attacked the liberal do-goodism of Johnson and the amoral realism of Nixon and Kissinger. Some pressed for rebuilding U.S. power, taking a harder line against the Soviet Union, and reasserting America's moral leadership in the world.[5]

Attitudes changed and institutions crumbled as fears grew and priorities shifted. At the height of the Cold War, Americans expressed greater trust in their government than any other people in the world. As a result of the Johnson/Nixon credibility gap, a once compliant media subjected the most innocent official statements to the most searching scrutiny. Nixon's abuses of power, revealed sensationally to an already agitated nation through the televised Watergate hearings, widened the gap to a chasm. The release of his White House tapes exposed a meanness and crudeness that degraded the office—"shabby, disgusting, immoral," Republican senator Hugh Scott fumed.[6] The imperial presidency, a foundation stone of Cold War foreign policy, in the wake of Vietnam and Watergate plummeted to its lowest point in prestige since the Harding scandals of the 1920s. Involvement of former CIA operatives in the Watergate burglary led to congressional investigations that produced sensational exposés of the agency's illegal surveillance of journalists, infiltration of the anti-war movement, assassination plots against Fidel Castro and Patrice Lumumba, and role in the overthrow of the Allende government. A once sacrosanct institution was badly tarnished in reputation and subjected to congressional oversight.[7] Cynicism and self-doubt marked the national mood.

Gerald R. Ford reaped the whirlwind sowed by his predecessors. A native of Michigan and star football player at the state university, Ford turned down a chance at pro football for Yale Law School. At Yale, he belonged to the isolationist America First organization, but, like many of his generation, he was converted by World War II. Whether "I was in Congress, vice president, or president," he later recalled, "I was an internationalist in foreign policy."[8] As president, he was often lampooned by

5. Ibid., 305–10.
6. Ibid., 20.
7. John R. Greene, *The Presidency of Gerald R. Ford* (Lawrence, Kans., 1995), 101–12.
8. Mieczkowski, *Ford*, 273.

television comedians—also a sign of the times—as a slow-witted stumble-bum who, in Lyndon Johnson's words, could not walk and chew gum at the same time. That image concealed a smart and tough politician who as House of Representatives minority leader understood the art of the deal. A respected, veteran congressman before replacing the scandal-besmirched Spiro Agnew as vice president, he had a vast knowledge of the workings of government. The only unelected president was honest and reliable, by his own admission a "Ford, not a Lincoln." Upon taking office he saw his essential tasks as healing the deep wounds opened by Vietnam and Watergate and maintaining continuity in foreign affairs.[9]

To the latter end, he retained Kissinger as national security adviser and secretary of state. The beneficiary of artful self-promotion and Nixon's self-destruction, "Super-K," then at the height of his prestige, was widely viewed as the essential person, the peerless diplomatic navigator needed to guide an unschooled president through troubled foreign policy waters. Kissinger had survived Watergate—no mean feat—but he had also made countless enemies who were ready to pounce at the first sign of vulnerability. In the Ford administration, he came under attack from liberals and conservatives inside and outside the administration. The tweedy, pipe-smoking Secretary of Defense James Schlesinger, his Harvard classmate and fellow academician, was equally intelligent—and vain. He needled Kissinger relentlessly and conspired against him with Congress. Schlesinger's replacement, the youthful Donald Rumsfeld, by Kissinger's own admission, was at least his equal in the cutthroat game of bureaucratic politics.[10] Mainly because of his role as an architect of detente, the indispensable man of 1974 two years later turned out to be a political liability for a president seeking election in his own right in a rapidly changing political environment.

The most dramatic change in the making of foreign policy in the mid-1970s was the role of Congress. Customarily in American politics, the legislature in postwar periods has sought to reclaim powers surrendered under military exigencies. With the Cold War seemingly in remission and Vietnam nearing an end, this was especially true of the Ford years. Dominated by Johnson, often stonewalled by Nixon, Congress set out with a vengeance to reinsert itself into the policy process. The rebellion began in the late 1960s with major challenges to the long-sacrosanct defense budget and assorted resolutions to end the war and limit its expansion in

9. Ford's career is recounted in Gerald R. Ford, *A Time to Heal: The Autobiography of Gerald R. Ford* (New York, 1979) and James Cannon, *Time and Chance: Gerald Ford's Appointment with History* (New York, 1994).

10. Henry Kissinger, *Years of Renewal* (New York, 1979), 175–82.

Indochina. Its first phase culminated with the 1973 War Powers Resolution that sought to restore to Congress some control over the executive's ability to commit military forces abroad by requiring that they be withdrawn within sixty days of deployment in the absence of legislative authorization.[11]

The rebellion had partisan undertones. Democrats controlled both houses of Congress and were naturally disposed to flex their muscles. It also reflected the growing potency of single-issue groups such as the powerful Israel lobby and a smaller but still influential organization of Greek-Americans. It was also ideological. Conservatives from both parties joined forces to challenge detente. But the initial thrust came from liberal internationalists, mostly Democrats, who sought to democratize U.S. foreign policy and restore its traditional idealism. Reacting against what they saw as the militarization of Cold War policies, these so-called new internationalists challenged exorbitant defense spending, military aid programs, overcommitment and interventionism abroad, and U.S. support for right-wing dictators. They favored economic cooperation and cultural exchanges and pressed for the defense of human rights in other countries. They used subcommittees to get around senior legislators who had long dominated major House and Senate committees, proposed amendments to appropriations bills to advance their agenda, and even paid for television time to promote their causes. They came very close to blocking Nixon's ABM proposal in 1969. They exposed secret U.S. military operations in Laos and Cambodia and sought to shut down the Pentagon's worldwide arms bazaar.[12]

In the broadest sense, a Congress that had generally rubber-stamped presidential initiatives since World War II now sought a position of "codetermination" in making foreign policy, by which it meant early and full consultation and even active participation in making decisions.[13] Increasingly assertive legislators opposed initiatives Ford and Kissinger considered vital and enacted their own measures undercutting established policies. Schooled in the realist tradition of European politics that emphasized

11. Jacob K. Javits, "The Debate over the War Powers Resolution, 1945–1970," and John H. Sullivan, "The Impact of the War Powers Resolution," in Michael Barnhart, ed., *Congress and United States Foreign Policy: Controlling the Use of Force in the Nuclear Age* (Albany, N.Y., 1987), 55–76.

12. Robert David Johnson, *Congress and the Cold War* (New York, 2006), xiv, xix, xx–xxi, 190–241.

13. Melvin Small, *Democracy and Diplomacy: The Impact of Domestic Politics on U.S. Foreign Policy, 1789–1994* (Baltimore, Md., 1996), 131; Thomas Franck and Edward Weisband, *Foreign Policy by Congress* (New York, 1979), 61.

insulating foreign policy from the destructive whims of public opinion and accustomed to having his way with Congress, Kissinger was especially ill suited to deal with the rebellion on Capitol Hill. He later lamented the supreme "irony that the Congress [Ford] genuinely loved and respected had harassed his foreign policy unmercifully from the beginning and encumbered it with unprecedented restrictions."[14]

Ford's ability to deal with Congress was significantly weakened during his first months in office. He assumed the presidency amid an outpouring of goodwill. His plain-spoken, down-to-earth manner and personal warmth won widespread praise. He set out at once to heal wounds left by Vietnam and Watergate. In his first speech, he vowed to be truthful and solemnly proclaimed that "our long national nightmare is over."[15] Making good on his promises of healing, he offered clemency to those Vietnam War draft evaders who submitted their cases to a federal board. Although well-intentioned, the move infuriated conservatives and fell short of what many liberals wanted, especially in light of his second major step, a "full, free, and absolute" pardon for Richard Nixon. Ford saw Nixon's pardon as essential to relegating the "long national nightmare" to the past. He was probably right, but the haste with which it was done and the lack of political preparation brought down a firestorm of criticism, including baseless but lingering charges of a sordid deal in which Ford gained office by promising to pardon his predecessor. Angry protestors shouted, "Jail Ford." The new president's approval rating plunged twenty-one points in less than a week—the worst drop in the history of the Gallup Poll. In the fall elections, the Republicans lost forty-three seats in the House and three in the Senate, increasing sizeable Democratic majorities to 147 and 23 respectively. An already rebellious Congress was further emboldened to take on Nixon's successor. The Ford presidency was crippled at the outset.[16]

II

Ford and Kissinger set relatively straightforward foreign policy goals: to uphold and where possible expand detente with the USSR; to protect America's international position against threats from enemies abroad and challenges from left and right at home. They achieved some early and ephemeral successes in negotiations with the Soviet Union, but little

14. Kissinger, *Years of Renewal,* 37, 1064.
15. Ford's "swearing-in" speech, August 9, 1974, can be found in www.ford/utexasedu/ LIBRARY/speeches/740001/html.
16. Greene, *Ford Presidency,* 39–52, 56.

else. From the beginning, they waged a desperate and ultimately futile rearguard action to defend established policies.

The new president had scarcely settled into the White House when Congress first thrust itself into a sensitive and significant foreign policy matter, setting the tone for the next two years. Since its independence in 1957, the ethnically divided island of Cyprus off the southern coast of Turkey had been the object of bitter conflict between NATO allies, Greece and Turkey. In June 1974, pro-Greek rebels overthrew a government that had attempted to maintain a precarious balance between the island's Greek majority and Turkish minority. Turkey responded a month later by invading Cyprus, using military equipment provided by the United States exclusively for self-defense. Angry Greeks attacked the U.S. embassy in Nicosia and killed the ambassador. Just two weeks after Ford assumed the presidency, the Cyprus crisis threatened the solidity of NATO. Even in the age of detente, some officials feared that Moscow might intrude in the strategically important eastern Mediterranean. When Kissinger could not resolve the dispute, the administration backed Turkey, an indispensable ally that provided essential military bases and a vital listening post for Soviet military activities. Ford and Kissinger also blamed Greece for provoking the Turkish invasion.[17]

Breaking with Cold War precedent, a rebellious Congress for the first time since the 1930s took foreign policy into its own hands. The ostensible reason was to uphold the letter of the law on military assistance. Congress was also responding to pressures from the Greek lobby. But what mainly drove the legislators was a pervasive post-Watergate distrust of the presidency and a determination to influence major foreign policy decisions.[18] The House of Representatives in the fall of 1974 twice voted to terminate military aid to Turkey. Ford both times vetoed the legislation, but he eventually accepted a compromise delaying the cutoff until early 1975. Turkey predictably retaliated by shutting down all U.S. military and intelligence installations except for one NATO air base. Ford later called it the "single most irresponsible, short-sighted foreign policy decision Congress had made in all the years I'd been in Congress."[19] The embargo lasted three years. It did nothing to solve the Cyprus conflict. In 1983, the northern part of the island established a separate government under Turkish rule. The Soviets did not exploit the crisis. Turkey and Greece both remained in NATO, but the embargo seriously damaged U.S. relations with Turkey for

17. Ibid., 117–19.
18. Franck and Weisband, Congress, 61.
19. Ford, Time to Heal, 302.

the short term. This huge early defeat for the Ford administration made plain the weakening of the imperial presidency. Kissinger's most serious foreign policy crisis, wrote pundit Robert Pastor, was not abroad but "in Washington with Congress."[20] Smelling blood, congressional rebels set out after bigger game—the Nixon-Kissinger policy of detente with the Soviet Union.

In truth, detente was in trouble when Ford took office. Soviet and American leaders held sharply divergent views of what it meant and became disillusioned when their unrealistic expectations were not met. The United States expected the Soviet Union to be content with the status quo once it became an accepted member of the world community; still certain that revolution was the wave of the future, Moscow saw no contradiction between its support for revolutionary groups and detente. In assessing the other's actions, each side applied what has been aptly called a "one-sided double standard." United States officials who had expected that detente would mitigate Soviet expansionist tendencies came to blame it for encouraging them. They failed to see how things they did might be viewed as threatening in Moscow. The two nations also fundamentally misunderstood each other's political processes. Soviet leaders placed excessive faith in U.S. presidents to work their will with Congress. Congress greatly exaggerated the United States' ability to influence Soviet internal policies.[21]

The congressional challenge to detente brought together hard-core Cold Warriors, human rights advocates, and friends of Israel. Democratic senator Henry "Scoop" Jackson assumed leadership of this unwieldy coalition. With a bland personality and plodding demeanor, Jackson appeared an unlikely candidate for the role of political firebrand. Known as the "senator from Boeing" for his close ties to the military-industrial complex in his home state of Washington, the doggedly persistent senator was moderately liberal on domestic issues but a hard line anti-Communist in foreign policy. He was egged on by his young staff assistant, Richard Perle, a charming— and ruthless—right-wing zealot and one-man pro-Israel lobby known as "the Prince of Darkness" for his take-no-prisoners approach to bureaucratic warfare.[22] Jackson hoped to ride anti-Soviet zeal and passionate support for Israel to the presidency in 1976. It was he and Democratic representative Charles Vanik of Ohio who had wrecked the 1972 Soviet-American trade

20. Johnson, *Congress and the Cold War*, 201.
21. Raymond Garthoff, *Détente and Confrontation: American-Soviet Relations from Nixon to Reagan* (Washington, 1985), 1069–73. The idea of a "one-sided double standard" is discussed on p. 1073.
22. Walter Isaacson, *Kissinger: A Biography* (New York, 1992), 612–13.

agreement by securing passage of the amendment requiring the USSR to permit unlimited emigration of Jews in return for most-favored-nation treatment. With Watergate consuming the nation's attention, Kissinger struggled to save a key component of detente by renegotiating with the Soviets—and Jackson—an agreement he thought had already been completed. He deeply resented congressional intrusion. He questioned the wisdom, indeed the legitimacy, of seeking to shape the internal policies of a sovereign state. The Soviets had already significantly increased the number of exit visas for Jews, and he protested—correctly—that his quiet diplomacy had produced major concessions. Nor was the issue important enough in his view to justify scuttling a major foreign policy venture. But the challenge was too serious and potentially too costly to ignore.

After months of complicated and prickly discussions—Jackson repeatedly caused problems by upping the ante—and with Ford now in the White House, Kissinger in the fall of 1974 finally patched together a characteristically convoluted deal in which Moscow would offer verbal assurances, to be set forth through an exchange of letters in which it was not directly involved, that sixty thousand Soviet Jews would be given exit visas each year. This quite extraordinary way of conducting diplomacy reflected the rising power of Jackson and Congress and the desperation of Ford and Kissinger. It was not enough. In a move driven by mischief or sheer ambition—perhaps both—Jackson destroyed Kissinger's handiwork by publicly claiming victory and making the Soviet assurances seem more definitive and binding than they were. The senator's feckless grandstand play naturally infuriated the Soviet leaders. They were further outraged when his congressional allies tacked on to the Soviet trade bill a $300 million limit on Export-Import Bank credits. In January 1975, they rejected the agreement. They subsequently stopped payments on their lend-lease debt. It was another stunning blow to Kissinger's reputation as a master diplomatic fixer, executive control of foreign policy, and, most important, detente.[23]

Fallout from the failed trade agreement contributed to the eventual breakdown of strategic arms limitations talks. SALT I had frozen the production of missiles at existing levels. This left the USSR with a sizeable advantage in numbers of ICBMs. But U.S. weapons were more accurate, and the United States had a much larger arsenal of MIRVs, a weapon described by one writer as "a hydra-headed beast that carries two or more nuclear warheads, each programmed to hit a different target."[24] Certain

23. Garthoff, Détente, 454–56.
24. Isaacson, Kissinger, 316.

that Nixon and Kissinger had again given away too much and perhaps opposed to the very idea of limitations on strategic arms, Jackson secured passage in late 1972 of a resolution requiring that future SALT agreements be based on the principle of equal numbers of missiles. On the surface, equality seemed equitable, but it was very difficult to implement because the two nations had quite different weapons systems. Soviet missiles were land-based, larger, and slower and required launchers with higher throw-weights. The U.S. weapons were smaller, faster, and more mobile and could be launched from aircraft and submarines. Working alone as always and without building a consensus behind him, Kissinger for nearly two years tried to get the Soviets to accept various formulas based on Jackson's principle of equality.[25]

Remarkably, in his first summit with Soviet leader Leonid Brezhnev, Ford seemed to achieve miracles. The two met near Vladivostok in late November 1974 in a military sanitarium Ford compared to "an abandoned YMCA camp in the Catskills." They got along famously, regaling each other with tales of their athletic exploits as young men. When Brezhnev readily accepted the president's proposal for an equal number of missiles, the shocked Americans adjourned outside to the bitter cold away from Soviet bugging devices to ponder what was going on and how to respond. Ford was "euphoric." After additional negotiations, the two sides seemed to achieve a huge victory for detente by agreeing that each should have 2,400 strategic delivery vehicles and 1,300 MIRVs.[26]

Like the trade agreement, the Vladivostok understanding ran into a political buzz saw at home. Kissinger and Ford had tailored their proposals to meet specifications set down by Jackson and hawks in the Pentagon, but the senator had no compunctions about opposing a deal based on principles he himself had demanded. In another of those concessions he must have come to regret, Kissinger had agreed before Vladivostok that the Soviet Backfire bomber, an aircraft Moscow insisted did not have strategic capability, be excluded from the negotiations. Jackson and other hawks now pinpointed that omission as a fatal flaw, again accusing the administration of selling out. Some Democratic liberals insisted that the numbers of missiles and MIRVs allowed were so high as to make the agreement meaningless. Kissinger's efforts to wriggle out of the Backfire concession infuriated his Soviet counterparts and did nothing to appease his congressional critics. The concurrent collapse of the trade talks created ill will on both sides that further damaged negotiations on strategic weapons. While Jackson

25. Greene, *Ford Presidency*, 124.
26. Isaacson, *Kissinger*, 626–28.

and his Senate allies delayed a vote on the agreement, subsequent discussions bogged down in differences over details. Largely because of problems with Congress, detente by the beginning of 1975 was in shambles.[27]

As Kissinger and Ford struggled to keep detente alive, America's eight-year war in Vietnam came to a painful end. Despite Nixon's claims of peace with honor, the January 1973 agreement, which permitted 150,000 North Vietnamese troops to remain in the South, was fatally flawed. Fighting continued. Negotiations for a new government quickly stalled. Nixon had hoped to enforce the agreement by keeping alive the threat of U.S. air intervention, but his ability to do so was increasingly limited by the paralyzing effects of Watergate and surging popular opposition to any form of reintervention in Indochina. Reflecting the mood of the nation, a war-weary Congress in 1973 cut off funds for air operations in Indochina. In September 1974, despite Kissinger's urgent warnings of a "corrosive effect on our interests beyond Indochina," Congress drastically reduced military and economic aid to South Vietnam. Runaway inflation at home evoked insistent demands for reducing expenditures. Critics pointed to the endemic waste and corruption in Saigon. It was time to terminate America's "endless support for an endless war," Democratic senator Edward Kennedy of Massachusetts proclaimed.[28]

Cuts in U.S. aid demoralized South Vietnam and encouraged North Vietnam to challenge a precarious status quo. The inescapable signs of waning U.S. support had a devastating effect on morale in a South Vietnamese army already reeling under enemy blows. The aid reductions heightened President Nguyen Van Thieu's already considerable economic and political difficulties. In late 1974, North Vietnamese regulars seized Phuoc Long northeast of Saigon. Encouraged by their success and by U.S. failure to respond, they struck the Central Highlands in March 1975. The end came with a suddenness that shocked even the leadership in Hanoi. When Thieu ordered an ill-considered withdrawal from the highlands, panic ensued. Much of the South Vietnamese army was captured or destroyed; thousands of civilians perished in a tragic mass retreat known as the "convoy of tears." Duplicating in the coastal cities of Hue and Da Nang its easy success in the highlands, North Vietnam threw all its forces into the "Ho Chi Minh Campaign" to "liberate" Saigon.[29]

The United States was stunned by the sudden collapse of South Vietnam but resigned to the outcome. The disinclination for further

27. Garthoff, Détente, 446–53; Isaacson, Kissinger, 628–29.
28. Herring, Longest War, 331.
29. Ibid., 332–33.

involvement was obvious. On the day Ban Me Thuot fell, Congress rejected Ford's request for an additional $300 million in military aid for South Vietnam. War-weary, pinched by recession at home, skeptical that any amount of U.S. assistance could alter the outcome, most Americans felt no generosity. The fall of Da Nang and Hue did nothing to alter such views. Ford gave no thought to employing U.S. air and naval power. To stiffen South Vietnamese morale and shift some of the blame to Congress, he asked for $722 million in emergency military assistance, setting off a final, bitter debate on the war. Clinging to the self-delusion that had marked U.S. involvement from the outset, the administration held out the chimera that additional aid might yet bring about a stalemate and negotiated settlement. Kissinger reiterated the shopworn warning that the impact of the fall of South Vietnam "on the United States in the world would be very serious indeed." Legislators retorted that no amount of money could save an army that refused to fight. Congress eventually appropriated $300 million and endorsed Ford's request to use U.S. troops for the evacuation of Americans and for humanitarian purposes. But it would do no more. "The Vietnam debate has run its course," Kissinger commented with finality on April 17.[30]

The certainty that the United States would not intervene extinguished the last glimmer of hope in South Vietnam. North Vietnamese troops advanced from Da Nang to the outskirts of Saigon in less than a month. Thieu resigned on April 21. "It is so easy to be an enemy of the United States, but so difficult to be a friend," he lamented.[31] On April 30, 1975, enemy tanks crashed through the gates of the presidential palace, and National Liberation Front soldiers triumphantly ran up their flag over a quickly renamed Ho Chi Minh City. A week earlier Ford had formally pronounced at Tulane University what had already become obvious: The Vietnam War was "finished as far as the United States was concerned." When he uttered the word *finished*, the crowd of mostly students jumped to its feet and erupted in prolonged cheering and applause.[32] Through Operation Frequent Wind, the United States extricated its own people from South Vietnam, along with, at Ford's insistence, 130,000 South Vietnamese who had supported U.S. efforts. Because of botched plans for withdrawal, many of those seeking to flee could not. The spectacle of U.S. Marines using rifle butts to keep frantic South Vietnamese from blocking escape routes provided a tragic epitaph for a quarter century of

30. *New York Times*, April 18, 1975.
31. Herring, *Longest War*, 336.
32. *New Orleans Times-Picayune*, April 23, 1975.

U.S. involvement in Vietnam. Ford recalled April 30, 1975, as "one of the saddest days in my life"; journalist Evan Thomas labeled it a "low moment in the American century."[33]

The fall of Saigon had a profound impact in the United States. For a people accustomed to ending wars with ticker tape parades, April 30, 1975, left a deep residue of frustration and anger. Americans generally agreed that the war had been a dark moment in their nation's history. Some comforted themselves that the United States should never have become involved in the first place, others that the war could have been won if properly fought. Still others regarded the failure to stand by an ally as a betrayal of American ideals. "It was the saddest day of my life when it sank in that we had lost the war," a Virginian lamented.[34] The fall of Vietnam came when the nation was preparing to celebrate the bicentennial of its birth, and the irony was painfully obvious. "The high hopes and wishful idealism with which the American nation had been born had not been destroyed," *Newsweek* observed, "but they had been chastened by the failure of America to work its will in Indochina."[35]

Ford showed admirable courage in dealing with the first influx of refugees from South Vietnam, part of the fallout from a lost war. American war-weariness, sometimes tinged with racism, evinced itself in often ugly antipathy to some of the most tragic victims of the war. Bucking popular opinion, the president set aside $2 million in emergency funds to help transport two thousand orphans to the United States. When Congress as part of its general assault on presidential prerogatives rejected a bill providing $327 million in aid for refugees, a furious president flew to San Francisco amid extensive publicity to personally welcome a flight of orphans. He gave a series of eloquent speeches appealing to Americans to live up to their own ideals of fair play and compassion. At least for the short term, he muted opposition in the country and Congress, helping to smooth the arrival of the first wave of Vietnamese immigrants.[36]

The administration was not so charitable in dealing with the new Socialist Republic of Vietnam. In an anomalous instance where the loser of a war imposed punitive terms on the winner for the reestablishment of diplomatic relations, the United States continued to treat Vietnam as an enemy. Few Americans were interested in reconciliation. On the other hand, a deep-seated bitterness, the legacy of frustration and defeat, posed

33. *Newsweek*, May 1, 2000, 37–42.
34. Herring, *Longest War*, 346–47.
35. *Newsweek*, April 28, 1975, 17.
36. Mieczkowski, *Ford*, 293–94.

a major obstacle to restoration of ties. Kissinger set the tone. Privately condemning the Vietnamese as "the most bloody minded bastards" he had ever dealt with, he insisted that the United States make no concessions. Geopolitical realities in time would force Hanoi to accept U.S. terms. The Ford administration thus extended to all of Vietnam the embargo applied during wartime to the North. It refused to consider the aid secretly promised by Nixon in the 1973 agreement and vetoed Vietnam's application for membership in the United Nations. Under pressure from Republican challenger Ronald Reagan, the normally easygoing Ford played to the galleries while campaigning in 1976, denouncing the Vietnamese as "pirates." It would be almost twenty years before the United States would establish relations with the nation that had defeated it.[37]

The humiliation, frustration, and anger that gripped the administration after the fall of Saigon was also manifest in its response to an incident in the Gulf of Thailand less than two weeks later. Claiming that the U.S. merchant ship *Mayaguez* had ventured into its territorial waters, the new, revolutionary government of Cambodia seized the vessel and its crew of forty. Suffering from post-Vietnam trauma and haunted by memories of North Korea's capture of the *Pueblo* in 1968, Ford and his advisers agreed they must act decisively: There "wasn't a dove in the place," one official recalled.[38] An embattled president saw a chance to prove his mettle. As always, Kissinger sought to mend tattered U.S. credibility. The administration never seriously considered negotiating with a Communist regime it had not recognized. It denounced Cambodia's "piracy," demanded return of the vessel and crew, mobilized military forces in the area, and heatedly debated whether to bomb Cambodia itself.

The United States recovered the ship and crew, made its point, and even enjoyed a moment of triumph, but as the result of a botched and costly operation that brought no real improvement to its international or domestic political position. Mistakenly believing that the crew was held on Koh Tang island off the southern coast of Cambodia, U.S. Marines landed on May 15, met unexpectedly fierce opposition from local Cambodian forces, and suffered heavy casualties in the initial assault: Eight helicopters were shot down, eighteen Marines killed—and it could have been much worse. Mainly as a punitive measure driven by political exigencies, the United States also bombed the Cambodian mainland—"Let's look

37. Herring, *Longest War*, 359–60; T. Christopher Jespersen, "The Bitter End and the Lost Chance in Vietnam: Congress, the Ford Administration, and the Battle over Vietnam, 1975–1976," *Diplomatic History* 24 (Spring 2000), 265–93.
38. Greene, *Ford Presidency*, 144.

ferocious," Kissinger snarled—a feel-good move that had no impact on the outcome.[39] The navy recovered the *Mayaguez*. At precisely the time the marines landed on Koh Tang, Cambodia voluntarily released the crew, permitting the administration to claim victory, a rare occurrence in those gloom-filled days. Ford's poll numbers shot up. For once, Congress praised his decisiveness: "It's nice to win one for a change," Kentucky representative Carroll Hubbard exclaimed.[40] The president's firm response probably helped secure release of the crew, but the bombing and invasion of Koh Tang obviously had no effect. The cost—carefully concealed from the American public—was high: a total of ninety casualties, including forty-one killed, three of them marines left behind and executed. The administration may have demonstrated its willingness to use force, but the glory was fleeting, and nothing changed in terms of its tattered global image and its shaky control over foreign policy.[41]

Congress asserted itself again later in the year with Angola, a most revealing case study of Cold War diplomacy in the era of detente and foreign policy in the Ford years. One of the last imperial powers to come to terms with decolonization, Portugal in 1975 finally conceded independence to its Angolan colony in southwest Africa. As with many other newly independent states, the heady reality of freedom left unresolved who would be in charge. Three major factions, divided along tribal as much as ideological lines, vied for power. As so often in the Cold War, a local conflict quickly escalated into a regional and then international crisis. Zaire and South Africa supported factions in the Angolan civil war, as did the Soviet Union and later Cuba, China, and the United States. Although Angola was rich in oil and minerals, neither the United States nor the USSR had major interests there. But a fear of Sino-American collaboration—which did not in fact exist—in support of the National Front for the Liberation of Angola (FNLA) faction spurred increased Soviet aid for the Popular Front for the Liberation of Angola (MPLA). Cuba seems to have intervened on its own initiative and in response to U.S. actions, although it undoubtedly consulted with the Soviet Union, eventually sending fifteen thousand troops. "The American stake was not *threatened* by the Soviet-Cuban involvement on the other side," author Raymond Garthoff has observed, "it was *created* by it."[42] Washington increasingly feared an MPLA victory. Ford and Kissinger believed that the United States in the aftermath of

39. Ibid., 150.
40. Mieczkoswki, *Ford*, 296.
41. Ralph Weterhahn, *The Last Battle: The Mayaguez Incident and the End of the Vietnam War* (New York, 2001), 253–66.
42. Garthoff, *Détente*, 521.

Vietnam must vigorously oppose Soviet adventurism and make clear its willingness to use force. The administration in July 1975 secretly and without consulting Congress approved $32 million for a CIA covert operation in collaboration with South Africa to bolster the FNLA and the National Union for the Total Independence of Angola (UNITA) and prevent an MPLA victory.

Congress had other ideas. When U.S. involvement came to light in the fall of 1975, Angola quickly became a volatile issue. The CIA had just been branded a "rogue elephant" by a congressional investigating committee headed by Idaho senator Frank Church for earlier covert operations and assassination plots. It was at this time in grave disrepute. United States cooperation with South Africa provoked loud protest. Congress saw yet another opportunity to challenge the administration's foreign policy. In an early example of what would be called the Vietnam Syndrome, liberals issued dire warnings that seemingly small-scale and innocent involvements in remote areas like Angola could produce Vietnam-like quagmires. Thus in December 1975, Congress by solid majorities passed legislation cutting off aid to Angola. Ford and Kissinger were outraged at this most blatant challenge to their authority, but Congress had the votes to override a veto, and they acquiesced. For the first time, Congress had stopped a covert operation.[43]

Angola had numerous important consequences. It provided another dramatic example of how weary the nation was of Cold War involvements and how eager Congress was to take on the executive. It revealed very different Soviet and American views of detente. The Kremlin saw itself acting as the United States had in Chile and the Middle East, continuing to expand its influence while pursuing detente. United States officials saw Soviet engagement in Angola and especially the use of what they viewed as Cuban proxy forces as exceeding the permissible bounds of detente. Kissinger's public highlighting of Soviet-Cuban involvement in Angola and a subsequent MPLA victory provided ammunition for those American conservatives who wanted a tougher line with Moscow. Angola was of no real importance to the United States. Additional U.S. aid would not have changed the outcome, and getting out caused no substantive damage to American interests. But from this point, Ford and Kissinger found themselves increasingly squeezed between liberals who wanted to curb the nation's involvement abroad and conservatives who sought to end detente, build up U.S. military power, and stand firmly against Soviet expansion.[44]

43. Greene, *Ford Presidency*, 115; Johnson, *Congress and the Cold War*, 221–23.
44. Garthoff, *Détente*, 519–36.

During the last year and a half of his short presidency, Ford lost ground at home and abroad. His commendable efforts to ease Cold War tensions became a political liability, a barrier to his efforts to secure election in his own right. A highly politicized summer 1975 flap over Russian writer Alexander Solzhenitsyn set the tone. The brilliant if irascible novelist's damning portrayal of Soviet crimes against their own people earned him a Nobel Prize for literature, a worldwide reputation as the regime's most eloquent dissident—and eventually expulsion. He was immediately adopted as a hero by hard-line anti-Communists in the United States. In June 1975, shortly before a scheduled meeting with Brezhnev at Helsinki, a group of right-wingers led by Senators Jesse Helms of North Carolina and Strom Thurmond of South Carolina in a blatantly political move declared Solzhenitsyn an honorary U.S. citizen and pressed Ford to receive him at the White House and attend a much publicized dinner in his honor. Heeding Kissinger, who warned of a threat to the upcoming summit, rather than his political advisers, Ford declined to meet with Solzhenitsyn on the grounds of a tight schedule, although he did extend an open invitation once he had returned from abroad. Having compelled Ford to put diplomatic expediency above principle, Helms and Thurmond dropped the issue, and Solzhenitsyn never sought a visit. The president's refusal to meet with the novelist did him no good at Helsinki and gave hard-liners at home another stick to flog him with.[45]

The Helsinki summit of July 30–August 1, 1975, is a classic example of a pivotal event whose short- and long-term consequences were strikingly different, even contradictory. Although it would eventually play a crucial role in ending the Cold War, its immediate effects were to further weaken detente and damage Ford at home. One of the largest such meetings ever, the conference included representatives from thirty-five nations and ratified the results of almost three years of intensive negotiations. Through the Conference on Security and Cooperation in Europe (CSCE), the Soviet Union sought recognition of its position in Eastern Europe. The Western Europeans hoped to advance the relative stability that had grown out of detente. With the United States, they also pushed for human rights and a freer flow of ideas, people, and information. Out of this mélange of often conflicting aspirations emerged by 1975 three sets of agreements, in diplomatic parlance, "baskets." A security basket included agreements to uphold basic human rights and "refrain from assaulting" the European boundaries established after World War II, a tacit concession to the Soviet position that stopped short of recognition. An economic basket provided for breaking

45. Greene, Ford Presidency, 151–52.

down inter-European barriers by tourism, expanded trade, and scientific and technical exchanges. A "Humanitarian and Other Fields" basket called for the freer flow of information, ideas, and people through travel, better access to media information, and reunification of families separated by the Cold War. A "Final Act" provided for monitoring observance of the agreements. The Soviet Union, Western Europeans, and United States were unhappy with some of the provisions but accepted the entire package to secure those items they considered most important.[46]

For Ford, Helsinki was a disaster. He had hoped to rejuvenate the SALT negotiations in private discussions with Brezhnev. In contrast to Vladivostok, however, their often angry exchanges produced nothing. Speaking to both Brezhnev and conservatives at home, he affirmed upon signing the CSCE agreements that the human rights provisions were for Americans "not clichés or empty phrases" but fundamental principles to which they were deeply devoted. Helsinki was warmly received in the Soviet Union and Western Europe but not in the United States. Before the meeting, conservatives had pleaded with Ford not to dignify it with his presence—even the *New York Times* had called the trip "misguided and empty."[47] Upon his return, Eastern European ethnic groups, still an important voting bloc, condemned him for a Yalta-like "betrayal of Eastern Europe." Reagan insisted that all Americans should be "against it"; Jackson denounced "yet another example of the sort of one-sided agreement that has become the hallmark of the Nixon-Ford administrations" and warned that the human rights provisions were unenforceable.[48] To Ford's dismay, members of his staff refused to defend Helsinki and sought to blame Kissinger. The effects of Helsinki were compounded later in the year when conservative critics twisted an informal, private explanation of U.S. Eastern European policy by Kissinger's deputy Helmut Sonnenfeldt into a so-called Sonnenfeldt Doctrine that, in Reagan's words, "put the seal of approval on the Red Army's World War II conquests."[49]

Instant appraisals of historical events are rarely on target. In this case, the attacks on Helsinki were also politically charged. In truth, the agreements so scorned in 1975 had the opposite effect of what was predicted. Instead of confirming Soviet control of Eastern Europe, they helped to undermine it and indeed eventually to bring about the fall of the USSR

46. Mieczkowski, *Ford*, 297–98.
47. Garthoff, *Détente*, 478.
48. Robert G. Kaufman, *Henry M. Jackson: A Life in Politics* (Seattle, 2000), 293.
49. Leo P. Ribuffo, "Is Poland a Soviet Satellite? Gerald Ford, the Sonnenfeldt Doctrine, and the Election of 1976," *Diplomatic History* 14 (Summer 1990), 394.

itself. West Germany negotiated at Helsinki a seemingly innocuous provision that would facilitate the reunification of Germany. The CSCE agreements encouraged rather than stifled dissident movements in Eastern Europe; they gave the governments of these countries some room to maneuver against the USSR and the means to chip away at Soviet control. Ironically, Reagan, one of the most bitter critics of Helsinki, as president would use it to press the Soviets to live up to the human rights principles contained in basket three. Although Ford could see the future no better than his critics, he later boasted that an agreement so viciously maligned was the "spark" that helped bring about the "demise of the Soviet Union."[50]

Facing a stiff electoral challenge the following year, Ford set out after Helsinki to regain control of U.S. foreign policy, restore popular confidence in his leadership, and head off a possible conservative challenge from Reagan. In October 1975, in what came to be known as the "Halloween Day Massacre," he asked Vice President Nelson Rockefeller, anathema to party conservatives, to take himself off the ticket for 1976. He fired the arrogant and cantankerous Schlesinger, who had publicly questioned detente and fed information to conservative critics such as Jackson. He replaced Schlesinger with White House chief of staff Rumsfeld. CIA director William Colby, who had spilled the agency's beans at the Church Committee hearings, gave way to Texan George H. W. Bush. Kissinger's star had fallen sharply since Ford took office. To balance the firing of Schlesinger, the president on November 2, 1975, appointed Gen. Brent Scowcroft national security adviser, leaving a disgruntled and no longer Super-K holding only the portfolio of secretary of state.[51]

These personnel changes brought no more than token political gains. Foreign policy issues were not in the forefront in 1976. The nation was spared foreign crises. The president clung doggedly to an internationalist foreign policy shed of detente, but he continued to be squeezed hard between left and right. Liberal Democrats were determined to destroy the imperial presidency and challenge old and new commitments abroad. But the mood of the country and Congress had shifted markedly to the right. Ford and Kissinger perceived only belatedly that conservative Democrats and especially Republicans represented the more serious immediate threat. Jackson's presidential campaign quickly imploded, but within the Republican Party Reagan mounted a formidable challenge and especially targeted Ford's foreign policy. He attacked detente, sneered that "Henry

50. Mieczkowski, *Ford*, 299.
51. Isaacson, *Kissinger*, 669–72.

Kissinger's recent stewardship of U.S. foreign policy has coincided with the loss of U.S. military supremacy," and warned that the administration had all but recognized Soviet domination of Eastern Europe. After a strenuous primary campaign, the president held off Reagan's challenge by a mere 117 delegate votes, squandering much money, energy, and political capital in the process.[52]

Foreign policy was not the decisive issue in the presidential campaign, nor even a major one. Americans had long since turned inward. A faltering economy that had not responded to Ford's initiatives loomed much larger in the minds of voters. The president could not shed the heavy baggage he still carried from the Nixon years. His opponent, the relatively unknown Democratic governor of Georgia, Jimmy Carter, cast himself as a Wilsonian moralist, sparing Ford further attacks from the right. But a colossal blunder in the debate with Carter on foreign policy did hurt Ford late in the campaign. Although he had prepared carefully for questions on detente, the president to the shock of his advisers—and listeners— answered a question regarding Helsinki by affirming that there was "no Soviet domination of Eastern Europe" and that the United States did not "concede that those countries are under the domination of the Soviet Union." What he meant, of course, was that the United States did not concede Soviet domination. But it came out wrong, and when given a chance to correct his blunder he compounded it by listing individual Eastern European countries that did not "consider themselves dominated by the Soviet Union." A media newly committed to "gotcha" journalism played up into a major issue a mistake that might otherwise have passed with little notice. Carter could not let pass a golden opportunity to attack Ford for the amorality of detente. The president stubbornly refused to issue a correction. Ford's statement, one of the great political blunders of recent years, cost him the debate and votes from Eastern European ethnic groups, although probably not the election—economic issues appear much more significant. It certainly raised doubts about his understanding and stewardship of U.S. foreign policy.[53] He lost to Carter in a very close contest.

III

By the time Carter took office, detente was moribund if not dead, and two competing views of U.S. foreign policy had emerged. The Committee on the Present Danger (CPD) pressed for military superiority and a tough

52. Greene, *Ford Presidency*, 164, 166, 168, 170–73.
53. Ribuffo, "Election of 1976," 398–403.

stance toward the USSR. Originally formed in 1950 to lobby for NSC-68, it was reborn in 1976 with Gerald Ford, ironically, as midwife. Responding to shrill conservative charges that the CIA had repeatedly underestimated Soviet capabilities and intentions, the president established a group called Team B to take another look. Composed of hard-liners such as Paul Nitze, Harvard historian Richard Pipes, and arms control official Paul Wolfowitz, Team B concluded in its report that the Soviet Union was seeking military superiority and indeed global hegemony and was exploiting detente to that end. As an outgrowth of Team B, the CPD sprang back into action. It was composed of retired military officers, conservative politicians, labor leaders, Jewish intellectuals, and an emerging group of so-called neo-conservatives, former liberals who had rebelled against the perceived cultural excesses of the 1960s. The CPD agitated for a massive defense buildup along the lines of NSC-68 that would give the United States absolute military superiority. Amply funded and very well connected, the group viewed Communism as an unmitigated evil, advocated its containment and ultimate destruction, and urged active steps to promote democracy abroad.[54]

The Trilateral Commission took a very different tack. Founded in 1973 by banker David Rockefeller, then chairman of the Council on Foreign Relations, the commission was an informal network of thoroughly establishmentarian business executives, academics, and government officials from the United States, Western Europe, and Japan. United States trilateralists believed that their country must adapt to recent changes in world politics and economics. The age of U.S. supremacy was over, they insisted, a new era of "complex interdependency" under way. The USSR was a sated superpower with enormous internal problems and an outdated ideology. Learning from America's failure in Vietnam and France's in Algeria, they insisted that military power had limited utility in a changing world. They believed that Nixon and Kissinger, in particular, had focused too narrowly on Soviet-American relations to the exclusion of other, more important matters. They set out to rebuild relations, neglected in the Nixon years, among the Western European nations, Japan, and the United States. To promote global stability and economic prosperity and check nuclear proliferation, the advanced nations must work together to promote human rights and to help Third World countries meet their economic needs, thus shifting the focus from East-West to North-South issues. The trilateralists also identified new "transnational" problems such as a looming

54. James Mann, *Rise of the Vulcans: The History of Bush's War Cabinet* (New York, 2004), 74; Richard A. Melanson, *American Foreign Policy Since the Vietnam War: The Search for Consensus from Nixon to Clinton* (Armonk, N.Y., 1996), 123.

scarcity of critical resources, the environment, and worldwide inflation. The subject of numerous conspiracy theories from the political left and right—the most exaggerated warned that the Trilateral Commission comprised a consortium of the industrial giants who sought to run the world—the group had its day briefly in the Carter years, when the president and many of his top foreign policy advisers were members.[55]

Where Ford had sought continuity in U.S. foreign policy, Carter was committed to change. A born-again Christian, surrounded by advisers scarred by Vietnam, he set out to restore morality to America's dealings with other nations and the United States to its customary position of world leadership. The first president elected in what some experts prematurely designated the post–Cold War era, he hoped also to shift the focus from East-West concerns to relations with the developing world. Carter attained some major successes. More than was appreciated at the time, he redirected U.S. foreign policy in important and enduring ways. By the end, however, his achievements were lost in an administration afflicted by mismanagement, burdened with unrelenting political opposition, and simply overwhelmed by events.

Carter's rise from obscurity to the presidency is a remarkable success story. A native of rural Georgia, he attended the U.S. Naval Academy, served in the navy, and became a protégé of the celebrated submariner Adm. Hyman Rickover. He returned to Georgia in 1953 to go into peanut farming and then politics. Elected governor in 1970, he served capably but gained little national attention: When he appeared on the popular television show *What's My Line?* the panelists could not guess what he did! The ambitious, upstart Georgian effectively exploited his status as a political outsider with a population weary of Beltway insiders and appealed to a broadly felt popular need for honesty in government. He took advantage of the Democrats' new and more open nominating process to win a series of primary victories over lackluster opponents such as Senators Jackson and Edward Kennedy. His southern origins, centrist politics, and lack of Washington connections helped him eke out a win over Ford. He brought to the White House no foreign policy experience. His views were formed in a crash course provided through Trilateral Commission meetings. A devoted Baptist and Sunday school teacher for much of his life, he still used in private the salty language learned in the navy. Intelligent, hardworking, and devoted to public service, a person of firm moral standards, he had a

55. Melanson, *Consensus*, 96–97; David J. Rothkopf, *Running the World: The Inside Story of the National Security Council and the Architects of American Power* (New York, 2004), 161–63.

tendency, as president, to micromanage and bog down in details. He lacked a sense of history and the ability to see how events and issues were connected. He did not have the charisma and persuasive powers to sell a nervous public on policies that were often sensible and realistic. At times, he manifested a shocking lack of political savvy.[56]

Carter's appointments to key foreign policy positions created additional problems. A West Virginian by birth, Secretary of State Cyrus Vance became a card-carrying member of the eastern foreign policy establishment. He served capably as secretary of the army and McNamara's top deputy under Johnson. A public servant of great integrity, he was deeply influenced by the Vietnam War. He was firmly committed to improving relations with the Soviet Union and Third World nations. Quiet in demeanor, discreet, he took a cautious and conciliatory approach toward the world and was alert to the complexity of international events. He was a consummate pragmatist and problem solver.[57] His White House counterpart, National Security Adviser Zbigniew Brzezinski, was in many ways his polar opposite. A Columbia University professor and prolific writer on international relations, Zbig, as he was known, brought to the position a résumé much like Kissinger's, although he lacked his predecessor's nimble mind, trademark wit, and ability to charm the media. Born in Poland, the son of a diplomat, he boasted, so the joke went, of being "the first Pole in 300 years in a position to really stick it to the Russians."[58] His butch haircut in an age of floppy hairstyles and sharp features gave physical evidence of the aggressive posture toward the Kremlin he would relentlessly push. Prickly and arrogant, he scorned Vance's "gentlemanly approach to the world." He advocated "architecture" in foreign policy, by which he meant clarity and certitude, as opposed to Kissinger's "acrobatics." He had served as executive director of the North American branch of the Trilateral Commission and helped to shape its views. He had a tendency to make grand geopolitical pronouncements, a "flair for making little fishes talk like big whales," according to former undersecretary of state George Ball.[59] A Vance-Brzezinski feud broke

---

56. Carter tells his own story in Jimmy Carter, *Keeping Faith: Memoirs of a President* (New York, 1982).

57. Gaddis Smith, *Morality, Reason and Power: American Diplomacy in the Carter Years* (New York, 1986), 41; Cyrus Vance, *Hard Choices: Critical Years in American Foreign Policy* (New York, 1983).

58. Walter LaFeber, *America, Russia, and the Cold War, 1945–1996* (8th ed., New York, 1997), 284.

59. James Bill, *The Eagle and the Lion: The Tragedy of American-Iranian Relations* (New Haven, Conn., 1988), 249; Zbigniew Brzezinski, *Power and Principle: Memoirs of the National Security Adviser, 1977–1981* (New York, 1985).

out early in the administration and worsened throughout, creating an institutionalized schizophrenia in policymaking, especially on Cold War issues,
an unfortunate situation with a foreign policy neophyte as president. With
the resurgence of Soviet-American tensions late in Carter's term, the
national security adviser gained the upper hand.

Carter's ambassador to the United Nations, Andrew Young, and First
Lady Rosalynn Carter deserve special mention. A youthful and prominent civil rights leader and follower of the late Martin Luther King Jr.,
Young was among the first African Americans to hold a top-level diplomatic position, an appointment of great symbolic importance for people
of color at home and abroad. Like many other African American leaders,
he linked the struggle for freedom in the United States with the fight
against colonialism abroad, especially in Africa, and he was one of the
first U.S. diplomats to disentangle southern African issues from the Cold
War. Often far out in front of Carter and the diplomatic establishment,
outspoken and at times quite undiplomatic in demeanor, Young sometimes got his boss in trouble with his candor. His unconventional behavior ultimately forced his resignation. While in office, however, he helped
to improve U.S. relations with the Third World and to engineer a major
shift in policies toward Africa.[60] The first lady also assumed an important
role in her husband's administration. Rosalynn Carter sometimes took
part in NSC briefings, sat in on top-level meetings, and advised the president on major issues. In the summer of 1977, she conducted an official
mission to Latin America, meeting with leaders of seven nations and discussing sensitive matters such as commercial issues, human rights, disarmament and nuclear proliferation, and the drug trade.[61]

Carter came to office promising basic changes in how things were done
and what was to be done. He went to great lengths to distinguish himself
from his discredited predecessors. He would play the dominant role in
shaping policy—there would be no Kissinger in his White House. Instead
of the obsessive secrecy, ultra-Byzantine processes, and undemocratic
methods of the Nixon-Kissinger era, he promised open diplomacy, adherence to American democratic principles, and cooperation with Congress.
He sought to formulate policies consistent with the values he believed

60. Thomas Borstelmann, *The Cold War and the Color Line: American Race Relations
in a Global Arena* (Cambridge, Mass., 2001), 250–52. On Young, see also Andrew J.
DeRoche, *Andrew Young: Civil Rights Ambassador* (Wilmington, Del., 2003).

61. Burton I. Kaufman and Scott Kaufman, *The Presidency of James Earl Carter* (2nd ed.,
Lawrence, Kans., 2006), 135–36; Kathy B. Smith, "The First Lady Represents America:
Rosalynn Carter in South America," *Presidential Studies Quarterly* 27 (Summer 1997),
514–39.

Americans held dear. He firmly believed that a more moral and democratic foreign policy would win strong popular support.[62] He vowed to work closely with the European allies and Japan. He recognized that the Cold War would continue to command U.S. attention, but he planned to give equal weight to other issues and to view the world through other than a Cold War prism. He hoped to redress what he considered the legitimate grievances of Third World nations, especially in Latin America and Africa. He placed enormous emphasis on promoting human rights and on curbing the lethal arms trade that threatened the peace and inflicted misery on the innocent. In short, Carter set out to change the policies that had been created in the late 1940s and modified only slightly thereafter.

By seeking to do too much too fast—and doing it in a notably amateurish manner—the administration got off to a singularly bad start. One of the president's first moves was to announce the beginning of troop withdrawals from South Korea. It is not clear exactly how he came to that decision. It reflected a widespread post-Vietnam aversion to military involvement abroad and Carter's personal desire to liquidate seemingly outdated Cold War commitments. He believed that the troops were more needed in Western Europe and that if necessary the United States could defend South Korea with air and naval power. The Park Chung Hee government exemplified the sort of repressive ally Carter found repugnant. South Korea's recent bribery of U.S. congressmen in a scandal known as "Koreagate" created the right climate for a drastic policy change. Carter's stubborn commitment to the policy after doubts were raised seems to have been based on his determination to carry out a campaign pledge.[63]

Thus, shortly after taking office—and without full consultation with allies—he announced the first withdrawal, setting off a firestorm in East Asia. South Korea naturally protested that the removal of U.S. troops would invite another North Korean invasion. Japan feared instability in Northeast Asia, fretted about its sizeable investments in South Korea, and questioned the reliability of U.S. security commitments. Many members of Congress opposed the decision and in light of Koreagate refused to appropriate funds for the military aid Carter hoped would palliate South Korea for the removal of troops. Within the bureaucracy, there was all-out rebellion. Carter would not reverse his decision, but in the face of rampant opposition at home and abroad Brzezinski developed a plan to delay the first withdrawal and reduce its size, making subsequent withdrawals unlikely. This early misstep had importance consequences, weakening Park's stature,

62. Melanson, Consensus, 91, 107.
63. Kaufman and Kaufman, Carter Presidency, 56–57.

leading eventually to his assassination, and making it impossible to reconsider withdrawing U.S. troops from South Korea for years to come.[64]

Carter also acted impulsively in the Middle East. Certain that bold measures were needed to move the interminable negotiations off dead center and minimizing the depth of the antagonisms among the various parties, he proposed a comprehensive Arab-Israeli settlement rather than continuing Kissinger's step-by-step approach. Reducing an enormously complex dispute to the simple formula of peace for land, he proposed that Israel's right to exist be guaranteed in return for its withdrawal from the occupied territories. Ignoring Vance's advice to move slowly and living up to his personal pledge for open diplomacy, he also came out publicly in May 1977 for a Palestinian homeland. His forthright if foolish approach to the most intractable of diplomatic problems won guarded support from some Arab leaders. Predictably, however, it provoked outrage in the American Jewish community and more importantly in Israel, where it helped produce an electoral victory by hard-liners led by former terrorist Menachem Begin and a subsequent toughening of Israeli policy on the West Bank. Carter's rash foray set back the peace process he had hoped to advance.[65]

Nowhere was Carter's early impulsiveness and ineptitude more on display than in relations with the Soviet Union. His approach was riddled with contradictions. He deliberately set out to downplay the centrality of Soviet-American relations while at the same time pursuing major negotiations with Moscow. He was undoubtedly sincere in his desire to decrease tensions. What he did not grasp was that other initiatives he was taking would inevitably increase them.[66] His Soviet policies were also complicated by sharp disagreements between Vance the pragmatist and Brzezinski the hard-liner.

Arms control was the first casualty. While vowing to look beyond the Cold War, Carter pushed ahead with a typically bold—and as it turned out wildly impractical—proposal to move beyond SALT and achieve reductions of rather than limits on nuclear weapons. However praiseworthy his commitment to openness, the real world of diplomacy requires at least a modicum of secrecy or at least discretion, and he infuriated Soviet leaders at the start by announcing his proposal publicly before explaining it to them privately. He proposed deep cuts in land-based missiles, where the

64. Don Oberdorfer, *The Two Koreas: A Contemporary History* (New York, 1997), 84–94.
65. Douglas Little, *American Orientalism: The United States and the Middle East Since 1945* (Chapel Hill, N.C., 2004), 288–89.
66. Garthoff, *Détente*, 564.

USSR had a clear-cut advantage, creating the impression that he was not serious.[67] This reckless plunge into an old Cold War thicket delayed serious negotiations on arms control and complicated dealings on other matters.

Carter also learned the hard way what should have been obvious: that his campaign for human rights could be a huge impediment to negotiations on arms control and other issues. The president somehow assumed that he could compartmentalize such matters. The Soviet leadership, not surprisingly, viewed protests about human rights violations as blatant interference in their internal affairs. Carter's timing could hardly have been worse. The administration first criticized the Soviet and Eastern European governments and praised dissidents at the very time it set forth its arms control proposals. It escalated support for dissidents and began issuing "report cards" on observance of Helsinki human rights provisions precisely when a nervous Kremlin was cracking down on dissent at home and within the satellites. Soviet leaders responded with more arrests and imprisonment of leading dissidents. They even expelled an American newsman covering dissent and charged Jewish dissenters with working for the CIA. The spat further strained relations already tense from the breakdown of detente in the Ford administration. Along with the deadlock over SALT, it delayed for several years a summit that might have headed off emerging problems. It set the tone for a steady deterioration of U.S.-Soviet relations over the next four years. Brzezinski later conceded that the administration in its early days tried to do "too much all at once."[68]

IV

Although Carter never quite mastered the intricacies of diplomacy, his administration did achieve some major successes in different parts of the world, moving boldly in new directions and taking important initiatives. The problem was that some of his achievements were not the sorts of things that brought visible and tangible benefits to the United States. Sometimes, in fact, he paid a high political price at home for doing the right thing abroad.

The Panama Canal treaties are a case in point. Negotiations to replace the one-sided Hay–Bunau-Varilla Treaty of 1903 had been going on sporadically since the 1964 riots, and the canal had become an issue in the 1976 campaign. Carter, ironically, had vowed that he would never surrender U.S. control, but once in office, he changed his mind. Experts

67. Ibid., 566.
68. John Lewis Gaddis, *Russia, the Soviet Union, and the United States: An Interpretive History* (2nd ed., New York, 1990), 300.

persuaded him that the canal, while still useful, was no longer vital to U.S. trade and security. Diplomats warned that without a settlement unrest in Panama could threaten U.S. control of the canal. Vance had witnessed firsthand the 1964 riots and was deeply committed to negotiations. Carter increasingly saw a treaty as an essential element of his new and more conciliatory approach to Latin America and the Third World in general, an "auspicious beginning for a new era," in his words.[69]

The United States secured an acceptable treaty in part because Panamanian dictator Gen. Omar Torrijos needed one as much as it did. His nation's economy was in shambles; unemployment had soared. Under fire from left-wing protestors on one side and the National Guard on the other, Torrijos desperately needed the treaty revenues to solidify his shaky position. In August 1977, Washington thus concluded a treaty favorable enough to present to a skeptical American public. Panama would take over territorial jurisdiction of the canal once the treaty was ratified and legal jurisdiction over a period of three years, but the United States would continue to operate the canal and be responsible for defending it until December 31, 1999. The ten thousand anxious "Zonians" could retain their jobs until they retired or died. Panama's major concession—crucial to the success of the treaty as far as North Americans were concerned—was that even after January 1, 2000, the United States could defend the canal's neutrality. Washington paid $40 million to sweeten the deal and threw in an attractive aid and trade package. Although it made significant concessions, the United States plainly gained from the treaty.[70]

In diplomacy as in war, Americans are disposed to accept nothing less than total victory, and the treaty proved a very hard sell. Public opinion polls showed powerful opposition; foes of the treaty were much more outspoken than its defenders. "The only people who give a damn are the ones who oppose it," a White House aide conceded.[71] The very idea of giving up the canal was anathema to most conservatives. "We bought it, we paid for it, it's ours and we're going to keep it," Reagan often roared, an applause line that blithely ignored late twentieth-century realities but touched deeply felt emotions. The U.S. military saw the treaties as yet another sign of the nation's weakness, offering further encouragement, in *New York Times* columnist Hanson Baldwin's words, to "penny-dictators

69. Mark T. Gilderhus, *The Second Century: U.S.-Latin American Relations Since 1989* (Wilmington, Del., 2000), 204.
70. Walter LaFeber, *The Panama Canal: The Crisis in Historical Perspective* (New York, 1979), 204–6.
71. Johnson, *Congress and the Cold War*, 236.

and minor aggressions everywhere."[72] Conservatives mounted a furious lobbying campaign against the treaty. On the other hand, major business organizations backed it as a way of promoting trade in Latin America. Religious groups supported it in order to shed "colonial positions of the nineteenth century."[73] A fierce debate raged across the country from August 1977 to April 1978 and in the Senate through the first months of 1978. The key to the administration's eventual narrow victory was the passage of two amendments carefully crafted and shepherded through the upper house by Democrat Robert Byrd of West Virginia and Republican Howard Baker of Tennessee. The first gave the United States explicit rights after the year 2000 to intervene militarily to keep the canal open and for U.S. ships to move to the head of the line in times of crisis. Originally a memorandum of understanding, this amendment was formally incorporated into the treaty after quite extraordinary negotiations between Senator Baker and Torrijos. Pro-treaty forces turned back seventy-seven amendments designed to cripple the document and ratified it by one vote more than the necessary two-thirds.[74]

Carter deserves much credit for the canal treaties. To be sure, the administration bungled its efforts to promote Senate approval. A massive public relations campaign had little impact; a major presidential speech promoting the treaties was labeled by one newspaper a "dud." Efforts to sway senators were typically disorganized and ineffectual. The administration also erred by acquiescing in an amendment giving the United States the right to take any action to keep the canal open.[75] This said, where his predecessors had equivocated, Carter fully committed the prestige of his office to negotiating and ratifying treaties giving up control over one of his nation's signal accomplishments. He showed great courage in going to Panama City for a signing ceremony in June 1978. Despite the political price he would pay, giving up the canal was the right thing to do, and Carter had the common sense and decency to see this. The treaties "symbolize our determination to deal with the developing nations of the world . . . on the basis of mutual respect and partnership," he proudly proclaimed.[76]

72. LaFeber, Panama Canal, 210.
73. Ibid., 214–16.
74. Ibid., 228–50.
75. Larry Grubbs, " 'Hands on Presidency' or 'Passionless Presidency?' Jimmy Carter and Ratification of the Panama Canal Treaties," SHAFR Newsletter 30 (December 1999), 1–17.
76. Kyle Longley, In the Eagle's Shadow: The United States and Latin America (Wheeling, Ill., 2002), 276.

Carter also completed the process of normalizing relations with China. Ironically, this long-overdue abandonment of an outdated Cold War position was driven in part by new Cold War considerations and itself significantly inflamed Soviet-American tensions in the late 1970s. Vance had hoped to pursue a balanced approach toward the two Communist powers, but Brzezinski relentlessly promoted closer ties with Beijing as a means to threaten Moscow. He skillfully maneuvered to wrest control of China policy from his archrival. As Soviet-American relations steadily deteriorated, he won over the president. The timing was right. A new Chinese leadership headed by Vice Premier Deng Xiaoping needed normalization with the United States to pursue its own domestic and foreign policy agenda. On a visit to Beijing in the spring of 1978, Brzezinski signaled U.S. interest in teaming up against a "common Soviet threat" and offered as bait indirect arms sales through Western Europe. He also expressed U.S. willingness to sever official relations with Taiwan, a crucial concession long demanded by Beijing. Without making formal pledges, China in oblique diplomatic language indicated it would not seek to absorb Taiwan by force, clearing away another major obstacle. Deng's visit to the United States in early 1979 was a major event. Carter hosted the most elegant gathering given for any foreign dignitary during his entire presidency. The diminutive Chinese leader appeared in a Washington arena with the Harlem Globetrotters basketball team, put on six-shooters and a huge ten-gallon hat at a Houston rodeo, and even visited Disneyland, a privilege denied Nikita Khrushchev. On March 1, 1979, almost thirty years after the Communists took power, diplomatic relations were officially restored.[77]

A diplomatic revolution of such magnitude was bound to have major repercussions. The U.S. ambassador awakened Chiang Kai-shek's son and successor Chiang Ching-kuo at 2:30 A.M. to give him several hours' notice before official announcements were made halfway across the world. Anti-American riots broke out in Taiwan. When Undersecretary of State Warren Christopher traveled to Taipei on a mission of mollification, his car was attacked by angry mobs throwing stones and sticking bamboo poles through the broken windows.[78] By contrast, normalization enjoyed broad support in the United States. In economic hard times, Americans again dreamed of tapping China's vast market. Some conservatives were seduced by the

77. Michael Schaller, *The United States and China in the Twentieth Century* (2nd ed., New York, 1990), 203–9; James Mann, *About Face: A History of America's Curious Relationship with China from Nixon to Clinton* (New York, 1999), 78–84, 97–98.
78. Mann, *About Face*, 94–95.

prospect of China joining an anti-Soviet coalition. But the remnants of the China lobby, joined by Sen. Barry Goldwater and Reagan, charged sellout of a loyal ally, denounced Carter's appeasement of an old foe, and warned that the sordid deal with China called "into question the honor—the very soul—of America's word in the field of foreign relations."[79] Congressional friends of Taiwan failed in a constitutional challenge to the president's authority to abrogate a treaty without the consent of the Senate, the Supreme Court once again upholding presidential prerogative. They did secure passage of a law guaranteeing future U.S. sales of defensive weapons to Taiwan and vaguely pledging U.S. support for its defense, embarrassing the Carter administration and infuriating the Chinese.

With Brzezinski in the driver's seat, the Carter administration in 1979 moved full throttle toward closer ties with China built around mutual opposition to the Soviet Union. The NSC ignored Vance's continued calls for balance and shut the State Department out of China policy. The administration stopped short of the alliance Deng apparently preferred but collaborated closely to thwart Moscow's perceived hegemonic aspirations. The USSR had become Vietnam's closest ally and chief benefactor after the fall of Saigon, arousing fears in Beijing. Even before normalization was consummated, Carter appears to have given Deng the green light to invade Vietnam—an ironic twist in that a decade earlier the United States had gone to war there to stop Chinese expansion in Southeast Asia. China became a major outpost for snooping on the Soviet Union. The United States removed export controls and sold China modern technology and eventually weapons. In a move of enormous symbolic importance, the administration in the summer of 1979 ignored the Jackson-Vanik amendment, winked at China's human rights violations, and offered most-favored-nation status and Export-Import Bank credits. Normalization was an obvious move, but in taking it the administration lost a necessary sense of balance and was enticed into a connection that compromised its ideals and damaged broader global interests. Mutual antipathy toward the Soviet Union proved a flimsy basis for a lasting Sino-American relationship.[80]

Carter also achieved a breakthrough of sorts in the Middle East, a treaty between Egypt and Israel negotiated under his direction, remarkable more for the fact that it happened than for its contents. Following his initial, disastrous descent into the quagmire of Middle Eastern diplomacy, a chastened president pulled back. A new opportunity seemed to present itself in September 1977 when Egypt's Anwar Sadat stunned the

79. Smith, *Morality, Reason, and Power*, 90–91.
80. Mann, *About Face*, 100–114.

world by journeying to Jerusalem for talks with Begin and a speech to the Knesset. But in the months that followed, the two sides seemed more at odds than ever. Sadat and Begin stopped speaking to each other. Fearing that any hope of negotiations might be lost, Carter staked his presidency on a bold diplomatic gambit, inviting Sadat and Begin to join him for a summit at Camp David. He also violated the first rule of summitry by bringing heads of state to a meeting to negotiate rather than to ratify agreements already worked out by others. He even drafted in his own hand the outlines of a possible settlement.[81]

Over thirteen days (September 5–17, 1978) of arduous and intense negotiations conducted under Carter's watchful eye, an agreement was finally reached. The participants worked in an environment "as self-contained as an ocean liner and as assertively American as Carter could make it," historian David Schoenbaum has written.[82] The president engaged the two antagonists in direct discussions until it became clear that their mutual antipathy rendered such an approach untenable. He and Vance then adopted the extraordinary technique of negotiating with their technical experts, who in turn dealt with their bosses. Real progress remained elusive. Sadat and Begin did agree that Israel would pull out of the Sinai in return for a peace treaty with Egypt. But the two sides quickly deadlocked over the explosive West Bank issue, Sadat insisting upon a homeland for Palestinians, Begin refusing to dismantle West Bank settlements or agree to a Palestinian state. With the talks near collapse, Carter pulled out a last-minute agreement. Sadat and Begin finessed the knotty West Bank problem by agreeing to work "for the resolution of the Palestinian problem in all its respects" over a five-year transitional period. Carter believed he had secured from Begin a promise not to build new settlements in the disputed area. The signatories also vaguely agreed, without specific reference to a Palestinian homeland, to "recognize the legitimate rights of the Palestinian people" and that "elected representatives of the inhabitants of the West Bank and Gaza should decide how they shall govern themselves."[83]

Camp David marked a significant milepost in an ancient conflict whose modern roots stretched back three decades. Egypt was the first Arab nation to recognize Israel's right to exist; Israel made important if vague and sharply qualified concessions. Carter viewed it as the most important

81. William B. Quandt, *Peace Process: American Diplomacy and the Arab-Israeli Conflict Since 1967* (rev. ed., Berkeley, Calif., 2001), 198–99.
82. David Schoenbaum, *The United States and the State of Israel* (New York, 1993), 260.
83. Ibid., 260–67; Little, *American Orientalism*, 289–93.

achievement of his presidency; the world hailed a major step forward. Begin and Sadat won the Nobel Peace Prize. Such settlements are rarely definitive, however. They are no more than individual steps in an ongoing process, as the Camp David Accords, to Carter's great disappointment, subsequently attested. It took another six months and a last-ditch Carter trip to Cairo and Tel Aviv simply to secure approval of what had previously been worked out. Begin reneged on his settlements "promise." As soon as the Israel-Egypt peace agreement was signed in March 1979, Israel resumed building settlements and refused even to talk about a Palestinian homeland until the Palestinians had conceded its sovereignty over the West Bank. Carter's public protest brought down on him the wrath of the Israel lobby. Sadat was bitterly disappointed with the outcome and isolated at home and among his Arab compatriots. The hopes of Camp David were thus crushed months before its author left office. The agreement starkly displayed the limits of the most dedicated and intense diplomacy. "This remarkable adventure in summit diplomacy achieved more than most its detractors have been willing to acknowledge," participant William Quandt has concluded, "and less than its most ardent proponents have claimed."[84]

Carter also pointed U.S. policy toward southern Africa in new directions. A product of the rural South, he had lived and worked with people of color since childhood. As an aspiring politician in an age of racial conflict, he had initially accommodated to segregation, but he grew with the times. His religion, basic morality, and sense of fairness brought forth a firm commitment to racial equality. As governor of Georgia, he actively promoted integration. The votes of African Americans helped him win the South—and thus the presidency—and he felt an obligation in domestic and foreign policy to push issues they considered important. Carter thus brought to the White House a firm commitment to improving U.S. relations with the non-white world. Like JFK, he took an especially keen interest in Africa. His 1978 trip to oil-rich Nigeria was the first visit to that continent by a sitting president. A newly potent African American political constituency, with whom Young had especially close ties, linked freedom at home and abroad, provided the president crucial support, and, on occasion, held his feet to the fire.[85]

In marked contrast to its predecessors, the Carter administration from the outset stood forth against apartheid and for black majority rule in

84. Quandt, *Peace Process*, 204.
85. Smith, *Morality, Reason, and Power*, 133–34; Borstelmann, *Cold War and the Color Line*, 243–48.

southern Africa. It stopped short of economic sanctions against the government of South Africa, recognizing the importance of U.S. investments there and rationalizing that American businesses in South Africa might help eliminate apartheid. Carter and his advisers also feared that a hard line could provoke more repression. At the same time, upon taking office the president publicly denounced white minority rule. In May 1977, Vice President Walter Mondale sternly scolded South Africa's prime minister, John Vorster, and warned that continued brutal enforcement of apartheid would seriously damage relations with the United States. When Pretoria tightened repression, the House of Representatives, with administration backing, passed a resolution sharply critical of apartheid. Young voted for a UN Security Council resolution calling for a mandatory arms embargo on a "racist regime" that threatened the peace, the first time sanctions had been imposed on a member nation.[86]

The administration took an even stronger and ultimately more decisive stand on Southern Rhodesia. In 1965, the white minority had defiantly declared independence from Britain to maintain its dominance over four million blacks. No nation recognized the rebellious Ian Smith regime. In marked contrast to policies toward South Africa, the United States joined Britain in imposing sanctions. On the other hand, die-hard southern segregationists like Democrats Helms and Virginia senator Harry Byrd Jr. sympathized with Smith and even compared Southern Rhodesia to their beloved Confederacy. In 1971, they joined conservatives like Goldwater in passing the Byrd Amendment that undercut sanctions by permitting imports of strategic materials such as chrome. Shortly after taking office, Carter boldly asked for and gained repeal of the Byrd Amendment as a "kind of referendum on American racism," in Young's words. The administration was not fooled by Smith's clever ploy to preserve white rule by adding moderate blacks to his government. Insisting that the elections had not been free and fair, it stood forth against Senate conservatives by refusing to lift the sanctions even after a Methodist bishop became the first black prime minister. It dismissed conservative arguments that Robert Mugabe's Popular Front was dominated by Communists. Carter held firm until September 1979, when new elections brought to power a government of Zimbabwe headed by Mugabe.[87] Southern Africa was the last bastion of white rule over people

86. Smith, *Morality, Reason, and Power*, 143–45; Borstelmann, *Cold War and the Color Line*, 254–55.
87. Andrew J. DeRoche, "Standing Firm for Principles: Jimmy Carter and Zimbabwe," *Diplomatic History* 23 (Fall 1999), 657–85.

of color. By standing firmly for principle in Southern Rhodesia, Carter led a successful assault against it.[88]

In Zaire and Angola, more conventional Cold War imperatives held sway. Invasions in March 1977 and May 1978 of Zaire's mineral-rich Katanga province, newly renamed Shaba, by Katangan rebels based in Angola assumed the form of classic Cold War crises where essentially local conflicts took on international implications and realpolitik prevailed over principle. In each case, the Carter administration backed the venal and brutally oppressive Zairean regime of Joseph Mobutu against insurgents allegedly controlled by the leftist government of Angola, the Soviet Union, and, most disturbing to Americans, Cuba. The incursions are still shrouded in uncertainty. The instigators were definitely anti-Mobutu Katangans who had sided with the victorious MPLA in Angola. They claimed to have leftist political views, but their interests were mainly local. The MPLA likely knew what they were doing and assisted them, but the Soviet role appears to have been quite limited. Careful study based on Cuban documents concludes that Castro did not instigate the invasions but rather sought to stop them for fear of provoking a Western response that might bolster the visibly shaky Mobutu regime or even topple the infant Angolan government.[89]

Alleged Cuban involvement eventually provoked a vocal U.S. response. Although Mobutu played the usually reliable red card, the Carter administration's reaction to the first invasion was notably cautious. The president had no use for the repulsive Mobutu. In the aftermath of Vietnam, no thought was given to direct U.S. intervention. The Cuban role was not clear. On the other hand, the United States had important economic interests in Zaire, and the administration was loath to do nothing. It thus provided Mobutu $2 million in non-lethal military supplies and encouraged French and Belgian support. By the second invasion, much had changed. Carter was under fire at home for his alleged weakness in foreign policy, the Cold War was heating up, and the hard-nosed Brzezinski had gained control. The Cuban role was still murky, but top U.S. officials cherry-picked from inconclusive intelligence those items emphasizing Cuban involvement. Carter used Cuba as a whipping boy to prove his toughness. Americans were eager to believe the worst of their insolent southern neighbor. The administration thus publicly and noisily blamed

88. Thomas Borstelmann, "The United States and the Final Years of White Rule in Zimbabwe," *Diplomatic History* 27 (January 2003), 155.
89. Piero Gleijeses, "Truth or Credibility: Castro, Carter, and the Invasion of Shaba," *International History Review* 18 (February 1996), 70–103.

Cuba for the second Shaba invasion and provided limited aid to Mobutu. "This may be a defensible enterprise," the *New York Times* opined, much too charitably as it turned out, but it "is not a noble or holy one."[90]

The Carter administration is remembered for its focus on human rights, and historians disagree sharply in assessing its record. Carter's defenders cite his emphasis on human rights as a major achievement of his presidency. Liberal detractors insist that he applied the policy inconsistently and often let expediency and geopolitics triumph over principle. Realists claim that a naive, do-gooder president permitted human rights concerns to interfere with more urgent national security considerations.[91]

Carter's human rights policy built on the work of others. A growing interest in the issue emerged out of 1960s activism. It spread across the world in the 1970s through private networks that reflected a phenomenon—what would be called globalization—that would dominate international life in the late twentieth century. Non-governmental organizations (NGO) such as Amnesty International and Human Rights Watch first began to define and call attention to the inviolable rights of individuals against state-sponsored repression. They employed the new technologies of the information age to collect, disseminate, and publicize information on abuses across the world. They pioneered direct mail fund-raising to expand their membership and operations and enlisted the support of benefactors such as the Ford and Rockefeller foundations. In an age of celebrities, they used prominent figures to get across their message. Congress passed legislation in the mid-1970s declaring it a "principal goal" of U.S. foreign policy "to promote the increased observance of internationally recognized human rights by all countries." It began to link the dispensing of foreign aid to the human rights records of recipient nations. "Human rights is suddenly chic," an activist proclaimed in 1977.[92]

Carter set out to put human rights at the top of the government's agenda. His interest in the issue sprang naturally from his Christian faith and his missionary impulse to do good in the world. It also seemed good politics given the post-Vietnam reaction against imperialism and realpolitik and the growing attention given human rights by liberals and conservatives. America's real strength, he insisted, resided more in what it stood

90. Ibid., 103.

91. For Carter's human rights policies, see Joshua Murachik, *The Uncertain Crusade: Jimmy Carter and the Dilemmas of Human Rights* (New York, 1986) and Sandy Vogelgesang, *American Dream, Global Nightmare: The Dilemma of Human Rights Policy* (New York, 1980).

92. Kenneth Cmiel, "The Emergence of Human Rights Politics in the United States," *Journal of American History* 86 (December 1999), 1248.

for than its vast military power. He firmly believed that the nation must pursue policies consistent with its traditional principles. He later recalled his hope that human rights "might be the wave of the future of the world" and his determination that the United States "be on the crest of the movement."[93] The Cold War, in his view, had forced compromises that undermined these principles, including the support of repressive dictatorships and anti-Communist interventionism. The nation's "commitment to human rights must be absolute," he affirmed in his inaugural address.[94]

It was, of course, much more difficult to implement human rights policies than to talk about them. The president and his advisers were not naive in their approach to the issue, as has often been charged. They recognized the difficulties of application in specific cases. They were painfully aware of the limits of U.S. power and understood that intrusion into the domestic affairs of other states could make things worse for victims of repression. They saw the need to balance human rights concerns with national security imperatives. Inevitably, there were inconsistencies and contradictions. The United States continued to make much of Soviet repression of Jews while turning a blind eye to China's human rights violations. It remained silent about the repression by important allies such as the Philippines, South Korea, and most notoriously Iran. Ignoring protests from human rights advocates and legislators, the administration did nothing to stop the murderous Pol Pot regime from committing genocide in Cambodia. Indeed, as part of its larger strategy of containing Soviet influence in Southeast Asia, it provided covert support to the Khmer Rouge after they were driven from power by the Soviet-backed government of Vietnam.[95]

The Carter administration focused on Latin America and especially its three largest countries, Chile, Brazil, and Argentina—with very limited results. The hemisphere appeared no longer threatened by Communism, and Carter hoped to shift there from a Cold War orientation to the North-South approach he preferred. All three countries were ruled by authoritarian governments notorious for their assault on human rights. Breaking sharply from Kissinger's tacit support, the Carter administration criticized Augusto Pinochet's gross human rights violations and cut back military aid. Pinochet responded by refusing to extradite three Chileans charged with murdering a political opponent in Washington. In Brazil, President Ernesto Geisel terminated the U.S. military aid program before it could

93. Carter, *Keeping Faith*, 144.
94. Carter inaugural address, January 20, 1977, www.bartleby.com/124/pres60.html.
95. Kenton Clymer, "Jimmy Carter, Human Rights, and Cambodia," *Diplomatic History* 27 (April 2003), 245–78.

be used as an instrument of pressure. Only in Argentina did the new approach achieve even limited gains. Human rights violations were especially egregious there, and Carter shortly after taking office cut U.S. foreign assistance by almost one-half. Responding to liberals in Congress, the administration also reduced military aid, blocked loans from an inter-American fund, and imposed trade restrictions. General Jorge Videla promised to restore civilian government, a commitment he did not keep. He did free some political prisoners.[96] In terms of changing conditions in individual countries, the Carter human rights campaign, much as in Latin America, had very limited impact. To its credit, the administration put human rights issues high on its agenda and institutionalized them by creating units in the bureaucracy to monitor abuses and recommend action. In 1978, it drafted a comprehensive statement of policy. Carter's emphasis on human rights contributed to improving the global image of the United States. It gave the issue international credibility, helping to set the agenda for world politics for the next decade.[97]

V

The beginning of the end for the Carter administration came in the fall of 1978 when revolution erupted in Iran. This first U.S. clash with Islamic radicalism—an unmitigated disaster for the nation and especially its president—was totally unexpected.[98] When Carter took office, Iran appeared one of America's closest and most reliable allies. Put in power by a U.S.-British sponsored coup in 1953, Reza Shah Pahlavi had used his nation's oil revenues to build up a modern military machine and initiate a top-down "White Revolution" that seemed to bring Western-style modernization to one corner of the turbulent Middle East. The shah maintained close ties with his U.S. patron and used Iran's strategic location and precious oil reserves to extort massive aid. Nixon had made Iran a pillar of American security interests in the Persian Gulf, fueling the shah's ambitions and filling his arsenal. Iran served as a key U.S. listening post to monitor Soviet nuclear tests and missile launches. Forty-five thousand Americans worked there. Carter had aroused concern in Tehran with his talk of promoting human rights and curbing arms sales, but, as in other geopolitically important areas, practicality trumped principle. Shortly

96. Gilderhus, *Second Century*, 206–8.
97. David F. Schmitz and Vanessa Walker, "Jimmy Carter and the Foreign Policy of Human Rights: The Development of a Post Cold War Foreign Policy," *Diplomatic History* 28 (January 2004), 119.
98. David Farber, *Taken Hostage: The Iran Hostage Crisis and America's First Encounter with Radical Islam* (Princeton, N.J., 2005), 4–5.

after taking office, he approved the sale of seven high-tech AWAC intelligence aircraft and 160 F-16 fighters. The shah visited Washington in late 1977 and greatly impressed the president, although on one ceremonial occasion they had to fight off tear gas wafting across the street from Lafayette Park, where police combated anti-shah demonstrators, most of them Iranian students. On New Year's Eve 1977, at the shah's sumptuous palace, Carter offered an effusive toast whose words would come back to haunt him: Iran, "under the great leadership of the Shah, is an island of stability in one of the more troubled areas of the world."[99]

Even as Carter spoke, rumblings could be heard of the revolution that within little more than a year would sweep the shah from power. The White Revolution enriched the few at the expense of the many. A lagging economy caused widespread distress among Iranians. Popular anger was fueled by opulent displays at the shah's court, rampant corruption among his inner circle, and the brutality of his secret police. Westernization threatened Islam and angered the clergy. A profound religious revival brought forth emotional protest; many Iranians in the face of rampant societal change turned to Islam for order and spirituality. Rioting broke out in 1977 in several cities and gradually spread across the country. The shah's attempts to silence dissent with brute force brought thousands of deaths and further outrage. His efforts to contain unrest by shuffling top officials, in the words of one of his diplomats, was like using first aid "where immediate surgery was required."[100] Because the United States had put the shah in power, helped keep him there, and encouraged his modernization policies, it became a handy target for revolutionaries. America was the "Great Satan" in the eyes of Islamic militants; the shah was "the American king."[101] Ill with cancer, the shah fled to Egypt exactly one year after Carter's toast, leaving behind a caretaker government. By this time, Iran verged on anarchy. Students ran the universities, workers the factories, and armed mobs exacted retribution. A series of moderate governments presided uneasily over the political maelstrom. Behind them loomed the scowling visage of the charismatic and bitterly anti-American Ayatollah Ruhollah Khomeini, then in exile, the nation's most revered religious leader and increasingly its most powerful political figure.

"President Carter inherited an impossible situation," historian Gaddis Smith has written, "and he and his advisers made the worst of it."[102]

99. Bill, *Eagle and Lion*, 233.
100. Ibid., 240.
101. Kenneth M. Pollack, *The Persian Puzzle: The Conflict Between Iran and America* (New York, 2004), 125.
102. Smith, *Morality, Reason, and Power*, 188.

Americans initially assumed that the shah, as before, could control the uprising. They disagreed whether he should use force or conciliation, Brzezinski not surprisingly favoring the former, Vance the latter, a debate that quickly became irrelevant. Even after the shah left the country, some top officials expected him to return; others counted on the military to take power. When neither happened, the administration sought to maintain contact with the moderates who succeeded the shah, not perceiving their lack of staying power or that ties with the United States could be fatal to them. The dispatch of a U.S. Army officer on a typically confused mission perhaps with the goal to engineer a military takeover seemed to confirm Iranian suspicions. The Islamic component of the revolution was beyond American comprehension. Ambassador William Sullivan urged the president to "think the unthinkable," but he refused to authorize contacts with Khomeini. As things went from bad to worse, U.S. officials played the blame game with each other. In truth no one knew what was happening or how to respond. With the country virtually in a state of anarchy, Khomeini returned to Tehran on February 1, 1979, to the adoring cheers of millions of well-wishers.[103]

Although probably nothing could have been done to head off or control the revolution, the United States might have done more to mitigate its anti-Americanism. It could have minimized its presence in Tehran— no more than "six men and a dog," one sensitive diplomat quipped.[104] It could have remained silent. But as Iranians increasingly denounced the United States, Americans responded in kind. Top U.S. officials issued threats. Congress passed anti-revolutionary resolutions. Senator Jackson again demonstrated a penchant for the perfectly mistimed misstatement by publicly proclaiming the revolution doomed. The most damaging mistake, made for the most humane of reasons and after months of agitation by such luminaries as Kissinger, David Rockefeller, and John McCloy, was Carter's reluctant October 1979 decision to admit the dying shah to the United States for medical treatment. That ill-fated move aroused profound suspicions among paranoid Iranian radicals of another 1953-like countercoup and provoked wild demonstrations in Tehran. Shortly after, Brzezinski met with moderate Iranian leader Mehdi Bazargan in Algiers, fueling revolutionary outrage and anxiety.[105]

The revolution abruptly changed from a serious problem for the United States to an all-out crisis on November 4, 1979, when young radicals

103. Kaufman and Kaufman, *Carter Presidency*, 158.
104. Bill, *Eagle and Lion*, 280.
105. Ibid., 285; Farber, *Taken Hostage*, 120–27.

stormed the U.S. embassy—the "Den of Spies"—and took hostage the sixty-six Americans still residing there. The immediate provocation was Carter's decision to allow the shah into the United States, but the hostage-takers also feared a CIA plot to restore him to power, suspicions encouraged by Jackson's statement and the Algiers meeting. Some former hostage-takers now admit, moreover, that their real purpose was to push the Bazargan government in more radical directions. They had no idea the takeover would lead to a prolonged crisis; some now concede it to have been a mistake.[106] Khomeini at first opposed the takeover, but when he recognized its popularity he exploited it to get rid of Bazargan and solidify his own power.

The crisis quickly took on a life of its own. Iran made demands for the hostages' release that Washington could not have met if it had wanted to, including the return of the shah for "revolutionary justice" and the surrender of his fortune. Threats from the United States only exacerbated tensions; the cessation of oil purchases and freezing of Iranian assets accomplished nothing. The crisis became the object of close international media scrutiny, keeping it constantly in the public eye. United States television news broadcasts solemnly counted off each day of captivity. Carter unwisely staked his political future on the outcome, vowing not to rest until the hostages were safely home. The more importance Carter attached to it, the more valuable the crisis became to the revolutionaries and the less likely any kind of settlement.[107] While Brzezinski pushed him to use force, the president explored without success every conceivable diplomatic channel. Americans at first rallied around their leader, as at the start of a war. His approval ratings rose. But as the crisis dragged on with no sign of an end, popular anger surged. Coming on top of America's failure in Vietnam and a steadily worsening economy, the hostage crisis came to symbolize for Americans a rising sense of impotence and belief that the nation had lost its mooring. The United States itself seemed hostage to forces it could not control.[108] The crisis aroused a fury that Americans directed first toward Iran and especially Khomeini, then against their unlucky president.

The hostage crisis came at a low point of Carter's chronically embattled presidency. The Organization of Petroleum Exporting Countries (OPEC) raised oil prices four times in five months in 1979. Shortages

---

106. Mark Bowden, "Among the Hostage Takers," *Atlantic Monthly*, December 2004, 77–96.
107. Pollack, *Persian Puzzle*, 161.
108. Farber, *Taken Hostage*, 1–2.

forced hour-long waits at gas stations. Increases in gasoline prices fueled price hikes across the board, causing inflation to rise at an annual rate of 14 percent. The liberal wing of his own party denounced Carter's budget proposals calling for austerity to combat inflation. Congress routinely shredded the administration's domestic programs. First brother Billy Carter, who carefully nurtured his redneck image and exploited his family connections, caused a mini-scandal (called, naturally, "Billygate") by maintaining dubious—and profitable—contacts with terrorist-sponsor Libya and speaking critically about Jews on national television.[109]

The president's efforts to deal with the emerging crisis only highlighted his seeming inability to do anything about them. In the early summer, the White House announced a major speech on the energy crisis only to cancel it thirty minutes before airtime. When finally given on July 15, the so-called malaise speech offered a remarkably candid assessment of what the president called a "crisis of confidence"—a "crisis that strikes at the very heart and soul of our national will." The speech earned good reviews from pundits, but its gloomy tone did nothing to lift the nation's spirits. A clumsily executed reshuffling of the cabinet and White House staff in the summer of 1979, while getting rid of troublemakers and incompetents, seemed further evidence of a government in disarray. Polls for the Democratic presidential nomination showed potential challenger Edward Kennedy leading Carter by a wide margin. The Carter presidency was "malleable and weak," pundits complained. The president would likely be a lame duck before the primaries began.[110]

Carter's foreign policy also came under fire. The administration did register major accomplishments in 1979, completing the process of normalization with China and making progress on SALT II negotiations with the USSR. But each of these gains came with domestic political costs. Chaos in the global economy, the Iranian revolution, the assassination of U.S. ambassador Adolph Dubs in Afghanistan in February, China's invasion of Vietnam later the same month, and the subsequent outbreak of civil war in Nicaragua created for Americans the sense that the world was both dangerous and hostile, the United States increasingly vulnerable.[111]

During the last half of 1979, Carter's critics zeroed in on SALT II. At a Vienna summit in June, Carter and Brezhnev finally signed the long-delayed treaty. Upon returning home, the president launched a major

109. Kaufman and Kaufman, *Carter Presidency*, 165–77, 228–30.
110. Farber, *Taken Hostage*, 143–44; Kaufman and Kaufman, *Carter Presidency*, 177–84.
111. Kaufman and Kaufman, *Carter Presidency*, 159–63.

campaign for its ratification. Critics wasted no time responding. Liberals protested that the treaty did not do enough to reduce nuclear armaments. Carter's inclusion of a new and enormously expensive missile system to appease Senate conservatives further angered liberals. The Committee on the Present Danger led the conservative charge. The CPD included leading hard-line Democrats, such as Nitze, who had been passed over by Carter for top-level positions and went after the treaty with a vengeance. Critics warned that SALT II put the United States at a disadvantage militarily and might lull Americans into a false sense of security. They questioned whether it could be properly monitored. In the Senate, the balance of power had shifted from those liberal internationalists who had bedeviled Ford to a loose, bipartisan coalition of conservatives whose ranks were strengthened by Republican and conservative gains in the 1978 elections. Howard Baker, who helped secure passage of the canal treaty, came out against SALT before Carter returned from Vienna. Democrat Sam Nunn of Georgia demanded sharp increases in overall defense spending in return for his support. Jackson predictably denounced the treaty as "appeasement in its purest form." Approval of the treaty was doubtful from the start; the embassy takeover further lowered its chances.[112]

Liberals' efforts to save their political skins added to Carter's difficulties. In September, Senate Foreign Relations Committee chairman Frank Church of Idaho, facing a strong conservative challenge for reelection, announced the "discovery" in Cuba of a brigade of Soviet troops that in fact had been there since 1962. Already on the ropes over Iran, Carter sought to ease popular fears by affirming that the brigade had "evidently" been in Cuba "some time" and in any event did not threaten the United States. To show their toughness, he and Vance insisted that it could not stay and beefed up U.S. military capabilities in the Caribbean, thus stoking the very fears they had attempted to calm. This tempest in a Cuban teapot dragged on for weeks, doomed SALT, infuriated the Soviets, and left the administration more vulnerable to conservative attack.[113]

The Soviet invasion of Afghanistan on December 27, 1979, pushed Carter into the camp of the hard-liners and provoked him to escalate the Cold War into its climactic phase. During most of the Soviet-American conflict, that isolated, landlocked nation had remained non-aligned. A 1973 coup brought to power a pro-Western government, which, five years later, was overthrown by leftist army officers. Following firmly established

112. Kaufman, *Jackson*, 385; Johnson, *Congress and the Cold War*, 243–46.
113. Garthoff, *Détente*, 828–29.

Cold War patterns, Moscow promptly sent aid and advisers to a potential client. Still in a detente frame of mind, the United States at first responded with remarkable equanimity, maintaining relations with the pro-Soviet regime and even sending limited assistance. United States policy changed in 1979. Allies Pakistan and Saudi Arabia pushed Washington to do something. In January, Carter authorized a covert operation providing aid to Islamic rebels, even though Brzezinski warned it might prompt large-scale Soviet intervention. Both men saw advantages in luring the USSR into the "Afghan trap."[114] By late 1979, Afghanistan's government was teetering from destructive internal rivalries and Islamic insurgents. Fearing its collapse, the Soviet Union intervened. The Kremlin acted reluctantly to protect what it viewed as a crucial buffer state. The Islamic revolution in nearby Iran seemed to endanger its own Muslim "republics." It especially feared China, which had close ties to Afghanistan's eastern neighbor, Pakistan. Perhaps more paranoid than their U.S. counterparts at this time, Soviet leaders took seriously alarmist KGB reports that the Afghan prime minister sought ties with the United States. Moscow thus sent a brigade of troops. Soon after, it overthrew the government and launched a costly and ultimately suicidal war against the insurgents.[115]

Viewing Soviet moves from a worst-case standpoint, Carter responded with a decisiveness quite out of character for his presidency. He was angered by the Kremlin's action, perhaps even took it personally since it seemed to prove that his original assessment of Soviet motives and goals had been wrongheaded. Already under fire at home from Cold Warriors and facing a tough campaign for renomination, he may have concluded that a hard-line policy was necessary to give him any chance for reelection. Whatever the precise reason, henceforth he was squarely in Brzezinski's camp. With the Middle East and crucial Persian Gulf region in turmoil, he viewed a Soviet takeover of Afghanistan as a dire threat to vital U.S. interests. In a notably alarmist speech on January 4, 1980, he condemned Soviet "aggression" and warned of the danger to Persian Gulf oil fields.[116]

To combat the Soviet intervention, he took a dazzling variety of steps. He drastically stepped up U.S. covert aid to the mujahideen rebels, laying

114. Mark Danner, "Taking Stock of the Forever War," New York Times Magazine, September 11, 2005, 49.
115. Martin Walker, The Cold War: A History (New York, 1994), 251–55; "The Soviet Union and Afghanistan, 1978–1989: Documents from Russian and East German Archives," Cold War International History Project Bulletin (Winter 1996–1997), 133–84.
116. Carter speech, January 4, 1980, www.presidency.ucsb.edu/ws/index.php?pid=32911 andst=andst1=.

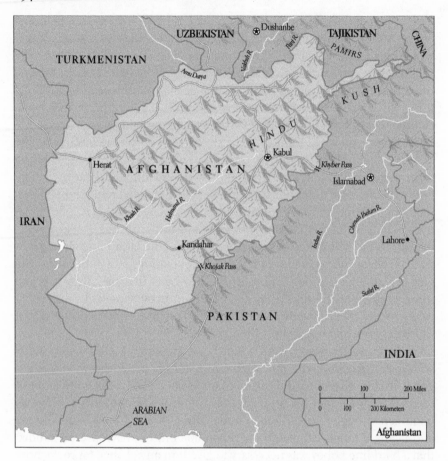

the basis for an assistance program that, as he and Brzezinski hoped, would in fact help make Afghanistan the Soviet Union's Vietnam.[117] He tabled the long-delayed SALT II agreement. Without giving much thought to their possible effectiveness, implications, or consequences, he instituted an array of punitive sanctions, embargoing the shipment of new technology to the Soviet Union and, over the loud protest of farm states, banning further grain sales. He later boycotted the Olympic Games scheduled for Moscow that summer. In his State of the Union address, he proclaimed what came to be called the Carter Doctrine, sternly warning that any attempt by an "outside force" to gain control of the Persian Gulf

---

117. William J. Daughtery, *Executive Secrets: Covert Operations and the Presidency* (Lexington, Ky., 2004), 189.

region would be "regarded as an assault on the vital interests of the United States" and would be "repelled by force." To back up his warnings, he initiated registration for the draft, asked for a 5 percent increase in military spending, proposed major aid for Pakistan, and beefed up the U.S. military presence in the Persian Gulf and Indian Ocean.[118] Much like Truman at the onset of the Korean War, he set out to shore up U.S. alliances, even in cases like the Western Hemisphere and South Asia where his actions compromised established policy on human rights and nuclear non-proliferation.

In a move that sent shock waves all the way to Moscow, Carter in January 1980 dispatched Secretary of Defense Harold Brown to Beijing to discuss the establishment of military ties. The United States to this point had scrupulously—and sensibly—avoided such steps. Some Americans hesitated to bolster Chinese military power while the status of Taiwan remained unresolved. Vance also correctly warned that, instead of forcing Moscow to be cooperative, cozying up to China would make working with the Soviet Union much more difficult.[119] Egged on by Brzezinski, Carter after Afghanistan threw caution to the winds. Brown made clear on arrival that he hoped to deal with "complementary actions in the field of defense as well as diplomacy." He arranged for the sale of non-lethal military equipment including radar and other high-tech electronic items long sought by the Chinese and denied the Soviets. He proposed that the two nations cooperate in sending arms to the Afghan insurgents and take joint action should Vietnam invade Thailand. The Chinese happily accepted U.S. electronic equipment but stopped well short of the de facto alliance Brown advocated, agreeing only to step up covert aid to the Afghan rebels. Later in the year, the United States opened preliminary discussions for the sale of military equipment. Disguised with a mustache grown especially for the occasion, CIA director Stansfield Turner secretly traveled to Beijing to discuss the sharing of intelligence. The 1980 tilt toward China ended any semblance of balance in U.S. relations with the two Communist powers.[120]

In July 1980, Carter approved Presidential Directive 59 (PD-59), a fundamental reassessment of U.S. nuclear strategy. The doctrine of mutual assured destruction had provided a measure of deterrence through the grim certainty that each nation could destroy the other's primary population centers. Nervous U.S. strategists increasingly feared, however, that

118. Garthoff, *Détente*, 945–57.
119. Mann, *About Face*, 110–11.
120. Ibid., 109–14.

an apparent Soviet lead in conventional weapons as well as qualitative and quantitative improvements in their nuclear arsenal gave them the means to target U.S. military installations and wage nuclear war short of annihilation. Their conclusion, outlined in PD-59, was equally disturbing but to them unavoidable: The United States must develop a strategy and the instruments to strike military as well as civilian targets. It must be able to fight and win a nuclear war. As significant for its era as NSC-68 for the 1950s, PD-59 also called for a huge boost in military spending and for the largest buildup of conventional and nuclear arms since the Truman years.[121]

The U.S. response to Afghanistan marked yet another major turning point in the Cold War. Carter's early 1980 initiatives constituted a clean break with policies pursued since the mid-1960s. The United States relegated detente to the scrap heap, sharply reescalated its Cold War rhetoric, and reinstituted policies of global containment reminiscent of the early days of the Soviet-American struggle. The sanctions initiated in haste took on a life of their own. Along with the scrapping of SALT II, the development of new missile systems, and the U.S. deployment of missiles to Europe, PD-59 appeared to Moscow to represent a menacing U.S. quest for nuclear superiority—"madness," *Tass* screamed; "nuclear blackmail," according to *Pravda*—reigniting the arms race and sending it to its most fearful level.[122]

As with the Korean War and other Cold War crises, the flare-up of 1979–80 stemmed at least in part from misperception and miscalculations on both sides. The Soviets saw themselves acting defensively in Afghanistan. The last thing they wanted was to spur a major U.S. rearmament program and drive Washington further into the arms of Beijing. Their move into Afghanistan thus took the form of a self-fulfilling prophecy, making a reality of the Sino-American collaboration that in their imagination had aroused grave concern about Afghanistan. The Soviet incursion deserved to be condemned and opposed. But at least in the beginning it was not truly an "invasion," as U.S. officials repeatedly charged. Nor did it represent the "greatest threat to world peace" since World War II, as Carter often affirmed, or the first step in a drive to the Persian Gulf. Americans seem to have found in Afghanistan an outlet for the frustrations that had built up in recent months. They were more comfortable with the clarity

121. Allan R. Millett and Peter Maslowski, *For the Common Defense: A Military History of the United States of America* (New York, 1984), 580; William E. Odom, "The Origins and Design of Presidential Directive-59: A Memoir," in Henry D. Sokoloski, *Getting MAD* (Carlisle Barracks, Pa., 2004), 175–96.
122. Kaufman and Kaufman, *Carter Presidency*, 231.

and certitude of a new era of confrontation than with the confused and uncertain state of detente. Whatever the cause, the Soviet move into Afghanistan and the U.S. overreaction provoked a new and especially dangerous phase of the Cold War.

Carter's political fortunes got no more than a short-term boost from his decisive moves. As in the first stages of the hostage crisis, the public initially rallied to their president. His poll numbers shot up. Although the grain embargo threatened to hurt farmers, Iowans overwhelmingly voted for Carter over Kennedy in that state's Democratic caucuses. But the president could never really overcome his reputation for indecisiveness. Indeed, Republicans and conservative Democrats insisted that his weakness and naïveté had brought about the situation he was forced to respond to.[123]

More important, during Carter's last months in office, everything seemed to fall apart. A crippling recession proved impervious to the numerous countermeasures attempted by Ford and Carter. In the summer of 1980, corporate profits dropped by almost 20 percent, one of the biggest downturns in the postwar period. Unemployment rose to almost 8 percent with forecasts that it might hit 10 percent by the end of the year. A sagging economy sparked racial violence from Boston to Miami. Eight years of hard times with no end in view left the nation in a surly and angry mood.[124]

There were more foreign policy setbacks. The European nations questioned Carter's hawkish response to Soviet military intervention in Afghanistan, opening new rifts in the Western alliance. The Camp David Accords, one of the president's major achievements, came apart at the seams. Israeli prime minister Begin defined Palestinian autonomy as narrowly as possible, stopping far short of the self-determination to which Sadat was committed. During 1980, Carter made several futile efforts to salvage his handiwork only to recognize that the agreements whose negotiation he had so painstakingly overseen were fundamentally flawed.[125] Closer to home, the administration's efforts to channel the Nicaraguan revolution in a moderate direction failed badly. The United States was no more successful using carrot and stick with embattled dictator Anastasio Somoza than it had been with the shah. Wisely, it refused to bail out his despicable regime when it crumbled, but its attempts to control the revolution through an unwieldy electoral device that would have limited the power of leftist rebels had no chance of success. The president at first tried to work with and even secure assistance for a new government headed by the

123. Ibid., 197.
124. Ibid., 221–22.
125. Ibid., 225–27.

Sandinistas, the dominant group whose choice of name (for rebel leader Augusto Sandino) made clear its political orientation and attitude toward the United States. While Congress dawdled with Carter's request for aid, the new government shifted to the left, secured assistance from Cuba and the Soviet Union, and established ties with leftist groups elsewhere in Central America. Carter came under fire from conservatives for allowing another Cuba in the hemisphere.[126]

The hostage crisis that at first worked in Carter's favor by the spring of 1980 had also turned against him. The crisis became the media event of its time. For months, it dominated the headlines and filled television screens, even late-night viewing, where ABC's new *Nightline* news program sometimes outdrew popular variety shows. Television especially played the story for maximum dramatic effect. Images of young Iranian women in strange clothing and bearded young men shouting anti-American slogans and burning U.S. flags piqued the emotions of an already frustrated and angry public. The loud demands of Iranian students in the United States that the shah be returned to Iran provoked from Americans counterdemands that all Iranians be deported. In time, the crisis became a rallying point for a bitterly divided people. It inspired popular songs such as "Go to Hell Ayatollah" and the more somber "Hostage Prayer." To show solidarity with the hostages, Americans kept their car lights on, rang church bells, and, following the example of another popular song, tied yellow ribbons around trees and light poles. In the early months, the solidarity extended to Carter, whose approval ratings soared. The president was the first to appreciate that American patience was limited, however, and by late March, with no end to the crisis in sight, he was in trouble again. It was in this context that he approved the ill-fated hostage rescue mission.[127]

No single event did more to highlight the nation's sense of impotence and destroy the Carter presidency than the botched attempt in April 1980 to rescue the hostages. Carter approved the plan out of desperation. It was the longest of long shots and risked the hostages being killed in retaliation or even escalation into a bloody war. In what was dubbed Operation Eagle Claw, eight helicopters from the aircraft carrier *Nimitz* in the Gulf of Oman were to rendezvous with C-130 transports at Desert One in the Iranian desert. A newly formed Delta Force rescue team would proceed to Tehran by helicopter and truck, seize the hostages,

126. Walter LaFeber, *Inevitable Revolutions: The United States in Central America* (New York, 1984), 241–42.
127. Farber, *Taken Hostage*, 141–71.

and return to an airfield for evacuation. In execution, a plan with virtu-ally no margin for error turned out to be Murphy's Law in operation, self-destructing almost from the start. In a bizarre and totally unexpected development, the would-be rescuers, landing at midnight, stumbled upon some Iranians crossing the desert in a ramshackle bus, blowing their cover. A blinding dust storm—the Iranians called it a *haboob*, and Khomeini hailed it as an act of Allah—hampered the desert landing and along with mechanical problems crippled all but four of the helicopters, forcing the mission to be aborted. To add to the embarrassment and tragedy, a helicopter crashed into a C-130 during evacuation, killing eight Americans, all of whom had to be left behind.[128]

The desert debacle had a huge impact for the unfortunate Carter. In terms of the immediate problem with Iran, it completely backfired, con-firming America's hostile intentions, strengthening the position of Khome-ini and the extremists, and providing a huge boost to Iranian nationalism.[129] At home, the nation once again initially backed the president, but as time went on and the details became known, frustrated Americans increasingly turned their anger against him. The Congress and allies complained about not being consulted. Vacationing in Florida, Vance had been delib-erately and entirely left out of the loop because of his known opposition to any military action. He quickly resigned, the first secretary of state since William Jennings Bryan in 1915 to leave office on a matter of princi-ple and only the third in U.S. history. Carter's approval rating plunged to 40 percent. "As things now stand," *Newsweek* opined, "the President's uncertain diplomatic strategy has left allies perplexed, enemies unim-pressed and the nation as vulnerable as ever in an increasingly dangerous world."[130]

The nation's lack of confidence in Carter's ability to lead cost him re-election. Given all the misfortunes that beset him, he hung remarkably close to Republican challenger Reagan up to Election Day. Had he been able to secure release of the hostages early in the campaign, he might still have snatched victory from the jaws of defeat. He seemed to achieve a breakthrough in negotiations that promised to gain freedom for the hostages several days before the election, but it did not produce immediate results and was of dubious value anyway since Republicans had warned of an eleventh-hour trick to sway the election. Reagan proved a more adept campaigner than Carter. He and his simple and

128. Mark Bowden, "The Desert One Debacle," *Atlantic Monthly*, May 2006, 62–77.
129. Bill, *Eagle and Lion*, 302–3.
130. Kaufman and Kaufman, *Carter Presidency*, 213.

sunny conservative message, delivered with charm, wit, and at times eloquence, contrasted sharply with a sitting president who seemed unable to
present a vision of any sort. Economic issues continued to loom largest
with the voters. In this area also, Carter failed the test. The result was a
Republican victory that in its magnitude shocked the experts. The actor-
turned-politician won 51 percent of the popular vote, 489 electoral votes
to a mere 49 for Carter. Republicans gained control of the Senate for the
first time since the early 1950s and made big gains in the House.[131]

CARTER HAS BEEN MUCH MALIGNED over the years for his handling
of U.S. foreign policy. Conservative publicists have made him, along with
1972 presidential candidate George McGovern, into living symbols of the
Democratic Party's alleged weakness on national security issues, an image that has dogged the party at election time for more than thirty years.
Like other such political myths, this one distorts the record. Carter had
the misfortune to serve in a complex and confusing time of transitions—
in foreign affairs, from Cold War to detente and back again, at home from
the liberal consensus to a more conservative outlook. Upon taking office,
he hoped to shift the focus of U.S. foreign policy from the Cold War to
North-South problems and human rights and to restore the United States
to what he considered its rightful position of moral leadership in the
world, a not unreasonable agenda in post-Vietnam, post-Watergate America. He sought also to further detente. His administration from the start
was hampered by his own inexperience and sometimes naïveté. His goals
were sometimes contradictory, and the Vance-Brzezinski feud gave a certain schizophrenic quality to some of his initiatives. Unschooled in the
complexities of international relations, he initially underestimated the
difficulties of dealing with the Soviet Union. His clumsy efforts to resolve
differences with Moscow were also repeatedly undercut by conservatives
in Congress. In part responding to their pressures, he overreacted to the
Soviet invasion of Afghanistan, reescalating Cold War tensions. It was he,
in fact, who initiated the military buildup, confrontational approach, and
covert action in Afghanistan that the Republicans took credit for and
claimed to be decisive in America's Cold War victory. Carter was thus
also unlucky. He did not even get the satisfaction of having the embassy
hostages released on his watch. Not until shortly after Ronald Reagan
took office on January 20, 1980, would they be set free.

131. Ibid., 239–46.

19

"A Unique and Extraordinary Moment"

Gorbachev, Reagan, Bush, and the End of the Cold War, 1981–1991

On November 11, 1983, millions of Americans gathered around their television sets to watch *The Day After*, a chilling account of the impact on ordinary people of a nuclear attack on the middle-American town of Lawrence, Kansas. Unbeknownst to these viewers, several days earlier, in response to NATO's annual Able Archer military exercises, a nervous Soviet government, convinced that a nuclear attack was imminent, went on full alert and put its nuclear-capable aircraft on standby. The world had come "frighteningly" close to the nuclear abyss, a Soviet defector later recalled.[1]

Incredibly, less than five years after this second most dangerous Cold War flash point, hard-core anti-Communist U.S. president Ronald Reagan and Soviet general secretary Mikhail Gorbachev strolled leisurely through Moscow's Red Square and declared themselves "old friends." When queried regarding his earlier, belligerent statements about the Soviet Union, Reagan dismissed them as from "another time, another place." Within three more years, the Communist governments in Eastern Europe had fallen, the Berlin Wall had been torn down, the Cold War declared ended, and the Soviet Union had collapsed. This swift and stunning transformation of the international system without war or violent revolution was without precedent. Reagan's successor, George H. W. Bush, aptly called it "a unique and extraordinary moment."[2]

Many Americans have been quick to claim credit for these breathtaking changes. It was the power of their ideals, they insist, that toppled the Iron

---

1. Martin Walker, *The Cold War: A History* (New York, 1993), 276–277; Robert M. Gates, *From the Shadows: The Ultimate Insider's Story of Five Presidents and How They Won the Cold War* (New York, 1996), 270–73.
2. Don Oberdorfer, *From the Cold War to a New Era: The United States and the End of the Soviet Union, 1983–1991* (Baltimore, Md., 1998), 353; the Bush quote is from David J. Rothkopf, *Running the World: The Inside Story of the National Security Council and the Architects of American Power* (New York, 2005), 260.

Curtain; the skill and strength of their policies, particularly under Reagan, that won the day. In this tale of virtue and heroism, Reagan's principled and outspoken stand against Communism and his massive defense buildup forced Soviet capitulation and won the Cold War.[3] There is, of course, some truth in such arguments. America's ideals—and even more, its popular culture—did influence people around the world. Reagan played an important role. But his policies were never as clear-cut as his proponents claim. They were often sloppily implemented. In the early years, they dangerously exacerbated Cold War tensions. It was only when he shifted toward conciliation that they began to produce results. His successor, George Bush, had the good sense to let history take its course. It is essential to look beyond the United States to comprehend the stunning transformation of 1981–91. More than anything else, it was the basic weakness of the Soviet system and the dramatic steps taken by the remarkable Gorbachev that produced these striking changes.

I

Ronald Wilson Reagan looms over the last quarter of the American Century as Woodrow Wilson the first and Franklin Roosevelt the second. Unlike Wilson, the former movie actor contributed nothing to the intellectual content of U.S. foreign policy. But like FDR, the hero of his youth, he touched the American psyche as few other politicians have. He restored the American spirit, scarred by Vietnam and Watergate and afflicted by a loss of confidence and self-esteem. He revived and gave eloquent expression to a messianic vision that resonated with Wilsonianism. Whether by luck or skill or some elusive combination of both, he presided over a rebirth at home and transformation abroad that set the stage for the end of the Cold War and America's emergence as a global power with a position of primacy unmatched since the days of Victorian England.

Reagan's life embodied the American dream, and therefore, perhaps naturally, he became one of its foremost exponents. A product of small-town midwestern America, often viewed as the quintessence of the nation, the young man known as "Dutch" first achieved notice in the 1930s by broadcasting over radio to regional households baseball games whose details he acquired by teletype. Sometimes, when the machine broke

---

3. See, for example, Peter Schweizer, *Reagan's War: The Epic Story of His Forty-Year Struggle and Final Victory over Communism* (New York, 2003). The triumphalist argument is critically evaluated in Robert J. McMahon, "American Foreign Policy during the Reagan Years," *Diplomatic History* 19 (Spring 1995), 367–84, and Jeremi Suri, "Explaining the End of the Cold War: A New Historical Consensus?" *Journal of Cold War Studies* 4 (Fall 2002), 60–92.

down, he made up the play-by-play as he went along. He moved easily from one form of media to another, starring in a series of B movies during the war years and after. A New Dealer, he anticipated the national shift to the right by adopting a fiercely anti-Communist position during 1950s investigations of leftist activities in Hollywood. He gained national prominence, wealth, and important political contacts as host for a popular television program and spokesperson for General Electric. He stirred the passions of conservatives in 1964 with a powerful speech supporting Goldwater for president. Undaunted by the Arizonan's disastrous defeat, in 1966 he unseated Edmund "Pat" Brown, the popular Democratic governor of California, launching a political career that after several setbacks led to the White House. By the time he went to Sacramento, he had put on full display the qualities that would make him an icon: rugged good looks; a genial and amiable disposition; and a mellifluous, soothing voice that earned the trust of his listeners. He had an instinctive feel for the mood of the American people. His sunny optimism was perfectly calculated to heal a wounded nation. Better than anyone else since John Kennedy, he articulated the nation's ideals and hallowed myths.[4] "Reagan's rhetoric wove a seamless tapestry of 'morality, heritage, boldness, heroism, and fairness' that offered a compelling, if rather fanciful, vision of a genuine national community," Richard Melason has written.[5]

Reagan brought to the presidency no foreign policy experience but deeply felt views. He had preached throughout his political career unrelenting opposition to Communist tyranny. He deplored the so-called Vietnam Syndrome that had allegedly sapped the United States of its sense of purpose and the defeatism and malaise that stamped the Carter years. Looking nostalgically to the days when the United States had been number one in the world, he sought to restore a position he thought had been squandered by lack of courage and will. He promised to rebuild the nation's faltering economy and its military arsenal to confront Communist adversaries and especially the USSR from a position of strength. Like the Committee on the Present Danger, he vowed to go beyond mere containment by exposing the evils of Communism, exploiting the Soviet Union's internal weaknesses, and backing insurgencies that aimed to overthrow leftist governments, thereby altering the status quo in America's favor.

4. Ronald Reagan, *An American Life: The Autobiography* (New York, 1990) tells the story. Garry Wills, *Reagan's America: Innocents at Home* (New York, 1987) offers an insightful analysis, focusing on the early years.
5. Richard A. Melanson, *American Foreign Policy Since the Vietnam War: The Search for Consensus from Nixon to Clinton* (Armonk, N.Y., 1996), 136–37.

The Reagan foreign policy was more complex than might appear on the surface, however. The president preferred people of action to intellectuals. But his idealism and instinctive unilateralism were tempered by a touch of pragmatism, the mainstream Republican internationalism espoused by secretaries of state Alexander M. Haig Jr. and George Shultz, and the hard-nosed Machiavellianism of CIA director William Casey. Reagan and the Californians who comprised his White House staff were in the most basic sense unilateralists. They knew little about the rest of the world. They had no faith in the United Nations and other international institutions. In his view of America, the president himself was a veritable Woodrow Wilson in greasepaint. He accepted as an article of faith the myth of American exceptionalism and repeatedly evoked John Winthrop's imagery of a "city on a hill," which he usually embellished by adding the adjective "shining." He had no doubt of the superiority of American ideals and institutions and was certain the rest of the world awaited them. He was also a throwback to Teddy Roosevelt. His code name Rawhide symbolized the western hero that he played in movies and that to him epitomized the nation. He believed the United States must have the courage of its convictions and be willing to fight for its ideals. But he was also a pragmatist.[6] As much as he deplored the Vietnam Syndrome, he recognized the deep-seated popular fears of military intervention abroad. His often bellicose rhetoric was moderated by caution in the use of power.

Reagan's unilateralist and messianic tendencies were also balanced by Haig and Shultz. The secretaries of state shared his anti-Communism and belief in a strong defense, but they were also committed to close cooperation with America's European allies and were more willing to negotiate with the Soviet Union and China. Casey on the other hand, shared the president's anti-communism and his penchant for action. Apparently with Reagan's blessing and sometimes without the knowledge of Shultz, he developed a worldwide program of covert operations to undermine Communist governments.[7]

Confusion of concept was joined by chaos in implementation. Reagan was grandly indifferent to detail. He often displayed a careless disregard for unpleasant facts and sometimes appeared to live in a Hollywood-like fantasy world. He was the sloppiest administrator since Franklin Roosevelt. His White House staff was totally inexperienced in foreign policy, and amateur night was a regular occurrence. Theoretically the orchestrator of

6. Lou Cannon, *President Reagan: The Role of a Lifetime* (New York, 1991), 185.
7. Bob Woodward, *Veil: The Secret Wars of the CIA, 1981–1987* (New York, 1987).

foreign policy, the National Security Council—by design—was plagued by weakness and chronic instability. Reacting against the dominant role played by Kissinger and Brzezinski, the president's team deliberately downgraded the NSC and appointed lesser lights to head it. Reagan had six different national security advisers in eight years.[8]

Conflict within the administration made the Vance-Brzezinski feud look like a love feast by comparison. Paraphrasing Air Force Gen. Curtis LeMay, hard-line NSC staffer Richard Pipes observed that while the Soviets were the adversary, "the enemy was State." For its part, Haig's State Department refused to share important documents with NSC.[9] Reagan was isolated from the NSC by White House advisers and his wife, Nancy, who feared that the ideologues who staffed it would reinforce his hard-line tendencies. Haig's efforts to crown himself the "vicar" of Reagan's foreign policy earned him the enmity of the White House staff, who sarcastically dubbed him CINCWORLD (commander in chief of the world)—and eventually got him fired. For more than six years, Shultz and Secretary of Defense Caspar Weinberger waged as acrimonious a power struggle as ever seen in Washington over such issues as arms reduction, the proper response to terrorism, and the employment of U.S. military forces abroad. The NSC staff and Casey conducted operations bitterly opposed by both Shultz and Weinberger—when they knew about them. The policy process suffered from an excess of democracy, James Baker later recalled, "a witches' brew of intrigue, elbows, egos, and separate agendas."[10] The most detached chief executive since Calvin Coolidge—whose portrait was restored to a place of prominence in his White House—Reagan refused to adjudicate the nasty disputes among his subordinates. He presided amiably over the chaos, reaping the whirlwind only in his second term when the ill-conceived and in some cases illegal shenanigans of his subordinates nearly made him a lame duck before his time. It was only in the last two years of his second term, following the Iran-Contra scandal, that some order was imposed on the policymaking process.

The Reagan policies reflected these conflicting forces. Anti-Communism was a constant. But the president's tough and occasionally bombastic talk was belied by a growing willingness to negotiate with the Soviets. Moreover, although the administration spoke loudly and through its massive arms buildup carried a big stick, it was generally cautious in sending military forces abroad. The major innovation was the so-called Reagan

8. Rothkopf, *Running the World*, 212–14.
9. Richard Pipes, *Vixi: Memoirs of a Non-Belonger* (New Haven, Conn., 2004), 153–54.
10. James A. Baker III, *Politics of Diplomacy: Revolution, War, and Peace, 1989–1992* (New York, 1995), 26–27.

Doctrine, a policy of using covert arms shipments to change the status quo in favor of the "free world." In that sense alone, it departed sharply from the policies of its predecessors.

The results were mixed. The Reagan administration engaged the United States in new and dangerous ways in the ever volatile Middle East. A not-so-covert war in Central America inflicted great destruction on that troubled region and came a cropper in the Iran-Contra scandal, for a time crippling the administration in its second term. On the positive side and to the dismay of his longtime conservative supporters, Reagan established the basis for a new relationship with the Soviet Union.

During the first term, the Cold War reescalated to a level of tension not equaled since the Cuban missile crisis. This process began with Carter, of course, but Reagan went well beyond his predecessor, openly repudiating detente and reasserting the moral absolutes of the Cold War as no one had since John Foster Dulles. Indeed, in the early years, Reagan seems to have reveled in unleashing verbal cannon shots against the Soviets. In a 1983 speech to Christian evangelicals, borrowing a phrase from the blockbuster 1977 movie *Star Wars*, he branded the Soviet Union "the evil empire" and accused it of being the "focus of evil in the modern world."[11] Moscow reserved for itself the right to "commit any crime, to lie, to cheat" to achieve its sinister goals, he said on another occasion. He once dismissed Marxism-Leninism as a "gaggle of bogus prophecies and petty superstitions" and predicted, correctly as it turned out, that communism would be remembered as a "sad and rather bizarre chapter in human history." He condemned the Soviets for shooting down a South Korean airliner in September 1983—an episode that revealed more about their nervousness and inept air defenses than their hostile intentions—insisting with no proof, and incorrectly as it turned out, that they knew all along it was a civilian aircraft. The president may have revealed his deepest instincts when he jokingly—and inadvertently—broadcast into an open radio microphone in August 1984: "My fellow Americans, I am pleased to tell you today that I've signed legislation that will outlaw Russia forever. We begin bombing in five minutes."[12]

During the first term, tough talk was sometimes backed by actions. The administration in 1981 threatened sanctions if the USSR used military force to put down mounting unrest in Poland. When the Polish government itself responded by instituting martial law—a "gross violation of

11. March 8, 1983, *Public Papers of the Presidents of the United States, Ronald Reagan, 1983* (Washington, 1983), 363–64.
12. Oberdorfer, *Cold War to New Era*, 85.

the Helsinki Pact," Reagan raged—the United States on Christmas Eve 1981 imposed sanctions on Poland.[13] Ironically, although the Soviet Union had not used force, the administration subsequently placed sanctions on it as well, terminating Aeroflot flights to U.S. cities, refusing to renew scientific exchange agreements, and in June 1982 banning the sale of equipment and technology for construction of a Soviet gas pipeline to Western Europe, an action taken without consulting European allies that outraged them. In a move that at least bordered on pettiness and spite, the administration revoked Soviet ambassador Anatoly Dobrynin's special parking place in the State Department garage.

From the beginning, however, the administration also displayed a pragmatic streak in dealing with the "evil empire." To appease U.S. farmers and satisfy his personal predilection for free trade, Reagan shortly after taking office scrapped Carter's embargo on grain shipments to the USSR. The administration's first major statement of Cold War strategy, National Security Decision Directive 75, approved in December 1982, was a compromise between hard-liners in the NSC and pragmatists in the Pentagon and the State Department. The United States would stand firmly against Soviet expansion. It would go beyond mere containment by using any means at its disposal to alter the Kremlin's behavior by inflicting costs that might exacerbate internal problems, increase reformist tendencies, and even bring about regime change. At the same time, the United States would negotiate agreements with the Soviet Union that served its interests.[14]

On crucial issues such as arms control, the administration in its early years was demonstrably hard-nosed. Here also, more than he was willing to admit, Reagan expanded on precedents set by Carter. Although he agreed to abide by its restrictions, he refused to resubmit to the Senate a "fatally flawed" SALT II agreement that did not provide for reductions in the two sides' nuclear arsenals. Even more than his predecessor, he rejected the doctrine of mutual assured destruction in favor of a strategy of deterrence through military superiority. Having used to advantage in the 1980 campaign the alleged "window of vulnerability" opened by a sustained Soviet buildup of nuclear and conventional weapons, the president vowed to seek "peace through strength." Ignoring campaign pledges to cut the federal budget, his administration expanded on Carter's huge buildup, increasing defense spending by 7 percent a year between 1981 and 1986. The cost was $2 trillion in the first six years and produced Pentagon spending estimated at an incredible $28 million an hour. It provided for major

13. Pipes, Vixi, 171.
14. Ibid., 188–203.

improvements in existing missiles and delivery systems, the addition of new systems such as the MX mobile land-based missile with ten independently targeted warheads, the humongous B-1 bomber that Carter had rejected, a six-hundred-ship navy capable of attacking Soviet ports in the event of war, and expanded salaries and benefits for military personnel.[15] The buildup even revived emphasis on civil defense, this time in the form of plans to shift people from cities to small towns in time of nuclear crisis.[16]

In part to mute increasingly outspoken anti-nuclear protest in the United States and Western Europe, the administration evinced a willingness to talk with the Soviets, but the positions it took raised doubts about its eagerness for substantive negotiations. The appointment of hard-liners to key positions reflected its approach. As a staff aide to "Scoop" Jackson, Richard Perle had wreaked havoc with SALT; as Reagan's assistant secretary of defense for international security policy, he was in a position to shape policy. Ironically, and especially revealing, Cold Warrior Paul Nitze, the author of NSC-68, became known as the Reagan administration's arms control dove!

On the two major issues of intermediate nuclear forces (INF) stationed in Europe or aimed at Europe and longer range strategic weapons, the Reaganites insisted on much larger cuts in Soviet forces than their own. In the INF negotiations, they set forth a so-called zero option, agreeing not to deploy Pershing and Tomahawk missiles in Europe if the Soviets would dismantle their SS-20 intermediate-range ballistic missiles (IRBMs, missiles with a range of 1,865 to 3,420 miles) and other intermediate-range missiles aimed at Western Europe. British and French missiles were exempted. The zero option also left out all sea- and air-based missiles, where the United States had a huge advantage. It was "loaded to Western advantage and Soviet disadvantage," Raymond Garthoff has concluded, "and it was clearly not a basis for negotiations aimed at reaching agreement."[17] When Nitze and his Soviet counterpart, after a secret July 1982 "walk in the woods," actually came up with a compromise, Perle and the hard-liners sabotaged it. Public U.S. statements that nuclear war was both feasible and "winnable" caused a furor in Europe and nervousness in the USSR.[18] Deployment of intermediate-range missiles in Europe in late 1983 provoked the Soviets to walk out of the talks.

15. Walker, Cold War, 266.
16. Paul S. Boyer, "Selling Star Wars: Ronald Reagan's Strategic Defense Initiative," paper delivered at Florida Atlantic University, February 2007, 7.
17. Raymond L. Garthoff, Détente and Confrontation: American-Soviet Relations from Nixon to Reagan (Washington, 1985), 1024.
18. Walker, Cold War, 267.

The result was the most contentious and least constructive arms control talks in many years.[19]

The two sides fared no better with strategic weapons. In this area, the administration sharply departed from its predecessors, abandoning arms *limitation* for *reduction*—especially on the Soviet side. The new acronym START (Strategic Arms Reduction Talks) signified the change. After months of bitter internal wrangling, the United States finally adopted a negotiating position. While setting as the eventual goal the reduction of warheads to five thousand on each side, it demanded substantial decreases in Soviet warheads and land-based launchers while leaving its own cruise missiles, bombers, and submarines unaffected. "You want to solve *your* vulnerability problem by making *our* forces vulnerable," a Soviet general complained. In the lengthy discussions that followed, the United States backed off only slightly, provoking charges of "old poison in new bottles."[20]

Reagan complicated matters still further with a bombshell speech in March 1983 proposing a Strategic Defense Initiative (SDI), a missile defense system employing lasers from space-based platforms that could intercept and destroy enemy missiles before they struck U.S. or allied soil. Controversial nuclear physicist, father of the hydrogen bomb, and ardent Cold Warrior Edward Teller first suggested the idea to the president in the fall of 1982. Reagan latched on to it with the unshakable faith that was an essential part of his being. It appealed to his longstanding and visceral hatred for nuclear weapons and the whole idea of MAD, which accepted Cold War stalemate—and which, he believed, the Soviets could not be trusted to adhere to. His enthusiasm may have been fed by a 1940 movie, *Murder in the Air*, in which he played FBI agent Brass Bancroft and U.S. scientists developed a secret weapon to neutralize enemy planes. He inserted the proposal into his speech before any discussion with allies and without full vetting from the bureaucracy—indeed, against the opposition of many top defense officials. He offered SDI to Americans as a "vision for the future," a way to render nuclear weapons "impotent and obsolete" and "offer hope for our children in the 21st century."[21]

SDI proved a typically Reaganesque stroke of political genius. Scientists and many national security experts promptly dismissed it as outrageously

---

19. Strobe Talbott, *Deadly Gambits: The Reagan Administration and the Stalemate in Nuclear Arms Control* (New York, 1984), 158.

20. Garthoff, *Détente*, 1026.

21. Boyer, "Selling Star Wars," 11–14; the fullest account is Frances FitzGerald, *Way Out There in the Blue: Reagan, Star Wars, and the End of the Cold War* (New York, 2000).

costly and wildly impractical and dubbed it "Star Wars" to highlight its chimerical nature. But it also touched a responsive chord with the public. Reagan shrewdly couched his appeal for SDI as a way to restore the sense of security Americans had enjoyed before World War II. He affirmed that the technological genius that had made the nation great could be used to keep it safe. By repeatedly and eloquently stressing that the United States would not exploit its invulnerability to the detriment of others—it would never be the aggressor—he played to Americans' traditional belief in their inno-cence. The SDI proposal immediately shifted the agenda of the national security debate, undercutting an international movement to freeze nuclear weapons at existing levels. Reagan's public approval ratings soared. SDI en-couraged public support for the rest of his enormously expensive defense program. It helped secure his reelection in 1984.[22]

SDI also intensified already pronounced Cold War tensions. It infuri-ated and alarmed Soviet leaders by raising the possibility that the United States could create a partially effective missile defense system that would give it a first-strike capability. At the end of 1983, the so-called Year of the Missile, for the first time in more than fifteen years, the two nations were not discussing arms control in any forum. By this time, Soviet-American relations had descended to their lowest point in years. Fears of nuclear Ar-mageddon had risen to their highest level since the Cuban missile crisis. In Western Europe and the United States, concern about nuclear war rose in proportion to the failure of the arms control talks. The Soviets were increasingly agitated by Reagan's inflammatory rhetoric, U.S. han-dling of arms control negotiations, and especially SDI. American officials expressed outrage at the September 1 downing of the South Korean air-liner, bitterly denouncing what they saw as a deliberate Soviet move. This incident "demonstrated vividly," Garthoff has written, "how deeply rela-tions between the two countries had plunged. Each was only too ready to assume the worst of the other and rush not only to judgment but also to premature indictment."[23] Later that month, a Soviet satellite mistakenly picked up the approach of five U.S. missiles, triggering a full nuclear alert. Perhaps only the bold and timely intervention of a forty-four-year-old lieutenant colonel who suspected an error and overrode the comput-ers averted a counterstrike that could have killed as many as one hundred million Americans.[24] In the tense and conflict-ridden atmosphere of late 1983, only a fool would have predicted that within five years the two Cold

22. Boyer, "Selling Star Wars," 15–19, 26–27.
23. Garthoff, Détente, 1016.
24. Washington Post, February 10, 1999.

War combatants would be negotiating major arms reduction agreements and within ten years the epic struggle would have ended.

II

Reagan's diplomacy was at its worst in the Middle East. United States policies lacked clear direction and purpose. They were often naive in conception and amateurish in execution. They veered between intervention and abstention. Designed on occasion to demonstrate America's toughness, they frequently underscored its weakness. The best that can be said is that the administration had the good sense—belatedly—to disentangle from a hopeless mess in Lebanon and to avoid rash actions elsewhere.

The tone was established at the outset. More divided on the Middle East than on any other issue, U.S. officials could not agree where to go with the Camp David peace process inherited from Carter. They therefore decided to put the Arab-Israeli dispute on hold. A "Hollywood poolside Zionist," in the words of David Schoenbaum, Reagan had long admired Israel's steadfast defense of its sovereignty. As an actor and rising politician, he had supported fair treatment of Jews. He had also become a spokesperson for an emerging group of zealously pro-Israel evangelical Christians. Thus, not surprisingly, the administration set out to revive the special relationship with Israel and repair the damage done by Carter's alleged evenhandedness. But its main concern in the Middle East, as elsewhere, was the Soviet Union. In the words of a top State Department official, the Arab-Israeli conflict should be put in a "strategic framework that recognizes and is responsible to the *larger threat* of Soviet expansionism." Ignoring the messy realities of Middle Eastern politics, Reagan officials reasoned that since Israel, Egypt, Jordan, and Saudi Arabia were all friends of the United States, they could be united in a "strategic consensus" to check Soviet advances in a vital region.[25]

The scheme was doomed to fail. The administration's proposed sale of advanced AWAC aircraft to Saudi Arabia to help defend against Iran and Iraq unleashed the full fury of the Israel lobby. Only after a prolonged and at times nasty debate did the Senate in late October approve the sale by a mere two votes. To appease Israel, the administration offered a memorandum of understanding providing for large U.S. purchases of Israeli products, joint military exercises, and "readiness activities." These moves antagonized the Arabs. In June 1981, Israeli jets bombed Iraq's

25. David Schoenbaum, *The United States and the State of Israel* (New York, 1993), 273–74.

Osiraq nuclear installation, a step that U.S. officials may have secretly applauded and even abetted but that had been taken without consultation and thus aroused concern about the consequences of Israeli independence. More seriously, despite U.S. appeals for restraint, Israel in December annexed the Golan Heights, an area it deemed essential to defend against Syria. The administration responded by rescinding the memorandum of understanding and shutting off military aid. "What kind of talk is this— 'penalizing' Israel?" Prime Minister Menachem Begin snarled. "Are we a banana republic?" Begin answered his own question six months later, again over U.S. protests, by invading Lebanon. "Boy, that guy makes it hard for you to be his friend," a befuddled Reagan moaned.[26] By then, U.S.-Israeli relations were as strained as at any time in years. America's Arab friends held it responsible for Israeli aggression. The strategic consensus collapsed amidst Middle Eastern recriminations. By late 1982, the administration was moving back toward the Camp David Accords.

A crisis in Lebanon thwarted any new initiatives. Using a terrorist assassination attempt against its ambassador to Britain as the pretext for a move it had long been considering, Israel in June 1982 invaded neighboring Lebanon to eliminate Syrian influence, strike a "knockout blow" against Yasser Arafat's Palestine Liberation Organization (PLO) based there, and establish a friendly Christian government. The attack came during a lull in terrorist activities and at a time when the threat to Israel had eased. It brought worldwide condemnation. The reaction was even more hostile when Israeli units drove into Beirut, igniting the powder keg of hatreds that was Lebanon. What Israel had hoped would be a quick and decisive strike became a quagmire, a modern nation with the most up-to-date military hardware combating fifteen thousand guerrillas in a city of one half million people in a war it could not win.[27]

Lebanon became for the United States, in the words of Reagan biographer Lou Cannon, a "case study of foreign policy calamity," a "catastrophe born of good intentions."[28] If it had not given Israel the go-ahead, the administration had at least left the light blinking a bright yellow. In the aftermath, reading from note cards, a coolly detached Reagan could do little more than scold an unrepentant Begin. To make the best of a bad situation, a deeply divided administration, without careful analysis or preparation, more or less adopted Israel's goals as its own, seeking to use the invasion to

26. Douglas Little, *American Orientalism: The United States and the Middle East Since 1945* (Chapel Hill, N.C., 2004), 111; Laurence L. Barrett, *Gambling with History: Reagan in the White House* (New York, 1984), 271.

27. Schoenbaum, *United States and Israel*, 286.

28. Cannon, *Reagan*, 390.

get Soviet-backed Syria out of Lebanon, weaken the PLO, make Lebanon genuinely independent, and persuade it to sign a peace treaty with Israel. The United States staunchly backed the efforts of Amin Gemayel to establish an independent Lebanese government. For the first time Reagan got tough with Begin, insisting that Israel stop bombing the Palestinians while they were withdrawing. "Menachem, this is a holocaust," he berated the Israeli leader. "Mr. President, I think I know what a holocaust is," Begin sarcastically retorted.[29] At the urging of new secretary of state George Shultz and over the vigorous objections of Weinberger and the military, Reagan, without a clear idea what they were to accomplish or how they would go about it, agreed in July 1982 to send a detachment of eight hundred U.S. Marines to join a multinational peacekeeping force in Lebanon.

"Lebanon is a harsh teacher," Middle East expert William Quandt has written. "Those who try to ignore its harsh realities . . . usually end up paying a high price."[30] As many as twenty-five armed factions waged unrelenting war with each other in a country made up of a bewildering array of political, religious, and ethnic groups: Maronite and other Christians, Sunni and Shiite Muslims, fierce Druze mountain tribesmen, an offshoot of the Shi'as, seventeen different sects in all. Arrival of U.S. forces in August 1982 was followed by a deceptive calm, but the country soon exploded. Israel sent Christian militia into West Beirut to root out remaining elements of the PLO, causing a bloody massacre of a thousand Palestinians that further destabilized Lebanon, drew widespread international criticism, and discredited both Israel and the United States. Supporting the ineffectual Gemayel plunged the United States into the middle of a hopelessly complicated civil war. In April 1983, a terrorist bomb blew up the U.S. embassy in Beirut, killing seventeen Americans. The United States responded with air attacks and naval bombardment against locations suspected of harboring terrorists. Withdrawn to their ships after their apparent initial success and then sent back into the maelstrom, the marines, now 1,400 strong, found themselves in the late summer of 1983 hunkered down in the midst of intense and hopelessly confused fighting in Beirut. In the early morning hours of October 23, 1983, a truck bomb with the explosive force of twelve thousand tons of TNT, the largest non-nuclear blast to this time, destroyed marine headquarters, killing 241 of its sleeping occupants. The normally buoyant Reagan recalled it as the "saddest day of my presidency, perhaps the saddest day of my life."[31]

29. Ibid., 401.
30. Ibid., 406.
31. Reagan, *American Life*, 437.

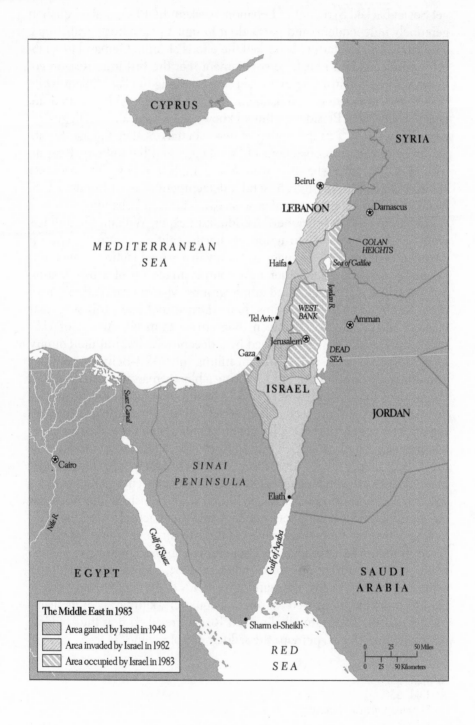

CYPRUS

SYRIA

Beirut ⊛

LEBANON

Damascus ⊛

MEDITERRANEAN
SEA

GOLAN
HEIGHTS

Haifa •

Sea of Galilee

Jordan R.

WEST
BANK

Tel Aviv •

⊛ Amman

Gaza •

Jerusalem ⊛

DEAD
SEA

ISRAEL

JORDAN

⊛ Cairo

SINAI
PENINSULA

Suez Canal

Nile R.

Elath •

Gulf of Suez

Gulf of Aqaba

SAUDI
ARABIA

EGYPT

The Middle East in 1983

Area gained by Israel in 1948
Area invaded by Israel in 1982
Area occupied by Israel in 1983

Sharm el-Sheikh •

RED
SEA

| 0 | 25 | 50 Miles |
| 0 | 25 | 50 Kilometers |

The bloody Sunday in Beirut ended the Lebanon intervention. Critical of the operation from the start, Weinberger and U.S. military leaders pushed for immediate evacuation of the marines. Shultz urged that they stay, and Reagan was reluctant to be pushed out. The administration thus set out to extricate them without losing face. It skillfully used the contemporaneous and successful invasion of tiny Grenada in the Caribbean to distract attention from the humiliation and grief of Beirut. But as the Lebanese army collapsed and pressures at home mounted for withdrawal, U.S. officials had little choice but to liquidate an ill-conceived venture. In February 1984, the marines were "redeployed" to their ships. Spokespersons now downplayed the importance of a country to which just recently they had attached the greatest significance. The United States had stuck "its hand into a thousand-year-old hornet's nest with the expectation that our mere presence might pacify the hornets," Army Col. Colin Powell, a top military adviser to Weinberger, later recalled.[32]

Powell and his boss immediately set out to prevent such deployments in the future. Over the next year, the two of them crafted a long list of conditions under which U.S. forces should be deployed. What came to be called the Weinberger or Powell Doctrine was an immediate response to the debacle in Lebanon and also to the secretary of defense's nasty, ongoing feud with Shultz over the commitment of military forces abroad. Weinberger later conceded that it also reflected the "terrible mistake" of sending forces to Vietnam without ensuring popular support and providing them the means to win. Made public in late 1984, the "doctrine" provided that U.S. troops must be committed only as a last resort and if it was in the national interest. Objectives must be clearly defined and attainable. Public support must be assured, and the means provided to ensure victory. The doctrine provoked a bloody fight within the Reagan administration— Shultz labeled it the "Vietnam Syndrome in spades." It was never given official sanction. But top military officers staunchly supported it, and as Joint Chiefs chairman in the 1990s Powell would fight vigorously for the application of what had become a doctrine bearing his name.[33]

The U.S. withdrawal left Lebanon more conflict-ridden than ever. Driven out of Beirut, the PLO scattered across the Middle East, and Arafat's position was badly damaged. The Israeli government was torn by internal crisis. Peace seemed more remote than before its ill-fated invasion.

32. Colin Powell, *My American Journey* (New York, 1996), 281.
33. Ibid., 302–3; Caspar W. Weinberger, *Fighting for Peace: Seven Critical Years in the Pentagon* (New York, 1990), 8–9, 31; George P. Shultz, *Turmoil and Triumph: My Years as Secretary of State* (New York, 1993), 649–51.

Libya and its mercurial leader, Muammar el-Qaddafi, proved yet another headache for the United States. A devout Muslim, passionately anti-colonial, the colonel had seized power in a 1969 coup that eliminated a pro-Western regime. Qaddafi entertained Nasser-like visions of leading the Arab world in triumph against the West; he had decidedly un-Nasser-like dreams of restoring Islamic fundamentalism. He closed down U.S. and British military bases, accepted Soviet aid, nationalized foreign holdings, and used oil revenues to finance terrorism and revolution. An inveterate foe of Israel, he supported Arab extremists in Syria and opposed moderates friendly to the United States in Egypt and Jordan. He also subverted his African neighbors Chad, Sudan, and Niger. By the mid-1970s, the colonel had moved to the top of America's enemies list. In 1980, Carter broke diplomatic relations.[34] Because Qaddafi took special delight in tweaking the American eagle's beak, the Reagan administration became obsessed with him. Haig labeled him a "cancer that had to be cut out," Reagan a "mad dog." The administration also saw his provocations as a pretext to demonstrate that the United States would no longer be pushed around.

In 1981, it took steps to housebreak the mad dog. The navy conducted "training exercises" in the Gulf of Sidra to challenge Qaddafi's claim to a 120-mile "Zone of Death" off Libyan shores. When Libyan planes attacked U.S. jets, the Americans, to the president's delight, shot them down. Qaddafi retaliated by widening his terrorist attacks. In response to intelligence reports of Libyan death threats against Reagan and other U.S. officials, some of them of dubious reliability, the administration prepared for military retaliation. A top-secret task force searched for ways to get rid of Qaddafi without violating restrictions against assassination of foreign leaders. It ordered all Americans out of Libya. In February 1982, the United States stopped purchasing Libyan oil.

The linkage of Qaddafi with international terrorism in Reagan's second term furnished the excuse for action long on the drawing board. Terrorism traditionally has been the weapon of the weak. The use of violence to further political aims, with innocent civilians often the victims, had roots as deep as humankind. The growing frustration of Arabs and especially Palestinians after the Six-Day War brought terrorism full force to the Middle East. Its proliferation in the 1970s elevated it to the top of U.S. foreign policy concerns.[35]

---

34. Little, *Orientalism*, 212–14.
35. "Terrorism," in Bruce W. Jentleson and Thomas G. Paterson, *Encyclopedia of U.S. Foreign Relations*, 4 vols. (New York, 1997), 4:186–91.

Reagan vowed "swift and effective retribution" against terrorists but found himself handcuffed in doing anything. The administration had been embarrassed by the way terrorists had driven it from Lebanon, and seven Americans were held captive there after the withdrawal. In June 1985, a TWA flight was hijacked, and in the full glare of publicity thirty-nine Americans were held captive for seventeen days. During the Christmas holidays, terrorists exploded bombs in airports in Rome and Vienna, killing five Americans. Reagan was stunned by the December attacks. Libya was a handy target. The smoking gun came in the form of intelligence linking Qaddafi to the December 1985 bombing of a West German discotheque in which one GI was killed, fifty injured.[36]

Claiming "irrefutable" evidence connecting Qaddafi to recent terrorist attacks, Reagan ordered retaliation. In the spring of 1986, the navy returned to the Gulf of Sidra and attacked Libyan naval forces and shore installations. In April, the administration ordered air attacks on Tripoli itself, allegedly in retaliation for Libyan sponsorship of terrorism and against facilities used to prepare terrorist activities. The real purpose was likely to eliminate Qaddafi. In either case, the bombing failed. The United States dropped ninety two-thousand-pound bombs, destroying Libya's air force and Qaddafi's residence. Thirty civilians died and many more were injured, provoking Libyan charges of terrorism against the United States. Qaddafi's house and the tent he often slept in were hit. Family members suffered injuries; a fifteen-month-old adopted daughter was killed. The colonel himself survived, perhaps, an air force officer lamented, because he had been in the toilet.[37]

The bombing of Tripoli had mixed results. In the immediate aftermath, the volatile Libyan leader was conspicuous by his silence, producing U.S. boasts that the bombing had shut him up. In any event, having made its point, the administration seemed willing to accord Qaddafi the inattention he deserved. The absence of further major terrorist attacks evoked claims that Reagan had effectively dealt with a major problem, but the truth appears more complicated. More important than the bombing in dealing with terrorism were the improved internal security measures taken by the Western European nations and their expulsion of Libyan diplomats and others suspected of belonging to terrorist networks. In addition, U.S. and European sanctions forced Syria to dismantle terrorist operations that were more significant than Libya's. The apparent lull in late 1986 was deceptive. The number of incidents actually increased the next year. Moreover, the

36. Reagan, *American Life*, 511, 514, 517–19.
37. Little, *Orientalism*, 248–49.

Western nations seemed only slightly better prepared to cope with terrorism than before, and their continuing vulnerability left open the possibility of new attacks at any time. When four Americans were kidnapped in 1987, Reagan publicly and ruefully conceded that there was little he could do. The December 1988 explosion of a Pan American airliner over Lockerbie, Scotland, from a terrorist bomb, later linked to Libya, underscored the stubborn persistence of a problem that vexed the administration like no other.

While attempting to tame Qaddafi with bombs, the administration also sought to open doors to Iran through the sale of arms, an ill-conceived, bumbling, and illegal ploy that damaged its credibility abroad and popularity at home.[38] In September 1980, Iran and Iraq plunged into a bloody struggle of attrition that would last almost nine years and cost an estimated seven hundred thousand dead, nearly two million wounded. The United States at first supported Saddam Hussein's Iraq, but as Iran faltered in the mid-1980s some officials found reasons to approach Tehran. Reagan was obsessed with recovering the seven hostages held by pro-Iranian extremists in Lebanon, and indications that Tehran might be able to influence their fate enticed him to trade arms for their release. He reportedly told friends that he was willing to go to prison to get the hostages out.[39] CIA director Casey believed that growing factionalism in Tehran might enable the United States to establish contacts among "moderates" that could be useful if the Khomeini government fell. As the USSR stepped up aid to Iraq, some Americans worried that an Iranian defeat would leave the Persian Gulf open to Soviet penetration. Others listened to Israelis who suggested that Iran might be brought around to a more moderate position. National Security Adviser Robert McFarlane, a lightweight notoriously lacking in foreign policy experience and political acumen, entertained grandiose visions of duplicating with Iran Kissinger's dramatic opening to China.[40]

Thus began an imbroglio that would temporarily cripple the Reagan presidency. The misadventure was made possible by Reagan's detachment, Shultz and Weinberger's inability to cooperate in stopping a venture both vigorously opposed, and the absence of a strong White House chief of staff to rein in misguided NSC zealots. Between the late summer

38. Cannon, *Reagan*, 589–738, provides a full analysis; the official report is in President's Special Review Board, *Tower Commission Report: The Full Text of the President's Special Review Board* (New York, 1987).
39. Cannon, *Reagan*, 541, 609–11, 630–31.
40. Ibid., 596, 613, 627–41.

of 1985 and the autumn of 1986, NSC operatives sold to Iran 2,004 TOW anti-tank missiles and fifty HAWK anti-aircraft missiles for assurances of assistance in securing the release of American hostages. The gambit violated the nation's announced policy of denying weapons to nations aiding terrorists and its arms embargo against Iran. U.S. officials did not inform Congress what they were doing, as the law required. They relied on Israel, which had its own interests in the matter, and on Manuchehr Ghorbanifar, a shady Iranian middleman who had failed numerous CIA lie detector tests and had been correctly called a "talented fabricator." At times the affair took on the trappings of farce, as when McFarlane and his assistant Marine Lt. Col. Oliver North, traveling under false passports, carried to Tehran a key-shaped cake and a Bible signed by Reagan as gestures of U.S. goodwill. On another occasion, North conducted a bizarre late-night tour of the White House for a member of Iran's Revolutionary Guard. The Americans overcharged the Iranians for many of the weapons and in some cases turned over old Israeli stocks, some, ironically, still bearing the Star of David. In the end, they were outmatched as bargainers, exchanging weapons for promises of the release of hostages from those they condescendingly dismissed as "rug merchants."[41]

What became known as "Irangate" produced, in Cannon's apt phrase, "a catastrophe" that "sometimes resembled a comic opera with tragic overtones and an unhappy ending."[42] The United States secured the release of only three hostages—three others were promptly taken to replace them. Reagan had repeatedly vowed not to deal with terrorists. When a Beirut newspaper broke the story in November 1986, his credibility was shattered. His lame efforts to justify a bad deal in terms of geopolitics fell flat. He had been so successful avoiding blame for anything that went wrong that he was known as the Teflon president, the man to whom nothing stuck. Irangate changed that, at least for a time. The president appeared ignorant or incompetent—or both. His administration descended into bitter infighting as beleaguered officials tried to save their skins. A long-restless Congress was spurred to go after a once invulnerable president. When it became known that proceeds from the arms sales were used to get around congressional restrictions against aiding U.S.-backed revolutionaries in Nicaragua, the administration was for a time reduced to impotence. Another president found himself stuck to the Iranian tar baby.

To keep oil flowing through the Persian Gulf, the administration in the summer of 1987 assembled in the Persian Gulf an armada of some thirty

41. Ibid., 640, 647–52.
42. Ibid., 639.

warships including the legendary battleship USS *Missouri*. The stated aims were to defend freedom of the seas and, of course, to deflect Soviet influence from a critical region. From the outset, the Persian Gulf intervention was surrounded by controversy. The Reagan administration never clearly explained why it acted. The cost was astronomical—$1 million a day. United States naval forces were bound by defensive rules of engagement and exposed to people the chief of naval operations admitted were "a little bit loony." On several occasions, the United States came close to getting sucked into the war. In May 1987, an Iraqi aircraft mistakenly attacked the USS *Stark*, killing thirty-seven sailors. A year later, a U.S. warship struck an Iranian mine and was disabled. The navy retaliated by putting out of action much of the tiny Iranian "fleet." In July 1988, nervous sailors aboard the USS *Vincennes* mistakenly shot down a civilian Iranian airliner, killing all of the 290 passengers and crew. Despite all these dangers, the convoy achieved valuable results. By helping numerous convoys steam safely through the gulf, the navy managed to sustain oil shipments from the Middle East to Western Europe and Japan. United States intervention contributed at least indirectly to the end of the Iran-Iraq war in July 1988.[43]

During 1988, world attention shifted back to the basics of Middle East politics. In late 1987, Palestinians in the Gaza Strip and West Bank territories occupied by Israel during the 1967 war launched a spontaneous and apparently leaderless series of sustained riots and demonstrations, including direct attacks on Israeli soldiers. Israel responded with repression, and by December 1988 more than three hundred Palestinians had been killed, seven thousand injured, and five thousand jailed in what came to be called the "uprising," or *intifada* (literally translated as shaking off). Initially reluctant to intrude in what was plainly an intractable and explosive problem, the Reagan administration saw no choice as the violence escalated. Revising old proposals to meet new circumstances, Shultz set forth a plan for an interim period of Palestinian "self-administration" in the occupied territories preliminary to a broader settlement between Israel and its Arab neighbors. PLO leader Yasser Arafat eventually agreed to a dialogue looking toward peace talks, but Israel continued to reject Shultz's proposals and set out to create more settlements in the occupied territories. After seven years of erratic U.S. involvement, and considerable frustration, the Middle East remained as volatile and dangerous as ever.[44]

43. Little, *Orientalism*, 250–52.
44. Ibid., 295–97.

III

In the April 1, 1985, issue of *Time* magazine, conservative columnist Charles Krauthammer hailed the emergence of a "Reagan Doctrine" of "overt and unashamed" aid to "freedom fighters" seeking to overthrow "nasty Communist governments."[45] Although it was given a name only in the second term, and then by a journalist, what came to be called the Reagan Doctrine was established policy from the start.[46] The administration's major innovation in foreign affairs, it marked a sharp departure from the dominant trends of Cold War foreign policy. John Foster Dulles had talked of rolling back Communist gains in Eastern Europe. The United States at times had attempted to destabilize and even overthrow leftist governments. But in general, containment had meant acquiescence in Communist governments already in power. The Reagan Doctrine was rooted in long-standing right-wing disdain for containment. It was pushed by conservative members of Congress and administration hardliners, especially CIA director Casey, as a way to exploit Soviet overextension, roll back recent gains, counter the noxious Brezhnev Doctrine, by which the Kremlin had claimed the duty to intervene anywhere socialism was threatened, and even undermine the USSR itself. Reagan enthusiasts claim great success for the doctrine, especially in Afghanistan, where they assign it a major role in America's Cold War victory.[47] In truth, the vigor of its implementation never matched the heat of its rhetoric. Even in Afghanistan, where it enjoyed some tactical success, its strategic impact has been overstated.

Although it is not generally included under the Reagan Doctrine, a non-military covert program in Poland stands as a modest success story. In Eastern Europe, generally, the CIA after 1982 had encouraged and helped finance protests, demonstrations, newspaper and magazine articles, and television and radio shows highlighting the evils of Soviet domination. Carter had initiated covert action in Poland. In June 1982, Reagan gained Pope John Paul II's blessings for an expanded program for the pontiff's native country. Casey and others considered Poland the weakest link in the Soviet bloc. The United States helped the non-Communist opposition group Solidarity stay in contact with the West and promote its cause inside Poland. United States funds purchased personal computers

45. *Time*, April 1, 1985.
46. James M. Scott, *Deciding to Intervene: The Reagan Doctrine and American Foreign Policy* (Durham, N.C., 1996), 19–21.
47. William J. Daugherty, *Executive Secrets: Covert Action and the Presidency* (Lexington, Ky., 2004), 189.

and fax machines and assisted Solidarity members in using them to publish newsletters and propaganda. The covert program helped keep Solidarity alive during the years of martial law and prepared it to seize power when the regime collapsed.[48]

Elsewhere, the Reagan Doctrine was applied unevenly and with mixed results. As part of its broader strategy of opposing Soviet expansionism and that of its clients, the administration furnished limited, covert aid to a disparate and unwieldy coalition of insurgents opposing the Vietnamese-imposed puppet government of Cambodia. No U.S. officials were eager for reintervention in former French Indochina. They also worried that aid might fall into the hands of the despicable Khmer Rouge, the most potent of the rebel factions. Assistance therefore remained very small, was distributed through the Association of Southeast Asian Nations (ASEAN), and had no more than a marginal effect on the diplomatic settlement that led to eventual Vietnamese withdrawal.[49]

In southern Africa, race and the Cold War defined U.S. policies. Reagan and his top advisers had little sympathy for black nationalism, linking the African National Congress with Communism. Rather than challenge apartheid, they claimed to follow a policy of "constructive engagement," but they said nothing when the South African government brutally cracked down on dissidents. Under the inspirational leadership of Archbishop Desmond Tutu, black protest in South Africa won rising international sympathy during the 1980s, along with growing demands for sanctions against the Pretoria government. In the United States, the drive for sanctions came mainly from private-sector pressure groups, with vocal support from college campuses. Responding to moral issues and political exigencies, Congress in 1986 passed over Reagan's veto a bill imposing broad sanctions. Shultz admitted that the domestic costs of leaving the South African government to its own devices far exceeded the benefits.[50]

The Reagan Doctrine was employed in southern Africa in a cautious and entirely practical manner. State Department pragmatists fended off heavy pressures from congressional conservatives and administration hardliners to assist a brutal right-wing rebel group in Mozambique. Indeed, ironically, as part of its regional strategy, the United States furnished limited aid to a leftist government.[51] In Angola, U.S. aid was employed to support a broader diplomatic effort to get Cuba and South Africa out, end the

---

48. Ibid., 186, 201–3.
49. Scott, *Reagan Doctrine*, 108–10.
50. Thomas Borstelmann, *The Cold War and the Color Line: American Race Relations in the Global Arena* (Cambridge, Mass., 2001), 260–61.
51. Scott, *Reagan Doctrine*, 207.

civil war, and secure independence for Namibia. The administration in 1985 initiated covert assistance through Zaire to UNITA's Jonas Savimbi, the darling of the American right. But as administered by the State Department, the assistance was used not to defeat the Soviet and Cuban-backed MPLA but through what Shultz called "stealth diplomacy" to encourage a diplomatic settlement. By helping achieve a military stalemate after Cuban and South African escalation, U.S. aid may have contributed to the withdrawal of outside powers and the beginning of negotiations. Continued assistance to Savimbi actually delayed an end to the Angolan civil war.[52]

The Reagan Doctrine enjoyed major success in Afghanistan, the largest covert operation to that time, but even here the administration's noisy rhetoric belied its generally cautious actions. The role of U.S. aid was less decisive than the Reaganites have claimed. Carter had initiated limited, covert assistance to the Afghan and foreign mujahideen fighting the Soviet invaders. From the outset, Casey pushed to "bleed" the Soviets in Afghanistan, but the administration moved slowly for fear that direct U.S. involvement might provoke Moscow to escalate the Afghan war or even attack Pakistan. Responding to mounting pressure from Congress and public lobbying groups, the administration increased aid to the Afghan "freedom fighters" in 1983 and 1984. But it was only in March 1985, in response to a threat of Soviet escalation, that Reagan ordered his advisers to do "what's necessary to win."[53] Aid jumped from $122 million in 1984 to $630 million in 1987. Working through Pakistani intelligence, the CIA provided rebel forces intelligence gathered from satellites and other sources, established training camps for Afghan fighters, and even helped plan some operations. In what is generally considered the decisive move, the administration in early 1986 provided the Afghans with lethal handheld Stinger anti-aircraft missiles. The Stingers at first exacted a devastating toll on Soviet helicopters and have been labeled the "silver bullet" that drove the USSR from Afghanistan.[54]

The allegedly decisive significance of the Stingers has swelled into one of the great myths of the Cold War. After heavy early losses, the Soviets developed countermeasures to neutralize the missiles. In any event, the new Soviet leader, Mikhail Gorbachev, largely out of a need for U.S. trade and technology, had decided to withdraw from Afghanistan even

---

52. Ibid., 121, 147.
53. Ibid., 47, 58.
54. Alan J. Kuperman, "The Stinger Missiles and U.S. Intervention in Afghanistan," *Political Science Quarterly* 114 , no. 2 (1999), 220, 244–45.

before the first Stingers arrived.[55] Like most military victories, moreover, the Reagan Doctrine's success in Afghanistan bore hidden costs in the form of what the CIA calls "blowback." The need for Pakistan's support in Afghanistan led the United States to turn a blind eye toward its nuclear program. The cultivation of heroin financed much of the war in Afghanistan, undermining the simultaneous U.S. "war" on drugs. As the CIA had feared, large numbers of Stingers ended up on the shelves of the international arms bazaar. Some were purchased back at grossly inflated cost. United States aid also helped ensure the eventual triumph of the fundamentalist Taliban regime in Afghanistan. The Islamic fighters the United States helped train would in time turn on their benefactors, launching deadly attacks against U.S. assets abroad and even the American homeland itself.[56]

The major Third World battleground was closer to home. Echoing John Kennedy twenty years earlier, ambassador to the United Nations Jeanne Kirkpatrick called Central America and the Caribbean the "most important place in the world for us." Reagan and Casey believed that the defeat of Communism in one area might cause the Soviet empire to crumble.[57] Determined to roll back perceived Communist gains in its own backyard, the United States employed the Reagan Doctrine in Nicaragua and used old-fashioned gunboat diplomacy in Grenada in an effort to topple leftist governments. In El Salvador, it used conventional Cold War methods to bolster a right-wing government against leftist insurgents. Although it refrained from large-scale military intervention except in Grenada, the administration invested great energy and resources in the region. Central America became the political and emotional cause célèbre of the 1980s, a source of unrelenting and bitter dispute between conservatives and liberals over the nation's proper role in the world. The Reagan administration achieved none of its main goals, but its intervention had a huge impact on the region.[58]

By the time Reagan took office, U.S. dominance of a traditional sphere of influence was being challenged from without and within. America's traditional economic hegemony was threatened by competition from Japan

55. Ibid., 235–53.
56. Ibid., 253–58; John Prados, "Notes on the CIA's Secret War in Afghanistan," *Journal of American History* 89 (September 2002), 466–71.
57. Michael Schaller, "Reagan and the Cold War," in Kyle Longley et al., *Deconstructing Reagan: Conservative Mythology and America's Fortieth President* (Armonk, N.Y., 2007), 25–26.
58. John H. Coatsworth, *Central America and the United States: The Clients and the Colossus* (New York, 1994), 166.

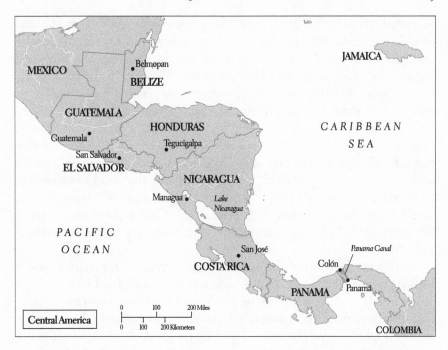

and Western Europe. Since the 1920s, the United States had relied on friendly military dictators such as Trujillo and Somoza to maintain order and protect its interests, but a half century later they too had come under fire. The worldwide economic crisis of the 1970s brought poverty and misery to the region and provoked mounting popular unrest. The Catholic Church had long been a bulwark of the established order, but in the 1970s, following principles set forth by Pope John XXIII, radical priests developed a liberation theology that encouraged the masses to assert themselves for democratic change.[59] Carter's human rights policy highlighted the abuses perpetrated by military governments; by cutting off military aid, it undermined their legitimacy and hence their authority. Before Carter left office, a coalition of revolutionaries had toppled the despised Anastasio Somoza in Nicaragua. As Reagan entered the White House, another threatened the government of El Salvador.

The administration's Central American policies developed from a jumble of conflicting ideas and forces. Cuba and the Soviet Union naturally

59. Kathleen M. Blee, "The Catholic Church and Central American Politics," in Kenneth M. Coleman and George C. Herring, eds., *The Central American Crisis: Sources of Conflict and the Failure of U.S. Policy* (Wilmington, Del., 1985), 55–71.

expressed sympathy for the revolutions in Nicaragua and El Salvador and provided limited assistance. Although they professed commitment to a pluralist democracy and a mixed economy, the Sandinistas—befitting their name—often took vocal anti-U.S. positions. "We have to be against the United States in order to reaffirm ourselves as a nation," one leader asserted.[60] Not surprisingly, therefore, Reagan and most of his top advisers expressed grave concern about a new "Soviet beachhead" in the hemisphere, "another Cuba." The president was also much taken with neo-conservative Kirkpatrick's 1980 article that attacked Carter's human rights policies for undermining friendly authoritarian governments that could evolve into democracies while indirectly encouraging totalitarian governments that would never change.[61] Many U.S. officials saw Central America as a place where the United States could reestablish its credibility in the aftermath of Vietnam.

There were also powerful constraints against intervention. Especially in its first months, the White House staff was determined not to let foreign policy interfere with passage of the president's economic program. Reagan himself was wary of intervention. His military advisers, still rebuilding the forces crippled by one disastrous Third World entanglement, were not disposed toward another. Polls made quite clear the public's lack of enthusiasm for sending U.S. troops to Central America. The mention of such a possibility was guaranteed to unloose a free-for-all in Congress.[62] Thus, while attaching rhetorical importance to the struggles in the Caribbean and Central America, the administration, except in Grenada, acted with some restraint. Even more than in the Middle East, moreover, Reagan's Central American policies reflected his administration's undisciplined managerial style.

Secretary of State Haig pushed Central America to the top of the foreign policy agenda before the Reaganites had settled into their offices. Viewing the region strictly in East-West terms, the hyper-energetic and volatile former Kissinger aide fired the department's Central American experts in the biggest purge since John Foster Dulles, replacing them with old Vietnam hands—the gang who couldn't shoot straight, they came to be called. He informed Reagan that tiny, impoverished El Salvador was "one you can win." Certain he had been given complete control over foreign policy, he

60. Stephen Kinzer, "Nicaragua: The Beleaguered Revolution," New York Times Magazine, August 28, 1983, 23.
61. William M. LeoGrande, Our Own Backyard: The United States in Central America, 1977–1992 (Chapel Hill, N.C., 1998), 54–56.
62. Cannon, Reagan, 344.

pushed for going to the source of the problem: Cuba. "You just give me the word," he bragged to the president in early 1981, "and I'll turn that fucking island into a parking lot." In February, the department released a white paper purporting to contain "definitive evidence" that Nicaragua, Cuba, and the Soviet Union were making El Salvador a key Cold War battleground.[63]

Although it stopped well short of Haig's recommendations, the administration made a substantial commitment in El Salvador. Haig's Cuban venture "scared the shit" out of even the hard-core anti-Communists around Reagan. His out-of-control, nationally televised statement that *he* was in control after a March 1981 assassination attempt on the president sealed his fate in the cabinet. The White House was also determined not to let Central America get in the way of the president's domestic program.[64] Still, the administration refused to leave El Salvador to its own devices. To support its regional anti-Communist offensive, it launched a major military buildup in neighboring Honduras and conducted much-publicized maneuvers in Central America. It increased military aid to El Salvador to $25 million and the number of U.S. military advisers to fifty-four. The goal shifted from ending the bloodshed and arranging a political settlement to defeating the insurgency, thus giving encouragement to the Salvadorean right, especially the notorious death squads who targeted even church leaders. Even these limited measures stirred memories of Vietnam, arousing sufficient protest in Congress and the country to underscore the difficulties of implementing a truly aggressive policy in Central America.[65]

Haig's "one you can win" brought much frustration for the United States and more misery for El Salvador. Throughout the first term, the administration engaged in a running battle with Congress over El Salvador, all the while implementing its policies, in former senator Sam Ervin's words, on the "windy side of the law."[66] The White House employed various subterfuges to adhere to its self-imposed limit of fifty-four advisers and increase military aid without congressional approval. Military assistance grew to more than $196 million in 1984. Massive economic aid helped cover the deficit caused by the government's military spending. Even with enormous U.S. support, the Salvadorean military could gain no more than a bloody stalemate. To appease Congress, the administration pushed for elections in El Salvador. In time, a crude, hybrid

63. LeoGrande, *Backyard*, 81–82, 86–88.
64. Cannon, *Reagan*, 344–45.
65. Walter LaFeber, "The Reagan Policy in Historical Perspective," in Coleman and Herring, *Central American Crisis*, 4–6.
66. LeoGrande, *Backyard*, 281.

form of democracy emerged there. The United States pinned its hopes on centrist José Napoleon Duarte, but the well-intentioned leader could neither control his military nor curb right-wing human rights abuses. He had little success implementing domestic reforms. Indeed, the austerity program Washington pushed on him in the mid-1980s imposed additional hardships on already impoverished people. The White House managed to get El Salvador off the front pages in the second term and could claim it had denied the insurgents victory. Without approval from the United States or his own military, however, Duarte could not end the war by negotiating with the insurgents. El Salvador remained wracked by violence, its economy in shambles.[67]

The administration's high-tech version of old-fashioned gunboat diplomacy in tiny Grenada in the fall of 1983 was more successful. With Cuban aid, the Marxist government of Maurice Bishop had built a twelve-thousand-foot jet runway on the 133-square-mile eastern Caribbean island and granted the Soviets permission to use it. Already nervous about a Cuba-Grenada-Nicaragua axis in the hemisphere, jittery U.S. officials were further alarmed in mid-October when extremists in the ruling party placed the government under house arrest and executed Bishop. Although Cuba had backed Bishop against those who killed him, an administration already obsessed with Grenada feared yet another "Soviet beachhead" in the Caribbean. Haunted by memories of Iran in 1979, the president worried that the eight hundred American medical students on the island might be taken hostage. Grenada also provided a much sought-after opportunity following the Lebanon debacle to burnish U.S. military credibility. Thus on October 25, Reagan dispatched a seven-thousand-man force to rescue the American students and "restore democracy" on Grenada.[68]

America's "lovely little war" (a phrase coined by a journalist) in Grenada did not come easily.[69] The United States lacked adequate intelligence, even accurate maps, for what was dubbed Operation Urgent Fury. Each of the military services insisted on a role. Coordination was poor at best, and the operation went off with anything but surgical precision. The landing force met stiff resistance from a small force of Cubans armed with obsolete weapons. Nine U.S. helicopters were lost; twenty-nine U.S. servicemen were killed, many from friendly fire and accidents, and more than one hundred wounded. The clumsy manner in which the mission was executed for a time left the students in harm's way. Ultimately, the operation succeeded

67. Ibid., 564–66; Coatsworth, *Central America*, 170–76.
68. Cannon, *Reagan*, 446–47; Richard A. Gabriel, *Military Incompetence: Why the American Military Doesn't Win* (New York, 1985), 149–50.
69. Cannon, *Reagan*, 448.

because it had to.[70] The vastly superior invading force rescued the students and took control of the island. Whatever the military flaws, Grenada was a huge political success. Reagan skillfully exploited the intervention to erase memories of Beirut. The administration exulted in what the president later called a "textbook success," reveled in this first rollback of Communism, and proclaimed that Grenada would send a clear message to Moscow, Havana, and especially Managua.[71]

Indeed, by the time of the Grenada operation, Nicaragua had become the focus of U.S. concern in Central America, a major test case for the Reagan Doctrine. In December 1981, at Casey's urging, Reagan authorized $20 million for a covert operation to organize and train in Honduras a five-hundred-man army of Nicaraguan "contras" (for counterrevolutionary). The stated purpose was to interdict Sandinista assistance for the Salvadoran insurgents, but top U.S. officials had more ambitious motives. The State Department hoped that a military threat might encourage the Sandinistas to negotiate, about what it was not entirely clear. Casey and the hawks wanted to "make the [Sandinista] bastards sweat."[72] For the president and many of his top advisers, the real aim was to overthrow the Sandinista government.

The not-so-covert war against Nicaragua grew steadily from 1981 to 1984. Reagan in time adopted the contras as his own, publicly referring to them as "our brothers" and the "moral equal of our Founding Fathers." He came to see Nicaragua as the major front in a global struggle "to repeal the infamous Brezhnev Doctrine, which contends that once a country has fallen into Communist darkness, it can never be allowed to see the light of freedom." The operation began with a small group of former officers from Somoza's National Guard. Supposedly limited to five hundred men, the contra force grew into a guerrilla army of ten thousand. Despite the increase in size, the contras never really threatened the government. They gained notoriety for repeated human rights abuses against peasants. The CIA took over operational control in late 1982. Agency operatives backed the contras' efforts the next year by attacking Nicaragua's fuel storage and mining its harbors. To intimidate Nicaragua, the United States in the summer and fall of 1983 conducted military operations in Honduras lasting six months and involving more than four thousand troops.[73]

70. Gabriel, *Military Incompetence*, 185.
71. Reagan, *American Life*, 455, 458; Cannon, *Reagan*, 449.
72. LeoGrande, *Backyard*, 331.
73. Ibid., 301–3, 317–18, 330–40, 363–64.

Even more than El Salvador, the widening war against Nicaragua provoked increasingly bitter debate in the country and Congress. Not persuaded of the urgency of the alleged Sandinista threat or the viability or legitimacy of the contras, and above all fearful of another Vietnam, Americans strongly opposed deepening involvement in Nicaragua. As early as October 1982, an already wary Congress forbade the use of U.S. funds to overthrow the Sandinista government, a restriction the administration readily dismissed by continuing to insist—disingenuously—that was not its intention. A more serious threat developed in 1984. Press reports of the CIA mining of Nicaraguan ports set off a furor and opened a sizeable credibility gap between the executive and Congress. A veteran of the glory days of the OSS in World War II, Casey had contempt for "those assholes on the Hill" and especially for congressional oversight of covert operations. From the outset, he had ignored, misled, or deceived legislators about Nicaragua. He mumbled almost unintelligibly—his voice had a "built-in scrambler," according to Weinberger—and when all else failed he gave answers no one could understand.[74] The realization after the mining operations that they had been repeatedly deceived on Nicaragua emboldened congressional foes of contra aid and infuriated even supportive legislators like Arizona senator Barry Goldwater. With a presidential election approaching, the administration in the summer of 1984 managed to get Nicaragua off the front pages by going through the motions of negotiating with the Sandinistas. But after months of often fractious debate, Congress in October passed another measure effectively cutting off funding for the contras. Reagan responded by instructing his subordinates to "do whatever you have to do to help these people keep body and soul together."[75]

The cutoff in aid and Reagan's open-ended instructions tested the ingenuity of NSC staffer Oliver North, a zealous marine labeled by one senator the only "five-star lieutenant colonel in the history of the military." Tireless, charming, not troubled by scruples about the truth or the law, North in the words of a colleague could "speak a blue haze of bull shit."[76] Utterly devoted to the president, he and his cohorts observed no bounds in carrying out what they thought were his wishes. Contemptuous of the institutions of government—their code name for the State Department was Wimp—North and his "cowboys," presumably with Casey's blessings, arranged an incredibly complex operation to implement policies outside the bureaucracy

74. Ibid, 300.
75. Schaller, "Reagan and the Cold War," 27.
76. LeoGrande, Backyard, 400.

and away from the scrutiny of Congress. In effect, they privatized U.S. foreign policy. With Reagan's knowledge and encouragement, NSC staffers solicited a total of $50 million from friendly governments such as Taiwan, Brunei, and Saudi Arabia, which alone contributed $32 million, and from right-wing U.S. citizens such as beer magnate Joseph Coors. In an early 1986 venture that North called a "neat idea" and Casey "the ultimate covert operation"—and that ultimately proved their undoing—they diverted to the contras funds from arms sold to Iran.[77] North used Project Democracy, an ostensibly private corporation established by Reagan to "cultivate the fragile flower of democracy" across the world, as the instrument of his operation. The "Enterprise," run by retired Air Force Gen. Richard Secord, had its own ships and airplanes and private landing strips throughout Central America, dummy corporations and secret banking accounts, and special highly sophisticated coding devices provided by North from the super-secret National Security Agency. Some of the operatives appear to have reaped handsome profits, and millions of dollars could not be accounted for. A $10 million contribution from the sultan of Brunei was mistakenly deposited in the account of a Geneva businessman.[78]

The administration's clumsy efforts to cover up its sins got it into more hot water. When the story of arms sales to Iran broke in November 1986, the Justice Department dawdled its investigation of NSC wrongdoing while North and his glamorous, equally zealous secretary, Fawn Hall, shredded thousands of "problem memos." National Security Adviser John Poindexter deleted five thousand e-mails (later retrieved). McFarlane doctored a "chronology" to obscure the president's role. Reagan at first alternated between denying knowledge of what had happened and blaming lapses of memory. "There was an awful lot going on and it's awfully easy to be a little short of memory," he confessed on one occasion. Testimony before a congressional committee investigating what came to be known as the Iran-Contra Affair subsequently revealed that he knew a great deal and had approved much. In time, he publicly boasted that funding the contras was "my idea to begin with."[79] The scandal at least temporarily crippled the Reagan presidency. The president's approval rating plummeted to 36 percent; in the fall elections, the Republicans lost control of the Senate. The Great Communicator escaped impeachment mainly because it could not be established that he had ordered the illegal actions.

77. Ibid., 407.
78. President's Special Review Board, *The Tower Commission Report* (New York, 1987), 51–61.
79. LeoGrande, *Backyard*, 638.

The war in Nicaragua ended through a bizarre, almost surreal, chain of events—despite rather than because of the United States. The architect of a cease-fire was Costa Rican president Oscar Arias Sánchez. Educated in the United States and Britain, a staunch anti-Communist who disliked the Sandinistas almost as much as the Reaganites, Arias feared that the contra war might escalate into a regional conflict. Small of stature, by reputation an intellectual, he proved a tough and creative diplomat. He devised a peace plan calling for a cease-fire, an end to outside aid, and democratization for Nicaragua. He locked the presidents of El Salvador and Honduras in a room until they went along, a trick he claimed to have learned from Franklin Roosevelt. He courageously stood up against bullying and threats from the United States; once when Reagan summoned him to the White House for a fifteen-minute lecture, Arias responded with a statement twice as long emphasizing that on Nicaragua the United States stood alone. In a strange gambit that backfired, the administration enlisted Democratic House of Representatives Speaker Jim Wright to draft a peace plan. When Wright backed Arias's proposals, an administration weakened by the Iran-Contra revelations had little choice but to go along. Defiant to the end, Reagan and his advisers counted on the Sandinistas to reject the plan and continued to seek to undermine it by securing additional contra aid. To Washington's shock, the Sandinistas went along because of Nicaragua's dire economic straits and in full expectation that they would win elections set for 1990. When Congress again rejected aid for the Nicaraguan rebels, the contras had no choice but to accept Arias's proposals. Despite persistent U.S. efforts at sabotage, a cease-fire was approved in March 1988. Although it did not bring peace, it did make war more difficult to wage.[80]

Once the most secure outpost of the U.S. empire, Central America during the Reagan years provided the most graphic example of the limits of U.S. power. Thinking it could win one in its own backyard, the United States set out in El Salvador and Nicaragua to exorcize the ghosts of Vietnam. The Reagan administration could claim victory in the narrow sense that the insurgents never gained power in El Salvador. Moreover, to the shock of everyone, the Sandinistas lost the 1990 election to a centrist coalition and willingly gave up power. In fact, the Reagan Doctrine ran aground in Central America. Despite millions of U.S. dollars, the insurgency dragged on in El Salvador, and the extreme right emerged victorious in March 1988 elections. Honduras was increasingly militarized and destabilized politically. Without the intervention of Arias and Wright, the

80. Ibid., 507–47.

elections that deposed the Sandinistas would never have taken place. The Reagan administration grossly exaggerated the Communist threat in Central America. It poured more than $5 billion into what became a "sterile regional bloodletting." At home, its misguided and often illegal policies polarized the political atmosphere and corrupted the political process. Abroad, it defied international institutions such as the UN and the World Court. Rarely in the history of U.S. foreign policy had so much zeal, energy, and money been invested in such a dubious and destructive cause. At the end, the White House's determination to back the contras "body and soul," in Reagan's words, seemed about little more than pride and stubborn commitment.[81]

The result for Central America was catastrophic, an estimated thirty thousand dead in Nicaragua (proportionately equal to the total U.S. killed in the Civil War, both World Wars, Korea, and Vietnam) and eighty thousand in El Salvador, many of them civilians. The United States "laid waste to Nicaragua," leaving an economy with 1,300 percent inflation and rampant unemployment.[82] The administration claimed some responsibility for the growth of democracy in Latin America as a whole, and during the 1980s seven civilian governments did come to power. But hemispheric leaders protested the "Centralamericanization" of U.S. policy and warned that a crisis caused by $420 billion of debt imperiled the fragile democratic gains and raised the threat of a new wave of extremism from left and right.[83]

IV

Had Reagan left office in 1987, his presidency would have gone down a failure, the victim of his own inattention and mismanagement so starkly manifested in Iran-Contra. In fact, even while he was reeling from setbacks in the Middle East and Central America, he was engaged in a dramatic and totally unexpected turnaround in relations with the Soviet Union. These initiatives would help bring about the *annus mirabilis* of 1989 when peace and freedom seemed to break out everywhere and a diplomatic revolution comparable to that of World War II began to take shape. In a little more than a year, Reagan rose from the ashes of scandal to heroic stature, the "man who ended the Cold War," in the exuberant

---

81. Kenneth M. Coleman and George C. Herring, eds., *Understanding the Central American Crisis: Sources of Conflict, U.S. Policy, and Options for Peace* (Wilmington, Del., 1991), 221–23.
82. LeoGrande, *Backyard*, 548.
83. Coleman and Herring, *Understanding the Central American Crisis*, 221–23.

words of one of his advisers.[84] A triumphalist myth took root among Reagan partisans that by standing forth boldly for freedom, confronting the Soviets across the world, and launching a military buildup they could not match, the former actor brought the "evil empire" to its knees.

The transformation in Soviet-American relations *was* sudden and momentous, and Reagan *did* play a major role, but its origins are much more complex than the triumphalists allow. Most decisive was the stunning volte-face engineered by Mikhail Gorbachev. In Reagan's first years, instability had gripped the Kremlin. The aged and infirm Brezhnev died in 1982 and was succeeded by former KGB head Yuri Andropov, who lasted but two years. Andropov's successor, Konstantin Chernenko, died little more than a year later. "How am I supposed to get anyplace with the Russians . . . ," Reagan quipped, "if they keep dying on me?"[85] Gorbachev brought stability and a new spirit to the Soviet government. Part of a generation of reform-minded officials, this onetime farm worker and aspiring actor broke sharply with the sclerotic patterns of his immediate predecessors. The child of peasants in the Caucasus, the self-confident, ambitious, and hard-driving Gorbachev combined a charm and sophistication so conspicuously lacking in most earlier Soviet leaders with toughness—a "nice smile but he's got iron teeth," said Foreign Minister Andrei Gromyko, who would later feel their bite.[86] Less ideological and more open-minded, he saw the need for major changes in foreign policy to make possible urgent domestic reforms. An incorrigible optimist, he set out to reform the Soviet system without destroying it, what he called *perestroika*, and to permit more openness, *glasnost*, without going all the way to democracy. In foreign policy, he determined to close what he called the "bleeding wound" in Afghanistan, shift to Eastern European Communist leaders responsibility for their own survival, and ease Cold War tensions in order to divert precious resources to domestic needs, secure desperately needed credits and technology from the West, and reduce the risk of nuclear war. Gorbachev's dramatic initiatives sprang more from internal exigencies than from external pressures.[87]

Reagan's change of heart evolved slowly and from a mix of motives. In a January 1984 speech, he conspicuously toned down the anti-Soviet rhetoric, spoke hopefully of peace, and in one of his more memorable passages wondered aloud what might happen if Ivan and Anya and Jim

---

84. Edwin Meese in McMahon, "Reagan Years," 370.
85. Reagan, *American Life*, 611.
86. Cannon, *Reagan*, 744.
87. Archie Brown, "Gorbachev and the End of the Cold War," in Richard K. Herrmann and Richard Ned Lebow, eds., *Ending the Cold War: Interpretations, Causation, and the Study of International Relations* (New York, 2004), 49–50.

and Sally (characters he made up) could sit down and talk together.[88] From the outset, he had viewed the military buildup as a means to nego-tiate from strength. He believed he had achieved that position by 1985 and, over the strong objections of hawks like Casey and Weinberger, was willing to test the waters.[89] Soviet-American tensions had escalated dan-gerously in Reagan's first three years in office, raising fears at home and among U.S. allies that in turn created pressures for more conciliatory policies. Nancy Reagan shared such concerns and regularly nudged her husband toward a more accommodating posture. The president felt cer-tain that his solid anti-Communist credentials would protect his right flank. After his overwhelming reelection in 1984, he was increasingly concerned about his place in history. Always inclined to reduce complex problems to the simplest terms, he had especially strong feelings on the nuclear issue. His reading of the Bible, especially its prophecies of the world ending in a climactic battle between good and evil at Armaged-don, aroused in him deeply emotional fears of nuclear war, a war that could "never be won and must never be fought," he told the Japanese Diet. He hoped to replace the doctrine of mutual assured destruction with one of "assured survival." He held conflicting visions of a world without nuclear weapons and one where people would be sheltered by the umbrella of nuclear defense, his cherished Star Wars.[90] Reagan's anti-nuclearism and his willingness to risk negotiations rather than his bluster and military buildup made possible the transformation in Soviet-American relations.[91]

With different personalities, the changes might have been delayed or never taken place, but what journalist Martin Walker has called an "ex-traordinary coincidence of two extraordinary men" played a vital role.[92] Personality was always more important to Reagan than the substance of policy. Encouraged by his friend British prime minister Margaret Thatcher, he concluded after their first meeting in late 1985 that Gor-bachev was a man he could work with.[93] He in turn worked his famous charm on his Soviet counterpart. Each leader "served the other's purpose," Cannon has noted. They initiated a private correspondence addressing

88. Oberdorfer, *Cold War to New Era*, 72.
89. Alan P. Dobson, "The Reagan Administration, Economic Warfare, and Starting to Close Down the Cold War," *Diplomatic History* 29 (June 2005), 547, 555.
90. Cannon, *Reagan*, 289–91, 475.
91. Daniel Deudney and John Ikenberry, "Who Won the Cold War?" *Foreign Policy* 87 (Summer 1992), 126–28, 132, 137.
92. Walker, *Cold War*, 291.
93. Oberdorfer, *Cold War to New Era*, 154.

a variety of issues. Despite strong differences between them and missteps along the way, they developed, in Reagan's words, a "kind of chemistry."[94] By the time Reagan left office, they were at ease with each other. The only discordant note was the frosty relationship between Nancy Reagan and Raisa Gorbachev, who seem to have taken an instant dislike to each other and never had second thoughts.

Events reinforced the two leaders' willingness to indulge in what Gorbachev called "new thinking." When Reagan learned of the Soviet reaction to NATO's Able Archer exercises during those extremely tense months in late 1983, he drew the obvious—but for Cold War adversaries often elusive—conclusion that the Soviets feared the United States as much as Americans feared them. This epiphany enabled him to put himself in their place and thus conclude that negotiations might be both feasible and productive.[95] The nuclear catastrophe at Chernobyl near Kiev in the summer of 1985 had a profound impact on both men. After a typically clumsy cover-up gave the Kremlin an international black eye, a chastened Gorbachev determined that *glasnost* was the route to take abroad as well as at home. Chernobyl reinforced Reagan's already emotional fears of a nuclear Armageddon and his determination to rid the world of nuclear weapons.[96]

Even with the commitment of the two heads of state, the path was littered with obstacles. Gorbachev faced stern opposition from his military advisers and hard-line civilians who attacked his "Capitulationist Line" toward the West. It took time for him to replace old-timers like Gromyko with his own people like Eduard Shevardnadze. He was never able to build a firm consensus around his "new thinking" and repeatedly had to outmaneuver his foes.[97] The deep divisions within the Reagan administration, especially on nuclear issues, enormously complicated the formulation of agreed-upon positions. Hard-liners like Weinberger, Casey, and arms control negotiator Kenneth Adelman fought bitterly with Shultz and the pragmatists. Differences between the two nations remained sharp even if no longer generally beyond resolution. On Afghanistan, for example, where they agreed in principle, they could still get tangled up in details. And on issues like SDI, which Gorbachev was determined to eliminate and Reagan to implement, the differences proved insurmountable.[98]

94. Cannon, *Reagan*, 740, 755.
95. Oberdorfer, *Cold War to New Era*, 67.
96. Cannon, *Reagan*, 756, 757.
97. Matthew Evangelista, "Turning Points in Arms Control," in Herrmann and Lebow, *Ending the Cold War*, 90–92.
98. Cannon, *Reagan*, 742–43, 758–59.

Moving in fits and starts through four summits in four years, the two leaders eventually registered signal achievements. At their first meeting in Geneva in November 1985, they agreed vaguely to seek 50 percent reductions in nuclear weapons—but on little else. At a hastily called October 1986 summit in Reykjavik, Iceland, only SDI seemed to stand in the way of truly astounding achievements. Before the meeting, Reagan had revived the "zero option" proposal to eliminate all intermediate-range nuclear forces (INF) in Europe. Gorbachev, who held the initiative throughout the period, countered with bold proposals for huge across-the-board cuts and the elimination of all nuclear weapons by the year 2000. During a "bizarre weekend" in a seaside house said to be haunted, he advanced the deadline by five years. The idea appealed to Reagan's anti-nuclearism. Their apparent accord "shocked" the negotiations into a "whole new dimension." After an extended late-night session, the initially stunned technical experts appeared to agree on terms. But Reagan flatly rejected Gorbachev's condition that SDI be confined to the laboratory. The Reykjavik summit broke up amidst great disappointment and without any agreement.[99]

Desperate for success and persuaded by physicist Andrei Sakharov that SDI would not work and in any event might be a bluff, Gorbachev subsequently isolated the INF issue and the two sides carved out a major agreement.[100] For the first time, they agreed on reducing the number of nuclear weapons in their arsenals, the Soviets giving up 1,836 missiles, the United States 859. Ironically, given earlier adamant Kremlin opposition to any kind of inspection, Gorbachev's verification proposals were so intrusive that the CIA and NSA balked, resulting in an agreement for on-site inspection. The INF treaty was signed with great fanfare in Washington at 1:45 P.M. on December 8, 1987, a time deemed especially propitious, it was later learned, by Nancy Reagan's astrologer. Reagan called it "a grand historical moment." It was also a godsend for a president beleaguered by Iran-Contra. It provoked noisy protests from hard-liners such as Perle, journalist William Buckley, and North Carolina senator Jesse Helms. Howard Phillips of the Conservative Caucus branded Reagan a "useful idiot for Soviet propaganda."[101]

Advances in superpower relations were not limited to nuclear weapons. The two nations opened bilateral discussions to defuse regional conflicts such as Nicaragua and Afghanistan. The hotline was upgraded and an agreement concluded on joint exploration of space. Jewish emigration

99. Walker, *Cold War*, 293–94.
100. FitzGerald, *Out There in the Blue*, 407–9.
101. Cannon, *Reagan*, 779–81.

remained a thorny problem, but Moscow and Washington discussed human rights issues openly and without the rancor of an earlier era. More emigrants left Russia for the United States and Israel. The two nations conspicuously cooperated in the UN Security Council in calling for a cease-fire in the Iran-Iraq war and jointly warned Libya against sending arms to Iran. Cultural interchange expanded well beyond the heyday of detente in the 1970s. Student exchanges reached down to the high school level and extended into new academic disciplines. Scholarly visits achieved new highs, and in the atmosphere of *glasnost* attained a new level of frankness, even in politically loaded subjects like the humanities.

In the last year of Reagan's presidency, there was growing talk of an end to the Cold War. The old rhetoric occasionally resurfaced, as when the president thundered at Berlin's Brandenburg Gate in June 1987, "Mr. Gorbachev, tear down this wall!"—a ringing statement designed to palliate his conservative critics and challenge the Soviet leader to take even more dramatic steps.[102] Human rights issues continued to vex superpower relations. But the other signs were more dramatic. "Gorby fever" infected Washington during the December 1987 summit, the ebullient Soviet premier drawing huge and enthusiastic crowds and on one occasion leaving his limousine like an American politician to press the flesh with curious onlookers. It was "as if he came from another planet," novelist Joyce Carol Oates exclaimed.[103] At the May 1988 Moscow summit, Reagan attracted large throngs. Insisting that the Soviet Union had changed rather than he, he still backed away from his 1983 "evil empire" speech. It was an "intensely symbolic moment," U.S. Kremlinologist Stephen Cohen observed, the most right-wing of postwar presidents going to Moscow and speaking in the most soothing tones.[104] The Moscow summit represented for all practical purposes the normalization of U.S.-Soviet relations. In a radical speech at the UN on December 7, 1988, another truly dramatic turning point, Gorbachev went much further. He conceded that Moscow had no monopoly on the truth. He appeared to foreswear the use of force as an instrument of diplomacy, setting forth instead a concept of "reasonable sufficiency for defense" and underscoring it by announcing the reduction of Soviet conventional forces by half a million troops and ten thousand tanks within the next year. Most shocking and significant, he opened the way for self-determination in Eastern Europe by proclaiming that "the principle of freedom of choice is mandatory." This scrapping of the Brezhnev

---

102. James Mann, "Tear Down That Myth," *New York Times*, June 10, 2007.
103. Oberdorfer, *Cold War to New Era*, 264–65.
104. *New York Times*, May 22, 1988.

Doctrine for what one Soviet official dubbed the Sinatra Doctrine (so named for crooner Frank Sinatra's song "My Way") effectively removed the central issue around which the Cold War had begun.[105]

Growing Soviet-American concord provided a foundation for resolving other conflicts. Reagan administration claims that aid to insurgent groups had made war more costly for Communist governments had some merit. But other factors were equally important. Giving higher priority to domestic matters, Gorbachev began to push Soviet client states to liquidate their wars. Soviet-American cooperation contributed to ending numerous conflicts and helped the UN to work as its founders had intended. War-weariness among the combatants themselves produced strong pressures for peace. The inability to play the superpowers off against each other denied them the means to fight. Thus in the summer and fall of 1988—what the New York Times labeled a "season of peace"—numerous belligerents moved to resolve seemingly interminable conflicts. Iran and Iraq agreed to a cease-fire. South Africa and Angola moved to end their fifteen-year-old conflict in Southwest Africa. Isolated in the international community and under pressure from Moscow, Vietnam set out to liquidate its ten-year occupation of Cambodia. The intifada ground on in the West Bank and Gaza, but at the UN in early December PLO leader Arafat appeared to meet long-standing U.S. terms, explicitly renouncing terrorism and implicitly recognizing Israel's right to exist. The "year of the dove" left many problems unattended; the initiatives undertaken did not always produce immediate results. Still, the peace moves were many and dramatic. Reagan left office in a strikingly different world than the one he had inherited from Carter.

V

Easily victorious over Democrat Michael Dukakis in a campaign in which foreign policy was suddenly peripheral, George Bush presided over the culmination of the revolution in world affairs set off by Gorbachev and Reagan. Sensing with the peaceful revolution that swept Eastern Europe in 1989 that events were moving in the right direction, he wisely allowed them to take their course, refusing to interfere or to gloat at the outcome. He struggled to find the right balance between liberation and the order he preferred, however, and at times seemed curiously out of touch with the spirit of human freedom that swept the world during his first years in office.

George Herbert Walker Bush brought to the White House a sometimes uneasy amalgam of eastern, moderate Republicanism and the new,

105. Evangelista, "Arms Control," 102–3; Walker, Cold War, 308–9.

more conservative Sun Belt variety.[106] Scion of a wealthy and prominent Connecticut family, a much decorated navy pilot in World War II, educated at Andover and Yale, he imbibed the Stimsonian ethos of hard work, modesty, competition, and public service. After graduation from college, he broke the mold by setting out for Texas to enter the oil business. Like many of his generation and class, he gravitated naturally to politics. Following two terms in Congress and a failed effort to win a Senate seat, he held a series of important positions that would earn him the title "résumé president": Nixon's ambassador to the UN; chairman of the Republican National Committee; de facto ambassador to China before normalization was completed; director of Central Intelligence. After losing the nomination to Reagan in 1980, in the interest of party unity he joined the ticket as vice presidential candidate. By his own admission lacking in "the vision thing," Bush was a doer rather than thinker. His views were thoroughly establishmentarian, although in his political campaigns he pandered to the increasingly potent right wing of his party by resigning from the Council on Foreign Relations and the Trilateral Commission. Like many of his generation, he found foreign policy "more fun." Certain that personal connections were what made diplomacy work, he traveled 1.3 million miles and visited sixty-five countries as vice president, cultivating ties with foreign leaders and also laying claim to the title "Rolodex President."[107]

More interested in the processes of government than in ideas and especially mindful of the destructive consequences of Reagan's chaotic managerial style, Bush put together a foreign policy team of generally like-minded men, many of them close friends. Like his boss, Secretary of State James A. Baker III came from wealth. A Texan educated at Princeton and an ex-marine, Baker met Bush through his Houston law practice. As Bush's campaign manager and Reagan's White House chief of staff and secretary of the treasury, he established a reputation as a shrewd political operative and master deal-maker. His close personal relationship to the president assured his position in the foreign policy inner circle. Secretary of Defense Dick Cheney was a last-minute replacement for Texas senator John Tower, who failed to gain congressional approval. Deeply conservative and almost pathologically secretive, the Wyoming native had been Gerald Ford's chief of staff and had served in Congress. The

106. David Halberstam, *War in a Time of Peace: Bush, Clinton, and the Generals* (New York, 2001), 71.

107. John Newhouse, "Shunning the Losers," *New Yorker*, October 26, 1992, 40; John Robert Greene, *The Presidency of George Bush* (Lawrence, Kans., 2000), 11–26.

Bush foreign policy apparatus was held together by national security adviser and Kissinger protégé Gen. Brent Scowcroft, who had held the same
position in Ford's last years. A workaholic, Scowcroft was notorious for
taking catnaps in meetings. Slight of build, happy with anonymity, the
former air force general became the president's alter ego, in journalist
Bob Woodward's words, the "model of the trustworthy, self-effacing
staffer."[108] The Bush team was not monolithic. The 1991 war in the Persian Gulf would expose major differences among them. But they shared
an innate caution and conservatism—"prudence" was the word the president preferred—a commitment to team play, and a passion for order.
They worked together more harmoniously than any group going back to
the Johnson administration. Especially in foreign policy, Bush adopted a
hands-on style, a marked contrast to his predecessor.

In its first months in office, the Bush administration was shaken by an
unexpected crisis in China, the country the president should have known
best. Ironically, despite Reagan's long-standing and vocal support for
Taiwan, U.S. relations with China during his presidency were remarkably harmonious. Reagan's early crusade against the "evil empire" easily
trumped his traditional sympathy for Taiwan, and the administration significantly expanded the ties created by Carter in 1979. The United States
provided the arms and technology eagerly sought by Beijing. The two nations actively collaborated in Cambodia and Afghanistan to undermine
pro-Soviet regimes. In the latter, to conceal its hand, the United States
purchased Chinese weapons that were shipped directly through Pakistan
to the rebels. It also subsidized breeding of the Chinese mules that became the backbone of mujahideen logistics. During the Reagan years,
China experienced its most intense period of Westernization, welcoming
U.S. influence and sending thousands of students to America to study. In
1987, opposite the Mao Zedong mausoleum in Beijing, Kentucky Fried
Chicken opened a two-story restaurant in the shape of a bucket bearing a
larger-than-life image of Colonel Sanders. One "reformist" Chinese official even proposed substituting knives and forks for chopsticks! After an
official visit in April 1984, Reagan referred to China as that "so-called
Communist country," a widely publicized off-the-cuff statement that reflected broader American delusions about the extent to which Westernization and reform had really taken hold there.[109]

108. Bob Woodward, The Commanders (New York, 1992), 18; Newhouse, "Losers," 40–41;
    Greene, Bush Presidency, 45–50.
109. James Mann, About Face: A History of America's Curious Relationship with China
    from Nixon to Clinton (New York, 1999), 134–47.

Bush and his advisers took office skeptical of Reagan's rapprochement with Moscow and eager to maintain close relations with China, but the shocking events in Beijing's Tiananmen Square in the spring of 1989 made it impossible to do so. Demonstrations that began innocently in December 1984 at Beijing University in protest against cutting off the electricity at 11:00 P.M. exploded over the next few years into a full-fledged, nationwide protest on the part of increasingly Westernized students seeking greater democracy and intellectual freedom from a regime determined to maintain the status quo. By 1989, the protests had spread to two hundred cities. In May, an increasingly nervous government imposed martial law. In early June, as the demonstrations swelled in Beijing, it sent tanks and units of the People's Liberation Army into Tiananmen Square to quell the protest. While a stunned world watched on television, the army brutally suppressed the demonstrators, some of them carrying plaster Statues of Liberty, killing as many as three thousand, wounding perhaps ten thousand more. A few U.S. commentators rationalized that the army was not trained to deal with domestic disturbance or that television had blown the events out of proportion, but Americans and other peoples worldwide were outraged by the naked display of military power.[110]

An administration caught completely off guard responded haltingly and with some confusion. Bush like everyone else was appalled by the bloodshed, but he also feared the regional impact of a destabilized China and valued U.S.-Chinese commercial ties. While he formally protested, an elitist president more comfortable with order than with democracy did not feel and therefore could not voice the anger felt throughout the world. The United States imposed tough sanctions, cutting off military ties, stopping arms sales, and working with other nations to deny China much-needed credits from the World Bank and other international lending institutions. The sanctions infuriated the Chinese without in any way slowing their crackdown on dissenters. The administration's statements and actions failed to stifle rising domestic protest against its China policy and indeed brought down on the president criticism from both liberals and conservatives.[111]

The dynamics of Sino-American relations changed completely after Tiananmen. The Bush administration never quite resolved the dilemma of how to take a firm stand on principle without compromising interests deemed vital. It doggedly persisted in trying to repair relations with the Chinese government, sending Scowcroft on two missions to Beijing.

110. Greene, *Bush Presidency*, 93–94.
111. Ibid., 94–95.

The first, in July 1989, was shrouded in secrecy greater than Kissinger's legendary 1971 trip. Its purpose was to make clear U.S. dismay at Tiananmen, and Scowcroft engaged in some tough talk. But his mere presence made plain U.S. eagerness to get back to normal, and his ill-chosen words in a banquet toast—reported worldwide on Cable News Network—seemed to endorse the Chinese position.[112]

At home the changes were equally significant. Throughout the 1970s, China policy had been the exclusive preserve of the White House; after Tiananmen new players got into the act. The forty-three thousand Chinese students in the United States organized a remarkably effective lobby to prevent their forced return to China. Democratic senator George Mitchell of Maine and representative Nancy Pelosi of California took a keen interest in China, on occasion getting support from conservatives like Jesse Helms. Pelosi sponsored a bill exempting the students from a regulation that required them to return home after a year. Misjudging congressional support and preferring that the students return to China, the administration at first did not take the legislation seriously, then tried to kill it. The bill passed the House unanimously, the Senate by voice vote. The White House attempted to stand up for executive prerogative without abandoning principle by vetoing it but giving the students the same privileges by executive order. The administration's domestic foes were not appeased, and Beijing refused to "swallow this bitter pill."[113]

A new and difficult era in U.S.-Chinese relations had begun. Architects of the old policy like Kissinger and Nixon continued to tout the old themes, but their rationale collapsed with the Berlin Wall and Communist regimes in Eastern Europe. With the Soviet Union no longer a threat, China lost its strategic centrality. In addition, the fall of the Eastern European dominoes made the Beijing government especially sensitive to the slightest U.S. intrusion into its internal affairs. The Bush administration persisted in trying to repair the widening rift, rationalizing that it was important to keep China from spreading nuclear weapons to other countries, an unpersuasive argument that seemed to reward China's bad behavior. The United States first eased and then removed most of the sanctions but got precious little in return. Scowcroft's second visit, in December 1989, provoked angry protest in the United States against what the *Washington Post* called appeasement of the "repressive and bloodstained Chinese government."[114] The following year, the Chinese students and Congress

112. Ibid., 95: Mann, *About Face*, 206–8.
113. Mann, *About Face*, 215.
114. Ibid., 223.

proposed using the Jackson-Vanik amendment to condition China's most-favored-nation status on its human rights record. Without sufficient votes in the Senate to override a certain Bush veto, the first effort died, but the debate signaled the beginning of a bitter annual struggle that would vex relations with China and provoke heated controversy in Washington to the end of the century.

Bush entered office also unprepared for the revolutions that swept Eastern Europe in the *annus mirabilis* 1989. He believed that Reagan had gone too far both in his early belligerence toward the Soviet Union and his later cozying up to Gorbachev. He feared that his predecessor's anti-nuclearism might denude U.S. defenses. He was suspicious of Gorbachev's intentions and worried that he might fail and be replaced by a hard-liner. The administration thus took office clinging to traditional Cold War views and prepared to contain a still unpredictable and possibly dangerous adversary.[115] Some adjustments were made by the spring. In a speech at Texas A&M University drafted by NSC staffer and Soviet specialist Condoleezza Rice, Bush proposed going "beyond containment." A subsequent NSC paper laid out conditions under which the United States would "welcome the Soviet Union back into the world order." Privately, however, the administration remained skeptical. And even its "beyond containment" approach was not sufficiently imaginative for the truly earthshaking events of the next twelve months.[116]

The Eastern European upheaval had little precedent in world history. Since 1948, the governments of that region had been controlled by local Communists beholden to the Soviet Union and tightly tied to Moscow through the Warsaw Pact and bilateral economic agreements. When they deviated, as with Hungary in 1956 or Czechoslovakia in 1968, the Kremlin swiftly and forcefully brought them into line. Gorbachev's grand design envisioned reform-minded Eastern European Communists instituting *perestroika*-like changes on their own, retaining voluntary ties with the Soviet Union, and leading all of Europe into a new era of interdependence and cooperation. His December 1988 speech to the United Nations—he called it a "Fulton in reverse," referring back to Churchill's 1946 Missouri speech—sent clear signals that conservative leaders could not count on Soviet protection and must adapt to survive.[117] In fact, by the end of 1989, while the Kremlin stood by and watched, most of those

115. Melanson, *Search for Consensus*, 212.
116. Oberdorfer, *Cold War to New Era*, 347–48; James W. Davis and William C. Wohlforth, "German Unification," in Herrmann and Lebow, *Ending the Cold War*, 150.
117. Vladislav Zubok, "New Evidence on the End of the Cold War," *Cold War International History Project Bulletin* 12/13 (Fall/Winter 2001), 9.

leaders had been replaced by non-Communists operating in democratic governments and looking west rather than east. The Eastern Europeans themselves were mainly responsible for this remarkable transformation. Gorbachev played a crucial role by doing nothing; U.S. involvement was incidental.[118]

Fittingly, the beginning of the end of the Cold War took place in Poland, where Soviet-American conflict had started. General Wojciech Jaruzelski was the East European leader Gorbachev most trusted and the first to enact reforms, but the result was not what either intended. Faced with rising discontent from martial law and economic stagnation, Jaruzelski in April 1989 legalized Solidarity and agreed to free elections. In the June voting, the first in Eastern Europe since the onset of the Cold War, anti-Communists won a resounding victory. With Gorbachev's blessing, a coalition government was formed in which the Communists reluctantly agreed to participate. A member of Solidarity was elected prime minister. Incredibly, the Communists had surrendered power and the Soviet Union did nothing.[119]

The shocking changes in Poland opened the floodgates to Eastern Europe. Hungary went still further, the Communists there reinventing themselves as social democrats, the first time a Communist party had voluntarily junked its ideology. In October 1989, on the anniversary of the 1956 uprising, Hungary declared itself a republic. Apparently with Soviet concurrence, the Budapest government also opened its borders, permitting the flight of thousands of disgruntled East Germans. Mass demonstrations in East Germany following an October Gorbachev visit forced out the recalcitrant hard-liner Eric Honeker. On November 9, his successor opened the Berlin Wall to passage without exit visas. Events quickly spun out of control. Citizens from the two Berlins embraced amidst the pop of fireworks and jubilant shouts of "The Wall is gone." Exultant youth danced on top of that most despised symbol of Cold War repression. Enterprising Berliners tore away at the structure with hand tools, saving pieces for souvenirs and, in the best tradition of capitalism, selling them to tourists. In neighboring Czechoslovakia, demonstrations led to a general strike. The Communist government first tried to suppress the uprising with force, then scrambled to adapt, then in the face of massive popular unrest simply resigned. On December 29, the parliament elected dissident poet Václav Havel prime minister, the process of radical change

118. Jacques Levesque, "The Emancipation of Eastern Europe," in Herrmann and Lebow, *Ending the Cold War*, 112–14.
119. Oberdorfer, *Cold War to New Era*, 361.

in Czechoslovakia occurring so smoothly that it was called the Velvet Revolution. Only in Bulgaria and Romania did the Communist governments fulfill Gorbachev's vision by instituting reforms to retain power.[120]

Bush handled these events with admirable dexterity, but, as with China, it was hard to find the right balance between promoting freedom and sustaining order. The administration responded with predictable—and appropriate—caution to the first signs of upheaval in Poland and Hungary. Conditioned by recent history, U.S. officials feared provoking revolts inside the Eastern European countries that would force Soviet leaders to act. Correctly recognizing that the key to change was Soviet acquiescence, U.S. officials saw their principal role as making it easy for Gorbachev to do this. There would be no gloating or celebration. "We're not there . . . to poke a stick in the eyes of Mr. Gorbachev," Bush told Poles during a June visit, but to "encourage the very kind of reforms he is championing, and more reforms." Underestimating the power of the revolutionary forces, the president during his Polish visit appeared more at ease with Jaruzelski than with Solidarity leader Lech Walesa. In Hungary, among Communists and reformers, he seemed to favor the former. When the Wall came down to thunderous cheers from across the world, the official U.S. response seemed out of touch. "I am not an emotional kind of guy," the president confessed.[121]

German unification was the key event of the end of the Cold War, and here the United States played a vital role. The major push came from the Germans themselves—*Wir sind ein Volk* (we are one people) was their battle cry. The flight of fifty thousand East Germans each month and the impending collapse of the East German economy underscored the need for action. Other Europeans retained vivid memories of World War II and feared the economic clout of a reunited Germany. "Except for the Germans," a Dutch official observed, "no one in Europe wants reunification."[122] The Soviet Union was especially nervous but unable to put on the brakes. His power slipping at home and his prestige and influence abroad, Gorbachev had lost the initiative. He desperately sought concessions to make the inevitable palatable, first proposing German neutrality, then insisting that a united Germany not be in NATO.

The U.S. government was divided, but Bush took the lead and in one of the more decisive moments of his presidency committed the United States to a unified Germany in NATO. He was sensitive to Soviet concerns. As a

120. Ibid., 363–86.
121. Ibid., 364. See also Mikhail Gorbachev et al., "Defrosting the Cold War," *New Perspectives Quarterly* 13 (Winter 1996), 20.
122. Oberdorfer, *Cold War to New Era*, 392.

means of "giving cover" to Gorbachev, Baker developed a "Two-plus-Four" scheme in which the two Germanys would work out arrangements on internal matters and then negotiate with the four postwar occupying powers on external matters. While the Germans pushed relentlessly toward unification, Baker and Bush at an April 1990 summit with Gorbachev agreed that the Red Army might remain in East Germany during a transitional period, offered aid for its redeployment to the USSR, and gave assurances on German boundaries, making unification acceptable. While complaining about being pushed out of Europe, Gorbachev acquiesced. Unification was set for October 1990.[123]

A crisis in Lithuania in 1990 posed the most difficult test in the emerging contest between freedom and order. As Eastern Europe escaped from the Soviet yoke, sentiment for independence mounted in Lithuania, since 1940 one of three Baltic States under Moscow's control. Already shaken by the Eastern European revolutions and fearful of a disastrous domino effect among the restive nationalities that made up the vast Soviet republic, Gorbachev firmly resisted the breakup of the union. Ignoring the Soviet leader, Lithuania declared its independence in March. The USSR responded with all means short of force, conducting menacing military maneuvers and imposing economic sanctions. The crisis posed a major dilemma for Washington. The United States had never recognized Soviet absorption of the Baltic States, the object of various "captive nation" resolutions passed with great fanfare by Congress in the early Cold War. Ethnic groups clamored for Baltic freedom. On the other hand, U.S. officials recognized the dangers to world order posed by a breakup or collapse of the Soviet Union, especially in the handling of nuclear weapons. Bush needed Gorbachev's support to consummate the German settlement. Recalling Hungary in 1956, the administration hesitated, in Condoleezza Rice's words, to "light a match in a gas-filled room."[124] Thus it contented itself with mild protests and ceased even those when Gorbachev warned that U.S. intrusion hindered his ability to resolve the crisis. Lithuanians protested another Munich; Congress agitated for Lithuanian freedom. In June, the Soviets and Lithuanians worked out a shaky stopgap solution.

While these dramatic events unfolded, the second phase of Soviet-American detente proceeded apace. A December 1989 "seasick summit" aboard warships off Malta in the stormy Mediterranean marked in important ways the end of the Cold War. Bush and Gorbachev bonded. By this time, the possibilities of future collaboration exceeded the dangers of

123. Ibid.,393–97, 415–17; Davis and Wohlforth, "German Reunification," 132–33.
124. Oberdorfer, Cold War to New Era, 404.

future conflict. "We don't consider you an enemy any more," the Soviet leader frankly conceded.[125] A meeting in Washington in May of the following year made quite clear the radical changes in the balance between the two superpowers since Gorbachev's last visit in 1987. To this point, the Soviet leader had held the initiative, but with the fall of Eastern Europe, the certainty of a united Germany in NATO, rebellion in the Soviet republics, and increasingly pressing domestic problems, Gorbachev was obviously on the defensive. Kremlinologists now questioned whether he was even in control and how long he might last. He came to Washington desperate merely to secure a trade agreement with the United States. The administration at first took a hard line, tying trade to freedom for Lithuania and the lifting of restrictions on emigration. Once assured of Soviet approval of German membership in NATO, however, Bush offered a trade agreement while making clear it would not go to Congress until the crisis in Lithuania was resolved. In December 1990, by executive order he waived the Jackson-Vanik amendment to permit Export-Import Bank credits. The two nations made no progress on strategic arms reduction, but they did work out expanded student exchanges and pledged to reach agreement on reducing land arms in Europe. Bush and Gorbachev established a close, even intimate working relationship. The question now was the value of agreements with a dynamic leader whose days seemed numbered.[126]

A short and seemingly decisive war in the Middle East in early 1991 underscored the dramatic changes in the international system and fixed the contours of what Bush would call a "new world order." On August 1, 1990, Iraqi dictator and onetime Soviet ally Saddam Hussein caught the world off guard by sending three divisions in a lightning strike into neighboring Kuwait. Until 1961, the smaller Arab kingdom had been part of Iraq. Saddam coveted Kuwait's long coastline and access to the sea. Short of cash from his eight-year war with Iran, he accused the Kuwaitis of exceeding production quotas and driving down the price of oil. The United States had also supported Iraq during much of its war with Iran. In a colossal miscalculation, the Bush administration reckoned that despite his bluster a war-weary Saddam would refrain from rash actions. It went out of its way to avoid pushing him in that direction. He was likely encouraged in his daring move by a July 25 conversation in which ambassador April Glaspie assured him that the United States sought better relations with

125. Raymond L. Garthoff, *The Great Transition: American-Soviet Relations and the End of the Cold War* (Washington, 1994), 406.
126. Oberdorfer, *Cold War to New Era*, 410–33.

Iraq and had "no opinion" on its border dispute with Kuwait. Iraqi forces quickly seized the capital of Kuwait City, giving Saddam control of 20 percent of the world oil supply.[127]

Saddam also miscalculated. Much as with Korea forty years earlier, the United States responded quickly, forcibly, and after remarkably little internal debate. Among the president's top advisers, only JCS chairman Gen. Colin Powell opposed the use of force. Deeply scarred by his two tours in Vietnam as a junior officer, he vigorously promoted adherence to what was now called the Powell Doctrine, insisting that the nation should go to war only to defend its most vital interests and then only as a last resort. He downplayed the importance of Kuwait. He insisted that U.S. objectives in the region could be achieved by containment and economic sanctions. The general stood alone. Top officials feared that an emboldened Iraq might threaten Israel and Saudi Arabia. Cheney doubted that sanctions would work and worried that absorption of Kuwait would give Iraq a stranglehold over Middle Eastern oil. As Truman and Acheson had done vis-à-vis Korea in June 1950, Scowcroft viewed Saddam's actions broadly in terms of the "ramifications of the aggression on the emerging post-Cold War world." To do nothing would send the wrong message to bad guys across the globe. Bush concurred. "This will not stand," he avowed, "this aggression against Kuwait."[128]

While hoping to cow Saddam into submission, the administration prepared, if necessary, to drive him from Kuwait with force. It imposed economic sanctions and applied diplomatic pressure but in full recognition that war might be necessary. Bush used his famous Rolodex and his personal ties with world leaders to assemble a broad coalition, including Syria, Egypt, and Saudi Arabia, to remove Iraq from Kuwait. Gorbachev was the key, and his assent left Saddam isolated. Throughout the fall of 1990, the United States mobilized in Saudi Arabia and the Persian Gulf an awesome array of air, sea, and land power, the fruits of Carter's and Reagan's military buildup. On November 29, it gained UN Security Council approval of a resolution authorizing the use of "all necessary means" if Iraq had not left Kuwait by January 15, 1991. The possibility of war provoked vigorous opposition in the United States, a revival in many ways of the Vietnam anti-war movement. The president wisely rejected Cheney's argument that congressional approval for war was unnecessary

---

127. Lawrence Freedman and Efraim Karsh, *The Gulf Conflict, 1990–1991: Diplomacy and War in the New World Order* (Princeton, N.J., 1993), 524.

128. James Mann, *Rise of the Vulcans: The History of Bush's War Cabinet* (New York, 2004), 184–86.

and might not be won. On January 12, after a heated debate suffused with references to Vietnam, Congress endorsed the use of force to uphold the UN resolution, 250–183 in the House, 52–47 in the Senate.[129] Drawing the wrong lessons about Iraqi military prowess from his recent war with Iran and about U.S. willingness to fight from Vietnam, Saddam remained defiant to the end.

Launched on January 16, 1991, Operation Desert Storm unveiled to the world a dazzling display of modern, high-technology military power. For five weeks, the air force and navy pounded Iraq with cruise missiles from B-52 bombers flown on thirty-hour round trips from Louisiana, Toma-hawk missiles fired from ships in the Persian Gulf, and laser-guided bombs dropped by Stealth F-117 aircraft. The attacks first targeted Iraq's communications networks, electrical power, and air bases. The bombing was not nearly as precise as portrayed on television. The collateral dam-age and civilian casualties were much worse than believed at the time. But the air war crippled Iraq's ability to fight. Coalition aircraft next "soft-ened up" Iraqi troop concentrations in Kuwait. The second phase of the war began on February 24 when U.S. Marines from bases in Saudi Arabia attacked Iraqi forces in Kuwait. Army units then executed a "left hook" across the western desert to catch the enemy in a trap. Coalition forces in-flicted huge losses on already demoralized Iraqi ground troops. Within a hundred hours, the fighting had stopped, apparently a resounding victory for the coalition and especially the United States.[130]

War is seldom so neat, however, and Desert Storm proved at best a par-tial success. Although Bush had publicly likened Saddam to Hitler, the administration declined to exploit its enormous military advantage to de-pose him. Regime change was never a goal, Scowcroft later admitted, simply a "hopeful byproduct."[131] The U.S. military permitted much of his Republican Guard forces to escape, thus facilitating his retention of power. The military command allowed him to keep his helicopters, which he used with lethal effect to suppress domestic opposition. As is customary in war, after the shooting had stopped, frustrated U.S. officials blamed each other, and there was plenty to go around. The United States, for good reasons, never seriously considered pushing on to Bagh-dad to topple Saddam's government. Such a move might have cost the support of Arab states, crucial to the coalition. Iraq's total defeat would leave a huge power vacuum in an especially volatile part of the world's

129. Freedman and Karsh, *Gulf Conflict*, 290–94.
130. Michael Gordon and Bernard Trainor, *The General's War* (Boston, 1995), 355–99.
131. Greene, *Bush Presidency*, 138.

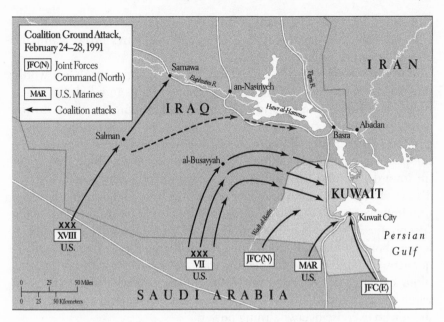

Coalition Ground Attack,
February 24–28, 1991

JFC(N) Joint Forces
        Command (North)

MAR   U.S. Marines

◄───── Coalition attacks

most explosive region, enhancing the position of Iran. United States forces might be tied down in an extended occupation and entangled in Iraqi politics in ways that made Vietnam look easy. "Once we cross over the line and start intervening in a civil war . . . ," Cheney admitted, "it raises the very real specter of getting us involved in a quagmire figuring out who the hell is going to govern Iraq."[132]

United States officials reasoned that destruction of a large part of Saddam's army would limit his capacity to make mischief and perhaps weaken his hold on power, but they did not even pursue this goal aggressively. Military commanders expected the Iraqis in Kuwait to stand and fight, and when they fled north instead the coalition did not adjust quickly enough. The army was slow to execute the left hook, permitting sizeable enemy forces to escape across the Euphrates. The United States agreed to end the ground war after that mere hundred hours—partly because the number had a "nice ring," also because television's depiction of a "turkey shoot" of fleeing Iraqis along the "highway of death" had created a public relations problem; continuing the slaughter would not be "chivalrous," Bush observed. Even then, whether destruction of all the Republican Guard forces in Kuwait would have been enough to topple

132. *Tampa Tribune*, May 19, 2007.

Saddam is doubtful. The main problem was the naive view shared by top U.S. officials that destroying just a part of Saddam's army would be enough to get rid of him.[133]

The Bush administration hoped that Saddam's crushing defeat would provoke a military coup, and they encouraged Iraqis to rebel, but when Shiites and Kurds rose up and Saddam brutally suppressed them during the cease-fire with mass murder using helicopter gunships and poison gas, the United States did nothing. Powell and the military wanted U.S. troops out as quickly as possible. Civilians worried that a Shiite Iraq might tilt toward Iran and that the Kurds' secessionist dreams could threaten Turkey. They most feared the disintegration of Iraq. Once again, order triumphed over freedom, the guiding principle, in Scowcroft's word, being "geopolitics."[134] The administration in truth never resolved its ambivalence about Saddam. It hoped to get rid of him but feared the consequences. The men who planned the military campaign with such meticulous care devoted scandalously little attention to what would happen when the war ended. They "failed to exploit the benefits that accrue to those who exercise overwhelming power."[135]

The full import of these failures would become obvious only later, and for the moment Americans relished a smashing and redemptive victory. A nervous nation had gone to war still haunted by Vietnam, and the thrashing administered to a supposedly formidable foe with minimal U.S. casualties brought forth enormous pride. The new volunteer army had proven its mettle; the performance of air power evoked awe. "The ghosts of Vietnam have been laid to rest beneath the sands of the Arabian desert," Bush himself crowed when it was over (prematurely, as it turned out).[136] The Gulf War put on graphic display America's military primacy in the post–Cold War world. The Soviet Union, only recently a superpower and once Iraq's sponsor, was relegated to the sidelines, involving itself only through several last-minute and ineffectual efforts to prevent war. Bush hailed a new world order in which Wilson's vision of maintaining peace through collective security would be accomplished by the instrumentation of a United Nations working as its framers intended under enlightened U.S. leadership. A grateful nation hailed its heroes with ticker tape parades.

133. Robert A. Divine, "The Persian Gulf War Revisited: Tactical Victory, Strategic Failure," *Diplomatic History* 24 (Winter 2000), 37.
134. Gordon and Trainor, *General's War*, 456; Mann, *Vulcans*, 193.
135. Gordon and Trainor, *General's War*, 477.
136. Arnold Isaacs, *Vietnam Shadows: The War, Its Ghosts, and Its Legacy* (Baltimore, Md., 1997), 65.

The finale to the upheaval of 1989–91 was the summer 1991 collapse of the Soviet Union itself, an event as momentous in its ramifications as it was anticlimactic in its occurrence. A visionary and dreamer, Gorbachev had hoped that reforming the Communist Party and the Soviet state would shake the USSR from its doldrums, stimulating political regeneration and economic revival. In fact, his reforms loosened the glue that held the vast Soviet empire together, unleashing powerful ethnic and nationalist forces among the diverse peoples that comprised the USSR. The dominoes fell from one end of the empire to the other, beginning, ironically, with a declaration of independence in June 1990 by the Russian republic. Humiliated by the "loss" of Eastern Europe, the reunification of Germany, the Gulf War, and the disintegration of the USSR, Soviet hardliners on August 18, 1991, two days before the signature of a treaty giving the remaining republics greater autonomy, placed Gorbachev under house arrest at his vacation spot in the Crimea and moved to take over the government. It was a bungled effort, halfheartedly executed by incompetents and drunkards. Hoping to restore the Communist Party to power and preserve what was left of the Soviet state, they accomplished the opposite. The flamboyant Boris Yeltsin, president of the Russian Republic, mounted a tank to rally anti-coup demonstrators in Moscow, outmaneuvered the plotters, and took power. An increasingly impotent Gorbachev hung on for a short time longer. In early December, Russia, Ukraine, and Belarus replaced the USSR with a loose Confederation of Independent States. Gorbachev resigned on Christmas. That day the hammer and sickle came down from atop the Kremlin for the last time and was replaced by the red and blue flag of the Russian Republic. "Never before," philosopher Sir Isaiah Berlin intoned, "has there been a case of an empire that caved in without a war, revolution, or an invasion."[137]

The Cold War ended in irony rather than celebration. United States officials watched the stunning events of summer 1991 with bewilderment and concern. Bush and his advisers feared that the fall of Gorbachev and the collapse of the USSR would set off rampant destabilization across the Soviet empire or lead to a restoration of the Communist old guard. Although Bush stopped well short of the massive infusion of economic assistance Gorbachev pleaded for, he tried other ways to help his friend. A START treaty was signed at the last summit in Moscow in early August, providing for sizeable reductions in the strategic arsenals of both countries. Proceeding to Kiev, the president warned restless Ukrainians of the

137. Walter LaFeber, *America, Russia, and the Cold War, 1945–1996* (8th ed., New York, 1997), 347.

dangers of "suicidal nationalism based on ethnic hatred" and emphasized that "freedom is not the same as independence," a statement conservative columnist William Safire branded the "chicken Kiev speech" and one widely viewed as favoring the USSR over self-determination. Scowcroft watched the denouement "feeling numb, disbelieving," at the "sheer incomprehensibility that such an epochal event could actually be occurring." He and Bush congratulated themselves on setting the "right tone" of encouraging reform without provoking a reaction.[138]

RONALD REAGAN AND GEORGE BUSH PRESIDED over one of the most remarkable periods of change in world history: the liberation of Eastern Europe; the end of the Cold War; and the collapse of the Soviet Union. These momentous events were not primarily a result of the massive Reagan defense buildup bankrupting the Soviet economy, as American "triumphalists" have argued. Soviet defense spending reflected more internal demands than U.S. policies; the Soviet economy collapsed primarily under its own weight, not external pressures.[139] America's "soft power" in the form of such things as rock-and-roll music and the glitter of Western consumer goods may have had a greater subversive effect than its military power.[140] The "historical wild card" in the great transformation, historian James Hershberg persuasively argues, was not Reagan but Mikhail Gorbachev, whose drastic reorientation of Soviet priorities set loose forces no one could control.[141] Reagan did contribute to the changes, but not in the way that is usually argued. He helped to restore a sense of national well-being, a necessary precondition for accommodation with the Soviet Union. His seemingly naive commitment to a nuclear-free world and his unique relationship with Gorbachev dramatically eased Soviet-American tensions, making it simpler for Gorbachev to relinquish control over Eastern Europe. Reagan's solid anti-Communist credentials permitted him to do what few other American leaders could have—effect a rapprochement with the nation he himself had only recently called an "evil empire." Although his administration was caught off guard by the rapidity and magnitude of change in the *annus mirabilis* and seemed to favor order over freedom, Bush had the good sense to let events take their course without the unwelcome intrusion of braggadocio.

138. Bush and Scowcroft, *World Transformed*, 563–565.
139. Richard Ned Lebow and Janice Gross Stein, "Reagan and the Russians," *Atlantic Monthly*, February 1994, 35–37.
140. Deudney and Ikenberry, "Cold War," 134–35.
141. *Washington Post*, June 27, 2004.

There was, of course, a darker side to the Reagan era. Flawed thinking, ideological zeal, and near scandalous mismanagement produced misguided and destructive policies. The president's absurd glorification of the Nicaraguan contras and obsession with a grossly exaggerated Soviet threat to Central America provoked debilitating political warfare at home and inflicted devastating destruction on that already benighted region. The muddled intrusions into the Middle East, also in response to an inflated Soviet threat, brought high costs and few gains. The two strands came together in the notorious Iran-Contra Affair that would be comical were it not so serious. Reagan and the zealots acting in his name displayed an open contempt for democracy, a disdain for Congress, and a blatant disregard for the law—in all, fourteen officials were charged with criminal offenses, including two national security advisers and the secretary of defense. They created what journalist Mark Danner has called an environment of "corrosive secrecy" to conceal what they were doing from the American people and Congress.[142] To evade restrictions on executive power, they employed private subcontractors and other subterfuges. Policies flawed in conception were often implemented in a most amateurish manner.

The United States "won" the Cold War in the sense that the other side gave up the fight, but, as is usually the case in war, victory did not come without cost. Despite nearly a half century of bitter struggle, the two superpowers managed to avoid direct conflict in what has been called the long peace. In their relentless pursuit of their own interests, however, the two sides put millions of people at risk of nuclear annihilation in 1962 and possibly again in 1983. For much of the Cold War, the world lived nervously under the nuclear mushroom cloud. Proxy wars in Korea, Vietnam, Afghanistan, Nicaragua, and elsewhere produced a body count of millions.[143] The United States experienced nothing to match the horrors of Stalin's gulags or Mao's Red Guards, but, especially during the McCarthy period, the Cold War produced rampant assaults on civil liberties. The Vietnam War, a direct by-product of the Cold War, divided Americans as nothing had since their civil war a century earlier, and the divisions persisted into the next century. The Cold War contributed to the so-called

142. Mark Danner, "How the Foreign Policy Machine Broke Down," *New York Times Magazine*, March 7, 1993, 32–34.

143. John Lewis Gaddis, *The Long Peace: Inquiries into the History of the Cold War* (New York, 1987). Warren Kimball's review of *Long Peace* notes that eight million people were killed in seventy wars between 1945 and 1988, many of them connected to the Cold War; *American Historical Review* 94 (June 1989), 921–22.

imperial presidency that reached its apogee with Richard Nixon and Ronald Reagan, producing in both cases abuses of power in the name of national security. The economic costs were especially high. The Reagan policies produced a short-lived boom but over the longer term had devastating effects on the U.S. economy. The massive defense budget was paid for by deficit spending and financed by foreign capital. The national debt soared to $2.7 trillion by 1989; 20 percent of it was held by foreign creditors. For the first time since World War I, the United States was a debtor nation. Focus on the Cold War deflected attention away from the infrastructure and such critical areas as education and social problems.[144]

For nearly fifty years, the Cold War was a major organizing principle of American life, providing for many a strange sense of certainty and reassurance. Its sudden and unexpected end left the nation unprepared for an uncertain era. "We were suddenly in a unique position," Scowcroft later recalled, "without experience, without precedent, and standing alone at the height of power."[145]

144. Thomas G. Paterson, *On Every Front: The Making and Unmaking of the Cold War* (New York, 1992), 194–95.
145. Bush and Scowcroft, *World Transformed*, 563–64.

20

"The Strength of a Giant"
America as Hyperpower, 1992–2007

After the end of the Cold War, the United States enjoyed a degree of world hegemony beyond George Washington's most extravagant dreams. Despite gloomy talk of decline in the 1970s and 1980s, America in the last years of the twentieth century boasted a seemingly invincible high-tech military machine, a robust computer-driven economy, and an array of "soft power" that gave it nearly incalculable influence over the planet's affairs. Not since Rome, it was argued, had any nation enjoyed such preeminence. The French, so often critical of the United States, coined a new word—*hyperpower*—to describe America's unprecedented status.[1]

Yet the attainment of such power did not bring the freedom from fear that Washington had envisioned. During the first part of the post–Cold War era, an uncertain nation focused on problems at home and used its vast power only with great reluctance. The terrorist attacks of September 11, 2001, made clear that even hyperpowers are vulnerable. And even after a smashingly successful 2003 military campaign against Iraq, the United States became bogged down in a confused and costly politico-military quagmire. Strategists pondered anew how the nation's vast power could best be used to protect its vital interests in a newly dangerous world.

I

For a fleeting moment in the early 1990s, peace and world order seemed within reach. The end of the Cold War and the sudden collapse of the Soviet Union removed the preceding half century's major causes of international tension and eased, if they did not eliminate altogether, the dread of a nuclear holocaust. The emergence of democracies and market economies in the former Soviet satellites, Latin America, and even South Africa offered the hope of a new age of global freedom and prosperity. The U.S.-led victory under the aegis of the United Nations in the Persian Gulf War seemed to hail the triumph of Woodrow Wilson's dream of collective security in which peace would be maintained and aggression repelled by international collaboration. President George H. W. Bush proclaimed a

---

1. William Safire, "On Language," *New York Times Magazine*, July 22, 2003.

new world order under U.S. leadership. State Department official Francis Fukuyama hailed the "end of history," the absolute triumph of capitalism and democracy over fascism and Communism, beyond which no great ideological conflicts could be imagined.[2]

It did not take long for such prophecies to be exposed as at best wishful thinking, at worst absolute folly. The Cold War had imposed a crude form of order on an inherently unstable world, and its end set loose powerful forces held in check for years. The two dominant trends of the post–Cold War world, integration and fragmentation, were each destabilizing; in a broader sense, they conflicted with each other.[3]

Almost without notice amidst the last climactic stages of the Cold War, the world changed radically in the 1980s, bringing people still closer together while setting off powerful new and often disruptive forces. A communications revolution—sometimes called the third industrial revolution—shattered old ways of thinking and doing things, challenging geopolitics itself. The development of computers and the Internet, cable television, satellite technology, and new high-speed jet aircraft created global networks that broke down old barriers and brought the world still closer together. These innovations made it impossible for governments to control information, as in the past, contributing to the collapse of the Soviet empire and in time the USSR itself. They empowered individuals and groups, enhancing the influence of non-state actors in international politics and economics. They permitted the globalization of trade in ways heretofore unimaginable, giving rise to new transnational corporations such as Nike that exploited cheap labor in developing countries to produce inexpensive, quality goods for an international market.[4]

Such was the impact of the communications revolution that Cable News Network (CNN) founder Ted Turner banned the use of the word *foreign* in his corporation's activities. By the mid-1990s, four of every five bottles of Coca-Cola were sold outside the United States, while high-quality European and Japanese goods flooded U.S. markets to satisfy the tastes of well-heeled and sophisticated consumers. Professional athletics became part of the process. National Basketball Association (NBA) games were telecast in 175 countries and broadcast in forty languages to six hundred million households. NBA mega-star Michael Jordan became the

2. Francis Fukuyama, *The End of History and the Last Man* (New York, 1992).
3. John Lewis Gaddis, "Toward the Post–Cold War World," *Foreign Affairs* 70 (Spring 1991), 102–5.
4. Joseph S. Nye Jr., *The Paradox of American Power: Why the World's Only Superpower Can't Go It Alone* (New York, 2002), 41–51.

"first great athlete of the wired world"; the paraphernalia of his Chicago Bulls—known in China as the "Oxen"—could be found even in Mongolia. A poll of Chinese high school students ranked Jordan with Zhou En-lai as the person they most admired.[5] In sports as elsewhere, globalization worked both ways. Seven-foot four-inch Yao Ming of China became an NBA star. European players increasingly joined the rosters of NBA and National Hockey League teams. But the United States dominated the export of culture. "American popular culture is the closest approximation there is today to a global lingua franca," sociologist Todd Gitlin observed in 1992.[6]

The revolutionary changes wrought by "globalization"—defined as worldwide networks of interdependence—raised profound concerns across the world. In fact, American popular culture often coexisted as a second culture alongside long-established local versions. In many instances, it was modified for indigenous tastes before being exported. In other regions, however, especially in Europe, the process was often simplistically viewed as Americanization and provoked angry reactions. Certain as ever of their own cultural superiority and the banality of the U.S. variety, French spokespersons raged against the corruption and trivialization of traditional high culture. France's cultural minister denounced plans for a European Disney World outside Paris as a "cultural Chernobyl." In the Middle East, Islamic fundamentalists railed against the degradation wrought by Satanist American popular culture and plotted terrorist attacks, ironically using instruments of globalization such as jetliners, the Internet, and cellular telephones, on the symbols of U.S. global dominance.[7]

A process that seemed to favor the United States also provoked alarm at home. Americans responded angrily to French protests. "We offer them the dream of a lifetime and lots of jobs. They treat us like invaders," said a Euro Disney spokesperson.[8] The growing "outsourcing" of jobs to cheaper labor markets made available to Americans less expensive consumer goods but also caused unemployment in U.S. manufacturing. An influx of Japanese capital in the early 1990s, including even the purchase of major communications networks, provoked nationalist fears of foreign

5. Walter LaFeber, *Michael Jordan and the New Global Capitalism* (New York, 1999), 14–15, 135; *New York Times*, April 21, 1996.
6. *New York Times*, May 3, 1992.
7. Thomas Friedman, *The Lexus and the Olive Tree: Understanding Globalization* (New York, 1999), offers a paean to globalization. A critical analysis is William Greider, *One World, Ready or Not: The Manic Logic of Global Capitalism* (New York, 1997).
8. *New York Times*, May 3, 1992.

control of crucial media outlets. College students organized nationwide protests against the way in which giant corporations like Nike, owing allegiance to no nation-state and beyond the control of any government, exploited workers in sweatshops in developing countries to produce maximum goods at minimum cost. Critics complained that globalization was widening an already yawning worldwide gap between rich and poor.

Coexisting uncomfortably alongside these new forces of integration were older, equally potent, and potentially even more disruptive forces of fragmentation: nationalism, ethnic rivalries, and tribal hatreds, forces, historian John Lewis Gaddis wrote in 1991, that were "resurrecting old barriers between nations and peoples—and creating new ones—even as others are tumbling."[9] The end of the Cold War took the lid off a pot that had been boiling for years. In Central and Eastern Europe, the Middle East, Central Asia, and Africa, fragile national loyalties gave way to fierce ethnic and tribal conflicts, secessionist movements, and vicious "ethnic cleansing." Most prominent in the 1990s were the brutal wars between Serbs, Croats, and Muslims in the former Yugoslavia, and conflicts between Sunni and Shiite Muslims and Kurds in the Middle East. The New York Times counted forty-eight such conflicts worldwide in 1993. New nations took shape almost as rapidly as during the heyday of decolonization. "Get ready for fifty new countries in the world in the next fifty years," a pessimistic Senator Daniel Patrick Moynihan of New York admonished in that same year, most of them "born in bloodshed." Wilson's dream of self-determination threatened to divide the world with conflict rather than bring it together in peace and harmony.[10]

Other commentators forecast even more gloomy scenarios. Some warned that the Cold War struggle between East and West would give way to conflict between North and South, the haves and the have-nots, the West and the rest. Runaway population growth in the developing countries portended a possibly disastrous drain on already scarce resources, environmental crises that could afflict the entire globe, and the rampant spread of crime, disease, and war. Others warned ominously of an assault on the borders of the developed countries through massive emigration. Still others admonished that the anarchy already gripping Africa would spread across the globe, the chaos in the less developed countries eventually contaminating the developed nations.[11] Although such predictions appeared unnecessarily pessimistic and may even have reflected a

9. Gaddis, "Post–Cold War World," 105.
10. New York Times, February 7, 1993.
11. Robert Kaplan, "The Coming Anarchy," Atlantic Monthly, February 1994, 44–76.

certain nostalgia for Cold War "order," it was clear that history had not ended. Conflict and disorder would continue to characterize the new era.

The position of the United States in the new world order was paradoxical. During the 1990s and beyond, America enjoyed a preponderance of power with little precedent in world history. Its economy was 40 percent larger than that of the second-rank nation, its defense spending six times that of the next six countries combined. What political scientist Joseph Nye called its "soft power"—the international appeal of its products, lifestyle, and values—gave the United States sway "over an empire on which the sun never sets."[12] Because of its wealth and relative security, it appeared to have unrivaled and unprecedented freedom of action. Neoconservative columnist Charles Krauthammer proclaimed with unabashed enthusiasm a "unipolar moment."[13]

Not surprisingly, the nation responded uncertainly to the new world order. Its contours were fuzzy at best, and Americans had no blueprint for dealing with it. "The central paradox of unipolarity," political scientist Stephen Walt observed, was that the United States "enjoys enormous influence but has little idea what to do with its power or even how much effort it should expend."[14] The absence of any obvious threat to its security removed any compelling inducement to assume leadership in solving world problems. Most Americans recognized that there could be no isolationism in a world shrunk by technology and bound by economic interdependence, but after forty years of global commitment and heavy Cold War expenditures, many of them yearned for what Warren Harding had called "normalcy" and relief from the burdens of world leadership. As in the aftermath of World Wars I and II, they preferred to focus on domestic problems. Support for foreign policy ventures waned. An always fickle public lost interest in the world. Both reflecting and shaping public opinion, the media drastically reduced coverage of events abroad. Sensing a "peace dividend," Congress slashed expenditures for foreign aid, diplomatic representation abroad, and international public information programs. Despite an overwhelming victory in the Gulf War, bitter memories of the Vietnam debacle continued to haunt the nation two decades after its end, adding yet another constraint. Military leaders were especially leery of so-called humanitarian

12. Nye, *Paradox*, 11.
13. Charles Krauthammer, "The Unipolar Moment," *Foreign Affairs* 70 (*America and the World*, 1990–1991), 23.
14. Stephen M. Walt, "Two Cheers for Clinton's Foreign Policy," *Foreign Affairs* 79 (March/April 2000), 65.

interventions to stop the bloodshed from burgeoning ethnic conflicts across the globe. With Gen. Colin Powell as chairman of a more powerful Joint Chiefs of Staff, the so-called Powell Doctrine first enunciated in the mid-1980s took the form of holy writ.

II

The halting response of the George H. W. Bush administration to the new world order it had proclaimed made clear the challenges of the post–Cold War era. Bush offered no concrete vision of America's future international role now that containment, which had guided policymakers during the Cold War, was no longer relevant. He was perhaps complacent after his triumphant leadership in the Persian Gulf. In his last year, he struggled with a stagnant economy and was politically crippled by enactment of the tax increase he had sworn not to endorse.[15]

The one serious effort to plot a post–Cold War strategy was quickly repudiated. A Defense Planning Guidance document drafted in Undersecretary of Defense Paul Wolfowitz's office under the supervision of Lewis "Scooter" Libby set forth a new vision for the United States as the world's lone superpower. The nation must maintain absolute military supremacy, the draft firmly asserted. It must prevent any power or combination of powers from challenging its position. The document was decidedly unilateralist, minimizing the significance of the UN and alliances. It pinpointed the spread of nuclear weapons as a major concern and suggested that the United States might have to act preemptively to head off that danger. Leaked to the press in March 1992, it provoked a brief furor. With the presidential primaries under way, the White House quickly distanced itself from the controversial draft. A toned-down revision paid lip service to collective security but never received official sanction. The document would be dusted off by another Bush administration after the turn of the century and become the underpinning for post-9/11 defense policy.[16]

After the Gulf War, the administration acted decisively only in the Middle East. From the outset, Bush and Secretary of State James Baker had made clear their determination to break the long-standing deadlock in Arab-Israeli negotiations. Israel must accept the principle of land for peace as specified in UN Resolution 242. It must "lay aside, once and for all, the unrealistic vision of a greater Israel," Baker boldly informed an American Israel Public Affairs Committee (AIPAC) gathering in

15. John Robert Greene, *The Presidency of George Bush* (Lawrence, Kans., 2000), 141–64.
16. James Mann, *Rise of the Vulcans: The History of Bush's War Cabinet* (New York, 2004), 209–15.

May 1989.[17] The end of the Cold War, the demise of the Soviet Union, and the defeat of Iraq seemed to strengthen the administration's hand. The Palestinians would no longer have an arms supplier. By easing the threat from Iraq, the United States presumably gained greater leverage with Israel. Working with moderate Palestinians in the West Bank rather than Arafat's PLO, the administration secured agreement of the major Arab states for a peace conference. Baker jawboned hard-line Israeli premier Yitzhak Shamir into attending. The conference, held in Madrid's Crystal Pavilion in late 1991, produced no substantive results, but it was enormously significant. Syria participated, a major breakthrough. For the first time, Palestinians spoke for themselves in an international forum. Ancient foes sat around a common table to discuss issues that had long divided them. The Madrid conference revived a peace process suspended for more than a decade.[18]

Baker and Bush also blocked Shamir's efforts to solidify Israel's position in the occupied territories. When they discovered that the prime minister was committed to building more than five thousand new houses, they held up legislation providing Israel $10 billion in loan guarantees to help settle recently arrived Soviet Jews. They also stood up to the Israel lobby. "The settlements are counterproductive to peace," Bush affirmed, "and everybody knows that."[19] The president warned he would veto any loan that did not include provisions for stopping the settlements. Bush's courageous stand helped drive Shamir from office. His successor, the more amenable Yitzhak Rabin, agreed to stop building new settlements in the West Bank and the Gaza Strip. Bush's timely and forceful diplomacy kept Middle East peace hopes alive.[20]

In dealing with Haiti and the former Yugoslavia, the Bush administration was far less assertive. In September 1991, the Haitian military overthrew the popularly elected government of Jean-Bertrand Aristide. Baker at first responded firmly: "This coup must not and will not succeed."[21] But the administration did nothing more than impose sanctions to back up its tough talk. It briefly considered and quickly rejected military intervention. Taking over Haiti would be easy, Powell asserted; getting out, very difficult.[22]

17. William B. Quandt, *Peace Process: American Diplomacy and the Arab-Israeli Conflict Since 1967* (rev. ed., Berkeley, Calif., 2001), 296.
18. Douglas Little, *American Orientalism: The United States and the Middle East Since 1945* (Chapel Hill, N.C., 2004), 297–99.
19. Ibid., 300.
20. Quandt, *Peace Process*, 312–14.
21. Thomas Friedman column, *New York Times*, May 31, 1992.
22. David Halberstam, *War in a Time of Peace: Bush, Clinton, and the Generals* (New York, 2001), 267–68.

The former Yugoslavia offered an even more glaring example of U.S. unwillingness to uphold the new world order. An unwieldy amalgam of six republics composed of conflicting ethnic and religious groups, the country had been held together by the force of Marshal Tito's personality and fear of the USSR. With the end of the Cold War, ethnic hatreds exploded, and the country knitted together after World War I began to unravel. Fanning the nationalist hatreds of his people, Slobodan Milosevic plotted to create a greater Serbia at the expense of other ethnic groups. In the summer of 1991, he set out to wrest lands from Croatia, laying siege to two major cities and subjecting helpless civilians to deadly bombardment and horrendous destruction. The next year, he joined Bosnian Serbs in military operations against Bosnia's Muslims. The former Yugoslavia would become the burning foreign policy issue of the decade.

The Bush administration had no inclination to stop the carnage. It was by no means clear at the beginning what horrors Milosevic would inflict. Throughout 1991, top officials were preoccupied with the Persian Gulf and the fall of the USSR. Intervention had no strong advocates within the administration. The military adamantly opposed the use of force in the Balkans. To scare off civilians, Powell deliberately exaggerated the number of troops that would be needed. With the end of the Cold War, Yugoslavia lost its geopolitical significance, and civilian leaders saw no compelling national interest there. Memories of Vietnam still held sway. The administration viewed the Balkans as a European problem, and at first Europeans seemed to agree. But even after Milosevic struck Bosnia in 1992 there was no interest in taking action. Despite growing warnings of a new Holocaust, the administration did nothing to halt Serbia's brutal "ethnic cleansing" of Croats and Muslims. "Where is it written that the United States is the military policeman of the world?" State Department spokesperson Margaret Tutwiler asked.[23] "We don't have a dog in that fight," her boss Baker curtly proclaimed after a trip to Yugoslavia in 1991. Baker admitted in 1992 that Bosnia had become a "humanitarian nightmare," but the administration would go no further than assist modest relief efforts and give verbal support to halting and ineffectual European peace efforts.[24]

In its last weeks in office, a lame-duck administration undertook a limited intervention in embattled Somalia in East Africa. Torn by struggle among competing warlords, with civilians the victims, Somalia by 1992

23. Friedman column, *New York Times*, May 31, 1992.
24. Klaus Larres, " 'Bloody as Hell': Bush, Clinton, and the Abdication of American Leadership in the Former Yugoslavia, 1990–1995," *Journal of European Integration History* 10 (July 2004), 192.

was a horrendous humanitarian disaster. Starvation was epidemic. Thousands had been killed in the fighting, and refugees poured out of the country. Illustrating a new phenomenon in world affairs, images of human misery were beamed around the globe on television, creating demands to do something—the so-called CNN effect. Responding to such appeals, the administration in the summer agreed to transport UN troops to provide food and medical assistance. Perhaps to compensate for his opposition to intervention in Bosnia, Powell endorsed the dispatch of thirty-five thousand U.S. troops on a strictly limited mission of mercy to feed the hungry and aid the suffering. Once some semblance of order was established, they would be replaced by UN forces. The mission at first seemed to work.[25] But the Bush administration never really determined whether it was committed to the new world order under U.S. leadership its rhetoric spoke of or, because of domestic preoccupations, preferred retrenchment and retreat. The post–Cold War world was full of surprises, Baker's successor, Lawrence Eagleburger, insisted, resulting in "pasted together diplomacy."[26]

Even more than its predecessor, the administration of William Jefferson Clinton found adjustment to the new world order vexing. Clinton's aides had salvaged a once floundering election campaign with the simple slogan "It's the economy, stupid." In many ways, this administration seemed more attuned to the new era, making clear from the outset its preference for domestic issues. Although a graduate of Georgetown University's School of Foreign Service and a Rhodes scholar, Clinton seemed the polar opposite of Bush. Having spent his political career in state politics, the former governor of Arkansas was plainly less experienced with and informed on foreign policy issues. Smart, gregarious, charming, a charismatic and natural-born politician, he was also notoriously undisciplined in his work habits and private life. His few campaign pronouncements on foreign policy hinted at more forthright leadership and a more active role in defending human rights in such volatile areas as the Balkans. At heart, however, Clinton was a domestic policy "wonk" with a full agenda. In the beginning, at least, he appeared to hope that his foreign policy team could hold the world at bay while he implemented domestic reforms.

His top foreign policy advisers, National Security Adviser Anthony Lake and Secretary of State Warren Christopher, a protégé of Cyrus Vance, came mainly out of the liberal Democratic mold—burned by Vietnam, nervous about unilateral intervention, committed to working

25. Mann, *Vulcans*, 222–23; Halberstam, *War*, 250–52.
26. *New York Times*, December 20, 1992.

through the UN and other international organizations. Although a Kissinger protégé, Lake followed the precedent set by Scowcroft, becoming "by design the most obscure member of the Clinton foreign policy team."[27] The new president's relations with his uniformed advisers were especially tenuous. Having avoided military service during the Vietnam era and actively protested the war, he was viewed with contempt by some of the top brass who served him. His early efforts to defend the rights of homosexuals in the military provoked seething opposition in the armed services.[28]

The Clinton administration was deeply committed to promoting domestic prosperity through expanding foreign trade. The president himself was an unabashed enthusiast for globalization, like the eighteenth-century *philosophes* viewing commerce as the essential instrument to promote free markets, democracy, and eventually peace and prosperity. "Since we don't have geopolitics any more," one Clinton adviser pronounced, "trade is the name of the game." In embassies across the world, diplomats turned their attention to economics. Clinton cashed in all his political chips to secure congressional passage in 1993 of the North American Free Trade Agreement (NAFTA). He also vigorously promoted the Asia-Pacific Economic Community as a modern economic NATO and the General Agreement on Tariffs and Trade (GATT). The Clinton administration eventually presided over an enormous expansion of U.S. foreign trade, sparking one of the nation's longest periods of economic growth.[29]

Trade expansion also brought huge short-term tradeoffs and costly job displacement. NAFTA contributed to the prosperity of the 1990s, but it also eliminated jobs in the nation's already moribund manufacturing sector. Promotion of trade also involved unprecedented and unwelcome intrusion into the internal affairs of other nations. Globalization provoked growing backlash abroad and among protest groups at home. In the 1999 "Battle of Seattle," fifteen hundred disparate groups waged warfare for days in the streets of that northwestern metropolis, disrupting the meeting of the newly formed World Trade Organization.[30]

Committed to protecting human rights as well as expanding trade, the administration quickly discovered the two could be incompatible. Exports were important to domestic prosperity. In the most prominent cases, the administration therefore bowed to expediency without totally abandoning

27. Jason DeParle, "The Man Inside Bill Clinton's Foreign Policy," *New York Times Magazine*, August 20, 1995, 34.
28. Halberstam, *War*, 204–7, 415–19.
29. David Rothkopf, *Running the World: The Inside Story of the National Security Council and the Architects of American Power* (New York, 2004), 306–10, 344–49.
30. Nye, *Paradox*, 41.

its principles. Two hundred thousand Americans were employed in the sale of some $9 billion worth of exports to China, for example. Millions of Americans depended on cheap imports of shirts, pants, and dresses to clothe their families. Yet that country's often gross abuses of human rights offended the sensibilities of pressure groups, many Washington officials, and members of Congress. Clinton had charged Bush with "coddling tyrants from Baghdad to Beijing."[31] In 1993, his administration authorized most-favored-nation treatment for China for one year but conditioned its extension on China's performance in five human rights areas. When Beijing stonewalled, U.S. business interests complained and Commerce Department officials warned that loss of the China trade would cause higher prices for American consumers. The administration caved in, the following year extending most-favored-nation treatment without any conditions or penalties for violations of the 1993 terms. Henceforth, the administration abandoned any serious effort to shape conditions inside China.[32]

Clinton also quickly discovered the painful truth that in foreign policy U.S. presidents do not have to seek trouble, it finds them. The administration was even less surefooted on the increasingly difficult questions of peacekeeping and humanitarian interventions. In the 1992 campaign and its early days, it sounded interventionist. Clinton attacked Bush's inaction on Bosnia and affirmed that "no national issue is more urgent than securing democracy's triumph around the world." Lake hinted at greater activism by coining such vague phrases as "enlargement of democracy" and "pragmatic neo-Wilsonianism."[33]

Once more, the administration beat a hasty retreat. Unable to persuade European allies to lift an arms embargo against Bosnia and in the face of Powell's steadfast opposition to intervention, it would approve no more than harmless NATO air strikes to defend embattled UN peacekeepers. It grudgingly agreed to expand the U.S./UN mission in Somalia to capture the ambitious and recalcitrant warlord Mohammed Farah Aidid. But when eighteen GIs were killed in bloody fighting in Mogadishu on October 3, 1993, exposing television viewers to the spectacle of an American corpse being dragged through the streets of the city, it immediately scaled back the U.S. role and promised an alarmed public and Congress that U.S. troops would be out in six months.[34] A week later, closer to home—and much more humiliating—American soldiers and technicians dispatched to Haiti

31. Rothkopf, *Running the World*, 348.
32. Ibid., 348–52; James Mann, *About Face: A History of America's Curious Relationship with China from Nixon to Clinton* (New York, 1999), 274–308.
33. *Newsweek*, May 5, 1994, 54; DeParle, "Man Inside," 35.
34. Mark Bowden, *Black Hawk Down* (New York, 1999).

aboard the USS *Harlan County* as part of a larger effort to unseat a cruel military government turned back in the face of armed mobs on the docks of Port-au-Prince jeering "Somalia! Somalia!"[35]

While rampant instability wracked the globe, the administration developed guidelines for humanitarian intervention critics dismissed as "self-containment."[36] The United States would intervene only where international security was gravely threatened, a natural disaster required urgent relief, or egregious violations of human rights occurred. Other nations must share the costs, but GIs would participate only under U.S. command. In response to proliferating UN commitments, the administration in May 1994 spelled out seventeen even more restrictive guidelines for support of that body's peacekeeping operations. Making clear after Somalia its distaste for UN enterprises, it vowed to commit troops only where vital U.S. interests were threatened. Congress must approve the mission and make funds available. There must be clearly stated objectives, a reasonable chance of success, and a strategy for completing the job. The crisis must pose a serious threat to international peace and security or involve major violations of human rights. Clinton also urged the UN to scale back its ambitions. "If the American people are to say yes to UN peacekeeping, the United Nations must know when to say no."[37] Parodying John F. Kennedy's inaugural address, critics claimed that Clinton's United States would "pay only some prices, fight only some foes, and bear only some burdens in the defense of freedom."[38]

Not surprisingly, the United States and the rest of the world looked the other way in 1994 when ethnic and tribal rivalries in Rwanda in Central Africa produced what writer Samantha Power has called "the fastest, most efficient killing spree of the twentieth century."[39] While the world did nothing, a vengeful Hutu tribe murdered an estimated eight hundred thousand rival Tutsis, in some cases with machetes. Even a relatively small intervention might have made a difference, but the world did nothing. Paralyzed by recent memories of Somalia and Haiti, the administration did not even discuss the possibility of intervention. As if to insulate themselves from guilt and responsibility, U.S. officials employed the euphemism "acts of genocide." They sought mainly to get Americans out of the country. Clinton later acknowledged that Rwanda had been his

35. Halberstam, *War*, 270–71.
36. Thomas Friedman column, *New York Times*, October 1, 1993.
37. Ibid.
38. Ibid.; *New York Times*, January 29, 1994; *Washington Post*, May 6, 1994.
39. Samantha Power, "Bystanders to Genocide," *Atlantic Monthly*, September 2001, 84.

administration's worst foreign policy mistake. "We never even had a staff meeting on it. . . . ," he conceded. "I blew it."[40]

The administration shifted gears in the fall of 1994. Liberals, many of them onetime opponents of the Vietnam War, increasingly urged the use of military force to prevent human suffering. Action-oriented analogies from Munich and the Holocaust now competed with the constraining Vietnam Syndrome as influences on policy decisions. After months of soul-searching, sanctions that hurt victims more than oppressors, and warnings that were ignored, the administration in September used the threat of a full-scale invasion of Haiti along with a peace mission composed of former president Jimmy Carter, the now civilian Colin Powell, and Georgia senator Sam Nunn to remove a brutal military dictatorship and restore to power the erratic—but elected—Aristide. Clinton justified the action as necessary to "restore democracy" and, more pragmatically, prevent a massive flight of Haitian refugees to U.S. shores. As U.S. paratroopers flew toward Haiti, the negotiators finally worked out a deal. This time, GIs met a warm reception. National Security Adviser Lake rode through the streets of Port-au-Prince in the back of a flatbed truck to boisterous shouts of *"bon jour."*[41] The intervention did not bring democracy to Haiti or lead to a new policy toward humanitarian intervention, but it spared some suffering and helped improve a badly tarnished Clinton image.

Although Clinton in 1992 had attacked Bush for inaction in the Balkans, his administration was no more eager to grapple with what came to be called "the problem from hell." Stories of rape, torture, executions, concentration camps, and indiscriminate shelling of civilians all under the anodyne rubric of "ethnic cleansing" provoked growing humanitarian outrage, but the potential costs of intervention and dubious prospects for success stood as insuperable barriers. Congress was leery. There was little public support. Until his departure from government in late 1993, Joint Chiefs chairman Powell stood as a powerful obstacle. The administration would do no more than air-drop food for besieged civilians, undertake "covert inaction" by facilitating arms shipments to Bosnian Muslims, and verbally support the European Community's lame efforts to arrange a diplomatic settlement. Europeans and Americans blamed each other for doing nothing.[42]

After years of hesitation, the United States in the summer of 1995 finally acted in the former Yugoslavia. By this time, the administration

40. David Remnick, "The Wanderer," *New Yorker*, September 18, 2006, 63.
41. DeParle, "Man Inside," 35; Bob Sacochis, *The Immaculate Invasion* (New York, 1999).
42. Larres, " 'Bloody as Hell,' " 196–97.

seemed to be falling apart. Its major domestic initiatives had been frustrated by an assertive newly elected Republican Congress led by conservative Georgia representative Newt Gingrich. Foreign policy appeared in such disarray that Christopher had to be talked out of resigning. His reputation in tatters, the president plainly faced trouble in the upcoming presidential election. In the Balkans, the Serb massacre of a supposedly UN-protected Bosnian Muslim enclave in the city of Srebrenica in July accompanied by some of the worst war crimes since World War II aroused worldwide outrage and galvanized a reticent Washington to action. Liberal and neo-conservative interventionists pressed the administration to do something. Majority Leader Bob Dole, a potential presidential foe in 1996, put together a Senate bloc for intervention. Humiliated by Somalia and Haiti, three years of inaction in the Balkans, and the increasingly blatant defiance of Milosevic, Clinton himself was moved to exclaim: "The United States cannot be a punching bag in the world any more."[43] Its "unique superpower status" was the "only hope for restoring a semblance of order and humanity to the Balkans."[44] Forceful moves might also help the president's reelection chances. The rise to power of France's hawkish Jacques Chirac in place of the pro-Serbian François Mitterand provided crucial international support. Finally, on July 1995, while chipping golf balls on the White House putting green, Clinton exploded: "I'm getting creamed. . . . We've got to find some kind of policy and move ahead."[45]

In August 1995, with full U.S. backing, NATO began intensive bombing of Bosnian Serb positions using the most modern military technology and eventually taking out Milosevic's communications center. This action shattered the aura of Serb invincibility. It forced a cease-fire in October and drove the warring parties to the conference table at Wright-Patterson Air Force Base in Dayton, Ohio. There, in late 1995, U.S. diplomat Richard Holbrooke brokered what journalist David Halberstam called "an imperfect peace to a very imperfect part of the world after an unusually cruel war."[46] The Dayton Accords divided Bosnia into autonomous Muslim-Croat and Serb regions and provided for a NATO force to maintain the precarious cease-fire. Clinton sent U.S. troops to participate in the peacekeeping mission; to cover his political flanks, he limited the commitment to twelve months (later extended).

43. Halberstam, War, 331.
44. Larres, " 'Bloody as Hell,' " 201.
45. Halberstam, War, 303–6, 317.
46. Ibid., 358; Larres, " 'Bloody as Hell,' " 200–201.

Clinton defeated Dole by a substantial margin in 1996, but foreign policy played no more than a peripheral part, and his reelection brought no
clarity to America's role in the world. With no clear external threat and
the nation prospering, there was little incentive for engagement. A band
of avidly nationalistic congressional Republicans flaunted their hostility
to the world. Some boasted of not having passports. House leader Richard
Armey of Texas claimed that he did not need to go to Europe because he
had been there—once! Gingrich's Contract with America, a much publicized political agenda for conservative Republicans, mentioned foreign
policy only in passing and stressed simply that America should maintain
a strong defense and GIs must not serve under UN command. The ascension of the arch-nationalist Jesse Helms to chairmanship of the once
prestigious Senate Foreign Relations Committee seemed to internationalists the cruelest of ironies.[47]

47. Max Frankel, "The Shroud," *New York Times Magazine*, November 17, 1994.

After January 1998, Clinton's presidency was increasingly crippled when he first denied, then, faced with incontrovertible evidence, admitted, an affair with a young White House intern, Monica Lewinsky, prompting his congressional foes to initiate impeachment proceedings.

The Clinton foreign policy team underwent major changes in the second term. Samuel "Sandy" Berger replaced Lake as national security adviser. An old friend and political soul mate of the president, Berger was a lawyer and political operative with little foreign policy experience. But he knew Clinton's mind better than anyone else. He was a consummate pragmatist untroubled by the lack of a strategic blueprint.[48] More important in terms of precedent—and policy—was the replacement of Christopher with UN ambassador Madeleine Albright, the first female secretary of state. The daughter of a Czech diplomat who escaped both the Nazi invasion and the Communist takeover, Albright claimed to know the meaning of Munich firsthand. The United States, in her view, must take responsibility for upholding world order. She was consistently the most hawkish of Clinton's advisers. "What's the point of having this superb military you're always talking about," she once berated Powell, "if we can't use it?" Described as the "ultimate independent woman," she had raised three daughters before launching a career. She bristled when reporters wrote about her appearance. Effective on television and in public, she won points at the White House during the 1996 campaign by telling an appreciative Cuban-American audience in Miami's Orange Bowl that the shooting down of a civilian aircraft by Fidel Castro's pilots was "not cojones but cowardice." By sheer force of personality, she became a key player, especially with regard to the Balkans.[49]

While the Clinton administration struggled to survive, southern Europe seethed with conflict. This time it was Kosovo, the most volatile area of a strife-torn part of the world. The region was populated mainly by Kosovar Albanians who were also Muslims. But Serbs viewed Kosovo as sacred ground because of their military defeat there in 1389 at the hands of the Turks, on which they blamed the fall of their empire. Left out of the Dayton discussions, Kosovo exploded soon after. In 1997, the Kosovars formed a Kosovo Liberation Army (KLA) to win their independence and mounted guerrilla warfare against local Serbs. The Serbs struck back with a vengeance, burning villages and murdering those Kosovars they could get their hands on. They moved slowly at first; "a village a day keeps

48. Halberstam, War, 404–9.
49. Elaine Sciolino, "Madeleine Albright's Audition," New York Times Magazine, September 22, 1996, 66–67, 87–88, 104.

NATO away" was their sardonic slogan. Their intent was nonetheless unmistakable, the results devastating. An especially bloody massacre at the
town of Racak in late 1998 where all adult males were marked for execution again provoked cries for international action. In Washington, the
killing gave ammunition to hawks and weakened foes of intervention.[50]

In early 1999, a still-reluctant administration once more decided to act.
The Senate acquitted Clinton of impeachment charges in February. Still
leery of a Balkans quagmire, most military leaders continued to resist intervention. Within and outside the government, however, pressures
mounted. Advocates increasingly compared the Serbs' ethnic cleansing
with the Holocaust. Albright passionately warned of another Munich and
derided the military's caution. So important and visible was her role that
the conflict came to be called "Madeleine's War."[51] In March, the United
States along with NATO finally went to war. If memories of World War II
pushed the administration to act, more recent and still-haunting recollec-
tions of Vietnam dictated the way it fought. Clinton hoped to replicate
the Bosnian experience, where modest bombing had forced Milosevic to
negotiate. To assuage fears in Congress and among European allies, the
administration again relied exclusively on air power. In what proved a
major miscalculation, the president even publicly affirmed: "I do not in-
tend to put our troops in Kosovo to fight a war."[52]

As always, the conflict in Kosovo proved more complex than anticipated. NATO commander U.S. Gen. Wesley Clark, another Rhodes
scholar from Arkansas, ran the war from Brussels and faced the unenvi-
able challenge of working out strategies acceptable to seventeen allies
and a divided Washington. His greatest problems were with the Pentagon. The allies underestimated Milosevic's determination. The bombing
was implemented gradually, and the Serbs stubbornly withstood it, evoking in some quarters memories of Vietnam. But Milosevic also misjudged
NATO's unwillingness to lose. Faced with that prospect, the allies at an
April meeting in Washington celebrating the alliance's fiftieth anniversary agreed to escalate the war. They drastically stepped up the bombing.
More important, they authorized preparations for the use of ground
troops. "All options are on the table," Clinton publicly affirmed.[53]

What U.S. military leaders called the Revolution in Military Affairs
worked dramatic results. It was a new kind of high-tech war, virtual war, it

50. Halberstam, War, 409–10.
51. Colin L. Powell with Joseph Persico, My American Journey (New York, 1995), 576.
52. Halberstam, War, 409, 423.
53. Ibid., 475.

seemed, fought by professional forces with no sacrifice required of the American people and minimal intrusion on their lives. Giant B-2 Stealth bombers that could not be seen from the ground flew fourteen hours from bases in Missouri to deliver large payloads of two-thousand-pound bombs guided by global positioning systems with remarkable accuracy to targets fifty thousand feet below. The bombing devastated Serb airfields and ground forces and eventually Belgrade itself, causing troops to mutiny and political opposition to form. In June, Milosevic conceded.[54] A war fought to minimize Western military losses killed an estimated ten thousand people, many of them civilians, turning on their head just-war principles of sparing noncombatants. The high-technology war fought in Kosovo cost the United States alone an estimated $2.3 billion, not the sort of price tag even a hyperpower can afford on a regular basis. The distinguished military historian John Keegan excitedly hailed the outcome as a "victory for air power and air power alone." In some ways it was, but the threat of ground troops and Russia's refusal to back the Serbs also contributed to the outcome.[55]

The war in Kosovo solved the immediate problem without providing a long-term solution. Milosevic was defeated, a major achievement, and in September 2000—with substantial U.S. assistance—those Serbs who had once cheered his nationalistic rantings voted him out of office. Indicted for war crimes while the fighting raged in Kosovo, he was subsequently tried at the UN's International Tribunal for the Former Yugoslavia and died before the proceedings were completed. Milosevic had used the start of the war to drive Albanians from Kosovo, producing more human suffering and millions of refugees. As the war ended, a vengeful KLA sought complete independence and expulsion of the remaining Serbs from Kosovo, making victims of those who had once been perpetrators and creating new political problems. Although he had gone to war with great reluctance and fought with the utmost caution, Clinton basked in NATO's victory. There was even talk of a Clinton Doctrine under which the United States would employ its power in cases of humanitarian disaster where the costs seemed manageable and prospects for success reasonable. In fact, the president never openly articulated such a policy. There was little public support. In any event, such wars proved not to be the norm in the new world order.[56]

54. Ibid., 457–60.
55. George C. Herring, "Analogies at War: The United States, the Conflict in Kosovo, and the Uses of History," in Albrecht Schnabel and Ramesh Thakur, eds., *Kosovo and the Challenge of Humanitarian Intervention* (Tokyo, 2000), 355.
56. G. John Ikenberry, "The Costs of Victory: American Power and the Use of Force in the Contemporary Order," in Schnabel and Thakur, *Kosovo*, 87–88.

Ironically, a president who had taken office with a full domestic agenda and little apparent interest in foreign policy ended his second term by becoming a foreign policy president. Frustrated at home by an unrelenting and fiercely partisan Republican opposition, he turned his attentions abroad, traveling to places where U.S. presidents had not gone before, Botswana, Slovenia, South Africa.[57] Pushed by war veterans in the Senate, he defied the die-hards by normalizing relations with Vietnam in 1995. Five years later, he became the first president to visit the former enemy. He stayed four days, longer than customary for such visits. In Hanoi and Ho Chi Minh City, he drew huge crowds. His triumphal visit represented for himself and his nation a sort of closure for a long and painful national experience.[58]

Clinton also took an active role in international peacemaking, even in such perennial trouble spots as Northern Ireland and the Middle East. He and his special envoy, former Senate majority leader George Mitchell, exerted great effort to broker a tenuous power-sharing agreement between Catholics and Protestants in embattled Northern Ireland. The deal fell apart before Clinton left office, but it marked a small step on the long road toward peace in that war-torn area.

In October 1993, Clinton had presided over the signing of the Oslo Accords, an agreement negotiated through Norwegian good offices calling for the PLO to recognize Israel and renounce terrorism and for Israel to turn over the Gaza Strip and the town of Jericho to a newly constituted Palestine Authority. That agreement was supposed to lead to further negotiations on the status of the West Bank and Jerusalem. The Oslo agreement immediately came under fire from extremists on both sides. In November 1995, Rabin was assassinated by a right-wing law student, ironically while making an appeal for peace. Clinton in his last years tried desperately to revive the peace process. In 1998, on the Eastern Shore of Maryland, he persuaded hard-line Israeli premier Benjamin Netanyahu to turn over more of the West Bank to Palestinians. Confronted with staunch opposition when he returned home, the prime minister reneged. During his last year in office, Clinton dragged new Israeli prime minister Ehud Barak and Arafat to Camp David for a meeting. Barak seemed flexible, but Arafat rejected any deal that did not provide for Israel's withdrawal from its pre-1967 borders. When war hero Ariel Sharon in September 2000 made much publicized and highly

57. Halberstam, War, 482–83.
58. George C. Herring, America's Longest War: The United States and Vietnam, 1950–1975 (4th ed., New York, 2002), 365, 367–68.

provocative visits to two of Islam's holiest places in Jerusalem, a new *intifada* erupted in the West Bank. The peace process was dead.[59]

The Clinton foreign policy legacy is surprisingly full given his administration's early hesitancy and his personal predilection for domestic policy. The United States collaborated with Russia to reduce nuclear inventories left from the Cold War. It opened a diplomatic dialogue with North Korea to check a rising nuclear threat. It enlarged NATO to include some of the former Soviet Union's Eastern and Central European satellites, rewrote the post–World War II peace treaty with Japan, and in 1996 sent warships to help defuse a dangerous crisis in the Taiwan Straits. The administration branched out in new directions. Activist first lady Hillary Clinton also traveled widely abroad, promoting the radical notion that women's rights had a place on the international agenda. In the second term, she gained support from Albright, who instructed diplomats to monitor women's rights internationally.[60]

In the realm of international politics, as Garry Wills has observed, Clinton was a "foreign policy minimalist, doing as little as possible as late as possible in place after place."[61] He apologized for U.S. inaction in Rwanda. In the Balkans, his administration at first stumbled badly, at very high human cost. To its credit, it eventually employed U.S. military power in collaboration with NATO to limit the bloodshed and work out shaky peace arrangements in Bosnia and Kosovo, even though there was little popular or congressional support for such interventions. In all, Clinton employed military forces eighty-four times in eight years.

Clinton's administration was the first to deal systematically with what would become the most pressing national security issue of the new century: international terrorism. It responded perfunctorily, normally with sporadic air strikes, against terrorist attacks on New York's World Trade Center in 1993, a U.S. Air Force barracks in Saudi Arabia in 1996, embassies in Kenya and Tanzania in 1998, and the destroyer USS *Cole* on the eve of the 2000 election. The president authorized the killing of al Qaeda terrorist leader Osama bin Laden, scoring one near miss with a missile. But he never seriously considered ground operations against bin Laden's base camp in Afghanistan or going after his host, the Taliban government. Behind the scenes, the administration worked with other governments to foil several major terrorist plots, including one against the Los Angeles airport on the eve of the millennium. It named the indefatigable and

59. Little, *American Orientalism*, 301–4.
60. *Newsweek*, April 7, 1997.
61. Garry Wills, "The Clinton Principle," *New York Times Magazine*, January 19, 1997, 44.

abrasive Richard Clarke as coordinator of counterterrorism operations. But there was no real sense of urgency and thus no strong incentive to take drastic action. "What's it gonna take, Dick?" a terrorism specialist asked Clarke prophetically. "Does Al Qaeda have to attack the Pentagon to get their attention?"[62]

In foreign as in domestic policy, the administration's major claims to success were in the realm of economics.[63] A timely bailout loan of $25 billion helped avert economic disaster in Mexico in 1995. By keeping U.S. markets open, the administration also helped contain the impact of the Asian economic meltdown of 1997. During the Clinton years, the United States concluded more than three hundred trade agreements. While the country enjoyed unparalleled prosperity, there was little sign that globalization was advancing prosperity in less developed nations or producing the stabilizing and democratizing results its enthusiasts claimed. On the contrary, by the end of the century it had provoked a strong backlash from labor unions and some liberals at home, and from leaders of developing nations who on the one hand resented the competitive edge enjoyed by the rich nations and on the other feared outside reformers who sought to impose on their shops labor and environmental standards.

The American mood at the end of the century was one of triumphalism and smug, insular complacency. According to a January 2000 poll, Americans ranked foreign policy twentieth in terms of importance. Following the lead of cable television, network news focused increasingly on entertainment and trivia and further slashed its coverage of events abroad. On college campuses, the teaching of foreign languages and area studies declined sharply. Defense spending remained at a remarkably high level through the 1990s—more than $325 billion in 1995. The United States maintained the capability to fight two major wars simultaneously. But the foreign affairs budget was sharply reduced. The United States was deeply in arrears to the UN and the World Health Organization. The State Department closed thirty embassies and twenty-five United States Information Agency libraries, provoking Christopher to protest that we "can't advance American interests by lowering the flag."[64] Foreign policy played no more than an incidental role in the 2000 presidential campaign. To foreigners, self-indulgent Americans seemed to revel in their prosperity, a minority of the world's population recklessly consuming a huge proportion of its resources. America was both admired

62. Rothkopf, *Running the World*, 385; *Washington Post Weekly*, January 7–13, 2002.
63. *Newsweek*, March 6, 1996.
64. *New York Times*, October 17, 1996.

and feared. Other peoples saw its ability to project its values abroad as a threat to their identities. The awesome display of U.S. military power in Kosovo worried allies as well as potential enemies. German chancellor Gerhard Schroeder fretted about the danger of U.S. unilateralism. A French diplomat observed in the spring of 1999 that the major danger in international politics was the American "hyperpower."[65]

III

After another period of stumbling and uncertainty, the new Republican administration of George W. Bush, son of the former president, would use the opportunity created by the devastating terrorist attacks of September 11, 2001, to effect the most revolutionary changes in U.S. foreign policy since the Truman Doctrine of 1947.

The younger Bush gave little hint in his campaign of what was to come. Compared to his father's deeply rooted internationalism, his experience and mindset were parochial. A graduate of Yale University and the Harvard Business School, he had traveled abroad very little, worked mostly in business, and in politics served only as governor of Texas. In the campaign, he emphasized the need for humility in dealing with other nations. He distanced himself from the Wilsonian idealist label he sought to pin on the Democrats and especially his opponent, Vice President Al Gore, expressing disdain for humanitarian interventions and "nation-building." "We don't need to have the 82nd Airborne escorting kids to kindergarten" in the Balkans, added his future national security adviser and foreign policy alter ego Condoleezza Rice, the first African American and first woman to hold that post. The United States must no longer be the "world's 911."[66]

Bush sought to make up for his own lack of preparation by naming what seemed a strong national security team. Appointment of the immensely popular Colin Powell as secretary of state, the first African American to hold that position, cheered internationalists perhaps more than it should have given his stalwart opposition to using force for humanitarian purposes. But the real power rested with Secretary of Defense Donald Rumsfeld and Vice President Dick Cheney. The two had worked together since the Nixon years. They shared their former boss's view that national security policy was the top priority. Gloomy in outlook and countenance, conservative in his politics, secretive almost to the point of

---

65. Ikenberry, "Costs of Victory," 97.
66. Michael C. Desch, "Liberals, Neocons, and Realcons: The Politics of Humanitarian Interentions," *Orbis* 46 (Fall 2001), 528.

being sinister, Cheney sought to restore to the presidency the power he believed had been lost through Watergate. He would become the most powerful vice president ever. The dynamic, hard-driving Rumsfeld was a master of bureaucratic warfare. The two men had been deeply disturbed by U.S. failure in Vietnam, the denouement of which they had witnessed from the Ford White House. They had opposed Kissinger's policy of detente. They believed that the United States must maintain absolute military supremacy and use its power to promote its own interests, not permitting the niceties of diplomacy or the scruples of allies to get in the way. Above all, they shared an especially assertive form of nationalism.[67] Less noticed at the outset but equally important was the presence in key second-level positions of neo-conservatives such as Paul Wolfowitz, "Scooter" Libby, and Douglas Feith, men who passionately believed that America's power must be used to reshape the world in its image.

From the start, the new administration took a decidedly unilateralist turn. Top officials expressed contempt for Clinton's bumbling internationalism. They believed that the United States, as the world's only superpower, could best protect its interests by shedding international constraints and acting alone, even preemptively if necessary, to eliminate potential threats. They revived and gave top priority to developing the missile defense system that Reagan had initiated, a project of dubious practicality and reliability that offered the allure of invulnerability but also violated treaties with the former Soviet Union. In the first months, they seemed to go out of their way to thumb their noses at other nations and international institutions. Bush spurned the Middle East peace process Clinton had nurtured. Without any prior consultation, Rice informed the European ambassadors that the Kyoto Protocol on global warming was dead, thus drastically weakening an admittedly flawed agreement the Clinton administration had helped negotiate but had not submitted to the Senate. The new administration also suspended talks with North Korea aimed at stopping the development of long-range missiles. State Department spokesperson Richard Haass euphemistically labeled it "a la carte multilateralism." "We'll look at each agreement and make a decision, rather than come out with a broad-based approach," he said.[68] Critics at home and abroad deplored the administration's rude manners and go-it-alone methods as a new isolationism.

In the early morning hours of September 11, 2001, an unusually clear and crisp late summer day, nineteen Arab terrorists operating under orders

67. Mann, *Vulcans*, 163.
68. *New York Times*, July 31, 2001.

from Osama bin Laden hijacked four commercial airliners and used them as missiles to strike New York's World Trade Center and the Pentagon. A planned attack on the Capitol or White House was thwarted when a revolt of courageous passengers forced a crash landing on Pennsylvania farmland. After two enormous explosions, Manhattan's landmark twin towers crumbled, killing 2,603 people, filling the city with smoke, and leaving a massive pile of rubble at what came to be called Ground Zero. The attack on the Pentagon left another 125 people dead; an additional 246 died on the aircraft.

The 9/11 attacks were not random acts of violence. Bin Laden's al Qaeda organization aimed to restore traditional Islam to its rightful place in the universe. The immediate goal was to eliminate the "near enemy," "apostate states" like Saudi Arabia, Egypt, Pakistan, and Jordan. Because the United States backed the rulers of these nations—indeed ensured their survival—it became the "far enemy." America's long-standing support for Israel and its "occupation" after 1991 of Saudi Arabia, site of Islam's most holy places, further branded it as the font of evil. Bin Laden and his followers hoped by striking the United States in a spectacular manner to rally jihadists across the world. By exposing U.S. vulnerability, they sought to destroy the aura of its power. They also hoped to goad it to invade a Muslim country where its killing of the faithful would provoke rage and rally more adherents. America might also bog down as the USSR had and be forced to abandon the "apostate" states.[69]

For the United States, September 11, 2001, ranks with Pearl Harbor as a colossal intelligence failure. After the fact, as with December 7, 1941, numerous clues pointed to a possible terrorist action and even to its type and target. Bin Laden was known to be responsible for earlier attacks on U.S. interests, most recently the *Cole*. Some of the hijackers had entered the United States illegally; the names of several were in databases with lists of potential terrorists. Some had violated the rules of their immigration status. Hijackers aroused suspicions by inquiring at flight schools about learning to fly passenger aircraft but admitting they would not need to know how to land. In 1998, an NSC counterterrorism group had carried out an exercise in which hijackers took over aircraft and loaded them with explosives to attack Washington. The World Trade Center had been the target of one terrorist explosion and was mentioned as a candidate for another. During the summer, U.S. intelligence intercepted al Qaeda communications promising that "something spectacular" was going to happen. "Bin

69. Mark Danner, "Taking Stock of the Forever War," *New York Times Magazine*, September 11, 2005, 50–51.

Laden Determined to Attack in U.S." screamed the headlines of one section of the CIA's August 6, 2001, President's Daily Briefing.[70]

A government lulled into a false sense of security by a decade of peace,
riven by bureaucratic rivalries, and focused on other matters missed the
signals. The various agencies responsible for counterterrorism, the FBI,
CIA, Defense Department, and NSC, did not communicate and, worse,
sometimes concealed information from each other, preventing them
from putting together the pieces of the puzzle. Despite a pattern of terrorist attacks up to the *Cole*, the agencies had not assigned high priority to
the issue and even sought to shift responsibility elsewhere. Top officials
were focused on missile defense and a possible threat from Iraq. They dismissed warnings of terrorist threats passed on during the transition. It was
a classic case of lack of interest, imagination, and communication leading
responsible officials to look past plain if not always distinct signs of a
deadly terrorist attack.[71]

Nine-eleven worked dramatic changes in the national psyche. For the
first time since 1814, the continental United States came under foreign attack. In one fiery moment, the intellectual and emotional baggage left
from Vietnam and the complacency that marked the 1990s were swept
aside in a surge of fear and anger. An already faltering economy suffered
further damage. In their shock and grief, Americans suddenly felt vulnerable. Speaking with a single voice for one of the few times since the 1964
Gulf of Tonkin Resolution, Congress granted the president sweeping new
authority to combat international terrorism.

An administration seemingly unfocused and floundering suddenly
found purpose and direction. Experts warned that terrorism represented
a new kind of non-state threat not to be dealt with by conventional
means, but Bush and his advisers responded in entirely traditional ways.
Confounding those who only recently had dismissed him as a lightweight, the president gave a powerful address before a joint session of
Congress, rallying the nation behind an all-out global war "to answer
these attacks and rid the world of evil." The analogue of war was familiar
to Americans and therefore reassuring, but it proved problematic in confronting a very different enemy. Responding slowly and deliberately,
the administration mobilized military forces to strike bin Laden and the

70. *New York Times*, July 25, 2004; *The 9/11 Commission Report: Final Report of the National Commission on Terrorist Attacks on the United States* (New York, 2004), 254–77;
Richard A. Clarke, *Against All Enemies: Inside America's War on Terror* (New York,
2004), 227–46.
71. *9/11 Commission Report*, 339–60.

fundamentalist Taliban regime that sheltered him in Afghanistan. In the parlance of the Old West, the president vowed to bring back the "evil one" dead or alive."[72]

September 11 evoked an outpouring of sympathy from abroad. "We are all Americans," the French newspaper *Le Monde* eloquently opined. "We are all New Yorkers." Officials who only recently had spurned collaboration with other nations now under Powell's leadership began cobbling together an unwieldy coalition composed of old allies such as Britain and France, former enemies Russia and China, and even pariah states such as Pakistan to attack on a variety of fronts and in different ways a new kind of foe and its backers, hinting, mistakenly as it turned out, that the summer's unilateralism was a thing of the past. The president's stark and tactless warning that "either you are with us or you are with the terrorists" more accurately reflected the direction the administration would take.[73]

The first phase of the war confounded military experts. Because of its forbidding geography, harsh climate, and fierce tribal rivalries, Afghanistan was historically a graveyard of great-power ambitions, most recently, of course, the Soviet Union's. Applying on a much larger scale the new high-tech methods of warfare used in the Balkans—"the first cavalry charge of the twenty-first century," Rumsfeld called it—the United States relied on air power and Afghan proxies to eliminate the despised and surprisingly weak Taliban and destroy bin Laden's training camps. Small numbers of U.S. special forces slipped into Afghanistan and sent signals to B-52 bombers to direct laser-guided bombs against suspected Taliban and al Qaeda bases. Americans on horseback worked with the friendly Northern Alliance to attack enemy fighters. In less than four months the Taliban was on the run and al Qaeda's operations in Afghanistan were crippled. Only one U.S. casualty was incurred from enemy fire. The United States in December 2001 installed Hamid Karzai as head of a new interim government. Administration supporters sneered at those who had warned of a quagmire.[74]

In fact, the war managers made crucial errors that turned tactical success into strategic failure. Properly worried about getting bogged down in Afghanistan and determined to convert the armed services to a new form of warfare, Rumsfeld and his civilian planners relied on air power and local forces to do what otherwise would have required large numbers of

---

72. September 20, 2001, www.whitehouse.gov/news/releases/2001/09/20010920-8.html.
73. Ibid.
74. Michael Kelly, "Myths of the Month," *Washington Post*, October 31, 2001; John Leo, "Quagmire, Schagmire," *U.S. News and World Report*, November 26, 2001, 52.

Americans. Without sufficient U.S. forces on the ground, bin Laden and Taliban leader Mullah Omar, along with numerous supporters, eluded capture near Tora Bora in December 2002 by paying off or evading Afghan fighters. They slipped away into the impenetrable mountains of Pakistan, an event of huge symbolic importance. Never enthusiastic about the job of reconstruction, the administration engaged in what critics called "nation-building lite," making inadequate preparations and providing insufficient funds for a formidable task. United States officials were already contemplating an invasion of Iraq, and preparations for that war diverted attention and resources from Afghanistan. Large parts of the country fell under the control of local warlords. Opium production regained its place as the nation's major cash crop. The government's authority barely extended beyond the capital, Kabul. Afghanistan, in time, disappeared from the front pages; an administration that had vowed to take the "evil one" stopped using bin Laden's name in public statements.[75]

While the war in Afghanistan lagged amid claims of victory, the White House unveiled a new national security doctrine. Even before the end of 2001, top officials had turned from the complicated task of destroying terrorist cells to the threat of weapons of mass destruction (WMD). To the shock of many observers, in his January 2002 State of the Union address, Bush identified an "axis of evil" composed of Iran, Iraq, and North Korea and sounded alarms that weapons of mass destruction produced by such rogue states might get into the hands of terrorists. He thus connected the global war on terrorism (GWOT in bureaucratese) with the danger of nuclear proliferation. Coming without any consultation, the speech caused consternation among major allies. In a June 2002 commencement address at West Point, the president affirmed that "in the world we have entered, the only path to safety is the path of action."[76]

In September, the administration issued the new doctrine. Prepared mainly in Rice's NSC and written, at Bush's instruction, in words "the boys in Lubbock" could understand, the strategy paper used 9/11 and the war on terrorism to elevate to doctrine ideas conservative and neoconservative Republicans had been discussing for years. It drew heavily on the 1992 Defense Planning Guidance Document repudiated by the first Bush administration. It manifested the influence of Wolfowitz and those

75. Seymour Hersh, "The Other War," New Yorker, April 12, 2004, 40–47; Michael Ignatieff, "Nation-Building Lite," New York Times Magazine, July 28, 2002, 26–31, 54, 57, 59.
76. The origins of the "axis of evil" phrase are discussed in David Frum, The Right Man: The Surprise Presidency of George Bush (New York, 2003), 238–45, 268–71.

neo-conservatives who viewed 9/11 as a "transformative" moment that put "events in much sharper relief."[77]

The new document combined ringing reaffirmations about spreading democracy with tough-minded statements about the use of U.S. power. It admitted to only one "sustainable model for national success: freedom, democracy, and free enterprise," vowed to "use this moment of opportunity to extend the benefits of freedom across the globe," and pledged to "defend liberty and justice because these principles are right and true for all peoples everywhere." The United States would do what was needed to prevent any single nation or combination of nations from challenging its military pre-eminence. The document paid lip service to cooperation with allies but also affirmed that the nation would "act apart when our interests and unique responsibility require." Threats must be met before they reached U.S. shores. The United States would not wait until it had "absolute proof" of danger from weapons of mass destruction. It would not "hesitate to act alone, if necessary, to exercise our right of self-defense by acting pre-emptively." The principles of military preeminence, unilateralism, and preemptive war departed sharply from the realism of the first Bush admin-istration and the basic principles that had guided Cold War strategies.[78]

The new doctrine provoked a varied and often emotional response. Conservatives cheered and insisted that what public intellectual Robert Kagan called a "Behemoth with a conscience" would not abuse its power. John Gaddis hailed a "truly 'grand' strategy" to transform the Middle East by bringing it into the modern world. The "world must be made safe for democracy," he concluded, "because otherwise democracy will not be safe in the world."[79] On the other side, the New York Times complained that what was already being called the Bush Doctrine struck a tone of arrogance worthy of the Roman Empire or Napoleon. "The boys in Lubbock may want to pause before signing on for the overly aggressive stance Mr. Bush has outlined," it concluded.[80] Harvard international relations specialist Stanley Hoffmann branded Cheney and Rumsfeld "High Noon sheriffs" and scored the Bush Doctrine as "Wilsonianism in boots."[81] Critics warned that the doctrine of preemption would encourage other nations to do the same, shattering any hope of world order.

77. Nicholas Lemann, "The War on What?" New Yorker, September 16, 2002, 44.
78. The text is in New York Times, September 20, 2002.
79. John Lewis Gaddis, "A Grand Strategy for Transformation," Foreign Policy 133 (No-vember/December 2002), 22.
80. New York Times, September 20, 2002.
81. Stanley Hoffmann, "The High and the Mighty," American Prospect, January 13, 2003, 28–29.

Long before releasing the new doctrine, the administration began to contemplate war with Iraq. Dictator Saddam Hussein had somehow survived the crushing defeat of 1991 and a decade of UN sanctions, a glaring irritant to those like Cheney who had hoped to topple him in the Gulf War. Even in the first days of the second Bush administration, there was talk of Iraq. On the night of September 12, 2001, a still-shaken president wandering the White House Situation Room asked Richard Clarke "to go back over everything. See if Saddam did this. . . . I want to know any shred."[82] Rumsfeld and Wolfowitz actually pressed for war with Iraq immediately after 9/11, but Powell urged focusing on Afghanistan, and Bush prudently concurred, although he did initiate war planning in November. Once the Afghan conflict appeared won, Iraq immediately resurfaced. Officials dismissed continued diplomatic pressure as too slow, a coup unlikely. Certain that Saddam had or would soon have weapons of mass destruction and fearing he might give them to terrorists, they were set on removing him. "A decision was not made," Haass later observed, "a decision happened, and you can't say when or how."[83]

"Why Iraq? Why now?" These were questions often asked in the days ahead, and the answers are as complex as the individuals who pushed for war. The easy response, of course, was oil, but the reasons went much deeper. For the neo-conservatives, war satisfied deep philosophical convictions as well as immediate practical concerns. The neo-cons, as they came to be called, included Wolfowitz, Defense Department adviser Richard Perle, and journalist William Kristol. Along with Cheney's chief of staff, Libby, Undersecretary of Defense Feith, and Undersecretary of State John Bolton, they formed a sort of "cabal" under the younger Bush. Utopian in outlook, they believed that the United States had a moral duty to oppose tyranny and spread democracy. In their view, Saddam Hussein was behind world terrorism and would soon have WMD. Many of them had close ties to Israel and insisted that Saddam's overthrow would make that vital ally more secure. They fervently believed that extending democracy to Iraq would set off a reverse domino effect throughout the Middle East, thereby eliminating a major breeding ground for terrorism.[84]

82. Clarke, *Against All Enemies*, 32.
83. George Packer, *The Assassins' Gate: America in Iraq* (New York, 2005), 45; Mann, *Vulcans*, 332–34; Bryan Burrough et al., "The Path to War," *Vanity Fair*, May 2004, 240.
84. Elizabeth Drew, "The Neocons in Power," *New York Review of Books*, June 12, 2003, 20–22. For Wolfowitz, see Bill Keller, "The Sunshine Warrior," *New York Times Magazine*, September 22, 2002, 48–54, 84, 86, 96. Also Jacob Heilbrun, *They Knew They Were Right: The Rise of the Neocons* (New York, 2007).

The neo-con position complemented the views of other top officials. Powell also wanted to get rid of Saddam, although he accepted war only as a last resort and insisted on international backing. By January 2003, he had concluded that war was inevitable and went along. Assertive nationalists Cheney and Rumsfeld saw a chance to complete the unfinished business of 1991, eliminate a nuisance and potential threat, and demonstrate the efficacy of modern, high-technology warfare. Cheney was even more alarmed by an anthrax scare in the United States in the fall of 2001 than by 9/11 and viewed Saddam Hussein's biological weapons as a threat for which the United States was completely unprepared.[85]

Advocates of war found a receptive audience in the White House. Thinking in mundane but for this administration crucial terms, White House political adviser Karl Rove saw in rallying the nation for war a chance to exploit the Democrats' post-Vietnam vulnerability on defense and national security issues, seal the Republican alliance with the Christian right, win the Jewish vote, help the party in the congressional elections, and build a permanent Republican majority.[86] Bush combined the Old West mentality of his native Texas with the missionary spirit of evangelical Christianity. He was neither a deep thinker nor particularly curious and could be remarkably ill-informed. Toppling Hussein would permit him to succeed where his father had failed and avenge the Iraqi dictator's 1993 attempt on his father's life. A born-again Christian, he saw the world in terms of good and evil and was certain he had been "called" to defend his country and extend "God's gift of liberty" to "every human being in the world."[87] His faith helped him choose a course. Once he had decided, there was no second-guessing. A war with Iraq would protect the security of the United States and eliminate a force for evil.

By the summer of 2002, after virtually no internal debate and apparently little discussion of whether war with Iraq might be counterproductive in terms of Afghanistan or the larger struggle with terrorism, an administration fixated on removing Saddam and carried away with hubris was deeply committed to war. Conflict was "inevitable," a high British official reported to his government; "intelligence and facts were being fixed

85. *Washington Post*, March 30, 2003. The importance of anthrax is noted in Jacob Weisberg, "Fishing for a way to Change the World," *Newsweek*, January 28, 2008, 31–32.

86. Elizabeth Drew, "The Enforcer," *New York Review of Books*, May 1, 2003, Internet version.

87. Bill Keller, "Reagan's Son," *New York Times Magazine*, January 26, 2003, 26–31, 43, 49; Frum, *Right Man*, 24–25; Ron Suskind, "Without a Doubt," *New York Times Magazine*, October 17, 2004, Internet version.

around the policy."[88] Outmatched in Bush's first term, Rice's NSC did not play its intended role of giving the president a variety of options and questioning proposals from the agencies. Intent on invading as soon as possible, Cheney, Rumsfeld, and the neo-cons refused to subject their assumptions to close scrutiny. They were certain of what they knew, even in the face of contrary evidence and inconvenient facts. They dismissed opposing views from what they called "the reality-based community." "We're an empire now," one official boasted, "and when we act we create our own reality."[89] They placed more stock in what they learned from the shady Ahmad Chalabi and other Iraqi exiles than in their own intelligence agencies (they also funded Chalabi's Iraqi National Congress to the tune of $36 million in 2002–3). They "cherry-picked" evidence that fit their preconceptions. They put subtle—and sometimes not so subtle—pressure on intelligence providers to come up with the right answers. Sometimes the providers tailored their assessments to fit their bosses' prejudices. CIA director George Tenet once famously called the case for weapons of mass destruction a "slam dunk," but in fact it was quite weak. There was no firm evidence that Saddam Hussein was close to acquiring WMD or indeed that he had anything to do with 9/11. But defeating Iraq seemed the next logical step in the larger war against terrorism, and preemptive war appeared justifiable.[90]

After Labor Day 2002, the administration mounted an all-out campaign for congressional and popular support. "From a marketing point of view you don't introduce new products in August," a White House aide quipped.[91] Bush and Cheney strong-armed Republicans and Democrats in Congress. Top officials kept up a steady drumbeat for war. There was "no doubt" that Saddam Hussein had weapons of mass destruction, Cheney insisted, even though there was considerable skepticism within the government and no solid evidence to back up the statement. He and Rice issued increasingly ominous (later to be proven false) statements that Saddam would acquire nuclear weapons "fairly soon." In a major speech in Cincinnati on October 7, Bush spoke of a "grave threat," affirmed that Saddam had given "shelter and support to terrorism," and warned that the "Iraqi regime . . . possesses and produces chemical and biological weapons" and was seeking nuclear weapons. Did it make any sense, he asked, concluding

88. The so-called Downing Street memo of July 21, 2002, was first published in the (London) *Sunday Times*, May 1, 2005.
89. Suskind, "Without a Doubt."
90. Burrough, "Path," 282; Michael Isikoff and David Corn, *Hubris: The Inside Story of Spin, Scandal, and the Selling of the Iraq War* (New York, 2006), chapters 2–11.
91. Isikoff and Corn, *Hubris*, 33.

with the administration's favorite scare-line (first used by Rice), "for the world to wait . . . for the final proof, the smoking gun that could come in the form of a mushroom cloud?"[92]

The campaign provoked no more than scattered opposition, some of it, interestingly, from the elder Bush's top advisers. James Baker urged concerted efforts to gain international support.[93] When Brent Scowcroft publicly warned that an invasion of Iraq could divert attention and resources from the more pressing war against terrorism, damage U.S. standing in the Middle East, and provoke an attack on Israel that could set off a regional "Armageddon"—the younger Bush's aides branded him "Neville," an obvious allusion to Chamberlain and Munich.[94] Prominent realist scholars questioned whether Iraq was the right war, insisted that Saddam could be contained, and warned of further destabilizing an already volatile Middle East.[95] In one of the most fascinating developments of the new century, energetic young activists used the Internet to mobilize liberal opposition to the war. By the end of the year, MoveOn.org had 1.3 million members worldwide, 900,000 in the United States. It raised millions of dollars to support liberal congressional candidates. In early 2003, it organized a "virtual" anti-war march on Washington.[96] Worldwide, an estimated ten million people protested the U.S. drive to war.

In a strange, almost surreal way, an administration intent on invading Iraq carried a reluctant nation toward its first preemptive war with remarkably little dissent. The White House equated patriotism with support for its policies. It skillfully exploited the anniversary of 9/11 to rally a still-anxious people. Discussions of war with Iraq were "dominated . . . by images of smoldering buildings in New York and Washington," the *New York Times* reported.[97] Surveys revealed that Americans were more worried about a stagnant economy than about Iraq. Some feared a long and costly war. Most seemed resigned to the inevitability of war rather than persuaded by the case for it. Still shaken by 9/11, they fell into line. Polls

92. Burroughs, "Path," 282.
93. *New York Times*, August 25, 2002.
94. *Wall Street Journal*, August 16, 2002; Jeffrey Goldberg, "Breaking Ranks," *New Yorker*, October 31, 2005, 58–60.
95. *New York Times* ad; Christopher Lehmann, "The War on What?" *New Yorker*, September 16, 2002, 36–44.
96. George Packer, "Smart-Mobbing the War," *New York Times Magazine*, March 9, 2003, 46–49.
97. *New York Times*, October 6, 2002.

indicated solid support, tempered by concern about casualties and insistence on gaining congressional and UN support.[98]

The administration easily secured congressional backing. Taking aim squarely at neo-cons like Perle—and perhaps by indirection the president—Vietnam veteran and Nebraska Republican senator Chuck Hagel protested that "many of those who want to rush this country into war and think it would be so quick and easy don't know anything about war."[99] But even those Republicans with doubts succumbed to White House appeals to "trust us." Divided among themselves, nervous about dissent in wartime, very much on the defensive against an aggressive executive and with midterm elections approaching, the Democrats failed to muster effective opposition. Leading senators such as John Kerry of Massachusetts and Hillary Rodham Clinton of New York challenged only the way a war should be fought, not the war itself, insisting that support must be secured from allies and the UN. West Virginia Democratic senator Robert Byrd's lonely and often eloquent dissent drew little attention. After brief discussion and with troops already pouring into the Persian Gulf, Congress in October 2002 gave the president blank-check authority to use U.S. military forces "against the continuing threat posed by Iraq" and to "enforce all relevant" UN Security Council resolutions on Iraq (77–23 in the Senate, 296–133 in the House). In the fall elections, the Republicans regained control of the Senate and increased their majority in the House. A debate mainly about how to go to war produced broad if not deep support for an administration firmly committed to invading Iraq. "There is no debate, no discussion, no attempt to lay out for the nation the pros and cons of this particular war," Byrd protested. "We stand passively mute . . . paralyzed by our own uncertainty, seemingly stunned by the sheer turmoil of events."[100]

The administration could not steamroll the UN as it had Congress. Over Rumsfeld's and Cheney's strenuous objections, Powell persuaded the president to secure UN support, a move he may have hoped would delay or even thwart the headlong rush to war. Bush's pledge to do so mollified critics at home and helped squelch a possibly searching domestic debate on the war, but it also produced major roadblocks. The United

98. Ibid., June 10, 2002, August 27, 2002, September 8, 2002, October 7, 2002; *USA Today*, September 18, 2002.

99. *New York Times*, August 26, 2002.

100. Thomas Ricks, *Fiasco: America's Military Adventure in Iraq* (New York, 2006), 88; Thomas Powers, "The Vanishing Case for War," *New York Review of Books*, December 9, 2003, 1–8.

States and its allies brought to the UN sharply divergent perspectives. Cheney, Rumsfeld, and the neo-cons preferred to go it alone. Viewing negotiations as a hindrance, top U.S. officials in late 2002 put on one of the most arrogant and inept diplomatic performances in the nation's history. Bush set the tone in a September speech at the UN by pointedly asking: "Will the United Nations serve the purposes of its founding, or will it be irrelevant?"[101] Among leading nations, only Britain firmly backed the United States. France initially accepted war as a last resort, Germany openly opposed it, and Russia, China, and Mexico expressed grave doubts. The administration's haughty demeanor squandered much of the international goodwill lavished upon the United States after 9/11. The Europeans were alarmed by Bush's "axis of evil" speech and preemptive war doctrine. They believed the administration was obsessed with Iraq and that Iraqi weapons of mass destruction could be eliminated without resorting to war.

The UN negotiations degenerated into a nasty and highly public spat between the United States on one side and France and Germany on the other. The administration blundered early on by rejecting outright a compromise French proposal for a war resolution that might have averted much of what followed. "Every good reason not to go to war was irrelevant," Rice tartly informed a French diplomat.[102] On January 20, 2003, what some U.S. officials called the "Day of Diplomatic Ambush," France issued a surprise announcement that it would not support war. French actions stunned Americans and undercut Powell's efforts to delay the war. They evoked an outburst of ally-bashing in the United States, with France the number one target. Playing to the most parochial of American instincts, Rumsfeld and other administration officials dismissed France and Germany as "old Europe." Long stereotyped by Americans as feminine and "sissy," the French provided a ready-made target.[103] To the glee of conservatives, the House of Representatives renamed the French fries on its cafeteria menu "freedom fries."[104]

To counter French obstructionism and an allied effort to delay war by additional inspections of Iraqi weapon sites, an agitated and increasingly impatient White House in late January assigned Powell to make the case for war. "You have the credibility to do this," Bush told him. "Maybe they'll believe you."[105] Scrapping a shoddy and polemical draft prepared

101. Karen DeYoung, *Soldier: The Life of Colin Powell* (New York, 2006), 411.
102. Burrough, "Path," 289.
103. *New York Times*, September 28, 2003.
104. Burrough, "Path," 289.
105. DeYoung, *Soldier*, 439.

in the vice president's office, Powell's aides hurriedly put together the best case they could. Although uneasy with the results and certain he was being used by the White House, the secretary played the dutiful soldier. His seventy-five-minute speech on February 5, 2003, complete with photographs, recordings, and even a small vial dramatically displayed to show how little anthrax it would take to cause enormous loss of life, warned of the "sinister nexus" between Saddam Hussein and al Qaeda and detailed evidence of Iraqi weapons of mass destruction (much of it dubious and soon discredited). Powell's speech persuaded few at the UN but had a major impact in the United States, as much because of who was speaking as what was said, helping to bring some skeptics around and clinch the case for others.[106]

At British prime minister Tony Blair's urging, the administration in February launched a last desperate effort to secure UN support. A French veto now likely if not indeed certain, U.S. officials set out to secure nine Security Council votes for war, thus exposing France as obstructionist. They fixed a tight deadline and demanded immediate answers. "It's time for people to show their cards, let the world know where they stand when it comes to Saddam," Bush proclaimed. Competing with France for votes, U.S. officials put tremendous pressure on Chile, Mexico, and three West African nations. "What can the Americans do to us?" an African diplomat asked. "Are they going to bomb us? Invade us?"[107] Nearly seven weeks of bullying and arm-twisting produced only the votes of Britain, Spain, and Bulgaria. On March 17, the United States and Britain declared the discussions ended. Two days later, President Bush announced the start of hostilities against Iraq. The United States would have its war, but without the support of close allies and the United Nations. It was a bold and risky move that would decisively affect the the Bush presidency and indeed world history.

IV

In contrast to this inept diplomacy, Operation Iraqi Freedom proved a textbook operation, once more displaying the fearsome power of America's high-tech military machine. Washington went to great lengths to publicize the contributions of the twenty-six nations that made up its "coalition of the willing," a pointed reference to those countries who refused to fight. Aside from British operations in southern Iraq, however, it was a U.S. show. A fierce bombing campaign knocked out communications,

106. Ibid., 440–51; Ricks, *Fiasco*, 93–94.
107. Paul Krugman in *New York Times*, March 19, 2003.

destroyed critical military installations, and softened up enemy forces, delivering "smart" bombs and missiles at the rate of a thousand per day.[108] On March 20, U.S. Army and Marine units drove north from Kuwait along two fronts. They met only sporadic resistance from shockingly inept and demoralized Iraq forces. British troops quickly seized Basra. The first Americans reached Baghdad on April 7, less than three weeks after the war began. Four days later, Iraqis toppled Saddam's statue in Baghdad, signifying the regime's collapse. The United States suffered only 109 casualties, Britain 31. On May 10, a jubilant Bush attired in full flight regalia landed on the deck of the aircraft carrier USS *Abraham Lincoln* in San Diego Bay. Standing beneath a banner boldly proclaiming "Mission Accomplished," the commander in chief hailed the triumph of his forces.

Celebrations of victory and talk of a new U.S. imperium quickly faded amidst fears of a quagmire. The first signs of trouble came with the fall of Baghdad. Instead of sending additional troops to secure the capital, Rumsfeld and Gen. Tommy Franks canceled deployment of the First Cavalry Division. The coalition did not have enough forces to maintain order, producing an orgy of lawlessness, violence, and looting, including the theft or destruction of priceless antiquities from the national museum. While U.S. troops stood by helplessly, looters picked the city clean, even pulling the copper pipe and electrical wire out of walls. Iraqis lost faith in U.S. authority. The one protected building was the oil ministry, confirming their suspicions that the invaders were mainly interested in seizing the nation's most valuable resource. Rumsfeld's typically brusque remarks that freedom was "untidy" and "stuff happens" were as insensitive as they were irresponsible.[109]

The occupiers did no better at providing essential services. In Baghdad, electricity worked only several hours a day, if at all. Telephones were dead, water in short supply and unsafe, sewage ran into the rivers, and hospitals were filled with patients and short of qualified workers and medical supplies. "It would be a tragic irony," wrote *New York Times* columnist Thomas Friedman, "if the greatest technological power in the history of the world came to the cradle of civilization with its revolutionary ideas and found itself defeated because it couldn't keep the electricity on."[110]

---

108. Rick Atkinson, *In the Company of Soldiers* (New York, 2004) is a lively account by an "embedded" journalist. Bernard E. Trainor and Michael R. Gordon, *Cobra II: The Inside Story of the Invasion and Occupation of Iraq* (New York, 2006) is more thorough and critical.

109. Packer, *Assassins' Gate*, 137–142; Ricks, *Fiasco*, 135–38.

110. *New York Times*, August 13, 2003.

Anarchy evolved into sustained guerrilla opposition. Elite Republican Guard soldiers melted away and armed themselves from huge stashes of guns and ammunition systematically scattered throughout the country before the invasion. By June, the number of attacks on U.S. troops and their Iraqi collaborators increased sharply. Bush's brash reaction to the insurgency—"Bring 'em on!"—seemed as foolhardy and inflammatory as Rumsfeld's response to the looting.

A war whose first stage was fought so effectively went sour so quickly because detailed planning for military operations was not matched by equally thorough preparation for the critical postwar period. To be sure, U.S. agencies and private charitable organizations spent months in planning. Some studies predicted the likelihood of looting and even a possible insurgency. But the president assigned responsibility to the Defense Department. As a result of crippling bureaucratic rivalries, bad advice, and fantastical assumptions, Rumsfeld, Wolfowitz, and Feith dismissed out of hand work produced elsewhere. An especially bitter struggle between State and Defense ensured that the former's massive and in many ways prophetic study would be tossed aside. Pentagon civilians began planning late and with inadequate staff and had no time to test their ideas. The neo-cons were also hoodwinked by the artful con-man Chalabi, who fed their illusions and manipulated them to advance his own interests. They believed their own wildly optimistic rhetoric that GIs, as in World War II, would be welcomed as liberators. One official spoke of a "cakewalk." The "planners" were confident that U.S. forces could overthrow the regime, turn over the government to Iraqi exiles, and get out within three months.[111]

Overly optimistic assumptions and a refusal to listen to others also produced gross miscalculations of what would be required to maintain the peace. Recent experience in the Balkans stressed the importance of going in heavy and trimming down. Army Chief of Staff Gen. Eric Shinseki insisted that several hundred thousand troops would be needed for postwar duties. Then at the height of his power and determined to validate his theories about the efficacy of small forces, Rumsfeld cut the figure in half and eased Shinseki into retirement. The coalition lacked sufficient forces to do the job.[112]

The U.S. Coalition Provisional Authority (CPA) made three early mistakes that immeasurably worsened an already bad situation. Headed by

111. James Fallows, "Blind into Baghdad," *Atlantic Monthly*, January/February 2004, 53–74; David Rieff, "Blueprint for a Mess," *New York Times Magazine*, November 2, 2003, 28–33, 44, 58, 76–78; Ricks, *Fiasco*, 85–111; Packer, *Assassins' Gate*, 100–148.
112. Fallows, "Blind into Baghdad," 66; Seymour Hersh, "Offense and Defense," *New Yorker*, April 7, 2003, 43–45.

J. Paul "Jerry" Bremmer, a hard-driving career diplomat, the organization was filled with young, zealous Republicans, eager to spread democracy but notoriously lacking in overseas experience and knowledge of Iraq. Most served only three months.[113] The CPA's de-Baathification project, designed to eradicate "Saddamism" by removing members of his ruling party, eliminated many of the people who had run the country. A decision to disband the Iraqi army and police force left thousands of soldiers and police officers angry, without employment, and *with* weapons. "That's another 350,000 Iraqis you're pissing off, and they've got guns," snorted one CIA operative.[114] Bremmer's decision to delay turning over the government to Iraqis provoked more anti-Americanism and fueled the insurgency.[115]

By the fall of 2003, U.S. troops faced a full-fledged and increasingly lethal opposition. The number of fighters was estimated as high as ten thousand. Foolishly dismissed by Rumsfeld as "dead-enders," their ranks included not only Baathist party members and Sunni Muslims who had backed Saddam and expected to be displaced under a new regime but also disaffected Shiites, the Sunnis' bitter rivals and the majority religious group, whose support Americans had expected. Jihadists from across the world slipped into the country to join the fight. By November, attacks numbered thirty-five per day; the insurgency spread from Baghdad throughout the country. Insurgents shifted from sniper attacks on individual GIs to ambushes of entire convoys and shooting down helicopters with rocket-propelled grenades and handheld missiles. To undermine international support, they attacked other coalition members and killed the chief UN envoy. Unprepared to deal with an insurgency, the U.S. Army struck back with conventional air and ground assaults that inflicted heavy civilian casualties and infuriated the population. The widespread violence further set back already glacial progress in reconstruction. The CPA increasingly huddled behind twelve-foot concrete barriers, the so-called Green Zone, "a bit of Belfast here, a bit of Cyprus there, here and there a sprinkling of the West Bank," one journalist described it.[116] United States military leaders admitted by late 2003 that they were fighting a classic guerrilla war; Rumsfeld conceded a "long, hard slog."

As the insurgency worsened, the rationale for war crumbled. No evidence was found to support administration claims of connections between

113. Packer, *Assassins' Gate*, 111.
114. Fallows, "Blind into Baghdad," 73; *Newsweek*, August 6, 2003, 35.
115. Ricks, *Fiasco*, 158–65. See also Roger Cohen in *New York Times*, August 17, 2007.
116. Mark Danner, "Delusions in Baghdad," *New York Review of Books*, December 18, 2003, 1–9.

Iraq and al Qaeda. Inspectors scoured the country for weapons of mass destruction and came up with nothing. In the meantime, critics discredited evidence employed to justify the nation's first preventive war. Often-used documents provided by a shadowy source called Curveball purporting to show that Saddam had attempted to buy uranium from Niger for nuclear weapons proved fabrications. United States spokespersons now claimed that removing Saddam had eliminated a bloody tyrant and made the world safer. A once invincible administration's credibility took a beating.[117]

The U.S. image was further tarnished by spring 2004 revelations of abuse of enemy detainees, especially at Baghdad's Abu Ghraib prison. By scrapping at the start of the conflict the 1949 Geneva Conventions setting standards for treatment of prisoners of war, the Bush administration opened the way for lower-level misconduct. As in so many other areas, the army's failure resulted from a hastily improvised reaction to unexpected events. Confronting an insurgency about whose sources and scale it knew next to nothing, it dumped into prisons thousands of captives, some mainly for interrogation. In Abu Ghraib, they were supervised by a demoralized reserve military police company that had expected to be home by late 2003. The unit perpetrated rampant abuse, graphically captured in photos taken by its members. Prisoners were left naked and chained to cells, piled naked on top of each other, made to wear women's underwear, and forced to simulate sexual acts. They were tortured in interrogation. The practices at Abu Ghraib violated a long U.S. tradition of humane treatment of prisoners. The pictures created a worldwide sensation. The army conducted a perfunctory investigation and punished only low-level people. The refusal to hold any top officials accountable became a Bush administration trademark, further tainting the war. "When you lose the moral high ground, you lose it all," one army general sadly reflected.[118]

The insurgency grew into a complex and, to Americans, unfathomable phenomenon made up of numerous often competing groups. Baathists and Sunni Muslims who had dominated the country for years fought furiously against what they saw as a U.S. effort to impose Shiite rule. They shifted from costly direct attacks against U.S. forces to improvised explosive devices (IED), which they used with deadly effectiveness against GIs and Shiites. Shiite militias also resisted U.S. rule. Foreign jihadists established in Iraq a

---

117. Powers, "Vanishing Case for War," 1–8; Isikoff and Corn, *Hubris*, 211–30. The story of Curveball is told in Bob Drogin, *Curveball: Spies, Lies, and the Con Man* (New York, 2007).

118. Ricks, *Fiasco*, 291.

new training ground for terrorism. After 2006, the insurgency was joined by rising sectarian violence. Kurds sought to create an autonomous region in the north. In Baghdad and other cities, Shiites mounted ethnic cleansing campaigns against Sunnis. The Bush administration finally admitted the existence of a civil war, but even those words did not convey the complexity of the struggle. Shiites fought each other and Sunnis; Sunnis fought the coalition and in some cases al Qaeda; the jihadists fought both. There was widespread criminal violence. A Shiite-dominated police force was infiltrated by militias who operated as death squads to force Sunnis out of Baghdad.[119] An estimated two million Iraqis fled the country to escape the violence, many of them middle-class people needed to get the country in operation. As many as two million more Iraqis became internal refugees.

The United States could not contain the rising violence or build a stable government. Saddam Hussein was finally captured in late 2003, tried by an Iraqi court, and later executed. The CPA nominally turned over the government to Iraqis in the summer of 2004. Elections were held, a National Assembly convened, a constitution drafted and approved, and a parliament established. But the new government was riddled with corruption and could not bring the disparate factions together or curb the violence. Iraqi troops remained untrained and generally unreliable and often participated in sectarian violence themselves.

Public support for the war at home began to decline in the spring of 2004 following the Abu Ghraib revelations and fierce fighting across Iraq. The drop occurred faster than in Korea and Vietnam, although the casualties were far fewer, mainly because Americans saw less at stake in Iraq than in these earlier wars. Once Saddam's weapons of mass destruction were not found, the ostensible reason for war evaporated. United States citizens were not enthused about spending blood and treasure to bring democracy to Iraq, the administration's public fallback rationale and the real reason for war in the minds of certain top officials.[120] By August 2007, three of four expressed pessimism about the conflict, six in ten believed the United States should have stayed out of Iraq, and only 23 percent approved Bush's handling of the war.

Despite the precipitous fall in support for the war and his rising unpopularity, the president refused to change course. Stubbornly optimistic, he continued to insist that the United States would remain until victory was secured. He refused to hold his advisers accountable even for

119. National Intelligence Estimate; *New York Times*, August 19, 2007.
120. John Mueller, "The Iraq Syndrome," *Foreign Affairs* 84 (November/December 2005), 44–46.

egregious mistakes and awarded medals to officials like CIA director Tenet and General Franks who bore substantial responsibility for the debacle. Although under intense fire, Rumsfeld hung on until after the Democrats regained control of both houses of Congress in 2006. The new Congress was bitterly divided on the war. Most members did not endorse an outright withdrawal, but by the summer of 2007 even some Republicans urged removing some forces from Iraq. Bush responded by sending thirty thousand additional troops to contain the rising violence.

The "surge" brought noticeable but tenuous gains. The troop increase and belated shift to a counterinsurgency strategy produced by late 2007 a decline in violence. Cooperation between the United States and Sunnis in Anbar province and with Shiite militia in the south brought some stability to those regions. In parts of Baghdad, life returned to normal; some refugees began to filter back into the country. Al Qaeda's power seemed on the wane. In some cases, however, good news resulted from bad. The relative quiet in Baghdad came from many Sunnis being driven from the city and others being ghettoized behind hastily constructed concrete "blast walls." Refugees returned not only because conditions had improved in Iraq but also because they were unwelcome in neighboring countries. Crime and corruption continued to flourish. Al Qaeda retained a stronghold in the north. The most glaring deficiency was the Shiite-dominated government's inability or unwillingness to bring together the country's bitterly divided ethnic and religious groups.[121]

At the start of 2008—a U.S. presidential election year—observers noted the huge disconnect between discussions of the war in Iraq and the United States. Top U.S. officials in Baghdad hailed the recent progress while stressing that it was "fragile" and that much more must be done to stabilize a war-shattered nation. They emphasized the need for a continued long-term U.S. military presence, speaking in terms of years, even a decade. As the presidential campaign geared up in the United States, politicians sought to appease public impatience. Republicans hinted that victory was near; Democrats pressed for troop withdrawals without discussing the possible consequences. The violence in Iraq apparently ebbing, the war lost its top priority; public attention shifted more and more to domestic issues, especially an increasingly shaky economy.[122]

The war in Afghanistan also continued to falter. The Bush administration had been no more enthusiastic about nation-building there than in Iraq. In any event, by late 2002, its attention and resources had shifted to

121. *New York Times*, December 2, 30, 2007.
122. Michael Gordon in *New York Times*, January 20, 2008.

Iraq. The United States provided no more funds in Afghanistan than had been given to earlier efforts in Bosnia or even the 1999 UN intervention in East Timor. Only forty thousand NATO and U.S. troops were deployed to maintain security and assist with reconstruction. One frustrated diplomat called Afghanistan "the most under-resourced nation-building effort in history." The central government exercised authority over little of the country. In most areas, local warlords held sway. More ominously, a revived and reinvigorated Taliban, funded partly by the lucrative opium trade, moved from safe havens in Pakistan into Afghanistan's southern provinces, exploiting popular disaffection with the government. They were not able to take large towns, but they mounted widening attacks, even in Kabul. The war in Afghanistan was by no means lost, but an opportunity to stabilize an important country seemed squandered.[123]

The cost of the wars for the United States was substantial. Nearly four thousand Americans had been killed in Iraq as of early 2008. Thousands more whose lives were spared by the miracles of modern medicine suffered horrible maiming wounds and severe psychological damage. The two wars strained the U.S. armed forces to the breaking point. A decline in enlistments, even with lowered standards and higher incentives, threatened the volunteer army concept, the mainstay of post-Vietnam national security policy. Popular disillusionment appeared likely to produce an Iraq Syndrome in the form of resistance to future military intervention abroad.[124] The Bush administration's attitudes and policies damaged the nation's image across much of the world and stirred virulent anti-Americanism. The economic costs were staggering, for both wars an estimated $800 billion, roughly 10 percent of all government expenditures. The addition of long-term medical care for veterans was predicted to drive the long-term cost as high as $3 trillion.[125]

The impact of the war on Iraq and the Middle East was profound. Estimates of Iraqi war dead ranged from fifty thousand to more than two hundred thousand through 2008. The influx of Iraqi refugees destabilized neighboring countries such as Jordan and Syria. The U.S. invasion and occupation of Iraq provoked fury in the Muslim world, undermining Washington's broader efforts against international terrorism. The one winner of the war was Iran, which no longer faced a strong Sunni nation to the south and had close ties with some Iraqi Shiites.[126]

123. *Newsweek*, October 2, 2006; *New York Times*, August 12, 20, 2002, December 16, 2007.
124. Mueller, "Iraq Syndrome," 53–54.
125. *Boston Globe*, August 1, 2007; *New York Times*, December 9, 2007, January 20, 2008.
126. *New York Times*, July 30, 2006.

The scorecard of the so-called Global War on Terror seemed also on the negative side. To be sure, the United States had not been struck since 9/11. Anti-terrorist forces across the world foiled numerous plots, notably in England and Scotland. But the war was far from won, and the United States was little safer than before 2001. Using the respite provided by the war in Iraq, al Qaeda revived and reconstituted itself and remained intent on striking the United States again. "We thank God for appeasing us with the dilemmas of Iraq and Afghanistan," bin Laden's deputy Ayman al-Zawahiri proclaimed in 2003.[127] Perhaps more important, the terrorist "movement" had transformed itself. The war in Iraq boosted recruitment among Muslims across the world. The Internet increasingly served as the major "training camp." Instead of al Qaeda, the United States and its allies faced a more diffuse and elusive al Qaedism, an international conglomeration of thousands of separate cells operating more or less on their own. "We have taken a ball of quicksilver and hit it with a hammer," one expert observed. Nine-eleven may not be replicated, but smaller attacks mounted by more amateurish terrorists seemed possible if not likely. A summer 2007 National Intelligence Estimate warned of a "heightened threat environment."[128]

As if Bush were chastened by these events, the tenor if not the essential thrust of his foreign policy changed in his second term. Powell resigned and was replaced by Rice. Her deputy Stephen Hadley took over as national security adviser; after Rumsfeld's departure, Robert Gates, her former NSC boss, became secretary of defense. Given the new foreign policy lineup and her especially close relationship with Bush, Rice emerged as a major player.[129] Amidst the wreckage of Iraq and Afghanistan, Bush's soaring second inaugural commitment to spread democracy and end tyranny in the world never got off the ground. On the contrary, elections in Palestine and Lebanon produced victories for Hamas and Hezbollah, militant movements tied closely to Iran. With "Madame Rice," as the president called her, in the lead, the United States set out to repair the damage to relations with the European allies done in the first term. Over loud protests from neo-cons like Bolton, the administration reopened negotiations with North Korea and made concessions that permitted a fragile agreement to halt its nuclear program.

127. Bruce Hoffman in *Washington Post*, September 9, 2007.
128. Mark Danner, "Taking Stock of the Forever War," *New York Times Magazine*, September 11, 2005, 47; Samantha Power, "Our War on Terror," *New York Times Book Review*, July 29, 2007, 8.
129. Rice's role is analyzed in Glenn Kessler, The *Confidante: Condoleezza Rice and the Creation of the Bush Legacy* (New York, 2007) and Elisabeth Bumiller, *Condoleezza Rice: A Biography* (New York, 2008).

The major second-term initiative was to infuse new life into the Arab-Israeli peace process. During his first years, Bush studiously refrained from involvement in this issue. When he spoke out, he usually sided with Israel. His late switch undoubtedly reflected his and Rice's hopes to leave a legacy for world peace and their willingness—both were avid football fans—to try the big play. It also resulted from changes in the region brought about partly by the invasion of Iraq. The rise of Iran as a major regional power with nuclear potential and its ties with Hamas and Hezbollah frightened Saudi Arabia and other predominantly Sunni nations, spurring what has been called an "alliance of fear."[130] Bush and Rice thus stepped onto perilous ground. The secretary of state visited the region eight times during 2007. She brought Israeli and Palestinian leaders, along with Saudi and Syrian representatives, to a conference in Annapolis, Maryland, in November. While maintaining a certain detachment, Bush made clear his commitment to a Palestinian state and his hopes for an agreement before he left office. The two sides agreed to work toward a settlement. But many thorny issues had to be resolved, especially the status of Jerusalem and the right of return of Palestinian refugees. The post-Annapolis talks deadlocked. The political weakness of the two major figures, Ohlmert and Abbas, along with Bush's reluctance to engage himself, left experts skeptical whether the "fifty-year headache" could be cured. Indeed, one commentator saw the conference less as producing peace than as "girding the region for conflict."[131]

A final assessment of the Bush legacy in foreign affairs lay in the lap of the future. Yet even if Iraq should emerge from its present chaos unified and stable, it is difficult to avoid the conclusion that it was the wrong war in the wrong place fought in the wrong way. It diverted attention and resources from the war in Afghanistan, what should have been the preeminent concern. Saddam Hussein was a cruel tyrant, to be sure, but his removal brought more misery to the Iraqi people, destabilized a critical region, and created a new training ground for terrorists. The Bush administration's dismissive attitude toward allies in the run-up to war, its scandalous incompetence in fighting the insurgency, and its abandonment of the Geneva Conventions, widespread use of torture, and detainment of suspects without recourse to the law compromised its claims to world leadership. The United States of 2008 bore little resemblance to the global behemoth of the turn of the century. It is one of the supreme ironies of recent history that leaders bent on per-

130. *New York Times*, September 17, 2007.
131. Michael Oren in *New York Times*, December 2, 2007.

petuating U.S. primacy squandered it through reckless use of the nation's power. Talk of unipolarity ended; pundits once more spoke of a nation in decline.

THE INTERNATIONAL SYSTEM WAS EXPERIENCING MAJOR CHANGES as the first decade of the twenty-first century neared an end, even, according to Fareed Zakaria, undergoing a "seismic shift in power and attitudes."[132] The European Union (EU) and China had joined the United States as economic great powers, competing for resources, markets, and influence across the world. The European market was now the world's largest. Europe's technology challenged that of the United States. The EU provided more foreign assistance to other countries than the United States and drew many countries into its commercial orbit. China appeared to be achieving in East Asia the sort of economic influence Japan sought in the 1930s. Its reach extended to Africa and Central Asia. Rising "Second World" nations such as Russia, India, Turkey, the Middle Eastern oil states, and Brazil might form the principal battleground of a new world order. Even beyond the Second World, economic growth was stunning in its scope and magnitude. Pundits spoke of the "end of the era of the white man," the "rise of the rest."[133]

Commentators also agreed that America's unipolar moment had ended. Indeed, Samantha Power observed, the erosion of U.S. strength was the "core fact of recent years."[134] Despite the costs of the wars in Afghanistan and Iraq, the United States in terms of its military spending and vast nuclear arsenal remained easily the world's strongest nation. In the "post-American world," however, military power seemed less important than economic clout, and the global economic position of the United States had changed significantly since the turn of the century. Along with the tax cuts enacted early in Bush's presidency, the wars in Afghanistan and Iraq produced soaring deficits. The national debt grew by more than $3 trillion. Once the world's greatest creditor, the United States became its greatest debtor, borrowing more than $800 billion per year from China, Japan, South Korea, and other nations. One of the most significant indicators of recent economic trends was the way in which other nations buoyed up the U.S. economy by pouring money into its corporations and financial institutions.

132. Fareed Zakaria, "The Rise of the Rest," Newsweek, May 12, 2008, 27.
133. Ibid.; Roger Cohen in New York Times, March 17, 2008. The importance of the Second World is discussed in Parag Khanna, "Waving Goodbye to Hegemony," New York Times Magazine, January 27, 2008, 37, 39, 40–41, 62.
134. Quoted in Cohen, New York Times, November 12, 2007.

The United States' decline was perhaps most evident in the area where the nation was once most dominant, its soft power, the sway of its ideals. This change resulted from an inevitable worldwide reaction against U.S. hegemony. It was also the product of competing sources of information. The United States no longer dominated world airwaves as it once did. Global viewers and listeners had many choices. The Arab television network al Jazeera, for example, reached 100 million households worldwide. But the decline also reflected recent U.S. actions. The Bush administration's policies provoked anti-Americanism across the world. Its mishandling of the conflict in Iraq as well as of Hurricane Katrina on its own Gulf Coast severely undermined its credibility. Perhaps most important in weakening U.S. claims to world leadership has been the huge gap between the principles its leaders proclaimed and the actions they took, especially in the much publicized mistreatment of captives. "Today, six years after the terrorist attacks produced a moment of global kinship, America is feared, loathed, and misunderstood across the world," journalist James Traub observed in late 2007.[135] America's decline may be temporary, as in the 1970s. It could certainly be slowed if not arrested by intelligent policies. But it may represent a longer-term trend.

Experts disagreed on whether the emerging world order would be peaceful or menacing and on how the United States should respond to it. Some insisted that terrorism remained the most urgent threat and that the United States, working with other nations, must vigorously combat it, even to the point of intervening in states that harbored terrorists.[136] Others warned that economic growth might spur a rising nationalism, especially among autocratic nations like China and Russia. The United States must therefore retain superior military power and must be prepared to use it to contain expansionist tendencies on the part of autocratic nations and to defend and extend democracy.[137] Still others played down the threats posed by terrorism and autocracy and argued that the new international system would be more benign, if also more complex and much messier. The United States must adapt by relearning the art of diplomacy and by reverting to the multilateralism that served it so well in the Cold War era. It must work closely with other nations to address urgent international problems. It must recommit itself to free trade and

135. James Traub, "Persuading Them," *New York Times Magazine*, November 25, 2007, 19–20.
136. This view is set forth in Philip Bobbitt, *Terror and Consent: The Wars for the Twentieth Century* (New York, 2008).
137. See, for example, Robert Kagan, *The Return of History and the End of Dreams* (New York, 2008).

open immigration. It must learn to function in a world where it can no longer call the shots. "For America to continue to lead the world, we will have to join it," Zakaria concluded.[138]

Even if in decline, the United States will remain a crucial player in world affairs, and in coping with the challenges of a new and complex era the nation has a rich foreign policy tradition to draw on: the pragmatism of the peacemakers of the American Revolution; the basic realism of George Washington, Alexander Hamilton, and John Adams; the practical idealism of Thomas Jefferson and Abraham Lincoln; the worldliness and diplomatic skill of John Quincy Adams; the remarkable cultural sensitivity of diplomats such as Townsend Harris and Dwight Morrow; the commitment to public service of Elihu Root and Henry Stimson; the noble aspirations for a better world espoused by Woodrow Wilson; the intuitive understanding of the way diplomacy works—and its limitations—and the "world point of view" manifested by Franklin Roosevelt in World War II; the coalition-building of Dean Acheson and the Wise Men of the Truman years and the George H. W. Bush administration during the first Gulf War; the strategic vision of Richard Nixon and Henry Kissinger; the ability to adapt and adjust displayed by Ronald Reagan; the efforts of countless men and women who sought to share with other peoples the best of their country and to educate their fellow citizens about the world.

Americans must also "disenthrall" themselves, to borrow Lincoln's apt word, from deeply entrenched ideas about their country and its place in the world. They must "think anew, and act anew."[139] They must cast away centuries-old notions of themselves as God's chosen people. In today's world, such pretensions cannot fail to alienate others. They should recognize the historical truth that the United States in its dealings with other people and nations has not been uniquely innocent and virtuous. It has done much good in the world, but in its drive to superpower status it has often violated its own principles and inflicted harm on other peoples. Unilateralism served the nation well for its first century and a half, but in the vastly shrunken and still very dangerous world of the twenty-first century, it is simply not viable. Most problems are global in scope and require multilateral solutions. The United States cannot resolve them by itself and on its terms, and efforts to do so, as the Iraq war has made clear, will likely be counterproductive. The United States must be more prudent in the use of

138. Fareed Zakaria, *The Post-American World* (New York, 2008).
139. Lincoln's Second Annual Message, December 1, 1862, in James C. Richardson, ed., *A Compilation of the Messages and Papers of the Presidents* (20 vols., Washington, 1897–1925), 7:3343.

its still quite considerable power. In the aftermath of Iraq and Afghanistan, it must not withdraw from a seemingly hostile and ungrateful world. But it must also recognize that power, no matter how great, has limits. The nation cannot rid the world of evil, as *it* defines evil; it cannot impose its way on other peoples by military force or diplomatic pressures. "The American idea can still resonate," columnist Roger Cohen recently observed. But, he adds, U.S. "leaders must embody it rather than impose it."[140] They must lead by example and especially by listening to other peoples and nations. The United States cannot dictate the shape of a new world order, but the way it responds to future foreign policy challenges can help ensure its security and well-being and exert a powerful influence for good or ill.

140. Cohen in *New York Times*, October 1, 2007.

Bibliographical Essay

The literature on the history of U.S. foreign relations is enormous, and I am including in this brief and highly selective listing only those works most valuable to me and most likely to be useful to nonspecialists. The indispensable bibliography is Robert L. Beisner, ed., *American Foreign Relations Since 1600* (2nd ed., 2 vols., Santa Barbara, Calif., 2003). Jerald A. Combs discusses trends in historical writing in *American Diplomatic History: Two Centuries of Changing Interpretations* (Berkeley, Calif., 1983). Michael J. Hogan, ed., *America in the World: The Historiography of American Foreign Relations Since 1941* (New York, 1995) covers recent historiography. Bruce W. Jentleson and Thomas G. Paterson, eds., *Encyclopedia of U.S. Foreign Relations* (4 vols., New York, 1997) is a valuable reference work. The State Department's *Foreign Relations of the United States* series, now publishing on the Nixon years, is an indispensable and splendidly edited collection of documents.

Numerous books set forth broad interpretations. George F. Kennan, *American Diplomacy, 1900–1950* (New York, 1951) outlines this scholar/diplomat's realist critique of U.S. foreign policy. William Appleman Williams, *The Tragedy of American Diplomacy* (3rd ed., New York, 1972) elaborates the highly influential interpretation of Open Door imperialism. Robert Dallek, *The American Style of Foreign Policy: Cultural Politics and Foreign Affairs* (New York, 1983) stresses domestic politics, and Michael H. Hunt, *Ideology and U.S. Foreign Policy* (New Haven, Conn., 1987) ideology. Walter A. McDougall, *Promised Land, Crusader State: The American Encounter with the World Since 1776* (New York, 1997) is a readable neorealist interpretation. In *Special Providence: American Foreign Policy and How It Changed the World* (New York, 2001), Walter Russell Mead uses key figures to elaborate different approaches to U.S. foreign policy. Paul

Kennedy's *Rise and Fall of the Great Powers* (New York, 1987) places the U.S. ascension to great-power status in the larger context of world politics and especially economics. Surveys of specific topics include Melvin Small, *Democracy and Diplomacy: The Impact of Domestic Politics on U.S. Foreign Policy* (Baltimore, Md., 1996), Ralph B. Levering, *The Public and American Foreign Policy, 1918–1978* (New York, 1978), Ole Holsti, *American Opinion and American Foreign Policy* (Ann Arbor, Mich., 1996), Alexander DeConde, *Ethnicity, Race, and American Foreign Policy* (Boston, 1992), and Alfred E. Eckes, *Opening America's Market: U.S. Foreign Trade Policy Since 1776* (Chapel Hill, N.C., 1995).

There are countless books analyzing U.S. relations with individual countries and regions. Some of the most useful for this study were Warren I. Cohen, *America's Response to China: An Interpretative History of Sino-American Relations* (4th ed., New York, 2000), Charles E. Neu, *The Troubled Encounter: The United States and Japan* (New York, 1975), Walter LaFeber, *The Clash: A History of U.S.-Japan Relations* (New York, 1997), Robert J. McMahon, *The Limits of Empire: The United States and Southeast Asia Since World War II* (New York, 1999), John Lewis Gaddis, *Russia, the Soviet Union, and the United States: An Interpretive History* (rev. ed., New York, 1990), David Schoenbaum, *The United States and the State of Israel* (New York, 1993), Howard F. Cline, *The United States and Mexico* (rev. ed., Boston, 1963), Karl M. Schmitt, *Mexico and the United States, 1821–1973: Conflict and Coexistence* (New York, 1974), Lars Schoultz, *Beneath the United States: A History of U.S. Policy Toward Latin America* (Cambridge, Mass., 1998), Mark T. Gilderhus, *The Second Century: U.S.–Latin American Relations Since 1889* (Wilmington, Del., 2000), Kyle Longley, *In the Eagle's Shadow: The United States and Latin America* (Wheeling, Ill., 2002), Douglas Little, *American Orientalism: The United States and the Middle East Since 1945* (Chapel Hill, N.C., 2002), and Michael B. Oren, *Power, Faith, and Fantasy: America in the Middle East, 1776 to the Present* (New York, 2007).

1776–1815: Max Savelle's *The Origins of American Diplomacy: The International History of Anglo-America, 1492–1763* (New York, 1967) is still valuable for the colonial background. Fred Anderson, *The War That Made America* (New York, 2005) is superb on the French and Indian War. Bradford Perkins, *The Creation of a Republican Empire, 1776–1865* (New York, 1993) and William Earl Weeks, *Building the Continental Empire: American Expansion from the Revolution to the Civil War* (Chicago, 1996) are excellent surveys of the beginnings of U.S. foreign policy.

Books that put Revolutionary War diplomacy in an international setting are Samuel Flagg Bemis, *The Diplomacy of the American Revolution* (rev. ed., Bloomington, Ind., 1957), Richard Van Alstyne, *Empire and Independence: The International History of the American Revolution* (New York, 1965), and Jonathan R. Dull, *A Diplomatic History of the American Revolution* (New Haven, Conn., 1985). Felix Gilbert, *The Beginnings of American Foreign Policy: To the Farewell Address* (New York, 1965) offers stimulating insights not only for the Revolutionary period but also for subsequent U.S. policies. Robert Middlekauff, *The Glorious Cause: The American Revolution, 1763–1789* (rev. ed., New York, 2005) is a richly detailed, readable account of the period. Major studies of key figures include James H. Hutson, *John Adams and the Diplomacy of the American Revolution* (Lexington, Ky., 1980) and Richard B. Morris, *The Peacemakers: The Great Powers and American Independence* (New York, 1965), which highlights John Jay's role. Gordon S. Wood, *The Americanization of Benjamin Franklin* (New York, 2004), Edmund S. Morgan, *Benjamin Franklin* (New Haven, Conn., 2002), and Stacy Schiff, *A Great Improvisation: Franklin, France, and the Birth of America* (New York, 2005) chronicle Franklin's major role. William Stinchcombe, *The American Revolution and the French Alliance* (Syracuse, N.Y., 1969) is a valuable monograph. James M. Merrell, "Declarations of Independence: Indian-White Relations in the New Nation," in Jack P. Greene, ed., *The American Revolution: Its Character and Limits* (New York, 1987) covers a much neglected dimension of the Revolution.

There is no up-to-date study of diplomacy during the Confederation period. The older surveys by Merrill Jensen, *The New Nation: A History of the United States During the Confederation, 1781–1789* (New York, 1950) and Richard B. Morris, *The Forging of the Union, 1781–1789* (New York, 1987), are still useful. Jack N. Rakove, *The Beginnings of National Politics: An Interpretive History of the Continental Congress* (New York, 1997) has much to say about foreign policy. Charles R. Ritcheson, *Aftermath of Revolution: British Policy Toward the United States, 1783–1795* (New York, 1971) provides a British perspective, and Frederick W. Marks III, *Independence on Trial: Foreign Affairs and the Making of the Constitution* (2nd ed., Wilmington, Del., 1986) stresses the importance of foreign policy in the making of the Constitution. David C. Hendrickson, *Peace Pact: The Lost World of the American Founding* (Lawrence, Kans., 2003) puts a new "internationalist" twist on the origins of the Constitution.

Stanley Elkins and Eric McKitrick's *The Age of Federalism: The Early American Republic, 1788–1800* (New York, 1993) provides a richly detailed and eminently readable introduction to the period. Lawrence S. Kaplan analyzes the roles of two key figures in *Alexander Hamilton: Ambivalent Anglophile* (Wilmington, Del., 2002) and *Thomas Jefferson: Westward the*

Course of Empire (Wilmington, Del., 1999). For Hamilton, see also John Lamberton Harper, *Alexander Hamilton and the Origins of American Foreign Policy* (Cambridge, Eng., 2004). Richard H. Kohn, *Eagle and Sword: The Beginnings of the Military Establishment in America* (New York, 1984) is excellent on military policy. Drew R. McCoy, *The Elusive Republic: Political Economy in Jeffersonian America* (Chapel Hill, N.C., 1980) illuminates the connection between landed and commercial expansion in republican ideology. Harry Ammon, *The Genet Mission* (New York, 1973) is the standard account. With somewhat different emphases, Samuel Flagg Bemis, *Jay's Treaty: A Study in Commerce and Diplomacy* (rev. ed., New Haven, Conn., 1962) and Jerald A. Combs, *The Jay Treaty: Political Battleground of the Founding Fathers* (Berkeley, Calif., 1970) analyze that controversial accord. For Anglo-American relations subsequent to the treaty, see Bradford Perkins, *The First Rapprochement: England and the United States, 1795–1805* (Berkeley, Calif., 1967). Samuel Flagg Bemis, *Pinckney's Treaty: America's Advantage from Europe's Distress, 1783–1800* (rev. ed., New Haven, Conn., 1960), remains the best account. The crisis with France is studied in Alexander DeConde, *Entangling Alliance: Politics and Diplomacy Under George Washington* (Durham, N.C., 1958) and *The Quasi-War: The Politics and Diplomacy of the Undeclared War with France, 1797–1801* (New York, 1966), and William Stinchcombe, *The XYZ Affair* (Westport, Conn., 1981).

Jefferson's leadership is evaluated critically in Forrest McDonald, *The Presidency of Thomas Jefferson* (Lawrence, Kans., 1976) and more favorably in Merrill Peterson, *Thomas Jefferson and the New Nation* (New York, 1970), still the best one-volume biography. Robert W. Tucker and David C. Hendrickson, *Empire of Liberty: The Statecraft of Thomas Jefferson* (New York, 1990) is a provocative realist critique. Robert J. Allison, *The Crescent Obscured: The United States and the Muslim World, 1776–1815* (New York, 1995) treats the Barbary wars in the context of American attitudes toward Islam. Peter S. Onuf, *Jefferson's Empire: The Language of American Nationhood* (Charlottesville, Va., 2000) is a stimulating analysis of Jefferson's expansionist vision. Alexander DeConde, *This Affair of Louisiana* (New York, 1976) is the standard study, but see also Sanford Levison and Bartholomew Sparrow, *The Louisiana Purchase and American Expansion, 1803–1898* (Lanham, Md., 2006) and Frank L. Owsley Jr. and Gene A. Smith, *Filibusters and Expansionists: Jeffersonian Manifest Destiny* (Tuscaloosa, Ala., 1997). Steven E. Ambrose, *Undaunted Courage: Meriwether Lewis, Thomas Jefferson, and the Opening of the American West* (New York, 1996) provides a stirring account of that exciting and enormously significant venture. The importance of the

Haitian revolution, which cannot be overestimated, is analyzed in David Geggus, *The Impact of the Haitian Revolution in the Atlantic World* (Columbia, S.C., 2001). The origins of the War of 1812 have been one of the more controversial topics in early U.S. diplomatic history. Bradford Perkins, *Prologue to War: England and the United States* (Berkeley, Calif., 1961) is critical of Jefferson and Madison. Roger H. Brown, *The Republic in Peril: 1812* (New York, 1971) stresses party politics, while Reginald Horsman, *The Causes of the War of 1812* (1962) emphasizes sectional issues. The best recent analysis is J.C.A. Stagg, *Mr. Madison's War: Politics, Diplomacy, and Warfare in the Early Republic, 1783–1830* (Princeton, N.J., 1983). Steven Watts, *The Republic Reborn: War and the Making of Liberal America, 1790–1820* (Baltimore, Md., 1987) highlights generational anxieties. Burton I. Spivak, *Jefferson's English Crisis: Commerce, Embargo, and the Republican Revolution* (Charlottesville, Va., 1979) is good on the embargo. Clifford L. Egan, *Neither Peace nor War: Franco-American Relations, 1803–1812* (Baton Rouge, 1983) and Peter P. Hill, *Napoleon's Troublesome Americans: Franco-American Relations, 1804–1815* (Washington, 2005) deal with that sometimes neglected aspect of the larger crisis. The Indian "problem" is discussed from the Indian perspective in R. David Edmunds, *The Shawnee Prophet* (Lincoln, Neb., 1983), and *Tecumseh and the Quest for Indian Leadership* (New York, 1984). Donald R. Hickey, *The War of 1812: A Forgotten Conflict* (Urbana, Ill., 1989) is the best scholarly study. Robert Allen Rutland, *The Presidency of James Madison* (Lawrence, Kans., 1990) provides a balanced analysis of that president's much criticized war leadership. The military aspects are analyzed from a British/Canadian perspective in George F. G. Stanley, *The War of 1812: Land Operations* (Ottawa, 1983).

1815–1861: Charles Sellers, *The Market Revolution: Jacksonian America, 1815–1846* (New York, 1991) and Daniel Walker Howe, *What Hath God Wrought: The Transformation of America, 1815–1848* (New York, 2007) provide detailed and lively accounts of the period with sharply divergent interpretations. Paul A. Varg, *United States Foreign Relations, 1820–1860* (East Lansing, Mich., 1979) is still useful. Noble Cunningham Jr., *The Presidency of James Monroe* (Lawrence, Kans., 1996), Mary Wilma Hargreaves, *The Presidency of John Quincy Adams* (Lawrence, Kans., 1985) and Donald R. Cole, *The Presidency of Andrew Jackson* (Lawrence, Kans., 1993) are scholarly analyses of these administrations. The activities of Adams, the most important figure in foreign policy, are discussed in the still-valuable Samuel Flagg Bemis, *John Quincy Adams and the Foundations of American Foreign Policy* (rev. ed., New York, 1973) and the more critical William Earl Weeks, *John Quincy Adams and American Global Empire* (Lexington, Ky., 1992) and James E. Lewis Jr., *John Quincy Adams: Policymaker for the Union* (Wilmington, Del., 2001). Robert V. Remini's *Henry Clay: Statesman for the Union* (New York, 1991) and *The Life of Andrew Jackson* (New York, 2001) are scholarly, highly readable biographies of two key leaders. Bradford Perkins discusses the budding Anglo-American accord in *Adams and Castlereagh: England and the United States, 1812–1823* (Berkeley, Calif., 1964). The Monroe Doctrine not surprisingly has inspired a sizeable literature. The background in terms of Russia can be found in the excellent Norman E. Saul, *Distant Friends: The United States and Russia, 1763–1867* (Lawrence, Kans., 1991) and in terms of Greece and Turkey in James A. Field Jr., *America and the Mediterranean World, 1776–1882* (Princeton, N.J., 1969). Arthur P. Whitaker, *The United States and the Independence of Latin America, 1800–1830* (New York, 1964) remains the standard work. Dexter Perkins's extensive writing on the subject is conveniently summarized in *A History of the Monroe Doctrine* (Boston, 1963). William W. Kaufman, *British Policy and Latin America, 1800–1830* (New Haven, Conn., 1951) is still useful. Ernest R. May, *The Making of the Monroe Doctrine* (Cambridge, Mass., 1976) stresses domestic politics. John M. Belohlavek, *"Let the Eagle Soar!" The Foreign Policy of Andrew Jackson* (Lincoln, Neb., 1985) is an excellent "revisionist" study. John H. Schroeder, *Shaping A Maritime Empire: The Commercial and Diplomatic Role of the American Navy, 1829–1861* (Westport, Conn., 1985) appraises the role of the Navy in nineteenth-century expansion. Theda Perdue and Michael D. Green, *The Cherokee Removal: A Brief History with Documents* (Boston, 1995) compile varied perspectives on this tragic episode.

Administrations from 1841 to 1861 are covered in Norma Lois Peterson, *The Presidencies of William Henry Harrison and John Tyler* (Lawrence, Kans., 1989), Paul H. Bergeron, *The Presidency of James K. Polk* (Lawrence, Kans., 1987), Elbert B. Smith, *The Presidencies of Zachary Taylor and Millard Fillmore* (Lawrence, Kans., 1988), Larry Gara, *The Presidency of Franklin Pierce* (Lawrence, Kans., 1991), and Elbert B. Smith, *The Presidency of James Buchanan* (Lawrence, Kans., 1975). Edward P. Crapol, *John Tyler: The Accidental President* (Chapel Hill, N.C., 2006) is an excellent recent biography of a neglected figure. The classic analysis of Manifest Destiny remains Albert K. Weinberg, *Manifest Destiny: A Study of Nationalist Expansionism in American History* (Baltimore, Md., 1935). Other major works include Frederick Merk, *Manifest Destiny and Mission in American History: A Reinterpretation* (New York, 1966), Thomas Hietala, *Manifest Design: Anxious Aggrandizement in Jacksonian America* (Ithaca, N.Y., 1985), and Anders Stephanson, *Manifest Destiny–American Expansion and the Empire of Right* (New York,

1995). Reginald Horsman, *Race and Manifest Destiny* (Cambridge, Mass., 1981) is indispensable. For Anglo-American relations in the 1840s, see Reginald Stuart, *United States Expansionism and British North America, 1775–1871* (Chapel Hill, N.C., 1988), Howard Jones and Donald Rakestraw, *Prologue to Manifest Destiny: Anglo-American Relations in the 1840s* (Wilmington, Del., 1997), and Howard Jones, *To the Webster-Ashburton Treaty: A Study in Anglo-American Relations, 1783–1843* (Chapel Hill, N.C., 1977). The crises with Britain over Oregon and Texas are expertly covered in Norman A. Graebner, *Empire on the Pacific: A Study in American Continental Expansion* (rev. ed., Claremont, Calif., 1989) and David M. Pletcher, *The Diplomacy of Annexation: Texas, Oregon and the Mexican War* (Columbia, Mo., 1973). Thomas M. Leonard, *James K. Polk: A Clear and Unquestionable Destiny* (Wilmington, Del., 2001) is an up-to-date study of that leading expansionist. Mexico's perspective can be gleaned from Enrique Krauze, *Mexico: Biography of a Nation-A History of Modern Mexico* (New York, 1997), Gene Brack, *Mexico Views Manifest Destiny, 1821–1846: An Essay on the Origins of the Mexican War* (Albuquerque, N.M., 1975), and William Depalo, *The Mexican National Army, 1822–1852* (College Station, Tex., 1997). K. Jack Bauer, *The Mexican War, 1846–1848* (New York, 1974) is a good military history. John M. Schroeder, *Mr. Polk's War: American Opposition and Dissent, 1846–1848* (Madison, Wisc., 1973) analyzes domestic opposition. Robert W. Johannsen, *To the Halls of the Montezumas: The Mexican War in the American Imagination* (New York, 1987) looks at literature, art, music, and the popular press to show the excitement and expansive vision aroused by the war. The most recent study of the Great United States Exploring Expedition is Nathaniel Philbrick, *Sea of Glory: America's Voyage of Discovery, the U.S. Exploring Expedition, 1838–1842* (New York, 2003). Arthur Power Dudden, *The American Pacific: From the Old China Trade to the Present* (New York, 1992) offers a readable overview of U.S. expansion into the Pacific region. Michael H. Hunt, *The Making of a Special Relationship: The United States and China to 1914* (New York, 1983) provides a good introduction to involvement in China. Jack L. Hammersmith, *Spoilsmen in a "Flowery Fairyland": The Development of the U.S. Legation in Japan, 1859–1906* (Kent, Ohio, 1998) is valuable for the Harris mission and its successors. For filibustering in South and Central America and the demise of Manifest Destiny, see Michael A. Morrison, *Slavery and the American West: The Eclipse of Manifest Destiny and the Coming of the Civil War* (Chapel Hill, N.C., 1997), Joseph A. Stout, *Schemers and Dreamers—Filibustering in Mexico, 1848–1921* (Fort Worth, Tex., 2002), Robert E. May, *Manifest Destiny's Underworld: Filibustering in Antebellum America* (Chapel Hill,

N.C., 2002), and Joseph A. Fry, *Dixie Looks Abroad: The South and U.S. Foreign Relations, 1789–1973* (Baton Rouge, La., 2002).

1861–1901: James M. McPherson, *Battle Cry of Freedom: The Civil War Era* (New York, 1988) is a splendid survey of that epic struggle, Charles P. Roland, *An American Iliad: The Story of the Civil War* (Lexington, Ky., 1991) an excellent shorter study. Robert E. May, ed., *The Union, the Confederacy and the Atlantic Rim* (Lafayette, Ind., 1995) includes essays by leading scholars on the international dimensions of the conflict. The best foreign policy survey is D. P. Crook, *Diplomacy During the American Civil War* (New York, 1975), a shorter version of *The North, the South, and the Great Powers, 1861–1865* (New York, 1974). The Union presidencies are covered in Philip S. Paludan, *The Presidency of Abraham Lincoln* (Lawrence, Kans., 1994) and Albert Castel, *The Presidency of Andrew Johnson* (Lawrence, Kans., 1979). Emory M. Thomas, *The Confederate Nation, 1861–1865* (New York, 1979) and Charles P. Roland, *The Confederacy* (Chicago, 1960) provide insights into southern diplomacy. Charles M. Hubbard, *The Burden of Confederate Diplomacy* (Knoxville, Tenn., 1998) is an up-to-date survey. Frank L. Owsley and Harriet C. Owsley, *King Cotton Diplomacy: Foreign Relations of the Confederate States of America* (2nd ed., Chicago, 1959) is the standard account. Howard Jones's *Union in Peril: The Crisis over British Intervention in the Civil War* (Chapel Hill, N.C., 1992) and *Abraham Lincoln and a New Birth of Freedom: The Union and Slavery in the Diplomacy of the Civil War* (Lincoln, Neb., 1999) are excellent, the latter especially on Lincoln's vision of a slavery-free Union. Doris Kearns Goodwin, *Team of Rivals: The Political Genius of Abraham Lincoln* (New York, 2005) highlights the extraordinary working relationship between the president and his secretary of state. R.J.M. Blackett, *Divided Hearts: Britain and the American Civil War* (Baton Rouge, La., 2001) is very good on British public opinion, which, he argues, was important in determining policy. Saul's *Distant Friends* is excellent on the Russo-American relationship. Martin B. Duberman, *Charles Francis Adams, 1807–1886* (Boston, 1961) and Joseph A. Fry, *Henry S. Sanford: Diplomacy and Business in Nineteenth Century America* (Reno, Nev., 1982) are fine biographies of two key Union diplomats. Post–Civil War expansion is treated in Ernest N. Paolino, *The Foundations of American Expansionism: William Henry Seward and U.S. Foreign Policy* (Ithaca, N.Y., 1973), Ronald J. Jensen, *The Alaska Purchase and Russian-American Relations* (Seattle, Wash., 1975), and Paul Holbo, *Tarnished Expansion: The Alaska Scandal, the Press, and Congress, 1867–1877* (Knoxville, Tenn., 1983).

Not surprisingly, the Gilded Age has drawn only modest attention from historians of U.S. foreign relations. Good surveys are John A. Garraty, *The*

New Commonwealth, 1877–1890 (New York, 1968) and Mark Wahlgren Summers, *The Gilded Age, or, The Hazard of New Functions* (New York, 1997). Broad studies of U.S. foreign policy, all emphasizing expansionist tendencies, are David Healy, *U.S. Expansionism: The Imperialist Surge in the 1890s* (Madison, Wisc., 1970), Charles C. Campbell, *The Transformation of American Foreign Relations, 1865–1900* (New York, 1976) and Milton Plesur, *America's Outward Thrust: Approaches to Foreign Affairs, 1865–1900* (DeKalb, Ill., 1971). Robert L. Beisner, *From the Old Diplomacy to the New, 1865–1900* (2nd ed., Arlington Heights, Ill., 1986) develops an interesting interpretation of what he calls "old paradigm diplomacy." Walter LaFeber's *The New Empire: An Interpretation of American Expansion, 1860–1898* (Ithaca, N.Y., 1963) and *The American Search for Opportunity, 1865–1913* (New York, 1993) emphasize economic forces, while David M. Pletcher, *The Diplomacy of Trade and Investment: American Economic Expansion in the Hemisphere, 1865–1900* (Columbia, Mo., 1998) questions the existence of a systematic policy of economic expansion. Eric T. L. Love, *Race over Empire: Racism and American Imperialism, 1865–1900* (Chapel Hill, N.C., 2004) is excellent. Ari Hoogenboom, *The Presidency of Rutherford B. Hayes* (Lawrence, Kans., 1988), Justus D. Doenecke, *The Presidencies of James A. Garfield and Chester A. Arthur* (Lawrence, Kans., 1981), Richard E. Welch Jr., *The Presidencies of Grover Cleveland* (Lawrence, Kans., 1988), and Homer E. Socolofsky and Allan B. Spetter, *The Presidency of Benjamin Harrison* (Lawrence, Kans., 1987) cover the administrations. David M. Pletcher, *The Awkward Years: American Foreign Relations Under Garfield and Arthur* (Columbia, Mo., 1962) is a valuable monograph. Edward P. Crapol, *James G. Blaine: Architect of Empire* (Wilmington, Del., 2000) is a fine biography of the period's most colorful and dynamic figure; David F. Healy, *James G. Blaine and Latin America* (Columbia, Mo., 2001) is also useful. Joseph A. Fry, *John Tyler Morgan and the Search for Southern Autonomy* (Knoxville, Tenn., 1992) skillfully covers the career of a southern expansionist. Norman E. Saul, *Concord and Conflict: The United States and Russia, 1867–1914* (Lawrence, Kans., 1996), is excellent on U.S. business activities in Russia. David L. Anderson, *Imperialism and Idealism: American Diplomats in China, 1861–1898* (Bloomington, Ind., 1985) is good on China policy, Stuart Creighton Miller, *The Unwelcome Immigrant: The American Image of the Chinese, 1785–1882* (Berkeley, Calif., 1969) on Chinese in the United States. The missionary movement took off during the Gilded Age. Among the best studies are Jane Hunter, *The Gospel of Gentility: American Women Missionaries in Turn-of-the-Century China* (New Haven, Conn., 1984), Patricia R. Hill, *The World Their Household: The American Women's Foreign Mission*

Movement and Cultural Transformation, 1870–1920 (Ann Arbor, Mich., 1985), and Sylvia M. Jacobs, ed., *Black Americans and the Missionary Movement in Africa* (Westport, Conn., 1982). Wayne Flynt and Gerald Berkeley, *Taking Christianity to China: Alabama Missionaries in the Middle Kingdom, 1850–1950* (Tuscaloosa, Ala., 1997) emphasizes the missionaries' selling of their work at home.

Eighteen nineties expansionism has drawn a great deal of attention. A readable recent survey of the period by a specialist in U.S. foreign relations is H. W. Brands, *The Reckless Decade: America in the 1890s* (New York, 1998). Interpretive studies include Julius W. Pratt, *Expansionists of 1898: The Acquisition of Hawaii and the Spanish Islands* (Baltimore, Md., 1936), Ernest R. May, *Imperial Democracy: The Emergence of America as a Great Power* (New York, 1961) and *American Imperialism: A Speculative Essay* (New York, 1968), LaFeber, *New Empire* and *Search for Opportunity*, Beisner, *Old Diplomacy to the New*, and Thomas Schoonover, *Uncle Sam's War of 1898 and the Origins of Globalization* (Lexington, Ky., 2003). Emily S. Rosenberg, *Spreading the American Dream: American Economic and Cultural Expansion, 1890–1945* (New York, 1982) covers a broader period and looks at cultural as well as economic and landed expansion. The once lampooned William McKinley has emerged as a key figure, the first modern president. Important works include H. Wayne Morgan, *William McKinley and His America* (Syracuse, N.Y., 1963) and especially Lewis L. Gould, *The Presidency of William McKinley* (Lawrence, Kans., 1980). Robert C. Hilderbrand, *Power and the People: Executive Management of Public Opinion in Foreign Affairs, 1877–1921* (Chapel Hill, N.C., 1981) is excellent on McKinley's innovations in management of the press.

The War of 1898 and the acquisition of overseas empire are analyzed from the perspective of gender in Kristin Hoganson, *Fighting for American Manhood: How Gender Politics Provoked the Spanish-American and Philippine-American Wars* (New Haven, Conn., 1998) and from a more traditional point of view in John L. Offner, *An Unwanted War: The Diplomacy of the United States and Spain over Cuba, 1895–1898* (Chapel Hill, N.C., 1992). *The Crisis of 1898: Colonial Redistribution and Nationalist Mobilization*, edited by Angel Smith and Emma Dávila-Cox (New York, 1998), contains valuable essays on numerous topics. Louis A. Pérez has challenged long-standing ideas about the war and its aftermath in *Cuba Between Empires, 1878–1902* (Pittsburgh, 1983), *Cuba and the United States: Ties of Singular Intimacy* (2nd ed., Athens, Ga., 1997), *On Becoming Cuban: Identity, Nationality, and Culture* (Chapel Hill, N.C., 1999), and the especially insightful *The War of 1898: The United States and Cuba in History and Historiography* (Chapel Hill, N.C., 1998). David F.

Trask, *The War with Spain in 1898* (2nd ed., Lincoln, Neb., 1996) is a good military history, Gerald F. Linderman, *The Mirror of War: American Society and the Spanish-American War* (Ann Arbor, Mich., 1974) a valuable social history. Robert Beisner, *Twelve Against Empire: The Anti-Imperialists, 1898–1900* (2nd ed., Chicago, 1985) is excellent on the debate over imperialism. The United States' involvement in the Philippines is broadly treated in H. W. Brands, *Bound to Empire: The United States and the Philippines* (New York, 1992) and Stanley Karnow, *In Our Image: America's Empire in the Philippines* (New York, 1989). The Philippines War is handled quite critically in Stuart Creighton Miller, *"Benevolent Assimilation": The American Conquest of the Philippines, 1899–1903* (New Haven, Conn., 1982) and more sympathetically in John M. Gates, *Schoolbooks and Krags: The United States Army in the Philippines, 1898–1902* (Westport, Conn., 1973) and Brian McAllister Linn, *The Philippine War, 1899–1902* (Lawrence, Kans., 2000), the most up-to-date and comprehensive study. Glenn Anthony May, *Battle for Batangas: A Philippine Province at War* (New Haven, Conn., 1991), an important local study, raises new questions and offers new interpretations. Richard E. Welch, *Response to Imperialism: The United States and the Philippine-American War, 1898–1902* (Chapel Hill, N.C., 1978) is good on the domestic reaction. Paul A. Kramer, *The Blood of Government: Race, Empire, the United States and the Philippines* (Chapel Hill, N.C., 2006) is an important new study. Thomas J. McCormick, *China Market: America's Quest for Informal Empire, 1893–1901* (Chicago, 1967) and Paul A. Varg, *The Making of a Myth: The United States and China, 1897–1912* (East Lansing, Mich., 1968) debate the role of economic interests in the Open Door policy and the importance of the policy itself.

1901–1921: Judy Crichton, *America 1900: The Turning Point* (New York, 1998) provides an interesting glimpse at turn-of-the-century America. A good recent biography of the major figure is H. W. Brands, *T. R.: The Last Romantic* (New York, 1997). Studies of Roosevelt's foreign policy include Howard K. Beale, *Theodore Roosevelt and the Rise of America to World Power* (New York, 1962), Raymond Esthus, *Theodore Roosevelt and the International Rivalries* (Waltham, Mass., 1970), Frederick Marks, *Velvet on Iron: The Diplomacy of Theodore Roosevelt* (Lincoln, Neb., 1979), Richard H. Collin, *Theodore Roosevelt: Culture, Diplomacy, and Expansionism: A New View of American Imperialism* (Baton Rouge, La., 1985), and Lewis L. Gould, *The Presidency of Theodore Roosevelt* (Lawrence, Kans., 1991). Surprisingly, there is no good biography of Root, one of the more important figures of twentieth-century America. Richard W. Leopold, *Elihu Root and the Conservative Tradition* (New York, 1954) is useful. Kenton J. Clymer, *John Hay: The Gentleman as Diplomat* (Ann Arbor, Mich., 1975) is good on another important and especially colorful person. The beginning of the modern foreign service is analyzed in Warren Frederick Ilchman, *Professional Diplomacy in the United States, 1779–1939* (Chicago, 1961) and Richard Hume Werking, *The Master Architects: Building the United States Foreign Service, 1890–1913* (Lexington, Ky., 1977). Studies of the peace movement include Charles DeBenedetti, *The Peace Reform in American History* (Bloomington, Ind., 1984), John W. Chambers, ed., *The American Peace Movement and United States Foreign Policy, 1900–1922* (Syracuse, N.Y., 1991), C. Roland Marchand, *The American Peace Movement, 1898–1918* (Princeton, N.J., 1973), and David S. Patterson, *Toward a Warless World: The Travail of the American Peace Movement, 1887–1914* (Bloomington, Ind., 1976). For relations with Britain, see Bradford Perkins, *The Great Rapprochement: England and the United States, 1895–1914* (Berkeley, Calif., 1968) and William N. Tilchin, *Theodore Roosevelt and the British Empire: A Study in Presidential Statecraft* (New York, 1997). For China, see Hunt, *Making of a Special Relationship*, and Delber L. McKee, *Chinese Exclusion Versus the Open Door Policy, 1900–1906* (Detroit, Mich., 1977). Saul's *Concord and Conflict* is good on the conflicts over Jewish immigration and trade, as is Gary Dean Best, *To Free a People: American Jewish Leaders and the Jewish Problem in Eastern Europe, 1890–1914* (Westport, Conn., 1982). Roosevelt's role in the Russo-Japanese War is covered in Raymond A. Esthus, *Double Eagle and Rising Sun: The Russians and Japanese at Portsmouth in 1905* (Durham, N.C., 1988) and Eugene P. Trani, *The Treaty of Portsmouth: An Adventure in American Diplomacy* (Lexington, Ky., 1969). For the expanding U.S. role in the Caribbean, see David F. Healy, *Drive to Hegemony: The United States in the Caribbean, 1898–1917* (Madison, Wisc., 1988) and Richard H. Collin, *Theodore Roosevelt's Caribbean: The Panama Canal, the Monroe Doctrine, and the Latin American Context* (Baton Rouge, La., 1990). International rivalries are covered in Nancy Mitchell, *The Danger of Dreams: German and American Imperialism in Latin America* (Chapel Hill, N.C., 1999) and Thomas D. Schoonover, *Germany in Central America: Competing Imperialism, 1821–1929* (Tuscaloosa, Ala., 1998). Walter LaFeber's *Search for Opportunity* and *The Panama Canal: The Crisis in Historical Perspective* (New York, 1979) are excellent. For U.S. colonial administration, see Pedro A. Cabán, *Constructing a Colonial People: Puerto Rico and the United States, 1898–1932* (Boulder, Colo., 1999) and Glenn Anthony May, *Social Engineering in the Philippines: The Aims, Execution, and Impact of American Colonial Policy, 1900–1913* (Westport, Conn., 1980), which finds little lasting impact from U.S. activities. Emily S. Rosenberg, *Financial Missionaries to the World: The Politics and Culture of Dollar Diplomacy, 1900–1930* (Durham, N.C., 2003) breaks new ground by analyzing the role of the ubiquitous U.S. financial advisers. Cyrus Veeser, *A World Safe for Capitalism: Dollar Diplomacy and America's Rise to World Power* (New York, 2002) is good on that topic.

Two excellent recent studies of the Great War by distinguished military historians are John Keegan, *The First World War* (New York, 2000) and Michael Howard, *The First World War* (London, 2003). The United States during the war period is covered in Robert H. Ferrell, *Woodrow Wilson and World War I, 1917–1921* (New York, 1985), Ellis W. Hawley, *The Great War and the Search for a Modern Order: A History of the American People and Their Institutions, 1917–1933* (2nd ed., New York, 1992), and Robert H. Zieger, *America's Great War* (Lanham, Md., 2000). David M. Kennedy, *Over Here: The First World War and American Society* (New York, 1980; rev. ed., 2004) focuses on the home front. Studies of Woodrow Wilson abound. Arthur Link was his authoritative biographer, and his *Woodrow Wilson: Revolution, War, and Peace* (Arlington Heights, Ill., 1979) summarizes his major arguments on Wilson's foreign policy. Other valuable studies include Kendrick Clements, *Woodrow Wilson, World Statesman* (Boston, 1987) and *The Presidency of Woodrow Wilson* (Lawrence, Kans., 1992), Lloyd E. Ambrosius, *Wilsonian Statecraft: Theory and Practice of Liberal Internationalism During World War I* (Wilmington, Del., 1991), a neo-realist critique, Frederick Calhoun, *Power and Principle: Armed Intervention in Wilson's Foreign Policy* (Kent, Ohio, 1986), which focuses on Wilson's military interventions, Thomas J. Knock, *To End All Wars: Woodrow Wilson and the Quest for a New World Order* (New York, 1992), which provides numerous insights into his ideas and foreign policy, Lloyd C. Gardner, *Safe for Democracy: The Anglo-American Response to Revolution, 1913–1923* (New York, 1987), and John A. Thompson, *Woodrow Wilson* (London, 2002), a balanced and thoughtful survey. Biographies of other key figures include William C. Widenor, *Henry Cabot Lodge and the Search for an American Foreign Policy* (Berkeley, Calif., 1980), Godfrey Hodgson, *Woodrow Wilson's Right Hand: The Life of Colonel Edward M. House* (New Haven, Conn., 2006), and Michael Kazin, *A Godly Hero: The Life of William Jennings Bryan* (New York, 2006), a needed revision of a much maligned secretary of state. Wilson's interventions in Central America and the Caribbean are critically analyzed in Bruce J. Calder, *The Impact of Intervention: The Dominican Republic During the United States Occupation of 1916–1926* (Austin, Tex., 1984), Hans Schmidt, *The United States Occupation of Haiti, 1915–1934* (New Brunswick, N.J., 1985), Mary

A. Renda, *Taking Haiti: Military Occupation and the Culture of U.S. Imperialism* (Chapel Hill, N.C., 2001), Brenda Gayle Plummer, *Haiti and the United States: The Psychological Moment* (Athens, Ga., 1992), and Michael Gobat, *Confronting an American Dream: Nicaragua Under U.S. Imperial Rule* (Durham, N.C., 2005). Wilson's involvement with Mexico is broadly covered in Mark T. Gilderhus, *Diplomacy and Revolution: U.S.-Mexican Relations Under Wilson and Carranza* (Tucson, Ariz., 1977). Robert E. Quirk, *An Affair of Honor: Woodrow Wilson and the Occupation of Veracruz* (Lexington, Ky., 1962) is readable and still useful. Friedrich Katz, *The Life and Times of Pancho Villa* (Stanford, Calif., 1998) is authoritative and much broader in coverage than might appear. John Mason Hart, *Empire and Revolution: The Americans in Mexico Since the Civil War* (Berkeley, Calif., 2002) is a first-rate study by a leading scholar of the Mexican revolution. The United States' entry into World War I was controversial from the outset. Ernest R. May, *The World War and American Isolation, 1914–1917* (Chicago, 1959), based on multi-archival research, and Ross Gregory, *The Origins of American Intervention in the First World War* (New York, 1971) are still valuable on U.S. involvement in the war. John W. Coogan, *The End of Neutrality: The United States, Britain, and Maritime Rights, 1899–1915* (Ithaca, N.Y., 1981) takes a broader approach to neutral rights issues and is more critical of U.S. policy. Anti-war opposition is analyzed in Frances H. Early, *A World Without War: How U.S. Feminists and Pacifists Resisted World War I* (Syracuse, N.Y., 1997).The armistice is covered in Bullitt Lowry, *Armistice 1918* (Kent, Ohio, 1997) and Klaus Schwabe, *Woodrow Wilson, Revolutionary Germany, and Peacemaking, 1918–1919: Missionary Diplomacy and the Realities of Power*, translated by Rita and Robert Kimber (Chapel Hill, N.C., 1985). A readable recent study of the Versailles peacemaking is Margaret Macmillan, *Paris 1919: Six Months That Changed the World* (New York, 2001). Arno J. Mayer, *Politics and Diplomacy at Peacemaking: Containment and Counterrevolution at Versailles, 1918–1919* (New York, 1967) is sweeping in scope and bold in interpretation. Erez Manela, *The Wilsonian Moment: Self-Determination and the International Origins of Anticolonial Nationalism* (New York, 2007) skillfully analyzes the reactions of oppressed people worldwide to Wilson's diplomacy. The problem of Bolshevik Russia at the peace conference is discussed in N. Gordon Levin Jr., *Woodrow Wilson and World Politics: America's Response to War and Revolution* (New York, 1968). The interventions in North Russia and Siberia are covered in Betty Miller Unterberger, *America's Siberian Expedition: A Study of National Policy* (Durham, N.C., 1959) and David Fogelsong, *America's Secret War Against Bolshevism: U.S. Intervention in the Russian Civil War* (Chapel Hill, N.C.,

1996). David W. McFadden, *Alternative Paths: Soviets and Americans, 1917–1920* (New York, 1992) deals with official and informal contacts during these years. Unterberger's *The United States, Revolutionary Russia, and the Rise of Czechoslovakia* (Chapel Hill, N.C., 1989) provides a valuable case study of the application of self-determination. Wilson's 1919–20 defeat is analyzed from various perspectives in Ralph Stone, *The Irreconcilables: The Fight Against the League of Nations* (Lexington, Ky., 1970), Lloyd E. Ambrosius, *Woodrow Wilson and the American Diplomatic Tradition: The Treaty Fight in Perspective* (New York, 1987), and Herbert F. Marguiles, *The Mild Reservationists and the League of Nations Controversy in the Senate* (Columbia, Mo., 1989). An authoritative recent study is John M. Cooper Jr., *Breaking the Heart of the World: Woodrow Wilson and the Fight for the League of Nations* (New York, 2001).

1921–1941: Selig Adler, *The Uncertain Giant: 1921–1941: American Foreign Policy Between the Wars* (New York, 1965) reflects the traditional view of an isolationist America rejecting global responsibilities. A more recent overview, Warren I. Cohen, *Empire Without Tears: America's Foreign Relations, 1921–1933* (New York, 1987) emphasizes the variety and extent of U.S. involvement in world affairs. Akira Iriye, *The Globalizing of America, 1913–1945* (New York, 1993) is an important study by a leading diplomatic historian. Joan Hoff Wilson, *American Business and Foreign Policy, 1921–1933* (Lexington, Ky., 1971) highlights a vital element of 1920s internationalism. For the presidential administrations, see Eugene P. Trani and David L. Wilson, *The Presidency of Warren G. Harding* (Lawrence, Kans., 1977) and Robert H. Ferrell, *The Presidency of Calvin Coolidge* (Lawrence, Kans., 1998) and *American Diplomacy in the Great Depression: Hoover-Stimson Foreign Policy* (New York, 1970). There are no up-to-date biographies of Charles Evans Hughes or Frank Kellogg. Waldo H. Heinrichs, *American Ambassador: Joseph C. Grew and the United States Diplomatic Tradition* (Boston, 1966) is especially good on foreign service and consular reform in the 1920s. David Schmitz, *Henry L. Stimson: The First Wise Man* (Wilmington, Del., 2001) and Jeffrey J. Matthews, *Alanson B. Houghton: Ambassador of the New Era* (Wilmington, Del., 2004) are first-rate short biographies of important figures. Robert D. Schulzinger, *The Wise Men of Foreign Affairs: The History of the Council on Foreign Relations* (New York, 1984) and Robert David Johnson, *The Peace Progressives and American Foreign Relations* (Cambridge, Mass., 1995) illustrate the varieties of 1920s internationalism. Three classic studies of U.S. involvement with European issues are Frank Costigliola, *Awkward Dominion: American Political, Economic, and Cultural Relations with Europe, 1919–1933* (Ithaca, N.Y., 1984), Michael J.

Hogan, *Informal Entente: The Private Structure of Cooperation in Anglo-American Economic Diplomacy, 1918–1928* (2nd ed., Chicago, 1991), and Melvyn P. Leffler, *The Elusive Quest: America's Pursuit of European Stability and French Security, 1919–1933* (Chapel Hill, N.C., 1979). Neal Pease, *Poland, the United States, and the Stabilization of Europe, 1919–1933* (New York, 1986) and Linda R. Killen, *Testing the Peripheries: U.S.-Yugoslav Economic Relations in the Interwar Years* (New York, 1994) are good on Eastern Europe. For the Washington Conference and disarmament, see Thomas H. Buckley, *The United States and the Washington Conference* (Knoxville, Tenn., 1970), Roger Dingman, *Power in the Pacific: The Origins of Naval Arms Limitation, 1914–1922* (Chicago, 1976), Stephen E. Pelz, *Race to Pearl Harbor: The Failure of the Second London Naval Conference and the Onset of World War II* (Cambridge, Mass., 1974), and Richard W. Fanning, *Peace and Disarmament: Naval Rivalry and Arms Control, 1922–1933* (Lexington, Ky., 1995). For the peace movement, see Charles Chatfield, *For Peace and Justice: Pacifism in America, 1914–1941* (Knoxville, Tenn., 1971), Charles DeBenedetti, *Origins of the Modern American Peace Movement, 1915–1929* (Millwood, N.Y., 1978), and Robert H. Ferrell, *Peace in Their Time: The Origins of the Kellogg-Briand Pact* (New Haven, Conn., 1952). Joseph H. Tulchin, *The Aftermath of War: World War I and U.S. Policy Toward Latin America* (New York, 1971) traces changes in Latin America policy during the early 1920s. Thomas F. O'Brien, *The Revolutionary Mission: American Enterprise in Latin America, 1900–1945* (Cambridge, Mass., 1996) and Michael L. Krenn, *U.S. Policy Toward Economic Nationalism in Latin America, 1917–1929* (Wilmington, Del., 1994) analyze the emerging conflict between U.S. economic expansion and revolutionary nationalism. Lester D. Langley, *The Banana Wars: An Inner History of American Empire, 1900–1934* (Lexington, Ky., 1983) has a chapter on Sandino and Nicaragua. Neill Macaulay, *The Sandino Affair* (Chicago, 1967) chronicles the guerrilla leader's resistance to the United States.

Good surveys of pre–World War U.S. policies are Robert A. Divine, *The Reluctant Belligerent: American Entry into World War II* (2nd ed., New York, 1979), Justus D. Doenecke and John E. Wilz, *From Isolation to War, 1931–1941* (Arlington Heights, Ill., 1991), and especially David Reynolds, *From Munich to Pearl Harbor: Roosevelt's America and the Origins of the Second World War* (Chicago, 2001), which breaks new ground in discussing the beginnings of national security policy. William E. Leuchtenburg, *Franklin D. Roosevelt and the New Deal* (New York, 1963) focuses on domestic affairs but gives ample attention to foreign policy. David M. Kennedy, *Freedom from Fear: The American People in Depression and War*

(New York, 1999), a prizewinning study, also gives extensive coverage to foreign policy. Robert Dallek, *Franklin D. Roosevelt and American Foreign Policy, 1932–1945* (New York, 1979) is the most comprehensive account. Frederick W. Marks III, *Wind over Sand: The Diplomacy of Franklin Roosevelt* (Athens, Ga., 1988) is highly critical. Robert Sherwood's classic *Roosevelt and Hopkins: An Intimate History* (rev. ed., New York, 1950) is still valuable. Irwin F. Gellman, *Secret Affairs: Franklin Roosevelt, Cordell Hull, and Sumner Welles* (New York, 2002) gives full coverage to the feud and its impact on policies. Robert S. McElvaine, *The Great Depression: America, 1929–1941* (New York, 1984) and Charles P. Kindelberger, *The World in Depression: 1929–1939* (Berkeley, Calif., 1986) are excellent on the depression, the latter especially on its international aspects. Christopher G. Thorne, *The Limits of Foreign Policy: The West, the League, and the Far Eastern Crisis, 1931–1933* (New York, 1973) is the standard account. Justus D. Doenecke, *When the Wicked Rise: American Opinion-Makers and the Manchuria Crisis of 1931–1933* (Cranbury, N.J., 1984) analyzes the U.S. response. FDR's Good Neighbor policy is studied in Bryce Wood, *The Making of the Good Neighbor Policy* (New York, 1961), Irwin F. Gellman, *Good Neighbor Diplomacy: United States Policies in Latin America, 1933–1945* (Baltimore, Md., 1979), and Frederick B. Pike, *FDR's Good Neighbor Policy: Sixty Years of Generally Gentle Chaos* (Austin, Tex., 1995). Eric Paul Roorda, *The Dictator Next Door: The Good Neighbor Policy and the Trujillo Regime in the Dominican Republic, 1930–1945* (Durham, N.C., 1998) highlights the downside of good neighborism. Recognition of the Soviet Union is covered in Normal E. Saul, *Friends or Foes? The United States and Soviet Russia* (Lawrence, Kans., 2006) and David Mayers, *The Ambassadors and American Soviet Policy* (New York, 1995). Edward M. Bennett's *Franklin D. Roosevelt and the Search for Security: American-Soviet Relations, 1933–1939* (Wilmington, Del., 1985) is still useful. For 1930s isolationism and neutrality policies, see Manfred Jonas, *Isolationism in America, 1935–1941* (Ithaca, N.Y., 1966), Warren I. Cohen, *The American Revisionists: The Lessons of Intervention in World War I* (Chicago, 1967), and Robert A. Divine, *The Illusion of Neutrality* (Chicago, 1962). An important aspect of the peace movement is analyzed in Linda K. Schott, *Reconstructing Women's Thoughts: The International League for Peace and Freedom Before World War II* (Stanford, Calif., 1997) and Carrie Foster, *The Women, the Warriors: The United States Section of the Women's International League for Peace and Freedom, 1915–1946* (Syracuse, N.Y., 1995). Brenda Gayle Plummer, *Rising Wind: Black Americans and U.S. Foreign Affairs, 1935–1960* (Chapel Hill, N.C., 1996) charts the rise of African American interest in foreign policy issues. Anglo-American relations are well covered in David Reynolds, *Creation of the Anglo-American Alliance, 1937–1941* (Chapel Hill, N.C., 1982) and B.J.C. McKercher, *Transition of Power: Britain's Loss of Global Preeminence to the United States, 1930–1945* (New York, 1999). Douglas Little, *Malevolent Neutrality* (Ithaca, N.Y., 1985) is good on the Spanish Civil War. Barbara Rearden Farnham, *Roosevelt and the Munich Crisis: A Study of Political Decisionmaking* (Princeton, N.J., 1997) sheds new light on that most memorable of crises. Jeffrey Record, *The Specter of Munich: Reconsidering the Lessons of Appeasing Hitler* (Dulles, Va., 2006) evaluates its lingering effects. Marvin Zahniser, *Then Came Disaster: France and the United States* (Westport, Conn., 2002) looks at the impact of the fall of France. Warren F. Kimball, *The Most Unsordid Act: Lend-Lease, 1941* (Baltimore, Md., 1969) is the standard work on that critical legislation. T. Christopher Jespersen, *American Images of China, 1931–1949* (Stanford, Calif., 1996) provides a valuable context for U.S.-East Asian policies. The best study of the road to war in Asia is Akira Iriye, *The Origins of the Second World War in Asia and the Pacific* (New York, 1987). Waldo Heinrichs, *Threshold of War: Franklin D. Roosevelt and American Entry into World War II* (New York, 1988) shows the connections between events in Europe and Asia and portrays the war much as FDR must have seen it. Justus D. Doenecke, *Storm on the Horizon: The Challenge to American Intervention, 1939–1941* (Lanham, Md., 2000) seeks to rehabilitate the anti-interventionists, and Steven Casey, *Cautious Crusade: Franklin D. Roosevelt, American Public Opinion, and the War Against Nazi Germany* (New York, 2001) is an up-to-date analysis of that important subject. The definitive study of the Pearl Harbor debacle is Gordon W. Prange, *At Dawn We Slept: The Untold Story of Pearl Harbor* (New York, 1981). Emily S. Rosenberg, *A Date Which Will Live: Pearl Harbor in American Memory* (Durham, N.C., 2003) looks at its longer-term effects.

1941–1961: Gerhard Weinberg, *A World at Arms: A Global History of World War II* (New York, 1994) is an extraordinary international history. Gaddis Smith, *American Diplomacy During the Second World War* (2nd. ed., New York, 1985) is a good introduction. Lloyd C. Gardner, *Economic Aspects of New Deal Diplomacy* (Madison, Wisc., 1964) was one of the first books to treat U.S. wartime diplomacy on a global basis. Warren F. Kimball's *The Juggler: Franklin D. Roosevelt as Wartime Statesman* (Princeton, N.J., 1991) and *Forged in War: Churchill, Roosevelt, and the Second World War* (New York, 1997) are indispensable for Big Three diplomacy. James MacGregor Burns, *Roosevelt: The Soldier of Freedom* (New York, 1970) is readable and still valuable. John Lewis Gaddis, *The United States and the Origins of the Cold War, 1941–1947* (New York, 1972) analyzes those wartime issues that produced the Cold War. Lloyd

C. Gardner, *Spheres of Influence: The Great Powers Partition Europe from Munich to Yalta* (Chicago, 1993) is excellent on those issues that most divided the Grand Alliance. Mark A. Stoler, *Allies and Adversaries: The Joint Chiefs of Staff, the Grand Alliance, and U.S. Strategy in World War II* (Chapel Hill, N.C., 2000) is also good on Anglo-American relations, especially as they pertain to military strategy. The divisive issue of colonialism is covered in Christopher Thorne, *Allies of a Kind: The United States, Britain, and the War Against Japan* (New York, 1978) and Wm. Roger Louis, *Imperialism at Bay: The United States and the Decolonization of the British Empire, 1941–1945* (New York, 1978). Randall Woods, *A Changing of the Guard: Anglo-American Relations, 1941–1946* (Chapel Hill, N.C., 1990) stresses economic issues. For U.S. relations with Stalin and the USSR, Vojtech Mastny, *Russia's Road to the Cold War: Diplomacy, Warfare, and the Politics of Communism, 1941–1945* (New York, 1979) and William Taubman, *Stalin's American Policy: From Entente to Detente to Cold War* (New York, 1982) are essential. For China, see Michael Schaller, *The U.S. Crusade in China, 1938–1945* (New York, 1979) and the colorful Barbara Tuchman, *Stillwell and the American Experience in China* (New York, 1970). Kenton J. Clymer, *Quest for Freedom: The United States and India's Independence* (New York, 1995) and Mark Lytle, *The Origins of the Iranian-American Alliance, 1941–1953* (New York, 1987) cover two important wartime topics. As the title suggests, David S. Wyman, *The Abandonment of the Jews: America and the Holocaust, 1941–1945* (New York, 1998) is highly critical of the United States. Henry L. Feingold, *Bearing Witness: How America and Its Jews Responded to the Holocaust* (Syracuse, N.Y., 1995) is important. For the founding of the United Nations organization, see Robert A. Divine, *Second Chance: The Triumph of Internationalism in America During World War II* (New York, 1967), Robert C. Hilderbrand, *Dumbarton Oaks: The Origins of the United Nations and the Search for Postwar Security* (Chapel Hill, N.C., 1990), and Stephen C. Schlesinger, *Act of Creation* (New York, 2003). John Dower, *War Without Mercy: Race and Power in the Pacific War* (New York, 1986) is superb on American and Japanese perceptions of each other. Akira Iriye, *Power and Culture: The Japanese-American War, 1941–1945* (Cambridge, Mass., 1981) offers a very different interpretation. Few issues in U.S. history have been more controversial than the dropping of the atomic bombs on Japan in August 1945. A good brief introduction is J. Samuel Walker, *Prompt and Utter Destruction: Truman and the Use of Atomic Bombs Against Japan* (Chapel Hill, N.C., 2004). One of the major revisionist works is Gar Alperovitz, *Atomic Diplomacy—Hiroshima and Potsdam: The Use of the Atomic Bomb and the Confrontation with U.S. Power* (rev. ed., New York, 1985). Martin J. Sherwin, *A World Destroyed: The Atomic Bomb and the Grand Alliance* (New York, 1977) is still valuable. Two major recent studies are Richard B. Frank, *Downfall: The End of the Japanese Empire* (New York, 1999) and Tsuyoshi Hasegawa, *Racing the Enemy: Stalin, Truman, and the Surrender of Japan* (Cambridge, Mass., 2005).

The Truman years mark a revolutionary period in U.S. foreign policy, and the writing on them has been voluminous. Alonzo L. Hamby, *Man of the People: A Life of Harry S. Truman* (New York, 1999) and Robert L. Beisner, *Dean Acheson: A Life in the Cold War* (New York, 2006) are the best biographies of two key figures. James Chace, *Acheson: The Secretary of State Who Created the American World* (New York, 1998) and Mark A. Stoler, *George C. Marshall: Soldier-Statesman of the American Century* (Boston, 1989) are also very good. Acheson's memoir, *Present at the Creation: My Years in the State Department* (New York, 1969) is a classic, as is George F. Kennan, *Memoirs, 1925–1950* (New York, 1967). Clark Clifford with Richard Holbrooke, *Counsel to the President: A Memoir* (New York, 1991) is especially valuable for connections between domestic and foreign policy. Walter Isaacson and Evan Thomas, *The Wise Men: Six Friends and the World They Made* (New York, 1986) is excellent on Truman's key advisers. Lloyd C. Gardner, *Architects of Illusion: Men and Ideas in U.S. Foreign Policy, 1941–1949* (Chicago, 1970) is insightful for lesser figures as well. Valuable general studies of the Cold War reflecting different points of view include Walter LaFeber, *America, Russia, and the Cold War, 1945–2005* (rev. ed., New York, 2008), Thomas G. Paterson, *On Every Front: The Making and Unmaking of the Cold War* (2nd ed., New York, 1992), which focuses on the Truman years, John Lewis Gaddis, *The Cold War: A New History* (New York, 2005), and Thomas J. McCormick, *America's Half Century: United States Foreign Policy in the Cold War* (Baltimore, Md., 1989). Vladislav Zubok and Constantine Pleshakov, *Inside the Kremlin's Cold War: From Stalin to Khrushchev* (Cambridge, Mass., 1996) is valuable for the Soviet side. Two superb up-to-date analyses of the Truman policies setting forth different interpretations are Melvyn P. Leffler, *A Preponderance of Power: National Security, the Truman Administration, and the Cold War* (Stanford, Calif., 1992) and the more critical Arnold A. Offner, *Another Such Victory: President Truman and the Cold War, 1945–1953* (Stanford, Calif., 2000). Robert L. Messer, *The End of Alliance: James F. Byrnes, Roosevelt, Truman, and the Origins of the Cold War* (Chapel Hill, N.C., 1982) is good for the immediate postwar period, Thomas G. Paterson, *Soviet-American Confrontation: Postwar Reconstruction and the Origins of the Cold War* (Baltimore, Md., 1973) on economic issues. Michael J. Hogan, *A Cross of Iron: Harry S. Truman and the Origins of the National Security State, 1945–1954* (New York, 1998) is essential. Important monographs on the reconstruction of Europe include Howard Jones, *"A New Kind of War": America's Global Strategy and the Civil War in Greece* (New York, 1989) and Lawrence S. Wittner, *American Intervention in Greece* (New York, 1982), which offer contrasting views on implementation of the Truman Doctrine, Michael J. Hogan, *The Marshall Plan: America, Britain, and the Reconstruction of Western Europe, 1947–1952* (New York, 1987), Irwin W. Wall, *The United States and the Making of Postwar France, 1945–1954* (New York, 1991), William I. Hitchcock, *France Restored: Cold War Diplomacy and the Quest for Leadership in Europe, 1944–1954* (Chapel Hill, N.C., 1998), Brian Angus McKenzie, *Remaking France: Americanization, Public Diplomacy, and the Marshall Plan* (New York, 2005), James Edward Miller, *The United States and Italy, 1940–1950: The Politics and Diplomacy of Stabilization* (Chapel Hill, N.C., 1986), John Lamberton Harper, *America and the Reconstruction of Italy, 1945–1948* (New York, 1986), Carolyn Woods Eisenberg, *Drawing the Line: The American Decision to Divide Germany* (New York, 1996), and Thomas Alan Schwartz, *America's Germany: John J. McCloy and the Federal Republic of Germany* (Cambridge, Mass., 1991). Richard Pells, *Not Like Us: How Europeans Have Loved, Hated, and Transformed American Culture Since World War II* (New York, 1997) looks at cultural interchange. Thomas Borstelmann, *Apartheid's Reluctant Uncle: The United States and Southern Africa in the Early Cold War Years* (New York, 1993), Peter L. Hahn, *Caught in the Middle East: U.S. Policy Toward the Arab-Israeli Conflict, 1945–1961* (Chapel Hill, N.C., 2004), and Robert J. McMahon, *Colonialism and Cold War: The United States and the Struggle for Indonesian Independence, 1945–1949* (Ithaca, N.Y., 1981) make clear the global impact of the Cold War. Mark Philip Bradley, *Imagining Vietnam and America: The Making of Postcolonial Vietnam, 1919–1950* (Chapel Hill, N.C., 2000) is an excellent cross-cultural analysis. Nancy Bernkopf Tucker, *Patterns in the Dust* (New York, 1983) covers U.S. domestic reaction to the fall of China. John Dower, *Embracing Defeat: Japan in the Wake of World War II* (New York, 1999) is superb on the occupation of Japan. Gregg Herken, *Winning Weapon: The Atomic Bomb in the Cold War, 1945–1950* (New York, 1980) and David Holloway, *Stalin and the Bomb: The Soviet Union and Atomic Energy, 1939–1956* (New Haven, Conn., 1994) discuss the origins of the nuclear arms race from U.S. and Soviet perspectives. Kai Bird and Martin J. Sherwin, *American Prometheus: The Triumph and Tragedy of J. Robert Oppenheimer* (New York, 2005) is superb. A good survey of the

Korean War is Burton I. Kaufman, *The Korean War: Challenges in Crisis, Credibility, and Command* (New York, 1986). William Stueck, *The Korean War: An International History* (Princeton, N.J., 1995) is more detailed and broader in perspective. Peter Lowe, *The Origins of the Korean War* (2nd ed., New York, 1997) and Allan R. Millett, *The War for Korea, 1945–1950: A House Burning* (Lawrence, Kans., 2005) are excellent on the beginnings. Bruce Cumings's *The Origins of the Korean War: Liberation and the Emergence of Separate Regimes, 1945–1947* (Princeton, N.J., 1981) and *The Origins of the Korean War: The Roaring of the Cataract, 1947–1950* (Princeton, N.J., 1990) are richly detailed and outspokenly revisionist. Chen Jian, *China's Road to the Korean War: The Making of the Sino-American Confrontation* (New York, 1994) and Rosemary Foot, *The Wrong War: American Policy and the Dimensions of the Korean Conflict, 1950–1953* (Ithaca, N.Y., 1985) and *A Substitute for Victory: The Politics of Peacemaking at the Korean Armistice Talks* (Ithaca, N.Y., 1990) are most valuable.

An excellent overview of the postwar era with chapters on the Eisenhower years is James T. Patterson, *Grand Expectations: The United States, 1945–1975* (New York, 1996). Stephen J. Whitfield, *The Culture of the Cold War* (2nd ed., Baltimore, Md., 1996) is also important for the domestic context. There is no up-to-date biography of Eisenhower. Chester J. Pach, *The Presidency of Dwight Eisenhower* (Lawrence, Kans., 1991) is an able survey. An early example of Eisenhower revisionism, Robert A. Divine, *Eisenhower and the Cold War* (New York, 1981) finds much to praise. Fred Greenstein, *The Hidden-Hand Presidency: Eisenhower as Leader* (New York, 1982) is another influential work of revisionism by a political scientist. Robert R. Bowie and Richard H. Immerman, *Waging Peace: How Eisenhower Shaped an Enduring Cold War Strategy* (New York, 1998) discusses the way policy was formulated as well as the policies. Townsend Hoopes, *The Devil and John Foster Dulles* (Boston, 1973) is highly critical of its subject; Frederick W. Marks III, *Power and Peace: The Diplomacy of John Foster Dulles* (Westport, Conn., 1993), quite positive. Richard H. Immerman, *John Foster Dulles: Piety, Pragmatism, and Power in U.S. Foreign Policy* (Wilmington, Del., 1999) strikes a persuasive balance. Peter A. Grose, *Gentleman Spy: The Life of Allen Dulles* (Boston, 1994) is a readable biography of the spymaster. H. W. Brands, *Cold Warriors: Eisenhower's Generation and American Foreign Policy* (New York, 1988) examines lesser but still important figures. Eisenhower's antagonist is capably analyzed in William Taubman, *Khrushchev: The Man and His Era* (New York, 2003) and Alexander Fursenko and Timothy Naftali, *Khrushchev's Cold War: The Inside Story of an American Adversary* (New York, 2006). Propaganda formed an important part of the Eisenhower policies. Walter L. Hixson, *Parting the Curtain: Propaganda, Culture, and the Cold War, 1945–1961* (New York, 1997) is an important overview. Kenneth Osgood, *Total Cold War: Eisenhower's Secret Propaganda Battles at Home and Abroad* (Lawrence, Kans., 2006) is exhaustively researched and comprehensive in coverage. Reinhold Wagnleitner, *Coca-Colonization and the Cold War: The Cultural Mission of the United States in Austria After the Second World War* (Chapel Hill, N.C., 1994) is a valuable study of an individual country. See also Penny von Eschen, *Satchmo Blows Up the World: Jazz, Race, and Empire During the Cold War* (Cambridge, Mass., 2005). For the Soviet invasion of Budapest, see Erich Lessing, *Revolution in Hungary: The 1956 Budapest Uprising* (London, 2006) and Victor Sebestyen, *Twelve Days: The Story of the 1956 Hungarian Revolution* (New York, 2006). Important regional and country studies include Marc Trachtenberg, *A Constructed Peace: The Making of the European Peace Settlement, 1945–1963* (Princeton, N.J., 1999), Hahn, *Caught in the Middle East*, Michelle Mart, *Eye on Israel: How America Came to View Israel as an Ally* (Albany, N.Y., 2006), Nathan J. Citino, *From Arab Nationalism to OPEC* (Bloomington, Ind., 2002), Diane B. Kunz, *The Economic Diplomacy of the Suez Crisis* (Chapel Hill, N.C., 1991), Wm. Roger Louis, *Ends of British Imperialism: The Scramble for Empire, Suez, and Decolonization* (London, 2007), and Salim Yaqub, *Containing Arab Nationalism: The Eisenhower Doctrine and the Middle East* (Chapel Hill, N.C., 2004) for the Middle East. On Iran, see Mary Ann Heiss, *Empire and Nationhood: The United States, Great Britain, and Iranian Oil, 1950–1954* (New York, 1997). For South Asia, see Robert J. McMahon, *The Cold War on the Periphery: The United States, India, and Pakistan* (New York, 1994), Andrew J. Rotter, *Comrades at Odds: The United States and India, 1947–1964* (Ithaca, N.Y., 2000), a stimulating cultural approach, and Dennis Merrill, *Bread and the Ballot: The United States and India's Economic Development, 1947–1963* (Chapel Hill, N.C., 1990). See also Nick Cullather, *Illusions of Influence: The Political Economy of United States-Philippine Relations, 1942–1969* (Stanford, Calif., 1994). Among the most valuable studies of early U.S. involvement in Vietnam are Lloyd C. Gardner, *Approaching Vietnam: From World War II to Dienbienphu* (New York, 1988), David L. Anderson, *Trapped by Success: The Eisenhower Administration and Vietnam* (New York, 1991), Kathryn Statler, *Replacing France: The Origins of American Intervention in Vietnam* (Lexington, Ky., 2007), and Mark Atwood Lawrence, *Assuming the Burden: Europe and the American Commitment to War in Vietnam* (Berkeley, Calif., 2005). Stephen G. Rabe, *Eisenhower and Latin America: The Foreign Policy of Anticommunism* (Chapel Hill, N.C., 1988) is a fine overview. For the Guatemalan coup, see Richard H. Immerman, *The CIA in Guatemala: The Foreign Policy of Intervention* (Austin, Tex., 1982), Piero Gleijeses, *Shattered Hope: The Guatemalan Revolution and the United States, 1944–1954* (Princeton, N.J., 1991), and Nick Cullather, *Secret History: The CIA's Classified Account of its Operations in Guatemala, 1952–1954* (Stanford, Calif., 1999). Kyle Longley, *The Sparrow and the Hawk: Costa Rica and the United States During the Rise of José Figueres* (Tuscaloosa, Ala., 1997) is a valuable account of a unique relationship. Thomas G. Paterson, *Contesting Castro: The United States and the Triumph of the Cuban Revolution* (New York, 1994) is excellent on this important topic. Civil rights and foreign relations became intricately connected during the postwar years. Carol Anderson, *Eyes off the Prize: The United Nations and the African American Struggle for Civil Rights, 1944–1955* (New York, 2003), Penny M. Von Eschen, *Race Against Empire: Black Americans and Anti-Colonialism, 1937–1957* (Ithaca, N.Y., 1997), Thomas Borstelmann, *The Cold War and the Color Line: American Race Relations in the Global Arena* (Cambridge, Mass., 2001), Mary L. Dudziak, *Cold War Civil Rights: Race and the Image of American Democracy* (Princeton, N.J., 2000), and Michael Krenn, *Black Diplomacy: African Americans and the State Department, 1945–1969* (Armonk, N.Y., 1999) shed much light on this important topic.

1961–1981: David Halberstam, *The Best and the Brightest* (New York, 1972) captures better than anything else the ethos of the 1960s. Robert Dallek, *An Unfinished Life: John F. Kennedy, 1917–1963* (New York, 2003) is up to date and sympathetic. James M. Giglio, *The Presidency of John F. Kennedy* (rev. ed., Lawrence, Kans., 2006) is good on domestic and foreign policy. Deborah Shapley, *Promise and Power: The Life and Times of Robert McNamara* (Boston, 1992) is useful for an influential member of JFK's foreign policy "team." Warren I. Cohen, *Dean Rusk* (Totowa, N.J., 1980) and Thomas Zeiler, *Dean Rusk: Defending the American Mission Abroad* (Wilmington, Del., 2000) are valuable for his secretary of state. Michael Beschloss, *The Crisis Years: Kennedy and Khrushchev, 1961–1963* (New York, 1991) is a good early analysis of Cold War issues. Thomas G. Paterson, ed., *Kennedy's Quest for Victory: American Foreign Policy, 1961–1963* (New York, 1989) contains essays dealing with the full range of foreign policy issues and is critical of the administration's aggressiveness. Lawrence Freedman, *Kennedy's Wars: Berlin, Cuba, Laos, and Vietnam* (New York, 2000) is excellent on these major crises. Valuable studies of specific topics include Howard Jones, *The Bay of Pigs* (New York, 2008), Jack M. Schick, *The Berlin Crisis, 1958–1962* (Philadelphia, 1971), Robert M. Slusser, *The Berlin Crisis of 1961: Soviet-American Relations and the*

Struggle for Power in the Kremlin, June-November 1961 (Baltimore, Md., 1973), especially good on Soviet policy, Warren Bass, *Support Any Friend: Kennedy's Middle East Policy* (New York, 2003), which emphasizes the origins of the U.S.-Israel alliance, Stephen G. Rabe, *The Most Dangerous Area of the World: John F. Kennedy Contains Communist Revolution in Latin America* (Chapel Hill, N.C., 1999) and *U.S. Intervention in British Guiana: A Cold War Story* (Chapel Hill, N.C., 2005), Frank A. Mayer, *Adenauer and Kennedy: A Study in German-American Relations, 1961–1963* (New York, 1996), and Gordon H. Chang, *Friends and Enemies: The United States, China, and the Soviet Union, 1948–1972* (Stanford, Calif., 1990). Economic issues are discussed in Diane B. Kunz, *Butter and Guns: America's Cold War Economic Diplomacy* (New York, 1997), Thomas W. Zeiler, *American Trade and Power in the 1960s* (New York, 1992), and Francis J. Gavin, *Gold, Dollars, and Power: The Politics of International Monetary Relations, 1958–1971* (Chapel Hill, N.C., 2004). Elizabeth Cobbs Hoffman, *All You Need Is Love: The Peace Corps and the Spirit of the 1960s* (Cambridge, Mass., 1998) is excellent, and Michael E. Latham, *Modernization as Ideology: American Social Science and "Nation Building" in the Kennedy Era* (Chapel Hill, N.C., 2000), is an important monograph on a major subject. The Cuban missile crisis is among the most analyzed events in U.S. history. Robert F. Kennedy's posthumously published memoir, *Thirteen Days: A Memoir of the Cuban Missile Crisis* (New York, 1969) conveys the mood. Graham Allison and Philip Zelikow, *Essence of Decision: Explaining the Cuban Missile Crisis* (rev. ed., Boston, 1999) is a classic analysis. Mark J. White, *The Cuban Missile Crisis* (Basingstoke, Eng., 1996), is critical of JFK. Alexansdr Fursenko and Timothy Naftali, *"One Hell of a Gamble": Khrushchev, Castro, Kennedy, 1958–1964* (New York, 1997) is an up-to-date account using Soviet sources. Vietnam was the last crisis of JFK's short tenure, and his policies and intentions have provoked great controversy. Andrew Preston, *The War Council: McGeorge Bundy, the NSC, and Vietnam* (Cambridge, Mass., 2006) is a recent study. Freedman, *Kennedy's Wars* and Fredrik Logevall, *Choosing War: The Lost Chance for Peace and Escalation of the War in Vietnam* (Berkeley, Calif., 1999) argue convincingly that JFK might have sought a solution other than military escalation.

A dynamic and fascinating personality, Lyndon Johnson has been the subject of excellent recent biographies by Robert Dallek, *Flawed Giant: Lyndon Johnson and His Times, 1961–1973* (New York, 1998) and Randall B. Woods, *Lyndon Johnson: Architect of American Ambition* (New York, 2006), which gets closer to the real LBJ. Johnson's tape recordings of his telephone conversations provide rich insights into his character and policies. The early recordings are selectively transcribed in Michael Beschloss, ed., *Taking Charge: The Johnson White House Tapes, 1963–1964* (New York, 1997) and *Reaching for Glory: Lyndon Johnson's Secret White House Tapes, 1964–1965* (New York, 2001). Monographic literature on LBJ's foreign policy is just beginning to appear. Collections of scholarly essays dealing with important topics include Robert A. Divine, ed., *Exploring the Johnson Years* (Austin, Tex., 1981), *The Johnson Years: Vietnam, the Environment, and Science* (Lawrence, Kans., 1987), and *The Johnson Years: LBJ at Home and Abroad* (Lawrence, Kans., 1994) and Mitchell B. Lerner, ed., *Looking Back at LBJ: White House Politics in a New Light* (Lawrence, Kans., 2005). Other useful volumes dealing with LBJ's foreign policy are Warren I. Cohen and Nancy Bernkopf Tucker, eds., *Lyndon Johnson Confronts the World, 1963–1968* (New York, 1994), Diane B. Kunz, ed., *The Diplomacy of the Crucial Decade: American Foreign Relations During the 1960s* (New York, 1994), and H. W. Brands, *The Wages of Globalism: Lyndon Johnson and the Limits of American Power* (New York, 1995). Among the few up-to-date scholarly monographs are Thomas Alan Schwartz, *Lyndon Johnson and Europe: In the Shadow of Vietnam* (Cambridge, Mass., 2003) and Mitchell Lerner, *The Pueblo Incident: A Spy Ship and the Failure of American Foreign Policy* (Lawrence, Kans., 2002), both of which give LBJ high marks for handling difficult situations. Carole Fink, Phillip Gassert, and Detlef Junker, eds., *1968: The World Transformed* (New York, 1998) is invaluable for the multiplicity of global happenings in that still quite unbelievable year. Three introductions to the Vietnam War are George C. Herring, *America's Longest War: The United States and Vietnam, 1950–1975* (New York, 2002), Marilyn B. Young, *The Vietnam Wars, 1945–1991* (New York, 1991), and A. J. Langguth, *Our Vietnam: The War, 1954–1975* (New York, 2000). The best treatment of LBJ's escalation is Logevall's *Choosing War*, which categorically rejects the notion that he had no choice but to act as he did. George C. Herring, *LBJ and Vietnam: A Different Kind of War* (Austin, Tex., 1994) and Lloyd C. Gardner, *Pay Any Price: Lyndon Johnson and the Wars for Vietnam* (Chicago, 1995) analyze Johnson's conduct of the war from different perspectives. Randall B. Woods, *Fulbright* (New York, 1995) and Kyle Longley, *Senator Albert Gore, Sr.* (Baton Rouge, La., 2004) are up-to-date biographies of leading "doves."

Tidbits from the Nixon and Kissinger papers have leaked out in recent years, and the trickle now seems to be surging into a flood. A source-based scholarly literature should not be far behind. In the meantime, it is necessary to rely largely on memoirs and those documents that have been declassified. Nixon's and Kissinger's memoirs are better than those of most top officials; Kissinger's breaks all records for size. *RN: The Memoirs of Richard Nixon* (New York, 1978) naturally defends a discredited president's policies but is also useful for diary entries and other revelations. *White House Years* (Boston, 1979) and *Years of Upheaval* (Boston, 1982) cover the Nixon period. They are rich in detail and especially noteworthy for candid and perceptive sketches of those people Kissinger worked with—and against. They are also staunchly defensive. There is no good up-to-date biography of Nixon. By contrast, Kissinger studies abound. Walter Isaacson, *Kissinger: A Biography* (New York, 1992) is detailed and readable. Jussi Hanhimäki, *The Flawed Architect: Henry Kissinger and American Foreign Policy* (New York, 2004) is thorough and based on some new documentation. Jeremi Suri, *Henry Kissinger and the American Century* (New York, 2007) is a valuable recent contribution. Robert Dallek, *Nixon and Kissinger: Partners in Power* (New York, 2007) is excellent, as is Melvin Small, *The Presidency of Richard Nixon* (Lawrence, Kans., 1999), which covers domestic and foreign policy. William P. Bundy, *A Tangled Web: The Making of Foreign Policy in the Nixon Presidency* (New York, 1998) is a critical study by a former Kennedy/Johnson administration official. Joan Hoff, *Nixon Reconsidered* (New York, 1994) praises Nixon's domestic policies and blames Kissinger for foreign policy failures. Raymond Garthoff, *Détente and Confrontation: American-Soviet Relations from Nixon to Reagan* (Washington, 1985) is thorough and indispensable for studying one of the administration's major achievements. Jeremi Suri, *Power and Protest: Global Revolution and the Rise of Détente* (Cambridge, Mass., 2003) places detente in the context of the worldwide upheavals of the 1960s. Also useful are John Newhouse, *Cold Dawn: The Story of SALT* (New York, 1973), a fine contemporary account by a journalist, Keith L. Nelson, *The Making of Détente: Soviet-American Relations in the Shadow of Vietnam* (Baltimore, Md., 1995), and for a Soviet perspective Anatoly Dobrynin, *In Confidence* (New York, 1993), a memoir by the longtime Cold War ambassador to Washington. For China, James Mann, *About Face: A History of America's Curious Relationship with China from Nixon to Clinton* (New York, 1999) is valuable, as is Margaret Macmillan, *Nixon and Mao: The Week That Changed the World* (New York, 2007). Abraham Rabinovich, *The Yom Kippur War: The Epic Encounter that Transformed the Middle East* (New York, 2004) is an up-to-date account. Jeffrey Kimball, *Nixon's Vietnam War* (Lawrence, Kans., 1998) is the best study of that topic. Kimball's *The Vietnam War Files: Uncovering the Secret History of Nixon-Era Strategy* (Lawrence, Kans., 2004) fills out parts of the story from recently declassified documentation. Larry Berman, *Vietnam: No Peace, No Honor* (New York, 2001) and Pierre

Asselin, *A Bitter Peace: Washington, Hanoi, and the Making of the Paris Agreement* (New York, 2002) are scholarly analyses of the flawed peace-making.

Scholarship on the Ford administration remains scant. *A Time to Heal: The Autobiography of Gerald R. Ford* (New York, 1979) and James Cannon, *Time and Chance: Gerald Ford's Appointment with History* (New York, 1994) are useful, as is Kissinger's *Years of Renewal* (New York, 1999). John R. Greene, *The Presidency of Gerald R. Ford* (Lawrence, Kans., 1995) and Yanek Mieczkowski, *Gerald Ford and the Challenges of the 1970s* (Lexington, Ky., 2005) treat Ford sympathetically. Robert David Johnson, *Congress and the Cold War* (New York, 2006) and Thomas Franck and Edward Wiesband, *Foreign Policy by Congress* (New York, 1979) deal with the congressional resurgence of the 1970s. Robert D. Kaufman, *Henry M. Jackson: A Life in Politics* (Seattle, 2000) portrays positively one of the leaders of the congressional rebellion. Garthoff's *Détente and Confrontation* is good on the breakdown of detente under Ford and Carter.

The Carter literature is similarly slim. Jimmy Carter, *Keeping Faith: Memoirs of a President* (New York, 1982), Cyrus Vance, *Hard Choices: Critical Years in American Foreign Policy* (New York, 1983), and Zbigniew Brzezinski, *Power and Principle: Memoirs of the National Security Adviser, 1977–1981* (New York, 1985) are basic sources. Andrew J. DeRoche, *Andrew Young: Civil Rights Ambassador* (Wilmington, Del., 2003) is a useful biography of an important figure. Burton I. Kaufman and Scott Kaufman, *The Presidency of James Earl Carter* (2nd ed., Lawrence, Kans., 2006) covers the entire administration and is excellent on foreign policy. Gaddis Smith, *Morality, Reason and Power: American Diplomacy in the Carter Years* (New York, 1986) is an early and still-useful attempt to make sense of the Carter foreign policy. The breakdown of detente and revivification of the Cold War are analyzed in Garthoff's *Détente and Confrontation* and Odd Arne Westad, ed., *The Fall of Détente: Soviet-American Relations During the Carter Years* (Boston, 1995). Piero Gleijeses, *Conflicting Missions: Havana, Washington, and Africa, 1959–1976* (Chapel Hill, N.C., 2002) uses Cuban sources to provide a persuasive revisionist account of conflicts in Angola and elsewhere. For the all-important issue of human rights, see Joshua Murachik, *The Uncertain Crusade: Jimmy Carter and the Dilemmas of Human Rights* (New York, 1980) and Sandy Vogelgesang, *American Dream, Global Nightmare: The Dilemma of Human Rights Policy* (New York, 1980). William Quandt, *Peace Process: American Diplomacy and the Arab Israeli Conflict Since 1967* (rev. ed., Berkeley, Calif., 2001), by a participant, is valuable for Camp David and its breakdown. The Iranian crisis is well covered in John D. Stempel, *Inside the Iranian Revolution* (Bloomington, Ind., 1981) and Kenneth M. Pollack, *The Persian Puzzle: The Conflict Between Iran and America* (New York, 2004). Its domestic impact is thoughtfully analyzed in David Farber, *Taken Hostage: The Iran Hostage Crisis and America's First Encounter with Radical Islam* (Princeton, N.J., 2005).

1981–2008: There is virtually no scholarly literature on the Reagan era. *An American Life: Ronald Reagan, The Autobiography* (New York, 1990) is bland and unrevealing, Douglas Brinkley, ed., *The Reagan Diaries* (New York, 2007) much more insightful. Alexander M. Haig Jr., *Caveat: Realism, Reagan, and Foreign Policy* (New York, 1984) vigorously defends the author's controversial role. George P. Shultz, *Turmoil and Triumph: My Years as Secretary of State* (New York, 1993) is very detailed and useful on numerous issues. Richard Pipes, *Vixi: Memoirs of a Non-Belonger* (New Haven, Conn., 2004) reveals the mood of Reagan's hard-line National Security Council. Lou Cannon, *President Reagan: The Role of a Lifetime* (New York, 1991) highlights Reagan's pragmatism. Garry Wills, *Reagan's America: Innocents at Home* (New York, 1987) is especially good on the pre-presidential career. Peter Schweizer, *Reagan's War—The Epic Story of his Forty Year Struggle and Final Triumph over Communism* (New York, 2003), as the title suggests, is a zealous affirmation of post–Cold War triumphalism. Kyle Longley et al., *Deconstructing Reagan: Conservative Mythology and America's Fortieth President* (Armonk, N.Y., 2007) offers a strong rebuttal from scholars writing on foreign policy and domestic issues. John Ehrman, *The Eighties: America in the Age of Reagan* (New Haven, Conn., 2005) is excellent on the domestic backdrop and Geoffrey Smith, *Reagan and Thatcher* (New York, 1991) on that special relationship. On Soviet-American relations, Garthoff, *Détente and Confrontation* is good on the first term and the sequel, *The Great Transition: American-Soviet Relations and the End of the Cold War* (Washington, 1994), on the second and beyond. Don Oberdorfer, *From the Cold War to a New Era: The United States and the End of the Soviet Union, 1983–1991* (New York, 1996) is a perceptive and readable account by a distinguished journalist. Richard Herrmann and Richard Ned Lebow, eds., *Ending the Cold War* (New York, 2004) contains excellent essays by leading international relations specialists on the end of the Cold War. Michael J. Hogan, ed., *The End of the Cold War: Its Meanings and Implications* (New York, 1992) is an early effort to explore the significance of that climactic event. Strobe Talbott, *Deadly Gambits: The Reagan Administration and the Stalemate in Nuclear Arms Control* (New York, 1984) is still useful for the first-term deadlock. Frances FitzGerald, *Way Out*

There in the Blue: Reagan, Star Wars, and the End of the Cold War (New York, 2000) tells the story of that most contentious issue in Soviet-American relations. William M. LeoGrande, *Our Own Backyard: The United States in Central America, 1977–1992* (Chapel Hill, N.C., 1998) is richly detailed and invaluable. Walter LaFeber, *Inevitable Revolutions: The United States in Central America* (rev. ed., New York, 1984) is indispensable for the roots of the 1980s crisis. James M. Scott, *Deciding to Intervene: The Reagan Doctrine and American Foreign Policy* (Durham, N.C., 1996) is a useful early study. Bob Woodward, *Veil: The Secret Wars of the CIA, 1981–1987* (New York, 1987) is entertaining and sometimes revealing but should be used with caution. Lawrence Freedman and Efraim Karsh, *The Gulf Conflict, 1990–1991* (Princeton, N.J., 1993) is a good early history of the first Gulf War. Michael Gordon and Bernard Trainor, *The Generals' War* (Boston, 1995) is an excellent military history.

George Bush and Brent Scowcroft, *A World Transformed: The Collapse of the Soviet Empire, the Unification of Germany, Tiananmen Square, the Gulf War* (New York, 1998) is an informative and quite remarkable joint memoir that reveals much about the working relationship of the authors. James A. Baker III, *The Politics of Diplomacy: Revolution, War and Peace, 1989–1992* (New York, 1995) fills in those stories and others from the perspective of the secretary of state. The George H. W. Bush administration is competently chronicled in John Robert Greene, *The Presidency of George Bush* (Lawrence, Kans., 2000).

David Halberstam, *War in a Time of Peace* (New York, 2001) is insightful on policymaking in the George H. W. Bush and Bill Clinton administrations, especially on the question of humanitarian interventions. David Rothkopf, *Running the World: The Inside Story of the National Security Council and the Architects of American Power* (New York, 2004) is particularly good on the Clinton administration, in which he served. Colin Powell with Joseph Persico, *My American Journey* (New York, 1995), Bill Clinton, *My Life* (New York, 2004), Warren Christopher, *Chances of a Lifetime* (New York, 2001), and Madeleine Albright, *Madame Secretary* (New York, 2003) provide useful detail.

James Mann, *Rise of the Vulcans* (New York, 2004) is essential for the mindset and rivalries among those who took power in the George W. Bush administration. Glenn Kessler, *The Confidante: Condoleezza Rice and the Creation of the Bush Legacy* (New York, 2007), and Elisabeth Bumiller, *Condoleezza Rice: A Biography* (New York, 2008), biographies by journalists, are valuable for Bush's national security adviser and secretary of state. Ivo H. Daalder and James M. Lindsay, *America Unbound: The Bush Revolution in American Foreign Policy* (Washington, 2003) is an early assessment of a controversial presidency. Robert Jervis, *American Foreign Policy in a New Era* (New York, 2005) is critical of the so-called Bush Doctrine. Robert Draper, *Dead Certain: The Presidency of George W. Bush* (New York, 2007) is an early attempt to assess a controversial presidency. Samuel P. Huntington, *The Clash of Civilizations and the Remaking of the World Order* (New York, 1996) anticipates the major conflict of the early twenty-first century. Lawrence Wright, *The Looming Tower: Al Qaeda and the Road to 9/11* (New York, 2006) helps understand an enigmatic enemy. Richard Clarke, *Against All Enemies* (New York, 2004) recounts the outspoken author's only partially successful efforts to engage the government on terrorism. Bob Woodward's trilogy, *Bush at War* (New York, 2003), *Plan of Attack* (New York, 2004), and *State of Denial* (New York, 2006) contains inside information and becomes increasingly critical of the Bush administration. Steve Coll, *Ghost Wars* (New York, 2004) covers the early years of the war in Afghanistan. The run-up to war in Iraq and the flimsy case it was built on are detailed in Michael Isikoff and David Corn, *Hubris: The Inside Story of Spin, Scandal, and the Selling of the Iraq War* (New York, 2006) and from Powell's viewpoint in Karen DeYoung, *Soldier: The Life of Colin Powell* (New York, 2006). Excellent early accounts of the Iraq War are Thomas Ricks, *Fiasco: America's Military Adventure in Iraq* (New York, 2006), Bernard E. Trainor and Michael R. Gordon, *Cobra II: The Inside Story of the Invasion of Iraq* (New York, 2006), and George Packer, *The Assassins' Gate: America in Iraq* (New York, 2005). An important work by an Iraqi political official is Ali A. Allawi, *The Occupation of Iraq: Winning the War, Losing the Peace* (New Haven, Conn., 2007). Seymour Hersh, *Chain of Command: The Road from 9/11 to Abu Ghraib* (New York, 2004) investigates the background of Abu Ghraib.

Index